lonely planet

Cuba

Havana p58
Varadero & Matanzas p198
Artemisa & Mayabeque p144
Valle de Viñales & Pinar del Río p173
Villa Clara p254
Ciego de Ávila p301
Cienfuegos p235
Trinidad & Sancti Spíritus p275
Camagüey p316
Isla de la Juventud (Special Municipality) p158
Las Tunas p335
Holguín p346
Granma p371
Santiago de Cuba p392
Guantánamo p429

Brendan Sainsbury,
Carolyn McCarthy

PLAN YOUR TRIP

ON THE ROAD

GLEN PHOTO/SHUTTERSTOCK ©

TRINIDAD, P277

MAURIZIO DE MATTEI/SHUTTERSTOCK ©

HAVANA, P58

DAYOWL/SHUTTERSTOCK ©

Contents

SANTA CLARA, P256

ON THE ROAD

ZOLTAN VARGA PHOTOGRAPHER/SHUTTERSTOCK ©

HAVANA, P58

AWL IMAGES LTD/SHUTTERSTOCK ©

CAYO COCO, P311

Contents

Welcome to Cuba

Timeworn but magnificent, dilapidated but dignified, fun yet maddeningly frustrating – Cuba is a country of indefinable magic.

Expect the Unexpected

Cuba is like a prince in a poor man's coat: behind the sometimes shabby facades, gold dust lingers. It's these rich dichotomies that make travel here the exciting, exhilarating roller-coaster ride it is. Trapped in a time warp and reeling from an economic embargo that has grated for more than half a century, this is a country where you can wave goodbye to everyday assumptions and expect the unexpected. If Cuba were a book, it would be James Joyce's *Ulysses*: layered, hard to grasp, frequently misunderstood, but – above all – a classic.

Cultural Heritage

Bereft of modern interference, Cuba's colonial cities haven't changed much since musket-toting pirates stalked the Caribbean. The atmosphere and architecture is particularly stirring in Havana, Trinidad, Remedios and Camagüey where grandiose squares and cobbled streets tell of opulence and intrigue. Yet, despite pockets of preservation, many buildings still lie ruined like aging dowagers waiting for a face-lift. With more funds, these heirlooms may yet rise again. Indeed, thanks to private investment, many of them have already been partially renovated, morphing into spectacular private homestays or retro-themed restaurants proudly showing off their weighty cultural heritage.

The Perfect Time to Visit

There's rarely been a better time to visit Cuba. Private enterprise is displaying the first buds of a creative spring, while the big-name brands from that well-known frenemy in the north have yet to dilute the cultural magic. As a result, the country is rife with experimentation. Here a free-spirited cafe where earnest students sit around debating Che Guevara's contribution to world revolution; there an avant-garde art studio where the furniture is as outlandish as the exhibits. From rural Viñales to urban Havana, it's as if the whole country is slowly awakening from a deep slumber. Come now and ride the wave.

Beyond the Beaches

The vast majority of Cuba's tourists gravitate to the attractive arcs of white sand that pepper the country's north coast and offshore islands. But, explore beyond the beaches and you're in a different domain, a land of fecund forests and crocodile-infested swamps, abandoned coffee plantations and rugged mountains as famous for their revolutionary folklore as their endemic species. Cuba, once observed German scientist Alexander von Humboldt, is a kind of Caribbean Galápagos where contradictory curiosities exist side by side. Get off the beaten path and seek them out.

Why I Love Cuba

By Brendan Sainsbury, Writer

For me, Cuba has always had the allure of a forbidden fruit. I love it for its uniqueness, creativity and survivalist spirit; but, above all, I love it because, despite 60 years of setbacks, it remains an upbeat and open place. Walk down the street with a Cuban friend and, within one block, you'll have received five handshakes, four kisses, three greetings of '*dime hermano!*' and at least two invites into someone's house for a *cafecito* (or something stronger). I've been lucky enough to visit 75 countries worldwide, but Cuba will always be my *número uno*.

For more about our writers, see p544

Above: Habana Vieja (p62), Havana

Cuba

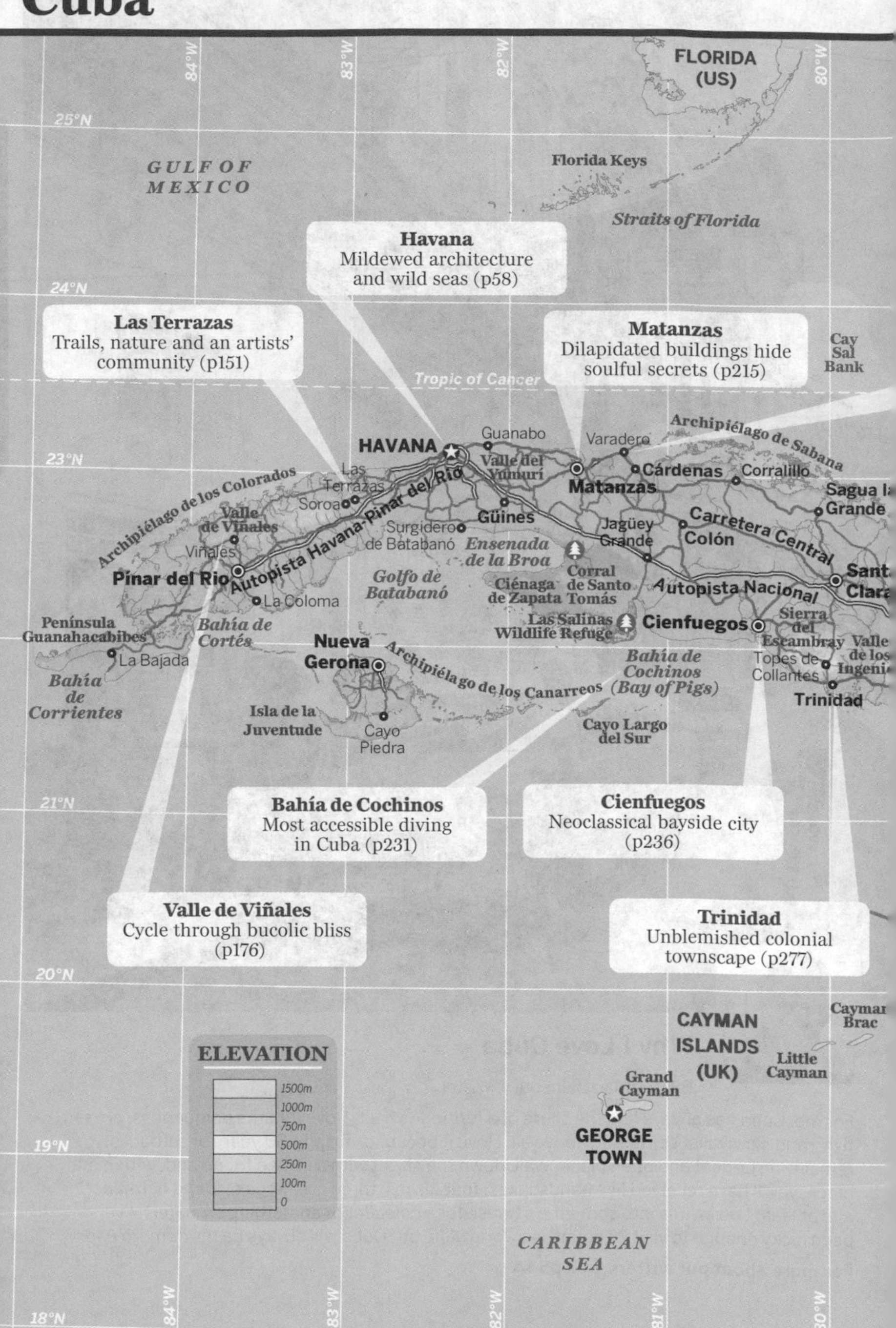
FLORIDA (US)
GULF OF MEXICO
Florida Keys
Straits of Florida
Havana
Mildewed architecture and wild seas (p58)
Las Terrazas
Trails, nature and an artists' community (p151)
Matanzas
Dilapidated buildings hide soulful secrets (p215)
Cay Sal Bank
Tropic of Cancer
Archipiélago de Sabana
HAVANA
Guanabo
Varadero
Valle del Yumurí
Matanzas
Cárdenas
Corralillo
Sagua la Grande
Archipiélago de los Colorados
Las Terrazas
Soroa
Valle de Viñales
Viñales
Güines
Surgidero de Batabanó
Jagüey Grande
Colón
Carretera Central
Pinar del Río
Autopista Havana-Pinar del Río
Ensenada de la Broa
Golfo de Batabanó
Corral de Santo Tomás
Ciénaga de Zapata
Autopista Nacional
Santa Clara
La Coloma
Península Guanahacabibes
Bahía de Cortés
Las Salinas Wildlife Refuge
Cienfuegos
Sierra del Escambray
Valle de los Ingenios
La Bajada
Nueva Gerona
Archipiélago de los Canarreos
Bahía de Cochinos (Bay of Pigs)
Topes de Collantes
Trinidad
Bahía de Corrientes
Isla de la Juventude
Cayo Piedra
Cayo Largo del Sur
Bahía de Cochinos
Most accessible diving in Cuba (p231)
Cienfuegos
Neoclassical bayside city (p236)
Valle de Viñales
Cycle through bucolic bliss (p176)
Trinidad
Unblemished colonial townscape (p277)
CAYMAN ISLANDS (UK)
Cayman Brac
Little Cayman
Grand Cayman
GEORGE TOWN
ELEVATION
1500m
1000m
750m
500m
250m
100m
0
CARIBBEAN SEA
25°N
24°N
23°N
21°N
20°N
19°N
18°N
84°W
83°W
82°W
81°W
80°W

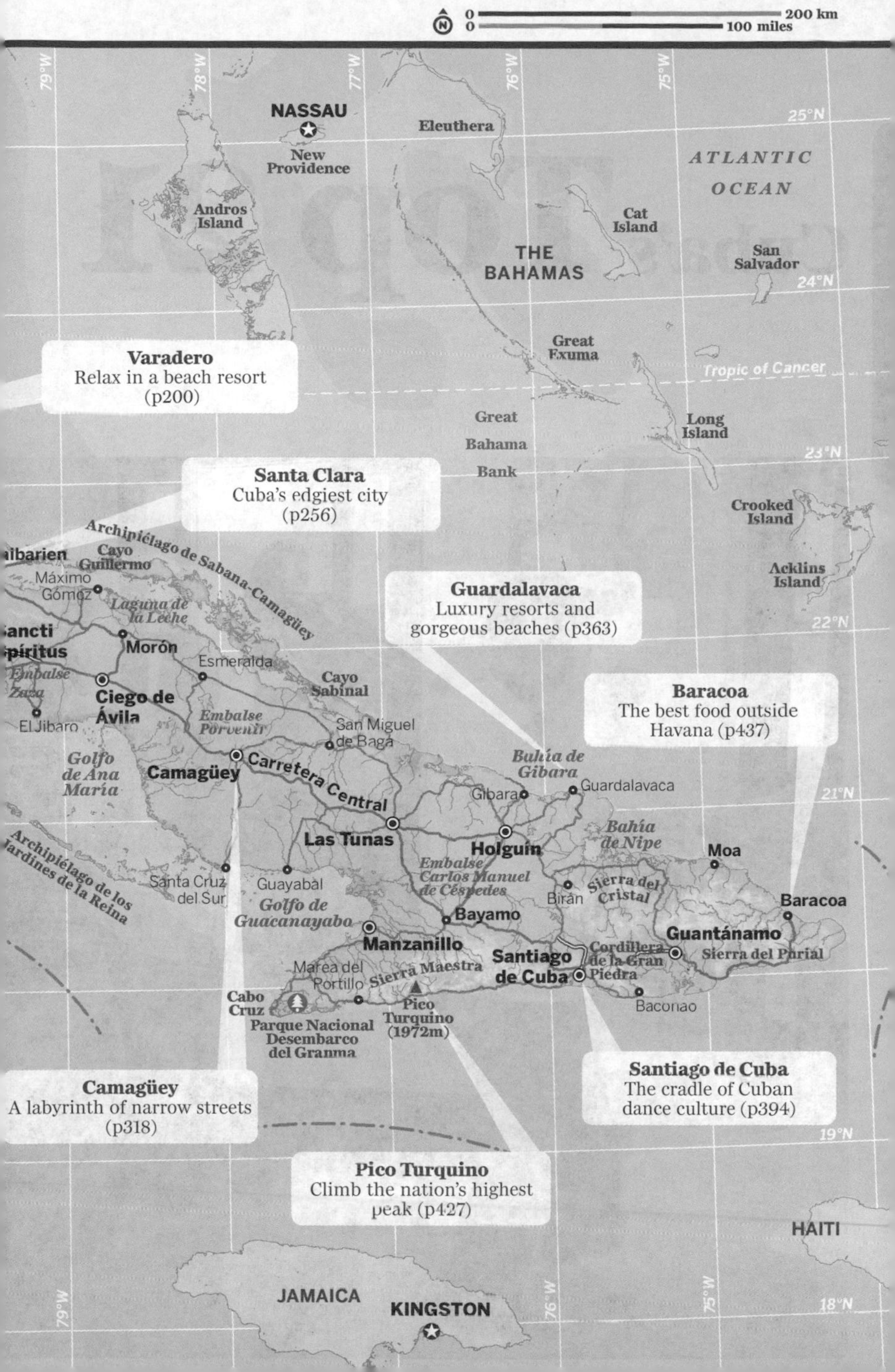

0 200 km
0 100 miles
NASSAU
New Providence
Eleuthera
ATLANTIC OCEAN
Andros Island
Cat Island
THE BAHAMAS
San Salvador
Great Exuma
Tropic of Cancer
Great Bahama Bank
Long Island
Crooked Island
Acklins Island
Varadero
Relax in a beach resort (p200)
Santa Clara
Cuba's edgiest city (p256)
Guardalavaca
Luxury resorts and gorgeous beaches (p363)
Baracoa
The best food outside Havana (p437)
Archipiélago de Sabana-Camagüey
Cayo Guillermo
Máximo Gómez
Laguna de la Leche
Morón
Esmeralda
Ciego de Ávila
El Jíbaro
Embalse Porvenir
Cayo Sabinal
San Miguel de Baga
Golfo de Ana María
Camagüey
Carretera Central
Bahía de Gibara
Guardalavaca
Gibara
Las Tunas
Holguín
Bahía de Nipe
Moa
Archipiélago de los Jardines de la Reina
Santa Cruz del Sur
Guayabal
Golfo de Guacanayabo
Embalse Carlos Manuel de Céspedes
Birán
Sierra del Cristal
Baracoa
Bayamo
Manzanillo
Guantánamo
Santiago de Cuba
Cordillera de la Gran Piedra
Sierra del Purial
Marea del Portillo
Sierra Maestra
Cabo Cruz
Pico Turquino (1972m)
Parque Nacional Desembarco del Granma
Baconao
Camagüey
A labyrinth of narrow streets (p318)
Santiago de Cuba
The cradle of Cuban dance culture (p394)
Pico Turquino
Climb the nation's highest peak (p427)
HAITI
JAMAICA
KINGSTON

Cuba's Top 21

1

Live-Music Scene

1 If you've been in Cuba for more than 10 minutes and still haven't heard any live music, you're clearly hanging out in the wrong bars. Welcome to one of the most musically diverse countries on the planet, where guitars still outnumber MP3-players and singing is seen as just another form of verbal communication. The traditional genres of *son* and salsa are merely one groove on a larger record. Cuba has been pushing the musical envelope for decades. From Benny Moré to hip-hop, the country bleeds syncopated rhythms.

Cafe Taberna (p110), Havana

Historic Habana Vieja

2 International observers regularly single out Cuba's healthcare system for universal praise. But, arguably one of the greatest achievements of the last 50 years is the piecing back together of Habana Vieja (p62). This detailed, meticulous, lovingly curated restoration process has created one of the historical wonders of the Americas, a kind of Latin American 'Rome' where the past can be peeled off in layers. Armed with a sharp eye and a lucid imagination, you can walk through Havana's cobbled streets and evoke the ghosts of mega-rich sugar barons and sabre-rattling buccaneers.

TERRY DONNELLY/ALAMY ©

2

DAN KOSMAYER/SHUTTERSTOCK ©

3

CHANTAL DE BRUIJNE/SHUTTERSTOCK ©

4

Eclectic Architecture

3 Cuba's architecture mirrors its heritage. Take a muscular slice of Spanish baroque, sprinkle in some French classicism, a generous dash of North American art deco and a hint of European art nouveau. Now add the sweat of Afro-Cuban slave labor, and a spark of creative modernism, and there you have it. Sometimes extreme, rarely constant, Cuban architecture retains certain binding threads, a definable 'Cuban-ness' that sets it apart from other genres. Visit the Unesco-listed cities of Havana (p62), Trinidad (p277; pictured), Cienfuegos (p236) and Camagüey (p318) and see.

Idyllic Beach Escapes

4 Cuba's beaches are famous for a reason – they're uncrowded, well endowed with tropical beauty, and extremely varied. There's the long, wide tourist-heavy beaches of Varadero (p200; pictured) backed by massive resorts; the wild, deserted eco-beaches of Península de Guanahacabibes where turtles lay their eggs; the little-visited black-sand beaches on the Isla de la Juventud where pirates once roamed; and the unashamedly nudist beaches of Cayo Largo del Sur where package tourists lounge with mojitos. Search around long enough and you're sure to find your own slice of nirvana.

Cuba's Casas Particulares

5 Stay in a private homestay and you quickly uncover the nuances of everyday Cuban life. Picture rocking chairs on porches, neighbors popping over for rum and cigars, roosters crowing at 5am, pictures of José Martí placed strategically above the TV set and animated conversations that go on well into the night and always seem to end with the words '*no es facil*' (it ain't easy). Some casas particulares are positively palatial, others remain refreshingly down-to-earth, all offer a candid and uncensored view of Cuba that no hotel could ever replicate.

5

Birdwatching

6 Crocodiles aside, Cuba has little impressive fauna, but the paucity of animals is more than made up for by the abundance of birdlife. Approximately 350 species inhabit the shores of this distinct and ecologically weird tropical archipelago, a good two dozen of them endemic. Look out in particular for the colorful *tocororo* (Cuban trogan; pictured), the *zunzuncito* (bee hummingbird), the critically endangered ivory-billed woodpecker and the world's largest flamingo nesting site. The Ciénaga de Zapata (p228) and the Sierra del Rosario Biosphere Reserve (p149) are two of many birdwatching highlights.

ELLIOTTE RUSTY HAROLD/SHUTTERSTOCK ©

6

Revolutionary Heritage

7 An improbable escape from a shipwrecked leisure yacht, handsome bearded guerrillas meting out Robin Hood–style justice and a classic David versus Goliath struggle that was won convincingly by the (extreme) underdogs: Cuba's revolutionary war reads like the pages of a barely believable movie script. But it all happened right here. Just to prove it, you can visit the revolutionary sites in person. Little has changed in more than 50 years at the disembarkation point of the *Granma* yacht and Fidel's wartime HQ at mountaintop Comandancia de la Plata (p381). Camagüey (p318)

Time-Warped Trinidad

8 Soporific Trinidad (p277) went to sleep in 1850 and never really woke up. This strange twist of fate is good news for modern travelers who can roam freely through the perfectly preserved mid-19th-century sugar town like voyeurs from another era. Though it's no secret these days, the time-warped streets still have the power to enchant with their grand colonial homestays, easily accessible countryside and exciting live music scene. But this is also a real working town loaded with all the foibles and fun of 21st-century Cuba.

7

8

SERGEY URYADNIKOV/SHUTTERSTOCK ©

LENA WURM/SHUTTERSTOCK ©

Diving & Snorkeling in the Caribbean

9 There will be protestations, no doubt, but let's say it anyway: Cuba is home to the best diving in the Caribbean. The reasons are unrivaled water clarity, virgin reefs and sheltered Caribbean waters that teem with fish. Accessibility for divers varies from the swim-out walls of the Bahía de Cochinos (Bay of Pigs; p230) to the hard-to-reach underwater nirvana of the Jardines de la Reina archipelago (p310). For repeat visitors, Punta Francés (p167) on Isla de la Juventud – host of an annual underwater photography competition – reigns supreme.

Ciénaga de Zapata's Wildlife

10 One of the few parts of Cuba that has never been truly tamed, the Zapata swamps (p227) are as close to pure wilderness as the country gets. This is the home of the endangered Cuban crocodile, various amphibians, the bee hummingbird and over a dozen different plant habitats. It also qualifies as the Caribbean's largest wetlands, protected in numerous ways, most importantly as a Unesco Biosphere Reserve and Ramsar Convention Site. Come here to fish, birdwatch, hike and see nature at its purest.

Cuban screech owl

Labyrinthine Streets of Camagüey

11 Get lost! No, that's not an abrupt putdown; it's a savvy recommendation for any traveler passing through the city of *tinajones* (clay pots), churches and erstwhile pirates – aka Camagüey (p318). A perennial rule-breaker, Camagüey was founded on a street grid that deviated from almost every other Spanish colonial city in Latin America. Here the lanes are as labyrinthine as a Moroccan medina, hiding Catholic churches, triangular plazas, and a growing ensemble of smart boutique hotels encased in restored colonial buildings.

12

DAVID SILVERMAN/GETTY IMAGES ©

13

14

Emerging Food Culture

12 Ever since new privatization laws lifted the lid off Cuba's creative pressure cooker in 2011, a culinary revolution has been in full swing. A country that once offered little more than rice and beans has rediscovered its gastronomic mojo with a profusion of new restaurants experimenting with spices, fusion and – perhaps best of all – a welcome re-evaluation of its own national cuisine. Havana (O'Reilly 304, p101; pictured above) leads the culinary field in number and variety of eating establishments, Viñales offers exquisite traditional plates, while isolated Baracoa rules for regional originality.

Cycling the Valle de Viñales

13 With less traffic on the roads than 1940s Britain, Cuba is ideal for cycling and there's no better place to do it than the quintessentially rural Valle de Viñales (p176). The valley offers all the ingredients of a tropical Tour de France: craggy *mogotes* (limestone monoliths), impossibly green tobacco fields, bucolic campesino huts and spirit-lifting viewpoints at every turn. The terrain is relatively flat and, if you can procure a decent bike, your biggest dilemma will be where to stop for your sunset-toasting mojito.

Cienfuegos' Classical Architecture

14 There's a certain *je ne sais quoi* about bayside Cienfuegos (p236), Cuba's self-proclaimed 'Pearl of the South.' Through hell, high water and an economically debilitating Special Period, this is a city that has always retained its poise. The elegance is best seen in the architecture, a homogeneous cityscape laid out in the early 19th century by settlers from France and the US. Dip into the cultural life around the city center and its adjacent garden suburb of Punta Gorda and absorb the Gallic refinement.

Santa Clara's Youthful Energy

15 Leave your preconceived notions about Cuba at the city limits. Santa Clara (p256) is everything you thought this country wasn't – progressive, creative, welcoming to people of all persuasions, enthusiastic about rock 'n' roll, and keen to push the boundaries of art in every direction. Being a university town helps. Youthful energy runs through Santa Clara like nowhere else in Cuba. Check out the drag shows at Club Mejunje, meet the arty students at the Casa de la Ciudad, or wander Parque Vidal in the evening when an orchestra is playing.

Las Terrazas' Eco-village

16 Back in 1968, when the fledgling environmental movement was a bolshie protest group for long-haired students in John Lennon glasses, the prophetic Cubans, concerned about the ecological cost of island-wide deforestation, came up with a good idea. After saving hectares of denuded forest from erosion by planting tree saplings on terraced slopes, a group of industrious workers built an eco-village, Las Terrazas (p151), and set about colonizing it with artists, musicians, coffee growers and an architecturally unique hotel. Fifty years later, the village is still there quietly practicing its Cuban-style sustainability.

Ebullient Festivals

17 Through war, austerity, rationing and hardship, the Cubans have retained their infectious *joie de vivre*. Even during the darkest days of the Special Period, the feisty festivals never stopped, a testament to the country's capacity to put politics aside and get on with the important business of living. The best shows involve fireworks in Remedios (p267), *folklórico* dancing in Santiago de Cuba (p406), movies in Gibara (p358) and every conceivable genre of music in Havana (p133; pictured). Arrive prepared to party.

Baracoa

18 Over the hills and far away on the easternmost limb of Guantánamo Province lies isolated Baracoa (p437), a small yet historically significant settlement, weird even by Cuban standards for its fickle Atlantic weather, eccentric local populace and unrelenting desire to be, well, different. Despite being hit hard by 2016's Hurricane Matthew, the town remains unbowed and open for business. Watch locals scale coconut palms, see bands play *kiribá*, the local take on *son* (Cuban music style), and, above all, enjoy the spicier, richer and more inventive food, starting with the sweet treat *cucurucho* (ice-cream cone).

17

18

CEM CANBAY/AGE FOTOSTOCK/ALAMY ©

CHRIS FOSSEY PHOTOGRAPHY/SHUTTERSTOCK ©

The Secrets of Matanzas

19 For too long the city of Matanzas (p215) has been overlooked by travelers, cast as an ugly cousin to nearby Varadero. But, things are gradually changing. Amid the bridges and rivers of this once great cultural city, flickers of its erstwhile beauty have started to re-emerge in revived classical music venues, a refurbished theater and a cutting-edge art co-op. Granted, there still isn't much of a tourist infrastructure. But, with a little time, Matanzas' gigantic historical legacy will teach you more about the real Cuba than 20 repeat visits to the resorts.

Folklórico in Santiago de Cuba

20 There's nothing quite as transcendental as the hypnotic beat of the Santería drums summoning up the spirits of the *orishas* (deities). But, while most Afro-Cuban religious rites are only for initiates, the drumming and dances of Cuba's *folklórico* (traditional Latin American dance) troupes are open to all. Formed in the 1960s to keep the ancient slave culture of Cuba alive, *folklórico* groups enjoy strong government patronage, and their energetic and colorful shows in Santiago de Cuba (p394), remain spontaneous and true to their roots.

Pico Turquino

21 The trek up Cuba's highest mountain, Pico Turquino (p427), is a mixture of endurance sport, nature tour and fascinating history lesson. Guides are mandatory for the tough two- to three-day 17km trek through the steep cloud forests of the Sierra Maestra (pictured) to the 1972m summit where you'll be greeted by a bronze bust of Cuban national hero, José Martí. Revolutionary buffs can make a side trip to Fidel's wartime jungle HQ, La Plata (p381), on the way up.

Need to Know

For more information, see Survival Guide (p501)

Currency

Cuban convertibles (CUC$) and Cuban pesos (MN$; *moneda nacional*).

Visas

Regular tourists require a *tarjeta de turista* (tourist card), valid for 30 days and usually provided with your flight package. Always check when booking.

Money

Cuba is primarily a cash economy. Non-US credit cards are accepted in resort hotels and some city hotels. There are a growing number of ATMs.

Cell Phones

Check with your service provider to see if your phone will work. You can use your own GSM or TDMA phones in Cuba, though you'll have to get a local chip and pay an activation fee (approximately CUC$30).

Time

Eastern Standard Time GMT/UTC minus five hours.

When to Go

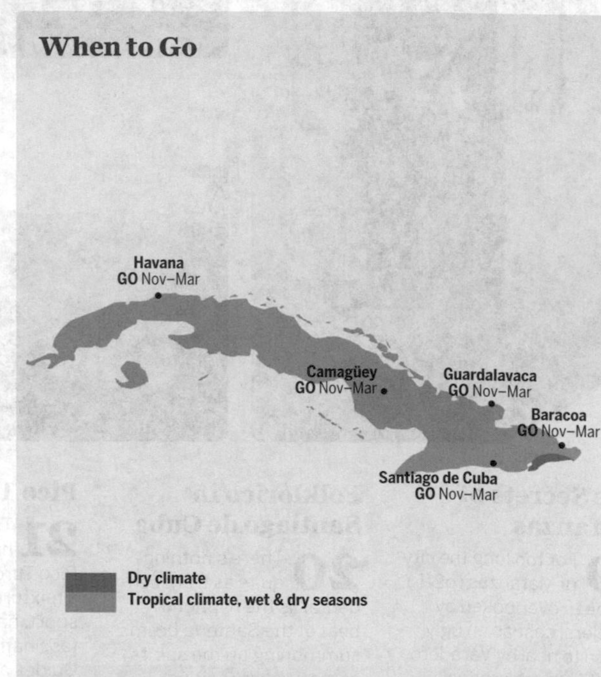

High Season

(Nov–Mar, Jul & Aug)

➡ Prices are 30% higher and hotels may require advance bookings.

➡ Prices are at their highest around Christmas and New Year.

➡ Weather is cooler and drier November to March.

Shoulder

(Apr & Oct)

➡ Look out for special deals outside of peak season.

➡ Prices and crowds increase over Easter.

Low Season

(May, Jun & Sep)

➡ Some resort hotels offer fewer facilities or shut altogether.

➡ There's a hurricane risk between June and November and a higher chance of rain.

Useful Websites

BBC (www.bbc.co.uk) Interesting correspondent reports on Cuba.

Cubacasas.net (www.cubacasas.net) Information, photos and contact details for casas particulares.

Info Cuba (www.cubainfos.net) Excellent collection of web pages focusing mainly on Cuba's resort areas.

La Habana (www.lahabana.com) Art, culture, business and travel in Havana.

Lonely Planet (www.lonelyplanet.com/cuba) Destination information, articles, hotel bookings, traveler forum and more.

Important Numbers

To call Cuba from abroad, dial your international access code, Cuba's country code (53), the city or area code (minus the '0,' which is used when dialing domestically between provinces), and the local number.

Emergency	☎106
Directory assistance	☎113
Police	☎106
Fire	☎105

Exchange Rates

Argentina	ARS$1	CUC$0.12
Australia	A$1	CUC$0.80
Canada	C$1	CUC$0.80
Europe	€1	CUC$1.12
Japan	¥100	CUC$0.85
Mexico	MXN$1	CUC$0.07
New Zealand	NZ$1	CUC$0.75
UK	£1	CUC$1.50
US	US$1	CUC$1.00

For current exchange rates see www.xe.com.

Daily Costs

Budget: Less than CUC$80

- Casa particulare: CUC$25–45
- Meal in government-run restaurant: CUC$10–15
- Museum entry: CUC$1–5

Midrange: CUC$80–170

- Midrange hotel: CUC$50–120
- Meal in paladar (private restaurant): CUC$15–25
- Víazul bus travel: Havana–Trinidad CUC$25

Top End: More than CUC$170

- Resort or historic hotel: CUC$200–300
- Car hire or taxi: CUC$60–70
- Evening cabaret: CUC$35–60

Opening Hours

Banks 9am to 3pm Monday to Friday

Cadeca money exchanges 9am to 7pm Monday to Saturday, 9am to noon Sunday. Many top-end city hotels offer money exchange late into the evening.

Pharmacies 8am to 8pm

Post offices 8am to 5pm Monday to Saturday

Restaurants 10:30am to 11pm

Shops 9am to 5pm Monday to Saturday, 9am to noon Sunday

Arriving in Cuba

Aeropuerto Internacional José Martí (Havana) There are no regular buses or trains running direct from the airport into the city center. Taxis cost CUC$25 to CUC$30 and take 30 to 40 minutes to reach most of the city center hotels. You can change money at the bank in the arrivals hall.

Other international airports Cuba has nine other international airports, but none of them has reliable public transport links; your best bet is always a taxi. Agree fares beforehand.

Getting Around

Buses are the most efficient and practical way of getting around.

Bus The state-run Víazul network links most places of interest to tourists on a regular daily schedule. Cubanacán runs a less comprehensive *conectando* service. Local buses are crowded and have no printed schedules.

Car Rental cars are quite expensive and driving can be a challenge due to the lack of signposts and ambiguous road rules.

Taxi Taxis are an option over longer distances if you are traveling in a small group. Rates are approximately CUC$0.55 per kilometer.

Train Despite its large train network, Cuban trains are slow, unreliable and lacking in comfort. For stoics only!

For much more on **getting around**, see p515

First Time Cuba

For more information, see Survival Guide (p501)

Checklist

➡ Check with your bank/ credit card company whether your debit and credit cards will work in Cuba.

➡ Print out a copy of your medical insurance to show at the airport.

➡ Check when booking your air ticket that the tourist card is included in your flight package.

➡ Book ahead for accommodation and bus tickets.

What to Pack

➡ Latin American Spanish dictionary/phrasebook

➡ Plug adaptors for European and US sockets

➡ Good money belt that fits snugly around your waist

➡ Basic first aid kit, pain killers and any required medications

➡ Insect repellent, sunscreen and sunglasses

➡ Stash of cash in euros, Canadian dollars or pound sterling

➡ Energy bars for long road trips

Top Tips for Your Trip

➡ For a glimpse of the real Cuba and a chance to put your money directly into the pockets of individual Cubans, stay in a casa particular (private homestay).

➡ Carry toilet paper and antiseptic hand-wash, and drink bottled water.

➡ Avoid driving in Havana. The city has various public transportation options and well priced taxis. Most neighborhoods are walkable.

➡ Thanks to heavy bureaucracy, answers to simple requests aren't always straightforward. Probe politely and ask at least five different people before you make important decisions.

➡ Bring a warm jumper for buses – the air-conditioning is often freezing.

➡ US travelers shouldn't rely on credit/debit cards – despite diplomatic talk, their use in Cuba still hasn't been activated.

➡ Book ahead for accommodation and transport, especially in peak season.

What to Wear

Cuba is a hot, humid country which, thankfully, has a casual approach to clothing. Locals generally opt for shorts, sandals and T-shirts; women favor tight-fitting Lycra, men looser *guayabera* shirts (invented in Cuba). There are only two nude beaches in Cuba, frequented almost exclusively by foreigners. Cinemas and theaters usually have a 'no shorts' rule for men.

Sleeping

While tourist numbers continue to climb hotel provision has lagged behind. Book accommodation in advance.

➡ **Casas particulares** Cuban homes that rent rooms to foreigners; an authentic and economic form of cultural immersion.

➡ **Campismos** Cheap, rustic accommodations in rural areas, usually in bungalows or cabins.

➡ **Hotels** All Cuban hotels are government-owned. Prices and quality range from cheap Soviet-era to high-flying colonial chic.

➡ **Resorts** Large international-standard hotels in resort areas that sell all-inclusive packages.

Money

Cuba has two currencies though the government is in the process of unifying them. At the time of writing, convertibles (CUC$) and pesos (*moneda nacional*; MN$) were both still in circulation. One convertible is worth 25 pesos. Non-Cubans deal almost exclusively in convertibles.

Bargaining

Cuba's socialist economy doesn't have a history of bargaining, though there may be some room for maneuver on prices at private enterprise markets.

Tipping

Tipping in Cuba is important. Since most Cubans earn their money in *moneda nacional* (MN$), leaving a small tip of CUC$1 (MN$25) or more can make a huge difference.

➡ **Resorts/hotels** Tip for good service with bellboys, room maids and bar/restaurant staff.

➡ **Musicians** Carry small notes for the ubiquitous musicians in restaurants. Tip when the basket comes round.

➡ **Tour guides** Depending on tour length, tip from a dollar for a few hours to more for extensive guiding.

➡ **Restaurants** Standard 10%, or up to 15% if service is excellent and/or you're feeling generous.

➡ **Taxis** Tip 10% if you are on the meter, otherwise agree full fare beforehand.

LEMBI/SHUTTERSTOCK ©

Casa particular, Viñales (p176)

Etiquette

Cuba is an informal country with few rules of etiquette.

➡ **Greetings** Shake hands with strangers; a kiss or double-cheek kiss is appropriate between people (men–women and women–women) who have already met.

➡ **Conversation** Although they can be surprisingly candid, Cubans aren't keen to discuss politics, especially with strangers and if it involves being openly critical of the government.

➡ **Dancing** Cubans don't harbor any self-consciousness about dancing. Throw your reservations out of the window and let loose.

Eating

➡ **Private restaurants** Although slightly pricier than their state-run equivalents, private restaurants nearly always offer the best, freshest food and the highest quality service.

➡ **Casas particulares** Cuban homestays invariably serve a massive breakfast for around CUC$5; some also offer an equally large and tasty dinner made from the freshest ingredients.

➡ **Hotels & resorts** The all-inclusives offer buffet food of an international standard but after a week it can get a bit bland.

➡ **State-run restaurants** Varying food and service from top-notch places in Havana to unimaginative rations in the provinces. Prices often lower than private places.

What's New

Havana's Retro Bars & Restaurants

Havana might not have the big food and drink chains of other countries, but it has seen a huge growth in independent coffee shops, restaurants and bars. The current penchant is for cool retro decor evoking the era of vinyl records and streamlined American cars that directly preceded the revolution.

New Boutique Hotels

State-run tourist operator Cubanacán has added half-a-dozen historic boutique hotels to its 'Encanto' brand in Cuba's provincial cities. Highlights include Hotel Arsenita in Gibara (p359), El Marqués in Camagüey (p324) and Hotel Caballeriza in Holguín (p353).

Commercial Flights from the US

Normal flight service between the US and Cuba was resumed in 2016. More than half-a-dozen airlines now run regular weekly flights between a variety of US and Cuban cities for qualifying American tourists.

Better Wi-Fi

In the last two years, Cuba has sprouted more than 200 wi-fi hot spots. Most provincial towns offer coverage in local parks and squares, while hotels of three-stars and up usually have a reasonable connection.

Cruise Ships

In May 2016, the *Adonia* became the first US cruise ship to dock in Cuba for five decades. Since then, the Cubans have given permission for five more lines to visit the country in 2017.

Gran Teatro de la Habana Alicia Alonso

Havana's finest theater and one of its most impressive eclectic buildings reopened after a lengthy renovation in 2016. Home to the Cuban ballet, it has been renamed in honor of the doyen of Cuban dance, Alicia Alonso. (p77)

Kitesurfing

Cuba's newest sport continues to make waves along the north coast and several new operators have opened for business renting gear and offering lessons. Havana, Varadero, Cayo Guillermo, Playa Santa Lucía and Guardalavaca are all active kite spots. (p44)

New Resorts

The resort building on the northern keys continues unabated with new hotels on Cayo Santa María, including the Valentín Perla Blanca (p272), as well as Cayo las Brujas and Cayo Guillermo.

Ice Cream

After 50 years of being monopolized by state-run ice-cream parlor La Coppelia, Havana is starting to produce a few private artisan ice-cream makers including Helad'oro, which knocks out impressive flavors made with local fruits, guava and mamey. (p98)

For more recommendations and reviews, see lonelyplanet.com/cuba

If You Like...

Architecture

Habana Vieja Like an old attic full of dusty relics, Havana is a treasure chest of eclectic architecture. (p62)

Cienfuegos Cuba's most architecturally homogeneous city is a love letter to French neoclassicism, full of elegant columns. (p236)

Camagüey An unusual street plan of labyrinthine lanes and baroque spires that hide a devout Catholic soul. (p318)

Trinidad One of the most beguiling and best-preserved towns in the Caribbean, tranquil Trinidad is a riot of colonial baroque. (p277)

Nightlife & Dancing

Santa Clara Where the 'next big thing' happens first; drag shows, rock 'n' roll music and everything in between. (p263)

Cabarets Cuba's flamboyant kitschy cabarets, like Havana's Tropicana, are something from opulent pre-revolutionary life that refused to die. (p133)

Casas de la Trova Cuba's old-fashioned spit-and-sawdust music houses are determined to keep the essence of traditional Cuban music alive. (p414)

Union of Cuban Writers and Artists (Uneac) Provincial free cultural centers full of latent artistic talent where everyone greets you like a long-lost friend. Leader of the pack Is El Hurón Azul in Havana. (p115)

Ruins

Gran Hotel & Balneario The elegant skeleton of this hotel and bathhouse sit totally abandoned in the middle of Matanzas Province. (p226)

Hacienda Cortina A surreal stately home surrounded by plant-rich, statue-filled grounds that's just been partially restored. (p189)

Antiguo Cafetal Angerona Romantic but little visited ruins of an old coffee farm just outside the town of Artemisa. (p147)

Sierra del Rosario Reserve The ruins of some of Cuba's oldest coffee farms lie within this Unesco Biosphere Reserve. (p151)

Presidio Modelo Cuba's creepiest prison with its huge circular cell-blocks is waiting to haunt you on La Isla de la Juventud. (p166)

Wildlife-Watching

Ciénaga de Zapata Take a boat trip to see a microcosm of Cuban wildlife, including the critically endangered Cuban crocodile. (p230)

Parque Nacional Alejandro de Humboldt Sky-high levels of endemism make Humboldt, home to the world's smallest frog, an ecological rarity. (p445)

Sierra del Chorrillo Non-indigenous exotic animals, including zebra and deer, in a quintessentially Cuban grassland setting. (p330)

Río Máximo Behold the largest colony of nesting flamingos in the world on Camagüey's north coast. (p326)

Guanahacabibes Crabs and iguanas do battle with 4WD traffic on the excursion to Cuba's western wilderness. (p195)

Diving & Snorkeling

Isla de la Juventud La Isla is famed for its clear water and hosts an underwater photography competition. (p160)

Jardines de la Reina Heavily protected archipelago with zero infrastructure protects some of the most unspoiled reefs in the Caribbean. (p310)

María la Gorda More than 50 easily accessible dive sites off Cuba's western tip make this small resort 'diver's central'. (p197)

Bahia de Cochinos Once infamous for another reason, the Bay of Pigs is today known for its easily accessible diving sites. (p233)

Playa Santa Lucía It's worth braving this rather tacky resort strip to experience the best diving on Cuba's north coast. (p332)

Relaxing at a Resort

Varadero The biggest resort in Cuba isn't to everyone's taste, but it's still insanely popular. (p200)

Cayo Coco An island getaway linked to the mainland by a causeway, Cayo Coco is low-rise and more subtle than Varadero. (p311)

Guardalavaca Three separate enclaves on Holguín's north coast offer three different price brackets, from expensive to bargain basement. (p363)

Cayerías del Norte The still-developing cayos of Villa Clara Province host Cuba's poshest resorts. (p271)

Cayo Largo del Sur Cuba's most isolated resort island isn't very Cuban, but its beaches are among the best in the nation. (p168)

Playa Santa Lucía Old and a little neglected, Camagüey's northern beach resort still offers the best bargains and excellent diving. (p331)

White-Sand Beaches

Playa Sirena Huge football field–sized beach on what is essentially a private tourist island with plenty of shady palms. (p169)

Top: 'Che with Child' (Estatua Che y Niño) by artist Casto Solano (p258), Santa Clara

Bottom: Street market, Trinidad (p277)

Varadero Twenty kilometers of unbroken beach – there's a reason why Varadero is the largest resort in the Caribbean. (p200)

Playa Las Tumbas On the western tip of Cuba, Las Tumbas, in the Guanahacabibes biosphere reserve, is practically virgin territory. (p195)

Playa Maguana Wind-whipped waves and bruised clouds all add to the ethereal ambience of Baracoa's finest beach. (p445)

Playa Pilar Hemingway's favorite is much-decorated in travel mags and backed by big dunes and a lobster-grilling beach shack. (p314)

Playa Bonita The only easily accessible beach on uninhabited Cayo Sabinal requires a boat transfer from Playa Santa Lucía. (p331)

Revolutionary History

Santa Clara 'Che City' is the home of Guevara's mausoleum, myriad statues and a fascinating open-air museum. (p256)

Bayamo The understated capital of Granma Province, where Cuba's first revolution was ignited in 1868. (p373)

Sierra Maestra Flecked with historical significance, including Castro's mountain-ridge HQ during the revolutionary war. (p381)

Santiago de Cuba The self-proclaimed 'City of Revolutionaries' was where Castro staged his first insurrection at Moncada Barracks. (p398)

Museo de la Revolución Cuba's most comprehensive museum is a one-stop immersion in all things revolutionary. (p76)

Indigenous Culture

Museo Chorro de Maita The most important archaeological site in Cuba; all pre-Columbian investigations should start here. (p363)

Museo Indocubano Bani Modest but enthusiastically curated museum in Cuba's archaeological 'capital' Banes. (p367)

Sendero Arqueológico Natural el Guafe Short trail in western Granma Province to a cave where a Taino water deity is carved in bare rock. (p389)

Museo Arqueológico 'La Cueva del Paraíso' Innovative museum in a cave close to some of Cuba's oldest pre-Columbian remains. (p437)

Boca de Guamá Slightly kitschy attempt to recreate a Taíno village and pass it off as a tourist hotel. (p228)

Cueva de Punta del Este Large collection of cave paintings rightly dubbed the 'Sistine Chapel of the Caribbean'. (p168)

Pirates & Forts

Havana's Forts Four of the finest examples of 16th-century military architecture in the Americas. (p75)

Castillo de San Pedro de la Roca del Morro Two hundred years in the making, Santiago's La Roca is today a Unesco World Heritage site. (p402)

Castillo de Nuestra Señora de los Ángeles de Jagua This little-visited bastion just outside Cienfuegos is 275 years old but still in remarkably good shape. (p239)

Baracoa Cuba's 'first city' has three stalwart forts that today serve as a museum, a hotel and a restaurant. (p438)

Matanzas Once breached by the British, Matanzas' little-visited Castillo de San Severino now harbors an interesting slave museum. (p217)

Live Music

Casas de la Música Havana's two Casas de la Música mix big-name live music with late-night dancing. (p113)

Casas de la Trova *Son* (Cuban music style) and boleros (ballads) give an old-fashioned lilt to these cultural houses in every Cuban provincial town. Our top pick is in Baracoa. (p443)

La Tumba Francesa Mysterious *folklórico* dance troupes in Guantánamo (p434) and Santiago de Cuba (p412) perform musical rites with a Haitian influence.

Street Rumba Salt-of-the-earth Havana (p113) and Matanzas (p221) specialize in mesmerizing drumming and dance rituals.

Jazz Cuba's best jazz venues are both in Havana's Vedado district: the Jazz Café (p113) and Jazz Club la Zorra y El Cuervo (p113).

Month by Month

TOP EVENTS

Festival Internacional de Cine Pobre, April

Carnaval de Santiago de Cuba, July

Festival Internacional de Ballet de la Habana, October

Las Parrandas, December

Festival Internacional de Jazz, December

January

The tourist season hits full swing, and the whole country has added buoyancy. Cold fronts bring occasionally chilly evenings.

Día de la Liberación

As well as seeing in the New Year with roast pork and a bottle of rum, Cubans celebrate January 1 as the triumph of the Revolution, the anniversary of Fidel Castro's 1959 victory.

Incendio de Bayamo

Bayamo residents remember the 1869 burning of their city with music and theatrical performances in an *espectáculo* (show) culminating in particularly explosive fireworks.

February

The peak tourist season continues and high demand can lead to overbooking, particularly in the rental-car market. Calm seas and less fickle weather promote better water clarity, making this an ideal time to enjoy diving and snorkeling.

Feria Internacional del Libro

First held in 1930, the International Book Fair is headquartered in Havana's Fortaleza de San Carlos de la Cabaña, but it later goes on the road to other cities. Highlights include book presentations, special readings and the prestigious Casa de las Américas prize. (p86)

Diving with Clarity

Calm conditions promote clear water for diving, particularly on Cuba's south coast. The country's prime diving nexuses, La Isla de la Juventud, and Playa Girón, have ideal conditions for underwater photography.

Habanos Festival

Trade fairs, seminars, tastings and visits to tobacco plantations draw cigar aficionados to Havana for this annual cigar festival with prizes, rolling competitions and a gala dinner.

March

Spring offers Cuba's best wildlife-watching opportunities, particularly for migrant birds. With dryer conditions, it is also an ideal time to indulge in hiking, cycling or numerous other outdoor activities.

Carnaval – Isla de la Juventud

The big annual party on the otherwise soporific Isla de la Juventud, a knees-up involving parades characterized by giant puppet-like heads, rodeo, sports competitions and perhaps just a little drinking. (p162)

Festival Internacional de Trova

Held since 1962 in honor of *trova* (international

poetic singing) pioneer Pepe Sánchez, this festival invades the parks, streets and music houses of Santiago de Cuba in a showcase of the popular verse/song genre.

Bird-Watching

March is a crossover period when migrant birds from both North and South America join Cuba's resident endemics en route for warmer or colder climes. There's no better time to polish off your binoculars.

April

Economy-seeking visitors should avoid the Easter holiday, which sees another spike in tourist numbers and prices. Otherwise April is a pleasant month with good fly-fishing potential off the south coast.

Semana de la Cultura

During the first week of April, Baracoa commemorates the landing of Antonio Maceo at Duaba on April 1, 1895, with a raucous carnival along the Malecón, expos of its indigenous music *nengon* and *kiribá,* and various culinary offerings.

Bienal Internacional de Humor

You can't be serious! Cuba's unique humor festival takes place in San Antonio de los Baños in out-of-the way Artemisa Province. Headquartered at the celebrated Museo del Humor, talented scribblers try to outdo each other by drawing ridiculous caricatures. Hilarious! (p146)

Festival Internacional de Cine Pobre

Gibara's celebration of low- and no-budget cinema has been an annual event since 2003, when it was inaugurated by late Cuban film director Humberto Sales. Highlights include film-showing workshops and discussions on moviemaking with limited resources.

May

Possibly the cheapest month of all, May is the low point between the foreign crowds of winter and the domestic barrage of summer. Look out for special deals offered by resort hotels and significantly cheaper prices all round.

Romerías de Mayo

This religious festival takes place in the city of Holguín during the first week of May and culminates with a procession to the top of the city's emblematic Loma de la Cruz, a small shrine atop a 275m hill. (p347)

Cubadisco

An annual get-together of foreign and Cuban record producers and companies, Cubadisco hosts music concerts, a trade fair and a Grammy-style awards ceremony that encompasses every musical genre from chamber music to pop.

Día Internacional Contra Homophobia y Transfobia

Cuba's biggest pride parade has been held in on May 17 since 2008. *Congas* (musical groups) wielding drums, trumpets and rainbow flags fan out along Havana's Calle 23, the climax of a three week LGBTIQ campaign that includes workshops, discussion groups and art expos.

June

The Caribbean hurricane season begins inauspiciously. A smattering of esoteric provincial festivals keeps June interesting. Prices are still low and, with the heat and humidity rising, travelers from Europe and Canada tend to stay away.

Festival Nacional de Changüí

Since 2003, Guantánamo has celebrated its indigenous music in this rootsy music festival held in May or June. Look out for Elio Revé Jr and his orchestra.

Jornada Cucalambeana

Cuba's celebration of country music, and the witty 10-line *décimas* (stanzas) that go with it, takes place about 3km outside unassuming Las Tunas at Motel el Cornito, the former home of erstwhile country-music king, Juan Fajardo 'El Cucalambé.' (p337)

Festival Internacional 'Boleros de Oro'

Organized by Uneac, Cuba's artists and writers union, the Boleros de Oro was created by Cuban composer and musicologist José Loyola Fernández in 1986 as a global celebration of this distinctive Cuban musical genre. Most events take place in Havana's Teatro Mella. (p115)

Fiestas Sanjuaneras

This feisty carnival in Trinidad on the last weekend in June is a showcase for the local *vaqueros* (cowboys), who gallop their horses through the narrow cobbled streets.

July

High summer is when Cubans vacation; expect the beaches, campismos (cheap, rustic accommodation) and cheaper hotels to be mobbed. The July heat also inspires two of the nation's hottest events: Santiago's Carnaval and the annual polemics of July 26.

Festival del Caribe and Fiesta del Fuego

The so-called Festival of Caribbean Culture, Fire Celebration in early July kicks off an action-packed month for Santiago with exhibitions, song, dance, poetry and religious-tinged rituals from all around the Caribbean.

Día de la Rebeldía Nacional

On July 26 Cubans 'celebrate' Fidel Castro's failed 1953 attack on Santiago's Moncada Barracks. The event is a national holiday and a chance for party leaders to deliver bombastic speeches. Expect *un poco* politics and *mucho* eating, drinking and being merry.

Carnaval de Santiago de Cuba

Arguably the biggest and most colorful carnival in the Caribbean, the famous Santiago shindig at the end of July is a riot of floats, dancers, rum, rumba and more. Come and join in the very *caliente* (hot) action.

August

While Santiago retires to sleep off its hangover, Havana gears up for its own annual celebration. Beaches and campismos still heave with holidaying Cubans while tourist hotels creak under a fresh influx of visitors from Mediterranean Europe.

Festival Internacional 'Habana Hip-Hop'

Organized by the Asociación Hermanos Saíz – a youth arm of Uneac – the annual Havana Hip-Hop Festival is a chance for the island's young musical creators to improvise and swap ideas.

Carnaval de la Habana

Parades, dancing, music, colorful costumes and striking effigies – Havana's annual summer shindig might not be as famous as its more rootsy Santiago de Cuba counterpart, but the celebrations and processions along the Malecón leave plenty of other city carnivals in the shade.

September

It's peak hurricane season. The outside threat of a 'big one' sends most Cubaphiles running for cover and tourist numbers hit a second trough. The storm-resistant take advantage of cheaper prices and near-empty beaches. But, beware – some facilities close down completely.

Fiesta de Nuestra Señora de la Caridad

Every September 8, religious devotees from around Cuba partake in a pilgrimage to the Basílica de Nuestra Señora del Cobre, near Santiago, to honor Cuba's venerated patron saint (and her alter ego, the Santería orisha, Ochún). (p424)

October

Continuing storm threats and persistent rain keep all but the most stalwart travelers away until the end of the month. While the solitude can be refreshing in Havana, life in the peripheral resorts can be deathly quiet and lacking in atmosphere.

Festival Internacional de Ballet de la Habana

Hosted by the Cuban National Ballet, this annual festival brings together dance companies, ballerinas and a mixed audience of foreigners and Cubans for a week of expositions, galas, and classical and contemporary ballet. It has been held in even-numbered years since its inception in 1960. (p86)

Festival del Bailador Rumbero

During the 10 days following October 10, Matanzas rediscovers its rumba roots in this festival with talented local musicians performing in the city's Teatro Sauto. (p218)

November

Get ready for the big invasion from the north – and an accompanying hike in hotel rates! Over a quarter of Cuba's tourists come from Canada; they start arriving in early November, as soon as the weather turns frigid in Vancouver and Toronto.

Benny Moré International Music Festival

The Barbarian of Rhythm is remembered in this biannual celebration (odd-numbered years) of his suave music, headquartered in the singer's small birth town of Santa Isabel de las Lajas in Cienfuegos Province. (p241)

Fiesta de los Bandas Rojo y Azul

Considered one of the most important manifestations of Cuban campesino (farmer) culture, this esoteric fiesta in the settlement of Majagua, in Ciego de Ávila Province, splits the town into two teams (red and blue) that compete against each other in boisterous dancing and music contests.

Marabana

The popular Havana marathon draws between 2000 and 3000 competitors from around the globe. It's a two-lap course, though there is also a half-marathon and 5km and 10km races.

Ciudad Metal

Decidedly edgy when it was first established in Santa Clara in 1990, this celebration of hardcore punk and metal sees Cuban bands setting up in the local baseball stadium and quite literally rocking the rafters.

December

Christmas and the New Year see Cuba's busiest and most expensive tourist spike. Resorts nearly double their prices and rooms sell out fast. The nation goes firework-crazy in a handful of riotous festivals. Book ahead!

Festival Internacional del Nuevo Cine Latinoamericano

Widely lauded celebration of Cuba's massive film culture with plenty of nods to other Latin American countries. Held at various cinemas and theaters across the city. (p86)

Festival Internacional de Jazz

The cream of Cuban music festivals arrives every December like a Christmas present. In the past it has attracted the greats, Dizzy Gillespie and Max Roach among them, along with a perfect storm of Cuban talent.

Las Parrandas

A firework frenzy that takes place every Christmas Eve in Remedios in Villa Clara Province, Las Parrandas sees the town divide into two teams that compete against each other to see who can come up with the most colorful floats and the loudest *bangs!* (p267)

Las Charangas de Bejucal

Didn't like Las Parrandas? Then try Bejucal's Las Charangas, Mayabeque Province's cacophonous alternative to the firework fever further east. The town splits into the exotically named *Espino de Oro* (Golden Thorn) and *Ceiba de Plata* (Silver Silk-Cotton Tree).

Procesión de San Lázaro

Every year on December 17, Cubans descend en masse on the venerated Santuario de San Lázaro in Santiago de las Vegas, on the outskirts of Havana. Some come on bloodied knees, others walk barefoot for kilometers to exorcize evil spirits and pay off debts for miracles granted. (p137)

Plan Your Trip
Itineraries

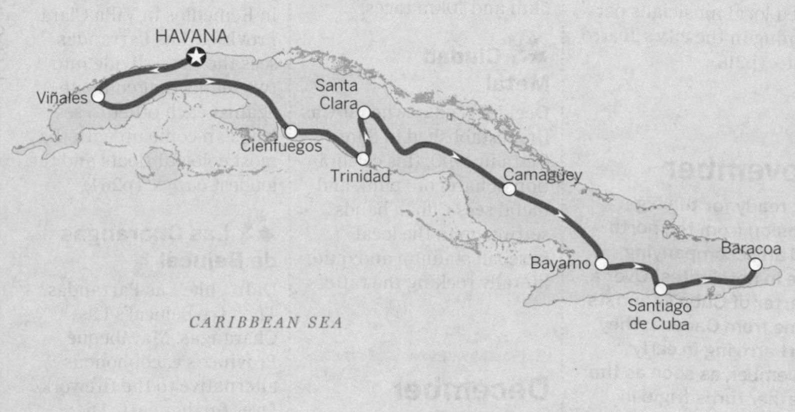

The Classic Itinerary

It's your first time in Cuba and you want to see as many eye-opening sights as possible countrywide. Even better, you don't mind a bit of road travel. This itinerary ferries you between the rival cities of Havana and Santiago, bagging most of the nation's historical highlights on the way. Víazul buses link all of the following destinations.

Fall in love with classic Cuba in **Havana**, with its museums, forts, theaters and rum. Three days is the bare minimum here to get to grips with the main neighborhoods of Habana Vieja, Centro Habana and Vedado.

Head west next to the bucolic bliss of **Viñales** for a couple of days of hiking, caving and relaxing on a rocking chair on a sun-kissed colonial porch. Daily buses connect Viñales with French-flavored **Cienfuegos**, an architectural monument to 19th-century neoclassicism. After a night of Gallic style and Cuban music, travel a couple of hours down the road to colonial **Trinidad**, with more museums per head than anywhere else in Cuba. The

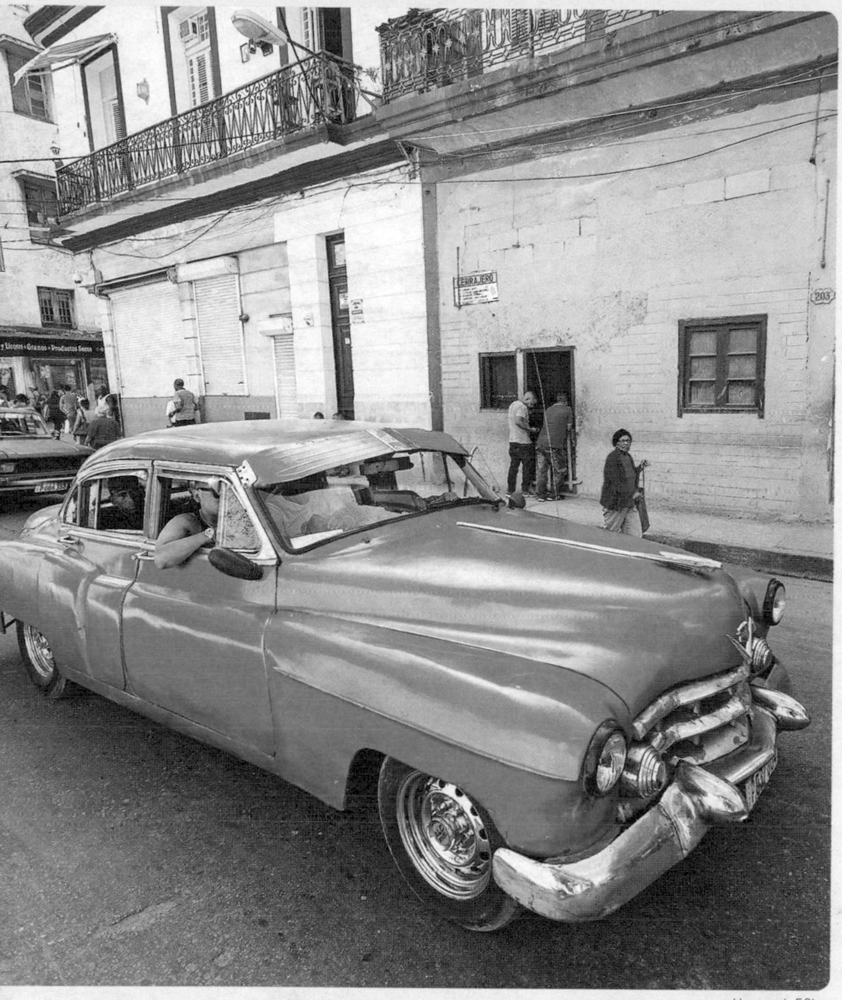

Havana (p58)

casas particulares (homestays) resemble historical monuments here, so stay three nights. On the second day you can break from the history and choose between the beach (Playa Ancón) or the natural world (Topes de Collantes).

Santa Clara is a rite of passage for Che Guevara pilgrims visiting his mausoleum but also a great place for luxurious private rooms and an upbeat nightlife. Check out Club Mejunje and have a drink in dive-bar La Marquesina. Further east, **Camagüey** invites further investigation with its maze of Catholic churches and giant *tinajones* (clay pots).

Laid-back **Bayamo** is where the revolution was ignited, and it has an equally sparky street festival should you be lucky enough to be there on a Saturday. Allow plenty of time for the cultural nexus of **Santiago de Cuba**, where seditious plans for rebellion have been routinely hatched. The Cuartel Moncada, Cementerio Santa Ifigenia and Morro Castle will fill a busy two days.

Save the best till last with a long, but by no means arduous, journey over the hills and far away to **Baracoa** for two days relaxing with the coconuts, chocolate and other tropical treats.

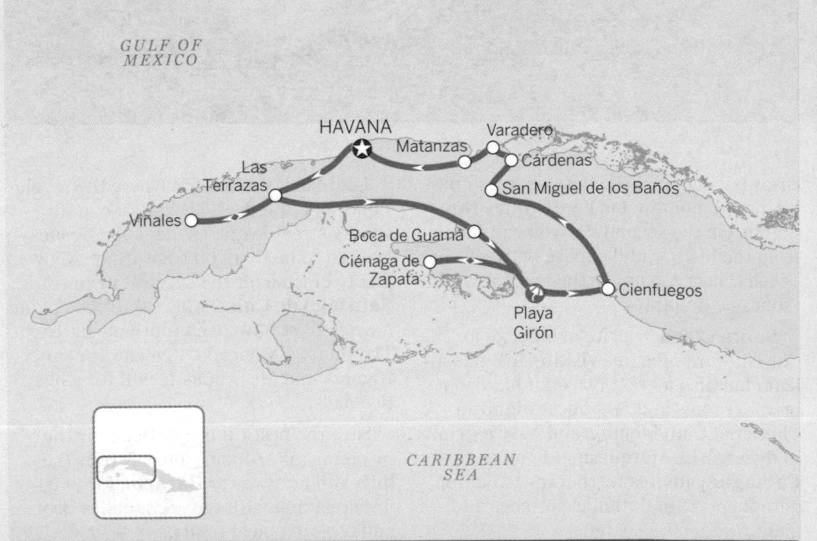
GULF OF MEXICO
HAVANA
Varadero
Matanzas
Cárdenas
Las Terrazas
San Miguel de los Baños
Viñales
Boca de Guamá
Ciénaga de Zapata
Cienfuegos
Playa Girón
CARIBBEAN SEA

Escape from Varadero

Varadero has some cheap packages and is a popular gateway into Cuba, but once you've pacified your partner/kids and had your fill of the beach, what else is there for a curious Cuban adventurer to do? Plenty. Víazul or Conectando buses link the following places.

Take a bus west, stopping off for lunch in **Matanzas**, where Cuban reality will hit you like a sharp slap to the face. Investigate the Museo Farmaceútico, take a peep inside the Teatro Sauto and buy a unique handmade book in Ediciones Vigía. For a slow approach to Havana, get on the Hershey train and watch as the lush fields of Mayabeque Province glide by. Book a night in a fine colonial hotel in **Havana** and spend the next day admiring the copious sights of the old quarter, Habana Vieja. Essential stops include the cathedral, the Museo de la Revolución and a stroll along the Malecón.

The next day, head west to **Las Terrazas**, an eco-resort that seems a million miles from the clamorous capital (it's actually only 55km). You can bathe and birdwatch at the same time in the Baños del San Juan and recuperate with a night in the Hotel Moka. An optional two-day extension of this itinerary lies further west in **Viñales**, a resplendent yet bucolic Unesco World Heritage Site where you can decamp to a casa particular, eat some of the best roast pork in Cuba (the world?), go for a hike and then slump into a rocking chair on a rustic colonial porch.

Going back east, keep on the green theme in **Boca de Guamá**, a reconstructed Taíno village and crocodile farm with boat trips to and around a tranquil lake. Procure a night or two of accommodations at a homestay in **Playa Girón**, where you can either dive or plan wildlife forays into the **Ciénaga de Zapata**. A couple of hours east lies the city of **Cienfuegos**, an elegant last stopover with fine boutique hotels and sunset cruises on the bay.

On the leg back to Varadero you can uncover a dustier, time-warped Cuba in half-ruined **San Miguel de los Baños** back in Matanzas Province, an erstwhile spa that harbors a grand abandoned hotel. Last stop before returning to your Varadero sunbed is **Cárdenas**, home to three superb museums.

Top: Beachfront hotel, Punta Gorda (p239)
Bottom: Eco-village, Las Terrazas (p151)

12 DAYS Around the Oriente

The Oriente is like another country; they do things differently here, or so they'll tell you in Havana. This circuit allows you to bypass the Cuban capital and focus exclusively on the culturally rich, fiercely independent eastern region. With poor transport links, a hire car is useful here.

Make your base in **Santiago de Cuba**, city of revolutionaries, culture and *folklórico* dance troupes. There's tons to do here pertaining to history (Morro Castle), music (Cuba's original Casa de la Trova) and religion (Basílica de Nuestra Señora del Cobre). On the second day, reserve time to explore east into the Parque Bacanao and the ruined coffee farms around **Gran Piedra**.

Regular buses travel east into the mountains of Guantánamo Province. Pass a night in **Guantánamo** to suss out the *changüí* music before climbing the spectacular road La Farola into **Baracoa**, where three days will bag you the highlights – beach time at Playa Maguana, a sortie into the Parque Nacional Alejandro de Humboldt and a day absorbing the psychedelic rhythms of the town itself.

Heading north via Moa is a tough jaunt, with taxis or rental cars required to get you to **Cayo Saetía**, an isolated key with an on-site hotel where lonesome beaches embellish a former hunting reserve.

Pinares del Mayarí sits in the pine-clad mountains of the Sierra Crystal amid huge waterfalls and rare flora. Hiking married with some rural relaxation seal the deal at the region's eponymous hotel. If you have half a day to spare, consider a side trip to **Museo Conjunto Histórico de Birán** to see the surprisingly affluent farming community that spawned Fidel Castro.

Take a day off in hassle-free **Bayamo** with its smattering of small-town museums before tackling **Manzanillo**, where Saturday night in the main square can get feisty. More-adventurous transport options will lead you down to Niquero and within striking distance of the largely deserted **Parque Nacional Desembarco del Granma**, famous for uplifted marine terraces and aboriginal remains. Linger in one of **Marea del Portillo's** low-key resorts before attempting the spectacular but potholed coast road back to Santiago.

Top: Castillo de San Pedro de la Roca del Morro (p402), Santiago de Cuba
Bottom: Casa Natal de Carlos Manuel de Céspedes (p373), Bayamo

STRAITS OF FLORIDA
Museo Conjunto Histórico de Birán
Pinares de Mayarí
Cayo Saetía
Manzanillo
Bayamo
Baracoa
Guantánamo
Gran Piedra
Santiago de Cuba
Parque Nacional Desembarco del Granma
Marea del Portillo
CARIBBEAN SEA

Cuba: Off the Beaten Track

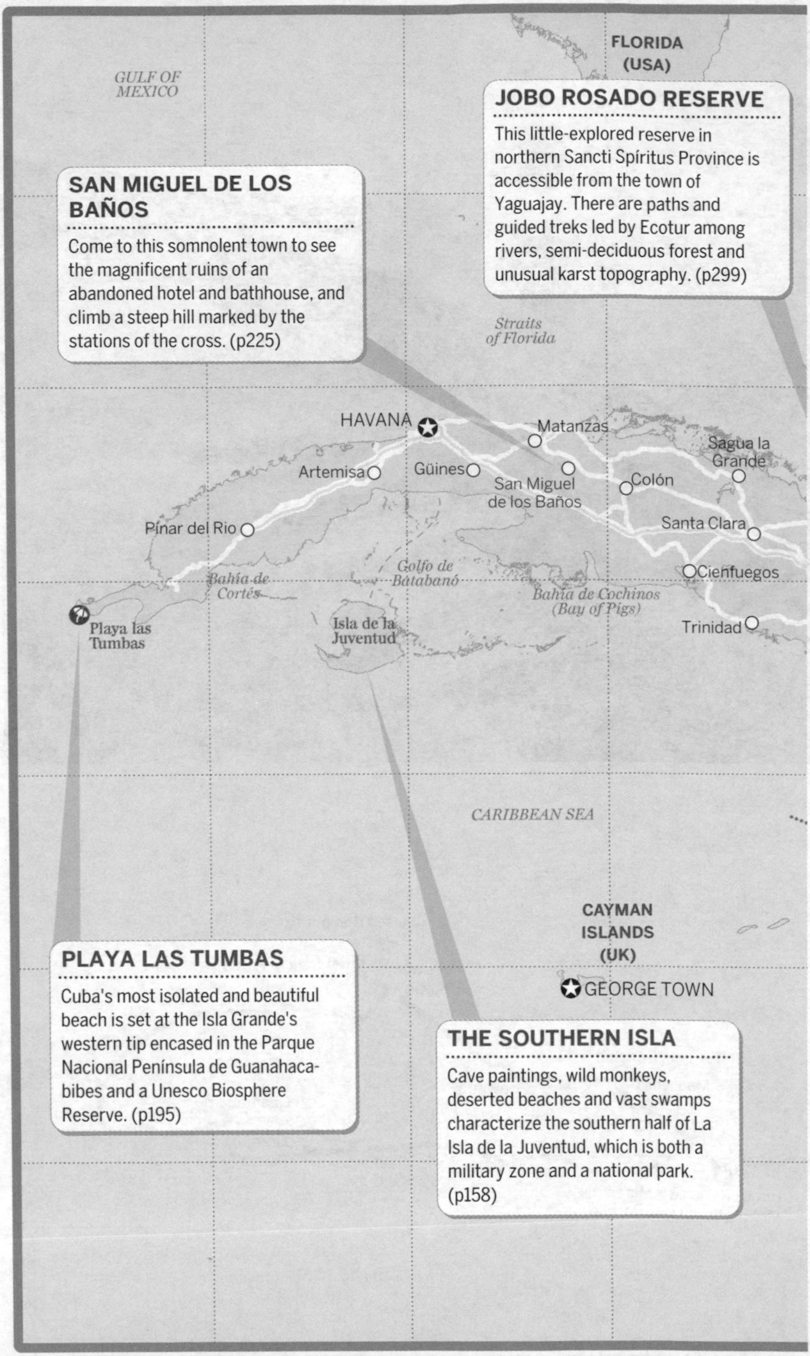

JOBO ROSADO RESERVE

This little-explored reserve in northern Sancti Spíritus Province is accessible from the town of Yaguajay. There are paths and guided treks led by Ecotur among rivers, semi-deciduous forest and unusual karst topography. (p299)

SAN MIGUEL DE LOS BAÑOS

Come to this somnolent town to see the magnificent ruins of an abandoned hotel and bathhouse, and climb a steep hill marked by the stations of the cross. (p225)

PLAYA LAS TUMBAS

Cuba's most isolated and beautiful beach is set at the Isla Grande's western tip encased in the Parque Nacional Península de Guanahacabibes and a Unesco Biosphere Reserve. (p195)

THE SOUTHERN ISLA

Cave paintings, wild monkeys, deserted beaches and vast swamps characterize the southern half of La Isla de la Juventud, which is both a military zone and a national park. (p158)

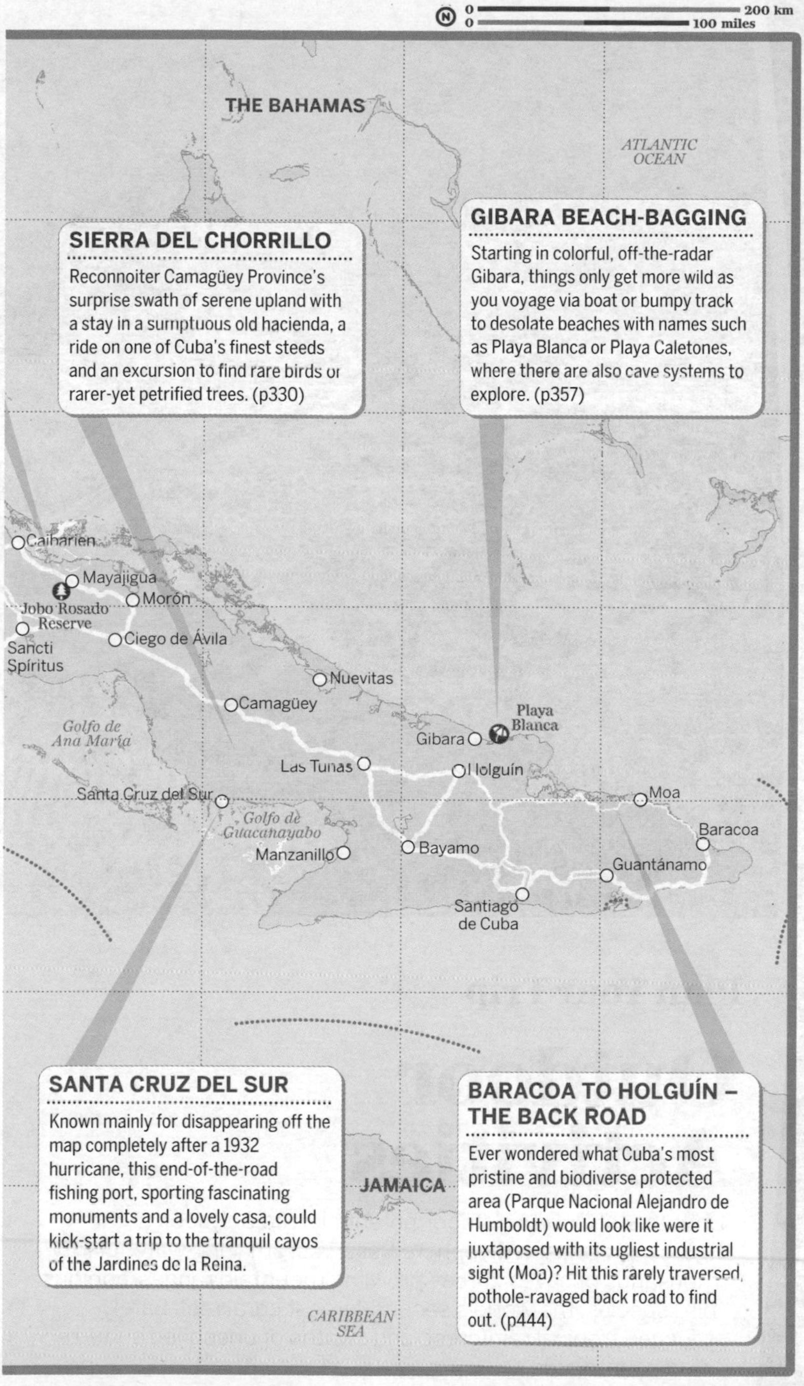

SIERRA DEL CHORRILLO

Reconnoiter Camagüey Province's surprise swath of serene upland with a stay in a sumptuous old hacienda, a ride on one of Cuba's finest steeds and an excursion to find rare birds or rarer-yet petrified trees. (p330)

GIBARA BEACH-BAGGING

Starting in colorful, off-the-radar Gibara, things only get more wild as you voyage via boat or bumpy track to desolate beaches with names such as Playa Blanca or Playa Caletones, where there are also cave systems to explore. (p357)

SANTA CRUZ DEL SUR

Known mainly for disappearing off the map completely after a 1932 hurricane, this end-of-the-road fishing port, sporting fascinating monuments and a lovely casa, could kick-start a trip to the tranquil cayos of the Jardines de la Reina.

BARACOA TO HOLGUÍN – THE BACK ROAD

Ever wondered what Cuba's most pristine and biodiverse protected area (Parque Nacional Alejandro de Humboldt) would look like were it juxtaposed with its ugliest industrial sight (Moa)? Hit this rarely traversed, pothole-ravaged back road to find out. (p444)

Diving, Jardines de la Reina (p310)

Plan Your Trip

Outdoor Activities

Doubters of Cuba's outdoor potential need only look at the figures: six Unesco Biosphere Reserves, amazing water clarity, thousands of caves, three sprawling mountain ranges, copious bird species, the world's second-largest coral reef, barely touched tropical rainforest, and swaths of unspoiled suburb-free countryside.

XAVIER XAFONT/VWPICS/ALAMY ©

Helpful Tips

Accessibility

Access to many parks and protected areas in Cuba is limited and can only be negotiated with a prearranged guide or on an organized excursion. If in doubt, consult **Ecotur** (☎7-273-1542; www.ecoturcuba.tur.cu) travel agency.

Private Guides

Since the loosening of economic restrictions in 2011, it has become legal for private individuals to set up as outdoor guides in Cuba, though, as yet, there are few full-blown non-government travel agencies. Most private guides operate out of casas particulares or hotels and many are very good. If you are unsure whether your guide is official, ask to see their government-issued license first.

Prebooking Tours

The following agencies organize outdoor tours from outside Cuba:

Scuba en Cuba (www.scuba-en-cuba.com) Diving trips.

Exodus (www.exodus.co.uk) Offers a 15-day walking trip.

WowCuba (www.wowcuba.com) Specializes in cycling trips.

Outdoor Opportunities

Travelers in search of adventure who've already warmed up on rum, cigars and all-night salsa dancing won't get bored in Cuba. Hit the highway on a bike, fish (as well as drink) like Hemingway, hike on guerrilla trails, jump out of an airplane or rediscover a sunken Spanish shipwreck off the shimmering south coast.

Thanks to the dearth of modern development, Cuba's outdoors is refreshingly green and free of the smog-filled highways and ugly suburban sprawl that infect many other countries.

While not on a par with North America or Europe in terms of leisure options, Cuba's facilities are well established and improving. Services and infrastructure vary depending on what activity you are looking for. The country's diving centers are generally excellent and instructors are of an international caliber. Naturalists and ornithologists in the various national parks and flora and fauna reserves are similarly conscientious and well qualified. Hiking has traditionally been limited and frustratingly rule-ridden, but opportunities have expanded in recent years, with companies such as Ecotur offering a wider variety of hikes in previously untrodden areas and even some multiday trekking. Cycling is refreshingly DIY, and all the better for it. Canyoning and climbing are new sports in Cuba that have a lot of local support but little official backing – as yet.

It's possible to hire reasonable outdoor gear in Cuba for most of the activities you will do, although it may not always be top quality. If you do bring your own supplies, any gear donated at the end of your trip to individuals you meet along the way (head lamps, snorkel masks, fins etc) will be greatly appreciated.

Boating & Kayaking

Boat rental is available on many of the island's lakes. Good options include the Laguna de la Leche, Laguna la Redonda and the Liberación de Florencia, in Ciego de Ávila Province, and Embalse Zaza in Sancti Spíritus Province. You can also rent rowboats and head up the Río Canímar near Matanzas, oaring between the jungle-covered banks of this mini-Amazon.

Kayaking as a sport is pretty low-key in Cuba, treated more as a beach activity in the plusher resorts. Most of the tourist beaches will have Náutica points that rent out simple kayaks, good for splashing around in but not a lot else.

Diving

If Cuba has a blue-ribbon activity, it is scuba diving. Even Fidel in his younger days liked to don a wetsuit and escape beneath the iridescent waters of the Atlantic or Caribbean (his favorite dive site was – apparently – the rarely visited Jardines de la Reina archipelago). Indeed, so famous was the Cuban leader's diving addiction that the CIA allegedly once considered an assassination plot that involved inserting an explosive device inside a conch and placing it on the seabed.

Excellent dive sites are numerous in Cuba. Focus on the area or areas where you want to dive rather than trying to cover multiple sites. The best areas – the Jardines de la Reina, María la Gorda and the Isla de la Juventud – are all fairly isolated, requiring travel time (and pre-planning). The more sheltered south coast, in particular Playa Girón, has the edge in terms of water clarity and dependable weather, though the north coast, offering easy access to one of the world's largest reefs, is no slouch.

What makes diving in Cuba special is its unpolluted ocean, clear water conditions (average underwater visibility is 30m to 40m), warm seas (mean temperature is 24°C), abundant coral and fish, simple access (including a couple of excellent swim-out reefs) and fascinating shipwrecks (Cuba was a nexus for weighty galleons in the 17th and 18th centuries, and rough seas and skirmishes with pirates sunk many of them).

USEFUL AGENCIES

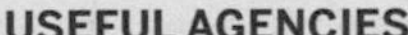

Ecotur (www.ecoturcuba.tur.cu) Runs organized hiking, trekking, fishing and birdwatching trips to some of the country's otherwise inaccessible corners. It has offices in every province and a main HQ (p120) in Havana.

Campismo Popular (www.campismopopular.cu) Runs Cuba's 80-plus campismos (rural chalets). It has Reservaciones de Campismo offices in every provincial capital.

Marlin Náutica y Marinas (www.nauticamarlin.tur.cu) State-run company that oversees many of Cuba's marinas. It also offers fishing, diving, boating and other water-based excursions.

Snorkeling, Bahía de Cochinos (p231)

Snorkeling

You don't have to go deep to enjoy Cuba's tropical aquarium. Snorkelers can glide out from the shore at Playa Girón in the Bay of Pigs, or Playa Coral and Playa Jibacoa on the north coast east of Havana. Otherwise, most dive operators can also organize snorkeling for cheaper rates.

Good boat dives for snorkeling happen around Isla de la Juventud and Cayo Largo especially, but also in Varadero and in the Cienfuegos and Guajimico areas. If you intend to do a lot of snorkeling, bring your own gear, as the rental stuff can be tattered and buying it in Cuba will mean you'll sacrifice both price and quality.

Fishing

Deep-Sea Fishing

Hemingway wasn't wrong. Cuba's fast-moving Gulf Stream along the north coast supports prime game fishing for sailfish, tuna, mackerel, swordfish, barracuda, marlin and shark pretty much year-round.

Beach, Varadero (p200)

Deep-sea fishing is a rite of passage for many and a great way to wind down, make friends, drink beer, watch sunsets and generally leave the troubles of the world behind. Not surprisingly, the country has great facilities for sport anglers, and every Cuban boat captain seems to look and talk as if he's walked straight from the pages of a Hemingway classic.

Cuba's best deep-sea fishing center is Cayo Guillermo, the small island (then uninhabited) that featured in Hemingway's *Islands in the Stream*. Papa may no longer be in residence, but there's still an abundance of fish. Another good bet is Havana, which has two marinas, one at Tarará and the other – better one – at Marina Hemingway to the west.

Elsewhere, all of Cuba's main resort areas offer deep-sea-fishing excursions for similar rates. Count on paying approximately CUC$310 per half-day for four people, including crew and open bar.

Fly-Fishing

Fly-fishing is undertaken mainly on shallow sand flats easily reached from the shoreline. Classic areas to throw a line are Las Salinas in the Ciénaga de Zapata, the protected waters surrounding Cayo Largo del Sur, parts of the Isla de la Juventud and – most notably – the uninhabited nirvana of the Jardines de la Reina archipelago. The archipelago is a national park and heavily protected. It is not unheard of to catch 25 different species of fish in the same day here.

A 'grand slam' for fly-fishers in Cuba is to bag tarpon, bonefish and permit in the same day; bag a snook as well and they call it a 'superslam.' The best fishing season in this part of Cuba is February to June. The remoteness of the many islands, reefs and sand flats means fishing trips are usually organized on boats that offer on-board accommodations. They are coordinated through a company called **Avalon** (www.cubandivingcenters.com).

The north coast hides a couple of good fly-fishing havens. Most noted are the still-uninhabited keys of Cayo Romano and Cayo Cruz in the north of Camagüey Province. Trips are coordinated by Avalon and based at an attractive lodge in the mainland town of Brasil.

ROSTISLAV AGEEV/SHUTTERSTOCK ©

Freshwater Fishing

Freshwater fishing in Cuba is lesser known than fly-fishing but equally rewarding, and many Americans and Canadians home in on the island's numerous lakes. Freshwater fly-fishing is superb in the vast Ciénaga de Zapata in Matanzas, where enthusiasts can arrange multiday catch-and-release trips. *Trucha* (largemouth bass) was first introduced into Cuba in the early 20th century by Americans at King's Ranch and the United Fruit Company. Due to favorable environmental protection, the fish are now abundant in many Cuban lakes. Good places to cast a line are the Laguna del Tesoro in Matanzas, the Laguna de la Leche and Laguna la Redonda in Ciego de Ávila Province, Embalse Zaza in Sancti Spíritus and Embalse Hanabanilla in Villa Clara – 7.6kg specimens have been caught here!

Kitesurfing

With stiff east-northeast winds fanning its jagged northern coastline, it was only a matter of time before the Cubans (and visiting tourists) woke up to the country's excellent kiteboarding potential. The sport is still relatively new in Cuba, although several good operators have now established themselves at various points along the north coast, offering equipment rental and courses. The main kitesurfing hubs are Havana (more specifically Tarará), Varadero and Cayo Guillermo. There are also small scenes at Playa Santa Lucía and Guardalavaca. Havana Kiteboarding Club (p139) maintains operations in Havana, Cayo Guillermo and Guardalavaca. Ke Bola Kiteboarding School (p202) is based in Varadero. There are several other multilingual operators at both sites.

DIVING CENTERS

In all, Cuba has 25 recognized diving centers spread over 17 different areas. The majority of the centers are managed by Marlin Náutica y Marinas (www.nauticamarlin.com), though you'll also find representation from **Gaviota** (☎7-204-5708; www.gaviota-grupo.com). Though equipment does vary between installations, you can generally expect safe, professional service with back-up medical support. Environmentally sensitive diving is where things can get wobbly, and individuals should educate themselves about responsible diving. As well as being Scuba Schools International (SSI), American Canadian Underwater Certification (ACUC) and Confédération Mondiale de Activités Subaquatiques (CMAS) certified, most dive instructors are multilingual, speaking a variety of Spanish, English, French, German and Italian. Because of US embargo laws, Professional Association of Diving Instructors (PADI) certification is generally not offered in Cuba.

Dives and courses are comparably priced island-wide, from CUC$25 to CUC$50 per dive, with a discount after four or five dives. Full certification courses are CUC$310 to CUC$365, and 'resort' or introductory dives cost CUC$50 to CUC$60.

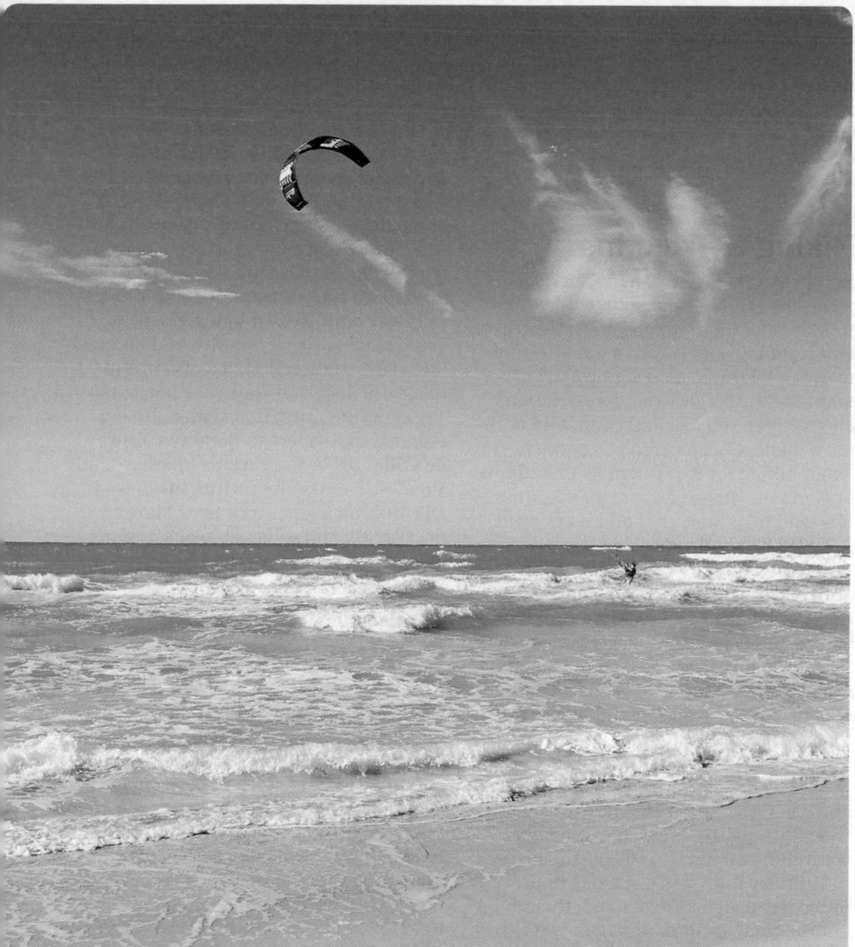

Top: Kitesurfing, Varadero (p200)

Bottom: Fishing, Baracoa (p437)

MATYAS REHAK/SHUTTERSTOCK ©

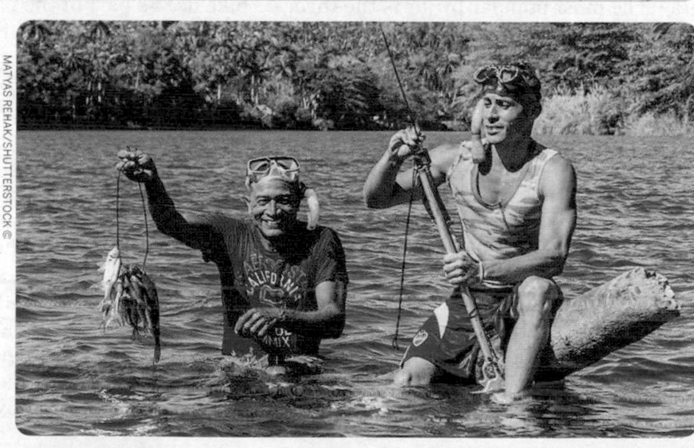

Three-hour basic courses cost from around CUC$150, and equipment rental starts at CUC$35 an hour, but there are various offers available. Kite operators can also help arrange accommodation packages at various beach-side hotels. Check the websites.

Hiking & Trekking

European hikers and North American wilderness freaks take note: while Cuba's trekking potential is enormous, the traveler's right to roam is restricted by badly maintained trails, poor signage, a lack of maps and rather draconian restrictions about where you can and cannot go without a guide. Cubans aren't as enthusiastic about hiking for enjoyment as Canadians or Germans. Instead, many park authorities tend to assume that all hikers want to be led by hand along short, relatively tame trails that are rarely more than 5km or 6km in length. You'll frequently be told that hiking alone is a reckless and dangerous activity, despite the fact that Cuba harbors no big fauna and no poisonous snakes. The best time of year for hiking is outside the rainy season and before it gets too hot (December to April).

The dearth of available hikes isn't always the result of nitpicking restrictions. Much of Cuba's trekkable terrain is in ecologically sensitive areas, meaning access is carefully managed and controlled.

Multiday hiking in Cuba has improved in the last couple of years and, though information is still hard to get, you can piece together workable options in the Sierra Maestra and the Sierra del Escambray. The most popular by far is the three-day trek to the summit of Pico Turquino. There are also long day hikes available in the forests around Soroa in Artemisa Province.

More challenging day hikes include El Yunque, a mountain near Baracoa; the Balcón de Iberia circuit in Parque Nacional Alejandro de Humboldt; and some of the hikes around Las Terrazas and Viñales.

Topes de Collantes probably has the largest concentration of hiking trails in its protected zone (a natural park). Indeed, some overseas groups organize four- to five-day treks here, starting near Lago Hanabanilla and finishing in Parque el Cubano. Inquire in advance at the Carpeta Central information office in Topes de Collantes if you are keen to organize something on behalf of a group.

Other, tamer hikes include Cueva las Perlas and Del Bosque al Mar in the Península de Guanahacabibes, the El Guafe trail in Parque Nacional Desembarco del Granma and the short circuit in Reserva Ecológica Varahicacos in Varadero. Some of these hikes are guided and all require the payment of an entry fee.

If you want to hike independently, you'll need patience, resolve and an excellent sense of direction. It's also useful to ask the locals in your casa particular. Try experimenting first with Salto del Caburní or Sendero la Batata in Topes de Collantes or the various hikes around Viñales. There's a beautiful, little-used DIY hike on a good trail near Marea del Portillo and some gorgeous options around Baracoa – ask the locals!

Cycling

Riding a bike in Cuba is *the* best way to discover the island in close-up. Decent, quiet roads, wonderful scenery and the opportunity to get off the beaten track and meet Cubans in rural areas make cycling here a pleasure, whichever route you take. For casual pedalers, daily bike rental is sometimes available and has become more widespread in recent years. Some hotels lend or rent bikes for about CUC$3 to CUC$7 per day. The bigger all-inclusive resorts in Varadero and Guardalavaca are the best bet as they sometimes include bike use as part of the package, although it's unlikely the bikes will have gears. If you're staying in a casa particular, your host will generally be able to rustle up something roadworthy. Some casa owners have even started renting out foreign-made bikes good enough for tackling rural day trips (bank on paying CUC$10 to CUC$15 a day).

Serious cyclists contemplating a multi-day Cuban cycling tour should bring their own bikes from home, along with plenty of spare parts. Since organized bike trips have long been common in Cuba, customs officials, taxi drivers and hotel staff are used to dealing with boxed bikes.

Cycling, Trinidad (p277)

Cycling highlights include the Valle de Viñales, the countryside around Trinidad, including the flat spin down to Playa Ancón, the quiet lanes that zigzag through Guardalavaca, and the roads out of Baracoa to Playa Maguana (northwest) and Boca de Yumurí (southeast). For a bigger challenge try La Farola between Cajobabo and Baracoa (21km of ascent), the bumpy but spectacular coast road between Santiago and Marea del Portillo – best spread over three days with overnights in Brisas Sierra Mar los Galeones and Campismo la Mula – or, for real wheel warriors, the insanely steep mountain road from Bartolomé Masó to Santo Domingo in Granma Province. For good private cycling tours around Havana and its environs, try CubaRuta Bikes (p87).

With a profusion of casas particulares offering cheap, readily available accommodation, cycle touring is a joy here as long as you keep off the Autopista and steer clear of Havana.

Off-road biking has not yet taken off in Cuba and is generally not permitted.

Horseback Riding

Cuba has a long-standing cowboy culture, and horseback riding is available countrywide in both official and unofficial capacities. If you arrange it privately, make sure you check the state of the horses and equipment first. Riding poorly kept horses is both cruel and potentially dangerous.

The state-owned catering company Palmares owns numerous rustic ranches across Cuba that are supposed to give tourists a feel for traditional country life. All of these places offer guided horseback riding, usually for around CUC$6 per hour. You'll find good ranchos in Florencia in Ciego de Ávila Province and Hacienda la Belén (p330) in Camagüey Province. Rancho la Guabina (p195) is a horse-breeding center near the city of Pinar del Río that offers both horse shows and horseback-riding adventures.

Trinidad and Viñales are two of the best and most popular places in Cuba for horse-riding.

Rock climbing, Viñales (p176)

Rock Climbing

The Valle de Viñales has been described as having the best rock climbing in the western hemisphere. There are more than 150 routes now open (at all levels of difficulty, with several rated as YDS Class 5.14) and the word is out among the climbing crowd, who are creating their own scene in one of Cuba's prettiest settings. Independent travelers will appreciate the free rein that climbers enjoy here.

Though you can climb year-round, the heat can be oppressive, and locals stick to an October–April season, with December to January being the optimum months. For more information, visit Cuba Climbing (www.cubaclimbing.com) or head straight to Viñales. It is important to note that, though widely practiced and normally without consequence, climbing in the Valle de Viñales is still not technically legal. While you're unlikely to get arrested or even warned, you undertake climbing activities at your own risk. Take extreme care and do not under any circumstances do anything that damages the delicate Parque Nacional Viñales ecosystem.

Caving

The karst landscapes of Cuba are riddled with caves – more than 20,000 and counting – and cave exploration is available to both casual tourists and professional speleologists.

The Gran Caverna de Santo Tomás (p183), near Viñales, is Cuba's largest cavern, with over 46km of galleries, and offers guided tours. The Cueva de los Peces (p232), near Playa Girón, is a flooded *cenote* (sinkhole) with colorful snorkeling. The Cuevas de Bellamar (p214) near Matanzas also has daily tours, while the bat-filled Cueva de Ambrosio (p201) in Varadero can be explored independently.

Caving specialists have virtually unlimited caves from which to choose. With advance arrangements, you can explore deep into the Gran Caverna de Santo Tomás or visit the Cueva Martín Infierno in Cienfuegos Province which has the world's largest stalagmite. The Cueva San Catalina, near Varadero, is famous for its unique mushroom formations.

Speleo-diving is also possible, but only for those already highly trained.

Plan Your Trip

Travel with Children

Cubans love kids and kids invariably love Cuba. Welcome to a culture where children still play freely in the street and waitstaff unconsciously ruffle your toddler's hair as they glide past your table on their way back to the kitchen. There's something wonderfully old-fashioned about kids' entertainment here, which is less about sophisticated computer games and more about messing around in the plaza with an improvised baseball bat and a rolled-up ball of plastic.

Cuba for Kids

There are certain dichotomies regarding child facilities in Cuba. On the one hand Cuban society is innately family-friendly, child-loving and tactile; on the other, economic challenges have meant that common 'Western' provisions such as pushchair ramps, changing tables and basic safety measures are often thin on the ground. The one place where you'll find generic international standards of service is in the modern resorts, most of which have dedicated and professionally run 'kids clubs.'

Children's Highlights

Forts & Castles

➡ **Fortaleza de San Carlos de la Cabaña** (p75) Havana's huge fort has museums, battlements and a nightly cannon ceremony with soldiers in period costume.

➡ **Castillo de San Pedro de la Roca del Morro** (p402) Santiago's Unesco-listed fort is best known for its exciting pirate museum.

Best Regions for Kids

Havana

The streets of Habana Vieja can't have changed much since the days of the *Pirates of the Caribbean*, so your kids' imaginations will be allowed to run wild in forts, squares, museums and narrow streets. Havana also has Cuba's largest amusement park (Isla del Coco), and its best aquarium (Acuario Nacional).

Varadero

Cuba's biggest resort has the largest – if most predictable – stash of specifically tailored kids' activities, including nighttime shows, organized sports, beach games and boat trips.

Trinidad

The south coast's southern gem is awash with economic casas particulares, an ideal opportunity for your kids to mix and mingle with Cuban families. Throw in an excellent beach (Playa Ancón), easily accessible snorkeling waters and a profusion of pleasant pastoral activities (horseback riding is popular) and you've got the perfect nonresort family option.

➡ **Castillo de la Real Fuerza** (p65) This centrally located Havana fort has a moat, lookouts and scale models of Spanish galleons.

Playgrounds

➡ **Parque Maestranza** (p63) Bouncy castles, fairground rides and sweet snacks overlooking Havana Harbor.

➡ **Isla del Coco** (p128) Huge, newish, Chinese-funded amusement park in Havana's Playa neighborhood.

➡ **Parque Lenin** (p137) More 'rustic' playground rides, boats, a minitrain and horses for rent in Havana.

Animal Encounters

➡ **Acuario Nacional** (p127) Various reproductions of Cuba's coastal ecosystems including a marine cave and a mangrove forest at the nation's main aquarium in Havana's Miramar district.

➡ **Criadero de Cocodrilos** (p423) Of the half-dozen croc farms spread across the country, the best is in Guamá, Matanzas Province.

➡ **Horseback riding** Possible all over Cuba and usually run out of rustic *fincas* (farms) in rural areas such as Pinar del Río and Trinidad.

Festivals

➡ **Las Parrandas** Fireworks, smoke and huge animated floats: Remedios' Christmas Eve party is a blast for kids *and* adults.

➡ **Carnaval de Santiago de Cuba** A colorful celebration of Caribbean culture with floats and dancing that takes place every July.

➡ **Carnaval de la Habana** More music, dancing and effigies, this time along Havana's Malecón in August.

Planning

Travelers with kids are not unusual in Cuba and the trend has proliferated in recent years with more Cuban-Americans visiting their families with offspring in tow; these will be your best sources for on-the-ground information. Be forewarned that physical contact and human warmth are so typically Cuban: strangers will effusively welcome your kids, give them kisses or take their hands with regularity. Chill, it's all part of the Cuban way.

Local children run around freely in Cuba and, with strong local community organizations, the safety of your child shouldn't be a problem as long as you take normal precautions. Be careful with the unforgiving motorized traffic, watch for unprotected roadworks and be aware of the general lack of modern safety equipment.

Your kids shouldn't need any specific pre-trip inoculations for Cuba, though you should check with your doctor about individual requirements before departing. Medicines are in short supply in Cuba, so take all you think you might need. Useful supplies include acetaminophen, ibuprofen, antinausea medicines and cough drops. Insect repellent is also helpful in lowland areas. Diapers and baby formula can be hard to find; bring your own. A copy of your child's birth certificate containing the names of both parents could also prove useful, especially if you have different surnames.

Car seats are not mandatory in Cuba, and taxi and rental-car firms don't carry them. Bring your own if you're planning on renting a car. High chairs in restaurants are also almost nonexistent, though waiters will try to improvise. The same goes for travel cribs. Cuba's pavements weren't designed with strollers in mind. If your child is small enough, carry him/her in a body harness.

Casas particulares are nearly always happy to accommodate families and are exceptionally child-friendly. Resort hotels are family-friendly too.

Dining

With a dearth of exotic spices and an emphasis on good, plain food, kids in Cuba are often surprisingly well accommodated. The family-oriented nature of life on the island certainly helps. Few eating establishments turn away children, and waiters and waitresses in most cafes and restaurants will, more often than not, dote on your boisterous young offspring and go out of their way to try to accommodate tastes. Rice and beans are good staples, and chicken and fish are relatively reliable sources of protein. The main absent food group – though your kid probably won't think so – is a regular supply of fresh vegetables.

Regions at a Glance

Cuba's provinces are splayed end to end across the main island, with the oft-forgotten comma of Isla de la Juventud hanging off the bottom. All of them have coast access and are embellished with beautiful beaches, the best hugging the north coast. Equally ubiquitous are the vivid snippets of history, impressive colonial architecture and potent reminders of the 1959 revolution. The country's highest mountain range, the Sierra Maestra, rises in the east with another significant range, the Sierra del Escambray, positioned south-central. Cuba's main wilderness areas are the Zapata swamps, the marine terraces of Granma, the tropical forests of Guantánamo and the uninhabited (for now) northern keys. Urban highlights include Havana, Santiago de Cuba, Camagüey and colonial Trinidad.

Havana

Museums
Architecture
Nightlife

Museos Históricos

The capital's 4-sq-km historic center has history wherever you look and museums dedicated to everything from chocolate to Simón Bolívar. Kick off with the Museo de la Revolución, garner more cultural immersion in the Museo de la Ciudad and schedule at least half a day for the fine Museo Nacional de Bellas Artes.

Eclectic Architecture

Havana's architecture is not unlike its flora and fauna: hard to categorize and sometimes a little, well, weird. Stroll the streets of Habana Vieja and Centro Havana and choose your own highlights.

Life is a Cabaret

Every Cuban music style is represented in Havana, from street rumba to glitzy cabaret, making it the best place in the country for live concerts, spontaneous busking and racy nightlife.

p58

Artemisa & Mayabeque Provinces

Beaches
Ecotourism
Coffee Ruins

Secret Beaches

Considering it's stuck on the main highway between Havana and Varadero, Mayabeque Province has its own unheralded and rather delightful beaches, spearheaded by Playa Jibacoa. Get there quick before the (planned) golf courses start springing up.

Small Footprints

The stark white eco-village of Las Terrazas was practicing environmentally friendly living long before the urgency of the Special Period or the adoption of eco-practices in the world outside. Today it carries on much as it has always done: quietly, confidently and – above all – sustainably.

Plantation Past

Las Terrazas has dozens of plantations, half-covered by encroaching jungle, while Artemisa has its own Antiguo Cafetal Angerona, a more refined, but no-less-weathered ruin that once functioned as a coffee plantation employing 450 slaves.

p144

Isla de la Juventud (Special Municipality)

Diving
Wildlife
History

Into the Blue

Outside the hard-to-access Jardines de la Reina archipelago, La Isla offers the best diving in Cuba and is the main reason many people come here. Ultra-clear water, abundant sea life and a protected marine park at Punta Francés are the high points.

Rejuvenated Fauna

If you missed it in the Ciénaga de Zapata, La Isla is the only other place in the world where you can view the Cuban crocodile in its natural state. It has been successfully reintroduced into the Lanier Swamps.

Cuba's Alcatraz

Not one but two of Cuba's verbose spokesmen were once imprisoned on the archipelago's largest outlying island that also doubled as a big jail: José Martí and Fidel Castro. Their former incarceration sites are riddled with historical significance.

p158

Valle de Viñales & Pinar del Río Province

Diving
Food
Flora & Fauna

Diver's Dream

Isolated at the westernmost tip of the main island, María la Gorda has long lured travelers for its spectacular diving, enhanced by electrically colored coral, huge sponges and gorgonians, and a knowledgeable but laid-back dive community.

Roast Pork

There's nothing like a true Cuban pork roast and there's no place better to try it than among the *guajiros* (country folk) of Viñales who offer up humongous portions of the national dish with trimmings of rice, beans and root vegetables.

Parks of Pinar

With more protected land than any other province, Pinar is a green paradise. Go hiking in Parque Nacional Viñales, spot a sea turtle in Parque Nacional Península de Guanahacabibes or train your binoculars on the feathered action around Cueva de los Portales.

p173

Varadero & Matanzas Province

Diving
Flora & Fauna
Beaches

Accessible Aquatics

Bahía de Cochinos (Bay of Pigs) might not have Cuba's best diving, but it certainly has its most accessible. You can glide off from the shore here and be gawping at coral-encrusted drop-off walls within a few strokes.

Swamp Life

In contrast to the resort frenzy on the north coast, Matanzas' southern underbelly is one of Cuba's last true wildernesses and an important refuge for wildlife, including Cuban crocodiles, manatees, bee hummingbirds and tree rats.

Sands of Varadero

Even if you hate resorts, there's still one reason to go to Varadero – an unbroken 20km ribbon of golden sand that stretches the whole length of the Península de Hicacos. It's arguably the longest and finest beach in Cuba.

p198

Cienfuegos Province

Architecture
Music
Diving

French Classicism

Despite its position as one of Cuba's newer cities, founded in 1819, Cienfuegos retains a remarkably homogenous urban core full of classical facades and slender columns that carry the essence of 19th-century France, where it drew its inspiration.

Benny Moré Trail

Benny Moré, Cuba's most adaptable and diverse musician, who ruled the clubs and dance halls in the 1940s and '50s, once called Cienfuegos the city he liked best. Come see if you agree and, on the way, visit the village where he was born.

Secrets of Guajimico

Welcome to one of Cuba's least-discovered diving spots, run out of a comfortable campismo on the warm, calm south coast and renowned for its coral gardens, sponges and scattered wrecks.

p235

Villa Clara Province

Beaches
History
Nightlife

Spectacular Keys

Cuba's newest resorts on the keys off the coast of Villa Clara hide some stunning and still relatively uncrowded beaches, including the publicly accessible Las Gaviotas on Cayo Santa María and the more-refined Playa el Mégano and Playa Ensenachos on Cayo Ensenachos.

Che Guevara

Love him or hate him, his legacy won't go away, so you might as well visit Santa Clara to at least try to understand what made the great *guerrillero* (warrior) tick. The city hosts Che's mausoleum, a museum cataloguing his life and the historic site where he ambushed an armored train in 1958.

Student Scene

The city of Santa Clara has the edgiest and most contemporary nightlife scene in Cuba, where local innovators are constantly probing for the next big thing.

p254

Trinidad & Sancti Spíritus Province

Museums
Hiking
Music

Revolution to Romance

Trinidad has more museums per square meter than anywhere outside Havana, and they're not token gestures either. Themes include history, furniture, counterrevolutionary wars, ceramics, contemporary art and romance.

Trails & Topography

Topes de Collantes has the most comprehensive trail system in Cuba and showcases some of the best scenery in the archipelago, with waterfalls, natural swimming pools, precious wildlife and working coffee plantations. Further trails can be found in the less-heralded Alturas de Banao and Jobo Rosado reserves.

Spontaneous Sounds

In Trinidad – and to a lesser extent Sancti Spíritus – music seems to emanate out of every nook and cranny, much of it spontaneous and unrehearsed. Trinidad, in particular, has the most varied and condensed music scene outside Havana.

p275

Ciego de Ávila Province

Fishing
Beaches
Festivals

Hemingway's Haunts

Cayo Guillermo has all the makings of a fishing trip extraordinaire: a warm tropical setting; large, abundant fish; and the ghost of Ernest Hemingway to follow you from port to rippling sea and back. Pack a box of beer and follow the Gulf Stream.

Pilar Paradise

Colorados, Prohibida, Flamingo and Pilar – the beaches of the northern keys lure you with their names as much as their reputations and, when you get there, there's plenty of room for everyone.

Fiestas & Fireworks

No other province has such a varied and – frankly – weird stash of festivals. Ciego is home to an annual cricket tournament, rustic country dancing, strange voodoo rites and explosive fireworks.

p301

Camagüey Province

Diving
Architecture
Beaches

Feeding Sharks

OK, the resorts aren't exactly refined luxury, but who cares when the diving's this good? Playa Santa Lucía sits astride one of the largest coral reefs in the world and is famous for its shark-feeding show.

Urban Maze

Camagüey doesn't conform to the normal Spanish colonial building manual when it comes to urban layout, but that's part of the attraction. Lose yourself in Cuba's third-largest city that, since 2008, has been a Unesco World Heritage site.

Limitless Sand

The beaches on the province's north coast are phenomenal. There's 20km-long Playa Santa Lucía, the Robinson Crusoe–like Playa Los Pinos on Cayo Sabinel, and the shapely curve of Playa los Cocos at the mouth of the Bahía de Nuevitas.

p316

Las Tunas Province

Beaches
Art
Festivals

Eco-Beaches

Hardly anyone knows about them, but they're still there. Las Tunas' northern eco-beaches are currently the preserve of local Cubans, seabirds and the odd in-the-know outsider. Come and enjoy them before the resort-building bulldozers wreck the tranquility.

City of Sculptures

Scout around the congenial streets of the provincial capital Las Tunas and you'll uncover an esoteric collection of revolutionary leaders, two-headed Taíno chiefs and oversize pencils crafted in stone.

Country Music

The bastion of country music in Cuba, Las Tunas hosts the annual Cucalambeana festival, where songwriters from across the country come to recite their quick-witted satirical *décimas* (verses).

p335

Holguín Province

Beaches
Ecotourism
Archaeology

Little-Known Beaches

Most tourists gravitate to the well-known beaches of Playa Pesquero and Guardalavaca that are backed by big resorts. Less touted, but equally *linda* (pretty), are Playa Caleta near Gibara and Las Morales near Banes.

Mountains & Keys

Strangely, for a province that hosts Cuba's largest and dirtiest industry (the Moa nickel mines), Holguín has a profusion of green escapes tucked away in pine-clad mountain retreats or hidden on exotic keys. Discover Cayo Saetía and Pinares de Mayarí.

Pre-Columbian Culture

Holguín preserves Cuba's best stash of archaeological finds. The region's long-lost pre-Columbian culture is showcased at the Museo Chorro de Maita and its adjacent reconstructed Taíno village. There are more artifacts on display at the Museo Indocubano Bani in nearby Banes.

p346

Granma Province

History
Hiking
Festivals

Revolutionary Sites

History is never as real as it is in Cuba's most revolutionary province. Here you can hike up to Castro's 1950s mountaintop HQ, visit the sugar mill where Céspedes first freed his slaves or ponder the poignant spot where José Martí fell in battle.

Bagging a Peak

With the Sierra Maestra overlaying two national parks, Granma has tremendous hiking potential, including the trek up to the top of the nation's highest peak, Pico Turquino.

Street Parties

Granma is famous for its street parties. Towns such as Bayamo and Manzanillo have long celebrated weekly alfresco shindigs with whole roast pork, chess tournaments and music provided by old-fashioned street organs.

p371

Santiago de Cuba Province

Dance
History
Festivals

Folklórico Groups

As magical as they are mysterious, Santiago's *folklórico* (Afro-Cuban folkdance) troupes are a throwback to another era when slaves hid their traditions behind a complex veneer of singing, dancing and syncretized religion.

Revolutionary Legacy

Cuba's hotbed of sedition has inspired multiple rebellions and many key sites can still be visited. Start at Moncada Barracks and head south through the birth houses of local heroes Frank País and Antonio Maceo, to the eerily named Museo de la Lucha Clandestina (Clandestine War Museum).

Caribbean Culture

Santiago has a wider variety of annual festivals than any other Cuban city. July is the top month, with the annual Carnaval preceded by the Festival del Caribe, celebrating the city's rich Caribbean culture.

p392

Guantánamo Province

Flora & Fauna
Hiking
Food

Endemic Eden

Guantánamo's historical isolation and complex soil structure has led to high levels of endemism, meaning you're likely to see plant and animal species here that you'll see nowhere else in the archipelago. Aspiring botanists should gravitate towards Parque Nacional Alejandro de Humboldt.

Unsung Trails

As Baracoa grows as an ecological center, hiking possibilities are opening up. Try the long-standing treks up El Yunque or into Parque Nacional Alejandro de Humboldt, or tackle newer trails around the Río Duaba or to the beaches near Boca de Yumurí.

Coconut & Cocoa

What do you mean you didn't come to Cuba for the food? Baracoa is waiting to blow away your culinary preconceptions with a sweet-and-spicy mélange of dishes concocted from the ubiquitous cocoa, coffee, coconuts and bananas.

p429

On the Road

Havana

☎7 / POP 2.1 MILLION

Includes ➡

Best Places to Eat

- Lamparilla 361 Tapas & Cervezas (p100)
- El Rum Rum de la Habana (p100)
- Doña Eutimia (p100)
- Café Laurent (p107)
- Starbien (p107)

Best Places to Sleep

- Hotel Saratoga (p92)
- Hotel Iberostar Parque Central (p92)
- Casavana Cuba (p94)
- Hostal Peregrino Consulado (p90)

Why Go?

No one could have invented Havana. It's too audacious, too contradictory, and – despite 50 years of withering neglect – too damned beautiful. How it does it is anyone's guess. Maybe it's the swashbuckling history still almost perceptible in atmospheric colonial streets; the survivalist spirit of a populace scarred by two independence wars, a revolution and a US trade embargo; or the indefatigable salsa energy that ricochets off walls and emanates most emphatically from the people. Don't come here with a long list of questions. Just arrive with an open mind and prepare for a long, slow seduction.

Awaiting you lies history piled up like wrecked treasure on a palm-fringed beach; an art culture threatening to out-create Paris or New York; cool new cafes full of denizens plotting the next cultural revolution; and old-fashioned neighborhoods alive with aromas, rhythms, gossip and candid snippets of Cuban life.

When to Go

- February is peak season, meaning there's extra life in the city and plenty of extracurricular activities, including a cigar festival and an international book fair.
- August is hot, but fun, especially if you time your visit to coincide with Havana's ostentatious Carnaval. However, Havana's summer heat can be stifling, so if you want to avoid it, come in October, a wonderfully quiet month when there's still plenty to do – such as enjoying the annual Festival Internacional de Ballet de la Habana.
- Busier (for a reason) is December, when people line up for the Festival Internacional del Nuevo Cine Latinoamericano, Cuba's premier movie shindig.

History

Havana was the most westerly and isolated of Diego Velázquez' original villas, and life was hard in the early days. The settlement was almost eradicated completely in 1538 when French pirates and local slaves razed it to the ground.

It took the Spanish conquest of Mexico and Peru to swing the pendulum in Havana's favor. The city's strategic location, at the mouth of the Gulf of Mexico, made it a perfect base for the annual 'treasure fleets' that regrouped in its sheltered harbor before heading east. Thus endowed, its ascension was quick and decisive, and in 1607 Havana replaced Santiago as the capital of Cuba.

The city was sacked again by French pirates led by Jacques de Sores in 1555. The Spanish replied by building La Punta and El Morro forts between 1558 and 1630 to reinforce an already formidable protective ring. From 1674 to 1740 a strong wall around the city was added. These defenses kept the pirates at bay but proved ineffective when Spain became embroiled in the Seven Years' War with Britain.

On June 6, 1762, a British army under the Earl of Albemarle attacked Havana, landing at Cojímar and striking inland to Guanabacoa. From there they drove west along the northeastern side of the harbor, and on July 30 they attacked El Morro from the rear. Other troops landed at La Chorrera, west of the city, and, by August 13, the Spanish were surrounded and forced to surrender. The British held Havana for 11 months.

The British occupation resulted in Spain opening Havana to freer trade. In 1765 the city was granted the right to trade with seven Spanish cities other than just Cádiz, and from 1818 Havana was allowed to ship its sugar, rum, tobacco and coffee directly to any part of the world. The 19th century was an era of steady progress: first came the railway in 1837, followed by public gas lighting (1848), the telegraph (1851), an urban transport system (1862), telephones (1888) and electric lighting (1890). The elephant in the room during this era of growth and advancement was the question of self-determination, coupled with slavery. Conflict beckoned. When the Ten Years' War broke out in 1868, the violence never reached Havana, where rich pro-colonial landholders maintained their power base. Similarly, the Independence War (1895–98) was also confined largely to the east, although this time general Antonio Maceo succeeded in leading a guerrilla column dangerously close to Havana before being killed in a skirmish at a farm near Santiago de las Vegas in 1896. What really changed Havana was not the war, but rather the post-war peace, when the city fell into the thrall of its new masters, the Americans.

By 1902 the city, nominally independent for the first time in its history, had a quarter of a million inhabitants. To provide space for its growing population, it expanded rapidly west along the Malecón into the wooded glades of formerly off-limits Vedado where a new gentrified neighborhood took root. The 20th-century colonizers weren't Spanish, but American. A large influx of rich Americans arrived in Havana at the start of the Prohibition era, taking advantage of Cuba's liberal drinking laws and the 'good times' began to roll with abandon.

Havana was awash with sugar money and the funds went into huge public works projects, including the building of an ornate presidential palace and a grandiose national assembly known as the Capitolio. But not all of the money was put to such good use. Corruption was rife in the nascent republic, which still relied heavily on US support, and a string of cash-embezzling presidents quickly abandoned big promises for cynical pragmatism. Things reached a head in 1933 when a group of non-commissioned officers staged a military revolt, led by an army sergeant named Fulgencio Batista, to topple the regime of democrat turned dictator Gerardo Machado. The event climaxed in a shoot-out between two opposing military factions in Havana's newly built Hotel Nacional.

By the 1950s, with Batista installed as 'strong man' president, Havana was a decadent gambling city frolicking amid all-night parties hosted by American mobsters and scooping fortunes into the pockets of disreputable 'businessmen' such as Meyer Lansky and Santo Trafficante. The action centered on the new district of Vedado where the Mob built luxury hotels including the Capri, Habana Hilton and the Riviera, each equipped with ostensibly 'clean' casinos. Behind the scenes, President Batista's henchmen were skimming between 10% and 30% of the profits. Meanwhile, Havana continued to expand outwards, most notably along the coast west of the Río Almendares into the Beverly Hills–like neighborhood known as Miramar.

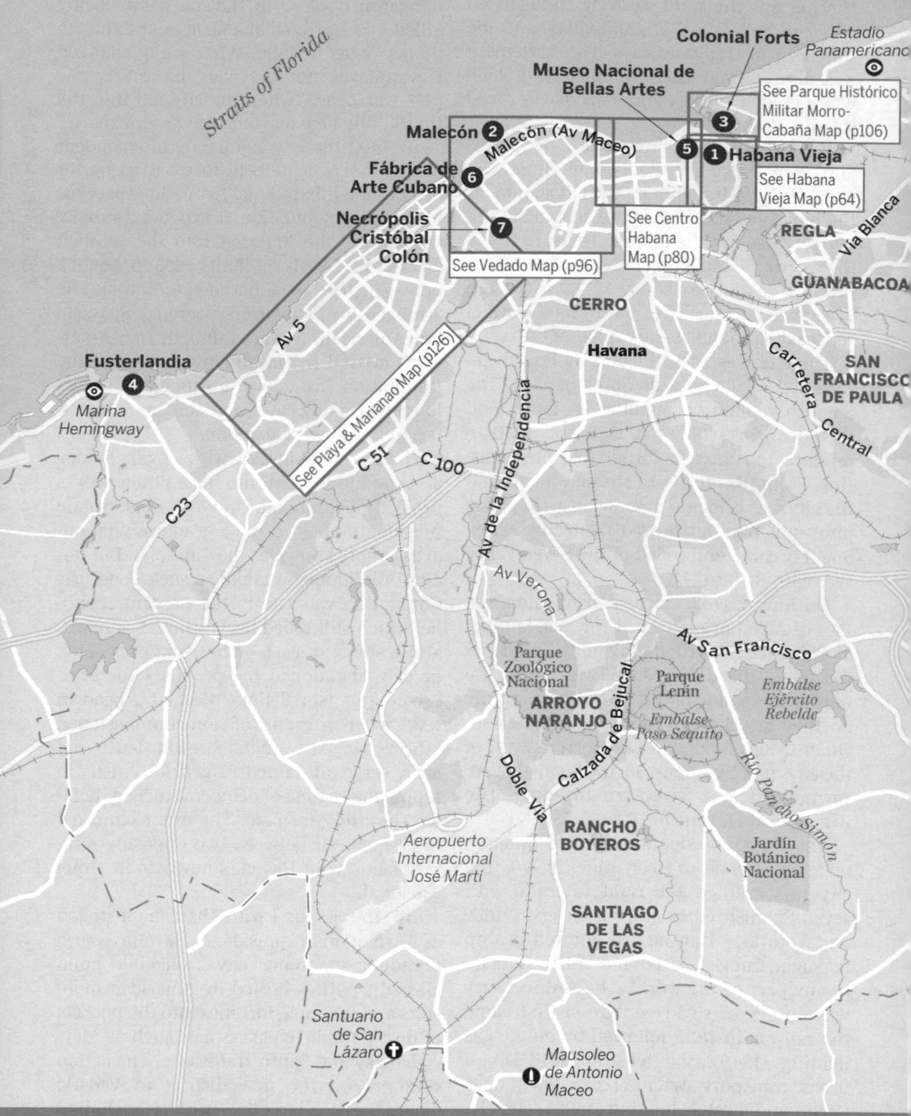

Havana Highlights

1 Habana Vieja (p62) Letting your imagination spill over on the evocative cobbled streets of 'Old Havana.'

2 Malecón (p76) Hanging out with the *habaneros* amid crashing waves and wandering troubadours.

3 Colonial Forts (p75) Seeing the sturdy bastions that once protected Havana from its cutthroat enemies.

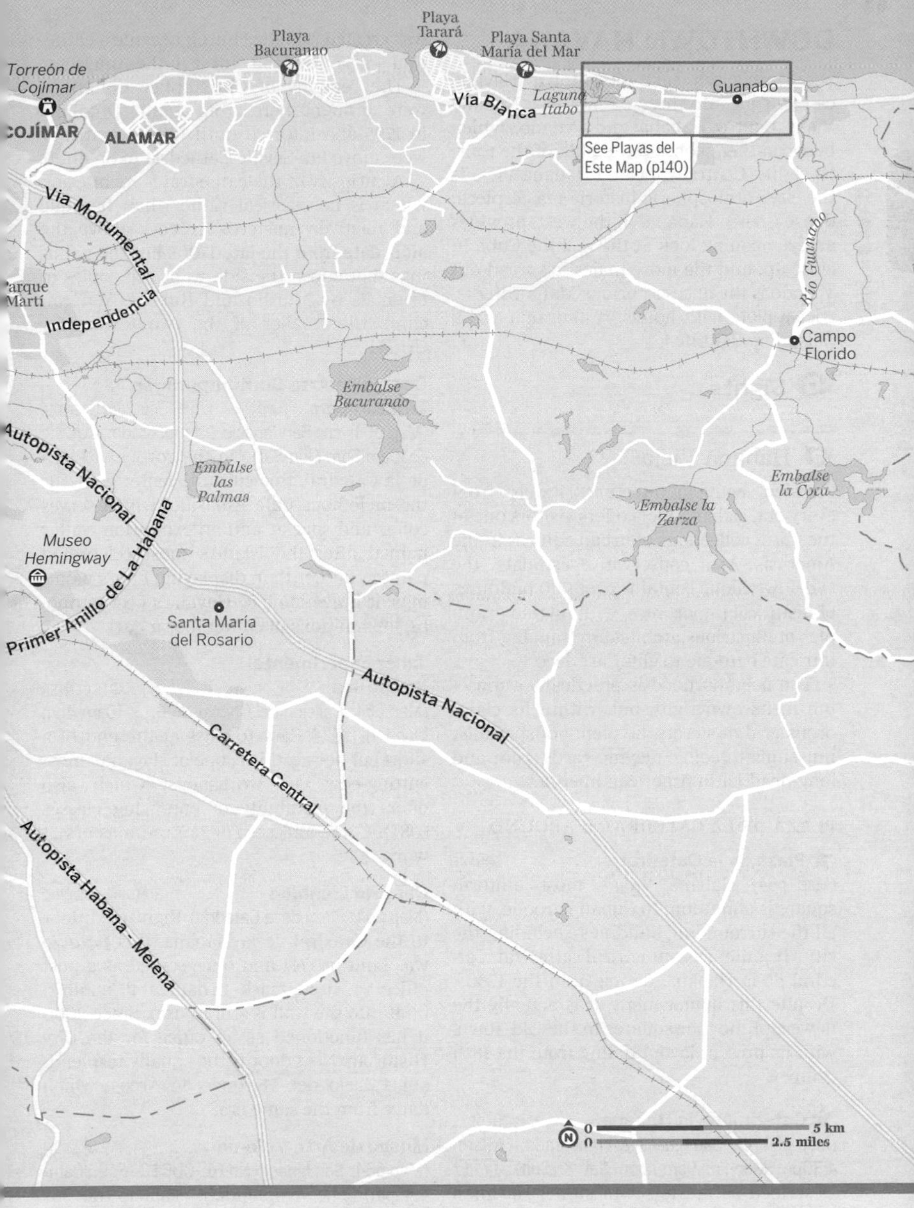

4 Fusterlandia (p124) Getting an insight into the amazing experimental street art of José Fuster.

5 Museo Nacional de Bellas Artes (p76) Cataloguing the dizzying breadth of Cuban art in this two-campus city-center museum.

6 Fábrica de Arte Cubano (p116) Listening to innovative music, viewing fabulous art and meeting creative people.

7 Necrópolis Cristóbal Colón (p83) Strolling among the beautiful dead in Havana's monumental graveyard.

DOWNTOWN HAVANA

For simplicity's sake downtown Havana can be split into three main areas: Habana Vieja, Centro Habana and Vedado, which between them contain the bulk of the tourist sights. Centrally located Habana Vieja is the city's atmospheric historic masterpiece; dense Centro Habana, to the west, provides an eye-opening look at the real-life Cuba in close-up; and the more majestic spread-out Vedado is the once-notorious Mafia-run district replete with hotels, restaurants and a pulsating nightlife.

Habana Vieja

Studded with architectural jewels from every era, Habana Vieja offers visitors one of the finest collections of urban edifices in the Americas. At a conservative estimate, the Old Town alone contains over 900 buildings of historical importance, with myriad examples of illustrious architecture ranging from intricate baroque to glitzy art deco.

The neighborhood is practically a museum in its own right, but, within its clamorous grid of streets, lie plenty of specialist museums to coins, playing cards, rum and long-dead Latin American liberators.

PLAZA DE LA CATEDRAL & AROUND

★Plaza de la Catedral SQUARE

(Map p64) Habana Vieja's most uniform square is a museum to Cuban baroque, with all the surrounding buildings, including the city's beguiling asymmetrical cathedral, Catedral de la Habana, dating from the 1700s. Despite this homogeneity, it is actually the newest of the four squares in the Old Town, with its present layout dating from the 18th century.

★Catedral de la Habana CATHEDRAL

(Map p64; cnr San Ignacio & Empedrado; ⌚9am-4:30pm Mon-Fri, 9am-noon Sat & Sun) FREE Described as music set in stone, Havana's incredible cathedral, which is dominated by two unequal towers and framed by a theatrical baroque facade, was designed by Italian architect Francesco Borromini. Construction of the church was begun by Jesuits in 1748 and work continued despite their expulsion in 1767. When the building was finished in 1787, the diocese of Havana was created and the church became a cathedral – it's one of the oldest in the Americas.

The remains of Christopher Columbus were brought here from Santo Domingo in 1795 and interred until 1898, when they were moved to Seville Cathedral in Spain.

A curiosity of the cathedral is its interior, which is neoclassical rather than baroque and relatively austere. Frescoes above the altar date from the late 1700s but the paintings that adorn the side walls are copies of originals by Murillo and Rubens. You can climb the smaller of the two towers for CUC$1.

Centro de Arte Contemporáneo Wifredo Lam CULTURAL CENTER

(Map p64; cnr San Ignacio & Empedrado; CUC$3; ⌚10am-5pm Mon-Sat) On the corner of Plaza de la Catedral, this cultural center contains the melodious Cafe Amarillo, which serves coffee and snacks, and an exhibition center named after the island's most celebrated painter. Rather than displaying Lam's paintings, it hosts some of Havana's best temporary exhibitions of contemporary art.

Taller Experimental de Gráfica ARTS CENTER

(Map p64; Callejón del Chorro No 6; ⌚10am-4pm Mon-Fri) FREE Easy to miss at the end of a short cul-de-sac, this is one of Havana's most cutting-edge art workshops, which also offers the possibility of engraving classes (p87). Come and see (or be) the masters at work.

Casa de Lombillo HISTORIC BUILDING

(Map p64; Plaza de la Catedral) Right next door to the Catedral de la Habana, this *palacio* was built in 1741 and once served as a post office (a stone-mask ornamental mailbox built into the wall is still in use). Since 2000 it has functioned as an office for the City Historian. Next door is the equally resplendent Palacio del Marqués de Arcos, which dates from the same era.

Museo de Arte Colonial MUSEUM

(Map p64; San Ignacio No 61; CUC$2; ⌚9:30am-4:45pm) The resplendent Palacio de los Condes de Casa Bayona in Plaza de la Catedral, built in 1720, today functions as the Museo de Arte Colonial, a small museum displaying colonial furniture and decorative arts. Among the finer exhibits are pieces of china with scenes of colonial Cuba, a collection of ornamental flowers, and many colonial-era dining-room sets.

LOCAL KNOWLEDGE

HABANA VIEJA – A PLAN OF ATTACK

Awash with museums, galleries, historic hotels and colonial plazas, Habana Vieja can be a bit overwhelming to first-time visitors. To tackle it properly, grab a cup of coffee (Plaza Vieja has some good spots), sit down with a map, and draw up a strategic plan of attack. The overriding motto: you won't have time to see everything.

Habana Vieja's essential business revolves around its four main squares, all clustered in close proximity to each other on the eastern side of the neighborhood. Intimate Plaza de la Catedral faces the not-to-be-missed cathedral and has some fine restaurants squeezed into a nearby alley. Shady Plaza de Armas (p63) is overlooked by the emblematic Museo de la Ciudad and Havana's oldest fort. Breezy Plaza de San Francisco de Asís (p66) has some thought-provoking public sculpture, while Plaza Vieja (p68) sports the most varied body of architecture and the best horde of after-dark bars and lounges.

Interesting connecting streets include Calle Oficos, Calle Obsipo (with a beautiful din of competing live music after 6pm) and Calle Mercaderes, with its historic ensemble of old shops. The rest of the quarter's dense grid is yours for the taking, a potluck of rusting 'yank tanks,' hole-in-the-wall restaurants and socialism on a shoestring. Anyone vaguely hip should gravitate toward Plaza del Cristo (p73), a dandy collection of spirited bars.

If you're in Havana for more than a day, a visit to the two forts (p75) on the opposite side of the harbor is essential. Early evening is a good time to arrive. The sunsets over the city from the ramparts are legendary.

Palacio de los Marqueses de Aguas Claras HISTORIC BUILDING
(Map p64; San Ignacio No 54) Situated on the western side of Plaza de la Catedral is this majestic one-time baroque palace, completed in 1760 and widely lauded for the beauty of its shady Andalucian patio. Today it houses the **Restaurante Paris** (meals CUC$15-20; ⏲noon-midnight).

Parque Maestranza PARK
(Map p64; Av Carlos Manuel de Céspedes; CUC$3; ⏲10am-5pm) A small-scale but fun kids playground (for children from four to 12) with inflatable castles and other games overlooking the harbor.

PLAZA DE ARMAS & AROUND

Plaza de Armas SQUARE
(Map p64) Havana's oldest square was laid out in the early 1520s, soon after the city's foundation, and was originally known as Plaza de Iglesia after a church – the Parroquial Mayor – that once stood on the site of the present-day Palacio de los Capitanes Generales.

The name Plaza de Armas (Square of Arms) wasn't adopted until the late 16th century, when the colonial governor, then housed in the Castillo de la Real Fuerza, used the site to conduct military exercises. Today's plaza, along with most of the buildings around it, dates from the late 1700s.

In the center of the square, which is lined with royal palms and hosts a daily (except Sundays) secondhand book market, is a marble statue of Carlos Manuel de Céspedes, the man who set Cuba on the road to independence in 1868. The statue replaced one of unpopular Spanish king Ferdinand VII in 1955.

Also of note, on the square's eastern aspect is the late 18th-century Palacio de los Condes de Santovenia (Calle Baratillo No 9), today the five-star Hotel Santa Isabel (p90).

★**Museo de la Ciudad** MUSEUM
(Map p64; Tacón No 1; CUC$3; ⏲9:30am-6pm) Even with no artifacts, Havana's city museum would be a tour de force, courtesy of the opulent palace in which it resides. Filling the whole west side of Plaza de Armas, the Palacio de los Capitanes Generales dates from the 1770s and is a textbook example of Cuban baroque architecture, hewn out of rock from the nearby San Lázaro quarries. A museum has resided here since 1968.

From 1791 until 1898 the palace was the residence of the Spanish captains general. From 1899 until 1902, the US military governors were based here, and during the first two decades of the 20th century the

Habana Vieja

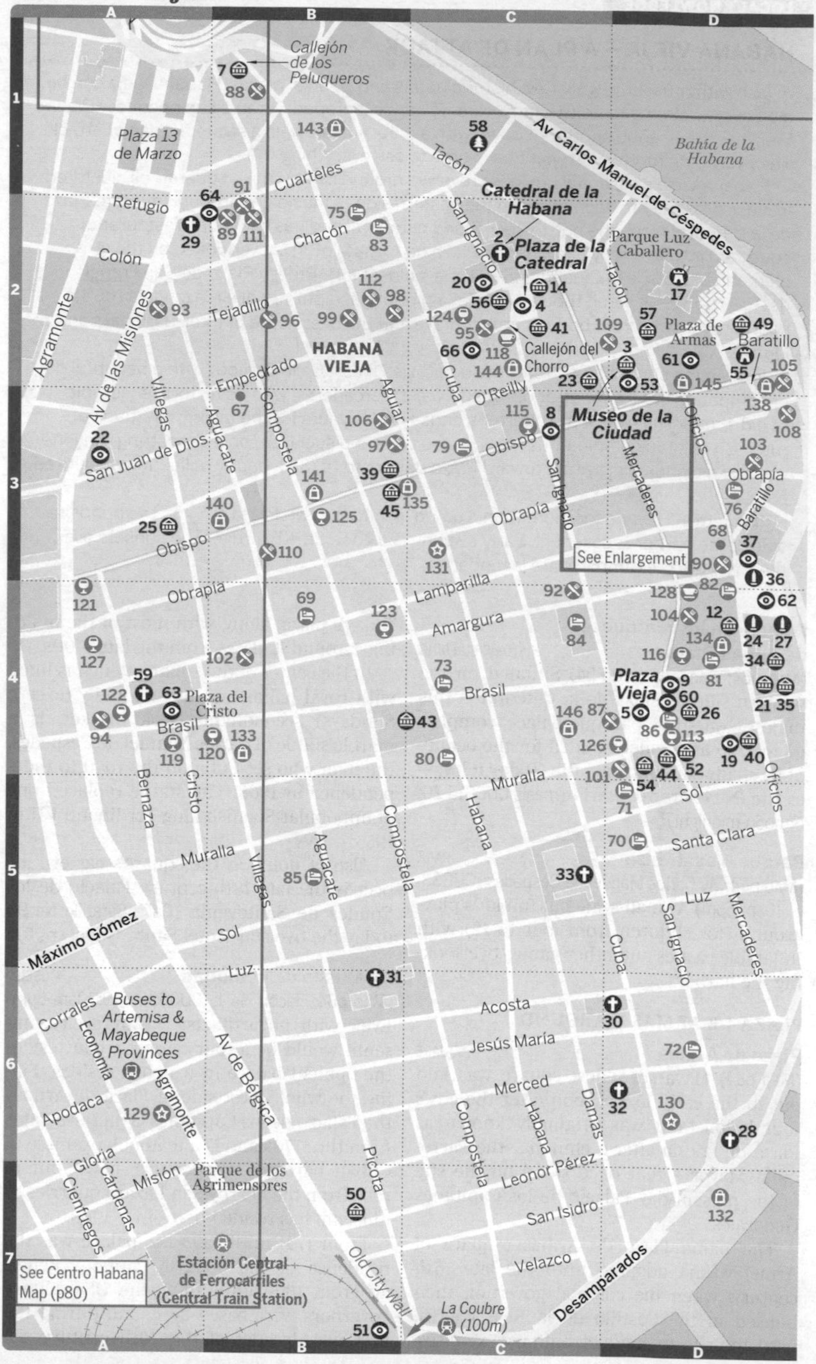
A
B
C
D
1
2
3
4
5
6
7
Callejón de los Peluqueros
Plaza 13 de Marzo
Av Carlos Manuel de Céspedes
Bahía de la Habana
Tacón
Cuarteles
Refugio
Chacón
Colón
Catedral de la Habana
Plaza de la Catedral
Parque Luz Caballero
San Ignacio
Tejadillo
Agramonte
Av de las Misiones
HABANA VIEJA
Empedrado
Callejón del Chorro
Plaza de Armas
Baratillo
Cuba
O'Reilly
Aguiar
Villegas
Aguacate
Compostela
Museo de la Ciudad
Obispo
Mercaderes
Oficios
San Juan de Dios
Obrapía
See Enlargement
Lamparilla
Amargura
Plaza del Cristo
Brasil
Plaza Vieja
Bernaza
Cristo
Muralla
Habana
Sol
Santa Clara
Luz
Máximo Gómez
Corrales
Buses to Artemisa & Mayabeque Provinces
Economía
Av de Bélgica
Acosta
Jesús María
Apodaca
Merced
Damas
Gloria
Misión
Cárdenas
Cienfuegos
Parque de los Agrimensores
Picota
Leonor Pérez
San Isidro
Estación Central de Ferrocarriles (Central Train Station)
Velazco
Desamparados
Old City Wall
La Coubre (100m)
See Centro Habana Map (p80)

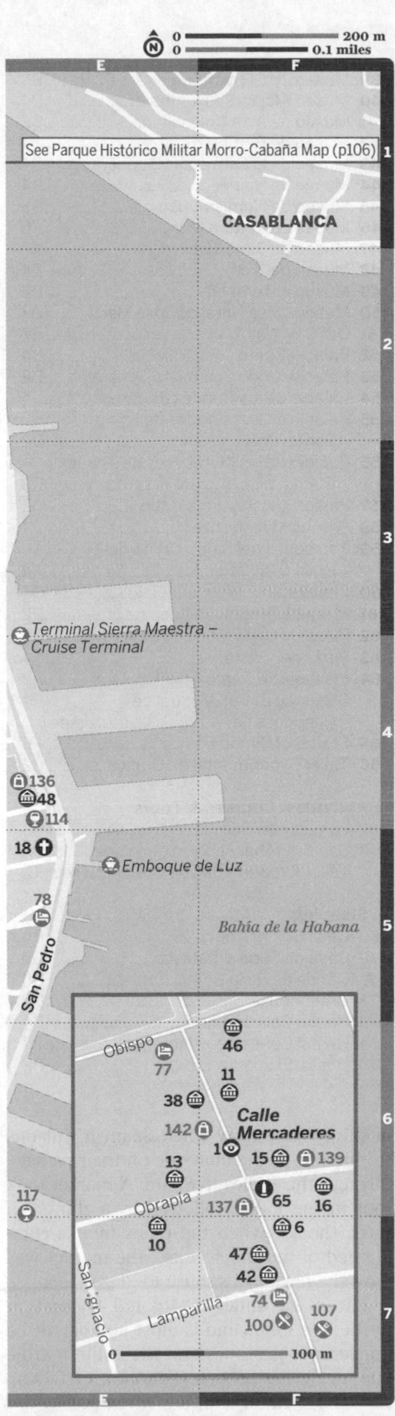

building briefly became the presidential palace. These days the museum is wrapped regally around a splendid central courtyard adorned with a white marble statue of Christopher Columbus (1862). Artifacts include period furniture, military uniforms and old-fashioned 19th-century horse carriages, while old photos vividly re-create events from Havana's roller-coaster history, such as the 1898 sinking of US battleship *Maine* in the harbor. It's better to body-swerve the pushy attendants and wander around at your own pace.

Castillo de la Real Fuerza FORT
(Map p64; Plaza de Armas; CUC$3; ⏲9am-5pm Tue-Sun) On the seaward side of Plaza de Armas is one of the oldest existing forts in the Americas, built between 1558 and 1577 on the site of an earlier fort destroyed by French privateers in 1555. Imposing and indomitable, the castle is ringed by an impressive moat and shelters the Museo de Navegación, which covers the history of the fort and Old Town, and its connections with the erstwhile Spanish Empire. Look out for the huge scale model of the *Santíssima Trinidad* galleon.

The west tower is crowned by a copy of a famous bronze weather vane called La Giraldilla. The original was cast in Havana in 1632 by Jerónimo Martínez Pinzón and is popularly believed to be of Doña Inés de Bobadilla, the wife of gold explorer Hernando de Soto. The original is now kept in the Museo de la Ciudad, and the figure also appears on the Havana Club rum label.

Palacio del Segundo Cabo HISTORIC BUILDING
(Map p64; O'Reilly No 4; ⏲9am-6pm Mon-Sat) FREE Wedged into Plaza de Armas' northwest corner, this beautiful baroque building was constructed in 1772 as the headquarters of the Spanish vice-governor. After several reincarnations as a post office, the palace of the Senate, the Supreme Court, and the National Academy of Arts and Letters, the building reopened in 2014 as a multifarious museum dedicated to Cuban-European cultural relations. An exposé on art nouveau architecture inhabited the ground floor at the time of research.

Museo el Templete MUSEUM
(Map p64; Plaza de Armas; CUC$2; ⏲8:30am-6pm) This museum is housed in the tiny neoclassical Doric chapel on the east side of Plaza de Armas, and was erected in 1828

Habana Vieja

Top Sights

1 Calle Mercaderes ... F6
2 Catedral de la Habana ... C2
3 Museo de la Ciudad ... D2
4 Plaza de la Catedral ... C2
5 Plaza Vieja ... D4

Sights

6 Armería 9 de Abril ... F7
7 Arte Corte ... B1
8 Calle Obispo ... C3
9 Cámara Oscura ... D4
10 Casa de África ... E7
11 Casa de Asia ... F6
12 Casa de Carmen Montilla ... D4
13 Casa de la Obra Pía ... E6
14 Casa de Lombillo ... C2
15 Casa de México Benito Juárez ... F6
16 Casa Oswaldo Guayasamín ... F6
17 Castillo de la Real Fuerza ... D2
18 Catedral Ortodoxa Nuestra Señora de Kazán ... E5
19 Centro Cultural Pablo de la Torriente Brau ... D4
20 Centro de Arte Contemporáneo Wifredo Lam ... C2
21 Coche Mambí ... D4
22 Edificio Bacardí ... A3
23 Edificio Santo Domingo ... C2
24 El Caballero de París ... D4
25 El Ojo del Ciclón ... A3
26 Fototeca de Cuba ... D4
27 Fuente de los Leones ... D4
28 Iglesia de San Francisco de Paula ... D6
29 Iglesia del Santo Ángel Custodio ... A2
30 Iglesia Parroquial del Espíritu Santo ... D6
31 Iglesia y Convento de Nuestra Señora de Belén ... B6
32 Iglesia y Convento de Nuestra Señora de la Merced ... D6
33 Iglesia y Convento de Santa Clara ... C5
34 Iglesia y Monasterio de San Francisco de Asís ... D4
35 Il Genio di Leonardo da Vinci ... D4
36 La Conversación ... D3
37 Lonja del Comercio ... D3
38 Maqueta de La Habana Vieja ... E6
39 Museo 28 Septiembre de los CDR ... B3
40 Museo Alejandro Humboldt ... D4
41 Museo de Arte Colonial ... C2
42 Museo de Bomberos ... F7
43 Museo de la Farmacia Habanera ... C4
44 Museo de Naipes ... D4
45 Museo de Numismático ... B3
46 Museo de Pintura Mural ... F6
47 Museo de Simón Bolívar ... F7
48 Museo del Ron ... E4
49 Museo el Templete ... D2
50 Museo-Casa Natal de José Martí ... B7
51 Old City Wall ... B7
52 Palacio Cueto ... D4
53 Palacio de los Capitanes Generales ... D2
54 Palacio de los Condes de Jaruco ... D4
55 Palacio de Los Condes de Santovenia ... D2
56 Palacio de los Marqueses de Aguas Claras ... C2
57 Palacio del Segundo Cabo ... D2
58 Parque Maestranza ... C1
59 Parroquial del Santo Cristo del Buen Viaje ... A4
60 Planetario ... D4
61 Plaza de Armas ... D2
62 Plaza de San Francisco de Asís ... D4
63 Plaza del Cristo ... A4
64 Plazuela de Santo Ángel ... A2
Statue of Carlos Manuel de Céspedes ... (see 61)
65 Statue of Simón Bolívar ... F6
66 Taller Experimental de Gráfica ... C2

Activities, Courses & Tours

67 La Casa del Son ... B3
68 San Cristóbal Agencia de Viajes ... D3
Taller Experimental de Gráfica ... (see 66)

Sleeping

69 Casa Colonial del 1715 ... B4
70 Casa de Pepe & Rafaela ... D5
71 Conde de Ricla Hostal ... D5
72 Greenhouse ... D6
73 Hostal Calle Habana ... C4
74 Hostal Conde de Villanueva ... F7
75 Hostal El Encinar ... B2

at the point where Havana's first Mass was held beneath a ceiba tree in November 1519. A similar ceiba tree has now replaced the original. Inside the chapel are three large paintings of the event by French painter Jean Baptiste Vermay (1786–1833).

PLAZA DE SAN FRANCISCO DE ASÍS & AROUND

Plaza de San Francisco de Asís SQUARE

(Map p64) Facing Havana harbor, the breezy Plaza de San Francisco de Asís first grew up in the 16th century when Spanish galleons stopped by at the quayside on their passage through the Indies to Spain. A market took root in the 1500s, followed by a church in 1608, though when the pious monks complained of too much noise, the market was moved a few blocks south to Plaza Vieja.

The plaza underwent a full restoration in the late 1990s and is most notable for its uneven cobblestones and the white marble Fuente de los Leones (Fountain of Lions), carved by Italian sculptor Giuseppe Gaggini

76 Hostal Valencia D3
77 Hotel Ambos Mundos E6
78 Hotel Armadores de Santander E5
79 Hotel Florida C3
80 Hotel Habana 612 C4
81 Hotel Los Frailes D4
82 Hotel Palacio del Marqués de San Felipe y Santiago de Bejucal D4
83 Hotel Palacio O'Farrill B2
84 Hotel Raquel C4
Hotel Santa Isabel (see 55)
85 Jesús & María B5
86 Penthouse Plaza Vieja D4

Eating

87 Café Bohemia D4
88 Café de los Artistas B1
89 Café del Ángel Fumero Jacqueline B2
90 Café del Oriente D3
91 Cafe Espada B2
92 Casa del Queso La Marriage C4
93 ChaChaChá A2
94 D'Next A4
95 Doña Eutimia C2
96 Donde Lis B2
97 El del Frente B3
98 El Rum Rum de la Habana B2
99 Helad'oro B2
100 La Imprenta F7
101 La Vitrola D4
102 Lamparilla 361 Tapas & Cervezas B4
103 Mama Inés D3
104 Mesón de la Flota D4
105 Nao Bar Paladar D2
106 O'Reilly 304 B3
107 Paladar Los Mercaderes F7
108 Restaurante el Templete D3
109 Restaurante la Dominica C2
Restaurante Paris (see 56)
110 Sandwichería La Bien Paga B3
111 Trattoria 5esquinas B2
112 Tres Monedas Creative Lounge B2

Drinking & Nightlife

113 Azúcar Lounge D4
114 Bar Dos Hermanos E4
Café el Escorial (see 86)
115 Café París C3
116 Café Taberna D4
117 Cervecería Antiguo Almacén de la Madera y Tabaco E6
118 Dulcería Bianchini II C2
119 El Chanchullero A4
120 El Dandy B4
121 El Floridita A4
122 El Patchanka A4
123 Espacios Old Fashioned B4
124 La Bodeguita del Medio C2
125 La Dichosa B3
126 La Factoria Plaza Vieja D4
127 Monserrate Bar A4
128 Museo del Chocolate D4

Entertainment

Basílica Menor de San Francisco de Asís (see 27)
Cinematógrafo Lumière (see 38)
129 El Guajirito A6
130 Gimnasio de Boxeo Rafael Trejo D6
131 Oratorio de San Felipe Neri C3

Shopping

Casa del Habano – Hostal Conde de Villanueva (see 74)
132 Centro Cultural Antiguos Almacenes de Deposito San José D7
133 Clandestina B4
134 Estudio Galería los Oficios D4
135 Fayad Jamás C3
136 Fundación Havana Club Shop E4
137 Habana 1791 F6
138 La Casa del Café D2
139 La Marca F6
140 Librería Venecia B3
141 Longina Música B3
142 Museo del Tabaco F6
143 Palacio de la Artesanía B1
144 Piscolabis Bazar & Café C2
145 Plaza de Armas Secondhand Book Market D2
146 Taller de Serigrafía René Portocarrero C4

in 1836. A more modern statue outside the square's famous church depicts El Caballero de París, a well-known street person who roamed Havana during the 1950s, engaging passersby with his philosophies on life, religion, politics and current events. The square's newest sculpture (added in 2012) is La Conversación by French artist Etienne, a modernist bronze rendition of two seated people talking.

Il Genio di Leonardo da Vinci MUSEUM
(Map p64; Churruca, btwn Oficios & Av Carlos Manuel de Céspedes; CUC$2; ⏲9:30am-4pm Tue-Sat) A permanent exposition in the San Francisco de Asís convent's Salón Blanco (use the separate entrance on the church's south side behind the Coche Mambí) that has cleverly built mock-ups of many of Leonardo's famous drawings (gliders, odometers, bikes, parachutes and tanks) – the antecedents to pretty much half the inventions in the modern world.

It's beautifully laid out with explanations in six languages, including Russian.

Museo del Ron MUSEUM

(Map p64; San Pedro No 262; incl guide CUC$7; 9am-5:30pm Mon-Thu, to 4:30pm Fri-Sun) You don't have to be an Añejo Reserva quaffer to enjoy the Museo del Ron in the Fundación Havana Club, but it probably helps. The museum, with its trilingual guided tour, shows rum-making antiquities and the complex brewing process, but lacks detail or passion. A not overgenerous measure of rum is included in the price.

There's a bar and shop on-site, but the savvy reconvene to Bar Dos Hermanos (p110) next door. The museum sits opposite Havana harbor.

Catedral Ortodoxa Nuestra Señora de Kazán CHURCH

(Map p64; Av Carlos Manuel de Céspedes, btwn Sol & Santa Clara) One of Havana's newer buildings, this beautiful gold-domed Russian Orthodox church was built in the early 2000s and consecrated at a ceremony attended by Raúl Castro in October 2008. The church was part of an attempt to reignite Russian-Cuban relations after they went sour in 1991.

Iglesia y Monasterio de San Francisco de Asís MUSEUM

(Map p64; Oficios, btwn Amargura & Brasil; museum CUC$2; 9am-6pm) Originally constructed in 1608 and rebuilt in baroque style from 1719 to 1738, this church/convent ceased to have a religious function in the 1840s. In the late 1980s crypts and religious objects were excavated, and many were later incorporated into the Museo de Arte Religioso, which displays religious paintings, silverware, woodcarvings and ceramics. Since 2005 part of the old monastery has functioned as a children's theater for the neighborhood's young residents. Some of Havana's best classical concerts are hosted in the old nave. For information on upcoming events check the listings in the *Bienvenidos* booklet, available in hotels and Infotur offices.

Lonja del Comercio ARCHITECTURE

(Map p64; Plaza de San Francisco de Asís) This large box-shaped building on Plaza de San Francisco de Asís is a former commodities market erected in 1909. The building was completely renovated in 1996 by Habaguanex and today it provides office space for foreign companies with joint ventures in Cuba. You can enter the Lonja to admire its central atrium and futuristic interior. It also houses a cafe-restaurant, El Mecurio, named after the bronze figure of the god Mercury that sits atop a dome on the roof.

Museo Alejandro Humboldt MUSEUM

(Map p64; cnr Oficios & Muralla; 9am-5pm Tue-Sat) FREE German scientist Alexander von Humboldt is often referred to as the 'second discoverer' of Cuba, but his huge Cuban legacy goes largely unnoticed by outsiders. This small museum displays a historical trajectory of his work collecting scientific and botanical data across the island in the early 1800s. It was getting a long-awaited clean-up at the time of research.

Coche Mambí MUSEUM

(Map p64; Churruca; 9am-2pm Tue-Sat) FREE To the side of the Palacio de Gobierno on Churruca is the Coche Mambí, a 1900 train car built in the US and brought to Cuba in 1912. Put into service as the Presidential Car, it's a palace on wheels, with a formal dining room and louvered wooden windows, and back in its heyday had fans cooling the interior with dry ice. You can peer inside.

Casa de Carmen Montilla GALLERY

(Map p64; Oficios No 164; 10:30am-5:30pm Tue-Sat, 9am-1pm Sun) An important art gallery, named after a celebrated Venezuelan painter who maintained a studio here until her death in 2004. Spread across three floors, the house exhibits the work of Montilla and other popular Cuban and Venezuelan artists. The rear courtyard features a huge ceramic mural by Alfredo Sosabravo.

PLAZA VIEJA & AROUND

★Plaza Vieja SQUARE

(Old Square; Map p64) Laid out in 1559, Plaza Vieja is Havana's most architecturally eclectic square, where Cuban baroque nestles seamlessly next to Gaudí-inspired art nouveau. Originally called Plaza Nueva (New Square), it was initially used for military exercises and later served as an open-air marketplace.

During the Batista regime an ugly underground parking lot was constructed here, but this monstrosity was demolished in 1996 to make way for a massive renovation project. Sprinkled liberally with bars, restaurants and cafes, Plaza Vieja today has its own microbrewery, the Angela Landa primary school, a beautiful fenced-in fountain and, on its west side, some of Havana's finest *vitrales* (stained-glass windows). Several new bars and cafes give it a sociable buzz in the evenings.

Planetario PLANETARIUM

(Map p64; ☎7-864-9544; Mercaderes No 311; CUC$10; ⊙10am-3pm Wed-Sun) Havana's planetarium includes a scale reproduction of the solar system inside a giant orb, a simulation of the Big Bang, and a theater that allows viewing of over 6000 stars. All pretty exciting stuff. It's only accessible by guided tours booked in advance. Tours take place Wednesday to Sunday and can be booked (in person) on Monday and Tuesday. There are four tours daily and two on Sunday.

Palacio Cueto HISTORIC BUILDING

(Map p64; cnr Muralla & Mercaderes) Kissing the southeast corner of Plaza Vieja is this distinctive Gaudí-esque building, which remains Havana's finest example of art nouveau. Its outrageously ornate facade once housed a warehouse and a hat factory before it was rented by José Cueto in the 1920s as the Palacio Vienna hotel. Habaguanex, the commercial arm of the City Historian's Office, is in the process of a seemingly interminable restoration; the building, constructed in 1906, has lain empty and unused since the early 1990s.

Palacio de los Condes de Jaruco GALLERY

(Map p64; Muralla No 107; ⊙10am-5pm Mon-Fri, 10am-2pm Sat) FREE This muscular mansion on Plaza Vieja's southwest corner is one of the square's oldest, constructed in 1738 from local limestone in a transitional *mudéjar*-baroque style. Rich in period detail, it is typical of merchant houses of the era. For many years it was the residence for the exalted Counts of Jaruco. Today it's the HQ of Cuba's main cultural foundation and harbors a small souvenir shop and an art gallery called La Casona.

Fototeca de Cuba GALLERY

(Map p64; www.fototecadecuba.com; Mercaderes No 307; ⊙10am-5pm Tue-Fri, 9am-noon Sat) FREE This photographic archive of Old Havana from the early 20th century onward was started by former City Historian Emilio Roig de Leuchsenring in 1937. There are an estimated 14,000 photos inside, and they have been instrumental in providing the visual pointers for the current restoration. Revolving photographic exhibitions are held. Check the website for upcoming events.

Museo de la Farmacia Habanera MUSEUM

(Map p64; cnr Brasil & Compostela; ⊙9am-5pm) FREE A few blocks east of Plaza del Cristo, this grand wood-paneled store founded in 1886 by Catalan José Sarrá has been restored as both a museum and a working pharmacy for the local population. The small museum section displays an elegant mock-up of an old drugstore with some interesting historical explanations.

Cámara Oscura LANDMARK

(Map p64; Plaza Vieja; CUC$2; ⊙9:30am-5pm Tue-Sun) On the northeastern corner of Plaza Vieja is this clever optical device providing live, 360-degree views of the city from atop a 35m-tall tower. Explanations are in Spanish and English.

Centro Cultural Pablo de la Torriente Brau CULTURAL CENTER

(Map p64; www.centropablo.cult.cu; Muralla No 63; ⊙9am-5:30pm Tue-Sat) FREE Tucked away behind Plaza Vieja, the 'Brau' is a leading cultural institution that was formed in 1996 under the auspices of the Unión de Escritores y Artistas de Cuba (Uneac; Union of Cuban Writers and Artists). The center hosts expositions, poetry readings and live acoustic music. Its Salón de Arte Digital is renowned for its groundbreaking digital art.

Museo de Naipes MUSEUM

(Map p64; Muralla No 101; ⊙9:30am-5pm Tue-Sun) FREE Encased in Plaza Vieja's oldest building is this quirky playing-card museum, with a 2000-strong collection that includes rock stars, rum drinks and round cards.

SOUTHERN HABANA VIEJA

Iglesia y Convento de Nuestra Señora de la Merced CHURCH

(Map p64; Cuba No 806; ⊙8am-noon & 3-5:30pm) Bizarrely overlooked by the tourist hordes, this baroque church in its own small square has Havana's most sumptuous ecclesiastical interior, as yet only partially restored. Beautiful gilded altars, frescoed vaults and a number of valuable old paintings create a sacrosanct mood. There's a quiet cloister adjacent.

Habana Vieja

WALKING TOUR OF OLD HAVANA

This easy 'four plaza' walking tour, though less than 2km in length, could fill a day with its museums, shops, bars and street theater. It highlights Havana's unique historical district, built up around four main squares.

Start at ❶ **Catedral de la Habana**, which anchors the Plaza de la Catedral. This compact square has bags of atmosphere and is always awash with interesting characters.

Then take Calle Empedrado followed by Calle Mercaderes to Plaza de Armas, once used for military exercises and still guarded by the ❷ **Castillo de la Real Fuerza**. The fort's museum is worth a quick look. Worth more time is the Museo de la Ciudad in the ❸ **Palacio de los Capitanes Generales**; eschew the on-site guides and wander alone.

Walk up ❹ **Calle Obispo** next, Havana's busy main drag, before turning left into ❺ **Calle Mercaderes**, where old shops and several museums make ambling a pleasure.

Turn left on Calle Amargura and dive into Plaza de San Francisco de Asís, dominated by ❻ **Iglesia y Monasterio de San Francisco de Asís**. Make a note of upcoming classical concerts (great acoustics!) and try to take in one of the church's two museums (Il Genio di Leonardo da Vinci is best). Turn right on Calle Brasil and you'll enter ❼ **Plaza Vieja**, home to a planetarium and several museum-galleries. And when you're museumed-out, crash at Factoria Plaza Vieja for a smooth microbrewed beer.

MUSEUMS

Dip into some of the museums you will pass on the way (in order):

Museo de Arte Colonial Colonial furniture

Museo de Navegación Maritime history

Museo de la Ciudad City history

Museo de Pintura Mural Frescos

Maqueta de la Habana Vieja Scale model of Havana

Museo de Naipes Playing cards

RICHARD CAVALLERI/SHUTTERSTOCK ©

Catedral de la Habana
The cathedral's interior was originally baroque, like its main facade. However, in the early 19th century, a renovation project redecorated the church's inner sanctum in a more sober classical tone.

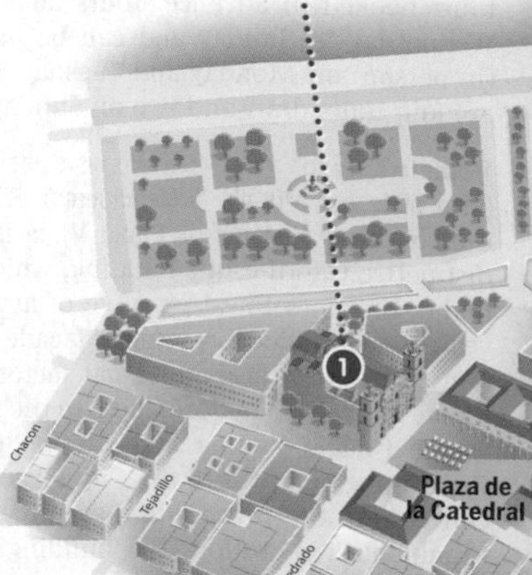

Palacio de los Capitanes Generales
An interesting feature of this sturdy building is the marine fossils embedded in its limestone walls. The street outside is lined with wooden bricks designed to deaden the sound of horses' hooves.

Calle Obispo
The lower section of Obispo is an architectural crossroads. The row of buildings on the south are the oldest townhouses in Havana, dating from the 1570s. Opposite is the Hotel Ambos Mundos, Hemingway's 1930s hangout.

HAILSHADOW/GETTY IMAGES ©

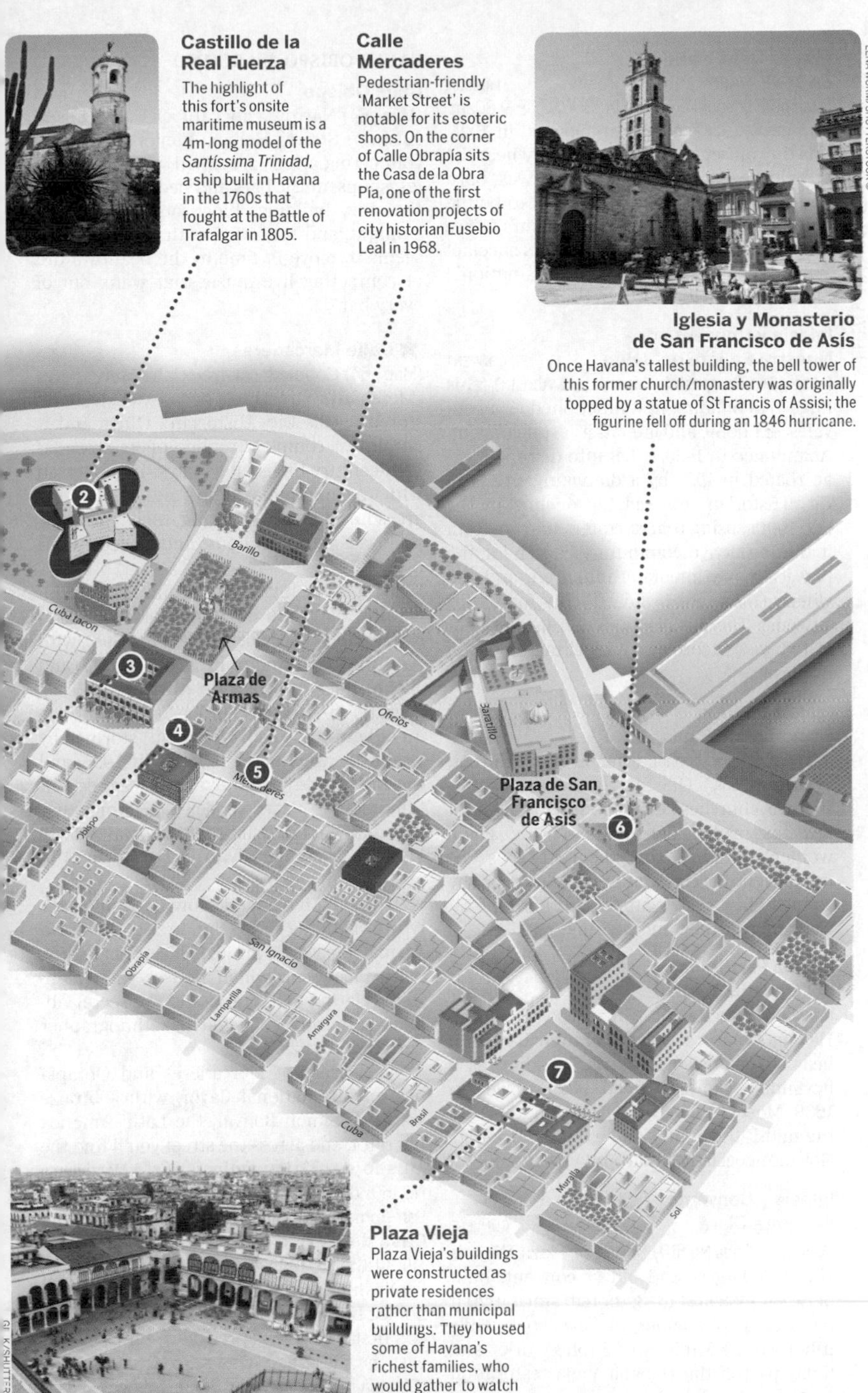

Castillo de la Real Fuerza
The highlight of this fort's onsite maritime museum is a 4m-long model of the *Santíssima Trinidad*, a ship built in Havana in the 1760s that fought at the Battle of Trafalgar in 1805.

Calle Mercaderes
Pedestrian-friendly 'Market Street' is notable for its esoteric shops. On the corner of Calle Obrapía sits the Casa de la Obra Pía, one of the first renovation projects of city historian Eusebio Leal in 1968.

Iglesia y Monasterio de San Francisco de Asís
Once Havana's tallest building, the bell tower of this former church/monastery was originally topped by a statue of St Francis of Assisi; the figurine fell off during an 1846 hurricane.

Plaza Vieja
Plaza Vieja's buildings were constructed as private residences rather than municipal buildings. They housed some of Havana's richest families, who would gather to watch the plaza's gory public spectacles, Including executions.

Museo-Casa Natal de José Martí MUSEUM

(Map p64; Leonor Pérez No 314; CUC$2; ⌚9:30am-5pm Tue-Sat, 9:30am-1pm Sun) Opened in 1925, this tiny museum, set in the house where the apostle of Cuban independence was born on January 28, 1853, is considered to be the oldest in Havana. The City Historian's Office took the house over in 1994, and its succinct stash of exhibits devoted to Cuba's national hero continues to impress.

Iglesia y Convento de Nuestra Señora de Belén CONVENT

(Map p64; Compostela, btwn Luz & Acosta) This huge 1718 building first functioned as a convalescent home and later as a Jesuit convent. Abandoned in 1925, it fell into disrepair, exacerbated in 1991 by a damaging fire. The City Historian reversed the decline in the late 1990s, using tourist coffers to transform it into an active community center for the physically and mentally impaired, and the elderly (there are 18 apartments for senior citizens). There is also a new museum dedicated to meteorology and climatology on five levels.

Iglesia de San Francisco de Paula CHURCH

(Map p64; cnr Leonor Pérez & Desamparados; ⌚concerts only) One of Havana's most attractive churches, this building is all that remains of the San Francisco de Paula women's hospital from the mid-1700s. Lit up at night for classical music concerts, the stained glass, heavy cupola and baroque facade are romantic and inviting.

Iglesia Parroquial del Espíritu Santo CHURCH

(Map p64; Acosta 161; ⌚8am-noon & 3-6pm) Havana's oldest surviving church has been heavily remodeled since its founding as a hermitage, built by freed black slaves in 1638. Most of the current edifice dates from the mid-19th century and exhibits Moorish, Gothic, neoclassical and Andaluz styles.

Iglesia y Convento de Santa Clara CONVENT

(Map p64; Cuba No 610) South of Plaza Vieja is Havana's largest and oldest convent, built between 1638 and 1643, though since 1920 it has served no religious purpose. For a while it housed the Ministry of Public Works, and today part of the Habana Vieja restoration team is based here. It was being renovated at the time of research.

CALLE OBISPO & AROUND

Calle Obispo AREA

(Map p64) Narrow, chockablock Calle Obispo (Bishop's Street), Habana Vieja's main interconnecting artery, is packed with art galleries, shops, music bars and people. Four- and five-story buildings block out most of the sunlight, and the swaying throng of people seems to move in time to the beautiful din of competing live music that wafts out of every bar.

★Calle Mercaderes AREA

(Map p64) Cobbled, car-free Calle Mercaderes (Merchant's Street) has been extensively restored by the City Historian's Office and is an almost complete replica of its splendid 18th-century high-water mark. Interspersed with the museums, shops and restaurants are some real-life working social projects, such as a maternity home and a needle-craft cooperative.

Most of the myriad museums are free, including the **Casa de Asia** (Calle Mercaderes No 111; ⌚10am-6pm Tue-Sat, 9am-1pm Sun), with paintings and sculpture from China and Japan; the **Armería 9 de Abril** (Calle Mercaderes No 157; ⌚9am-5pm Tue-Sat, 1-5pm Mon), an old gun shop (now museum) stormed by revolutionaries on the said date in 1958; and the **Museo de Bomberos** (cnr Mercaderes & Lamparilla; ⌚10am-6pm Mon-Sat), which has antediluvian fire equipment dedicated to 19 Havana firefighters who lost their lives in an 1890 railway fire.

Just off Mercaderes down Obrapía, it's worth slinking into the gratis **Casa de África** (Obrapía No 157; ⌚9:30am-5pm Tue-Sat, 9:30am-1pm Sun), which houses sacred objects relating to Santería and the secret Abakuá fraternity collected by ethnographer Fernando Ortíz.

The corner of Mercaderes and Obrapía has an international flavor, with a bronze statue of Simón Bolívar, the Latin America liberator, and across the street you'll find the **Museo de Simón Bolívar** (Calle Mercaderes No 160; donations accepted; ⌚9am-5pm Tue-Sat, 9am-1pm Sun) dedicated to Bolívar's life. The **Casa de México Benito Juárez** (Obrapía No 116; CUC$1; ⌚10:15am-5:45pm Tue-Sat, 9am-1pm Sun) exhibits Mexican folk art and plenty of books, but not a lot on Señor Juárez (Mexico's first indigenous president) himself. Just east is the **Casa Oswaldo Guayasamín** (Obrapía No 111; ⌚9am-4:30pm Tue-Sun) FREE, now a museum, but once the studio of the great Ecuadorian artist who painted Fidel in numerous poses.

Mercaderes is also characterized by its restored shops, including a perfume store and a spice shop. Wander at will.

El Ojo del Ciclón GALLERY

(Map p64; ☎7-861-5359; O'Reilly No 501, cnr Villegas; ⏲10am-7pm) FREE Just when you think you've seen the strangest, weirdest, surrealist and most avant-garde art, along comes the 'eye of the cyclone' to give you plenty more. The abstract gallery displays the work of Cuban visual artist Leo D'Lázaro and it's pretty mind-bending stuff – giant eyes, crashed cars, painted suitcases and junk reborn as art. Think Jackson Pollock meets JRR Tolkien at a Psychedelic Furs gig.

Some of the art is semi-interactive. You can hit a punchbag, play a bizarre game of table football, or hang your bag on a masked metal scarecrow.

Plaza del Cristo SQUARE

(Map p64) In the space of just a few years, Habana Vieja's once overlooked 'fifth' square has become *the* coolest place to hang out, courtesy of its edgy assortment of bars and shops and occasional live concerts. A little apart from the historical core, it hasn't benefited from a full restoration yet, which is possibly part of its charm.

The square's chunkiest edifice is the **Parroquial del Santo Cristo del Buen Viaje** (⏲9am-noon), a recently renovated 18th-century church where sailors once came to pray before embarking on long voyages.

Edificio Santo Domingo MUSEUM

(Map p64; Mercaderes, btwn Obispo & O'Reilly; ⏲9:30am-5pm Tue-Sat, 9:30am-1pm Sun) FREE The block behind Plaza de Armas was the original home of Havana's university, which stood on this site between 1728 and 1902. The university was once part of a convent. The contemporary modern office block you see today was built by Habaguanex in 2006 over the skeleton of an uglier 1950s office, the roof of which was used as a helicopter landing pad. It's been ingeniously refitted using the convent's original bell tower and baroque doorway – an interesting juxtaposition of old and new.

Many of the university's arts faculties have reinhabited the space, and a small museum/art gallery displays a scale model of the original convent and various artifacts that were rescued from it.

Maqueta de La Habana Vieja MUSEUM

(Map p64; Mercaderes No 114; CUC$1.50; ⏲9am-6:30pm; 👪) Herein lies a 1:500 scale model of Habana Vieja complete with an authentic soundtrack meant to replicate a day in the life of the city. It's incredibly detailed and provides an excellent way of geographically acquainting yourself with the city's historical core.

Also here is a small cinema, the **Cinematógrafo Lumière** (CUC$2), that shows nostalgia movies for senior citizens, and educational documentaries about the restoration for visitors.

Casa de la Obra Pía HISTORIC BUILDING

(Map p64; Obrapía No 158; CUC$1.50; ⏲10:30am-5:30pm Tue-Sat, 9:30am-2:30pm Sun) One of the more muscular sights around Calle Mercaderes is this typical Havana aristocratic residence originally constructed in 1665 and rebuilt in 1780. Baroque decoration – including an intricate portico made in Cádiz, Spain – covers the exterior facade. The house today functions as a decorative arts museum; there are some colonial artifacts displayed inside. It is also HQ for a local sewing and embroidery cooperative.

Museo 28 Septiembre de los CDR MUSEUM

(Map p64; Obispo, btwn Aguiar & Habana; CUC$2; ⏲8:30am-5pm) A venerable building on Obispo that dedicates two floors to a rather one-sided dissection of the nationwide Comites de la Defensa de la Revolución (CDR; Committees for the Defense of the Revolution). Commendable neighborhood-watch schemes, or grassroots spying agencies? Sift through the propaganda and decide.

Museo de Numismático MUSEUM

(Map p64; Obispo, btwn Aguiar & Habana; CUC$1.50; ⏲9am-5pm Tue-Sat, 9:30am-12:45pm Sun) This numismatist's heaven brings together various collections of medals, coins and banknotes from around the world, including a stash of 1000 mainly American gold coins (1869–1928) and a full chronology of Cuban banknotes from the 19th century to the present.

Museo de Pintura Mural MUSEUM

(Map p64; Obispo, btwn Mercaderes & Oficios; ⏲10am-6pm) FREE A simple museum that exhibits some beautifully restored original frescoes in the Casa del Mayorazgo de Recio, popularly considered to be Havana's oldest surviving house. It was being renovated at the time of research.

LA LOMA DEL ÁNGEL & AROUND

Plazuela de Santo Ángel PLAZA

(Map p64) This lovely, intimate plaza behind the Iglesia del Santo Ángel Custodio (p74) has benefited from a recent beautification project that has installed several private restaurants, along with a statue of the fictional heroine Cecilia Valdés, who is watched over by a bust of the author who created her, Cirilo Villaverde.

Edificio Bacardí LANDMARK

(Bacardí Bldg; Map p64; Av de las Misiones, btwn Empedrado & San Juan de Dios; ⏲hours vary) Finished in 1929, the magnificent Edificio Bacardí is a triumph of art deco architecture with a whole host of lavish finishes that somehow manage to make kitsch look cool. Hemmed in by other buildings, it's hard to get a full panoramic view of the structure from street level, though the opulent bell tower can be glimpsed from all over Havana.

There's a bar in the lobby, and for CUC$1 you can usually travel up to the tower for an eagle's-eye view.

Arte Corte MUSEUM

(Map p64; ☎7-861-0202; www.artecorte.org; Aguiar No 10, btwn Peña Pobre & Av de las Misiones; ⏲noon-6pm Mon-Sat) FREE It's hard to classify Arte Corte. Is it a hairdressers? Yes. Is it a museum? Yes, of sorts. Is it the initiator of an inspired community project? Yes, most certainly. The brainchild of Gilberto Valladares, aka 'Papito,' this novel hairdressing salon doubles as a small museum to the barber's art. Even better, with a little help from his friends (including the City Historian), Papito's barber theme has taken over the whole street, unofficially rechristened as Callejón de los Peluqueros (Hairdresser's Alley).

Nearby there's a kids park with barber-themed apparatus, and Figaros restaurant, named after the main character in *The Barber of Seville*.

Statue of General Máximo Gómez MONUMENT

(Map p80; cnr Malecón & Paseo de Martí) On a large traffic island overlooking the mouth of the harbor is a rather grand depiction of Máximo Gómez, a war hero from the Dominican Republic who fought tirelessly for Cuban independence in both the 1868 and 1895 conflicts against the Spanish. The impressive statue of him sitting atop a horse was created by Italian artist Aldo Gamba in 1935 and faces heroically out to sea.

Iglesia del Santo Ángel Custodio CHURCH

(Map p64; Compostela No 2; ⏲during Mass 7:15am Tue, Wed & Fri, 6pm Thu, Sat & Sun) Originally constructed in 1695, this church

CECILIA VALDÉS

The Plazuela de Santo Ángel, the small cobbled square behind the Iglesia del Santo Ángel Custodio, was immortalized in the seminal novel *Cecilia Valdés o la loma del ángel* by Cuban author Cirilo Villaverde. First published in 1839, the book is regarded as the finest Cuban novel of the 19th century, although it took another 43 years before a heavily revised version was released internationally through a publisher in New York. Controversial for its time, the novel documents the issues of class, slavery, love and incest in Havana society in the 1830s. The plot revolves around Cecilia Valdés, the beautiful illegitimate daughter of a slave-trader who falls in love with her half-brother. The climatic final scene, involving a murder of passion, takes place in the Plazuela de Santo Ángel, just outside the church.

The novel was subsequently made into a zarzuela (Spanish-style opera) in the 1930s and adapted for a 1982 film directed by Humberto Solás.

In commemoration of the book, a bust of Cirilo Villaverde (placed on the side of one of the Plazuela's buildings) has looked over the square since 1946 and was joined in 2014 by a life-sized statue of his literary heroine, Cecilia Valdés, the work of Cuban artist Erig Rebull. The more recent sculpture was the cherry on the cake for a community renovation project that has breathed new life into the surrounding neighborhood known colloquially as 'La Loma del Ángel' (Angel Hill). With a raft of new restaurants, bars and artists studios, it is now one of Habana Vieja's most salubrious quarters.

was pounded by a ferocious hurricane in 1846, after which it was entirely rebuilt in neo-Gothic style. Among the notable historical and literary figures that have passed through its handsome doors are 19th-century Cuban novelist Cirilo Villaverde, who set the main scene of his novel *Cecilia Valdés o la loma del ángel* here. Other notables include Félix Varela and José Martí, who were baptized in the church in 1788 and 1853 respectively.

Castillo de San Salvador de la Punta FORT

(Map p80; CUC$2; ⌚museum 9:30am-5pm Tue-Sat, 9:30am-noon Sun) One in a quartet of forts defending Havana harbor, La Punta was designed by the Italian military engineer Bautista Antonelli and built between 1589 and 1600. It underwent comprehensive repairs after the British shelled it during their successful 1762 Havana raid. During the colonial era a chain was stretched 250m to the castle of El Morro every night to close the harbor mouth to shipping.

The castle's museum is really just a few information boards chronicling its history (in Spanish), but there are good views from the battlements where you can also admire the huge Parrott cannons dating from the mid-19th century.

Parque Histórico Militar Morro-Cabaña

Havana's two largest forts sit on the opposite (eastern) side of the harbor to Habana Vieja, but are included in this Unesco World Heritage Site (Map p106; ⌚10am-10pm).

★Fortaleza de San Carlos de la Cabaña FORT

(Map p106; before/after 6pm CUC$6/8; ⌚10am-10pm) This 18th-century colossus was built between 1763 and 1774 on a long, exposed ridge on the east side of Havana harbor to fill a weakness in the city's defenses. In 1762 the British had taken Havana by gaining control of this strategically important ridge, and it was from here that they shelled the city mercilessly into submission. In order to prevent a repeat performance, the Spanish king Carlos III ordered the construction of a massive fort that would repel future invaders.

Measuring 700m from end to end and covering a whopping 10 hectares, it is the largest Spanish colonial fortress in the Americas. The impregnability of the fort meant that no invader ever stormed it, though during the 19th century Cuban patriots faced firing squads here. Dictators Machado and Batista used the fortress as a military prison, and immediately after the revolution Che Guevara set up his headquarters inside the ramparts to preside over another catalog of grisly executions (this time of Batista's officers).

These days the fort has been restored for visitors, and you can spend at least half a day checking out its wealth of attractions. As well as bars, restaurants, souvenir stalls and a cigar shop (containing the world's longest cigar), La Cabaña hosts the **Museo de Fortificaciones y Armas** (entry incl in La Cabaña ticket; ⌚10am-10pm) and the engrossing **Museo de Comandancia del Che** (entry incl in La Cabaña ticket; ⌚10am-10pm). The nightly 9pm *cañonazo* ceremony is a popular evening excursion in which actors dressed in full 18th-century military regalia reenact the firing of a cannon over the harbor. You can visit the ceremony independently or as part of an organized excursion.

★Castillo de los Tres Santos Reyes Magnos del Morro FORT

(Map p106; El Morro; CUC$6; ⌚10am-6pm) This wave-lashed fort with its emblematic lighthouse was erected between 1589 and 1630 to protect the entrance to Havana harbor from pirates and foreign invaders (French corsair Jacques de Sores had sacked the city in 1555).

Perched high on a rocky bluff above the Atlantic, the fort has an irregular polygonal shape, 3m-thick walls and a deep protective moat, and is a classic example of Renaissance military architecture.

For more than a century the fort withstood numerous attacks by French, Dutch and English privateers, but in 1762 after a 44-day siege a 14,000-strong British force captured El Morro by attacking from the landward side. The Castillo's famous **lighthouse** (CUC$2; ⌚10am-6pm) was added in 1844.

Aside from the fantastic views over the sea and the city, El Morro also hosts a **maritime museum** (entry incl in El Morro ticket; ⌚10am-6pm) that includes a riveting account of the fort's siege and eventual surrender to the British in 1762 using words (in English and Spanish) and paintings.

Centro Habana

Centro Habana's crowded residential grid offers an uncensored look at Cuba without the fancy wrapping paper. On its potholed but perennially action-packed streets, old men engage in marathon games of dominoes, Afro-Cuban drums beat out addictive rumba rhythms, and sorrily soiled buildings give intriguing hints of their illustrious previous lives. Juxtaposed against this ebullient but spectacularly dilapidated quarter is the very different world of Parque Central and El Prado, a busy tourist-heavy zone crammed with Havana's poshest hotels and some of its finest museums.

★Museo Nacional de Bellas Artes MUSEUM

(Map p80; www.bellasartes.cult.cu; each CUC$5, combined entry to both CUC$8, under 14yr free; ⌚9am-5pm Tue-Sat, 10am-2pm Sun) Spread over two campuses, the Bellas Artes is arguably the finest art gallery in the Caribbean. The 'Arte Cubano' building contains the most comprehensive collection of Cuban art in the world, while the 'Arte Universal' section is laid out in a grand eclectic palace overlooking Parque Central, with exterior flourishes that are just as impressive as the art within.

The **Museo Nacional de Bellas Artes – Arte Cubano** (Trocadero, btwn Agramonte & Av de las Misiones; ⌚9am-5pm Tue-Sat, 10am-2pm Sun) displays purely Cuban art and, if you're pressed for time, is the better of the duo. Works are displayed in chronological order starting on the 3rd floor and are surprisingly varied. Artists to look out for are Guillermo Collazo, considered to be the first truly great Cuban artist; Rafael Blanco, with his cartoonlike paintings and sketches; Raúl Martínez, a master of 1960s Cuban pop art; and the Picasso-like Wifredo Lam.

Two blocks away, arranged inside the fabulously eclectic Centro Asturianos (a work of art in its own right), the **Museo Nacional de Bellas Artes – Arte Universal** (San Rafael, btwn Agramonte & Av de las Misiones; ⌚9am-5pm Tue-Sat, 10am-2pm Sun) exhibits international art from 500 BC to the present day on three separate floors. Its undisputed highlight is its Spanish collection with some canvases by Zurbarán, Murillo, de Ribera and a tiny Velázquez. Also worth perusing are the 2000-year-old Roman mosaics, Greek pots from the 5th century BC and a suitably refined Gainsborough canvas (in the British room).

★Malecón WATERFRONT

(Map p80) The Malecón, Havana's evocative 7km-long sea drive, is one of the city's most soulful and quintessentially Cuban thoroughfares, and long a favored meeting place for assorted lovers, philosophers, poets, traveling minstrels, fishers and wistful Florida-gazers. The Malecón's atmosphere is most potent at sunset when the weak yellow light from creamy Vedado filters like a dim torch onto the buildings of Centro Habana, lending their dilapidated facades a distinctly ethereal quality.

Laid out in the early 1900s as a salubrious oceanside boulevard for Havana's pleasure-seeking middle classes, the Malecón expanded rapidly eastward in the century's first decade with a mishmash of eclectic architecture that mixed sturdy neoclassicism with whimsical art nouveau. By the 1920s the road had reached the outer limits of burgeoning Vedado, and by the early 1950s it had metamorphosed into a busy six-lane highway that carried streams of wave-dodging Buicks and Chevrolets from the gray hulk of the Castillo de San Salvador de la Punta to the borders of Miramar. Today the Malecón remains Havana's most authentic open-air theater, sometimes dubbed 'the world's longest sofa,' where the whole city comes to meet, greet, date and debate.

Fighting an ongoing battle with the corrosive effects of the ocean, many of the thoroughfare's magnificent buildings now face decrepitude, demolition or irrevocable damage. To combat the problem, 14 blocks of the Malecón have been given special status by the City Historian's Office in an attempt to stop the rot.

The Malecón is particularly evocative when a cold front blows in and massive waves crash thunderously over the sea wall. The road is often closed to cars at these times, meaning you can walk right down the middle of the empty thoroughfare and get very wet.

★Museo de la Revolución MUSEUM

(Map p80; Refugio No 1; CUC$8, guided tours CUC$2; ⌚9:30am-4pm) This emblematic museum resides in the former Presidential Palace, constructed between 1913 and 1920 and used by a string of Cuban presidents, culminating in Fulgencio Batista. The world-famous Tiffany's of New York decorated the interior, and the shimmering Salón de los Espejos (Hall of Mirrors) was designed to resemble the eponymous room at the Palace of Versailles.

The museum itself descends chronologically from the top floor, focusing primarily on the events leading up to, during, and immediately after the Cuban revolution. It presents a sometimes scruffy but always compelling story told in English and Spanish, and tinted with *mucho* propaganda.

The palace's sweeping central staircase, guarded by a bust of José Martí, still retains the bullet holes made during an unsuccessful attack on the palace in March 1957 by a revolutionary student group intent on assassinating President Fulgencio Batista.

The stairs take you up to the 2nd floor and several important exhibit-free rooms, including the Salón Dorado (decorated in Louis VI style and once used for banquets), the Despacho Presidencial (president's office where Fidel Castro was sworn in in 1959), and the capilla (chapel, with a Tiffany chandelier).

In front of the building is a fragment of the former city wall, as well as an SAU-100 tank used by Castro during the 1961 Bay of Pigs battle. In the space behind you'll find the Pavillón Granma, containing a replica of the 18m yacht that carried Fidel Castro and 81 other revolutionaries from Tuxpán, Mexico, to Cuba in December 1956. The boat is encased in glass and guarded 24/7, presumably to stop anyone from breaking in and sailing off to Florida in it. The pavilion is surrounded by other vehicles associated with the revolution, including planes, rockets and an old postal van used as a getaway car during the 1957 attack.

Paseo de Martí HISTORIC SITE

(El Prado; Map p80) Construction of this stately European-style boulevard – the first street outside the old city walls – began in 1770, and the work was completed in the mid-1830s during the term of Captain General Miguel Tacón (1834–38). The original idea was to create a boulevard as splendid as any found in Paris or Barcelona (El Prado owes more than a passing nod to Las Ramblas). The famous bronze lions that guard the central promenade at either end were added in 1928.

Notable Prado buildings include the neo-Renaissance **Palacio de los Matrimonios** (Paseo de Martí No 302), the streamline-modern Teatro Fausto (p115) and the neoclassical **Escuela Nacional de Ballet** (cnr Paseo de Martí & Trocadero), Alicia Alonso's famous ballet school.

These days, the Prado hosts a respected alfresco art market on weekends and countless impromptu soccer matches during the week.

Although officially known as Paseo de Martí, the street is almost universally referred to by its old name: 'Prado.'

Gran Teatro de la Habana Alicia Alonso THEATER

(Map p80; Paseo de Martí No 458) The ornate neo-baroque Centro Gallego, erected as a Galician social club between 1907 and 1914, has has an architectural style best described as a style without style that becomes baroquism. Still standing the test of time, the theater was renovated in 2015 and now sparkles afresh from its perch in Parque Central. Ask about guided tours at the box office.

The original Centro Gallego was built around the existing Teatro Tacón, which opened in 1838 with five masked Carnaval dances. This connection is the basis of claims by the present 2000-seat theater that it's the oldest operating theater in the western hemisphere. History notwithstanding, the architecture is brilliant, as are many of the weekend performances.

Capitolio Nacional LANDMARK

(Map p80; cnr Dragones & Paseo de Martí) The incomparable Capitolio Nacional is Havana's most ambitious and grandiose building, constructed after the post-WWI sugar boom ('Dance of the Millions') gifted the Cuban government a seemingly bottomless bank vault of sugar money. Similar to the Washington, DC, Capitol building, but actually modeled on the Panthéon in Paris, the building was initiated by Cuba's US-backed dictator Gerardo Machado in 1926 and took 5000 workers three years, two months and 20 days to construct at a cost of US$17 million.

Formerly it was the seat of the Cuban Congress, then from 1959 to 2013 it housed the Cuban Academy of Sciences and the National Library of Science and Technology. At the time of research it was being restored and was due to reopen in 2018 as the home of Cuba's national assembly.

Constructed with white Capellanía limestone and block granite, the entrance is guarded by six rounded Doric columns atop a staircase that leads up from Paseo de Martí (Prado). Looking out over the Havana skyline is a 62m stone cupola topped with a replica of 16th-century Florentine sculptor Giambologna's bronze statue of Mercury in the Palazzo de Bargello. Set in the floor directly below the dome is a copy of a 24-carat diamond. Highway distances between Havana and all sites in Cuba are calculated from this point.

The entryway opens up into the Salón de los Pasos Perdidos (Room of the Lost Steps; so named because of its unusual acoustics), at the center of which is the statue of the republic, an enormous bronze woman standing 11m tall and symbolizing the mythic Guardian of Virtue and Work.

Taller Comunitario José Martí GALLERY
(Map p80; Paseo de Martí, btwn Neptuno & Virtudes; ⏲10am-6pm) This is the operations center for Yulier Rodríguez (aka Yulier P) and several other modern Cuban artists, most of whom dabble in graffiti art – still an exciting new genre in Havana. Yulier's paintings, characterized by their gaunt alien-like figures, have recently started to embellish many of Havana's ruined buildings. You'll spot several of them decorating the porch outside this workshop-gallery.

Convento & Iglesia del Carmen CHURCH
(Map p80; cnr Calzada de la Infanta & Neptuno; ⏲7:30am-noon & 3-7pm Tue-Sun) This little-visited church's craning bell-tower dominates the Centro Habana skyline and is topped by a huge statue of Nuestra Señora del Carmen, but the real prizes lie inside: rich Seville-style tiles, a gilded altarpiece, ornate woodcarving and swirling frescoes. Surprisingly, the church was only built in 1923 to house the Carmelite order. The building is considered 'eclectic.'

El Barrio Chino AREA
(Map p80) One of the world's more surreal Chinatowns, Havana's Barrio Chino is notable for its gaping lack of Chinese people, most of whom left as soon as a newly inaugurated Fidel Castro uttered the word *'socialismo.'* Nevertheless, it's worth a wander on the basis of its novelty and handful of decent restaurants.

The first Chinese arrived as contract laborers on the island in the late 1840s to fill in the gaps left by the decline of the transatlantic slave trade. By the 1920s Havana's Chinatown had burgeoned into the biggest Asian neighborhood in Latin America, a bustling hub of human industry that spawned its own laundries, pharmacies, theaters and grocery stores. The slide began in the early 1960s when thousands of business-minded Chinese relocated to the US. Recognizing the tourist potential of the area in the 1990s, the Cuban government invested money and resources into rejuvenating the district's distinct historical character with bilingual street signs, a large pagoda-shaped arch at the entrance to Calle Dragones, and incentives given to local Chinese businesspeople to promote restaurants. Today most of the action centers on the narrow Calle Cuchillo and its surrounding streets.

Hotel Inglaterra HISTORIC BUILDING
(Map p80; Paseo de Martí No 416) Havana's oldest hotel first opened its doors in 1856 on the site of a popular bar called El Louvre (the hotel's alfresco bar still bears the name). Facing leafy Parque Central, the building exhibits the neoclassical design features in vogue at the time, complemented by a lobby beautified with Moorish tiles. At a banquet here in 1879, José Martí made a speech advocating Cuban independence, and much later US journalists covering the Spanish-Cuban-American War stayed at the hotel.

Iglesia del Sagrado Corazón de Jesús CHURCH
(Map p80; Av Simón Bolívar, btwn Gervasio & Padre Varela; ⏲hours vary) A little out on a limb but well worth the walk is this inspiring marble creation with a distinctive white steeple – it's one of Cuba's few Gothic buildings. The church is rightly famous for its magnificent stained-glass windows, and the light that penetrates through the eaves first thing in the morning (when the church is deserted) gives the place an ethereal quality.

Parque de los Enamorados PARK
(Map p80) In Parque de los Enamorados (Lovers' Park), surrounded by streams of speeding traffic, lies a surviving section of the colonial Cárcel or Tacón Prison, built in 1838, where many Cuban patriots including José Martí were imprisoned. A brutal place that sent prisoners to perform hard labor in the nearby San Lázaro quarry, it was demolished in 1939, with this park dedicated to the memory of those who had suffered so horribly within its walls. Two tiny cells and a chapel are all that remain.

Behind the park, the beautiful wedding-cake-like building (art nouveau with a dash of eclecticism) flying the Spanish flag is the old **Palacio Velasco** (Cárcel No 51), now the Spanish embassy.

Beyond that, on a traffic island, is the Memorial a los Estudiantes de Medicina, a fragment of wall encased in marble marking the spot where eight Cuban medical students were shot by the Spanish in 1871 in reprisal for allegedly desecrating the tomb of a Spanish journalist.

Old City Wall HISTORIC SITE

(Map p64) In the 17th century, anxious to defend the city from attacks by pirates and overzealous foreign armies, Cuba's paranoid colonial authorities drew up plans for the construction of a 5km-long city wall. Built between 1674 and 1740, the wall on completion was 1.5m thick and 10m high, running along a line now occupied by Av de las Misiones and Av de Bélgica.

Among the wall's myriad defenses were nine bastions and 180 big guns aimed toward the sea. The only way in and out of the city was through 11 heavily guarded gates that closed every night and opened every morning to the sound of a solitary gunshot. From 1863 the walls were demolished, but a few segments remain, the largest of which stands on Av de Bélgica close to the train station.

Parque Central PARK

(Map p80) Diminutive Parque Central is a verdant haven from the belching buses and roaring taxis that ply their way along Paseo de Martí (Prado). The park, long a microcosm of daily Havana life, was expanded to its present size in the late 19th century after the city walls were knocked down. The 1905 marble statue of José Martí at its center was the first of thousands to be erected in Cuba.

Hard to miss over to one side is the group of baseball fans who linger 24/7 at the famous Esquina Caliente, discussing form, tactics and the Havana teams' prospects in the playoffs.

Parque de la Fraternidad PARK

(Map p80) Leafy Parque de la Fraternidad was established in 1892 to commemorate the fourth centenary of the Spanish landing in the Americas. A few decades later it was remodeled and renamed to mark the 1927 Pan-American Conference. The name is meant to signify American brotherhood, hence the many busts of Latin and North American leaders that embellish the green areas, including one of US president Abraham Lincoln.

Today the park is the terminus of numerous metro bus routes, and is sometimes referred to as 'Jurassic Park' because of the plethora of photogenic old American cars now used as *colectivos* (collective taxis) that congregate here.

Fuente de la India MONUMENT

(Map p80; Paseo de Martí) Save a glance for this white Carrara marble fountain, carved by Giuseppe Gaggini in 1837 for the Count of Villanueva, now situated on a traffic island in front of Hotel Saratoga. It portrays a regal indigenous woman adorned with a crown of eagle's feathers and seated on a throne surrounded by four gargoylesque dolphins.

In one hand she holds a horn-shaped basket filled with fruit, in the other, a shield bearing the city's coat of arms – a golden key between two mountains, a sun above the sea, three stripes emblazoned on a white background, and a royal palm.

Asociación Cultural Yoruba de Cuba MUSEUM

(Map p80; Paseo de Martí No 615; CUC$5; ⏲9am-4:30pm Mon-Sat) To untangle the confusing mysteries of the Santería religion, its saints and their powers, decamp to this museum-cum-cultural-center. Aside from sculpted models of the various *orishas* (deities), the association also hosts *tambores* (Santería drum ceremonies) on Friday and Saturday at 6pm (CUC$5). Check the noticeboard at the door. Note that there's a church dress code for the *tambores* (no shorts or tank tops).

Real Fábrica de Tabacos Partagás FACTORY

(Map p80; San Carlos No 816, btwn Peñalver & Sitios; tours CUC$10; ⏲tours every 15min 9am-1pm Mon-Fri) One of Havana's oldest and most famous cigar factories, the landmark Real Fábrica de Tabacos Partagás was founded in 1845 by Spaniard Jaime Partagás. Since 2013, the factory has moved from its original building behind the Capitolio to this location just off Calle Padre Varela in Centro Habana. Tickets for factory tours must be bought beforehand in the lobby of the Hotel Saratoga (p92).

Centro Habana

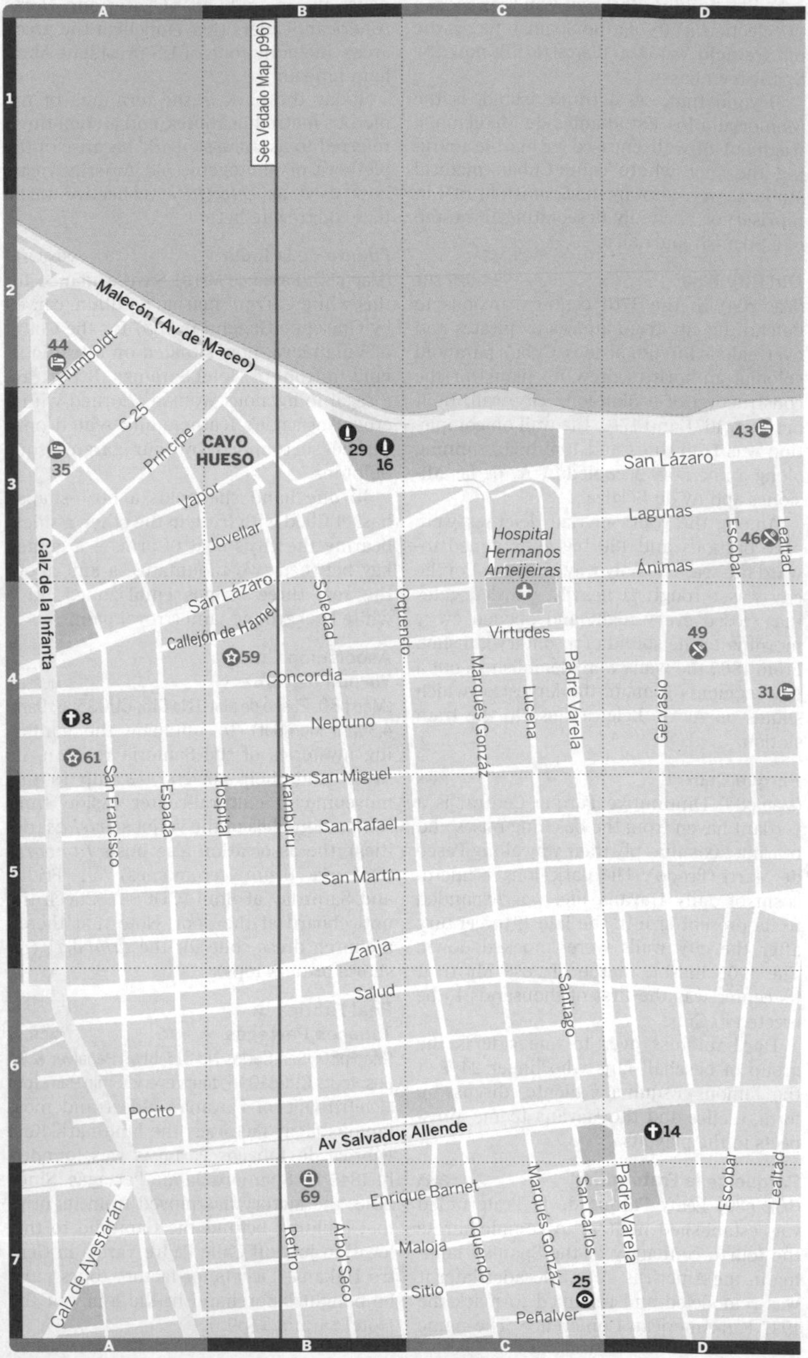

See Vedado Map (p96)

A B C D

1 2 3 4 5 6 7

CAYO HUESO

Malecón (Av de Maceo)

Humboldt

C 25

Príncipe

Vapor

Jovellar

San Lázaro

Callejón de Hamel

Calz de la Infanta

Soledad

Oquendo

Concordia

Neptuno

San Miguel

San Rafael

San Martín

Zanja

Salud

Pocito

Av Salvador Allende

Enrique Barnet

Maloja

Sitio

Peñalver

Calz de Ayestarán

Retiro

Árbol Seco

Marqués Gonzáz

San Carlos

Padre Varela

Escobar

Lealtad

San Francisco

Espada

Hospital

Aramburu

Hospital Hermanos Ameijeiras

Virtudes

Lucena

Santiago

Gervasio

Lagunas

Ánimas

44 35 29 16 43 46 49 31 59 8 61 14 69 25

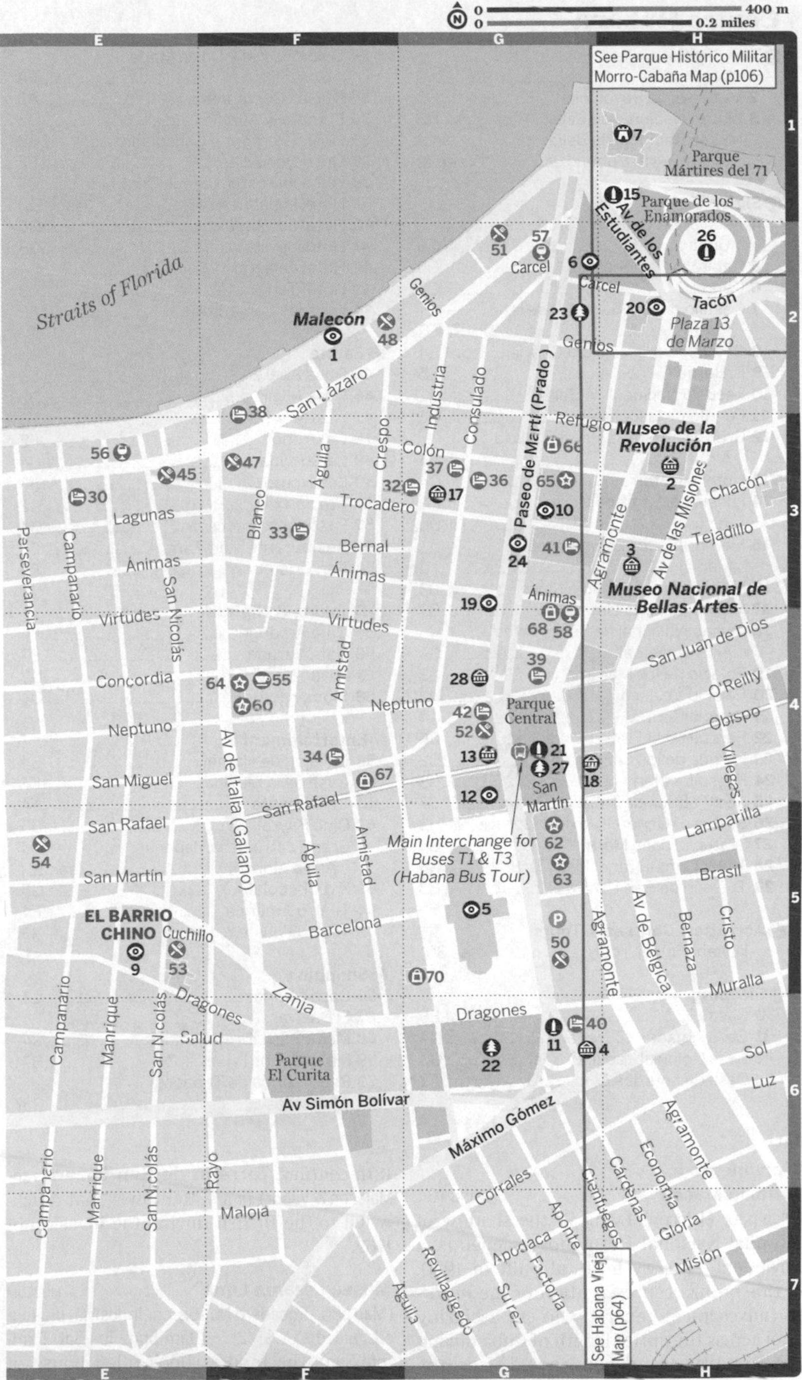

0 400 m
0 0.2 miles
See Parque Histórico Militar Morro-Cabaña Map (p106)
Parque Mártires del 71
Parque de los Enamorados
Av de los Estudiantes
Straits of Florida
Malecón
Carcel
Genios
Tacón
Plaza 13 de Marzo
San Lázaro
Paseo de Martí (Prado)
Refugio
Museo de la Revolución
Colón
Trocadero
Lagunas
Bernal
Ánimas
Virtudes
Chacón
Tejadillo
Museo Nacional de Bellas Artes
Av de las Misiones
Agramonte
San Juan de Dios
O'Reilly
Obispo
Concordia
Neptuno
Parque Central
San Miguel
San Rafael
San Martín
Main Interchange for Buses T1 & T3 (Habana Bus Tour)
Lamparilla
Brasil
Av de Bélgica
Bernaza
Cristo
Villegas
EL BARRIO CHINO
Cuchillo
Barcelona
Zanja
Dragones
Salud
Muralla
Parque El Curita
Sol
Luz
Av Simón Bolívar
Máximo Gómez
Corrales
Maloja
Aponte
Apodaca
Factoría
Suárez
Revillagigedo
Cienfuegos
Cárdenas
Economía
Gloria
Misión
See Habana Vieja Map (p64)
Perseverancia
Campanario
San Nicolás
Manrique
Rayo
Av de Italia (Galiano)
Blanco
Águila
Amistad
Crespo
Industria
Consulado
HAVANA

Centro Habana

Top Sights

1 Malecón F2
2 Museo de la Revolución H3
3 Museo Nacional de Bellas Artes H3
Museo Nacional de Bellas Artes – Arte Cubano (see 3)

Sights

4 Asociación Cultural Yoruba de Cuba G6
5 Capitolio Nacional G5
6 Cárcel G2
7 Castillo de San Salvador de la Punta H1
8 Convento & Iglesia del Carmen A4
9 El Barrio Chino E5
10 Escuela Nacional de Ballet G3
11 Fuente de la India G6
12 Gran Teatro de la Habana Alicia Alonso G4
13 Hotel Inglaterra G4
14 Iglesia del Sagrado Corazón de Jesús D6
15 Memorial a los Estudiantes de Medicina H1
16 Monumento a Antonio Maceo B3
17 Museo Lezama Lima G3
18 Museo Nacional de Bellas Artes – Arte Universal G4
19 Palacio de los Matrimonios G3
20 Palacio Velasco H2
21 Parque Central G4
22 Parque de la Fraternidad G6
23 Parque de los Enamorados G2
24 Paseo de Martí G3
25 Real Fábrica de Tabacos Partagás C7
26 Statue of General Máximo Gómez H2
27 Statue of José Martí G4
28 Taller Comunitario José Martí G4
29 Torreón de San Lázaro B3

Activities, Courses & Tours

Havana Super Tour (see 30)

Sleeping

30 Casa 1932 E3
31 Casa Amada D4
32 Casa Colonial Yadilis & Yoel G3
33 Casa de Lourdes & José F3
34 Dulce Hostal – Dulce María González F4
35 Duplex Cervantes A3
36 Eumelia & Aurelio G3
37 Hostal Peregrino Consulado G3
38 Hotel Deauville F2
39 Hotel Iberostar Parque Central G4
Hotel Inglaterra (see 13)
40 Hotel Saratoga G6
41 Hotel Sevilla G3
42 Hotel Telégrafo G4
43 Hotel Terral D3
44 Lourdes Cervantes A2

Eating

45 Casa Abel E3
46 Casa Miglis D3
47 Castas y Tal F3
48 Castropol F2
49 La Guarida D4
50 Los Nardos G5
51 Nazdarovie G2
52 Pastelería Francesa G4
53 Restaurante Tien-Tan E5
54 San Cristóbal E5

Drinking & Nightlife

55 Café Arcangel F4
56 Café Neruda E3
57 Prado No 12 G2
58 Sloppy Joe's G4

Entertainment

59 Callejón de Hamel B4
60 Casa de la Música F4
61 Cine Infanta A4
62 Cine Payret G5
Gran Teatro de la Habana Alicia Alonso (see 12)
63 Kid Chocolate G5
64 Teatro América F4
65 Teatro Fausto G3

Shopping

66 Casa Guerlain G3
67 El Bulevar F4
68 Memorias Librería G4
69 Plaza Carlos III B7
70 Real Fábrica de Tabacos Partagás G5

Monumento a Antonio Maceo MONUMENT

(Map p80; Malecón) Lying in the shadow of Hospital Nacional Hermanos Ameijeiras, a Soviet-era 24-story hospital built in 1980, is this bronze representation of the *mulato* (mixed race) general who cut a blazing trail across the entire length of Cuba during the First War of Independence. The nearby 18th-century **Torreón de San Lázaro** (cnr Malecón & Vapor) is a watchtower that quickly fell to the British during the invasion of 1762.

Museo Lezama Lima MUSEUM

(Map p80; Trocadero No 162, cnr Industria; unguided/guided CUC$1/2; 9am-5pm Tue-Sat, 9am-1pm Sun) The modest book-filled house of the late Cuban man of letters, José Lezama Lima, is an obligatory pit stop for anyone attempting to understand Cuban literature beyond Hemingway. Lima's magnum opus was the rambling classic, *Paradiso,* and he wrote most of it here.

Vedado

Majestic, spread-out Vedado is Havana's once-notorious Mafia-run district. During Cuba's 50-year dalliance with the US, this was the city's commercial hub and, in many ways, it still is; although these days the nightlife is less tawdry, the casinos have become discos, and the hotels seem more like historical relics than havens of luxury.

Aside from its small clutch of modernist *rascacielos* (skyscrapers), Vedado is a largely leafy residential quarter bisected by two wide Parisian-style boulevards and anchored by the bombastic Plaza de la Revolución and the beautifully eerie Necrópolis Cristóbal Colón.

★Necrópolis Cristóbal Colón — CEMETERY

(Map p96; CUC$5; 8am-6pm, last entry 5pm) Havana's main cemetery (a national monument), one of the largest in the Americas, is renowned for its striking religious iconography and elaborate marble statues. Far from being eerie, a walk through these 57 hallowed hectares can be an educational and emotional stroll through the annals of Cuban history. A map (CUC$1) showing the graves of assorted artists, sportspeople, politicians, writers, scientists and revolutionaries is for sale at the entrance.

Enter via the splendid Byzantine-Romanesque gateway, the Puerta de la Paz; the tomb of independence leader General Máximo Gómez (1905) is on the right (look for the bronze face in a circular medallion). Further along past the first circle, and also on the right, are the firefighters monument (1890) and neo-Romanesque Capilla Central (1886), in the center of the cemetery. Just northeast of this chapel is the graveyard's most celebrated (and visited) tomb, that of **Señora Amelia Goyri** (cnr Calles 1 & F), better known as La Milagrosa (the miraculous one), who died while giving birth on May 3, 1901. The marble figure of a woman with a large cross and a baby in her arms is easy to find due to the many flowers piled on the tomb and the local devotees in attendance. For many years after her death, her heartbroken husband visited the grave several times a day. He always knocked with one of four iron rings on the burial vault and walked away backwards so he could see her for as long as possible. When the bodies were exhumed some years later, Amelia's body was uncorrupted (a sign of sanctity in the Catholic faith) and the baby, who had been buried at its mother's feet, was allegedly found in her arms. As a result, La Milagrosa became the focus of a huge spiritual cult in Cuba, and thousands of people come here annually with gifts, in the hope of fulfilling dreams or solving problems. In keeping with tradition, pilgrims knock with the iron ring on the vault and walk away backwards when they leave.

As important as La Milagrosa among the Santería community, the so-called tomb of 'Hermano José' marks the grave of a woman called Leocadia Pérez Herrero, a black Havana medium known for her great acts of charity among the poor in the early 20th century. Leocadia claimed that she consulted with a mythical Santería priest called Hermano José who encouraged and guided her in her generous charitable acts. As a spiritual and superstitious person, she always kept a painting of Hermano José's image in her house and, when she died in 1962, the canvas was buried alongside her. Today followers of Santería venerate Hermano José and regularly come to Leocadia's grave to ask for charitable favors. In keeping with Santería tradition, they often leave flowers, glasses of rum, half-smoked cigars or sacrificed chickens on the grave.

Also worth looking out for are the graves of novelist Alejo Carpentier (1904–80), scientist Carlos Finlay (1833–1915), the Martyrs of Granma and the Veterans of the Independence Wars.

★Museo Napoleónico — MUSEUM

(Map p96; San Miguel No 1159; CUC$3; 9:30am-5pm Tue-Sat, 9:30am-12:30pm Sun) Without a doubt one of the best museums in Havana and, by definition, Cuba, this magnificently laid-out collection of 7000 objects associated with the life of Napoleon Bonaparte was amassed by Cuban sugar baron Julio Lobo and politician Orestes Ferrara.

Highlights include sketches of Voltaire, paintings of the Battle of Waterloo, china, furniture, an interesting re-creation of Napoleon's study and bedroom, and one of several bronze Napoleonic death masks made two days after the emperor's death by his personal physician, Dr Francisco Antommarchi. It's set over four floors of a beautiful Vedado mansion next to Havana University and has stunning views from its 4th-floor terrace.

Hotel Nacional HISTORIC BUILDING

(Map p96; cnr Calles O & 21; ⊙free tours 10am & 3pm Mon-Fri, 10am Sat) Built in 1930 as a copy of the Breakers Hotel in Palm Beach, Florida, the eclectic art deco/neoclassical Hotel Nacional is a national monument and one of Havana's architectural emblems.

The hotel's notoriety was cemented in October 1933 when, following a sergeants' coup by Fulgencio Batista that toppled the regime of Gerardo Machado, 300 aggrieved army officers took refuge in the building hoping to curry favor with resident US ambassador Sumner Welles, who was staying here. Much to the officers' chagrin, Welles promptly left, allowing Batista's troops to open fire on the hotel, killing 14 of them and injuring seven. More were executed later, after they had surrendered.

In December 1946 the hotel gained infamy of a different kind when US mobsters Meyer Lansky and Lucky Luciano used it to host the largest ever get-together of the North American Mafia, who gathered here under the guise of a Frank Sinatra concert.

These days the hotel maintains a more reputable face and the once famous casino is long gone, though the spectacular Parisian cabaret is still a popular draw. Nonguests can admire the Moorish lobby, stroll the breezy grounds overlooking the Malecón or partake in a free guided hotel tour.

Museo de Artes Decorativas MUSEUM

(Map p96; Calle 17 No 502, btwn Calles D & E; CUC$3; ⊙9:30am-4pm Tue-Sat) One of Havana's best museums is something of a lost treasure half-hidden in the Vedado neighborhood. The decorative arts museum is replete with fancy rococo, Asian and art deco baubles. Equally interesting is the building itself, of French design, commissioned in 1924 by the wealthy Gómez family who built the Manzana de Gómez shopping center in Centro Habana.

Memorial a José Martí MONUMENT

(Map p96; Plaza de la Revolución; CUC$3; ⊙9:30am-4pm Mon-Sat) Center stage in Plaza de la Revolución is this monument, which at 138.5m is Havana's tallest structure. Fronted by an impressive 17m marble statue of a seated Martí in a pensive *Thinker* pose, the memorial houses a museum – the definitive word on Martí in Cuba – and a 129m lookout reached via a small CUC$2 lift (broken at last visit) with fantastic city views.

Parque Lennon PARK

(Map p96; cnr Calles 17 & 6) There are two similarly named parks in Havana – one named for the Russian communist leader and this other one, dedicated to the more benign, but no less iconic, ex-Beatle. The park is anchored by a hyper-realistic statue of the musician unveiled by Fidel Castro in 2000 on the 20th anniversary of his death. Since the statue's glasses were repeatedly stolen, a security guard has been employed to watch it.

The guard usually maintains a discreet distance and will produce said spectacles should you wish to take a picture.

Plaza de la Revolución SQUARE

(Map p96) Conceived by French urbanist Jean Claude Forestier in the 1920s, the gigantic Plaza de la Revolución (known as Plaza Cívica until 1959) was part of Havana's 'new city,' which grew up between 1920 and 1959. As the nexus of Forestier's ambitious plan, the square was built on a small hill (the Loma de los Catalanes) in the manner of Paris' Place de l'Étoile, with various avenues fanning out toward the Río Almendares, Vedado and the Parque de la Fraternidad in Centro Habana.

Surrounded by gray, utilitarian buildings constructed in the late 1950s, the square today is the base of the Cuban government and a place where large-scale political rallies are held. In January 1998, one million people (nearly one-tenth of the Cuban population) crammed into the square to hear Pope John Paul II say Mass.

The ugly concrete block on the northern side of the plaza is the Ministerio del Interior, well known for its huge mural of Che Guevara (a copy of Alberto Korda's famous 1960 photograph) with the words *Hasta la Victoria Siempre* (Always Toward Victory) emblazoned underneath. In 2009 a similarly designed image of Cuba's other heroic *guerrillero,* Camilo Cienfuegos, was added on the adjacent telecommunications building. Its wording reads: *Vas Bien Fidel* (You're going well Fidel).

On the eastern side is the 1957 **Biblioteca Nacional José Martí** (⊙8am-9:45pm Mon-Sat) FREE, which sometimes has a photo exhibit in the lobby, while on the west is the Teatro Nacional de Cuba (p115).

Tucked behind the Memorial a José Martí are the governmental offices housed in the heavily guarded Comité Central del Partido Comunista de Cuba.

Av de los Presidentes MONUMENT
(Map p96) Statues of illustrious Latin American leaders line the Las Ramblas–style Calle G (officially known as Av de los Presidentes), including Salvador Allende (Chile), Benito Juárez (Mexico) and Simón Bolívar. At the top of the avenue is a huge marble Monumento a José Miguel Gómez, Cuba's second president. At the other end, the monument to his predecessor – Cuba's first president – Tomás Estrada Palma (long considered a US puppet) has been toppled, with just his shoes remaining on the original plinth.

Guarding the entrance to Calle G on the Malecón is the equestrian **Monumento a Calixto García** (cnr Malecón & Av de los Presidentes), paying homage to the valiant Cuban general who was prevented by US military leaders in Santiago de Cuba from attending the Spanish surrender in 1898. Twenty-four bronze plaques around the statue provide a history of García's 30-year struggle for Cuban independence.

Hotel Habana Libre NOTABLE BUILDING
(Map p96; Calle L, btwn Calles 23 & 25) This classic modernist hotel – the former Havana Hilton – was commandeered by Castro's revolutionaries in 1959 just nine months after it had opened, and was promptly renamed the Habana Libre. During the first few months of the revolution, Fidel ruled the country from a luxurious suite on the 24th floor.

A 670-sq-meter Venetian tile mural by Amelia Peláez is splashed across the front of the building, while upstairs Alfredo Sosa Bravo's *Carro de la revolución* utilizes 525 ceramic pieces. There are some good shops and an interesting photo gallery, displaying snaps of the all-conquering *barbudas* (literally 'bearded ones') lolling around with their guns in the hotel's lobby in January 1959.

Monumento a las Victimas del Maine MONUMENT
(Map p96; Malecón) West beyond the Hotel Nacional is a monument (1926) to the 266 American marines who were killed when the battleship USS *Maine* blew up mysteriously in Havana harbor in 1898. The American eagle that once sat on top was decapitated during the 1959 revolution.

Quinta de los Molinos GARDENS, LANDMARK
(Map p96; cnr Av Salvador Allende & Luaces; guided tour CUC$5; ⏲by tour 10am Tue & Sat) The former stately residence of Independence War general Máximo Gómez, the Quinta sits amid lush grounds that have been managed as botanical gardens since 1839. While the former Gómez residence is currently closed, the grounds have recently reopened as a botanical garden with 160 tree species, 40 bird species and the tiny colorful polymita snails that are endemic to Cuba. There's also a butterfly enclosure, the first of its type in the country. Guided visits only.

Museo de Danza MUSEUM
(Map p96; Línea No 365, cnr Av de los Presidentes; CUC$2; ⏲10am-6pm Mon-Sat) A dance museum in Cuba – well, there's no surprise there. This well-laid-out exhibition space in an eclectic Vedado mansion collects objects from Cuba's rich dance history, with many artifacts drawn from the collection of ex-ballerina Alicia Alonso.

Universidad de la Habana UNIVERSITY
(Map p96; cnr Calles L & San Lázaro) Founded by Dominican monks in 1728 and secularized in 1842, Havana University began life in Habana Vieja before moving to its present site in 1902. The existing neoclassical complex dates from the second quarter of the 20th century, and today some 30,000 students here take courses in social sciences, humanities, natural sciences, mathematics and economics.

Perched on a Vedado hill at the top of the famous *escalinata* (stairway), near the Alma Mater statue, the university's central quadrangle, the Plaza Ignacio Agramonte, displays a tank captured by Castro's rebels in 1958. Directly in front is the Librería Alma Mater (library) and, to the left, the **Museo de Historia Natural Felipe Poey** (CUC$1; ⏲9am-noon & 1-4pm Mon-Fri Sep-Jul), the oldest museum in Cuba, founded in 1874 by the Royal Academy of Medical, Physical and Natural Sciences. Many of the stuffed specimens of Cuban flora and fauna date from the 19th century. Upstairs is the **Museo Antropológico Montané** (CUC$1; ⏲9am-noon & 1-4pm Mon-Fri Sep-Jul), established in 1903, with a rich collection of pre-Columbian Indian artifacts including the wooden 10th-century Ídolo del Tabaco.

Edificio Focsa LANDMARK

(Focsa Bldg; Map p96; cnr Calles 17 & M) Unmissable on the Havana skyline, the modernist Edificio Focsa was built between 1954 and 1956 in a record 28 months using pioneering computer technology. In 1999 it was listed as one of the seven modern engineering wonders of Cuba. With 39 floors housing 373 apartments, it was, on its completion in June 1956, the second-largest concrete structure of its type in the world, constructed entirely without the use of cranes.

When it fell on hard times in the early 1990s, the upper floors of the Focsa became nests for vultures, and in 2000 an elevator cable snapped, killing one person. Rejuvenated once more after a restoration project, this skyline-dominating Havana giant nowadays contains residential apartments and – in the shape of top-floor restaurant La Torre (p108) – one of the city's most celebrated eating establishments.

US Embassy LANDMARK

(Map p96; Calzada, btwn Calles L & M) Arguably the world's most famous US embassy and certainly its newest, this modernist seven-story building with the high security fencing on the Malecón was formerly the US Interests Section, set up by the Carter administration in the late 1970s. In July 2015 the US embassy reopened again for the first time in 54 years thanks to the political thaw instigated by the Obama administration.

The embassy faces the Plaza Tribuna Anti-Imperialista (also known as Plaza de la Dignidad), once a site of major protests directed against the Americans. The mass of flagpoles was put up by the Cubans to block out an electronic message board mounted on the former Interests Section that flashed up messages, or propaganda, depending on which side of the fence you're on (!).

Edificio López Serrano LANDMARK

(Map p96; Calle L, btwn Calles 11 & 13) Tucked away behind the US Interests Section is this art deco tower, which looks like the Empire State Building with the bottom 70 floors chopped off. One of Havana's first *rascacielos* (skyscrapers) when it was built in 1932, the López Serrano building now houses apartments.

Gran Synagoga Bet Shalom SYNAGOGUE

(Map p96; Calle I No 251, btwn Calles 13 & 15; ⌚hours vary) Cuba has three synagogues servicing a Jewish population of approximately 1500. The main community center and library are located here, where the friendly staff are happy to tell interested visitors about the fascinating and little-reported history of the Jews in Cuba.

Festivals & Events

Havana has a packed program of annual events. There's a summer Carnaval, multiple music festivals (including the much lauded December Festival Internacional de Jazz), sports events such as the Marabana (marathon), and big international occasions that pull in famous names from abroad.

Feria Internacional del Libro LITERATURE

(www.filcuba.cult.cu; ⌚Feb) Headquartered in La Cabaña fort, this annual book fair kicks off in Havana in February before going on tour around the country.

Carnaval de la Habana CULTURAL

(⌚Jul/Aug) Parades, dancing, music, colorful costumes and striking effigies – Havana's annual summer shindig might not be as famous as its more rootsy Santiago de Cuba counterpart, but the celebrations and processions along the Malecón leave plenty of other city carnivals in the shade.

Festival Internacional de Ballet de la Habana DANCE

(www.festivalballethabana.cu; ⌚Oct) Cuba demonstrates its ballet prowess at this annual festival, with energetic leaps and graceful pirouettes starting in late October.

Festival Internacional del Nuevo Cine Latinoamericano FILM

(www.habanafilmfestival.com; ⌚Dec) Widely lauded celebration of Cuba's massive film culture, with plenty of nods to other Latin American countries. Held at various cinemas and theaters across the city.

Tours

★**Havana Super Tour** TOURS

(Map p80; ☎52-65-71-01; www.campanario63.com; Campanario No 63, btwn San Lázaro & Lagunas; tours CUC$35) One of Havana's first private tour companies, Super Tour runs all its trips in classic American cars. The two most popular are the art deco architectural tour and the 'Mob tour,' uncovering the city's pre-revolution Mafia haunts. If you're short on time, the full-blown Havana day

HISTORICAL JIGSAW

Never in the field of architectural preservation has so much been achieved by so many with so few resources. You hear plenty about the sterling performance of the Cuban education and healthcare systems in the international press, but relatively little about the remarkable work that has gone into preserving the country's valuable but seriously endangered historical legacy, most notably in Habana Vieja.

A work in progress since the late 1970s, the piecing back together of Havana's 'old town' after decades of neglect has been a foresighted and startlingly miraculous process considering the economic odds stacked against it. The genius behind the project is Eusebio Leal Spengler, Havana's celebrated City Historian who, unperturbed by the tightening of the financial screws during Cuba's Special Period, set up Habaguanex in 1994, a holding company that earns hard currency through tourism and re-invests it in a mix of historical preservation and city-wide urban regeneration. By safeguarding Havana's historical heritage, Leal and his cohorts have attracted more tourists to the city and earned a bigger slice of revenue for Habaguanex to plough back into further restoration work and much-needed social projects.

Eschewing the temptation to turn Havana's old quarter into a historical theme park, Leal has sought to rebuild the city's urban jigsaw as an authentic 'living' center that provides tangible benefits for the neighborhood's 91,000-plus inhabitants. As a result, schools, neighborhood committees, care-homes for seniors, and centers for children with disabilities sit seamlessly alongside the cleaned-up colonial edifices. Every time you put your money into a Habana Vieja hotel, museum or restaurant, you are contributing, not just to the quarter's continued restoration, but to a whole raft of social projects that directly benefit the local population.

Today, the City Historian's Office splits its annual tourist income (reported to be in excess of US$160 million) between further restoration (45%) and social projects in the city (55%), of which there are now over 400. So far, one quarter of Habana Vieja has been returned to the height of its colonial-era splendor, with ample tourist attractions including 20 Habaguanex-run hotels, four classic forts and more than 30 museums.

tour (CUC$150) will whip you around all of the city's key sights.

★San Cristóbal Agencia de Viajes CULTURAL
(Map p64; ☎7-863-9555; www.cubaheritage.com; Oficios No 110, btwn Lamparilla & Amargura; ⏲8:30am-5:30pm Mon-Fri, to 12:30pm Sat) A travel agency representing the City Historian's Office, operating out of Habana Vieja's classic hotels. Its income helps finance restoration and it offers the best tours in Havana. Highlights are the 'Historical Center Conservation' tour, from Christ to Lennon (a tour of Havana's sculptures), and 'Eclecticism and Modernity' (an architectural tour).

★CubaRuta Bikes CYCLING
(Map p96; ☎52-47-66-33; www.cubarutabikes.com; Calle 16 No 152; city tour CUC$29) This was Havana's first decent bicycle-hire and tour company when it started in 2013. Its guided cycling tours have proved to be consistently popular, particularly the three-hour classic city tour, which takes in the Bosque de la Habana, Plaza Vieja, Plaza de la Revolución, the Malecón and more. Book via phone or email at least a day in advance. It also offers sturdy well-maintained bikes for rent.

Courses

Aside from Spanish-language courses, Havana offers a large number of learning activities for aspiring students. Dancing and art classes are the most popular and in recent years several private businesses have started to offer facilities for both.

★La Casa del Son DANCING, LANGUAGE
(Map p64; ☎7-861-6179; www.bailarencuba.com; Empedrado No 411, btwn Compostela & Aguacate; per hour from CUC$10) A highly popular private dance school based in an attractive 18th-century house. It also offers lessons in Spanish language and percussion. Very flexible with class times.

Taller Experimental de Gráfica ART
(Map p64; ☎7-862-0979; Callejón del Chorro No 6) Offers classes in the art of engraving.

Individualized instruction costs CUC$25 for one day; CUC$250 for one week. Make arrangements at least a few days in advance.

Club Salseando Chévere DANCING
(www.salseandochevere.com; cnr Calles 49 & 28; per hour from CUC$25) One of Havana's best dance schools specializing in salsa lessons, but it can also guide you through rumba, *chachachá*, mambo and more. It's based out of El Salón Chévere (p133), a popular dance club in Parque Almendares.

Conjunto Folklórico Nacional de Cuba DANCING
(Map p96; ☎7-830-3060; www.folkcuba.cult.cu; Calle 4 No 103, btwn Calzada & Calle 5) Teaches highly recommended classes in *folklórico* dance, including esoteric forms of Santería and rumba. It also teaches percussion. Classes start on the third Monday in January and the first Monday in July, and cost CUC$500 for a 15-day course. An admission test places students in classes of four different levels.

Universidad de la Habana LANGUAGE
(Map p96; ☎7-832-4245, 7-831-3751; www.uh.cu; Calle J No 556, Edificio Varona, 2nd fl) The university's FLEX (School of Foreign Languages) faculty offers Spanish courses year-round, beginning on the first Monday of each month. Costs start at CUC$200 for 40 hours (two weeks) and go on up to a nine-month intensive course (CUC$1798). You must first sit a placement test to determine your level (graded one to five).

It is always best to make arrangements before you travel. For the FLEX page on the university website choose 'Facultades' and then 'Lenguas Extranjeras.'

Paradiso CULTURAL
(Map p96; ☎7-832-9538; www.paradiso.es; Calle 19 No 560) A cultural agency that offers an astounding array of courses of between four and 12 weeks on everything from Afro-Cuban dance to ceramics workshops. Check the website for a full list of options.

Sleeping

With literally thousands of casas particulares (private houses) letting out rooms, you'll never struggle to find accommodation in Havana. Rock-bottom budget hotels can match casas for price, but not comfort. There's a dearth of decent hotels in the midrange price bracket, while Havana's top-end hotels are plentiful and offer oodles of atmosphere, even if the overall standards can't always match facilities elsewhere in the Caribbean.

Habana Vieja

★**Greenhouse** CASA PARTICULAR $
(Map p64; ☎7-862-9877; fabio.quintana@infomed.sld.cu; San Ignacio No 656, btwn Merced & Jesús María; r CUC$30-40; ❄) A fabulous Old Town casa run by Eugenio and Fabio, who have added superb design features to their huge colonial home. Check out the terrace fountain and the backlit model of Havana on the stairway. There are seven rooms in this virtual hotel packed with precious period furnishings and gorgeous wooden beds; two of them share a bathroom.

Hostal Calle Habana CASA PARTICULAR $
(Map p64; ☎7-867-4081; www.hostalcallehabana.com; Habana No 559, btwn Brasil & Amargura; r CUC$30-40; ❄) This is one of a new wave of private casas that realistically qualify as small hotels. It's well managed and beautifully maintained with a small cafe (guests only) out front, and a profusion of art, plants and tiles throughout. The four rooms are clean and uncluttered, but punctuated with tasteful lamps and bright paintings.

For the price, it's possibly the best bargain in the city.

Hostal El Encinar CASA PARTICULAR $
(Map p64; ☎7-860-1257; www.hostalperegrino.com; Chacón No 60 Altos, btwn Cuba & Aguiar; r incl breakfast CUC$35-50; ❄) This outpost of Centro Habana's popular Hostal Peregrino (p90) is like a little hotel for independent travelers. Eight rooms all with private bathrooms are approaching boutique standard with classy tilework, hairdryers, TVs and minibars. There's a comfortable lounge area and a delightful roof terrace overlooking the bay and La Cabaña fort.

Jesús & María CASA PARTICULAR $
(Map p64; ☎7-851-1378; jesusmaria2003@yahoo.com; Aguacate No 518, btwn Sol & Muralla; r CUC$30; ❄) An old-school casa where you have to walk through the family sitting room ducking deftly beneath the TV in order to get to your room. Inside, the house morphs into something bigger, with an ample terrace equipped with rockers where you can enjoy an equally ample breakfast.

The five spotless rooms come with safe boxes and comfortable beds.

Casa Colonial del 1715 CASA PARTICULAR $
(Map p64; ☎7-864-1914; rozzo99@gmail.com; Lamparilla No 324, btwn Aguacate & Compostela; r CUC$30-35; ❄) This lovely mint-green colonial house stands out amid the superficial scruffiness of Calle Lamparilla. The bright tone is continued inside with a wonderful patio set off by a collection of a dozen or more international flags, a welcome that is matched by the congenial owners. There are three clean rooms and fine breakfasts.

Penthouse Plaza Vieja CASA PARTICULAR $
(Map p64; ☎7-861-0084; Mercaderes No 315-317; r CUC$60; ❄) A private penthouse in a historic central square – this place would cost thousands anywhere else, but in Havana you can still bag it for CUC$60. Fidel and Bertha's two rooms high above Plaza Vieja share a leafy terrace guarded by a Santería shrine.

Casa de Pepe & Rafaela CASA PARTICULAR $
(Map p64; ☎7-862-9877; San Ignacio No 454, btwn Sol & Santa Clara; r CUC$30-35; ❄) A wonderful sunny yellow colonial house just off Plaza Vieja, with antiques and Moorish tiles throughout. The two rooms have balconies, wooden shutters and gorgeous bathrooms. The house is currently being run by the younger generation of the original family. They are great hosts.

Conde de Ricla Hostal HOTEL $$
(Map p64; ☎52-91-63-23; www.condedericlahostal.com; San Ignacio No 402, btwn Sol & Muralla; d/ste CUC$100/150; ❄) It might not be obvious to first-timers in Cuba, but this place is rather unique; it's an early attempt at a truly *private* hotel as opposed to a casa particular (up until now all Cuban hotels have been government-owned). The five rooms pass the test – all are large, clean and equipped with minimalist boutique touches despite the colonial setting.

Big bonus: breakfast in La Vitrola (p101) downstairs (owned by the same family) is included.

★**Hotel Los Frailes** HISTORIC HOTEL $$$
(Map p64; ☎7-862-9383; www.habaguanexhotels.com; Brasil No 8, btwn Oficios & Mercaderes; d/ste CUC$200/230; ❄@📶) There's nothing austere about Los Frailes (The Friars), despite the monastic theme (staff wear hooded robes), inspired by the nearby San Francisco de Asís convent. Instead, this is the kind of hotel you'll look forward to coming back to after a long day, to recline in large, historical rooms in your monkish dressing gown, with candlelight flickering on the walls.

An added perk is the resident woodwind quartet in the lobby; the musicians are so good that they regularly lure passing tour groups for impromptu concerts.

Hostal Conde de Villanueva HOTEL $$$
(Map p64; ☎7-862-9293; www.habaguanexhotels.com; Mercaderes No 202; s/d CUC$235/305; ❄@📶) If you want to splash out on one night of luxury in Havana, check out this highly lauded colonial hotel. Restored under the watchful eye of the City Historian in the late 1990s, the Villanueva has been converted from a grandiose city mansion into a thoughtfully decorated hotel with nine bedrooms spread around an attractive inner courtyard (complete with resident peacock).

Upstairs suites contain stained-glass windows, chandeliers, arty sculptures and – in one – a fully workable whirlpool bathtub.

Hotel Florida HOTEL $$$
(Map p64; ☎7-862-4127; www.habaguanexhotels.com; Obispo No 252; d/ste CUC$245/305 incl breakfast; ❄@📶) They don't make them like this anymore. The Florida is an architectural extravaganza built in the purest colonial style, with arches and pillars clustered around an atmospheric central courtyard. Habaguanex has restored the 1836 building with loving attention to detail: the amply furnished rooms retain their original high ceilings and wonderfully luxurious finishes.

Anyone with even a passing interest in Cuba's architectural heritage will want to check out this colonial palace, complemented with an elegant cafe and a popular bar-nightspot (from 8pm).

Hotel Raquel HOTEL $$$
(Map p64; ☎7-860-8280; www.habaguanexhotels.com; cnr Amargura & San Ignacio; d/ste CUC$280/330; ❄@📶) Encased in a dazzling 1908 palace (that was once a bank), the Hotel Raquel gives you historical hallucinations with its grandiose columns, sleek marble statues and intricate stained-glass ceiling. Behind its impressive architecture, the Raquel offers well-presented if noisy rooms, a small gym/sauna, friendly staff and a great central location.

Painstakingly restored, the reception area in this marvelous eclectic building is a tourist sight in its own right – it's replete with priceless antiques and intricate art nouveau flourishes.

Hotel Armadores de Santander HISTORIC HOTEL **$$$**
(Map p64; ☎7-862-8000; www.habaguanexhotels.com; Luz No 4, cnr San Pedro; d/ste CUC$235/305; ❄@📶) The Santander down by the harbor has a tangible nautical feel. You almost expect some old Spanish sailor to come strolling into the thin mahogany bar and start singing a sea shanty. The 32 rooms are variable. The split-level suites with their stained glass and spiral staircases are well worth the investment. The sundeck overlooking the harbor is another highlight.

Hotel Habana 612 HISTORIC HOTEL **$$$**
(Map p64; ☎7-867-1039; www.habaguanexhotels.com; Habana No 612; r CUC$200; ❄@📶) One of Habana Vieja's newer and smaller hotels, this 12-room place overlays minimalist design in an old colonial building. The artistic theme is 'tools,' which are stamped everywhere – indeed, the reception clock looks like something designed by Da Vinci. Rooms are large; the front ones have small balconies but get a bit of street noise.

Hotel Palacio del Marqués de San Felipe y Santiago de Bejucal HOTEL **$$$**
(Map p64; ☎7-864-9191; www.habaguanexhotels.com; cnr Oficios & Amargura; d CUC$360; ❄@📶) Cuban baroque meets modern minimalist in one of Habaguanex' more expensive offerings, and the results are something to behold. Spreading 27 rooms over six floors in the blustery Plaza de San Francisco de Asís, this place is living proof that Habana Vieja's delicate restoration work is getting better and better.

Hotel Palacio O'Farrill HOTEL **$$$**
(Map p64; ☎7-860-5080; www.habaguanexhotels.com; Cuba No 102-108, btwn Chacón & Tejadillo; d/ste CUC$235/305; ❄@📶) Not an Irish joke, but one of Havana's most impressive period hotels, the Hotel Palacio O'Farrill is a staggeringly beautiful colonial palace that once belonged to Don Ricardo O'Farrill, a Cuban sugar entrepreneur who was descended from a family of Irish nobility. Compared to the lavish communal areas, the bedrooms are plainer and more modest.

Taking the Emerald Isle as its theme, this hotel has plenty of greenery in its plant-filled 18th-century courtyard. The 2nd floor, which was added in the 19th century, provides grandiose neoclassical touches, while the 20th-century top floor merges seamlessly with the magnificent architecture below.

Hotel Ambos Mundos HOTEL **$$$**
(Map p64; ☎7-860-9529; www.habaguanexhotels.com; Obispo No 153; s/d CUC$235/305; ❄@📶) This pastel-pink Havana institution was Hemingway's hideout and where he's said to have penned his seminal guerrilla classic *For Whom the Bell Tolls* (Castro's bedtime reading during the war in the mountains). Small, sometimes windowless rooms suggest overpricing, but the lobby bar is classic enough (follow the romantic piano melody) and drinks in the rooftop restaurant one of Havana's finest treats.

It's an obligatory pit stop for anyone on a world tour of 'Hemingway once fell over in here' bars.

Hostal Valencia HOTEL **$$$**
(Map p64; ☎7-867-1037; www.habaguanexhotels.com; Oficios No 53; d/ste CUC$220/240 incl breakfast; ❄@📶) Slap-bang in the historic core, Valencia is decked out like a Spanish *posada* (inn), with hanging vines, doorways big enough to ride a horse through and a popular on-site paella restaurant. One of the cheaper Habana Vieja offerings, it's an excellent old-world choice, with good service and atmosphere aplenty. You can almost see the ghosts of Don Quixote and Sancho Panza floating by.

Hotel Santa Isabel HOTEL **$$$**
(Map p64; ☎7-860-8201; www.habaguanexhotels.com; Baratillo No 9; r incl breakfast CUC$360; ❄@📶) Considered one of Havana's finest hotels, as well as one of its oldest (operations began in 1867), Hotel Santa Isabel is housed in the Palacio de los Condes de Santovenia (p63), the former crash pad of the counts of Santovenia. This three-story, five-star baroque beauty has 17 regular rooms full of historic charm, with attractive Spanish-colonial furniture and paintings by contemporary Cuban artists.

🛏 Centro Habana

★Hostal Peregrino Consulado CASA PARTICULAR **$**
(Map p80; ☎7-861-8027; www.hostalperegrino.com; Consulado No 152, btwn Colón & Trocadero; r

incl breakfast CUC$35-50; ❄@) Julio Roque is a pediatrician who, along with his wife Elsa, has expanded his former two-room casa particular into a growing web of accommodations. His HQ, Hostal Peregrino, offers three rooms a block from Paseo de Martí (Prado) and is one of the most professionally run private houses in Cuba. Super-helpful Julio and Elsa are fluent in English and a mine of local information.

Extra services include airport pick-up, internet, laundry and cocktail bar. The family offers three more places: one in Habana Vieja, one in Calle Lealtad and a beautiful new house in Vedado. They're all bookable through the same number.

★Casa 1932 CASA PARTICULAR $
(Map p80; ☎7-863-6203, 52 64-38-58; www.casahabana.net; Campanario 63, btwn San Lázaro & Lagunas; r CUC$30-40; ❄@) The charismatic owner, Luis Miguel, is an art deco fanatic who offers his house as both boutique private homestay and museum to the 1930s, when his preferred architectural style was in vogue. Collectibles, including old signs, mirrors, toys, furniture and stained glass, will make you feel like you've walked into a Clark Gable movie. There are three comfortable rooms and huge breakfasts.

The biggest bonus, however, is Luis Miguel, a mine of local history and culture who runs his own tour company Havana Super Tour (p86).

Casa Colonial Yadilis & Yoel CASA PARTICULAR $
(Map p80; ☎7-863-0565; www.casacolonialyadilisyyoel.com; Industria No 120 Altos, btwn Trocadero & Colón; r CUC$30-35; ❄) A magic formula: take a solid-pink colonial house in the thick of Centro Habana's street life, throw in four well-maintained, spacious rooms, an ample terrace and lavish breakfasts, then add charming English-speaking hosts Yoel and Yadilis, who go above and beyond with tips and local information. The result: a casa that's highly professional and refreshingly down-to-earth.

The couple also own a second house nearby with a sea-view roof terrace.

Casa de Lourdes & José CASA PARTICULAR $
(Map p80; ☎7-863-9879; Águila 168b, btwn Ánimas & Trocadero; r CUC$30; ❄) Located in the midst of Centro, this place with wonderful hosts has en suite rooms and set-you-up-for-the-day breakfasts. If you like good old-fashioned hospitality and the feeling that you're staying with a tight-knit Cuban family, look no further.

Lourdes Cervantes CASA PARTICULAR $
(Map p80; ☎7-879-2243; lourdescervantesparades@yahoo.es; Calzada de la Infanta No 17 Apt 10, btwn Calles 23 & Humboldt; r CUC$30; ❄📶) On the border of Vedado and Centro Habana, just a baseball swing from the Hotel Nacional and Malecón, this 1st-floor apartment offers two large rooms with balconies. The bathroom is large but shared. Lourdes is a great hostess and fluent in English and French.

Casa Amada CASA PARTICULAR $
(Map p80; ☎7-862-3924; www.casaamada.net; Lealtad No 26, Altos, btwn Neptuno & Concordia; r CUC$30-40; ❄) A huge house with gracious hosts that offers five rooms (all with private bathrooms) and a communal roof terrace. An enclosed balcony out front overlooks the gritty cinematic street life that is Centro Habana.

Eumelia & Aurelio CASA PARTICULAR $
(Map p80; ☎7-867-6738; eumelialonchan@gmail.com; Consulado No 157, btwn Colón & Trocadero; r CUC$30; ❄) New bathrooms, minibars and digitally controlled air-con feature in this pleasant family house close to Paseo de Martí (Prado). There are five double rooms and a shared terrace.

Dulce Hostal – Dulce María González CASA PARTICULAR $
(Map p80; ☎7-863-2506; Amistad No 220, btwn Neptuno & San Miguel; r CUC$25; ❄) This house is all about the lovely hostess, Dulce, who has been renting out just one room in her neocolonial house for well over a decade. Nothing has changed – it's still as clean, friendly, welcoming and down-to-earth as it was on day one.

Duplex Cervantes APARTMENT $$
(Map p80; ☎52-54-36-29, 7-879-5486; duplexcervantes@gmail.com; Espada No 7 Apt 312, btwn Calle 25 & Calzada de Infanta; apt CUC$100-150; P❄) You won't find many of these in Havana, yet. A renovated, tastefully minimalist duplex apartment with three bedrooms, two bathrooms, lounge-dining room, kitchen and balcony. And you don't have to sacrifice on location either: you're still deep in the heart of the 'hood. English, French and Italian are spoken by the friendly owners and large breakfasts go for CUC$5 extra.

Prices depend on the season and the number in your party.

Hotel Deauville HOTEL **$$**

(Map p80; ☎7-866-8812; Av de Italia No 1, cnr Malecón; s/d CUC$82/124; P ❄ @ 🛜 🏊) Despite its perfect location on the Malecón, this old dowager is just that. A former Mafia gambling den, the Deauville doesn't really match up to the stellar views.

Deauville is currently reborn in sea-blue and already showing the effects of the corrosive sea water, with the handy facilities (money exchange, wi-fi and car rental are available here) fighting a losing battle, and worn-out rooms a good few years past their renovation date.

★Hotel Iberostar Parque Central HOTEL **$$$**

(Map p80; ☎7-860-6627; www.iberostar.com; Neptuno, btwn Agramonte & Paseo de Martí; r from CUC$450; P ❄ @ 🛜 🏊) With the exception of perhaps the Hotel Saratoga, the Iberostar is Havana's best international-standard hotel, with service and business facilities on par with top-ranking five-star facilities elsewhere in the Caribbean. Although the fancy lobby and classily furnished rooms may lack the historical riches of Habana Vieja establishments, the ambience here is far from antiseptic.

Bonus facilities include a full-service business center, a rooftop swimming pool/fitness center/Jacuzzi, an elegant lobby bar, the celebrated El Paseo restaurant, plus excellent international telephone and internet links. There's also an even swankier, newer wing across Calle Virtudes, connected to the rest of the hotel by an underground tunnel. As well as state-of-the-art rooms, the wing includes its own luxurious restaurant, cafe and reception area.

★Hotel Saratoga HOTEL **$$$**

(Map p80; ☎7-868-1000; www.saratogahotel-cuba.com; Paseo de Martí No 603; r CUC$506-1204; P ❄ @ 🛜 🏊) The glittering Saratoga is an architectural work of art that stands imposingly at the intersection of Paseo de Martí (Prado) and Dragones, with fantastic views over toward the Capitolio. Sharp, if officious, service is a feature here, as are the extra-comfortable beds, power showers, a truly decadent rooftop swimming pool and an exquisite hotel bar.

Not surprisingly, there's a price for all this luxury. The Saratoga is eye-wateringly expensive, especially if you plump for the presidential suite. Then again, it's perhaps the best hotel in Cuba.

Hotel Terral BOUTIQUE HOTEL **$$$**

(Map p80; ☎7-860-2100; www.habaguanexhotels.com; Malecón, cnr Lealtad; s/d CUC$235/305; ❄ @ 🛜) A boutique hotel on Havana's semi-ruined sea drive that looks out across the water at Florida and compares notes. Despite being built (and run) by the City Historian's Office, Terral is not historic. On the contrary, the 14 ocean-facing rooms are chic, clean-lined and minimalist. A sinuous glass-fronted cafe-bar downstairs offers inviting sofas and great coffee.

Hotel Sevilla HOTEL **$$$**

(Map p80; ☎7-860-8560; www.hotelsevilla-cuba.com; Trocadero No 55, btwn Paseo de Martí & Agramonte; s/d incl breakfast CUC$260/340; P ❄ @ 🛜 🏊) Al Capone once hired out the whole 6th floor, Graham Greene used room 501 as a setting for his novel *Our Man in Havana*, and the Mafia requisitioned it as operations center for their pre-revolutionary North American drugs racket. Nowadays the Moorish Sevilla still packs a punch, with its ostentatious lobby that could have been ripped straight out of Granada's Alhambra.

Spacious, comfortable rooms have seen regular updating and the 9th-floor restaurant where you're serenaded by a violin over breakfast is an 'experience,' but you're paying more for history here than modern facilities or snappy service.

Hotel Telégrafo HOTEL **$$$**

(Map p80; ☎7-861-4741, 7-861-1010; www.hoteltelegrafo-cuba.com; Paseo de Martí No 408; d/ste CUC$235/305; ❄ @ 🛜) This bold royal-blue beauty on the northwest corner of Parque Central juxtaposes old-style architectural features (the original building hails from 1888) with futuristic design flourishes; these include big, luxurious sofas, a huge winding central staircase and an intricate tile mosaic emblazoned on the wall of the downstairs bar. The rooms are large and elegant.

Hotel Inglaterra HOTEL **$$$**

(Map p80; ☎7-860-8595; www.hotelinglaterra-cuba.com; Paseo de Martí No 416; s/d CUC$204/320; ❄ @ 🛜) There's no doubting that the Inglaterra is a Havana icon, the city's oldest hotel, where José Martí once stayed the night. But, while the tiled Moorish lobby is still magnificent and the busy El Louvre bar out front a beehive of music and

FORESTIER & THE BEAUTIFICATION OF HAVANA

Paris and Havana share at least one thing in common aside from the Panthéon-mimicking Capitolio building – landscape architect Jean-Claude Nicolas Forestier.

Fresh from high-profile commissions in the French capital, Forestier arrived in Havana in 1925 to draw up a master-plan to link the city's fast-growing urban grid. The landscaper – a strong advocate of the 'city beautiful' movement – spent the next five years sketching broad tree-lined boulevards, Parisian-style squares and a harmonious city landscape designed to accentuate Havana's iconic monuments and lush tropical setting.

Central to the plan was a civic center (to be called Plaza de la República) located on the Loma de Catalanes, a hill that stood at the southern edge of Vedado, from which a series of avenues would radiate outwards in the manner of Paris' Place de l'Étoile. Forestier envisaged that the civic center would be embellished with fountains and gardens and anchored by a huge memorial to José Martí. To the west, the space would link to a grand network of parks that followed the course of the Río Almendares.

The onset of the Great Depression coupled with political unrest in Cuba in the 1930s put the brakes on many of Forestier's plans, although a few of his ideas were adopted before his death in 1930. These included the lush Av del Puerto by the harbor, the famous staircase in front of the university and the reimagining of the 'Prado.'

It took another 25 years before the Frenchman's Parisian vision for Havana was finally realized, with vast construction projects enacted in the 1950s. The civic center ultimately became Plaza de la Revolución, with its grand Martí Memorial, while the wide avenues were built as Paseo and Av de los Presidentes (Calle G), both adorned with tree-lined central walkways and heroic busts and statues.

Forestier is sometimes seen as Havana's Baron Haussmann (the civic planner who redesigned Paris in the 1860s), but unlike Haussmann, who tore down much of medieval Paris, Forestier was adamant about not disturbing the city's old quarter, Habana Vieja. For that we have much to thank him for.

action, the Inglaterra remains a better place to hang out than stay.

Despite regular renovations, the dark, lackluster and often viewless rooms are easily outshone by the beautiful but deceptively promising communal areas.

Verdado

★Central Yard Inn CASA PARTICULAR $
(Map p96; ☎7-832-2927; centralyardinn@gmail.com; Calle I, btwn Calles 21 & 23; r CUC$30-40; P ❄) Some of Havana's state-run hotels could learn a lot from this highly professional casa particular located in the middle of Vedado's nightlife zone. The yard in question is a stunner, beautified with plenty of greenery and a fountain, and surrounded by four hotel-standard rooms.

It's hard to believe, but this place is the result of a recent renovation project that melds perfectly with the existing house. The owners speak English and offer five-star meals and service.

★La Colonial 1861 CASA PARTICULAR $
(Map p96; ☎7-830 1861; www.lacolonial1861.com; Calle 10 No 60, btwn Calles 3 & 5; d/f CUC$55/80; ❄) It's unusual to find a house this old in western Vedado, so make the most of the 1861, whose five private rooms (one is family-sized) are a riot of wrought iron, stained glass and mosaic floor tiles. The house is self-contained, with its own patio, common areas and antique furniture, and the owner is very knowledgeable about Havana's brilliant art scene.

La Casa de Ana CASA PARTICULAR $
(Map p96; ☎7-833-5128; www.anahavana.com; Calle 17 1422, btwn Calles 26 & 28; CUC$30-35; ❄ @) Don't be put off by the out-of-the-way location (western Vedado); there's plenty going on in this neck of the woods and the highly professional Casa de Ana will put you straight on everything from cheap transportation to where to find the best mojitos. Rooms are modern and clean, and service goes well beyond the call of duty. Book well in advance.

Marta Vitorte CASA PARTICULAR $
(Map p96; ☎7-832-6475; www.casamartainhavana.com; Calle G No 301 Apt 14, btwn Calles 13 & 15; r CUC$40-60; P ❄) Marta has lived in this craning apartment block on Av de los

Presidentes since the 1960s. One look at the view and you'll see why – the glass-fronted wraparound terrace that soaks up 270 degrees of Havana's pock-marked panorama makes it seem as if you're standing atop the Martí monument. Not surprisingly, her four rooms are deluxe, with lovely furnishings, minibars and safes.

Then there are the breakfasts, the laundry, the parking space, the lift attendant... Get the drift? Marta also rents two self-contained luxury apartments nearby (CUC$100 to CUC$180).

Mercedes González CASA PARTICULAR **$**
(Map p96; ☎7-832-5846; Calle 21, btwn Av de los Presidentes & Calle H; r CUC$35-45; ❄) Mercy's four rooms at this long-standing renter spread across two 1st-floor apartments just off Av de los Presidentes have a passionate following. It's no surprise why. The hostess is lovely, and the rooms and common areas (with an extensive book collection) have a refined art deco feel. Mercy offers a good breakfast and can help with trip planning.

Doña Lourdes CASA PARTICULAR **$**
(Map p96; ☎7-830-9509; Calle 17 No 459, btwn Calles E & F; r CUC$30-35; ❄) Opposite the Museo de Artes Decorativas, this small unassuming place is in a pleasant tucked-away nook. There's one rented room located upstairs in a typically regal early 20th-century Vedado residence, with a large communal balcony overlooking the street.

Casa Lizette CASA PARTICULAR **$**
(Map p96; ☎7-830-1226; lizette2602@gmail.com; Calle 3 No 580, btwn Calles 8 & 10; r CUC$35; ❄) A relatively modern, self-contained house with private entry in western Vedado, a block from the Malecón and handily placed for nearby restaurants and the fabulous Fábrica de Arte Cubano. Lizette's three rooms share a communal dining room and lounge and there's access to a terrace with rocking chairs out back.

Casa Amada Malecón CASA PARTICULAR **$**
(Map p96; ☎7-832-9659; www.casaamada.net; Calzada No 15, btwn Calles M & N; r CUC$30-40; ❄) So close to the US embassy you can practically smell the hamburgers, this casa (affiliated to a similar one in Centro Habana) is big on the inside and has several plushly renovated rooms sequestered away behind a slim patio.

★Casavana Cuba CASA PARTICULAR **$$**
(Map p96; ☎58-04-92-58; www.casavanacuba.com; Calle G No 301, 5th fl, btwn Calles 13 & 15; r CUC$50-90; ❄) When casas particulares start to look like four-star hotels you know you're onto something. Encased in a *rascacielo* (skyscraper) in Vedado, Casavana's huge rooms are positively luxurious, with precious furniture and floors so polished you can virtually see your face in them. Behold the carved wooden beds and then drink in the wondrous views from your personal balcony.

The accommodation is spread over two floors (floors 5 and 11) in a 20-story apartment building on Av de los Presidentes. It's a little pricier than your average casa, but well worth it. Book online.

Hotel Paseo Habana HOTEL **$$**
(Map p96; ☎7-836-0808; cnr Calles 17 & A; s/d CUC$112/125; ❄@📶) First things first: the Hotel Paseo Habana is not actually in Paseo, rather it's one block east on the corner of Calle A. It used to be a bit of a bargain, but, after hiking up its prices it's harder to overlook the dodgy water pressure, missing light fittings and peeling paintwork. The best part is the front terrace with its rocking chairs and wi-fi.

Hotel Vedado HOTEL **$$**
(Map p96; ☎7-836-4072; www.hotelvedadocuba.com; Calle O No 244, btwn Calles 23 & 25; s/d CUC$70/125; P❄@📶🏊) Hotel Vedado is ever popular with the tour-bus crowd, with regular refurbishments that never quite break the three-star barrier despite an OK pool (rare in Havana), passable restaurant and not-unpleasant rooms.

Elsewhere the patchy service, perennially noisy lobby and almost total lack of character will leave you wondering if you wouldn't have been better off staying in a local casa particular – for a third of the price.

★Hotel Nacional HOTEL **$$$**
(Map p96; ☎7-836-3564; www.hotelnacionaldecuba.com; cnr Calles O & 21; s/d CUC$338/468; P❄@📶🏊) The cherry on the cake of Cuban hotels and flagship of the government-run Gran Caribe chain, the neoclassical/neocolonial/art deco (let's call it eclectic) Hotel Nacional is as much a city monument as it is an international accommodation option. Even if you haven't got the money to stay here, find time to sip at least one minty mojito in its exquisite oceanside bar.

Steeped in history and furnished with rooms with plaques that advertise details of illustrious past occupants, the towering Havana landmark sports two swimming pools, a sweeping manicured lawn, a couple of lavish restaurants and its own top-class nighttime cabaret, the Parisién (p115). While the rooms might lack some of the fancy gadgets of deluxe Varadero, the ostentatious communal areas and the ghosts of Winston Churchill, Frank Sinatra, Lucky Luciano and Errol Flynn that haunt the Moorish lobby make for a fascinating and unforgettable experience.

Hotel Meliá Cohiba HOTEL **$$$**

(Map p96; ☎7-833-3636; www.meliacuba.com; Paseo, btwn Calles 1 & 3; s/d CUC$527/600; P ❄ @ ᯤ ≋) Cuba's most business-like city hotel is an oceanside concrete giant built in 1994 (it's the only building from this era on the Malecón) that will satisfy the highest of international expectations with its knowledgeable, consistent staff and modern, well-polished facilities. After a few weeks in the Cuban outback you'll feel like you're on a different planet here.

For workaholics there are special 'business-traveler rooms,' and 59 units have Jacuzzis. On the lower levels gold-star facilities include a shopping arcade, one of Havana's plushest gyms and the ever-popular Habana Café (p116).

Hotel Capri HOTEL **$$$**

(Map p96; ☎7-839 7200; cnr Calles 21 & N; s/d CUC$290/350; P ❄ @ ᯤ ≋) After spending over a decade as a rotting ruin, one of Havana's most famous hotels was reborn as a quieter, less notorious version of its former self in 2014. And, rather like *The Godfather*, the sequel is better. The 19-story Capri has a sharp minimalist lobby and a rooftop pool. The rooms are slick and modern but not ostentatious.

The views from the higher-up rooms are expansive.

Built in modernist style with Mafia money in 1957, the hotel in its (brief) heyday, was owned by mobster Santo Trafficante, who used American actor George Raft as his debonair front-man. When Castro's guerrillas came knocking in January 1959, Raft allegedly told them where to stick it and slammed the door in their faces.

The hotel has also featured in two movies; Carol Reed's *Our Man in Havana* and Mikhail Kalatozov's *Soy Cuba* (in an astounding 'tracking shot'). It was also the setting for Michael Corleone's meeting with Hyman Roth in *The Godfather: Part II*, though, due to the embargo, Coppola shot the scenes in the Dominican Republic.

Hotel Habana Libre HOTEL **$$$**

(Map p96; ☎7-834-6100; www.meliacuba.com; Calle L, btwn Calles 23 & 25; d/ste CUC$464/495, incl breakfast; P ❄ @ ᯤ ≋) This icon of the Havana skyline opened in March 1958 on the eve of Batista's last waltz. Originally the Havana Hilton, it was commandeered by Castro's rebels in January 1959, who turned it into their temporary HQ. Now managed by Spain's Meliá chain it is by turns spectacular (behold the views!) and sloppy (old-school TVs, slow wi-fi, shaky elevators).

The hotel's communal areas easily outshine the slightly outdated rooms. The 25th-floor cabaret El Turquino (p115) with its retractable roof is a city institution.

Hotel Riviera HOTEL **$$$**

(Map p96; ☎7-836-4051; www.hotelhavanariviera.com; cnr Paseo & Malecón; s/d CUC$200/280; P ❄ @ ≋) Meyer Lansky's magnificent Vegas-style palace has leapt back into fashion with its gloriously retro lobby almost unchanged since 1957. Though luxurious 50 years ago, the 354 rooms are now looking a little rough around the edges and struggle to justify their price tag, but you can readily dampen the dreariness in the fabulous 1950s-style pool, gambling-era bar and good smattering of restaurants.

The hotel was taken over by the Spanish Iberostar chain in 2016, so some improvements can be expected.

Hotel ROC Presidente HOTEL **$$$**

(Map p96; ☎7-838-1801; www.roc-hotels.com; cnr Calzada & Calle G; s/d CUC$225/300; P ❄ @ ᯤ ≋) This art-deco-influenced hotel on Av de los Presidentes wouldn't be out of place on a street just off Times Sq in New York. Built the same year as nearby Hotel Victoria (1928), the Presidente is similar but larger, with more officious staff. Unless you're a walker or fancy getting some elbow exercise on Havana's crowded bus system, the location can be awkward.

Hotel Victoria HOTEL **$$$**

(Map p96; ☎7-833-3510; www.hotelvictoriacuba.com; Calle 19 No 101; s/d CUC$160/240 incl breakfast; ❄ @ ≋) Looking perkier after a recent modernizing refurb, this well-heeled and oft-overlooked Vedado option looks a

Vedado

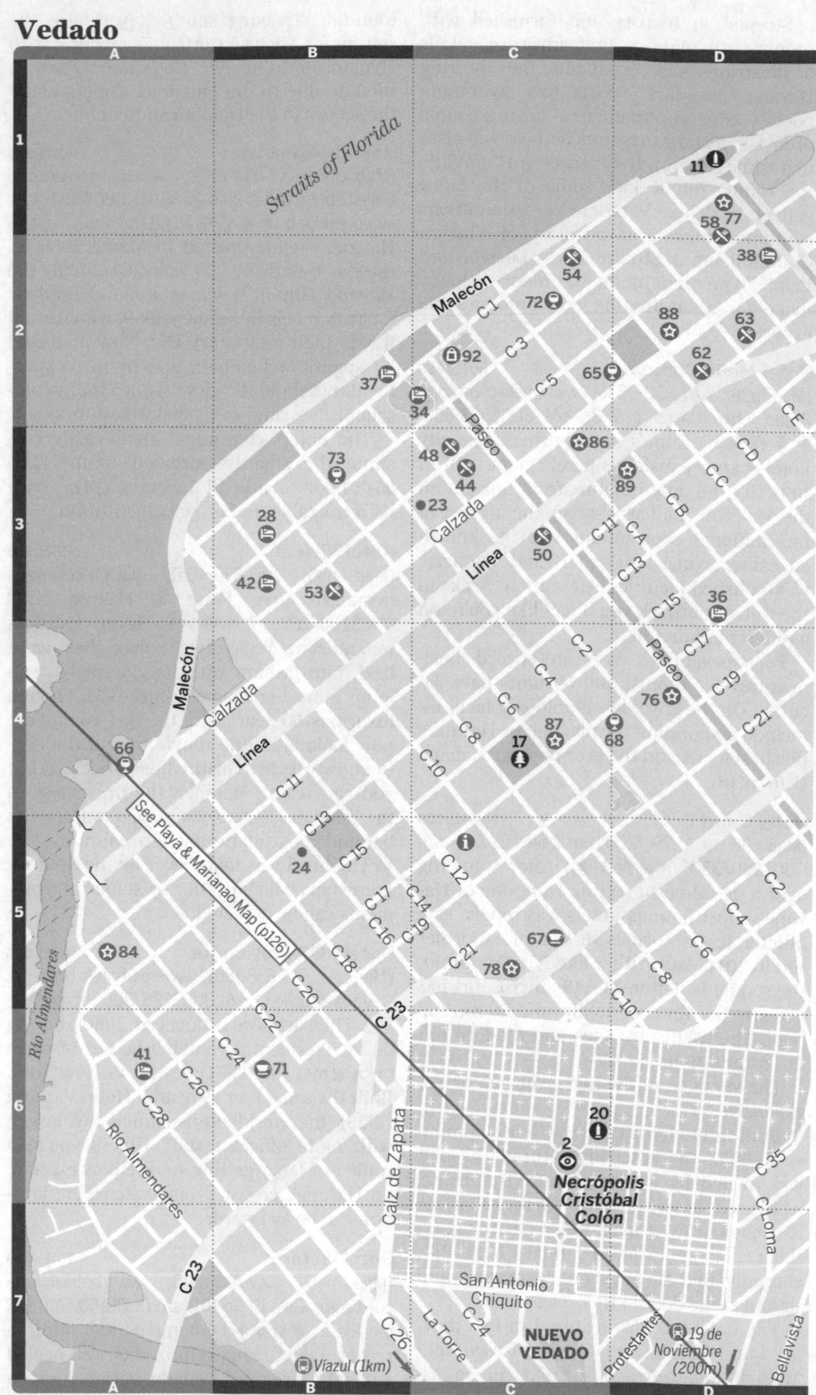

Straits of Florida
Malecón
Calzada
Línea
Paseo
Necrópolis Cristóbal Colón
San Antonio Chiquito
NUEVO VEDADO
Río Almendares
Calz de Zapata
La Torre
Protestantes
Bellavista
C Loma
See Playa & Marianao Map (p126)
Víazul (1km)
19 de Noviembre (200m)

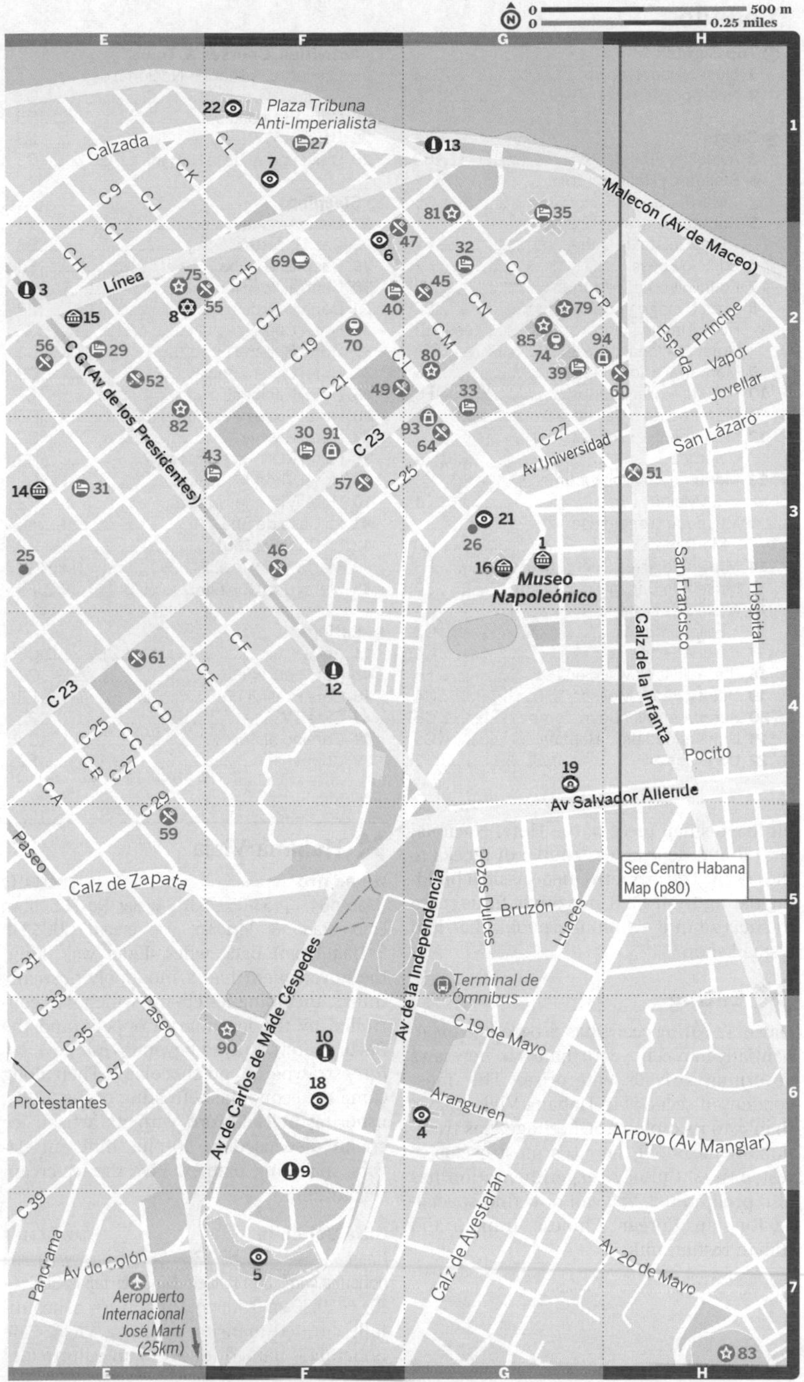
0 500 m
0 0.25 miles
E
F
G
H
1
2
3
4
5
6
7
Plaza Tribuna
Anti-Imperialista
Calzada
Malecón (Av de Maceo)
Línea
C G (Av de los Presidentes)
C 23
C 25
C 27
Av Universidad
San Lázaro
Jovellar
Vapor
Príncipe
Espada
San Francisco
Hospital
Calz de la Infanta
Pocito
Museo
Napoleónico
Av Salvador Allende
See Centro Habana
Map (p80)
Paseo
Calz de Zapata
Pozos Dulces
Bruzón
Luaces
Av de la Independencia
Av de Carlos de Máde Céspedes
Terminal de
Ómnibus
C 19 de Mayo
Aranguren
Arroyo (Av Manglar)
Calz de Ayestarán
Av 20 de Mayo
Av de Colón
Panorama
Aeropuerto
Internacional
José Martí
(25km)
Protestantes

Vedado

Top Sights
1 Museo Napoleónico G3
2 Necrópolis Cristóbal Colón C6

Sights
3 Av de los Presidentes E2
4 Biblioteca Nacional José Martí G6
5 Comité Central del Partido Comunista de Cuba F7
6 Edificio Focsa F2
7 Edificio López Serrano F1
8 Gran Synagoga Bet Shalom E2
Hotel Habana Libre .... (see 33)
Hotel Nacional .... (see 35)
9 Memorial a José Martí F6
10 Ministerio del Interior F6
11 Monumento a Calixto García D1
12 Monumento a José Miguel Gómez F4
13 Monumento a las Víctimas del Maine G1
Museo Antropológico Montané .... (see 16)
14 Museo de Artes Decorativas E3
15 Museo de Danza E2
16 Museo de Historia Natural Felipe Poey G3
17 Parque Lennon C4
18 Plaza de la Revolución F6
19 Quinta de los Molinos G4
20 Señora Amelia Goyri Tomb C6
21 Universidad de la Habana G3
22 US Embassy F1

Activities, Courses & Tours
23 Conjunto Folklórico Nacional de Cuba C3
24 CubaRuta Bikes B5
25 Paradiso E3
26 Universidad de la Habana G3

Sleeping
27 Casa Amada Malecón F1
28 Casa Lizette B3
29 Casavana Cuba E2
30 Central Yard Inn F3
31 Doña Lourdes E3
32 Hotel Capri G2
33 Hotel Habana Libre G2
34 Hotel Meliá Cohiba C2
35 Hotel Nacional G1
36 Hotel Paseo Habana D3
37 Hotel Riviera B2
38 Hotel ROC Presidente D2
39 Hotel Vedado G2
40 Hotel Victoria F2
41 La Casa de Ana A6
42 La Colonial 1861 .... B3
Marta Vitorte .... (see 29)
43 Mercedes González F3

Eating
44 Atelier C3
45 Café Laurent G2
46 Café Presidente F3
47 Café TV F2
48 Camino al Sol C3
49 Coppelia F2

bit like a small piece of the Hotel Nacional cut off and deposited a couple of blocks to the south. The attractive neoclassical building dating from 1928 amazingly finds room to squeeze in a swimming pool, a bar and a small shop.

Eating

Havana's eating scene has progressed exponentially in recent years thanks to new laws governing private enterprise. The most condensed scene is in Habana Vieja. Playa, thanks to its diplomatic heritage, has traditionally harbored the city's most exclusive restaurants. Culinary experimentation has also proliferated. You can now find specialist Russian, Korean, Chinese, Iranian and Italian restaurants.

Habana Vieja

Helad'oro ICE CREAM $

(Map p64; ☎53-05-91-31; Aguiar No 206, btwn Empredrado & Tejadillo; ice cream CUC$2-4; ⏰11am-10pm) Back when Fidel was 'king,' the government had a monopoly on many things, including ice cream, which was controlled by the legendary Coppelia and the flavors rarely strayed beyond *fresa y chocolate* (strawberry and chocolate). Then along came the economic defrosting of the 2010s, ushering in Helad'oro with its artisan ice cream dispensed in 30-plus different flavors, including mamey. Viva the ice-cream revolution!

Café Bohemia TAPAS, CAFE $

(Map p64; ☎7-836-6567; www.havanabohemia.com; San Ignacio No 364; tapas CUC$6-10; ⏰10:30am-9:30pm) Inhabiting a beautifully curated mansion on Plaza Vieja, Café Bohemia – named for a Cuban culture and arts magazine – manages to feel appropriately bohemian, but also serves great cocktails, tapas and extremely addictive cakes.

There's also a boutique apartment (CUC$80) and en suite bedroom (CUC$45) available for rent.

D'Next CAFETERIA $

(Map p64; 7-860-5519; Brasil No 512, btwn Av de las Misiones & Bernaza; snacks CUC$3-6; 8:30am-midnight) The plastic black and red diner seats of D'Next provide a welcome pew for knackered travelers who've overdosed on Che Guevara. One chunky chicken sandwich and guava fruit shake later and you'll be back on the revolutionary bandwagon, probably relieved to escape from the cafe's ear-splitting reggaeton music.

Cafe Espada BREAKFAST $

(Map p64; 7-801-5561; cnr Cuarteles & Espada; breakfast CUC$4-6; 8am-11pm) Refined but casual, the Espada is reminiscent of one of those tiny corner bistros in Paris where service is quick and you feel as comfortable with your nose in a book as with a cocktail. It's perfect for a light breakfast or a fleeting *merienda* (light tea) in-between museum visits.

Café del Ángel Fumero Jacqueline CAFE $

(Map p64; 7-862-6562; Compostela No 1, cnr Cuarteles; breakfast CUC$4-6; 8am-11pm) Guarding the heavenly small square behind the Iglesia del Santo Ángel Custodio (the result of a foresighted community project), the highly minimalist Fumero is part cocktail bar, part ladies clothing boutique, and also one of the best breakfast spots in Habana Vieja. Pull up an alfresco chair for eggs, waffles and super-hot coffee.

Casa del Queso La Marriage CHEESE $

(Map p64; 7-866-7142; cnr San Ignacio & Amargura; cheeseboard CUC$1-3; 10am-10pm) In a country that until recently produced just one rubbery, tasteless cheese, a multifarious cheese shop is a big deal. You can extinguish bad memories of peso pizza and the 'Special Period' over plates of gouda, blue and cheddar, washed down with a fruity Chilean red wine.

Sandwichería La Bien Paga SANDWICHES $

(Map p64; Aguacate No 259; sandwiches CUC$1-2; ⏲9am-6pm) Jumping into a niche still underrepresented in Havana, this casual sandwich shop beloved by locals makes up savory snacks as you wait in a space barely big enough to swing a small kitten. A classic 'Cuban' (ham, cheese, pork and pickles) goes for a giveaway CUC$2.

★El Rum Rum de la Habana SEAFOOD, SPANISH $$

(Map p64; ☎7-861-0806; Empedrado No 256, btwn Cuba & Aguiar; mains CUC$7-13; ⏲noon-midnight) In Cuba, eating establishments are full of rum (the vital ingredient for mojitos) *and rum rum* (local term for gossip). And gossip we must, because El Rum Rum is the talk of Habana Vieja – an ambitious new restaurant run by a cigar sommelier that pays homage to seafood, Spanish gastronomy, cigars and throat-warming shots of the hard stuff.

The restaurant is split into three areas. A front bar decked out like a Spanish tavern, an artier inner sanctum, and a patio for cigar smokers. A suave, non-obtrusive house band do the rounds of all three. If you're struggling for choices, opt for the paella or the inky black rice with octopus.

★Lamparilla 361 Tapas & Cervezas TAPAS $$

(Map p64; ☎52-89-53-24; Lamparilla No 361, btwn Aguacate & Villegas; tapas CUC$3-12; ⏲noon-midnight) What makes a new restaurant just...click? Come to this nascent place on Lamparilla (never really a happening street – until now) and try to work out the secret. Maybe it's the perfect tapa-sized lasagna, the crisp sautéed vegetables served in ceramic dishes, the rich espresso-flavored crème brûlée, or the table menus written on dried palm leaves.

Other important little details about 361 are its genuine friendliness (they greet you with sincerity even five minutes before closing time), and the fact that it manages to be trendy without being pretentious. The open-to-the-street interior is small but thoughtfully decorated.

★Doña Eutimia CUBAN $$

(Map p64; Callejón del Chorro 60c; mains CUC$9-12; ⏲noon-10pm) Keep it simple. The secret at Doña Eutimia is that there *is* no secret. Just serve decent-sized portions of incredibly tasty Cuban food. The *ropa vieja* – shredded beef – and minced beef *picadillo* both deserve mentions. Doña Eutimia was the first

FROM RUSSIA WITH LOVE

American and Spanish culture is widely represented in Havana, but evidence of Cuba's 30-year *amistad* (friendship) with the Russians is less obvious.

For an early hint, study the traffic. Contrary to what glossy coffee-table books would have you believe, the most common car in Cuba isn't an Eisenhower-era Chevy or an antediluvian Oldsmobile, but the slightly less sexy Russian Lada, closely followed by its oft-forgotten cousin, the ghastly Moskvitch. Raising the profile of both cars up a notch is the fact that many antique American automobiles often run on Lada or Moskvitch engines due to the unavailability of spare parts in Cuba.

Soviet subtleties are also present in the city's architecture, especially in the utilitarian apartment blocks constructed in the 1970s and '80s by Cuba's *micro brigadas* (small armies of workers responsible for building much of the post-revolution housing). One building that particularly stands out (like a sore thumb) is the **Russian Embassy** (Av 5 No 6402, btwn Calles 62 & 66) in Miramar, which looks like a giant concrete robot. Its unusual design has been described as everything from constructivist to thuggish. Equally monolithic is the Hospital Nacional Hermanos Ameijeiras (p120) on the Malecón, a building which wouldn't look out of place in Moscow.

While you won't find too many Cubans longing for a return to the era of collective farms and nuclear brinkmanship, there has been a small outbreak of Soviet nostalgia in Havana of late. A notable Soviet-phile is Nazdarovie (p103), a new private restaurant on the Malecón. Serving Russian food, it's decked out with Soviet propaganda posters from the 1970s and encourages customers to order in the native Russian language.

private restaurant to grace this small cul-de-sac near the cathedral.

Now, there are at least five other restaurants and a rugby scrum of *jinteros* (hustlers) trying to lure you in (avoid them and you'll save money).

★Trattoria 5esquinas ITALIAN $$
(Map p64; ☎7-860-6295; Habana No 104, cnr Cuarteles; mains CUC$5-11; ⊙11am-11pm) Best Italian restaurant in Havana? There are a few contenders, but 5esquinas is making a strong claim. It has the full trattoria vibe right down to the open glow of the pizza oven and the aroma of roasted garlic. Visiting Italians won't be disappointed with the seafood pasta (generous on the lobster) or the crab and spinach cannelloni. Round it off with tiramisu.

The restaurant is situated, as the name suggests, on a junction of five streets in the Santo Ángel quarter.

El del Frente INTERNATIONAL $$
(Map p64; ☎7-863-0206; O'Reilly No 303; mains CUC$8-13; ⊙noon-midnight) When the owners of O'Reilly 304 realized that they had no room to expand their increasingly popular restaurant they opened up another one directly across the street and humorously called it El del Frente ('the one in front'). It's more of the same culinary genius with a few bonuses – a roof terrace, retro 1950s design features and heady gin cocktails.

Partake in the lobster tacos, spaghetti and meatballs, or practically anything else on the menu. Book ahead; it's insanely popular. Now the boys need *another* restaurant.

ChaChaChá INTERNATIONAL $$
(Map p64; ☎7-867-2450; Av de las Misiones No 159, btwn Tejadillo & Chacón; mains CUC$7.50-14; ⊙noon-2am) Spanking new in 2016, ChaChaChá has presented a good opening dance. The food is a smattering of international fare, with early kudos to the sizzling fajitas and the well-executed pasta dishes. There's an attractive interior with a mezzanine, retro-1950s Mob-era decor, vinyl records serving as place-mats and a bistro-style open-fronted location luring people fresh out of the Museo de la Revolución and Bellas Artes.

The conclusion: ChaChaChá is off to a flying start.

Donde Lis CUBAN $$
(Map p64; ☎7-860-0922; www.dondelis.com; Tejadillo No 163, btwn Habana & Compostela; mains CUC$5-12; ⊙noon-midnight) The Lis' interior is like a modern love letter to Havana; iconography from the Rat Pack era of the 1950s, reproduced 20th-century tropical art and bright colors splashed onto old colonial walls. The menu is a carefully cultivated mélange of different flavors presenting Cuban staples with modern twists – octopus with guacamole, lobster enchilados – along with some Italian and Spanish cameos.

O'Reilly 304 INTERNATIONAL $$
(Map p64; ☎52-64-47-25; O'Reilly No 304; meals CUC$8-13; ⊙noon-midnight) Thinking up the name (the restaurant's address) can't have taken much imagination, so it is perhaps a little ironic that O'Reilly 304 serves up some of the most imaginative cuisine in Havana. Exquisite seafood with crispy veg is presented on metal pans set into wooden trays, while the cocktails and tacos are fast becoming legendary.

The small interior is cleverly laid out to make the most of a mezzanine floor, while the walls are adorned with bold, edgy art – think nudes, screen prints and studies of fallen matadors.

Mesón de la Flota TAPAS $$
(Map p64; ☎7-863-3838; Mercaderes No 257, btwn Amargura & Brasil; tapas CUC$3-6; ⊙noon-midnight) This nautically themed tapas bar-restaurant might have been transported from Cádiz' Barrio de Santa María, so potent is the atmosphere. Old-world tapas include *garbanzos con chorizo* (chickpeas with sausage), calamari and tortilla, but there are also more substantial seafood-biased *platos principales* (main meals).

For music lovers the real drawcard is the nightly *tablaos* (flamenco shows), the quality of which could rival anything in Andalucía. Sit back and soak up the intangible spirit of *duende* (the climactic moment in a flamenco concert inspired by the fusion of music and dance).

La Vitrola BREAKFAST, INTERNATIONAL $$
(Map p64; ☎52-85-71-11; Muralla No 151, cnr San Ignacio; breakfast CUC$4-7; ⊙8:30am-midnight) A retro 1950s place with live music on the corner of Plaza Vieja that routinely gets swamped by tourists in the evening. Unbeknownst to many, La Vitrola is actually far better for its quieter alfresco breakfasts of fruit, coffee, toast and generous omelets.

Café de los Artistas INTERNATIONAL **$$**
(Map p64; ☎7-866-2418; Callejón de los Peluqueros; mains CUC$6-10; ⏰10am-1am) You'll probably find more tourists than artists here, but no matter. The restaurant's location in the community-fostered Callejón de los Peluqueros lends it a certain edge, aided by arty black-and-white photos, good all-over-the-map food and involved management. Bag a seat outside if you can and order something light with a cocktail.

Tres Monedas Creative Lounge INTERNATIONAL **$$**
(Map p64; ☎7-862-7206; Aguiar No 209, btwn Empedrado & Tejadillo; snacks CUC$2-5, mains CUC$8-15; ⏰noon-midnight) Behind Habana Vieja's grubby facades lie havens of arty magnificence, no more so than in Tres Monedas, a 'creative lounge'/cafe/restaurant where the decor designed by artist and owner Kadir López flaunts images of gaudy 1950s Havana – old Coke adverts, Esso signs and bottletop-shaped bar stools. The food is notable for its artistic presentation and it usually tastes as good as it looks.

Nao Bar Paladar SEAFOOD **$$**
(Map p64; ☎7-867-3463; Obispo No 1; meals CUC$6-12; ⏰noon-midnight) No 1 on Havana's main drag, Nao occupies a 200-year-old building near the docks that plays on its seafaring theme. The small upstairs space is good for main courses (seafood dominates); the downstairs bar and outdoor seating excels in snacks, including possibly the best warm baguettes in Cuba (try one stuffed with *jamón-serrano*).

Mama Inés CUBAN **$$**
(Map p64; ☎7-862-2669; Obrapía No 62; meals CUC$8-14; ⏰noon-10:30pm Tue-Sun) Mama's is run by Fidel Castro's ex-chef Erasmo, whose CV lists a veritable who's who of celebrity 'lefties' he's cooked for, from Hollywood actors to South American strongmen. Swept up in Cuba's culinary revolution, he's chucked his hat in the private sphere with this unpretentious (considering his résumé) restaurant, set in gorgeous colonial digs just off Calle Oficios.

The food is good, honest Cuban grub done well. Try the *ropa vieja*, octopus or roast pork, all served with traditional rice and beans.

Restaurante la Dominica ITALIAN **$$**
(Map p64; O'Reilly No 108; meals CUC$7-11; ⏰noon-midnight) Back in the Fidel era, this was one of Havana's few decent Italian restaurants, but in recent years it has been usurped by better private competition. That said, La Dominica – with its wood-fired pizza oven and al dente pasta – still delivers the Mediterranean goods in an elegantly restored dining room with alfresco seating on Calle O'Reilly.

Professional house bands serenade diners with a slightly more eclectic set than the obligatory Buena Vista Social Club staples.

Restaurante la Divina Pastora INTERNATIONAL **$$**
(Map p106; Parque Histórico Militar Morro-Cabaña; mains CUC$10-18; ⏰noon-11:30pm) Near Dársena de los Franceses and a battery of 18th-century cannons lies one of the more progressive outlets of Cuban cooking. Eschewing the iron rations of yore, La Divina Pastora offers creamy soups, grilled octupus, pesto-doused vegetables and excellent seafood (its specialty).

As it's state-run by Gaviota, the service can be patchy, but the food and views across the harbor usually make up for any shortfalls.

Paladar Los Mercaderes CUBAN, INTERNATIONAL **$$$**
(Map p64; ☎7-861-2437; Mercaderes No 207; meals CUC$12-20; ⏰11am-11pm) This private restaurant in a historic building has to be one of Cuba's most refined paladares for ambience, service *and* food, both Cuban and international. Follow a staircase strewn with flower petals to a luxurious 1st-floor dining room where musicians play violins and fine international dishes combine meat with exotic sauces. *Muy romántico!*

Restaurante el Templete SEAFOOD **$$$**
(Map p64; Av Carlos Manuel de Céspedes No 12; mains CUC$15-30; ⏰noon-11pm) Welcome to a rare Cuban breed: a state-run restaurant that can compete with the nascent private sector. The Templete's specialty is fish, and special it is: fresh, succulent and cooked simply without the pretensions of celebrity-chef-producing nations.

Sure, it's a little *caro* (expensive), but the quality is good and it serves all sorts of hard-to-get varieties – mahimahi, grouper and sole among them.

La Imprenta INTERNATIONAL **$$$**
(Map p64; Mercaderes No 208; meals CUC$10-17; ⏰noon-midnight) This attractive restaurant has a resplendent interior filled with memo-

rabilia from the building's previous incarnation as a printing works. The food isn't quite as spectacular although service is thorough and the menu offers previously unheard-of Cuban innovations such as al dente pasta, creative seafood medleys and a stash of decent wines.

Paladar Doña Carmela CUBAN **$$$**
(Map p106; ☎7-867-7472; Calle B No 10; mains CUC$15-35; ⏰noon-11pm) On the eastern side of the harbor in the small community near the forts, this private eating option is generally full of tourists on their way to the nightly *cañonazo* ceremony. Book ahead. The food is good, if pricey. Bank on dishes such as octopus in garlic and whole roast pork cooked in a wood oven. Tables are arranged in a very pleasant garden.

Café del Oriente CARIBBEAN, FRENCH **$$$**
(Map p64; Oficios 112; meals CUC$20-30; ⏰noon-11pm) A posh elegant side to Havana greets you as you walk through the door at this long-standing state-run establishment in Plaza de San Francisco de Asís. Smoked salmon, caviar (yes, caviar!), goose-liver pâté, lobster thermidor, steak au poivre, cheese plate and a glass of port. Plus service in a tux, no less. There's just one small problem: the price. But what the hell?

Centro Habana

Pastelería Francesa CAFE **$**
(Map p80; Parque Central No 411; snacks CUC$1-2; ⏰8am-midnight) This cafe has all the ingredients of a Champs-Élysées classic: a great location (in Parque Central), waiters in waistcoats, and delicate pastries displayed in glass cases. But the authentic French flavor is diminished by grumpy staff and the swarming *jineteras* (female touts) who roll in with foreign tourists for cigarettes and strong coffee.

Nazdarovie RUSSIAN **$$**
(Map p80; ☎7-860-2947; www.nazdarovie-havana.com; Malecón No 25, btwn Prado & Cárcel; mains CUC$10-12; ⏰noon-midnight) Cuba's 31-year dalliance with bolshevism is relived in this new and highly popular restaurant in prime digs overlooking the Malecón. Upstairs, the decor is awash with old Soviet propaganda posters, brotherly photos of Fidel and Khrushchev and slightly less bombastic Russian dolls. The menu is in three languages (to get in the real spirit, try ordering in Russian).

Choices are simple but classic: beef stroganoff, chicken kiev and borscht are all listed and they're all good. For cocktails try the James Bond option: a vodka martini (shaken, not stirred). From Russia with love.

Castas y Tal CUBAN **$$**
(Map p80; ☎7-864-2177; Av de Italia No 51, cnr San Lázaro; mains CUC$6-9; ⏰noon-midnight) In its short life the C&T has gone from old-school paladar (ensconced in someone's 11th-floor apartment) to trendy bistro-style restaurant. High-quality and adventurous food, such as lamb with Indian masala, or chicken in orange sauce, comes backed up with Cuban classics (lashing of rice and beans are served on the side). It's all beautifully presented, too.

Castropol SPANISH **$$**
(Map p80; ☎7-861-4864; Malecón 107, btwn Genios & Crespo; mains CUC$9-20; ⏰6pm-midnight) Castropol is run by the local Spanish Asturianas society, and its reputation has expanded in line with its fleshed-out restaurant space over the last few years. Word is now out that the venerable two-story establishment with its upstairs balcony overlooking Havana's dreamy sea drive serves some of the best Spanish and Caribbean food in Havana.

Pizza, pasta and the like are served downstairs. Upstairs is a little posher, with paella, *garbanzos fritos* (fried chickpeas), prawns in a tangy sauce, and generous portions of lobster pan-fried in butter.

Casa Abel INTERNATIONAL **$$**
(Map p80; ☎7-860-6589; San Lázaro No 319, cnr San Nicolás; mains CUC$7-16; ⏰noon-midnight) Rum and cigars dominate the proceedings at Casa Abel. Several food dishes on the menu contain meats marinated in Cuba's favorite tipple (including chicken marinated in rum and then smoke-roasted with beer!), while on the floor above the dining room you can puff away till your heart's content (or lament) in a smoking room, with *puros* (cigars) chosen from a special menu.

Casa Miglis SWEDISH **$$**
(Map p80; ☎7-864-1486; www.casamiglis.com; Lealtad No 120, btwn Ánimas & Lagunas; mains CUC$6-12; ⏰noon-1am) There's a place for everything in Havana these days, even Swedish-Cuban fusion food. Emerging improbably from a kitchen in the battle-scarred tenements of Centro Habana, comes *toast skagen* (prawns on toast), ceviche, couscous,

DON'T MISS

THE BACK ALLEYS OF HAVANA

Havana has a handful of easy-to-miss *callejones* (back alleys), each brushed with its own distinctive personality. Here is the leading quartet:

Callejón del Chorro

Habana Vieja's culinary alley was once a forgotten cul-de-sac that contained nothing more than a graphic artist's co-op at one end. Now it is a beehive of mega-popular private restaurants packed with alfresco seating and guarded by a gauntlet of over-keen waiters. Notwithstanding, the Chorro, which sits pretty just off Plaza de la Catedral, contains some of Havana's best restaurants, including Doña Eutimia (p100).

Callejón de Hamel

Havana's most famous back alley is located in a small sub-neighborhood of Centro Habana called Cayo Hueso and is dedicated to street art, live music, Afro-Cuban folklore and Santería.

Callejón Espada

Named after a reformist 19th-century Havana bishop, Espada cuts diagonally across the Habana Vieja grid in the increasingly genteel Santo Ángel neighborhood. Reclaimed as a community project a few years ago, its repaved sidewalks are often filled with seniors playing dominoes, or tourists sitting outside one of several new restaurants that furnish Cinco Esquinas de Santo Ángel where Espada merges with Calles Cuarteles and Habana.

Callejón de los Peluqueros

This small 100m stretch of Calle Aguiar on the north side of Habana Vieja has been improbably transformed into a hairdressing-themed art project by a local barber named Gilberto Valladares, aka 'Papito,' in tandem with the City Historian's Office. Anchored by Papito's own salon, which doubles as a museum called Arte Corte (p74), the street has been augmented by an art studio, a clothes boutique, several restaurants and a kids' playground.

and the *crème de la crème:* melt-in-your-mouth meatballs with mashed potato.

The owner's Swedish (no surprise) and the decor (empty picture frames, chairs attached to the wall) has a touch of IKEA minimalism about it.

Los Nardos SPANISH **$$**
(Map p80; ☎7-863-2985; Paseo de Martí No 563; mains CUC$4-10; ⏲noon-midnight) An open secret opposite the Capitolio, but easy to miss (look out for the queue), Los Nardos is a semi-private restaurant operated by the Spanish Asturianas society. The dilapidated exterior promises little, but the leather and mahogany decor and generous-sized dishes inside suggest otherwise – Los Nardos is touted in some quarters as one of the best cheap eateries in the city.

The menu includes lobster in a Catalan sauce, garlic prawns with sautéed vegetables and an authentic Spanish paella. Service is attentive, there are usually more Cubans than tourists, and the prices, for what you get, are mind-bogglingly cheap.

Restaurante Tien-Tan CHINESE **$$**
(Map p80; ☎7-863-2081; Cuchillo No 17, btwn Rayo & San Nicolás; meals CUC$7-12; ⏲10:30am-11pm) One of Barrio Chino's best authentic Chinese restaurants, Tien-Tan ('Temple of Heaven') is run by a Chinese-Cuban couple and serves up an incredible 130 different dishes. Try chop suey with vegetables or chicken with cashew nuts and sit outside in action-packed Cuchillo, one of Havana's most colorful and fastest-growing 'food streets.'

★San Cristóbal CUBAN **$$$**
(Map p80; ☎7-867-9109; San Rafael, btwn Campanario & Lealtad; meals CUC$9-18; ⏲noon-midnight Mon-Sat) San Cristóbal was knocking out fine food long before the leader of the free world dropped by in March 2016, although the publicity garnered from

President Obama's visit probably helped. Crammed into one of Centro Habana's grubbier streets, the restaurant has a museum-worthy interior crowded with old photos, animal skins, and a Santería altar flanked by pictures of Maceo and Martí.

The menu is Cuban with a touch of Spain. Obama had the *solomillo* (sirloin), while the First Lady had *tentación habanero* (fajitas with fried plantains).

La Guarida INTERNATIONAL **$$$**

(Map p80; ☎7-866-9047; www.laguarida.com; Concordia No 418, btwn Gervasio & Escobar; mains CUC$15-22; ⏰noon-3pm & 7pm-midnight) Only in Havana! The entrance to the city's most legendary private restaurant greets you like a scene out of a 1940s film noir. A decapitated statue at the bottom of a grand but dilapidated staircase leads up past drying lines of clothes to a wooden door, behind which lie multiple culinary surprises.

La Guarida's lofty reputation was first fermented in the 1990s when it was used as a location for the Oscar-nominated film *Fresa y Chocolate*. Not surprisingly, the food is still up there with Havana's best, shoehorning its pioneering brand of Nueva Cocina Cubana into dishes such as rabbit pâté and oxtail risotto. Reservations recommended.

Vedado

El Biky CAFETERIA **$**

(Map p96; ☎7-870-6515; cnr Calzada de la Infanta & San Lázaro; sandwiches & burgers CUC$2-5; ⏰8am-11pm) Havana needs more places like El Biky, a kind of upscale diner with quick service, cozy booths, walls covered in retro 1950s photos and the option to choose either a snack or a full meal. There's an affiliated bakery next door selling the best chocolate croissants in Havana (which you can have brought in to your table).

Café Presidente INTERNATIONAL **$**

(Map p96; ☎7-832-3091; cnr Av de los Presidentes & Calle 25; breakfast CUC$4-6.50; ⏰9am-midnight) With its red awnings and huge glass windows doing a good impersonation of a Champs-Élysées bistro, the Presidente delivers the goods on Havana's very own Champs-Élysées, Av de los Presidentes. It's the kind of place where you won't feel awkward popping in for a quick milk shake or plate of pasta, but it also does killer breakfasts and coffee.

Camino al Sol VEGETARIAN **$**

(Map p96; Calle 3 363, btwn Paseo & 2; CUC$1-4; ⏰10am-6pm Mon-Sat; ✍) In a country where the national dish is pork and no meal is considered complete without meat, this vegetarian hole-in-the-wall is truly a find. The chef uses locally grown vegetables such as eggplant, okra, corn and yuca to make anything from a pie to a veggie burger. The homemade pasta is especially delicious.

This spot is ideal for lunch, but be prepared to stand up as seating is limited.

La Catedral INTERNATIONAL **$**

(Map p96; ☎7-830-0793; Calle 8 No 106, btwn Calzada & Calle 5; meals CUC$4-6; ⏰noon-11pm) It's not anywhere near the cathedral nor does it look particularly ecclesial, but no matter. The best thing about La Catedral is that, by offering very reasonable prices, it attracts a local Cuban clientele and not just tourists. The restaurant tackles a number of culinary genres – including pizza, tapas and a tremendous *tres leches* cake – and in big portions too.

If the size of the dishes defeat you, they will bag them up for you to go.

Restaurant Bar Razones CUBAN, INDIAN **$**

(Map p96; ☎7-832-8732; Calle F No 63, btwn Calles 3 & 5; mains CUC$4-7; ⏰noon-midnight) Since Havana no longer has a pure Indian restaurant, it's left for Razones to pick up the spicy pieces, bravely inserting a couple of curry dishes onto its multifarious menu. It also does interesting things with lobster (flavored with pineapple sauce and even coffee extract). The clientele is mainly Cuban, meaning the prices aren't too steep.

Topoly IRANIAN **$**

(Map p96; ☎7-832-3224; www.topoly.fr; Calle 23 No 669, cnr Calle D; small plates CUC$4-7; ⏰10am-midnight) Cuba finds solidarity with Iran in Havana's first Iranian restaurant, corralled in a lovely collonaded mansion on arterial Calle 23. Sit on the wraparound porch beneath iconic prints of Gandhi, José Martí and Che Guevara, and enjoy pureed eggplant, lamb *brochetas* (shish kebabs), fantastic coffee, and tea in ornate silver pots. Belly dancers entertain on selected evenings.

Waoo Snack Bar INTERNATIONAL **$**

(Map p96; Calle L No 414, cnr Calle 25; snacks CUC$3-7; ⏰noon-midnight) Wow! The Waoo Snack Bar truly impresses with its wooden wraparound bar, happening locale close to

Parque Histórico Militar Morro-Cabaña

Parque Histórico Militar Morro-Cabaña

Top Sights

Sights

Eating

Calles 23 and L, and quick offerings you might want to savor – think carpaccio, cheese plates and coffee with accompanying desserts.

La Chucheria AMERICAN $

(Map p96; Calle 1, btwn Calles C & D; snacks CUC$2-7; 7am-midnight) Clinging to its perch close to the Malecón, this sleek sports bar looks as if it floated mockingly across the straits from Florida like a returning exile. But you can forget about politics momentarily as you contemplate pizza toppings, sandwich fillings and the best ice cream and fruit milk shakes in Havana.

The restaurant's diminutive interior, with its clear plastic chairs and flat-screen TVs replaying Messi's latest match-winner, demonstrates how the line between *socialismo* and *capitalismo* is becoming ever more blurred.

Toke Infanta y 25 BURGERS $

(Map p96; 7-836-3440; cnr Calzada de la Infanta & Calle 25; snacks CUC$2-4; 7am-midnight) Sitting pretty amid the bruised edifices of Calzada de la Infanta on the cusp of Vedado and Centro Habana, Toke lures enamored *habaneros* (and tourists) with cool neon, smart color accents, economical *hamburguesas* (hamburgers) and chocolate brownies. It's become known as a gay-friendly spot lately due to its location next to a couple of nightclubs.

Coppelia ICE CREAM $

(Map p96; cnr Calles 23 & L; ice cream from MN$40; 10am-9:30pm Tue-Sat) The Coppelia, Havana's celebrated ice-cream parlor housed in a flying-saucer-like structure in a park in Vedado, is as celebrated for its massive queues as much as it is for its ice cream. Insanely popular since opening in

1966 (through some very rough economic times), this state-run institution is about far more than mere ice cream.

Relationships have been forged here, fledgling novels drafted, birthday parties celebrated and Miami-bound escape plots hatched. The ultimate accolade came in 1993 when the Coppelia served as a location and major plot device in the Oscar-nominated Cuban movie *Fresa y Chocolate* (the film's title alludes to two flavors of Coppelia ice cream: strawberry and chocolate).

As a tourist visiting the Coppelia, you'll probably be directed by a security guard into a smaller convertible-paying outdoor section, but dodge the directives. Queueing is an integral part of Coppelia folklore, as traditional as the table-sharing, the cheap ice cream (you'll pay in Cuban pesos), and the uncensored people-watching opportunities that abound inside.

Café TV FAST FOOD $

(Map p96; cnr Calles N & 19; mains CUC$4.50; ⏲11am-3am Mon-Sat, 11am-midnight Sun) Hidden in the bowels of Edificio Focsa, this TV-themed cafe is a funky dinner/performance venue lauded by those in the know for its cheap food and hilarious comedy nights. If you're willing to brave the frigid air-con and rather foreboding underground entry tunnel, head here for fresh burgers, healthy salad, pasta and chicken cordon bleu.

★Starbien INTERNATIONAL $$

(Map p96; ☎7-830-0711; Calle 29 No 205, btwn Calles B & C; lunch CUC$12; ⏲noon-5pm & 7pm-midnight) The ingredients: an elegant tucked-away Vedado mansion, an authentic Cuban welcome, complimentary bites to start you off, a great wine list, never-miss-a-beat service, and chicken in pineapple sauce. And it's all yours for CUC$12 if you bag the lunchtime special four-course menu. So get over to Calle 29 near Plaza de la Revolución.

★Café Laurent INTERNATIONAL $$

(Map p96; ☎7-832-6890; Calle M No 257, 5th fl, btwn Calles 19 & 21; meals CUC$10-15; ⏲noon-midnight) Talk about a hidden gem. The unsigned Café Laurent is a sophisticated fine-dining restaurant encased, incongruously, in a glaringly ugly 1950s apartment block next to the Focsa Building. Starched white tablecloths, polished glasses and lacy drapes furnish the bright modernist interior, while sautéed pork with dry fruit and red wine, and seafood risotto headline the menu. Viva the culinary revolution!

Mediterraneo Havana MEDITERRANEAN $$

(Map p96; ☎7-832-4894; www.medhavana.com; Calle 13 No 406, btwn Calles F & G; mains CUC$9-18; ⏲noon-midnight) Allying themselves with the *granja a la mesa* (farm-to-table) movement and utilizing a couple of agricultural co-ops in Guanabacoa, the Med serves primarily Italian food with a few nods to Spain in a pleasant Vedado residence. Run by two Cuban-Sardinian friends, it hits most of the right notes, with pasta dishes that aren't afraid to go out of the box.

Try the penne in brandy or the truffle risotto and make a note about the crème caramel for dessert. Compliments must also go to the service, which is warm but discreet.

El Idilio CUBAN $$

(Map p96; ☎7-830-7921; cnr Av de los Presidentes & Calle 15; meals CUC$6-11; ⏲noon-midnight) A bold, adventurous, neighborhood joint in Vedado with checkered tablecloths, Idilio epitomizes the Cuban culinary scene as it spreads its wings and flies. Anything goes here: pasta, ceviche and Cuban standards, or opt for the seafood medley peeled freshly off the barbecue before your very eyes.

Paladar Mesón Sancho Panza MEDITERRANEAN $$

(Map p96; ☎7-831-2862; Calle J No 508, btwn Calles 23 & 25; mains CUC$5-12; ⏲noon 11pm) Appropriately situated next to Parque Don Quijote, Paladar Mesón Sancho Panza doesn't let down its loyal literary *compañero*. Fine Spanish-influenced food is served in a lovely semi-alfresco restaurant adorned with ponds and plant-covered trellises, and there's a cake case that could make skipping dessert difficult. Set yourself up with paella, lasagna or *brochetas* (kebabs) first.

Bonus: there's occasional live flamenco.

Versus 1900 INTERNATIONAL $$$

(Map p96; ☎7-835-1852; www.versus1900.com; Línea No 504, btwn Calles D & E; mains CUC$7-24; ⏲noon-midnight) Opened in late 2015, Versus 1900 shows how Cuban restaurants are moving the yardstick ever forward. Set inside a large detached house and making good use of the multifarious space including interior rooms, front terrace and rooftop, the place is exquisitely decorated (antique, but uncluttered) and delivers an interesting menu that includes rabbit, duck and Peruvian soup.

The best and most unique part is on the roof at super-cool Chill Out (p112), a trance-y bar with sofas, poufs and four-poster recliners.

Atelier CUBAN $$$
(Map p96; ☎7-836-2025; Calle 5 No 511, Altos, btwn Paseo & Calle 2; meals CUC$12-25; ⊙noon-midnight) The first thing that hits you here is the stupendous wall art – huge, thought-provoking, religious-tinged paintings. You'll also notice the antique wooden ceiling, Moorish-style roof terrace and old-school elegance (even the plates are interesting). At some point you'll get around to the food – Cuban with a French influence – scribbled onto an ever-changing menu. Try the duck (the specialty) if it's on, or the rabbit.

Decameron INTERNATIONAL $$$
(Map p96; ☎7-832-2444; Línea No 753, btwn Paseo & Calle 2; mains CUC$12-18; ⊙noon-midnight;) Nondescript from the outside, but far prettier within, thanks largely to its famous collection of antique clocks (don't be late now!), the Decameron is an old stalwart paladar that was always good, still is good and probably always will be good. The food is Cuban with international inflections. People rave about the savory tuna tart; ditto the sweet lemon tart.

On top of that there's a decent wine selection, powerful cocktails and the kitchen is sympathetic to vegetarians.

Le Chansonnier FRENCH $$$
(Map p96; ☎7-832-1576; www.lechansonnierhabana.com; Calle J No 257, btwn Calles 13 & 15; meals CUC$12-20; ⊙12:30pm-12:30am) A great place to dine if you can find it (there's no sign), hidden away in a faded mansion turned private restaurant whose revamped interior is dramatically more modern than the front facade. French wine and French flavors shine in house specialties such as rabbit with mustard, eggplant gratin and spare ribs. Opening times vary and it's often busy; phone ahead.

VIP Havana MEDITERRANEAN $$$
(Map p96; ☎7-832-0178; Calle 9 No 454, btwn Calles E & F; mains CUC$15-21; ⊙noon-3am) You don't have to be a very important person to eat at VIP Havana, but it probably helps. This is Havana posing as Miami, with a large central bar on the restaurant floor, drink shelves backlit with neon strip-lights, and old black-and-white movies showing (silently) on a massive cinema screen.

VIP's atmosphere manages to be refined but not at all snobby, while the food does good renditions of Cuba's default lobster along with an enthusiastically lauded paella. A small, but important detail: it also has what are possibly Cuba's finest *baños* (toilets).

La Torre FRENCH, CARIBBEAN $$$
(Map p96; ☎7-838-3088; Edificio Focsa, cnr Calles 17 & M; mains CUC$15-30; ⊙11:30am-12:30am) Havana's tallest restaurant is perched high above Vedado on the 36th floor of the skyline-hogging Focsa building. The lofty fine-dining extravaganza has sweeping city views that rarely disappoint, although the food sometimes does.

Back in the day, government-run Torre was a legend, a colossus of French-Cuban haute cuisine. These days, there are plenty of other (private) places that have usurped it in both novelty and value for money. But, oh, the view!

Drinking & Nightlife

Havana's cafe scene has entered an interesting stage. Bland international franchises have yet to gain a foothold but, with more freedom to engage in private business, local entrepreneurs are directing their artistic creativity into a growing number of bohemian bars and cafes.

Habana Vieja

★**El Dandy** BAR, CAFE
(Map p64; ☎7-867-6463; www.bareldandy.com; cnr Brasil & Villegas; ⊙8am-1am) The jury's still out on Havana's trendiest bar-cafe, but there's little doubt that it's the dandiest. Proving itself to be 'unduly devoted to style, neatness, and fashion in dress and appearance,' El Dandy is a vortex of strong coffee, powerful cocktails and (something not always included in the hipster rule book) warm, unpretentious service.

It also acts as a mini photo gallery, with subject matter dedicated to the two great balletic themes of dance and boxing adorning the walls.

★**Azúcar Lounge** LOUNGE
(Map p64; ☎7-860-6563; Mercaderes No 315; ⊙11am-midnight) How to make an old square trendy: stick a low-lit, chill-out bar with IKEA-style couches on the upper floor of

one of its oldest houses. Sprinkle said bar with avant-garde art and weird light fixtures. Offer lavish cocktails and hypnotic trance music. Call it Azúcar (sugar).

★ El Chanchullero BAR

(Map p64; www.el-chanchullero.com; Brasil, btwn Bernaza & Christo; ⌚1pm-midnight) '*Aquí jamás estuvo Hemingway*' (Hemingway was never here) reads the sign outside roguish Chanchullero, expressing more than a hint of irony. It had to happen. While rich tourists toast Hemingway in La Bodeguita del Medio, hip Cubans and foreigners who think they're hip pay far less for better cocktails in their own boho alternative.

Squeeze inside the clamorous, graffiti-ridden dive bar interior where the music rocks in 4/4 time rather than 6/8. Stuff that in your cigar and smoke it, Ernesto!

El Patchanka BAR

(Map p64; ☎7-860-4161; Bernaza No 162; ⌚1pm-1am) Live bands rock the rafters, locals knock back powerful CUC$2 mojitos, and earnest travelers banter about Che Guevara's contribution to modern poster art in this new dive bar in Plaza del Cristo that already looks comfortably lived in. Cultural interaction is the key here. By keeping the prices low (lobster for CUC$6!), Patchanka attracts everyone.

The walls are decorated with graffiti from around the world along with a cartoonish pirate ship sporting the name 'Patchanka' – the Spanish term for fusion-rock. It fits like a coat.

Museo del Chocolate CAFE

(Map p64; cnr Amargura & Mercaderes; ⌚9am-9pm) Chocolate addicts beware, this unmissable place in Habana Vieja's heart is a lethal dose of chocolate, truffles and yet more chocolate (all made on the premises). Situated – with no irony intended – in Calle Amargura (literally, Bitterness Street), it's more a cafe than a museum, with a small cluster of marble tables set amid a sugary mélange of chocolate paraphernalia.

Not surprisingly, everything on the menu contains one all-pervading ingredient: have it hot, cold, white, dark, rich or smooth – the stuff is divine, whichever way you choose.

Espacios Old Fashioned BAR

(Map p64; ☎7-861-3895; www.barrestaurantespaciosoldfashioned.com; Amargura No 258, btwn Habana & Compostela; ⌚noon-midnight) The new offshoot of the hip Miramar restaurant, Espacios inhabits a smaller abode in Habana Vieja, but, like its bigger sibling, adorns its walls with avant-garde art. You can eat here, but we recommend it as a place to sink a glass or cup of something containing caffeine, alcohol or perhaps just juice, while checking out the art – and artists.

Musicians roll in at about 10:30pm.

Cervecería Antiguo Almacén de la Madera y Tabaco BEER HALL

(Map p64; cnr Desamparados & San Ignacio; ⌚noon-midnight) Down on the docks lies Havana's largest brewpub, which makes and serves three Austrian-style beers in an old lumber and tobacco warehouse. The interior is huge, recalling the ambience of an Oktoberfest beer tent, so it never feels overcrowded.

There's barbecued food on offer plus a central stage for live music, but this place is best for its beer – CUC$2 for a half liter, or CUC$12 for a 3L theatrical beer tower.

Dulcería Bianchini II CAFE

(Map p64; ☎7-862-8477; www.dulceria-bianchini.com; San Ignacio No 68; ⌚9am-9pm) Cubans seemed to have long forgotten about the Spanish *merienda* – that lovely afternoon pause for hot drinks and cake. Then along came Bianchini, with its sweet snacks and excellent coffee, to remind everyone why tea time matters. This tiny bohemian abode is squeezed into Habana Vieja's jam-packed 'culinary alley' near the cathedral. Dodge the menu-touting hustlers and order a coffee.

La Bodeguita del Medio BAR

(Map p64; Empedrado No 207; ⌚11am-midnight) Made famous thanks to the rum-swilling exploits of Ernest Hemingway (who by association instantly sends the prices soaring), this is Havana's most celebrated bar. A visit here has become de rigueur for tourists who haven't yet cottoned on to the fact that the mojitos are better and (far) cheaper elsewhere.

Past visitors have included Salvador Allende, Fidel Castro, Nicolás Guillén, Harry Belafonte and Nat King Cole, all of whom have left their autographs on La Bodeguita's wall – along with thousands of others (save for the big names, the walls are repainted every few months). These days the clientele is less luminous, with package tourists from Varadero outnumbering beatnik bohemians. Purists claim the mojitos have lost their Hemingway-esque shine in recent years. Only one way to find out…

LGBTIQ HAVANA

The revolution had a hostile attitude toward homosexuality in its early days. While the Stonewall riots were engulfing New York City, Cuban homosexuals were still being sent to re-education camps by a government that was dominated by macho, bearded ex-guerrillas dressed in military fatigues.

But since the 1990s the tide has been turning, spearheaded somewhat ironically by Mariela Castro, daughter of current president, Raúl Castro, and the director of the Cuban National Center for Sex Education in Havana.

An important landmark for the LGBT community was reached in June 2008 when the Cuban government passed a law permitting free sex-change operations to qualifying citizens courtesy of the country's famously far-sighted health system. In November 2012 Cuba elected its first transgender person to public office when Adela Hernández (a woman) won a municipal seat in Villa Clara Province.

Havana's LGBT scene has taken off in the last few years. The focus of gay life is on the cusp of Centro Habana and Vedado in the 'triangle' that stretches between Calzada de la Infanta, Calle L and Calle 23 (La Rampa). Calle 23 at its intersection with the Malecón has long been a favored meeting spot for gay people, while Cine Yara and the Coppelia park opposite are well-known cruising spots. Nightlife centers on gay-friendly venues such as the Pico Blanco (p112) club in Hotel St John's and Cabaret Las Vegas (p112), both known for their drag shows. Sandwiched between the two is a pleasant little cafe called Toke Infanta y 25 (p106). Also worth a trip is the Café Cantante Mi Habana (p112) in Cuba's National Theater, which has a gay party on Saturday nights.

In more discriminatory days, Havana's only gay beach was Mi Cayito, a quiet secluded stretch of Playa Boca Ciega in Playas del Este. The beach remains popular. You can now also enjoy gay film nights at the Icaic headquarters on the corner of Calles 23 and 12 in Vedado and, since 2009, an annual gay parade along Calle 23 in mid-May. Legally, lesbians enjoy the same rights as gay men, though there is a less evident lesbian 'scene.'

El Floridita BAR

(Map p64; Obispo No 557; ⏲11am-midnight) El Floridita was a favorite of expat Americans long before Hemingway dropped by in the 1930s, hence the name (which means 'Little Florida'). Bartender Constante Ribalaigua invented the daiquiri soon after WWI, but it was Hemingway who popularized it and ultimately the bar christened a drink in his honor: the Papa Hemingway Special (a grapefruit-flavored daiquiri).

Hemingway's record – legend has it – was 13 doubles in one sitting. Any attempt to equal it at the current prices (CUC$6 for a shot) will cost you a small fortune – and a huge hangover.

La Factoria Plaza Vieja BAR

(Map p64; cnr San Ignacio & Muralla; ⏲11am-midnight) Havana's original microbrewery occupies a boisterous corner of Plaza Vieja and sells smooth, cold, homemade beer at sturdy wooden benches set up outside on the cobbles or indoors in a bright, noisy beer hall. Gather a group together and you'll get the amber nectar in a tall plastic tube drawn from a tap at the bottom. There's also an outside grill.

Café Taberna BAR

(Map p64; cnr Brasil & Mercaderes; ⏲noon-midnight) Founded in 1772 and still glowing after a 21st-century makeover, this drinking and eating establishment is a great place to prop up the (impressive) bar and sink a few cocktails before dinner. The music, which gets swinging around 8pm, doffs its cap, more often than not, to one-time resident mambo king Benny Moré. Skip the food.

Bar Dos Hermanos BAR

(Map p64; San Pedro No 304; ⏲24hr) This once-seedy, now polished bar down by the docks broadcasts a boastful list of former rum-slugging patrons on a plaque by the door: Federico Lorca, Marlon Brando, Errol Flynn and Hemingway (of course) among them. With its long wooden bar and salty seafaring atmosphere, it still spins a little magic.

Café París BAR
(Map p64; Obispo No 202; 24hr) Things never stand still at this rough-hewn Habana Vieja dive bar, known for its live music and gregarious tourist-heavy atmosphere. On good nights, the rum flows and spontaneous dancing erupts.

Monserrate Bar BAR
(Map p64; Obrapía No 410; noon-midnight) A couple of doors down from the famous Hemingway drinking haunt of El Floridita, Monserrate is a Hemingway-free zone, meaning the daiquiris are half the price.

Café el Escorial CAFE
(Map p64; Mercaderes No 317, cnr Muralla; 9am-9pm) Once the only cafe on Plaza Vieja, this state-run staple encased in a finely restored colonial mansion has been usurped by new private competition. Granted, the caffeine infusions are still pretty good – *café cubano, café con leche,* frappé, coffee liquor and even *daiquirí de café* are all available – but the cakes are often as dry as the service.

La Dichosa BAR
(Map p64; cnr Obispo & Compostela; 10am-midnight) It's hard to miss rowdy La Dichosa on busy Calle Obispo. Small and cramped, with at least half the space given over to the resident band, this is a good place to sink a quick mojito.

Centro Habana

★Café Arcangel CAFE
(Map p80; 5-268-5451; Concordia No 57; 8:30am-6:30pm Mon-Sat, 8:15am-1pm Sun) Excellent coffee, fine *tortas* (cakes), suave non-reggaeton music and Charlie Chaplin movies playing on loop in a scarred Centro Habana apartment – what more could you want?

Sloppy Joe's BAR
(Map p80; cnr Agramonte & Ánimas; noon-3am) This bar, opened by young Spanish immigrant José García (aka 'Joe') in 1919, earned its name due to its dodgy sanitation and a soggy *ropa vieja* (shredded-beef) sandwich. Legendary among expats before the revolution, it closed in the '60s after a fire, but was reincarnated in 2013 beneath the same noble neoclassical facade. And it's still serving decent cocktails and soggy sandwiches. Granted, it's tourist-ville these days, but the interior is equally true to its predecessor, as old black-and-white photos (most of which feature Sinatra with a glass in his hand) on the wall testify.

Café Neruda BAR
(Map p80; Malecón No 203, btwn Manrique & San Nicolás; 11am-11pm) A romantically disheveled place on the Malecón, named after the famous Chilean man of letters, Pablo Neruda, it's better for its drinks than its food menu. Spend a poetic afternoon writing your own verse as the waves splash over the sea wall.

Prado No 12 BAR
(Map p80; Paseo de Martí No 12; noon-11pm) A slim flat-iron building on the corner of Paseo de Martí (Prado) and San Lázaro that serves drinks and simple snacks, Prado No 12 resembles Havana in a 1950s time warp. Soak up the atmosphere of the city here after a sunset stroll along the Malecón.

Vedado

★Café Mamainé CAFE, BAR
(Map p96; 7-832-8328; Calle L No 206, btwn Calles 15 & 17; 8am-midnight Mon-Thu, 8am-3am Fri-Sun) Art and coffee go together like Fidel and Che in this wonderfully reimagined eclectic mansion with an interior decked out with revolving local art, much of it made from recycled 'junk.' Flop down on a cushion on the wooden mezzanine, order a strong coffee or cocktail and chat with the person next to you (probably an artist).

★Café Madrigal BAR
(Map p96; Calle 17 No 302, btwn Calles 2 & 4; 6pm-2am Tue-Sun) Vedado flirts with bohemia in this dimly lit romantic bar that might have materialized serendipitously from Paris' Latin Quarter in the days of Joyce and Hemingway. Order a *tapita* (small tapa) and a cocktail, and retire to the atmospheric art nouveau terrace where the buzz of nighttime conversation competes with the racket of vintage American cars rattling past below.

La Juguera JUICE BAR
(Map p96; Calle 6, btwn Calles 1 & 3; 9am-7pm Mon-Sat, 9am-1pm Sun) Tucked away behind a residential building, this spot offers dozens of fresh juice combinations and also a great slice of Cuban life, as it is very popular among locals. If you are staying nearby and want to take some fresh juice home, it also sells by the liter.

Make sure you bring some small change as a glass of juice is generally around CUC$6.

Chill Out BAR

(Map p96; Línea No 504, btwn Calles D & E; ⊙7pm-3am) Chill Out doesn't need much more explanation beyond its name. It's the trance-y, super-cool rooftop bar at Versus 1900 (p107), with sofas, poufs and four-poster recliners. The ideal after-party haunt in Vedado.

Gabanna Café BAR

(Map p96; cnr Calle 3 & C; ⊙5pm-3am) Sleek, small, trendy, and embellished with black-and-white overtones, this à la mode cocktail bar is what the modern Havana scene is all about. Beautiful people sip equally attractive cocktails in its small, supercool interior.

Bar-Restaurante 1830 CLUB

(Map p96; cnr Malecón & Calle 20; ⊙noon-1:45am) If you want to salsa dance, this is *the* place to go. After the Sunday night show literally everyone takes to the floor. It's at the far west end of the Malecón with a water-facing terrace. Skip the food.

Cuba Libro CAFE

(Map p96; ☎7-830-5205; cnr Calles 24 &19; ⊙11am-8pm Mon-Sat; 👪) 🍃 Cafe, book vendor, socially responsible community resource, and a great place for Cubans and non-Cubans to interact; Cuba Libro wears many different hats. Although it's a bit of a walk from the main sights, it's a good place to find out more about Havana below the radar. Grab a juice or coffee and join the discussion.

Aside from selling secondhand books, the cafe displays emerging Cuban art, gives out free condoms, provides toys for kids and follows sustainable practices.

Café Fresa y Chocolate CAFE

(Map p96; Calle 23, btwn Calles 10 & 12; ⊙9am-11pm) No ice cream here, just movie memorabilia. This is the HQ of the Cuban Film Institute and a nexus for coffee-quaffing students and art-house movie addicts. It's not fancy, but you can debate the merits of Almodóvar over Scorsese on the pleasant patio before disappearing next door for a film preview.

Café Cantante Mi Habana CLUB

(Map p96; ☎7-879-0710; cnr Paseo & Calle 39; ⊙8pm-3am) Below the Teatro Nacional de Cuba (side entrance), this is a hip disco that offers live salsa music and dancing, as well as bar snacks and food. It has earned a reputation as being *the* place to go to meet cool, trendy Cubans in a laid-back *jintero*-free environment. On Saturdays, it hosts a gay party called Divino, with drag show.

No shorts, T-shirts or hats may be worn, and no under-18s are allowed. The cover is CUC$10.

Piano Bar Delirio Habanero CLUB

(Map p96; ☎7-878-4275; cnr Paseo & Calle 39; ⊙from 6pm Tue-Sun) This sometimes suave, sometimes frenetic lounge upstairs in Teatro Nacional de Cuba hosts everything from young rap artists to smooth, improvised jazz. The sharp red-accented bar and performance space abut a wall of glass overlooking Plaza de la Revolución – it's impressive at night with the Martí memorial alluringly backlit. The cover charge is between CUC$5 and CUC$10.

The scene usually gets swinging in the small hours with a largely Cuban clientele. Bring your dancing shoes.

Cabaret Las Vegas CLUB

(Map p96; Calzada de la Infanta No 104, btwn Calles 25 & 27; ⊙10pm-4am) The Vegas was once a rough and slightly seedy local music dive, but these days it's better known for its late-night drag shows. With the demise of Humboldt 25, it's become one of Havana's most reliable gay clubs. Entry is CUC$5.

Pico Blanco CLUB

(Map p96; Calle O, btwn Calles 23 & 25; ⊙from 9pm) An insanely popular nightclub, the Pico Blanco is on the 14th floor of the medi-

BEST HOTEL BARS

Hotel Nacional (p94) Mojitos on the terrace at the Hotel Nacional is a not-to-be-missed Havana experience.

Hotel Saratoga (p92) Beautiful decor, refined ambience and very expensive drinks.

Hotel Armadores de Santander (p90) Dark mahogany wood and a seafaring atmosphere down by Havana's harborside.

Hotel Ambos Mundos (p90) Hemingway's old hotel is a romantic place to order a cocktail and offer your requests to the house pianist.

ocre Hotel St John's in Vedado. The program can be hit or miss. Some nights it's karaoke and cheesy boleros (ballads). another it's drag queens and boys in tight T-shirts. It's primarily Cuban with some hustlers. Entry is CUC$5 to CUC$10.

Bar-Club Imágenes BAR
(Map p96; Calzada No 602; ⏲10pm-3am) This small, darkly lit piano bar attracts something of an older Cuban crowd with its regular diet of boleros (ballads) and *trova* (traditional music), though there are also comedy shows; check the schedule posted outside.

Club la Red CLUB
(Map p96; cnr Calles 19 & L; ⏲10pm-2am) A local neighborhood disco with the occasional bemused foreigner thrown in. Entry costs CUC$3 to CUC$5.

☆ Entertainment

Although it may have lost its pre-revolutionary reputation as a dazzling casino quarter, Vedado is still *the* place for nightlife in Havana. Cabaret, jazz, classical music, dance and cinema are offered in abundance and it's invariably of a high standard. Entertainment in Habana Vieja is emerging from a Rip Van Winkle–like slumber and becoming increasingly hip. Centro's nightlife is edgier and more local.

Live Music

Jazz Club la Zorra y El Cuervo LIVE MUSIC
(Map p96; ☎7-833-2402; cnr Calles 23 & O; CUC$5-10; ⏲from 10pm) Havana's most famous jazz club (The Vixen and the Crow) opens its doors nightly at 10pm to long lines of committed music fiends. Enter through a red British phonebox and descend into a diminutive and dark basement. The scene here is hot and clamorous and leans toward freestyle jazz.

Callejón de Hamel LIVE MUSIC
(Map p80; ⏲from noon Sun) Aside from its funky street murals and psychedelic art shops, the main reason to come to Havana's high temple of Afro-Cuban culture in Centro Habana is the frenetic rumba music that kicks off every Sunday at around noon.

For aficionados, this is about as raw and hypnotic as it gets, with interlocking drum patterns and lengthy rhythmic chants powerful enough to summon up the spirit of the *orishas* (Santería deities). Due to a liberal sprinkling of tourists these days, some argue that the Callejón has lost much of its basic charm. Don't believe them. This place still rocks – and rumbas!

Jazz Café LIVE MUSIC
(Map p96; ☎7-838-3302; top fl, Galerías de Paseo, cnr Calle 1 & Paseo; cover after 8pm CUC$10; ⏲noon-2am) This upscale joint, located improbably in a shopping mall overlooking the Malecón, is a kind of jazz supper club, with dinner tables and a decent menu. At night, the club swings into action with live jazz, *timba* and, occasionally, straight-up salsa. It's definitely the suavest of Havana's jazz venues.

Basílica Menor de San Francisco de Asís CLASSICAL MUSIC
(Map p64; Plaza de San Francisco de Asís; tickets CUC$3-8; ⏲from 6pm Thu-Sat) Plaza de San Francisco de Asís' glorious church, which dates from 1738, has been reincarnated as a 21st-century museum and concert hall. The old nave hosts choral and chamber music two to three times a week (check the schedule at the door) and the acoustics inside are famously good. It's best to bag your ticket at least a day in advance.

Café Teatro Bertolt Brecht LIVE MUSIC
(Map p96; ☎7-832-9359; cnr Calles 13 & I; tickets CUC$3) A live-music venue beloved by Havana's trendy youth for the weekly concerts headlined by the legendary music collective Interactivo (Wednesdays at midnight-ish). If you're curious about Cuban culture – and its future – roll up for an evening here. Be prepared to queue.

Submarino Amarillo LIVE MUSIC
(Map p96; cnr Calles 17 & 6; ⏲2-7:30pm & 9pm-2am Tue-Sat, 2-10pm Sun, 9pm-2am Mon) You can't escape the Beatles in Cuba; their iconic status is epitomized in clubs such as this one, which abuts Parque Lennon and hosts all types of live music as long as it's in 4/4 time and a subgenre of 'rock.' Look out for top Cuban band Los Kents. Afternoons are more laid-back, when you can nibble tapas while watching surreal '60s videos.

Casa de la Música LIVE MUSIC
(Map p80; Av de Italia, btwn Concordia & Neptuno; CUC$5-25; ⏲5pm-3am) One of Cuba's best and most popular nightclubs and live-music venues. All the big names play here, from Bamboleo to Los Van Van – and you'll pay peanuts to see them. Of the city's two Casas de la Música, this Centro Habana version is a little edgier than its Miramar

LOCAL KNOWLEDGE

WATCHING SPORT

As economic standards nosedived during the early 1990s, the nation's sporting prowess moved in the other direction, peaking at the 1992 Barcelona Olympics when Cuba (the world's 106th-largest nation) came fifth in the overall medals table with 14 gold. The Cubans continue to excel in baseball, boxing, volleyball and high jump (Javier Sotomayor has held the world record since 1993). Soccer is a growing sport attracting an ever-expanding fan base, particularly since the 2014 FIFA World Cup. Havana's main sporting stadiums are located in the peripheral municipalities of Playa, Cerro and Habana del Este. Going to a game is an experience. No bookings are required; just turn up, pay the nominal ticket price and find a (hard) seat.

Estadio Latinoamericano (Map p96; Zequiera No 312, Cerro; tickets CUC$2) The largest stadium in the country holds 55,000 and was built before the revolution in 1946. It's the home of Havana's Los Industriales baseball team. Entrance to games costs small change. The season is from late October to April with playoffs running until May.

Estadio Pedro Marrero (cnr Av 41 & Calle 46, Kohly) This slightly down-at-heel Playa stadium holds 28,000 spectators and is home to FC Ciudad de La Habana, the city's main soccer team, who have won the Campeonato Nacional de Fútbol six times.

Estadio Panamericano The shabby Estadio Panamericano was built for the 1991 Pan American Games. It was fitted with a new athletics track in 2008 but still looks neglected and unloved. It's used mainly for athletics and soccer.

Coliseo de la Ciudad Deportiva (cnr Av de la Independencia & Vía Blanca, Cerro) This multiuse 15,000-capacity indoor sports arena opened in 1958. It's the headquarters of the national men's volleyball team, and in 2016 the surrounding grounds hosted the Rolling Stones' first Cuban rock concert.

counterpart (some say it's too edgy), with big salsa bands and not much space. It was getting a makeover at the time of research.

El Guajirito LIVE MUSIC

(Map p64; ☎7-863-3009; Agramonte No 660, btwn Gloria & Apodeca; show CUC$30; ⏰9:30pm) Some label it a tourist trap but this restaurant-cum-entertainment-space bivouacked upstairs in a deceptively dilapidated Havana tenement plays some of the most professional Buena Vista Social Club music you'll ever hear. Indeed, this *is* a Buena Vista Social Club of sorts.

True, there are plenty of tour-bus escapees crowding out the tables, and yes the food's a little anemic, but the musicianship of the horn-blasting, drum-thumping, lung-stretching band, most of whom are of pensionable age, ought to have the likes of Compay Segundo smiling down from the great gig in the sky.

El Gato Tuerto LIVE MUSIC

(Map p96; Calle O No 14, btwn Calles 17 & 19; drink minimum CUC$5; ⏰noon-6am) Once the HQ of Havana's alternative artistic and sexual scene, the 'one-eyed cat' is now a nexus for middle-aged karaoke singers who come here to knock out rum-fueled renditions of traditional Cuban boleros (ballads). It's hidden just off the Malecón in a quirky two-story house with turtles swimming in a front pool.

The upper floor is taken up by a restaurant, while down below late-night revelers raise the roof in a chic nightclub.

Oratorio de San Felipe Neri LIVE MUSIC

(Map p64; cnr Aguiar & Obrapía; CUC$2; ⏰performances at 7pm) The Neri has had many incarnations since its founding in 1693; first as a church under various religious orders (Oratorianas, Capuchinos, Carmelitas), then as a bank, and, since 2004, as one of Havana's top venues for classical music (mainly choral).

Teatro Amadeo Roldán THEATER

(Map p96; ☎7-832-1168; cnr Calzada & Calle D; per person CUC$10) Constructed in 1922 and burnt down by an arsonist in 1977, this wonderfully decorative neoclassical theater was rebuilt in 1999 in the exact style of the original. Named after the famous Cuban composer and the man responsible for bringing Afro-Cuban influences into modern classical music, the theater is one of Havana's grandest, with two different auditoriums.

The Orquesta Sinfónica Nacional plays in the 886-seat Sala Amadeo Roldán, while soloists and small groups are showcased in the 276-seat Sala García Caturla. It was being renovated at the time of research.

El Hurón Azul LIVE MUSIC
(Map p96; ☎7-832-4551; www.uneac.org.cu; cnr Calles 17 & H; ⏲hours vary) If you want to rub shoulders with some socialist celebrities, hang out at Hurón Azul, the social club of Uneac (Union of Cuban Writers and Artists). Replete with priceless snippets of Cuba's under-the-radar cultural life, most performances take place outside in the garden. Wednesday is Afro-Cuban rumba, Saturday is authentic boleros (ballads), and alternate Thursdays there's jazz and *trova*. You'll never pay more than CUC$5.

El Turquino LIVE MUSIC
(Map p96; Hotel Habana Libre, Calle L, btwn Calles 23 & 25; CUC$10; ⏲from 10:30pm) Spectacular shows in a spectacular setting on the 25th floor of the Hotel Habana Libre. The retractable roof slides back and everyone hits the dance floor around midnight.

Theater

★Gran Teatro de la Habana Alicia Alonso THEATER
(Map p80; ☎7-861-3077; cnr Paseo de Martí & San Rafael; per person CUC$20; ⏲box office 9am-6pm Mon-Sat, to 3pm Sun) Havana's fabulously renovated 'great' theater is open again and offering up the best in Cuban dance and music. It's specialty is ballet (it's the HQ of the Cuban National Ballet), but it also stages musicals, plays and opera. Check the noticeboard for upcoming events.

Teatro Nacional de Cuba THEATER
(Map p96; ☎7-879-6011; cnr Paseo & Calle 39; per person CUC$10; ⏲box office 10am-5pm & before performances) One of the twin pillars of Havana's cultural life, the Teatro Nacional de Cuba on Plaza de la Revolución is the modern rival to the Gran Teatro in Centro Habana. Built in the 1950s as part of Jean Forestier's grand city expansion, the complex hosts landmark concerts, foreign theater troupes and La Colmenita children's company.

The main hall, Sala Avellaneda, stages big events such as musical concerts or Shakespeare plays, while the smaller Sala Covarrubias along the back puts on a more daring program (the seating capacity of the two halls combined is 3300). The 9th floor is a rehearsal and performance space where the newest, most experimental stuff happens. The ticket office is at the far end of a separate single-story building beside the main theater.

Teatro Mella THEATER
(Map p96; ☎7-833-8696; Línea No 657, btwn Calles A & B) Occupying the site of the old Rodi Cinema on Línea, the Teatro Mella offers one of Havana's most comprehensive programs, including an international ballet festival, comedy shows, theater, dance and intermittent performances from the famous Conjunto Folklórico Nacional. If you have kids, come to the 11am Sunday children's show.

The adjacent Jardines del Mella is a good place to chill with a drink before or after a performance.

Teatro América THEATER
(Map p80; Av de Italia No 253, btwn Concordia & Neptuno) Housed in a classic art deco *rascacielo* (skyscraper) on Av de Italia (Galiano), the América seems to have changed little since its theatrical heyday in the 1930s and '40s. It plays host to variety, comedy, dance, jazz and salsa; shows are normally held on Saturday at 8:30pm and Sunday at 5pm.

The interior was recently renovated and is worth perusing for its curvaceous art deco-ness.

Sala Teatro Hubert de Blanck THEATER
(Map p96; ☎7-830-1011; Calzada No 657, btwn Calles A & B) This theater is named for the founder of Havana's first conservatory of music (1885). The Teatro Estudio based here is Cuba's leading theater company. You can usually see plays in Spanish on Saturdays at 8:30pm and on Sundays at 7pm. Tickets are sold just prior to the performance.

Teatro Fausto THEATER
(Map p80; Paseo de Martí No 201) Rightly renowned for its side-splitting comedy shows, Fausto is a classic example of late streamlined art deco. It was being renovated at the time of research.

Cabaret

★Cabaret Parisién CABARET
(Map p96; ☎7-836-3564; Hotel Nacional, cnr Calles 21 & O; entry CUC$35; ⏲9pm) One rung down from Marianao's world-famous Tropicana, but cheaper and closer to the city center, the nightly Cabaret Parisién in the Hotel Nacional is well worth a look, especially if you're staying in or around Vedado. It's the usual mix of frills, feathers and semi-

naked women (and men), but the choreography is first class and the costumes wonderfully flamboyant.

Doors open at 9pm. There's a warm-up band and one cocktail is included.

Habana Café CABARET
(Map p96; Paseo, btwn Calles 1 & 3; CUC$20; ⏲ from 9pm) A hip and trendy nightclub-cum-cabaret-show at the Hotel Meliá Cohiba laid out in 1950s American style, but with salsa music. After 1am the tables are cleared and the place rocks to 'international music' until the cock crows. Excellent value.

Cultural Centers

★ Fábrica de Arte Cubano LIVE PERFORMANCE
(Map p96; ☎7-838-2260; www.fabricadearte cubano.com; cnr Calle 26 & 11; CUC$2; ⏲ 8pm-3am Thu-Sun) The brainchild of Afro-Cuban fusion musician X-Alfonso, this is one Havana's finest new art projects. An intellectual nexus for live music, art expos, fashion shows and invigorating debate over coffee and cocktails, there isn't a pecking order or surly bouncers in this converted cooking-oil factory in Vedado. Instead you can mingle with the artists, musicians and mainly Cuban clientele for electrifying 'happenings' that kick off at 8pm Thursday to Sunday in the Bauhaus-like interior. Check the website for upcoming acts.

Centro Cultural El Gran Palenque DANCE
(Map p96; Calle 4 No 103, btwn Calzada & Calle 5; CUC$5; ⏲ 3-6pm Sat) Founded in 1962, the high-energy Conjunto Folklórico Nacional de Cuba specializes in Afro-Cuban dancing (all of the drummers are Santería priests). See them perform here, and dance along during the regular Sábado de Rumba – three full hours of mesmerizing drumming and dancing. This group also performs at Teatro Mella and internationally.

A major festival called FolkCuba unfolds here biannually, during the second half of January and the first half of July.

Casa de la Amistad LIVE PERFORMANCE
(Map p96; ☎7-830-3114; Paseo No 416, btwn Calles 17 & 19; ⏲ 11am-11pm) Rocking cultural and musical events are held in this elegant mansion built in 1926 by Juan Pedro Baró, a rich landowner involved in a scandalous marriage with high-society belle Catalina Lasa. There's also a restaurant and bar.

Casa de las Américas LIVE PERFORMANCE
(Map p96; ☎7-838-2706; www.casa.co.cu; cnr Calles 3 & G) A powerhouse of Cuban and Latin American culture set up by Moncada survivor Haydee Santamaría in 1959, offering conferences, exhibitions, a gallery, a bookstore, concerts and an atmosphere of erudite intellectualism. The Casa's annual literary award is one of the Spanish-speaking world's most prestigious. See the website for the schedule of upcoming events.

Cinemas

Cine Yara CINEMA
(Map p96; cnr Calles 23 & L) The first date (and first kiss) of many an enamored *cubano* has taken place at this classic modernist cinema on Vedado's main crossroads. It's also a major venue in the December film festival.

Cine 23 & 12 CINEMA
(Map p96; ☎7-833-6906; Calle 23, btwn Calles 12 & 14) One of a clutch of well-maintained cinemas on ICAIC's Vedado movie strip, this is one of the HQs of Havana's film festival.

Cine Infanta CINEMA
(Map p80; Calzada de la Infanta No 357) A multiplex cinema that's plush by Cuban standards, Infanta is an important venue during December's international film festival.

Cine la Rampa CINEMA
(Map p96; Calle 23 No 111) Ken Loach movies, French classics, Cuban film festivals – catch them all at this Vedado staple, which houses the Cuban film archive.

Cine Payret CINEMA
(Map p80; Paseo de Martí No 505) Opposite the Capitolio, Cine Payret is Centro Habana's largest and oldest cinema, erected in 1878. Plenty of American movies play here. It was being renovated at the time of research.

Sports

Kid Chocolate SPECTATOR SPORT
(Map p80; Paseo de Martí) A boxing club directly opposite the Capitolio, which usually hosts matches on Friday at 7pm.

Gimnasio de Boxeo Rafael Trejo SPECTATOR SPORT
(Map p64; ☎7-862-0266; Cuba No 815, btwn Merced & Leonor Pérez) Boxing is hugely popular in Cuba and the country has a long list of Olympic gold medals to demonstrate its skills. Boxing enthusiasts should check out this gym where you can see fights on Friday

at 7pm (CUC$1), or drop by any day after 4pm to watch the training (or even train yourself).

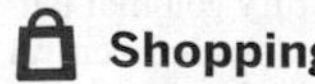

Shopping

Sixty years of *socialismo* didn't do much for Havana's shopping scene. That said, there are some decent outlets for travelers and tourists, particularly for those after the standard Cuban shopping triumvirate of rum, cigars and coffee. Art is another lucrative field. Havana's art scene is cutting edge and ever changing, and browsers will find many galleries in which to while away hours.

Habana Vieja

★Clandestina CLOTHING

(Map p64; ☎53-81-48-02; Villegas No 403; ⏲10am-8pm) Progressive private shops are still in their infancy in Havana, but this is one of the best, set up by a Cuban artist in the mid-2010s and selling its clothes (many of them recycled), bags and accessories under the banner *99% Cuban design*. Viva the private boutique.

★Centro Cultural Antiguos Almacenes de Deposito San José ARTS & CRAFTS

(Map p64; cnr Desamparados & San Ignacio; ⏲10am-6pm Mon-Sat) Havana's open-air handicraft market sits under the cover of an old shipping warehouse in Desamparados. Check your socialist ideals at the door. Herein lies a hive of free enterprise and (unusually for Cuba) haggling. Possible souvenirs include paintings, *guayabera* shirts, woodwork, leather items, jewelry and numerous apparitions of the highly marketable El Che.

There are also snacks, cleanish toilets and a tourist information representative

UNDERSTANDING JOSÉ MARTÍ

'Two fatherlands, have I; Cuba and the Night,' wrote poet, journalist, philosopher and all-round Renaissance man José Martí in 1882, perfectly summing up the dichotomies of late 19th-century Cuba, still as relevant today as they were 130 years ago.

Ironically, Martí – the brains behind Cuba's Second Independence War – remains the one figure who binds Cubans worldwide, a potent unifying force in a country fractiously divided by politics, economics and 145km of shark-infested ocean.

Born in Havana in 1851, Martí spent well over half his life outside the country he professed to love in sporadic exile, shunting between Spain, Guatemala, Venezuela and the US. But his absence hardly mattered. Martí's importance was in his words and ideas. An accomplished political commentator and master of aphorisms, he was responsible, in many ways, for forming the modern Cuban identity and its dream of self-determination. It's difficult to meet a Cuban today who can't eloquently quote stanzas of his poetry. Similarly, there is barely a town or village across the country that doesn't have a statue or plaza named in his honor. The homage extends to the exile community in the US where the Cubans have named a radio station after him. Indeed, Martí is venerated all across the American continent where he is often viewed as the ideological successor to Simón Bolívar.

A basic understanding of Martí and his far-reaching influence is crucial to understanding contemporary Cuba. Havana, the city of his birth, is dotted with poignant monuments, but there are important sites elsewhere. The following are the bare essentials:

Memorial a José Martí (p84) This giant tower (the tallest in Havana) has a massive statue of el Maestro at its foot and a comprehensive museum inside.

Museo-Casa Natal de José Martí (p72) Modest but lovingly curated birth house of Cuba's national hero.

Museo Finca el Abra (p160) Small poignant house on the Isla de la Juventud where Martí was briefly imprisoned in 1870.

Cementerio Santa Ifigenia (p402) The apostle's beautiful mausoleum in Santiago de Cuba has a grand guard-changing ceremony every 30 minutes.

Dos Ríos Obelisk (Dos Rios) Simple but appropriate monument marking where Martí died in battle in 1895 near Bayamo.

from the San Cristóbal agency. It's as popular with Cubans as it is with tourists.

Piscolabis Bazar & Café HOMEWARES
(Map p64; San Ignacio 75, btwn Callejón del Chorro & O'Reilly; 9:30am-7:30pm Mon-Sun) Perfectly located just steps from Havana's 18th-century cathedral, this eclectic shop is run by a group of Cuban artists of various disciplines and features a wide range of decorative and functional items for the home, as well as jewelry and some clothing. The designers make modern creations from iconic objects of Cuba's past.

Librería Venecia BOOKS
(Map p64; Obispo No 502; 10am-10pm) A nice little private secondhand bookshop in Obispo where you might uncover all number of mysteries. It's particularly good for its old Cuban posters, which steer clear of the clichéd Che Guevara poses.

Casa del Habano – Hostal Conde de Villanueva CIGARS
(Map p64; Mercaderes No 202; 10am-6pm) One of Havana's best cigar shops, with its own roller, smoking room and expert staff.

Plaza de Armas Secondhand Book Market BOOKS
(Map p64; cnr Obispo & Tacón; 9am-7pm) This long-standing book market convenes under the leafy boughs in Plaza de Armas. It stocks old, new and rare books, including Hemingway, some weighty poetry and plenty of written pontifications from Fidel. There's no market if it rains or on important holidays.

BEST PLACES TO BUY CIGARS

La Casa del Habano Quinta (p134) The top choice of all cigar aficionados also has an affiliated bar and restaurant.

Casa del Habano – Hostal Conde de Villanueva (p118) Smoke shop in a historic Havana hotel known for its expert staff and rollers.

Real Fábrica de Tabacos Partagás – Shop (p119) The factory's moved, but the shop is still open in a building behind the Capitolio Nacional.

Museo del Tabaco (p119) Small museum and shop in Habana Vieja's antique shopping street, Calle Mercaderes.

Palacio de la Artesanía GIFTS & SOUVENIRS
(Map p64; Cuba No 64; 9am-7pm) If only all shopping malls could be this attractive! Encased in a former 18th-century colonial palace and gathered around a shaded central patio, this place offers one-stop shopping for souvenirs, cigars, crafts, musical instruments, CDs, clothing and jewelry at fixed prices. Join the gaggles of tour-bus escapees and fill your bag.

La Marca TATTOO
(Map p64; 7-801-2026; www.lamarcabodyart.com; Obrapía 108C, btwn Oficios & Mercaderes; 11am-7pm Mon-Sat) Should you want a more permanent memento of your time in Cuba, La Marca is the only licensed tattoo shop on the island. The parlor is run by a group of young Cuban artists who maintain an international level of cleanliness and hygiene, and they sometimes host exhibitions from some of Cuba's leading artists.

La Casa del Café COFFEE
(Map p64; cnr Baratillo & Obispo; 9am-5pm) For a range of coffee and a decent taster cup, pop into La Casa del Café just off Plaza de Armas.

Fundación Havana Club Shop DRINKS
(Map p64; San Pedro No 262; 9am-9pm) Havana Club rum, right from the source.

Habana 1791 PERFUME
(Map p64; Mercaderes No 156, btwn Obrapía & Lamparilla; 9:30am-6pm) A specialist shop that sells perfume made from tropical flowers, Habana 1791 retains the air of a working museum. Floral fragrances are mixed by hand – you can see the petals drying in a laboratory out the back.

Taller de Serigrafía René Portocarrero ART
(Map p64; 7-862-3276; Cuba No 513, btwn Brasil & Muralla; 9am-4pm Mon-Fri) Paintings and prints by young Cuban artists are exhibited and sold here (from CUC$30 to CUC$150). You can also see the artists at work. Budding artists should ask about courses.

Estudio Galería los Oficios ART
(Map p64; Oficios No 166; 10am-5:30pm Mon-Sat) Pop into this gallery to see the large, hectic but intriguing canvases by Nelson Domínguez, whose workshop is upstairs.

Museo del Tabaco CIGARS
(Map p64; Mercaderes No 120; ⏲10am-5pm Mon-Sat) At Museo del Tabaco you can gawp at various indigenous pipes and idols and buy some splendid smokes.

Fayad Jamás BOOKS
(Map p64; Obispo, btwn Habana & Aguiar; ⏲9am-7pm Mon-Sat, to 1pm Sun) This bookstore, a throwback to the 1920s, was refurbished by Habaguanex to fit in with its Old Town surroundings. Editions are mainly in Spanish, but there are some interesting cultural magazines, including *Temas*.

Longina Música MUSIC
(Map p64; Obispo No 360, btwn Habana & Compostela; ⏲10am-7pm Mon-Sat, 10am-1pm Sun) This place on Obispo has a reasonable selection of CDs, plus musical instruments such as bongos, guitars, maracas, *güiros* (gourds) and *tumbadoras* (conga drums). It often places loudspeakers in the street outside to grab the attention of passing tourists.

Centro Habana

★Memorias Librería BOOKS
(Map p80; ☎7-862-3153; Ánimas No 57, btwn Paseo de Martí & Agramonte; ⏲9am-5pm) A shop full of beautiful old artifacts, the Memorias Librería opened in 2014 as Havana's first genuine antique bookstore. Delve into its gathered piles and you'll find wonderful rare collectibles including old coins, postcards, posters, magazines and art deco signs from the 1930s. Priceless!

Real Fábrica de Tabacos Partagás CIGARS
(Map p80; Industria No 520, btwn Barcelona & Dragones; ⏲9am-7pm) Confusingly, the cigar shop affiliated with Havana's main cigar factory is still housed here on the ground floor of the original building behind the Capitolio; the factory (p79) itself has moved a couple of kilometers away. Naturally, it sells some of Havana's best smokes.

Plaza Carlos III SHOPPING CENTER
(Map p80; Av Salvador Allende, btwn Arbol Seco & Retiro; ⏲10am-6pm Mon-Sat) After Plaza América in Varadero, this is probably Cuba's flashiest shopping mall – and there's barely a tourist in sight. The place has taken a step up in recent years – once empty shelves are now full with consumer goods. For something with a unique Cuban touch, pop into Baracoa, a chocolate shop.

Casa Guerlain PERFUME
(Map p80; Paseo de Martí157, btwn Refugio & Colón) If there was any doubt of how chic Havana is these days, look no further than the newest addition to the Prado. This exclusive perfume parlor reopened on the same premises as the original 1917 shop and sells high-end perfume and cosmetics. With the prices out of reach for most Cubans, this shop caters largely to a foreign clientele.

El Bulevar SHOPPING STREET
(Map p80; San Rafael, btwn Paseo de Martí & Av de Italia) The pedestrianized part of Calle San Rafael near the Hotel Inglaterra is Havana's *búlevar* shopping street. Come here for peso snacks, 1950s shopping nostalgia and to see how average Cubans shop.

Vedado

Bazar Estaciones GIFTS & SOUVENIRS
(Map p96; ☎7-832-9965; Calle 23 No 10, btwn Calles J & I; ⏲10am-9pm) This is a lovingly curated new private shop selling some interesting and unique souvenirs (not the standard government-branded stuff). It's on the upper floor of a Vedado mansion right on the main drag.

Instituto Cubano del Arte e Industria Cinematográficos GIFTS & SOUVENIRS
(Map p96; Calle 23, btwn Calles 10 & 12; ⏲10am-5pm) The best place in Havana for rare Cuban movie posters and DVDs. The shop is inside the ICAIC (Cuban Film Institute) building and accessed through the Café Fresa y Chocolate (p112).

Librería Centenario del Apóstol BOOKS
(Map p96; Calle 25 No 164; ⏲10am-5pm Mon-Sat, 9am-1pm Sun) Great assortment of used books with a José Martí bias in downtown Vedado.

Andare – Bazar de Arte GIFTS & SOUVENIRS
(Map p96; cnr Calles 23 & L; ⏲10am-6pm Mon-Fri, to 2pm Sat) A fabulous selection of old movie posters, antique postcards, T-shirts and, of course, all the greatest Cuban films on videotape are sold at this shop inside the Cine Yara.

Galerías de Paseo SHOPPING CENTER
(Map p96; cnr Calle 1 & Paseo; ⏲9am-6pm Mon-Sat, to 1pm Sun) Across the street from the Hotel Meliá Cohiba, this supposedly

upscale shopping center was getting an overdue upgrade at the time of research. It sells well-made clothes and other consumer items to tourists and affluent Cubans, and also hosts the peerless Jazz Café (p113).

La Habana Sí GIFTS & SOUVENIRS

(Map p96; cnr Calles 23 & L; 10am-10pm Mon-Sat, to 7pm Sun) This shop opposite the Hotel Habana Libre has a good selection of CDs, cassettes, books, crafts and postcards.

 Information

EMERGENCY

Asistur (7-866-4499, emergency 7-866-8527; www.asistur.cu; Paseo de Martí No 208; 8:30am-5:30pm Mon-Fri, 8am-2pm Sat) Emergency help for tourists. Someone on staff should speak English; the emergency center here is open 24 hours.

INTERNET ACCESS

Cuba's internet service provider is national phone company Etecsa. Etecsa runs various *telepuntos* (internet-cafes-cum-call-centers) in Habana: the main ones are in Centro Habana (Águila No 565, cnr Dragones; 8:30am-7pm) and Habana Vieja (Habana No 406, cnr Obispo; 9am-7pm). The drill is to buy a one-hour user card (CUC$2) with a scratch-off user code and *contraseña* (password), and either help yourself to a free computer or use it on your own device in one of the city's 30-plus wi-fi hot spots. Most Havana hotels that are rated three stars and up also have wi-fi. You don't generally have to be a guest to use it.

Popular wi-fi hot spots in Havana include La Rampa (Calle 23 between L and Malecón) in Vedado, the corner of Av de Italia and San Rafael in Centro Habana, and the Miramar Trade Center in Playa.

MEDICAL SERVICES

There are 10 international pharmacies in Havana selling products in convertibles (CUC$). The handiest for travelers are at Hotel Habana Libre (p95) and Hotel Sevilla (p92).

Centro Oftalmológico Camilo Cienfuegos (7-832-5554; Calle L No 151, cnr Calle 13, Vedado; 24hr) Head straight here if you have eye problems.

Farmacia Taquechel (7-862-9286; Obispo No 155; 9am-6pm) In Habana Vieja.

Hospital Nacional Hermanos Ameijeiras (Map p80; 7-877-6053; San Lázaro No 701) Special hard-currency services, general consultations and hospitalization. Enter via the lower level below the parking lot off Padre Varela (ask for CEDA in Section N).

MONEY

The quickest and most hassle-free places to exchange money are in Cadecas. There are dozens of them across Havana and they usually have much longer opening hours and quicker service than banks.

Banco de Crédito y Comercio Vedado (cnr Línea & Paseo; 9am-3pm Mon-Fri); Vedado (7-870-2684; Airline Bldg, Calle 23; 9am-3pm Mon-Fri). Expect lines.

Banco Financiero Internacional Habana Vieja (7-860-9369; cnr Oficios & Brasil; 9am-3pm Mon-Fri); Vedado (Hotel Habana Libre, Calle L, btwn Calles 23 & 25; 9am-3pm Mon-Fri)

Banco Metropolitano Centro Habana (7-862-6523; Av de Italia No 452, cnr San Martín; 9am-3pm Mon-Fri); Vedado (7-832-2006; cnr Línea & Calle M; 9am-3pm Mon-Fri); Habana Vieja (cnr Cuba & O'Reilly; 9am-3pm Mon-Fri)

Cadeca Centro Habana (cnr Neptuno & Consulado; 8am-12:30pm, 1-3pm, 4-6:30pm & 7-10pm); Habana Vieja (cnr Oficios & Lamparilla; 8am-7pm Mon-Sat, to 1pm Sun); Vedado (cnr Calles 23 & J; 7am-2:30pm & 3:30-10pm); Vedado (Mercado Agropecuario, cnr Calles 19 & A; 7am-6pm Mon-Sat, 8am-1pm Sun); Vedado (Hotel Meliá Cohiba, Paseo, btwn Calles 1 & 3; 8am-8pm).

TOILETS

Havana isn't over-endowed with clean and accessible public toilets. Most tourists slip into upscale hotels if they're caught short. Even there, restrooms often lack toilet paper, soap and door locks. Make sure you tip the lady at the door.

TOURIST INFORMATION

State-run Infotur books tours and has maps, phonecards and useful free brochures.

Pretty much every hotel in Havana has some type of state-run tourist information desk.

Infotur offices in downtown Havana:

Habana Vieja (7-863-6884; cnr Obispo & San Ignacio; 9:30am-noon & 12:30-5pm)

Habana Vieja (Map p64; 7-866-4153; Obispo No 524, btwn Bernaza & Villegas; 9:30am-5:30pm)

TRAVEL AGENCIES

Cubatur (7-832-9538; cnr Calles 23 & L, Vedado; 8am-8pm) Also in most of the main hotels.

Ecotur (7-649-1055; www.ecoturcuba.tur.cu; Calle 13 No 18005, btwn Av 5 & Calle 182, Playa; 9am-5pm Mon-Fri) Naturalistic excursions mostly outside Havana.

Gaviota (7-867-1194; www.gaviota-grupo.com; 9am-5pm) In all Gaviota hotels.

HAVANA SCAMS

Tourist scams are the bane of travelers in many cities, and Havana is no exception, although the city rates more favorably than plenty of other Latin American metro areas. Some Cuban con tricks are familiar to anyone who has traveled internationally. Agree on taxi fares before getting in a cab, don't change money on the street, and always check your bill and change in restaurants. Cuba's professional tricksters are called *jinteros* (literally, jockeys). They are particularly proficient in Havana where their favorite pastime is selling knock-off cigars to unsuspecting tourists.

Cuba's dual currency invites scammers. Although the two sets of banknotes look very similar, there are actually 25 *moneda nacional* (MN$; sometimes called Cuban pesos) to every Cuban convertible (CUC$). Familiarize yourself with the banknotes early on (most banks have pictorial charts) and double-check all money transactions to avoid being left seriously out of pocket. One popular trick is for young men in the street to offer to change foreign currency into Cuban convertibles at very favorable rates, but as you'll be given back *moneda nacional*, it will be only worth one-twenty-fifth of the value when you take them into a shop.

Casas particulares (private homestays) attract *jinteros* who prey on both travelers and casa owners. A common trick is for a *jintero* to pose falsely as a reputed casa particular owner who a traveler has booked in advance (including those listed by Lonely Planet), and then proceed to lead you to a different house where they will extract CUC$5 to CUC$10 commission (added to your room bill). On some occasions, travelers are not aware they have been led to the wrong home. There have even been reports of people writing bad reviews online.

If you've prebooked a casa, or are using Lonely Planet to find one, make sure you turn up without a commission-seeking *jintero*.

Another scam is the illicit sale of cheap cigars, usually perpetuated by hissing street salesmen around Centro Habana and Habana Vieja. It is best to politely ignore these characters. Any bartering is not worth the bother. Cigars sold on the street are almost always substandard – something akin to substituting an expensive French wine with cheap white vinegar. Instead, buy your cigars direct from the factory or visit one of the numerous Casas del Habano that are scattered throughout the city.

San Cristóbal Agencia de Viajes (Map p64; ☎7-863-9555; www.cubaheritage.com; Oficios No 110, btwn Lamparilla & Amargura; ⊙8:30am-5:30pm Mon-Fri, to 12:30pm Sat) Office of the City Historian tours.

Getting There & Away

AIR

Aeropuerto Internacional José Martí (www.havana-airport.org; Av Rancho Boyeros) is at Rancho Boyeros, 25km southwest of Havana via Av de la Independencia. There are four terminals here. Terminal 1, on the southeastern side of the runway, handles only domestic Cubana flights. Terminal 2 is 3km away via Av de la Independencia and receives flights and charters from the US. All other international flights use Terminal 3, a well-ordered, modern facility at Wajay, 2.5km west of Terminal 2. Charter flights, mainly to Cuban destinations, are from the Caribbean Terminal (also known as Terminal 5) at the northwestern end of the runway, 2.5km west of Terminal 3. Terminal 4 handles freight. Check carefully which terminal you'll be using.

Aerogaviota (☎7-203-0668; www.aerogaviota.com) is a Cuban airline run by the government tourist agency, handling mainly domestic flights to places like Holguín.

Most airlines, including national carrier **Cubana de Aviación** (☎7-649-0410; www.cubana.cu; ⊙8:30am-4pm Mon-Fri, to noon Sat), have offices in the **Airline Building** (Calle 23 No 64) in Havana's Vedado district.

BOAT

There are currently no international ferries calling at Havana.

Buses connecting with the hydrofoil service to the Isla de la Juventud leave from the **Terminal de Ómnibus** (Map p96; ☎7-878-1841; cnr Av de la Independencia & Calle 19 de Mayo, Vedado), near Plaza de la Revolución, but they're often late. It's advisable to reserve and buy your bus-boat combo ticket at least a day in advance. Tickets are available at the **Naviera Cubana Caribeña (NCC) Kiosk** (☎7-878-1841; ⊙7am-noon), and cost CUC$50 for the boat and MN$5 for the bus. Bring your passport.

BUS

Víazul (☎7-881-5652, 7-881-1413; www.viazul.com; Calle 26, cnr Zoológica, Nuevo Vedado; ⏰7am-9:30pm) covers most destinations of interest to travelers, in safe, air-conditioned coaches. Most buses are direct except those to Guantánamo, Baracoa, Remedios and Cayo Santa María. You board all Víazul buses at their inconveniently located terminal 3km southwest of Plaza de la Revolución. This is where you'll also have to come to buy tickets from the Venta de Boletines office. Buses get busy particularly in peak season (November through March), so it's wise to book up to a week in advance. You can also book online. Full bus schedules are available on the website. Some casa particular owners may offer help with prearranging bus tickets.

The Víazul bus terminal is in the suburb of Nuevo Vedado, and taxis will charge between CUC$5 and CUC$10 for the ride to central Havana. There are no direct metro buses from central Havana. If you take the P-14 from the Capitolio, you'll have to get off on Av 51 and walk the last 500m or so.

A newer alternative to the increasingly crowded Víazul buses is Conectando run by **Cubanacán** (☎7-537-4090; www.cubanacan.cu), which offers six itineraries linking Havana with Viñales, Trinidad, Varadero and Santiago de Cuba. The smaller buses, which run daily, pick up from various hotels and charge similar prices to Víazul. Tickets can be reserved at Infotur or with any Cubanacán hotel rep or at Infotur offices.

Buses (Map p64) to points in Artemisa and Mayabeque Provinces leave from Apodaca No 53, off Agramonte, near the main train station. They go to Güines, Jaruco, Madruga, Nueva Paz, San José, San Nicolás and Santa Cruz del Norte, but expect large crowds and come early to get a peso ticket.

TAXI

Full buses are the norm in Cuba these days, as public transportation hasn't yet caught up with the increase in tourist numbers. To counter the shortfall, many travelers are turning to *colectivos* (shared taxis). Taxis charge approximately CUC$0.50 to CUC$0.60 per kilometer. This translates as around CUC$90 to Varadero, CUC$90 to Viñales, CUC$150 to Santa Clara, CUC$120 to Cienfuegos and CUC$160 to Trinidad. A *colectivo* can take up to four people, meaning you can share the cost. *Colectivos* can usually be organized through your casa particular, at an Infotur office or by negotiating at a standard pick-up point. It's also usually pretty easy to arrange a *colectivo* at the Víazul bus terminal.

TRAIN

Trains to most parts of Cuba depart from **La Coubre station** (Túnel de la Habana), while the **Estación Central de Ferrocarriles** (Central Train Station; ☎7-861-8540, 7-862-1920; cnr Av de Bélgica & Arsenal) is being refurbished until 2018 or later. La Coubre is on the southwestern side of Habana Vieja; from the main station, head down Calle Egido toward the harbor and turn right. The ticket office is located 100m down the road on the right-hand side. If it's closed, try the Lista de Espera office adjacent, which sells tickets for trains leaving immediately. Kids under 12 travel half-price.

VÍAZUL BUS DEPARTURES FROM HAVANA

Check the most up-to-date departure times on www.viazul.com.

DESTINATION	COST (CUC$)	DURATION (HR)	DEPARTURES
Bayamo	44	13	12:30am, 6:30am, 3pm
Camagüey	33	9	12:30am, 6:30am, 9:30am, 3pm, 7:45pm
Ciego de Ávila	27	7	12:30am, 6:30am, 3pm, 7:45pm
Cienfuegos	20	4	7am, 10:45am, 2:15pm
Holguín	44	12	9:30am, 3pm, 7:45pm
Las Tunas	39	11½	12:30am, 6:30am, 9:30am, 3pm, 7:45pm
Matanzas	7	2	6am, 8am, 1pm, 5:30pm
Pinar del Río	11	3	8:40am, 11:25am, 2pm
Sancti Spíritus	23	5¾	12:30am, 6:30am, 3pm
Santa Clara	18	3¾	12:30am, 6:30am, 9:30am, 3pm, 7:45pm
Santiago de Cuba	51	15	12:30am, 6:30am, 3pm
Trinidad	25	5-6	7am, 10:45am, 2:15pm
Varadero	10	3	6am, 8am, 1pm, 5:30pm
Viñales	12	4	8:40am, 11:25am, 2pm

At the time of research, Cuba's main train (No 11), the Tren Francés (still using its increasingly dilapidated French SNCF carriages), was running every fourth day between Havana and Santiago, stopping in Santa Clara and Camagüey. It leaves Havana at 6:13pm and arrives in Santiago the following morning at 10:05am. There are no sleeper cars or air-con. Tickets cost CUC$30 for 1st class (which is nothing like usual 1st class). Bring plenty of food, water and toilet paper (the toilets are legendary – for all the wrong reasons). The journey, without delays, takes 16 hours.

The other train services are the No 15 to Guantánamo (CUC$32) leaving every fourth day at 6:53pm; the No 13 to Bayamo (CUC$25.50) and Manzanillo (CUC$27.50) leaving every fourth day at 7:25pm; and the No 7 to Sancti Spíritus (CUC$15) leaving every other day at 9:21pm.

Trains to Cienfuegos (CUC$12) and Pinar del Río (CUC$7) leave from 19 de Noviembre station every other day.

The above information is only a rough approximation; services are routinely delayed or canceled. Always double-check scheduling and which terminal your train will leave from.

Getting Around

TO/FROM THE AIRPORT

Public transportation from the airport into central Havana is practically nonexistent. A standard taxi will cost you approximately CUC$20 to CUC$25 (30 to 40 minutes).

BOAT

Passenger ferries shuttle across the harbor to Regla and Casablanca, leaving every 15 or 20 minutes from the recently refurbished terminal **Emboque de Luz** (Map p64), at the corner of San Pedro and Santa Clara, on the southeast side of Habana Vieja. The fare is a flat 10 centavos, but foreigners are often charged CUC$1. There's a quick bag search before you get on.

Cruise ships dock at the **Terminal Sierra Maestra – Cruise Terminal** (Map p64), adjacent to Plaza de San Francisco de Asís on the cusp of Habana Vieja.

BUS

The handy hop-on, hop-off **Habana Bus Tour** (Map p80) runs on two routes: T1 and T3 (route T2 had been suspended at the time of research). The main stop is in Parque Central opposite the Hotel Inglaterra. This is the pick-up point for bus T1, which runs from Habana Vieja via Centro Habana, the Malecón, Calle 23 and Plaza de la Revolución to La Cecilia at the west end of Playa; and bus T3, which runs from Centro Habana to Playas del Este (via Parque Histórico Militar Morro-Cabaña).

Bus T1 is an open-top double-decker. Bus T3 is an enclosed single-decker. All-day tickets for T1/T3 are CUC$10/5. Services run from 9am to 7pm and routes and stops are clearly marked on all bus stops. Beware: these bus routes and times have been known to change. Check the latest route maps at the bus stop in Parque Central.

Havana's metro bus service calls on a relatively modern fleet of Chinese-made 'bendy' buses and is far less dilapidated than it used to be. These buses run regularly along 17 different routes, connecting most parts of the city with the suburbs. Fares are 40 centavos (five centavos if you're using convertibles), which you deposit into a small slot in front of the driver when you enter. Cuban buses are crowded and little used by tourists. Guard your valuables closely.

All bus routes have the prefix P before their number:

P-1 La Rosita–Playa (via Virgen del Camino, Vedado, Línea, Av 3)

P-2 Alberro–Línea y G (via Vibora and Ciudad Deportiva)

P-3 Alamar–Túnel de Línea (via Virgen del Camino and Vibora)

P-4 San Agustín–Terminal de Trenes (via Playa, Calle 23, La Rampa)

P-5 San Agustín–Terminal de Trenes (via Lisa, Av 31, Línea, Av de Puerto)

P-6 Reparto Eléctrico–La Rampa (via Vibora)

P-7 Alberro–Capitolio (via Virgen del Camino)

P-8 Reparto Eléctrico–Villa Panamericano (via Vibora, Capitolio and harbor tunnel)

P-9 Vibora–Hospital Militar (via Cuatro Caminos, La Rampa, Calle 23, Av 41)

P-10 Vibora–Playa (via Altahabana and Calle 100)

P-11 Alamar–Vedado (via harbor tunnel)

P-12 Santiago de las Vegas–Capitolio (via Av Boyeros)

P-13 Santiago de las Vegas–Vibora (via Calabazar)

P-14 San Agustín–Capitolio (via Lisa and Av 51)

P-15 Alamar/Guanabacoa–Capitolio (via Av Boyeros and Calle G)

P-16 Santiago de las Vegas–Vedado (via Calle 100 and Lisa)

PC Hospital Naval–Playa (via Parque Lenin)

Infotur offices publish a free map of Havana metro bus routes called *Por La Habana en P*.

CAR

There are lots of car-rental offices in Havana, so if you're told there are no cars or there isn't one in your price range, try another office or agency. All agencies have offices at Terminal 3 at Aeropuerto Internacional José Martí. Otherwise, there's a car-rental desk in any three-star (or higher) hotel. Prices vary depending on the make of car, rental period and season. The cheapest you'll get is around CUC$55 per day. An average medium-sized rental would be closer to CUC$75 per day.

Cubacar has desks at most of the big hotels, including Meliá Cohiba, Meliá Habana, Iberostar Parque Central, Habana Libre and Sevilla.

Rex Rent a Car (7-836-7788; www.rex.cu; cnr Línea & Malecón, Vedado; 9am-5pm) rents fancy cars for extortionate prices.

Servi-Cupet gas stations are in Vedado at Calles L and 17; Malecón and Calle 15; Malecón and Paseo near the Riviera and Meliá Cohiba hotels; and on Av de la Independencia (northbound lane) south of Plaza de la Revolución. All are open 24 hours a day.

TAXI

Taxis hang around outside all the major tourist hotels, outside the two main bus stations and at various city-center nexus points such as Parque Central and Parque de la Fraternidad. You're never far from a taxi in Havana.

The most common taxis are the yellow cabs of **Cubataxi** (7-796-6666; Calle 478, btwn Av 7 & 7B). Other taxis might be Ladas, old American cars or modern Toyotas.

Always agree a fare before you get in. The cheapest official cabs charge around CUC$1 as the starting fare, then CUC$0.50 per kilometer.

Since 2011 legal private taxis have become more common, although they're often older yellow-and-black Ladas. You've got more chance haggling here, but agree on the fare before getting into the car. If you're non-Cuban you'll be expected to pay in convertibles (CUC$).

Shared Cuban taxis (usually old American cars) charge in *moneda nacional* and run on several well-established routes in Havana.

The small yellow egg-shaped 'Coco taxis' are a well-known tourist rip-off.

OUTER HAVANA

Beyond its jaunty downtown, Havana supports another 12 municipalities. Most visitors with time to spare hit the diplomatic and convention quarter of Playa in the west or head to the sandy beaches of Playas del Este in the east. Less frequented are the historic but undone neighborhoods of Guanabacoa and Regla, and the unkempt greenery of Parque Lenin near the airport.

Playa & Marianao

Playa, west of Vedado across the Río Almendares, is a large, complex municipality. For the sake of clarity, it can be split into several contrasting sub-neighborhoods. Gracious Miramar is a leafy diplomatic quarter of broad avenues, weeping laurel trees and fine private restaurants; Cubanacán, further west, plays host to scientific fairs, business conventions, and biotechnological and pharmaceutical research institutes; Jaimanitas, hugging the shoreline, broadcasts the street-art extravaganza Fusterlandia; while Santa Fé is anchored by the Marina Hemingway, Havana's premier, if slightly decrepit, boat marina. The separate municipality of Marianao is south of Playa.

Sights

★Fusterlandia PUBLIC ART

(cnr Calle 226 & Av 3) FREE Where does art go after Gaudí? For a hint, head west from central Havana to the seemingly low-key district of Jaimanitas, where Cuban artist José Fuster has turned his home neighborhood into a masterpiece of intricate tilework and kaleidoscopic colors – a street-art extravaganza that makes Barcelona's Park Güell look positively sedate. Imagine Gaudí on steroids relocated to a tropical setting.

The result is what is unofficially known as Fusterlandia, an ongoing project first hatched around 20 years ago that has covered several suburban blocks with whimsical but highly stylized public art. The centerpiece is Fuster's own house, **Taller-Estudio José Fuster** (cnr Calle 226 & Av 3; 9am-4pm Wed-Sun) FREE, a sizable residence decorated from roof to foundations by art, sculpture and – above all – mosaic tiles of every color and description. The overall impression defies written description (just GO!), a fantastical mishmash of spiraling walkways, rippling pools and sunburst fountains. The work mixes homages to Picasso and Gaudí with snippets of Gauguin and Wifredo Lam, elements of magic realism, strong maritime influences, Santería, the curvaceous lines of modernisme, plus a large dose of Fuster's own Cubanness, which runs through almost everything. Look for the Cuban flags, a mural of the *Granma* yacht, and the words 'Viva Cuba' emblazoned across eight chimney pots.

Fusterlandia stretches way beyond Fuster's own residence. Over half the neighborhood has been given similar artistic treatment, from street signs to bus stops to the local doctor's house. Wandering around its quiet streets is a surreal and psychedelic experience.

Jaimanitas is located just off Quinta Avenida (Av 5) in the far west of Playa, sandwiched between Club Havana and Marina Hemingway. A taxi from central Havana will cost CUC$12 to CUC$15.

Iglesia Jesús de Miramar CHURCH
(cnr Av 5 & Calle 82; ⏲9am-noon & 4-6pm) Despite its modernity, Playa cradles Cuba's second-largest church, an aesthetically pleasing neo-Romanesque structure topped by a giant dome. Built in 1948, it protects Cuba's largest pipe organ and – best of all – a set of truly amazing stations of the cross painted directly onto the walls by Spaniard Cesareo Hombrados Oñativia in the 1950s.

La Casa de las Tejas Verdes HISTORIC BUILDING
(☎7-212-5282; Calle 2 No 308, btwn Avs 3 & 5; ⏲by appointment) FREE Emerging from the tunnel under the Río Almendares, your first glimpse of Miramar is the so-called 'house of the green tiles,' a subtle hint of the eclecticism to come: this is the only example of Queen Anne architecture in Cuba. The house was built in 1926, and, for most of its existence, was the home of a semi-famous Havana socialite, Luisa Rodríguez Faxas, who lived here from 1943 to 1999.

After Faxas' death the house was passed to the Cuban government who restored and opened it as an architectural study center in 2010. It's not strictly a museum, but management runs free tours by appointment on selective days; phone ahead.

Marina Hemingway MARINA
(cnr Av 5 & Calle 248) Havana's premier marina was constructed in 1953 in the small coastal community of Santa Fé. After the revolution it was nationalized and named after Castro's favorite *Yanqui*. The marina has four 800m-long channels, a dive center, a motley collection of shops and restaurants, and two hotels (one currently disused), so it's only worth visiting if you're docking your boat or utilizing the water-sports facilities.

Like much of Cuba's infrastructure, the place retains a strangely abandoned air and is crying out for a renovation.

Club Habana HISTORIC BUILDING
(☎7-204-5700; Av 5, btwn Calles 188 & 192; day pass CUC$20; ⏲9am-7pm) This fabulously eclectic 1928 mansion in Flores once housed

LATIN AMERICA'S OLDEST ART ACADEMY

In 1816 the reformist bishop of Havana, Juan Diaz de Espada, invited a French neoclassical painter named Jean Baptiste Vermay to Cuba with instructions to restore several important works of art in Havana's cathedral (legend has it that Espada originally asked romantic master Goya, but the Spaniard was otherwise engaged and thus got a French friend to recommend Vermay instead). Vermay arrived, carried out his work diligently and, after striking up a friendship with the Cuban poet José María Heredia, elected to stay. It was a fortuitous decision. In 1818, Vermay, with the help of Bishop Espada, inauspiciously opened the **Academia Nacional de Bellas Artes 'San Alejandro'** (cnr Av 31 & Calle 100, Marianao), Cuba's first art academy, a body that continues to operate to this day, making it the oldest artistic institution in Latin America.

Installed initially in Habana Vieja with Vermay as its first director, the San Alejandro moved to Centro Habana in the 1850s. Despite only welcoming whites in its early days, it quickly became a fertile breeding ground for Cuban painters.

Numerous illustrious names had soon passed through its doors, including José Martí, Victor Manuel Valdés, sculptor Rita Longa, pop artist Raúl Martínez and future rebel commander Camilo Cienfuegos. However, by the 1920s the academy and the climate it fostered had become increasingly staid and bogged down with copying European landscapes. Several former alumni traveled to France where they had their eyes opened by Picasso and Gauguin, and subsequently came together in the Vanguardia, a movement that served as a sharp slap to the creeping orthodoxy of the San Alejandro.

The academy subsequently reevaluated itself and adapted. In 1962 the campus was moved to Marianao, where it still resides in a monumental building at the entrance to the Ciudad Libertad (a former military barracks converted into educational establishments after the revolution). While no longer the only art school in Havana, the San Alejandro remains its most storied artistic institution and today runs various exchange projects with schools abroad.

Playa & Marianao

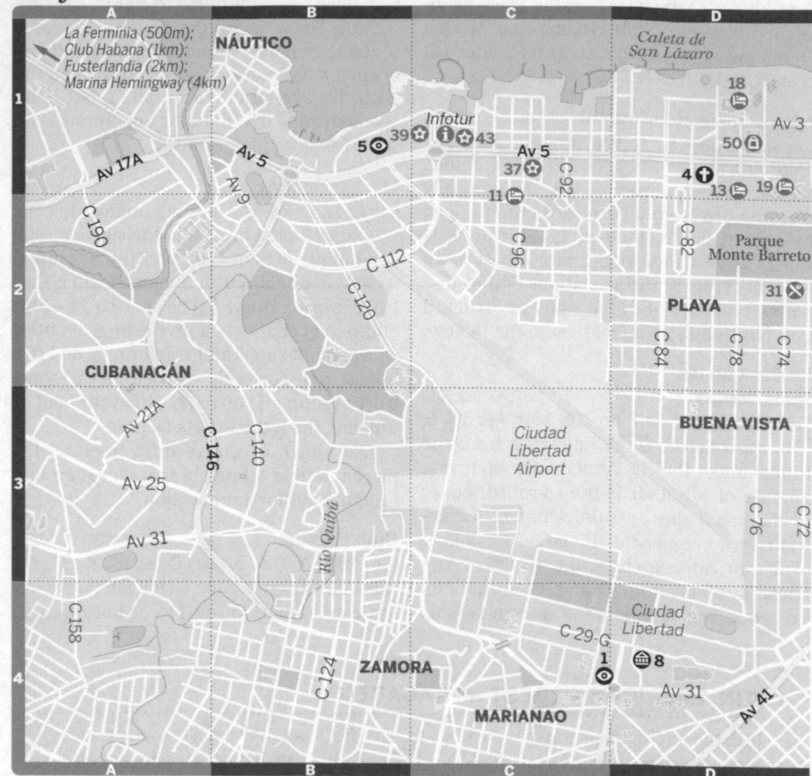

the Havana Biltmore Yacht & Country Club. These days the establishment seems to have swung full circle and it is again a popular hangout for foreign correspondents and diplomats. The club has its own beach, swimming pool, tennis courts, bar, boutiques and health club. Annual membership is costly, but should you wish to hobnob spontaneously with the high and mighty, you can get a daily pass for CUC$20.

In the 1950s the establishment gained brief notoriety when it famously denied entry to Cuban president Fulgencio Batista on the grounds that he was 'black.' Castro had better luck when he dropped by for dinner some 30 years later and the club remains one of the few places where he dined in public.

Parque Almendares PARK

Running along the banks of the Río Almendares, below the bridge on Calle 23, is this welcome oasis of greenery and fresh air in the heart of the chaotic city. Parque Almendares might not be the Bois de Boulogne (witness the stray dogs and half-wrecked toilets), but it *is* a work in progress and far healthier than it was a decade ago. Benches now line the river promenade and plants grow profusely, though the river water is far from crystal clear.

The park has a stash of so-so facilities, including an antiquated miniature golf course, the Anfiteatro Parque Almendares (a small outdoor performance space), a playground and a dinosaur park containing stone reproductions of the monstrous reptiles.

Museo de la Alfabetización MUSEUM

(cnr Av 29e & Calle 76; 8am-noon & 1-3pm Tue-Fri, 8am-noon Sat) FREE The former Cuartel Colombia military airfield at Marianao is now a school complex called Ciudad Libertad. Pass through the gate to visit this inspiring museum, which describes the 1961 literacy campaign, when 100,000 youths aged 12 to

18 spread out across Cuba to teach reading and writing to farmers, workers and seniors.

In the center of the traffic circle, opposite the entrance to the complex, is a tower in the form of a syringe in memory of Carlos Juan Finlay, who discovered the cause of yellow fever in 1881.

Fundación Naturaleza y El Hombre MUSEUM
(☎7-209-2885; Av 5b No 6611, btwn Calles 66 & 70; CUC$2; ⏲8:30am-3pm Mon-Fri) This tiny museum seems to confirm the old adage that 'small is beautiful,' displaying artifacts from a 17,422km canoe trip from the Amazon source to the sea, led by Cuban intellectual and anthropologist António Núñez Jiménez in 1987. Exhibits in this astounding array of items include one of Cuba's largest photography collections, books written by the prolific Núñez Jiménez, his beloved canoe, and a famous portrait of Fidel by Ecuadorian painter Oswaldo Guayasamín. The museum is part of a nonprofit foundation and one of Havana's most rewarding.

Acuario Nacional AQUARIUM
(☎7-202-5872; cnr Av 3 & Calle 62; adult/child CUC$10/7; ⏲10am-6pm Tue-Sun) Founded in 1960, the national aquarium is a Havana institution that gets legions of annual visitors. Despite its rather scruffy appearance, this place leaves most other Cuban *acuarios* (aquatic centers) in the shade (which isn't saying much). Saltwater fish are the specialty, but there are also sea lions and dolphins, including hourly dolphin shows. Note, that dolphin performances are widely criticized by animal welfare groups who claim the captivity of such complex marine mammals is debilitating and stressful for the animals.

La Maqueta de la Capital MUSEUM
(Calle 28 No 113, btwn Avs 1 & 3; CUC$3; ⏲9:30am-5pm Mon-Fri) Havana itself is somewhat dilapidated in parts and so, ironically, is this huge

Playa & Marianao

Sights

1 Academia Nacional de Bellas Artes 'San Alejandro' ... C4
2 Acuario Nacional ... E1
3 Fundación Naturaleza y El Hombre ... E2
4 Iglesia Jesús de Miramar ... D1
5 Isla del Coco ... B1
6 La Casa de las Tejas Verdes ... H2
7 La Maqueta de la Capital ... G1
8 Museo de la Alfabetización ... D4
9 Parque Almendares ... G3
10 Russian Embassy ... E1

Activities, Courses & Tours

Club Salseando Chévere ... (see 41)

Sleeping

11 Casa Guevara Alba ... C2
12 Complejo Cultural La Vitrola ... G1
13 Four Points Habana ... D1
14 H10 Habana Panorama ... E1
15 Hotel Copacabana ... E1
16 Hotel el Bosque ... G3
17 Hotel Kohly ... G3
18 Hotel Meliá Habana ... D1
19 Memories Miramar ... D1
20 Starfish Montehabana ... E2
21 Villa Teresa ... E1

Eating

Cafetería Betty Boom ... (see 2)
Casa Española ... (see 24)
22 Casa Pilar ... F1
23 Club Su Miramar ... F1
Doctor Café ... (see 7)
24 Dos Gardenias ... F2
25 El Aljibe ... G2
26 El Tocororo ... G1
27 Espacios ... G2
28 La Carboncita ... F1
29 La Casa del Gelato ... F1
30 La Cocina de Lilliam ... E2
31 La Corte del Príncipe ... D2
32 La Esperanza ... G1
33 La Fontana ... E1
34 Paladar Vista Mar ... G1
35 Pan.com ... F2

Drinking & Nightlife

36 Café Fortuna Joe ... G1

Entertainment

37 Café Miramar ... C1
38 Casa de la Música ... G2
39 Circo Trompoloco ... C1
40 Don Cangrejo ... G1
41 El Salón Chévere ... G3
42 Estadio Pedro Marrero ... F3
43 La Cecilia ... C1
44 Salón Rosado Benny Moré ... F3
45 Teatro Karl Marx ... H1
46 Tropicana Nightclub ... E4

Shopping

47 Alma Shop ... G2
Egrem Tienda de Música ... (see 12)
48 La Casa del Habano Quinta ... G2
49 La Maison ... G2
50 Miramar Trade Center ... D1

1:1000 scale model of the city that looks like it could do with a good dusting. The model was originally created for urban-planning purposes, but is now a tourist attraction. It is going through a protracted renovation, but can usually still be viewed.

Nearby, the two parks on Av 5, between Calles 24 and 26, with their immense banyan trees and shady lanes, are an atmospheric pocket.

Isla del Coco AMUSEMENT PARK
(Av 5 & Calle 112, Playa; CUC$5; noon-8pm Fri-Sun) A huge Chinese-built amusement park in western Playa with big wheels, bumper cars, roller coasters, the works.

Activities

Marlin Náutica WATER SPORTS
(www.nauticamarlin.tur.cu; Av 5 & Calle 248, Marina Hemingway, Barlovento) There are several water activities available at Marina Hemingway in Barlovento, 20km west of central Havana. Marlin Náutica runs fishing trips for four anglers and four hours of deep-sea fishing for around CUC$310, including tackle and an open bar; marlin season is June to October. Catamaran tours of Havana's littoral (CUC$60) are also available (four-person minimum). It's usually easier to book with a tour agency in the city center.

La Aguja Marlin Diving Center DIVING
(7-209-3377; Av 5 & Calle 248, Marina Hemingway, Barlovento) Between Marlin Náutica and the shopping center at Marina Hemingway, this center offers scuba diving for CUC$40 per dive. Initiation courses are CUC$25. Departures are at 9am daily. A diving excursion to Playa Girón where the diving's much better can also be arranged.

Sleeping

Playa's hotels are the preserve of diplomats, the convention crowd and people whose flights have been bumped. There are a couple of good ones amongst the dross, but the general location is detached from Havana's main sights and you'll need taxis or strong legs to get around.

Casa Guevara Alba CASA PARTICULAR **$**
(7-202-6515; mt_alba@yahoo.es; Av 5f No 9611, btwn Calles 96 & 98; r CUC$35; P ❄) A welcome homestay close to Playa's main hotel zone that outsmarts most of the other hotels when it comes to price, service and comfort. On offer are two apartments with bedrooms, sitting rooms, use of kitchen, outdoor terraces and bathrooms. It's modern for Cuba, but still has plenty of character.

Complejo Cultural La Vitrola HOTEL **$**
(7-202-7922; Calle 18 No 103, btwn Avs 1 & 3; r CUC$30; ❄) Imagine staying at London's Abbey Road recording studios. Well, this is the Cuban equivalent. The Egrem studios – working space for Cuba's top musical artists – now has a lovely on-site hotel with five rooms that have bright interiors and song lyrics painted on the walls. Hang around in the downstairs Bar Bilongo and you might even bump into Silvio Rodríguez.

Villa Teresa CASA PARTICULAR **$$**
(7-202-2799; marlene7667@yahoo.es; Ave 1 No 4401, cnr Calle 44; r incl breakfast CUC$100; P ❄) A new private rental opposite the Hotel Copacabana in a conspicuously modern lily-white house that looks as if it's just been towed in from the Florida Keys. The four tastefully decorated rooms are boutique-hotel-worthy with good art, large beds and fully stocked minibars. Breakfast in the open-plan dining area and lounge is included.

Hotel Club Acuario HOTEL **$$**
(7-204-6336; Aviota & Calle 248; s/d CUC$80/119 all-inclusive; P ❄ @) Don't come to Marina Hemingway for the hotels. With El Viejo y el Mar perennially on hiatus, the only real option is the strung-out Acuario, Havana's only all-inclusive option outside Playas del Este, splayed between two harbor channels and infested with cheap out-of-date furnishings. If you're booked for an early-morning dive, it might just qualify; otherwise stay in Havana and commute.

Hotel Copacabana HOTEL **$$**
(7-204-1037; Av 1, btwn Calles 44 & 46; s/d CUC$100/140; P ❄ @) Slightly better than some of its tired Playa competitors thanks to a 2010 refurbishment, though there's still an inherent dankness about the Copacabana, despite its fine oceanside location. Best feature? There are two pools – one of them a saltwater affair that drains into the sea.

★Hotel Meliá Habana HOTEL **$$$**
(7-204-8500; www.meliacuba.com; Av 3, btwn Calles 76 & 80; s/d CUC$527/600; P ❄ @) Ugly outside but beautiful within, Miramar's gorgeous Hotel Meliá Habana is one of the city's best-run and best-equipped accommodation options. The 409 rooms (some of which are wheelchair-accessible) are positioned around a salubrious lobby with abundant hanging vines, marble statues and gushing water features. Outside, Cuba's largest and most beautiful swimming pool lies next to a desolate, rocky shore.

Throw in polite service, an excellent buffet restaurant and the occasional room discount, and you could be swayed. But the price...?

H10 Habana Panorama HOTEL **$$$**
(7-204-0100; www.h10hotels.com; cnr Av 3 & Calle 70; s/d CUC$260/320; P ❄ @) This flashy 'glass cathedral' on Playa's rapidly developing hotel strip opened in 2003. The rather strange aesthetics – acres of blue-tinted glass – improve once you step inside the monumental lobby where space-age elevators whisk you promptly up to one of 317 bright rooms, offering great views over Miramar and beyond.

Extra facilities include a business center, a photo shop, numerous restaurants and a spacious and shapely swimming pool. But the Panorama is almost too big: its scale makes you feel small and gives the place a rather deserted and antiseptic feel.

Memories Miramar HOTEL **$$$**
(7-204-3583/4; www.memoriesresorts.com; cnr Av 5 & Calle 74; s/d CUC$250/350; P ❄ @) This hotel is now onto its third name change. The facilities at this 427-room giant built in 2000 are fair enough: big rooms, decent breakfasts, serviceable business facilities and a large attractive pool area. Where it falls down is in the nitty-gritty. With better attention to ongoing maintenance and more of a desire to go above and beyond for service issues, it might justify its four stars.

There are plenty of sporty extras if the isolated location starts to grate, including tennis courts, said swimming pool, sauna, gym and games room.

Hotel el Bosque HOTEL $$$

(7-204-9232; www.hotelelbosquehabana.com; Calle 28a, btwn Calles 49a & 49c, Kohly; s/d CUC$142/225;) El Bosque is one arm of the Gaviota-run Kohly-Bosque *complejo* (complex). Clean and friendly, it lies on the banks of the Río Almendares surrounded by the Bosque de La Habana – the city's green lungs. The decor is a little behind the fashion curve and, like most Havana hotels it's hugely overpriced, although the wooded grounds deaden the blow a little.

Hotel Kohly HOTEL $$$

(7-204-0240; www.hotelkohly.com; cnr Calles 49a & 36, Kohly; s/d CUC$117/189;) The Kohly, in western Playa, makes up for its utilitarian exterior with a few handy extras including a swimming pool, bowling alley, gym and on-site pizzeria.

Four Points Habana HOTEL $$$

(7-214-1470; www.fourpointshavana.com; Av 5, btwn Calles 76 & 80; r incl breakfast CUC$400-600;) Four Points completes a trio of expensive accommodations behind the Miramar Trade Center. While there are plenty of facilities, including large rooms, gym, pool, restaurants and a business center, the lack of maintenance, patchy service and weirdly un-Cuban personality struggle to justify the price. It's recently been taken over by the Sheraton group, so hopefully the new owners will turn the page.

Starfish Montehabana HOTEL $$$

(7-206-9595; www.starfishresorts.com; Calle 70, btwn Avs 5a & 7; r from CUC$225;) This Miramar giant opened in 2005 with the promise of something a little different. However, with its overbearing concrete stairways and boxy Lego-land architecture, it was something of an ugly duckling from the start. Lack of maintenance in the ensuing years hasn't brightened its allure. It's an apart-hotel with 101 apartments with living rooms and fully equipped kitchens.

If you're not up to cooking, the restaurant does an OK breakfast and dinner buffet (both extra). Elsewhere the facilities, rather like the service, are a bit moldy. A bonus – guests share the gym, pool and tennis courts with the four-star Memories Miramar (p129) next door.

Eating

Playa has been a bastion of some of Cuba's best private restaurants since the 1990s and many of the old stalwarts continue to impress despite an abundance of new competition. There are also some surprisingly good state-run restaurants, many of them developed to satisfy the taste buds of the diplomatic crowd. It's worth the taxi fare of CUC$5 to CUC$10 from the city center to eat out here.

La Casa del Gelato ICE CREAM $

(52-42-08-70; Av 1 No 4215, btwn Calles 42 & 44; ice cream CUC$2-4; 11am-11pm) Miramar has always seemed to be one step ahead of the rest of Havana in the culinary stakes, sporting posh dining options when the rest of the city was still on iron rations. Now they've moved the goalposts again with this fabulous ice-cream parlor that smells of waffles, sells multiple flavors and even has a Nespresso coffee machine.

Cafetería Betty Boom FAST FOOD $

(53-92-94-12; cnr Av 3 & Calle 60; snacks CUC$2.50-5; 11am-2:30am) Inhabiting the space once occupied by 'El Garage,' Betty Boom offers a similar concept: cheap but good fast food (hot dogs, sandwiches, shakes and salads) in a retro 1950s diner interior where the waitresses dress like 1930s cartoon character Betty Boop. Opening hours are generous, as are the portions. There's a small outdoor terrace.

Pan.com FAST FOOD $

(7-204-4232; cnr Av 7 & Calle 26; snacks CUC$1-4; 10am-midnight) Not an internet cafe but a haven of Havana comfort food, with hearty sandwiches, cheap burgers and ice-cream milk shakes to die for. Join the diplomats under the breezy front canopy.

★Espacios TAPAS, INTERNATIONAL $$

(7-202-2921; Calle 10 No 513, btwn Avs 5 & 7; tapas CUC$3-6; noon-6am) A fabulously chilled tapas bar that occupies an unsignposted house in Miramar where hip people come to consume cocktails and art. Select from an internationally inspired menu while mingling with Havana's brainy and beautiful, a healthy mix of in-the-know expats and Cubans with artistic sensibilities.

The house is filled with interesting nooks and an attractive patio. The interior walls act as a de facto art gallery hung with avant-garde paintings.

El Aljibe CARIBBEAN $$

(7-204-1583/4; Av 7, btwn Calles 24 & 26; mains CUC$12-15; noon-midnight) On paper a humble state-run restaurant, but in reality a rip-roaring culinary extravaganza, El Aljibe has been delighting both Cuban and foreign diplomats' taste buds for years. The furore surrounds the gastronomic mysteries of just one dish: the obligatory *pollo asado* (roast chicken), which is served up with as-much-as-you-can-eat helpings of white rice, black beans, fried plantain, french fries and salad.

The accompanying bitter orange sauce is said to be a state secret.

Paladar Vista Mar SEAFOOD **$$**
(☎7-203-8328; www.restaurantevistamar.com; Av 1 No 2206, btwn Calles 22 & 24; mains CUC$8-15; ⊙noon-midnight Mon-Sat) The Vista Mar has been around for eons in paladar years (since 1996). It inhabits the 2nd-floor family room turned restaurant of a private residence, which faces the sea. The seaside ambience is embellished by a beautiful swimming pool that spills its water into the ocean. If enjoying delicious seafood dishes overlooking the crashing ocean sounds enticing, read no more, and book a table!

Casa Pilar SPANISH **$$**
(www.facebook.com/casapilarhabana; Calle 36 No 103, btwn Avs 1 & 3; mains CUC$10-20; ⊙noon-2am) Tapas bar and Spanish restaurant in one, Casa Pilar serves up dishes that have the true taste of a Spanish kitchen with a slight Cuban flare. Try the *garbanzos* (chickpeas) with *ropa vieja* (shredded beef). The gin and tonics are among the best in Havana, and the restaurant's terrace on the 2nd floor is the ideal place to enjoy them.

Club Su Miramar KOREAN **$$**
(☎7-206-3443; Calle 40a No 1115, btwn Avs 1 & 3; mains CUC$9-14; ⊙noon-3am) Havana's restaurant scene in the last few years has been an exciting potluck of 'what's next?' We've already had Cuba's first Russian, Iranian and Indian restaurants. Now we have its first Korean place. You're halfway to Seoul in Club Su with the decor – a fragrant garden and tranquil terrace with sliding doors into an Asian-minimalist domain. The food's not far behind.

The smoked salmon makes a good awayday from normal Cuban cuisine and the *gimbab* is suitably exotic, while the aromatic rice is imported from Korea.

El Cucalambe CUBAN **$$**
(Calle 226; mains CUC$5-9; ⊙noon-11pm) Jaimanitas, aka Fusterlandia, has recently sprouted a pretty good restaurant to serve the regular deluge of visitors. It's decorated, not surprisingly, with cutting-edge art and named (perhaps more surprisingly) for an erstwhile Las Tunas poet. The food, headlined by spit-roasted pork, also has a Las Tunas bent. Tables with ceramic eating utensils are set around a pleasant outdoor patio.

La Carboncita ITALIAN **$$**
(Av 3 No 3804, btwn Calles 38 & 40; pasta & pizza CUC$7-8; ⊙noon-midnight) The food appears mysteriously from the garage of this Miramar house turned Italian restaurant with both indoor and outdoor front porch seating, but there's nothing mechanical about the flavors. On the contrary, the pasta is homemade by the Italian owner and you can choose from a multitude of authentic sauces including pesto. The thin-crust pizzas are good too.

Casa Española SPANISH **$$**
(☎7-206-9644; cnr Calle 26 & Av 7; meals CUC$8-14; ⊙noon-11pm) A medieval parody built in the Batista-era by the silly-rich Gustavo Gutiérrez y Sánchez, this crenellated castle in Miramar has found new life as a Spanish-themed restaurant cashing in on the Don Quixote legend. The ambience is rather fine, if you don't mind suits of armor watching you as you tuck into paella, Spanish omelet or *lanja cerdo al Jerez* (pork fillet).

Papa's Complejo Turístico CARIBBEAN, CHINESE **$$**
(cnr Av 5 & Calle 248; meals CUC$5-10; ⊙noon-3am) There's all sorts of stuff going on at this joint in the Marina Hemingway, from beer-swilling boatmen to warbling *American Idol* wannabes hogging the karaoke machine. The eating options are equally varied, with a posh Chinese place (with dress code) and an outdoor *ranchón* (rustic, open-sided restaurant). Good fun if there's enough people.

Dos Gardenias CARIBBEAN **$$**
(cnr Av 7 & Calle 28; mains CUC$7-10; ⊙noon-11pm) You can choose from a grill or a pasta restaurant in this complex, which is famous as a *bolero* (ballad) music hot spot. Stick around to hear the singers belting out ballads later on.

Restaurante la Cova ITALIAN **$$**
(☎7-209-7289; cnr Av 5 & Calle 248; meals CUC$8; ⊙noon-midnight) Part of the Pizza Nova chain, this place, like much of the Marina Hemingway, has seen better days. It's OK if you're short on options (which you will be). There's an affiliated cafe next door.

★La Fontana BARBECUE $$$
(☎7-202-8337; www.lafontanahavana.info; Av 3a No 305; mains CUC$20-28; ⊙noon-midnight) La Fontana, encased in a hard-to-find but beautiful house in Playa, is one of the best restaurants in Havana, a position it has enjoyed pretty much since its inception in 1995 (back in Cuba's culinary Stone Age). The secret: the restaurant has progressed with the times, adding space, dishes and multiple quirks like fish ponds and live jazz.

These days there are four separate areas to drink and dine in, each with a different ambience, including a new lounge bar and the ever-popular fern-filled terrace.

Fontana is famed for its barbecue or, more to the point, its full-on charcoal grill. Huge portions of meat and fish are served up so go easy on the starters, which include lobster ceviche, tuna tartar, and beef carpaccio with rocket.

La Corte del Príncipe ITALIAN $$$
(☎52-55-90-91; cnr Av 9 & Calle 74; mains CUC$15-20; ⊙noon-3pm & 7pm-midnight Tue-Sun) Possibly the most Italian of Italian restaurants in Havana is this lovely semi-alfresco nook run by an expat Italian who plies the best of his country's famous cuisine. The menu's a potluck inscribed on a blackboard, but there are regular appearances from eggplant parmigiano and *vitello tonnato* (veal in tuna sauce). Shiny fresh vegetables in display baskets add to the allure.

It's a little out of the way, but the word is out. Book ahead.

La Cocina de Lilliam FUSION $$$
(☎7-209-6514; www.lacocinadelilliam.com; Calle 48 No 1311, btwn Avs 13 & 15; meals CUC$15-30; ⊙noon-3pm & 7-11pm Tue-Sat) A legend long before Cuban food became legendary, Lilliam's was once one of Havana's only posh private restaurants – the long-standing diplomat's choice. These days it's got more competition, but maintains its prominence with classy service, secluded ambience and freshly cooked food to die for.

The experience is as much about the surroundings as the food. The restaurant is set in an illustrious villa in Miramar and you are served in a garden with trickling fountains and lush tropical plants. The menu changes regularly, but there's usually good steak, octopus and pork options.

La Esperanza INTERNATIONAL $$$
(☎7-202-4361; Calle 16 No 105, btwn Avs 1 & 3; meals CUC$8-17; ⊙7-11pm Mon-Sat) The unassuming Esperanza was being gastronomically creative long before the 2011 reforms made life for chefs a lot easier. The interior of this vine-covered house is a riot of quirky antiques, old portraits and refined 1940s furnishings, while the food from the family kitchen includes such exquisite dishes as *pollo luna de miel* (chicken flambéed in rum) and lamb brochettes.

Doctor Café CUBAN $$$
(☎7-203-4718; Calle 28, btwn Avs 1 & 3; mains CUC$12-20; ⊙noon-midnight) Exotic dishes such as ceviche, red snapper and grilled octopus are served in either a fern-filled patio or cooler indoor dining area; this doctor is obviously getting the treatment spot on. The menu is from all over the globe, although the fish off the grill is the highlight. Unusually for Cuba it often has good desserts, including key lime pie!

El Tocororo CARIBBEAN $$$
(☎7-202-4530; Calle 18 No 302; meals CUC$12-35; ⊙noon-11:45pm) Once considered – along with El Aljibe (p130) – to be one of Havana's finest government-run restaurants, El Tocororo has lost ground to its competitors in recent years and is often criticized for being overpriced. Nonetheless the candlelit tables and grandiose interior are still worth a visit, while the menu, with such luxuries as lobster's tail and (occasionally) ostrich, still has the ability to surprise.

La Ferminia STEAK $$$
(☎7-273-6786; Av 5 No 18207, Flores; meals from CUC$15; ⊙noon-midnight) The out-of-the-way Ferminia is old-school Havana posh. During rougher economic times it drew in diplomats and famous visitors in spades (Fidel Castro ate here), but today it struggles to emulate the raft of newer, cooler competition. The semi-elegant interior has seen better days, while the food revolves around steak done Argentinian-style.

Drinking & Nightlife

Playa is spread out and thus doesn't really encourage bar crawls. Many of the neighborhood's famously plush restaurants also have excellent bars – of note are Espacios (p130) and La Fontana (p132). You can also down a few rums or *cervezas* at Club Habana (p125) or Marina Hemingway (p125).

★Café Fortuna Joe BAR
(☎54-13-37-06; cnr Calle 24 & Av 1, Miramar; ⊙9am-midnight) There are a lot of seriously

weird (in a good way) places to drink coffee in Havana, but Café Fortuna Joe takes some beating, mainly because of its original seating. Forget the mismatched chairs so beloved by hipsters elsewhere. Fortuna's seating arrangements include a horse carriage, an old car, a bed and a cushioned toilet. We kid you not. The coffee and service here are excellent, and it also serves food.

There's another smaller Cafe Fortuna nearby at Av 3 and Calle 28.

☆ Entertainment

El Salón Chévere DANCE

(☎52-64-96-92; cnr Calles 49 & 28; CUC$6-10; ⊙11pm-3am) Go into the woods at Parque Almendares to find one of Havana's most popular open-air discos, where a mix of Cubans and non-Cubans come to dance salsa. You can also take salsa lessons here through Club Salseando Chévere (p88).

Tropicana Nightclub CABARET

(☎7-267-1871; Calle 72 No 4504, Marianao; tickets from CUC$75; ⊙from 10pm) A city institution since its 1939 opening, the world-famous Tropicana was one of the few bastions of Havana's Las Vegas–style nightlife to survive the revolution. Immortalized in Graham Greene's 1958 classic *Our Man in Havana,* the open-air cabaret show here has changed little since its 1950s heyday, with scantily clad *señoritas* descending from palm trees to dance Latin salsa amid bright lights.

It's easily Havana's most popular cabaret and de rigueur on the bus tour circuit (read: lots of tourists), none of which takes away from the magnificence of the spectacle.

You'll need a taxi to get here. Book tickets in advance through Infotur (p134) or any top-end hotel.

Café Miramar LIVE MUSIC

(Av 5 No 9401, cnr Calle 94; cover CUC$2) Miramar's slick new jazz club wouldn't cut ice with bebop-era jazz greats who would smirk at the sanitized air and no-smoking rule, but it doesn't seem to bother today's young innovators. The club is encased in the Cine Teatro Miramar and belongs to government agency ARTex. Things usually get jamming at 10pm-ish and there's cheap food.

Salón Rosado Benny Moré LIVE MUSIC

(El Tropical; ☎7-206-1281; cnr Av 41 & Calle 46, Kohly; varies; ⊙9pm-late) If you're looking for something inherently Cuban, tag along with the local *habaneros* for some very *caliente* action at this outdoor venue known colloquially as El Tropical. The long-standing club hosts live music and has changed its spots over the years – these days it's less Benny Moré and more Pupy y Los Que Son Son with occasional reggaeton thrown in.

Dancing is de rigueur, unless you can escape to one of the balconies for a drink. Entry prices and show nights vary – check the local grapevine first.

Casa de la Música LIVE MUSIC

(☎7-202-6147; Calle 20 No 3308, cnr Av 35, Miramar; CUC$5-20; ⊙from 10pm Tue-Sat) Launched with a concert by renowned jazz pianist Chucho Valdés in 1994, this Miramar favorite is run by national Cuban recording company Egrem, and the programs are generally a lot more authentic than the cabaret entertainment you'll see at the hotels.

Platinum players such as NG la Banda, Los Van Van and Aldaberto Álvarez y Su Son play here regularly; you'll rarely pay more than CUC$20. It has a more relaxed atmosphere than its Centro Habana namesake.

Teatro Karl Marx LIVE MUSIC

(☎7-209-1991; cnr Av 1 & Calle 10, Miramar) Sizewise the Karl Marx puts other Havana theaters in the shade, with a seating capacity of 5500 in a single auditorium. The very biggest events happen here, such as the closing galas for the jazz and film festivals, and rare concerts by *trovadores* like Silvio Rodriguez.

Don Cangrejo LIVE MUSIC

(Av 1 No 1606, btwn Calles 16 & 18, Miramar; cover CUC$5; ⊙11pm-3am) The daytime restaurant of the Cuban fisheries becomes party central particularly on Friday night, with alfresco live music (big-name acts) and an atmosphere akin to an undergraduate fresher's ball. It's crowded and there are queues.

La Cecilia LIVE MUSIC

(☎7-204-1562; Av 5 No 11010, btwn Calles 110 & 112; ⊙noon-midnight) This place has long been a staple with the diplomatic crowd, but better than the food (meals CUC$12 to CUC$20) is the big-band music, which blasts out on weekend nights inside its large but atmospheric courtyard.

Circo Trompoloco CIRCUS

(www.circonacionaldecuba.cu; cnr Av 5 & Calle 112, Playa; CUC$5-10; ⊙7pm Fri, 4pm & 7pm Sat & Sun; 👪) Havana's permanent 'Big Top' with a weekend matinee features strongmen, contortionists and acrobats.

OFF THE BEATEN TRACK

SANTA MARÍA DEL ROSARIO

Santa María del Rosario, 19km southeast of central Havana, is an old colonial town founded in 1732. Unlike most other towns from that period, it has not become engulfed by modern suburbs, but stands alone in the countryside. The charms of this area were recognized by one of Cuba's greatest living painters, Manuel Mendive, who selected it for his personal residence. You can also see the local countryside in Tomás Gutiérrez Alea's film *La última cena*, a metaphorical critique of slavery.

Also called the Catedral de los Campos de Cuba, the **Iglesia de Nuestra Señora del Rosario** (Calle 24, btwn 31 & 33; 8am-6pm Tue-Sun), on Santa María del Rosario's old town square, was built in 1760 in classic baroque style. It's known for its gleaming gold interior made up of a gilded mahogany altar and some equally sumptuous side altars fashioned in the churrigueresque style. It is one of suburban Havana's most attractive secrets.

From the Capitolio in Centro Habana take metro bus P-7 to Cotorro and then bus 97, which runs from Guanabacoa to Santa María del Rosario.

Shopping

★**La Casa del Habano Quinta** CIGARS
(7-214-4737; cnr Av 5 & Calle 16, Miramar; 10am-6pm Mon-Sat, to 1pm Sun) Arguably Havana's top cigar store – and there are many contenders. The primary reasons: it's well stocked, with well-informed staff, a comfy smoking lounge, a decent on-site restaurant and a welcome lack of tourist traffic.

Alma Shop ARTS & CRAFTS
(53-5-264-0660; www.almacubashop.com; Calle 18 No 314, btwn Avs 3 & 5; 10am-4pm Mon-Sat) Whether you're searching for jewelry, embroidered cushions or a vintage cigar humidor, this is a great place to pick up a high-quality gift or souvenir. Owner Alex Oppmann has traveled across Cuba to carefully select pieces made by local artisans; each item is unique and handmade using natural or recycled materials.

La Maison CLOTHING
(Calle 16 No 701, Miramar; 9am-5pm) The Cuban fashion fascination is in high gear at this large boutique selling designer clothing, shoes, handbags, jewelry, cosmetics and souvenirs. It also holds regular fashion shows.

Miramar Trade Center SHOPPING CENTER
(Av 3, btwn Calles 76 & 80, Miramar; hours vary) Cuba's largest and most modern shopping and business center houses myriad stores, airline offices and embassies.

Egrem Tienda de Música MUSIC
(Calle 18 No 103, Miramar; 9am-6pm Mon-Sat) There's a small CD outlet hidden here in leafy Miramar at the site of Havana's most celebrated recording studios.

Information

MEDICAL SERVICES

Clínica Central Cira García (7-204-4300; Calle 20 No 4101; 9am-4pm Mon-Fri, emergencies 24hr) Emergency, dental and medical consultations for foreigners.

Farmacia Internacional Miramar (7-204-4350; cnr Calles 20 & 41, Playa; 9am-5:45pm) Across the road from Clínica Central Cira García.

MONEY

Banco Financiero Internacional (Sierra Maestra Bldg, cnr Av 1 & Calle 0, Miramar; 9am-3pm Mon-Fri) Has an ATM.

Cadeca Playa (7-204-9087; cnr Av 3 & Calle 70; 9am-5pm Mon-Sat, 9am-noon Sun) and Miramar (Av 5a, btwn Calles 40 & 42, Miramar; 9am-5pm Mon-Sat, 9am-noon Sun) Handy money exchanges with minimal queues.

POST

DHL (cnr Av 1 & Calle 26, Miramar; 8:30am-6pm Mon-Fri, 8am-2pm Sat) For important mail it's best to use DHL.

Post Office (Calle 42 No 112, btwn Avs 1 & 3, Miramar; 8-11:30am & 2-6pm Mon-Fri, 8-11:30am Sat)

TOURIST INFORMATION

Infotur (cnr Av 5 & Calle 112, Playa; 8:30am-noon & 12:30-5pm Mon-Sat) Oddly located but highly informative Infotur office.

Getting There & Away

BUS

The best way to get to Playa from Centro Habana and Vedado is on the Habana Bus Tour T1, which plies most of the neighborhood's highlights all the way to **La Cecilia** (p133) on Av 5 in Cubanacán

(CUC$10 for an all-day ticket). Plenty of metro buses also make the trip, though they often detour around the residential neighborhoods; P-1 and P-10 buses are the most useful.

CAR

Cubacar has offices at the **Hotel Meliá Habana** (☎7-204-3236; ⌚9am-5pm) and **Marina Hemingway** (☎7-835-0000; ⌚9am-5pm). Rental costs depend on the type of car and duration of rent – take CUC$70 per day as an average. **Vía Rent a Car** (☎7-204-3606; cnr Avs 47 & 36, Kohly; ⌚9am-5pm) has an office opposite the Hotel el Bosque.

Regla & Guanabacoa

Regla and Guanabacoa are two small towns on the eastern side of Havana harbor that got swallowed up during Havana's urban growth. Slow-paced and little visited by tourists, the municipalities retain an independent-minded and culturally distinct spirit.

There are other spirits here too. Guanabacoa is sometimes called *el pueblo embrujado* ('the bewitched town') for its strong Santería traditions, while Regla – another Santería hotbed – was known as the Sierra Chiquita (Little Sierra, after the Sierra Maestra) in the 1950s for its bolshie revolutionary politics.

Sights

Regla

★Iglesia de Nuestra Señora de Regla CHURCH

(⌚7:30am-6pm) As important as it is diminutive, Iglesia de Nuestra Señora de Regla, which sits close to the boat dock in Regla, has a long and colorful history. Inside on the main altar you'll find La Santísima Virgen de Regla.

The virgin, represented by a black Madonna, is venerated in the Catholic faith and associated in the Santería religion with Yemayá, the *orisha* of the ocean and the patron of sailors (always represented in blue). Legend claims that this image was carved by St Augustine 'The African' in the 5th century, and that in AD 453 a disciple brought the statue to Spain to safeguard it from barbarians. The small vessel in which the image was traveling survived a storm in the Strait of Gibraltar, so the figure was recognized as the patron of sailors. In more recent times, rafters attempting to reach the US have also evoked the protection of the Black Virgin.

To shelter a copy of the image, a hut was first built on this site in 1687 by a pilgrim named Manuel Antonio. But this structure was destroyed during a 1692 hurricane. A few years later a Spaniard named Juan de Conyedo built a stronger chapel, and in 1714 Nuestra Señora de Regla was proclaimed patron of the Bahía de la Habana. In 1957 the image was crowned by the Cuban Cardinal in Havana cathedral. Every year on September 7 thousands of pilgrims descend on Regla to celebrate the saint's day, and the image is taken out for a procession through the streets.

The current church dates from the early 19th century and is always busy with devotees from both religions stooping in silent prayer before the images of the saints that fill the alcoves. In Havana, there is probably no better (public) place to see the layering and transference between Catholic beliefs and African traditions.

Museo Municipal de Regla MUSEUM

(Martí No 158; CUC$2; ⌚9am-5pm Mon-Sat, 9am-noon Sun) If you've come across to see Regla's church, you should also check out this important museum. Don't be put off by its superficial dinginess – there's some valuable relics inside. Located a few blocks up the main street from the ferry, it records Regla's history and Afro-Cuban religions. Don't miss the Palo Monte *ngangas* (cauldrons) and the masked Abakuá dancing figurines.

There's also an interesting, small exhibit on Remigio Herrero, first *babalawo* (priest) of Regla, and a bizarre statue of Napoleon with his nose missing.

Estatua de Cristo MONUMENT

(Map p106; Casablanca) This impossible-to-miss statue on a rise on the harbor's eastern side was created by Jilma Madera in 1958. It was promised to President Batista by his wife after the US-backed leader survived an attempt on his life in the Presidential Palace in March 1957, and was (ironically) unveiled on Christmas Day 1958, one week before the dictator fled the country. As you disembark the Casablanca ferry, follow the road uphill for about 10 minutes until you reach the monument.

Colina Lenin MONUMENT

From Regla's boat dock, head straight (south) on Martí past Parque Guaicanamar, and turn left on Albuquerque and right on 24 de Febrero, the road to Guanabacoa. About 1.5km from the ferry you'll see a high metal stairway that gives access to Colina Lenin, one of two monuments in Havana to Vladimir Ilyich Ulyanov (better known to his friends and enemies as Lenin).

The monument was conceived in 1924 by the socialist mayor of Regla, Antonio Bosch, to honor Lenin's death (in the same year). Above a monolithic image of the man is an olive tree planted by Bosch, surrounded by seven lithe figures. There are fine harbor views from the hilltop.

Guanabacoa

Ermita de Potosí CHURCH
(cnr Calzada Vieja Guanabacoa & Potosí; 8am-5pm) Inexplicably, barely anyone visits this, the oldest church in Cuba still standing in its original perch. The existing structure dates from around 1675 and is a simple *mudéjar* design with a single belltower and a wooden ceiling. It sits in an eerie graveyard atop a hill in Guanabacoa and is in remarkably good condition following a 21st-century restoration.

Museo Municipal de Guanabacoa MUSEUM
(Martí No 108; CUC$2; 9am-5:30pm Tue-Sat, 9am-1pm Sun) Guanabacoa's main museum, like Regla's, is an important shrine to Santería, though you'll need to see past the rundown facilities and impassive 'guides' to appreciate it. The collection is small but concise; rooms are dedicated to the various Santería deities with a particular focus on the *orisha* Elegguá. Equally fascinating are rare artifacts from the Palo Monte and Abakuá religions.

The museum has another arm further west along Calle Martí in the **Museo de Mártires** (Martí No 320; 10am-6pm Tue-Sat, 9am-1pm Sun) FREE, which displays historical material relevant to the revolution and its local 'martyrs.'

Iglesia de Guanabacoa CHURCH
(cnr Pepe Antonio & Adolfo del Castillo Cadenas; parochial office 8-11am & 2-5pm Mon-Fri) This church, in Parque Martí in the center of Guanabacoa, is also known as the Iglesia de Nuestra Señora de la Asunción, and was designed by Lorenzo Camacho and built between 1721 and 1748 with a Moorish-influenced wooden ceiling.

Eating

La Brisilla CUBAN $$
(Cruz Verde, btwn Santa Ana & Segui; mains CUC$6-10; noon-midnight) Unsignposted, hard to find and, consequently, almost 100% local, this is a rare private restaurant in Guanabacoa, where the food culture doesn't seem to have moved on much since the not-so-tasty '90s. You'll have to ask the way in Spanish to get here, but when/if you make it, the rabbit in red wine and succulent lobster will leave you feeling as pleased as you'll be surprised.

In Calle Cruz Verde, La Brisilla is the pleasant stone-fronted house with two lions on a parapet.

Drinking & Nightlife

Centro Cultural Recreativo los Orishas BAR
(7-794-7878; Martí No 175, btwn Lamas & Cruz Verde; 10am-2am) Situated in the hotbed of Havana's Santería community in Guanabacoa, this bar-restaurant used to host live rumba music on weekends, including regular visits from the Conjunto Folklórico Nacional, though it seemed to have limited its program at last visit. The walled garden bar is surrounded by Afro-Cuban sculptures of various Santería deities.

Getting There & Away

BUS

Metro bus P-15 from the Parque de la Fraternidad in Centro Habana goes to Regla and Guanabacoa, stopping at the main train terminal in Habana Vieja on the way.

FERRY

Regla is easily accessible on the passenger ferry that departs every 20 minutes (CUC$0.25) from the **Emboque de Luz** (p123) at the intersection of San Pedro and Santa Clara in Habana Vieja. Bicycles are readily accepted via a separate line that boards first.

FOOT

You can walk uphill from Regla where the Havana ferry docks to Guanabacoa (or vice versa) in about 45 minutes, passing the Colina Lenin monument on the way.

Parque Lenin & Around

Spread out like a fan on three sides of downtown, Havana's little-visited suburban municipalities hide a handful of disparate sights that can make interesting half-day and day trips from the city center. Santiago de las Vegas and Santa María del Rosario are former rural settlements that have been incorporated into the larger metropolis without losing their soporific airs; San Francisco de Paula trades off its association with famous former resident, Ernest Hemingway; Arroyo Naranjo encircles the city's largest green space, Parque Lenin, and hosts Havana's expansive botanical gardens.

Sights

★Museo Hemingway MUSEUM

(☎7-692-0176; cnr Vígia & Singer; CUC$5; ⏰10am-4:30pm Mon-Sat) In 1940, American novelist Ernest Hemingway bought the Finca la Vigía, a villa on a hill in San Francisco de Paula, 15km southeast of Havana, where he lived continuously for 20 years. When he departed, tired and depressed, for the US in 1960 soon after the Castro revolution, he generously donated his house to the 'Cuban people.' It is now a museum and almost unchanged since the day he left.

To prevent the pilfering of objects, visitors are not allowed inside the house (La Casona), but there are enough open doors and windows to allow a proper glimpse into Papa's universe. Inside the house there are books everywhere (including beside the toilet), a large Victrola and record collection, and a disturbing array of trophy animal heads.

A three-story tower next to the main house contains a tiny typewriter, a telescope and a comfortable lounger, and offers suitably inspiring views north toward the distant city. In the heavily wooded grounds below you'll encounter the swimming pool where Ava Gardner once swam naked, a cockfighting ring and Hemingway's beloved fishing boat, *Pilar*, grounded on what was once his tennis court.

To reach San Francisco de Paula, take metro bus P-7 (Alberro) from Parque de la Fraternidad in Centro Habana. Tell the driver you're going to the museum. You get off in San Miguel del Padrón; the house entrance is on Calle Vigía, 200m east of the main road, Calzada de Guines.

Jardín Botánico Nacional GARDENS

(Carretera del Rocio; CUC$4; ⏰10am-5pm Wed-Sun) Havana's curiously under-visited 600-hectare botanical garden suffers from an out-of-town location and poor transport links (get a taxi). It opened in 1984 after 16 years of development and is hailed for its collection of 250 species of palm trees, ethno-botanical crop displays and tranquil Japanese Garden (1992). Multilingual guided tours are conducted on a mini-train (not as tacky as it sounds), or in your own vehicle should you have one (the guide will come with you).

Between November and February, the garden is an excellent spot for observing migratory birds. It is also known for its vegetarian Restaurante el Bambú (p138), which serves a meat-free buffet daily. There's a separate *ranchón* (rustic, open-sided restaurant) serving à la carte meat dishes for carnivores.

Santuario de San Lázaro CHURCH

(Carretera San Antonio de los Baños; ⏰7am-6pm) You can make your own journey to the site of Cuba's biggest annual pilgrimage, tucked away in the village-like Havana suburb of Rincón. The saint inside the church is San Lázaro (represented by the *orisha* Babalú Ayé in the Santería religion), the patron saint of healing and the sick. Hundreds come to light candles and lay flowers daily. Thousands come on December 17 to pray for respite from illnesses or to give thanks for cures.

There's a small museum displaying a raft of previous offerings to San Lázaro in a chapel next door.

Parque Lenin PARK

(⏰hours vary) Parque Lenin, in Arroyo Naranjo municipality, 20km south of central Havana, is the city's largest recreational area. Constructed between 1969 and 1972 on the orders of Celia Sánchez, a long-time associate of Fidel Castro, it is one of the few developments in Havana from this era. The 670 hectares of green parkland and beautiful old trees surround an artificial lake, the Embalse Paso Sequito, just west of the much larger Embalse Ejército Rebelde, which was formed by damming the Río Almendares.

Although the park itself is attractive enough, its mishmash of facilities has fallen on hard times since the 1990s. Taxi drivers complain it's *muy abandonado* and wax nostalgic about when 'Lenin' was an idyllic weekend getaway for scores of pleasure-seeking Havana families. These days the place retains a neglected and surreal air. Help has long been promised, though words tend to be louder than actions. To date, some Chinese investment has filtered through, but it's a big job that's still a long way from completion. Around 95% of the current visitors are Cubans who come here mainly at weekends.

Most of the park's attractions are open 9am to 5pm Tuesday to Sunday, and admission to the park itself is free. You can sometimes rent a rowboat on the Embalse Paso Sequito. Horse-riding is also popular, but hire your mounts from the Centro Ecuestre (p138) rather than the army of hustlers who hang around outside the entrance and who often ride maltreated horses.

To get to the park, the P-13 will get you close, but to catch it you have to first get to Vibora. The best way to do this is to get on the P-9 at Calles 23 and L in Vedado.

Mausoleo de Antonio Maceo MONUMENT

FREE On a hilltop at El Cacahual, 8km south of Aeropuerto Internacional José Martí via Santiago de las Vegas, is the little-visited mausoleum of the hero of Cuban independence, General Antonio Maceo, who was killed in the Battle of San Pedro near Bauta on December 7, 1896. An open-air pavilion next to the mausoleum shelters a historical exhibit.

Activities

Centro Ecuestre HORSE RIDING

(Parque Lenin; 9am-5pm) The stables in the northwestern corner of Parque Lenin are run by environmental agency Flora y Fauna. They generally offer horse-riding for around CUC$12 per hour from their equestrian center. If you'd like to ride in the park, go with these guys, not the touts at the park entrance who often ride maltreated horses.

Club de Golf la Habana GOLF

(Carretera de Venta, Km 8 Reparto Capdevila, Boyeros; 8am-8pm, bowling alley noon-11pm) A curiosity as much as a place to swing a nine-iron, this golf club lies between Vedado and the airport and is one of only two in Cuba. There are nine holes on the rough-and-rutted par-35 course. Green fees are CUC$20 for nine holes; clubs, cart and caddie cost extra. The club also has tennis courts and a bowling alley

Originally called the Rover's Athletic Club, it was established by a group of British diplomats in the 1920s, and the diplomatic corps is largely the clientele today. Fidel and Che Guevara played a round here once as a publicity stunt soon after the Cuban missile crisis in 1962. The photos of the event are still popular. Che – an ex-caddy – apparently won.

Poor signposting makes the club hard to find and most taxi drivers get lost looking: ask locals for directions to the *golfito* or Dilpo Golf Club.

Eating

La Ceiba PARRILLA $

(cnr Av San Francisco & Primer Anillo de la Habana; mains MN$75-150; 11:30am-9:45pm) La Ceiba is a thatched *ranchón* at the northern entrance to Parque Lenin close to where the galloping horse hustlers congregate. Come here for the *parrillada* (giant barbecue) and watch as selective meats send up aromatic plumes of smoke while you sit nursing a cold beer. Cheap, simple and very Cuban.

Casa 1740 CUBAN $

(María Capote, Parque Lenin; mains MN$50-70; 9am-5pm Wed-Sun) One of Parque Lenin's quieter eating options is set in a small house south of the lake and is air-conditioned to replicate a chilly day in Canada. Food is straight up *comida criolla* (Creole food). You can't go wrong with the *ropa vieja* (shredded beef) at MN$60 (CUC$2.40).

Restaurante el Bambú VEGETARIAN $$

(Jardín Botánico Nacional; buffet CUC$12; 1-3pm;) This was once the only example of vegetarian dining in Havana, and has long been a leading advocate for the benefits of a meatless diet (a tough call in the challenging economy of Cuba). The all-you-can-eat lunch buffet is served alfresco, deep in the botanical gardens, with the natural setting paralleling the wholesome tastiness of the food.

Gorge on soups and salads, root vegetables, tamales and eggplant caviar.

Las Ruinas CARIBBEAN $$

(Cortina de la Presa, Parque Lenin; mains CUC$6-10; 11am-midnight Tue-Sun) Once celebrated for its architecture (a modernist structure incorporating the ruins of a sugar mill), Las Ruinas had become a ruin itself by the 2010s. Work was in progress at the time of research to spruce it up and restore the eye-catching stained glass by Cuban artist René Portocarrero, as well as the food.

Entertainment

Rodeo Nacional RODEO

(7-643-8089; Parque Lenin; 4pm Sun) In an arena in Parque Lenin, Rodeo Nacional, the biggest rodeo in Cuba, is held on Sundays (but not *every* Sunday, so check ahead). Rodeos in Cuba attract few tourists but are classic Cuban affairs and a great insight into rural culture. The big one, held here every March, is the Boyeros Cattlemen's International Fair.

Getting There & Away

BUS

Metro bus P-12 from Parque de la Fraternidad or bus P-16 from outside Hospital Nacional Hermanos Ameijeiras just off the Malecón go to Santiago de las Vegas. To reach San Francisco de Paula (for Museo Hemingway), take metro bus P-7 (Alberro) from the Parque de la Fraternidad in Centro Habana. Tell the driver you're going to the museum. You get off in San Miguel del Padrón. For Parque Lenin, the P-13 will get you close, but to catch it you have to first get to Vibora. The best way to do this is to get on the P-9 at Calles 23 and L in Vedado.

TAXI

Cars to Havana's outer regions charge anywhere between CUC$15 and CUC$25 depending on the destination.

Habana del Este

Habana del Este is home to Playas del Este, a multiflavored if slightly unkempt beach strip situated 18km east of Habana Vieja. While the beaches here are sublime, the accompanying resorts aren't exactly luxurious. Rather, Playas del Este has a timeworn and slightly abandoned air, and aspiring beach loungers might find the ugly Soviet-style hotel piles more than a little incongruous. But for those who dislike modern tourist development or are keen to see how Cubans get out and enjoy themselves, Playas del Este is a breath of fresh air.

Sights

Eastern Havana doesn't have much in the way of specific sights: the multiflavored beaches provide the main draw. Stretching from west to east in an almost unbroken 15km strip are Bacuranao, Tarará, El Mégano, Santa María del Mar, Boca Ciega and Guanabo.

Cojímar AREA

Situated 10km east of Havana is the little port town of Cojímar, famous for harboring Ernest Hemingway's fishing boat *El Pilar* in the 1940s and 1950s. These days it's an obligatory stop on any 'Hemingway-wos-'ere' tour, with groups arriving primarily to visit the historic if mediocre Restaurante la Terraza (p141) where Ernesto once sank daiquiris.

Overlooking the harbor is Torreón de Cojímar (1649), an old Spanish fort presently occupied by the Cuban Coast Guard. It was the first fortification taken by the British when they attacked Havana from the rear in 1762. Next to this tower and framed by a neoclassical archway is a gilded bust of Ernest Hemingway, erected by the residents of Cojímar in 1962.

Alamar AREA

East across the river from Cojímar is a large housing estate of prefabricated apartment blocks built from 1971 by *micro brigadas* (small armies of workers who built post-revolution housing). This is the birthplace of Cuban rap, and the annual hip-hop festival is still centered here. It is also the home of one of Cuba's largest and most successful urban agricultural gardens, the Organopónico Vivero Alamar.

Activities

Havana Kiteboarding Club KITESURFING

(☎58-04-96-56; www.havanakite.com; Plaza Cobre, btwn 12 & 14, Tarará) At Tarará, where conditions for kiteboarding are excellent, this Italian-run operator offers lessons (CUC$155 for two hours) and board rental (CUC$60 per hour), and can organize accommodation packages in the adjacent Villa Tarará (p140).

Marlin Náutica Tarará WATER SPORTS

(☎7-796-0240; cnr Av 8 & Calle 17, Tarará) Yacht charters, deep-sea fishing and scuba diving are offered at the Marina Tarará, 22km east of Havana. It's generally easier to organize activities at a hotel tour desk in Havana before heading out. Prices are similar to those at Marina Hemingway.

Sleeping

Guanabo

Gilberto & Blanca CASA PARTICULAR $

(☎7-796-2171; gilberto@nauta.cu; Av 5 No 47012, btwn Calles 470 & 472; s/d CUC$25/35; ❄) A friendly retired couple has this pleasant bungalow on Guanabo's main drag, with four rooms sharing two bathrooms. Ideal for families or groups of friends.

Playas del Este

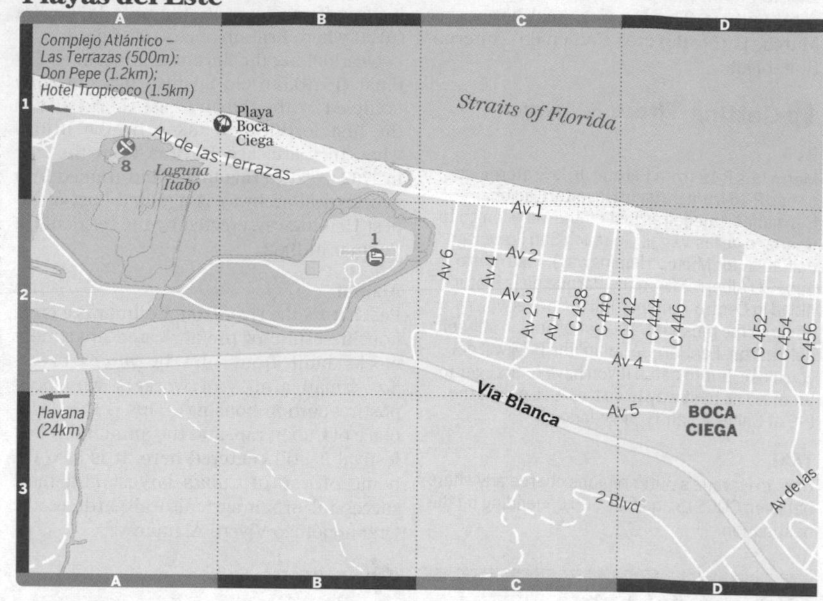

Playas del Este

Sleeping

1 Bravo Club Hotel Arenal B2
2 Gilberto & Blanca F2
3 Hostal Elena Morina F3
4 Hostal Las Terrazas de Teresa F2

Eating

5 Chicken Little H2
6 El Cubano E2
7 Il Piccolo H1
8 Mi Cayito A1
9 Restaurante 421 ..... E3

Drinking & Nightlife

10 Bar Luna G2
11 Cabaret Guanimar E2

Hostal Las Terrazas de Teresa CASA PARTICULAR $
(7-796-6860; Calle 472 No 7B07, btwn Avs 7b & 9; apt CUC$35; P ❄) The three rooms here are realistically mini-apartments with their own kitchens and eating areas. Teresa has put a lot of work into renovating her house and the gray stone brickwork lends the spacious rooms a handsome glow. The terraces on different levels are great for relaxing with a drink.

Hostal Elena Morina CASA PARTICULAR $
(7-796-7975; Calle 472 No 7B11, btwn Avs 7b & 9; r CUC$30; P ❄) *Hay Perro* reads the sign, but don't worry, the pit bull that resides here is friendly (really), as is the hostess Elena, who once lived in Italy. There's great coffee and five decent rooms with a leafy patio a few blocks back from the beach.

Playas del Este

Villa Tarará BUNGALOW $
(7-798-2072; Via Blanca Km 16; 1/2/3/4-bed bungalows CUC$62/71/98/108) The Villa Tarará is part of a planned resort town conceived and built in the 1940s that has gone through various incarnations in the years since (Che Guevara once lived here). It's located 16km east of Havana on a pleasant scoop of beach next to a marina and consists of a huge stash of beach houses of varying sizes and quality.

Beware: this isn't a typical resort. There aren't any good restaurants, little entertainment and the place retains a soporific, vaguely abandoned air. However, it makes a decent base if you're here to kiteboard – nearby Havana Kiteboarding Club (p139) is on the beach and the winds and waves are perfect.

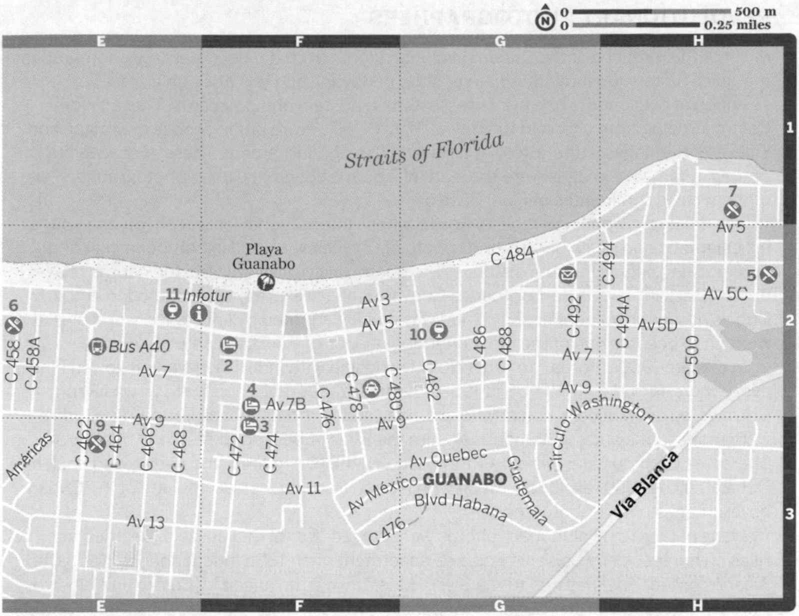

Hotel Tropicoco RESORT **$$**
(☎7-797-1371; cnr Av de las Terrazas & Av de las Banderas; s/d/tr CUC$79/122/163 all-inclusive; P❄@≋) Run by Cubanacán and trying hard to impersonate a grounded ship, this big blue monster is an architectural disaster inside and out. Pity the poor travelers who book this online without looking at photos first! The main (only) benefit for the terribly unfussy is the price (cheap) and the location (you could hit a big home run onto the beach from here).

Bravo Club Hotel Arenal RESORT **$$$**
(☎7-797-1272; Laguna Boca Ciega; s/d/tr CUC$150/250/320 all-inclusive; P❄@≋) Back after a six-year hiatus, the Arenal has re-established itself as Playas del Este's best hotel (although this isn't saying much). Situated aside a small lagoon with boardwalk access to a lovely slice of beach, it lacks the panache of Cuba's northern *cayos* (keys), though its slightly iffy architecture has, at least, received a welcome sprucing up. The clientele is primarily Italian.

Complejo Atlántico – Las Terrazas APARTMENT, HOTEL **$$$**
(☎7-797-1494; Av de las Terrazas, btwn Calles 11 & 12; s/d/tr CUC$116/250/320 all-inclusive; P❄@≋) An amalgamation of a beach hotel and an old *aparthotel,* this place offers 60 or so apartments (with kitchenettes) along with the fair-to-middling Atlántico hotel, one of only three all-inclusives in the city of Havana. Rooms are clean and the beach is lovely, but, take note, this isn't high-end Varadero. Manage your expectations.

Eating

Cojímar

Restaurante la Terraza SEAFOOD **$$**
(Calle 152 No 161; meals CUC$7-15; ⏲noon-11pm) Another photo-adorned shrine to the ghost of Hemingway, Restaurante la Terraza specializes in seafood and does a roaring trade from the hordes of Papa fans who get bused in daily. The food is surprisingly mediocre, although the terrace dining room overlooking the bay is pleasant. More atmospheric is the old bar out front, where mojitos haven't yet reached El Floridita rates.

Guanabo

★**Il Piccolo** ITALIAN **$$**
(☎7-796-4300; cnr Av 5 & Calle 502; pizzas CUC$7-9; ⏲noon-11pm) This Guanabo old-school private restaurant has been around for eons

REVOLUTIONARY PHOTOGRAPHERS

Much of the romance of the Cuban revolution stems from the documentary photographs that told its story. Go into any souvenir shop in Havana and you'll see an attractive selection of black-and-white prints recreated on posters and postcards. There's Fidel Castro jumping from a tank in the Bay of Pigs, Che Guevara puffing coolly on a cigar, and Fidel and Hemingway tête-à-tête at a Havana fishing tournament. These evocative but propaganda-heavy images were the work of a quartet of great Cuban photographers, all of them close confidantes of Fidel Castro.

The most renowned was Alberto Korda, whose international fame rests on one image: his enigmatic and much copied 1960 photo of Che Guevara clad in bomber jacket and beret looking angrily into the distance. The photo, taken at the funeral for victims of a bomb attack in Havana harbor (hence Guevara's angry expression), seemed to embody Cuba's nascent revolutionary spirit and was quickly adopted by leftists the world over. It went on to become one of the most enduring images of the 20th century.

In the late 1950s, Korda formed a close friendship with Fidel Castro and followed him everywhere, including to the US in 1959. Another photographer on that trip was Raúl Corrales, an avowed communist whose artistic shots, though not as famous as Korda's, were more subtle and spontaneous. A third member of this group of Cuban photographers was Osvaldo Salas, who was impressed by the young firebrand and moved back to Cuba after the 1959 revolution. Along with his son Roberto, he became one of the Cuban government's official photographers.

Many of Cuba's revolutionary photos were staged. A shot of a posse of bearded guerrillas on horseback by Corrales was a re-enactment of an 1895 Independence War battle. A series called 'Fidel Returns to the Sierra Maestra' was arranged by Castro and Alberto Korda in the 1960s for the Cuban newspaper *Revolución*. Nonetheless the graphic power of the images endures. Korda's iconic Che image still appears on coins, banknotes and tourist T-shirts, while depictions of Fidel, Che and Camilo Cienfuegos have turned up on everything from revolutionary billboards to the pop art of Raúl Martínez.

and is a bit of an open secret among *habaneros,* some of whom consider its thin-crust wood-oven pizzas to be the best in Cuba. Out of the way and a little more expensive than Playas del Este's other numerous pizza joints, it's well worth the journey (take a horse and cart on Av 5).

Restaurante 421 INTERNATIONAL, CUBAN **$$**
(☎53-05-69-00; Calle 462 No 911, btwn Avs 9 & 11; mains CUC$5-12; ⏲9am-1am) Ask a local about food preferences in Guanabo and they'll probably direct you up the steep hill behind the main roundabout to this newish perch that has a surprisingly wide selection of Cuban favorites mixed with international dishes, including paella and the inevitable pizza. Sit indoors or outside and enjoy attentive service amid a perfect fusion of food and people.

Chicken Little INTERNATIONAL **$$**
(☎7-796-2351; Calle 504 No 5815, btwn Calles 5b & 5c; mains CUC$6-9; ⏲noon-11pm) Forgive them the kitschy name – Chicken Little could yet make it big. Defying Guanabo's ramshackle image, this deluxe restaurant has polite waitstaff with welcome cocktails who'll talk you through a menu of pesto chicken, chicken in orange and honey and – surprise – some jolly fine lobster.

El Cubano CUBAN **$$**
(☎7-796-4061; Av 5, btwn Calles 456 & 458; mains CUC$6-9; ⏲11am-midnight) This is a spick-and-span place on Guanabo's western Boca Ciega end, with a full wine rack (French and Californian), checkered tablecloths and a good version of chicken cordon bleu. There's a nightly disco at 10pm.

Playas del Este

Mi Cayito CUBAN **$**
(☎7-797-1339; Av de las Terrazas, Itabo; mains CUC$4-8; ⏲10am-6pm) A small bar-restaurant reached via a raised boardwalk that overlooks Laguna Itabo, a small lagoon abutting Playa Boca Ciega. It's a quiet spot surrounded by nature selling solid if unremarkable Cuban food.

Don Pepe SEAFOOD $

(Av de las Terrazas; mains CUC$5-7; ⌚10am-11pm) When the Guanabo pizza gets too much, head to this thatched-roof, beach-style restaurant about 50m from the sand. It specializes in seafood.

Drinking & Nightlife

Bar Luna BAR

(Av 5, btwn Calles 482 & 484; ⌚8am-3am) New and privately run, Bar Luna is also a restaurant, but with its luminously lit interior and open terrace overlooking the street it's probably best utilized for its drinks and nighttime action. This being Guanabo, you can expect to see plenty of foreign men of a certain age and their Cuban escorts.

Cabaret Guanimar CLUB

(cnr Av 5 & Calle 468; ⌚9pm-3am Tue-Sat) This outdoor club in Guanabo is really just a disco with a dancing show (at 11pm) and a heavy assemblage of *jintero/as* (touts). Don't expect the Tropicana. Entry per couple is CUC$10.

Entertainment

Centro Cultural Enguayabera ARTS CENTER

(Calle 162, btwn Avs 7a & 7b, Alamar; ⌚9am-11pm) In an old shirt factory, abandoned in the 1990s when it became a rubbish dump and public urinal, is this new state-sponsored community arts project in lowly Alamar, inspired by the Fábrica de Arte Cubano (p116) in Vedado. It bivouacs numerous funky venues under its cultural umbrella, including three small cinemas, a literary cafe, a theater and a crafts outlet.

The place is a shot in the arm for oft-forgotten Alamar, the ugly collection of '70s apartment blocks that gave birth to Cuban hip-hop and can now concentrate on fostering plenty more urban creativity. The center offers free entry and a wi-fi zone.

Information

MEDICAL SERVICES

Pharmacy (☎7-796-7146; cnr Av 5, btwn Calles 472 & 474; ⌚9am-6pm Mon-Fri) In Guanabo; basics only.

MONEY

Banco de Crédito y Comercio (Paseo Panamericano; ⌚8:30am-3pm Mon-Fri, to 11am Sat) Changes money and gives cash advances.

Banco Popular de Ahorro (Av 5 No 47810, btwn Calles 478 & 480; ⌚9am-3pm Mon-Fri) In Guanabo; has an ATM.

Cadeca (Av 5 No 47612, btwn Calles 476 & 478; ⌚8am-6pm)

POST

Post Office (Av 5, btwn Calles 490 & 492; ⌚9am-5pm Mon-Sat)

TOURIST INFORMATION

Infotur (Av de las Terrazas, Edificio los Corales, btwn Calles 10 & 11; ⌚8:15am-4:15pm) Helpful government tourist office just behind Playa Santa María del Mar.

Infotur (Av 5, btwn Calles 468 & 470; ⌚8:15am-4:15pm) Helpful government tourist office on Guanabo's main drag.

Getting There & Away

BUS

Habana Bus Tour's T3 bus runs a service every 40 minutes from Parque Central to Playa Santa María del Mar, stopping at Tarará, Club Mégano, Hotel Tropicoco and Club Atlántico. It doesn't go as far as Guanabo. All-day tickets cost CUC$5. Bus A40 stops at the roundabout at Calle 462 and Av 5 in Guanabo before heading into Havana where it terminates near Habana Vieja's central train station. It's usually crowded but costs only CUC$0.05 and runs every 20 minutes.

CAR

You can find **Cubacar** car-rental branches at Hotel Tropicoco (☎7-797-1650; cnr Av de las Terrazas & Av de las Banderas; ⌚9am-5pm) and in Guanabo (☎7-214-0090; cnr Calle 464 & Av 5; ⌚9am-5pm).

Servi-Cupet gas stations are located in Guanabo (cnr Av 5 & Calle 464; ⌚24hr) and west of Bacuranao (Vía Blanca; ⌚24hr).

TAXI

A car from Centro Habana to Playas del Este costs between CUC$15 and CUC$20 depending on your bargaining skills.

Artemisa & Mayabeque Provinces

☎ 47 (48 IN LAS TERRAZAS & SOROA) / POP 885,545

Includes ➡

Best Places to Eat

- El Romero (p153)
- Casa del Campesino (p153)
- San Miguel (p148)
- Don Oliva (p147)

Best Places to Sleep

- Maité Delgado (p150)
- Castillo de las Nubes (p150)
- Hotel Moka (p153)
- Memories Jibacoa Beach (p156)

Why Go?

Leap-frogged by almost all international visitors, Cuba's two smallest provinces, created by dividing Havana Province in half in 2010, are the preserve of more everyday concerns – like growing half of the crops that feed the nation, for example. But in among the patchwork of citrus and pineapple fields lie a smattering of small towns that will satisfy the curious and the brave.

The most interesting corner is Las Terrazas and Soroa, Cuba's most successful ecoproject and an increasingly important nexus for trekking and birdwatching. East of Havana, Jibacoa's beaches are the domain of a trickle of Varadero-avoiding tourists who guard their secret tightly. Wander elsewhere and you'll be in mainly Cuban company (or none at all) contemplating sugar-plantation ruins, weird one-of-a-kind museums, and improbably riotous festivals. For a kaleidoscope of the whole region take the ridiculously slow Hershey train through the nation's proverbial backyard and admire the view.

When to Go

- The provinces' attractions vary considerably climate-wise. Because of their unique geographical situation, Soroa and Las Terrazas have a microclimate: more rain and minimum monthly temperatures 2°C to 3°C colder than Havana.
- The big parties around here are December for the carnivalesque frivolity of Bejucal's Las Charangas and April for the International Humor Festival in San Antonio de los Baños.
- December through April is best for the beaches at Playa Jibacoa.

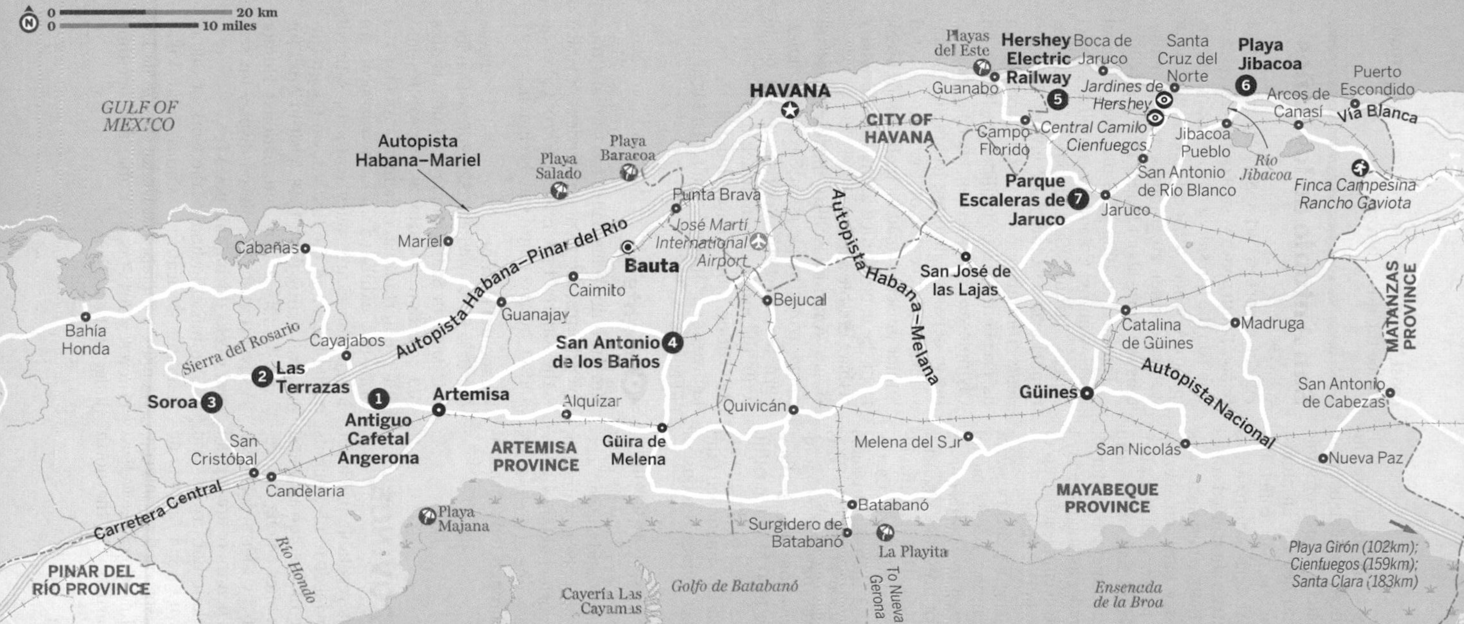

Artemisa & Mayabeque Provinces Highlights

1. **Antiguo Cafetal Angerona** (p147) Roaming the abandoned ruins of a once-mighty coffee plantation.
2. **Las Terrazas** (p151) Going green at Cuba's primary ecovillage, where the slopes have been replanted with trees, orchids, painters and poets.
3. **Soroa** (p148) Hiking in the 'rainbow of Cuba' amid giant ferns and diminutive orchids.
4. **Museo del Humor** (p146) Seeing the funny side of San Antonio de los Baños.
5. **Hershey Electric Railway** (p155) Escaping the tourist trails on the still-functioning electric railway of an erstwhile chocolate czar.
6. **Playa Jibacoa** (p154) Bagging a beach retreat where you can snorkel direct from the shore.
7. **Parque Escaleras de Jaruco** (p156) Feasting with a view and weekending Havana folk amid the heights of Mayabeque.

History

Havana was originally founded on the site of modern-day Surgidero de Batabanó in 1515 but rapidly relocated; the region's role in shaping Cuba was to become an almost exclusively agricultural one, with coffee and sugar the key crops. Western Artemisa was the center of the country's short-lived coffee boom from 1820 until 1840, when sugar took over as the main industry. Large numbers of slaves were recruited to work on the plantations during the second half of the 19th century, when Cuba became the center of the Caribbean slave trade; as such, the area became a focus for the events leading up to the abolition of slavery in the 1880s.

The success of the sugar industry swept over into the 20th century: sweets mogul Milton S Hershey turned to Mayabeque as a dependable source for providing sugar for his milk chocolate in 1914. This lucrative industry would later suffer under Fidel Castro, once the Americans and then the Russians ceased to buy Cuba's sugar at over-the-odds prices. The region was hard-hit economically, and this deprivation was perhaps best epitomized by the 1980 Mariel Boatlift, when a port on the coast west of Havana became the stage for a Castro-sanctioned (and Jimmy Carter–endorsed) mass exodus of Cubans to Florida.

A major step against the area's downturn was taken in 1968. Neglected land in western Artemisa Province, around the very coffee plantations that had once sustained it, was reforested and transformed into a pioneering ecovillage – now one of the region's economic mainstays through the tourism it has generated.

ARTEMISA PROVINCE

In many ways a giant vegetable patch for Havana, Artemisa Province's fertile delights include the ecovillage of Las Terrazas and the outdoor action on offer among the scenic forested slopes of the Sierra del Rosario mountain range. Then there are myriad mystery-clad coffee-plantation ruins and the ever-inventive town of San Antonio de los Baños, which has spawned an internationally renowned film school as well as some of Cuba's top artists. On the north coast, good beaches and great back roads entice the adventurous.

San Antonio de los Baños

POP 35,980

Full of surprises, artsy San Antonio de los Baños, 35km southwest of central Havana, is Cuba on the flip side, a hard-working municipal town where the local college churns out wannabe cinematographers and the museums are more about laughs than crafts.

Founded in 1986 with the help of Nobel Prize–winning Colombian novelist Gabriel García Márquez, San Antonio's Escuela Internacional de Cine y TV invites film students from around the world to partake in its excellent on-site facilities, including an Olympic-sized swimming pool for practicing underwater shooting techniques. Meanwhile, in the center of town, an unusual humor museum makes a ha-ha-happy break from the usual stuffed animal/revolutionary artifact double act.

San Antonio is also the birthplace of *nueva trova* music giant Silvio Rodríguez, born here in 1946. Rodríguez went on to write the musical soundtrack to the Cuban Revolution almost single-handed. His best-known songs include 'Ojalá,' 'La Maza' and 'El Necio.'

Sights

San Antonio de los Baños has several attractive squares, the most resplendent of which is the square at the intersection of Calles 66 and 41, overseen by a stately church.

Museo del Humor MUSEUM

(cnr Calle 60 & Av 45; CUC$2; 10am-6pm Tue-Sat, 9am-1pm Sun) Unique in Cuba is this fun selection of cartoons, caricatures and other entertaining ephemera. Among the drawings exhibited in a neoclassical colonial house are saucy cartoons, satirical scribblings and the first known Cuban caricature, dating from 1848. Visit in April for extra laughs at the International Humor Festival (entries remain on display for several weeks during this period).

The museum houses the work of Cuba's foremost caricaturist, Carlos Julio Villar Alemán, a member of Uneac (Unión de Escritores y Artistas de Cuba) and one-time judge at the festival.

A few times monthly music and ballet are also staged here.

Galería Provincial Eduardo Abela GALLERY
(Calle 58 No 3708, cnr Calle 37; ⌚noon-8pm Mon-Fri, 8am-8pm Sat, 8am-noon Sun) FREE This bold and groundbreaking art gallery is anything but provincial. The first room focuses on painting while others showcase poignant black-and-white photography. The gallery is named after city son Eduardo Abela, a Cuban artist perhaps most famous for creating El Bobo (The Fool), a cartoon character who poked fun at the Gerardo Machado dictatorship of the 1920s and '30s.

Sleeping & Eating

San Antonio's main shopping strip is Av 41, and there are numerous places to snack on peso treats along this street. Full-blown restaurants are thinner on the ground, but there's at least one goodie.

Hotel Las Yagrumas HOTEL $$
(☎47-38-44-60; Calle 40 y Final Autopista; s/d from CUC$38/52; P ❄ ≋) A hotel of untapped potential, Las Yagrumas, 3km north of San Antonio de los Baños, overlooks the picturesque but polluted Río Ariguanabo. Its 120 rooms with balcony and terrace (some river facing) are popular with peso-paying Cubans as opposed to foreign tourists, but many fixtures are falling apart. Sports facilities are better; there's table tennis and a gigantic pool (nonguests pay CUC$6).

Boat trips take off on the nearby river. A motor boat will take you on an 8km spin for CUC$3, while rowing boats go for CUC$1 an hour.

Don Oliva CUBAN $
(☎47-38-23-70; Calle 62 No 3512, btwn Calles 33 & 35; mains CUC$3-5; ⌚noon-11pm Tue-Sun) Quite possibly the cheapest lobster in Cuba is served on Don Oliva's secluded covered patio; the price comes in at around CUC$5, and it's not bad either. Not surprisingly this is a refreshingly untouristed private restaurant with prices displayed in *moneda nacional*. Opt for the seafood.

Drinking & Nightlife

Taberna del Tío Cabrera CLUB
(Calle 56 No 3910, btwn Calles 39 & 41; ⌚2-5pm Mon-Fri, 2pm-1am Sat & Sun) An attractive garden nightclub that puts on occasional comedy shows organized in conjunction with the Museo del Humor (opposite). The clientele is a mix of townies, folk from surrounding villages and film-school students.

Getting There & Away

Hard to get to without a car, San Antonio is supposedly connected to Havana's Estación 19 de Noviembre (CUC$1.50, one hour, four trains a day), but check well ahead. Otherwise, a taxi should cost CUC$35 one-way from central Havana (45 minutes).

Artemisa

POP 57,160

Becoming the capital of Artemisa Province in 2010 didn't exactly transform Artemisa into a tourist mecca: this farming town's days of affluence and appeal lie firmly embedded in the past. Having once attracted notables such as Ernest Hemingway and the Cuban poet Nicolás Guillén, and having grown wealthy on the back of 19th-century sugar and coffee booms, Artemisa's importance declined when the bottom fell out of the sugar and coffee industries. It's known today as the Villa Roja (Red Town) for the famous fertility of its soil, which still yields a rich annual harvest of tobacco, bananas and sugarcane.

Artemisa has no accommodations for tourists: Soroa is the nearest option. As if in compensation, it has one of provincial Cuba's nicest *bulevares* (pedestrianized shopping streets) recently given an injection of government money.

Sights

★Antiguo Cafetal Angerona HISTORIC SITE
(⌚dawn-dusk) FREE The Antiguo Cafetal Angerona, 5km west of Artemisa on the road to the Autopista Habana–Pinar del Río (A4), was one of Cuba's earliest *cafetales* (coffee farms). Erected between 1813 and 1820 by Cornelio Sauchay, Angerona once employed 450 slaves tending 750,000 coffee plants. Behind the ruined mansion lie the slave barracks, an old watchtower from which the slaves were monitored, and multiple storage cellars. Receiving few visitors, it's a great place to take creative photos as you quietly contemplate Cuba's past.

The quiet, atmospheric walls and arches surrounded by sugarcane and gnarly trees have the feel of a latter-day Roman ruin. Look for the stone-pillared gateway and sign on the right after you leave Artemisa.

The estate is mentioned in novels by Cirilo Villaverde and Alejo Carpentier, and James A Michener devotes several pages to it in *Six Days in Havana*.

Mausoleo a los Mártires de Artemisa MAUSOLEUM
(☎47-36-32-76; Av 28 de Enero; ⊙9am-5pm Tue-Sun) FREE Revolution buffs may want to doff a cap to the Mausoleo a los Mártires de Artemisa. Of the 119 revolutionaries who accompanied Fidel Castro in the 1953 assault on the Moncada Barracks, 28 were from Artemisa or this region. Fourteen of the men buried below the cube-shaped bronze mausoleum died in the assault or were killed soon after by Batista's troops. The other Moncada veterans buried here died later in the Sierra Maestra. A small subterranean museum contains combatants' photos and personal effects.

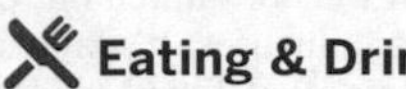

Eating & Drinking

Because it receives practically zero tourists, Artemisa's private restaurants are cheap and orientated primarily toward Cubans. Notwithstanding, there are a couple of good ones.

Los Nardis CUBAN $
(cnr Calle 49 & Calle 42; mains CUC$3-6; ⊙noon-midnight Tue-Sun) Unsignposted thus hard-to-find private restaurant a block from the main drag (Av 28 de Enero) that serves unadorned Cuban dishes featuring *mucho* rice and beans.

San Miguel CUBAN $
(Calle 45 No 4811, btwn Calle 48 & Calle 50; mains CUC$2-4; ⊙10am-11pm) Cute paladar (privately owned restaurant) serving unusual (for Artemisa) dishes including crab and *bistec uruguayo* (Uruguayan steak). Favored by locals.

Cafe Cubita CAFE
(Búlevar, btwn Maceo & General Gómez; ⊙10am-10pm Sun-Thu, 10am-midnight Fri & Sat) This is one of the best outlets of Cuba's reinvigorated coffee chain, with comfortable seating, a comprehensive coffee menu and table service. Bonus: it does cheap (CUC$1 to CUC$2) toasted sandwiches on fresh Cuban bread. Practically everyone opts for the *café helado* (coffee ice-cream milk shake).

Getting There & Away

The bus station is on the Carretera Central in the center of Artemisa (local buses only).

Artemisa train station (Av Héroes del Moncada) is four blocks east of the bus station. There are supposed to be two trains a day from Havana (CUC$2.20, two hours) at noon and midnight, but don't bank on it.

Soroa

POP 7200

Known appropriately as the 'rainbow of Cuba,' Soroa, a gorgeous natural area and tiny settlement 85km southwest of Havana, is the closest mountain resort to the capital. Located 8km north of Candelaria in the Sierra del Rosario, the easternmost and highest section of the Cordillera de Guaniguanico, the region's heavy rainfall (more than 1300mm annually) promotes the growth of tall trees and orchids. The area gets its name from Jean-Pierre Soroa, a Frenchman who owned a 19th-century coffee plantation in these hills. One of his descendants, Ignacio Soroa, created the park as a personal retreat in the 1920s, and only since the revolution has this luxuriant region been developed for tourism.

While it shares the same abundant flora as Las Terrazas, Soroa is generally quieter and receives less tourists. It's a great area to explore by bike.

Sights

All Soroa's sights are conveniently near Hotel & Villas Soroa (p150), where you can organize horseback riding and a variety of hikes into the surrounding forest and a couple of local communities. Alternatively, ask at your casa particular. Other trails lead to a rock formation known as Labyrinth de la Sierra Derrumbada and an idyllic bathing pool, the Poza del Amor (Pond of Love). The hotel is the main information point for the area.

Finca Excelencia FARM
(Carretera Soroa Km 11; ⊙dawn-dusk) FREE Fitting right into the ecological rainbow of Soroa is this private farm that has recently opened its gates to curious travelers. Stroll through the diligently tilled sloping grounds and feast your eyes upon 140 va-

rieties of fruit (blended into juices and smoothies) and over 300 types of orchids. Higher up sit two *miradores* (lookouts) that teeter over tremendous views painted with a hundred different shades of green. The quietly inspiring owner will happily show you round.

Orquideario Soroa GARDENS
(Carretera Soroa Km 9; CUC$3; ⌚8:30am-4:30pm) Tumbling down a landscaped hillside garden next door to Hotel & Villas Soroa (p150) is a labor of love built by Spanish lawyer Tomás Felipe Camacho, in memory of his wife and daughter in the late 1940s. Camacho traveled round the world to amass his collection of 700 orchid species (the largest in Cuba), including many endemic plants. Though he died in the 1960s, the Orquideario, connected to the University of Pinar del Río, lives on with guided tours in Spanish or English.

Salto del Arco Iris WATERFALL
(Carretera Soroa Km 8; CUC$3; ⌚9am-6pm) This is a 22m waterfall on the Arroyo Manantiales. The entrance to the park encompassing it is to the right just before the Hotel & Villas Soroa (p150). A path corkscrews to two viewpoints above and below the falls, at their most impressive in the May-to-October rainy season and at other times a trickle. You can swim here.

Activities

This part of the Sierra del Rosario is one of the best birdwatching sites in western Cuba after the Ciénaga de Zapata. You don't have to venture far from Hotel & Villas Soroa (p150) to see species such as the tocororo or Cuban trogon and the entertaining Cuban tody. Guided tours, arranged through the hotel, are from between CUC$6 and CUC$8 per hour.

You can arrange and pay for the hikes at Hotel & Villas Soroa (p150) or at most local casas particulares.

★Mirador Loma El Mogote HIKING
(Carretera Soroa Km 8) Starting at the Baños Romanos (p150), take the signposted well-trodden path 2km uphill to the Mirador, a rocky crag with an incredible sweeping panorama of all Soroa and the coastal flats beyond. Hungry turkey vultures circle below you.

OFF THE BEATEN TRACK

NORTH COAST BEACHES

The coastline along the north of Artemisa is occasionally visited for its little-used back road from Havana through to Bahía Honda and on to Pinar del Río Province (mostly by cyclists). The monstrous, and highly polluted, main settlement here, Mariel, is best known for the 125,000 Cubans who left for Florida in the 1980 Mariel Boatlift. But east of Mariel are a couple of decent (and unpolluted) beaches.

Playa Salado is a largely deserted beach with some 15 dive sites lying offshore, mostly accessed via excursion groups from Havana. Playa Baracoa, a few kilometers further east, is more developed. Big dudes near the shoreline lean on old American cars sipping beer while fishers throw lines from the rocky shore. A couple of basic beach shacks sell food, but there are no notable accommodations in the area.

El Brujito HIKING
(per person CUC$15) This hike goes to the tiny village of El Brujito, still inhabited by the descendants of slaves who once worked on a former French-run coffee plantation. It's the area's longest walk at around 15km. You'll need around seven hours to complete it with a guide.

Ruinas de los Cafetales Franceses HIKING
(per person CUC$12) Adjacent to Las Terrazas, Soroa also sits within the region's former coffee-growing area and the ruins of several French coffee farms – La Independencia, La Esperanza and La Merced – can be seen during this four-hour hike that pitches northeast from the Villa Soroa.

La Rosita HIKING
(per person CUC$12) For some great birdwatching, head out on this, one of the more adventurous trails in Soroa, to the former ecovillage of La Rosita (itself sadly destroyed by a recent hurricane), perched in the hills beyond the Hotel & Villas Soroa (p150). Nevertheless, this is one of the all-too-rare, hands-on opportunities to experience rural life as Cubans do – without the 'acting up' to tourists. It's around 8km long.

OFF THE BEATEN TRACK

BAHÍA HONDA

The wild, whirling road north from Soroa along the coast to either Bahía Honda and the north of Pinar del Río Province (west) or Havana (east) is surprisingly low-key and bucolic. You'll feel as if you're 1000km from the busy capital here. Forested hills give way to rice paddies in the shaded river valleys as you breeze past a picturesque succession of thatched farmhouses, craning royal palms and machete-wielding *guajiros* (rural workers). It makes a tough but highly rewarding cycling route.

Bahía Honda itself is a small bustling town with a pretty church. Despite its relative proximity to Havana, you'll feel strangely isolated here, particularly as the road deteriorates after Soroa.

Baños Romanos SWIMMING

(Carretera Soroa Km 8; per hr CUC$5) Roman they're not, but this stone bathhouse on the opposite side of the stream from the Salto del Arco Iris (p149) car park has a pool of cold sulfurous water. Ask at Hotel & Villas Soroa about the baths and massage treatments.

Sleeping & Eating

Nearly every house along the road from Candelaria to Soroa rents rooms and, with the recent opening of the Castillo de las Nubes, there are now two hotels. Soroa makes an excellent alternative base for visiting Las Terrazas and, in its own way, is equally beautiful.

All the accommodation places in Soroa provide food, with the casas particulares offering the best nosh. Good job, too, as there aren't many stand-alone restaurants.

★ **Maité Delgado** CASA PARTICULAR $

(52-27-00-69; yeisondelg@nauta.cu; Carretera Soroa Km 7; r CUC$25-30; P ❄) A bright family casa within easy walking distance of the Soroa sights, Maité's is a slice of rustic heaven with rocking chairs on the porch, a verdant garden and five funky rooms decked out in designer decor. Comfort in *el campo* (the countryside). English is spoken and dinner is prepared on request.

Don Agapito CASA PARTICULAR $

(58-12-17-91; donagapitosoroa@nauta.cu; Carretera Soroa Km 8; r CUC$20-25; P ❄) Two fantastic well-lit, super-clean rooms and some professional touches, including a personalized giant map of the province, make a stopover at this Soroa casa particular right next to the Orquideario (p149) a real pleasure. The food is equally marvelous. Check out the garden with its own plant-festooned mini-cave!

Hotel & Villas Soroa RESORT $$

(48-52-35-34; Carretera Soroa Km 9; s/d/tr incl breakfast CUC$59/88/115; P ❄ 📶 🏊) You can't knock the setting of this place nestled in a narrow valley amid stately trees and verdant hills (though you might wonder about the juxtaposition of these scattered block-like cabins against such a breathtaking natural backdrop). Isolated and tranquil, there are 80 rooms in a spacious complex just shouting distance from the forest, along with an inviting pool, a small shop and an ordinary restaurant.

The hotel also has four-, six- and eight-person casas to rent (from CUC$60 to CUC$120). Elsewhere on the campus there's a disco and an office where you can arrange and pay for numerous activities, including hiking and birdwatching.

Castillo de las Nubes BOUTIQUE HOTEL $$$

(Castle of the Clouds; 48-52-35-34; s/d/ste CUC$150/175/250; P ❄ 📶 🏊) A romantic faux-European castle with a circular tower on a hilltop 1.5km up a rough road beyond the Orquideario Soroa (p149), the Castillo de las Nubes was built by wealthy farmer Antonio Arturo Bustamante in 1940, but was quickly abandoned after the revolution. In 2016, it reopened as a six-room boutique hotel with a bar-restaurant, small pool and expansive Soroa views in every direction.

Restaurante el Salto CUBAN $

(Carretera Soroa Km 8; mains CUC$5-12; 9am-7pm; P) This simple place next to the Baños Romanos is one of the few independent eating options outside Soroa's hotels and casas particulares. It serves basic Cuban food, high on bulk, if low on taste.

Getting There & Away

The Havana–Viñales Víazul (www.viazul.com) bus stops in Las Terrazas, but not Soroa; you can cover the last 16km in a taxi for CUC$15

(15 minutes). If staying at a casa particular, ask about lifts. Transfer buses (not to be depended upon) sometimes pass through Soroa between Viñales and Havana. Inquire at Hotel & Villas Soroa, or at Infotur in Viñales (p182) or Havana (p120).

The only other access to Soroa and the surrounding area is with your own wheels: car, bicycle or moped. The Servi-Cupet gas station is on the Autopista at the turnoff to Candelaria, 8km below Soroa.

Las Terrazas

POP 1200

The pioneering ecovillage of Las Terrazas dates back to a reforestation project in 1968. Today it's a Unesco Biosphere Reserve, a burgeoning activity center (with a canopy tour) and the site of the earliest coffee plantations in Cuba. Not surprisingly, it attracts day-trippers from Havana by the busload.

Over-nighters can stay in the community's sole hotel, the mold-breaking Hotel Moka, an upmarket ecoresort built between 1992 and 1994 by workers drawn from Las Terrazas to attract foreign tourists. Close by, in the picturesque whitewashed village that overlooks a small lake, there's a vibrant art community with open studios, woodwork and pottery workshops. But the region's biggest attraction is its verdant natural surroundings, which are ideal for hiking, relaxing and birdwatching.

Sights

Cafetal Buenavista HISTORIC SITE

FREE The most moving ruins in Las Terrazas are about 1.5km up the hill from the Puerta las Delicias (p154) eastern gate, and accessible by road. Cafetal Buenavista is Cuba's oldest (now partially restored) coffee plantation, built in 1801 by French refugees from Haiti. Ruins of the quarters of some of the 126 slaves held by the French-Cuban owners here can be seen alongside the driers.

The attic of the master's house (now a restaurant) was used to store the beans until they could be carried down to the port of Mariel by mule. There are decent views from here, best appreciated on the Sendero las Delicias hike (p153) which incorporates the *cafetal*.

The huge *tajona* (grindstone) out the back once extracted coffee beans from their shells. The beans were then sun-dried on huge platforms.

Casa-Museo Polo Montañez MUSEUM

(9am-5pm Mon-Fri) FREE The former lakeside house of local *guajiro* musician Polo Montañez, regarded as one of Cuba's finest-ever folk singers, is now a small museum containing various gold records and assorted memorabilia. It's right in Las Terrazas village, overlooking the lake.

Polo's most famous songs include 'Guajiro Natural' and 'Un Montón de Estrellas'; they captured the heart of the nation between 2000 and 2002 with simple lyrics about love and nature. His stardom was short-lived, however: he died in a car accident in 2002.

San Pedro & Santa Catalina HISTORIC SITE

FREE These 19th-century coffee-estate ruins are down a branch road at La Cañada del Infierno (Trail to Hell), midway between the Hotel Moka (p153) access road and the Soroa side entrance gate. A kilometer off the main road, just before the ruins of the San Pedro coffee estate, a bar overlooks a popular swimming spot. After this it's another kilometer to Santa Catalina.

A trail leads on from here to Soroa.

Hacienda Unión HISTORIC SITE

FREE About 3.5km west of the Hotel Moka (p153) access road, the Hacienda Unión is another partially reconstructed coffee-estate ruin that features a country-style restaurant, a small flower garden known as the Jardín Unión, and **horseback riding** (per hour CUC$6).

La Plaza PLAZA

(9am-5pm) In the middle of Las Terrazas village at the top of a large knoll, this minimall encompasses a cinema, a cafe, a library and a small ecomuseum that gives an overview of the community's short history. All are generally open throughout the day, or can become so if you ask at the Oficinas del Complejo (p154).

Galería de Lester Campa GALLERY

(daily, hours vary) FREE Several well-known Cuban artists are based at Las Terrazas, including Lester Campa, whose work has been exhibited internationally. Pop into his lakeside studio-gallery, on the right-hand side a few houses after Casa-Museo Polo Montañez.

Activities

The Sierra del Rosario has some of the best hikes in Cuba. However, they're all guided, so you can't officially do any of them on your own (nonexistent signposting deters all but the hardiest from trying). On the upside, most of the area's guides are highly trained, which means you'll emerge from the experience both fitter and wiser. There were four different hikes available at last visit, each costing CUC$19 per person. Book at the Oficinas del Complejo (p154) or Hotel Moka.

★ Sendero la Serafina HIKING

(per person CUC$19) The easy 6.4km La Serafina loop starts and finishes near the Rancho Curujey. It's a well-known paradise for birdwatchers (there are more than 70 species on show). Halfway through the walk you will pass the ruins of the Cafetal Santa Serafina, one of the first coffee farms in the Caribbean. Reserve three hours for this guided excursion.

Baños del San Juan SWIMMING

(incl lunch CUC$15; ⏲9am-7pm) It's hard to envisage more idyllic natural swimming pools than those situated 3km to the south of Hotel Moka (opposite) down an undulating paved road. These *baños* (baths) are surrounded by naturally terraced rocks, where the clean, bracing waters cascade into a series of pools.

Riverside, there are a handful of open-air eating places, along with changing rooms, showers and overnight **cabins** (☎48-57-86-00; s/d CUC$15/25), though the spot still manages to retain a sense of rustic isolation.

El Taburete HIKING

(per person CUC$19) This 5.6km hike has the same start/finish point as El Contento, but follows a more direct route over the 452m Loma el Taburete where a poignant monument is dedicated to the 38 Cuban guerrillas who trained in these hills for Che Guevara's ill-fated Bolivian adventure.

As with the El Contento hike, you'll have to walk 5km along a quiet road to get back to the start, or arrange a taxi (around CUC$3).

Book and pay at the Oficinas del Complejo (p154) or Hotel Moka.

El Contento HIKING

(per person CUC$19) This 7.6km ramble takes you through the reserve's foothills between the Campismo el Taburete (rustic accommodation for Cubans only) and the Baños del San Juan (p152), taking in two coffee-estate ruins: San Ildelfonso and El Contento. You'll have to hike 5km along a quiet road to get back to the start or arrange a taxi (around CUC$3).

BIRTH OF AN ECOPROJECT

Back in 1968, when the nascent environmental movement was a prickly protest group led by hippies with names like 'Swampy,' the forward-thinking Cubans – concerned about the ecological cost of island-wide deforestation – came up with an idea.

The plan involved taking a 50-sq-km tract of degraded land in Cuba's western mountains that had once supported a network of French coffee farms and reforesting it on terraced, erosion-resistant slopes. In 1971, with the first phase of the plan completed, the workers on the project were tasked to create a reservoir, and on its shores construct a small settlement of white houses to provide much-needed housing for the area's disparate inhabitants.

The result was Las Terrazas, Cuba's first ecovillage, a thriving community of 1200 inhabitants whose self-supporting, sustainable settlement today includes a hotel, myriad artisan shops and a vegetarian restaurant, and uses small-scale organic farming techniques. The project was so successful that, in 1985, the land around Las Terrazas was incorporated into Cuba's first Unesco Biosphere Reserve, the Sierra del Rosario.

In 1994, as the tourist industry was expanded to counteract the economic effects of the Special Period, Las Terrazas opened Hotel Moka, an environmentally congruous hotel designed by minister of tourism and green architect Osmani Cienfuegos, brother of the late revolutionary hero Camilo.

Now established as Cuba's most authentic ecoresort, Las Terrazas operates on guiding principles that include energy efficiency, sustainable agriculture, environmental education and a sense of harmony between buildings and landscape. Far from being degraded, the hills around Las Terrazas these days attract the country's most diverse and abundant birdlife.

Sendero las Delicias HIKING
(per person CUC$19) This 3km route runs from Rancho Curujey to the Cafetal Buenavista (p151), incorporating some fantastic views and plenty of birdwatching opportunities. Book and pay at the Oficinas del Complejo (p154) or Hotel Moka.

Tours

Canopy Tour ZIPLINING
(per person CUC$35) Cuba's original canopy tour has recently expanded from three to six ziplines that catapult you over Las Terrazas village and the Lago del San Juan like a turkey vulture in flight. The total 'flying' distance is 1600m. Professional instructors maintain high safety standards. To book the ziplining, get in touch with the Oficinas del Complejo (p154) near Rancho Curujey.

Sleeping

The ecofriendly Hotel Moka is Las Terrazas' emblematic hotel. From here, you can also book five rustic cabins 3km away in **Río San Juan** (single/double CUC$15/25) or arrange **tent camping** (CUC$12). There are also three **villas** (single/double CUC$105/120) available for rent in the village.

There are a couple of casas particulares on the eastern approach road, a kilometer or so outside the park entrance gate (p154).

Villa Duque CASA PARTICULAR $
(53-22-14-31; Carretera a Cayajabos Km 2, Finca San Andrés; r incl breakfast CUC$25; P) Ecotourism doesn't have to come at a cost. Those on a budget might wish to check out this farmhouse 2km before the eastern entrance of Las Terrazas, which has two spick-and-span rooms, a fridge full of beer, a wraparound balcony and breakfast included in the price. The fresh country smells come free of charge, too.

★**Hotel Moka** RESORT $$$
(48-57-86-00; s/d/tr all-inclusive CUC$158/180/247; P) Cuba's only *real* ecohotel might not qualify for the four stars it advertises, but who's arguing? With its trickling fountains, blooming flower garden and resident tree growing through the lobby, Moka would be a catch in any country. The 26 bright, spacious rooms have fridges, satellite TV and bathtubs with a stupendous view (there are blinds for the shy).

Equipped with a bar, restaurant, shop, pool and tennis court, the hotel also acts as an information center for the reserve and can organize everything from hiking to fishing.

Eating

Las Terrazas has a scattered collection of country-style restaurants, open to the elements and purveying simple *comida criolla* (Creole food). In the village itself there are some more esoteric offerings, including a bona fide vegetarian restaurant – a rarity in Cuba.

Casa del Campesino CARIBBEAN $
(mains CUC$5-8; 9am-9pm; P) Of the *ranchón*-style restaurants dotted around, this one adjacent to the Hacienda Unión (p151), about 3.5km west of the Hotel Moka access road, is a visitor favorite. The only proviso: you'd better like rice and beans.

El Romero VEGETARIAN $
(mains CUC$3-7; noon-9pm;) One of Cuba's few full-blown eco-restaurants, El Romero specializes in vegetarian fare, uses solar energy, homegrown organic vegetables and herbs, and keeps its own bees. You'll think you've woken up in San Francisco when you browse the menu replete with hummus, bean pancake, pumpkin and onion soup, and extra-virgin olive oil.

Rancho Curujey CARIBBEAN $
(snacks CUC$2-5; 9am-9pm; P) This *ranchón*-style set-up offers beer and snacks under a small thatched canopy overlooking Lago Palmar. The Serafina (opposite) and Las Delicias trailheads are here.

Fonda de Mercedes CUBAN $$
(mains CUC$6-8; 9am-9pm) On a terrace beside her home in an apartment block beneath Hotel Moka, Mercedes has been serving up vegetable soup and hearty home-cooked meat and fish dishes for years.

Casa de Botes SEAFOOD $$
(mains CUC$5-9; 9am-10pm) The community's fish specialist is suspended on stilts above Lago del San Juan where you can work up an appetite on a kayak first.

Drinking & Nightlife

Patio de Maria CAFE
(9am-10pm) Patio de María is a small, brightly painted coffee bar that might just qualify for the best brew in Cuba. The secret comes in the expert confection and the fact

that the beans are grown about 20m away from your cup in front of the flowery terrace. Frappés are also available.

Information

Las Terrazas is 20km northeast of Hotel & Villas Soroa (p150) and 13km west of the Havana–Pinar del Río Autopista at Cayajabos. There are toll gates at both entrances to the Biosphere Reserve (entry CUC$4 per person). The eastern toll gate, Puerta las Delicias, is a good source of information on the park, while the best place to get information and arrange excursions is at the **Oficinas del Complejo** (48-57-85-55, 48-57-87-00; 8am-5pm), adjacent to Rancho Curujey, or at Hotel Moka (p153), perched behind trees above the village. Both places act as nexus points for the reserve.

Getting There & Away

Two Víazul (www.viazul.com) buses a day currently stop at the Rancho Curujey (p153) next door to Las Terrazas; one at 10am bound for Pinar del Río and Viñales (CUC$8, 2¼ hours), the other at 4pm heading to Havana (CUC$6, 1½ hours). Occasional transfer buses, which run when they have enough passengers, pass through bound for Havana or Viñales. Inquire at Hotel Moka (p153) or contact the Viñales office of Infotur (p182).

MAYABEQUE PROVINCE

Tiny Mayabeque, now the country's smallest province, is a productive little place, cultivating citrus fruit, tobacco, grapes for wine and the sugarcane for Havana Club rum, the main distillery of which is in Santa Cruz del Norte. Tourists, predominantly Cubans, come here principally for the sandy coast in the northeast, drawn by the good-value resorts that back onto beautiful beaches for a fraction of the price of a Varadero vacation. Inland amid the workaday agricultural atmosphere lie some luxuriant scenic treats: landscaped gardens, the picturesque protected area of Jaruco, Cuba's most spectacular bridge, and *the* classic Cuban train journey transecting the lot.

Playa Jibacoa Area

Playa Jibacoa is the Varadero that never was, or the Varadero yet to come – depending on your hunch. For the time being it's a mainly Cuban getaway, with a coastal branch road from the main Vía Blanca highway winding by two small all-inclusive resorts, a hotel-standard campismo (cheap rustic accommodation) and several other shoreline sleeping options thrown in for good measure. Punctuated by a series of small but splendid beaches and blessed with good snorkeling accessible direct from the shore, Jibacoa is backed by a lofty limestone terrace overlooking the ocean. The terrace offers excellent views and some short DIY hikes.

The Vía Blanca, running between Havana and Matanzas, is the main transport artery in the area, although few buses make scheduled stops here, making Playa Jibacoa a more challenging pit stop than it should be. Just inland are picturesque farming communities and tiny time-warped hamlets linked by the Hershey Electric Railway.

Sights

Puente de Bacunayagua BRIDGE

Marking the border between Havana and Matanzas Provinces, this is Cuba's longest (314m) and highest (103m) bridge. Begun in 1957 and finally opened by Fidel Castro in September 1959, it carries the busy Vía Blanca across a densely wooded canyon that separates the Valle de Yumurí from the sea. There's a snack bar and observation deck (8am to 10pm) on the Havana side of the bridge, where you can sink some drinks in front of one of Cuba's most awe-inspiring views.

You'll be looking out over hundreds of royal palm trees standing like ghostly sentries on the sheering valley slopes and, in the distance, dark, bulbous hills and splashes of blue ocean.

The snack bar and observation deck are a favorite stopping-off point for tour buses and taxis, and aside from hiring a car, these are your only means of visiting.

Central Camilo Cienfuegos LANDMARK

Standing disused on a hilltop like a huge rusting iron skeleton, this former sugar mill, 5km south of Santa Cruz del Norte, was one of Cuba's largest and a testimony to the country's previous production clout. Opened in 1916, it once belonged to the Philadelphia-based Hershey Chocolate Company, which used the sugar to sweeten its world-famous chocolate. The Hershey Electric Railway (box opposite) used to transport produce and workers between

OFF THE BEATEN TRACK

THE HERSHEY TRAIN

'Cow on the line,' drawls the bored-looking ticket seller. 'Train shut for cleaning,' reads a scruffy hand-scrawled notice. To *habaneros*, the catalog of daily transport delays is tediously familiar. While the name of the antique Hershey Electric Railway might suggest a sweet treat to most visitors, in Cuba it signifies a more bitter mix of bumpy journeys, hard seats and interminable waits.

Built in 1921 by US chocolate 'czar' Milton S Hershey (1857–1945), the electric-powered railway line was originally designed to link the American mogul's humungous sugar mill in Mayabeque Province with stations in Matanzas and the capital. Running along a trailblazing rural route, it soon became a lifeline for isolated communities cut off from the provincial transport network.

In 1959 the Hershey factory was nationalized and renamed Central Camilo Cienfuegos after Cuba's celebrated rebel commander. But the train continued to operate, clinging unofficially to its chocolate-inspired nickname. In the true tradition of the post-revolutionary 'waste not, want not' economy, it also clung to the same tracks, locomotives, carriages, signals and stations.

While a long way from *Orient Express*–style luxury, an excursion on today's Hershey train is a captivating journey back in time to the days when cars were for rich people and sugar was king. For outsiders, this is Cuba as the Cubans see it. It's a microcosm of rural life with all its daily frustrations, conversations, foibles and – occasionally – fun.

The train seemingly stops at every house, hut, horse stable and hillock between Havana and Matanzas (CUC$2.80, four hours). Getting off is something of a toss-up. Beach bums can disembark at Guanabo (CUC$0.75, 1¼ hours) and wander 2km north for a taste of Havana's rustic eastern resorts. History buffs can get off at Central Camilo Cienfuegos (CUC$1.40, two hours) and stroll around the old Hershey sugar-mill ruins. You can also alight at Jibacoa (CUC$1.65, 2½ hours) for Playa Jibacoa's tucked-away beach paradise and at indeterminate stops through the beautiful Valle de Yumurí. *¡Buen viaje!*

Havana, Matanzas and the small town that grew up around the mill.

While the train still runs three times a day (and stops in the Jibacoa town center), the mill was closed in July 2002.

Jardines de Hershey GARDENS

These overgrown gardens, formerly owned by the famous American chocolate tycoon Milton Hershey who ran the nearby, former sugar mill, Central Camilo Cienfuegos, are charmingly wild these days with attractive paths, abundant green foliage and a beautiful river, plus a couple of thatched-roof restaurants. It's a serene spot for lunch and a stroll. The gardens are approximately 1km north of Camilo Cienfuegos train station on the Hershey train line. From Playa Jibacoa, it's a pleasantly walkable 4km south of Santa Cruz del Norte.

Activities

Playa Jibacoa is the only resort area in northern Cuba where you can snorkel and dive directly from the shore. You can borrow snorkeling gear for free if you're staying in Memories Jibacoa Beach (p156) and swim off from the beach. The resort also has a dive center offering immersions from CUC$25.

There is good snorkeling from the beach facing Campismo los Cocos (p156); heading westward along the coast you'll find unpopulated pockets where you can don a mask or relax under a palm.

The **Finca Campesina Rancho Gaviota** (☎47-61-47-02; incl meal CUC$8; ⏰10am-5pm) is an activities center, 12km inland from Puerto Escondido via the pretty, palm-sprinkled Valle de Yumurí, which is usually incorporated in day trips from Matanzas and Varadero. The hilltop ranch overlooks a reservoir and offers horseback riding, kayaking and cycling, plus a massive feast of local Cuban fare. Huts showcase various elements of Cuban agriculture, such as coffee and sugarcane – with tastings.

For self-drivers getting to the *ranchón*, take the inland road for 2km to Arcos de Canasí and turn left at the fork for another 10km to the signpost.

Sleeping

Casas particulares are coming to Playa Jibacoa; they line the Matanzas end of the coast road after the last of the hotels. Look out for the blue-and-white *Arrendador Divisa* stickers.

Campismo los Cocos CAMPISMO **$**
(☎47-29-52-31; www.campismopopular.cu; s/d CUC$30/45; P ❄ ≋) The newest and nicest of Cubamar's 80 or more campismo sites, Los Cocos has facilities to match a midrange hotel and a beachside setting that emulates the big shots in Varadero. Ninety self-contained cabins are clustered around a pool set in the crook of the province's low, steplike cliffs.

Facilities include a small library, a medical post, an à la carte restaurant, a games room, rooms for travelers with disabilities and walking trails (up to a lookout on the limestone terrace backing the site). The downsides: poor maintenance since the 2006 opening and blaring music around the pool.

Villa Jibacoa RESORT **$$**
(☎47-29-52-05; www.gran-caribe.com; Vía Blanca Km 60; s/d all-inclusive CUC$120/150; P ❄ @ ≋) This small, well-landscaped resort has great snorkeling and large spick-and-span rooms in cute concrete bungalows. Posh it isn't. Instead it's marketed as a three-star and is popular with repeat-visit package tourists from Canada.

★**Memories Jibacoa Beach** RESORT **$$$**
(☎47-29-51-22; www.memoriesresorts.com; r all-inclusive from CUC$175; P ❄ @ ≋) Who knew? One of Cuba's best all-inclusive resorts isn't in Varadero (or any other resort strip for the matter), but in the more tranquil confines of Jibacoa. The secret? This 250-room resort doesn't try too hard. The trickling fountains, 24-hour pool and narrow but idyllic beach are elegantly unpretentious.

Then there's the joy of the surf and turf surroundings – snorkeling from the shore (with gear lent free to guests), an on-site dive center (immersions from CUC$25), and trekking into the uplifted terraces just inland. Formerly SuperClub Breezes, the resort was last renovated in 2012. Coming from Matanzas, the turnoff is 13km west of the Puente de Bacunayagua (p154).

Getting There & Away

The best – some would say the *only* – way to get to Playa Jibacoa is on the Hershey Electric Railway (p155) from Casablanca train station in Havana to **Jibacoa Pueblo** (CUC$1.65, 2½ hours). There's no bus to the beach from the station and traffic is sporadic, so bank on hiking the last 5km – a not unpleasant walk if you don't have too much gear.

Jaruco

POP 18,107

Jaruco, set back from the coast between Havana and Matanzas, is a good day trip for travelers with a car, moped or bike who want to give the beaches a body-swerve and instead sample quintessential rural Cuba.

Jaruco village is a wash of pastel-hued houses bunched along steeply pitching streets that wouldn't look amiss in the Peruvian Andes. The Parque Escaleras de Jaruco, 6km west, is even more precipitous, with its jungle-like vegetation and unmarked, narrow and winding roads. The protected area, featuring forests, caves and strangely shaped limestone cliffs, is the main reason for visiting the region.

Habaneros come here for bucolic weekend breaks Thursday through Sunday, the park's only official opening days, but with a minor road bisecting the park between Tapaste (off the Autopista Nacional) and Jaruco, you can slip in any time. This forgotten oasis has outstanding *miradores* (viewpoints) over Mayabeque Province.

Eating

A handful of Jaruco's restaurants open up from Thursday to Sunday and blare out cheesy music, which can disrupt the serenity.

El Criollo CUBAN **$**
(mains CUC$3-6; ⏲11:30am-5pm Thu-Sun) The best of the handful of Parque Escaleras de Jaruco's restaurants is the pleasant *ranchón*-style El Criollo, where you'll pay in pesos for various pork- and fish-focused offerings.

Getting There & Away

It's 32km to Jaruco from Guanabo in a southeasterly direction via Campo Florido, and you can make it a loop by returning through Santa Cruz del Norte, 18km northeast of Jaruco via

WORTH A TRIP

LAS CHARANGAS DE BEJUCAL

The journeyman town of Bejucal, like many settlements in Mayabeque Province, is not exactly overflowing with interesting things to do – unless you time your visit to coincide with Las Charangas on December 24, which compete with Las Parrandas of Remedios and Santiago's Carnival as Cuba's most cacophonous and colorful festival.

As in Remedios, the town splits into two competing groups, the Ceiba de Plata (Silver Ceiba) and the Espina de Oro (Golden Thorn), who hit the streets laughing, dancing and singing among outrageously large, dazzling floats and the famous Bejucal *tambores* (drums). The climax comes with the building of 20m-high towers made of brightly lit artistic displays in the main plaza, to the accompaniment of the music of the traditional conga. The displays mix tradition with topical news stories referencing everything from Santería deities to global warming. Las Charangas dates back to the early 1800s when the parading groups were split between creoles and black slaves (the racial discriminations no longer exist), making it one of Cuba's oldest festivals.

There's no real accommodation in town for travelers, but at 40km from Havana, Bejucal is in easy day-tripping reach. The only option for reaching Bejucal other than train is by taxi or private car (for around CUC$35 one-way, 40 minutes).

Central Camilo Cienfuegos. A taxi from Havana costs CUC$35 one-way (40 minutes).

It's possible to get to Jaruco on a branch line of the Hershey Electric Railway, a slow and ponderous journey. Take the train to Camilo Cienfuegos (CUC$1.40, two hours) then change onto a train south to Jaruco station (CUC$1, 30 minutes, eight trains a day).

Surgidero de Batabanó

POP 22,313

Spanish colonizers founded the original settlement of Havana on the site of Surgidero de Batabanó on August 25, 1515, but quickly abandoned it in favor of the north coast. Looking around the decrepit town today, with its tumbledown clapboard houses and grubby beachless seafront, it's not difficult to see why. The only reason you're likely to end up in this fly-blown port is during the purgatorial bus-boat trip to the Isla de la Juventud. Should there be unforeseen delays, either staying within the port confines or cabbing it back to Havana, however depressing, are preferable to spending any time in the town itself.

Fidel Castro and the other Moncada prisoners disembarked here on May 15, 1955, after Fulgencio Batista granted them amnesty. They made a quick getaway.

Eating

Surprise! The semi-abandoned afterthought of Surgidero de Batabanó has recently sprouted an OK restaurant.

Los Dos Hermanos CUBAN $

(Calle 68 No 521; mains CUC$2-5; noon-10pm) In a cute clapboard house that was once an elegant hotel lies the best answer to any ferry delay. Dos Hermanos serves straight-up Cuban nosh quickly and without unnecessary ceremony. Dig in; your next decent meal (if you're heading to La Isla) could be a long way away.

Getting There & Away

The ferry from Surgidero de Batabanó to the Isla de la Juventud (p165) is supposed to leave daily at 1pm with an additional sailing at 4pm on Friday and Sunday (two hours). It is highly advisable to buy your bus-boat combo ticket (CUC$50.20) in Havana from the office at the main Astro bus station (p121) rather than turning up and doing it here. More often than not convertible tickets are sold out to bus passengers.

For self-drivers, there's a **Servi-Cupet gas station** (Calle 64 No 7110, btwn Avenidas 71 & 73) in Batabanó town. The next Servi-Cupet station east is in Güines.

Isla de la Juventud (Special Municipality)

☎46 (45 ON CAYO LARGO DEL SUR) / POP 86,420

Includes ➡

Best Places to Eat

- ➡ Restaurante Tu Isla (p163)
- ➡ Restaurante Toti (p163)
- ➡ Ranchón Playa Sirena (p171)
- ➡ Restaurante El Abra (p164)

Best Places to Sleep

- ➡ Tu Isla (p163)
- ➡ Sol Cayo Largo (p170)
- ➡ Villa Choli (p163)
- ➡ Hotel Pelícano (p171)

Why Go?

A historic refuge from the law for everyone from 16th-century pirates to 20th-century gangsters, La Isla is perhaps the quirkiest castaway destination you ever will see. Dumped like a crumpled apostrophe 100km off mainland Cuba, this pine-tree-clad island is the Caribbean's sixth-largest. But the Cayman Islands this isn't. Other tourists? Uh-uh. And if you thought mainland Cuba's towns were time-warped, try blowing the dust off island capital Nueva Gerona, where the main street doubles as a baseball diamond, and the food 'scene' is stuck in the Special Period. Yet, if you make it here, you're in for a true adventure. The main lure is diving some of the Caribbean's most pristine reefs, but otherwise get used to being becalmed with the coral, the odd crocodile and a colorful history that reads like an excerpt from *Treasure Island*.

Further east, Cayo Largo del Sur is La Isla's polar opposite, a manufactured tourist enclave renowned for its wide, white-sand beaches.

When to Go

- ➡ The beach life, diving and snorkeling are highlights of La Isla, Cayo Largo or any of the other mini-paradises in the Archipiélago de los Canarreos. The hottest times are the best: July to August along with the cooler-but-balmy high season in December to April.
- ➡ Always-spirited Nueva Gerona ups the ante for its biggest party, Carnaval, in March.
- ➡ The best time for diving in the waters off the Isla de la Juventud is January to May when water clarity is good and the seas are generally calm.

Isla de la Juventud (Special Municipality) Highlights

1. **Nueva Gerona** (p160) Getting the lowdown on local life in the petite, sleepy island capital.
2. **Sierra de las Casas** (p161) Climbing the steep hills above Nueva Gerona to see the city (and island) splayed out below.
3. **Presidio Modelo** (p166) Exploring the ominous prison where Fidel Castro was once incarcerated.
4. **Cueva de Punta del Este** (p168) Seeing ancient cave paintings in the rarely visited militarized zone on the Isla de la Juventud.
5. **Punta Francés** (p167) Diving amid wrecks, walls, coral gardens and caves at, arguably, the best dive sites in Cuba.
6. **Playa Tortuga** (p169) Watching turtles nesting on the moonlit beaches of Cayo Largo del Sur.
7. **Playa Sirena** (p169) Trekking along the wide, white (sometimes nudist) beaches to Cayo Largo del Sur's finest stretch of sand.

History

La Isla's star-studded history starts with its first settlers, the Siboney, a pre-ceramic civilization who came to the island around 1000 BC via the Lesser Antilles. They named their new homeland Siguanea and created a fascinating set of cave paintings, which still survive in Cueva de Punta del Este.

Columbus arrived in June 1494 and promptly renamed the island Juan el Evangelista, claiming it for the Spanish crown. But the Spanish did little to develop their new possession, which was knotted with mangroves and surrounded by shallow reefs.

Instead La Isla became a hideout for pirates, including Francis Drake and Henry Morgan. They called it Parrot Island, and their exploits are said to have inspired Robert Louis Stevenson's novel *Treasure Island*.

In December 1830 the Colonia Reina Amalia (now Nueva Gerona) was founded, and throughout the 19th century the island served as a place of imposed exile for independence advocates and rebels, including José Martí. Twentieth-century dictators Gerardo Machado and Fulgencio Batista followed this Spanish example by sending political prisoners – Fidel Castro included – to the island, which had by then been renamed a fourth time as Isla de Pinos (Isle of Pines).

As the infamous 1901 Platt amendment placed Isla de Pinos outside the boundaries of the 'mainland' part of the archipelago, some 300 US colonists also settled here, working the citrus plantations and building the efficient infrastructure that survives today (albeit a tad more dilapidated). By the 1950s La Isla had become a favored vacation spot for rich Americans, who flew in daily from Miami. Fidel Castro abruptly ended the decadent party in 1959.

In the 1960s and 1970s, thousands of young people from across the developing world volunteered to study here at specially built 'secondary schools' (although their presence is almost non-existent today). In 1978 their role in developing the island was officially recognized when the name was changed for the fifth time to Isla de la Juventud (Isle of Youth).

ISLA DE LA JUVENTUD

Large, very detached and set to a slow metronome, La Isla is both historically and culturally different to the rest of the Cuban archipelago. Mass sugar and tobacco production never existed here, and until the Castro revolution, the island yielded to a greater American influence. Eclectic expat communities, which call on Cayman Island, American and Japanese ancestry, have even thrown up their own musical style, a sub-genre of Cuban *son* known as *sucu sucu*. Today the island, bereft of the foreign students that once populated its famous schools, is sleepy but extravagantly esoteric: with a prison masquerading as a museum and scuppered ships just waiting for you to dive down to – or to party in! The opportunities for getting (way) off the beaten track will appeal to divers, escape artists, adventurers and committed contrarians.

Nueva Gerona

POP 47,038

Flanked by the Sierra de las Casas to the west and the Sierra de Caballos to the east, Nueva Gerona is a small, unhurried town that hugs the left bank of the Río las Casas, the island's only large river. Its museums and vivacious entertainment scene will detain, entertain and drain you for a day or two before you trundle out to explore the swashbuckling south, and it has almost 100% of the island's somewhat scant services.

Sights

Museo Finca el Abra MUSEUM

(Carretera Siguanea Km 2; CUC$1; 9am-5pm Tue-Sat, to noon Sun) On October 17, 1870, the teenage José Martí spent nine weeks of exile at this farm before his deportation to Spain. Legend has it that the revolutionary's mother forged the shackles he wore here into a ring, which Martí wore to his death. Set below the Sierra de las Casas, the old hacienda's surroundings are as much of an attraction as the museum. It's signed off the main road to Hotel Colony (a continuation of Calle 41), 3km southwest of Nueva Gerona.

The house is still occupied by descendants of Giuseppe Girondella, who hosted Martí here. A dirt road just before the museum leads north to the island's former marble quarry, clearly visible in the distance.

El Pinero MONUMENT

(Calle 28, btwn Calle 33 & river) Two blocks east of Parque Guerrillero Heroico, you'll see

ISLA DE LOS CASINOS?

Oh, what could have been. Charles 'Lucky' Luciano, the 'Boss of Bosses' of the mafia world of the 1940s and 1950s, having sized up the Isla de los Pinos (as Isla de la Juventud was then known), decided in about 1946 that the isle was ripe for conversion into a gambling destination to rival Monte Carlo. American narcotics agents tracked down Luciano, who consequently had to flee Cuba, but his partner-in-crime Meyer Lansky did proceed with the scheme. In 1958, a Hilton Hotel with a casino was duly opened (now the Hotel Colony). But the days of decadence were short-lived. The coming of Fidel Castro a year later put a stop to gambling in Cuba for good. At least, that is the official line. However, merchandise produced to celebrate the opening of La Isla to high-stakes gaming can still be found in Cuban shops today.

a huge black-and-white ferry set up as a tatty memorial next to the river. This is El Pinero, the original boat used to transport passengers between La Isla and the main island. On May 15, 1955, Fidel and Raúl Castro, along with the other prisoners released from Moncada, returned to the main island on this vessel.

These days it's a meeting point for young reggaeton fanatics (read: very loud music).

Museo Municipal MUSEUM

(Calle 30, btwn Calles 37 & 39; CUC$1; ⏲9am-4:30pm Tue-Sun) In the former Casa de Gobierno (1853), the Museo Municipal houses a small historical collection that romps through the best of the island's past. It begins with a huge wall-mounted map of La Isla and continues through themed *salas* (rooms) relating to aboriginals, pirates, US occupiers (most interestingly including gangster Charles 'Lucky' Luciano) and some local art.

Nuestra Señora de los Dolores CHURCH

(cnr Calles 28 & 39) On the northwest side of Parque Guerrillero Heroico, this dinky, Mexican colonial-style church was built in 1926, after the original was destroyed by a hurricane. In 1957 the parish priest, Guillermo Sardiñas, left Nueva Gerona to join Fidel Castro in the Sierra Maestra, the only Cuban priest to do so.

Museo Casa Natal Jesús Montané MUSEUM

(cnr Calles 24 & 45; ⏲9:30am-5pm Tue-Sat, 8:30am-noon Sun) FREE This museum documents the life of revolutionary Jesús Montané, who was born here, took part in the Moncada Barracks attack in 1953, fought alongside Fidel in the Sierra Maestra, and served in the post-1959 government. It's a small but fascinating place and well worth 20 minutes of your time.

Activities

The area around Nueva Gerona is a good area to discover on bicycle, with beaches, and the big three attractions of the Presa El Abra reservoir, Museo Finca el Abra and the Presidio Modelo all only a few kilometers from the town center. The folk at Villa Choli (p163) in Nueva Gerona organize bike rental.

Sierra de las Casas HIKING

Behold the view from the northernmost face of the craggy Sierra de las Casas! From the west end of Calle 22, a few hundred meters along a dirt track, a sinuous trail on the left heads toward the hills, at the foot of which is a deep cave and a local swimming hole. Beyond here a trail ascends steeply for around 1.5km to the mountaintop.

The view from the summit is amazing, taking in half the island, though the final stretch of the ascent is a bit closer to rock scrambling than hiking. For the sure-footed only.

Presa El Abra WATER SPORTS

(Carretera Siguanea; ⏲noon-5:30pm) Where have all the folk from Nueva Gerona gone? Gone to cool off in Presa El Abra, every one. On a scalding La Isla afternoon, you'd best join them. With verdant shores (perfect for picnics), this wide *presa* (reservoir) has Nueva Gerona's best restaurant (p164), plus various craft for aquatic shenanigans, including kayaks (CUC$1.50 per hour) and aquatic bicycles (CUC$3 per hour).

Nueva Gerona

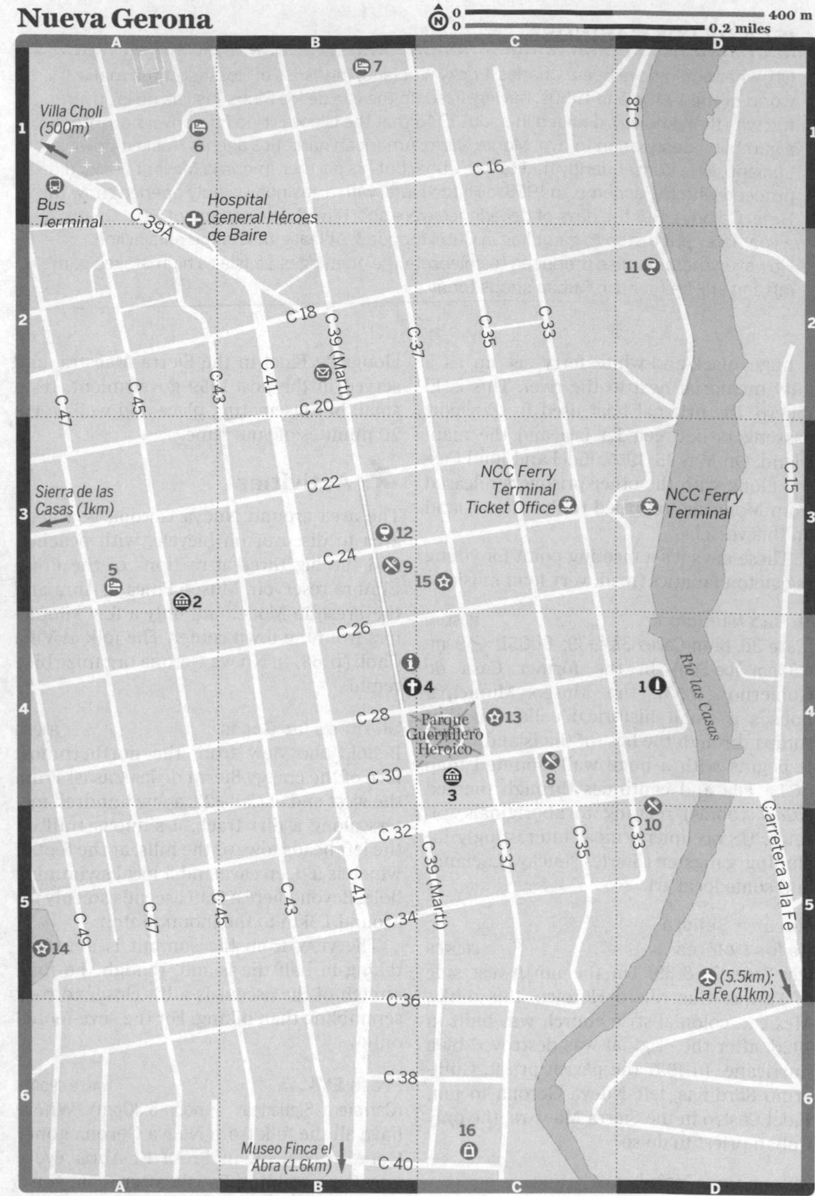

Festivals & Events

Carnaval Pinero CARNIVAL

(Mar) This is the big one. Get over here for a knees-up that includes parades with giant puppet-like heads, rodeo, sports competitions and perhaps just a little drinking. Held over three days in mid-March.

Sleeping

Casas particulares are your only town-center options and will provide meals;

Nueva Gerona

Sights

1 El Pinero ... D4
2 Museo Casa Natal Jesús Montané ... A3
3 Museo Municipal ... C4
4 Nuestra Señora de los Dolores ... B4

Sleeping

5 Tu Isla ... A3
6 Villa Mas – Jorge Luis Mas Peña ... A1
7 Villa Peña ... B1

Eating

8 Cubalse Supermarket ... C4
9 El Cochinito ... B3
10 Restaurante Río ... D5
Restaurante Tu Isla ... (see 5)

Drinking & Nightlife

11 Disco la Movida ... D2
El Pinero ... (see 1)
12 La Rumba ... B3

Entertainment

13 Cine Caribe ... C4
14 Estadio Cristóbal Labra ... A5
15 Uneac ... C3

Shopping

16 Centro Experimental de Artes Aplicadas ... C6

the owners will invariably meet arriving ferries. Nueva Gerona's two run-down state-operated hotels are south of town and barely worth a glance.

★Tu Isla CASA PARTICULAR $
(☎46-50-91-28; Calle 24, btwn Calles 45 & 47; r CUC$15-20; ❄ 🌊) This fabulous casa is worthy of any city on mainland Cuba. Run by a passionate *pinero* who knows and loves his island, it evokes La Isla's swashbuckling maritime history with wonderful murals, anchor motifs and six hotel-worthy rooms (three have private balconies). Furthermore it touts spacious terraces, a plunge pool and a brilliant 3rd-floor rooftop restaurant. *Tu Isla* (your island), indeed!

Villa Choli CASA PARTICULAR $
(☎46-32-31-47, 52-48-79-16; Calle C No 4001a, btwn Calles 6 & 8; r CUC$25; P ❄ @) Four serviceable rooms split between two floors with TV, internet access, secure parking space, delicious food and – possibly the highlight – a great terrace with rockers and a hammock. A second terrace opens for alfresco grill-ups on occasion. There are bicycles for rent, and port pickup/tickets can be arranged. The convivial host Ramberto is an excellent cook.

Villa Mas – Jorge Luis Mas Peña CASA PARTICULAR $
(☎46-32-35-44; negrin@infomed.sld.cu; Calle 41 No 4103 apt 7, btwn Calles 8 & 10; r CUC$20-25; ❄) Forget the rather ugly apartment-block setting; there are two above-average rooms here with refurbished marble bathrooms. Good meals are served on a rooftop terrace. It's in the northern part of town behind the hospital.

Villa Peña CASA PARTICULAR $
(☎46-32-23-45; cnr Calles 10 & 37; r CUC$15-20; ❄) A comfortable, secure option in a pretty bungalow near the hospital with two clean rooms, meals and friendly owners who'll be pleased to see you.

Motel el Rancho el Tesoro HOTEL $
(☎46-32-30-35; Autopista Nueva Gerona-La Fe Km 2; s/d CUC$25/30; P ❄) Oh dear! This lackluster motel with a castellated frontage lies in a wooded area near the Río las Casas, 3km south of town. Inside, it's like a museum to kitsch with 34 sizeable rooms propped up by a paltry state restaurant.

Eating

As far as food goes, La Isla is still living in the 1990s, bar a couple of welcome new exceptions. After one night of fruitless searching, most travelers sensibly elect to dine in their casa particular. Small sandwich and churros vendors set up on Martí (Calle 39) and peso ice-cream sellers appear spontaneously in the windows of various private houses.

★Restaurante Tu Isla CUBAN $
(Calle 24, btwn Calles 45 & 47; mains CUC$4-8; ⏰7pm-midnight Sun-Thu, to 2am Fri & Sat) This rooftop restaurant above the casa particular of the same name serves good Cuban classics with an Italian twist. The decor is nautical and traditional live music gets going most nights.

Restaurante Toti CUBAN $
(Reparto Chacón; mains CUC$2-5; ⏰noon-midnight) Lobster fresh off the grill for CUC$5 and a guitar duo serenading you as you dine? Sound too good to be true? It all happens at Toti, a deliciously modest private restaurant in the Chacón neighborhood up by the Presidio Modelo.

Restaurante El Abra CUBAN $
(Carretera Siguanea Km 4; meals CUC$1-4; ⏲ noon-5:30pm; P) An open-air place on delightful Presa El Abra, 4km southwest of the center, this is where *pineros* go on weekends to partake in *comida criolla* (Creole food), spontaneous dancing and water sports. Pork (would you believe it?) is a favorite for the grill-ups, but there are good fish options too. Or simply sip a cold beer and salute the view.

Restaurante Río SEAFOOD $
(Calle 32, btwn Calle 33 & river; MN$20-50; ⏲ noon-10pm; ❄) A dog-eared establishment by the river which, on a good day, serves fresh fish from the river and the sea (Nueva Gerona is one of the few places in Cuba where you can eat both) in *moneda nacional*. It has an outside terrace with a stereo blasting out the latest Cuban pop and an air-conditioned interior.

El Cochinito CARIBBEAN $
(cnr Calles 39 & 24; mains CUC$3-7; ⏲ noon-10pm Thu-Tue) The ominously named 'little pig' offers *desperados* pork concoctions in a smart but disturbing interior decorated with pigs' heads (some appear to be squealing).

Cubalse Supermarket SUPERMARKET $
(Calle 35, btwn Calles 30 & 32; ⏲ 9:30am-6pm Mon-Sat) Sells life-saving Pringles and biscuits.

Drinking & Nightlife

Call it pent-up boredom, but Nueva Gerona likes a party. Venues on and around Calle 39 are pretty gritty. Others (eg El Pinero) are less 'venues' and more outdoor get-togethers.

El Pinero CLUB
(Calle 28, btwn Calle 33 & river; ⏲ from around 9pm) Extremely loud music and most of the town's teenagers and 20-somethings converge by the historic boat for alfresco dancing. Drink and snack stalls also set up shop. Fridays and Saturdays are liveliest.

La Rumba CLUB
(Calle 24, btwn Calles 37 & 39; ⏲ 10pm-2am) Buy your drinks in the cage-like bar next door then head to the courtyard and hectic disco round the corner. If you don't dance hard, you'll stand out here.

Disco la Movida CLUB
(Calle 18; ⏲ from 11pm) For a little atmospheric booty-shaking, join the throngs of locals dancing in an open-air locale hidden among the trees near the river.

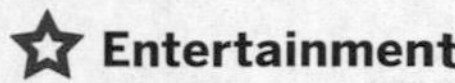

Entertainment

Uneac CULTURAL CENTER
(Calle 37, btwn Calles 24 & 26) Your best bet for a non-reggaeton night out is this nicely renovated colonial house with patio, bar and suave live music.

Cine Caribe CINEMA
(cnr Calles 37 & 28) If you're at a loose end, check the noticeboard at the cinema in Parque Guerrillero Heroico.

Estadio Cristóbal Labra SPECTATOR SPORT
(cnr Calles 32 & 53) Nueva Gerona's baseball stadium, Estadio Cristóbal Labra is seven blocks west of Calle 39. Ask at your local casa particular for details of upcoming games (staged from October to April).

Shopping

Calle 39, also known as Calle Martí, is a pleasant pedestrian mall shaded by greenery and decorated with sculptures by local artists. The shop displays aren't quite so handsome.

Centro Experimental de Artes Aplicadas ARTS & CRAFTS
(Calle 40, btwn Calles 39 & 37; ⏲ 8am-4pm Mon-Fri, to noon Sat) Near the Museo de Historia Natural. Makes artistic ceramics.

Information

INTERNET ACCESS

Etecsa Telepunto (Calle 41 No 2802, btwn Calles 28 & 30; per hr CUC$4.50; ⏲ 8:30am-7:30pm) Has internet terminals and sells cards for wi-fi (CUC$1.50 per hour).

MEDICAL SERVICES

Hospital General Héroes de Baire (☎ 46-32-30-12; Calle 39a) Has a recompression chamber.

MONEY

Banco Popular y Ahorro (cnr Calles 39 & 26; ⏲ 8am-7pm Mon-Fri) Has an ATM.

Cadeca (Calle 39 No 2022; ⏲ 8:30am-6pm Mon-Sat, to 1pm Sun) ATM.

POST

Post office (Calle 39 No 1810, btwn Calles 18 & 20; ⏲ 8am-6pm Mon-Sat)

TOURIST INFORMATION

Ecotur (☎ 46-32-71-01; reservas.ij@occ.ecotur.tur.cu; Calle 39, btwn Calles 26 & 28; ⏲ 8am-4pm Mon-Fri) Organizes trips into the militarized zone (where the Cueva de Punta del Este cave paintings and Cocodrilo are located)

GETTING TO ISLA DE LA JUVENTUD BY BOAT

Getting to La Isla by boat is an unnecessarily complicated and confusing affair. Few foreigners attempt it, while the trickle who do probably feel a bit like Columbus stumbling ashore when they arrive.

Bus-boat combo tickets are sold from the Naviera Cubana Caribeña (NCC) kiosk in Havana's main Terminal de Ómnibus (p121) for Astro buses (*not* the Víazul terminal). The bus takes you to the seedy port of Surgidero de Batabanó, from where boats depart for Nueva Gerona. It is wise to book tickets at least a day in advance. Beware, even the reservation process can take several hours. Tickets cost MN$5 for the 90-minute bus journey and CUC$50 for the 2½-hour ferry ride. Note, it's not possible to buy a return ticket in Havana, meaning you'll have to go through the whole ticket-buying rigmarole again in Nueva Gerona (preferably as soon as you arrive). Theoretically there is supposed to be one boat a day from Batabanó at 1pm, with a second boat running on Fridays and Saturdays at 4pm. However, in practice, boats often run late or are cancelled. Check ahead.

You'll need to get to the bus terminal at least two hours before departure to confirm your ticket. Be prepared for queues.

On arrival at the port in Surgidero de Batabanó, more lines usher you through airport-style security and into a waiting room for a likely period of one to two hours before the boat departs.

Do not show up independently in Batabanó with the intention of buying a ferry ticket direct from the dock. Although technically possible, a number of travelers have come unstuck here, being told that the tickets have been sold out through the NCC kiosk in Havana. Furthermore, bedding down overnight in Batabanó holds little appeal for travelers.

The return leg is equally problematic. Procure your ticket as early as possible (preferably the day you arrive) from the **ticket office** (cnr Calle 24 & Calle 33; ⌚8am-5:30pm) across the street from Nueva Gerona's **NCC ferry terminal** (☎46-32-44-15, 46-32-49-77; cnr Calles 31 & 24). The ferry leaves for Surgidero de Batabanó daily at 8am (CUC$50), but you'll need to get there at least two hours beforehand to tackle the infamous queues. A second boat is supposed to leave at 1pm on Fridays and Saturdays (with a check-in time of 10:30am).

Before reserving tickets, ask if there are sufficient bus connections from Surgidero de Batabanó to Havana and, importantly, that you have a reservation.

Don't take anything as a given until you have booked your ticket. Isla boat crossings, rather like Cuban trains, tend to be late, break down or get canceled altogether.

Traveling in either direction you'll need to show your passport. You'll also want to carry plenty of your own refreshments.

and to Punta Francés; also offers four-day packages to Cayo Largo del Sur. Day passes to the Southern Military Zone are available here (CUC$21 including an obligatory guide).

Getting There & Away

AIR

The most hassle-free and (often) cheapest way to get to La Isla is to fly. Unfortunately, most people have cottoned onto this, so flights are usually booked out days in advance.

Rafael Cabrera Mustelier Airport (airport code GER) is 5km southeast of Nueva Gerona.

Cubana Airlines (☎46-32-42-59; www.cubana.cu; Rafael Cabrera Mustelier Airport) flies here from Havana at least twice daily from as little as CUC$35 one-way. There are no international flights.

There are no flights from Isla de la Juventud to Cayo Largo del Sur.

Getting Around

BUS

Ecotur can organize trips/transfers from Nueva Gerona to the diving areas and into the militarized zone. A taxi (easily arranged through your casa or hotel) from Nueva Gerona to Hotel Colony should cost approximately CUC$30 to CUC$35.

There are less reliable local buses: buses 431 and 436 to La Fe (26km) and 440 to Hotel Colony (45km) leave from the terminal, a glorified

DON'T MISS

DIVING OFF THE ISLA DE LA JUVENTUD

Protected from sea currents off the Gulf of Mexico and blessed with remarkable coral and marine life, Isla de la Juventud offers some of the Caribbean's best diving: 56 buoyed and little-visited dive sites here will make you truly feel like a castaway. The dive sites are an underwater adventure park of everything from caves and passages to vertical walls and coral hillocks, while further east, in an area known as Bajo de Zambo, you can dive to the remains of some 70-odd shipwrecks.

The International Diving Center (opposite), run from Marina Siguanea just south of Hotel Colony on the island's west coast, is the center of diving operations. The establishment has a modern on-site recompression chamber along with the services of a dive doctor. It's from here that you can be transported out to the National Maritime Park at Punta Francés (opposite).

Boat transfers to Punta Francés take 90 minutes and deliver you to a gorgeous stretch of white-sand beach, from which most main dive sites are easily accessible. The cream of the crop is Cueva Azul (advanced), a trench of cerulean blue with a small cueva (cave) about 40m down, followed by Pared de Coral Negro (intermediate), a wall of black coral. You'll see lots of fish, including tarpon, barracuda, groupers, snooks and angelfish, along with sea turtles.

Diving costs start at CUC$43 for one immersion. Inquire at Hotel Colony (opposite) about diving and other nautical activities on offer first.

bus stop, opposite the cemetery on Calle 39a, just northwest of the hospital. Other useful buses are the 204 departing for Chacón (Presidio Modelo), Playa Paraíso and Playa Bibijagua, and the 203 bound for the airport.

CAR

Cubacar (☎46-32-44-32; cnr Calles 32 & 39; ⏰7am-7pm) rents cars from CUC$60 with insurance and, as you'll need your own vehicle to enter the military zone (unless on an organized tour), is the best bet for arranging transport here. Be warned: there aren't many cars available.

The **Oro Negro gas station** (cnr Calles 39 & 34) is in the center of town.

HORSE CARTS

Horse *coches* (carts) often park next to the Cubalse supermarket on Calle 35. You can easily rent one at CUC$10 per day for excursions to the Presidio Modelo, Museo Finca el Abra, Playa Bibijagua and other nearby destinations. If you've got the time, you can be sure the driver will.

East of Nueva Gerona

Sights

★ Presidio Modelo NOTABLE BUILDING

(CUC$1; ⏰8:30am-4:30pm Tue-Sat, 9am-1pm Sun) Welcome to the island's most impressive yet depressing sight. Located near Reparto Chacón, 5km east of Nueva Gerona, this striking prison was built between 1926 and 1931, during the repressive regime of Gerardo Machado. The four six-story and rather scary-looking yellow circular blocks were modeled after those of a notorious penitentiary in Joliet, Illinois, and could hold 5000 prisoners at a time.

During WWII, assorted enemy nationals who happened to find themselves in Cuba (including 350 Japanese, 50 Germans and 25 Italians) were interned in the two rectangular blocks at the north end of the complex.

The Presidio's most famous inmates, however, were Fidel Castro and the other Moncada rebels, who were imprisoned here from October 1953 to May 1955. They were held separately from the other prisoners, in the hospital building at the south end of the complex.

In 1967 the prison was closed and the section where Castro stayed was converted into a museum. There is one room dedicated to the history of the prison and another focusing on the lives of the Moncada prisoners. Admission to the now skeletal circular blocks (the most moving part of the experience) is free.

Playa Bibijagua BEACH

This unusual beach on the island's north coast, 4km to the east of Chacón, sports black sand rather than white and pine trees rather than palms. Facilities begin and end with a peso restaurant, but there's plenty of low-key Cuban ambience. It's an easy bike ride from Nueva Gerona.

Playa Paraíso BEACH

About 2km north of Chacón (about 6km northeast of Nueva Gerona), Playa Paraíso is a dirty brown beach with good currents for water sports. The wharf was originally used to unload prisoners heading to the Presidio Modelo.

Cementerio Colombia CEMETERY

The cemetery here contains the graves of Americans who lived and died on the island during the 1920s and 1930s. It's about 7km east of Nueva Gerona and 2km east of Presidio Modelo. Bus 38 passes by.

South of Nueva Gerona

The Isla's largely uninhabited interior is sprinkled with pine and palm trees and retains a strange, understated beauty. Now and then you'll encounter abandoned Soviet-era buildings, the international schools for which the island was once famous.

Sights

Punta Francés BEACH

This beach is the location of the National Maritime Park, accessible by a 90-minute boat ride from the marina just south of Hotel Colony. The white-sand beach is ground zero for divers who head for the reefs just offshore. However, it's also a fine place to lounge, swim, snorkel and enjoy a pristine paradise. Non-divers are welcome to use the boat. There's a small beach-shack restaurant.

Criadero Cocodrilo CROCODILE FARM

(CUC$3; 7am-5pm) This farm has played an important part in crocodile conservation in Cuba over the last few years and the results are interesting to see. Harboring more than 500 crocodiles of all shapes and sizes, the *criadero* (hatchery) acts as a breeding center, raising and then releasing groups of crocs back into the wild when they reach a length of about 1m.

To get to the *criadero* turn left 12km south of La Fe just past Julio Antonio Mella.

The center is similar to the one in Guamá in Matanzas, although the setting here is infinitely wilder.

La Jungla de Jones GARDENS

(CUC$3; dawn-dusk) Situated 6km west of La Fe several kilometers off the main road (look for the sign), Jungla de Jones is a 'botanical garden' containing more than 80 tree varieties, established by two American botanists, Helen and Harris Jones, in 1902. The highlight is the aptly named Bamboo Cathedral, an enclosed space surrounded by huge clumps of craning bamboo that only a few strands of sunlight manage to penetrate. Paths wind through the overgrown grounds and past the ruins of the Jones' erstwhile residence.

Beyond the gate, you'll be met by a couple of local farmers, who'll offer to show you round.

Activities

International Diving Center DIVING

(46-39-82-82 ext 166) Run from Marina Siguanea 1km south of Hotel Colony, this is the Isla de la Juventud's center of dive operations. The dive boat leaves for Punta Francés at 9am (a 90-minute transfer), so arrive around 8am if you want to organize an excursion. Immersions cost CUC$43.

Sleeping

Hotel Colony HOTEL $$

(46-39-81-81; s/d rooms CUC$32/50, bungalows CUC$40/70; P) Looking more like a hospital than a hotel from the outside, the Colony, 46km southwest of Nueva Gerona, originated in 1958 as part of the Hilton chain, but was confiscated by the revolutionary government. Today the complex has a mix of dull out-of-fashion rooms and large, bright newer bungalows. The clientele is split between foreign divers and Cubans belting out recorded music.

The water off the hotel's white-sand beach is shallow, with sea urchins littering the bottom. Take care if you decide to swim. A safer bet is the Colony's noisy pool. A long wharf stretches out hopefully into the Caribbean, though it's half-ruined these days. Snorkeling in the immediate vicinity of the hotel is mediocre, but the sunsets are to die for.

Getting There & Away

Transport is tough on La Isla, and bus schedules make even the rest of Cuba seem efficient. Bus 440 travels daily to Hotel Colony from Nueva Gerona (departing from opposite the cemetery next to the hospital). It departs at around 7am and returns at about 5pm. Otherwise, your best bet to get to Hotel Colony is by taxi (approximately CUC$35 from the airport), moped or rental car.

The Southern Military Zone

If the La Isla de la Juventud is Cuba's last frontier, the Southern Military Zone is a frontier on the frontier. Don't expect tanks and military bastions here. Instead what you'll find is deserted beaches, caves full of ancient pictographs, a turtle sanctuary, the Caribbean's tallest lighthouse and the Lanier swamps, Cuba's second-largest wetland and home to a population of American crocodiles.

The southern Isla is also replete with other unusual wildlife. Look out for monkeys, deer, lizards and turtles.

As the entire southern portion of La Isla beyond Cayo Piedra is a military zone, you must first procure a one-day pass and guide (CUC$21) from Ecotur (p164) in Nueva Gerona. There are further fees for entry to the Cueva de Punta del Este, Playa Larga, Cocodrilo and the Sea Turtle Breeding Center (CUC$3.60 each). The obligatory guides speak Spanish, English, German, French and Italian (subject to availability). Hiring your own vehicle can be organized with Cubacar (p166) in Nueva Gerona (from CUC$60 to CUC$100). Traveling in the military zone is not possible without a guide or an official pass, so don't arrive at the Cayo Piedra checkpoint without either. As the whole excursion can wind up being rather expensive, it helps to split the transportation costs with other travelers. For more up-to-date advice on the region inquire at Ecotur in Nueva Gerona. Cuban nationals require 72 hours notice to enter the military zone.

Sights

Cueva de Punta del Este CAVE

The Cueva de Punta del Este, a national monument 59km southeast of Nueva Gerona, has been called the 'Sistine Chapel' of Caribbean Indian art. Long before the Spanish conquest (experts estimate around AD 800), Indians painted some 235 pictographs on the walls and ceiling of several caves. The largest has 28 concentric circles of red and black, and the paintings have been interpreted as a solar calendar. Discovered in 1910, they're considered the most important of their kind in the Caribbean.

There's a small visitor center and meteorological station. The long, shadeless white beach nearby is another draw (for you and the mosquitoes – bring repellent).

Playa Larga BEACH

Playa Larga is the star of La Isla's south-coast beaches, lying about 12km south of the village of Cayo Piedra. The long strip of white sand fronting a (usually) calm sea is clean, inviting and practically virgin. There are no facilities.

Cocodrilo VILLAGE

The friendly village of Cocodrilo lies 50km west of Playa Larga. Barely touched by tourism, and with a population of just 750, Cocodrilo was formerly known as Jacksonville, and was colonized in the 19th century by families from the Cayman Islands. You still occasionally meet people here who can converse in English. Through the lush vegetation beside the potholed road one catches glimpses of cattle, birds, lizards and beehives. The rocky coastline, sporadically gouged by small, white sandy beaches lapped by crystal-blue water, is magnificent.

Sea Turtle Breeding Center FARM

(CUC$1; 8am-6pm) One kilometer west of Cocodrilo, the breeding center does an excellent job in conserving one of Cuba's rarest and most endangered species. Rows of green-stained glass tanks teem with all sizes of turtles. The turtles are then released back into the wild again.

CAYO LARGO DEL SUR

If you came to Cuba to witness colonial cities, exotic dancers, asthmatic Plymouths and peeling images of Che Guevara, then 38-sq-km Cayo Largo del Sur, 114km east of Isla de la Juventud, will hugely disappoint. If, instead, you booked tickets while dreaming of glittering white sandy expanses, coral reefs teeming with fish, fabulous all-inclusive resorts and lots of fleshy Canadians and Italians wandering around naked, then this diminutive tropical paradise is the place for you.

No permanent Cuban settlement has ever existed on the Cayo. Instead, the island was developed in the early 1980s purely as a tourism enterprise. Cayo Largo del Sur is largely frequented by Italian tourists – several resorts here cater exclusively to them. The other all-inclusives are less picky. The heavenly beaches surpass most

NATURISM ON CAYO LARGO DEL SUR

Naturism isn't part of the culture in Cuba, hence the only recognizable clothes-optional beaches are on the isolated holiday isle of Cayo Largo del Sur where, aside from a revolving army of flown-in hotel workers, no Cubans officially live.

Safe places to get naked on Cayo Largo include pockets of the main Lindarena beach in front of the tourist hotels as well as the east end of Playa Paraíso. More secluded is Playa Mal Tiempo on the headland between Playas Paraíso and Lindarena. Discretion is the key. None of the resorts on the island officially tolerate nudism within their grounds, and you'd be wise to cover up before visiting the beach bar. Nonetheless, naturism has a strong following among Playa Largo's tourists, many of whom are French-Canadian.

The only other bastion of public nudity in Cuba is similarly isolated Cayo Santa María (p271) in Villa Clara Province, where a small stretch of beach on the western edge of the island near the Hotel Meliá Buenavista is popular with naturists.

Note, unlike in Jamaica or other Caribbean countries, there are no full-blown naturist resorts in Cuba.

visitors' expectations of Caribbean paradise and are renowned for their size, emptiness and nesting turtles. There's also a profusion of iguanas and birdlife, including hummingbirds and flamingos.

Sights

★Playa Sirena — BEACH

Cayo Largo's (and, perhaps, Cuba's) finest beach is the broad westward-facing Playa Sirena, where 2km of powdery white sand is wide enough to accommodate several football pitches. Tourists on day trips from Havana and Varadero are often brought here. Thanks to calm seas, nautical activities (kayaks, catamarans) are available. Set back from the beach there's a *ranchón*-style bar and restaurant (p171), along with showers and toilets. It is the only Cayo Largo beach with shade.

Just southeast is Playa Paraíso, a narrower and less shady but nonetheless wonderful strip of sand, serviced by a small **bar** (sandwich CUC$3-4; ⏲9am-5pm).

Vivero de Crocodrilos — WILDLIFE RESERVE

(donations accepted; ⏲dawn-dusk) A beautiful, old building on Cayo Largo? You'd better believe it. Just past the turn-offs to the Sol resorts, the stone tower marking the Vivero de Crocodrilos dates from 1951 – the island's first construction. Here, you can meet real Cubans, who will show you the few animals that reside in and around the small lagoon – Kimbo the croc, Lola the iguana and a couple of turtles.

You can also climb the rickety ladder for decent views. This is where the plants that decorate your hotel grounds are grown.

Cayo Rico — ISLAND

A big day-trip destination is this island between Cayo Largo and Isla de la Juventud. Boat excursions to the beaches leave from the hotels (for around CUC$69 per person). Rico also has a simple beach restaurant that serves lunch (included). Cheaper excursions also leave from Marina Internacional Cayo Largo (p170).

Playa los Cocos — BEACH

You can head up the island's east coast via this beach, where there is good snorkeling, but no shade or facilities. The paved road gives out after Playa Blanca.

Playa Tortuga — BEACH

Beyond Playa los Cocos at the far end of the island is this beach, where sea turtles lay their eggs in the sand in the summer.

Granja de las Tortugas — NATURE RESERVE

(Combinado; CUC$1; ⏲8am-noon & 1-5:45pm) A small, often-closed complex beyond the airstrip on the northwest end of the island in the settlement of Combinado. From May to September guides here can organize night-time turtle-watching on the Cayo's beaches, one of only two places in Cuba where this is possible.

Activities

There are numerous activities available on the island, including snorkeling (from CUC$19), windsurfing, sailing and tennis. Of note is a boat adventure in the mangroves (CUC$29; you drive the boat) and the popular sunset catamaran cruise (CUC$73). You can also organize day trips to Havana and Trinidad (CUC$179 to

Cayo Largo del Sur

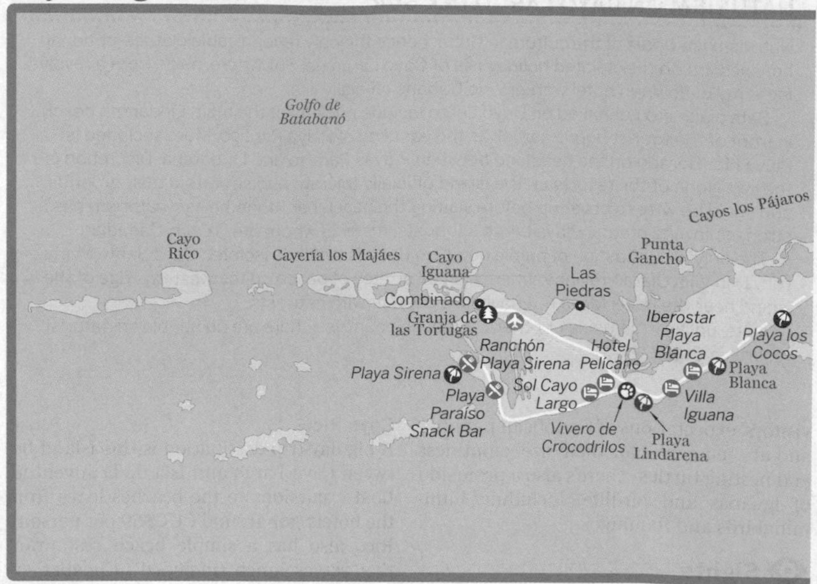

CUC$199). Ask to book any of the above at the hotels.

The island's best hike is from Playa Sirena round to Sol Cayo Largo along the beach (7km) or vice versa. A broken path follows the dune ridge for much of the way if the tide is high. You can also procure a bicycle if you're staying in one of the resorts and head east beyond the Playa Blanca Beach Resort to some of the island's remoter beaches.

Marina Internacional Cayo Largo DIVING, FISHING
(☎45-24-81-33; Combinado) Just beyond the turtle farm in Combinado, this is the departure point for deep-sea fishing trips (CUC$369 for four hours for a minimum of four people) and diving (CUC$50 for one immersion including hotel transfer). Prices are more expensive here because you can't shop around. Transfers from the marina to Playa Sirena are free for island guests and depart during the morning.

Sleeping & Eating

Cayo Largo del Sur's hotels face the 4km Playa Lindarena on the island's south side. Though largely shadeless, the beach is gorgeous and rarely crowded (although the sea can be choppy). Day-trippers can buy day passes to the Sol and Pelicano resorts starting from CUC$50 including lunch. Aside from the four large resorts, there are four small hotels reserved for Italian tourists.

Of the all-inclusives, the Sol Cayo Largo (p170) serves the best food.

For an away-day from the buffets, there's a restaurant on Playa Sirena and a couple in the small administrative center of Combinado.

Villa Marinera RESORT $$
(☎45-24-80-80; Combinado; s/d all-inclusive CUC$80/120; P ❄ 🛜 🏊) The Marinera, an offshoot of the Iberostar Playa Blanca, is a little different to other Cayo Largo resorts. Rather than hugging the wide southern beach, it resides in the small administrative 'town' of Combinado. In this sense, it's ideal for people focused mainly on the water activities that leave from the adjacent marina.

There are 22 cabins and guests have access to all the facilities at the Playa Blanca (a twice-daily shuttle links the hotels).

★ Sol Cayo Largo RESORT $$$
(☎45-24-82-60; www.meliacuba.com; s/d all-inclusive from CUC$215/310; P ❄ @ 🛜 🏊) The Meliá's only property on the cayo is four-star Sol Cayo Largo, with its Greek-temple-

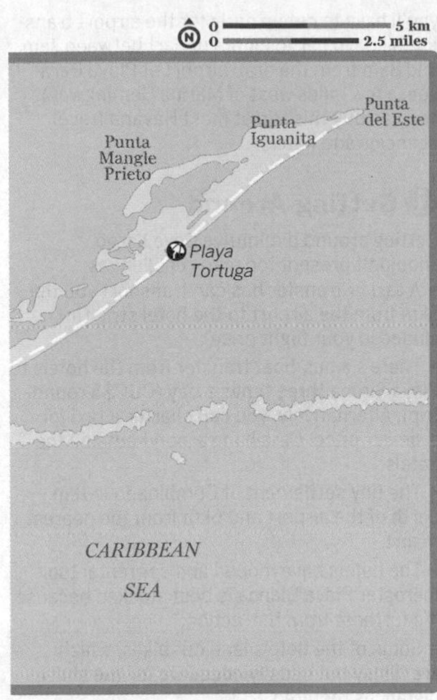

like lobby and trickling Italianate fountains. The beach out here is fantastic (and nudist) and the brightly painted (but not luxurious) rooms all have terraces with sea views. To date, it's Cayo Largo's most exclusive resort and great if you want to escape the families and poolside bingo further east.

Check out the on-site spa and gym.

Villa Iguana RESORT **$$$**
(☎45-24-81-11; r all-inclusive from CUC$185; P ❄ @ ✆ ≈) Salvaged from the wreckage of Hurricane Michelle in 2001 and reopened after 15 years in 2016, the Iguana is a small modest place by modern Cuban all-inclusive standards. Its 196 rooms mix old refurbished units with new wooden cabins linked by boardwalks. It styles itself as a 3½-star and is adults only.

Iberostar Playa Blanca RESORT **$$$**
(☎45-24-80-80; s/d all-inclusive CUC$135/185; P ❄ @ ✆ ≈) One of only two four-star hotels on Cayo Largo, this 306-room pile is set apart from the rest of the gang on an expansive stretch of Playa Blanca. Rather drab architecture is augmented by three different dining options, an array of sporting activities and – a rarity in Cuba – poolside music that opts for classical over skull-splitting reggaeton.

There's an individual touch, too. Artworks by leading Cuban artist Carlos Guzmán decorate the public areas, and the suites in the upper echelons with their mezzanine sleeping areas could hold their own in Greenwich Village. Well, nearly. Some shade wouldn't go amiss, though.

Hotel Pelícano RESORT **$$$**
(☎45-24-82-33; www.gran-caribe.com; s/d all-inclusive CUC$235/335; P ❄ @ ✆ ≈) This Spanish-style resort, flush on the beach 5km southeast of the airport, has 307 rooms in a series of three-story buildings and two-story duplex *cabañas* (cabins) built in 1993. This is the island's largest resort (by one room!) and its most beloved. Facilities include a nightclub and many family-friendly concessions. Low-season prices drop to almost half: book online.

★**Ranchón Playa Sirena** SEAFOOD **$$$**
(lunch buffet CUC$20; ⌚9am-5pm) A rather fetching beach bar amid the Playa Sirena palm trees, with Latino Tom Cruises tossing around the cocktail glasses. Good food is also served here, and a buffet (CUC$20) happens if enough tourists are around. It offers no-nonsense, salt-of-the-earth *comida criolla* (Creole food) and good grilled *pargo* (red snapper) for CUC$12.

Drinking & Nightlife

Taberna el Pirata CAFE, CLUB
(Combinado; ⌚24hr) Taberna el Pirata is primarily a haunt for boat hands, resort workers and the odd escaped tourist alongside Marina Internacional Cayo Largo. Icy beer, throat-burningly strong coffee, sandwiches and chips in pleasant environs.

Shopping

Casa de Habano CIGARS
(☎45-24-82-11; ⌚8am-8pm) Buy cigars at this shop in Combinado.

Information

DANGERS & ANNOYANCES

Due to dangerous currents, swimming is occasionally forbidden. This will be indicated by red flags on the beach. Mosquitoes can be a nuisance, too.

MEDICAL SERVICES

Clínica Internacional (☎45-24-82-38; ⌚24hr) In the admin village of Combinado.

MONEY

You can change money at the hotels; otherwise Combinado houses the island's main bank, **Bandec** (8:30am-3pm Mon-Sat, 8am-noon Sun).

TOURIST INFORMATION

There's a **Cubatur** (45-24-82-58) in the Hotel Pelícano and further information offices in the Sol Cayo Largo (p170) and Playa Blanca (p171) resorts.

Getting There & Away

Vilo Acuña International Airport is a bright-enough place with a big snack bar and a souvenir stand. Several charter flights arrive directly from Canada and Italy weekly.

For pop-by visitors, daily flights from Havana to Cayo Largo del Sur with **Aerogaviota** (7-203-8686; Av 47 No 2814, btwn Calles 28 & 34, Kohly, Havana) or **Cubana de Aviación** (7-649-0410; www.cubana.cu; Airline Building, Calle 23 No 64, Vedado; 8:30am-4pm Mon-Fri, to noon Sat), cost from CUC$149 for a return trip. Included will be airport transfer at both ends and a boat trip from Cayo Largo's marina (but you don't have to go). The island makes a viable day trip from Havana, although you'll have to get up early for the airport transfer (all Cayo Largo flights depart between 7am and 8am from the drab airport at Playa Baracoa, a few miles west of Marina Hemingway). You can buy this trip at most Havana travel agencies and hotels.

Getting Around

Getting around diminutive Cayo Largo shouldn't present too many challenges:

- A taxi or transfer bus can transport you the 5km from the airport to the hotel strip (included in your flight price).
- There's a bus-boat transfer from the hotels to Playa Sirena three times a day (CUC$5 round-trip). Alternatively, you can charter a taxi for a similar price. Cars hang around outside the hotels.
- The tiny settlement of Combinado is 1km north of the airport and 6km from the nearest resort.
- The hotels have moped and car rental too; Iberostar Playa Blanca is best stocked because it's furthest from the 'action.'
- Some of the hotels lend out bikes, which are flimsy but usually adequate for the short distances required.

Valle de Viñales & Pinar del Río Province

☎48 / POP 595,000

Includes ➡

Best Places to Eat

- Tres Jotas (p181)
- El Olivo (p180)
- Balcón del Valle (p181)
- Café Ortuzar (p192)

Best Places to Sleep

- Casa Daniela (p178)
- Hotel los Jazmines (p180)
- Terra Mar 1910 (p192)
- Villa los Reyes (p178)

Why Go?

Tobacco is still king on Cuba's western fingertip, a rolling canvas of rust-red oxen-furrowed fields, thatched tobacco-drying houses and sombrero-clad *guajiros* (country folk).

The crucible of this emerald land is the Valle de Viñales, a Unesco World Heritage Site framed by a backdrop of distinctive *mogotes* (limestone monoliths) that nigh-on beseech you to get hiking. Playing a tuneful second fiddle is the Península de Guanahacabibes, an uninhabited wilderness chock-a-block with fertile ecosystems that abut a swath of 50-plus offshore dive sites.

People primarily come here to be close to nature, basing themselves in the serene hassle-free village of Viñales. From here, huge cave complexes call for torch-lit exploration, tobacco plantations offer expert fact-finding tours, beaches invite lazy contemplation, and every horizon seems to be filled with a host of quintessential 'come to the Cuban countryside' images. So follow the fragrant aroma of tobacco and come.

When to Go

- Come from May through August to see prized wildlife, such as the Guanahacabibes turtles and thousands of red crabs.
- November through February is the tobacco-growing season and a good time to visit the plantations speckled with their deep-green plants.
- December through March is ideal beach weather. Calm seas also create good conditions for diving at María la Gorda.
- July through early November is the hurricane season. Beware, in the last decade several big storms have hit the province, usually in August or September.

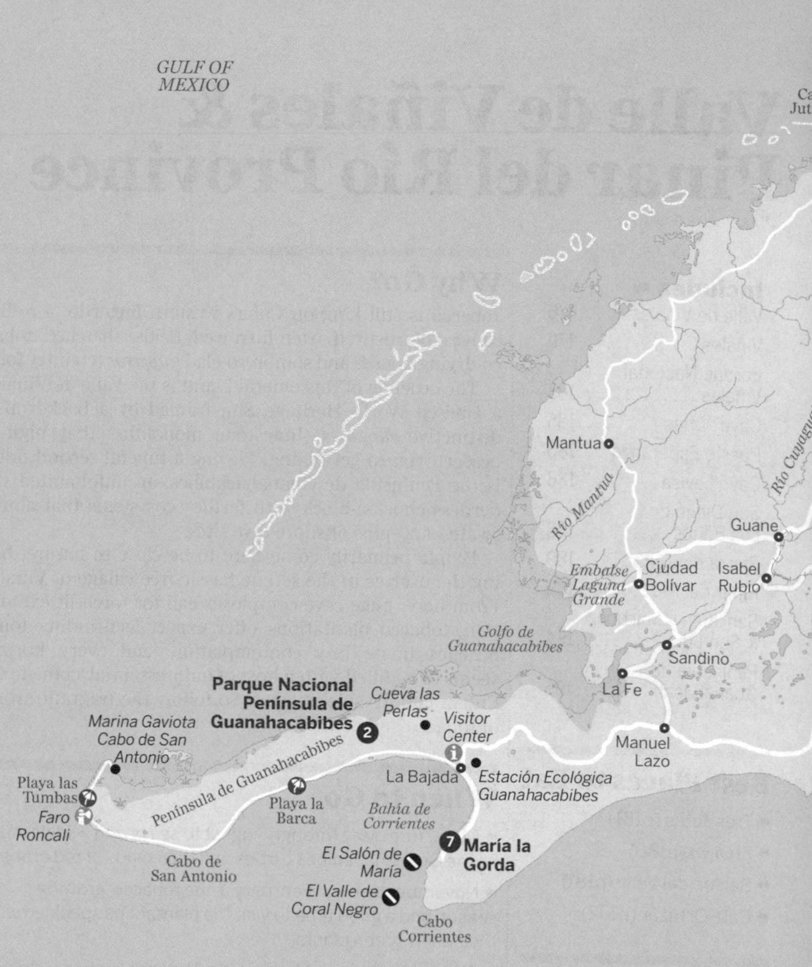

Valle de Viñales & Pinar del Río Province Highlights

1 **Parque Nacional Viñales** (p183) Seeing, smelling and tasting the agricultural beauty of this wonderfully authentic Unesco World Heritage Site.

2 **Parque Nacional Península de Guanahacabibes** (p195) Going turtle-watching on virgin beaches on the western fingertip of the Cuban mainland.

3 **Valle de Palmarito** (p185) Riding a horse or hiking up with the *guajiros* into this pastoral valley in the Parque Nacional Viñales.

4 **Gran Caverna de Santo Tomás** (p183) Getting gobsmacked by the grottos of one of Latin America's largest subterranean cave systems.

5 Cayo Levisa (p186)
Recharging your batteries on this dreamy key accessible only by boat.

6 Hacienda Cortina (p189)
Walking around the recently restored, but still agreeably outlandish ruins of this huge rural estate.

7 María la Gorda (p196)
Dipping down under the azure waters of one of Cuba's clearest and most colorful diving sites.

VALLE DE VIÑALES

Embellished by soaring pine trees and bulbous limestone cliffs that teeter like top-heavy haystacks above placid tobacco plantations, Parque Nacional Viñales is one of Cuba's most magnificent natural settings. Wedged spectacularly into the Sierra de los Órganos mountain range, this 11km-by-5km valley was recognized as a national monument in 1979, with Unesco World Heritage status following in 1999 for its dramatic steep-sided limestone outcrops (known as *mogotes*), coupled with the vernacular architecture of its traditional farms and villages.

Viñales offers opportunities for fine hiking, rock climbing and horseback trekking. On the accommodations front, it boasts first-class hotels and some of the best casas particulares (rooms in private homes) in Cuba. Despite drawing in day-trippers by the busload, the area's well-protected and spread-out natural attractions have somehow managed to escape the frenzied tourist circus of other less well-managed places, while the atmosphere in and around the town remains refreshingly hassle-free.

Valle de Viñales

Viñales

POP 27,806

When Pinar del Río's greenery starts to erupt into craggy *mogotes* (limestone monoliths) and you spy a cigar-chewing *guajiro* driving his oxen and plough through a rust-colored tobacco field, you know you've arrived in Viñales. Despite its longstanding love affair with tourism, this slow, relaxed, wonderfully traditional settlement is a place that steadfastly refuses to put on a show. What you see here is what you get – an agricultural town where front doors are left wide open, everyone knows everyone else, and a night out on the tiles involves sitting on a *sillón* (rocking chair) on a rustic porch analyzing the Milky Way.

People don't come to Viñales for the music or the mojitos, they come to dip indulgently into the natural world, hiking, horse-riding or cycling through some of the most wonderful landscapes in Cuba. Join them.

Sights

Finca Raúl Reyes FARM

(Map p179; dawn-dusk) FREE Finca Raúl Reyes, 1km north of the town center, is a tobacco plantation where you can enjoy fruit, coffee, *puros* (cigars) and a dose of throat-warming rum. From here, you can also hike up to Cueva de la Vaca, a cave that carves a tunnel through the *mogotes:* from the cave mouth, unforgettable valley vistas roll out before you.

El Jardín Botanico de las Hermanas Caridad y Carmen Miranda GARDENS

(Map p179; Salvador Cisneros; donations accepted; 8am-5pm) Just opposite the Servi-Cupet gas station as Cisneros swings north out of town, you'll spot an outlandish, vine-choked gate beckoning you in. This is the entrance to a sprawling garden, work on which began in 1918. Cascades of orchids bloom alongside plastic doll heads, thickets of orange lilies grow in soft groves and turkeys run amok. Knock on the door of the Little

THE VALLEYS OF VIÑALES

Viñales craggy *mogotes* (limestone monoliths) divide the area up into five main valleys.

Viñales

The beautiful main valley is a feast for the eyes best viewed from the Hotel los Jazmines (p180) at sunset. Herein lives most of the area's population and infrastructure, and several of the main sights, including the hard-to-miss Mural de la Prehistoria (p183). The valley supports Viñales' quintessential tobacco landscape and has been heavily modified by agriculture. The hard limestone *mogotes* to the north are all that remains of a huge cave system that used to cover the whole region. At some point, millions of years ago, the soft roofs of the caves collapsed leaving only the harder walls and pillars standing.

Palmerito

The Palmerito (usually referred to as the Valle de la Guasasa on maps) lies directly to the north of Viñales and is easily accessible on foot from the town. The valley's rust-red soil supports numerous tobacco plantations and is studded with distinctive thatched-roof tobacco-drying houses. Since serious floods in the 1980s, no one has lived permanently in the valley. Instead, farmers commute in and out daily from Viñales, mostly on horseback. Much of the work in the fields is still done by plow and oxen (tractors are restricted). The Palmerito also hides several caves, including one in which you can swim. The valley is notorious for hosting cock-fights.

San Vicente

From the south you enter the narrow San Vicente valley through the jaws of two mogotes on the road to Puerto Esperanza. The valley is known for its caves – including the Cueva del Indio (p184) and Cueva de San Miguel (p184) – and its tourist hotel, which is the starting point for various trails. It offers good birdwatching.

Ancón

This quiet northern valley is usually accessed from the Rancho San Vicente (p185) area north of Viñales. It is crossed by the Ancón River, which yields the freshwater crayfish served in several Viñales restaurants. The valley supports a small settlement and a coffee plantation. It is a good cycling destination from Viñales.

Silencio

The 'silent' valley is considered the best place in Viñales to sit and enjoy a sunset over the *mogotes*. It's also where most of the region's tobacco is grown and, thanks to wide, relatively flat tracks, is popular with cyclists. There are several lakes to explore and a couple of farms open to visitors.

Red Riding Hood cottage and someone will probably emerge to show you around.

Gallería de Arte GALLERY
(Map p179; ⏲7am-noon, 1-7pm & 8-11pm) FREE A tiny art gallery next to the Casa de la Cultura in the Viñales town center. Worth a stop on a rainy day!

Iglesia del Sagrado Corazón de Jesús CHURCH
(Map p179) This tiny cream-colored church on the main square has benefited from a recent (by Cuban standards) renovation.

Museo Municipal MUSEUM
(Map p179; Salvador Cisneros No 115; CUC$1; ⏲8am-5pm Mon-Sat, to 4pm Sun) Positioned halfway down Cisneros, Viñales' pine-lined main street, the Museo Municipal occupies the former home of independence heroine Adela Azcuy (1861–1914) and tracks the local history. Five different guided hikes leave from here daily; check times at the museum a day prior

La Casa del Veguero FARM
(Map p176; Carretera a Pinar del Río Km 24; ⏲10am-5pm) To learn about the local

tobacco-growing process, stop by this tobacco plantation just outside Viñales on the road south to Pinar del Río and see a fully functional *secadero* (drying house) in which tobacco leaves are cured from February to May. The staff give brief explanations, and you can buy loose cigars (the unbranded variety most Cubans smoke) here at discount prices. There's a restaurant too.

Tours

Cubanacán TOURS

(Map p179; 48-79-63-93; Salvador Cisneros No 63c; 9am-7pm Mon-Sat) Cubanacán organizes perennially popular day trips to Cayo Levisa (CUC$39), Cayo Jutías (CUC$15), Gran Caverna de Santo Tomás (CUC$20) and María la Gorda (CUC$35). Official park hikes leave from here daily (CUC$8).

Sleeping

★ Casa Daniela CASA PARTICULAR $

(Map p179; 48-69-55-01; casadaniela@nauta.cu; Carretera a Pinar del Río; r CUC$25; P) Run by a former doctor and his wife, who must have had formidable bedside manners if their hospitality in this surgically clean casa is anything to judge by, this orange house has expanded into a sizeable residence without losing its local intimacy. There are six rooms, a pool, a roof terrace and a shady outside yard for the obligatory Viñales relaxation.

The breakfasts cooked up by the couple's hardworking son are worth the stay alone.

Casa Papo y Niulvys CASA PARTICULAR $

(Map p179; 48-69-67-14; papoyniulvys@gmail.com; Rafael Trejo No 18a; r CUC$30; P) One of the few houses in Viñales with a front garden, this place gives you room to swing on a hammock as well as rock on a rocking chair on the front porch. Rooms are small but recently decorated in a modern style. It's a dreamily tranquil spot in this increasingly busy town. Book well ahead – it gets busy.

Villa Los Reyes CASA PARTICULAR $

(Map p179; 48-79-33-17; http://villalosreyes.com; Salvador Cisneros No 206c; r CUC$25-30; P@) A great modern house with five rooms (including a new block out back), all amenities, a secluded patio where a restaurant serves some original Cuban-fusion food, and one of the town's best roof terraces. Hostess, Yarelis, was a biologist at the national park and host, Yoan, has Viñales running through his veins.

The couple are known for their excellent tours, including a popular sunrise tour to Los Aquáticos (p183) and a sunset tour to the Valle del Silencio.

Villa Juanito El Joyero CASA PARTICULAR $

(Map p179; 48-69-59-33; milay.rivera@nauta.cu; Adela Azcuy Norte No 53; r CUC$25-30;) If you just want a simple, decent house replete with traditional Viñales hospitality away from the main street bustle, this bright-orange bungalow will suit. The rental room comes with two beds, a minibar and a pleasant back patio. Small is beautiful in this neck of the woods.

La Auténtica CASA PARTICULAR $

(Map p179; 48-69-58-38; Salvador Cisneros No 125; r CUC$30) Giving a plush new brushstroke to Viñales' main drag, La Auténtica is like a mini-hotel with four new rooms encased in a large one-story house that adds modern adornments to a traditional base. Unlike other Viñales casas, the owners don't live on-site, meaning you're free to roam between the various common areas, including a spacious back patio equipped with comfy chairs.

Casa Haydée Chiroles CASA PARTICULAR $

(Map p179; 52-54-89-21; casahaydee@nauta.cu; Rafael Trejo No 139; r CUC$25) With six rooms split between two adjacent houses and a lovely lush communal back patio where you can rock beneath the stars on your *sillón* (rocking chair), this house reflects all the best attributes of Viñales. Even better, the daughter of the owner works at the Infotur office (p182), meaning English and French are spoken and recommendations are well-informed.

Villa El Niño CASA PARTICULAR $

(Map p179; 48-69-66-66; casaelninoalexander@nauta.cu; Adela Azcuy No 9; r CUC$25;) Lovely green abode with multiple terraces and swing-chairs on Calle Adela Azcuy away from the noise of main drag Salvador Cisneros. It offers four small but adequate rooms and plenty of chill-out space.

Casa Nenita CASA PARTICULAR $

(Map p179; 48-79-60-04; emiliadiaz2000@yahoo.es; Salvador Cisneros Internal No 1; r CUC$35-40; P) Nenita's has quietly become one of Cuba's top casas particulares. While its out-of-center location might deter some,

Viñales

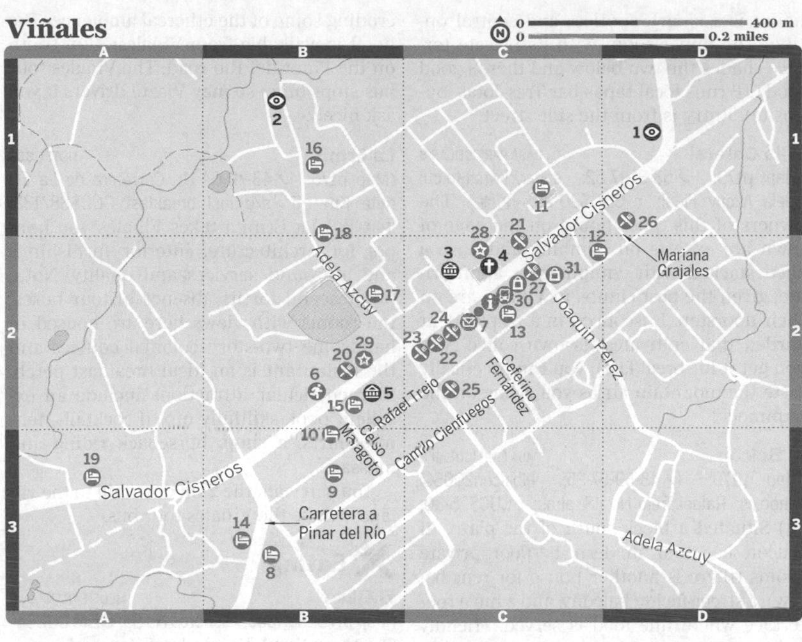

Viñales

Sights

1 El Jardín Botanico de las Hermanas Caridad y Carmen Miranda D1
2 Finca Raúl Reyes B1
3 Galería de Arte C2
4 Iglesia del Sagrado Corazón de Jesús C2
5 Museo Municipal B2

Activities, Courses & Tours

6 Bike Rental Point B2
7 Cubanacán C2

Sleeping

8 Casa Daniela B3
9 Casa Haydée Chiroles B3
10 Casa Jean-Pierre B3
11 Casa Nenita C1
12 Casa Papo y Niulvys C2
13 El Balcón C2
14 Hostal Doña Hilda B3
15 La Auténtica B2
16 Villa Cafetal B1
17 Villa El Niño B2
18 Villa Juanito El Joyero B1
19 Villa Los Reyes A3

Eating

20 Cocinita del Medio B2
21 El Barrio C2
22 El Olivo C2
23 La Cuenca C2
24 La Dulce Vida C2
25 La Esquinita C2
26 Restaurant La Berenjena D1
27 Tres Jotas C2

Entertainment

28 Centro Cultural Polo Montañez C2
29 Patio del Decimista B2

Shopping

30 Los Vegueros C2
31 Mercado de Artesanía C2

the eight rooms are above par and, when augmented by the amazing restaurant, pool and roof terrace, give you a luxurious launchpad from which to go *mogote*-hopping. Nenita's battered fish has even featured in recipe books. Finding the place can be tricky, however – it's behind the *policlinico* (hospital).

Casa Jean-Pierre CASA PARTICULAR $
(Map p179; ☎48-79-33-34; cnr Celso Maragoto & Salvador Cisneros; r CUC$25; P ❄) Jean-Pierre's recently renovated tangerine-hued

house is a smart, spotless and central option. The upper room with its private terrace shades the two below and there's good food (JP runs local tapas bar Tres Jotas, opposite). Entry is from the side street.

Villa Cafetal CASA PARTICULAR $
(Map p179; 53-31-17-52; edgar21@nauta.cu; Adela Azcuy Final; r CUC$20-25; P ❄) The owners of this quiet house on the edge of town are experts on climbing and have a shed stacked with equipment – appropriate, given the best climbs in Viñales are on their doorstep. Ensconced in a resplendent garden that cultivates its own coffee (yes, you get it for breakfast), you can practically taste the mountain air as you swing on the hammock.

El Balcón CASA PARTICULAR $
(Map p179; 48-69-67-25; elbalcon2005@yahoo.es; Rafael Trejo No 48, altas; r CUC$25-30; ❄) Situated a block south of the plaza, El Balcón has four modern 1st-floor private rooms (there is another house for rent below), a street-facing balcony, and a huge roof terrace where fine food is served. Friendly owners Mignelys and Juanito speak English.

Hostal Doña Hilda CASA PARTICULAR $
(Map p179; 48-79-60-53; flavia@correodecuba.cu; Carretera a Pinar del Río No 4 Km 25; r CUC$25; ❄) One of the first houses in town on the road from Pinar del Río, Hilda's house has three rooms with porches and rockers. More importantly, this unpretentious place is classic Viñales – just like the perennially smiling hostess – with divine food. The mojitos are among Cuba's very best. Ask here about dance classes.

★ Hotel los Jazmines HOTEL $$$
(Map p176; 48-79-64-11; Carretera a Pinar del Río; s/d incl breakfast CUC$88/138; P ❄ 🏊) Prepare yourself: the vista from this pastel-pink colonial-style hotel is one of the best in Cuba. Open the shutters of your classic valley-facing room and drink in the shimmering sight of magnificent *mogotes,* oxen-ploughed red fields and palm-frond-covered tobacco-drying houses. While no five-star palace, Jazmines benefits from its unrivaled location and a gloriously inviting swimming pool.

Handy extras include an international medical clinic, a massage room and a small shop/market. The setting comes at a cost: bus tours stop off here almost hourly, thus eroding some of the ethereal ambience. The hotel is walkable from Viñales: 4km south on the Pinar del Río road. The Viñales tour bus stops here; so may Víazul drivers if you ask nicely.

La Ermita HOTEL $$$
(Map p176; 48-79-64-11; Carretera de La Ermita Km 1.5; s/d incl breakfast CUC$88/138; P ❄ 🏊) La Ermita takes Viñales' top honors for architecture, interior furnishings and all-round services and quality. Notably peaceful for its absence of tour buses, the rooms with views here are housed in handsome two-story colonial edifices and the restaurant is an ideal breakfast perch. Extracurricular attractions include an excellent pool, skillfully mixed cocktails, tennis courts, a shop, horseback riding and massage.

You can walk the 2km downhill to the village or take the Viñales tour bus.

Eating

El Olivo MEDITERRANEAN $
(Map p179; Salvador Cisneros No 89; pasta CUC$4-6; noon-11pm) Viñales' most popular restaurant, as the perennial queue outside will testify, serves tremendous lasagna and pasta dishes, backed up by other Med classics such as duck *à l'orange.* The joker in the pack is rabbit with herbs in a dark chocolate sauce.

Restaurant La Berenjena VEGETARIAN $
(Map p179; 52-54-92-69; Mariana Grajales, btwn Salvador Cisneros & Rafael Trejo; mains CUC$4-7; 10am-10pm;) A commendable attempt to fill a void in Cuba's food market – ie vegetarianism – La Berenjena (meaning 'aubergine' or 'eggplant') inhabits a lovely blue-and-white house with an awning-covered terrace out front. This is a genuine eco-restaurant plying fruit shakes, vegetable lasagne, crepes, soups, aubergines (of course), and a few meat dishes for those who can't be swayed.

Furthermore it uses recycled rainwater, makes its own honey and uses ingredients from its own vegetable garden.

La Esquinita FAST FOOD $
(Map p179; cnr Rafael Trejo & Adela Azcuy; snacks CUC$1-3; 10am-11pm) A welcome new addition in a town where on-the-go outdoor activities are popular is this quick walk-up cafe that grills simple sandwiches for you to

take away. An added bonus are the chocolate-filled churros, arguably Viñales' finest dessert.

El Barrio MEDITERRANEAN $

(Map p179; ☎48-69-69-27; Salvador Cisneros No 58a; mains CUC$3-7; ⏰9:30am-10:30pm) This grungily cool joint is cornering a new market in Viñales: the right-round-the-clock market. Breakfast here, lunch here, knock back cocktails here. The tapas and the pizza are good, the pasta less so. An animated clientele of travelers keeps the terrace buzzing.

★Tres Jotas TAPAS $$

(Map p179; ☎53-31-16-58; Salvador Cisneros No 45; tapas CUC$2-6; ⏰8am-2am) Who knew that Viñales, long a bastion of *cerdo asado* (whole roast pig), also produces huge crayfish fresh from the Ancón River? For a reminder, pop into 3J's, a tapas bar cum restaurant cum cocktail lounge cum breakfast cafe run by the affable Jean-Pierre, who tirelessly welcomes guests at the door.

The signature dish is *camarones del río* (shrimp), but you can warm up with an array of Spanish-style tapas, including croquettes, herb-spiked cheese and cured ham. The dimly lit interior is cool without being over the top, and the atmosphere is always electric.

★Balcón del Valle CUBAN $$

(Map p176; Carretera a Pinar del Río; mains CUC$8; ⏰noon-midnight) With three deftly constructed wooden decks overhanging a panorama of tobacco fields, drying houses and craggy *mogotes,* this aptly named restaurant (translation: Balcony of the Valley) has food that stands up to its sensational views. The unwritten menu gives a three-way choice between chicken, pork and fish, all prepared country-style with copious trimmings. It's 3km outside Viñales towards Hotel los Jazmines.

La Dulce Vida ITALIAN $$

(Map p179; Salvador Cisneros No 71b; mains CUC$5-14; ⏰noon-10pm) The 'sweet life' Spanish style is another successful Viñales take on Italian food and does noteworthy pasta dishes – just choose your pasta shape and your sauce. Backing it up are some Cuban staples. The small interior is reminiscent of a simple trattoria in Puglia, and there are cushioned benches to sink into outside. Good desserts too!

La Cuenca INTERNATIONAL $$

(Map p179; ☎48-69-69-68; Salvador Cisneros No 97, cnr Adela Azcuy; mains CUC$5-12; ⏰11am-10:30pm) Looking less rustic than some of its Viñales brethren, La Cuenca's narrow covered terrace and funky black-and-white

CLIMBING IN VIÑALES

You don't need to be Reinhold Messner to recognize the unique climbing potential of Viñales, Cuba's mini-Yosemite. Sprinkled with steep-sided *mogotes* (limestone monoliths) and blessed with whole photo-albums' worth of stunning natural vistas, climbers from around the world have been coming here for over a decade to indulge in a sport that has yet to be officially sanctioned by the Cuban government.

Viñales' climbing remains very much a word-of-mouth affair. There are no printed route maps and no official on-the-ground information (indeed, most state-employed tourist reps will deny all knowledge of it). If you are keen to get up onto a rock face, your first points of reference should be the comprehensive website of Cuba Climbing (www.cubaclimbing.com), along with the book *Cuba Climbing* by Aníbal Fernández and Armando Menocal (2009). Once on the ground, the best nexus for climbers are the casas of Oscar Jaime Rodríguez and Villa Cafetal in Viñales. Ask any local for directions to either.

Viñales has numerous well-known climbing routes, including the infamous 'Wasp Factory,' and a handful of skillful Cuban guides, but there's no official equipment hire (bring your own) and there are no adequate safety procedures in place. Everything you do is at your own risk, and this includes any sticky situations you may encounter with the authorities, who don't currently sanction climbing (although they generally turn a blind eye). Climbing in Viñales is expected to become an official activity in the near future, so check the latest situation on the ground. Also consider that in the meantime, unregulated climbing in a national park area has the potential to damage endangered flora and ecosystems, so proceed with caution and care.

interior are rather tempting. The food is all over the map, from Spanish tapas to rack of lamb, although some dishes (rabbit with chocolate) seem to mimic nearby culinary king, El Olivo. If you're not lingering long, the coffee and cocktails are famously good.

Cocinita del Medio CUBAN **$$**
(Map p179; Salvador Cisneros, btwn Celso Marago-to & Adela Azcuy; platters CUC$10; noon-11pm) Sometimes simple is best. It's easy to miss La Cocinita, which looks more like someone's house than a restaurant, but, what it lacks in fancy decor, it makes up for in generous platters of grilled meat and fish – generous in both size and in seasoning. Eat here at least once.

Entertainment

Centro Cultural Polo Montañez LIVE MUSIC
(Map p179; cnr Salvador Cisneros & Joaquin Pérez; after 9pm CUC$1; music from 9pm-2am) Named for the late Pinar del Río resident-turned-*guajiro* hero and legendary folk singer, Polo Montañez, this open-to-the-elements patio off the main plaza is a bar-restaurant with a full-blown stage that comes alive after 9pm.

Patio del Decimista LIVE MUSIC
(Map p179; Salvador Cisneros No 102; music from 7pm) The ebullient and long-standing Patio del Decimista serves up live music, cold beers, snacks and great cocktails.

Shopping

Mercado de Artesanía ARTS & CRAFTS
(Map p179; Joaquin Pérez; 10am-7pm) This private-enterprise market sells Cuba-themed arts and crafts and sets up in Calle Joaquin Pérez every day.

Los Vegueros CIGARS, RUM
(Map p179; 48-79-60-80; Salvador Cisneros No 57; 9am-9pm) A hot selection of cigars – with a roller often in residence – and rum too.

Information

INTERNET ACCESS

Etecsa Telepunto (Ceferino Fernández No 3; internet per hr CUC$1.50; 8:30am-7pm Mon-Sat, to 5pm Sun) Three terminals in a tiny office; it also sells cards for wi-fi. The main square has good wi-fi reception.

MEDICAL SERVICES

Clinica (48-79-33-48; Salvador Cisneros interior)

Farmacia Internacional (48-79-64-11; Hotel los Jazmines, Carretera a Pinar del Río) Pharmacy in Hotel los Jazmines.

MONEY

Banks in Viñales have long queues. Arrive early or consider changing money in Pinar del Río

Banco de Crédito y Comercio (Salvador Cisneros No 58; 8am-noon & 1:30-3pm Mon-Fri, 8-11am Sat) Has two ATMs.

Cadeca (cnr Salvador Cisneros & Adela Azcuy; 8:30am-4pm Mon-Sat) Quickest service.

POST

Post Office (Map p179; Ceferino Fernández 14, cnr Salvador Cisneros; 9am-6pm Mon-Sat)

TOURIST INFORMATION

Infotur (Map p179; Salvador Cisneros No 63b; 8:15am-4:45pm)

Getting There & Away

BUS

The well-ordered **Víazul ticket office** (Map p179; Salvador Cisneros No 63a; 8am-noon & 1-3pm) is opposite the main square in the same building as Cubataxi. Daily Víazul buses depart from here for Havana at 8am and 2pm (CUC$12, 3¼ hours). At 6:45am another bus heads to Cienfuegos (CUC$32, eight hours) and Trinidad (CUC$37, 9½ hours). All buses stop at Pinar del Río (CUC$6, 30 minutes)

Conectando buses run by Cubanacán (p178), and departing from outside the Cubanacán office, have daily transfers to Havana, Trinidad and Cienfuegos. Book a day ahead. Prices are the same as Víazul.

Daily transfer buses run to Cayo Levisa (CUC$39 including lunch and boat transfer), Cayo Jutías (CUC$15) and María la Gorda (CUC$35). Prices include return fare.

CAR & MOPED

To reach Viñales from the south, take the long and winding road from Pinar del Río; the roads from the north coast are not as sinuous, but due to their condition, are way more time-consuming. The remote mountain road from the Península de Guanahacabibes through Guane and Pons is one of Cuba's most spectacular routes. Allow a lot of travel time.

Car hire can be arranged at **Cubacar** (48-79-60-60; Salvador Cisneros No 63c; 9am-7pm) in the Cubanacán office.

Mopeds can be rented for CUC$26 a day at the Bike Rental Point (p184) next to Restaurante la Casa de Don Tomás.

TAXI

Víazul buses are often fully booked days in advance. The solution? A *collectivo* (shared) taxi. These can be booked at the office that **Cubataxi** (☎48-79-31-95; Salvador Cisneros No 63a) shares with Víazul. Prices per person, if taxis are full (four people), are Havana (CUC$20), Varadero (CUC$30), Cienfuegos (CUC$35) and Trinidad (CUC$40).

Getting Around

The Viñales Bus Tour is a hop-on, hop-off minibus that runs nine times a day between the valley's spread-out sites. Starting and finishing in the town plaza, the whole circuit takes 65 minutes, with the first bus leaving at 9am and the last at 4:50pm. There are 18 stops along the route, which runs from Hotel los Jazmines to Hotel Rancho San Vicente, and all are clearly marked with route maps and timetables. All-day tickets cost CUC$5 and can be purchased on the bus.

There's a Servi-Cupet gas station at the northeast end of the main street, Salvador Cisneros.

Parque Nacional Viñales

Parque Nacional Viñales' extraordinary cultural landscape covers 150 sq km and supports a population of 25,000 people. A mosaic of *mogote*-studded settlements grows coffee, tobacco, sugarcane, oranges, avocados and bananas on some of the oldest, most tradition-steeped landscapes in Cuba.

Sights

Gran Caverna de Santo Tomás CAVE

(CUC$10; ⌚9am-3pm) Welcome to Cuba's largest cave system and the second-largest on the American continent. There are over 46km of galleries on eight levels, with a 1km section accessible to visitors. There's no artificial lighting, but headlamps are provided for the 90-minute guided tour. Highlights include bats, stalagmites and stalactites, underground pools, interesting rock formations and a replica of an ancient native Indian mural.

Wear suitable shoes and be aware that the cave requires some steep climbs and scrambling over slippery rocks. Most people visit the cave on an organized trip from Viñales (CUC$20).

Los Aquáticos VILLAGE

A kilometer beyond the turn-off to Dos Hermanas and the Mural de la Prehistoria, a dirt road twists up to the mountain community of Los Aquáticos, founded in 1943 by followers of visionary Antoñica Izquierdo, who discovered the healing power of water when the campesinos of this area had no access to conventional medicine. They colonized the mountain slopes and two families still live there. Los Aquáticos is accessible only by horse or on foot. Guided tours can be organized in most of Viñales' casas particulares.

You can also go it alone. Although no signs mark the path, there are plenty of homesteads en route where you can ask the way. From the main road follow a dirt road for approximately 400m before branching left and heading crosscountry. You should be able to pick out a blue house halfway up the mountain ahead of you. This is your goal. Once there, you can admire the view, procure grown-on-site coffee and chat to the amiable owners about the water cure. After your visit, you can make a loop by returning via Campismo Dos Hermanas and the Mural de la Prehistoria cliff paintings; it's a wonderfully scenic route (the complete Los Aquáticos–Dos Hermanas circuit totals 6km from the main highway).

Mural de la Prehistoria PUBLIC ART

(Map p176; incl drink CUC$3; ⌚9am-6pm) Four kilometers west of Viñales village on the side of Mogote Pita is a 120m-long painting. Leovigildo González Morillo, a follower of Mexican artist Diego Rivera, designed it in 1961 (the idea was hatched by Celia Sánchez, Alicia Alonso and Antonio Núñez Jiménez). On a cliff at the foot of the 617m-high Sierra de Viñales, the highest portion of the Sierra de los Órganos, this massive mural took 18 people four years to complete.

The huge snail, dinosaurs, sea monsters and humans on the cliff symbolize the theory of evolution and are either impressively psychedelic or monumentally horrific, depending on your viewpoint. You don't really have to get up close to appreciate the artwork, but the admission fee is waived if you take the overpriced, CUC$15 lunch at the on-site restaurant (p185). Horses are usually available here (CUC$5 per hour) for various excursions.

Cueva del Indio CAVE

(Map p176; CUC$5; 9am-5:30pm;) In a pretty nook 5.5km north of Viñales village, this cave is very popular with tourists. An ancient indigenous dwelling, the cave was rediscovered in 1920. After a short 200m walk, you're transferred to a motor boat to ply the final 400m along an underground river. The cave is electrically lit and the experience underwhelming. Exit through the gift shop. Good for kids.

El Memorial 'Los Malagones' MONUMENT

(CUC$1) Los Malagones, from the community of El Moncada, was the first rural militia in Cuba. It comprised 12 men who rooted out a counterrevolutionary band from the nearby mountains in 1959. A mausoleum and memorial fountain inaugurated in 1999 contains niches dedicated to the 12 militiamen (all but two are now dead).

It is crowned by a stone recreation of their leader, Leandro Rodríguez Malagón. The water features are designed to replicate (with unerring accuracy) the sound of machine-gun fire. A tiny museum is on site.

Cueva de San Miguel CAVE

(Map p176; incl drink CUC$3; 9am-5:30pm) This is a small cave at the jaws of the Valle de San Vicente, with the cave entrance serving as a bar/nightspot. Your entrance fee gets you into a gaping cave that engulfs you for a brief, kind-of-absorbing 10-minute tour before dumping you a tad cynically in the El Palenque de los Cimarrones restaurant on the other side.

Activities

Cycling

Despite the sometimes hilly terrain, Viñales is one of the best places in Cuba to cycle (most roads follow the valleys and are relatively flat). Traffic on the roads is still light, and the scenery is a conveyor belt of natural beauty. Many casas now offer cheap bike rentals. Some also offer bike tours. Ask around.

Bike Rental Point CYCLING

(Map p179; Salvador Cisneros No 140; bike hire per hr/day CUC$1/10) Offers modern bikes with gears. Located next door to the Restaurante la Casa de Don Tomás. (Many casa particular owners also rent bikes for similar prices.)

Hiking

★Coco Solo & Palmarito Mogotes HIKING

(Map p176) This walk starts on a spur road about 100m south of the entrance to La Ermita hotel and progresses for 8km, taking in the Valle del Silencio, the Coco Solo and Palmarito *mogotes* and the Mural de la Prehistoria. There are good views and ample opportunities to discover the local flora and fauna, including a visit to a tobacco *finca* (farm).

It returns you to the main road back to Viñales.

San Vicente/Ancón HIKING

(Map p176) The trail around the more remote Valle Ancón enables you to check out still-functioning coffee communities in a valley surrounded by *mogotes*. It's an 8km loop.

Tradiciones de Viñales HIKING

(Map p176) Starting just east of Hotel los Jazmines, this bucolic 5.7km loop ushers you up through woods to a hilltop *mirador* (lookout) and returns you via typically delightful tobacco-plantation scenery.

Cueva El Cable HIKING

(Map p176) A 10km hike into a local cave typical of Viñales' karst topography. It starts in the Valle de San Vicente near the Cueva del Indio (p184).

Maravillas de Viñales HIKING

A 6km loop beginning 1km northeast of El Moncada and 13km from the Dos Hermanas turnoff, this hike takes in endemic plants, orchids and the biggest leaf-cutter ant hive in Cuba (so they say).

Horseback Riding

The lush hills and valleys (and the *guajiros*, indeed) around town lend themselves to horseback riding, particularly the Valle de Palmarito and the route to Los Aquáticos. Most casas particulares can hook you up with a guide. Riding a horse will mean you see more in a shorter space of time. It's particularly useful in the wet season (April to October) when the trails can be muddy.

Swimming

It is possible to swim in a natural pool by torchlight at La Cueva de Palmarito in the Valle de Palmarito. This place is a doable hike/horseback ride from Viñales. You can swim at the pools in all three of the valley's

LOCAL KNOWLEDGE

VIÑALES HIKES & GUIDES

The Parque Nacional Viñales has added a considerable number of new hikes to its repertoire in recent years. There are now around 15 routes and maps are displayed at the visitor center. It is best to go with a guide as signposting is terrible. Prices for guides are around CUC$10 per person but depend on distance and group size.

Aside from the park guides, almost every casa particular in Viñales will be able to hook you up with a private guide who can pretty much custom-build any trip you want. Eternally popular is the loop around the Valle de Palmarito, which starts and ends in the village and takes in a coffee plantation, tobacco house and the Cueva de Palmarito where swimming by torchlight is possible.

Other favorites are the hikes to Los Aquáticos and the Valle del Silencio.

hotels for CUC$8 (including CUC$7 drinks cover).

Sleeping

Campismo Dos Hermanas CAMPISMO $
(Cubamar; Map p176; ☎48-79-32-23; www.campismopopular.cu; Mogote Dos Hermanas; d/tr CUC$30/45;) Trapped between the sheer-sided jaws of two mogotes (it takes its name from the Mogote Dos Hermanas, which lies about 1km to the west) and in view of the Mural de la Prehistoria is one of Cubamar's best international campismos. Bonuses include a restaurant, a pool, a geological museum, horseback riding and nearby hiking trails. The only incongruity is the loud music that spoils the tranquil ambience of this beautiful valley.

Hotel Rancho San Vicente HOTEL $$$
(Map p176; ☎48-79-62-01; Carretera a Esperanza Km 33; s/d CUC$88/138; P) After Viñales' two spectacularly located hotels, you probably thought it couldn't get any better, but Rancho San Vicente goes close. Situated 8km north of the village, this bucolic scattering of cabins nestled in a grove has just been extended – a more modern 22-room block lies just across the road, and jolly nice it is too.

There are two pools and a restaurant, plus a spa with massage facility on-site. Birdwatching walks can be organized.

Eating

La Carreta MEDITERRANEAN $$
(Map p176; Carretera a Esperanza Km 36; mains CUC$10-15; ⊙10am-5pm) A carreta is a simple oxen-drawn cart, but there's nothing basic about how this restaurant transports you up its steep steps and into the privileged pantheons of wonderful Cuban food laced with Mediterranean influences. The classic dish? Lamb with red-wine sauce. It's 2km north of Hotel Rancho San Vincente.

Finca San Vicente CUBAN $$
(Map p176; Carretera a Esperanza Km 32½; mains CUC$10; ⊙noon-3pm) A large, but reasonable rural restaurant typical of the Viñales area, Finca San Vicente serves a slap-up CUC$10 lunch. If there are enough people, it serves whole roast pork with all the trimmings. It's ever popular with tour buses.

Restaurante Mural de la Prehistoria CUBAN, INTERNATIONAL $$$
(set lunch CUC$15; ⊙8am-7pm) Steep but almost worth it, the Mural's humongous set lunch – tasty pork roasted and smoked over natural charcoal – ought to keep you fueled at least until tomorrow's breakfast.

Information

Parque Nacional Viñales Visitors Center
(Map p176; ☎48-79-61-44; Carretera a Pinar del Río Km 22; ⊙8am-6pm) Located 3km south of Viñales, the visitor center is equipped with a good set of maps, trail information and natural history pertaining to the park. Park wardens are always on hand and hikes and other activities can be arranged here.

THE NORTHERN COAST

Cayo Jutías

Pinar del Río's most discovered 'undiscovered' beach is the 3km-long blanket of sand that adorns the northern coast of Cayo Jutías, a mangrove-covered key situated approximately 65km northwest of Viñales and attached to the mainland by a short *pedraplén* (causeway). Jutías – named for its indigenous tree rats – vies with Cayo Levisa to the east for the title of the province's most picturesque beach, and while the latter might be prettier, the former has no overnight accommodation and thus greater tranquility.

The Cayo's access road starts about 4km west of Santa Lucía. Ten minutes after crossing the causeway the Faro de Cayo Jutías appears; this metal lighthouse was built by the US in 1902 and makes for an interesting walk along the abutting mangrove-studded sands. The road kinks sharp left to culminate at the main Jutías beach, caressed by crystal-clear water, 12.5km from the coastal highway.

Activities

Jutías has a small dive center that rents out kayaks for CUC$1 per hour, runs snorkeling trips for CUC$12 and other boat trips for CUC$10 to CUC$25, plus organizes diving from CUC$37 for one immersion (there are seven dive sites nearby). Beyond the initial arc of sand, the beach continues for 3km; you can hike barefoot through the mangroves.

Eating

Restaurante Cayo Jutías SEAFOOD **$$**

(Cayo Jutías; mains CUC$7-10; 10am-5:30pm) The open-sided Restaurante Cayo Jutías right on the beach specializes in local seafood.

Getting There & Away

Transfer buses from Viñales cost CUC$15 and will give you six hours' beach time. Otherwise you will have to make your own transport arrangements. The fastest, and by far the prettiest, route is via Minas de Matahambre, through rolling pine-clad hills.

Puerto Esperanza

POP 7000

Becalmed at the end of a long, bumpy road, the fishing village of Puerto Esperanza (Port of Hope), 6km north of San Cayetano and 25km north of Viñales, isn't sleepy so much as veritably slumbering. The clocks haven't worked here since...oh...1951. According to town lore, the giant mango trees lining the entry road were planted by slaves in the 1800s. A long pier pointing out into the bay, a favored perch for catatonic fishers, is tempting for a jump into the ocean.

Puerto Esperanza has a loyal following of ultra-independent travelers who are keen to see a side of Cuba where few foreigners care to tread. Rich in money it isn't. Rich in wild off-the-cuff experiences it is. Come here to spin with local cyclists through craggy hills and end up on an unkempt beach fishing for your dinner.

Activities

Itineraries? Forget them. Relax. Read. Eat lobster. Discover some transcendental Santería ritual, chat to the old timers with the fishing rods or tour your neighbor's tobacco plantation in search of pungent peso cigars. Eat more lobster.

The people at Casa Teresa can custom-make horse-riding and cycling jaunts around the locality and beyond.

Sleeping

Casa Teresa Hernández Martínez CASA PARTICULAR **$**

(48-79-37-03; Calle 4 No 7; r incl breakfast CUC$25) The charismatic Teresa is as colorful as her six bright and clean rooms furnished in lurid pink, blue and green. She also runs a private restaurant in a jungle-like garden out back, where fish (seafood plate CUC$10) and lobster headline the menu. Local activities from cycling trips to horse-riding can be arranged here.

Getting There & Away

You'll need your own wheels to get to Puerto Esperanza. There's a handy Servi-Cupet gas station at San Cayetano. The road on to Cayo Jutías deteriorates to dirt outside San Cayetano: expect a throbbing backside if you're on a bike or moped.

Cayo Levisa

More frequented than its rival Cayo Jutías, and perhaps more splendid, Cayo Levisa sports a beach-bungalow-style hotel, a basic restaurant and a fully equipped diving center, yet still manages to feel relatively isolated. Separation from the mainland obviously helps. Unlike other Cuban keys, there's no causeway here, and visitors must make the 35-minute journey by boat from Palma Rubia. It's a worthwhile trip: 3km of sugar-white sand and sapphire waters earmark

Cayo Levisa as Pinar del Río's best beach. American writer Ernest Hemingway first 'discovered' the area, part of the Archipiélago de los Colorados, in the early 1940s after he set up a fishing camp on Cayo Paraíso, a smaller coral island 10km to the east. These days Levisa attracts up to 100 visitors daily as well as the 50-plus hotel guests. While you won't feel like an errant Robinson Crusoe here, you should find time (and space) for plenty of rest and relaxation.

Activities

Levisa has a small marina offering scuba diving for CUC$40 per immersion, including gear and transport to the dive site. Fourteen dive sites are peppered off the coast. These include the popular La Corona de San Carlos (San Carlos' Crown), the formation of which allows divers to get close to marine life unobserved, and Mogotes de Viñales, so called for its towering coral formations, which are said to bear a likeness to mogotes: the precipitous limestone hills outside Viñales. La Cadena Misteriosa (Mysterious Chain) is a shallow reef where some of the most colorful fish hereabouts – including barracudas and rays – can be seen. Snorkeling plus gear costs CUC$12 and a sunset cruise goes for the same price. Kayaking and aqua biking are also possible.

Sleeping

Casa Mario & Antonia CASA PARTICULAR $

(☎52-28-30-67; Palma Rubia; r CUC$25) Ideal for resort-phobes or people who miss the last boat to the cayo, Mario and Antonia's place is a slice of rustic heaven where genuine Cuban hospitality makes up for any lack of modern appliances. The small, simple house has two bedrooms for rent, great food and a quiet bucolic setting. The boat dock is a five-minute walk away.

Hotel Cayo Levisa HOTEL $$$

(☎48-75-65-01; www.hotelcayolevisa-cuba.com; s/d incl meals CUC$106/172; ❄) With an idyllic tropical beach just outside your front door, you won't worry about the slightly outdated *cabañas* (cabins) and dull food choices here. Expanded to a 60-room capacity a couple of years back, the Levisa's newer wooden cabins (all with bathroom) are an improvement on the old concrete blocks. Service has pulled its socks up too. Book ahead, as this place is isolated and popular.

Getting There & Away

The dock for embarkations to Cayo Levisa is around 21km northeast of La Palma or 40km west of Bahía Honda. Take the turnoff to Mirian and proceed 4km through a large banana plantation to reach the coastguard station at Palma

FROM GUANAHATABEYS TO GUAJIROS

The pre-Columbian history of western Cuba is synonymous with the Guanahatabeys, a group of nomadic Indians who lived in caves and procured their livelihood largely from the sea. Less advanced than the other indigenous peoples who lived on the island, the peaceful, passive Guanahatabeys developed more or less independently of the Taíno and Siboney cultures further east. These people were extinct by the time the Spanish arrived in 1492.

Post-Columbus the Spanish left rugged Pinar del Río largely to its own devices, and the area developed lackadaisically only after Canary Islanders began arriving in the late 1500s. Originally called Nueva Filipina (New Philippines) for the large number of Filipinos who came to the area to work the burgeoning tobacco plantations, the region was renamed Pinar del Río in 1778, supposedly for the pine forests crowded along the Río Guamá. By this time the western end of Cuba was renowned for its tobacco and already home to what is now the world's oldest tobacco company, Tabacalera, dating from 1636. Cattle ranching also propped up the economy. The farmers who made a living from the delicate and well-tended crops here became colloquially christened *guajiros*, a native word that means – literally – 'one of us.' By the mid-1800s, Europeans were hooked on tobacco and the region flourished. Sea routes opened up and the railway was extended to facilitate the shipping of the fragrant weed.

These days tobacco, along with tourism, keeps Pinar del Río both profitable and popular, with Viñales now the third-most-visited tourist destination in Cuba after Havana and Varadero.

Rubia, where there is a snack bar (10am to 6pm) and the departure dock for the island. The Cayo Levisa boat leaves daily at 10am, 2pm and 6pm and returns 9am, 12:30pm and 5pm. It costs CUC$35 per person round-trip (including boat, three drinks and buffet lunch). Should you miss the boat, you can hire a water taxi for an extra CUC$10.

From the Cayo Levisa dock you cross the mangroves on a wooden walkway to the Hotel Cayo Levisa and the gorgeous beach along the island's north side. If you are without a car, the easiest way to get here is via a day excursion from Viñales, great value at CUC$39 including the boat and lunch.

SAN DIEGO DE LOS BAÑOS & AROUND

San Diego de Los Baños

POP 6269

Sitting 130km southwest of Havana, this nondescript town just north of the Carretera Central is popularly considered the country's best spa location. As with other Cuban spas, its medicinal waters were supposedly 'discovered' in the early colonial period when a sick slave stumbled upon a sulfurous spring, took a revitalizing bath and was miraculously cured. Thanks to its proximity to Havana, San Diego's fame spread quickly and a permanent spa was established in 1891. During the early 20th century American tourists flocked here, leading to the development of the current hotel-bathhouse complex in the early 1950s.

Despite numerous possibilities for tourism, San Diego's scruffy bathhouse with its creepy sanatorium ambience isn't everyone's cup of tea. More alluring is the attractive natural region to the west known as the Sierra de Güira, an area replete with pine, mahogany and cedar forests. It's a favorite spot for birdwatchers.

Sights

Balneario San Diego HOT SPRINGS
(shared/private baths CUC$2/4; 8am-5pm) Thermal pools, hot springs, recuperation center; there are many terms to describe San Diego's famous bathhouse, but 'spa' isn't one of them . Whatever you do, don't come here expecting fluffy towels, fancy facials and the alluring whiff of eucalyptus oil. Reopened in 2015 after a lengthy closure, the famous *balneario* still looks like something out of *One Flew Over the Cuckoo's Nest*. Nevertheless, baths in thermal waters (30°C to 40°C), along with massages and acupuncture are all available.

Perennially popular with Cubans undergoing courses of medical treatment, the bathhouse is open to all-comers yet only receives the odd curious tourist. Prepare for an all-pervading stench of sulfur.

Activities

Julio César Hernández BIRDWATCHING
(52-48-66-31; carpeta@mirador.sandiego.co.cu) Birdwatching and trekking trips into Parque la Güira with qualified guide Julio César Hernández can be organized at Hotel Mirador. You'll need your own wheels. Possible feathered sightings include the bee hummingbird, the Cuban pygmy owl and the Cuban soltaire. It's one of the best birding spots in Cuba.

Sleeping & Eating

Villa Julio & Cary CASA PARTICULAR $
(48-54-80-37; Calle 29 No 4009; r CUC$20-25;) One of the town's few casas, this place is an agreeable nook with a small garden, colorful mural and porches (with rockers) guarding clean, tidy rooms. Within spitting distance of the *balneario*.

Hotel Mirador HOTEL $$
(48-77-83-38; Calle 23 Final; s/d incl breakfast CUC$68/78;) The Mirador is a low-key stopoff. Predating the Revolution by five years, the hotel was built in 1954 to accommodate spa-seekers headed for the adjacent Balneario San Diego. Well-tended terraced gardens slope up to rooms that match the pretty exterior: crisp, cozy and looking for the most part onto balconies with garden and *balneario* views.

Downstairs there's a pleasant swimming pool and an outdoor grill that does whole roast pig on a spit. There's also a proper restaurant *con una vista* (with a view) inside, serving Cuban cuisine.

Getting There & Away

The area is only accessible by car or bicycle.

The town is on a kink in the Carretera Central and around 10km north of the Autopista. There's a Servi-Cupet gas station at the entrance to San Diego de los Baños from Havana.

A taxi from Havana will cost about CUC$60, from Viñales about CUC$25.

Sierra de Güira

With rough roads and precious little accommodation, the untamed Sierra de Güira, a medley of limestone karst cliffs and swooping pockets of forest west of San Diego de los Baños, is off the tourist radar. This didn't prevent it becoming a retreat for the Revolution's most renowned figures in the past and, to this day, a host of rare birdlife.

Sights

★Hacienda Cortina HISTORIC SITE

(dawn-dusk) A grand crenelated entry gate a few kilometers west of San Diego de los Baños announces the surreal, long-abandoned grounds of Hacienda Cortina. The brainchild of wealthy lawyer José Manuel Cortina, this rich-man's-fantasy-made-reality was built as a giant park during the 1920s and 1930s, with Cortina plonking a stately home in its midst. After nigh-on a century of neglect, in 2014 refurbishment money arrived out of the blue and the hacienda has been partially restored.

There's a lot to take in at this tropical pleasure dome, although most of it is yet to be fully appreciated by foreign visitors (most passers-by are Cuban). A driveway from the grandiose entrance leads up to a cluster of attractively restored buildings, including a restaurant, swimming pool and hotel (Cubans only). From here a staircase leads down through a French-style garden adorned with colorful buds and statues of Carrera marble. Beyond, lie the ruins of Cortina's erstwhile mansion, partially restored and incorporating another open-air bar-restaurant.

On either side, the extensive plant-rich grounds spread out to incorporate an artificial boating lake, several ornamental bridges, plus Japanese and Chinese gardens complete with pagodas. It's a spirit-lifting and beautiful domain and would be even more so if the various eating joints didn't insist on playing ear-splitting music.

The hacienda grounds fan out beyond into the wild 25,000-hectare Parque la Güira.

Cueva de los Portales CAVE

(CUC$2; 8am-5pm) During the October 1962 Cuban Missile Crisis, Ernesto 'Che' Guevara transferred the headquarters of the Western Army to this vast and spectacular cave, 11km west of Parque la Güira and 16km north of Entronque de Herradura on the Carretera Central. The cave is set in a beautiful remote area among steep-sided vine-covered *mogotes* (limestone monoliths) and was declared a national monument in the 1980s.

Within the cavemouth, a small outdoor museum exhibits Che's roughshod artifacts including his bed and the table where he played chess (while the rest of the world stood at the brink of nuclear Armageddon). Three other caves called El Espejo, El Salvador and Cueva Oscura are further up the hillside. This area is brilliant birdwatching turf: birding tours can be arranged at San Diego de los Baños' Hotel Mirador (p188), or you can ask staff at the cave entrance. There's a good campismo (Cuban guests only) outside the cave with a bar-restaurant open to all-comers. You'll need your own wheels to get here.

Getting There & Away

The area is only accessible by car.

By car, the road across the mountains from San Diego de los Baños to the Cueva de los Portales is beautiful, but narrow and full of potholes. But it is drivable in a normal car, just. The approach from Entronque de Herradura is an easier drive. There's a Servi-Cupet gas station at the entrance to San Diego de los Baños from Havana.

PINAR DEL RÍO AREA

Pinar del Río

POP 191,660

Surrounded by beautiful verdant countryside and enriched by its proximity to the world's best tobacco-growing terrain, the city of Pinar del Río emits a strange energy, exacerbated by its famous *jinteros* (touts), who can abrade the most thick-skinned traveler. As a result, the place probably has more detractors than fans, especially since the bucolic *jintero*-free paradise of Viñales is so close by. But a stopover here needn't be purgatorial. There's a good tobacco factory to visit, some weirdly interesting architecture, and a hot, frenetic after-dark scene if you're up for it.

Despite this, Pinar often feels like a city in the slow lane, an urban backwater that has become the butt of countless

Pinar del Río

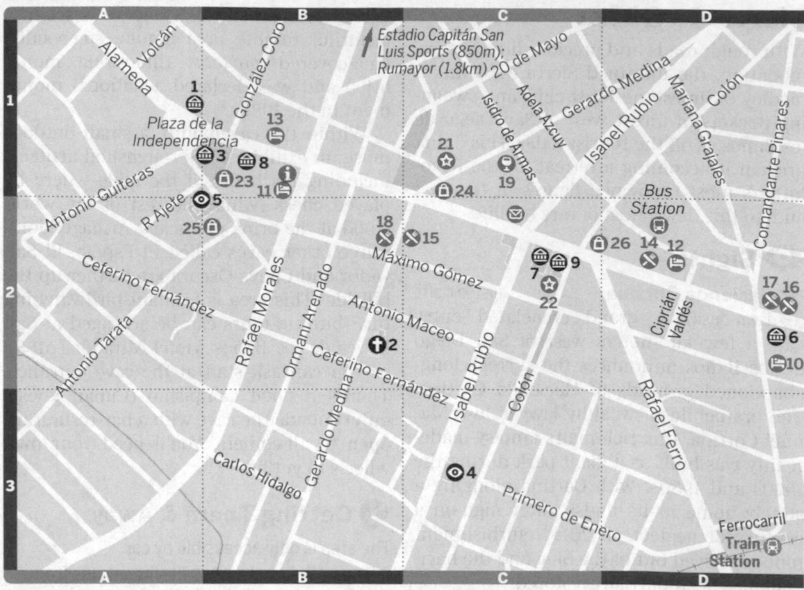

Pinar del Río

Sights

1 Casa Taller A1
2 Catedral de San Rosendo B2
3 Centro Provincial de Artes Plásticas Galería B1
4 Fábrica de Bebidas Casa Garay C3
5 Fábrica de Tabacos Francisco Donatien A2
6 Museo de Historia Natural D2
7 Museo Provincial de Historia C2
8 Palacio de los Matrimonios B1
9 Teatro José Jacinto Milanés C2

Sleeping

10 Gladys Cruz Hernández D2
11 Hotel Vueltabajo B1
12 Pensión El Moro D2
13 Terra Mar 1910 .... B1

Eating

14 Café Ortuzar D2
15 Casa del Té La Beisbolera C2
16 El Gallardo D2
17 El Mesón D2
18 Panadería Doña Neli B2

Drinking & Nightlife

19 Café Pinar C1
20 Disco Azul E2

Entertainment

21 Casa de la Música C1
22 La Piscuala C2

Shopping

23 Casa del Habano B1
24 Fondo Cubano de Bienes Cultural C1
25 La Casa del Ron B2
26 Todo Libro Internacional C2

jokes about the supposedly easy-to-fool *guajiros* (country folk from Pinar del Río Province), who are popularly portrayed as simple-minded rural hicks. Not so. Check out the local art, for starters, or pop by in July for the Carnaval.

Sights

Palacio de los Matrimonios HISTORIC BUILDING
(Martí, btwn Rafael Morales & Plaza de la Independencia; with guide CUC$1) Wow! West on Martí, the grand neoclassical facades give way to the gushingly opulent in the shape of this

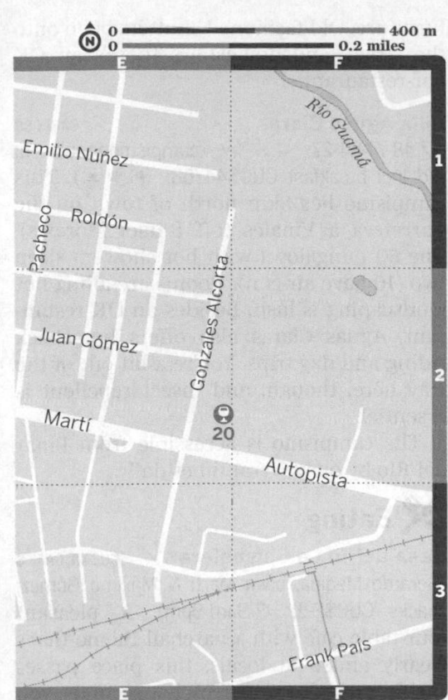

building dating from 1924, now primarily a wedding venue. That said, the amiable guards will let you look around the lavish interior, which includes a plethora of artwork, much of it Chinese in origin.

Casa Taller GALLERY

(Martí No 160, Plaza de la Independencia; hrs vary) FREE The Plaza de la Independencia is the hub of the art scene. First and foremost, on the northwest side, is the workshop-gallery of renowned Cuban artist Pedro Pablo Oliva. The key point of the gallery is to promote and encourage artistic talent in Pinar del Río; several local artists have work displayed. Stop by most days for a browse.

Fábrica de Tabacos Francisco Donatien FACTORY

(Antonio Maceo Oeste No 157; CUC$5; 9am-1:30pm Mon-Fri) You can observe people busily rolling some of Pinar's (read: the world's) finest cigars in this factory, which is now tobacco central on the tourist circuit.

Smaller than the Partagás factory in Havana, you get a more intimate insight here, though the foibles are the same – robotic guides, rushed tours and the nagging notion that it's all a bit voyeuristic. There's an excellent cigar shop opposite.

Museo de Historia Natural MUSEUM

(Martí Este No 202; CUC$1, camera CUC$1; 9am-5pm Mon-Sat, 9am-1pm Sun) A mad but magnificent neo-Gothic-meets-Moorish-meets-Hindu-meets-Byzantium mansion built by local doctor and world traveler Francisco Guasch in 1914. Once you've got over the shock of the whimsical exterior (gargoyles, turrets and sculpted seahorses), the decrepit exhibits inside will slow your pulse right down again. The giant stone T-Rex in the garden is fun though.

Teatro José Jacinto Milanés HISTORIC BUILDING

(48-75-38-71; Martí Este No 60, btwn Colón & Isabel Rubio) Often included in a set of seven classic 19th-century Cuban provincial theaters, the 540-seat Milanés dates from 1845, making it one of Cuba's oldest. It reopened in 2006 after lengthy renovations and, with its three-tiered auditorium, antique seats, and Spanish-style patio and cafe, is well worth a look.

Museo Provincial de Historia MUSEUM

(Martí Este No 58, btwn Colón & Isabel Rubio; CUC$1; 8am-10pm Tue-Sat, to noon Sun) A museum collecting the history of the province from pre-Columbian times to the present, including Enrique Jorrín ephemera (Jorrín was the creator of the *cha-cha-chá*). It has recently reopened after a renovation.

Centro Provincial de Artes Plásticas Galería GALLERY

(Antonio Guiteras, Plaza de la Independencia; 8am-9pm Mon-Sat) FREE This top-notch Pinar gallery on Plaza de la Independencia houses many local works. Bonus: there are some interesting new murals adorning the buildings outside in the square.

Fábrica de Bebidas Casa Garay FACTORY

(Isabel Rubio Sur No 189, btwn Ceferino Fernández & Frank País; CUC$1; 9am-3:30pm Mon-Fri, to 12:30pm Sat) Workers here use a secret recipe to distill sweet and dry versions of the city's signature liquor, Guayabita del Pinar guava brandy. Whistle-stop 15-minute multilingual factory tours are topped off with a taste of the brew in the sampling room. There's a shop adjacent.

Catedral de San Rosendo CHURCH

(Antonio Maceo Este No 3) The city's understated cathedral is four blocks southeast of the cigar factory. It dates from 1883 and its faded-pink exterior is overdue a paint-job. As with most Cuban churches, the interior is often closed. Get a peek during Sunday-morning service.

Festivals & Events

Carnaval CARNIVAL

(Jul) Carnaval in early July features a procession of *carrozas* (carriages) through the streets with couples dancing between the floats. It's a big, drunken dance party.

Sleeping

★Terra Mar 1910 CASA PARTICULAR $

(48-75-58-42; Martí No 140, btwn Rafael Morales & González Coro; s/d/q CUC$35/40/60;) A newly opened accommodation and dining option right on Pinar del Río's main street, this place is run by a Cuban who has lived in Brussels (hence the Belgian flag outside). There are six rooms and a restaurant spread around an attractive colonial residence. One room has a king-sized bed; another has a huge hot tub/bath.

The restaurant specializes in fish grilled on the barbecue and wi-fi can be picked up on the front porch.

Pensión El Moro CASA PARTICULAR $

(48-77-43-35; moro75@nauta.cu; Adela Azcuy No 46, btwn Colón & Ciprián Valdés; r CUC$20-25;) Two bright little apartments – one down, one up – opposite the Víazul bus station. The inviting kitchen with its breakfast bar is shared between both. The upper room is ultimately best, as it's right alongside a roof terrace. English spoken.

Gladys Cruz Hernández CASA PARTICULAR $

(48-77-96-98; casadegladys@gmail.com; Av Comandante Pinares Sur No 15, btwn Martí & Máximo Gómez; r CUC$20-25;) Gladys' unmissable purple house is one of the most dependable places in Pinar del Río, if top-notch colonial rooms and sunny service are what you like for the night. There are two rooms with recently redone tiled bathrooms. Rooms have a fridge and TV, and there's an attractive rear patio. It's near the train station.

Hotel Vueltabajo HOTEL $$

(48-75-93-81; cnr Martí & Rafael Morales; s/d incl breakfast CUC$82/97;) A colonial throwback with high ceilings and striped Parisian window awnings, this dustily atmospheric hotel has rooms so spacious you almost think the owners must've run out of furniture. Old-fashioned shutters open onto the street, and downstairs there's an OK bar-restaurant.

Villa Aguas Claras CABIN $$

(48-77-84-27; www.campismopopular.cu; s/d incl breakfast CUC$44/58;) This campismo lies 8km north of town on the Carretera a Viñales (off Rafael Morales). The 50 bungalows with hot showers sleep two (10 have air-con). Rooms are ailing but landscaping is lush. Besides an OK restaurant, Aguas Claras also offers horseback riding and day trips. You're a bit out of the way here, though, and insect repellent is essential.

The campismo is accessible from Pinar del Río by bus several times daily.

Eating

Casa del Té La Beisbolera CUBAN, CAFE $

(Gerardo Medina, btwn Martí & Máximo Gómez; snacks CUC$2-5; 9am-9pm) A pleasant four-table cafe with a baseball theme that's clearly aimed at locals, this place passes the first test (good coffee). For seconds, you can move on down the menu past the eggs, smoothies, tea and burgers and onto the mains – headlined by chicken. Very simple. Very Pinar.

El Mesón CUBAN $

(48-75-28-67; Martí Este 205; meals CUC$4-6; 11am-11pm) This rather good private restaurant serves up liberal helpings of simple *comida criolla* (Creole food), heavy on the rice and beans, with plenty of Cuban company.

El Gallardo CUBAN $

(48-77-84-92; Martí Este 207; MN$40-125; 11am-11pm;) A rather lavish entrance leads back to a more typical *ranchón*-style main eating area. Great food, particularly the fish, but why the rather grotesque gnomes? Pay in pesos.

Panadería Doña Neli BAKERY $

(cnr Gerardo Medina Sur & Máximo Gómez; snacks CUC$0.50-1; 7am-7pm) For your daily bread.

★Café Ortuzar CUBAN, INTERNATIONAL $$

(Martí 127; 3-course meal CUC$15; 11:30am-midnight;) Slurp a coffee in the streetside cafe or gravitate to the elegant air-conditioned, two-floor interior for the city's best eating experience, where abstract pictures of the province's famous *guajiros* watch on while you eat the CUC$15 three-course meals – a proud part of the new wave of rich, refined Cuban cuisine.

Drinking & Nightlife

Café Pinar LIVE MUSIC
(Gerardo Medina Norte No 34; cover CUC$3; 10am-2am) This spot gets the local youth vote and is also the best place to meet other travelers (if there are any around). Situated on a lively stretch of Calle Gerardo Medina, it features bands playing at night on the open patio, and light menu items such as pasta, chicken and sandwiches available during the day. Mondays and Saturdays are the best nights.

Disco Azul CLUB
(cnr Gonzales Alcorta & Autopista; CUC$5; from 10pm Tue-Sun) A drab hotel, but a kicking disco – this glittery nightclub in Hotel Pinar del Río, on the edge of town coming from the Autopista, is the city's most popular.

Entertainment

La Piscuala CULTURAL CENTER
(cnr Martí & Colón) Peaceful patio alongside the Teatro José Jacinto Milanés (p191). Check the schedule posted outside for nightly cultural activities.

Estadio Capitán San Luis Sports SPECTATOR SPORT
(48-75-38-95; Herryman, btwn Rafael Morales & San Luis; MN$1; matches 7pm Tue-Thu & Sat, 4pm Sun) From October to April, exciting baseball games happen at this stadium on the north side of town. Pinar del Río is one of Cuba's best teams, often challenging the Havana–Santiago monopoly (and national champions in 2011 and 2014). Pop by evenings to see the players going through a training session.

Casa de la Música LIVE MUSIC
(Gerardo Medina Norte No 21; CUC$1; concerts nightly at 9pm) After warming up at nearby Café Pinar, many revelers cross the street for more live music here.

Rumayor CABARET
(48-76-30-51; Carretera a Viñales Km 1; cover charge CUC$5; noon-midnight) Reports vary on the nocturnal action at this state-run restaurant and entertainment center on the edge of the city (on the Viñales road). There's so-so food during the day and a rather rugged nighttime disco from Tuesday through Sunday heating up around 10pmish. The kitschy Sunday cabaret isn't the Tropicana, but it ain't half bad.

Shopping

Casa del Habano CIGARS
(Antonio Maceo Oeste No 162; 9am-5pm Mon-Sat) Opposite the Fábrica de Tabacos Francisco Donatien tobacco factory, this store is one of the better outlets of this popular government cigar chain, with a patio bar, an air-conditioned shop and a smoking room.

Todo Libro Internacional BOOKS
(cnr Martí & Colón; 8am-noon & 1:30-6pm Mon-Fri, 8am-noon & 1-4pm Sat) Selection of maps, books and office supplies next door to the Cubanacán office.

La Casa del Ron ARTS & CRAFTS, RUM
(Antonio Maceo Oeste No 151; 9am-4:30pm Mon-Fri, to 1pm Sat & Sun) Near the Fábrica de Tabacos Francisco Donatien, sells souvenirs, CDs and T-shirts, plus plenty of the strong stuff.

Fondo Cubano de Bienes Cultural ARTS & CRAFTS
(cnr Martí & Gerardo Medina; 9am-4:30pm Mon-Fri, 8:30am-3:30pm Sat) The most interesting selection of regional handicrafts, although revenue goes almost exclusively to the government rather than the makers themselves.

Information

DANGERS & ANNOYANCES

For a relatively untouristed city Pinar del Río has plenty of *jinteros* (unsolicited touts). The majority are young men who hang around Calle Martí, offering everything from paladar (privately owned restaurant) meals to 'guided tours' of tobacco plantations. Most will back off at your first or second *'no me moleste, por favor,'* but bolder ones have been known to mount bicycles and accost tourist cars (identifiable by their purple/brown number plates) when they stop at traffic lights. Although they're generally nonaggressive, it's best to be firmly polite from the outset and not invite further attention.

INTERNET ACCESS

Etecsa Telepunto (cnr Gerardo Medina & Juan Gómez; per hr CUC$1.50; 8:30am-7:30pm) Telephone and internet access.

MEDICAL SERVICES

Farmacia Martí (Martí Este No 50; 8am-11pm)

Hospital Provincial León Cuervo Rubio (☎78-75-44-43; Carretera Central) Two kilometers north of town.

MONEY

Banco Financiero Internacional (Gerardo Medina Norte No 46; ⏲8:30am-3:30pm Mon-Fri) Opposite Casa de la Música.

Cadeca (Martí No 46; ⏲8:30am-5:30pm Mon-Sat) No queues.

POST

Post Office (Martí Este No 49; ⏲8am-8pm Mon-Sat)

TOURIST INFORMATION

Cubanacán (☎48-75-01-78, 48-77-01-04; Martí No 109, cnr Colón; ⏲8am-6pm) Come here to arrange tours of local tobacco plantations and find out about the so-called 'Ruta del Tabaco.' It also arranges tickets for Conectando buses (a back-up for Víazul).

Infotur (☎48-72-86-16; Hotel Vueltabajo, cnr Martí & Rafael Morales; ⏲9am-5:30pm Mon-Fri) At the Hotel Vueltabajo, and one of the city's most helpful sources of information.

Getting There & Away

BUS

The city's **bus station** (Adela Azcuy, btwn Colón & Comandante Pinares) is conveniently close to the center. Pinar del Río is on the **Víazul** (www.viazul.com) network, with all services to Havana and destinations east originating in Viñales. There are departures to Havana at 8:35am and 2:35pm (CUC$11, 2½ hours). The later Havana bus also stops in Las Terrazas. Buses to Viñales leave at 11:45am, 2:25pm, 3:30pm and 5:25pm (CUC$6, 45 minutes).

Conectando buses running most days offer services to Havana and Viñales. You'll need to book ahead with Cubanacán; ask here about other transfers to Cayo Levisa, Cayo Jutías and María la Gorda.

TAXI

Private taxis hanging around outside the bus station will offer prices all the way to Havana. It's worth considering if you can find someone to share the fare with.

TRAIN

Before planning any train travel, check the station blackboards for canceled/suspended/rescheduled services. From the **train station** (cnr Ferrocarril & Comandante Pinares Sur; ⏲ticket window 6:30am-noon & 1-6:30pm) there's a painfully slow train to Havana (CUC$6.50, 5½ hours) every other day. You can buy your ticket for this train the day of departure; be at the station a good hour before departure. Local trains go southwest to Guane via Sábalo (CUC$2, two hours).

Getting Around

Cubacar (☎48-75-93-81; Hotel Vueltabajo, cnr Martí & Rafael Morales; ⏲9am-5pm) has an office at Hotel Vueltabajo. Mopeds can be rented from Cubanacán.

Servicentro Oro Negro (Carretera Central) is opposite the Hospital Provincial on the Carretera Central. There's another on Rafael Morales Sur at the south entrance to town.

Horse carts (MN$1) on Isabel Rubio near Adela Azcuy go to the Hospital Provincial and out onto the Carretera Central. Bici-taxis cost MN$5 around town.

San Juan y Martínez & San Luis

If Cuba is the world's greatest tobacco producer and Pinar del Río its tobacco-growing heartland, then the verdant San Luis region southwest of the provincial capital is the heart of the heartland. Few deny that the pancake-flat farming terrain around the smart town of San Juan y Martínez churns out the crème de la crème of the world's tobacco, and the agricultural scenery is suitably picturesque. The Cuban tourist ministry have recently starting promoting the area as the 'Ruta del Tabaco' and several tobacco farms are now open to visitors.

Sights

Vega Quemado del Rubi FARM

(☎58-20-38-39; Comunidad de Obeso; tours CUC$2; ⏲9am-5pm) The tobacco farm of Hector Luis Prieto is one of the most popular on the current Ruta del Tabaco circuit. In 2007, Prieto was Cuba's youngest ever winner of the prestigious *Hombre Habano* award given annually to the nation's best tobacco producer. His 6-hectare farm, which rears around 250,000 tobacco plants a year, offers detailed tours and horseback-riding, and also maintains a restaurant for lunch and a couple of cozy blue-and-white wooden cabins for overnight accommodation (CUC$45 to CUC$50).

Alejandro Robaina Tobacco Plantation FARM

(☎48-79-74-70; CUC$2; ⏲9am-5pm) The famous Robaina *vegas* (fields), in the rich Vuelta Abajo region southwest of Pinar del Río, have been growing quality tobacco since 1845, but it wasn't until 1997 that a brand of cigars known as Vegas Robaina was first launched to wide international acclaim. The former owner Alejandro Robaina, who made the brand so famous, died in April 2010. But the show must go on, and does at the plantation today. It's been open to outside visitors for some years.

With some deft navigational skills, you can roll up to the farm and get the lowdown on the tobacco-making process from delicate plant to aromatic wrapper: tours are 25 minutes long.

To get there, take the Carretera Central southwest out of Pinar del Río for 12km, turn left toward San Luis and left again after approximately 3km at the Robaina sign. This rougher track continues for 1.5km to the farm. Do not hire a *jintero* (hustler) to lead you, as they often take you to the wrong farm. Tours are available every day. The tobacco-growing season runs from November to February, and this is obviously the best time to visit. Plants only reach an impressive height from December.

Rancho la Guabina RANCH

(☎48-75-76-16; Carretera de Luis Lazo Km 9.5; ⏰horse shows at 10am & 4pm Mon, Wed & Fri) A former Spanish farm spread over 1000 hectares of pasture, forest and wetlands, the Rancho la Guabina is a jack of all trades and a master of at least one. You can partake in horseback riding here, go boating on a lake, or enjoy a scrumptious Cuban barbecue. The big drawcard for most, though, is the fantastic horse shows.

The *rancho* is a long-standing horse-breeding center that raises fine Pinto Cubano and Appaloosa horses, and mini-rodeo-style shows run on Monday, Wednesday and Friday from 10am to noon and from 4pm to 6pm. Agencies in Viñales and Pinar del Río run excursions here starting at CUC$29, or you can arrive on your own. It's a great place to enjoy the peaceful *guajiro* life. Limited accommodations are available.

Getting There & Away

Your own wheels are best in this area. If you're visiting the tobacco plantations, taxis can easily be organized in Viñales or Pinar del Río. Enquire at Cubataxi (p183) in Viñales.

Península de Guanahacabibes

As the island narrows at its western end, you fall upon the low-lying and ecologically rich Península de Guanahacabibes. One of Cuba's most isolated enclaves, it once provided shelter for its earliest inhabitants, the Guanahatabeys. A two-hour drive from Pinar del Río, this region lacks major tourist infrastructure, meaning it feels far more isolated than it is. There are two reasons to come here: a national park (also a Unesco Biosphere Reserve) and an international-standard diving center at María la Gorda.

Although the park border straddles the tiny community of La Fe, the reserve entrance is at La Bajada.

It's a 120km round-trip to Cuba's westernmost point from La Bajada. The lonesome Cabo de San Antonio is populated by a solitary lighthouse (Faro Roncali), the Gaviota Marina and Villa Cabo San Antonio. Abutting the hotel is Playa las Tumbas, Cuba's most isolated beach, where you can swim.

Parque Nacional Península de Guanahacabibes

If you want to see Cuba how Columbus must have seen it, come to the Península de Guanahacabibes, the flat and deceptively narrow finger of land that points toward Mexico on the island's western tip. Protected by a national park and a Unesco Biosphere Reserve, this place is practically virgin territory. Picture miles of limestone karst guarded by iguanas, lagoons full of petrified trees and sun-bathing crocodiles, rare birds fluttering through veritable forests of palm trees, and storm-lashed beaches where even Robinson Crusoe would have felt lonely.

In summer sea turtles come ashore at night to lay their eggs (the only part of mainland Cuba where this happens), while April sees swarms of *cangrejos colorados* (red-and-yellow crabs) crawling across the peninsula's rough central road only to be unceremoniously crushed under the tires of passing cars. The area is also thought to shelter important archaeological sites relating to the pre-Columbian Guanahatabey people.

Sights

★Playa las Tumbas BEACH

If they gave out Academy Awards for Cuban beaches, Las Tumbas might just win, edging out Playa Sirena on Cayo Largo del Sur (too many tourists) and Playa Pilar on Cayo Guillermo (recently blemished by an ugly hotel). It's certainly the nation's most isolated beach, 60km from the nearest population and backed only by a quiet 16-room hotel.

Faro Roncali LIGHTHOUSE
On the far western tip of Cuba sits the nation's oldest lighthouse, which was constructed by slaves and Chinese laborers in 1849. It was named after the then governor of Cuba, the Spaniard, Federico Roncali Ceruti.

Activities

Península de Guanahacabibes is a paradise for divers, eco-travelers, conservationists and birdwatchers. Feathered species on display here include parrots, tocororos (Cuba's national bird), woodpeckers, owls, tody flycatchers and *zunzuncitos* (bee hummingbirds). Animal-wise there are *jutías* (tree rats), iguanas, turtles and a population of around 30 American crocodiles.

Diving

Centro Internacional de Buceo DIVING
(☎48-77-13-06; María la Gorda) Diving is María la Gorda's raison d'être and the prime reason people come to Cuba's western tip. The nerve center is this well-run base next to the eponymous hotel at the Marina Gaviota. Good visibility and sheltered offshore reefs are highlights, plus the proximity of the 32 dive sites to the shore.

Couple this with the largest formation of black coral in the archipelago and you've got a recipe for arguably Cuba's best diving reefs outside the Isla de la Juventud.

A dive here costs CUC$40 (night dive CUC$50), plus CUC$10 for equipment. The center offers a full CMAS (Confédération Mondiale des Activités Subaquatiques; World Underwater Activities Federation) scuba certification course (CUC$365, four days) and snorkelers can hop on the dive boat for CUC$15.

Among the 50 identified dive sites in the vicinity, divers are shown El Valle de Coral Negro, a 100m-long black-coral wall, and El Salón de María, a cave 20m deep containing feather stars and brilliantly colored corals. The concentrations of migratory fish can be incredible. The furthest entry is only 30 minutes by boat from shore.

Marina Gaviota Cabo de San Antonio DIVING
(☎48-75-01-18) Cuba's most westernmost boat dock is 4km beyond Playa las Tumbas at the end of the Península Guanahacabibes. The marina has fuel, boat mooring, a small restaurant, a shop and easy access to 27 diving sites. The Villa Cabo San Antonio is nearby.

Guided Hikes

It's a long drive from Pinar del Río to the national park entrance, so to avoid potential disappointment, phone ahead and reserve a guide for park activities through the visitor center (opposite).

The park currently offers three different excursions. Independent travelers with a reservation at Villa Cabo San Antonio are also granted access.

Del Bosque al Mar HIKING
(guide CUC$6) Leaving from near the Estación Ecológica Guanahacabibes, this 1.5km trail passes a lagoon where you can view resident birdlife, and takes in some interesting flora including orchids, as well as a crystal clear *cenote* (sinkhole) for swimming.

At 90 minutes it's rather short for such an immense park, but the guides are highly trained and informed, and tours can be conducted in Spanish, English or Italian.

Cueva las Perlas HIKING
(guide CUC$8) The three-hour 3km-round-trip trek to the 'pearl cave' traverses deciduous woodland replete with a wide variety of birds, including tocororos, *zunzuncitos* and woodpeckers. You'll clock evidence of indigenous occupants from former centuries en route. After 1.5km you come to the cave itself, where you can spy (and hear) screech owls: it's a multi-gallery cavern with a lake of which 300m is accessible to hikers.

Turtle-Watching

Guanahacabibes is still a park in tentative development, but includes turtle-monitoring opportunities among its limited stash of organized excursions. The turtle program has been running since 1998 under the direction of environmental researchers and with involvement from the local population (primarily schoolchildren). In recent years, outsiders have been allowed to participate. Approximately 1500 nesting green turtles lay their eggs on half a dozen of the peninsula's south-facing beaches between June and August, and willing participants are invited to observe, monitor and aid in the process. In 2013, a record 900 turtle nests were recorded. To take part, inquire in advance at the visitor center (details opposite) at La Bajada. Tours take place nightly between 10pm and 2am in season, and there are observa-

WORTH A TRIP

JOURNEY TO THE END OF THE ISLAND

The five-hour tour to Cuba's isolated and practically virgin western tip at Cabo de San Antonio is superb. Along the way you'll see jungles of palms, deserted beaches, iguanas, crocodiles (if you're lucky), *cenotes* (sinkholes) and petrified forests. The responsibility is yours to supply transport and sufficient gas, water and food, so you'll need a taxi or your own wheels.

During most of the 120km round-trip through the Parque Nacional Península de Guanahacabibes, you'll have dark, rough *diente de perro* (dog's teeth) rock on one side and the brilliant blue sea on the other. Iguanas will lumber for cover as you approach and you might spy small deer, *jutías* (tree rats) and lots of birds. Beyond the lighthouse is deserted Playa las Tumbas, where you'll have time to swim should you desire.

Thanks to the upgraded road surface, any hire car can make this trip. The five-hour excursion costs CUC$10 per person with guide, plus the CUC$80 or so you'll need to hire a car (there's car rental at Hotel María la Gorda). Besides the beaches and exotic flora, there's a chance to see crocodiles, explore a bat-ridden cave and climb a wooden *mirador* to spy Cuba's north and south coasts. Near Playa La Barca, a recently wrecked ship adds romance to the proceedings.

tion shelters at Playa La Barca, the main turtle-watching beach. The release of baby turtles begins in mid-September.

Sleeping

Hotel María la Gorda HOTEL **$$**
(☎48-77-81-31; www.hotelmarialagorda-cuba.com; s/d/tr incl breakfast CUC$62/85/106; P ❄ @) This is among Cuba's remotest hotels, and the isolation has its advantages. The adjoining palm-fringed beach is pretty (if a little rocky), but 90% of people come here to dive; reefs and vertical drop-offs beckon just 200m from the hotel. María la Gorda (literally 'Maria the Fatso') is on the Bahía de Corrientes, 150km southwest of Pinar del Río.

Room-wise you get a choice of three beach-hugging pink-concrete, motel-type buildings or, further back, either attractive white two-floor apartment blocks or rustic wooden cabins connected by walkways. Far from being a posh resort, María la Gorda is an easygoing place where hammocks are strung between palm trees, cold beers are sipped at sunset and dive talk continues into the small hours.

Buffet meals cost CUC$15 for lunch or dinner; reports on the food vary. There are two restaurants and a beach bar. A small shop sells water and basic provisions. There's a steep CUC$10 (including a sandwich) charge to visit Hotel María la Gorda and its adjoining 5km beach for nonguests, although sneaking down for free beach time wouldn't be hard if you forgo the sandwich.

Villa Cabo San Antonio CABIN **$$**
(☎48-75-76-55; Playa las Tumbas; r incl breakfast CUC$118; P ❄) A 16-villa complex on the almost-virgin Península de Guanahacabibes behind idyllic Playa las Tumbas, set 3km beyond the Faro Roncali (Roncali Lighthouse) and 4km shy of the Gaviota Marina. It's a friendly and surprisingly well-appointed place, with satellite TV, car rental, bike/quad hire and a modest restaurant.

Ask about their lavish Casa Leñador designed by Faro Roncali, a CUC$160-per-night house sleeping nine and with a private pool.

Information

Visitor Center (☎48-75-03-66; La Bajada; 8:30am-3pm)

Getting There & Away

BUS

A transfer bus (return CUC$35) operates between Viñales and María la Gorda most days, but check and book ahead. It is scheduled to leave Viñales at 7am and arrive at the peninsula at 9:30am. The return leg leaves María la Gorda at 5pm and arrives in Viñales at 7pm. Reserve at Cubanacán (p178) in Viñales or Infotur (p194) in Pinar del Río.

CAR

Vía Gaviota (☎48-77 81 31; Hotel María la Gorda) has an office at Hotel María la Gorda, offering car hire from around CUC$75 per day for a small car. The road into the national park has recently been upgraded and is passable in a normal car.

Varadero & Matanzas Province

☎45 / POP 692,536

Includes ➡

Best Places to Eat

- ➡ Varadero 60 (p210)
- ➡ Salsa Suárez (p208)
- ➡ Paladar Nonna Tina (p209)
- ➡ El Chiquirrín (p220)

Best Places to Sleep

- ➡ Hostal Azul (p218)
- ➡ Casa Julio y Lidia (p233)
- ➡ Casa Mary y Àngel (p203)
- ➡ Royalton Hicacos Resort (p206)

Why Go?

With a name translating as 'massacres,' Matanzas Province conceals an appropriately tumultuous past beneath its modern-day reputation for glam all-inclusive holidays. In the 17th century pillaging pirates ravaged the region's prized north coast, while three centuries later, more invaders grappled ashore in the Bahía de Cochinos (Bay of Pigs) under the dreamy notion that they were about to liberate the nation.

The Bahía de Cochinos attracts more divers than mercenaries these days, while sunbathers rather than pirates invade the northern beaches of Varadero, the vast Caribbean resort and lucrative economic 'cash cow' that stretches 20km along the sandy Península de Hicacos.

Providing a weird juxtaposition is the scruffy city of Matanzas, the music-rich provincial capital that has gifted the world with rumba, *danzón* (ballroom dance), countless grand neoclassical buildings and Santería (the province is the veritable cradle of Afro-Cuban religion). Tourists may be scant here outside of Varadero but soulful, only-in-Cuba experiences are surprisingly abundant.

When to Go

- ➡ December through April the all-inclusive hotels in the tourist set-piece – Varadero – hike prices for the *temporada alta* (high season), the best time for beach-basking.
- ➡ Hit Matanzas city around October 10 for the annual rumba festival, Festival del Bailador Rumbero.
- ➡ November to April are the best months for birdwatching in the Ciénaga de Zapata.

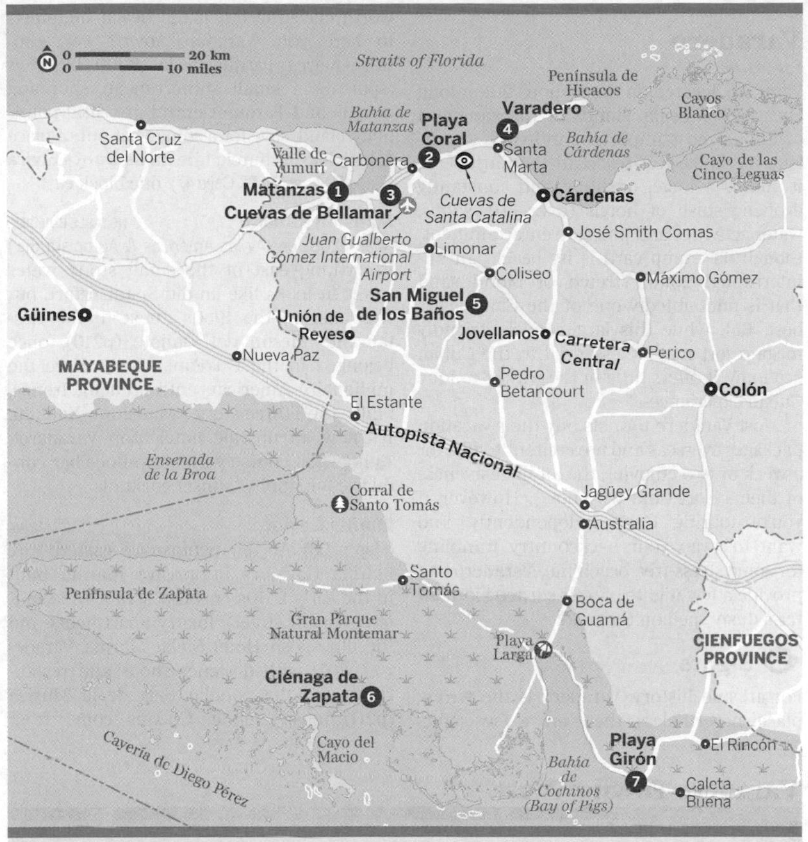

Varadero & Matanzas Province Highlights

1. **Matanzas** (p215) Unlocking the buried secrets of the long-neglected but slowly re-emerging 'Athens of Cuba.'
2. **Playa Coral** (p214) Indulging in a rare opportunity to dive and snorkel from the shore at this north coast beach.
3. **Cuevas de Bellamar** (p214) Delving into Cuba's deepest cave system just outside Matanzas.
4. **Varadero** (p202) Finding your own private nirvana on the sandy expanses of Cuba's longest beach.
5. **San Miguel de los Baños** (p225) Admiring forgotten grandeur in long abandoned bathhouses.
6. **Ciénaga de Zapata** (p228) Exploring the vast, varied vegetation zones in one of Cuba's last true wildernesses.
7. **Playa Girón** (p231) Discovering the plunging dropoffs and colorful coral walls of Cuba's most accessible dive zone.

NORTHERN MATANZAS

Home to Cuba's largest resort area (Varadero) and one of its biggest ports (Matanzas), the northern coastline is also Matanzas Province's main population center and a hub for industry and commerce. Despite this, the overriding feel is distinctly green, and most of the region is undulating farmland – think a cross between North American prairie and the UK's Norfolk Broads – occasionally rupturing into lush, dramatic valleys like the Valle de Yumurí, or sinking into enigmatic caves outside Matanzas.

Varadero

POP 27,630

Varadero, located on the sinuous 20km-long Hicacos Peninsula, stands at the vanguard of Cuba's most important industry – tourism. As the largest resort in the Caribbean, it guards a huge, unsubtle and constantly evolving stash of hotels (over 60), shops, water activities and poolside entertainment; though its trump card is its beach, an uninterrupted 20km stretch of blond sand that is undoubtedly one of the Caribbean's best. But, while this large, tourist-friendly mega-resort may be essential to the Cuban economy, it offers little in the way of unique Cuban experiences.

Most Varadero tourists buy their vacation packages overseas and are content to idle for a week or two enjoying the all-inclusiveness of their resort (and why not?). However, if you're touring Cuba independently, and want to swap your backcountry rambling for some stress-free beach life, Varadero can provide a few nights of well-earned sloth after a dusty spell on the road.

Sights

For art and history, Varadero is the wrong place; nevertheless, there are a few sights worth checking out if the beach life starts to bore you. Varadero town's two central squares, Parque de las 8000 Taquillas (sporting a small subterranean shopping center) and Parque Central are disappointingly bland, save for a somewhat out-of-place colonial-style church, **Iglesia de Santa Elvira** (Map p204; cnr Av 1 & Calle 47), one block east.

Mansión Xanadú NOTABLE BUILDING

(Map p208; cnr Av las Américas & Autopista Sur) Everything east of the small stone water tower (it looks like an old Spanish fort, but was built in the 1930s), next to the Restaurante Mesón del Quijote (p210), once belonged to the Du Pont family. Here the millionaire American entrepreneur, Irenée, built the three-story Mansión Xanadú. It's now an upscale hotel atop Varadero's 18-hole golf course with a top-floor bar conducive for sipping sunset cocktails.

Marina Gaviota MARINA

(Map p208) At the peninsula's eastern tip, Marina Gaviota's impressive marina built in the early 2010s encompasses a wide *malecón* (main street), luxury apartments and the ultra-posh Hotel Meliá Marina Varadero (p207) with designer shops and restaurants, and the popular Sala de la Música (p211) music venue. Cubans come from

Varadero Town – West

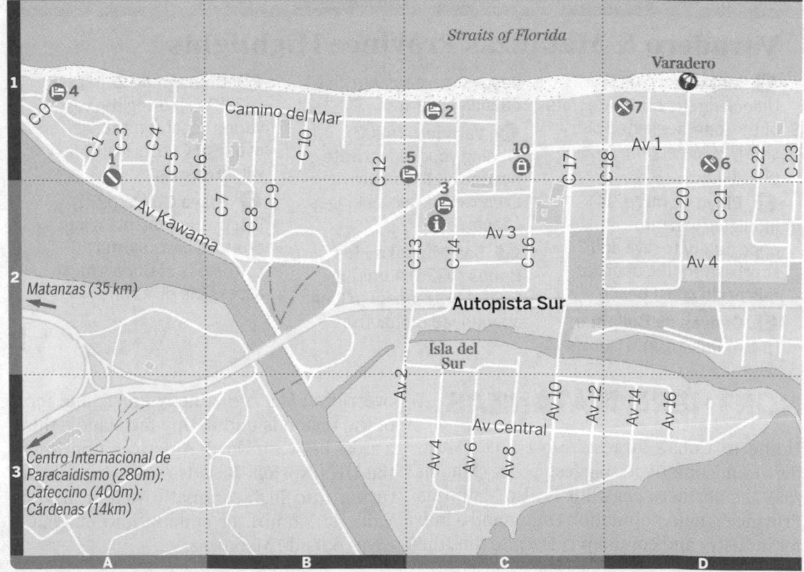

miles around to marvel: it's a little bit more of Florida that's found its way across the water and the only marina in Cuba worthy of international rating.

Parque Josone PARK
(Map p204; cnr Av 1 & Calle 58; 9am-midnight;) If you're set on sight-seeing in Varadero, ensconce yourself in this pretty green oasis. These landscaped gardens date back to 1940 and take their name from the former owners, José Fermín Iturrioz y Llaguno and his wife Onelia, who owned the Arechabala (p224) rum distillery in nearby Cárdenas and built a neoclassical mansion here: the Retiro Josone.

Expropriated after the revolution, the mansion became a guesthouse for visiting foreign dignitaries. The park is now a public space for the enjoyment of all – you may see Cuban girls celebrate their *quinceañeras* (15th-birthday celebrations) here. Josone's expansive, shady grounds feature a lake with rowboats (per person per hour CUC$0.50) and water-bikes (per hour CUC$5), atmospheric eateries, resident geese, myriad tree species and a minitrain (ride CUC$1). There's a public swimming pool (CUC$2) in the south of the park and the odd ostrich lurking nearby. Good music can be heard nightly.

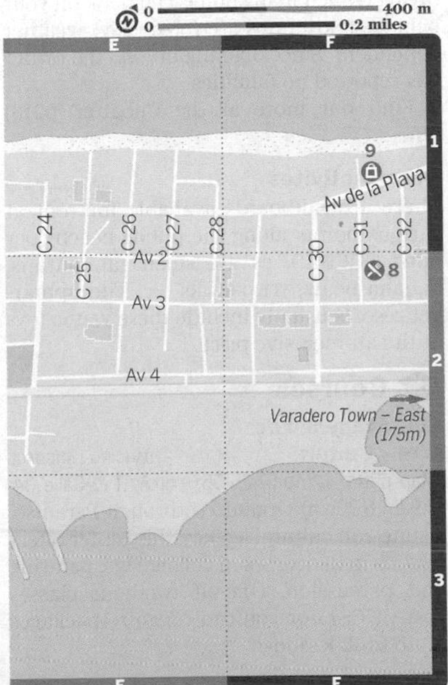

Cueva de Ambrosio CAVE
(Map p208; Autopista Sur; CUC$5; 9am-4:30pm) For something completely different in Varadero's tourist circus, decamp to this large cave 500m beyond the Club Amigo Varadero on the Autopista Sur. It's known for its 47 pre-Columbian drawings, discovered in a recess in 1961 and thought to be around 2000 years old. The black-and-red drawings feature the same concentric circles seen in similar paintings on the Isla de la Juventud, perhaps a form of solar calendar. You'll be given a torch at the entrance and told to mind the bats!

Museo Municipal de Varadero MUSEUM
(Map p204; Calle 57; CUC$1; 10am-7pm) Walking up Calle 57 from Av 1, you'll see many typical wooden beach-houses with elegant wraparound porches. The most attractive of the bunch, Varadero's Museo Municipal, has been turned into a balconied chalet displaying period furniture and a snapshot of the resort's history. It's more interesting than you'd think.

Activities

Diving & Snorkeling

Varadero has several excellent dive centers, although, this being tourist-ville, the prices are double those in the Bahía de Cochinos on Matanzas Province's south coast. Additionally, all of the 21 dive sites around the Península de Hicacos require a boat transfer of approximately one hour. Highlights include reefs, caverns and a Russian patrol boat sunk for diving purposes in 1997. The nearest shore diving is 20km west at Playa Coral (p214). The centers also offer day

Varadero Town – West

Activities, Courses & Tours
1 Barracuda Scuba Diving Center A1

Sleeping
2 Casa Menocal C1
3 Hotel Acuazul C2
4 Hotel Club Kawama A1
5 Villa Sunset C1

Eating
6 La Vaca Rosada D1
7 Lai-Lai D1
8 Salsa Suárez F2

Shopping
9 Casa del Habano F1
10 Gran Parque de la Artesania C1

excursions to superior sites at the Bahía de Cochinos (p231) (one/two immersions with transfer CUC$50/70) – or you could bus it there yourself and dive unrushed with local instructors, including an overnight stay at a local casa for just a fraction more.

Note that when the weather is inclement on the north coast, divers are often bussed over to more sheltered Bahía de Cochinos in the south.

Barracuda Scuba Diving Center DIVING

(Map p200; ☎45-61-34-81; Av Kawama, btwn Calle 2 & Calle 3; ⌚8am-7pm) Varadero's top scuba facility is the mega-friendly, multilingual Barracuda Scuba Diving Center. Diving costs CUC$50 per dive with equipment, cave diving is CUC$80 and night diving costs CUC$65. Packages of multiple dives work out cheaper. Barracuda conducts introductory resort courses for CUC$70, and American Canadian Underwater Certificate (ACUC) courses starting at CUC$250, plus many advanced courses. Snorkeling at Playa Coral (p214) with guide is CUC$36.

When a north wind is blowing and diving isn't possible in the Atlantic, you can be transferred to the Caribbean coast in a minibus (90-minute drive); this costs a total of CUC$55/75 for one/two dives. Other popular trips include Cueva de Saturno (p215) for cave diving and Playa Coral for snorkeling.

Golf

Varadero Golf Club GOLF

(Map p208; ☎45-66-77-88; www.varaderogolfclub.com; Mansión Xanadú; green fees 18-holes CUC$100; ⌚7am-7pm) While it's no Pebble Beach, golfers can have a swinging session at this uncrowded and well-landscaped club: Cuba's first and only fully fledged 18-hole course (par 72). The original nine holes created by the Du Ponts are between Hotel Bella Costa and Du Pont's Mansión Xanadú; another nine holes added in 1998 flank the southern side of the three Meliá resorts.

Bookings for the course are made through the pro shop next to the Mansión Xanadú (p206; now a cozy hotel with free, unlimited tee time). Bizarrely, golf carts (CUC$30 per person) are mandatory.

Kitesurfing

Ke Bola Kiteboarding School KITESURFING

(Map p208; ☎52-64-43-76; Varadero Beach; kite rent per hour/day CUC$35/190; ⌚noon-6pm) Kiteboarding school and equipment rental based on the beach between Hotels Laguna Azul and La Ocean El Patriarca (p207). Beginners courses are offered from CUC$55 per hour. The beach here is ample with stiff winds.

Skydiving

Centro Internacional de Paracaidismo SKYDIVING

(☎45-66-28-28; http://skydivingvaradero.com; Carretera Vía Blanca Km 1.5; skydive per person CUC$190) For those with a head for heights, Varadero's greatest thrill has to be skydiving at this base at the old airport just west of Varadero. The terminal is 1km up a dirt road, opposite Marina Acua. Skydivers take off in an Antonov AN-2 biplane and jump from 3000m using a two-harness parachute with an instructor strapped in tandem on your back.

After 35 seconds of free fall the parachute opens and you float tranquilly for 10 minutes down onto Varadero's white sandy beach. The center also offers less spectacular (but equally thrilling) ultralight flights at various points on the beach. Prices for skydiving are CUC$190 per person with CUC$80 extra for video. If you are already a qualified skydiver, solo jumps (CUC$60) are also available on production of the relevant certification.

A day's notice is usually required for skydiving (which many hotels can book on your behalf), and jumps are (obviously) weather dependent. Since opening in 1993 the center has reported no fatalities.

Find out more at the Cubatur (p213) office.

Other Activites

There are sailboards available for rent at various points along the public beach (per hour CUC$10), as are small catamarans, banana boats, sea kayaks etc. The upmarket resorts usually include these water toys in the all-inclusive price.

Courses

ABC Academia de Arte y Cultura DANCING, LANGUAGE

(Map p204; ☎45-61-25-06; cnr Av 1 & Calle 34; ⌚9am-6:30pm) Organized through Paradiso, a state-run cultural agency, this center offers lessons in dance, Spanish language, painting and percussion. One-off two-hour classes cost CUC$15 or you can organize packages of up to 12 lessons.

Tours

Tour desks at all the main hotels churn out a regular diet of nautical or sporting activities and arrange organized sightseeing excursions from Varadero. They are perennially popular with the all-inclusive set.

Standard days trips include sunset cruises, a 4WD safari to the Valle de Yumurí, boat trips on the Río Canímar and a whole range of bus tours to places as far away as Santa Clara, Trinidad, Viñales and, of course, Havana.

Boat Adventure BOATING
(Map p208; ☎45-66-84-40; per person CUC$41; ⏰9am-4pm) This two-hour guided trip, leaving from a separate dock next to the Marlin Marina Chapelín, is a speedy sortie through the adjacent mangroves on two-person motorboats to view myriad forms of wildlife, including curious crocs. Bookings for all these watery excursions can also be made at most of the big hotels.

Marlin Marina Chapelín (Aquaworld) BOAT TOUR, WATER SPORTS
(Map p208; ☎45-66-75-50; Autopista Sur Km 12; ⏰8am-4pm) Aquaworld Marina Chapelín organizes Varadero's nautical highlight in the popularity stakes: the Seafari Cayo Blanco, a seven-hour sojourn (CUC$109) from Marina Chapelín to nearby Cayo Blanco and its idyllic beach. The trip includes an open bar, lobster lunch, two snorkeling stops, live music and hotel transfers.

There's also five hours of deep-sea fishing: CUC$310 for four people (price includes hotel transfers, open bar and licenses; nonfishing companions pay CUC$30).

Sleeping

Varadero Town

★**Beny's House** CASA PARTICULAR $
(Map p204; ☎45-61-17-00; www.benyhouse.com; Calle 55, btwn Av 1 & Av 2; r incl breakfast CUC$35; P ❄) Why would you want to blow hundreds of dollars on an all-inclusive when you can pay CUC$35 a night to stay at Beny's house? It's within spitting distance of the beach and you can converse with one of Varadero's great characters.

There's everything you need here: landscaped garden, patio, three smart rooms with queen-size beds and flatscreen TVs, restaurant specializing in fish, and – best of all – Beny himself.

Casa Mary y Ángel CASA PARTICULAR $
(Map p204; ☎45-61-23-83; marisabelcarrillo@yahoo.com; Calle 43 No 4309, btwn Av 1 & Av 2; d/tr CUC$35/40; ❄) The array of shady terraces at this leading private accommodation option will have hotels hereabouts looking

VARADERO'S HOTELS IN A NUTSHELL

Varadero's confusingly large hotel zone can, for simplicity's sake, be broken into four broad segments.

The accommodations in the spread-out Cuban town (Varadero town) at the west end of the peninsula consist of older budget hotels wedged in among the shops, banks, bars and vintage beach-houses. Since 2011, town residents have been able to legally rent out rooms to foreigners and over 20 casas particulares have now taken root.

The section from Calle 64 northeast to the golf course is punctuated by a thin strip of hodgepodge architecture, from kitschy Holiday Camp to bloc-style Soviet-esque. Selling cheap packages to mainly foreign tourists, many of these hotels are already looking dated after only three or four decades in operation.

East of the Mansión Xanadú (p200) is a cluster of large single-structure hotels with impressive lobbies and multiple stories, built mostly in the early 1990s. The tallest is the spectacular 14-story Blau Varadero (p206), designed to resemble an Aztec pyramid.

The nearer you get to the east end of the peninsula, the more it starts to look like a Florida suburb. Contemporary Cuban all-inclusive resorts favor detached one-to-three story blocks that are laid out like mini-towns and spread over multiple acres. Most of these sprawling resorts have been built since 2000 and it is here that you'll find Varadero's largest (the 1025-room Memories Varadero; p207) and most exclusive (Blau Marina Palace's Planta Real; p206) accommodations, although every year brings tidings of new resorts opening with new never-seen-before attributes.

Varadero Town – East

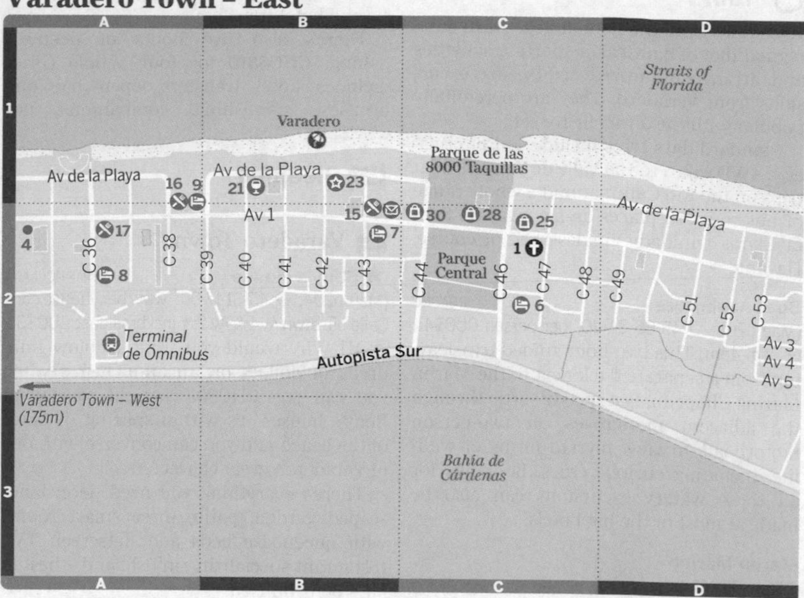

Varadero Town – East

Sights
1 Iglesia de Santa Elvira C2
2 Museo Municipal de Varadero E2
3 Parque Josone E2

Activities, Courses & Tours
4 ABC Academia de Arte y Cultura A2

Sleeping
5 Beny's House E2
6 Casa Marlén y Javier C2
7 Casa Mary y Ángel B2
8 Hostal Sol RyA A2
9 Hotel los Delfines A1
10 Hotel Starfish Cuatro Palmas F2
11 Papo's House E2
12 Starfish Las Palmas F2

Eating
13 Dante E2
14 La Fondue F2
15 La Rampa B2
16 Paladar Nonna Tina A1
17 Restaurante Esquina Cuba A2
18 Restaurante La Barbacoa F2
Restaurante Mallorca .... (see 14)
19 Varadero 60 .... F3
20 Waco's Club E3

Drinking & Nightlife
Calle 62 .... (see 14)
21 La Bodeguita del Medio B1

Entertainment
22 Beatles Bar-Restaurant F2
23 Casa de la Música B1
24 Centro Cultural Comparsita F2

Shopping
25 ARTex C2
Casa de las Américas .... (see 29)
26 Casa del Habano F2
27 Casa del Ron F2
28 Centro Comercial Hicacos C2
29 Galería de Arte Varadero F2
30 Librería Hanoi C2
Taller de Cerámica Artística .... (see 29)

enviously over their shoulders – as will the three gleaming, well-appointed rooms. Breakfast will run to several courses, and to several hours if the rich, strong coffee has anything to do with it. Best of all are the hosts – warm, welcoming and full of local info.

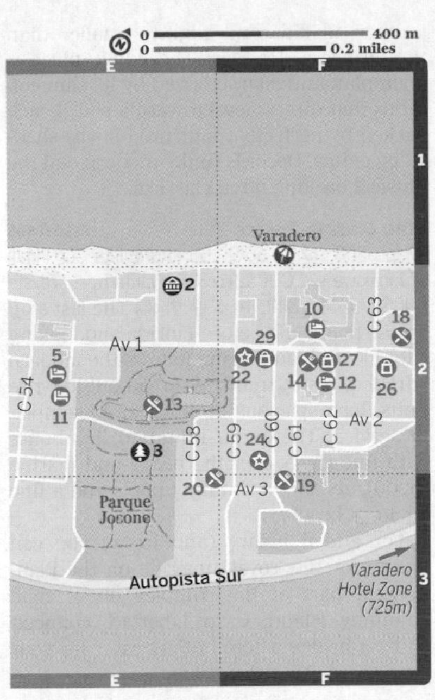

Casa Marlén y Javier CASA PARTICULAR $
(Map p204; ☎45-61-32-86; Av 2, btwn Calles 46 & 47; r CUC$30-35; ❄) A superb house with three rooms on a quiet back street, with hosts that are among Varadero's favorites with travelers. There is a *ranchón-* (rustic, open-sided restaurant) style rooftop terrace where meals are served. English spoken.

Papo's House CASA PARTICULAR $
(Map p204; ☎45-61-26-40; papomoreno89@yahoo.es; Calle 55 No 114, btwn Av 1 & Av 2; r CUC$35; P❄) You're in for a treat. Papo's is one of the few houses in Cuba decorated with antique Louis XV furniture, at least in some of the rooms, meaning it has a strong following among French travelers. It's right next to Parque Josone (p201) and, like everywhere in Varadero, close to the beach. There's a wi-fi hotspot on the adjacent street.

Hostal Sol RyA CASA PARTICULAR $
(Map p204; ☎45-61-29-25; rafael.g@nauta.cu; Calle 36 No 117, btwn Av 1 & Autopista; CUC$35-40; ❄) Handy little homestay right next to the Víazul bus station (p213) with one independent apartment (with bunk beds and ideal for families) and another normal double room. Rooms have all mod cons and there's plenty of local information on hand.

Casa Menocal CASA PARTICULAR $
(Map p200; ☎45-60-31-64; Calle 14 No 1, cnr Callejón del Mar; s/d/tr CUC$35/45/50; ❄) Traditional grey-stone Varadero house right on a dreamy slice of beach. Five rooms with roof beams and traditional 1940s feel. Book ahead.

Villa Sunset CASA PARTICULAR $
(Map p200; ☎52-39-45-42; adrylopfer@yahoo.es; Calle 13, btwn Av 1 & Av Camino del Mar; r incl breakfast CUC$45; ❄) The sedate four-room Villa Sunset comes with a large well-appointed kitchen and the absence of on-site owners (not uncommon in Varadero casas particulares) means it sits somewhere between fancy boutique hostel and self-catering apartment. A good option for families, with a garden at the rear.

Starfish Las Palmas HOTEL $$
(Map p204; ☎45-66-70-40; www.starfishresorts.com; Calle 62, btwn Av 1 & Av 2; s/d with breakfast CUC$90/120; P❄📶) Varadero introduced a welcome new concept in November 2016 with the opening of this new Starfish hotel. It's not an all-inclusive, it's not a casa particular; rather it's a kind of mid-range, boutique, standard hotel spread over several buildings in the eastern part of town.

Rooms are fresh and clean with earthy tones and mini-balconies and you can procure a CUC$20 day-pass for the **Starfish Cuatro Palmas** (Map p204; Av 1, btwn Calles 60 & 62; s/d all-inclusive CUC$135/220; P❄@📶🏊) across the road. The hotel is stretched across several street blocks with the reception on Calle 62.

Hotel los Delfines RESORT $$
(Map p204; ☎45-66-77-20; www.islazul.cu; cnr Av de la Playa & Calle 39; s/d all-inclusive from CUC$110/125; ❄@🏊) The Delfines is unusual for Varadero in that it's a cheap all-inclusive that inhabits the town itself rather than the spread-out hotel zone to the east. If you're used to Meliá-style luxury, then this 103-room resort probably isn't your bag, but, if you don't mind sharing a cozier more modest hotel with both foreign *and* Cuban guests, it could cut ice.

The hotel abuts a lovely scoop of wide protected beach and there are plenty of shops and restaurants around should you tire of the all-inclusive package.

Hotel Acuazul HOTEL $$
(Map p200; ☎45-66-71-32; Av 1, btwn Calle 13 & Calle 14; s/d all-inclusive CUC$102/124;

) Not fussy? Then head for this cheap-ish all-inclusive at the west end of the peninsula, whose architecture is a little Russian and where the ambience is more Cuban than international. If the buffet gets boring (and it will), there are plenty of private restaurants nearby.

Hotel Club Kawama RESORT **$$$**
(Map p200; 45-61-44-16; www.gran-caribe.cu; cnr Av 1 & Calle 1; s/d all-inclusive from CUC$124/170;) A venerable old 1930s hacienda-style building, the sprawling Kawama was the first of the 60-plus hotels to inhabit this once-deserted peninsula more than 70 years ago. The service struggles here and facilities are a bit haggard despite recent renovations, but optimists will still detect some silver linings in the 235 colorful rooms which blend artfully into the sliver of beach that's Varadero's western extremity.

All-inclusive prices include everything from tennis to aquabike usage.

Varadero Hotel Zone

★**Royalton Hicacos Resort** RESORT **$$$**
(Map p208; 45-66-88-51, 45-66-88-44; www.royaltonresorts.com; Punta Hicacos; ste all-inclusive CUC$420;) Having a more understated look (and more personable service) than many of its neighbors has made Royalton Hicacos one of the most appealing resorts on the end-point of the peninsula, with vast *ranchón*-style public areas and babbling water features lending a mellifluous air. Bedrooms, done up in sunny yellows and oranges, have king beds and huge bathrooms. No kids.

Paradisus Princesa del Mar RESORT **$$$**
(Map p208; 45-66-72-00; www.meliacuba.com; Carretera las Morlas Km 19.5; s/d CUC$389/555;) With a big asking price, you going to have high expectations of this adults-only Meliá resort. Despite its size (630 rooms), it's certainly heavy on the romantic theme with luxury beds around the pool, a big spa complex, loungers scattered under the palm trees and plenty of honeymooners strolling around contentedly hand-in-hand. It's certainly paradise – or 'paradisus' – for some.

Paradisus Varadero RESORT **$$$**
(Map p208; 45-66-87-00; www.meliacuba.com; Autopista Sur; s/d CUC$372/585;) More five-star Meliá luxury, this Paradisus is open to kids and slightly smaller than the 'Princesa del Mar.' The whole place is open-plan and characterized by its slim columns that direct views toward a wide beach backed by perfectly manicured lawns shaded by palms. Decor is funky-modern and the musical backing often classical.

Blau Marina Palace RESORT **$$$**
(Map p208; 45-66-99-66; Autopista Sur Final; all-inclusive s/d CUC$211/338, Planta Real s/d/ste CUC$279/448/848;) The last stop on the peninsula before Florida and looking a lot like it, Blau Marina follows the modern Varadero resort trend, ie spread-out low-rise units, lush spacious grounds and exemplary service. There's an imitation lighthouse with fine views over the beach and marina (p200), acres of swimming pools and a fine adjacent beach.

For added luxury (and irony) you can plump for the 'royal' upgrade on the Planta Real part of the complex on a small adjoining island, Cayo Libertad, connected by a bridge where butlers cater for your every need. Ah....*socialismo!*

Blau Varadero RESORT **$$$**
(Map p208; 45-66-75-45; Carretera de las Morlas Km 15; all-inclusive s/d CUC$228/375;) Suspend your judgment on Varadero's tallest and most architecturally unsubtle resort. Trying hard to imitate an Aztec pyramid from the outside (why?), the interior is nothing short of spectacular; a 14-story enclosed courtyard embellished by hundreds of hanging plants, some falling for over 80m. Huge rooms are surgically clean and the higher ones have the best views in Varadero.

Downstairs, you're in resort land, so expect loquacious poolside entertainers, beer in plastic cups and iffy Michael Jackson theme nights.

Mansión Xanadú RESORT **$$$**
(Map p208; 45-66-73-88; www.varaderogolfclub.com; cnr Av las Américas & Autopista Sur; s/d all-inclusive CUC$198/264;) Varadero's most intriguing, intimate lodging is in the grand former residence of US chemical-entrepreneur Irenée Du Pont, where eight lavish rooms tempt guests. The first large-scale building on the peninsula's eastern end and an outstanding jewel in a bland architectural desert, Mansión Xanadú still displays the millions of dollars' worth of Cuban marble and furnishings commissioned by Du Pont in the 1930s.

Rates here include unlimited tee time at the adjoining golf club (p202).

Meliá Las Américas RESORT $$$
(Map p208; ☎45-66-76-00; Autopista Sur Km 7; all-inclusive s/d CUC$274/395; P ❄ @ ≋) The smaller, more grown-up alternative to the Meliá Marina Varadero next door, Las Américas has a no-kids policy, a nice slice of palm-tree-embellished beach and fancy chandeliers. With 225 rooms, it's too large to be intimate, though there's a more refined ambience here than in the other resort giants nearby.

Sol Palmeras RESORT $$$
(Map p208; ☎45-66-70-09; www.meliacuba.com; Carretera de las Morlas; s/d all-inclusive CUC$230/338; P ❄ @ ᯤ ≋) For a Meliá this is quite an old hotel (1980s) and the architecture doesn't exactly take your breath away. However, the hotel was in the midst of a bit-by-bit renovation at last visit, with the revamped family bungalows looking rather handsome inside. Repeat visitors (and there are many) regularly applaud the excellent service here.

La Ocean Varadero El Patriarca RESORT $$$
(Map p208; ☎45-66-81-66; www.oceanvaradero.com; Autopista Sur Km 18; s/d CUC$222/359; P ❄ @ ᯤ ≋) Named for a nearby giant cactus that the hotel developers mercifully didn't bulldoze, the Patriarca has a few worthy quirks. The room units are wooden rather than concrete, there's a lovely intimate almost Moorish patio beside the lobby, and poolside 'entertainers' keep a lower profile than elsewhere. Then there's the beach – pure bliss!

Meliá Marina Varadero RESORT $$$
(Map p208; ☎45-66-73-30; www.meliacuba.com; Autopista Sur Final; s/d all-inclusive from CUC$347/496; P ❄ @ ᯤ ≋) No, that's not a beached cruise liner, but a brand-new Meliá! Part of the plushly redeveloped Marina Gaviota (p200), this has several key advantages over its competitors up at this eastern end of the peninsula: gleaming marina views, plus access to a host of eateries and shops within the marina complex that makes the stay that little bit more varied than at the other all-inclusives.

There's no beach here (a walkway over the road connects you to one however) and reports on the rooms vary, but, if you can't make it to Miami, this is as close as you'll get in Cuba. The hotel also offers some non-all-inclusive apartments.

Meliá Varadero RESORT $$$
(Map p208; ☎45-66-70-13; Carretera las Morlas; all-inclusive s/d CUC$180-240/340-400; P ❄ @ ᯤ ≋) Twice as big as its sister hotel Meliá Las Américas, and happy to cater to families, the 490-room Meliá Varadero immediately impresses with its cylindrical vine-draped lobby. Perched on a small rocky promontory, the beach is set to one side and offers plenty of shade. Unlike many of its Varadero brethren it offers guests free bike use. And psst: the restaurants here are superior to its supposedly more illustrious sister; the Japanese restaurant Sakura is first-class.

Memories Varadero RESORT $$$
(Map p208; ☎45-66-70-09; www.memoriesresorts.com; Autopista Sur Km 18; all-inclusive s/d CUC$208/340; P ❄ @ ≋) By the time you reach the end of the peninsula all of the strung-out resorts appear to merge into one – this one. The Memories (opened 2008, changed its name 2012) is a kind of identikit of a modern beach hotel: 1025 rooms, international cuisine, wall-to-wall entertainment, and lots of sunburned Europeans whizzing around on golf-carts.

Hotel Tuxpán RESORT $$$
(Map p208; ☎45-66-75-60; www.cubanacan.cu; Av las Américas Km 2; s/d all-inclusive from CUC$87/140; P ❄ @ ᯤ ≋) Concrete-block architecture and palm-fringed beaches make jarring bedfellows that are all too common in Varadero. But the Tuxpán is famous for other reasons, such as its disco, La Bamba (p211), purportedly one of the resort's hottest. For those not enamored with Soviet architectonics, the beautiful beach is never far away, and the hotel is cheap!

Be Live Experience Varadero RESORT $$$
(Map p208; ☎45-66-82-80; www.belivehotels.com; Av las Américas Km 2; all-inclusive 2-/3-/4-/5-/6-bed villas CUC$176/249/314/395/447; P ❄ @ ≋) The recently re-branded Villa Cuba looks suspiciously like an airport (right down to the observation tower), but, inside, feels more like a 1970s holiday camp. The advantage here is the multitude of room sizes; villas range from two to six bedrooms, although the color scheme might have been thrown together by a hyperactive five-year-old let loose with Lego bricks.

Varadero Hotel Zone

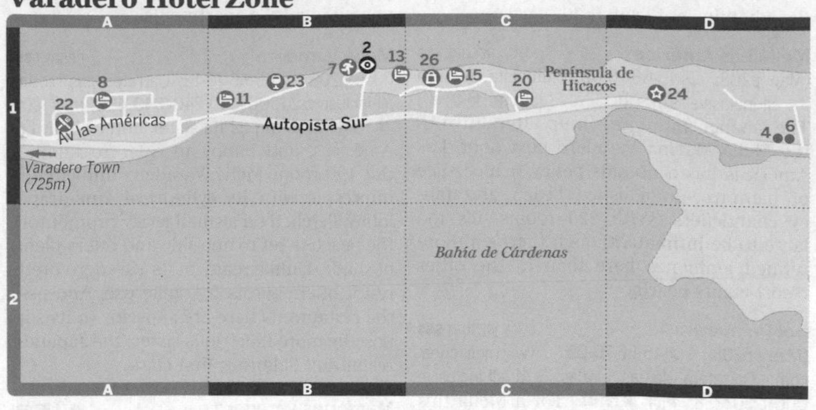

Varadero Hotel Zone

Sights

1 Cueva de Ambrosio F1
2 Mansión Xanadú B1
3 Marina Gaviota H2

Activities, Courses & Tours

4 Boat Adventure D1
5 Ke Bola Kiteboarding School G1
6 Marlin Marina Chapelín (Aquaworld) D1
7 Varadero Golf Club B1

Sleeping

8 Be Live Experience Varadero A1
9 Blau Marina Palace H2
10 Blau Varadero E1
11 Hotel Tuxpán B1
12 La Ocean Varadero El Patriarca G1
Mansión Xanadú .... (see 2)
13 Meliá Las Américas B1
14 Meliá Marina Varadero G2
15 Meliá Varadero C1
16 Memories Varadero G1
17 Paradisus Princesa del Mar G1
18 Paradisus Varadero F1
19 Royalton Hicacos Resort F1
20 Sol Palmeras C1

Eating

21 Kike-Kcho G2
22 Restaurante Mesón del Quijote A1

Drinking & Nightlife

Bar Mirador Casa Blanca .... (see 2)
Discoteca la Bamba .... (see 11)
La Isabelica Casa del Café .... (see 3)
23 Palacio de la Rumba B1

Entertainment

24 Cabaret Cueva del Pirata D1
25 Club Mambo E1
Sala de la Música la Marina .... (see 3)

Shopping

26 Plaza América C1

Eating

Varadero Town

La Rampa CUBAN $

(Map p204; ☎45-60-24-14; Calle 43, btwn Av 1 & Av de la Playa; mains CUC$4.50-10.50; ⊙noon-11pm)
A modest private place that's family-run and rightly lauded for its thoroughly decent food. Seating is half inside and half out. The lobster tails are recommended (and amazingly cheap).

★**Salsa Suárez** INTERNATIONAL $$

(Map p200; ☎45-61-41-94; Calle 31 No 103, btwn Av 1 & Av 3; mains CUC$8-12; ⊙10:30am-11pm; 🖉)
With possibly the most all-encompassing menu of Varadero's new private restaurants, Salsa Suárez impresses with its salubrious greenery-covered patio and ultra-professional never-miss-a-beat service. Food influences are all over the map (tapas, quesadillas, risotto, sushi and good old Cuban fare), but it's consistently good, right down to the details – complementary bread baskets and excellent Italian-style coffee.

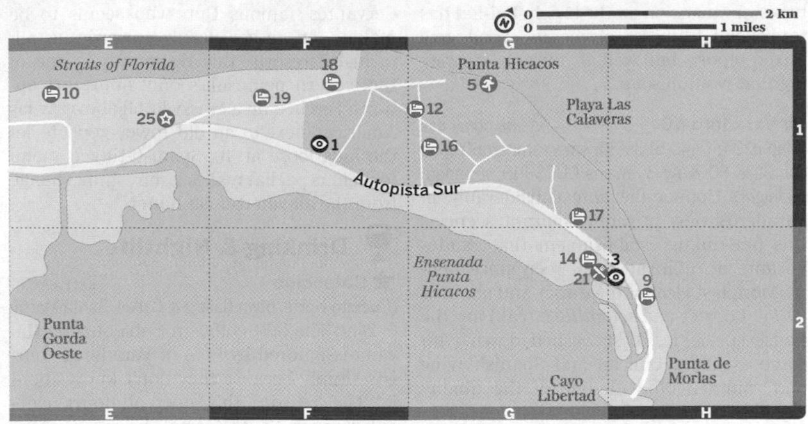

Restaurante La Barbacoa STEAK $$
(Map p204; ☎45-66-77-95; cnr Calle 64 & Av 1; steaks CUC$11-15; ⊙noon-11pm) Varadero's best state-run restaurant is a steakhouse that serves ridiculously cheap steak and lobster in an old-world decor (stag's heads, horsey paraphernalia) staffed by very straight-faced waiters.

Paladar Nonna Tina ITALIAN $$
(Map p204; ☎45-61-24-50; www.paladarnonnatina.it; Calle 38, btwn Av 1 & Av de la Playa; pizza & pasta CUC$6-10; ⊙noon-11pm;) Veteran Cuba visitors will remember an era when the word 'pasta' was a euphemism for 'mush.' But, times have changed and, thanks to inspired new restaurants such as Italian-owned Nonna Tina, the term 'al dente' is no longer an untranslatable foreign term. You'll find proof in this restaurant's pretty front garden where traveling Italophiles enjoy wood-fired thin-crust pizza, pesto linguine and proper *cappuccini*.

La Vaca Rosada SEAFOOD $$
(Map p200; ☎45-61-23-07; Calle 21, btwn Av 1 & Av 2; mains CUC$7.50-23; ⊙6:30-11pm Tue-Sun) If it's not raining, the 'pink cow' is worth an evening of your time. The place is set on an atmospheric rooftop terrace and serves surf and turf dishes, with a cameo appearance from good old thin-crust pizza.

La Fondue SWISS $$
(Map p204; cnr Av 1 & Calle 62; mains CUC$7-13; ⊙noon-midnight) Locals rate this fondue-focused restaurant as one of the best state-run joints in town and, while it's a welcome change from rice and beans, is not quite up to Swiss standards in the melted-cheese stakes. Nonetheless, the little hot cauldrons can make a worthwhile away-day from the hotel buffet.

Restaurante Mallorca SPANISH $$
(Map p204; Av 1, btwn Calle 61 & Calle 62; mains CUC$10; ⊙noon-midnight) This is an intimate venue with a bias toward Spanish cuisine (chorizo, garbanzos, etc) that's renowned for its paella. It's surprisingly spacious inside, with a well-stocked bar (with a good South American wine selection) and generous servings and service.

Dante ITALIAN $$
(Map p204; ☎45-66-77-38; Parque Josone; pizza CUC$7.50; ⊙noon-10:45pm) Going strong since 1993, Dante takes its name from an entrepreneurial chef who continues to rustle up delectable Italian fare to complement the serene lakeside setting in Parque Josone (p201). Antipasto starts at CUC$6; Varadero's most impressive wine stash also awaits. It's living proof that some state-run restaurants in Cuba can still compete.

Restaurante Esquina Cuba CUBAN $$
(Map p204; cnr Av 1 & Calle 36; mains CUC$8-13; ⊙noon-11pm) This place was one-time favorite of Buena Vista Social Club luminary Compay Segundo, and the man obviously had taste. It's worth it for the pork special (CUC$13) with lashings of beans, rice and plantain chips under the gaze of the great Cuban ephemera that line the walls – and the resident American car.

Lai-Lai CHINESE $$
(Map p200; cnr Av 1 & Calle 18; mains CUC$6-10; ⊙noon-11pm) An old stalwart set in a

two-story mansion on the beach, Lai-Lai has traditional Chinese set menus. Food gets mixed reports but, well, if you've been craving that wonton soup...

★Varadero 60 INTERNATIONAL **$$$**
(Map p204; ☎45-61-39-86; www.varadero60.com; cnr Calle 60 & Av 3; mains CUC$9-19; ⏰noon-midnight) Upping the ante considerably in Varadero's new private-restaurant scene is this fine-dining establishment that exudes an aura of refinement not seen since Benny Moré last cleared his throat and shouted *'Dilo'!* Lobster and *solomillo* (steak) are the house specialties, best washed down with some excellent Chilean and Spanish wine and rounded off with one of the quality cigars or rums on offer.

In almost a decade of repeat visits to Cuba, we've rarely seen such impeccable service. There's double meaning in the name – it's on Calle 60 and its theme is 1960s advertisements, which adorn the walls of the elegant interior.

Waco's Club INTERNATIONAL **$$$**
(Map p204; ☎52-97-14-08, 45-61-21-26; Av 3, btwn Calle 58 & Calle 59; mains CUC$12-28; ⏰noon-11pm; 👪) Travelers rate this sequestered-away spot, which was once Varadero's Club Náutico. The restaurant is clearly aiming high with its impressive international menu (nothing as wacko as you might think with a name like this, but all well-presented and flavorsome) and refined upstairs dining terrace. The specialty is the lobster done numerous ways, including *langosta Varadero* (flambéed in rum).

Varadero Hotel Zone

Kike-Kcho SEAFOOD **$$$**
(Map p208; ☎45-66-41-15; Autopista Sur y Final; mains CUC$15-30; ⏰noon-11pm) A posh 'floating' restaurant in the Marina Gaviota (p200), Kike-Kcho pushes its lobster, which is caught locally and stored on-site meaning it's ultra-fresh. It's backed up by all number of other fish species – cod, tuna, hake, eels, you name it. It's a great location, but food somehow lacks the 'soul' of Varadero's privately run places.

Restaurante Mesón del Quijote SPANISH **$$$**
(Map p208; Reparto la Torre; mains CUC$8-16.50; ⏰noon-midnight; 👪) Next to a statue of Cervantes' famous Don who seems to be making off rather keenly toward the all-inclusive resorts, this restaurant is one of the eastern peninsula's only nonresort options. Perched on a grassy knoll above Av las Américas next to an old tower good to let the kids loose at, its Spanish-tinged menu (delicious paella) makes a refreshing change from the all-you-can-eat buffet.

Drinking & Nightlife

★Cafeccino CAFE, BAKERY
(Circuito Norte, btwn Calle J & Calle I, Santa Marta; ⏰24hr) The best coffee in Cuba outside Havana is ignored by 99% of Varadero's tourists simply because they don't know about it. The reason: this open-all-hours cafe-bakery is in Santa Marta, the small settlement at the southwest end of the peninsula. Cafeccino is also notable for its cakes. The *tres leches* is better than any cake they serve in the five-star hotels hereabouts.

★Bar Mirador Casa Blanca BAR
(Map p208; Mansión Xanadú, Av las Américas; CUC$2; ⏰11am-midnight) On the top floor of Mansión Xanadú (p206), Bar Mirador Casa Blanca is Varadero's ultimate romantic hangout where happy hour conveniently coincides with sunset cocktails.

La Bodeguita del Medio BAR
(Map p204; Av de la Playa, btwn Calle 40 & Calle 41; ⏰10:30am-11:30pm) Varadero seems to have sprouted a copy of Hemingway's favorite Havana dive bar, aka La Bodeguita del Medio, a cool place where musicians strum on the courtyard and punters add graffiti to the walls inside while sipping afternoon mojitos. The question is – can you *really* successfully make a boho dive-bar into a chain?

There's decent *comida criolla* (Creole food) should you be hungry.

La Isabelica Casa del Café COFFEE
(Map p208; Marina Gaviota, Autopista Sur Final; snacks/sweets from CUC$2; ⏰9am-11pm) In the Miami-esque Marina Gaviota (p200) at the eastern end of the peninsula, you get a Miami-esque cafe. The Isabelica tries to impress Starbucks-starved tourists with its Ikea-like sofas and coffee-growing scenes on the walls, but the coffee is pretty average.

Palacio de la Rumba CLUB
(Map p208; Av las Américas Km 2; CUC$10; ⏰10pm-3am) Overall, the most banging

night out on the peninsula if you like a drink or six. There's live salsa music at weekends and a good mix of Cubans and tourists. Admission includes your drinks. It's located by the Hotel Bella Costa.

Calle 62 BAR
(Map p204; cnr Av 1 & Calle 62; ⏲8am-2am) Set in the transition zone between old and new Varadero, this simple snack bar attracts clientele from both ends. It's good for a cheese sandwich during the day, and the ambience becomes feistier after dark with live salsa-music going on until midnight.

Discoteca la Bamba CLUB
(Map p208; Hotel Tuxpán, Av las Américas Km 2; CUC$10; ⏲10pm-4am) Varadero's most modern video disco is at Hotel Tuxpán (p207), in eastern Varadero. It plays mostly Latin music and is considered 'hot.'

☆ Entertainment

★Beatles Bar-Restaurant LIVE MUSIC
(Map p204; cnr Av 1 & Calle 59; ⏲1pm-1am) A *roquero's* delight on the edge of Parque Josone (p201), honoring the previously banned Beatles in a bar that evokes the swinging spirit of the decidedly un-Cuban 1960s. Simple food and beer are served but the real draw is the live rock 'n' roll kicking off alfresco at 10pm Monday, Wednesday and Friday. Varadero's best night out!

Count on energetic covers of Led Zep, the Stones, Pink Floyd and you-know-who.

Sala de la Música la Marina LIVE MUSIC
(Map p208; Marina Gaviota, Autopista Sur Final; CUC$10-15; ⏲10pm-late) A new-ish place at the Marina Gaviota (p200) complex that's (obviously) heavy with tourists. Most nights it's a disco with a live DJ. On Saturdays it usually has a live band playing *Buena Vista Social Club* music. It's pleasantly modern with white lounge sofas and an upstairs terrace with marina views.

Club Mambo LIVE MUSIC
(Map p208; Av las Américas; CUC$10; ⏲11pm-2am Mon-Fri, to 5am Sat & Sun) Cuba's 1950s mambo craze lives on at this quality live-music venue – arguably one of Varadero's hippest and best. Situated next to Club Amigo Varadero in the eastern part of town, the CUC$10 entry includes all your drinks. A DJ spins when the band takes a break, but this place is all about live music.

There's a pool table if you don't feel like dancing.

Cabaret Cueva del Pirata CABARET
(Map p208; ☎45-66-77-51; Autopista Sur; CUC$10; ⏲10:30pm-3am Mon-Sat) A kilometer east of the Hotel Sol Elite Palmeras, Cabaret Cueva del Pirata presents scantily clad dancers in a Cuban-style floor show with a buccaneer twist (eye patches, swashbuckling moves). This cabaret is inside a natural cave and once the show is over, the disco begins. It's a popular place, attracting a young crowd. Monday's the best night. Book through your hotel.

Casa de la Música LIVE MUSIC
(Map p204; cnr Av de la Playa & Calle 42; CUC$10; ⏲10:30pm-3am Wed-Sun) Aping its two popular Havana namesakes, this place has some quality live acts and a definitive Cuban feel. It's in town and attracts a local crowd who pay in pesos. Non-Cubans pay in convertibles.

Centro Cultural Comparsita CULTURAL CENTER
(Map p204; Calle 60, btwn Av 2 & Av 3; CUC$1-5; ⏲10pm-3am) An ARTex cultural center on the edge of Varadero town, offering concerts, shows, dancing, karaoke and plenty of local flavor. Check the current schedule taped on the door.

Shopping

Casa del Ron ALCOHOL
(Map p204; cnr Av 1 & Calle 62; ⏲9am-9pm) The best selection of rum in Varadero as well as tasting opportunities in a venerable old building. It gives a through-the-ages look at Cuba's spirited relationship with the drink, including a scale model of Matanzas' Santa Elena distillery to admire as you sup.

Casa del Habano CIGARS
(Map p200; Av de la Playa, btwn Calle 31 & Calle 32; ⏲9am-6pm) *The* place for cigars: it has top-quality merchandise from humidors to perfume, and helpful service. There's also a small bar-tasting room abutting a quiet slice of beach. This branch is in the center of Varadero town.

Casa de las Américas BOOKS, MUSIC
(Map p204; cnr Av 1 & Calle 59; ⏲9am-7pm) A retail outlet of the famous Havana cultural institution, this place sells CDs, books and art.

Gran Parque de la Artesanía MARKET
(Map p200; Av 1, btwn Calle 15 & Calle 16; ⏲9am-7pm) Open-air artisans market with private vendors selling mainly Cuba-themed crafts.

Casa del Habano CIGARS
(Map p204; ☎45-66-78-43; cnr Av 1 & Calle 63; ⏲9am-9pm) Your quintessential cigar stop. It also serves a wicked cup of coffee in the upstairs cafe. This shop is at the east end of Varadero town, closer to the resort strip.

Galería de Arte Varadero ART
(Map p204; Av 1, btwn Calle 59 & Calle 60; ⏲9am-7pm) Antique jewelry, museum-quality silver and glass, paintings and other heirlooms from Varadero's bygone bourgeois days are sold here. As most items are of patrimonial importance, everything is already conveniently tagged with export permission.

Taller de Cerámica Artística ARTS & CRAFTS
(Map p204; Av 1, btwn Calle 59 & Calle 60; ⏲9am-7pm) Next door to Galería de Arte Varadero (p212) and Casa de las Américas (p211), you can buy fine artistic pottery that's made on the premises. Most items are in the CUC$200 to CUC$250 range.

ARTex GIFTS & SOUVENIRS
(Map p204; Av 1, btwn Calle 46 & Calle 47; ⏲9am-8pm) Showcases CDs, T-shirts, musical instruments and more.

Centro Comercial Hicacos SHOPPING CENTER
(Map p204; Parque de las 8000 Taquillas; ⏲10am-10pm) Varadero town's modern subterranean mall in Parque de las 8000 Taquillas is small by American standards, but serves the basics including souvenirs, cigars, a spa/gym and a small market.

Plaza América SHOPPING CENTER
(Map p208; Autopista Sur Km 7; ⏲10am-8:30pm) Built in 1997, but already looking dated, Cuba's first bona fide shopping mall is one of Varadero's less-inspired architectural creations, though it serves its purpose. Useful outlets include a pharmacy, bank, a music store, fashion stores, restaurants and various souvenir shops.

Librería Hanoi BOOKS
(Map p204; cnr Av 1 & Calle 44; ⏲9am-8:30pm) Books in English, from poetry to politics.

Information

DANGERS & ANNOYANCES

Crime-wise, Varadero's dangers are minimal. Aside from getting drunk at the all-inclusive bar and tripping over your bath mat on the way to the toilet, you haven't got too much to worry about. Watch out for mismatched electrical outlets in hotels. In some rooms, a 110V socket might sit right next to a 220V one. They should be labeled, but aren't always.

Out on the beach, a red flag means no swimming allowed, due to the undertow or some other danger. A blue jellyfish known as the Portuguese man-of-war, most common in summer, can produce a bad reaction if you come in contact with its long tentacles. Wash the stung area with vinegar and seek medical help if the pain becomes intense or you have difficulty breathing. Theft of unguarded shoes, sunglasses and towels is routine along this beach.

EMERGENCIES

Asistur (☎45-66-72-77; Av 1 No 103, cnr Calle 30; ⏲9am-4:30pm Mon-Fri) Tourist-oriented emergency assistance in Central Varadero.

INTERNET ACCESS

Most Varadero hotels have internet access, so buy your internet card at reception or at the **Etecsa Telepunto** (cnr Av 1 & Calle 30; ⏲8:30am-7pm).

There's a wi-fi hotspot on Calle 54.

MEDICAL SERVICES

Many large hotels have infirmaries that can provide free, basic first aid.

Clínica Internacional Servimed (☎45-66-77-11; cnr Av 1 & Calle 60; ⏲24hr) Also has a pharmacy.

Farmacia Internacional (☎45-66-80-42; Plaza América, Autopista Sur Km 7; ⏲9am-9pm) In the Plaza América.

Farmacia Internacional (☎45-61-44-70; Av Kawama, cnr Calle 4; ⏲9am-9pm) At the west end of the peninsula near Hotel Club Kawama (p206).

MONEY

In Varadero, European visitors can pay for hotels and meals in euros. If you change money at your hotel front desk, you'll sacrifice 1% more than at a bank.

Banco de Ahorro (Calle 36, btwn Av 1 & Autopista Sur; ⏲8:30am-4pm Mon-Fri) Popular ATM.

Banco de Crédito y Comercio (Av 1, btwn Calle 35 & 36; ⏲9am-7pm Mon-Fri, to 5pm Sat & Sun) ATM.

Banco Financiero Internacional (Autopista Sur Km 7; ⏲9am-noon & 1-6pm Mon-Fri,

9am-6pm Sat & Sun) Money exchange in Plaza América (opposite) in the Hotel Zone.

Cadeca (cnr Av de la Playa & Calle 41; ⌚8:30am-6pm Mon-Sat, to noon Sun)

POST

Many of the larger Varadero hotels have branch post offices.

Post Office (Map p204; Av 1, btwn Calles 43 & 44; ⌚8am-6pm Mon-Sat)

TOURIST INFORMATION

Every all-inclusive hotel in Varadero has a tourist-info desk.

Cubatur (☎45-66-72-16; cnr Av 1 & Calle 33; ⌚8:30am-6pm) Reserves hotel rooms nationally; organizes bus transfers to Havana hotels and excursions to Península de Zapata (p227) and other destinations. Can act as a general information point, too.

Infotur (Map p200; ☎45-66-29-61; cnr Av 1 & Calle 13; ⌚8:30am-4pm) Main office is next to Hotel Acuazul, but they have a desk in most large resorts.

Getting There & Away

AIR

Juan Gualberto Gómez International Airport (☎45-61-30-16, 45-24-70-15) is 20km from central Varadero toward Matanzas and another 6km off the main highway. Airlines here include Thomson Airways from London; Cubana from Buenos Aires and Toronto; Air Berlin from Düsseldorf, American Airlines from Miami; TUI Airlines from Amsterdam; and Air Transat and WestJet from various Canadian cities.

BUS

The **Terminal de Ómnibus** (Map p204; cnr Calle 36 & Autopista Sur) has daily air-con Víazul buses (www.viazul.com) to a few destinations. Warning: they fill up fast. Book ahead!

All five daily Havana buses stop at Matanzas (CUC$6, one hour) and Juan Gualberto Gómez International Airport (CUC$6, 25 minutes).

The Trinidad bus stops in Cienfuegos (CUC$16, 4½ hours).

The Santiago bus also stops in Santa Clara (CUC$11, 3¼ hours), Sancti Spíritus (CUC$17, five hours), Ciego de Ávila (CUC$19, 6¼ hours), Camagüey (CUC$25, eight hours), Las Tunas (CUC$33, 10 hours), Holguín (CUC$38, 11¼ hours) and Bayamo (CUC$41, 13 hours).

For Cárdenas, you can go on local bus 236 (CUC$1), which departs every hour or so from next to a small tunnel marked Ómnibus de Cárdenas outside Varadero's Terminal de Ómnibus. Don't rely on being able to buy tickets for non-Víazul buses from Varadero to destinations in Matanzas Province and beyond: the official line is tourists can't take them, and tourists in Varadero are generally recognizable from Cubans. With decent Spanish you could get lucky.

Cubanacán's Conectando runs a handy bus service between hotels in Varadero and hotels in Havana (bookable through hotel receptions). There's also a daily service between Varadero and Trinidad via Cienfuegos. Prices are similar to Víazul. Book tickets at least a day in advance through Infotur.

CAR

You can hire a car from practically every hotel in Varadero, and prices are pretty generic between different makes and models. Once you've factored in fuel and insurance, a standard car will cost you approximately CUC$70 to CUC$80 a day.

Aside from the hotel reps, you can try the **Cubacar** (☎45-66-81-96; cnr Av 1, btwn Calle 21 & 22; ⌚9am-5pm) office in town or car rental offices at the airport.

There's a **Servi-Cupet gas station** on the Autopista Sur at Calle 17 (cnr Autopista Sur & Calle 17; h24hr), and another at Calle 54 (Autopista Sur & Calle 54).

If heading to Havana, you'll have to pay the CUC$2 toll at the booth on Vía Blanca upon leaving.

TAXI

With Víazul buses in high demand, *colectivos* (shared taxis) are picking up the slack. You can book one directly by phoning **Cuba Taxi** (☎45-61-05-55), asking at your casa particular, or hanging around at the Víazul bus station. There are usually other passengers seeking lifts when fully booked buses are due to leave, so you can club together.

BUSES FROM VARADERO

DESTINATION	COST (CUC$)	DURATION (HR)	DEPARTURE TIME
Havana	10	3	8am, 12pm, 2pm, 4pm, 6pm
Santa Clara	11	3	7:25am, 9pm
Santiago de Cuba	49	15¼	9pm
Trinidad	20	6¼	7:25am
Viñales	22	7¼	8am

Getting Around

BICYCLE

Bikes are an excellent way of getting off the Hicacos Peninsula and discovering a little of the Cuba outside. Rentals are available at most of the all-inclusive resorts, and bikes are usually lent as part of the package. Some casas particulares will be able to rent (or lend) you basic bicycles. Ask around.

BUS

Varadero Beach Tour (all-day tickets CUC$5; 9am-9pm) is a handy open-top double-decker tourist bus with 45 hop-on, hop-off stops linking all the resorts and shopping malls along the entire length of the peninsula. It utilizes well-marked stops with route and distance information. Buy tickets on the bus itself.

A gimmicky toy train connects the three large Meliá resorts.

Local buses 47 and 48 run from Calle 64 to Santa Marta, south of Varadero on the Autopista Sur; bus 220 runs from Santa Marta to the far eastern end of the peninsula. There are no fixed schedules. Fares are small change. You can also utilize bus 236 to and from Cárdenas, which runs the length of the peninsula.

HORSE CARTS

A state-owned horse-and-cart trip around Varadero costs around CUC$10 for a full two-hour tour – plenty of time to see the sights.

TAXI

Metered tourist taxis in Varadero charge a CUC$1 starting fee plus CUC$1 per kilometer (same tariff day and night). Coco-taxis (*coquitos* or *huevitos* in Spanish) charge less with no starting fee. A taxi to Cárdenas/Havana (15 minutes/2¼ hours) will be about CUC$20/85 one way. Taxis hang around all the main hotels and the bus station (p213), or you can phone Cuba Taxi (p213).

Varadero to Matanzas

The 40-minute drive along the wide, smooth 36km sweep of the Vía Blanca Hwy, heading between the cities of Matanzas and Varadero, passes many of northern Matanzas' most magnificent sights: subterranean swimming holes, superb snorkeling and boat trips on hidden rivers. You could spend the best part of a day lingering for aquatic diversions at the Río Canímar and Playa Coral, and there's a full-on cabaret in the evenings.

Sights & Activities

Parque Turístico Río Canímar RIVER

Boat trips on the Río Canímar, 8km east of Matanzas, are a truly magical experience. Gnarly mangroves dip their jungle-like branches into the ebbing water and a warm haze caresses the regal palm trees as your boat slides 12km upstream from the Vía Blanca bridge to a riverside *ranchón* called 'La Arboleda,' where you can have lunch and go horse-riding.

Four-person self-drive motor boats (first hour CUC$35, each additional hour CUC$10), or kayaks (first hour CUC$10, each additional hour CUC$5) can be rented to get upstream. The rental point is on the east side of the river by the Vía Blanca bridge. It takes roughly 25 minutes to reach La Arboleda with a motor boat.

Most Varadero hotels have tour agencies offering this trip (look for the Río Canímar 'Back to Nature' tour).

Playa Coral BEACH

Your closest bet for shore snorkeling in the Varadero area is Playa Coral, on the old coastal road (about 3km off the Vía Blanca) halfway between Matanzas and Varadero. You can snorkel solo from the beach, but it's far better (and safer) to enter from the Flora y Fauna Reserve (8am to 5pm), 400m east of the beach. Professional Ecotur provide guides to take you out to the reef 150m offshore (one hour CUC$10).

There are a reported 300 species of fish here and visibility is a decent 15m to 20m. Diving is on offer, too (immersion CUC$35).

The flora and fauna reserve also incorporates the **Laguna de Maya** (P) 2km inland from Playa Coral. A package including all the activities is offered for CUC$25 and can be organized through most Varadero hotels or the Barracuda Scuba Diving Center (p202). Most of the coast hereabouts is a gray-white coral shelf, but there are beaches just west of Playa Coral.

Cuevas de Bellamar CAVE

(45-25-35-38, 45-26-16-83; admission CUC$10, camera CUC$5; 9am-5pm; P) Cuba's oldest tourist attraction, according to local propaganda, lies 5km southeast of Matanzas and is 300,000 years old. There are 2500m of caves here, discovered in 1861 by a Chinese workman in the employ of Don Manuel

Santos Parga. The entrance is through a small museum, and a 45-minute Cuevas de Bellamar visit leaves almost hourly starting at 9:30am. The caves on show include a vast 12m stalagmite and an underground stream; cave walls glitter eerily with crystals. Well-maintained, well-lit paths mean it's easy for kids to imbibe the stupendous geology, too. Outside the Cuevas de Bellamar are two restaurants and a playground.

To get there, take bus 12 from Matanzas' Plaza Libertad.

Cueva de Saturno CAVE

(☎45-25-38-33, 45-25-32-72; incl snorkel gear CUC$5; ⊙8am-6pm) One kilometer south of the Vía Blanca by the side of the road to Varadero's International airport (p213), is the freshwater Cueva de Saturno, a highly popular (read: crowded) subterranean cave with a pool billed as a snorkeling and/or swimming spot. The water's about 20°C and the maximum depth is 22m, though there are shallower parts. There's a snack bar and equipment rental post on-site.

Castillo del Morrillo CASTLE, MUSEUM

(CUC$1; ⊙9am-5pm Tue-Sun) On the western side of the Río Canímar bridge, 8km east of Matanzas, a road runs 1km down to a cove presided over by the four guns of this yellow-painted castle (1720). The castle is now a museum dedicated to the student leader Antonio Guiteras Holmes (1906–35), who founded the revolutionary group Joven Cuba (Young Cuba) in 1934.

After serving briefly in the post-Machado government, Guiteras was forced out by army chief Fulgencio Batista and shot on May 8, 1935. A bronze bust marks the spot where he was executed.

Sleeping

Hotel Canimao HOTEL $$

(☎45-26-10-14; Carretera Matanzas-Varadero Km 5; r incl breakfast CUC$45-65; P ❄ ≋) Perched above the Río Canímar 8km east of Matanzas, the Canimao has 160 rooms with little balconies that look like they were last updated during the Cold War – by Soviet interior designers. It's handy for Río Canímar excursions, the Cuevas de Bellamar or to visit the Tropicana Matanzas, but otherwise you're isolated here. There's a 'meh' restaurant.

Entertainment

Tropicana Matanzas CABARET

(☎45-26-53-80; Carretera Matanzas-Varadero Km 5; CUC$35; ⊙10pm-2am Tue-Sat) Capitalizing on its success in Havana and Santiago de Cuba, the famous Tropicana cabaret has a branch 8km east of Matanzas, next to the Hotel Canimao. You can mingle with the Varadero bus crowds and enjoy the same entertaining formula of lights, feathers, flesh and frivolity in the open air.

Matanzas

POP 152,408

Matanzas is like a sunken galleon left at the bottom of the ocean. Most casual visitors to Cuba sail right over the top of it (usually on a tour bus to Varadero), but, a few curious adventurers dive down and discover that this ostensibly scruffy city is still full of priceless treasure. Go back a few generations and Matanzas was a very different place. During the 18th and 19th centuries, the city developed a gigantic literary and musical heritage, and was regularly touted as the 'Athens of Cuba.' Two pivotal Cuban musical forms, *danzón* and rumba, were hatched here, along with various religions of African origin. Matanzas also hosts one of Cuba's finest theaters, and was the birthplace of some of its most eloquent poets and writers. Despite the contemporary aura of decay, the cultural riches haven't disappeared. You just need patience, imagination and a Sherlock Holmes hat to disentangle them.

Sights

★**Taller-Galería Lolo** GALLERY

(☎45-26-08-54; Calle 97, cnr Calle 288) Imagine. You're tramping through Matanzas' tatty streets wondering whether the 'Athens of Cuba' moniker is just a local joke when you stumble upon this artist's collective by the river, guarded by epic surreal sculptures seemingly made out of bits of a salvaged ship. You go inside for plenty more artistic apparitions from the cutting edge of Matanzas' cultural custodians. Within minutes, you'll be emailing your *amigos* back home to tell them about Lolo, a not-to-be-missed art gallery-workshop intent on putting Matanzas back where it should be – alongside Havana on the cultural map.

Matanzas

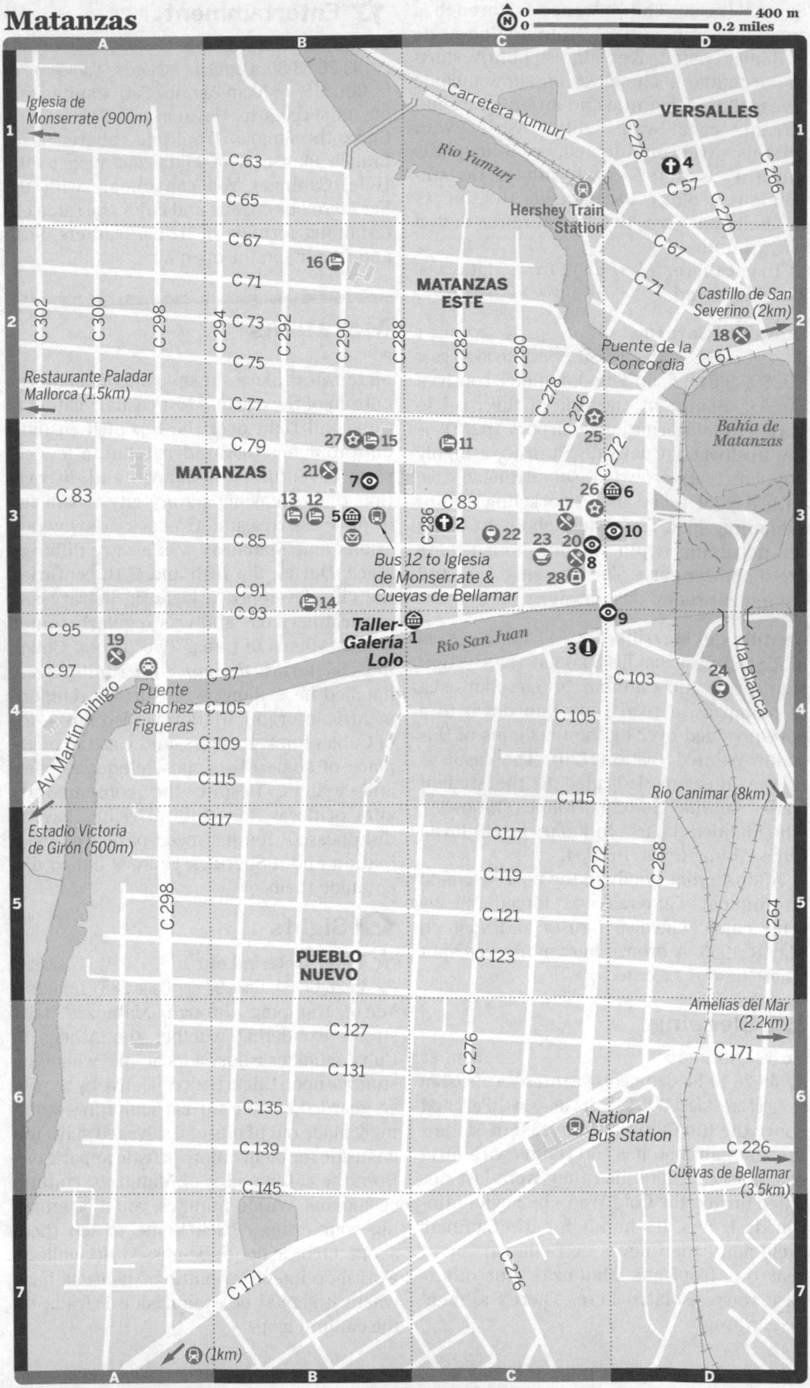

0 400 m
0 0.2 miles
Iglesia de Monserrate (900m)
Restaurante Paladar Mallorca (1.5km)
Estadio Victoria de Girón (500m)
Carretera Yumurí
Río Yumurí
Hershey Train Station
VERSALLES
MATANZAS ESTE
MATANZAS
PUEBLO NUEVO
Castillo de San Severino (2km)
Puente de la Concordia
Bahía de Matanzas
Bus 12 to Iglesia de Monserrate & Cuevas de Bellamar
Taller-Galería Lolo
Río San Juan
Puente Sánchez Figueras
Av Martín Dihigo
Vía Blanca
Río Canímar (8km)
Amelias del Mar (2.2km)
National Bus Station
Cuevas de Bellamar (3.5km)
(1km)
C 63
C 65
C 67
C 71
C 73
C 75
C 77
C 79
C 83
C 85
C 91
C 93
C 95
C 97
C 105
C 109
C 115
C117
C 119
C 121
C 123
C 127
C 131
C 135
C 139
C 145
C 171
C 103
C 57
C 61
C 226
C 302
C 300
C 298
C 294
C 292
C 290
C 288
C 286
C 282
C 280
C 278
C 276
C 272
C 270
C 268
C 266
C 264

Matanzas

Top Sights
1 Taller-Galería Lolo C4

Sights
2 Catedral de San Carlos Borromeo C3
3 Che Mural C4
4 Iglesia de San Pedro Apóstol D1
5 Museo Farmaceútico B3
6 Museo Histórico Provincial D3
7 Parque Libertad B3
8 Plaza de la Vigía C3
9 Puente Calixto García D4
10 Teatro Sauto D3

Sleeping
11 Evelio & Isel C3
12 Hostal Alma B3
13 Hostal Azul B3
14 Hostal Río B3
15 Hotel Velazco B3
16 Villa Soñada B2

Eating
17 Café Atenas C3
18 El Chiquirrín D2
19 Mercado la Plaza A4
20 Plaza la Vigía C3
21 Restaurante Romántico San Severino B3

Drinking & Nightlife
22 ACAA C3
Bistro Kuba .... (see 13)
23 Café Mambo Jambo C3
24 Ruinas de Matasiete D4

Entertainment
25 Centro Cultural Comunitario Nelson Barrera C3
26 Museo Histórico Provincial C3
27 Sala de Conciertos José White B3
Teatro Sauto .... (see 10)

Shopping
28 Ediciones Vigía C3

★Iglesia de Monserrate CHURCH

(Calle 306; 26) For a mappable view of mildewed Matanzas on one side and the broccoli green Valle de Yumurí on the other, climb 1.5km northeast of the center up Calle 306 to this renovated church dating from 1875. The lofty bastion perched high above the city was built by colonists from Catalonia in Spain, as a symbol of their regional power.

The lookout near here has a couple of *ranchón*-style restaurants good for skull-splitting music and basic refreshments. Come in the early morning, however, and the views offer a whole new perspective on this deceptively beautiful city.

Plaza de la Vigía SQUARE

The original Plaza de Armas still remains as Plaza de la Vigía (literally 'lookout place'), a reference to the threat from piracy and smuggling that Matanzas' first settlers faced. This diminutive square was where Matanzas was founded in the late 17th century and numerous iconic historical buildings still stand guard.

Teatro Sauto THEATER

(45-24-27-21; Plaza de la Vigía) The defining symbol of the city according to Mexican painter (and admirer) Diego Rivera, the Teatro Sauto (1863) on Plaza de la Vigía's south side is one of Cuba's finest theaters and famous for its superb acoustics. The lobby is graced by marble Greek goddesses and the ceiling in the main hall bears paintings of the muses.

Three balconies enclose this 775-seat theater, which features a floor that can be raised to convert the auditorium into a ballroom. The original theater curtain is a painting of Matanzas' Puente de la Concordia, and notables like Soviet dancer Anna Pavlova have performed here. The theater will reopen, after a long restoration, in 2017.

Castillo de San Severino FORT

(Av del Muelle; CUC$2; 10am-7pm Tue-Sat, 9am-noon Sun) Northeast of Versalles lies this formidable bastion, built by the Spanish in 1735 as part of Cuba's defensive ring. It was tested early on by the British; during their 1762 invasion, they mercilessly bombarded it. Rebuilt in the 1770s, it became an offloading point for slaves. Later, Cuban patriots were imprisoned within the walls – and sometimes executed. San Severino remained a prison until the 1970s and in more recent times has become the modest slavery-themed Museo de la Ruta de los Esclavos.

The castle itself has great views of the Bahía de Matanzas, but could offer a lot more to inspire curious visitors.

Catedral de San Carlos Borromeo CHURCH

(Calle 282, btwn Calle 83 & Calle 85; 8am-noon & 3-5pm Mon-Sat, 9am-noon Sun) Standing back from the disorganized melee of Calle 83 behind shady Plaza de la Iglesia is Matanzas' main church, a neoclassical structure with two unequal towers founded in 1693 (although the existing building dates from the 1730s). Despite being made a cathedral in 1912, the church suffered terribly from years of neglect in the 20th century. It reopened in 2016 after eight years of renovation. The interior is relatively plain, but handsome all the same, and has once again become a hub of local life.

Museo Farmacéutico MUSEUM
(Calle 83 No 4951; CUC$3; ⏲10am-5pm Mon-Sat, to 4pm Sun) Museo Farmacéutico, on the park's south side, is one of Matanzas' showcase sights. Founded in 1882 by the Triolett family, the antique pharmacy was the first of its type in Latin America and still looks much as it did in the 1880s. The fine displays include all the bottles, instruments and suchlike used in the trade. The included guided tour will explain the rest.

Puente Calixto García BRIDGE
If you've only got time to see *one* bridge (there are 21 in total) in Cuba's celebrated 'city of bridges,' gravitate toward this impressive steel structure built in 1899, spanning the Río San Juan with its kayaks floating lazily by. Just south is an eye-catching Che Mural while the northern side leads directly into Plaza de la Vigía.

Museo Histórico Provincial MUSEUM
(cnr Calles 83 & 272; CUC$2; ⏲9am-5pm Tue-Sun) Also known as Palacio del Junco (1840), this double-arched edifice on the Plaza de la Vigía showcases the full sweep of Matanzas' history from pirate incursions to the cruel reign of slavery. There's a huge statue of unpopular Spanish king Ferdinand VII on a side patio, made in Italy in the 1830s.

Parque Libertad SQUARE
A few blocks directly west of Plaza de la Vigía is Parque Libertad with several of Matanzas' most stimulating sights, including a 'liberty' statue depicting an open-armed woman, her wrists bearing broken chains, and a bronze statue (1909) of José Martí.

Iglesia de San Pedro Apóstol CHURCH
(cnr Calles 57 & 270, Versalles) Dominating the scruffy Versalles neighborhood is this fine neoclassical church that was recently refurbished inside and out. The interior is bright with cream-colored arches but little ornamentation.

Festivals & Events

Festival del Bailador Rumbero DANCE
During the 10 days following October 10, Matanzas rediscovers its rumba roots at this festival, currently held in a small park outside Museo Histórico Provincial (p222), while the Teatro Sauto (p221) is being restored. The festival coincides with the anniversary of the city's founding (October 12), a multiday party which includes celebrations of luminaries who have made the city what it is (or was).

Sleeping

★Hostal Azul CASA PARTICULAR $
(☎45-24-24-49; hostalazul.cu@gmail.com; Calle 83 No 29012, btwn Calle 290 & Calle 292; r CUC$25-30; ❄) With a front door large enough to ride an elephant through, this handsome blue house dating from the 1890s has original tiled floors, an antique wooden spiral staircase and four castle-sized rooms set around a spacious alfresco patio.

Even better, multilingual owner, Joel, is a true gent and happy to offer his sturdy 1984 Lada for taxi duty. And best? Possibly the spacious period bar with its soaring wooden ceiling (10am to 10pm), with live music in the evenings, making this one extremely atmospheric address.

Villa Soñada CASA PARTICULAR $
(☎45-24-27-61; mandy_rent_habitaciones@yahoo.com; Calle 290 No 6701, cnr Santa Isabel; r CUC$25-30; ❄) The 'villa of dreams,' set four blocks north of Matanzas' main square, has an attractive facade topped by a huge terrace guarded by sculpted lions. The rooms are modern with glass bricks, lots of space (one has two levels), mini-bars and super-slick bathrooms. Inside and out, there are plenty of nooks to relax and the breakfasts and dinners (at extra cost) are fabulous and plentiful.

Hostal Río CASA PARTICULAR $
(☎45-24-30-41; hostalrio.cu@gmail.com; Calle 91 No 29018, btwn Calle 290 & Calle 292; r CUC$25-30; ❄) This house is owned by the parents of Joel, star of nearby Hostal Azul; the overriding color here is *amarillo* (yellow) rather than *azul* (blue). There are two comfortable rooms with high ceilings in colonial digs.

ABAKUÁ

A secret all-male society, a language understood only by initiates, a close-knit network of masonic-like lodges, and the symbolic use of the African leopard to denote power: the mysterious rites of Abakuá read like a Cuban Da Vinci Code.

In a country not short on foggy religious practices, Abakuá is perhaps the least understood. It's a complicated mixture of initiations, dances, chants and ceremonial drumming that testifies to the remarkable survival of African culture in Cuba since the slave era.

Not to be confused with Santería or other syncretized African religions, Abakuá's traditions were brought to Cuba by enslaved Efik people from the Calabar region of southeastern Nigeria in the 18th and 19th centuries. With practitioners organizing themselves into 'lodges' or *juegos*, the first of which was formed in the Havana suburb of Regla in 1836, Abakuá acted as a kind of African mutual aid society, originally made up primarily of black dock workers whose main goal was to help buy their tribal brethren out of slavery.

In the early days, Abakuá lodges were necessarily anti-slavery and anti-colonialist and were suppressed by the Spanish. Nonetheless, by the 1860s, the lodges were increasingly admitting white members and finding that their strength lay in their secretiveness and invisibility.

Today, there are thought to be over 100 Abakuá lodges in Cuba, some up to 600-strong, based primarily in Havana, Matanzas and Cárdenas (the practice never penetrated central or eastern Cuba). Initiates are known as *ñáñigos* and their intensely secret ceremonies take place in a temple known as a *famba*. Although detailed information about the brotherhood is scant, Abakuá is well-known to the outside world for its masked dancers called *Ireme* (devils) who showcase their skills in various annual carnivals and were instrumental in the development of the *guaguancó* style of rumba. Cuba's great abstract artist, Wilfredo Lam, used Abakuá masks in his paintings, and composer, Amadeo Roldán, incorporated its rhythms into classical music.

While there is a strong spiritual and religious element to the brotherhood (forest deities and the leopard symbol are important), it differs from the more widespread Santería religion in that it is does not hide its deities behind Catholic saints. Cuban anthropologist, Fernando Ortíz Fernández, once referred to Abakuá societies as a form of 'African masonry' while other researchers have suggested it acts like a separate state within a nation with its owns laws and language. The casual Cuban word *'asere'* (meaning 'mate') is actually derived from the Abakuá term for 'ritual brother.'

Meals are served at Hostal Azul two blocks away.

Evelio & Isel CASA PARTICULAR **$**
(☎45-24-30-90; evelioisel@yahoo.es; Calle 79 No 28201, btwn Calle 282 & Calle 288; r CUC$20-25; P ❄) Rooms at this 2nd-floor apartment have TV, security boxes, balconies and underground parking. Congenial owner Evelio is a font of knowledge about the Matanzas music scene.

Hostal Alma CASA PARTICULAR **$**
(☎45-29-08-57; hostalalma63@gmail.com; Calle 83 No 29008, btwn Calle 290 & Calle 292; r CUC$25-30; ❄) A house with *mucha alma* (a lot of soul), Mayra's place has Seville-invoking *azulejos* (tiles), relaxing rocking chairs, and rainbow *vitrales* (stained-glass windows) that refract colored light across the tiled floors. You can enjoy a welcome cocktail on one of its two colossal terraces while surveying Matanzas' semi-ruined rooftops. There are three spiffy rooms.

Hotel Velazco HOTEL **$$**
(☎45-25-38-80; Calle 79, btwn Calle 290 & Calle 288; s/d CUC$85/128; ❄@🛜) This lovely period hotel harks back to the early years of the Cuban Republic – the original 1902 fin-de-siècle style blends seamlessly with the horses, carts and antediluvian autos in the square outside. A beautiful mahogany bar lures you in; 17 elegant rooms (with flat-screen TVs and wi-fi) practically force you to stay.

Eating

★El Chiquirrín

INTERNATIONAL $

(☎45-24-38-77; Calle Laborde No 27013; mains CUC$2.50-6.50; ⏲12:30pm-11pm Tue-Sun) A pianist plays romantically on a baby grand, chefs work artistically behind a glass partition in the kitchen, and a waiter carves Chateaubriand at your table. New York? Paris? No, the former culinary wasteland of Matanzas. A testament to how things are changing in Cuba is this charming new restaurant facing the bay in the city's Versalles quarter.

Starched table cloths play host to well-executed Cuban food backed up by pizza and pasta and – like all good restaurants – they'll bring you a complementary snack while you wait.

Amelias del Mar

CUBAN, INTERNATIONAL $

(☎45-26-16-53; Via Blanca No 22014, Playa; mains CUC$2-7; ⏲noon-2am Thu-Tue) Amelias del Mar brings tongue-in-cheek creativity to standard Cuban 'international' food through flashy presentation and then serves the concept in a neat open-air patio doubling as a lively bar. Here chicken fajitas become delicious *trapos de viejas,* or old lady's rags; shrimps are *cuerpos revisitados* – unearthed corpses. The sign outside just says 'Snack Bar,' but it's so much more than that.

Restaurante Romántico San Severino

INTERNATIONAL $

(Calle 290, btwn Calle 279 & Calle 283; mains CUC$4.50-6.50; ⏲6-11pm) Parque Libertad (p218) now has a stand-out restaurant up a steep flight of steps on the west side. Colonial interior, good service and excellent shrimp-stuffed fish filets.

Plaza la Vigía

CAFE $

(cnr Plaza de la Vigía & Calle 85; snacks CUC$2-3; ⏲11am-11pm) Burgers and draft beer rule the menu, while young student-types dominate the clientele in this throwback bar that looks like a scene from a Parisian art nouveau poster, circa 1909. The ultimate anti-Varadero escape!

Café Atenas

CARIBBEAN $

(Calle 83 No 8301; CUC$2-5; ⏲10am-10pm) Settle down on the *terraza* (terrace) with the local students, taxi drivers and hotel workers on a day off, and contemplate everyday life on Plaza de la Vigía. Decent sandwiches; grilled meats.

Restaurante Paladar Mallorca

INTERNATIONAL $$

(☎45-28-32-82; Calle 334, btwn Calle 77 & Calle 79; mains CUC$8-14; ⏲12:30-9:30pm Wed-Sun; 👪) The Mallorca out in Los Mangos neighborhood northwest of the center impresses with adventurous dishes such as fish in balsamic-cream glaze, and some of Cuba's best piña coladas. Presentation is very nouveau and there are surprise touches such as a kid's menu, handwash brought to your table and live minstrel music.

Drinking & Nightlife

Café Mambo Jambo

CAFE

(Calle 85 No 27414; ⏲10:30am-6pm) New dinky little cafe full of antique radios and old album covers that serves strong coffee, frappuccinos and basic snacks. Clientele is a mix of arty students and old ladies fresh from a makeover at the local hairdressers.

ACAA

BAR

(Asociación Cubana de Artistas y Artesanos; Calle 85, btwn Calle 282 & Calle 284; ⏲10am-late) What begins as a glam-looking art-supplies shop and exhibition venue leads back into a courtyard reminiscent of bohemian Paris, where artsy culture vultures sit around slurping strong coffee and conversing animatedly. A rooftop bar gets going after dark, often with live music as an accompaniment.

Bistro Kuba

BAR

(Calle 83, btwn Calles 292 & 290; ⏲11am-2am) The tables in this cool dinky bar light up to show old city landmarks. Cocktails are incredible, ditto the espresso. If you're peckish there are ham and cheese tasting platters. The crowd's 95% Cuban and there's live music several nights per week.

Ruinas de Matasiete

BAR

(cnr Vía Blanca & Calle 101; ⏲10am-10pm, club 10pm-2am) The city's famed drinking hole is a frenetic (too frenetic for some) place housed in the ruins of a 19th-century, bay-facing warehouse. Drinks and grilled meats are served on an open-air terrace, but a better reason to come here is to hear live music (9pm Friday to Sunday; cover charge CUC$3).

Entertainment

★Sala de Conciertos José White

CONCERT VENUE

(☎45-26-70-32; Calle 79, btwn Calle 290 & Calle 288) Restoration of this 1876 building abut-

LOCAL KNOWLEDGE

RUMBA IN MATANZAS

'Without rumba there is no Cuba, and without Cuba there is no rumba,' runs a Cuban saying. Matanzas certainly gave birth to one of Cuba's defining musical forms and occupies a pivotal place both in the history and in the future development of music in the country.

Rumba originated here in the city's African *cabildos*, secret brotherhood councils formed among slaves brought over from West Central Africa during the 19th century to work Cuba's plantations. These brotherhoods came together in the port backstreets to worship their *orishas* (deities) and keep their traditions alive. So rumba in Matanzas began, and rapidly spread: the music of a repressed and displaced people remembering their roots through music. It was the outlet through which initially Afro-Cubans, but later other subjugated groups from deprived backgrounds, expressed fears and hopes about their position in society.

Matanzas is responsible for most of the main forms of rumba. The most ancient variety, Rumba Yambú, stems from the Versalles district in the late 19th century, and has a slower, smoother pace. Rumba Guaguancó is more modern and sensual, emulating the mating ritual between a rooster and a hen, and uses conga drums. Then there is Rumba Columbia, named after an old bus stop outside Matanzas, performed only by men because of its dangerous moves. Only recently recognized as a sub-genre, there is also Batá-rumba, invented and best exemplified by contemporary group AfroCuba de Matanzas. Percussion here is provided by hourglass-shaped Batá drums, a ritual instrument of Nigeria's Yoruba people.

Masters of the first three of these forms are Los Muñequitos de Matanzas, formed almost 60 years ago, when an inspired impromptu jamming session on bottles in a bar in the city's Barrio Marina persuaded various locals they could gel as a group. And gel they did. Originally named Guaguancó Matancero, their first A-side 'Los Muñequitos' (little comics) was so popular that that was how the group became known.

Los Muñequitos de Matanzas and AfroCuba de Matanzas are descended from the early days of *cabildos*, with Lucumí and Kongo origins. But the music they are making now is as much about re-evaluating the roots of music as remembering the roots of their ancestors. A great example is AfroCuba's groundbreaking collection of songs, *The Sign and the Seal*, which uses a focus on traditional *orishas* to seemingly push the boundaries of music itself. Songs are dedicated to such deities as Agayú – in Yoruba culture, an uninhabited space or wilderness – while another explores Oshún, the source of rivers, water and life. In returning to the building blocks of a culture, the album revisits the building blocks of music; it reassembles sound as the universe (the relationship with which is the cornerstone of Yoruba beliefs) reassembles sound.

Better than reading about the city's rumba is listening to some and both of the groups mentioned here perform in Matanzas. An incredible ingredient to the city is that, in the home of rumba, its two most renowned exponents can still be found indulging in a spot of low-key jamming here. The best bet to catch rumba is the great alfresco performances that take place at 4pm on the third Friday of every month outside the Museo Histórico Provincial (p222).

ting Hotel Velazco (p219) was completed in 2014 and every inch, flourish and cornicing of its former glory is well worth a lingering look. Fitting for a building that formerly hosted the city symphony orchestra, classical music makes up the majority of its performances, although there is also that made-in-Matanzas dance *danzón* (ballroom dance) performed here. A courtyard bar complements proceedings.

Teatro Sauto THEATER

(☎45-24-27-21; Plaza de la Vigía) On the threshold of reopening (some time in 2017) after a lengthy renovation, the Sauto certainly has clout: performances have been held here since 1863. If you're lucky, you might catch the Ballet Nacional de Cuba or the Conjunto Folklórico Nacional de Cuba (rumba).

Centro Cultural Comunitario Nelson Barrera CULTURAL CENTER
(cnr Calles 276 & 77, Marina; ⊙9am-5pm Tue-Sun) A good starting point for anyone interested in Matanzas' Afro-Cuban history lies in this Marina-neighborhood cultural center. Inquire about upcoming events and you could get lucky with religious processions, drum sessions, or just shooting the breeze with some *hombres* from the *barrio*.

Museo Histórico Provincial CULTURAL CENTER
(Palacio del Junco; cnr Calles 83 & 272; CUC$2; ⊙10am-6pm Tue-Fri, 1-7pm Sat, 9am-noon Sun) Check the board outside this building for events ranging from theater to *danzón* performances to rumba, with listings for the month ahead.

Estadio Victoria de Girón SPECTATOR SPORT
(Av Martín Dihigo) From October to April, baseball games take place at this stadium, home of beloved local team the Cocodrilos. It's 1km southwest of the **market** (cnr Calles 97 & 298).

Shopping

Ediciones Vigía BOOKS
(Plaza de la Vigía, cnr Calle 91; ⊙9am-5pm Mon-Sat) To the southwest of Plaza de la Vigía (p217) is a unique book publisher founded in 1985, that produces high-quality handmade paper and first-edition books on a variety of topics. The books are typed, stenciled and pasted in editions of 200 copies. Visitors are welcome in the Dickensian workshop where they can purchase beautiful numbered and signed copies (CUC$5 to CUC$40).

Information

INTERNET ACCESS

Etecsa Telepunto (cnr Calles 83 & 282; per hour CUC$1.50; ⊙8:30am-7:30pm) sells phone and internet cards.

There's wi-fi in the park outside the cathedral (p217) opposite or in Parque Libertad (p218).

MEDICAL SERVICES

Servimed (☎45-25-31-70; Hospital Faustino Pérez, Carretera Central Km 101; ⊙24hr) Clinic by hospital, just southwest of Matanzas.

MONEY

Banco de Crédito y Comercio (Calles 85 No 28604, btwn Calle 286 & 288; ⊙9am-5pm) ATM.

Cadeca (Calle 286, btwn Calles 83 & 85; ⊙8am-6pm Mon-Sat, 8am-noon Sun)

POST

Post Office (cnr Calles 85 & 290; ⊙8am-5pm Mon-Sat)

Getting There & Away

AIR

Matanzas is connected to the outside world through Juan Gualberto Gómez International Airport (p213), aka Varadero airport, 20km east of town.

BICYCLE

Matanzas is reachable by bike from Varadero. The 32km road is well-paved and completely flat, bar the last 3km into the city starting at the Río Canímar bridge. Bike hire is available at some Varadero all-inclusive hotels.

BUS

All buses to Matanzas, long distance and provincial, use the **National Bus Station** (cnr Calles 131 & 272, Pueblo Nuevo), in the old train station south of the Río San Juan.

Matanzas has decent connections, although for destinations like Cienfuegos and Trinidad you need to change at Varadero, taking the first Varadero bus of the day then waiting for the afternoon Varadero–Trinidad bus.

Víazul (www.viazul.com) has five daily departures to Havana (CUC$7, two hours, 9am, 12:55pm, 2:50pm, 4:50pm and 6:50pm); the 9am bus continues to Viñales. There are also five departures to Varadero (CUC$6, one hour, 8am, 10:05am, 12:05pm, 3:05pm and 7pm), also calling at the airport (CUC$6, 25 minutes).

CAR

The nearest car rental to the center is **Cubacar** (☎45-25-32-46; cnr Calles 127 & 204, Playa) in the Playa neighborhood.

TAXI

Taxis hang around the bus station and in Parque Libertad (p218). For a *colectivo* (shared taxi) to destinations south and east, you might be better off heading to Varadero bus station (p213) and looking for a ride-share there.

TRAIN

Matanzas has two train stations. The main **train station** (☎45-29-16-45; Calle 181) is in Miret, at the southern edge of the city. Most trains between Havana and Santiago de Cuba stop here, but services are slow, grubby and unreliable. In theory, there are half a dozen daily trains to Havana (CUC$3, 1½ hours). The Santiago de Cuba train (CUC$27; 13½ hours) should leave in the evening every three or four days. Latest train information is plastered on pieces of paper in the waiting room. Get here well in advance to beat the bedlam.

The **Hershey Train Station** (☎45-24-48-05; cnr Calle 55 & Calle 67) is in Versalles, an easy 10-minute walk from Parque Libertad (p218). There are three trains a day to Casablanca station in Havana (CUC$2.80, four hours) via Canasí (CUC$0.85, one hour), Jibacoa (CUC$1.10, 1½ hours; for Playa Jibacoa), Hershey (CUC$1.40, two hours; for Jardines de Hershey) and Guanabo (CUC$2, three hours). Departure times from Matanzas are 4:39am, 12:09am (an express service that should take three hours in total) and 4:25pm.

The train usually leaves on time, but often arrives in Havana's Casablanca station (just below La Cabaña fort on the east side of the harbor) one hour late. This is the only electric railway (p155) in Cuba. It's a scenic trip if you're not in a hurry, and a great way of reaching the little-visited attractions of Mayabeque Province.

Getting Around

Bus 12 links Plaza Libertad with the Cuevas de Bellamar and the Iglesia de Monserrate.

The **Oro Negro gas station** (cnr Calles 129 & 210) is 4km outside central Matanzas on the Varadero road. If you're driving to Varadero, you will pay a CUC$2 highway toll between Boca de Camarioca and Santa Marta (no toll between Matanzas and the airport).

Bici-taxis congregate next to the Mercado la Plaza and can take you to most of the city's destinations for one to two Cuban pesos. A taxi to Juan Gualberto Gómez International Airport (p213) should cost CUC$25 to CUC$30 (20 minutes), with Varadero fares (CUC$30; 40 minutes) a bit more again.

Cárdenas

POP 109,552

Without the bright lights of Varadero or the rejuvenated historic and cultural legacy of Matanzas, Cárdenas can appear downright shabby. Looking like a sepia-toned photo from another era, this dilapidated town is home to countless resort-based waiters, front-desk clerks and taxi drivers, but with barely a restaurant, hotel or motorized cab to serve it.

Cárdenas has nevertheless played an episodic role in Cuban history. In 1850 Venezuelan adventurer Narciso López and a ragtag army of American mercenaries raised the Cuban flag here for the first time, in a vain attempt to free the colony from its Spanish colonizers. Other history-making inhabitants followed, including revolutionary student leader José Antonio Echeverría, who was shot during an abortive raid to assassinate President Batista in 1957. This rich past is showcased in three fabulous museums stationed around Parque Echeverría, the city's main plaza, which today constitute the key reason to visit.

Sights

★Museo Oscar María de Rojas — MUSEUM

(cnr Av 4 & Calle 13; CUC$5; 9am-6pm Mon-Sat, 9am-1pm Sun) Cuba's second-oldest museum (after the Museo Bacardí in Santiago) offers a selection of weird artifacts, including a strangulation chair from 1830, a face mask of Napoleon, the tail of Antonio Maceo's horse, Cuba's largest collection of snails and, last but by no means least, some preserved fleas – yes fleas – from 1912.

The museum is set in a lovely colonial building and staffed with knowledgeable official guides.

Museo de Batalla de Ideas — MUSEUM

(Av 6, btwn Calle 11 & Calle 12; CUC$2; 9am-5pm Tue-Sat, 9am-noon Sun) The newest of Cárdenas' three museums offers a well-designed and organized overview of the history of US–Cuban relations, replete with sophisticated graphics. Inspired by the case of Elián González, a boy from Cárdenas whose mother, stepfather and 11 others drowned attempting to enter the US by boat in 1999, the museum is the solid form of Castro's resulting *batalla de ideas* (battle of ideas) with the US government.

The displays' themes naturally center round the eight months during which Cuba and the US debated the custody of Elián – but it extends also to displays on the quality of the Cuban education system and a courtyard containing busts of anti-imperialists who died for the revolutionary cause. The exhibit that most epitomizes the purpose of the museum, however, is possibly the sculpture of a child in the act of disparagingly throwing away a Superman toy.

Museo Casa Natal de José Antonio Echeverría — MUSEUM

(Av 4 Este No 560; incl guide CUC$5; 10am-5pm Tue-Sat, 9am-1pm Sun) This museum has a macabre historical collection including the original garrote used to execute Narciso López by strangulation in 1851. Objects relating to the 19th-century independence wars are downstairs, while the 20th-century revolution is covered upstairs, reached via a beautiful spiral staircase.

In 1932 José Antonio Echeverría was born here, a student leader slain by Batista's police in 1957 after a botched assassination attempt in Havana's Presidential Palace. There's a statue of him in the eponymous square outside.

Arechabala Rum Factory FACTORY

(cnr Calle 2 & Av 13) To the northwest of the center of Cárdenas, in the industrial zone, is this famous rum factory founded by Spanish immigrant José Arechabala in 1878. Arechabala concocted Havana Club, Cuba's second most iconic rum (after Bacardí) until the family business was requisitioned by the Cuban government in 1959. Arechabala left for the US, but failed to register the Havana Club trademark, which was picked up by the Cuban government in 1976.

Arechabala (and its international partner Bacardí) has recently been entangled in a trademark dispute with the Cuban government and partner Pernod Ricard over the rights to sell Havana Club in the US. The factory still operates but no tours are available.

Flagpole Monument MONUMENT

(cnr Av Céspedes & Calle 2) No, not just any old flagpole. Follow Av Céspedes past Catedral de la Inmaculada Concepción to its northern end and you will see *this* flagpole is attached to a monument and commemorates the first raising of the Cuban flag on May 19, 1850.

Catedral de la Inmaculada Concepción CHURCH

(Av Céspedes, btwn Calle 8 & Calle 9) Parque Colón is the city's other interesting square, five blocks north of Parque Echeverría. Here stands the main ecclesiastical building of Cárdenas. Built in 1846, it's noted for its stained glass and purportedly the oldest statue of Christopher Columbus in the western hemisphere.

Dating from 1862, Cristóbal Colón, as he's known in Cuba, stands rather authoritatively with his face fixed in a thoughtful frown and a globe resting at his feet. It's Cárdenas' best photo op.

Sleeping

Down the road Varadero flaunts 60 hotels (and counting). Here in humble Cárdenas there are precisely zero. Fortunately, Cárdenas sports a couple of good (if notoriously hard-to-find) casas particulares.

Hostal Ida CASA PARTICULAR $

(☎45-52-15-59; ida83@nauta.cu; Calle 13, btwn Av 13 & Av 15; r CUC$35; P ❄) Don't let the tatty street setting put you off here. Inside this plush apartment (with private entrance and garage) you'll find a stunning living room/kitchenette, and a decadently furnished bedroom/bathroom that might have floated over from a decent Varadero hotel. Ample breakfasts (CUC$5).

Ricardo Domínguez CASA PARTICULAR $

(☎52-89-44-31; yaniamaria82@nauta.cu; cnr Avs 31 & Calle 12; r CUC$35; P ❄) Ricardo's place is 1.5km northwest of Parque Echeverría and worth tracking down. The spick-and-span white terracotta-roofed house is cocooned within a large, leafy garden and seemingly just plucked from one of Miami's more tasteful suburbs. Three rooms available.

Eating

Half the chefs in Varadero probably come from Cárdenas, which adds irony to the city's dire restaurant scene. A couple of new paladares (privately owned restaurants) have raised the game slightly.

There are many convertible supermarkets and stores near the cast-iron 19th-century market hall Plaza Molocoff (opposite), where you can get cheap peso snacks.

★**Don Qko** CUBAN $

(☎45-52-45-72; Av Céspedes No 1000, cnr Calle 21; mains CUC$3-8; ⏲noon-11pm Wed-Mon) Don Qko is one of those well-executed but defiantly local private restaurants peculiar to Cuba's provincial towns (Cárdenas and Matanzas excel in them) which isn't specifically aimed at netting tourist money. As a result, the prices are reasonable, the food unashamedly home-style and the ambience 90% Cuban. Learn a bit of Spanish and pop by.

Studio 55 CAFE $

(Calle 12, btwn Av 4 & Av 6; light mains CUC$3-5; ⏲noon-midnight Mon-Thu, to 2am Fri & Sat) Soak up the industrial-chic vibe and order great burgers at this rather trendy spot on the main square, which is good for well-executed fast food ordered from menus designed like DVD cases. A great addition to Cárdenas' rather scant food scene.

Restaurant Don Ramón INTERNATIONAL $
(Av 4, btwn Calle 12 & Calle 13; mains CUC$6-8; ⌚11am-10pm; ❄) Overlooking Parque Echevería, the lovely Don Ramón woos you with its old-style colonial charm. For a varied sit-down meal, there's nowhere better in Cárdenas. Elect for the filet mignon and choose something off the specialized gin menu.

Plaza Molocoff MARKET $
(cnr Av 3 Oeste & Calle 12) Plaza Molocoff is a whimsical two-story cast-iron market hall with a glittery 16m-high silver dome built in 1859. It's still the city vegetable market but is crying out for a face-lift.

☆ Entertainment

Casa de la Cultura CULTURAL CENTER
(Av Céspedes No 706, btwn Calle 15 & Calle 16; ⌚hours vary) Housed in a beautiful but faded colonial building with stained glass and an interior patio with rockers. Search the handwritten advertising posters for rap *peñas* (performances), theater and literature events.

ℹ Information

INTERNET ACCESS

Parque Echeverría is also a wi-fi hotspot.

Etecsa Telepunto (cnr Av Céspedes & Calle 12; per hour CUC$1.50; ⌚8:30am-7:30pm) Telephone and internet access.

MEDICAL SERVICES

Centro Médico Sub Acuática (☎45-52-21-14; Carretera a Varadero Km 2; per hour CUC$80; ⌚8am-4pm Mon-Sat, doctors on-call 24hr) Two kilometers northwest on the road to Varadero at Hospital Julio M Aristegui; has a Soviet recompression chamber dating from 1981.

Pharmacy (Calle 12 No 60; ⌚24hr)

MONEY

Banco de Crédito y Comercio (cnr Calle 9 & Av 3)

Cadeca (cnr Av 1 Oeste & Calle 12)

ℹ Getting There & Away

It's simplest to go to Varadero to get onward bus connections because whilst the Varadero–Santiago de Cuba **Víazul** (www.viazul.com) bus does pass through, it doesn't officially stop here. Varadero also has many more daily bus services to places such as Trinidad and Havana.

Bus 236 to/from Varadero leaves hourly from the corner of Av 13 Oeste and Calle 13 (50 centavos, but tourists are usually charged CUC$1, 30 minutes). A taxi for the same journey costs CUC$15 to CUC$20 (15 minutes).

ℹ Getting Around

'Coches' (horse-carriages) are how one gets around Cárdenas. The main route is northeast on Av Céspedes from the **bus station** (cnr Av Céspedes & Calle 22) and then northwest on Calle 13 to the hospital, passing the stop of bus 236 (to Varadero) on the way. Pay with your smallest CUC$ coin.

For self-drivers, the **Servi-Cupet gas station** (cnr Calle 13 & Av 31 Oeste) is opposite an old Spanish fort on the northwest side of town, on the road to Varadero.

When asking for directions, beware that Cárdenas residents often use the old street names rather than the new street-naming system (numbered *calles* and *avenidas*). Double-check if uncertain.

San Miguel de los Baños & Around

Nestled in the interior of Matanzas Province amid rolling hills punctuated by vivid splashes of bougainvillea, San Miguel de los Baños is an atmospheric old spa town that once rivaled Havana for elegant opulence. Once, that is. Flourishing briefly as a destination for wealthy folk seeking the soothing medicinal waters that were 'discovered' here in the early 20th century, San Miguel saw a smattering of lavish neoclassical villas shoot up; they still line the town's arterial Av de Abril today. But the boom times didn't last. Just prior to the Revolution, pollution from a local sugar mill infiltrated the water supply and the resort quickly faded from prominence. Now, it's a curious mix between an architectural time capsule from a bygone era and the boarded-up mansion in Charles Dickens' *Great Expectations*.

👁 Sights

★**Finca Coincidencia** FARM
(☎45-81-39-23; Carretera Central, btwn Coliseo & Jovellanos) FREE Enhance your taste for bucolic provincial life, away from the razzmatazz of Matanzas Province's north coast at this ecological farm 14km northeast of San Miguel de los Baños and 6km east of Colesio on the Carretera Central. Chill in the grounds replete with mango and guava trees, participate in ceramics classes and look around gardens where 83 types of plants are cultivated.

OFF THE BEATEN TRACK

THE GRAN HOTEL – CUBA'S NOBLEST RUIN

Cuba has its fair share of abandoned ruins, but few are as noble as the erstwhile Gran Hotel and its elegant bathhouse in central Matanzas Province. Closeted in the soporific town of San Miguel de los Baños, a mere 50km south of Varadero, the hotel sits like a withered time capsule not yet brought to order by earnest restoration teams or officious security guards. As a result, kids still play football amid the parapets and patios, and curious travelers can stroll unhindered through overgrown grounds feeling a little like Pip in Charles Dickens' *Great Expectations*.

The 'Gran' was built as a hotel and spa in the 1920s by a rich Cuban lawyer named Manuel Abril Ochoa who was intent on attracting Cuba's wealthy to the region's thermal waters.

Ochoa prophetically assigned engineer Alfredo Colley to head the project. Fresh from working on Monte Carlo's palatial casino in southern France, Colley designed the hotel as a close copy with four lavish towers and a central sweeping staircase. The adjoining bathhouses were rendered in terracotta brick and displayed a whimsical blend of Roman, Moorish and art nouveau influences.

Opened in 1929, the Gran and its *balneario* (spa) were popular in their early days – so much so that the small town quickly spawned three further hotels to accommodate the flood of guests. Yet, despite losing its opulence soon after the revolution and being totally abandoned in the 1970s, the hotel and its surroundings retain a quiet unexpected beauty enhanced by the almost total lack of visitors. Plans to restore the site are regularly touted, but, as yet, nobody has had the heart to tamper with the disintegrating yet magnificent ruins.

The owner, Héctor Correa is an ecological genius who grows practically everything he consumes. He also maintains a small ceramics workshop and has constructed a quirky sculpture garden amid the mango trees – pride of place goes to the life-sized Charlie Chaplin. For those seeking total rural immersion, accommodation and meals (around CUC$10) are also available.

★Gran Hotel & Balneario RUINS
A gorgeous ruin lying truly abandoned in the middle of small-town Cuba, that's heavy with atmosphere and still shines (despite the mildew) with a perceptible beauty. Between the 1920s and 1950s, this grand edifice functioned as an expensive bathhouse and hotel. These days it hosts birds nests, weeds and – who knows? – the ghosts of guests past.

There's no entry fee and barely any other visitors. Just slip inside and enjoy the magic on your own while you still can.

Loma de Jacán HILL
Looming above San Miguel de los Baños are the steep slopes of Loma de Jacán, a glowering hill with 448 steps embellished by faded murals of the Stations of the Cross. When you reach the small chapel on top you can drink in the town's best views with the added satisfaction that you are standing at the highest point in the province. The views are tremendous.

Sleeping

Finca Coincidencia CASA PARTICULAR $
(☎45-81-39-23; Carretera Central, btwn Coliseo & Jovellanos; r CUC$20-25; P ❄) Possibly the best rural hideout in Cuba. Three simple but lovely rooms on an ecological farm (p225) and ceramics workshop where pretty much everything (including your coffee, milk and coffee cup) are made in house. This is the life.

Getting There & Away

To get to San Miguel de los Baños, follow Rte 101 from Cárdenas to Colesio where you cross the Carretera Central; the town is situated a further 8km to the southwest of Colesio. A taxi from Cárdenas (25 minutes) should cost CUC$20 to CUC$25 – bargain hard.

For cyclists, it makes for a pleasant day-ride from Cárdenas (42km out-and-back) or, if you're fit, Varadero town (80km out-and-back).

PENÍNSULA DE ZAPATA

A vast, virtually uninhabited swampy wilderness spanning the entirety of southern Matanzas, the 4520-sq-km Península de Zapata quickens the pulses of wildlife-watchers and divers alike with the country's most important bird species and some of the most magical offshore reef diving secreted in its humid embrace. Most of the peninsula is a protected zone, safeguarded nationally as the Gran Parque Natural Montemar, and internationally as the Ciénaga de Zapata Unesco Biosphere Reserve.

The sugar-mill town of Australia in the northeast of the peninsula marks the main access point to the park. Just south of here is one of the region's big tourist money-spinners, the cheesy yet oddly compelling Boca de Guamá, a reconstructed Taíno village.

The road hits the coast at Playa Larga, home to the peninsula's best beaches, at the head of the Bahía de Cochinos where propaganda billboards still laud Cuba's historic victory over the *Yanquis* in 1961.

Getting There & Away

Daily **Víazul** (www.viazul.com) buses ply the peninsula with official stops in Playa Larga and Playa Girón. Otherwise you'll need a rental car or taxi. The flat terrain is excellent for cycling.

Central Australia & Around

No, you haven't just arrived Down Under. About 1.5km south of the Autopista Nacional, on the way to Boca de Guamá, is the large disused Central Australia sugar mill, built in 1904, now home to a small museum, along with a rather absurd rural 'farm.' It's a viable stopover if you're on the way to Playa Girón or Cienfuegos.

Sights

Museo Comandancia de las FAR MUSEUM
(CUC$1; 9am-5pm Tue-Sat) During the 1961 Bay of Pigs invasion, Fidel Castro had his headquarters in the former office of the sugar mill, but today the building is devoted to this revolutionary museum. You can see the desk and phone from where Fidel commanded his forces, along with other associated memorabilia. Outside is the wreck of an invading aircraft shot down by Fidel's troops.

The concrete memorials lining the road to the Bahía de Cochinos mark the spots where defenders were killed in 1961. The museum and its monuments acts as a kind of twin to the much better Museo de Playa Girón (p231).

Finca Fiesta Campesina PARK
(CUC$1; 9am-6pm; P) Approximately 400m on your right after the Central Australia exit on the Autopista Nacional, is a kind of mini-zoo-meets-country fair with labeled examples of Cuba's typical flora and fauna. The highlights of this slightly seedy place are the coffee (some of the best in Cuba and served with a sweet wedge of sugarcane), the bull-riding and the hilarious if slightly infantile games of guinea-pig roulette overseen with much pizzazz by the gentleman at the gate.

It's the only place in Cuba – outside the cockfighting – where you encounter any form of open gambling.

Sleeping & Eating

Motel Batey Don Pedro CABIN $
(45-91-28-25; Carretera a Península de Zapata; s/d CUC$36/54; P) A sleepy motel with 12 rooms in thatched blue-and-white double units with ceiling fans, crackling TVs and patios – and a random frog or two in the bathroom. It's further down the Finca Fiesta Campesina track, just south of the Península de Zapata turnoff at Km 142 on the Autopista Nacional at Jagüey Grande.

The motel is designed to resemble a 'peasant' settlement. For food, the best option is the Finca Fiesta Campesina next door.

Pío Cuá CARIBBEAN $$
(Carretera de Playa Larga Km 8; meals CUC$8-20; 11am-5pm; P) A favorite with Guamá-bound tour buses, this huge place is set up for big groups, but retains fancy decor with lots of stained glass. Shrimp, lobster or chicken meals are pretty good. It's 8km from the Autopista Nacional turnoff, heading south from Australia.

Boca de Guamá

Boca de Guamá may be a tourist creation, but as resorts around here go it's among the more imaginative. Situated about halfway between the Autopista Nacional at Jagüey Grande and the famous Bahía de Cochinos, it takes its name from native Taíno chief Guamá, who made a last stand against the Spanish in 1532 (in Baracoa). The big attraction is the boat trip through mangrove-lined waterways and across Laguna del Tesoro (Treasure Lake) to a 'recreation' of a Taíno village. Fidel once holidayed here and had a hand in developing the Taíno theme. You'll soon be struggling to draw parallels with pre-Columbian Cuba, however: raucous tour groups and even louder rap music welcome your voyage back in time. Arranged around the dock the boats depart from are a cluster of restaurants, expensive snack bars, knickknack shops and a crocodile farm. The palm-dotted grounds make a pleasant break from the surrounding swampy heat.

Sights

Laguna del Tesoro LAKE

This lake is 5km east of Boca de Guamá via the Canal de la Laguna, accessible only by boat. On the far (east) side of the 92-sq-km body of water is a tourist resort named Villa Guamá, built to resemble a Taíno village, on a dozen small islands.

A sculpture park next to the mock village has 32 life-size figures of Taíno villagers in a variety of idealized poses. The lake is called 'Treasure Lake' due to a legend about some treasure the Taíno supposedly threw into the water just prior to the Spanish conquest (not dissimilar to South American El Dorado legends). The lake is stocked with largemouth bass, so fishers frequently convene.

Criadero de Cocodrilos CROCODILE FARM

(☎45-91-56-66; Carretera a Playa Larga; adult/child incl drink CUC$5/3; ⏲9:30am-5pm) On your right as you come into Boca de Guamá from the Autopista, the Criadero de Cocodrilos is a highly successful crocodile-breeding facility run by the Ministerio de la Industria Pesquera. Two species of crocodiles are raised here: the native *Crocodylus rhombifer* (*cocodrilo* in Spanish, or Cuban crocodile), and the *Crocodylus acutus* (*caimán* in Spanish), which is found throughout the tropical Americas.

Rock up here and you could get a guided tour (in Spanish), taking you through each stage of the breeding program. Prior to the establishment of this program in 1962 (considered the first environmental protection act undertaken by the revolutionary government), these two species of marsh-dwelling crocodiles were almost extinct.

The breeding has been so successful that across the road in the Boca de Guamá complex you can buy stuffed baby crocodiles or dine, legally, on crocodile steak.

If you buy anything made from crocodile leather at Boca de Guamá, be sure to ask for an invoice (for the customs authorities) proving that the material came from a crocodile farm and not wild crocodiles. A less controversial purchase would be one from the site's **Taller de Cerámica** (⏲9am-6pm Mon-Sat).

Sleeping

Villa Guamá CABIN **$$**

(☎45-91-55-51; s/d half-board CUC$67/100; ❄🏊) This place was built in 1963 on the east side of the Laguna del Tesoro, about 8km from Boca de Guamá by boat (cars can be left at the crocodile farm; CUC$1). The 50 thatched *cabañas* (cabins) with bath and TV are on piles over the shallow waters.

The six small islands bearing the units are connected by wooden footbridges to other islands with a bar, *cafetería*, overpriced restaurant and a swimming pool containing chlorinated lake water. Rowboats are available for rent, and the birdwatching at sunrise is reputedly fantastic. You'll need foreign-made insect repellent if you decide to stay. Breakfast and dinner are included in the room price; the 20-minute ferry transfer (adult/child CUC$12/6) isn't.

Getting There & Around

A passenger **ferry** (adult/child CUC$12/6, 20 minutes) departs Boca de Guamá for Villa Guamá – across Laguna del Tesoro – four times a day. Speedboats depart more frequently and whisk you across to the pseudo-Indian village in just 10 minutes any time during the day for CUC$12 per person round-trip (with 40 minutes waiting time at Villa Guamá, two-person minimum). In the morning you can allow yourself more time on the island by going one way by launch and returning by ferry.

Gran Parque Natural Montemar

The largest *ciénaga* (swamp) in the Caribbean, Ciénaga de Zapata is protected on multiple levels as the Gran Parque Natural Montemar, a Unesco Biosphere Reserve and a Ramsar Convention Site. Herein lies one of Cuba's most diverse ecosystems, a steamy mix of wildlife-rich wetlands and briny salt flats. Crowded onto a vast, practically uninhabited peninsula (essentially two swamps divided by a rocky central tract) are 14 different vegetation formations including mangroves, wood, dry wood, cactus, savannah, selva and semideciduous. The extensive salt pans and marshes make Zapata the best birdwatching spot in Cuba, as well as a haven for crocodiles, and an excellent spot for catch-and-release fishing.

The main industry today is tourism and ecotourists are arriving in increasing numbers to take advantage of several expertly-led excursions. Access is only possible with a guide.

Activities

There are six main excursions into Gran Parque Natural Montemar, with an understandable focus on birdwatching. Itineraries are flexible.

Transport is not usually laid on; it's best to arrange beforehand. Cars (including chauffeur-driven 4WDs) can be rented from Cubacar (p234) in Playa Girón. Another option is a taxi.

Activities, excursions and transport options can be discussed at Playa Larga's National Park Office (p230); **La Finquita** (45-91-32-24; Autopista Nacional Km 142; 9am-5pm Mon-Sat, 8am-noon Sun), at the Playa Larga turn-off on the Autopista Nacional; or at most of Playa Girón's casas particulares.

★Reserva de Bermejas BIRDWATCHING
(per person CUC$15) This is, arguably, Cuba's best birding trip which takes you with a qualified park ornithologist around the Reserva de Bermejas. Here, it is possible to see an astounding 21 of Cuba's 28 endemic bird species including the prized *ferminia* (Zapata wren), *cabrerito de la ciénaga* (Zapata sparrow) and *gallinuela de Santo Tomás* (Zapata rail). Inquire at the National Park Office (p230) or ask around Playa Larga for a private guide. Reserve four hours for the 3km walk.

Sendero Enigma de las Rocas HIKING
The park's newest hike has quickly established itself as one of its most popular thanks to its proximity to the village of Playa Girón (p231). Most travelers get to the start point several kilometers northwest of the village in a horse and cart. The trail itself is 4km round-trip, but reserve half a day with a guide to enjoy the rich flora and fauna. At the end of the trail there is a *cenote* (sinkhole) where you can swim.

PENINSULA SHUTTLE SERVICE

Complementing the Havana–Cienfuegos–Trinidad Víazul bus (www.viazul.com) which runs through the Zapata peninsula, but with a history of altering (or canceling) its schedule, there is a twice-daily hop-on, hop-off shuttle bus linking all of the area's key sights. The service starts at Hotel Playa Girón at 9am, heads out to Caleta Buena and then back past Punta Perdiz, Cueva de los Peces and Hotel Playa Larga to Boca de Guamá at 10am. The shuttle then leaves Boca de Guamá at 10:30am for the reverse journey. The service is repeated in the afternoon with departure times of 1pm from Hotel Playa Girón and 3:30pm from Boca de Guamá. A ticket for the day costs CUC$3 per person.

Schedules are subject to change, so check when you arrive in the destination.

Cayo Venado BIRDWATCHING
(per person CUC$20) Cayo Venado is essentially an optional extension of the Las Salinas excursion (two hours extra) where you'll be transported by boat to said cayo for a low-down on the exotic fauna and the birdlife that call it home.

Laguna de las Salinas BIRDWATCHING
(4hr-tour per person CUC$15) One of the most popular excursions is to this *laguna* where large numbers of migratory waterfowl can be seen from November to April: we're talking 10,000 pink flamingos at a time, plus 190 other feathered species. The road to Las Salinas passes through forest, swamps and lagoons (where aquatic birds can be observed). Guides (and vehicle) are mandatory to explore the refuge.

The 22km trip lasts over four hours but you may be able to negotiate for a longer visit.

Señor Orestes Martínez García BIRDWATCHING
(52-53-90-04, 45-98-75-45; chino.zapata@gmail.com; excursions per person CUC$10-20) Garnering a reputation as the Zapata peninsula's

most knowledgeable resident birdwatcher, this *señor* can take you on more personalized, and reportedly highly rewarding, ornithological forays into the *ciénaga*. He runs a casa particular in the village Caletón near Playa Larga.

Río Hatiguanico BIRDWATCHING
(per person CUC$15) Switching from land to boat, this three-hour 14km river-trip runs through the densely forested northwestern part of the peninsula. You'll have to dodge branches at some points, while at others the river opens out into a wide delta-like estuary. Birdlife is abundant and you may also see turtles and crocodiles. You need independent transport (try Cubacar; p234) to cover the 90km to the start point.

Santo Tomás OUTDOORS
(per person CUC$20) It's also worth asking about this trip, available December through April, beginning 30km west of Playa Larga in the Gran Parque's only real settlement (Santo Tomás) and proceeds along a tributary of the Hatiguanico – walking or boating, depending on water levels. It's another good option for birdwatchers.

Playa Larga

Playa Larga, several kilometers south of Boca de Guamá at the head of the Bahía de Cochinos (Bay of Pigs), was one of two beaches invaded by US-backed exiles on April 17, 1961 (although Playa Girón, 35km further south, saw far bigger landings). Nowadays, it's the best base for exploring the Zapata peninsula, Cuba's largest wilderness area, and is also known for its diving (although Playa Girón makes a better base for the latter activity). There's a cheapish resort here, a scuba-diving center, and a smattering of casas particulares in the adjacent beachside village of Caletón.

Activities

Club Octopus International Diving Center DIVING
(45-98-72-25, 45-98-72-94; per dive CUC$35) The Club Octopus International Diving Center is 200m west of Villa Playa Larga. Most of the actual dive sites are further south in and around Playa Girón (p233). Costs start at CUC$25 for one immersion.

Sleeping

Casa Kirenia CASA PARTICULAR $
(45-98-73-68; kirenia800320.roque@nauta.cu; r CUC$25-30;) You can't miss the bright-orange facade of Caletón's brightest, orangest house – and also one of its best. Three spotless rooms are light with plenty of space to spread out, there's excellent food and drink, and the hosts are extremely welcoming (and can help organize local nature activities).

Hostal Enrique CASA PARTICULAR $
(45-98-74-25; enriqueplayalarga@gmail.com; r CUC$25-40;) Located smack in the middle of the village of Caletón is one of area's better casas, a humongous place with 14 rooms all with private bathrooms, a dining area (serving large portions of food), a rooftop terrace and a path from the back garden leading to the often-deserted Caletón beach. Enrique can help arrange diving and birdwatching at distinctly cheaper prices than the hotels hereabouts.

Villa Playa Larga HOTEL $$
(45-98-72-94; s/d incl breakfast CUC$67/100; P) On a small scimitar of white-sand beach by the road, just east of the village of Caletón, this hotel has huge rooms in detached bungalows with bathroom, sitting room, fridge and TV. There are also eight two-bedroom family bungalows and an on-site restaurant. However, it's all rather dowdy and in need of more regular maintenance.

Information

National Park Office (45-98-72-49; 8am-4:30pm) The National Park Office covering Gran Parque Natural Montemar (p228) is at the north entrance to Playa Larga on the road from Boca de Guamá. The staff here is knowledgeable, helpful and multilingual (Spanish, English and German) and can help you organize activities and transport for the park.

Getting There & Away

There's a thrice-daily **Víazul** (www.viazul.com) bus from Havana that heads onto Playa Girón (CUC$6, 30 minutes), Cienfuegos (CUC$7, 1¾ hours) and Trinidad (CUC$12, 2¾ hours). It stops at the main road junction, 400m west of the Villa Playa Larga. There's only one daily bus in the opposite direction toward Havana (CUC$13, 3¼ hours), and another to Varadero (CUC$12, three hours). Note: buses are usually full. Book in advance, preferably at the ticket office (p234) in Playa Girón.

Playa Girón

The sandy arc of Playa Girón nestles peacefully on the eastern side of the infamous Bahía de Cochinos (Bay of Pigs), backed by one of those gloriously old-fashioned Cuban villages where everyone knows everyone else. Notorious as the place where the Cold War almost got hot, the beach is actually named for a French pirate, Gilbert Girón, who met his end here by decapitation in the early 1600s at the hands of embittered locals. In April 1961 it was the scene of another botched raid, the ill-fated, CIA-sponsored invasion that tried to land on these remote sandy beaches in one of modern history's classic David-and-Goliath struggles. Lest we forget, there are still plenty of propaganda-spouting billboards dotted around rehashing past glories.

These days Girón, with its clear Caribbean waters, precipitous offshore dropoff and multitude of private home-stays, is one of the best places in Cuba to go diving and snorkeling.

Sights

Museo de Playa Girón MUSEUM
(CUC$2, camera CUC$1; 8am-5pm) This museum with its gleaming glass display cases evokes a tangible sense of the history of the famous Cold War episode that

DON'T MISS

DIVING IN THE BAHÍA DE COCHINOS

While the Isla de la Juventud and María la Gorda head most Cuban divers' wish lists, the Bahía de Cochinos has some equally impressive underwater treats. There's a huge dropoff running 30m to 40m offshore for over 30km from Playa Larga down to Playa Girón, a fantastic natural feature that has created a 300m high coral encrusted wall with amazing swim-throughs, caves, gorgonians and marine life. Even better, the proximity of this wall to the coastline means that the region's 30-plus dive sites can be easily accessed without a boat – you just glide out from the shore. Good south-coast visibility stretches from 30m to 40m and there is a handful of wrecks scattered around.

Organizationally, Playa Girón is well set up with highly professional instructors bivouacked at five different locations along the coast. Generic dive prices (immersion CUC$25, night dive CUC$35, five dives CUC$100, or open-water courseCUC$365) are some of the cheapest in Cuba. Snorkeling is CUC$5 per hour.

The International Scuba Center (p233), at Villa Playa Girón, is the main diving headquarters here. Casa Julio y Lidia (p233) in Playa Girón is another great source of information on diving.

La Guarandinga, a colorfully painted 'divers bus,' picks up tourists at locations in Playa Girón every morning and heads to Playa el Tanque, the best nearby dive spot, on the Playa Larga road: particularly good for learners because you start off in shallow water.

Eight kilometers southeast of Playa Girón is Caleta Buena (p233), a lovely sheltered cove perfect for snorkeling and kitted out with another diving office. Black coral ridges protect several sinkholes and underwater caves teeming with the oddly shaped sponges for which the area is renowned: a great opportunity for speleo-scuba diving! Because saltwater meets freshwater, fish here are different to other sites. Admission to the beach is CUC$15 and includes an all-you-can-eat lunch buffet and open bar. Beach chairs and thatched umbrellas are spread along the rocky shoreline. Snorkel gear is CUC$3.

More underwater treasures can be seen at the Cueva de los Peces (p232), a sinkhole (or *cenote*), about 70m deep on the inland side of the road, almost exactly midway between Playa Larga and Playa Girón. There are lots of bright, tropical fish, plus you can explore back into the darker, spookier parts of the *cenote* with snorkel/dive gear (bring torches). There's a handy restaurant and an on-site dive outfit.

Just beyond the Cueva de los Peces is Punta Perdiz (p233), another phenomenal snorkeling/scuba-diving spot with the wreck of a US landing craft (scuttled during the Bay of Pigs invasion) to explore. The shallow water is gemstone-blue here and there's good snorkeling right from the shore. There's a smaller on-site diving concession. Non-water-based activities include volleyball and chances to play the amiable custodians at dominoes. Beware the swarms of mosquitoes and *libélulas* (enormous dragonflies).

unfolded within rifle-firing distance of this spot in 1961. Across the street from Villa Playa Girón (p233), it offers two rooms of artifacts from the Bay of Pigs skirmish plus numerous photos with (some) bilingual captions.

The mural of victims and their personal items is harrowing and the tactical genius of the Cuban forces comes through in the graphic depictions of how the battle unfolded. The 15-minute film about the 'first defeat of US imperialism in the Americas' is CUC$1 extra. A British Hawker Sea Fury aircraft used by the Cuban Air Force is parked outside the museum; round the back are other vessels used in the battle.

Cueva de los Peces DIVE SITE

(⌚8am-5pm) If you don't fancy diving in the sea, head to the Cueva de los Peces, a 70m-deep *cenote* (sinkhole) on the inland side of the coast road halfway between Playa Larga (p230) and Playa Girón. It's a pretty spot as popular with swimmers as snorkelers for spotting tropical fish. The brave can glide into the darker parts of the underwater cave with diving gear. Hammocks swing languidly around the crystal clear pool, while the beach opposite calls to you.

There's a handy restaurant and an on-site dive outfit that also rents snorkeling gear (CUC$3).

THE US AND THE BAY OF PIGS

What the Cubans call Playa Girón, the rest of the world has come to know as the Bay of Pigs 'fiasco,' a disastrous attempt by the Kennedy administration to invade Cuba and overthrow Fidel Castro.

Conceived in 1959 by the Eisenhower administration and headed up by deputy director of the CIA, Richard Bissell, the plan to initiate a program of covert action against the Castro regime was given official sanction on March 17, 1960. There was but one proviso: no US troops were to be used in combat.

The CIA modeled their operation on the 1954 overthrow of the left-leaning government of Jacobo Árbenz in Guatemala. However, by the time President Kennedy was briefed on the proceedings in November 1960, the project had mushroomed into a full-scale invasion backed by a 1400-strong force of CIA-trained Cuban exiles and financed with a military budget of US$13 million.

Activated on April 15, 1961, the invasion was a disaster from start to finish. Intending to wipe out the Cuban Air Force on the ground, US planes painted in Cuban Air Force colors (and flown by Cuban-exile pilots) missed most of their intended targets. Castro, who had been forewarned of the plans, had scrambled his air force the previous week. Hence, when the invaders landed at Playa Girón two days later, Cuban Sea Furies (light aircraft) were able to promptly sink two of the US supply ships and leave a force of 1400 men stranded on the beach.

To add insult to injury, a countrywide Cuban rebellion that had been much touted by the CIA never materialized. Meanwhile a vacillating Kennedy told Bissell he would not provide the marooned exile soldiers with US air cover.

Abandoned on the beaches, without supplies or military back-up, the invaders were doomed. There were 114 killed in skirmishes and a further 1189 captured. The prisoners were returned to the US a year later in return for US$53 million worth of food and medicine.

The Bay of Pigs failed due to a multitude of factors. First, the CIA had overestimated the depth of Kennedy's personal commitment and had made similarly inaccurate assumptions about the strength of the fragmented anti-Castro movement inside Cuba. Second, Kennedy himself, adamant all along that a low-key landing should be made, had chosen a site on an exposed strip of beach close to the Zapata swamps. Third, no one had given enough credit to the political and military know-how of Fidel Castro or to the extent to which the Cuban Intelligence Service had infiltrated the CIA's supposedly covert operation.

The consequences for the US were far-reaching. 'Socialism or death!' a defiant Castro proclaimed at a funeral service for seven Cuban 'martyrs' on April 16, 1961. The revolution had swung irrevocably toward the Soviet Union.

Punta Perdiz DIVE SITE
(incl lunch CUC$15; ⏱10am-5pm) Punta Perdiz is a snorkeling and diving spot, 10km north of Playa Girón, where you can glide out from the shore in fish-tank clarity water to a world of coral and tropical treasure. There's a boat-shaped restaurant perched on the rocky shoreline, volleyball nets, sun-loungers, gear rental and a dive center. For CUC$15 you can use the place all day and partake in the buffet lunch (noon-3pm). It's an easy, flat cycle ride from Playa Girón village.

Caleta Buena BEACH
(⏱9:30am-4pm) Eight kilometers southeast of Playa Girón is Caleta Buena, a lovely protected cove perfect for snorkeling and kitted out with another diving office. The CUC$15 admission includes an all-you-can-eat lunch buffet and open bar. There are beach chairs and thatched umbrellas dotting the rocky shoreline and enough space in this remote place to have a little privacy. Snorkel gear is CUC$3.

Activities

All things considered Girón could offer the best diving in Cuba. The reasons? Well, a) it's relatively close to Havana; b) most of the dives are directly off-shore and don't need boat transfers; c) at CUC$25 an immersion, the diving is cheap; d) water clarity is excellent; and e) there's a plenitude of good diving instructors, many of whom also rent rooms.

International Scuba Center DIVING
(☎45-98-41-10, 45-98-41-18; Villa Playa Girón) The International Scuba Center, at Villa Playa Girón (p233), is the main diving headquarters. This is the best place for coordinating dives in the area. It's well-run and offers dives from CUC$25 per immersion.

Sleeping

★ **Casa Julio y Lidia** CASA PARTICULAR $
(☎45-98-41-35; lidia.aguero@nauta.cu; r CUC$30; P ❄) Owner Julio is the most experienced dive instructor hereabouts, meaning his modern house with two plush rooms is a useful option for divers. The huge rooms are equipped with some of the most comfortable beds and softest sheets in Cuba. The food is spectacular. It's the second house on the left as you're entering Playa Girón from the west.

Hostal Luis CASA PARTICULAR $
(☎45-98-42-58; hostalluis@yahoo.es; r incl breakfast CUC$30-50; P ❄) The first house on the road to Cienfuegos is also the Playa Girón's premier casa. Instantly recognizable by the blue facade and the two stone lions guarding the gate, youthful Luis and his wife offer eight spotless rooms both here and in another just-renovated house opposite. They'll help you organize any number of local activities.

Ivette & Ronel CASA PARTICULAR $
(☎45 98 41 29; micha@infomed.sld.cu; r CUC$30; P ❄) The first house on the left (if entering Playa Girón from the west), Ivette and Ronel's benefits from having a casa-owner-cum-dive-master at the helm. Five rooms and a small animal farm out back with *jutías* (tree rats) and crocs.

KS Abella CASA PARTICULAR $
(☎45-98-43-83; r CUC$25-30; ❄) The *señor* is a former chef at Villa Playa Girón now trying out his seafood specialties on his casa guests. The two-bedroom casa (with roof terrace) is the impressive red-and-cream bungalow a few houses up the Cienfuegos road from Hostal Luis (opposite).

Villa Playa Girón RESORT $$
(☎45-98-41-10; s/d all-inclusive CUC$66/99; P ❄ 🏊) On a beach imbued with historical significance lies this very ordinary hotel. Always busy with divers, the villa has clean, basic rooms that are often a long walk from the main block. The beach is a 50m dash away, though its allure has been spoiled somewhat by the construction of a giant wave-breaking wall.

Eating

Bar-Restaurante El Cocodrilo INTERNATIONAL $$
(☎52-82-96-86; mains CUC$5-10; ⏱11:30am-10:30pm) The ultimate après-dive spot in Playa Girón is an opened-sided beach-shack-style place opposite the approach road to Hotel Playa Girón. It looks fun from the outside and doesn't usually disappoint. Warm up with a cocktail at the bar and then move onto pork and chicken, or the billiard table, however the mood takes you.

Bahía de Cochinos

Information

Cadeca (⏲8:30am-noon & 12:30-4pm Mon-Fri, 8:30-11:30am Sat) Opposite Museo de Playa Girón

Getting There & Away

There's a daily **Víazul** (www.viazul.com) bus to Havana (CUC$13, 3¼ hours) at 5:35pm and two departures to Trinidad (CUC$13, three hours) at 10:15am and 2:35pm, both of which call at Cienfuegos (CUC$7, 1½ hours). The bus stop and ticket office is opposite the Museo de Playa Girón.

Getting Around

BICYCLE

Many of the local casas particulares rent (or lend) basic bikes; they're perfectly adequate for the Playa Girón area's flat roads and a great way to link with the various beaches and dive sites, most of which are less than 10km away.

BUS

A small hop-on, hop-off **shuttle bus** (CUC$3, 2½ hours for the full run) links Playa Girón with most of the local dive and nature sites in the area, including Caleta Buena (p233) to the south and Playa Larga (p230) and Boca de Guamá (p227) to the north. It passes twice a day; check times at your casa/hotel.

La Guarandinga is the unique open-sided dive bus that picks up in Playa Girón village every morning (around 8:30am) and takes divers to the various local dive sites. It returns again in the evening. Tell your casa owner if you want it to stop.

CAR & MOPED

Cubacar (☎45-98-41-26; Villa Playa Girón; ⏲9am-5pm) has a car-rental office at Villa Playa Girón or you can hire a moto for CUC$26 per day.

East of **Caleta Buena** (p233), the coastal road toward Cienfuegos is not passable in a normal car; backtrack and take the inland road via Rodas.

Cienfuegos Province

☎43 / POP 108,825

Includes ➡

Best Places to Eat

➡ Restaurante Villa Lagarto (p245)

➡ Paladar Aché (p245)

➡ Restaurante Las Mamparas (p245)

➡ Casa Prado Restaurante (p245)

Best Places to Sleep

➡ Bella Perla Marina (p241)

➡ Hotel la Unión (p242)

➡ Angel y Isabel (p242)

➡ Hostal Palacio Azul (p243)

Why Go?

Bienvenue (welcome) to Cienfuegos, Cuba's Gallic heart, which sits in the shadow of the crinkled Sierra del Escambray like a displaced piece of Paris on Cuba's untamed southern coastline. French rather than Spanish colonizers were the pioneers in this region, arriving in 1819 and bringing with them the ideas of the European Enlightenment, which they industriously incorporated into their fledgling neoclassical city: the result today is a dazzling treasure box of 19th-century architectural glitz.

Beyond the city, the coast is surprisingly underdeveloped, a mini-rainbow of emerald greens and iridescent blues, flecked with coves, caves and coral reefs. The province's apex is just inland at El Nicho, arguably the most magical spot in the Sierra del Escambray.

Though ostensibly Francophile and white, Cienfuegos' once-muted African 'soul' gained a mouthpiece in the 1940s with local-born Mambo king Benny Moré and in the Catholic-Yoruba Santería brotherhoods, which still preserve their slave-era traditions in the town of Palmira.

When to Go

➡ High season between January and April sees beach lovers and divers hit the Caribbean coast.

➡ Despite the imminent hurricane season in August and September, partygoers enjoy the Cienfuegos Carnaval and the biannual Benny Moré festival.

➡ Wet-season road conditions between August and October makes travel tougher at El Nicho in the Sierra del Escambray.

Cienfuegos Province Highlights

1. **Parque José Martí** (p243) Strolling amid grand eclectic 19th-century architecture in Unesco-listed Cienfuegos.

2. **Punta Gorda** Enjoying a perfect sundowner in a once priceless, still handsome hotel, yacht club or private residence on this gorgeous peninsula.

3. **El Nicho** (p250) Escaping to the jungle-like landscapes of the Sierra del Escambray to cool down underneath an invigorating waterfall.

4. **Palmira** (p250) Tracking the legends of the Santería religion in this unlikely Afro-Cuban outpost.

5. **Jardín Botánico de Cienfuegos** (p240) Beholding the astounding collection of plants and trees at Cuba's oldest botanical garden.

6. **Castillo de Nuestra Señora de los Ángeles de Jagua** (p239) Visiting one of the only military bastions on Cuba's south coast.

7. **Laguna Guanaroca** (p241) Spotting pink flamingos and pelicans at this little-visited protected area.

Cienfuegos

POP 165,113

In his song 'Cienfuegos,' Benny Moré described his home city as the city he liked best. He wasn't the settlement's only cheerleader. Cuba's so-called 'Pearl of the South' has long seduced travelers from around the island with its elegance, enlightened French airs and feisty Caribbean spirit. If Cuba has a Paris, this is most definitely it.

Arranged around the country's most spectacular natural bay, Cienfuegos is a nautical city founded in 1819 by French émigrés, whose homogeneous grid of elegant classical architecture earned it a Unesco World Heritage Site listing in 2005. Geographically, the city is split into two distinct parts: the colonnaded central zone with its stately Paseo del Prado and graceful park; and Punta Gorda, a thin knife of land slicing into the bay with a clutch of outrageously eclectic palaces built by the moneyed classes in the 1920s.

History

Cienfuegos was founded in 1819 by a pioneering French émigré from Louisiana named Don Louis D'Clouet. Sponsoring a scheme to increase the population of whites on the island, D'Clouet invited 40 families from New Orleans and Philadelphia, and Bordeaux in France to establish a fledgling settlement known initially as Fernandina de Jagua. Despite having their initial camp destroyed by a hurricane in 1821, the unperturbed French settlers rebuilt their homes and – suspicious, perhaps, that their first name had brought them bad luck – rechristened the city Cienfuegos after the then governor of Cuba.

With the arrival of the railway in 1850 and the drift west of Cuban sugar growers after the War of Independence (1868–78), Cienfuegos' fortunes blossomed, and local merchants pumped their wealth into a dazzling array of eclectic architecture that harked back to the neoclassicism of their French forefathers.

D-day in Cienfuegos' history came on September 5, 1957, when officers at the local naval base staged a revolt against the Batista dictatorship. The uprising was brutally crushed, but it sealed the city's place in revolutionary history.

Modern-day Cienfuegos retains a plusher look than many of its urban counterparts. And now with some much-needed Unesco money on board, as well as the city's growing industrial clout, the future for Cienfuegos and its fine array of 19th-century architecture looks bright.

Sights

City Center

★Teatro Tomás Terry THEATER
(Map p238; ☎43-51-33-61, 43-55-17-72; Av 56 No 270, btwn Calles 27 & 29; tours CUC$2; ⌚9am-6pm) Sharing French and Italian influences, this theater on the northern side of Parque José Martí is grand from the outside (look for the gold-leafed mosaics on the front facade), but even grander within. Built between 1887 and 1889 to honor Venezuelan industrialist Tomás Terry, the 950-seat auditorium is embellished with Carrara marble, hand-carved Cuban hardwoods and whimsical ceiling frescoes.

In 1895 the theater opened with a performance of Verdi's *Aida* and it has witnessed numerous landmarks in Cuban music, as well as performances by the likes of Enrico Caruso and Anna Pavlova, and pulsates with plays and concerts still.

Museo Provincial MUSEUM
(Map p238; cnr Av 54 & Calle 27; CUC$2; ⌚10am-6pm Tue-Sat, 9am-1pm Sun) The main attraction on the south side of Parque José Martí, this dignified museum proffers a microcosm of Cienfuegos' history. The frilly furnishings of refined 19th-century French-Cuban society form the majority of displays, but there's also a rare insight into the province's prehistory. Go upstairs for the highlight: the mirrored work *Como ven los hombres de la guerra*, via which you get a close-up on the room's incredible ceiling murals.

Catedral de la Purísima Concepción Church CHURCH
(Map p238; Av 56 No 2902; ⌚7am-noon Mon-Fri) On the eastern side of Parque José Martí, Cienfuegos' cathedral dates from 1869 and is distinguished by its French stained-glass windows in an otherwise austere interior that is awaiting restoration. Chinese writing discovered on columns is thought to date from the 1870s. The cathedral is nearly always open; you can also join the faithful for a service (7:30am weekdays, 10am Sundays).

Arco de Triunfo LANDMARK
(Map p238; Calle 25, btwn Avs 56 & 54) The Arch of Triumph on the western edge of Cienfuegos' serene central park catapults the plaza into the unique category: there is no other building of its kind in Cuba. Dedicated to Cuban independence, the Francophile monument ushers you through its gilded gateway toward a marble statue of revolutionary and philosopher José Martí.

Casa de la Cultura Benjamin Duarte HISTORIC BUILDING
(Map p238; Calle 25 No 5401; ⌚8:30am-midnight) FREE On the western side of Parque José Martí the former Palacio de Ferrer (1918) is a riveting neoclassical building with Italian marble floors and – most noticeably – a rooftop cupola equipped with a wrought-iron staircase. The downside? The stairs up are invariably closed – and otherwise there's only dingy art within.

Palacio de Gobierno HISTORIC BUILDING
(Map p238; Av 54, btwn Calles 27 & 29) Most of Parque José Martí's south side is dominated by this grandiose, silvery-gray building where the provincial government (Poder Popular Provincial) operates. The Palacio de Gobierno doesn't allow visitors, but you can steal a look at the palatial main staircase through the front door. It's in wonderful condition.

Casa del Fundador HISTORIC BUILDING
(Map p238; cnr Calle 29 & Av 54) On the southeastern corner of Parque José Martí stands the city's oldest building, once the residence of city founder Louis D'Clouet and now a souvenir store. El Bulevar (p248), Cienfuegos' quintessential shopping street, heads

Central Cienfuegos

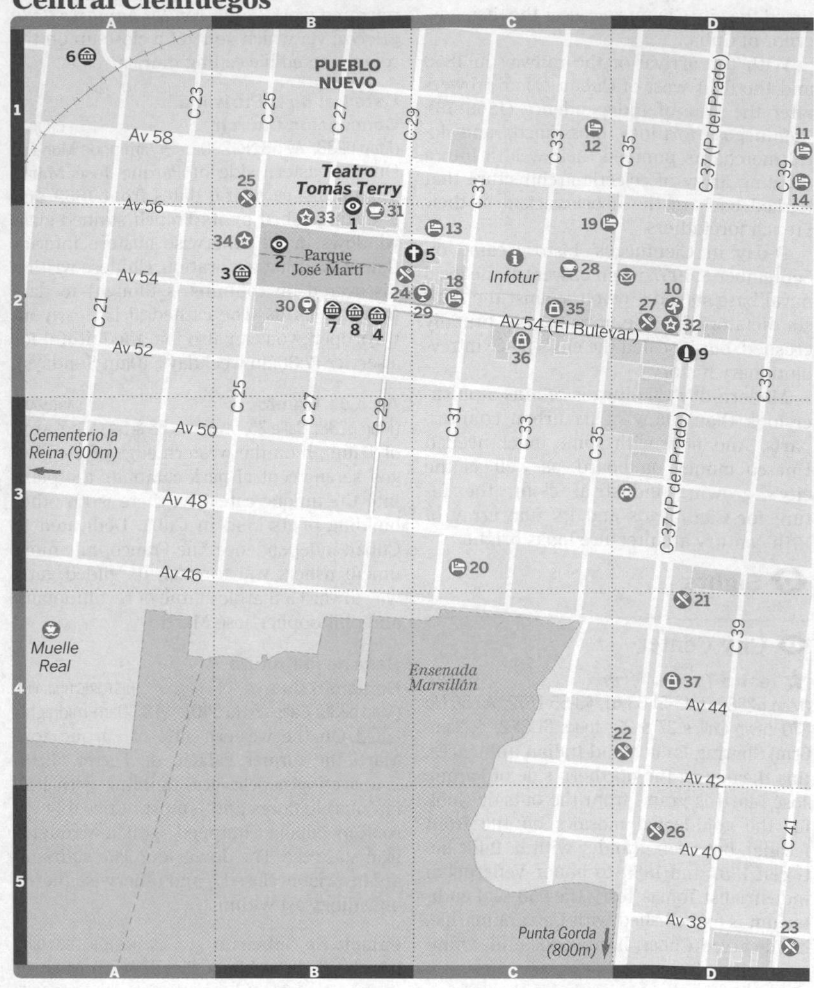

east from here to link up with Paseo del Prado.

Statue of Benny Moré MONUMENT

(Map p238; cnr Av 54 & Calle 37) Before you hit the Malecón, at the intersection of Av 54 and Paseo del Prado you can pay your respects to this life-sized likeness of the Cienfuegos-born musician with his trademark cane.

Museo Histórico Naval Nacional MUSEUM

(Map p238; cnr Av 60 & Calle 21; 9am-4:30pm Tue-Sun) FREE Across the railway tracks, five blocks northwest of Parque José Martí, is this eye-catching rose-pink museum, dating from 1933. It's housed in the former headquarters of the Distrito Naval del Sur, and is approached by a wide drive flanked with armaments dating from different eras. It was here in September 1957 that a group of sailors and civilians staged an unsuccessful uprising against the Batista government. The revolt is the central theme of the museum. The ramparts offer great bay views.

★Cementerio la Reina CEMETERY

(43-52-15-89; cnr Av 50 & Calle 7; 8am-5pm) FREE A listed national monument, the city's

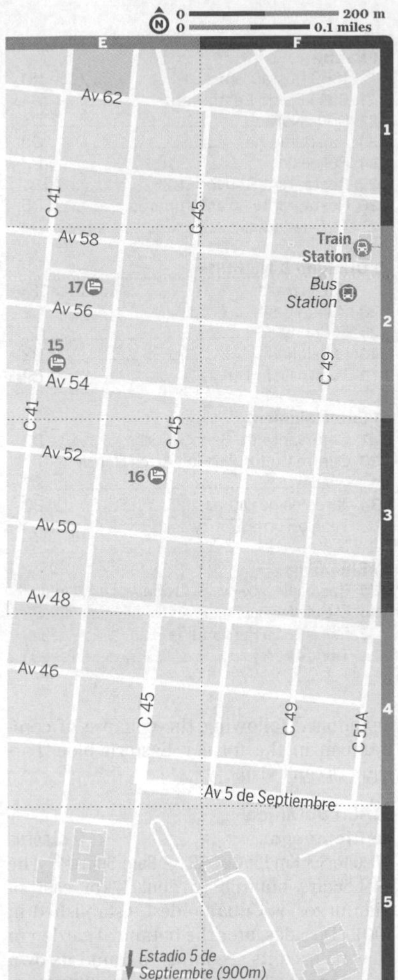

oldest cemetery was founded in 1837, and is lined with the graves of Spanish soldiers who died in the Wars of Independence. La Reina is the only cemetery in Cuba where bodies are interred above ground (in the walls) due to the high groundwater levels. It's an evocative place if you're into graveyards (tours are available). Look for the marble statue called Bella Durmiente: a tribute to a 24-year-old woman who died in 1907 of a broken heart. Approach is via the slum-like Av 50: a long, hot walk or horse-cart ride via the sorry-looking collection of trains passing as the Parque de Locomotivas.

Punta Gorda

Malecón WATERFRONT

(Map p244) Keep heading south on Paseo del Prado and the street becomes the Malecón as it cuts alongside one of the world's finest natural bays, offering exquisite vistas. Like all sea drives (Havana's being the archetype), this area comes alive in the evening when poets come to muse and couples to canoodle.

Palacio de Valle HISTORIC BUILDING

(Map p244; Calle 37, btwn Avs 0 & 2; ⏲9:30am-11pm) FREE The ultimate in kitsch comes near the end of Calle 37 when, with a sharp intake of breath, you'll stumble upon the *Arabian Nights*–like Palacio de Valle. Built in 1917 by Acisclo del Valle Blanco, a Spaniard from Asturias, the structure resembles an outrageously ornate Moroccan casbah.

Batista planned to convert this colorful riot of tiles, turrets and stucco into a casino, but today it's an (aspiring) upscale restaurant with an inviting terrace bar.

Centro Recreativo la Punta PARK

(Map p244; ⏲9am-10pm Sun-Fri, to midnight Sat) Lovers come to watch the sunset amid sea-framed greenery at the gazebo on the extreme southern tip of this park. The bar is also popular with local police officers.

Outside Town

Necrópolis Tomás Acea CEMETERY

(☎43-52-52-57; Av 5 de Septiembre; CUC$1; ⏲8am-5pm) One of two national-monument-listed resting places in Cienfuegos, the Acea is classed as a 'garden cemetery' and is entered through a huge neoclassical pavilion (1926) flanked by 64 Doric columns modeled on the Parthenon in Greece. This cemetery contains a monument to the marine martyrs who died during the abortive 1957 Cienfuegos naval uprising. Compared to the Cementerio la Reina (p238), it's newer and better maintained. It's 2km east of the city center along Av 5 de Septiembre.

Castillo de Nuestra Señora de los Ángeles de Jagua FORT

(CUC$5; ⏲8am-6pm) Predating the city of Cienfuegos by nearly a century, this fort, to the west of the mouth of Bahía de Cienfuegos, was designed by José Tontete in 1738 and completed in 1745. At the time it was

Central Cienfuegos

Top Sights
1 Teatro Tomás Terry B2

Sights
2 Arco de Triunfo B2
3 Casa de la Cultura Benjamin Duarte.... B2
4 Casa del Fundador............ B2
5 Catedral de la Purísima Concepción Church............ C2
6 Museo Histórico Naval Nacional............ A1
7 Museo Provincial............ B2
8 Palacio de Gobierno B2
9 Statue of Benny Moré D2

Activities, Courses & Tours
Cubanacán............ (see 29)
10 Cubatur D2

Sleeping
11 Bella Perla Marina............ D1
12 Casa Amigos del Mundo............ C1
13 Casa de la Amistad............ C2
14 Casa las Golondrinas............ D1
15 Claudio & Ileana E2
16 Hostal Colonial Pepe & Isabel E3
17 Hostal Mailé............ E2
18 Hotel la Unión C2
19 Lagarto Ciudad............ C2
20 Villa María C3

Eating
1869 Restaurant............ (see 18)
21 Casa Prado Restaurante D4
22 Doña Nora D4
23 Paladar Aché............ D5
24 Polinesio B2
25 Restaurant Bouyón 1825............ B1
26 Restaurante Las Mamparas D5
27 Te Quedarás............ D2

Drinking & Nightlife
Bar Terrazas .... (see 18)
28 Cubita Café............ C2
29 El Benny............ C2
30 El Palatino............ B2
31 Teatro Café Terry B2

Entertainment
32 Café Cantante Benny Moré............ D2
33 Centro Cultural de las Artes Benny Moré B2
34 Jardines de Uneac............ B2
Teatro Tomás Terry .... (see 1)

Shopping
35 Casa del Habano 'El Embajador' C2
36 El Bulevar............ C2
37 Librería 'La Fernandina'............ D4
Tienda Terry............ (see 1)

the third most important fortress in Cuba, after those of Havana and Santiago de Cuba.

Extensive renovation in 2010 gave the castle the makeover it sorely needed. In addition to a cracking view of the bay and a basic museum outlining the history of nuclear energy in Cienfuegos (!!), the castle also has a reasonably atmospheric restaurant down below.

Passenger ferries from the castle ply the waters to Cienfuegos (CUC$1, 40 minutes) twice daily, leaving Cienfuegos at 8am and 1pm and returning at 10am and 3pm. Another ferry leaves frequently to a landing just below the Hotel Pasacaballo in Rancho Luna (CUC$0.50, 15 minutes).

Juragua Nuclear Power Plant LANDMARK
Across the bay from Cienfuegos with its dome clearly visible from the city is the infamous, but never completed, Juragua nuclear power plant, a planned joint venture between Cuba and the Soviet Union that was conceived in 1976 and incorporated the ominous disused apartment blocks of the adjacent Ciudad Nuclear. Only 288km from Florida Keys, construction met with strong opposition from the US and was abandoned following the collapse of communism in the former Eastern bloc. Foreigners can't visit.

Jardín Botánico de Cienfuegos GARDENS
(Cicuito Sur Km 15; CUC$2; 8am-5pm) The 94-hectare botanic garden, 17km east of Cienfuegos, is Cuba's oldest, established in 1901. (Decades later the botanical garden in Havana used its seedlings to found its own green space.) The garden houses 2000 species of trees, including 23 types of bamboo, 65 types of fig and 150 different palms. It was founded by US sugar baron Edwin F Atkins, who initially intended to use it to study different varieties of sugarcane, but instead began planting exotic tropical trees.

You can explore the gardens independently or with a multilingual free guide. If you reserve ahead, you can also partake in a special 7am birdwatching excursion.

To reach the gardens, you'll need your own wheels or a taxi (around CUC$20 return with a wait). The cheapest method is to go with an organized excursion; Cubanacán (p241) in Cienfuegos runs trips for CUC$10. Drivers coming from Cienfuegos should turn right (south) at the junction to Pepito Tey.

Laguna Guanaroca LAKE

(☎43-54-81-17; incl tour CUC$10; ⊙8am-3pm) Laguna Guanaroca is a mangrove-rimmed saline lake southeast of Cienfuegos. It's second only to Las Salinas on the Península de Zapata as a bird magnet, and is Cienfuegos Province's only *area protegida* (natural protected area). Trails lead to a viewing platform where flamingos, pelicans and tocororos (trogons or Cuba's national bird) are regular visitors.

Plant life includes pear, lemon and avocado trees, as well as the güira, the fruit used to make maracas. Tours take around two hours and include a short hike and a boat trip to the far side of the lake. Arrive early to maximize your chances of seeing a variety of birds.

The reserve entrance is 12km from Cienfuegos, off the Rancho Luna road on the cut-through to Pepito Tey. A taxi there and back with a wait costs around CUC$15.

Activities

Base Náutica Club Cienfuegos WATER SPORTS

(Map p244; ☎43-52-65-10; Calle 35, btwn Avs 10 & 12; ⊙10am-6pm) At this nautical base at Club Cienfuegos you can organize all manner of aquatic activities from boat trips to kayaking and windsurfing, starting from CUC$12 per person. It also has a tennis court (there is no fence, so get used to lots of ball retrieving) and an amusement center with bumper cars and video games. The swimming pool costs CUC$8 per person.

Marlin Marina Cienfuegos FISHING, SAILING

(Map p244; ☎43-55-16-99; http://nauticamarlin.tur.cu/en; Calle 35, btwn Avs 6 & 8; ⊙11am-8:45pm) Hook up with this 36-berth marina a few blocks north of Hotel Jagua to arrange deep-sea fishing trips. Prices start at CUC$200 for four people for four hours. Local bay excursions are also available (CUC$12 to CUC$16), including a Castillo de Jagua one. Book through Cubatur (p248) or Cubanacán.

Tours

Cubanacán TOURS

(Map p238; ☎43-55-16-80; Av 54, btwn Calles 29 & 31) Cubanacán's helpful Cienfuegos office organizes interesting local tours, including bay boat trips (CUC$12) and the ever-popular El Nicho excursion (CUC$35), plus other hard-to-reach places such as Jardín Botánico de Cienfuegos (from CUC$10) and the local cigar factory (CUC$5). Other possible excursions include diving at Rancho Luna, Península de Zapata and the 'El Purial' trip to some little-known waterfalls and hikes at El Güije.

Festivals & Events

Benny Moré International Music Festival MUSIC

(⊙Nov) This festival remembers the province's biggest all-time hero, singer Benny Moré. In recent years, it has been held annually in November, both in town and in nearby Santa Isabel de las Lajas.

Sleeping

In contrast to other Cuban cities where the state-run hotels are often a joke, Cienfuegos has at least four good ones ranging from re-imagined colonial to slickly modern. The casas particulares are equally fitting of the refined bayside setting. Those at Punta Gorda are more removed, generally more atmospheric and pricier.

City Center

★Bella Perla Marina CASA PARTICULAR $

(Map p238; ☎43-51-89-91; bellaperlamarina@yahoo.es; Calle 39 No 5818, cnr Av 60; r/ste CUC$30/70; P❄@) Long popular for its city-center location and warm hospitality, Bella Perla is what you might call a 'boutique' casa particular. The house, with two standard rooms and a stunning rooftop suite, has taken on fortress-like dimensions in recent years with a gorgeous two-level, plant-filled terrace crowning everything. The antique beds are fit for royalty and it even has a full-sized billiards table.

Owner, Waldo, has a new, equally exquisite house called Auténtica Perla nearby.

Lagarto Ciudad CASA PARTICULAR $

(Map p238; ☎43-52-23-09; www.lagartociudad.com; Calle 35 No 5607, btwn Avs 56 & 58; r CUC$35-40; ❄@) A classic, eclectic Cienfuegos building dating from the 1920s and stuffed with all the city's calling cards: columns, antique beds, tiled floors, *vitrales* (stained glass windows) and chandeliers. Name a hotel where you can get all this for CUC$40. The food is good too, and English is spoken. Book online.

Villa María CASA PARTICULAR $
(Map p238; ☎54-16-66-74; odalys.villamaria@nauta.cu; Calle 31 No 4606a, btwn Avs 46 & 48; r CUC$40) New private place affiliated with a quiet restaurant that is more boutique hotel than casa particular. A lot of work has been put into the six smart rooms which are gleaming white with a few designer accents. The family owners are very involved and the attractive cafe-restaurant is a great place to repose even if you're not staying.

Hostal Mailé CASA PARTICULAR $
(Map p238; ☎43-52-53-85; mailebarcelo@yahoo.es; Ave 56a No 4116, btwn Calles 41 & 43; r CUC$25; ❄) Hostess Mailé always has a smile, which lends extra quality to this relatively modest house in an equally modest Cienfuegos backstreet. Once inside the lean structure, things open out with deceptively large rooms (as clean and well-equipped as any local hotel) and a sun-dappled roof terrace where you can enjoy breakfast and/or sunset cocktails.

Hostal Colonial Pepe & Isabel CASA PARTICULAR $
(Map p238; ☎43-51-82-76; hostalcolonial isapepe@gmail.com; Av 52 No 4318, btwn Calles 43 & 45; r CUC$25-35; ❄) Ex-teacher Pepe greets you with a smile as wide as the Bahía de Cienfuegos at his deceptively large colonial house, which incorporates five modern rooms set around two long, narrow upstairs and downstairs terraces. Each room has a queen bed and an extra pull-down single Murphy bed, and two come with additional living room or kitchen space.

Casa Amigos del Mundo CASA PARTICULAR $
(Map p238; ☎43-55-55-34; Av 60, btwn Calles 33 & 35; r CUC$25) The two ground-floor rooms are set a long way back from the road here, making them some of the quietest in central Cienfuegos, and are complemented by an inviting, newly completed roof terrace.

Casa las Golondrinas CASA PARTICULAR $
(Map p238; ☎43-51-57-88; drvictor61@yahoo.es; Calle 39, btwn Avs 58 & 60; r CUC$25-30; ❄) Run by a doctor and his wife, this is a gorgeous renovated colonial house with three ample rooms. There's a lot of TLC in the restoration, from the colonnaded front room to the long, plant-bedecked roof terrace where guests can relax with food and/or cocktails. The owners also rent city bikes (CUC$5 per day) and good hybrids with gears (CUC$15 per day).

Casa de la Amistad CASA PARTICULAR $
(Map p238; ☎43-51-61-43; casaamistad@correocuba.cu; Av 56 No 2927, btwn Calles 29 & 31; r CUC$25; P❄) Friendship's the word in this venerable colonial house stuffed full of family heirlooms just off Parque José Martí. Hostess Leonor has been renting for eons and has welcomed travelers from all over the world. There are two well-kept rooms, a lovely roof terrace and several resident cats.

Claudio & Ileana CASA PARTICULAR $
(Map p238; ☎43-51-97-74; Av 54 No 4121, btwn Calles 41 & 43; r CUC$20-25; ❄) A hospitable couple (both doctors) renting a polished place with two bedrooms and all mod cons near the bus station and within walking distance of the Unesco-listed city center.

★**Hotel la Unión** BOUTIQUE HOTEL $$$
(Map p238; ☎43-55-10-20; www.hotellaunioncuba.com; cnr Calle 31 & Av 54; s/d CUC$130/190; ❄@📶🏊) Barcelona, Naples, Paris? There are echoes of all these cities in this plush, colonial-style hotel with its European aspirations and splendid Italianate pool, fit for a Roman emperor. Tucked away in a maze of marble pillars, antique furnishings and two tranquil inner courtyards are 46 well-furnished rooms with balconies either overlooking the street or a mosaic-lined patio.

You'll also find a gym, hot tub and local art gallery. Service is refreshingly efficient: there's an airy roof terrace that showcases live salsa plus a well-regarded downstairs **restaurant** (mains CUC$10; ⏰7:30-9am & noon-2pm & 7-9:45pm; ❄).

Punta Gorda

Casa los Delfines CASA PARTICULAR $
(Map p244; ☎43-52-04-58; Calle 35 No 4e; r CUC$35; P❄) Right at the southern tip of Punta Gorda, Casa los Delfines (the dolphins) enjoys all of the benefits of this idyllic strip, backing directly onto the calm shallow bay with the Sierra del Escambray beckoning in the distance. The two rooms with minibars are cozy and light-filled, not that you'll be spending much time in them in this setting. Cocktails on the terrace are obligatory.

Angel y Isabel CASA PARTICULAR $
(Map p244; ☎43-51-15-19; Calle 35 No 24, btwn Av 0 & Litoral; r CUC$35; ❄) Location, location, location. One of many architecturally accomplished abodes on that coveted mansion-studded final stretch of Punta Gorda.

At the back of the turreted main house are three rooms facing onto a patio that abuts the bay. It even has its own private little boat dock. Bliss.

Villa Lagarto – Maylin & Tony CASA PARTICULAR **$**
(Map p244; ☎43-51-99-66; villalagartocuba@gmail.com; Calle 35 No 4b, btwn Avs 0 & Litoral; r CUC$40;) Established as one of Cienfuegos' leading restaurants, the Lagarto also rents out three rooms cocooned on a delightful terrace, all with king-sized beds, hammocks and glinting views of the bay. While the bayside setting is magnificent, the restaurant gets busy. If it's intimacy and privacy you're after, look elsewhere.

Perla del Mar BOUTIQUE HOTEL **$$$**
(Map p244; ☎43-55-10-03; Calle 37, btwn Avs 0 & 2; s/d/tr CUC$90/150/210;) Opened in September 2012, Perla del Mar takes the 'historical boutique' hotel theme of the nearby Palacio Azul and updates it to the 1950s. The nine rooms have a sleek modernist feel, and two alfresco hot tubs are invitingly positioned overlooking the bay. Stairs lead up to a made-for-sunbathing terrace.

Hostal Palacio Azul HOTEL **$$$**
(Map p244; ☎43-58-28-28; Calle 37 No 201, btwn Avs 12 & 14; d CUC$271-286; P) A palace posing as a hotel rather than a hotel posing as a palace, the Palacio Azul was one of the first big buildings to grace Punta Gorda on its construction in 1921. Its seven renovated rooms are named after flowers and sparkle with plenty of prerevolutionary character.

You'll find an intimate on-site restaurant called El Chelo and a graceful rooftop cupola with splendid views.

Hotel Jagua HOTEL **$$$**
(Map p244; ☎43-55-10-03; Calle 37 No 1, btwn Avs 0 & 2; s/d/tr CUC$110/180/210; P) It's not clear what Batista's brother had in mind when he erected this modern concrete giant on Punta Gorda in the 1950s, though making money was probably the prime motivation. Still, the Jagua is a jolly good hotel – airy and surprisingly plush

CIENFUEGOS' FRENCH-INSPIRED ARCHITECTURE

C'est vrai, the elegant bayside city of Cienfuegos is Cuba's most Gallic corner. Its innate Frenchness is best exemplified not in its cuisine, where rice and beans still hold sway over *bœuf à la Bourguignonne*, but in its harmonious neoclassical architecture. With its wide, paved streets laid out in an almost perfect grid, Cienfuegos' enlightened 19th-century settlers sought to quash slums, promote hygiene and maximize public space using a system of urban planning later adopted by Baron Haussmann in Paris in the 1850s and '60s. Porches, pillars and columns are the city's most arresting architectural features, with its broad Parisian-style main avenue (Prado) which runs north–south for over 3km embellished with neat lines of well-proportioned colonnaded facades painted in an array of pastel colors.

Although founded by French émigrés in 1819, most of Cienfuegos' surviving neoclassical buildings date from between 1850 and 1910. By the early 20th century, eclectic features had begun to seep into the architecture. One of the first to break the mold was the Palacio Ferrer (now Casa de la Cultura Benjamin Duarte) in Parque José Martí, built in 1917, whose uncharacteristically decorative cupola started a craze for eye-catching rooftop lookouts.

The flamboyance continued in the 1920s and '30s on the upscale Punta Gorda Peninsula, where filthy-rich sugar merchants invested their profits in ever more ostentatious mansions, turning the neighborhood into a mini-Miami. You can track the evolution as you head south on Calle 37 past the regal Palacio Azul and the wedding-cake Club Cienfuegos to the baroque-meets-Moorish Palacio de Valle, possibly Cuba's most riotously eclectic building.

Cienfuegos' city center was declared a World Heritage Site by Unesco in 2005 for both the beauty of its architecture and the progressiveness of its urban planning, which was considered revolutionary in 19th-century Latin America. Money has since gone into livening up the main square and Parque José Martí and its environs, where various interpretive signboards pinpoint the most important buildings.

Punta Gorda

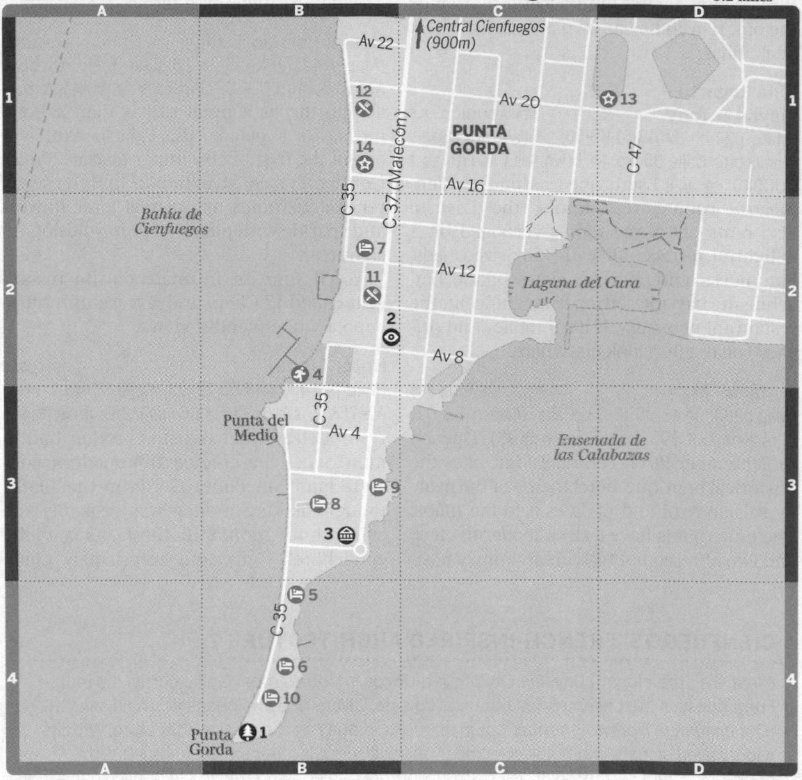

Punta Gorda

Sights
1 Centro Recreativo la Punta B4
2 Malecón B2
3 Palacio de Valle B3

Activities, Courses & Tours
Base Náutica Club Cienfuegos .... (see 11)
4 Marlin Marina Cienfuegos B2

Sleeping
5 Angel y Isabel B4
6 Casa los Delfines B4
7 Hostal Palacio Azul B2
8 Hotel Jagua B3
9 Perla del Mar B3
10 Villa Lagarto – Maylin & Tony B4

Eating
11 Club Cienfuegos B2
El Marinero .... (see 11)
12 Finca del Mar B1
Palacio de Valle .... (see 3)
Restaurante Café Cienfuegos .... (see 11)
Restaurante Villa Lagarto .... (see 10)

Drinking & Nightlife
Bar la Terraza .... (see 11)

Entertainment
13 Estadio 5 de Septiembre D1
14 Patio de ARTex – El Cubanismo B1

with modern common areas hung with revolving avant-garde art. Upper rooms (there are seven floors) are best.

Eating

Cienfuegos has some truly memorable dining options, particularly on Punta Gorda, and it has recently upped the ante in quantity and quality now that cruise ships dock at the port several times weekly.

City Center

Restaurante Las Mamparas INTERNATIONAL $
(Map p238; 43-51-89-92; Calle 37 No 4004, btwn Avs 40 & 42; mains CUC$3-6; noon-10:30pm) The usually busy Mamparas is named for the antique swing doors found in Cuba's colonial houses. There aren't many in evidence here, but the ambience is nice and the hearty food – mainly Cuban-biased with lashings of rice and beans – is unbelievably economical.

Polinesio SANDWICHES $
(Map p238; Calle 29, btwn Avs 54 & 56; mains CUC$5-12; 11am-10pm) Right under the portals in Parque José Martí, this is a salubrious setting for a cold beer or snack.

★ **Paladar Aché** SEAFOOD $$
(Map p238; 43-52-61-73; Av 38, btwn Calles 41 & 43; mains CUC$10-15; noon-10:30pm Mon-Sat; P) One of only two surviving private restaurants from the austere 1990s, Aché has taken on the young new opposition and is still abreast of the pack. Interesting decor includes caged birds, the seven dwarfs re-created as garden gnomes and a wall relief map of Cienfuegos' cultural icons. Roast pork headlines the comprehensive menu.

Casa Prado Restaurante INTERNATIONAL $$
(Map p238; 52-62-38-58; www.casapradorestaurant.com; Calle 37 No 4626, btwn Avs 46 & 48; mains CUC$4-11; 11:30am-10:30pm) A highly economical Cienfuegos restaurant that serves what is perhaps the largest and quickest seafood paella you'll see in Cuba. It has a cozy downstairs, plus a roof terrace with occasional live music. Ring the bell on the Prado to get in.

Doña Nora INTERNATIONAL $$
(Map p238; 43-52-33-31; Calle 37, btwn Avs 42 & 44; mains around CUC$10; 8am-3pm & 6-11pm) One floor up is a long way in these chunky, colonial Paseo del Prado houses, so the views from this busy little place, should you be lucky enough to bag a table by the balcony, are great for people-watching. Food is outstanding here with a French twist (rabbit in wine sauce), and the joint fills up fast.

Restaurant Bouyón 1825 PARRILLA $$
(Map p238; 43-51-73-76; Calle 25 No 5605, btwn Avs 56 & 58; mains around CUC$10; 11am-11pm) Handily situated just off the main square, this private restaurant specializes in meat cooked *a la parrillada* (on the barbecue). Avowed carnivores will revel in the hearty mixed grill, which includes four different meats and is complemented by some robust Chilean reds.

Te Quedarás INTERNATIONAL $$$
(Map p238; 58-26-12-83; Av 54, btwn Calles 35 & 37; mains CUC$10-18; noon-midnight) *Te quedarás* means 'you will stay,' and you probably will if you can bag a seat on the small, narrow wrought-iron balcony overlooking El Bulevar with a shaved-ice daiquiri as the live band breaks into something by Benny Moré (preferably 'Te Quedarás,' which was one of his more popular songs).

The restaurant is something of a shrine to Moré, and it has a lovely ambience with a mahogany bar, mambo-era black-and-white photos and those elegant Cienfuegos columns. The food is almost secondary, but it delivers, especially the prawns.

Punta Gorda

Club Cienfuegos SEAFOOD $$
(Map p244; 43-51-28-91; Calle 37, btwn Avs 10 & 12; noon-10:30pm) When in Cienfuegos, it's practically obligatory to go to Club Cienfuegos, if not for the food (it's state-run) then for the wedding-cake architecture, sunset views and bygone yacht-club ambience.

That said, there are plenty of food options here: **Bar la Terraza** (11am-10pm Sun-Fri, 11am-2am Sat) for cocktails and beer; **El Marinero** (snacks CUC$3-7; noon-3pm), a smart sea-level establishment for snacks and light lunches; and the top-floor **Restaurante Café Cienfuegos** (mains CUC$12-17; 6-10pm), a more refined, adventurous place where the steak or paella almost emulate the food in a private restaurant.

Palacio de Valle SEAFOOD $$
(Map p244; cnr Calle 37 & Av 2; mains CUC$7-12; 10am-10pm) The food doesn't have as many decorative flourishes as the eclectic architecture, but the setting is so unique it would be a shame to miss it. Seafood dominates the menu downstairs; if you aren't enthralled, use the rooftop bar here for a pre-dinner cocktail or post-dinner cigar.

Restaurante Villa Lagarto INTERNATIONAL $$$
(Map p244; 43-51-99-66; www.villalagarto.com; Calle 35 No 4b, btwn Av 0 & Litoral; mains

CUC$10-18; ⌚noon-11pm) The truly wondrous bayside setting at Largarto (the lizard) is emulated by the food and made even more memorable by some of the fastest yet most discreet service you'll see in Cuba. With its excellent *brochetas* (shish kebabs), lamb and roast pork, Lagarto is at the vanguard of Cuba's emerging private dining sector and could hold its own in Miami – easily!

Finca del Mar SEAFOOD **$$$**
(Map p244; Calle 35, btwn Avs 18 & 20; mains CUC$10-20; ⌚noon-midnight) A fine restaurant by any yardstick in terms of service and food – seafood, including lobster and octopus, is the specialty – but with its pricey dishes and abundance of tourists, this might not be everyone's Cuban dream night out. It's ever popular with the new breed of cruisers. Most Cubans find it too expensive.

Drinking & Nightlife

Cienfuegos has a pretty suave drinking scene and many of its bars are close to the water. Excellent drinking perches (especially at sunset) can be found at Club Cienfuegos and the upstairs bar of the Palacio de Valle.

Teatro Café Terry CAFE
(Map p238; Av 56 No 2703, btwn Calles 27 & 29; ⌚9am-10pm) Cafe, souvenir stall and nightly music venue, this small space wedged between the Teatro Tomás Terry and the neoclassical Colegio San Lorenzo is the most atmospheric place to flop down and observe the morning exercisers in Parque José Martí. The side patio, covered by a canopy of flowers, reveals its true personality in the evenings, with great live music ranging from *trova* (traditional music) to jazz.

El Palatino BAR
(Map p238; Av 54 No 2514, btwn Calles 25 & 27; ⌚noon-midnight) Liquid lunches were invented with El Palatino in mind – a darkwood bar set in one of the city's oldest buildings on the southern side of Parque José Martí. Impromptu jazz sets sometimes erupt, but prepare to be hit up for payment at the end of song number three.

Bar Terrazas BAR
(Map p238; cnr Av 54 & Calle 31; ⌚10am-midnight) Re-create the dignified days of old with a mojito upstairs at the Hotel la Unión; live salsa music usually kicks off around 10pm.

Cubita Café CAFE
(Map p238; Av 56, btwn Calles 33 & 35; ⌚24hr) Strong, thick coffee for trained Cuban palates, or weak lattes for those reared on Starbucks, plus some ultra-sweet cakes.

El Benny CLUB
(Map p238; Av 54 No 2907, btwn Calles 29 & 31; per couple CUC$8; ⌚10pm-3am Tue-Sun) It's difficult to say what the Barbarian of Rhythm, Benny Moré, would have made of this disco-club named in his honor. Bring your dancing shoes, stock up on the rum and Cokes, and come prepared for music that's more techno than mambo.

☆ Entertainment

★ Patio de ARTex – El Cubanismo LIVE MUSIC
(Map p244; cnr Calle 35 & Av 16; ⌚6pm-2am) A highly recommendable and positively heaving patio in Punta Gorda where you can catch *son* (Cuba's popular music), salsa, *trova* (traditional music) and a touch of Benny Moré nostalgia live in the evenings as you mingle with *cienfuegueños*. Alternatively, stand on the Malecón and you'll often hear the music drifting across the bay.

Teatro Tomás Terry LIVE MUSIC, THEATER
(Map p238; ☎43-51-33-61, 43-55-17-72; Av 56 No 270, btwn Calles 27 & 29; ⌚10pm-late) Best theater in Cuba? The Tomás Terry is certainly a contender. The building is worth a visit in its own right, but you'll really get to appreciate this architectural showpiece if you come for a concert or play; the box office is open 11am to 3pm daily and 90 minutes before show time.

Centro Cultural de las Artes Benny Moré LIVE PERFORMANCE
(Map p238; Av 56, btwn Calles 25 & 27; ⌚10am-11pm) A new state-run cultural center with a bar and dancing space within. A noticeboard out front displays what's showing on any given night, though it's mostly traditional music. Tuesdays at 5pm are a weekly homage to Benny Moré.

Café Cantante Benny Moré LIVE MUSIC
(Map p238; cnr Av 54 & Calle 37; ⌚6pm-2am) This is where you might get some suave Benny tunes, especially after hours. A tatty restaurant by day, this place blacks out the blemishes in the evenings when it mixes up mean cocktails and tunes into live traditional music. Dress up a bit for this.

Jardines de Uneac LIVE MUSIC
(Map p238; Calle 25 No 5413, btwn Avs 54 & 56; CUC$2; ⏲10am-2am) Uneac's a good bet in any Cuban city for live music in laid-back environs. Here it's quite possibly Cienfuegos' best venue, with an outdoor patio hosting Afro-Cuban *peñas* (musical performances), *trova* and top local bands such as the perennially popular Los Novos.

Estadio 5 de Septiembre SPECTATOR SPORT
(Map p244; ☎43-51-36-44; Av 20, btwn Calles 45 & 51a) From October to April, the provincial baseball team – nicknamed Los Elefantes – plays matches here. Its best-ever national series finish was fourth in 1979.

Shopping

Most of Cienfuegos' shops hug the main drag Av 54 (known colloquially as El Bulevar), which mixes souvenir outlets with traditional shops selling cheap goods in the local currency. A few more esoteric private shops have recently sprung up on Calle 37 (Paseo del Prado).

★ **Librería 'La Fernandina'** BOOKS, VINTAGE
(Map p238; ☎43-51-70-37; Calle 37 No 4404, btwn Avs 44 & 46; ⏲10am-8pm) This is the first shop in Cuba we've seen selling a (secondhand) copy of George Orwell's *Nineteen Eighty-Four* – a true revolutionary! As well as books, it stocks retro magazines, 1950s curiosities and other pieces of sunken treasure.

Tienda Terry GIFTS & SOUVENIRS
(Map p238; Av 56 No 270, btwn Calles 27 & 29; ⏲9am-6pm) A good bet for bongos, books and Che Guevara T-shirts.

BENNY MORÉ

No one singer encapsulates the gamut of Cuban music more eloquently than Bartolomé 'Benny' Moré. A great-great-grandson of a king of the Congo, Moré was born in the small village of Santa Isabel de las Lajas in Cienfuegos Province in 1919. He gravitated to Havana in 1936 where he earned a precarious living selling damaged fruit on the streets. He then played and sang in the smoky bars and restaurants of Habana Vieja's tough dockside neighborhood, where he made just enough money to get by.

His first big break came in 1943 when his velvety voice and pitch-perfect delivery won him first prize in a local radio singing competition and landed him a regular job as lead vocalist for a Havana-based mariachi band called the Cauto Quartet.

His meteoric rise was confirmed two years later when, while singing at a regular gig in Havana's El Temple bar, he was spotted by Siro Rodríguez of the famed Trío Matamoros, then Cuba's biggest *son*-bolero (ballad) band. Rodríguez was so impressed that he asked Moré to join the band as lead vocalist for an imminent tour of Mexico. In the late 1940s, Mexico City was a proverbial Hollywood for young Spanish-speaking Cuban performers. Moré was signed up by RCA records and his fame spread rapidly.

Moré returned to Cuba in 1950 a star, and was quickly baptized the Prince of Mambo and the Barbarian of Rhythm. In the ensuing years, he invented a brand new hybrid sound called *batanga* and put together his own 40-piece backing orchestra, the Banda Gigante. With the Banda, Moré toured Venezuela, Jamaica, Mexico and the US, culminating in a performance at the 1957 Oscars ceremony. But the singer's real passion was always Cuba. Legend has it that whenever Benny performed in Havana's Centro Gallego hundreds of people would fill the parks and streets to hear him sing.

With his multitextured voice and signature scale-sliding glissando, Moré's real talent lay in his ability to adapt and seemingly switch genres at will. As comfortable with a tear-jerking bolero (ballad) as he was with a hip-gyrating rumba, Moré could convey tenderness, exuberance, emotion and soul, all in the space of five tantalizing minutes. Although he couldn't read music, Moré composed many of his most famous numbers, including 'Bonito y sabroso' and the big hit 'Que bueno baila usted.' When he died in 1963, more than 100,000 people attended his funeral. No one in Cuba has yet been able to fill his shoes.

Moré fans can follow his legend in the settlement of Santa Isabel de las Lajas, a few kilometers west of Cruces on the Cienfuegos–Santa Clara road, where there's a small museum. Regular buses (local, not Víazul) run to Santa Isabel de las Lajas from Cienfuegos' bus station.

Casa del Habano 'El Embajador' CIGARS
(Map p238; cnr Av 54 & Calle 33; ⌚9am-5:30pm Mon-Sat) The best spot for smokes, rum and coffee, all encased in a rather refined interior.

El Bulevar STREET
(Map p238; Av 54) Cienfuegos' main drag – known officially as Av 54, but colloquially as El Bulevar – is an archetypal Cuban shopping street with not a chain store in sight. The best traffic-free stretch runs from Calle 37 (Paseo del Prado) to Parque José Martí, full of shops of all shapes and sizes.

ℹ Information

INTERNET ACCESS

Hotel la Unión and Parque Martí are wi-fi hot spots.

Etecsa Telepunto (Calle 31 No 5402, btwn Avs 54 & 56; per hour CUC$1.50; ⌚8:30am-7pm) Buy scratch cards here.

MEDICAL SERVICES

Clínica Internacional (☎43-55-16-22; Av 10, btwn Calles 37 & 39) Excellent new-ish center catering to foreigners and handling medical (including dental) emergencies, with a 24-hour pharmacy.

Hotel la Unión Pharmacy (☎43-55-10-20; cnr Calle 31 & Av 54; ⌚24hr) The pharmacy here is aimed at international tourists.

MONEY

Banco de Crédito y Comercio (Bandec; cnr Av 56 & Calle 31; ⌚9am-5pm Mon-Fri) Has ATMs.

Cadeca (Av 56 No 3316, btwn Calles 33 & 35; ⌚9am-5pm Mon-Fri) Change cash for convertibles or Cuban pesos.

POST

Post office (Map p238; Av 56 No 3514, btwn Calles 35 & 37; ⌚9am-5pm Mon-Fri)

TOURIST INFORMATION

Cubanacán (Map p238; ☎43-55-16-80; Av 54, btwn Calles 29 & 31) First stop for organized excursions.

Cubatur (Map p238; ☎43-55-12-42; Calle 37 No 5399, btwn Avs 54 & 56; ⌚9am-6pm Mon-Sat) Organizes excursions.

Infotur (Map p238; Calle 56 No 3117, btwn Avs 31 & 33; ⌚8:30am-5pm) Maps and brochures.

Paradiso (☎43-51-18-79; www.paradisonline.com; Av 54 No 3301, btwn Calles 33 & 35; ⌚9am-6pm Mon-Sat) Most tours of the local city and surrounds cost CUC$5 to CUC$16.

ℹ Getting There & Away

AIR

Jaime González Airport (☎43-55-22-35; Carretera a Caonao Km 3), 5km northeast of Cienfuegos, receives weekly international flights from Miami and Canada (many of them seasonal). There are no connections to Havana.

BUS

Cienfuegos' **bus station** (Map p238; ☎43-51-57-20, 43-51-81-14; Calle 49, btwn Avs 56 & 58) is clean and well organized. A Víazul office on the lower level (down the stairs and left) issues tickets; for local buses to Rancho Luna, Santa Isabel de las Lajas and Palmira for CUC$1-ish, plus other destinations, check the blackboard on the lower level (down the stairs to the right, where the ticket counters have more Cuban-style waits for service).

Varadero buses also call at Santa Clara (CUC$6, 1½ hours). The Cayo Santa María bus calls at Santa Clara and Remedios.

To reach other destinations, you have to connect in Trinidad or Havana. Note that when heading to Trinidad from Cienfuegos, buses originating further west may be full.

TRAIN

The **train station** (☎43-52-54-95; cnr Av 58 & Calle 49; ⌚ticket window 8am-3:30pm Mon-Fri, to 11:30am Sat) is across from the bus station,

BUSES FROM CIENFUEGOS

Víazul buses serve the following destinations. Check www.viazul.com for updates.

DESTINATION	COST (CU$)	DURATION (HR)	DEPARTURES
Cayo Santa María	16	4¼	9:45am
Havana	20	5	9:20am, 4:05pm
Playa Girón	7	1½	4:05pm
Trinidad	6	1¾	11:40am, 2:30pm, 4:05pm
Varadero	16	5	8:35am, 3:30pm

but with a traveling time to Havana of 10 hours (versus three by bus), you have to be a serious rail geek to want to enter or exit Cienfuegos by the comically slow *ferrocarril*. Havana-bound trains allegedly leave at 7am on alternate days: check departure times well in advance.

Getting Around

BOAT

A 120-passenger ferry runs to the Castillo de Jagua (CUC$1, 40 minutes) from the **Muelle Real** (Map p238; cnr Av 46 & Calle 25). Take note – this is a Cuban commuter boat, not a sunset cruise. Check at the port for current schedules. It's supposed to run at 8am and 1pm.

A smaller ferry (CUC$0.50, 15 minutes) also makes the short jump across the harbor mouth between the *castillo* and Rancho Luna's Hotel Pasacaballo. Last departure from the *castillo* is 8pm.

BICYCLE

Cienfuegos is a great cycling city with a strong sporting culture, and bikes are a good way to connect with the spread-out sights on Punta Gorda. Some casas particulares now rent out bikes. Try Casa las Golondrinas (p242).

CAR & MOPED

The **Servi-Cupet gas station** (cnr Calle 37 & Av 16) is in Punta Gorda. There's another station 5km northeast of Hotel Rancho Luna.

Cubacar (Hotel Jagua, Calle 37, btwn Avs 0 & 2; 9am-5pm) rents mostly manual transmission cars and has an office at Hotel Jagua.

HORSE CARTS

Horse carts and bici-taxis ply Calle 37 charging Cubans one peso a ride and foreigners CUC$1. It's a pleasant way to travel between town, Punta Gorda and the cemeteries.

TAXI

There are plenty of cabs in Cienfuegos. Most hang around outside Hotel Jagua and Hotel la Unión or linger around the bus station. Bici-taxis patrol the Malecón and will ferry you to/from Punta Gorda for about CUC$3. Negotiate. A taxi to the airport from downtown should cost CUC$6. Check the **Cubataxi** (Map p238; 43-55-11-72; Av 50, btwn Calles 35 & 37) office for latest prices.

Around Cienfuegos

Rancho Luna

Rancho Luna is a diminutive, picturesque beach resort 18km south of Cienfuegos, close to the jaws of Bahía de Cienfuegos. It has two midrange, low-key hotel complexes, but it's also possible to stay in a scattering of casas particulares on the approach road to the Hotel Faro Luna. Protected by a coral reef, the coast has good snorkeling. The beach isn't Varadero-standard sand; then again, it isn't Varadero-standard noise or incessant development, either.

Activities

Dive Center DIVING
(43-54-80-40; Carretera Pasacaballos Km 18; dives from CUC$35, open-water certification CUC$365) This dive center next door to the Hotel Faro Luna visits 30 sites within a 20-minute boat ride. There are caves, profuse marine life and dazzling coral gardens (dubbed Notre Dame by divers for their sheer, vast beauty). From November to February harmless whale sharks frequent these waters.

Other underwater sights include six sunken ships and remnants of a transmission cable once linking Cuba with Spain and laid by the Brits in 1895.

Courses

Academia Cienfuegos LANGUAGE
(www.formationcuba.com; Carretera Faro Luna) This Spanish-language school is one of the best in Cuba, running courses for one or two weeks from a base in the Hotel Faro Luna, with cultural activities offered too. See website for prices.

Sleeping

Rancho Luna has two hotels – one is all-inclusive and both are reasonably priced. Even better value for money are the dozen or so casas particulares that pepper the tiny village.

★ **Casa Larabi** CASA PARTICULAR $
(43-54-81-99; casa.larabi1@gmail.com; Carretera Faro Luna; r CUC$35; P) Possibly the most whimsical house in the whole province, the impossible-to-miss Larabi – painted turquoise, purple and pink (it works!) – jumps out at you on the approach road to the Hotel Faro Luna. Inside is a riot of museum-worthy antique furniture and botanical-garden-worthy plants. The icing on the cake: a wonderful pink terrace with sea views.

OFF THE BEATEN TRACK

PALMIRA

If you're interested in Santería and its affiliated mysteries, stop by the amiable town of Palmira, 8km north of Cienfuegos, a town famous for its Santería brotherhoods, including the societies of Cristo, San Roque and Santa Barbara. A brief exposé of their raison d'être can be found at the **Museo Municipal de Palmira** (☎43-54-45-33; Villuendas No 41; CUC$1; ⏰10am-6pm Tue-Sat, 10am-1pm Sun) on the main plaza. Cubanacán (p241) in Cienfuegos sometimes runs tours here. The main religious festivals are held in early December.

There are four fabulous rooms and great food. English spoken.

Hotel Rancho Luna RESORT $$
(☎43-54-80-12; Carretera Rancho Luna Km 18; s/d all-inclusive CUC$75/120) Rancho Luna might not offer Varadero levels of comfort and a good refurb wouldn't go amiss, but it has a loyal following among budget-conscious travelers (especially Canadians), many of whom have been coming here for years. The advantages over more expensive north-coast resorts? It's quiet and there's a beautiful Unesco-listed city 15 minutes away. Daily free shuttles head into town.

Hotel Faro Luna RESORT $$$
(☎43-54-80-30; Carretera Faro Luna; s/d CUC$80/120; P ❄ @ ≋) The dark horse of Cuba's south coast, Faro Luna is a refreshingly unpretentious place and one of only two hotels to grace what is possibly Cuba's most un-resort-like resort area. Unlike its neighbor, Hotel Rancho Luna, the Faro doesn't offer all-inclusive packages, but the in-house restaurant does an OK dinner enhanced by the setting.

The hotel is popular with language-course groups from Canada. There's a dive center (p249) next door.

Getting There & Away

Theoretically, there are half-a-dozen local buses from Cienfuegos daily, but this is Cuba – prepare for waits and chalked-up schedules. The Jagua ferry runs from the dock directly below Hotel Pasacaballo several times daily; more sporadic is the boat from Castillo de Jagua back to Cienfuegos (which runs between all three points, departing from the dock here at 10am and 3pm only at the time of research). Most reliable is a taxi; a one-way fare to Cienfuegos should cost around CUC$10 – taxis wait outside Hotel la Unión (p242). Bargain hard.

The two Rancho Luna hotels lay on a daily free shuttle to and from Cienfuegos.

An even better way to get here is zipping along from Cienfuegos on a bicycle.

El Nicho

While Cienfuegos Province's share of the verdant Sierra del Escambray is extensive (and includes the range's highest summit, 1156m Pico de San Juan), access is limited to a small protected area around El Nicho, a segment of the Parque Natural Topes de Collantes.

The beautiful road to El Nicho via Cumanayagua is legendary for its twists and turns. *'Tienes mas curvas de la carretera por Cumanayagua'* (you have more curves than the road to Cumanayagua) is reportedly a compliment to *chicas* (girls) hereabouts. The falls make a popular and worthwhile day trip from Cienfuegos, but don't expect to have the place to yourself.

Sights

El Nicho PARK
(CUC$10; ⏰8am-5pm) El Nicho, an outlying segment of the Topes de Collantes Natural Park, is the name of a beautiful waterfall on the Río Hanabanilla and the protected zone that surrounds it. People come here to view the falls, swim in one of two natural pools and navigate a couple of short, steep but well-defined trails that end at a *mirador* (lookout point) offering views over lush mountains and the distant Embalse Hanabanilla. The area is known for its birdwatching potential. You can relax afterwards at a large farm-style **restaurant** (mains CUC$5.50; ⏰noon-5pm).

Getting There & Away

There's no reliable public transportation to El Nicho. Hiring a taxi in Cienfuegos (about CUC$50 with a two-hour wait) is the best bet. Half-day tours can be organized through the excellent Cubanacán (p241) in Cienfuegos, which also offers an El Nicho trip with onward transportation to Trinidad.

With your own wheels, you can drive through the mountains on a reasonable road to the Embalse Hanabanilla area in Villa Clara Province.

Caribbean Coast

Heading east toward Trinidad in Sancti Spíritus Province, postcard views of the Sierra del Escambray loom ever closer until their ruffled foothills almost engulf the coast road, while offshore hidden coral reefs offer excellent diving.

Activities

Guajimico Diving Center DIVING
(43-42-06-46; Carretera de Trinidad Km 42) Unusually for a campismo, Villa Guajimico has its own dive center with 16 dive sites situated atop an offshore coral ridge nearby. Guajimico means 'place of the fishes' in the language of the indigenous tribes that once lived here, and the dive sites harbor some exotic marine life. All are close to the shore and six are located in a serene forest-rimmed inlet. Ask for latest prices and deals at reception.

Hacienda la Vega HORSEBACK RIDING
(Carretera de Trinidad Km 52; per hour CUC$6) On the main road, approximately 9km east of Villa Guajimico, this bucolic cattle farm is surrounded by fruit trees and has an attached restaurant serving Cuban staples (CUC$5 to CUC$10) – a good place to relax over a shady lunch. Unhurried travelers can hire horses and canter down to the nearby beach, Caleta de Castro, where the snorkeling is excellent (BYO gear).

Sleeping & Eating

Villa Guajimico CABIN $
(43-42-06-46; Carretera de Trinidad Km 42; s CUC$22-25, d CUC$38-44; P) This is one of Cubamar's most luxurious campismos. The 51 attractive cabins with their idyllic seaside setting have facilities matching most three-star hotels and act as a nexus for scuba divers. Also offered are bike hire, car rental, various catamaran or kayaking options and short hiking trails. Cienfuegos–Trinidad buses pass by. It's also popular with Cubans.

Villa Yaguanabo CABIN $$
(43-54-19-05; Carretera de Trinidad Km 55; s/d incl breakfast CUC$78/92; P) Something of an unheralded (if overpriced) place located too close to Trinidad to delay most of the drive-by traffic, Villa Yaguanabo sits on a sublime stretch of coast at the mouth of the Río Yaguanabo. Basic but clean motel rooms look out on a quiet swath of tan-colored beach.

Using the surprisingly salubrious hotel as a base, you can catch a boat (CUC$3) for a 2km ride upriver to the Valle de Iguanas, where you'll find thermal waters, horseback-riding and a small trail network in the foothills of the verdant Sierra del Escambray. There's a private restaurant (Casa Verde) on the main road opposite the hotel offering all right lunch and dinner options.

ROSTISLAV AGEEV/SHUTTERSTOCK ©

1. Statue of José Martí (p79) In Parque Central, Havana, this was the first of thousands of statues of the independence hero.

2. Ruins of the Iglesia de Santa Ana (p280) Located in the perfectly preserved Spanish colonial settlement of Trinidad.

3. Iglesia de Nuestra Corazón de Sagrado Jesús (p325) This church in Camagüey has ornate stained glass, decorative ironwork and arches.

4. Havana (p62) There are more than 900 buildings of historical importance, from intricate baroque to glitzy art deco, in Habana Vieja.

LENA WURM/SHUTTERSTOCK ©

HEIKONEUMANNPHOTOGRAPHY/SHUTTERSTOCK ©

3

LENA WURM/SHUTTERSTOCK ©

Villa Clara Province

☎42 / POP 803,690

Includes ➡

Best Places to Eat

- Restaurant Florida Center (p262)
- La Piramide (p269)
- La Taberna (p270)
- Restaurante Casona Jover (p262)

Best Places to Sleep

- Hostal Camino del Príncipe (p268)
- Meliá Buenavista (p272)
- 'Villa Colonial' – Frank & Arelys (p267)
- Iberostar Ensenachos (p272)

Why Go?

What is that word hanging in the air over Villa Clara, one of the nation's most diverse provinces? 'Revolution,' perhaps? And not just because Che Guevara liberated its capital, Santa Clara, from Batista's corrupt gambling party to kick-start the Castro brothers' 58-year (and counting) stint in power. Oh, no. Ultra-cultural Santa Clara is guardian of the Cuban avant-garde (having the nation's only drag show and its main rock festival). Meanwhile, the picturesque colonial town of Remedios and the beach-rimmed Cayerías del Norte beyond are experiencing Cuba's most drastic contemporary tourist development.

This region is indelibly stamped with Che's legacy and associated sights. Yet it should also win your heart for hosting the nation's most frenzied street party (Remedios), for its highs among the glimmering Escambray peaks and their adventure possibilities (around Embalse de Hanabanilla), and for its lows along the lolling white-sand strands off its northern coast (Cayo Santa María).

When to Go

- There's no better time to visit Villa Clara than December. Specifically, Christmas Eve. Swap your cold Christmas for the Caribbean's hottest street party in Remedios. Book ahead, it gets busy.
- Head over to the Cayerías del Norte for the start of the high season (December through March), when the chances of the skies raining on your beach parade are as low as they get.
- November is a good time to visit Santa Clara to engage in the joys of one of Cuba's most unique and revolutionary festivals, the Ciudad Metal (a celebration of Cuban rock music).

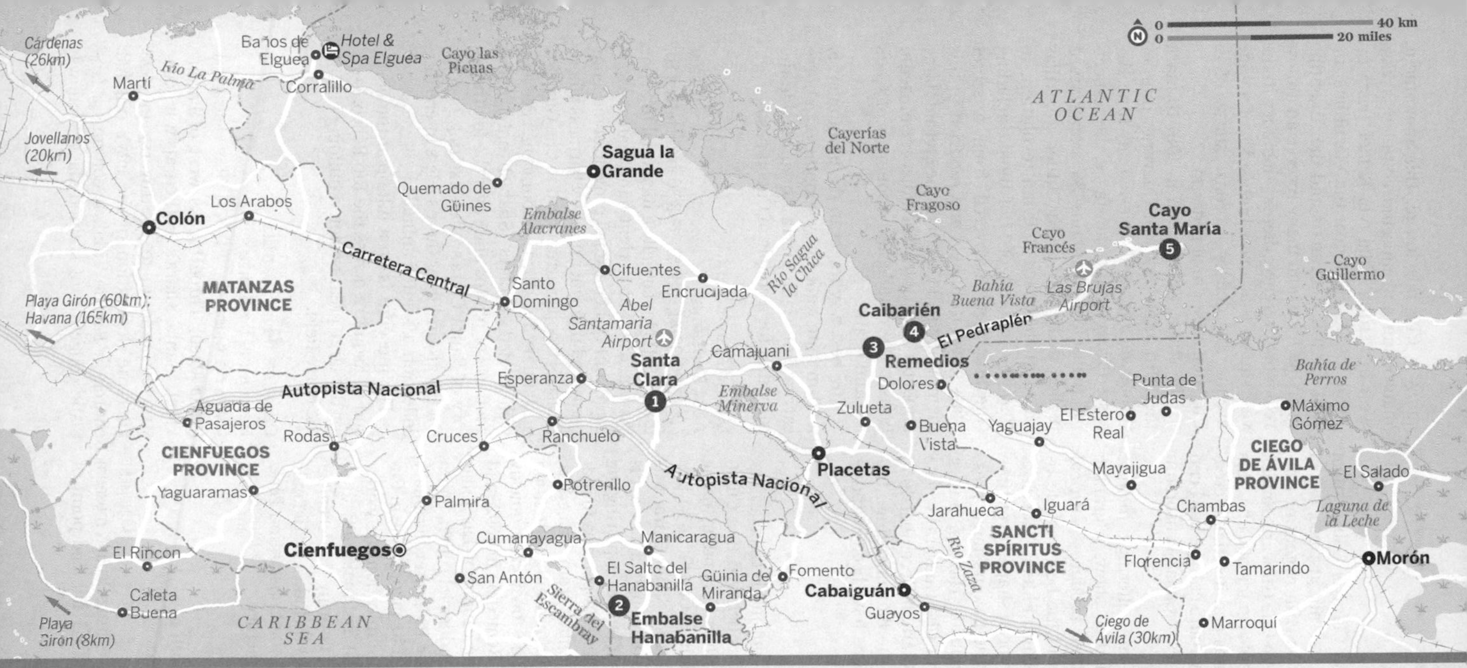

Villa Clara Province Highlights

❶ **Santa Clara** (p256) Staying in a palatial casa particular while plugging into the electric nightlife at the legendary Club Mejunje and tracing the legend at the monument to Ernesto Che Guevara.

❷ **Embalse Hanabanilla** (p265) Hiking the trails, bathing in the pools and soaking up the solitude at this lovely lake surrounded by mountains.

❸ **Remedios** (p266) People-watching from a cafe in this recently rejuvenated but, as yet, unspoiled colonial town.

❹ **Caibarién** (p270) Seeing what the Villa Clara tourist board forgot to mention in this ramshackle yet heart-warming waterside settlement.

❺ **Cayo Santa María** (p271) Basking on the balmy sands of Playa Las Gaviotas, one of Cayo Santa María's last remaining public-access beaches.

Santa Clara

POP 239,000

Sorry Havana. Santa Clara is Cuba's most revolutionary city – and not just because of its historical obsession with Argentine doctor turned *guerrillero* Che Guevara. Smack bang in the geographic center of Cuba, this is a city of new trends and insatiable creativity, where an edgy youth culture has been testing the boundaries of Cuba's censorship police for years.

Unique Santa Clara offerings include Cuba's only official drag show, a graphic artists' collective that produces satirical political cartoons, and the best rock festival in the country: Ciudad Metal. The city's fiery personality has been shaped over time by the presence of the nation's most prestigious university outside Havana, and a long association with Che Guevara, whose liberation of Santa Clara in December 1958 marked the end of the Batista regime. Little cultural revolutions have been erupting here ever since.

History

A good 10,000 miles out in his calculations, Christopher Columbus believed that Cubanacán (or Cubana Khan, an Indian name that meant 'the middle of Cuba'), an Indian village once located near Santa Clara, was the seat of the khans of Mongolia; hence his misguided notion that he was exploring the Asian coast. Santa Clara proper was founded in 1689 by 13 families from Remedios, who were tired of the unwanted attention of passing pirates. The town grew quickly after a fire emptied Remedios in 1692, and in 1867 it became the capital of Las Villas Province. A notable industrial center, Santa Clara was famous for its prerevolutionary Coca-Cola factory and its pivotal role in Cuba's island-wide communications network.

Santa Clara was the first major city to be liberated from Batista's army in December 1958. Today, industries include a textile mill, a marble quarry and the Constantino Pérez Carrodegua tobacco factory.

Sights

★Conjunto Escultórico Comandante Ernesto Che Guevara MONUMENT

(Plaza de la Revolución; mausoleum & museum 9:30am-4pm Tue-Sun) FREE The end point of many a Che pilgrimage, this monument, mausoleum and museum complex is 2km west of Parque Vidal (via Rafael Tristá on Av de los Desfiles), near the Víazul bus station. Even if you can't stand the Argentine guerrilla for whom many reserve an almost religious reverence, there's poignancy in the vast square that spans both sides of a wide avenue, guarded by a bronze statue of El Che atop a 16m-high pedestal.

The statue was erected in 1987 to mark the 20th anniversary of Guevara's murder in Bolivia, and can be viewed any time. Accessed from behind the statue, the respectful mausoleum contains 38 stone-carved niches dedicated to the other guerrillas killed in the failed Bolivian revolution. In 1997 the remains of 17 of them, including Guevara, were recovered from a secret mass grave in Bolivia and reburied in this memorial. Fidel Castro lit the eternal flame on October 17, 1997. The adjacent museum houses the details and ephemera of Che's life and death.

The best way to get to the monument is a 20-minute walk, or by hopping on a horse carriage on Calle Marta Abreu outside the cathedral for a couple of Cuban pesos.

Museo Provincial Abel Santamaría MUSEUM

(42-20-30-41; CUC$1; 8:30am-5pm Mon-Fri, to noon Sat) Not actually a memorial to Señor Santamaría (Fidel's right-hand man at Moncada), but rather a small provincial museum quartered in former military barracks where Batista's troops surrendered to Che Guevara on January 1, 1959. The comprehensive and well-labeled displays (Spanish only) make good use of photos and cover the full trajectory of Santa Clara's often exciting history. On the ground floor there's a less interesting collection of stuffed animals.

The museum is on a hilltop at the north end of Esquerra across the Río Bélico. Look for the large cream-colored building behind the horse field.

Catedral de las Santas Hermanas de Santa Clara de Asís CATHEDRAL

(Marta Abreu) Three blocks west of Parque Vidal, Santa Clara's cathedral was constructed amid huge controversy in 1923 after the demolition of the city's original church in Parque Vidal. It contains a fantastic collection of stained-glass windows, some notable art deco influences and a mythical white statue of Mother Mary known (unofficially) as La Virgen de la Charca (Virgin of the Pond).

The statue was discovered in a ditch in the 1980s, having mysteriously disappeared shortly after the cathedral's consecration in 1954. It returned to grace the cathedral in 1995.

La Casa de la Ciudad CULTURAL CENTER
(☎42-20-55-93; cnr Independencia & JB Zayas; ⏲8am-5pm) FREE The pulse of the city's progressive cultural life, hosting art expositions (including an original Wifredo Lam sketch), Noches del Danzón (traditional dance nights), a film museum and impromptu music events. It recently reopened after a refurbishment.

Parque Vidal SQUARE
A veritable alfresco theater named for Colonel Leoncio Vidal y Caro, who was killed here on March 23, 1896, Parque Vidal was encircled by twin sidewalks during the colonial era, with a fence separating blacks and whites. Scars of more recent division are evident on the facade of mint-green Hotel Santa Clara Libre on the park's west side: it's pockmarked by bullet holes from the 1958 battle for the city between Guevara and Batista's government troops.

Today all the colors of Cuba's cultural rainbow mix in one of the nation's busiest and most vibrant urban spaces, with old men in *guayabera* shirts gossiping on the shaded benches and young kids getting pulled around in carriages led by goats. Find time to contemplate the statues of local philanthropist Marta Abreu and the emblematic *El niño de la bota* (Boy with a Boot), a long-standing city symbol. Since 1902, the municipal orchestra has played rousing music in the park bandstand at 8pm every Thursday and Sunday.

Monumento a la Toma del Tren Blindado MONUMENT
(boxcar museum CUC$1; ⏲boxcar museum 8:30am-5pm Mon-Sat) History was made at the site of this small boxcar museum on December 29, 1958, when Ernesto 'Che' Guevara and a band of 18 rifle-wielding revolutionaries barely out of their teens derailed an armored train using a borrowed bulldozer and homemade Molotov cocktails.

The battle lasted 90 minutes and improbably pulled the rug out from under the Batista dictatorship, ushering in 50 years of Fidel Castro. The museum – east on Independencia, just over the river – marks the spot where the train derailed and ejected its 350 heavily armed government troops. The celebrated bulldozer is mounted on its own plinth at the entrance.

Fábrica de Tabacos Constantino Pérez Carrodegua FACTORY
(Maceo No 181, btwn Julio Jover & Berenguer; CUC$4; ⏲9-11am & 1-3pm) Santa Clara's tobacco factory, one of Cuba's best, makes a quality range of Montecristos, Partagás and Romeo y Julieta cigars. Tours here are lo-fi compared to those in Havana, and so the experience is a lot more interesting and less rushed. Buy tickets in advance at the Hotel Santa Clara Libre (p261).

Across the street is La Veguita (p263), the factory's diminutive but comprehensively stocked sales outlet, staffed by a friendly, ultra-professional team of cigar experts. You can buy cheap rum here, and the bar brews exquisite coffee.

Teatro la Caridad THEATER, HISTORIC BUILDING
(cnr Marta Abreu & Máximo Gómez) Many are deceived by the relatively austere neoclassical facade. But toss CUC$1 to whoever is manning the door and you'll serendipitously discover why the 1885 Teatro la Caridad is one of the three great provincial theaters of the colonial era.

The ornate interior is almost identical to the Tomás Terry in Cienfuegos and the Sauto in Matanzas: three tiers, a U-shaped auditorium and decadent marble statues. The rich ceiling fresco by Camilo Zalaya provides the pièce de résistance.

Museo de Artes Decorativas MUSEUM
(Parque Vidal No 27; CUC$2; ⏲9am-6pm Sun-Thu, 1-10pm Fri & Sat) Something of a sleeping beauty on Parque Vidal, this 18th-century mansion turned museum is packed with period furniture from a whole gamut of styles that seem to ape Cuba's architectural heritage. Look for baroque desks, art nouveau mirrors, art deco furniture and Veláquez' epic *Rendición de Brega*, reproduced on a china plate. Live chamber music adds to the romanticism in the evenings.

Iglesia de Nuestra Señora del Carmen CHURCH
(Carolina Rodríguez) The city's oldest church is five blocks north of Parque Vidal. It was

Santa Clara

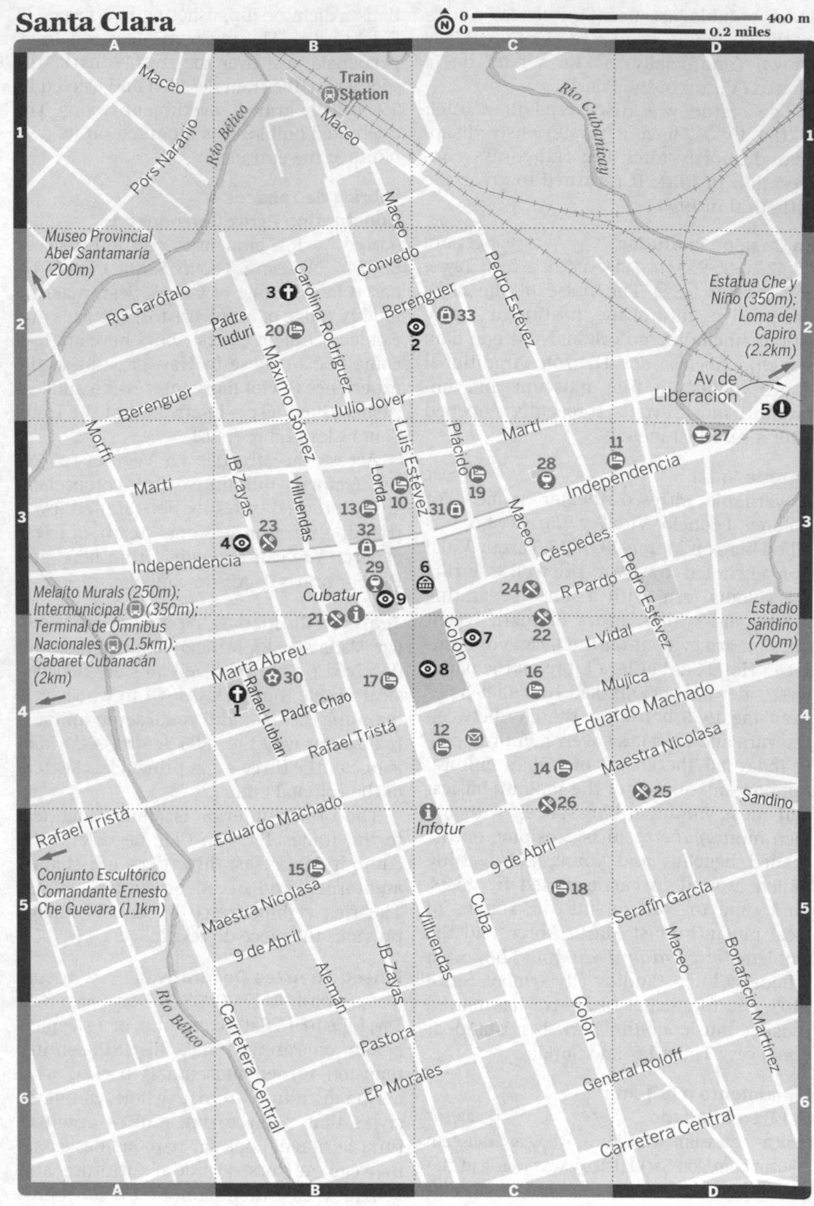

built in 1748, with a tower added in 1846. During the War of Independence, it stood in as a jail for Cuban patriots. A modern cylindrical monument facing it commemorates the spot where Santa Clara was founded in 1689 by 13 refugee families from Remedios.

Estatua Che y Niño MONUMENT

(Av Liberación) Far more intimate and intricate a monument than its big brother on the other side of town, this statue in front of the Officina de la Provincia (PCC) four blocks east of Tren Blindado shows El Che

Santa Clara

Sights
1 Catedral de las Santas Hermanas de Santa Clara de Asís B4
2 Fábrica de Tabacos Constantino Pérez Carrodegua C2
3 Iglesia de Nuestra Señora del Carmen B2
4 La Casa de la Ciudad B3
5 Monumento a la Toma del Tren Blindado D2
6 Museo de Artes Decorativas C3
7 Palacio Provincial C4
8 Parque Vidal C4
9 Teatro la Caridad B3

Sleeping
10 Authentica Pérgola B3
11 Casa Mercy 1938 .... D3
12 Hostal Alba C4
13 Hostal Familia Sarmiento B3
14 Hostal Florida Terrace C4
15 Hostal Marilin & Familia B5
16 Hotel América C4
17 Hotel Santa Clara Libre B4
18 La Casona Jover C5
19 Mary & Raicort C3
20 Olga Rivera Gómez B2

Eating
21 Dinos Pizza B4
22 El Alba C4
23 El Gobernador B3
24 Empire C3
25 Panadería Doña Neli D4
26 Restaurant Florida Center C4
Restaurante Casona Jover .... (see 18)

Drinking & Nightlife
27 Cafe-Museo Revolución D3
28 El Bar Club Boulevard C3
La Marquesina .... (see 9)
29 Santa Rosalia B3

Entertainment
30 Club Mejunje B4

Shopping
31 ARTex C3
32 Boulevard B3
33 La Veguita C2

with a baby (symbolizing the next generation) on his shoulder.

Looking closer you'll see smaller sculptures incorporated into the revolutionary's uniform depicting junctures in his life, including likenesses of the 38 men killed with Guevara in Bolivia concealed within the belt buckle.

Loma del Capiro LANDMARK
Two blocks east of the *Estatua Che y niño,* a road to the right leads to Santa Clara's best lookout, the distinctive Loma del Capiro. The crest is marked by a flag and a series of stakes supporting the metallic but recognizable face of, you've guessed it, Che Guevara.

The hill was a crucial vantage point for his forces during the 1958 liberation of Santa Clara.

Palacio Provincial NOTABLE BUILDING
(Parque Vidal) The eastern side of Parque Vidal is guarded by the thick columns of the neoclassical Palacio Provincial (1902), today home to the **Martí library** (9am-5pm) and a rare-book collection.

Festivals & Events

Santa Clara's renegade annual offerings include Miss Trasvesti, a Miss World-type event with transvestite contestants in March, and November's Ciudad Metal, when headbanging to the country's leading rock acts happens at various venues citywide.

Sleeping

★ **Hostal Familia Sarmiento** CASA PARTICULAR $
(42-20-35-10; www.santaclarahostel.com; Lorda No 56, btwn Martí & Independencia; r CUC$25-35;) The Sarmiento offers two options directly opposite each other: a traditional family-run casa particular and a smart new boutique-style hotel. The latter has its own reception, 24-hour bar and room service amid minimalist design features. Between the properties there are eight rooms, all with private bathrooms.

Hostess Elizabeth is a fantastic cook, while host Carlos is a driver, keen photographer and mine of information on Cuba. English is spoken and wi-fi is available on-site.

★ **Hostal Florida Terrace** CASA PARTICULAR $
(42-22-15-80; florida.terrace59@gmail.com; Maestra Nicolasa No 59, btwn Maceo & Colón; r CUC$30-35; P) This finely decorated hotel-like place is affiliated with Restaurant Florida Center across the road and

THE LIFE & TIMES OF CHE GUEVARA

Few 20th-century figures have successfully divided public opinion as deeply as Ernesto Guevara de la Serna, whose remains are now interred in a mausoleum (p256) in Santa Clara. Better known to his friends (and enemies) as El Che, he has been revered as an enduring symbol of Third World freedom and celebrated as the hero of the Sierra Maestra – and yet he was also the most wanted man on the CIA hit list. The image of this handsome and often misunderstood Argentine physician turned *guerrillero* is still plastered over posters and tourist merchandise across Cuba. But what would the man himself have made of such rampant commercialization?

Born in Rosario, Argentina, in June 1928 to a bourgeois family of Irish-Spanish descent, Guevara was a delicate and sickly child who developed asthma at the age of two. It was an early desire to overcome this debilitating illness that instilled in the young Ernesto a willpower that would dramatically set him apart from other men.

A pugnacious competitor in his youth, Ernesto earned the name 'Fuser' at school for his combative nature on the rugby field. Graduating from the University of Buenos Aires in 1953 with a medical degree, he shunned a conventional medical career in favor of a cross-continental motorcycling odyssey, accompanied by his old friend and colleague Alberto Granado. Their nomadic wanderings – well documented in a series of posthumously published diaries – would open Ernesto's eyes to the grinding poverty and stark political injustices all too common in 1950s Latin America.

By the time Guevara arrived in Guatemala in 1954 on the eve of a US-backed coup against Jacobo Arbenz' leftist government, he was enthusiastically devouring the works of Marx and nurturing a deep-rooted hatred of the US. Deported to Mexico for his pro-Arbenz activities in 1955, Guevara fell in with a group of Cubans that included Moncada veteran Raúl Castro. Impressed by the Argentine's sharp intellect and never-failing political convictions, Raúl – a long-standing Communist Party member himself – decided to introduce Che to his charismatic brother, Fidel.

The meeting between the two men at Maria Antonia's house in Mexico City in June 1955 lasted 10 hours and ultimately changed the course of history. Rarely had two characters needed each other as much as the hot-headed Castro and the calmer, more ideologically polished Che. Both were favored children from large families, and both shunned the quiet life to fight courageously for a revolutionary cause. Similarly, both men had little to gain and much to throw away by abandoning professional careers for what most would have regarded as narrow-minded folly.

In December 1956 Che left for Cuba on the *Granma* yacht, joining the rebels as the group medic. One of only 12 or so of the original 82 rebel soldiers to survive the catastrophic landing at Las Coloradas, he proved himself to be a brave and intrepid fighter who led by example and quickly won the trust of his less reckless Cuban comrades. As a result Castro rewarded him with the rank of Comandante in July 1957, and in December 1958 Che repaid Fidel's faith when he masterminded the battle of Santa Clara, an action that effectively sealed a historic revolutionary victory.

Guevara was granted Cuban citizenship in February 1959 and soon assumed a leading role in Cuba's economic reforms as president of the National Bank and minister of industry. His insatiable work ethic and regular appearance at enthusiastically organized volunteer worker weekends quickly saw him cast as the living embodiment of Cuba's New Man.

But the honeymoon wasn't to last. Disappearing from the Cuban political scene in 1965 amid many rumors and myths, Guevara eventually materialized again in Bolivia in late 1966 at the head of a small band of Cuban *guerrilleros*. After the successful ambush of a Bolivian detachment in March 1967, he issued a call for 'two, three, many Vietnams' in the Americas. Such bold proclamations could only prove his undoing. On October 8, 1967, Guevara was captured by the Bolivian army. Following consultations between the army and military leaders in La Paz and Washington, DC, he was shot the next day in front of US advisors. His remains were eventually returned to Cuba in 1997.

has more floors (four) than most casas particulares have rooms. The smart colonial decor has art deco echoes, offering plenty to admire, and the six rooms with antique beds are top drawer. It has an upstairs bar and *mirador* (lookout) with some of Santa Clara's best views.

English, French and Italian spoken.

Casa Mercy 1938 CASA PARTICULAR $
(☎42-21-69-41; casamercy@gmail.com; Independencia No 253, btwn Estévez & Gutiérrez; r CUC$30-35; ❄📶) The name might hark back to another age, but this wonderful neocolonial house only opened recently after a restoration. The details are spectacular; check out the Seville-style fountain that sets off the central patio. The house is self-contained (the owners live elsewhere) but diligently staffed and comes with two large rooms and plenty of communal space – including that patio.

Authentica Pérgola CASA PARTICULAR $
(☎42-20-86-86; carmen64@yahoo.es; Luis Estévez No 61, btwn Independencia & Martí; r CUC$30; ❄) The Pérgola is set around an Alhambra-esque patio draped in greenery and crowned by a fountain, from where several large rooms lead off. Pretty much everything here is antique, including in the bedrooms. There's a beautiful roof-terrace restaurant open to all called La Aldaba.

La Casona Jover CASA PARTICULAR $
(☎42-20-44-58; almiqui2009@yahoo.es; Colón No 167, btwn 9 de Abril & Serafín García; r CUC$30-35; ❄) With five large colonial rooms set well back from the road and a terrace stuffed with a profusion of plants ripe for contemplation, the Jover fits comfortably into Santa Clara's top accommodation bracket.

Hostal Marilin & Familia CASA PARTICULAR $
(☎42-20-76-55; marilin1103@gmail.com; 116 Maestra Nicolasa, btwn Alemán & JB Zayas; r CUC$25-30; ❄📶) A charming addition to the accommodation scene with three bedrooms (one big enough for families), a leafy back courtyard, a front terrace, and – most uniquely – a classic cigar-smoking room. Owner Marilin is an experienced cigar expert and knows all about the nuances of Cohibas, Montecristos et al.

Olga Rivera Gómez CASA PARTICULAR $
(☎42-21-17-11; Evangelista Yanes No 20, btwn Máximo Gómez & Carolina Rodríguez; r CUC$25; ❄) From the fabulous roof terrace, guests are spoiled with vistas of Santa Clara's prettiest church; below, the two rooms are large and clean.

Mary & Raicort CASA PARTICULAR $
(☎42-20-70-69; Placído No 54, btwn Independencia & Martí; r CUC$20-25; ❄) A charming 1st-floor house with two rooms (one with balcony) for rent and possibly Santa Clara's fruitiest *desayuno* (breakfast). Steep stairs ascend to a gorgeously done roof terrace. Bubbly hostess Mary is the other main reason to stay!

Hostal Alba CASA PARTICULAR $
(☎42-29-41-08; Eduardo Machado No 7, btwn Cuba & Colón; r CUC$30-35; ❄) This architectural stunner with lovely antique beds, original tilework and a patio serves amazing breakfasts and is just one block from the main square. The congenial owner, Wilfredo, is chef at Restaurante Florida Center – enough said!

Villa Los Caneyes HOTEL $$
(☎42-20-45-13; cnr Av de los Eucaliptos & Circunvalación de Santa Clara; s/d CUC$85/120; P❄@🏊) Recently spruced up, this out-of-town option should now be a serious consideration, particularly if you like peace and quiet. A mock-indigenous village, Los Caneyes has 95 thatched *bohios* (bungalows) in suitably verdant grounds replete with abundant birdlife, good on-site restaurant, pool, well-stocked bar and souvenir shop. It's 3km from Santa Clara and a favorite with organized coach tours.

To get here, follow the continuation of Martha Abreu over the Carretera Central.

Hotel Santa Clara Libre HOTEL $$
(☎42-20-75-48; Parque Vidal; s/d CUC$62/70) It might be Santa Clara's tallest building, but the rooms and facilities aren't so highly regarded. Notwithstanding, the hotel has a history. Bullet holes are still visible on the facade – the result of the battle in 1958 between Che Guevara's guerrillas and flailing government troops.

Hotel América HOTEL $$$
(☎42-20-15-85; Mujica, btwn Colón & Maceo; r CUC$156; ❄@🏊) The first hotel in the city center that you'd recommend to your friends rather than your enemies, the 27-room América, which opened in 2012, can't quite claim a 'boutique' moniker. But it's new, keen to please and has some interesting details (check out the metal staircase

balustrades). It has a decent bar (open to nonguests) and a small outdoor pool.

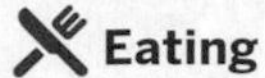

Eating

Empire SANDWICHES **$**
(cnr R Pardo & Maceo; sandwiches CUC$0.80-1.50; 10am-2am) Perched in a busy corner, this is a simple privately owned cafe aimed mainly at locals. It's a great place for a grilled cheese sandwich and a *café bombón* (espresso with condensed milk). Service comes with a smile.

El Alba CUBAN **$**
(42-20-39-35; cnr Maceo & R Pardo; MN$35-95; noon-11pm) Cheap food and large portions sold in Cuban pesos without undue ceremony. Good if you're on a budget

El Gobernador CUBAN **$**
(cnr Independencia & JB Zayas; mains CUC$3-8; 11am-5pm & 7-11:30pm) In this new era of competition from independents, state-run eateries have to perform better, and this one does. In a glamorous former state office, furnished in somber colonial splendor and hung with original artwork, El Gobernador's food was never going to *quite* live up to the ambience in which it is served, but hey, decent meat and fish dishes nevertheless.

Panadería Doña Neli BAKERY **$**
(cnr Maceo Sur & 9 de Abril; bread/snacks around CUC$1; 7am-6pm) This joyous bakery amid the austere shopfronts on Calle Maceo has plenty of tables available where you can relax with a piece of aromatic fruit cake and the best cappuccino in Santa Clara.

Dinos Pizza CAFETERIA **$**
(Marta Abreu No 10, btwn Villuendas & Cuba; pizzas CUC$3-6; 10am-10pm) The Santa Clara branch of this Cuban mini-chain has a pleasant bar, air-conditioning and friendly, helpful staff. It's generally packed with young students and serves OK pizza for those on a budget (or in a hurry).

★ **Restaurant Florida Center** CUBAN, FUSION **$$**
(42-20-81-61; Maestra Nicolasa No 56, btwn Colón & Maceo; mains CUC$10-15; 6-8:30pm) The Florida has been Santa Clara's best restaurant for at least a decade. The food is as good as the experience. Diners eat in a colonial, plant-festooned, candlelit courtyard full of interesting antiques. Owner Ángel is as active as his waitstaff, advising on the profusion of dishes in French, English, Italian and Spanish. The highlight: lobster with prawns in a tangy tomato sauce.

Restaurante Casona Jover INTERNATIONAL **$$**
(42-20-44-58; Colón No 167, btwn 9 de Abril & Serafín García; mains CUC$8; noon-10pm) A long-standing casa particular renter who's decided to give it a go in the culinary sphere, the Jover is encased in a lovely 1867 colonial house with a patio and specializes in honey chicken. Give it a try!

Drinking & Nightlife

Thanks to its large student population, Santa Clara has some of Cuba's best nightlife outside Havana – and it's not just the usual suspects. The city has an established gay scene and a strong contingent of *roqueros* (rock musicians). Most of the nightlife is on or around Parque Vidal, although there are a couple of outlying strongholds, including a new cabaret venue.

★ **La Marquesina** BAR
(Parque Vidal, btwn Máximo Gómez & Lorda; 9am-1am) You can chinwag and neck a cold bottled beer with locals of all types in this legendary dive bar under the porches of the equally legendary Teatro la Caridad on the corner of Parque Vidal. The clientele is a potpourri of Santa Clara life – students, bohemians, cigar-factory workers and the odd off-duty bici-taxi rider. Live music erupts regularly.

Cafe-Museo Revolución CAFE
(Independencai No 313; 11am-11pm) You say you want a revolution... Well, Santa Clara's a good place to start. It's already had one, successfully ignited by Che Geuvara in 1958. This new cafe pays homage to Santa Clara's (and Cuba's) revolutionary past with photos, old uniforms and other ephemera lovingly curated by the owner. The coffee and milk shakes are pretty revolutionary too.

Santa Rosalia BAR
(Máximo Gómez, btwn Independencia & Marta Abreu; 11am-2am) The Santa Rosalia styles itself as a state-run *complejo* (complex); there's a restaurant, a bar and a music venue on-site. We're recommending it for the latter (although the food isn't bad by state standards, you can eat far better in Santa Clara). The colonial building is a joy and the patio out back is large and atmospheric after dusk. Live bands kick off at 10pm-ish.

LOCAL KNOWLEDGE

MELAÍTO – SATIRE & STREET ART

While *socialismo* in Cuba hasn't always been a bundle of laughs, the revolution didn't snuff out political humor completely – at least not in Santa Clara, home of *Melaíto*, a periodical that, for over 50 years, has provided a pulpit for some of Cuba's best caricaturists and graphic artists. Founded in 1968 as a lighthearted propaganda supplement to support the upcoming 'Zafra de Diez Millones' (10-million-tonne sugar harvest), the magazine was named after one of its early characters, a hapless Chinese-Cuban cane-cutter called Melaíto. With the sugar harvest over, the magazine worked hard to build on its new-found popularity, tackling more general political themes with satire and wit. By the 1970s it had become a regular monthly supplement to the local Villa Clara newspaper, *Vanguardia*, a position it holds to this day thanks primarily to the talent of its humorists, cartoonists and artists, who are some of the finest in Cuba.

In the last few years, *Melaíto* has widened its reach to include the internet and street art. The magazine's distinctive cartoons regularly pop up in public spaces in Santa Clara and a whole building on the Carretera Central has been dedicated to **murals** (Carretera Central, btwn Vidaurreta & Carlos Pichardo) of its work. The cartoons change regularly. At last visit the theme was decidedly anti-war, depicting soldiers with doves in their rifles and taking a satirical glance at Cuba's fragile relationship with the US.

El Bar Club Boulevard CLUB
(Independencia No 2, btwn Maceo & Pedro Estévez; CUC$2; 10pm-2am Mon-Sat) This much-talked-about cocktail lounge has live bands and dancing, plus the odd comedy show. It generally gets swinging around 11pm.

☆ Entertainment

★Club Mejunje LIVE MUSIC
(Marta Abreu No 107; 4pm-1am Tue-Sun;) Urban graffiti, children's theater, transvestites, old crooners belting out boleros (ballads), tourists dancing salsa. You've heard about 'something for everyone,' but this is ridiculous. Welcome to Club Mejunje, set in the ruins of an old roofless building given over to sprouting greenery. It's a local – nay, national – institution, famous for many things, not least Cuba's first official drag show (every Saturday night).

Roll in any day of the week (except Monday) and enjoy an unforgettable 'only in Santa Clara' moment.

Cabaret Cubanacán CABARET
(Carretera Central, btwn Caridad & Venecia; cover CUC$5; 10am-3pm Wed-Sun) This new but slightly-out-of-town cabaret venue has a late-night disco preceded by a Cuban-style singing and dancing 'show' at weekends. It's one of Santa Cara's suaver nights out.

Estadio Sandino SPECTATOR SPORT
(9 de Abril Final) From October to April, you can catch baseball games in this stadium east of the center via Calle 9 de Abril. Villa Clara, nicknamed Las Naranjas (the Oranges) for their team strip, are one of Cuba's better baseball teams and were last national series champions in 2013.

Shopping

Independencia, between Maceo and JB Zayas, is the pedestrian shopping street called the Boulevard by locals. It's littered with all kinds of shops and restaurants and is the bustling hub of city life.

La Veguita CIGARS, RUM
(42-20-89-52; Maceo No 176a, btwn Julio Jover & Berenguer; 9am-7pm Mon-Sat, 11am-4pm Sun) Sales outlet for Fábrica de Tabacos Constantino Pérez Carrodegua that is staffed by a friendly team of cigar experts. You can also buy cheap rum here, and the bar out the back sells good coffee. It's across the street from the tobacco factory (p257).

ARTex GIFTS & SOUVENIRS
(Independencia, btwn Luis Estévez & Plácido; 9am-5pm Mon-Sat, to noon Sun) On Santa Clara's pedestrianized 'Boulevard,' this outlet sells handicrafts and the usual souvenirs, including plenty of the obligatory Che Guevara T-shirts and mugs.

Information

INTERNET ACCESS

Etecsa Telepunto (Marta Abreu No 55, btwn Máximo Gómez & Villuendas; internet per hour

CUC$1.50; ⌚8:30am-7pm) Eight internet terminals and three phone cabins.

Parque Vidal Wi-fi hot spot.

MEDICAL SERVICES

Farmacia Internacional (Parque Vidal; ⌚8:30am-5pm) In Hotel Santa Clara Libre.

Hospital Arnaldo Milián Castro (☎42-46049; btwn Circumvalación & Av 26 de Julio) Southeast of the city center, just northwest of Santa Clara's *circumvalación* (ring road). It's the best all-round option for foreigners; often called Hospital Nuevo.

MONEY

Banco Financiero Internacional (Cuba No 6, cnr Rafael Tristá; ⌚9am-3pm Mon-Fri) Has an ATM.

Cadeca (cnr Rafael Tristá & Cuba; ⌚8:30am-8pm Mon-Sat, to 11:30am Sun) On the corner of the main square, this is the best place to change money. Long opening hours.

POST

Post Office (Colón No 10, btwn Machado & Parque Vidal; ⌚8am-6pm Mon-Sat, to noon Sun)

TOURIST INFORMATION

Cubanacán (☎42-20-51-89; Colón, cnr Maestra Nicolasa; ⌚8am-8pm Mon-Sat)

Cubatur (☎42-20-89-80; Marta Abreu No 10, btwn Máximo Gómez & Villuendas; ⌚9am-noon & 1-8pm) Book tobacco factory tours here.

Infotur (☎42-20-13-52; Cuba No 68, btwn Machado & Maestra Nicolasa; ⌚8:30am-5pm) Handy maps and brochures in multiple languages.

Getting There & Away

AIR

Santa Clara's **Abel Santamaría Airport** (☎42-22-75-25; off Rte 311) receives several weekly flights from Montreal, Toronto and Calgary, plus a Copa Airlines flight to Panama City on Tuesday/Sunday, and is now the country's third-most-important airport. There are no flights to Havana.

BUS

The **Terminal de Ómnibus Nacionales** (☎42-20-34-70), which is also the Víazul bus station, is 2.5km west of the center, out on the Carretera Central toward Matanzas, or 500m north of the Che monument. Tickets for air-conditioned Víazul buses are sold at a special 'foreigners' ticket window at the station entrance.

The Santiago de Cuba bus travels via Sancti Spíritus (CUC$6, 1¼ hours), Ciego de Ávila (CUC$9, 2½ hours), Camagüey (CUC$15, 4½ hours), Holguín (CUC$26, 7¾ hours) and Bayamo (CUC$26, 9¼ hours).

The Cayo Santa María bus also stops in Remedios (CUC$7, one hour) and Caibarién (CUC$7, 1¼ hours).

The **intermunicipal bus station** (Carretera Central), west of the center via Calle Marta Abreu, has cheap local buses to Remedios, Caibarién and Manicaragua (for Embalse Hanabanilla). Transportation could be by bus or truck, gets overcrowded and isn't 100% reliable.

Casa owners usually know schedules, or will find them out on your behalf.

TAXI

Colectivos (shared taxis) hang around the Terminal de Ómnibus Nacionales to drum up custom for the journey to Havana. The best time to catch them is just before the scheduled Víazul departures. They'll whisk you to addresses in Central Havana in three hours for CUC$35 (less if you bargain hard), but they only leave when full (four people).

TRAIN

The **train station** (☎42-19591) is straight up Luis Estévez from Parque Vidal on the north side of town. The **ticket office** (Luis Estévez Norte No 323) is across the park from the train station.

Notoriously erratic trains pass by en route to Santiago de Cuba via Camagüey. In the other direction, they run to Havana, usually via Matanzas. Due to their fickle nature and depressingly bad facilities, few foreigners use them.

Getting Around

Horse carriages congregate outside the cathedral on Marta Abreu and will angle for CUC$1

BUSES FROM SANTA CLARA

DESTINATION	COST (CUC$)	DURATION (HR)	DEPARTURES
Cayo Santa María	13	2½	11:30am
Havana	18	4	3:35am, 8:40am, 4:50pm
Santiago de Cuba	33	12½	12:10am, 1:45am, 9:50am, 7pm
Trinidad	8	3½	10:30am, 5:15pm
Varadero	11	3¼	7:50am, 4:55pm

OFF THE BEATEN TRACK

HIKING AROUND LAKE HANABANILLA

The Sierra del Escambray is riddled with walking trails. The most accessible and well-publicized routes emanate out of Topes de Collantes in Sancti Spíritus Province and are well traipsed by tourists based in nearby Trinidad. Far less crowded are the trails that surround Embalse Hanabanilla in Villa Clara Province, most of which require a boat transfer from the Hotel Hanabanilla (p266). The hotel has more information on the trails and a (very) rough relief map stuck on the wall. Private guides wait outside the hotel.

Ruta Natural por la Rivera A 3.4km trail that follows the contours of the lake, passing coffee plantations and humid foliage replete with butterflies.

Montaña por Dentro A 17km hike connecting Embalse Hanabanilla to El Nicho waterfall on the Cienfuegos side of the Sierra del Escambray. Get a guide, as it's poorly marked.

Un Reto a Loma Atahalaya A 12km all-encompassing walk that incorporates a climb up the 700m-high Loma Atahalaya (with broad views north and south), a waterfall and a local campesino house. It finishes at a cave, La Cueva de Brollo.

per ride. Bici-taxis (from the northwest of the park) cost the same. Taxis from the center to the Terminal de Ómnibus Nacionales/airport cost CUC$3/15.

CAR & MOPED

Cars can be rented from **Cubacar** (☎42-21-81-77; Marta Abreu, btwn JB Zayas & Alemán; ⏲9am-5pm), which has offices in town, or **Rex** (☎42-22-22-44; ⏲8:30am-5:30pm), which has an office at the airport.

There's a **gas station** (cnr Carretera Central & Calle 9 de Abril) southwest of the city center.

TAXI

Private cabs loiter in front of the Terminal de Ómnibus Nacionales and will offer you lifts to Remedios and Caibarién. A state taxi to the same destinations will cost approximately CUC$30/35 respectively. To get to Cayo Santa María, bank on CUC$70 to CUC$80 one-way. Negotiate prices for return rides with waiting time. Drivers generally congregate in Parque Vidal outside Hotel Santa Clara Libre.

Embalse Hanabanilla

Embalse Hanabanilla, Villa Clara's main gateway to the Sierra del Escambray, is a 36-sq-km reservoir nestled picturesquely amid traditional farms and broccoli-toned hills. The glittering lake is fjord-like and comes stocked with a famed supply of record-breaking bass. Fishers, boaters and nature lovers are well catered for, with several excursions and some rewarding seldom-trodden hikes available. The area is best accessed by boat from the Hotel Hanabanilla on the reservoir's northwestern shore, some 80km by road south of Santa Clara. Tourism in the region is still in its infancy.

Activities

Fishing

Whopping 9kg largemouth bass have been caught on the lake, and fishing trips can be organized at the hotel: for two people with a guide, prices start at CUC$50 for four hours.

Boat Trips

Boats ferry passengers over to Casa del Campesino (p266), which offers coffee, fresh fruit and a taste of bucolic Cuban life (with lunch if desired). Another popular boat trip is to the **Río Negro Restaurant** (mains CUC$5-6; ⏲9am-5pm) perched atop a steep stone staircase overlooking the lakeshore, 7km away. You can enjoy *comida criolla* (Creole food) surrounded by nature, and hike up to a mirador (lookout). Another 2km by boat from the Río Negro Restaurant is a tiny quay; disembark for the 1km hike to the Arroyo Trinitario waterfall, where you can swim. A couple of other trails lead off from here. Depending on duration and passenger numbers, return trips will be CUC$10 to CUC$20 per person.

A lesser-known seasonal boat trip runs to the spectacular El Nicho waterfall (p250), in Cienfuegos Province, via the southwestern arm of the lake. Bank on CUC$35 return.

You can organize these activities at the Hotel Hanabanilla or book a day excursion (around CUC$33 from Santa Clara; CUC$69 from Cayo Santa María). Outside the hotel gates, locals offer all the above trips for cheaper prices.

Sleeping & Eating

Hotel Hanabanilla HOTEL **$$**
(42-20-84-61; Salto de Hanabanilla; s/d CUC$72/83; P) Another page from the utilitarian school of Cuban architecture that blemished many a beauty spot in the 1970s, the 125-room Hanabanilla has attempted regular refurbs in the years since, though none have fully eradicated its incongruous ugliness. However, closer inspection reveals well-kept facilities inside, including an à la carte restaurant, a swimming pool, a vista-laden bar and lake-facing rooms with small balconies.

Peaceful during the week but packed with mainly Cuban guests at weekends, it is your only accommodation for miles and the best base for lakeside activities. To get here from Manicaragua, proceed west on route 152 for 13km. Turn left at a junction (the hotel is signposted) and follow the road 10km to the hotel.

Casa del Campesino CUBAN **$$**
(lunch CUC$8; lunch) Roll up on a boat (there's no road connection) to this traditional wooden abode above Embalse Hanabanilla where the men will be out back cutting down fruit with machetes while the ladies rustle up rice, pork and beans over huge steaming pots in the outdoor kitchen. The food is as delicious as the setting.

Getting There & Away

The chalked-up bus schedule in Santa Clara advertises daily buses to Manicaragua (but check ahead). Theoretically, there are buses from Manicaragua on to Embalse Hanabanilla, but the only practical access is by car, bike or moped. Taxi drivers in Santa Clara will energetically offer the trip (about CUC$50 one-way). Negotiate hard if you want the driver to wait while you participate in excursions.

Remedios

POP 45,836

A small, tranquil town that goes berserk every Christmas Eve in a cacophonous firework festival known as Las Parrandas, Remedios is one of Cuba's lesser-glimpsed colonial highlights. Some historical sources claim it is Cuba's second-oldest settlement (founded in 1513), although it is officially listed at number eight after Santiago and proudly celebrated its quincentennial in 2015. The anniversary has transformed Remedios from a slightly scruffy stopover on the way to Cayo Santa María into a mini-Trinidad replete with handsome boutique hotels, a beautifully restored central square (Plaza Martí) and several decent eating joints. However, the bulk of Cuba's culture-seeking tourists have yet to cotton on to Remedios' glorious rebirth. Come now before they find out.

Sights

★ **Parroquia de San Juan Bautista de Remedios** CHURCH
(Camilo Cienfuegos No 20; donations accepted; 9am-noon & 2-5pm Mon-Sat) One of the island's most interesting and oldest ecclesiastical buildings, Remedios' main church dates from around 1550, although much of the current structure is the result of extensive 18th-century renovations. The wooden *mudéjar* ceiling was once the hull of a boat while the gold-leaf high altar is carved from Cuban cedar in classic baroque style. The church's main curiosity is a rare carving of a pregnant *Inmaculada concepción* made in Seville, Spain.

Other important statues include *San Salvador* (north side) and *Carmen* (south side), depicting the two neighborhood patrons represented in the town's December Parrandas festival. The statue of the *Vigen del Cobre* (Cuba's patron saint) is the second oldest in Cuba after the Santiago original.

Entrance to the church is through the small rear door. Get one of the assistants to show you around, as its precious artifacts deserve a full explanation.

Museo de las Parrandas Remedianas MUSEUM
(Andrés del Río No 74; CUC$1; 9am-6pm) Visiting this recently renovated and relocated museum two blocks off Parque Martí is no substitute for the real-life revelry on December 24, but what the hell? It maintains a photo gallery that usually recaps the previous year's *parrandas,* along with historical information on the tradition, including scale models of floats and depictions of how the fireworks are made.

DON'T MISS

LAS PARRANDAS

Sometime during the 18th century, the priest at Remedios' cathedral, Francisco Vigil de Quiñones, had the bright idea of providing local children with cutlery and crockery and getting them to run about the city making noise in a bid to increase Mass attendance in the lead-up to Christmas. He could not have imagined what he was starting. Three centuries later and *parrandas*, as these cacophonous rituals became known, have developed into some of the best-known Caribbean street parties. Peculiar to the former Las Villas region of Cuba, *parrandas* take place only in towns in Villa Clara, Ciego de Ávila and Sancti Spíritus Provinces, and the biggest party erupts annually in Remedios on December 24.

Festivities kick off at 10pm, with the city's two traditional neighborhoods (El Carmen and El Salvador) grouping together to outdo each other with displays of fireworks and dance, from rumba to polka. The second part of the party is a parade of vast floats, elaborate carnival-like structures, only with the fancifully dressed people in the displays standing stock still as the tractor-towed artworks traverse the streets. Further fireworks round off the revelry.

The *parrandas* aren't confined to Remedios. Other towns in former Las Villas Province (now Ciego de Ávila, Sancti Spíritus and Villa Clara) stage their own seasonal shenanigans. Though each is different, there are some generic party tricks, such as fireworks, decorative floats and opposing neighborhoods competing for the loudest, brightest and wildest stunts. Camajuani, Caibarién, Mayajigua and Chambas all have (almost) equivalently raucous *parrandas* celebrations.

Note that Remedios is booked out months in advance for Las Parrandas. If you can't get in for the Christmas Eve revelries, come earlier. Smaller parties kick off in the town from December 8 onward.

Iglesia de Nuestra Señora del Buen Viaje CHURCH

(Alejandro del Río No 66) On Parque Martí (the only plaza in Cuba with two Catholic churches), the 18th-century Iglesia de Nuestra Señora del Buen Viaje is in the middle of a long-overdue restoration. It is named after a statue of the Virgin Mary taken there by sailors in 1600.

Museo de Música Alejandro García Caturla MUSEUM

(Parque Martí No 5) Between the churches in the main square is the former house of Alejandro García Caturla, a Cuban composer and musician who lived here from 1920 until his murder in 1940. Caturla was a pioneer who integrated Afro-Cuban rhythms into classical music and also served as a lawyer and judge. The house hosts occasional impromptu concerts. The museum was on hiatus at last visit.

Sleeping

Remedios has a quartet of boutique hotels (two of them new in 2016) set in rejuvenated historical buildings and run by Cubanacán's 'Encanto' brand. Like Trinidad, most of the casas particulares inhabit beautiful colonial-era buildings.

Book well ahead in December, especially from the 20th onward when Las Parrandas hits full throttle.

★'Villa Colonial' – Frank & Arelys CASA PARTICULAR $

(☎42-39-62-74; www.cubavillacolonial.com; Maceo No 43, cnr Av General Carrillo; r CUC$30; ❄@📶) Frank & Arelys' wonderful colonial house is their pride and joy – and it shows. The four independent rooms have their own entrance, private bathroom, dining area (with stocked fridge), and living room with massive windows protected by iron *rejas* (bars) and adorned with decorative *mamparas* (swing-doors). There's internet connection, and fine wines and food can be rustled up at short notice. A rooftop terrace is the icing on the cake.

Hostal Casa Richard CASA PARTICULAR $

(☎42-39-66-49; hostalcasarichard@gmail.com; Maceo No 52, btwn Av General Carrillo & Fe del Valle; r CUC$30; ❄) Long-term renters with three rooms that include plenty of extras (hairdryers, soaps, umbrellas). The rooms open onto a lovely uncluttered patio (unless you

Remedios

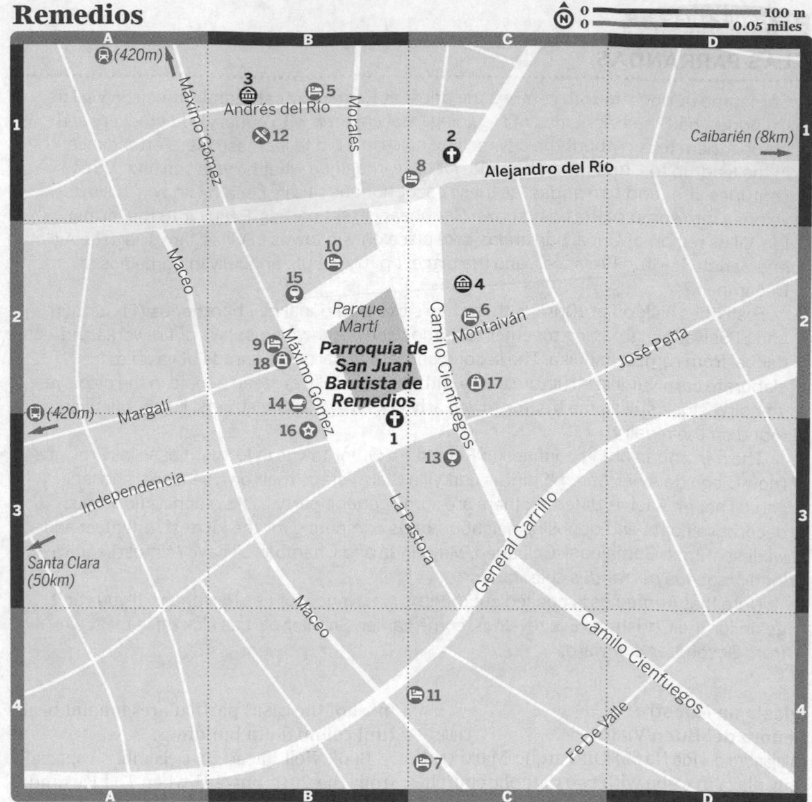

count the lush avocado tree), complete with the essential rocking chairs. Owner Richard is extremely obliging and a great source of local knowledge. If he's full, he can recommend another family house nearby.

Hostal Buen Viaje CASA PARTICULAR **$**
(☎42-39-65-60; hostal.buenviaje@gmail.com; Andrés del Río No 20; r CUC$30; ❄) Longstanding colonial renter near the church of the same name with a courtyard that will transport you back 150 years. The house offers three bedrooms with large beds and even larger breakfasts. The very friendly owners speak English. Not surprisingly, it gets a lot of repeat visits.

La Paloma CASA PARTICULAR **$**
(☎42-39-54-90; Parque Martí No 4; r CUC$25; P ❄) Sharing prime frontage on Remedios' main square along with three of the town's historic hotels, this casa, which dates from 1875, also shares plenty of antique trimmings with tilework and furnishings that would be worth zillions anywhere else.

The three rooms have been upgraded with modern fittings, including massive shower units, art deco beds, and doors big enough to ride a horse through. There's also an on-site restaurant.

★Hostal Camino del Príncipe BOUTIQUE HOTEL **$$**
(☎42-39-51-44; Camilo Cienfuegos No 9, btwn Montaiván & Alejandro del Río; s/d CUC$98/144; ❄) A mark of Remedios' recent progression, this new hotel with its elegant white pillars holding up a handsome terracotta facade is one of Cuba's best boutique offerings. Loaded with the kind of low-key charm the town is famous for, it successfully melds modern comfort with old-world glory. Ask for a room overlooking the square.

Remedios

Top Sights
1 Parroquia de San Juan Bautista de Remedios B3

Sights
2 Iglesia de Nuestra Señora del Buen Viaje C1
3 Museo de las Parrandas Remedianas B1
4 Museo de Música Alejandro García Caturla C2

Sleeping
5 Hostal Buen Viaje B1
6 Hostal Camino del Príncipe C2
7 Hostal Casa Richard C4
8 Hostal Real C1
9 Hotel Mascotte B2
10 La Paloma B2
11 'Villa Colonial' – Frank & Arelys C4

Eating
12 La Piramide B1

Drinking & Nightlife
13 Driver's Bar C3
14 El Louvre B2
15 Taberna de los 7 Juanas B2

Entertainment
16 Centro Cultural las Leyendas B3

Shopping
17 Plaza Isabel II Artesania C2
18 Tres Reyes B2

Hostal Real BOUTIQUE HOTEL $$
(Camilo Cienfuegos, cnr Alejandro del Río; s/d CUC$90/120) The addition of this colonial-style hotel on Parque Martí brings Remedios' haul of boutique hotels to four – and what an attractive quartet it is. Like its three cohorts, the Real is intimate, authentic and tastefully done, meaning Remedios is one of the few towns in Cuba where hotels can compete with casas particulares in quality (if not price).

Hotel Mascotte BOUTIQUE HOTEL $$
(☎42-39-53-41; Parque Martí; s/d CUC$90/120; ❄@) Take an eloquent colonial Remedios theme and stick it inside a small 'Encanto' hotel (the boutique branch of the Cubanacán chain) and the results are pretty impressive, as this long-standing 10-room gem on the main plaza demonstrates.

Eating

La Piramide CUBAN $$
(☎42-39-54-21; Andrés del Río No 9; 3-course meals CUC$13; ⏰10:30am-2:30pm & 6:30-10:30pm Wed-Mon) Remedios doesn't have many private eateries, but the ones it does have are good. For proof, sample the surf and turf *brochetas* (shish kebabs) in this diminutive little haven of good taste.

Drinking & Nightlife

Driver's Bar BAR
(José Peña No 61, cnr Camilo Cienfuegos; ⏰10am-midnight) Once a dive, the Driver's recently had a radical rethink. A local artist has given it a throwback 1950s feel with a strong focus on automobiles. Vintage car enthusiasts and the local bici-taxi *muchachos* tend to congregate here, meaning the prices are cheap and the atmosphere 90% Cuban. Roll up and order a mojito.

Taberna de los 7 Juanas BAR
(Parque Martí, cnr Máximo Gómez; ⏰10am-midnight) Remedios' 500th anniversary has bequeathed the city many good things, not least this new place across the square from long-standing default bar, El Louvre (which needed a bit of competition). The service is sharp, the location sublime and the beer plentiful. It even has its own wine cellar.

El Louvre CAFE, BAR
(Máximo Gómez No 122; ⏰7:30am-midnight) With a gravitational pull on Remedios' scattering of tourists, El Louvre is, so locals proclaim, the oldest bar in the country in continuous service (since 1866) – and who are *you* to argue? The bar was good enough for Spanish poet Federico García Lorca, who heads the list of famous former patrons. It does basic food too.

Entertainment

In December, during Las Parrandas and its affiliated events, Remedios offers up some of the best entertainment in Cuba. At other times the scene is more low-key.

Centro Cultural las Leyendas CULTURAL CENTER
(Máximo Gómez, btwn Margalí & Independencia) Next door to El Louvre is an ARTex cultural

center with music till 1am from Wednesday to Saturday.

Shopping

Plaza Isabel II Artesania ARTS & CRAFTS
(Camilo Cienfuegos No 13; ⏲7am-6pm) Among the usual Che Guevara key rings, this place sells some genuine only-in-Remedios mementos. Of note are the abstract musical instruments and the Parrandas masks made with seashells.

Tres Reyes CIGARS
(cnr Máximo Gómez & Margali; ⏲9am-5pm) Heavily air-conditioned cigar shop selling Cuba's best smokes along with a selection of other fairly predictable souvenirs.

Getting There & Away

BUS

The **bus station** (Av Cespedes, btwn Margalí & La Fragua) is on the southern side of town at the beginning of the 45km road to Santa Clara.

There's one daily Viazul bus to Cayo Santa María (CUC$6, 1½ hours) via Caibarién leaving at 12:40pm, and one in the other direction calling at Santa Clara (CUC$7, 1¼ hours), Cienfuegos (CUC$11, three hours) and Trinidad (CUC$14, 4¼ hours) that leaves at 4pm. Check ahead, as times sometimes change.

TAXI

A state taxi from the bus station to Caibarién will cost roughly CUC$5; to Santa Clara or Cayo Santa María the fare is CUC$30 to CUC$35. Bici-taxis run from the bus station to Parque Martí for small change.

Caibarién

POP 37,902

After metropolitan Santa Clara and the colonial splendor of Remedios, this once-busy, now-bypassed shipping port on Cuba's Atlantic coast might come as a shock with its crumbling old buildings trying hard to hang onto their former gentility. Since the piers slumped into the sea and the provincial sugar mills closed down, Caibarién's economic foundations have shifted to tourism: the town supplies most of the staff who work in Cayo Santa María's hotels.

Caibarién is also famous for its *cangrejo* (crab), the best in Cuba, and crackling December *parrandas* allegedly second only to Remedios in explosiveness.

For those keen to catch a glimpse of the cayos and their beaches without shelling out the expensive all-inclusive prices, Caibarién makes a cheap and friendly alternative base.

Sights

Museo de Agroindustria Azucarero Marcelo Salado MUSEUM
(☎42-35-38-64; Carretera Caibarién-Remedios Km 3.5; CUC$3, with train ride CUC$9; ⏲9am-4pm Mon-Sat) FREE Three kilometers past the crab statue on the Remedios road lies this former sugar mill (decommissioned in 1998), which is now a museum. Of the four preserved sugar mills in Cuba, it's probably the best. On the campus, you'll find potted histories of slave culture, the sugar industry, and pre-diesel locomotives. There's a video of Cuba's sugar industry, models of figures toiling to harvest the product, and lots of original machinery. A guide talks you through the process and dispatches gratis *guarapo* (sugarcane juice).

An added bonus is the extensive collection of locomotives (the place is also known as the Museo de Vapor, or Museum of Steam), featuring Latin America's largest steam engine, and there are steam train rides daily.

Crab Statue MONUMENT
(cnr Av 9 & Circuito Norte) The entrance to Caibarién is guarded by a giant crustacean, the town's symbol, designed by Florencio Gelabert Pérez and erected in 1983.

Museo Municipal María Escobar Laredo MUSEUM
(cnr Av 9 & Calle 10; CUC$1; ⏲10am-6pm Mon-Fri, 2-10pm Sat, 9am-1pm Sun) Even humble Caibarién had a heyday (although it was a while ago): find out more about it here in one of the city's most elegant buildings, the former Liceo (1926), in the main square.

Sleeping & Eating

Virginia's Pension CASA PARTICULAR $
(☎42-36-33-03; Ciudad Pesquera No 73; r CUC$25-30; P❄) A stalwart amid Caibarién's growing assemblage of casas particulares, this place, run by the charismatic Virginia Rodríguez, has kept up with the pace. Food here is a highlight, including Virginia's special seafood stew and the obligatory *cangrejo* (crab).

La Taberna CUBAN $
(Calle 10 No 921; MN$150-200; ⏲11am-11pm) The narrow entrance gives little away, but rather like Dr Who's Tardis, La Taberna is bigger

inside than out. Walk in through the narrow bar done out with a buccaneering theme, pass the mini dance floor and stage (disco and live bands at weekends) and enter the real revelation – the restaurant.

Dramatically decorated with more pirates, the menu leans toward seafood (prawns and lobster dominate). As Caibarién is mainly local, the prices are in *moneda nacional*, meaning the lobster clocks in at just CUC$8.

Information

Cadeca (Calle 10 No 907, btwn Avs 9 & 11; 8:30am-4pm Mon-Sat)

Havanatur (42-35-11-71; Av 9, btwn Calles 8 & 10; 9am-5pm Mon-Sat) Can arrange accommodation on Cayo Santa María.

Getting There & Away

BUS

National carrier Víazul has one daily bus to Cayo Santa María (CUC$6, 1¼ hours), departing at 12:50pm. In the other direction there's one daily bus that stops in Remedios (CUC$3, 10 minutes), Santa Clara (CUC$7, 1½ hours) and Cienfuegos (CUC$11, three hours), before terminating in Trinidad (CUC$14, 4½ hours). It departs Caibarién at 3:50pm from outside the Servi-Cupet gas station at the entrance to town.

Several local buses a day go to Remedios, Santa Clara and Yaguajay from Caibarién's old blue-and-white **bus and train station** (Calle 6) on the western side of town.

CAR & MOPED

The Servi-Cupet gas station is at the entrance to town from Remedios, behind the crab statue.

TAXI

A one-way taxi to Villa los Brujas on Cayo Santa María costs about CUC$25; it's a shade more to the Cayo Santa María hotel strip or Santa Clara.

Cayerías del Norte

Cuba's newest tourist project splays across a scattered archipelago of pancake-flat keys off the north coast of Villa Clara Province. While avoiding some of the erstwhile architectural hideousness of other Cuban resorts, development here is wide-reaching and rapid, and sits a little awkwardly alongside the Buenavista Unesco Biosphere Reserve, which it abuts. The keys were still a mosquito-infested wilderness until 1998 when the first hotel went up. As of 2017, there are over a dozen almost identical all-inclusive resorts (and more on the way) supporting a clientele that's 85% Canadian. Located on three different keys – Cayo las Brujas, Cayo Ensenachos and Cayo Santa María – linked by an impressive 48km causeway called El Pedraplén, the enclave aims at the luxury end of the market.

For day-trippers, the Cayerías have a couple of public-access beaches, water activities bookable through the Gaviota-run marina, and a small fauna refuge. Resorts sell day-use passes from around CUC$70.

Sights

Refugio de Fauna Cayo Santa María — NATURE RESERVE

You can forge your own way into what's left of Cayo Santa María's natural habitat in this fauna refuge. The gate (sometimes unmanned) with various signage is at a bend in the main road just after the Hotel Cayo Santa María. Trails include the Aguada del Bagá (1.2km), the Ensenada de Santa María (1.7km) and Punta Amanecer (5.6km).

It's lightly trodden (most tourists seem to prefer organized day trips).

Playa Las Gaviotas — BEACH

(Cayo Santa María; CUC$4) One of the few public beaches left on Cayo Santa María not connected to a resort, Playa Las Gaviotas is located inside a nature reserve at the far east of the island. Pay your entry fee in the car park and follow a 700m trail to the beach, which is usually refreshingly quiet and popular with kiteboarders.

San Pascual — HISTORIC SITE

FREE One of the area's oldest and oddest curiosities is the *San Pascual*, a San Diego tanker built in 1920 that got wrecked in 1933 on the far side of Cayo Francés, just west of Cayo las Brujas. Later the ship was used to store molasses, and later still it was opened up as a rather surreal hotel-restaurant (now closed).

The journey out to see the ship is included in snorkeling excursions and sunset cruises.

Activities

Every hotel offers the same organized activities for the same prices, all administered by state-run company, Gaviota. Most are water-based, including diving, snorkeling and fishing. Jeep safaris head to the mainland daily, and there are also tours of Remedios and Santa Clara. For those who'd prefer a DIY experience, there are several walking trails in the Refugio de Fauna Cayo Santa María (p271).

Marina Gaviota WATER SPORTS
(42-35-00-13; Cayo las Brujas) Most water-based activities are funneled through the hotels, but you can also arrange them directly at the marina on Cayo las Brujas. Highlights include a day-long catamaran cruise with snorkeling (CUC$85), a sunset cruise (CUC$59) and deep-sea fishing (CUC$295 for four people). Diving to one of 24 offshore sites is also offered (CUC$65 for two immersions). Activities can be canceled during inclement weather.

Sleeping

The cayos have over a dozen all-inclusive resorts, most of them on Cayo Santa María. All the resorts offer comfortable accommodation in two- or three-story buildings spread over expansive grounds. All have pools and gyms; most have tennis courts. Three, including the plush Meliá Buenavista, are adults only. Gaviota, a company owned by the Cuban government, runs the whole show.

★ **Meliá Buenavista** RESORT $$$
(42-35-07-00; www.meliacuba.com; Punta Madruguilla, Cayo Santa María; s/d all-inclusive CUC$360/450;) Small really is beautiful at the Buenavista, where 105 rooms (a bairn by cayo standards) are located apart from the other hotels at the western end of Cayo Santa María where, on a quiet sunset-facing beach, wine is brought to you by obliging butlers. Welcome to a veritable romantic heaven (no kids allowed) where you feel guilty even raising your voice.

★ **Iberostar Ensenachos** RESORT $$$
(42-35-03-00; www.iberostar.com; Cayo Ensenachos; r all-inclusive CUC$300-600;) A top-end paradise reminiscent of a Maldives private island getaway, this is the only hotel on tiny Cayo Ensenachos and greedily bags two of Cuba's best beaches (Playas Ensenachos and Mégano). One portion of the hotel is adults only. The decor is refined, with Alhambra-esque fountains and attractive natural foliage. Guests are accommodated in pretty 20-unit blocks; each unit has its own private concierge.

Royalton Cayo Santa María RESORT $$$
(42-35-09-00; www.royaltonresorts.com; Cayo Santa María; s/d all-inclusive CUC$228/298;) The favorite of many on the cayos, the Royalton lays on the romantic theme pretty strong with lots of lace-curtain four-poster sunbeds around the swimming pool. It is relatively small by Santa María standards (122 rooms), adults only, and popular with the Canadian honeymoon set. Cuba's best resort? Some might say.

Ocean Casa del Mar RESORT $$$
(42-35-08-50; www.oceanhotels.net; Cayo Santa María; s/d all-inclusive CUC$150/221;) New in 2016, the Ocean, with its gleaming modern three-story accommodation blocks, resembles a plush Miami suburb. There are some interesting touches like tiles in the lobby, heavy drapes and wooden (as opposed to plastic) sun-loungers, but with a clientele that's 90% Canadian, you're more likely to end up discussing ice hockey than the poetry of José Martí. It's at the east end of the cayo, near Perla Blanca beach.

Valentín Perla Blanca RESORT $$$
(42-35-06-21; www.valentinhotels.com; Cayo Santa María; d all-inclusive CUC$270;) The adults-only Valentín is one of the newer resorts on Cayo Santa María. Its rooms are set in white three-story apartment-style blocks; the overall look is clean-lined minimalist with sharp color accents. It's a little quieter than some of the more family-orientated resorts, especially if you stroll east onto public-access Playa Las Gaviotas.

Sol Cayo Santa María RESORT $$$
(42-35-02-00; www.meliacuba.com; Cayo Santa María; s/d all-inclusive from CUC$167/238;) Differentiating between Cayo Santa María's resorts isn't easy: they share more similarities than differences. The Sol, however, broadcasts a few minor quirks including rocking chairs on room verandas; secluded, leafy grounds; and one- and two-story wooden accommodation blocks embellished with lattice-work and brown balustrades. Otherwise, it's more of the same.

Meliá Las Dunas RESORT $$$
(42-35-03-01; www.meliacuba.com; Cayo Santa María; r all-inclusive CUC$350;) This monster-sized resort with 925 rooms (the biggest on the cayos) offers many things, although intimacy isn't one of them. It's more lush than some of the other places, with plenty of palm trees and tropical vegetation. Beds are comfortable and the staff are uniformly excellent.

Cayo Santa María Area

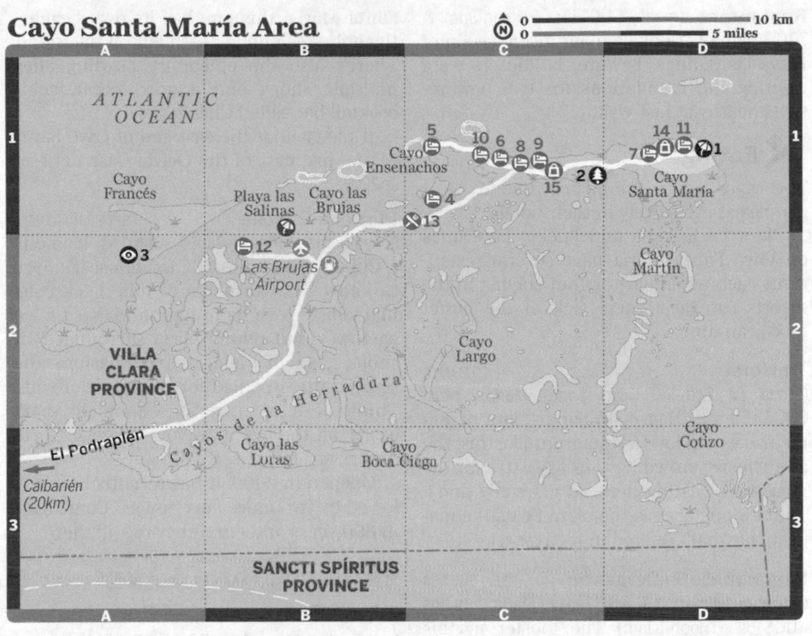

Cayo Santa María Area

Sights
1 Playa Las Gaviotas ... D1
2 Refugio de Fauna Cayo Santa María ... C1
3 San Pascual ... A2

Activities, Courses & Tours
Marina Gaviota ... (see 12)

Sleeping
4 Iberostar Ensenachos ... C1
5 Meliá Buenavista ... C1
6 Meliá Las Dunas ... C1
7 Ocean Casa del Mar ... D1
8 Playa Cayo Santa María ... C1
9 Royalton Cayo Santa María ... C1
10 Sol Cayo Santa María ... C1
11 Valentín Perla Blanca ... D1
12 Villa las Brujas ... B2

Eating
Farallón Restaurant ... (see 12)
13 Restaurante 'El Bergantín' ... C1
Trattoria ... (see 15)

Entertainment
Jazz Bar ... (see 15)

Shopping
14 Las Terrazas del Atardecer ... D1
15 Plaza La Estrella ... C1

Playa Cayo Santa María RESORT $$$
(☎42-35-08-00; www.gaviota-grupo.com; Cayo Santa María; s/d all-inclusive CUC$150/245;) With 769 rooms, the Playa is a big beast that offers pretty reasonable rates compared to the nearby competition. If you're just here for the day, you can bag a day pass (adult/child CUC$70/35) and gorge greedily on the all-you-can-eat lunch buffet.

Villa las Brujas HOTEL, RESORT $$$
(☎42-35-01-99; www.gaviota-grupo.com; Cayo las Brujas; r CUC$128; P) Atop a small, relatively untamed headland crowned by a statue of a *bruja* (witch), Villa las Brujas is the cayo's oldest (1999), smallest and most modest resort. If you can't abide sprawling all-inclusives, you may well love this quiet non-manicured place situated amid tangled mangroves and evoking the air of a tropical *Wuthering Heights* when a cold front blows in.

The 24 spacious if slightly mottled cabins are equipped with coffee machines, cable TV and massive beds, while the **Farallón**

Restaurant (meals CUC$15; ⏲noon-3pm & 7-10:30pm) overlooks a magnificent scoop of Playa las Salinas. Beware: bulldozers were clearing the foundations for two new resorts nearby at last visit.

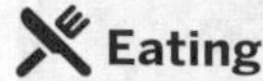

Eating

The cayos are an all-inclusive zone. Most people eat exclusively in their hotels.

Plaza La Estrella and Pueblo las Dunas on Cayo Santa María have several restaurants each where visitors not staying in the resorts (or vacationers sick of the buffet food) can dine.

Trattoria ITALIAN **$**
(Plaza La Estrella, Cayo Santa María; pizza CUC$3.50-5; ⏲11am-4pm) Santa Clara or Remedios would love a restaurant like this; the all-inclusive crowd have to pay extra for the pleasure of eating here, so generally don't. That's a mistake, as the pizza beats the majority of what's offered in the resorts.

Restaurante 'El Bergantín' SEAFOOD **$$$**
(Acuario-Delfinario, Cayo Santa María; mains CUC$15; ⏲noon-10pm) The lobster in this Gaviota-run restaurant might not be the cheapest in Cuba, but it's undoubtedly the freshest, courtesy of the on-site lobster nursery; yes, the clawed creatures are literally living within fishing-line distance of your table, and they're divine.

☆ Entertainment

The resorts lay on their own (sometimes cheesy) in-house entertainment, ranging from magic shows to fashion parades around the swimming pool. The three 'plaza' shopping centers have discos; Plaza La Estrella has a **jazz bar** (⏲8pm-2am) and a piano bar.

Shopping

There are three mini shopping centers on Cayo Santa María, euphemistically known as 'plazas' or 'pueblos,' which host a standard amalgam of forgot-your-holiday-gear shops along with a trio of Casa del Habano cigar stores and various alfresco craft markets.

Las Terrazas del Atardecer SHOPPING CENTER
(Cayo Santa María) The newest of the three shopping/entertainment centers on Cayo Santa María, this one has its own beach – the only free public beach left on the island. There's also the obligatory bowling alley, multiple shops and a good ocean-facing cocktail bar called Chachacha's.

It's located at the east end of Cayo Santa María, just east of the Ocean Casa del Mar (p272).

Plaza La Estrella SHOPPING CENTER
(Cayo Santa María; ⏲9am-7:30pm) Welcome to a Cuban town full of…Canadians. It's hard to know what to make of this mock colonial village with its imitation Manaca Iznaga tower and phony plaza surrounded by shops, a bowling alley, spa-gymnasium, and restaurants designed for the resort crowds. Think of it as a curious anomaly that's easier on the eye than your average North American shopping mall.

Opened in 2009, it has recently been followed by two more faux 'towns.' Come back in 300 years and see if they're still there.

ℹ Getting There & Away

AIR

Las Brujas Airport (☎42-35-00-09) has mainly charter flights to Havana with Aerogaviota. Most tourists arrive at Abel Santamaría Airport near Santa Clara and transfer from there.

BUS

Viazul (p264) extended their bus service to Cayo Santa María in 2015. There's now a daily bus to and from Trinidad (CUC$20, 5¾ hours) that also stops in Caibarién (CUC$6, 1¼ hours), Remedios (CUC$6, 1½ hours) and Santa Clara (CUC$13, three hours). Once on the cayos, it stops at most of the hotels. The bus departs Cayo Santa María at 2:40pm.

TAXI

The one-way fares from Caibarién/Remedios/Santa Clara by taxi are approximately CUC$30/35/70 to Cayo Santa María (depending on which hotel you're aiming for). Bargain hard – particularly if you want to get a return fare with waiting time.

ℹ Getting Around

Panoramic Bus Tour is a double-decker open-topped hop-on, hop-off bus that links the Delfinario on Cayo Ensenachos with all the Cayo Santa María hotels several times daily. A daily pass costs CUC$2.

Trinidad & Sancti Spíritus Province

☎41 / POP 465,500

Includes ➡

Best Places to Eat

- La Redaccion Cuba (p285)
- Vista Gourmet (p284)
- Esquerra (p285)
- Restaurante San José (p284)

Best Places to Sleep

- Iberostar Grand Hotel (p282)
- Casa Muñoz – Julio & Rosa (p281)
- Hostal del Rijo (p296)
- Casa El Suizo (p281)
- El Capitan (p289)

Why Go?

This small but well-endowed province is Cuba at its loveliest, also guarding a precious chunk of the country's fantastical historical legacy. Sancti Spíritus Province boasts nature worth exploring. The best on Cuba's underwhelming south coast, Playa Ancón is a stunner. And then there are mountains. Outside Trinidad, the haunting Escambray offers outstanding hiking on a network of picturesque trails.

A postcard come alive, Trinidad is one of the most intact colonial towns in the Americas, with red-tile roofs, cobblestone streets and pastel houses with castle-sized colonial doors. Its underdog rival, the city of Sancti Spíritus offers a more intangible, crumbling allure. In 2014, both celebrated their 500th anniversaries to much fanfare and an invigorated shine on their finest architecture.

But there's even more: a surprisingly varied cache of oft-overlooked curiosities, including lightly trodden eco-parks, a seminal museum dedicated to guerrilla icon Camilo Cienfuegos, and the Unesco-protected Bahía de Buenavista.

When to Go

- Trinidadians don't wait long after Christmas to rediscover their celebratory style. The popular Semana de la Cultura Trinitaria (Trinidad Culture Week) takes place during the second week of January and coincides with the city's feted anniversary.
- The quiet month of May is a good time to visit this province, as you can avoid both the crowds and bad weather during the quiet off-season.
- Stick around until June and you'll witness Trinidad's second big annual shindig, the Fiestas Sanjuaneras, a local carnival where rum-fueled horsemen gallop through the streets. Take cover!

Trinidad & Sancti Spíritus Province Highlights

1. **Trinidad** (p277) Visiting museums and basking in the colonial comfort of gorgeous casas particulares and well-heeled restaurants.
2. **Valle de los Ingenios** (p289) Climbing the tower at the Manaca Iznaga for a killer view of the Unesco-listed sites throughout this lush valley.
3. **Sancti Spíritus** (p293) Strolling without an itinerary around this city's recently renovated colonial streets.
4. **Jobo Rosado Reserve** (p299) Exploring the woodlands, waterfalls and war history in this rich reserve.
5. **Playa Ancón** (p288) Renting a house in La Boca to enjoy the sunset hours on the sands of this popular beach.
6. **Salto del Caburní** (p291) Hiking to a frigid natural bathing pool and diving in!
7. **Horseback Riding** (p280) Visiting the cowboy-cool countryside around Trinidad.

Trinidad

POP 73,500

Trinidad is one of a kind, a perfectly preserved Spanish colonial settlement where the clocks stopped in 1850 and – apart from a zombie invasion of tourists – have yet to restart. Huge sugar fortunes amassed in the nearby Valle de los Ingenios during the early 19th century created the illustrious colonial-style mansions bedecked with Italian frescoes, Wedgwood china and French chandeliers.

Declared a World Heritage Site by Unesco in 1988, Cuba's oldest and most enchanting 'outdoor museum' attracts busloads of visitors. Yet the cobblestone streets, replete with leather-faced *guajiros* (country folk), snorting donkeys and melodic troubadours, retain a quiet air. Come nightfall, the live-music scene is particularly good.

Trinidad is also ringed by sparkling natural attractions. Twelve kilometers south lies platinum-blond Playa Ancón, the best beach of Cuba's south coast. Looming 18km to the north, the purple-hued shadows of the Sierra del Escambray (Escambray Mountains) offer a lush adventure playground with hiking trails and waterfalls.

History

In 1514 pioneering conquistador Diego Velázquez de Cuéllar founded La Villa de la Santísima Trinidad on Cuba's south coast, the island's third settlement after Baracoa and Bayamo. In 1518, Velázquez' former secretary, Hernán Cortés, passed through the town recruiting mercenaries for his all-conquering expedition to Mexico, and the settlement was all but emptied of its original inhabitants. Over the ensuing 60 years it was left to a smattering of the local Taíno people to keep the ailing economy alive through a mixture of farming, cattle-rearing and a little outside trade.

Reduced to a small rural backwater by the 17th century and cut off from the colonial authorities in Havana by dire communications, Trinidad became a haven for pirates and smugglers who conducted a lucrative illegal slave trade with British-controlled Jamaica.

Things began to change in the early 19th century when the town became the capital of the Departamento Central, and hundreds of French refugees fleeing a slave rebellion in Haiti arrived, setting up more than 50 small sugar mills in the nearby Valle de los Ingenios. Sugar soon replaced leather and salted beef as the region's most important product; by the mid-19th century the area around Trinidad was producing a third of Cuba's sugar.

The boom ended rather abruptly during the Independence Wars, when the surrounding sugar plantations were devastated by fire and fighting. The industry never fully recovered. By the late 19th century the focus of the sugar trade had shifted to Cienfuegos and Matanzas Provinces, and Trinidad slipped into an economic coma.

The tourist renaissance began in the 1950s, when President Batista passed a preservation law that recognized the town's historical value. In 1965 the town was declared a national monument, and in 1988 it became a Unesco World Heritage Site.

Sights

In Trinidad, all roads lead to Plaza Mayor, the town's remarkably peaceful main square, located at the heart of the *casco histórico* (old town) and ringed by a quartet of impressive buildings.

★Museo Histórico Municipal MUSEUM

(☎41-99-44-60; Simón Bolívar 423; CUC$2; ⏰9am-5pm Sat-Thu) Trinidad's main museum, this grandiose mansion just off Plaza Mayor belonged to the Borrell family from 1827 to 1830. Later it passed to a German planter named Kanter, or Cantero, for whom it's now named. The rundown exhibits could use a full makeover but the city panoramas from the tower, reached by rickety stairs, is alone worth the price of admission.

Reputedly, Dr Justo Cantero acquired vast sugar estates by poisoning an old slave trader and marrying his widow, who also suffered an untimely death. Cantero's ill-gotten wealth is well displayed in the stylish neoclassical decoration of the rooms. Visit before 11am, when the tour buses start rolling in.

Plaza Mayor SQUARE

Trinidad's remarkably peaceful main square is located in the heart of the *casco histórico* and is the town's most photographed spot.

Iglesia Parroquial de la Santísima Trinidad CHURCH

(⏰11am-12:30pm Mon-Sat) Despite its unremarkable facade, this church on the northeastern side of Plaza Mayor graces countless

Trinidad

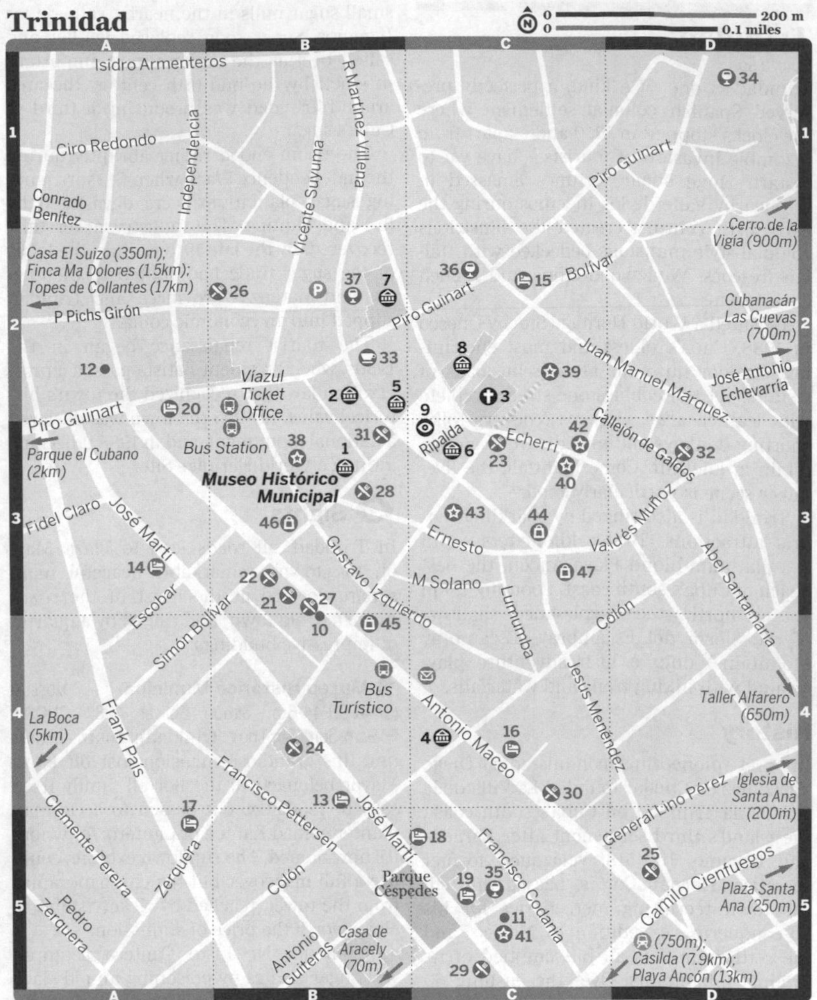

Trinidad postcards. Rebuilt in 1892 on the site of a church destroyed in a storm, it mixes 20th-century touch-ups with artifacts dating to the 18th century, such as the venerated Christ of the True Cross (1713), second altar from the front to the left.

Plaza Santa Ana PLAZA

(Camilo Cienfuegos; 11am-10pm) Located on the eponymous square, which delineates Trinidad's northeastern reaches, is a former Spanish prison (1844) that has been converted into the Plaza Santa Ana tourist center. The complex includes an art gallery, handicraft market, ceramics shop, bar and restaurant.

Maqueta de Trinidad MUSEUM

(41-99-43-08; cnr Colón & Maceo; CUC$1, city tour CUC$5; 9am-5pm Mon-Sat, to 1pm Sun) Opened in 2014 and encased in the beautifully restored Casa Frias, this scale model of Trinidad's *casco histórico* displays amazing attention to detail (try to pick out your casa particular). A resident guide will fill you in on what's what with a conductor-like stick. Also offers city tours in English and Spanish.

Trinidad

Top Sights

1 Museo Histórico Municipal B3

Sights

2 Casa Templo de Santería Yemayá B2
3 Iglesia Parroquial de la Santísima Trinidad C2
4 Maqueta de Trinidad C4
5 Museo de Arqueología Guamuhaya B2
6 Museo de Arquitectura Trinitaria C3
7 Museo Nacional de la Lucha Contra Bandidos B2
8 Museo Romántico C2
9 Plaza Mayor C3

Activities, Courses & Tours

10 Las Ruinas del Teatro Brunet B4
11 Paradiso C5
12 Trinidad Travels A2

Sleeping

Casa de Victor .... (see 12)
13 Casa Gil Lemes B4
14 Casa Muñoz – Julio & Rosa A3
15 El Rústico C2
16 Hostal Colina C4
17 Hostal José & Fatima A5
18 Hotel La Ronda C5
19 Iberostar Grand Hotel C5
20 Nelson Fernández Rodríguez A2

Eating

21 Cubita Restaurant B3
22 Dulcinea B3
23 Esquerra C3
24 Galería Comercial Universo B4
25 Guitarra Mia D5
26 La Ceiba B2
27 La Redaccion Cuba B3
28 Mesón del Regidor B3
29 Paraito C5
Restaurant El Dorado .... (see 20)
30 Restaurante San José C4
31 Sol Ananda B3
32 Vista Gourmet D3

Drinking & Nightlife

33 Café Don Pepe B2
34 Disco Ayala D1
35 El Floridita C5
36 Taberna La Botija C2
37 Taberna la Canchánchara B2

Entertainment

38 Bar Yesterday B3
39 Casa de la Música C2
40 Casa de la Trova C3
41 Casa Fischer C5
42 Palenque de los Congos Reales C3
43 Rincon de la Salsa C3

Shopping

44 Arts & Crafts Market C3
45 Casa del Habano B4
46 Galería La Paulet B3
47 Taller Instrumentos Musicales C3

Plans to turn Casa Frias into a full-on cultural center continue developing.

Casa Templo de Santería Yemayá MUSEUM

(R Martínez Villena 59, btwn Simón Bolívar & Piro Guinart; hours vary) FREE You will need some luck to find this religious center in action. While no Santería museum can replicate the ethereal experience of Regla de Ocha (also known as Santería, Cuba's main religion of African origin), this house tries with a Santería altar to Yemayá, Goddess of the Sea, laden with myriad offerings of fruit, water and stones.

The house is presided over by *santeros* (priests of the Afro-Cuban religion Santería), who'll emerge from the back patio and surprise you with some well-rehearsed tourist spiel. On the goddess's anniversary, March 19, ceremonies are performed day and night.

Museo Nacional de la Lucha Contra Bandidos MUSEUM

(41-99-41-21; Echerri 59; CUC$1; 9am-5pm Tue-Sun) The most recognizable building in Trinidad, the dilapidated pastel-yellow bell tower occupies the former convent of San Francisco de Asís. Since 1986, it's a museum with photos, maps, weapons and objects relating to the struggle against the various counterrevolutionary bands that took a leaf out of Fidel's book and operated illicitly out of the Sierra del Escambray between 1960–65.

The fuselage of a US U-2 spy plane shot down over Cuba is also on display. You can climb the bell tower for good views.

Museo Romántico MUSEUM

(41-99-43-63; Echerri 52; CUC$2; 9am-5pm Tue-Sun) Across Calle Simón Bolívar is the glittering Palacio Brunet. The ground floor was built in 1740, and the upstairs was added in 1808. In 1974 the mansion was converted into a museum with 19th-century furnishings, a fine collection of china and various other period pieces. Pushy museum staff may materialize out of the shadows for a tip.

The shop adjacent has a good selection of photos and books in English.

Museo de Arquitectura Trinitaria MUSEUM
(☎41-99-32-08; Ripalda 83; CUC$1; ⊙9am-5pm Sat-Thu) Another public display of wealth sits on the southeastern side of Plaza Mayor in a museum showcasing upper-class domestic architecture of the 18th and 19th centuries. Housed in buildings erected in 1738 and 1785 and joined in 1819, the museum was once the residence of the wealthy Iznaga family.

Iglesia de Santa Ana CHURCH
(Plaza Santa Ana, Camilo Cienfuegos) Grass grows around the domed bell tower, and the arched doorways were bricked up long ago, but the shell of this ruined church (1812) defiantly remains. Looming like a time-worn ecclesiastical stencil, it looks ghostly after dark.

Museo de Arqueología Guamuhaya MUSEUM
(☎41-99-32-08; Simón Bolívar 457; CUC$1; ⊙9am-5pm Tue-Sat) On the northwestern side of Plaza Mayor is this odd mix of stuffed animals, native bones and vaguely incongruous 19th-century kitchen furniture.

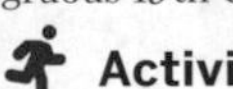

Activities

Ride a bike to one of Cuba's outstanding beaches, work up a sweat on a couple of DIY hikes, or get a different perspective astride a horse.

If you are booking an excursion in the region, check to see that transportation is included. It's not included with snorkel and dive trips.

Centro Ecuestre Diana HORSEBACK RIDING
(☎41-99-36-73; www.trinidadphoto.com; riding CUC$26-30) This unique equestrian center offers nature excursions and riding lessons with helmets on a *finca* (farm) on the edge of town. It's not set up for walk-ins; inquire first with Julio at Casa Muñoz. Visits include huge country-style meals that are a hit. It's also a rescue center promoting better equine care and humane horse-training techniques.

In winter, Julio uses his horse-whispering techniques to pacify wild, untrained horses.

Parque el Cubano HIKING
(CUC$10) This pleasant spot within a protected park consists of a *ranchón* (farm-style restaurant) serving *pez gato* (catfish) from the on-site fish farm. Take the Huellas de la História trail (3.6km) to the refreshing Javira Waterfall. With a stop for lunch in the *ranchón* (thatched-roof restaurant) it can make an excellent day trip.

Cubatur (p287) leads trips with motorized transportation, or you can hire a taxi from Trinidad (CUC$30 round-trip).

The hike to El Cubano from Trinidad is approximately 16km. Go west out of town on the Cienfuegos road. Pass the 'Welcome to Trinidad' sign and cross a bridge over the Río Guaurabo. A track on your left leads back under the bridge and up a narrow, poorly paved road for 5km to Parque el Cubano.

Finca Ma Dolores FARM, HOTEL
(☎41-99-64-81; Carretera de Cienfuegos Km 1.5) This rustic Cubanacán hotel runs boat trips down the Río Guaurabo to La Boca (CUC$5), and hosts sporadic *fiestas campesinas* (country fairs). Horseback riding may be offered in the future. You can arrive here by taxi (CUC$5) via Trinidad.

Cerro de la Vigía HIKING
For a good workout and broad vistas of Trinidad, the Valle de los Ingenios and the Caribbean littoral, walk up Simón Bolívar between the Iglesia Parroquial and the Museo Romántico to the destroyed 18th-century hermitage, part of a former Spanish military hospital turned luxury hotel. From here it's 30 minutes further up the hill to the radio transmitter (180m).

Tours

With its sketchy public transportation and steep road gradients making cycling arduous, it's easiest to visit the extensive natural park of Topes de Collantes on a day tour.

Guided walking tours of Trinidad organized by the City Historian's Office run from the Maqueta de Trinidad (p278) daily for CUC$10.

Trinidad Travels HIKING, HORSEBACK RIDING
(☎52-82-37-26; www.trinidadtravels.com; Antonio Maceo No 613a) One of the best private guides is English- and Italian-speaking Reinier at Trinidad Travels. He leads all kinds of excursions, including hiking in the Sierra del Escambray and horseback riding

in the nearby countryside. Spanish lessons are also offered. He's based at Casa de Victor (p282).

Courses

Las Ruinas del Teatro Brunet DRUMMING, DANCE
(Antonio Maceo No 461, btwn Simón Bolívar & Zerquera; lessons per hour from CUC$5) The roofless ruins of an 1840-vintage theater is now an entertainment space where you can take drumming and dance lessons (inquire within for times).

Paradiso CULTURAL TOUR
(www.paradiso.cu; General Lino Pérez 306, Casa ARTex; to Valle de los Ingenios CUC$15; ⏲8am-5pm Mon-Sat, to noon Sun) This tour desk in Casa Fischer has some interesting courses, including salsa, percussion, Spanish and cultural topics such as Cuban architecture and Afro-Cuban culture. These courses last four hours and are taught by cultural specialists. There are also the best-priced tours of the area, including the Valle de los Ingenios and Trinitopas waterfall. A city night tour travels via horse-drawn carriage (CUC$20).

The courses require a minimum number of six to 10 people, but you can always negotiate.

Festivals & Events

Semana Santa RELIGIOUS
(Holy Week; ⏲Mar or Apr) Semana Santa is important in Trinidad and on Good Friday thousands of people form a procession through the center.

Sleeping

Almost every house seems to be a casa particular. Arriving by bus or walking the streets with luggage, you'll be besieged by *jinteros* (touts) working for commissions, or by casa owners. Take your time and shop around.

A boutique five-star hotel, Pansca Trinidad, is due to open soon. The much stalled project will integrate part of Ermita de Nuestra Señora de la Candelaria de la Popa, the ruins of a mid-18th-century church, into the hotel.

★Casa Muñoz – Julio & Rosa CASA PARTICULAR $
(☎41-99-36-73; www.trinidadphoto.com; José Martí No 401, cnr Escobar; d/tr/apt CUC$40/45/50, photography tour CUC$25; P ❄) A stunning colonial home with outstanding warmth, English-speaking assistance and a few gentle dogs on-site. There are three huge rooms and a two-level apartment. Delicious food is served on the patio. Book early. It's insanely popular with licensed US people-to-people groups. Julio is an accomplished photographer offering courses on documentary photography, religion and life in Cuba's new economic reality.

The owner, also a horse whisperer, offers horseback riding through the Centro Ecuestre Diana.

★Casa El Suizo CASA PARTICULAR $
(☎53-77-28-12; P Pichs Girón No 22; r CUC$40; P ❄) Away from the hustle of the center and handily located for excursions by the Trinidad–Cienfuegos road, this spacious lodging feels more like an inn, with five large rooms each featuring private terraces. Installations are new, with safe, hair dryer and wi-fi on the way. English and German are spoken. The only downside is longer walking distances from central attractions.

It is also adding a *ranchon* (thatched restaurant).

Nelson Fernández Rodríguez CASA PARTICULAR $
(☎41-99-38-49; www.hostalcasanelsontrinidad.com; Piro Guinart No 226, btwn Maceo & Gustavo Izquierdo; r CUC$30; ❄) Nelson's place above the lovely Restaurant El Dorado (p284) bears all the hallmarks of a fine Trinidadian homestay – lush patio, romantic terrace and Unesco-standard colonial splendor. Four rooms are available, as well as two across the street (run by the same family).

El Rústico CASA PARTICULAR $
(☎41-99-30-24; Juan Manuel Márquez No 54a, btwn Piro Guinart & Simón Bolívar; s/d/tr CUC$25/30/35; ❄) These upstairs rooms above the El Criollo restaurant (guests get

BOOKING SERVICE

To do it yourself, use online, English-language booking service **Trinidad Rent** (☎41-99-36-73, 52-90-08-10; www.trinidadrent.com), which curates some of the best casas in Trinidad. Utilizing photos, you can reserve the room of your choosing, and it can also be used to book tours. Handy if you don't want to deal with cash.

discounts) are a pleasant, breezy surprise, with attractive, immaculate spaces and hair dryers in the bathrooms. The roof terrace is a nice bonus. It's one cobbled block from Plaza Mayor.

Hostal José & Fatima CASA PARTICULAR **$**
(☎41-99-66-82; hostaljoseyfatima@gmail.com; Zerquera No 159, btwn Frank País & Pettersen; r CUC$30-35; ❄📶) Highly popular casa with five rooms and colonial trimmings, including a terrace. The helpful hosts can hook you up with many local activities. There's also an adorable dachshund keen on dog lovers.

Casa Gil Lemes CASA PARTICULAR **$**
(☎41-99-31-42; carlosgl3142@yahoo.es; José Martí No 263, btwn Colón & Zerquera; r CUC$35-40; ❄) This gorgeous casa was one of Trinidad's first, listed in Lonely Planet's 1st edition *Cuba* guidebook in 1997. Marvel at the noble arches, religious statues and a classic patio with fountain, real hummingbirds and sea serpents. It's often booked, though the addition of two more rooms for a total of four should help. The cost of a renovated room is slightly higher.

Hostal Colina CASA PARTICULAR **$**
(☎41-99-23-19; Antonio Maceo 374, btwn General Lino Pérez & Colón; r CUC$30; ❄) Another place that leaves you struggling for superlatives. Although the house dates from the 1830s, it has a definitive modern touch, giving you the feeling of being in a plush Mexican hacienda. Three pastel-yellow rooms give out on to a patio where you can sit at the plush wooden bar and catch mangoes and avocados as they fall from the trees.

Casa de Victor CASA PARTICULAR **$**
(☎41-99-64-44; hostalsandra@yahoo.es; Maceo No 613a; r CUC$25; ❄) Handy to the bus station, Victor's place has three rooms with TV, air-conditioning and private bathrooms. The best are upstairs. Guests share spacious open-air terraces decorated with potted plants.The location is surprisingly quiet, with a tall wall of recycled ceramic pots circling the garden.

Casa de Aracely CASA PARTICULAR **$**
(☎41-99-35-58; General Lino Pérez No 207, btwn Frank País & Miguel Calzada; r CUC$30; ❄) Had enough of the colonial splendor? Head away from the tourist frenzy to General Lino Pérez, where Aracely rents two upstairs rooms with a private entrance, a very quiet flower-bedecked patio and a splendid roof terrace.

Finca Ma Dolores HOTEL **$$**
(☎41-99-64-81; Carretera de Cienfuegos Km 1.5; s/d CUC$45/67, s/d cabin CUC$53/75; P❄🏊) Trinidad goes rustic with the out-of-town Finca Ma Dolores, 1.5km west on the road to Cienfuegos and Topes de Collantes. It's equipped with hotel-style rooms and cabins. Cabins are the better option, try for one with a porch overlooking the Río Guaurabo.

On nights when groups are present, there's a *fiesta campesina* (country fair) with country-style Cuban folk dancing at 8:30pm (guests/nonguests free/CUC$10, including one drink). It also has a swimming pool, a *ranchón* restaurant, and boat and horseback-riding tours.

★Iberostar Grand Hotel BOUTIQUE HOTEL **$$$**
(☎41-99-60-70; www.iberostar.com; cnr José Martí & General Lino Pérez; d incl breakfast from CUC$400; ❄@📶) Start in the fern-filled tiled lobby and browse the courtyard surrounded by three floors of rooms in a remodeled 19th-century colonial. The five-star Grand oozes luxury. Forget the standard all-inclusive tourist formula. Instead there's privacy, refinement and an appreciation for local history. Details shine from a cool cigar bar to 36 rooms with designer toiletries, in-room minibars, safes and coffee makers.

It's one of a handful of Spanish-run Iberostar's Cuban hotels.

Cubanacán Las Cuevas HOTEL **$$$**
(☎41-99-61-33; reservas@cuevas.co.cu; Finca Santa Ana; s/d incl breakfast CUC$90/130; P❄📶🏊) Perched on a hill above town, Las Cuevas serves a steady stream of bus tours. While the setting is lush, the rooms – arranged in scattered two-storied units – are a little less memorable, as is the breakfast. There's value added with the swimming pool, well-maintained gardens and panoramic views.

You can visit the murky Cueva la Maravillosa, accessible down a stairway, where you'll see a huge tree growing out of a cavern (CUC$1). The hotel is accessed via a steep road that climbs northeast from the Iglesia de Santa Ana.

Hotel La Ronda BOUTIQUE HOTEL **$$$**
(☎41-99-61-33; José Martí No 238; s/d CUC$143/170; ❄@📶🏊) A slight improvement on Trinidad's best casas particulares, it's also considerably pricier. Guests enjoy

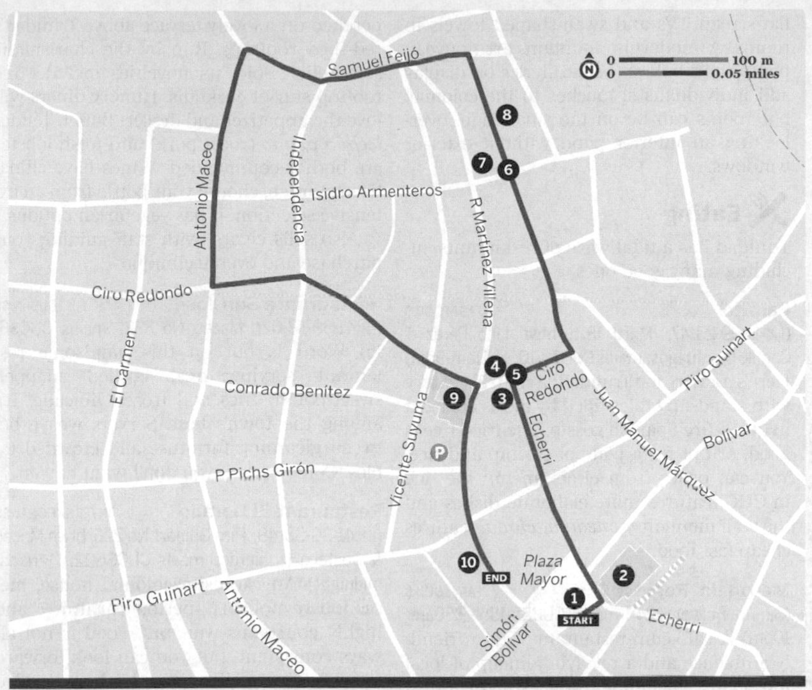

City Walk
Photographic Trinidad

START PLAZA MAYOR
END CASA TEMPLO DE SANTERÍA YEMAYA
LENGTH 2KM; 1½ HOURS

Soft evening light, striking colonial architecture and street scenes that have more in common with the 1850s than the 2010s create an ideal prowling ground for photographers.

Early evening, when the sunlight is less intense and the shadows longer, is a good time to undertake this walk. Start in **1 Plaza Mayor** (p277), the colonial square that features in a thousand different postcards. With local life continuing at a lazy pace around you, there's always a new way of snapping it with the **2 Iglesia Parroquial de la Santísima Trinidad** (p277) as backdrop.

The classic shot is looking northwest along cobbled Calle Echerri past colonial edifices to the tower of the **3 Convento de San Francisco de Asís**. Walk a block northwest and try to capture the small sunlit **4 park** opposite the convent with some human silhouettes. At the end of Echerri, stand back from the **5 T-Junction** with Calle Ciro Redondo and wait...and wait. Something interesting will pass at the end of the street – a horse, a 1951 Plymouth, a bicycle.

Turn right on Ciro Redondo, left on Calle Juan Manuel Márquez and wander toward the shabbier, no less photogenic **6 Barrio Los Tres Cruces**. Slices of Trinidadian life play out here. Look out for ladies in curlers, cowboys, people dragging pigs, kids playing stickball in the neighborhood's **7 plaza**, and old men sitting in doorways. A row of rainbow-colored, single-story **8 houses** in Calle Juan Manuel Márquez are given extra luminescence by the slanting evening sun. On Calle Samuel Feijó, horses and riders often congregate with the shadowy Sierra del Escambray looming behind them.

More street life awaits back on Calle Ciro Redondo. Strike up a conversation, flash a smile and capture the moment. Outside the iconic **9 Taberna la Canchánchara** (p285) there's nearly always a 1958 Chevy being used as a communal seat, or perhaps a baseball backstop. Pass the **10 Casa Templo de Santería Yemayá** (p279) dedicated to the *orisha* (Yoruba god) of the sea. With dusk falling you're back in Plaza Mayor.

flat-screen TVs and swan-shaped towels in rooms. A modernist fountain, art nouveau photos and bolero (ballad) lyrics on display add individualistic touches to the colonial, but rooms can be on the small side, overlooking an interior patio without exterior windows.

Eating

Trinidad has a tidal wave of restaurants, including many good ones.

Paraito FAST FOOD **$**
(☎41-99-23-47; Martí 181b, btwn Lino Pérez & Camilo Cienfuegos; mains CUC$3-10; ⊙11am-9pm) Here's a rarity for Trinidad: a no-frills eatery with stand-up tables filled by locals engaged in quick-fire Spanish gossip. The fried rice is good, or opt for a plate of shrimp and rice. You can order from either menu: the one in CUC features more elaborate dishes and the wall menu in *moneda nacional* features cheap fast food.

Mesón del Regidor FAST FOOD **$**
(Simón Bolívar 424; mains CUC$5-15; ⊙10am-10pm) A cafe-cum-restaurant with a friendly ambience and a revolving lineup of local musicians, including the best *trovadores* (traditional singer-songwriters), who'll drop by during the day and serenade you with a song over grilled-cheese sandwiches and *café con leche* (coffee with milk). Savor the surprise.

Dulcinea CAFE **$**
(cnr Antonio Maceo & Simón Bolívar; snacks CUC$1-4; ⊙7:30am-10pm) The former Begonias cafe has long been a daytime nexus for Trinidad's transient backpacker crowd, meaning it's a good place to swap tips and *jinetero* stories. Reborn as a bakery and cake shop, it retains its busy street-corner atmosphere, cleanish toilets, and five or six cheap – but always crowded – internet terminals (CUC$3 for 20 minutes).

Galería Comercial Universo SUPERMARKET **$**
(cnr José Martí & Zerquera) Mini shopping center that includes a variety of shops for most of your immediate needs including Trinidad's best (and most expensive) grocery store. Head here for yogurt, lifesaving biscuits and pharmacy goods.

★**Vista Gourmet** CUBAN, INTERNATIONAL **$$**
(☎41-99-67-00; Callejón de Galdos; mains CUC$13; ⊙noon-midnight; 🍃) A slick private option perched on a lovely terrace above Trinidad's red-tiled rooftops. Run by the charismatic sommelier Bolo, its novelties include free rooftop sunset cocktails. Hungry diners will love the appetizer and dessert buffet. Tender *lechón asado* (roast pork) and fresh lobster are both recommended. Wines have climatized storage, choose your bottle from an extensive selection. It has vegetarian options.

Also sells cigars, with staff guiding your purchase and even technique.

Restaurante San José CUBAN **$$**
(☎41-99-47-02; Maceo No 382; mains CUC$6-15) Word is out on this handsome restaurant serving fresh grilled snapper, sweet-potato fries and frozen limeade. It's among the town's best. Servers weave between gleaming furniture and crowded tables. Come early if you don't want to wait.

Restaurant El Dorado INTERNATIONAL **$$**
(☎41-99-38-49; Piro Guinart No 226, btwn Maceo & Gustavo Izquierdo; meals CUC$6-12; ⊙noon-midnight) An exquisite colonial house, meticulously polished period furniture, and highly courteous waitstaff. Food is not always consistent, but you can look forward to beef strips, well-seasoned fish and grilled turkey, rounded off with some professional touches such as a complimentary bread basket and starters.

Cubita Restaurant INTERNATIONAL **$$**
(☎54-30-63-76; Antonio Maceo No 471; mains CUC$8-15; ⊙11am-midnight) When good food and fine service conspire, it can be a highly pleasurable experience – and one which, until recently, had been hard to find in Trinidad. Fighting hard in a highly competitive field, La Cubita has inventive starters, complimentary salads, some wonderfully marinated brochettes and highly discreet service. It's run by Trinidad's famous ceramic-makers.

Guitarra Mia CUBAN **$$**
(☎41-99-34-52; Jésus Menéndez No 19, btwn Camilo Cienfuegos & Lino Pérez; mains CUC$10-15; ⊙12:30-11pm) Drift a few blocks from the *centro histórico* and crowds disperse without any measurable drop in food quality. Music is the theme in this interesting nook, never short of a quintet or passing troubadour. From the menu, the *tostones* (plantain pan-fried in oil) stuffed with minced crab linger longest in the memory.

There's also *ropa vieja* (shredded lamb in this case) and natural juices. Write your comments on the door (literally) on the way out.

La Ceiba CUBAN **$$**
(P Pichs Girón No 263; meals CUC$12-18; ⏲noon-11pm) Set in a back patio under a giant ceiba tree, this upscale cafe specializes in *pollo meloso* (chicken in honey and lemon sauce). Order Trinidad's favorite cocktail, the *canchánchara* (a lemony rum drink), in ceramic cups and bask in the tranquility. Service is hovering but attentive and the setting can't be beat. Mains include sides, salad and fruit plate.

Sol Ananda INTERNATIONAL **$$**
(☎41-99-82-81; Rubén Martínez Villena No 45, cnr Simón Bolívar; mains CUC$9-18; ⏲11am-11pm;) Fine 18th-century china, grandfather clocks, even an antique bed: Sol Ananda in Trinidad's Plaza Mayor is, on first impressions, more museum than restaurant. Situated in one of the town's oldest houses (dating from 1750) it tackles an ambitious cross-section of global food from traditional Cuban (excellent lamb *ropa vieja*) to South Asian (fish kofta and samosas). Good vegetarian options.

★**La Redaccion Cuba** INTERNATIONAL **$$$**
(☎41-99-45-93; www.laredaccioncuba.com; Maceo No 463; mains CUC$8-17) With bare-bones brickwork more Brooklyn than Cuba, this new French-run offering provides a dose of comfort for travelers with culinary homesickness. Think huge lamb burgers with yam chips, pasta tossed with lobster and herbs, and stone-oven cooked meals. For solo travelers, there's a huge shared table in the center conducive to making friends. Otherwise, reserve ahead. It's popular.

Esquerra CUBAN **$$$**
(☎41-99-34-34; Rosario No 464; mains CUC$8-18; ⏲noon-11pm) With a prime location on the cobblestone plaza, this elegant restaurant serves well-prepared Cuban fare. It differs from the competition with specialty flavors – spicy criollo tomato sauce, meunière and Catalan sauces that give a boost to fish or pork. Shrimp cocktail is a standout, as is service. There's also a nice intimate courtyard option.

Drinking & Nightlife

★**Taberna La Botija** BAR
(cnr Juan Manuel Márquez & Piro Guinart; ⏲24hr) While other restaurants send their waitstaff out into the street to fish for customers, La Botija crams half the town into its lively corner bar without even trying. The key: a warm talk-to-your-neighbor atmosphere, cold beer served in ceramic mugs and the best house band in Trinidad (think jazz meets soul over a violin). The food ain't bad either.

Café Don Pepe CAFE
(☎41-99-35-73; cnr Piro Guinart & Martínez Villena; ⏲8am-11pm) In an adorable colonial courtyard decorated with modern graffiti, the best coffee in Trinidad is served in ceramic mugs with a square of Baracoan chocolate.

Taberna la Canchánchara BAR
(cnr Rubén Martínez Villena & Ciro Redondo; ⏲10am-midnight) This place is famous for its eponymous house cocktail made from rum, honey, lemon and water. Local musicians regularly drop by for off-the-cuff jam sessions, and it's not unusual for the *canchánchara*-inebriated crowd to break into spontaneous dancing. Note that hours can be sporadic.

Disco Ayala CLUB
(CUC$10; ⏲10pm-3am) A slightly tacky cabaret with an indigenous theme that takes place in a cave up on the hill behind the Ermita Popa church. A frenetic disco, usually thick with *jineteras,* kicks off afterwards. Entry includes as many mojitos as you care to sink.

To get there follow Calle Simón Bolívar from Plaza Mayor up to the Ermita de Nuestra Señora de la Candelaria de la Popa. The disco is 100m further along on your left.

El Floridita BAR
(General Lino Pérez No 313; ⏲24hr) A cheap state-run copy of Havana's much-hyped Hemingway bar, although this one peddles its daiquiris for a reasonable price. A life-sized statue of the revered writer props up the bar.

☆ Entertainment

Get ready for the best Cuban nightlife outside Havana.

★**Casa de la Música** CLUB
(Cristo; cover CUC$2) One of Trinidad's (and Cuba's) classic venues, this casa is an alfresco affair that congregates on the sweeping staircase beside the Iglesia Parroquial off Plaza Mayor. A good mix of tourists and locals take in the 10pm salsa show here. Alternatively, full-on salsa concerts are held

in the casa's rear courtyard (also accessible from Juan Manuel Márquez).

★**Casa de la Trova** LIVE MUSIC
(Echerri No 29; CUC$1; ⌚9pm-2am) Trinidad's spirited casa retains its earthy essence despite the high package-tourist-to-Cuban ratio. Local musicians to look out for here are Semillas del Son, Santa Palabra and the town's best *trovador* (traditional singer-songwriter), Israel Moreno.

Rincon de la Salsa CLUB
(☎53-91-02-45; Zerquera, btwn Martínez Villena & Ernesto; ⌚10pm-2am) A fun live-music venue aimed at those practicing their salsa steps. It can also connect travelers to dance teachers for private lessons during the daytime.

Palenque de los Congos Reales LIVE MUSIC
(cnr Echerri & Av Jesús Menéndez) A must for rumba fans, this open patio on Trinidad's music alley has an eclectic menu incorporating salsa, *son* (Cuban popular music) and *trova* (traditional poetic singing). The highlight, however, is the 10pm rumba drumming with soulful African rhythms and energetic fire-eating dancers.

Casa Fischer CULTURAL CENTER
(ARTex; General Lino Pérez No 312, btwn José Martí & Francisco Codania; show CUC$1) The local ARTex patio cranks up at 10pm with a salsa orchestra (on Tuesday, Wednesday, Thursday, Saturday and Sunday) or a folklore show (Friday). If you're early, kill time at the art gallery (free) and chat to the staff at the on-site Paradiso office about salsa lessons and other courses.

Bar Yesterday LIVE MUSIC
(Gustavo Izquierdo, btwn Piro Guinart & Simón Bolívar; ⌚4pm-midnight) They've changed the beat to 4/4 time in the old Casa de la Rumba where the decor is dedicated exclusively to the Beatles, including four life-sized statues. But there's nothing 'yesterday' about the audience, most of whom are barely out of their teens. Beatlemania redux?

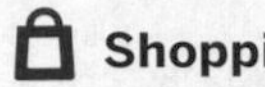

Shopping

Open-air markets are set up all over town. See local painters at work – and buy their paintings too. The town is full of picture-crammed, open-windowed workshops.

Galería La Paulet ART
(Simón Bolívar No 411) Interesting selection of probing, mainly abstract art by local artists.

Casa del Habano CIGARS
(cnr Antonio Maceo & Zerquera; ⌚9am-7pm) Dodge the street hustlers and satisfy your alcoholic (rum) and tobacco vices here.

Arts & Crafts Market CRAFTS, SOUVENIRS
(Av Jesús Menéndez; ⌚9am-6pm) This open-air market in front of the Casa de la Trova is the place to buy souvenirs, especially textiles and crochet work. Avoid buying black coral or turtle-shell items, made from endangered species. They are forbidden entry into many countries.

Taller Alfarero CERAMICS
(☎41-99-31-46; Andrés Berro No 51, btwn Pepito Tey & Abel Santamaría; ⌚8am-noon & 2-5pm Mon-Fri) FREE Trinidad is known for its pottery. In this large factory, teams of workers make trademark Trinidad ceramics from local clay using a traditional potter's wheel. You can watch them at work and buy the finished product.

Taller Instrumentos Musicales MUSICAL INSTRUMENTS
(cnr Av Jesús Menéndez & Valdés Muñoz) Musical instruments are made here and sold in the adjacent shop.

ℹ Information

DANGERS & ANNOYANCES

Thefts, though still relatively uncommon, are not unheard of in Trinidad. Incidents usually

VÍAZUL BUS DEPARTURES FROM TRINIDAD

DESTINATION	COST (CUC$)	DURATION (HR)	DEPARTURES
Cienfuegos	6	1½	7:30am, 8:15am, 3pm, 4pm
Havana	25	6⅓	8:15am, 4pm
Santa Clara	8	3	7:30am
Santiago de Cuba	33	12	8am
Varadero	20	6	7:30am, 3pm

occur late at night when travelers have had a few drinks. To avoid being a potential target for thieves, make sure that you are alert and on your guard, particularly when returning to your hotel or casa after a night out. A little bit of caution can go a long way.

INTERNET ACCESS

There's public wi-fi in Plaza Mayor and on the steps leading to the Casa de la Musica.

Dulcinea (Antonio Maceo No 473; internet per hour CUC$4.50; ⏲9am-8:30pm) Half a dozen terminals on the corner of Simón Bolívar. Crowded.

Etecsa Telepunto (cnr General Lino Pérez & Francisco Pettersen; internet per hour CUC$1.50; ⏲8:30am-7pm) Modern, if slow, computer terminals. Not too crowded.

MEDICAL SERVICES

Trinidad has a hospital and pharmacy services.

General Hospital (☎41-99-32-01; Antonio Maceo No 6) Southeast of the city center.

Servimed Clínica Internacional Cubanacán (☎41-99-62-40; General Lino Pérez No 103, cnr Anastasio Cárdenas; ⏲24hr) There is an on-site pharmacy selling products in convertibles.

MONEY

There are banking services and a currency-exchange house.

Banco de Crédito y Comercio (José Martí No 264; ⏲9am-3pm Mon-Fri) Has an ATM.

Cadeca (Maceo, btwn Camilo Cienfuegos & Lino Perez; ⏲8:30am-5pm) Money changers.

POST

Post Office (Antonio Maceo No 418, btwn Colón & Zerquera; ⏲9am-6pm Mon-Sat)

TOURIST INFORMATION

The agencies in Trinidad usually have a line – try to go early.

Cubatur (☎41-99-63-14; Antonio Maceo No 447; ⏲8am-8pm) Good for general tourist information, plus hotel bookings and excursions. Goes to the Valle de los Ingenios (CUC$35) and Salto del Caburní in Topes de Collante (CUC$30). Snorkeling excursions go to Cayo Iguanas (CUC$45) and Cayo Blanco (CUC$50). State taxis congregate outside.

Infotur (☎42-99-82-58; Gustavo Izquierdo No 112; ⏲9am-5pm) Useful for general information on the town, its surroundings and Sancti Spíritus Province.

Getting There & Away

BUS

The centrally located **bus station** (Piro Guinart No 224) has buses for nationals and the more reliable Víazul service aimed at foreign travelers. The **Víazul ticket office** (☎41-99-44-48; ⏲8:30am-4pm) is further back in the station.

With Víazul, Varadero departures can deposit you in Jagüey Grande (CUC$15, three hours) with stops on request in Jovellanos, Colesio and Cárdenas. The Santiago de Cuba departure goes through Sancti Spíritus (CUC$6, 1½ hours), Ciego de Ávila (CUC$9, 2¾ hours), Camagüey (CUC$15, 5¼ hours), Las Tunas (CUC$22, 7½ hours), Holguín (CUC$26, eight hours) and Bayamo (CUC$26, 10 hours). There's also a bus to Playa Santa Lucía at 10am (CUC$23, 6½ hours).

The Cubanacán Conectando tourist shuttle service has direct links daily with Havana (CUC$25). There's no office. Inquire at Infotur.

TRAIN

Train transportation out of Trinidad is awful even by Cuban standards. The town hasn't been connected to the main rail network since a hurricane downed a bridge in the early 1990s.

The tourist route up the Valle de los Ingenios is currently closed for repairs. Check with the train station or tour agencies for updates.

The **train terminal** (Lino Pérez final) is in a pink house across the train tracks on the western side of the station.

Getting Around

BICYCLE

Casas particulares can help organize bike rentals with a local. Just don't expect the latest Shimano gears. Trinidad to Playa Ancón is a pleasant and flat 30-minute ride; Trinidad to Topes de Collantes is akin to a tough stage in the Tour de France.

BUS

Trinidad has a handy hop-on, hop-off tourist-oriented minibus, **Bus Turístico** (all-day ticket CUC$5), similar to Havana's and Viñales', linking its outlying sights.

CAR & MOPED

Car rental prices fluctuate depending on season, car type and length of hire. The rental agencies at the Playa Ancón hotels rent cars and mopeds (CUC$25 per day).

Cubacar (☎41-99-66-33; General Lino Perez, btwn Codania & Maceo; per day CUC$70) rents cars and scooters.

The Oro Negro gas station is at the entrance to Trinidad from Sancti Spíritus, 1km east of Plaza Santa Ana. The **Servi-Cupet gas station** (⏲24hr), 500m south of Trinidad on the road to Casilda, has an El Rápido snack bar attached.

Guarded parking is available in certain areas around the *casco histórico*. Ask at your hotel or casa particular, where staff can arrange it.

TAXI

State-owned taxis tend to congregate outside the Cubatur office on Antonio Maceo. A cab to Sancti Spíritus (70km) should cost approximately CUC$40.

Taxi Cuba (☎41-99-80-80) Official taxi. Round-trip services to area attractions require some negotiation depending on wait times.

Playa Ancón & Around

A ribbon of white beach on Sancti Spíritus' iridescent Caribbean shoreline, Playa Ancón is often considered as the finest arc of sand on Cuba's south coast. The beach has three all-inclusive hotels and a well-equipped marina with catamaran trips to nearby coral keys. While it can't compete with the north-coast giants of Varadero, Cayo Coco and Guardalavaca, Ancón has one trump card: Trinidad, Latin America's sparkling colonial diamond, lies just 12km to the north.

Between Playa Ancón and Trinidad lies half-forgotten La Boca, a small fishing village at the mouth of the Río Guaurabo with a pebbly beach shaded by flowering acacias. If you like lazy rocking-chair tranquility, fresh lobster, raspberry-ripple sunsets and bantering in Spanish with the local fishers, it's bliss.

The one paved road crosses a tidal flat teeming with birdlife visible in the early morning. Be warned: sand fleas are famously ferocious at sunrise and sunset.

Activities

Cyclists can ride from Trinidad to Hotel Club Amigo Ancón – it's 18km via Casilda, or 16km on the much nicer coastal road via La Boca. The hotel pool is also open to nonguests and you can usually nab the ping-pong table undetected.

Marina Trinidad FISHING, SNORKELING
(☎41-99-82-60; www.nauticamarlin.com; half-day deep-sea fishing CUC$300; ⏲8am-5pm) The marina is a few hundred meters north of Hotel Club Amigo Ancón. Romantic types might want to check out the sunset cruise, enthusiastically recommended by readers. The marina runs an all-day snorkeling-and-beach tour to Cayo Iguanas. Travel agencies in Trinidad also sell these tours with 24 hours' notice. A four-hour deep-sea fishing tour includes transportation, gear and guide.

Cayo Blanco International Dive Center DIVING
(Marina Trinidad; single dive CUC$35, open-water course CUC$320; ⏲8am-5pm) Diving out of the marina, Cayo Blanco International Dive Center offers single/multiple dive packages as well as open-water courses. Cayo Blanco, a reef islet 25km southeast of Playa Ancón, has 22 marked scuba sites where you'll see black coral and bountiful marine life. To reserve, head to the desk inside Hotel Club Amigo Ancón nearby.

Sleeping

Ancón's three hotels offer all-inclusive rates. Those on tighter budgets might consider a homestay in the seaside village of La Boca.

Playa Ancón

Hotel Club Amigo Ancón RESORT $$
(☎41-99-61-20/29; asubdirector@brisastdad.co.cu; s/d/tr all-inclusive CUC$67/89/122; P ❄ @ ≋) Built during Cuba's 30-year flirtation with Soviet architectonics, the Ancón wouldn't win any beauty contests. Indeed, this steamship-shaped seven-story concrete pile contrasts with the natural beauty of Ancón beach. Installations are tired and food gets bad reports. Some like the lack of pretension and low prices; others, like Groucho Marx, suspect a club that would have them as a member.

Brisas Trinidad del Mar RESORT $$$
(☎41-99-65-00; reserva5@brisastdad.co.cu; s/d all-inclusive CUC$115/184; P ❄ @ ≋) Although a kitschy attempt to re-create Trinidad in a resort environment, Brisas wins kudos for rejecting monolithic architecture in favor of low-rise colonial-style villas. The swath of beach is stunning and the massage, sauna, gym and tennis courts handy for the sports-minded. However, after barely a decade in operation, the quality of this place suffers from poor maintenance and service.

La Boca

Hostal Idel & Domingo CASA PARTICULAR $
(☎41-99-86-34; Av del Mar No 9; r CUC$30; P ❄) The queen of kitsch, Idel is a lovely grandma offering simple rooms. This is La Boca life personified, with rockers and hammocks on a wraparound porch within sight of the sea, and two simple rooms with

Trinidad Area

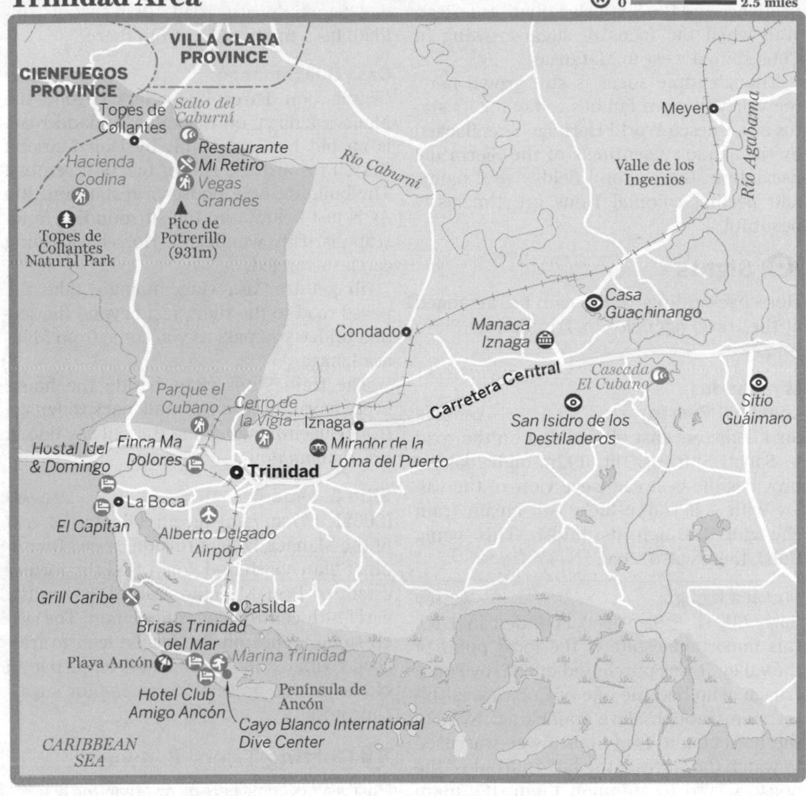

all you need (fan, air-con, fridge and double bed) to keep you *muy contente*.

★El Capitan CASA PARTICULAR **$$**
(☎41-99-30-55; capitancasanovatrinidad@yahoo.es; Playa Boca 82; d/tr incl breakfast CUC$60/70; ❄) With true B&B style, this modern beach house provides a great escape. Owners Yile and Maikel have four smart guest rooms, each with refrigerator and safe, facing a terrace where breakfast is served. There's also a sprawling seafront garden with shade – prime relaxation territory. Budget travelers can ask for the room without sea view and save CUC$15.

Eating

Grill Caribe CARIBBEAN **$$**
(meals CUC$5-23; ⏰8am-8pm) On a lovely beach, this open-air restaurant serves fresh seafood. There's fish and shrimp or lobster served with sides. Strict vegetarians will be disappointed here. It's a great sunset spot.

Getting There & Away

From Trinidad, you can get here in less than 15 minutes by car or a leisurely 40 minutes on a bike. A shuttle bus run by Transtur links Ancón to Trindad four times daily (CUC$5). Otherwise, it's a pleasant bike ride or a cheap taxi to the beach (CUC$8) or La Boca (CUC$5).

Valle de los Ingenios

Trinidad's immense wealth was garnered not in the town itself, but in a verdant valley 8km to the east. The Valle de los Ingenios (or Valle de San Luis) still contains the ruins of dozens of 19th century sugar mills, including warehouses, milling machinery, slave quarters, manor houses and a fully functioning steam train. Most of the mills were destroyed during the War of Independence and the Spanish-Cuban-American War, when the focus of sugar-growing in Cuba shifted west to Matanzas.

Though some sugar is still grown here, the valley is more famous today for its status as a Unesco World Heritage Site. Backed by the shadowy sentinels of the Sierra del Escambray, the pastoral fields, royal palms and peeling colonial ruins are timelessly beautiful.

Sights

Horseback-riding tours can be arranged at the travel agencies in Trinidad or Playa Ancón.

Mirador de la Loma del Puerto VIEWPOINT
Six kilometers east of Trinidad on the road to Sancti Spíritus, this 192m-high lookout provides the best eagle-eye view of the valley with – if you're lucky – a steam train chugging through its midst. This being Cuba, there's also a bar.

Manaca Iznaga MUSEUM
(tower CUC$1; 9am-4pm) Founded in 1750, this important estate is the focal point of the valley. It was purchased in 1795 by Pedro Iznaga, who became one of Cuba's wealthiest men through slave trafficking. Next to the hacienda, a 44m-high tower was used to watch the slaves – the bell in front of the house served to summon them. It's 16km northeast of Trinidad.

Today you can climb to the top of the tower for pretty views, followed by a reasonable lunch (from noon to 2:30pm) in the restaurant-bar in Iznaga's former colonial mansion. Don't miss the huge sugar press out back.

San Isidro de los Destiladeros HISTORIC SITE
(CUC$1; 9am-5pm) After lengthy excavations, the ruins of this once grand sugar mill are accessible to the public. Dating from the early 1830s and sophisticated for its time, the mill belongs to the pre-industrial age and functioned primarily with slave labor. After ceasing production in 1890, the main buildings – a hacienda, a three-story bell-tower, slave quarters and some cisterns – fell into ruin.

Renovation is ongoing and has been criticized by some who think the ruins should have been left as, well, ruins. San Isidro is accessed by branching right off the Trinidad–Sancti Spíritus road, 10km east of Trinidad. It's a further 2km from there.

Casa Guachinango LANDMARK
(9am-5pm) Three kilometers beyond the Manaca Iznaga, on the valley's inland road, is an old hacienda built by Don Mariano Borrell toward the end of the 18th century. The building now houses a restaurant. Río Ay is just below, and the surrounding landscape is truly wonderful. Horseback riding can be arranged.

To get to Casa Guachinango, take the paved road to the right, just beyond the second bridge you pass as you come from Manaca Iznaga.

The train stops right beside the house every morning. You can walk back to Iznaga from Guachinango along the railway line in less than an hour.

Sitio Guáimaro LANDMARK
(CUC$1; 7am-7pm) Seven kilometers east of the Manaca Iznaga turnoff, travel for another 2km south and you'll find the former estate of Don Mariano Borrell, a wealthy early 19th-century sugar merchant. The seven stone arches on the facade lead to frescoed rooms, now a restaurant featuring an old-fashioned press or *traipiche* for sugarcane juice.

Getting There & Away

Most visitors come here on an organized bus tour from Trinidad. You can also take a taxi (CUC$30 to CUC$40 round-trip with wait).

Trinidad's train plying the Valle de los Ingenios is currently out of action. Contact Cubatur (p287) in Trinidad for information on schedules and service interruptions. Tour desks at the Ancón hotels sell the same train tour for slightly more, including bus transfers to Trinidad.

Alternatively, a horseback-riding tour from Trinidad should take in most (if not all) of the sights.

Topes de Collantes

The Sierra del Escambray is Cuba's second-largest mountain range. The beautiful crenellated hills are rich in flora and surprisingly isolated. With the best network of hiking trails in Cuba, these jungle-clad forests harbor vines, ferns and eye-catching epiphytes.

In late 1958, Che Guevara camped here on his way to Santa Clara. Almost three years later, CIA-sponsored counterrevolutionary groups operated a cat-and-mouse guerrilla campaign from the same vantage point.

Not strictly a national park, Topes is a heavily protected 200-sq-km area straddling three provinces. The umbrella park contains Parque Altiplano, Parque Codina, Parque Guanayara and Parque el Cubano. A fifth enclave, El Nicho in Cienfuegos Province, is administered by the park authority.

The park name comes from its largest settlement, a 1937 health resort founded by dictator Fulgencio Batista for his sick wife. A tuberculosis sanatorium turned health 'resort' began construction in the late '30s and opened in 1954.

Sights

Museo de Arte Cubano Contemporáneo MUSEUM

(CUC$2; 8am-8pm) Believe it or not, Topes de Collantes' monstrous sanatorium once harbored a veritable Louvre of Cuban art, containing works by Cuban masters such as Tomás Sánchez and Rubén Torres Llorca. Raiding the old collection in 2008 inspired provincial officials to open this infinitely more attractive museum, which displays over 70 works in six *salas* (rooms) spread over three floors. The museum is on the main approach road from Trinidad, just before the hotels.

Plaza de las Memorias MUSEUM

(8am-5pm) FREE Topes' token museum is this quaint little display housed in three small wooden abodes just down from the Casa Museo del Café. It tells the history of the settlement and its resident hotels.

Casa Museo del Café MUSEUM

(7am-7pm) Coffee has been grown in the Sierra del Escambray for more than two centuries. In this small rustic cafe you can fill in the gaps on its boom-bust history while sipping the aromatic local brew called Cristal Mountain. Just up the road, stroll through Jardín de Variedades del Café, a garden with 25 varieties of coffee plants.

Activities

Topes has the best network of hiking trails in Cuba. Wear good, sturdy shoes. A recent relaxation in park rules means you can now tackle most of them solo, although you'll need wheels to reach some of the trailheads.

BEST SWIMMING HOLES

Poza del Venado Sendero 'Centinelas del Río Melodioso'

Salto del Caburní Topes de Collantes

La Solapa de Genaro (p299) Jobo Rosado

Cascada Bella (p293) Alturas de Banao

★ Sendero 'Centinelas del Río Melodioso' HIKING

(entry CUC$10, tour incl lunch CUC$47) The least accessible but the most rewarding hike by far from Topes de Collantes is this 6km round-trip hike in Parque Guanayara. The trail begins in cool, moist coffee plantations and descends steeply to El Rocío waterfall, where you can enjoy a bracing shower. Following the course of the Río Melodioso, pass another inviting waterfall and swimming pool, Poza del Venado, before emerging into the gardens of Casa la Gallega, a traditional rural hacienda.

Normally, a light lunch can be organized at the hacienda and camping is sometimes permitted in the lush grounds. It's 15km from the Centro de Visitantes along a series of steep and heavily rutted tracks. Logistics aren't easy. Organize this excursion with a guide from the Centro de Visitantes, or in an organized tour from Trinidad with Cubatur.

★ Salto del Caburní HIKING, SWIMMING

(CUC$10) The classic Topes hike, easily accessed on foot from the hotels, goes to this 62m waterfall that cascades over rocks into cool swimming holes before plunging into a chasm where macho locals dare each other to jump. Be warned: at the height of the dry season (March to May) there may be low water levels.

The entry fee is collected at the toll gate to Villa Caburní, just down the hill from the Kurhotel near the Centro de Visitantes (it's a long approach on foot). Allow an hour down and 1½ hours back up for this 5km (round-trip) hike. Some slopes are steep and can be slippery after rain.

Gruta Nengoa HIKING, SWIMMING

(CUC$10) A newly developed 2.6km trail centered on a grotto and 12m-high waterfall with some good opportunities for birdwatching and swimming. The trailhead is located 16km from Topes, just south of the village of Cuatro Vientos.

Hacienda Codina HIKING
(CUC$10) At the hacienda, the Sendero de Alfombra Mágica is a 1.2km circular trail through orchid and bamboo gardens and past the Cueva del Altar. There are also mud baths, a restaurant and a scenic viewpoint. It's 8km from Topes by a rough road (the 4km 4WD track begins on a hilltop 3km down the road toward Cienfuegos and Manicaragua).

Alternatively, hike La Batata trail and continue 1.5km past the cave to arrive at the hacienda. Ask for directions at the Centro de Visitantes first and hire a guide.

Sendero Jardín del Gigante HIKING
(CUC$10) Those pressed for time can get a taste of Topes' ecosystems with this ideal 1.2km ramble. It starts at the Plaza de las Memorias and finishes just downhill in the Parque la Represa on the Río Vega Grande. En route you can count 300 species of trees and ferns, including the largest *caoba* (mahogany) tree in Cuba.

The small restaurant at the entrance to the garden is in a villa built by Fulgencio Batista's wife, whose love for the area inspired her husband to build the Topes resort.

Vegas Grandes HIKING, SWIMMING
(CUC$10) This 2km waterfall trail begins at the apartment blocks known as Reparto el Chorrito on the southern side of Topes de Collantes, near the entrance to the resort as you arrive from Trinidad. Allow a couple of hours to hike and enjoy a refreshing dip.

It's possible to continue to the Salto del Caburní with a guide. The paths are poorly signposted.

Sendero la Batata HIKING
(CUC$10) This 6km out-and-back trail to a small cave containing an underground river starts at a parking sign just downhill from Casa Museo del Café. When you reach another highway, go around the right side of the concrete embankment and down the hill. Keep straight or right after this point (avoid trails to the left). Allow an hour each way.

Sleeping

Villa Caburní CABIN $
(☎41-54-01-80; per person incl breakfast CUC$14; P ❄) It's all about location, in this case, a verdant park setting. With 29 Swiss-chalet-style cabins (some still being renovated), all with solar panels, this is a screaming good deal. Each has hot water and refrigerator. Breakfast is served in a dated on-site bar-cafeteria. It sits just behind the Centro de Visitantes.

Hotel los Helechos HOTEL $
(☎41-54-03-30; s/d incl breakfast CUC$51/64; P ❄ ≋) Never 100% at home in its verdant natural surroundings, this clumsy chocolate-box building with its wicker furnishings and holiday-camp-style villas still looks a bit awkward. Not helping matters are the unattractive indoor pool, poky steam baths (if they're working), journeyman restaurant and kitschy local disco (in a natural park of all places!).

The saving grace is the restaurant's delicious home-baked bread – surely the best in Cuba.

Eating

Bar-Restaurante Gran Nena CUBAN $
(☎41-54-03-38; Carretera Principal; mains CUC$4-6; ⏱10am-9pm) An ambient setting where Cuban food that's just OK is served (slowly) under a traditional open-sided sitting area. Bananas, papayas, avocados, oranges and peaches all grow abundantly in the adjacent sloping garden and you can follow a trail through them to a hidden cave.

The restaurant is next door to the Museo de Arte Cubano Contemporáneo (p291).

Restaurante Mi Retiro CARIBBEAN $$
(Carretera de Trinidad; meals CUC$6-9; ⏱8am-11pm) Situated 3km back down the road to Trinidad, Restaurante Mi Retiro does fair-to-middling *comida criolla* (Creole food) to the sound of the occasional traveling minstrel.

Information

Centro de Visitantes (⏱8am-5pm) Near the sundial at the entrance to the hotel complexes; it's the best place to procure maps, guides and trail info.

Getting There & Away

Without a car, it's very difficult to get to Topes de Collantes and harder still to get around to the various trailheads. Your best bet is a taxi (CUC$40 to CUC$60 return with a wait), an excursion from Trinidad (from CUC$35) or a hire car.

The road between Trinidad and Topes de Collantes is paved, but very steep. It's slippery when wet.

OFF THE BEATEN TRACK

ALTURAS DE BANAO

Still well off the radar, this ecological reserve hides a little-explored stash of mountains, waterfalls, forest and steep limestone cliffs. In the Guamuhaya mountain range, the reserve's highest peak is 842m. Foothills are replete with rivers, abundant plant life, including epiphyte cacti, and the ruins of a handful of pioneering 19th-century farmhouses.

The park headquarters is at Jarico, 3.5km up a beaten track leading off the Sancti Spíritus–Trinidad road. It incorporates a *ranchón*-style restaurant, visitors center and chalet with eight double rooms.

Within shouting distance is the Cascada Bella waterfall and a natural swimming pool. From Jarico the 6km La Sabina trail leads to an eponymous biostation and La Sabina Chalet. Guided day hikes (CUC$3) are charged separately from entry to the reserve.

For drivers, a spectacular 44km road continues right over the mountains from Topes de Collantes to Manicaragua via Jibacoa (occasionally closed, so check in Trinidad before setting out). It's also possible to drive to/from Cienfuegos via Sierrita on a partly paved, partly gravel road (4WD only).

Sancti Spíritus

POP 105,200

In any other country, this attractive colonial city would be a cultural tour de force. But cocooned inside illustrious Sancti Spíritus Province, second fiddle to Trinidad, visitors barely give it a glance. For many therein lies the attraction. Sancti Spíritus is Trinidad without the touts. You can dine, listen to boleros (ballads) on the plaza or search for a casa particular without hassle.

Founded in 1514 as one of the seven original villas of Diego Velázquez, Sancti Spíritus was moved to its present site on the Río Yayabo in 1522. Yet audacious corsairs continued to loot the town until well into the 1660s.

Sancti Spíritus has made its contributions. It concocted the dapper *guayabera*, Latin America's favorite men's shirt, cultivated *guayaba* (guava) fruit and built a quaint humpbacked bridge reminiscent of Yorkshire, England. The city underwent intense beautification in 2014 to celebrate its 500th anniversary.

Sights

★Casa de la Guayabera MUSEUM

(☎41-32-22-05; guayabera@hero.cult.cu; San Miguel 60; CUC$1; ⏲10am-5pm Tue-Sun) The favored uniform of South American strongman presidents and blushing grooms at Mexican beach weddings, the *guayabera* shirt was purportedly 'invented' in Sancti Spíritus by the wives of agricultural workers who sewed the trademark pockets into the garments so that their men could safely store their tools and packed lunches. This new museum honors the iconic shirts displaying *guayaberas* worn by Hugo Chávez, Gabriel García Márquez and Fidel.

The complex, set on a lovely riverside patio in front of the city's famous packhorse bridge, also has a bar and lovely garden where social and cultural events take place (open to the public) after hours. Those who want to order a *guayabera* need to wait two days for its completion.

★Puente Yayabo LANDMARK

Looking like something out of an English country village, this quadruple-arched bridge is Sancti Spíritus' signature sight. Built by the Spanish in 1815, it carries traffic across the Río Yayabo and is now a national monument. For the best view (and a mirror-like reflection) hit the outdoor terrace at the Taberna Yayabo.

It's flanked by cobblestone streets – the most arresting is narrow Calle Llano, where old ladies peddle live chickens door to door, and neighbors gossip noisily in front of pastel houses. Also worth a wander are Calle Guairo and Calle San Miguel.

Parque Serafín Sánchez SQUARE

While not Cuba's shadiest or most atmospheric square, pretty Serafín Sánchez is full of understated Sancti Spíritus elegance. Metal chairs laid out inside the pedestrianized central domain are usually commandeered by cigar-smoking grandpas and flirty young couples with their sights set on some ebullient local nightlife.

There's plenty to whet the appetite on the square's south side, where the stately

Sancti Spíritus

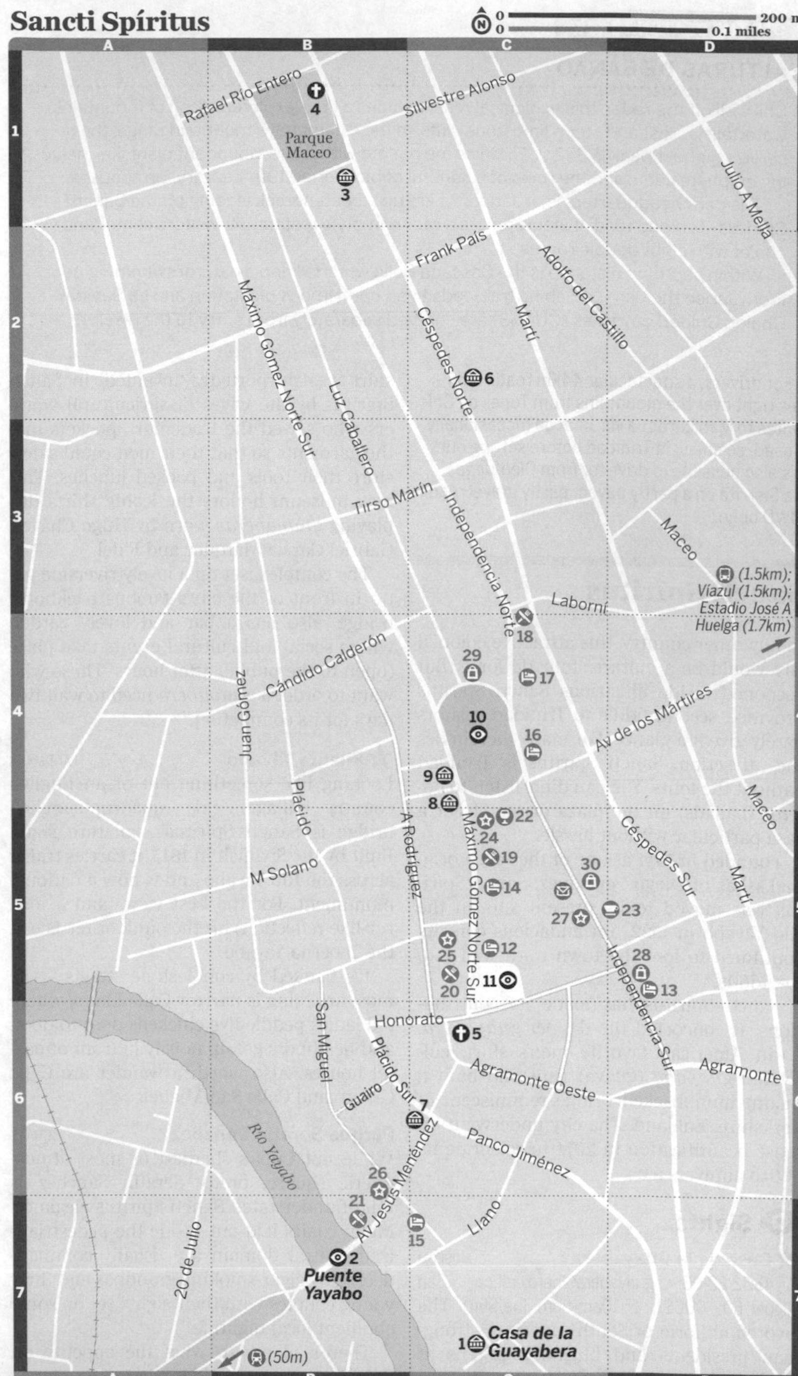

Sancti Spíritus

Top Sights
1 Casa de la Guayabera C7
2 Puente Yayabo B7

Sights
3 Fundación de la Naturaleza y El Hombre B1
4 Iglesia de Nuestra Señora de la Caridad B1
5 Iglesia Parroquial Mayor del Espíritu Santo C6
6 Museo Casa Natal de Serafín Sánchez C2
7 Museo de Arte Colonial C6
8 Museo de Ciencias Naturales C4
9 Museo Provincial C4
10 Parque Serafín Sánchez C4
11 Plaza Honorato C5

Sleeping
12 Hostal del Rijo C5
13 Hostal Don Florencio D5
14 Hostal Paraíso C5
15 Hostal Yayabo C7
16 Hotel Plaza C4
17 'Los Richards' – Ricardo Rodríguez C4

Eating
18 Dulce Crema C4
19 El 19 .... C5
20 Mesón de la Plaza C5
Restaurante la Fuente .... (see 12)
21 Taberna Yayabo B7

Drinking & Nightlife
22 Café ARTex C5
23 Cafe Colga'o D5

Entertainment
24 Casa de la Cultura C5
25 Casa de la Trova Miguel Companioni C5
26 Teatro Principal B6
27 Uneac C5

Shopping
28 Boulevard D5
29 La Perla C4
30 Librería Julio Antonio Mella C5

Casa de la Cultura (p298) often exports its music on to the street. Next door the columned Hellenic beauty that today serves as the **Biblioteca Provincial Rubén Martínez Villena** (41-32-77-17; Máximo Gómez Norte No 1; 9am-5pm) was built originally in 1929 by the Progress Society.

The magnolia-colored grande dame on the square's northern side is the former La Perla hotel, which lay rotting and unused for years before being turned into a three-level government-run shopping center.

Fundación de la Naturaleza y El Hombre — MUSEUM

(41-32-83-42; Cruz Pérez No 1; recommended donation CUC$2; 10am-5pm Mon-Fri) Replicating its equally diminutive namesake in Miramar, Havana, this museum on Parque Maceo chronicles the 17,422km canoe odyssey from the Amazon to the Caribbean in 1987 led by Cuban writer and Renaissance man Antonio Nuñez Jiménez (1923–98). Some 432 explorers made the journey through 20 countries, from Ecuador to the Bahamas, in the twin dugout canoes *Simón Bolívar* and *Hatuey*. The latter measures over 13m and is the collection's central, prized piece.

The visit is made much more interesting if you speak Spanish. Beware of sporadic opening hours.

Iglesia Parroquial Mayor del Espíritu Santo — CHURCH

(Agramonte Oeste No 58; 9-11am & 2-5pm Tue-Sat) Overlooking Plaza Honorato is this beautiful blue church that underwent a Lazarus-like renovation for the 2014 anniversary. Originally constructed of wood in 1522 and rebuilt in stone in 1680, it's said to be the oldest church in Cuba still standing on its original foundations.

The best time to take a peek at the simple but soulful interior is during Sunday morning Mass (10am). A small donation will go a long way.

Museo de Arte Colonial — MUSEUM

(41-32-54-55; Plácido Sur No 74; CUC$2; 9am-5pm Tue-Sat, 8am-noon Sun) This small museum had a 2012 refurb and displays 19th-century furniture and decorations in an imposing 17th-century building that once belonged to the sugar-rich Iznaga family.

Plaza Honorato — SQUARE

Formerly known as Plaza de Jesús, this tiny square was where the Spanish authorities once conducted grisly public hangings. Later on, it hosted a produce market, and scruffy peso stalls still line the small connecting lane to the east. The north side of the square is now occupied by a boutique hotel.

Museo Provincial MUSEUM
(41-32-74-35; Máximo Gómez Norte No 3; CUC$1; 9am-5pm Tue-Sun) One of those vaguely comical Cuban museums where guides follow you from room to room as if you're about to make off with the crown jewels. In reality the collection is less distinguished, logging the history of Sancti Spíritus with a dusty stash of ephemera that includes English china, cruel slave artifacts and the inevitable revolutionary M-26/7 paraphernalia.

Iglesia de Nuestra Señora de la Caridad CHURCH
(Céspedes Norte No 207) Across from the Fundación de la Naturaleza y El Hombre is the city's second church, the recipient of a handsome 2014 paint job. Its internal arches are a favored nesting spot for Cuban sparrows, who seem unfazed by the church interior's continuing state of disrepair.

Museo Casa Natal de Serafín Sánchez MUSEUM
(41-32-77-91; Céspedes Norte No 112; CUC$1; 9am-5pm Tue-Sat) Serafín Sánchez was a local patriot who took part in both Wars of Independence and went down fighting in November 1896. The museum cataloguing his heroics is good for a 20-minute browse.

Museo de Ciencias Naturales MUSEUM
(41-32-63-65; Máximo Gómez Sur No 2; CUC$1; 9am-5pm Tue-Sun) Not much of a natural-history museum, this colonial house just off Parque Serafín Sánchez has a stuffed crocodile (which will scare the wits out of your kids) and some shiny rock collections.

Sleeping

Sancti Spíritus' gracious boutique sleeping establishments are branded as Encanto hotels, belonging to the Cubanacán chain. They are complemented by a handful of pleasant casas particulares.

In Town

★Hostal Paraíso CASA PARTICULAR $
(41-33-46-58; Máximo Gómez Sur No 11, btwn Honorato & M Solano; r CUC$25;) The best budget option in town, this central colonial draped in ferns is home to a nice family with a puttering dachshund. Try for one of the two outstanding rooms on the breezy roof deck. The house dates from 1838, with huge bathrooms, powerful showers and uplifting greenery.

Hostal Yayabo CASA PARTICULAR $
(mobile 53-53-00-70; liosmany.gomez@nauta.cu; Jesus Menendez No 109; r CUC$25;) Nuris and her young family host guests in their riverside home. There's a motorcycle in the living room and a bubblegum-pink bedroom with satin bedspread that would be the envy of any Barbie princess. Guests can cook and there's a riverside terrace.

'Los Richards' – Ricardo Rodríguez CASA PARTICULAR $
(41-32-26-56; gisel.rios@nauta.cu; Independencia Norte No 28 Altos; r CUC$25-30;) A dark unkempt stairway off the main square gives way to a dated but clean 2nd-floor apartment. The two front rooms are enormous. There are four guest rooms, numerous beds, indoor bar, private dining area and fridge. The best part: the wrought-iron protected balconies overlooking the theatrics of the main square.

It can also arrange excursions to Alturas de Banao.

Hostal Don Florencio BOUTIQUE HOTEL $$
(41-32-83-06; rperurena@islazulssp.tur.co.cu; Independencia Sur; s/d CUC$102/122;) Sancti Spíritus doesn't often get one over on Trinidad, but it does have a better collection of hotels. This beauty has bright spaces, antique furnishings and two inviting Jacuzzis in the cool central patio. Service can be a little lax. It's popular with tour groups.

★Hostal del Rijo BOUTIQUE HOTEL $$$
(41-32-85-88; rperurena@islazulssp.tur.co.cu; Honorato del Castillo No 12; s/d incl breakfast CUC$102/122;) Even committed casa particular fans will have trouble resisting this meticulously restored 1818 mansion situated on quiet (until the Casa de la Trova opens) Plaza Honorato. Sixteen huge, plush rooms – many with plaza-facing balconies – are equipped with everything a romance-seeking Cuba-phile could wish for, including satellite TV, complimentary shampoos and chunky colonial furnishings.

Downstairs in the elegant courtyard restaurant you'll be served the kind of sumptuous, unhurried breakfast that keeps you lingering.

Hotel Plaza BOUTIQUE HOTEL $$$
(41-32-71-02; rperurena@islazulssp.tur.co.cu; Independencia Norte No 1; s/d incl breakfast CUC$102/122;) On the edge of Parque Serafín Sánchez, this is courtside seating to great people-watching. Public spaces, such

as the romantic patio bar, shine. Rooms are large and spread over two stories, with fluffy bathrobes, an in-room safe and chunky furnishings. Popular with tour groups.

Outside Town

Hotel Zaza HOTEL $
(☎41-32-70-15; ypuerta@islazulssp.tur.co.cu; Finca San Jose Km 5.5, Lago Zaza; s/d incl breakfast CUC$25/33; P ❄ ≋) Perched above expansive Embalse Zaza, 5km east of Sancti Spíritus, this scruffy rural retreat looks more like a utilitarian apartment block transplanted from Moscow than a hotel – not that this discourages the armies of bass fishers who descend on the lake in droves (four-hour fishing trips go for CUC$40).

For nonfishers there's a swimming pool and boat trips on the lake (one-hour cruise CUC$20 for two people).

Villa Rancho Hatuey HOTEL $$
(☎41-36-13-15; gniubo@islazulssp.tur.co.cu; Carretera Central Km 384; s/d CUC$76/85; P ❄ @ ≋) A veritable Islazul gem accessible from the southbound lane of Carretera Central. Rancho Hatuey spreads 76 rooms in two-story cabins across expansive landscaped grounds set back from the road. Catch some rays around the swimming pool or grab a bite in the on-site restaurant while observing Canadian bus groups and Communist Party officials from Havana mingling in awkward juxtaposition.

Eating

Never rated highly for its private restaurants, Sancti Spíritus has a couple of good ones since privatization laws were relaxed. The state sector has some equally strong contenders.

Dulce Crema ICE CREAM $
(cnr Independencia Norte & Laborni; ice cream CUC$1-2; ⊙8am-10pm) What, no Coppelia? Dulce Crema is Sancti Spíritus' long-standing provincial stand-in and is actually – ahem – better. Alternatively, hang around long enough in Parque Serafín Sánchez and a DIY ice-cream man will turn up with his ice-cream maker powered by a washing-machine motor.

Mesón de la Plaza CARIBBEAN, SPANISH $
(Máximo Gómez Sur No 34; mains CUC$4-7; ⊙noon-3pm & 6-10pm) Long a solid option, this state-run restaurant occupies a 19th-century mansion that once belonged to a rich Spanish tycoon. You can tuck into classic Spanish staples such as *potaje de garbanzos* (chickpeas with pork) and some chewable beef while appetizing music drifts in from the Casa de la Trova next door.

★**Taberna Yayabo** CUBAN, SPANISH $$
(☎41-83-75-52; Jesús Menéndez No 106; meals CUC$6-12; ⊙9am-10:45pm) With an excellent riverside location, wine cellar and wonderful service, there's reason to linger at this pleasant state-run restaurant. Sure, you might be bombarded by a steady stream of '80s hits, but there are also tapas such as *serrano* ham carved on-site and cheeses – items not easily found on the island. The resident sommelier brims over with enthusiasm.

It also has cigars. Cocktails are notable. Try the *cunyaya,* a mix of lemon drops, *guarapo* (sugarcane), honey and aged rum.

El 19 INTERNATIONAL $$
(Máximo Gómez No 9, btwn Manolo Solano & Honorato del Castillo; meals CUC$8-12; ⊙6:30am-10pm) The stylish and centrally located El 19 specializes in sirloin steak, a dish largely unavailable in Cuba until recently. It is delivered to your table by eager-to-please servers.

Restaurante la Fuente INTERNATIONAL $$
(Honorato No 12; meals CUC$6-9; ⊙7am-11pm) Quiet colonial ambience in the impressive central courtyard of the Rijo or on the lovely terrace. Choose from an international menu with filet mignon and chicken in white-wine sauce or a sandwich menu. Service is good, and there is a notable selection of desserts, drinks and coffee.

Drinking & Nightlife

★**Cafe Colga'o** CAFE
(☎mobile 54-33-62-37; Independencia Sur No 9c; ⊙4pm-midnight Fri-Wed) It doesn't get more underground than this Cuban-Italian cafe with no on-street signs. Follow a staircase to this 9th-floor apartment sporting tiny tables with floor cushions and balcony views. It's filled with local youth grooving to an eclectic music mix, sipping espresso drinks and eating cheap sandwiches sold in *moneda nacional.* Costing mere cents, the coffee flan is outstanding.

Café ARTex CLUB
(M Solano; CUC$1-3; ⊙10pm-2am Tue-Sun) On an upper floor on Parque Serafín Sánchez, this place has more of a nightclub feel than the usual ARTex patio. It offers dancing, live music and karaoke nightly, and a Sunday

matinee at 2pm. Thursday is reggaeton (Cuban hip-hop) night, and the cafe also hosts comedy. Clientele is mainly under 25.

Entertainment

Sancti Spíritus has a wonderful evening ambience: cool, inclusive and unpretentious. There are also numerous cultural centers with live music.

★Uneac LIVE MUSIC
(Independencia Sur No 10) There are friendly nods as you enter, handshakes offered by people you've never met, and a starry-eyed crooner on stage blowing kisses to his girlfriend(s) in the audience. Uneac concerts always feel more like family gatherings than organized cultural events, and Sancti Spíritus' is one of the nicest 'families' you'll meet.

★Casa de la Trova Miguel Companioni LIVE MUSIC
(Máximo Gómez Sur No 26; ⏲from 9pm) Another of Cuba's famous *trova* (traditional poetic singing) houses, this kicking folk-music venue in a colonial building off Plaza Honorato is on a par with anything in Trinidad. But here the crowds are 90% local and 10% tourist.

Casa de la Cultura LIVE MUSIC
(☎41-32-37-72; M Solano No 11) Numerous cultural events that at weekends spill out into the street and render the pavement impassable. It's situated on the southwest corner of Parque Serafin Sánchez.

Teatro Principal THEATER
(☎232-5755; Av Jesús Menéndez No 102) This landmark architectural icon next to the Puente Yayabo was recently given a comprehensive clean-up. It has weekend matinees (at 10am) with kids' theater.

Estadio José A Huelga SPECTATOR SPORT
(Circunvalación) From October to April, baseball games are held at this stadium, 1km north of the bus station. The provincial team Los Gallos (the Roosters) last tasted glory in 1979.

Shopping

Boulevard STREET
The city's revived shopping street, Calle Independencia Sur, is traffic-free and lined with statues, sculptures and myriad curiosity shops. Check out the opulent Colonia Española Building, once a whites-only gentlemen's club, now a mini department store. The *agropecuario* (vegetable market) is unusually located right in the city center.

A flea market inhabits Calle Honorato just off Independencia and all around are *vendutas* (small private shops or stalls), illustrating the recent economic relaxation.

La Perla SHOPPING CENTER
(☎41-32-81-71; Parque Serafín Sánchez; ⏲9am-4pm) Three levels of austerity-busting shopping behind a beautifully restored magnolia colonial edifice on Parque Serafín Sánchez.

Librería Julio Antonio Mella BOOKS
(Independencia Sur No 29; ⏲8am-5pm Mon-Sat) Revolutionary (mainly in Spanish) reading material for erudite travelers in a store opposite the post office.

Information

INTERNET ACCESS

There's wi-fi on the plaza and in all hotels.

Etecsa Telepunto (Independencia Sur No 14; internet per hour CUC$1.50; ⏲8:30am-7:30pm) Two rarely busy computer terminals, plus wi-fi scratchcards for sale.

MEDICAL SERVICES

Sancti Spíritus has the services of a major city.

Farmacia Especial (Independencia Norte No 123; ⏲24hr) Pharmacy on Parque Maceo.

Hospital Provincial Camilo Cienfuegos (☎41-32-40-17; Bartolomé Masó No 128) 500m north of Plaza de la Revolución.

Policlínico Los Olivos (☎41-32-63-62; Circunvalación Olivos No 1) Hospital near the bus station. Will treat foreigners in an emergency.

MONEY

There are plenty of ATMs and a money-exchange office.

Banco Financiero Internacional (☎41-32-84-47; Independencia Sur No 2; ⏲9am-3pm Mon-Fri) On Parque Serafín Sánchez.

Cadeca (☎41-33-61-84; Independencia Sur No 31; ⏲9am-5pm Mon-Sat) Lose your youth in this bank's line.

POST

Post Office (☎41-32-47-01; Independencia Sur No 8; ⏲9am-6pm Mon-Sat)

TOURIST INFORMATION

There's very little in the way of tourist information. Visit the Infotur (p287) in Trinidad for information on destinations in the province.

VÍAZUL BUS DEPARTURES FROM SANCTI SPÍRITUS

DESTINATION	COST (CUC$)	DURATION (HR)
Bayamo	21	7
Camagüey	10	3
Ciego de Ávila	6	1¼
Havana	23	5
Santa Clara	6	1¼
Santiago de Cuba	28	8
Trinidad	6	1¼

Getting There & Away

BUS

The provincial **bus station** (Carretera Central) is 2km east of town. Air-conditioned and punctual, **Víazul** (☎41-32-41-42; www.viazul.com; Carretera Central) buses serve numerous destinations.

Five daily departures for Santiago de Cuba also stop in Ciego de Ávila, Camagüey, Las Tunas and Bayamo. Five daily Havana buses stop at Santa Clara. The link to Trinidad leaves at a sleep-reducing 5:40am.

TRAIN

There are two train stations serving Sancti Spíritus. For Havana use the main **train station** (☎41-32-79-14; Av Jesús Menéndez No 92; to Havana CUC$14; ⏲tickets 7am-2pm Mon-Sat), southwest of the Puente Yayabo, an easy 10-minute walk from the city center.

Points east are served out of Guayos, 15km north of Sancti Spíritus, including Holguín (8½ hours), Santiago de Cuba (10¼ hours) and Bayamo (8¼ hours). If you're on the Havana–Santiago de Cuba cross-country express and going to Sancti Spíritus or Trinidad, get off at Guayos.

The ticket office at the Sancti Spíritus train station can sell you tickets for trains departing Guayos, but you must find your own way to the Guayos train station (CUC$10 in a taxi).

TRUCKS & TAXIS

Trucks to Trinidad, Jatibonico and elsewhere depart from the bus station. A state taxi to Trinidad will cost you around CUC$40.

Getting Around

Parking in Parque Serafín Sánchez is relatively safe. Ask in hotels Rijo and Plaza, and they will often find a man to stand guard overnight for CUC$1 to CUC$3.

Cubacar (☎41-32-85-33; Calle Maximo Gomez 9; ⏲9am-4pm) There is a Cubacar car-rental booth on the northeast corner of Parque Serafín Sánchez; prices for daily car hire start at around CUC$70.

Servi-Cupet Gas Station (Carretera Central) 1.5km north of Villa los Laureles, toward Santa Clara.

Northern Sancti Spíritus

For every 1000 tourists that visit Trinidad, a small handful gets to see the province's narrow northern corridor, which runs between Remedios, in Villa Clara, and Morón, in Ciego de Ávila.

The landscape is comprised of karstic uplands characterized by caves and covered in semideciduous woodland, juxtaposed with a flat, ecologically valuable coastal plain protected in the hard-to-visit but worthwhile Parque Nacional Caguanes.

Activities

Parque Nacional Caguanes HIKING, BOATING

Strict conservation measures mean public access to Parque Nacional Caguanes with its caves, aboriginal remains and flamingos is limited but not impossible. There is a basic biological station on the coast accessible by a rough road due north of Mayajigua but, rather than just turn up, your best bet is to check details first at the Villa San José del Lago (p300) or at Ecotur's handy public office in Trinidad (☎41-99-84-16; Simón Bolívar 424).

The one advertised excursion is Las Maravillas que Atesora Caguanes (2½ hours), which incorporates a path to the Humboldt, Ramos and Los Chivos caves and a boat trip around the Cayos de Piedra.

Jobo Rosado NATURE RESERVE

This 40-sq-km managed-resource area is still little-explored by independent travelers, although organized groups come here. Organize guided hikes through Ecotur or at

WORTH A TRIP

MUSEO NACIONAL CAMILO CIENFUEGOS

This excellent **museum** (☎41-55-26-89; CUC$1; ⊙8am-4pm Tue-Sat, 9am-1pm Sun) at Yaguajay, 36km southeast of Caibarién, was opened in 1989 and is eerily reminiscent of the Che Guevara monument in Santa Clara. Camilo fought a crucial battle in this town on the eve of the revolution's triumph, taking control of a local military barracks (now the Hospital Docente General, opposite the museum).

The museum is directly below a modernist plaza embellished with a 5m-high statue of El Señor de la Vanguardia (Man at the Vanguard). It contains an extremely well-curated display of Cienfuegos' life intermingled with facts and mementos from the revolutionary struggle. A replica of the small tank 'Dragon I,' converted from a tractor for use in the battle, stands in front of the hospital. Out back the Mausoleo de los Mártires del Frente Norte de las Villas is dedicated to the soldiers who died in the skirmish.

Villa San José del Lago. Highlights include La Solapa de Genaro, a 1km hike through tropical savanna to a gorgeous set of waterfalls and swimming holes. The Cueva de Valdés walk (800m) goes through semideciduous woodland to a cave.

The reserve includes the Sierra de Meneses-Cueto, a hill range running across the north of the province that acts as a buffer zone for the heavily protected Bahía de Buenavista.

As in the Sierra Maestra, history is intertwined with the ecology here. General Máximo Gomez battled through these hills during the Spanish-Cuban-American War. In 1958, Camilo Cienfuegos' rebel army (column No 2) pitched their final command post here. An imaginative monument by sculptor José Delarra marks the spot.

Rancho Querete FARM

(⊙9am-4pm Tue-Sun) The nexus for the Jobo Rosado Reserve is just off the main road a few kilometers east of Yaguajay and is equipped with a bar-restaurant, natural swimming hole, biological station and small 'zoo' (roosters mainly). Guided hikes can be organized here.

Sleeping

Villa San José del Lago HOTEL $

(☎41-54-61-08; Antonio Guiteras, Mayajigua; d incl breakfast/meals CUC$20/45; P❄≈) Once popular with vacationing Americans, this novel spa is just outside Mayajigua in northern Sancti Spíritus Province. The tiny rooms are set in a variety of two-story villas, nestled beside a small palm-fringed lake with pedal boats and two resident flamingos. It's famous for its thermal waters (32°C), first used by injured slaves in the 19th century, now for holidaying Cubans.

The 67 rooms are no-frills, but the setting, wedged between the Sierra de Jatibonico and Parque Nacional Caguanes, is magnificent and makes a good base for some of Cuba's lesser-known excursions. There's a restaurant and snack bar on-site.

Information

Ecotur (☎41-55-49-30; Pedro Díaz No 54, Yaguajay) The best information portal for the region, one block north of the Caibarién–Morón road in Yaguajay.

Getting There & Away

A Víazul bus used to ply this northern route, but it wasn't running at last visit, meaning you're on your own with a bike, hire car or taxi.

Ciego de Ávila Province

☎33 / POP 424,400

Includes ➡

Best Places to Eat

- ➡ Restaurante Maité la Qbana (p307)
- ➡ Lenny's Lobster Shack (p313)
- ➡ Ranchón Playa Pilar (p314)
- ➡ Rancho Flamingo (p313)

Best Places to Sleep

- ➡ Alojamiento Maité (p307)
- ➡ Meliá Cayo Coco (p311)
- ➡ Iberostar Daiquirí (p315)
- ➡ Colonial Cayo Coco (p312)

Why Go?

Diminutive Ciego de Ávila's finger-in-the-dyke moment came during the late 19th-century Cuban Wars of Independence: it became the site of an impressive fortified wall, the Trocha, built to keep out rebellious eastern armies from the prosperous west. Today, the province continues to be the cultural divide between Cuba's Oriente and Occidente. Most tourists come here for the ambitious post–Special Period resort development of Cayo Coco and Cayo Guillermo. The brilliant tropical pearls that once seduced Ernest Hemingway have had their glorious beaches spruced up and daubed with over a dozen exclusive resorts.

Away from the tourist hordes, the province has been harboring intriguing secrets for more than a century. Various non-Spanish immigrants first arrived here in the 19th century from Haiti, Jamaica, the Dominican Republic and Barbados, bringing with them myriad cultural rites still practiced in cricket matches, folk-dancing, explosive fireworks and more.

When to Go

- ➡ Beachgoers should descend on the cayos between November and March for drier weather that, while cool by Cuban standards, is still pleasantly warm.
- ➡ Head for the countryside in November for the Fiesta de los Bandas Rojo y Azul, a folkloric throwback to Spanish times celebrated in rural Majagua.
- ➡ Morón's Aquatic Carnival kicks off in September, in the channel leading to Laguna de la Leche.

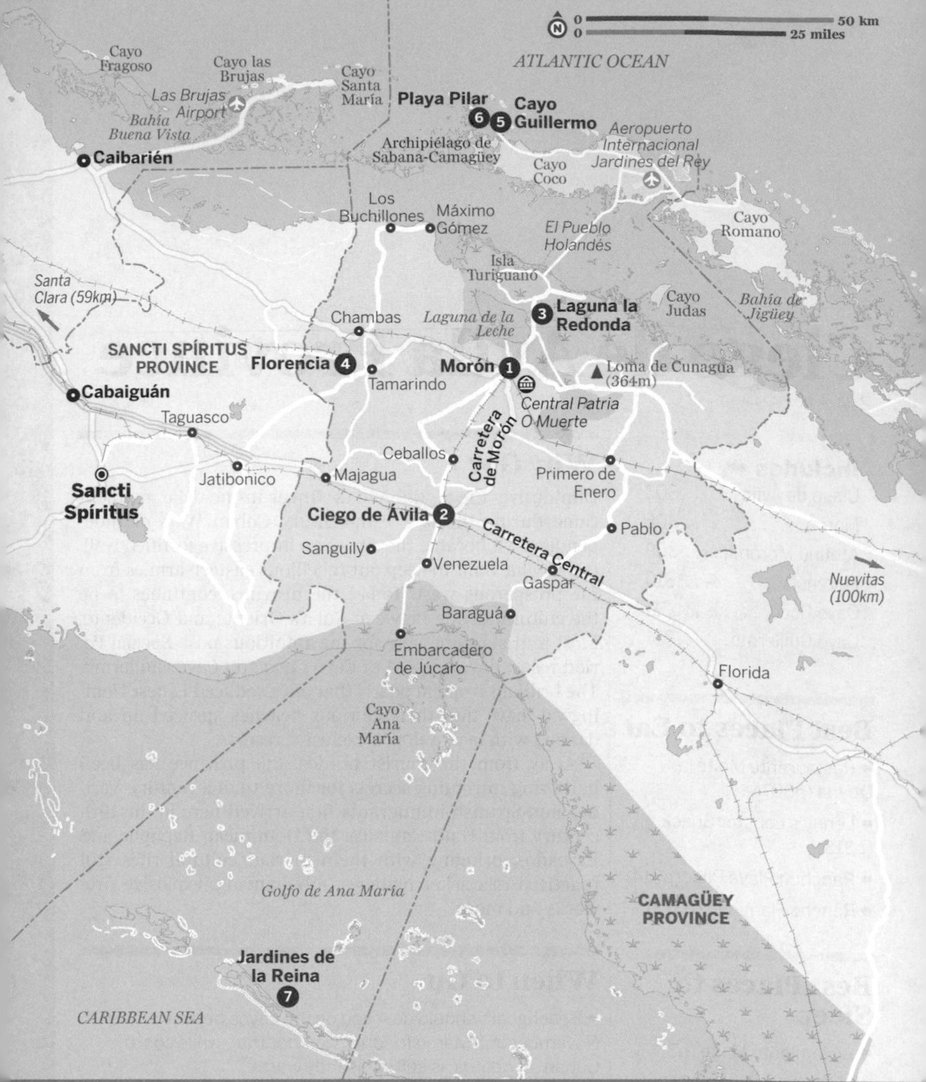

ATLANTIC OCEAN
0 50 km
0 25 miles
Cayo Fragoso
Cayo las Brujas
Las Brujas Airport
Bahía Buena Vista
Cayo Santa María
Playa Pilar
6
5
Cayo Guillermo
Archipiélago de Sabana-Camagüey
Aeropuerto Internacional Jardines del Rey
Cayo Coco
Caibarién
Los Buchillones
Máximo Gómez
El Pueblo Holandés
Cayo Romano
Isla Turiguanó
Santa Clara (59km)
Cayo Judas
Bahía de Jigüey
Chambas
Laguna de la Leche
3 Laguna la Redonda
SANCTI SPÍRITUS PROVINCE
Florencia 4
Morón 1
Tamarindo
Loma de Cunagua (364m)
Cabaiguán
Central Patria O Muerte
Taguasco
Carretera de Morón
Ceballos
Primero de Enero
Jatibonico
Majagua
Sancti Spíritus
Ciego de Ávila 2
Pablo
Carretera Central
Sanguily
Venezuela
Gaspar
Nuevitas (100km)
Baraguá
Embarcadero de Júcaro
Florida
Cayo Ana María
Golfo de Ana María
CAMAGÜEY PROVINCE
Jardines de la Reina
7
CARIBBEAN SEA

Ciego de Ávila Province Highlights

❶ **Morón** (p306) Staying in a private homestay in this hard-working Cuban town.

❷ **Parque de la Ciudad** (p303) Marveling at how waste ground got transformed into one of Cuba's most interesting city parks.

❸ **Laguna la Redonda** (p309) Taking the controls of a speedboat through the mangrove-fringed channels of this freshwater lake.

❹ **Florencia** (p310) Taking to the hills on horseback in the bucolic paths and lanes of northern Ciego.

❺ **Cayo Guillermo** (p314) Following 'Papa' Hemingway and taking to the waters of the Gulf Stream for deep-sea fishing or kiteboarding.

❻ **Playa Pilar** (p314) Finding out if this is really the finest beach in Cuba.

❼ **Jardines de la Reina** (p310) Exploring the clear seas of Cuba's finest diving archipelago from a floating hotel.

Ciego de Ávila

POP 110,400

Orgullo (pride) surges through Ciego de Ávila in improbably large doses for a settlement of such diminutive stature. But proud or not, Ciego isn't one of Cuba's more interesting provincial capitals, although its colonnaded streets are attractive enough. Founded in 1840, the city grew up originally in the 1860s and '70s as a military town behind the defensive Morón–Júcaro (Trocha) line; it later became an important processing center for the region's lucrative sugarcane and pineapple crops (the pineapple is the local mascot). Ciego's inhabitants refer to their city as 'the city of porches,' a reference to the ornate, colonnaded house-fronts which characterize the center.

Famous *avileños* include Cuban pop-art exponent Raúl Martínez and local socialite Ángela Hernández, the rich widow of Señor Jiménez who helped finance many of the city's early 20th-century neoclassical buildings, including the Teatro Principal.

Ciego are currently Cuba's best baseball team, having won the national series thrice since 2012.

Sights

Ciego de Ávila has endeavored to ensure it waylays you, with a recently reconfigured three-block boulevard, appealing parks, and museums which promulgate a relatively low-key history in an interesting and relevant way.

Parque de la Ciudad PARK

() The once scrubby wasteland between Hotel Ciego de Ávila (p304) and the city center, on the northwestern edge of town, is now a vast park featuring an artificial lake, the Embalse la Turbina, with boating available, children's playgrounds and good eateries. With its offbeat attractions and amiable understatedness, it's one of Cuba's most interesting urban regeneration projects.

It's also testimony to the wonders achievable with scrap: old steam trains have been dusted off in homage to Ciego's transport history; there's impressive *artes plásticos* (art pieces) including an elephant statue fashioned from old car parts; and, among the eating possibilities, an old Aerocaribbean aircraft converted into a restaurant.

The lake fills a hole left by an old quarry that used to provide stone for the Trocha defensive wall in the 1860s and the Carretera Central in the 1920s.

Museo Provincial Simón Reyes MUSEUM

(cnr Honorato del Castillo & Máximo Gómez; CUC$1; 9am-5pm Tue-Sat, 8am-noon Sun) One of Cuba's best-presented municipal museums, this mustard-yellow building with a typical *avileño* porch is one convertible well spent. Riveting exhibits include a scale model of La Trocha, detailed information on Afro-Cuban culture and religion, and explanations on the province's rich collection of traditional festivals. There are also indigenous artifacts from the nearby Los Buchillones (p308) archaeological site

Museo de Artes Decorativas MUSEUM

(cnr Independencia & Marcial Gómez; CUC$1; 9am-5pm Mon-Thu, 1-9pm Sat, 9am-noon Sun) Cuba's most beautiful beds? Not in Varadero, nor in one of the island's classic colonial stop-offs, but downstairs at this modest museum. The thoughtful collection contains items from a bygone age, such as a working Victrola (Benny Moré serenades your visit) and antique pocket watches. Up top, the exhibits impress with ornate oriental art: check the striking Chinese screen.

Come here for piano recitals at 3pm on Saturdays.

Parque Martí SQUARE

All Ciego roads lead to this textbook colonial park laid out in 1877 in honor of then king of Spain, Alfonso XII, but renamed in the early 20th century for newly martyred Cuban national hero, José Martí. Here you'll find a 1947 church, the **Iglesia Católica** (Independencia, btwn Marcial Gómez & Honorato del Castillo), and a 1911 **Ayuntamiento** (City Hall; no visitors).

Centro de Promoción Cultural Guiarte GALLERY

(Independencia No 65; 8am-9pm Tue-Fri & Sun, 8am-11pm Sat) FREE On Calle Independencia, this gallery has works by Raúl Martínez, Cuba's king of pop art, on permanent display, alongside works by other local artists.

Sleeping

★ **Villa Jabón Candado** CASA PARTICULAR $

(33-22-58-54; cnr Chico Valdés & Abraham Delgado; r CUC$20-25; P) Tired cyclists and drivers, look no further: here's a bright-pink detached place that's easy to find, with owners who have accrued years of experience in the trade. The two rooms are clean, with the

Ciego de Ávila

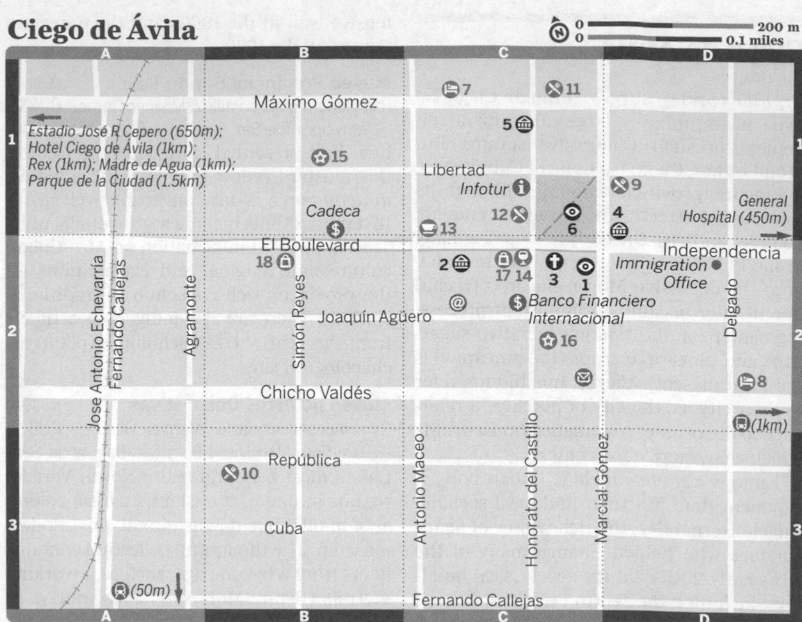

upstairs (balcony included) being the best, and there's a carport.

María Luisa Muñoz Álvarez CASA PARTICULAR $
(52-39-39-95; Máximo Gómez No 74, btwn Honorato del Castillo & Antonio Maceo; r CUC$25; P ❄) Two clean rooms off a looong corridor culminating in a patio equals textbook private-rental standard, with no real quirks. Only a block from the center.

Hotel Ciego de Ávila HOTEL $
(33-22-80-13; Carretera a de Ceballos Km 1.5; s/d incl breakfast CUC$32/44; P ❄ @ ≈) Where have all the tourists gone? Cayo Coco probably, leaving this Islazul staple the domain of Cuban sports teams and workers on government-sponsored vacation time. Located 2km from the city center and overlooking Parque de la Ciudad, it has bog-standard rooms, a noisy swimming-pool area and boring breakfasts, but the staff seem friendly.

Eating

Fonda la Estrella CUBAN $
(33-26-61-86; Honorato del Castillo No 34, cnr Máximo Gómez; mains CUC$2-3; noon-10pm) Serving what is possibly the cheapest edible *ropa vieja* (spicy stewed beef) in Cuba, La Fonda (as it's always known), is a tiny corner bar where none of the dishes on the laconic menu break CUC$3. And everything comes with rice and beans. A budget traveler's paradise.

El Camarote INTERNATIONAL $
(República No 183, btwn Reyes & Agramonte; mains CUC$2-4; 6:30-11pm) Despite its strategic geographical position, Ciego isn't oozing good private restaurants – yet. For some respite, pop into this modest little place three blocks from the Carretera Central for pizza, tacos, spaghetti or the house special: grilled fish topped with prawns, bechamel and – er – cheese.

Madre de Agua CUBAN $
(Parque de la Ciudad; mains MN$25-150; noon-10pm) The *restaurante flotante* (floating restaurant) is raised on stilts above the waters of Embalse la Turbina in Parque de la Ciudad, Ciego's commendable urban-regeneration project. It sells basic, but OK, Cuban nosh in pesos. The setting is lovely.

Solaris FUSION $
(33-22-34-24; Doce Plantas Bldg, cnr Honorato del Castillo & Libertad; mains CUC$1-5; 11am-11pm; ❄) City-center joint on the 12th floor of the rather ugly Doce Plantas building that recently reopened after a year-long

Ciego de Ávila

Sights

Sleeping

Eating

Drinking & Nightlife

Entertainment

Shopping

refurbishment. Excellent city views, and it has now added a terrace and a *parrillada* (barbecue). As before, cordon bleu (chicken stuffed with ham and cheese), which it refers to as 'Gordon Bleu,' headlines the menu.

Don Ávila CARIBBEAN **$$**
(Marcial Gómez, cnr Libertad; mains CUC$1-5; ⌚11am-11pm; ❄) Plaza-abutting Don Ávila impresses with its regal ambience, on-site cigar outlet, old-gents-style bar, typically friendly *avileño* service and cheap prices. The *comida criolla* (Creole food) is less spectacular but plentiful.

Drinking & Nightlife

Piña Colada BAR
(cnr Independencia & Honorato del Castillo; ⌚3pm-2am) Proudly mixing Caribbean cocktails with Antarctic air-con since 2011.

La Fontana CAFE
(cnr Independencia & Antonio Maceo; ⌚6am-2pm & 3-11pm) Ciego's long-standing coffee institution has seen better days. Still if you just want a *cafecito* will no ceremony, milk, take-out cup or wi-fi, it can probably oblige.

Entertainment

Teatro Principal THEATER
(cnr Joaquín Agüero & Honorato del Castillo) One block south of Parque Martí, the grand Teatro Principal more than compensates for the park's lack of illustrious edifices. Built in 1927 with help from local financier Ángela Hernández de Jiménez, it purportedly has the island's best (theatrical) acoustics. Check the poster board for performances.

Estadio José R Cepero SPECTATOR SPORT
(Máximo Gómez) October to April, baseball games take place to the northwest of Ciego's center. The town's Tigres have experienced a dramatic turnaround in fortune of late and are currently Cuba's best team, bagging the Cuban National Series in 2012, 2015 and 2016.

Casa de la Trova Miguel Ángel Luna LIVE MUSIC
(Libertad No 130; ⌚noon-6pm & 9pm-1am Tue-Sun) In the dice-roll of traditional musical entertainment, Ciego's *trova* (national poetic singing) house scores a magic six with polished Thursday-night regional *trovadores* in a pleasant colonial setting.

Shopping

La Época GIFTS & SOUVENIRS
(Independencia, btwn Antonio Maceo & Honorato del Castillo; ⌚9am-5pm Mon-Sat) This is an ARTex souvenir store rather than the well-known Cuban department store. It's on two levels selling everything from arty parasols to Cuban flags.

Librería Juan A Márquez BOOKS
(Independencia Oeste No 153, cnr Simón Reyes; ⌚9am-5pm Mon-Fri, 9am-noon Sat) Revolutionary tomes for ardent lefties.

Information

INTERNET ACCESS

Etecsa Telepunto (Joaquín Agüero No 62; internet per hour CUC$1.50; ⌚8:30am-7pm) Sells internet cards.

Parque Martí A wi-fi hotspot.

MEDICAL SERVICES

General Hospital (☎33-22-40-15; Máximo Gómez No 257)

MONEY

Banco Financiero Internacional (cnr Honorato del Castillo & Joaquín Agüero Oeste; ⏰9am-3pm Mon-Fri)

Cadeca (Independencia Oeste No 118, btwn Antonio Maceo & Simón Reyes; ⏰8:30am-12:30pm)

POST

Post Office (cnr Chicho Valdés & Marcial Gómez; ⏰8am-5pm Mon-Sat)

TOURIST INFORMATION

Infotur (☎33-20-91-09; Doce Plantas Bldg, cnr Honorato del Castillo & Libertad; ⏰9am-noon & 1-6pm) Possibly Cuba's friendliest, most informative Infotur office.

Getting There & Away

BUS

The **bus station** (Carretera Central), situated about 1.5km east of Ciego de Ávila's center, has multiple daily Víazul (www.viazul.com) services.

Santiago de Cuba buses also stop at Camagüey (CUC$6, 1½ hours), Las Tunas (CUC$12, 4½ hours), Holguín (CUC$17, 5¼ hours) and Bayamo (CUC$17, six hours). Havana buses also stop at Sancti Spíritus (CUC$6, 1½ hours) and Santa Clara (CUC$9, 2½ hours). Book ahead online or in person at the terminal.

TAXI

The common procedure when a Víazul bus is full is to hang around outside the bus station and wait for a *colectivo* (shared taxi). More often than not, you'll find other travelers with a similar conundrum. Up to four people can share a Cubataxi; the going rate is around CUC$0.55 per kilometer.

TRAIN

The **train station** (☎33-22-33-13) is six blocks southwest of Ciego de Ávila's center. Ciego is on the main Havana–Santiago railway line. There are sporadic trains to Havana (CUC$15.50, 7½ hours), Bayamo (CUC$10.50, seven hours), Camagüey (CUC$3.50, 2¼ hours), Holguín (CUC$11, seven hours), Guantánamo (CUC$17, 9½ hours) and Santiago de Cuba (CUC$14, 9¼ hours). There are also four trains daily to Morón (CUC$1, one hour).

The timetable is notoriously fickle and the trains tatty at best. Check at least a day before you want to leave.

Getting Around

The **Carretera a Morón gas station** (Carretera a Morón) is just before the bypass road, northeast of the town center. The **Oro Negro gas station** (Carretera Central) is near the bus station.

Rex (Hotel Ciego de Ávila, Carretera a Ceballos; ⏰8:30am-7:30pm) can help with vehicle and moped rental.

Morón

POP 59,200

Despite its slightly removed position 35km north of Cuba's arterial Carretera Central, Morón remains an important travel nexus (thanks to its railway) and acts as a viable base camp for people not enamored with resort-heaving Cayo Coco.

Founded in 1543, three centuries before provincial capital Ciego de Ávila, Morón is known island-wide as the Ciudad del Gallo (City of the Cockerel), for a 'cocky' bullying official in the colonial era who eventually got his comeuppance. The city has architecture to match its years, with more, better-preserved examples of those Ciego de Ávila column-flanked facades.

Also in evidence are some excellent casas particulares and a surprisingly varied list of things to do in the surrounding countryside. The city itself is easy-going and compact. Many independent travelers love it.

Sights

Morón is famous for its emblematic cockerel, which stands guard on a roundabout opposite the Hotel Morón on the southern edge of town. It's named after a 'cocky' and abusive 16th-century official who got his just deserts at the hands of locals and was driven

BUSES FROM CIEGO DE ÁVILA

DESTINATION	COST (CUC$)	DURATION (HR)	DEPARTURES
Havana	27	6½	12:50am, 2:25am, 5:50am, 2pm, 3:40pm
Santiago de Cuba	24	8½	3am, 4:30am, 10:45am, 1:15pm, 10:20pm
Trinidad	9	2¾	4:25am
Varadero	19	6½	4:55am

out of town. The cock crows (electronically) at 6am every morning.

Terminal de Ferrocarriles NOTABLE BUILDING
(Train Station; Vanhorne, btwn Av de Tarafa & Narciso López) Morón has long been central Cuba's main railway crossroads and exhibits the most elegant railway station outside Havana. Built in 1923, the building's edifice is neocolonial, though inside the busy ticket hall hides a more streamlined art deco look. Equally eye-catching is the stained-glass skylight. Like many things in provincial Cuba, it's crying out for a sympathetic restoration.

Museo Caonabo MUSEUM
(Martí No 374, btwn Cervantes & Antuña; CUC$1; 9am-5pm Mon-Sat, 8am-noon Sun) In among the teeming sidewalks and peeling colonnades, this well-laid-out museum of history and archaeology is housed in Morón's former bank, an impressive neoclassical building dating from 1919. There is a rooftop *mirador* (lookout) with a good view out over town.

Central Patria o Muerte HISTORIC SITE
(Patria; incl tour CUC$3; 8am-5pm) Cuba's sugar industry is preserved at this huge, rusting ex-sugar mill founded in 1914 in the village of Patria, 3km south of Morón. Guides explain the sugar-milling process from slave times to the factory's decommissioning in 2001. For an extra CUC$4, a 1920 Philadelphia-made Baldwin steam train can take you on a 5km ride through cane fields to Rancho Palma, a bucolic *finca* (farm) with a bar-restaurant where you can sample *guarapo* (pressed cane juice).

The mill and its 263-strong workforce were passed over to the Americans in 1919, and it remained in Yanqui hands until nationalization in 1960.

Sleeping

★Alojamiento Maité CASA PARTICULAR $
(33-50-41-81; maite68@enet.cu; Luz Caballero No 40b, btwn Libertad & Agramonte; r CUC$25-30; P ❄ @ ≋) Surely one of the most professionally run casas in Cuba, Maité's place is reason alone to visit Morón. Relax by the small pool, or on the breezy roof terrace, or in one of the large well-appointed rooms equipped with complimentary bathroom bags, well-stocked minibars (with wine) and starched white sheets (changed daily).

Best of all is the tireless host and her staff who will not only make your stay memorable, they'll convince you that Morón is one of the most underrated small towns in Cuba.

There are five rooms. Book ahead.

Alojamiento Vista al Parque CASA PARTICULAR $
(33-50-41-81; yio@hgm.cav.sld.cu; Luz Caballero No 49d Altos, btwn Libertad & Agramonte; r CUC$25-30; P ❄ @) There's comfort and slick service in this lovely pale-blue house with three rooms (two of them apartments) with a couple of terraces and views across the well-tended park. It's run by Idolka (who speaks some English) and is affiliated to Alojamiento Maité opposite.

Casa Belkis CASA PARTICULAR $
(33-50-57-63; Cristobal Colón No 37; r CUC$20-25; ❄) Just one haughty colonial room but it's a whopper, and with a view onto Parque los Ferrocarriles in possibly the most idyllic location in town. Just northeast of the train station (p308).

La Casona de Morón HISTORIC HOTEL $
(33-50-22-36; Colón No 41; s/d CUC$34/45; P ❄ ≋) Ostensibly scruffy, Morón is a town of many secrets and here's one of them – a beautiful yellow-and-white plantation house with a two-level wraparound porch made into a small hotel. There are eight simple rooms, attractive colonial embellishments and a lovely outside pool in shady grounds. It has long been favored by Morón's small but active hunting and fishing fraternity.

Eating

Restaurante Maité la Qbana INTERNATIONAL $$
(33-50-41-81; Luz Caballero No 40, btwn Libertad & Agramonte; mains CUC$10-15; noon-11pm;) Maité is a highly creative cook whose international dishes, prepared with *mucho amor*, will leave you wondering why insipid all-inclusive buffets ever got so popular. Prepare for al dente pasta, fine wine, homemade cakes and paella that has visiting *valencianos* reminiscing about their homeland. It's a good idea to reserve early.

Don Papa CUBAN $$
(Enrique Varona No 56, btwn Calles 5 & 6; mains CUC$7; noon-midnight) Despite being draped with international flags, Don Papa is 100% *cubano*. The food here is simply delicious and also abundant. Meat, fish and lobster come with lashings of root vegetables, plantains, rice and beans and there's a 'side order' of live music. It's a modest place in a

OFF THE BEATEN TRACK

LOS BUCHILLONES

Tucked away on Ciego de Ávila Province's northwest coastline, the Los Buchillones archaeological site was originally excavated during the 1980s after fishermen began discovering implements such as ax handles and needles in the surrounding swamps.

What became apparent was that Los Buchillones was the location of a sizeable Taíno settlement of between 40 and 50 houses, pre-dating European arrival in the region. Everything from *cemíes* (Taíno deities to various Gods of rain, cassava and the like) to canoes to house structures have been subsequently recovered from the excavation site, most of which remains a waterlogged work in progress. The mud at the bottom of the shallow lagoon here was what preserved the artifacts so well and yielded the most significant stash of pre-Columbian relics anywhere in the Greater Antilles.

Many of the artifacts can be seen in either the **Museo Municipal** (Agramonte No 80, btwn Calixto García & Martí; CUC$1; ⌚8am-5pm Mon-Thu, 8am-9pm Fri, 1-9pm Sat, 9am-noon Sun) in Chambas or in Ciego de Ávila's Museo Provincial Simón Reyes (p303). However, anyone with a passing interest in pre-Columbian Cuba should make the trip to the poignant site, complete with a small museum displaying finds, halfway between the fishing village of Punta Alegre and Punta San Juan. A handful of trains pass Chambas, from where Los Buchillones is a 35km drive (public transportation is scarce) through Parque Nacional Caguanes.

backstreet stapled to the side of an average Morón house.

Drinking & Nightlife

Discoteca Morón CLUB
(Hotel Morón, Av de Tarafa; ⌚10pm-late) Young, raucous entertainment-seekers test the patience of sleep-deprived paying guests at the Hotel Morón.

Entertainment

Casa de la Trova Pablo Bernal LIVE MUSIC
(Martí No 169; ⌚8pm-11pm) Vibrant alfresco music house with popular Wednesday comedy night.

Information

INTERNET ACCESS

You'll find internet at Morón's **Etecsa** (El Centro Multiservicio de Morón; cnr Martí & Céspedes; per hour CUC$1.50; ⌚8:30am-7:30pm), and the park outside is a wi-fi hot spot.

MEDICAL SERVICES

Hospital Multiclínica Roberto Rodríguez (☎33-50-50-11; Zayas, btwn Libertad & Teneria; ⌚24hrs) Centrally located, three blocks east of Martí.

MONEY

There are several ATMs on the main street, Calle Martí.

Cadeca (cnr Martí & Gonzalo Arena; ⌚9am-4:40pm Mon-Sat, 9am-noon Sun) Money-changing facilities.

TOURIST INFORMATION

Information on Lagunas de la Leche and la Redonda can be procured at **Cubatur** (Martí No 169; ⌚9am-5pm) in the Casa de la Trova. It is also possible to arrange tours to Florencia (p310).

Getting There & Away

BUS

Morón is, somewhat unfairly, a transport conundrum with no Víazul bus connections. The nearest buses stop in the city of Ciego de Ávila, from where a taxi will cost around CUC$15 to CUC$20 (40 minutes).

Morón's **bus station** (Martí No 12) is a block back towards the center (north) from the train station and has local buses which are sadly not a lot of good for travelers.

TRAIN

Morón was once an important rail terminus, and the glorious **train station** (Vanhorne, btwn Av de Tarafa & Narciso López) is legendary, but the trains aren't (late, unreliable and in poor state of repair). There are supposedly three to four daily trains to Ciego de Ávila (CUC$1, one hour) where you can pick up services on Cuba's main Havana–Santiago line (or a bus). There are also connections to Camagüey (CUC$3, four hours, daily) and Santa Clara (CUC$4, six hours, every other day).

Getting Around

The roads from Morón northwest to Caibarién (112km) and southeast to Nuevitas (168km) are good. Rental cars are in short supply and it pays to reserve a vehicle several days ahead of when you need it: try **Cubacar** (☎33-50-22-30; Hotel Morón, Av de Tarafa; ⏲9am-5pm). The **Servi-Cupet gas station** (Carretera a Ciego de Ávila; ⏲24hr) is one block south of Hotel Morón.

For taxis, ask your casa particular owner or try outside the train station. Bank on paying around CUC$0.55 per kilometer for out-of-town journeys.

We wouldn't recommend the local buses.

Around Morón

Laguna de la Leche & Laguna la Redonda

Aquatic action creates significant waves at these two large natural lakes just north of Morón, where fish are abundant and you can hire your own motor boat to make a splash in the mangroves. Both lakes offer food, fishing trips and various boating options. Smaller Redonda is on the Cayo Coco day-trip circuit and has better tourist infrastructure. Closer to Morón, the expansive Laguna de la Leche guards a more local scene.

Sights

★Laguna la Redonda LAKE
(⏲9am-5pm) Anglers, listen up: 12km north of Morón, off the Cayo Coco road, this mangrove-rimmed, 4-sq-km lake has the island's best square-kilometer density of bass and trout. Four hours of fishing costs CUC$70. Boat trips are available too, and take in narrow, foliage-covered tributaries – as close to the Amazon as the province comes. You'll even be allowed to take the wheel if you want! But if you're not a fishing fanatic, just rock up at the decent, rustic bar-restaurant for a drink or fish meal with a lake view.

Laguna de la Leche LAKE
Laguna de la Leche (Milk Lake), named for its reflective underwater lime deposits, is Cuba's largest natural lake (66 sq km). Its water content is a mixture of fresh and salt water, and anglers flock here to hook the abundant stocks of carp, tarpon, snook and tilapia. Guided fishing trips (CUC$70 for four hours) can be arranged at the main southern-shore entrance.

For a little more you can keep your catch and cook it on a mobile barbecue aboard a ship. Nonfishing boat excursions (CUC$20 for 45 minutes) are also available.

The lake is also the venue for the annual Morón Aquatic Carnival, usually held in September.

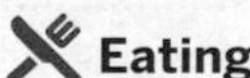

Eating

Restaurant Laguna la Redonda FISH $
(mains CUC$4-8; ⏲10am-5pm) This restaurant at the entrance to Laguna la Redonda is good for *comida criolla* or a drink with a lake view. Try the house specialty, a fillet of fish called *calentico* – great with ketchup and Tabasco.

La Atarraya FISH $
(mains CUC$2-7; ⏲noon-6pm) Raised on stilts in a clapboard building off the southern shoreline of Laguna de la Leche, you'll find one of Cuba's best local fish restaurants. The insanely cheap menu is headlined by *paella valenciana* and *pescado monteroro* (fish fillet with ham and cheese), while the ambience is ebulliently local.

Entertainment

Cabaret Cueva CABARET
(Laguna de la Leche; ⏲10pm-late Thu-Sun) Locals willingly hitch, walk or carpool to make the 6km trip from Morón to this cabaret, held in a cave on the southern shores of Laguna de la Leche.

Loma de Cunagua

Rising like a huge termite mound above the surrounding flatlands, **Loma de Cunagua** (CUC$5; ⏲9am-4pm), a wild, foliage-covered *loma* (hill), is a protected (since 1985) flora and fauna reserve harboring a *ranchón*-style restaurant, a small network of trails and excellent birdwatching opportunities. At 364m above sea level, it's Ciego de Ávila Province's highest point and views over land and ocean are expansive.

The reserve's short bushy trails are ideal places to spot tocororos (Cuban trogons), *zunzunes* (bee hummingbirds) and the like, and guides are usually multilingual and highly knowledgeable.

For independent travelers wishing to access the reserve, it's best to phone ahead rather than just turn up. Visits are normally arranged through **Ecotur** (☎33-30-81-63; Hotel Sol Cayo Coco; ⏲9am-5pm) on Cayo Coco, who will subsequently ensure that a naturalist guide is on hand to lead you around the (unsignposted) trails and explain the unusual flora and fauna.

OFF THE BEATEN TRACK

JARDINES DE LA REINA

The uninhabited Jardines de la Reina is a 120km-long mangrove-forest and coral-island system situated 80km off the south coast of Ciego de Ávila Province and 120km north of the Cayman Islands. The local marine park measures 3800 sq km, and is virgin territory left more or less untouched since the time of Columbus. It's the best place to dive in Cuba (nay, the Caribbean), but only allows a tiny trickle of visitors in annually on half-a-dozen live-aboard boats.

Commercial fishing in the area has been banned, and with a permanent local population of precisely zero inhabitants, divers must stay on board a two-story, eight-bedroom houseboat called *Hotel Flotante Tortuga,* or venture in from the port of Embarcadero de Júcaro (on the mainland) aboard one of five well-appointed yachts.

The flora consists of palm trees, pines, sea grapes and mangroves, while the fauna – aside from tree rats and iguanas – contains an interesting variety of resident birds, including ospreys, pelicans, spoonbills and egrets. Below the waves the main attraction is sharks (whale and hammerhead) and this, along with the pristine coral and the unequaled clarity of the water, is what draws divers from all over the world.

Getting to the Jardines is not easy – or cheap. The only way in is on a diving excursion with the Italian-run **Avalon** (www.cubandivingcenters.com). One-week dive packages, which include equipment, seven nights of accommodation, guide, park license, 12 dives and food and drink, cost from CUC$3250 and up. Ask for a quote via the website. Another company, **Windward Islands Cruising Company** (www.windward-islands.net), incorporates the western tip of the archipelago into its one-week Cuba cruises.

You'll need a car (or taxi) to reach the reserve, which is located 18km east of Morón (signposted). After paying your entry fee at the gate, a 7km-long unpaved leads to the summit from where the walks start. A couple of **cabins** (☎33-30-81-63; r CUC$30) offer basic overnight accommodation for those in search of some rural tranquility. There's also a simple restaurant and lookout tower.

Florencia

Ringed by gentle hills, the somnolent town of Florencia, 40km west of Morón, was named after Florence in Italy – early settlers claimed the surrounding countryside reminded them of Tuscany. In the early 1990s the Cuban government constructed a hydroelectric dam, the Liberación de Florencia, on the Río Chambas and the resulting lake has created an unexpectedly beautiful juxtaposition of water and greenery. With its low-key rural activities and nearby nature reserve at Boquerón, Florencia makes an excellent day trip from Morón.

Activities

There are two trips that can be organized in the Florencia area. The first is a horse-ride and hike in the hills surrounding the lake to a tobacco-growing farm, followed by a boat-ride to the lake's sole island with its rustic restaurant for lunch, relaxation and kayaking.

The other is a horse-ride/hike in the nearby Boquerón nature reserve following the course of the Río Jatibonico where you can swim and explore some caves.

To organize either excursion, it's best to phone ahead to **La Esquinita** (☎33-55-92-94; cnr Martí & Agramonte; ⏲9am-8pm).

Eating

Restaurante Presa de Florencia CUBAN $

(mains CUC$3.50-5; ⏲9am-5pm) A traditional open-sided restaurant under a thatched shelter on a small island in the middle of the Florencia reservoir. It serves straight-up Cuban food using whatever ingredients are available that day. Price is usually included in excursion packages which can be organized in either Cubatur (p308) in Morón or La Esquinita (above).

Getting There & Away

There are no regular public transportation options to Florencia beyond the local trucks and buses which run on sketchy schedules. Your best bet is to use a rental car or to hire a taxi in Morón (rough cost one-way CUC$25, one hour).

Cayo Coco

Situated in the Archipiélago de Sabana-Camagüey, or the Jardines del Rey (King's Gardens) as travel brochures prefer to call it, Cayo Coco is Cuba's fourth-largest island, a 370-sq-km beach-rimmed key that is unashamedly dedicated to tourism. The area north of the Bahía de Perros (Bay of Dogs) was uninhabited before 1992, when the first hotel – the Cojímar – went up on adjoining Cayo Guillermo. The bulldozers haven't stopped buzzing since.

Cayo Coco largely resembles Cayo Santa María to the west (which it predates), although the latter is now larger in terms of hotel capacity and star-rating. Since 1988, the island has been connected to the mainland by a 27km causeway slicing across the Bahía de Perros. There are also causeways from Cayo Coco to Cayo Guillermo in the west and to Cayo Romano in the east, as well as an international airport.

Sights & Activities

Cayo Paredón Grande ISLAND
(Map p312) East of Cayo Coco, a road crosses over to Cayo Romano (technically Camagüey Province) and turns north to Cayo Paredón Grande and Faro Diego Velázquez, a 52m lighthouse dating from 1859. This area has a couple of isolated beaches, including much-lauded Playa los Pinos, and is good for fishing. Get there soon! It's touted for future hotel development.

Rocarena CLIMBING
(Map p312; ☎33-30-21-29; Av de los Hoteles; CUC$25; ⏲9am-9pm; 👪) A rather ingeniously designed climbing extravaganza designed mainly for kids and teens, although adults can partake. Tons of pulleys, tightropes, swings, climbing walls and a mini bungee jump will keep you occupied for a couple of hours. There are expert guides and good safety harnesses. It's just west of Hotel Sol Cayo Coco.

Centro Internacional de Buceo Blue Diving DIVING
(Map p312; http://nauticamarlin.tur.cu/en; Meliá Cayo Coco) On the beach inside the Meliá Cayo Coco resort. Dives cost from CUC$45 for one immersion, and an introductory course in the swimming pool costs CUC$70 and includes one open-water dive. The diving area stretches for over 10km mainly to the east, and there are six certified instructors with the capacity for 30 divers per day.

Beware: the sea is choppy here, so dives are often canceled.

Marina Marlin Aguas Tranquilas FISHING
(Map p312; http://nauticamarlin.tur.cu/en) Cayo Coco's main marina is on the south-facing shore near the Meliá Cayo Coco and offers deep-sea fishing outings (CUC$310 per four hours).

Sleeping

Cayo Coco is an all-inclusive zone with all of the resorts enjoying direct beach access. Facilities vary from three- to five-star, but are fairly generic. There is no Cuban settlement on the island and thus no private homestays for rent. The best bet for indie travelers is the rustic but cheap Sitio la Güira.

Sitio la Güira CABIN $
(Map p312; ☎33-39812; cabaña CUC$25; ❄) Backpackers aren't well catered for on Cuba's resort islands, except perhaps at this simple abode, an imitation of an erstwhile charcoal-burner's camp. Four pseudo-rustic *bohíos* (thatched huts) with private bathrooms and – get this – air-con (to dissuade the mosquitoes apparently) are available for rent. There's a *ranchón*-style restaurant and bar on-site.

★ Meliá Cayo Coco RESORT $$$
(Map p312; ☎33-29555; www.meliacuba.com; s/d all-inclusive CUC$265/378; P❄@📶🏊) This intimate resort on Playa las Coloradas, at the hotel strip's eastern end, is everything you'd expect from Spain's Meliá chain. For a luxury twist try staying in one of the elegant white bungalows perched on stilts in a lagoon. Prices are high, but the Meliá is unashamedly classy and a 'no kids' policy enhances the tranquility.

Pullman Cayo Coco RESORT $$$
(Map p312; ☎33-30-44-00; www.accorhotels.com; r all-inclusive from CUC$350; P❄@📶🏊) The Cayo's newest five-star opened in December 2015 and has bagged a large slice of once tranquil Playa las Coloradas. It comes in two different flavors – a family section and one for adults only – and early reports are good with punters hailing the service, beach and strong (for Cuba) wi-fi. However, like all new all-inclusives, it still seems a bit bare and antiseptic like some kind of characterless Toronto suburb (with a beach).

Cayo Coco & Cayo Guillermo

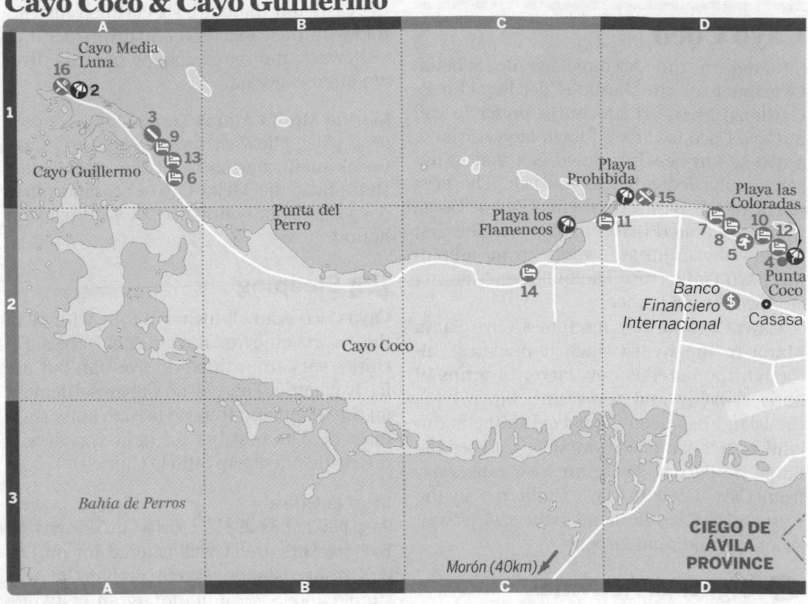

Cayo Coco & Cayo Guillermo

Sights
1 Cayo Paredón Grande F2
2 Playa Pilar A1

Activities, Courses & Tours
Boat Adventure ...... (see 6)
Centro Internacional de Buceo Blue Diving ...... (see 10)
3 Centro Internacional de Buceo Coco Diving A1
Ecotur ...... (see 10)
4 Marina Marlin Aguas Tranquilas D2
Marina Marlin Cayo Guillermo ...... (see 6)
5 Rocarena D2

Sleeping
6 Casa Gregorio A1
7 Colonial Cayo Coco D2
8 Hotel Tryp Cayo Coco D2
9 Iberostar Daiquirí A1
10 Meliá Cayo Coco D2
11 Meliá Jardines del Rey D2
12 Pullman Cayo Coco D2
13 Secortel Club Cayo Guillermo A1
14 Sitio la Güira C2

Eating
15 Lenny's Lobster Shack D1
Rancho Flamingo ...... (see 11)
16 Ranchón Playa Pilar A1

Shopping
Plaza Los Flamencos ...... (see 11)

Information
Clínica Internacional Cayo Coco ...... (see 7)

Meliá Jardines del Rey RESORT **$$$**
(Map p312; ☎33-30-43-00; www.meliacuba.com; s/d all-inclusive CUC$186/232; P ❄ @ ☎ ≋) The big kahuna of Cuba resorts (1176 rooms), this five-star place, which opened in 2014, constitutes a small town with golf carts to get around, maps to aid navigation and more restaurants than the nearby city of Morón. Common areas feature earthy woods and Ikea-like minimalism, while rooms are punctuated with some welcome color accents and decorated in a bold contemporary style.

Colonial Cayo Coco RESORT **$$$**
(Map p312; ☎33-30-13-11; www.hotelescubanacan.com; s/d all-inclusive CUC$148/190;

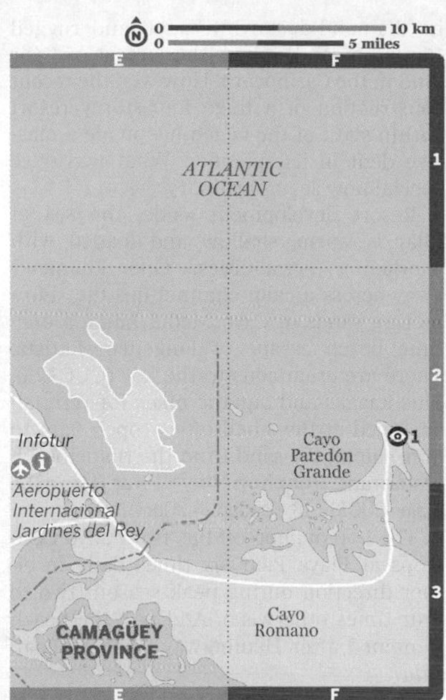

(P ❄ @ Wi-Fi pool) The Spanish-colonial villas with attractively tiled public areas lend the Colonial a cloistered, refined air – a pleasant break from the standard unadorned design of the usual Cuban all-inclusives.

This was the island's first hotel when it opened in 1993 (ancient history by Cayo Coco standards) and it remains handsomer than a lot of its younger siblings.

Hotel Tryp Cayo Coco RESORT **$$$**
(Map p312; ☎33-30-13-00; www.meliacuba.com; s/d all-inclusive CUC$173/216; P ❄ @ Wi-Fi pool) The family choice. Tryp is a quintessential all-inclusive with a meandering pool, myriad bars and nightly tourist shows. Facilities are good, although overzealous poolside 'entertainers' lend the place a holiday-camp feel at times. The 500-plus rooms – in sunny three-story apartment blocks – are big, with balconies and huge beds, although finishes are a little worn. The four-star rating is generous.

Eating

Amid the ubiquitous as-much-as-you-can-eat hotel buffets in Cayo Coco, there are a few indie restaurants, mainly fronting the beaches.

Rancho Flamingo CARIBBEAN **$**
(Map p312; Playa los Flamencos; mains CUC$4-10; ⏰10am-7:30pm; P) Eat exquisite seafood, drink cold beer, swim, sunbathe, drink more beer...you get the picture. The Flamingo guards a small scoop of public beach in the shadow of Cuba's largest resort.

Lenny's Lobster Shack SEAFOOD **$$**
(Map p312; Playa Prohibida; mains CUC$7-15; ⏰10am-7:30pm) Named unofficially after a Canadian tourist and regular patron, Lenny's is a beautiful opened-sided thatched rondavel on hotel-free Playa Prohibida decorated with old Canadian license plates and famed for one dish – the lobster, prawn and fish medley – CUC$15 (!) well-spent. The house band, Coco Indio, is usually augmented by several passing diners.

Shopping

Plaza Los Flamencos SHOPPING CENTER
(Map p312) New shopping plaza just outside the entrance to the Meliá Jardines del Rey with souvenir and clothes shops, a bowling alley and a spa open to all comers.

Information

MONEY

All of Cayo Coco's resorts have money exchanges. Rates are marginally better than the bank.

Banco Financiero Internacional (Map p312; Rotunda, 4 Caminos; ⏰8:30am-5pm Mon-Sat)

MEDICAL SERVICES

Clínica Internacional Cayo Coco (Map p312; ☎33-30-21-58; Colonial Cayo Coco; ⏰9am-5pm) Provides medical treatment. Located at Colonial Cayo Coco.

TOURIST INFORMATION

Infotur (Map p312; ☎33-30-91-09; www.infotur.cu; Jardines del Rey Airport; ⏰8:30am-5pm) Has a helpful office at the airport, as well as desks at the main hotels. Ciego de Ávila's Infotur (p306) office has bundles of information on Cayo Coco, too.

Getting There & Away

AIR

Cayo Coco's **Aeropuerto Internacional Jardines del Rey** (Map p312; ☎33-30-91-65) can process 1.2 million visitors annually. Weekly flights arrive here from Canada, the UK, the US, France, Argentina and more. There's a daily service to and from Havana (about CUC$110; three hours with stop), usually via Holguín, with Aerogaviota (www.aerogaviota.com).

TAXI

A taxi to Cayo Coco from Morón will cost about CUC$40 (one hour); from Ciego de Ávila, CUC$60 (1¾ hours). You pay a CUC$2 fee to enter the causeway.

Getting Around

Getting around both Cayo Coco and Cayo Guillermo has become infinitely easier since the introduction of a Transtur hop-on, hop-off, open-topped double-decker bus. The service varies according to season, but expect a minimum service of two buses per day in either direction, with six scheduled for peak times. The bus runs east–west between Pullman Cayo Coco and Playa Pilar, stopping at all Cayo Coco and Cayo Guillermo hotels. An all-day pass costs CUC$5. The full journey takes 50 minutes with stops.

You can rent a car or moped in any of the hotels with **Cubacar** (www.cubacar.info; per day from CUC$70).

Some of the hotels also have (free) bicycles available, although they might not be Tour de France worthy.

Cayo Guillermo

Ah, Cayo Guillermo: haunt of pink flamingos, agreeably blond beaches and Cuba's second-most famous Ernesto after Mr Guevara – Señor Hemingway. It was Hemingway who initiated Guillermo's early publicity drive, describing it radiantly in his posthumously published Cuban novel *Islands in the Stream* (1970). Development of the northern cayos took off here in 1993 when the first of six all-inclusive resorts, Villa Cojímar, received its formative guests. Long a prized deep-sea fishing spot, 13-sq-km Guillermo has recently morphed into Cuba's most prized kiteboarding spot thanks to its stiff north-coast winds. The mangroves off the south coast remain home to pink flamingos and pelicans, and there's a tremendous diversity of tropical fish and crustaceans on the Atlantic reef.

Would Hemingway like it today? Probably not. Notwithstanding, a statue of the laconic writer, who once revered Guillermo for its solitude and fishing, guards the entry bridge.

Sights & Activities

Playa Pilar BEACH

(Map p312) This much sought-after strip of sand is regularly touted as Cuba's (and the Caribbean's) best beach, courtesy of its diamond-dust white sand and rugged 15m-high sand dunes (the largest of their kind in the Caribbean). However, the recent construction of a huge four-storey resort within sight of the beach has made a massive dent in its splendor. What was once special now seems ordinary.

Resort development aside, the sea at Pilar is warm, shallow and loaded with snorkeling possibilities. One kilometer away across a calm channel lies the shimmering sands of Cayo Media Luna, a one-time beach escape of Fulgencio Batista. There are excursions to the key (CUC$25), plus kayaks and aquatic bikes for rent, all arranged at the small office (open 9am to 3pm) along the sand from the rustic beach restaurant, **Ranchón Playa Pilar** (Map p312; mains CUC$12-18; ⌚10am-4:30pm).

The hop-on, hop-off bus from Cayo Coco stops at Playa Pilar six times daily in either direction during peak season (two to four times otherwise). And yes, the beach is named after Hemingway's fishing boat, *Pilar*.

Marina Marlin Cayo Guillermo FISHING

(Map p312; ☎33-30-15-15; http://nauticamarlin.tur.cu/en) On the right of the causeway as you arrive from Cayo Coco, this 36-berth marina is one of Cuba's certified international entry ports. You can organize deep-sea fishing for mackerel, pike, barracuda, red snapper and marlin in Hemingway's former playground on large boats that troll 5km to 13km offshore. Prices start at CUC$310 per half-day (four persons).

Centro Internacional de Buceo Coco Diving DIVING

(Map p312; www.amazingcocodiving.com) Recently relocated from Cayo Coco to Cayo Guillermo (based at the Meliá Cayo Guillermo). Multilingual (four languages) dives from CUC$45 for one immersion.

Tours

Boat Adventure BOATING

(Map p312; 2hr boat trip CUC$46) This popular activity has its own separate dock on the left-hand side of the causeway as you enter Guillermo. The two-hour motorboat trip (with a chance to operate the controls) takes you through the key's natural mangrove channels. Trips leave four times daily starting from 9am.

CUBA'S KITESURFING CAPITAL

You'll glimpse the many multicoloured sails as you approach Cayo Guillermo before anything else comes into focus. The latest craze, kiteboarding, has now taken off all over northern Cuba, but many of the experts claim this small isle so loved by Hemingway has the best combo of wind, waves and kite-friendly hotels. There are several operators based here, including the Italian-run **Havana Kiteboarding Club** (☎58-04-96-56 ; www.havanakite.com ; Plaza Cobre , btwn 12 & 14, Tarará), who operate out of the Secortel Club Cayo Guillermo. A basic kiteboarding lesson costs around CUC$150; weekly courses start at around CUC$650. Equipment rental is in the vicinity of CUC$60 for the first hour. If you're a serious kiter, the cost of renting per week probably outweighs the costs of bringing your own gear from abroad. The main launch point for boarders is Playa el Paso and the most kite-friendly hotels are the Secortel and Sol Cayo Guillermo. Both of these places have large lawns that are ideal for laying out your equipment.

Sleeping

Casa Gregorio HOTEL $

(Map p312; d incl breakfast CUC$25; P ❄ ≋) The opening of a budget hotel, aimed as much at Cubans as foreigners, is an usual occurrence in these parts. The Gregorio (named for Hemingway's old fishing partner), sits next to the marina at the entrance to Cayo Guillermo and offers a small selection of simple but smart rooms set around a small, if sometimes noisy, pool.

Dinner can be procured at the on-site restaurant and the beach is a short walk through the mangroves.

★Iberostar Daiquirí HOTEL $$$

(Map p312; ☎33-30-16-50; www.iberostar.com; r all-inclusive CUC$160-200; P ❄ ≋) Plenty of shade, a lily pond, and a curtain of water cascading in front of the pool bar add up to make the Daiquirí the pick of the bunch in Guillermo right now. The 312 rooms are encased in attractive colonial-style apartment blocks that actually show some architectural imagination, and the thin slice of paradisiacal beach is straight out of the brochure.

Secortel Club Cayo Guillermo HOTEL $$$

(Map p312; ☎33-30-17-12; www.clubcayoguillermo.com; s/d all-inclusive CUC$107/187; P ❄ @ ≋) This three-star, economically priced resort is the oldest hotel on the Sabana-Camagüey archipelago (opened in 1993) and has had more name changes than the British royal family. It comprises a low-key collection of salmon-colored bungalows in a quiet beachside location.

Part of the hotel is block-booked by Italian tour companies; the rest is increasingly popular with kiteboarders who lay out their kites under the palm trees on the resort's lush lawns. Lessons and board hire can be organized here.

Getting There & Away

The hop-on, hop-off bus carries people to and from Cayo Coco, stopping at all Cayo Guillermo hotels and terminating at Playa Pilar. All-day tickets costs CUC$5. It runs five to six times a day in either direction. A taxi between Cayos Guillermo and Coco should cost CUC$10 to CUC$15 (25 minutes).

For onward transportation from Cayo Coco, you'll need your own wheels or a taxi.

Camagüey Province

☎32 / POP 782,500

Includes ➡

Best Places to Eat

- ➡ Casa Austria (p326)
- ➡ El Paso (p326)
- ➡ Mesón del Príncipe (p327)
- ➡ El Bucanero (p334)

Best Places to Sleep

- ➡ El Marqués (p324)
- ➡ Hotel Camino de Hierro (p324)
- ➡ Los Vitrales (p323)
- ➡ Hotel Avellanada (p324)
- ➡ The Point of Pilots (p334)

Why Go?

Neither Occidente nor Oriente, Camagüey is Cuba's provincial contrarian, a region that likes to go its own way in political and cultural matters – and usually does – defying expectations in Havana and Santiago. These seeds were sown in the colonial era, when Camagüey's preference for cattle ranching over sugarcane meant less reliance on slave labor and more enthusiasm to eliminate the whole system.

Today Cuba's largest province is a mostly pancake-flat pastoral landscape of grazing cattle, lazy old sugar mill towns and, in the south, a few low-but-lovely hill ranges. It's flanked by Cuba's two largest archipelagos: Sabana-Camagüey in the north and Jardines de la Reina in the south, both almost virgin in places, though development is already underway in the cays to the north.

With its alluring architecture, illustrious citizens of note and cosmopolitan airs, the staunchly Catholic capital of Camagüey is the star attraction.

When to Go

- ➡ In February, Camagüeyans celebrate the Jornada de la Cultura Camagüeyana (Days of Camagüeyan Culture) to mark the city's founding in 1514.
- ➡ For outdoor enthusiasts, March is prime time for viewing migratory birds passing through the little-developed northern keys.
- ➡ At Playa Santa Lucía, divers can watch the amazing underwater shark-feeding show held seasonally between the months of June and January, with the best beach weather from November on.
- ➡ Held the first week of October, Camagüey showcases some more of its cultural prowess with the Festival Nacional de Teatro (National Theater Festival).

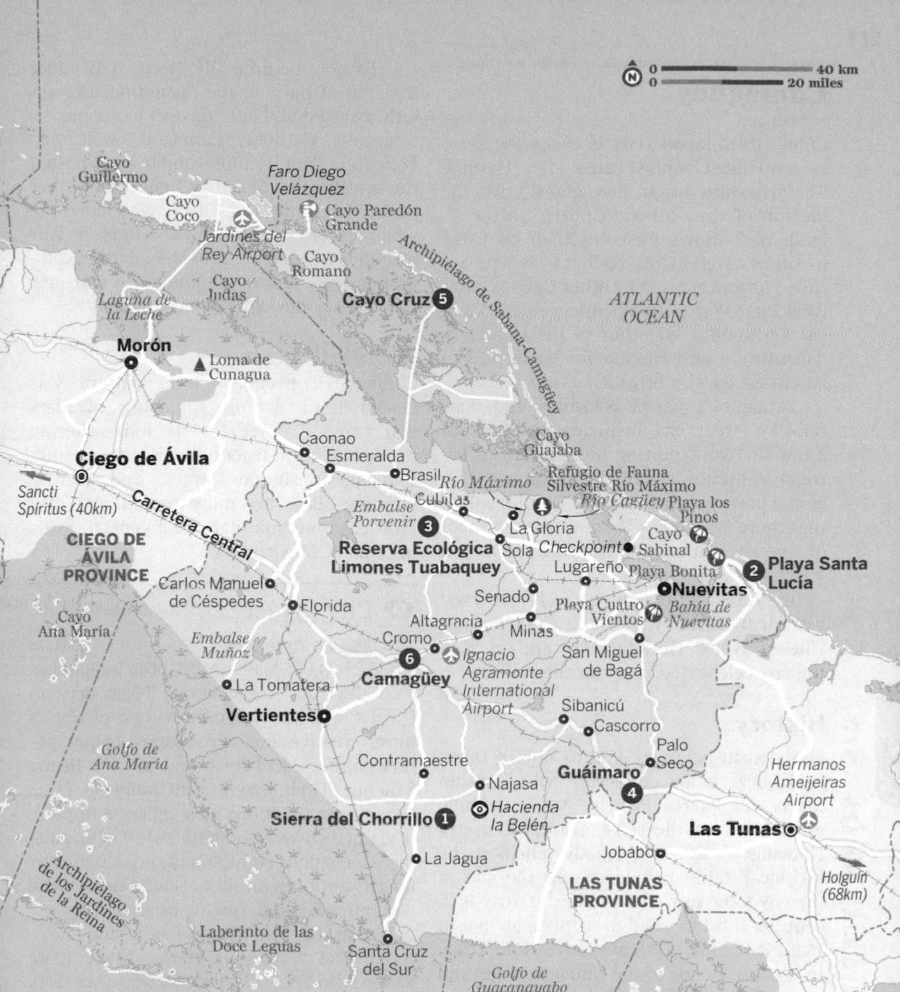

Camagüey Province Highlights

1. **Sierra del Chorrillo** (p330) Retreating into these verdant hills harboring rare birdlife and petrified forests.
2. **Playa Los Cocos** (p333) Swimming off the white-sand beach and soaking up the culture of the tiny village of La Boca.
3. **Reserva Ecológica Limones Tuabaquey** (p329) Checking out the caves, craters and natural gorge of one of Cuba's newest reserves.
4. **Guáimaro** (p331) Making a history stop in the city of emancipation, where Cuba's first constitution was signed.
5. **Cayo Cruz** (p334) Fly-fishing for tarpon and bonefish in the shallow flats off the key.
6. **Camagüey heritage** (p318) Walking the winding streets of the city to visit artist studios, explore intricate churches and soak up vibrant local life.

Camagüey

POP 301,000

Cuba's third-largest city is easily the suavest and most sophisticated after Havana. The arts shine bright here and it's also the bastion of the Catholic Church on the island. Well known for going their own way in times of crisis, its resilient citizens are called *agramontinos* by other Cubans, after local First War of Independence hero Ignacio Agramonte, coauthor of the Guáimaro constitution and courageous leader of Cuba's finest cavalry brigade.

Camagüey's pastel colonials and warren-like streets are inspiring. Get lost for a day or two exploring hidden plazas, baroque churches, riveting galleries and congenial bars and restaurants. The flip side is that there is a higher-than-average number of *jinteros* (touts) who can dog you as you stroll.

In 2008, Camagüey's well-preserved historical center was made Cuba's ninth Unesco World Heritage Site and in 2014 the city celebrated its quincentennial.

History

Founded in February 1514 as one of Diego Velázquez' hallowed seven 'villas,' Santa María del Puerto Príncipe was originally established on the coast near present-day Nuevitas. A series of bloody rebellions by the local Taíno people caused the site of the city to be moved twice in the early 16th century. It established in its present spot in 1528. Its name was changed to Camagüey in 1903, in honor of the camagua tree from which all life is descended, according to an indigenous legend.

Despite continued attacks by corsairs, Camagüey developed quickly in the 1600s with an economy based on sugar production and cattle-rearing. Acute water shortages in the area forced the townsfolk to make *tinajones* (clay pots) to collect rainwater. Even today Camagüey is known as the city of *tinajones* – the pots now ornamental.

Besides swashbuckling independence hero Ignacio Agramonte, Camagüey has produced several personalities of note, including poet and patriot Nicolás Guillén and eminent doctor Carlos J Finlay, the man largely responsible for discovering the causes of yellow fever. In 1959 the prosperous citizens quickly fell foul of the Castro revolutionaries when local military commander Huber Matos (Fidel's one-time ally) accused El Líder Máximo of burying the revolution. He was duly arrested and later thrown in prison.

Loyally Catholic, Camagüey welcomed Pope John Paul II in 1998 and in 2008 hosted the beatification of Cuba's first saint, 'Father of the Poor' Fray José Olallo, who aided the wounded of both sides in the 1868–78 War of Independence. In 2014 the city was comprehensively renovated (and given four new hotels) in honor of its quincentennial.

Sights

Camagüey's peculiar street pattern was designed to confuse pillaging invaders and provide cover for its long-suffering residents (or so legend has it). As a result, Camagüey's sinuous streets and narrow, winding alleys are more reminiscent of a Moroccan medina than the geometric grids of Lima or Mexico City.

City Center

★Casa de Arte Jover GALLERY

(32-29-23-05; Martí No 154, btwn Independencia & Cisneros; 9am-noon & 3-5pm Mon-Sat) FREE Camagüey is home to two of Cuba's most creative and prodigious contemporary painters, Joel Jover and his wife Ileana Sánchez. Their magnificent home in Plaza Agramonte functions as a gallery and piece of art in its own right, with a slew of original pieces, resident chihuahuas and delightfully kitschy antiques on show. Guests can browse and purchase high-quality original art.

The artists also keep a studio and showroom, the **Estudio-Galería Jover** (Calle Ramón Pinto 109; 9am-noon & 3-5pm Mon-Sat), in Plaza San Juan de Dios, which is also free to visit.

Museo Casa Natal de Ignacio Agramonte MUSEUM

(32-28-24-25; Av Agramonte No 459; CUC$2; 9am-5pm Tue-Fri, 9am-4pm Sat, to 1pm Sun) The birthplace of independence hero Ignacio Agramonte (1841–73), the cattle rancher who led the Camagüey area's revolt against Spain. The house – an elegant colonial building in its own right – tells of the oft-overlooked role of Camagüey and Agramonte in the First War of Independence. The hero's gun is one of his few personal possessions displayed.

In July 1869, rebel forces under Agramonte bombarded Camagüey. Four years later he was killed in action at the age of 32.

Cuban folk singer Silvio Rodríguez lionized this hero, nicknamed 'El Mayor' (the major), on his album *Días y flores*. It's opposite Iglesia de Nuestra Señora de la Merced, on the corner of Independencia.

Plaza San Juan de Dios SQUARE
(cnr Hurtado & Calle Ramón Pinto) Looking more Mexican than Cuban (Mexico was capital of New Spain so the colonial architecture was often superior), Plaza San Juan de Dios is Camagüey's most picturesque and beautifully preserved corner. Its eastern aspect is dominated by the Museo de San Juan de Dios, formerly a hospital. Behind the square's arresting blue, yellow and pink building facades lurk worthwhile restaurants.

Parque Ignacio Agramonte SQUARE
(cnr Martí & Independencia) Camagüey's most dazzling square in the heart of the city invites relaxation with rings of marble benches and an equestrian statue (c 1950) of Camagüey's precocious War of Independence hero, Agramonte.

Casa de la Diversidad MUSEUM
(32-29-25-98; Cisneros No 150; CUC$1; 10am-6pm Mon-Fri, 9am-9pm Sat, 8am-noon Sun) Impossible to miss due to its eclectic facade (a mix of Moorish and neoclassical elements), this museum's best exhibit is the building itself. Four exhibition rooms dedicated to slavery, costumes, art and architecture are explored relatively quickly, but it's worth savoring the ornate lobby with soaring pillars. Pride of place, however, goes to the toilets (yes, *toilets*!) where intricate frescos have been uncovered. The ladies' is the most ornate.

Museo de San Juan de Dios MUSEUM
(Plaza San Juan de Dios; CUC$2; 9am-5pm Tue-Sat, to 1pm Sun) Housed in a former hospital administered by Father José Olallo, the friar who became Cuba's first saint, the museum chronicles Camagüey's history and exhibits some local paintings. Its front cloister dates from 1728 and a unique triangular rear patio with Moorish touches was built in 1840. Ceasing to function as a hospital in 1902, it served as a teachers' college, a refuge during the 1932 cyclone and the Centro Provincial de Patrimonio responsible for restoring local monuments.

At the time of update, the museum was under renovation.

Centro de Interpretacion de la Ciudad ARCHITECTURE
(La Maqueta; 32-22-12-35; Martí; CUC$1; 9am-6pm Mon-Sat, 9am-1pm Sun) Cuba loves its *maquetas* (scale models) and Camagüey is no exception. This one offers a good overview of the twisting streets of the city.

Casa Natal de Nicolás Guillén CULTURAL CENTER
(Hermanos Agüero No 58; 9am-5pm) FREE This modest house gives visitors a small insight into Cuba's late national poet and his books, and today doubles as the Instituto Superior de Arte, where local students come to study music. At the time of writing, this center was closed for renovation.

Casa Finlay MUSEUM
(32-29-67-45; Cristo, btwn Cisneros & Lugareño; CUC$1; 9am-5pm Mon-Fri, 8am-noon Sat) Dr Carlos J Finlay (1833–1915), Camagüey's other hero, made medical breakthroughs in discovering how mosquitoes transmit yellow fever. Calling this place – his birth house – a museum is a stretch, but on a good day staff can enlighten you on his life story and scientific feats. There's a splendidly grizzled indoor patio.

West of the City Center

★Plaza del Carmen SQUARE
(Hermanos Agüero, btwn Honda & Carmen) Around 600m west of the frenzy of República sits another sublimely beautiful square, one less-visited than the central plazas. It's backed on the eastern side by the masterful Iglesia de Nuestra Señora del Carmen, one of the prettiest city churches.

Little more than a decade ago Plaza del Carmen was a ruin, but it's now restored to a state better than the original. The cobbled central space has been infused with giant *tinajones* (clay pots), atmospheric street lamps and unique life-sized sculptures of *camagüeyanos* going about their daily business (reading newspapers and gossiping, mostly).

★Martha Jiménez Pérez GALLERY
(32-25-75-59; Martí 282, btwn Carmen & Onda; 8am-8pm) FREE In Cuba's ceramics capital, the studio-gallery of Martha Jiménez Pérez shows the work of one of Cuba's greatest living artists. See everything from pots to paintings being produced here. The studio overlooks Pérez' magnum opus, Plaza del Carmen''s alfresco statue of three

Camagüey

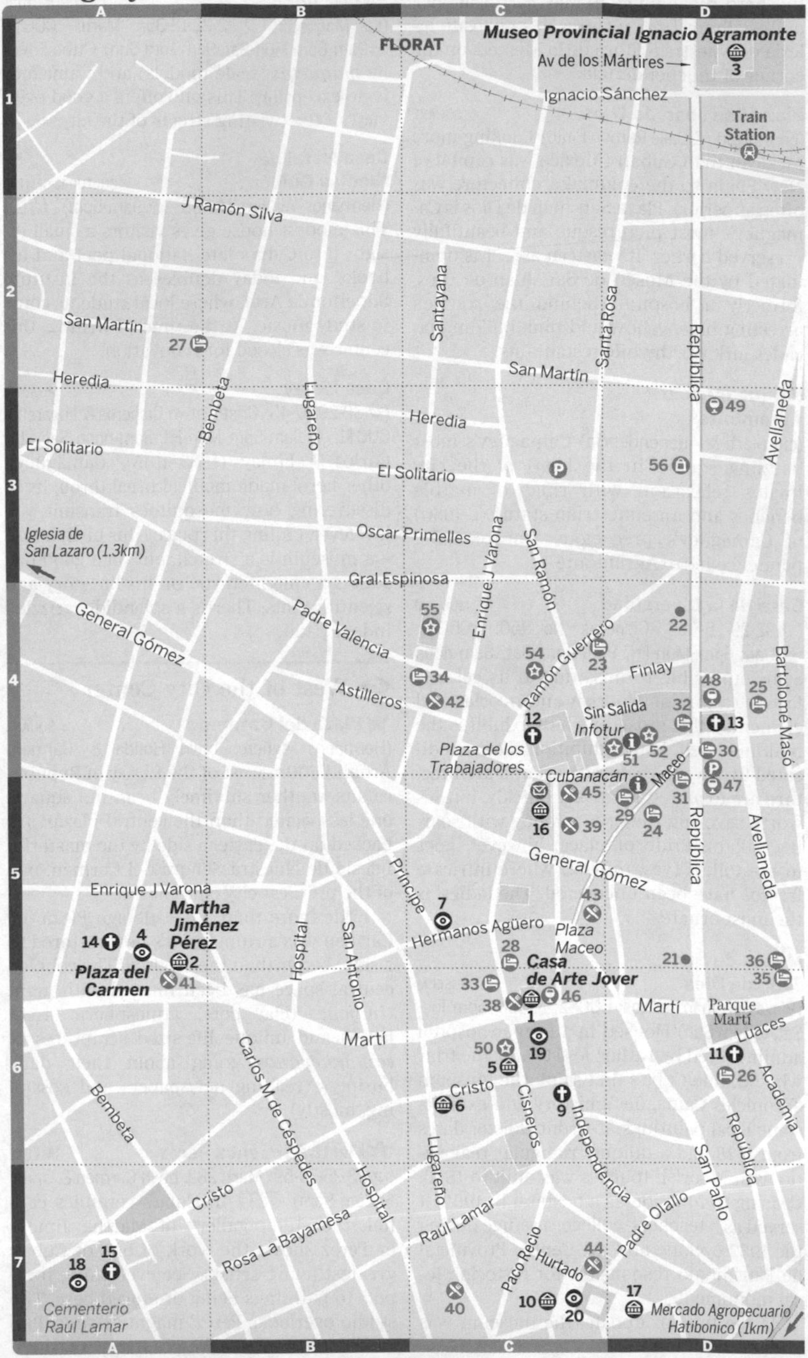

A B C D

1 2 3 4 5 6 7

FLORAT

Museo Provincial Ignacio Agramonte

3

Av de los Mártires

Ignacio Sánchez

Train Station

J Ramón Silva

San Martín

27

Heredia

Bembeta

Lugareño

Santayana

Santa Rosa

República

San Martín

Heredia

49

El Solitario

El Solitario

56

Avellaneda

Iglesia de San Lazaro (1.3km)

Oscar Primelles

Enrique J Varona

San Ramón

Gral Espinosa

General Gómez

Padre Valencia

55

22

54

Ramón Guerrero

23

Finlay

34

Astilleros

42

48

25

Bartolomé Masó

12

Sin Salida

32

13

Infotur

Plaza de los Trabajadores

51

52

30

Cubanacán

Maceo

45

31

47

29

16

39

24

República

Avellaneda

General Gómez

Príncipe

Enrique J Varona

Martha Jiménez Pérez

7

43

14

4

2

Hermanos Agüero

Plaza Maceo

28

Plaza del Carmen

41

Casa de Arte Jover

21

36

35

33

Hospital

San Antonio

38

1

46

Martí

Parque Martí

Martí

Luaces

19

50

11

5

26

Carlos M de Céspedes

Bembeta

6

Cristo

9

Academia

Cisneros

Independencia

República

Lugareño

San Pablo

Cristo

Hospital

Raúl Lamar

Padre Olallo

Rosa La Bayamesa

Paco Recio

44

Hurtado

15

18

17

40

10

20

Cementerio Raúl Lamar

Mercado Agropecuario Hatibonico (1km)

A B C D

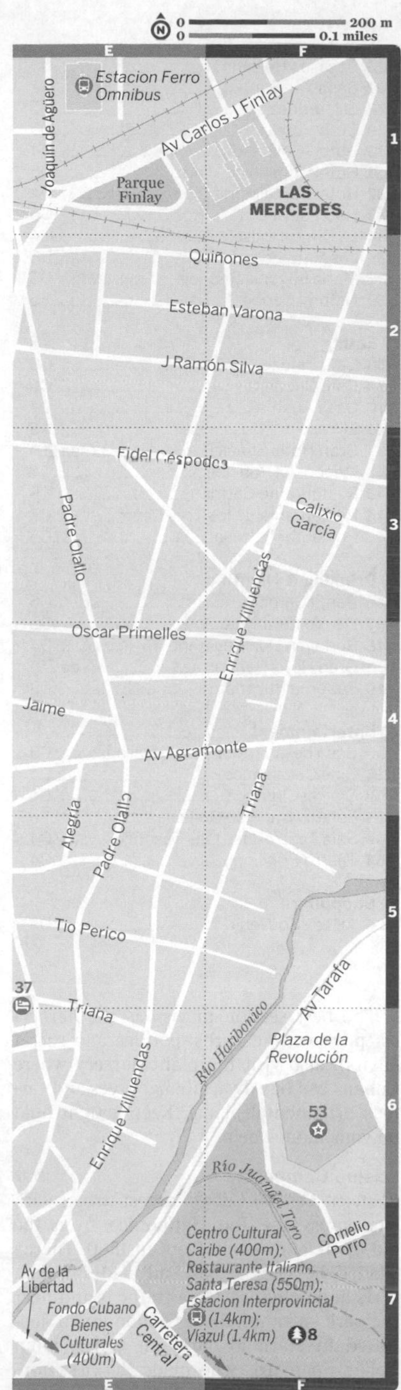

gossiping women entitled *Chismosas* (gossipers). The *chismosas* also feature in many of her paintings inside.

Necropolis de Camagüey CEMETERY
(Plaza del Cristo; 7am-6pm) FREE This sea of elaborate, lop-sided, bleached-white Gothic tombs makes up Cuba's most underrated cemetery, secreting the resting place of Camagüey-born independence hero Ignacio Agramonte, among others. It might not quite have the clout of Havana's Cementerio Colón but isn't too far behind in its roll call of famous incumbents.

Agramonte lies halfway down the second avenue on the left after the entrance (the blue-painted tomb). Harder to find are the tombs of Camagüey freedom-fighters Tomás Betancourt or Salvador Cisneros Betancourt (one time President of Cuba); show up for tours which depart from the entrance behind Iglesia de San Cristo de Buen Viaje (early to mid-morning is best).

North of the City Center

★Museo Provincial Ignacio Agramonte MUSEUM
(32-28-24-25; Av de los Mártires No 2; CUC$2; 9am-5pm Tue-Fri, 9am-4pm Sat, to 1pm Sun) Named (like half of Camagüey) after the exalted local War of Independence hero, this cavernous museum, just north of the train station, is in a Spanish cavalry barracks dating from 1848. There's some impressive artwork upstairs, including much by Camagüey natives, as well as antique furniture and old family heirlooms.

The art collection features both 19th- and early 20th-century art such as the haunting work of *camagüeyano* Fidelio Ponce, and *artes plasticos* (modern art) by nationally renowned figures like Alfredo Sosabravo.

South & East of the City Center

El Lago de los Sueños PARK
The so-called 'lake of dreams' is as an out-of-town escape from Camagüey's urban maze. It uses the same inventive (if slightly kitschy) methodology employed by a similar venture in Ciego de Ávila. The bizarro pièce de résistance is an ice-cream parlor encased in the fuselage of an old Soviet plane. Runner up is the antediluvian train carriage turned restaurant.

Camagüey

Top Sights

1 Casa de Arte Jover C6
2 Martha Jiménez Pérez A5
3 Museo Provincial Ignacio Agramonte D1
4 Plaza del Carmen A5

Sights

5 Casa de la Diversidad C6
6 Casa Finlay C6
7 Casa Natal de Nicolás Guillén C5
8 Casino Campestre F7
9 Catedral de Nuestra Señora de la Candelaria C6
Centro de Interpretacion de la Ciudad .... (see 1)
10 Estudio-Galería Jover C7
11 Iglesia de Nuestra Corazón de Sagrado Jesús D6
12 Iglesia de Nuestra Señora de la Merced C4
13 Iglesia de Nuestra Señora de la Soledad D4
14 Iglesia de Nuestra Señora del Carmen A5
15 Iglesia de San Cristo del Buen Viaje A7
16 Museo Casa Natal de Ignacio Agramonte C5
17 Museo de San Juan de Dios D7
18 Necropolis de Camagüey A7
19 Parque Ignacio Agramonte C6
20 Plaza San Juan de Dios C7

Activities, Courses & Tours

21 Camaguax Tours D5
22 Ecotur D4

Sleeping

23 Alba Ferraz C4
24 Casa Angelito D5
25 Casa Láncara D4
26 Casa los Helechos D6
27 Casa Yaneva A2
28 El Marqués C5
29 Gran Hotel D5
30 Hotel Avellanada D4
31 Hotel Camino de Hierro D5
32 Hotel Santa María D4
33 Hotel Sevillana C6
34 La China House C4
35 Los Vitrales D6
36 Maria Eugenia Requejo D5
37 Natural Caribe E5

Eating

38 Café Ciudad C6
39 Café Cubanitas C5
40 Casa Austria C7
41 El Paso A6
Gran Hotel Snack Bar .... (see 29)
42 Mesón del Príncipe C4
43 Restaurante Carmen C5
44 Restaurante de los Tres Reyes C7
45 Restaurante la Isabella C5

Drinking & Nightlife

46 Bar El Cambio C6
47 Bar Yesterday D5
48 Bodegón Don Cayetano D4
Gran Hotel Bar Terraza .... (see 29)
49 Taberna Bucanero D3

Entertainment

50 Casa de la Trova Patricio Ballagas C6
51 Cine Casablanca D4
52 Cine el Circuito D4
53 Estadio Cándido González F6
54 Sala Teatro José Luis Tasende C4
55 Teatro Principal C4

Shopping

56 ARTex Souvenir D3

Elsewhere, you can enjoy the lake, go for a boat ride or even stroll along a specially constructed *malecón* (main street). There are copious places to eat.

Mercado Agropecuario Hatibonico MARKET

(Carretera Central; 7am-6pm) If you visit just one market in Cuba, make it this muddy one. Beside the murky Río Hatibonico just off the Carretera Central, and characterized by its *pregones* (singsong, often comic, offering of wares) ringing through the stalls, this is a classic example of Cuban-style free enterprise juxtaposed with cheaper but lower-quality government stalls.

The best section to visit is the *herberos* (purveyors of herbs, potions and secret elixirs); also visit the plant nursery where Cubans can buy dwarf mango trees and various ornamental plants. Keep a tight hold on your money belt.

Casino Campestre PARK

(Carretera Central) Cuba's largest urban park sits across the Río Hatibonico from the old town, and was laid out in 1860. There's shaded benches, a baseball stadium, concerts and activities. On a traffic island near the park entrance, there's a monument dedicated to Mariano Barberán and Joaquín Collar, Spaniards who made the first nonstop flight between Seville, Spain and Camagüey, Cuba, in 1933.

The pair made the crossing in their plane Cuatro Vientos, but tragically the plane disappeared when flying to Mexico a week later. Ubiquitous bici-taxis are on hand to pedal you around.

Tours

★ Camaguax Tours TOURS
(☎32-28-73-64, 58-64-23-28; www.camaguax.com/en; República 155 No 7; ⌚8:30am-5:30pm) A private agency with English- and French-speaking guides and myriad quality offerings throughout the province with a cultural or adventure focus. Hits include a city tour, sugarcane farm visits, hiking and caving. There's excursions to Sierra del Chorrillo, Reserva Nacional Limones Tuabaquey and Río Máximo. Uses 4WD vehicles for rough roads and has overnight options.

Ecotur TOURS
(☎32-24-49-57; República No 278; ⌚8am-noon & 1-4:30pm Mon-Sat) Can arrange excursions to the Hacienda la Belén in the Sierra del Chorrillo and Reserva Ecológica Limones Tuabaquey. Read the fine print as you book since some outings don't include transport. The office is inside the Complejo Turístico Bambú.

Festivals & Events

Festival Nacional de Teatro PERFORMING ARTS
(www.festivalteatro.pprincipe.cult.cu; ⌚late Sept-early Oct) Camagüey showcases the best Cuban theater has to offer at the Festival Nacional de Teatro (National Theater Festival).

San Juan Camagüeyano CARNIVAL
(⌚Jun 24-29) The annual carnival, known as the San Juan Camagüeyano, runs from June 24 to 29 and includes dancers, floats and African roots music.

Sleeping

The city is undergoing a boom in boutique-hotel accommodations, with two more planned to open in the near future.

★ Los Vitrales CASA PARTICULAR $
(Emma Barreto & Rafael Requejo; ☎32-29-58-66, mobile 52-94-25-22; requejobarreto@gmail.com; Avellaneda No 3, btwn General Gómez & Martí; r CUC$30; P ❄) A former convent, this enormous, painstakingly restored colonial house sports broad arches, high ceilings and dozens of antiques. The helpful owner Rafael is an architect and it shows. Three rooms with good water pressure are arranged around a shady patio draped in lush gardens that are a highlight. There's over-the-top breakfasts and dinners with special orders available (vegetarians welcome).

Touts often lead guests astray to another 'Vitrales' – be sure to call ahead for taxi pickup and confirm your reservation a day ahead.

La China House CASA PARTICULAR $
(☎32-28-30-28, mobile 54-65-92-40; houselachina@gmail.com; Padre Valencia No 57; r $25; ❄) In front of the Teatro Principal, this impeccably kept 2nd-story apartment features modern art and colonial style. There are two rooms with leather headboards, TV and electric showers. Friendly host Misleydi offers dinner and can arrange massage, salsa and guitar classes. With some English.

Natural Caribe CASA PARTICULAR $
(☎32-29-14-17, mobile 52-76-75-98; requejoarias@nauta.cu; Avellaneda No 8; r CUC$30; ❄) Tropical minimalism sets the tone for this sleek renovated colonial. Cleverly designed by a local architect, it wouldn't look out of place in a New York loft, albeit one with a tropical courtyard strewn with ferns. Breakfasts are large. The roof terrace is undergoing renovations to add a barbecue and lounge area.

Two rooms and a terrace integrate light, space, water and sustainable building materials.

Casa Láncara CASA PARTICULAR $
(☎32-28-31-87; aledino@nauta.cu; Avellaneda No 160; r CUC$30; ❄ 📶) A dose of Seville with beautiful blue-and-yellow *azulejos* (tiles), this welcoming colonial is overseen by Andalusian fanatic Alejandro and his wife, Dinorah. The two rooms are hung with original local art and there's a roof terrace all within spitting distance of the Soledad church. They are in the process of building a gorgeous lodging across the street.

Maria Eugenia Requejo CASA PARTICULAR $
(☎32-25-86-70; Avellaneda No 3-A; r CUC$30; ❄ 📶) An offshoot of Los Vitrales run by the daughter of the owner, this ultramodern apartment is good for families or those who want some privacy.

Casa los Helechos CASA PARTICULAR $
(☎32-29-48-68, 52-31-18-97; v.manuel@nauta.cu; República No 68; r CUC$30; ❄) *Helechos* means 'ferns' and plenty occupy the long interior patio of this pleasant colonial house. There's a sizeable room with two beds and its own private kitchen, perfect for families.

Casa Yaneva CASA PARTICULAR $
(☎32-29-79-31; www.casayaneva.com; San Martin No 763; CUC$30; ❄📶) A gleaming option that's a bit of a walk from the center, perhaps best for those with a rental car. Eva knows tourism and provides three very clean and secure rooms, though they are small, with safe and refrigerator. There's also an interior patio.

Casa Angelito CASA PARTICULAR $
(☎32-29-82-71; Maceo No 62 altos; CUC$25; P❄) Angelito jokes that he's the cozier, cheaper alternative to the Gran Hotel in front. Climb the stairs to this 2nd-floor accommodation with small, modest rooms off a large terrace. Hang out sipping a cocktail or take breakfast among the plants. It's an affable family home and very central.

Alba Ferraz CASA PARTICULAR $
(☎32-28-30-81; jose.collot5477@gmail.com; Ramón Guerrero No 106; r CUC$25-30; ❄) A home with lovely, multigenerational hosts. Two rooms open onto a rather grand colonial courtyard bedecked with plants. There's a roof terrace and your host, Alba, can arrange dance and guitar lessons for guests. Alba can also arrange a taxi pickup from the bus station or airport.

★**El Marqués** BOUTIQUE HOTEL $$$
(☎32-24-49-37; ventas@ehoteles.cmg.tur.cu; Cisneros No 222; s/d incl breakfast CUC$120/160; ❄@📶) Simply lovely, this six-room colonial is a treasure trove of character. Rooms shoot off a central courtyard with rod-iron furniture, each door guarded by a Martha Jiménez Pérez sculpture on a pedestal. Bedrooms feature satellite TV, safe and air-conditioning. There's period furniture and quiet throughout. Also features a small bar with 24-hour service and hot tub.

It's part of the exclusive E hotel brand managed by Cubanacán.

★**Hotel Camino de Hierro** BOUTIQUE HOTEL $$$
(☎32-28-42-64; ventas@ehoteles.cmg.tur.cu; Plaza de la Solidaridad; s/d CUC$115/140; ❄@) Among the best of Camagüey's boutique hotels, it occupies an attractive city center building that was once an office for the Cuban *ferrocarril* (railway). So goes the railway theme. There's also lovely colonial furniture and romantic balconies. Guests enjoy a 24-hour bar and a pleasant patio privy to all the downtown action.

It's part of the exclusive E hotel brand managed by Cubanacán.

Hotel Avellanada BOUTIQUE HOTEL $$$
(☎32-24-49-58; ventas@ehoteles.cmg.tur.cu; República No 226; s/d CUC$115/140; ❄@) Named for a notable 19th-century, Cuban woman writer, this ground-floor hotel emanates class. The colonial has a large interior patio lined with columns, patterned tiles and a portrait of Gertrudis herself, famed for her stories of love, feminist stance and antislavery messages. Rooms feature a safe, minibar, TV and big windows. If you want to splurge, book the fabulous minisuite.

It's part of the exclusive E hotel brand managed by Cubanacán.

Hotel Sevillana BOUTIQUE HOTEL $$$
(☎32-24-49-37; Calle Cisneros, btwn Hermanos Agüero & Martí; s/d CUC$120/160; ❄@) In a gorgeous 1920's mansion decked with stained glass and chandeliers. Great spaces include a huge courtyard with a spurting fountain and a rooftop terrace with hot tubs. Compared to all this, rooms are less impressive, though adequate. There's a small on-site restaurant too.

It's part of the exclusive E hotel brand managed by Cubanacán.

Hotel Santa María BOUTIQUE HOTEL $$$
(Ignacio Agramonte, cnr República; s/d incl breakfast CUC$120/160; ❄@📶) An attractive boutique hotel with elegant common areas depicting scenes of Camagüey and sculptures by Martha Jiménez Pérez. The 31 rooms come equipped with safe, TV and minibar and suites feature claw-foot tubs. The roof garden restaurant has good views outdoors. There's one room with wheelchair access.

Gran Hotel HOTEL $$$
(☎32-29-20-93; Maceo No 67, btwn Av Agramonte & General Gómez; s/d incl breakfast CUC$132/152; ❄@🏊) This time-warped, city center hotel classic dates from 1939. A haughty pre-revolutionary atmosphere stalks the 72 clean rooms reached by a marble staircase or ancient lift replete with cap-doffing attendants. There are bird's-eye, citywide views from the 5th-floor restaurant or gorgeous rooftop bar.

CAMAGÜEY'S CHURCHES

If Cuba has a Catholic soul, it undoubtedly resides in Camagüey, where ecclesial spires rise above the narrow tangle of streets.

The Cathedral

Any exploration of Camagüey's religious history should begin at the **Catedral de Nuestra Señora de la Candelaria** (Cisneros 168), rebuilt in the 19th century on the site of an earlier chapel dating from 1530. The cathedral, which is named for the city's patron saint, was fully restored with funds raised from Pope John Paul II's 1998 visit. While not Camagüey's most eye-catching church, it is noted for its noble Christ statue that sits atop a craning bell tower. You can climb the tower for CUC$1.

The Eclectic

The **Iglesia de Nuestra Señora de la Merced** (Plaza de los Trabajadores), dating from 1748, is arguably Camagüey's most impressive colonial church. Local myth tells of a miraculous figure that floated from the watery depths here in 1601; it's been a place of worship ever since. The active convent in the attached cloister is distinguished by its two-level arched interior, spooky catacombs and the dazzling Santo Sepulcro, a solid-silver coffin.

The Baroque

Gleaming after a much-lauded 2007 renovation, **Iglesia de Nuestra Señora de la Soledad** (cnr República & Av Agramonte) is a massive baroque structure dating from 1779. Its picturesque cream-and-terracotta tower predates the rest of the church and is an attention-grabbing landmark on the city skyline. Inside there are ornate baroque frescoes and the hallowed font where Ignacio Agramonte was baptized in 1841.

The Neo-Gothic

One of Cuba's rare neo-Gothic churches beautifies Parque Martí, a few blocks east of Parque Ignacio Agramonte. The triple-spired **Iglesia de Nuestra Corazón de Sagrado Jesús** (cnr República & Luaces) is technically from an architectural subgenre called Catalan Gothic and dazzles with its ornate stained glass, decorative ironwork and pointed arches.

The Twin Towers

The **Iglesia de Nuestra Señora del Carmen** (Plaza del Carmen), a twin-towered baroque beauty dating from 1825, is another church that shares digs with a former convent. The Monasterio de las Ursalinas is a sturdy arched colonial building with a pretty, cloistered courtyard that once provided shelter for victims of the furious 1932 hurricane. Today it is the City Historian's offices.

The San Lázaro

The **Iglesia de San Lazaro** (cnr Carretera Central Oeste & Calle Cupey) is a beautiful (if diminutive), cream-colored church dating from 1700, although as interesting is the nearby cloistered hospital constructed a century later by virtuous Franciscan monk Padre Valencia to nurse leprosy victims. It's 2km west of the center.

The Diminutive

The **Iglesia de San Cristo del Buen Viaje** (Plaza del Cristo), next door to the necropolis and overlooking a quiet square, is one of the least visited of Camagüey's ecclesial octet, but it is worth a peek if you're exploring the Necropolis de Camagüey (behind). An original chapel was raised here in 1723, but the current structure is of mainly 19th-century vintage.

A piano bar is accessed through the lobby and an elegant renaissance-style swimming pool shimmers out back.

Eating

Restaurante Carmen CUBAN $

(☎32-28-79-02; Maceo No 6; mains CUC$2-12;

OFF THE BEATEN TRACK

REFUGIO DE FAUNA SILVESTRE RÍO MÁXIMO

These little known and hard to reach wetlands sit between the Ríos Máximo and Cagüey on the northern coast of Camagüey Province. There are flamingos, migratory water fowl, American crocodiles and a healthy population of West Indian manatees. It has been protected since 1998 as a *refugio de fauna silvestre* (wildlife refuge) and, more recently, as a Ramsar Convention Site.

Yet the Río Máximo delta faces a precarious future due to human and agricultural contamination coupled with occasional droughts. Once the largest flamingo nesting ground in the world, the population has been largely depleted due to contamination.

The area is roadless and hard to reach, but trips in can sometimes be organized via Ecotur (p323) or Camaguax Tours (p323) in Camagüey.

11am-11pm; ❄) With a Siberian chill thanks to hyperactive air-conditioning, this popular restaurant on the pedestrian stretch of Maceo brims with locals at midday. Most come for the cheap lunch specials – get yours early because they usually run out. It's consistent, with a diverse menu that ranges from sandwiches to stewed meat with rice.

Mercado Agropecuario Hatibonico MARKET **$**
(Carretera Central; 7am-6pm) Located alongside the fetid Río Hatibonico, this is a classic example of a Cuban market where government (lower quality, but cheaper price) and private (vice versa) produce is sold side by side. Chew on peso sandwiches and fresh *batidos* (fruit shakes, sold in jam jars) and buy fruit and vegetables grown within 500m of where you stand.

There's a good herb section and the market also sells an excellent selection of fruit and vegetables. Watch out for pickpockets.

Café Ciudad CAFE **$**
(32-25-84-12; Plaza Agramonte, cnr Martí & Cisneros; snacks CUC$2-5; 10am-10pm; wi-fi) Camagüey has made Agramonte-like efforts to carve culinary quality into its historical inheritance. This lovely plaza-hugging colonial cafe melds grandiosity with great service, emulating anything in Havana Vieja. Try the *jamón serrano* (cured ham) or savor a superb *café con leche* under the louvers. The picture occupying one wall shows the exact continuation of the old street.

Restaurante Italiano Santa Teresa ITALIAN **$**
(32-29-71-08; Av de la Victoria No 12, btwn Padre Carmelo & Freyre; meals CUC$3-7; noon-midnight) An Italian feast-in-waiting. Divine pizza, great ice cream and more-than-passable espresso on the patio definitely make this a spot to savor.

Café Cubanitas CAFE **$**
(cnr Independencia & Av Agramonte; snacks CUC$1-3; 24h) Just off Plaza de los Trabajadores, Cubanitas is alfresco and lively. And it really does stay open all hours, offering cold beer and 3am *ropa vieja* (shredded beef and vegetables in a tomato salsa).

Gran Hotel Snack Bar FAST FOOD **$**
(Maceo No 67, btwn Av Agramonte & General Gómez; snacks CUC$1-4; 9am-11pm) Has coffee, sandwiches, chicken and ice cream. The hamburgers (when available) are good and the atmosphere is 1950s retro.

★ **Casa Austria** EUROPEAN **$$**
(32-28-55-80; Lugareño No 121, btwn San Rafael & San Clemente; meals CUC$5-14; 7:30am-11:30pm; ❄) Locals line up for strudel and decadent cakes at this Austrian-run cafe. After so much *comida criolla* (Creole food), travelers embrace the international menu featuring chicken cordon bleu, schnitzel and garbanzos stewed in tomato sauce with bacon. It's all good. The setting, stuffed with heavy colonial furniture, is a bit claustrophobic, but there's patio dining as well.

★ **El Paso** INTERNATIONAL **$$**
(32-27-43-21; Hermanos Agüero No 261, btwn Carmen & Honda; meals CUC$5-10; 9am-11pm) Finally, a private restaurant with all-day hours, plus a funky interior and an enviable Plaza del Carmen location. There's flavorful *ropa vieja* (spiced shredded beef), heaping bowls of *arroz con pollo a la chorrillana* (chicken, rice prunes and peppers in a ceramic bowl). Try *pan patato* for dessert – consisting of cassava and coconut.

The restaurant has a lovely patio and 2nd-floor terrace seating. It also has a full wine and cocktail menu.

Mesón del Príncipe CUBAN $$
(☎52-40-45-98; Astilleros No 7; meals CUC$4-12; ⏲noon-midnight) Elegant restaurant that offers an affordable fine-dining experience in a typically refined Camagüeyan residence. It is places like this that have put Camagüey at the cutting edge of Cuba's new culinary revolution – a notch above Santiago.

Restaurante la Isabella ITALIAN $$
(☎32-24-29-25; cnr Av Agramonte & Independencia; mains CUC$5-12; ⏲11am-4pm & 6:30-10pm) This hip restaurant was opened during a visit by delegates from Gibara's iconic film festival, Festival Internacional del Cine Pobre, in 2008. Blending Italian food (pizza, lasagna, fettuccine) with a maverick movie-themed decor and director-style seats, the restaurant occupies the site of Camagüey's first ever cinema.

Restaurante de los Tres Reyes CARIBBEAN $$
(☎32-28-68-12; Plaza San Juan de Dios No 18; meals CUC$8-12; ⏲10am-10pm) A handsome, state-run place set in beautiful colonial digs on Plaza San Juan de Dios that sells mainly chicken dishes. Ruminate on Camagüey life by one of the giant iron-grilled windows out front or enjoy greater privacy on a plant-bedecked interior patio.

Drinking & Nightlife

Maybe it's the pirate past, but Camagüey has great tavern-style drinking houses.

Gran Hotel Bar Terraza BAR
(Maceo No 67, btwn Av Agramonte & General Gómez; ⏲1pm-2am) The aesthete's choice. At the top of the Gran Hotel, its cocktail maestro will prepare you mojitos and daiquiris while you gaze at the city's premier vista – all Camagüey laid bare before you. Duck below to the swimming pool for the bizarrely addictive water ballet shows, happening several times weekly at 9:15pm.

Bodegón Don Cayetano BAR
(☎32-29-19-61; República No 79; ⏲noon-11pm) This casual Spanish-style taverna, nestled beneath Iglesia de Nuestra Señora de la Soledad, is best used as a drinking option. There's a decent wine collection but better food elsewhere. Tables spill into the adjacent alley.

Bar Yesterday BAR
(☎32-24-49-43; República No 222; ⏲noon-midnight Mon-Fri, to 1am Sat & Sun) This Beatles-themed bar has a large inner patio and life-sized bronze sculptures of the fab four. Locals come for snacks and chilly brews.

Bar El Cambio BAR
(cnr Independencia & Martí; ⏲7am-late) The Hunter S Thompson choice. A dive bar with graffiti-splattered walls and interestingly named cocktails, this place consists of one room, four tables and bags of atmosphere.

Taberna Bucanero BAR
(☎32-25-34-13; cnr República & Fidel Céspedes; ⏲24hr) The beer drinker's choice. Fake pirate figures and Bucanero beer on tap characterize this swashbuckling tavern, faintly reminiscent of a British pub.

☆ Entertainment

★**Teatro Principal** THEATER
(☎32-29-30-48; Padre Valencia No 64; tickets CUC$5-10; ⏲shows 8:30pm Fri & Sat, 5pm Sun) If a show's on, GO! Second only to Havana in its ballet credentials, the Camagüey Ballet Company, founded in 1971 by Fernando Alonso (ex-husband of number-one Cuban dancing diva, Alicia Alonso), is internationally renowned and performances are the talk of the town. Also of interest is the wonderful theater building of 1850 vintage, bedizened with majestic chandeliers and stained glass.

Casa de la Trova Patricio Ballagas LIVE MUSIC
(☎32-29-13-57; Cisneros No 171, btwn Martí & Cristo; CUC$3; ⏲7pm-1am) An ornate entrance hall gives way to an atmospheric patio where old crooners sing and young couples *chachachá*. One of Cuba's best *trova* (traditional poetic singing) houses, where regular tourist traffic doesn't detract from the old-world authenticity. Tuesday's a good night for traditional music. Cover includes one drink.

Centro Cultural Caribe CABARET
(☎32-29-81-12; cnr Narciso Montreal (Calle 1) & Freyre; tickets CUC$3-6; ⏲10pm-2am, to 4am Fri & Sat) Some say it's the best cabaret outside Havana and, at this price, who's arguing? Book your seat (from the box office on the same day) and pull up a pew for an eyeful of feathers and a few frocks. There's a trousers-and-shirt dress code.

Estadio Cándido González SPECTATOR SPORT
(☎32-29-31-40; Av Tarafa; ⏲7:15pm games Oct-Apr) Baseball games are held at this stadium

alongside Casino Campestre. Team Camagüey, known as the Alfareros (the Ceramicists), have long been underdogs but recent seasons have seen them winning more games.

Sala Teatro José Luis Tasende THEATER
(☎32-29-21-64; Ramón Guerrero No 51; ⏲shows 8:30pm Sat & Sun) For serious live theater, head to this venue, which has quality Spanish-language performances.

Cine Casablanca CINEMA
(☎32-29-22-44; Av Agramonte No 428) A 1940s-era cinema reopened as a multiplex.

Cine el Circuito CINEMA
(☎32-25-65-43; Av Agramonte) Former cinema reincarnated in 2014 as a fount of video-art, with a 3D room. The on-site Galería Pixel shows revolving documentary films.

Shopping

Calle Maceo is Camagüey's top shopping street, with a number of souvenir shops, bookstores and department stores on an attractive pedestrian boulevard.

Fondo Cubano Bienes Culturales ARTS & CRAFTS
(Av de la Libertad No 112; ⏲8am-6pm Mon-Sat) Sells all kinds of artifacts in a pleasantly nontouristy setting, just north of the train station.

ARTex Souvenir GIFTS & SOUVENIRS
(República No 381; ⏲9am-5pm) Che T-shirts, mini-*tinajones*, Che key rings, CDs, Che mugs. Get the picture?

Information

DANGERS & ANNOYANCES

Camagüey's hardworking *jinteros* (touts) are experts at making a buck off tourists. Many travelers have been offered help finding their casa particular, only to later realize they have been led to a different house (usually with less-desirable facilities). Or someone outside your reserved house will tell you it's under renovation or closed. Ring the bell to be sure.

Try to book accommodation in advance, ideally arranging a pickup from the station or airport. Particularly at these places, be wary of strangers approaching and offering 'services' (eg to be your guide). Bici-taxis at the bus station can be particularly predatory.

INTERNET ACCESS

There's public wi-fi (with scratchcard-code access) at Parque Ignacio Agramonte and between Plaza los Trabajadores and Iglesia de Nuestra Señora de la Soledad.

Etecsa Telepunto (☎32-25-15-59; República, btwn San Martín & José Ramón Silva; internet per hr CUC$1.50; ⏲8:30am-7pm) Camagüey is light on wi-fi, so grab one of the dozen terminals here. Visitors can buy a scratch card for wi-fi.

MEDICAL SERVICES

Policlínico Integral Rodolfo Ramirez Esquival (☎32-28-14-81; cnr Ignacio Sánchez & Joaquín de Agüero) North of the level crossing from the Hotel Plaza; it will treat foreigners in an emergency.

Policlínico José Martí (☎32-29-78-10; Luaces No 1; ⏲24hr) A centrally located hospital.

MONEY

Banco de Crédito y Comercio (☎32-29-25-31; cnr Av Agramonte & Cisneros; ⏲9am-3pm Mon-Fri) Has an ATM.

Banco Financiero Internacional (☎32-29-48-46; Independencia, btwn Hermanos Agüero & Martí; ⏲9am-3pm Mon-Fri) With an ATM.

Cadeca (☎32-29-52-20; República No 84, btwn Oscar Primelles & El Solitario; ⏲8:30am-8pm Mon-Sat, 9am-6pm Sun) Money changing.

POST

Post Office (☎32-29-39-58; Av Agramonte No 461, btwn Independencia & Cisneros; ⏲9am-6pm Mon-Sat)

TOURIST INFORMATION

Infotur (☎32-25-67-94; www.facebook.com/camaguey.travel; Ignacio Agramonte; ⏲8:30am-5:30pm) Very helpful information

VÍAZUL BUS DEPARTURES FROM CAMAGÜEY

DESTINATION	COST (CUC$)	DURATION (HR)	DAILY DEPARTURES
Havana	33	9	12:35am, 6:30am, 11:05am, 2:25pm, 11:45pm
Holguín	11	3	12:30am, 4:30am, 6:25am, 1:20pm, 6:40pm
Santiago de Cuba	18	6	12:30am, 6:25am, 9:30am, 1:20pm, 4pm
Trinidad	15	4½	2:45am
Varadero	24	8¼	3:10am

OFF THE BEATEN TRACK

RESERVA ECOLÓGICA LIMONES TUABAQUEY

One of Cuba's newest reserves, these heavily wooded **uplands** (CUC$6) occupy the Sierra de Cubitas in northern Camagüey Province. The star attraction is Cuba's most important indigenous art: pre-Columbian cave paintings at Cueva Pichardo and Cueva María Teresa. Its Hoyo de Bonet is a unique 300m-wide, 90m-deep natural karstic depression covered in vegetation with a cool, humid microclimate replete with trippy giant ferns. The rich birdlife includes an abundance of toccorros and cartacubas known to produce a symphony of birdsong.

Paths fan out to caves, craters and a narrow natural gorge called the Paso de los Paredones, with sheer 40m-high walls. Historical infamy is recalled nearby: a post marks the spot where, in February 1869, a group of *mambises* (19th-century Cuban independence fighters) successfully saw off a Spanish attack.

Walking on the trails is permitted with a guide only. Guided tours of the reserve can be arranged at Ecotur (p323) or with private agencies in Camaguey. There is a visitor center and accommodation in cabins.

The reserve lies approximately 35km north of the city of Camagüey on the main (bumpy) road between Morón and Nuevitas. The turnoff is near the village of Cubitas.

office hidden in a gallery near Casablanca cinema.

TRAVEL AGENCIES

Cubanacán (☎32-28-78-79; Maceo No 67, Gran Hotel) The best place for information in the city center.

Getting There & Away

AIR

Air connections to the United States continue to grow. **Air Transat** (www.airtransat.com) and **Sunwing** (www.sunwing.ca) fly in the all-inclusive crowd from Toronto, who are hastily bussed off to Playa Santa Lucía.

BUS & TRUCK

The **Estacion Ferro Omnibus** (regional bus station) near the train station, has trucks to regional destinations (CUC$2) including Playa Santa Lucía, paid in Cuban pesos. Arrive at 5am to be ensured a spot for beach-bound trucks.

Long-distance **Víazul** (☎32-27-03-96; www.viazul.com; Carretera Central Este, at Calle Peru) buses depart from the **Estacion Interprovincial** (Bus Station; Carretera Central), 3km southeast of the center. There's also one daily departure to Playa Santa Lucía at 2:45pm (CUC$8, 1¾ hours).

Passenger trucks (charging tourists around CUC$1) to Las Tunas, Ciego de Ávila and nearby towns also leave from this station. Arriving before 9am will greatly increase your chances of having a spot.

CAR

A taxi to Playa Santa Lucía should cost around CUC$60 to CUC$70 one way: bargain hard.

TRAIN

The **train station** (☎tickets 32-28-47-66; cnr Avellaneda & Av Carlos J Finlay; to Santiago/Havana CUC$11/19) is more conveniently located than the bus station – though its service isn't as convenient. Every fourth day the Tren Francés leaves for Santiago at around 3:19am and for Havana, stopping in Santa Clara, at around 1:47am.

Schedules change frequently: check at the station a couple of days before you intend to travel. Slower *coche motor* (cross-island) trains also serve the Havana–Santiago route, stopping at places such as Matanzas and Ciego de Ávila.

Going east there are daily services to Las Tunas, Manzanillo and Bayamo. Heading north there are (theoretically) four daily trains to Nuevitas and four to Morón.

Getting Around

BICI-TAXIS

Bicycle taxis are found around most of the city's squares, with the main contingent in Plaza de los Trabajadores. They should cost five pesos, but drivers will probably ask for payment in convertibles.

CAR

Car-rental prices start around CUC$70 a day plus gas, depending on the make of car and hire duration. Try **Cubacar** (☎32-29-74-72; www.transturcarrental.com; Casino Campestre).

Guarded parking (CUC$2 for 24 hours) is available for those brave enough to attempt Camagüey's maze in a car. Ask at your hotel or casa particular for details.

There are two **Servi-Cupet gas stations** (Carretera Central; ⌚24hr) near Av de la Libertad. Driving in Camagüey's narrow one-way streets is a sport akin to base-jumping. Experts only!

HORSE CARTS

Horse carts shuttle along a fixed route (CUC$1) between the regional bus station and the train station. You may have to change carts at Casino Campestre, near the river.

Florida

POP 73,600

A million metaphoric miles from Miami, the hard-working sugar-mill town of Florida, 46km northwest of Camagüey on the Ciego de Ávila road, is a viable overnighter if you're driving around central Cuba and are too tired to negotiate the labyrinthine streets of Camagüey after dark (a bad idea, whatever your physical or mental state). There's a working rodeo and an Etecsa telephone office.

The one hotel here is worthwhile in a pinch: **Hotel Florida** (☎32-51-46-70; Carretera Central, Km 534; s/d CUC$23/36; P❄🏊) is a two-story hotel, 2km west of the center of town that has 74 adequate rooms, some partially renovated. The entry drive is potholed, which sort of sets the tone for the place, but the staff are friendly and the price comparable to a casa particular. Inside there's a thatched restaurant serving *criolla*-style food.

If not here, the many options of Camagüey are less than an hour away.

Getting There & Away

Florida is 46km from Camagüey. If you are stopping here, chances are that you have your own rental car. But you can find passenger trucks going between Florida and Camagüey.

For drivers there's a Servi-Cupet gas station in the center of town on Carretera Central.

Sierra del Chorrillo

This protected area 36km southeast of Camagüey contains three low hill ranges: the Sierra del Chorrillo, the Sierra del Najasa and the Guaicanámar (highest point: 324m). Visitors access the area through Hacienda la Belén, a ranch turned nature reserve with a zoo, petrified forest and excellent birdwatching.

Sights

Hacienda la Belén RANCH

(entry CUC$6; Sendero las Aves hike CUC$7) Nestled in grassy uplands, this handsome country ranch was built by a Peruvian architect during WWII. It is now run as a nature reserve by Ecotur. It's one of the best places in Cuba to view rare bird species such as the Cuban parakeet, the giant kingbird and the Antillean palm swift. There's also nonindigenous exotic animals such as zebras, deer, bulls and horses, and visitors can hike Sendero las Aves for a fee.

Another curiosity is a three-million-year-old petrified forest spread over 1 hectare. To find the petrified forest, drive several kilometers past the hacienda entrance to the road junction and bear right to reach a dead end at a factory. There's also a far-larger fossilized tree nearby.

Sleeping

Motel la Belén MOTEL $

(☎reservations 32-24-49-57; s/d CUC$13/20, full board CUC$29/40; ❄🏊) Simple and countrified in that spartan, semiabandoned Cuban way, Motel la Belén reclines within the hacienda grounds and is equipped with a swimming pool, restaurant, TV room and clean, air-conditioned rooms. Glorious landscapes are within stone-chucking distance. Reserve via Ecotur (p323) in Camagüey.

Getting There & Away

Tours from Camagüey visit the area. Otherwise, you can come by rental car. Drive 24km east of Camagüey on Carretera Central, then 30km southeast following signs to Najasa. If approaching from Las Tunas, another potholed road to Najasa branches south off the Carretera Central in Sibanicú. The hacienda is 8km beyond Najasa along a rutted road. Alternatively, negotiate a rate with a taxi in Camagüey.

Cayo Sabinal

Though slated for development, Cayo Sabinal, 22km to the north of Nuevitas, is still virgin territory in part. The 30km-long coral key with marshes is favored by flamingos and iguanas. The land cover is mainly flat and characterized by marshland and lagoons. The fauna consists of tree rats, wild boar and a large variety of butterflies. It's astoundingly beautiful.

WORTH A TRIP

GUÁIMARO: THE CITY OF EMANCIPATION

Guáimaro would be just another nameless Cuban town if it wasn't for the famous Guáimaro Assembly of April 1869, which approved the first Cuban constitution and called for the emancipation of slaves. The assembly elected Carlos Manuel de Céspedes as president.

If you are a history buff, stop here. The events of 1869 are commemorated by a large monument erected in 1940 in Parque Constitución. Around the base of the monument are bronze plaques with likenesses of José Martí, Máximo Gómez, Carlos Manuel de Céspedes, Ignacio Agramonte, Calixto García and Antonio Maceo, the stars of Cuban independence. The park also contains the mausoleum of Cuba's first – and possibly greatest – heroine, Ana Betancourt (1832–1901) from Camagüey, who fought for women's emancipation alongside the abolition of slavery during the First War of Independence. Also be sure to stop at the **Museo Histórico** (Constitución 85 btwn Libertad & Máximo Gómez, Guáimaro; admission CUC$1; ⊙9am-5pm Mon-Fri), with a couple of rooms given over to art and history.

Guáimaro is on the Carretera Central between Camagüey and Las Tunas. A number of Víazul buses pass through daily. Speak to the driver if you want to get off.

Sights

Fuerte San Hilario FORT

Cayo Sabinal has quite some history for a wilderness area. Following repeated pirate attacks in the 17th and 18th centuries, the Spanish built a fort here (1831) to keep marauding corsairs at bay. The fort later became a prison and, in 1875, witnessed the only Carlist uprising (a counter-revolutionary movement in Spain that opposed the reigning monarchy) in Cuba - ever.

Faro Colón LIGHTHOUSE

(Punta Maternillo) Erected in 1848, Faro Colón is one of the oldest lighthouses still operating on the Cuban archipelago. As a result of various naval battles fought in the area during the colonial era, a couple of Spanish shipwrecks - *Nuestra Señora de Alta Gracia* and the *Pizarro* - rest in shallow waters nearby, providing great fodder for divers.

Activities

Playa Bonita BEACH

(day tour adult/child CUC$59/36) Of Cayo Sabinal's 30km of beaches, this one has top billing. It's frequented by daily catamaran excursions from Playa Santa Lucía offering lunch at a rustic *ranchón* (ranch).

Getting There & Away

There is a dirt road to the cay, but a security checkpoint is currently curtailing access while the island is under construction. The 2km causeway linking the key to the mainland was the first of its kind constructed in Cuba and the most environmentally destructive.

Access Cayo Sabinal via a catamaran tour from Playa Santa Lucia that visits Playa Bonita. Trips run most days and include transfers and lunch. Book through the Playa Santa Lucía hotels.

Currently, the only access to the island is via a catamaran tour from Playa Santa Lucía.

Playa Santa Lucía

With 20 km of golden sand, this beach, 112km northeast of Camagüey, competes with Varadero as Cuba's longest. Travelers generally come here to dive the north coast's best and most accessible coral reef, lying just a few kilometers offshore. Another highlight is the beach itself - a tropical idyll, most of it still deserted - though it collects seaweed even in the radius of the hotels. This isolated resort strip has seen better days, with many hotels sporting a cheap holiday-camp feel.

The swimming, snorkeling and diving are exceptional, however, and the four all-inclusive resorts are well-priced for snowbirds. In peak season, the clientele is primarily Canadian. The flat surroundings feature flamingos, scrubby bushes and the odd grazing cow. Backed by wetlands, mosquitoes can be a huge annoyance, particularly at dusk. Prepare accordingly.

Activities

Playa Santa Lucía is a diving destination extraordinaire and the world's second-longest coral reef after Australia's Great Barrier Reef.

The 35 scuba sites take in six Poseidon ridges, the Cueva Honda dive site, shipwrecks, and the abundant marine life, including several types of rays at the entrance to the Bahía de Nuevitas. A much-promoted

Playa Santa Lucía

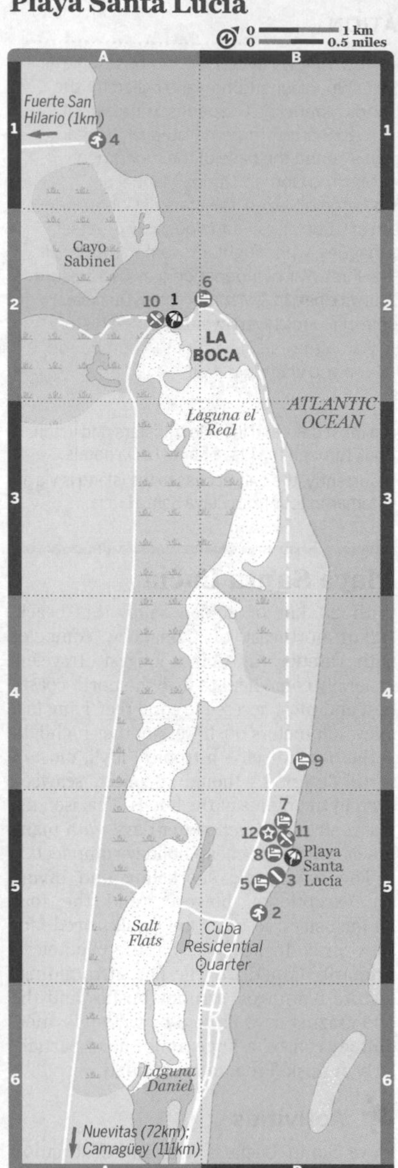

Playa Santa Lucía

Sights
1 Playa los Cocos......A2

Activities, Courses & Tours
2 Catamaran to Playa Bonita......B5
3 Centro Internacional de Buceo Shark's Friends......B5
4 Playa Bonita......A1

Sleeping
5 Brisas Santa Lucía......B5
6 Casa Betty......B2
7 Club Brava Caracol......B5
8 Club Santa Lucía......B5
9 Islazul Tararaco......B4
The Point of Pilots......(see 6)

Eating
10 El Bucanero......A2
11 Restaurante Luna Mar......B5

Entertainment
12 Mar Verde Centro Cultural......B5

highlight is the hand-feeding of 3m-long bull sharks from June to January.

The hotels can organize other water activities, including kayaking, deep-sea fishing and kitesurfing (the last from November to April).

★Catamaran to Playa Bonita BOATING

(adult/child CUC$59/36) Fulfill your deserted-island fantasy traveling on a 14-passenger catamaran to remote Playa Bonita on Cayo Sabinal. Included is a 45-minute snorkel session and lunch with an open bar. It departs Playa Santa Lucía at 9:30am and returns at 4:20pm. Bring plenty of sunscreen.

Book the trip through Marlin, which has aquatic activity centers in every hotel.

Centro Internacional de Buceo Shark's Friends DIVING

(☎32-36-51-82; www.nauticamarlin.com; Av Tararaco; shark feeds CUC$69, dives from CUC$30) Shark's Friends is a professional outfit with dive masters speaking English, Italian and German. The center, on the beach between Brisas Santa Lucía and Gran Club Santa Lucía, offers dives, open-water certification and shark feeds.

November through January is the best time for the shark feeding or dive boats go out every two hours between 9am and 3pm daily (though the last dive is contingent on demand). The open-water course costs CUC$315; a resort course is CUC$74. It also has snorkeling excursions.

Sleeping

The small hotel strip begins 6km northwest of the roundabout at the entrance to Santa

Lucía. The four big ones are Cubanacán resorts whose star ratings and quality decrease as you head northwest. Due to Playa Santa Lucía's size and isolation, it's good to book a room beforehand.

Casas particulares may be found in the village located southeast of the hotels where beach access is inferior.

Islazul Tararaco HOTEL $
(☎32-33-63-10; s/d CUC$33/36; ❄) Bargain hunters can thank Changó for the Tararaco, the strip's oldest hotel (it actually predates the revolution). Every room has a TV and a little patio, and is within stone-chucking distance of the beach. Víazul buses to Camagüey arrive and depart from the driveway.

Brisas Santa Lucía RESORT $$$
(☎32-33-63-17; s/d/tr all-inclusive CUC$143/190/193; P❄@📶🏊) With 412 rooms in several three-story buildings, Brisas covers a monstrous 11 hectares. It boasts the strip's top rating – a hugely flattering four stars. That comes with an overly jaunty holiday camp atmosphere of mic-happy pool entertainers and a show where everything is repeated in three languages: not for everyone. There's special kids programming.

Club Brava Caracol RESORT $$$
(☎32-33-63-02; s/d all-inclusive CUC$89/139; P❄@📶🏊) Sleek remodeled rooms with comfortable beds and Caribbean colors give style points to this resort. The kids program makes it the beach's family favorite. Choose your room wisely: shows and taped music on the central stage could keep you up unwillingly and not all in-room safes work. Ocean-view rooms are more expensive.

Gran Club Santa Lucía RESORT $$$
(☎32-33-61-09; s/d all-inclusive CUC$86/133; P❄@📶🏊) Gran Club is one of the better strip options, with 249 colorfully painted rooms in well-maintained two-story blocks. There's also prettily landscaped grounds and poolside action. Discoteca la Jungla is the not-overly-inspiring nightclub that offers an evening music/comedy show (which tries way too hard to be funny).

Eating

Aside from the hotel buffets, your choices are limited. There's an El Rápido on the roundabout at the western end of the hotel strip that serves cheap (for a reason) fast food.

Restaurante Luna Mar SEAFOOD $$
(Playa Santa Lucía; mains CUC$7-20; ⏰noon-9pm) This place, flush up against the beach and wedged between Gran Club Santa Lucía and Club Amigo Caracol, offers a seafood menu in an easy-to-reach setting.

Entertainment

Resort entertainment dominates the nightlife here. If you aren't interested definitely bring earplugs.

Mar Verde Centro Cultural CULTURAL CENTER
(☎32-33-62-05; Mar Verde Centro Commercial; CUC$1; ⏰10pm-3am) The Mar Verde Centro Cultural has a pleasant patio bar and a cabaret with live music nightly.

Information

MEDICAL SERVICES

Clínica Internacional de Santa Lucía (☎32-33-63-60; Ignacio Residencial No 14) A well-equipped Cubanacán clinic for emergencies and medical issues. There's also a pharmacy here.

MONEY

Cadeca (Mar Verde Centro Commercial; ⏰9am-4pm) In the Mar Verde shopping center.

TOURIST INFORMATION

For tour agencies, Cubanacán, which owns four of the five hotels here, is well represented with a desk in each hotel. There's a good Cubatur office just outside Gran Club Santa Lucía.

Getting There & Away

Víazul (www.viazul.com) travels to Camagüey daily at 11am (CUC$9, 1¾ hours) from the entrance of Hotel Tararaco.

You can also taxi between Camagüey and Playa Santa Lucía (approximately CUC$70 one way).

The Servi-Cupet gas station is at the southeastern end of the strip, near the access road from Camagüey. Another large Servi-Cupet station, with a snack bar, is just south of Brisas Santa Lucía.

Rent cars or mopeds via Cubacar (p329), with desks in all the hotels.

Playa los Cocos

This comma of beach at the end of 20km-long Playa Santa Lucía, 7km from the hotels at the mouth of the Bahía de Nuevitas, is a stunner, with yellow-white sand and iridescent jade water. Sometimes flocks of pink flamingos are visible in Laguna el Real, behind this beach. The small Cuban

CAYOS & CAUSEWAYS

In any other country, the necklace of beach-embellished cayos (keys) that lies between Cayo Coco and Playa Santa Lucía would have been requisitioned by the biggest, richest hotel chains. But in Cuba, due to a mix of economic austerity and nitpicking government bureaucracy, they are largely untouched, though hotels are in the works for several cays. In-the-know fishers ply the waters out as far as Cayo Cruz. The flats, lagoons and estuaries off Camagüey's north coast are fly-fishing heaven (bonefish, permit and tarpon are concentrated in a designated fishing area of just under 350 sq km that's invariably deserted). The fishing season runs from November to August and no commercial fishing is allowed.

Rough causeways and roads were built across Camagüey's cayos in the late 1980s in preparation for Cuba's next big tourist project – a plan that, due to the Special Period economic meltdown, never got off the ground. Instead, the islands and their unblemished waters have remained the preserve of in-the-know fisherfolk, resolute birdwatchers and those in search of splendid solitude. Running west to east are Cayo Paredón Grande, home to the checkered lighthouse Faro Diego Velázquez, a sultry beach and bevies of day-trippers from Cayo Coco; Cayo Romano, Cuba's third-largest island and a haven for flamingos, mangroves and blood-thirsty mosquitoes; Cayo Guajaba, an untouched roadless wilderness; and Cayo Sabinal, which has a rough road and a trio of unblemished beaches, plus an old Spanish fort and lighthouse. Tucked away to the north is 800m-long Cayo Confites, where a 21-year-old Fidel Castro hid out in 1947 in preparation for an abortive plot to overthrow the dictatorial regime of Rafael Trujillo in the Dominican Republic (Fidel jumped ship in the Bay of Nipe and swam 15km to shore carrying his weapon).

You'll need a sturdy car or a bike to penetrate these potholed northern wildernesses. Entry points to Cayo Romano are from Cayo Coco, or Brasil in northwestern Camagüey Province. Cayo Cruz is accessed via a causeway from Cayo Romano. Cayo Sabinal is linked to the mainland by a small causeway northwest of Nuevitas. There are police checkpoints, so you'll need your passport.

settlement here is known as La Boca. This is a fine swimming spot, with views of the Faro Colón (lighthouse) on Cayo Sabinal, but beware of tidal currents further out. Avoid swimming on the ocean-facing beaches where there are sea urchins.

Sleeping & Eating

There's dining at two restaurants here. Meals are also available at casas particulares.

★The Point of Pilots CASA PARTICULAR $

(mobiles 53-41-46-60, 55-44-88-21; La Boca No 16; r CUC$25) A stone's throw from the water, this freshly painted, marine-blue house on a sandy alley has the world's nicest hosts. There's three ship-shape rooms, one very small. Owners will also provide seafood meals if you arrange ahead.

Casa Betty CASA PARTICULAR $

(La Boca No 38; r CUC$25) Basic but well-located, this seafront cottage has just two rooms. The savory smells wafting from the tiny kitchen reveal its secondary purpose – as a paladar (privately owned restaurant). You can get seafood, grilled or deep-fried (mains CUC$5 to CUC$10), at all hours here, not such a good sign for lodgers but great for hungry beachgoers.

★El Bucanero SEAFOOD $$

(32-36-52-26; Playa los Cocos; meals CUC$8-12; 10am-10pm) With a prime beach setting, this thatched seafood hut is in its own class. Call it simple and fresh. The house special of lobster and prawns is enhanced immeasurably by the setting. There's also deck chairs for rent, and with fresh coconut juice and cold beer at the ready, it's not a bad spot to hunker down.

Getting There & Away

A horse and carriage from the Santa Lucía hotels to Playa los Cocos is CUC$20 round-trip plus the wait.

You can also walk it, jog it or bike it (free gearless, but adequate, bikes are available at all the resorts). It's 12km by road and 8km by the coast (impassable to cars, with a five-minute sandy section that horse carts and cyclists must walk).

Las Tunas Province

☎31 / POP 526,000

Includes ➡

Best Places to Eat

➡ La Negra (p338)
➡ Ristorante La Romana (p339)
➡ La Sicilia (p342)
➡ El Bodegón de Polo (p342)

Best Places to Sleep

➡ Villa Carolina (p342)
➡ Mayra Busto Méndez (p337)
➡ Hostal Melina (p337)
➡ Casa Karen & Roger (p337)
➡ Brisas Covarrubias (p342)

Why Go?

Most travelers say hello and goodbye to Las Tunas Province in the time that it takes to drive across it on the Carretera Central – one hour on a good day. But, hang on a second! With laid-back, leather-skinned cowboys and poetic country singers, the province is known for daredevil rodeos and Saturday-night street parties. Here barnstorming entertainment is served up at the drop of a sombrero.

Although historically associated with the Oriente, Las Tunas Province shares many attributes with Camagüey in the west. The flat grassy fields of the interior are punctuated with sugar mills and cattle ranches, while the eco-beaches on the north coast remain wild and lightly touristed by aradero standards.

In this low-key land of the understated and underrated, accidental visitors can enjoy the small-town charms of the provincial capital, or head north to beaches off the old mill town Puerto Padre where serenity rules.

When to Go

➡ Avoid the wettest months of June and October, when more than 160mm of average precipitation inundates the streets.

➡ During the hottest months of July and August, locals take to the beaches for vacations; visitors usually prefer cooler months.

➡ Las Tunas has many festivals for a small city; the best is the Cuban country-music festival Jornada Cucalambeana in June.

➡ La Festival Internacional de Magia Anfora, held in the provincial capital in November, draws pro magicians from around the world to demonstrate their craft.

➡ The National Sculpture Exhibition, an event befitting the so-called 'City of Sculptures,' happens in February.

Las Tunas Province Highlights

❶ **Parque 26 de Julio** (p339) Checking out the Cuban version of the lasso-wielding cowboy in this Las Tunas fairground hosting the city's celebrated rodeo twice a year.

❷ **Playa la Herradura** (p342) Enjoying this unkempt village beach while nary a resort spoils its tranquil sands.

❸ **Puerto Padre** (p341) Lingering awhile in this friendly, unpretentious and out-on-a-limb seaside town.

❹ **Jornada Cucalambeana** (p337) Rolling into El Cornito in June to experience some country crooning at the music festival.

❺ **Las Tunas** (p336) Enjoying some slick private enterprise in the capital's Italian restaurants.

❻ **Punta Covarrubias** (p342) Diving in a dozen sites with largely undiscovered reefs off this pristine beach.

Las Tunas

POP 163,500

La Victória de Las Tunas (as it's officially known) is a sleepy agricultural town anointed provincial capital. It has long held a sleazy reputation for being the Oriente's capital of sex tourism. But thanks to good private lodgings, welcoming locals and a handy location on Cuba's arterial Carretera Central, handfuls of road-weary travelers drop by and are pleasantly surprised. Missing here are the touts that exasperate tourists in other destinations. It's a window into real provincial life.

Referred to as the 'city of sculptures,' Las Tunas is certainly no Florence. But what it lacks in grandiosity it makes up for in small-town quirks. You can see an authentic country rodeo here, admire a statue of a two-headed Taíno chief, go wild at one of the city's riotous Saturday-night street parties or wax lyrical at the weird and witty Jornada Cucalambeana, Cuba's leading country-music festival.

Sights

Memorial a los Mártires de Barbados

MUSEUM

(Lucas Ortíz No 344; 10am-6pm Mon-Sat) FREE Las Tunas' most evocative sight is in the former home of Carlos Leyva González, an Olympic fencer killed in the nation's worst terrorist atrocity: the bombing of a Cubana airliner in 1976. Individual photos of victims of the attack line the museum walls, providing poignant reminders of the fated airplane.

On October 6, 1976, Cubana de Aviación Flight 455, on its way back to Havana from Guyana, took off after a stopover in Barbados' Seawell airport. Nine minutes after clearing the runway, two bombs went off in the cabin's rear toilet causing the plane to crash into the Atlantic Ocean. All 73 people on board – 57 of whom were Cuban – were killed. The toll included the entire Cuban fencing team fresh from a clean sweep of gold medals at the Central American Championships. At the time, the tragedy of Flight 455 was the worst ever terrorist attack in the western hemisphere.

Memorial Vicente García MUSEUM
(☎31-34-51-64; Vicente García No 7; CUC$1; ⊙9am-5pm Tue-Sat, 8am-2pm Sun) A colonial-era structure near the eponymous park that commemorates Las Tunas' great War of Independence hero who captured the town from the Spanish in 1876, and torched it 21 years later when the colonizers sought to reclaim it. The building was once García's house, but only a small exposed section of floor tiles remains from the original structure. The museum's four rooms are best navigated with a guide who'll fill in the many historical gaps.

Museo Provincial General Vicente García MUSEUM
(☎31-34-51-64; cnr Francisco Varona & Ángel de la Guardia; CUC$1; ⊙8am-4:30pm Tue-Sun) Housed in the royal-blue town hall with a clock mounted on the front facade, the provincial museum documents local *tunero* history. A member of staff will happily lead you through the exhibits.

El Cornito FOREST
(Carretera Central Km 8; ⊙9am-5pm) The bamboo woods around Motel el Cornito, about 6km outside town, offer a welcome, shady diversion from the scorching city bustle. You'll find *ranchón*-style restaurants (favoring the usual booming reggaeton music), the site of the old farmhouse of great Las Tunas poet Juan Cristóbal Nápoles Fajardo (aka El Cucalambé) and a reservoir.

Back toward the main road, there's a zoo, a fun park and a motocross circuit. A taxi here costs CUC$5 to CUC$7 return.

Festivals & Events

Bienal de Escultura Rita Longa SCULPTURE
(⊙Feb) Held in February in even-numbered years in this so-called 'City of Sculptures.'

Jornada Cucalambeana MUSIC
(⊙Jun) Cuba's biggest celebration of country music, where local lyricists impress each other with their 10-line *décima* verses. It happens in June, just outside Las Tunas, by Motel el Cornito.

Sleeping

★**Hostal Melina** CASA PARTICULAR $
(☎31-34-35-03; Av Frank País 55; r CUC$25; P ❄) With a warm welcome, this 1970s home sparkles with care. Gape at the gold lamé bed covers. Two guest rooms behind the house offer ample privacy and space, with flat-screen TVs and refrigerators. There's also a private covered patio and roof deck, and breakfasts are huge.

★**Mayra Busto Méndez** CASA PARTICULAR $
(☎31-34-42-05, mobile 52-71-30-84; mayra.busto@nauta.cu; Hirán Durañona No 16, btwn Frank País & Lucas Ortíz; r CUC$25; P ❄) A very helpful and secure casa particular with personalized attention. The sheen coming off the furnishings in this immaculate bungalow might dazzle you. There are two guest rooms, one enormous, and renovations underway to update the bathrooms. To find it, let the taxi know that it's a dead-end street (*calle sin salida*).

Casa Karen & Roger CASA PARTICULAR $
(☎31-34-28-73; kyl@itu.sld.cu; Lico Cruz No 93; r CUC$25; ❄) With sleek, modern design that's a rare find in Cuba, this second-story home with two spacious rooms is a welcome addition. There's original art on the walls, bold colors and an excellent roof terrace. The family has young children and a small dog.

Hotel Cadillac HOTEL $$
(☎31-37-27-91; cnr Ángel de la Guardia & Francisco Vega; s/d incl breakfast CUC$72/86; ❄) A Las Tunas hotel that doesn't give you flashbacks to the Khrushchev and Brezhnev years. Opened in 2009, this rehabilitated, centrally located 1940s building features eight rooms, including a lovely corner suite, with safe and minibar. There are flat-screen TVs, up-to-the-minute bathrooms and a dash of old-fashioned prerevolutionary class. Out front is the lively Cadillac Snack Bar (p339).

Eating

Los Hermanos ITALIAN $
(☎mobile 54-86-45-14; Varona No 284; mains CUC$2-6) Cheap and good, this is the locals' choice for Italian fare such as garlicky pesto. Skip the underwhelming dessert.

Las Tunas

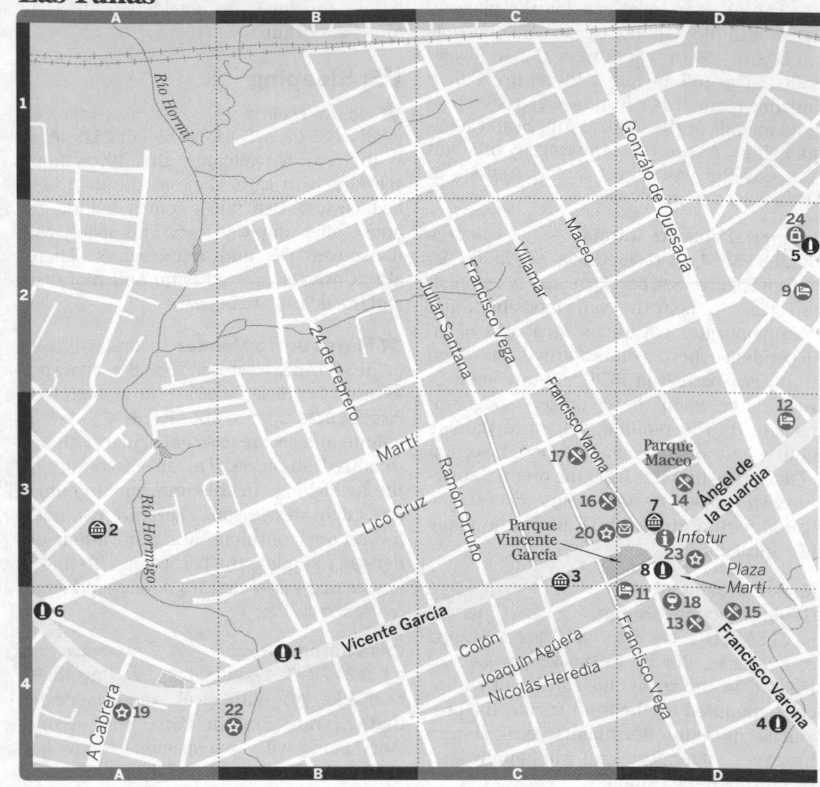

Caché INTERNATIONAL $
(☎31-99-55-57; Francisco Varona, btwn Nicolás Heredia & Joaquin Agüera; sandwiches & burgers CUC$2-5; ⊙noon-2am) Proof that things are changing in Cuba, this swanky cocktail bar/cafe/restaurant attempts to bring the taste of Miami to Las Tunas – of all places! The dimly lit, air-conditioned interior is dressed to impress with leather seats, dexterous cocktail waiters and a menu heavy with deluxe burgers and club sandwiches.

Locals favor the tasty fried *croquetas*.

La Patrona CUBAN $
(☎31-34-05-11; Custodio Orive No 94; meals CUC$3-4; ⊙11am-11pm) A largely local place with highly reasonable prices and equally reasonable food. The mains are primarily *comida criollla* (Creole food), but it also does eggs and pasta for cheap.

Restaurante la Bodeguita CARIBBEAN $
(☎31-37-15-36; Francisco Varona No 293; meals CUC$5; ⊙noon-11pm) A Palmares state-run joint, meaning that it's a better bet than the usual peso parlors. You'll get checkered tablecloths, a limited wine list and what the Cuban government calls 'international cuisine' – read spaghetti and pizza. Try the chicken breast with mushroom sauce.

★La Negra CUBAN $$
(☎31-39-81-48, mobile 52-71-30-72; www.restaurantelanegra.com; Israel Santos 41; mains CUC$5-12; ⊙11am-11pm) Among provincial Cuba's best eats, this private home with a leafy courtyard serves up stunning Cuban classics. Crisp plantain shavings, fragrant pork stir-fry (*fajita de cerdo*) and shrimp *criollo*, served with a creamy tomato sauce, do not disappoint. Chef Vladimir works wonders with subtle sauces, olive oil and fresh ingredients. It's a short taxi ride from downtown.

Las Tunas

Sights

1 La Fuente de Las Antilles B4
2 Memorial a los Mártires de Barbados A3
3 Memorial Vicente García C3
4 Mestizaje D4
5 Monumento a Alfabetización D2
6 Monumento al Trabajo A4
7 Museo Provincial General Vicente García D3
8 Statue of José Martí D3

Sleeping

9 Casa Karen & Roger D2
10 Hostal Melina E2
11 Hotel Cadillac D4
12 Mayra Busto Méndez D3

Eating

13 Caché D4
14 La Patrona D3
15 Los Hermanos D4
16 Restaurante la Bodeguita C3
17 Ristorante La Romana C3

Drinking & Nightlife

Cadillac Snack Bar .... (see 11)
18 Casa del Vino Don Juan D4

Entertainment

19 Cabaret el Taíno A4
20 Casa de la Cultura C3
21 Estadio Julio Antonio Mella F1
22 Parque 26 de Julio B4
23 Teatro Tunas D3

Shopping

Fondo Cubano de Bienes Culturales .... (see 23)
24 Galería Taller Escultura Rita Longa D2

★ Ristorante La Romana ITALIAN **$$**
(☎31-34-77-55; Francisco Varona No 331; meals CUC$6-9; ⏱12:45-11pm) Drop by this new Roman abode on the main boulevard where the olive oil's extra virgin, the pasta's homemade and the coffee's Lavazza. The food – including the starter bruschettas – is *molta ottima*, according to Las Tunas' Italian visitors. There's also a cheaper menu with Cuban specialties. Great atmosphere.

Drinking & Nightlife

Cadillac Snack Bar CAFE
(cnr Ángel de la Guardia & Francisco Vega; ⏱9am-11pm) This offshoot of the Hotel Cadillac (p337) has tables on a terrace overlooking the Plaza Martí action and serves decent cappuccinos.

Casa del Vino Don Juan BAR
(cnr Francisco Varona & Joaquín Agüera; ⏱9am-midnight) Wine tasting in Las Tunas probably sounds about as credible as food rationing in Beverley Hills, yet here it is; only 7 pesos for a shot of the local poison, a sickly sweet red called Puerto Príncipe. Go just to say you've been there.

Entertainment

★ Parque 26 de Julio FAIRGROUND
(Av Vicente García; ⏱9am-6pm Sat & Sun) FREE Located in Parque 26 de Julio where Vicente García bends into Av 1 de Mayo. It kicks off every weekend with a market, music, food stalls and kids' activities.

Teatro Tunas THEATER
(☎31-34-50-10; cnr Francisco Varona & Joaquín Agüera) This recently revitalized theater shows quality movies and some of Cuba's best touring entertainment including flamenco, ballet and plays.

Casa de la Cultura CULTURAL CENTER
(☎31-34-35-00; Vicente García No 8) The best place for the traditional stuff with concerts, poetry and dance. The action spills out into the street on weekend nights.

Cabaret el Taíno THEATER
(☎31-34-38-23; cnr Vicente García & A Cabrera; per couple CUC$1; ⏲9pm-2am Tue-Sun) This large thatched venue at the west entrance to town has the standard feathers, salsa and pasties show on Saturdays and Sundays.

Estadio Julio Antonio Mella SPECTATOR SPORT
(☎31-34-84-03; Frank Pais) October to April is baseball season. Las Tunas plays at this stadium near the train station. Los Magos (the Wizards) haven't produced much magic of late and usually compete with the likes of Ciego de Ávila for bottom place in the East League.

Shopping

Galería Taller Escultura Rita Longa ART
(☎31-34-29-69; cnr Av 2 de Diciembre & Lucas Ortíz; ⏲9am-5pm Mon-Sat) The small gallery pulls together some fine local work for perusal or purchase.

Fondo Cubano de Bienes Culturales ARTS & CRAFTS
(☎31-34-69-83; cnr Ángel de la Guardia & Francisco Varona; ⏲9am-noon & 1:30-5pm Mon-Fri, 8:30am-noon Sat) This store sells fine artwork, ceramics and embroidered items opposite the main square.

Information

MEDICAL SERVICES

Casas particulares can help visitors get home doctor visits.

Hospital Che Guevara (☎31-34-50-12; cnr Avs CJ Finlay & 2 de Diciembre) A kilometer from the highway exit toward Holguín.

SCULPTURE VULTURES

It might not be Florence, but Las Tunas has an eclectic, sometimes eccentric collection of urban sculptures, more than 150 of them in fact, dating back to a pioneering sculpture expo that was held in the city in 1974. For a small but precocious precis of the town's new young talent, check out the Galería Taller Escultura Rita Longa, while true sculpture vultures should visit in February (even-numbered years) for the Bienal de Escultura Rita Longa (p337) – a celebration of all things sculpted.

Las Tunas' most important and emblematic statue is Rita Longa's La Fuente de Las Antilles. First unveiled in 1977, it was elemental in reviving Cuba's sculpturing traditions and making Las Tunas its HQ. The sculpture comprises a huge fountain filled with elaborate interwoven figures symbolizing the emergence of the Greater Antilles' indigenous peoples from the Caribbean Sea. Cuba is represented by an *India dormida* (sleeping Taíno woman). The work reawakened interest in indigenous-themed art in Cuba and has spawned other complex sculptures, such as Mestizaje, a multifaced representation of Cuba's mixed races in the Parque de la India near the bus station.

In the central hub of Plaza Martí is another Longa work, an inventive bronze statue of the 'apostle of Cuban independence,' José Martí, which doubles as a solar clock. It was opened in 1995 to commemorate the 100th anniversary of Martí's death.

Elsewhere in town you'll find sculptures with revolutionary themes. The 8m-high abstract **Monumento al Trabajo** (cnr Carretera Central & Martí) by José Peláez pays cubist homage to Cuban workers, while the pencil-like **Monumento a Alfabetización** (Lucas Ortíz) marks the 1961 act passed in Las Tunas to stamp out illiteracy.

Further afield, the Janus-inspired Cacique Maniabo y Jibacoa is a two-headed Taíno chief looking in opposite directions, which dominates the surroundings at the rustic Motel el Cornito 6km west of town. Also at El Cornito is the Columna Taina, a kind of native totem pole, along with Las Tunas' newest sculpture, the Cornito al Toro (2013), a legendary bull made out of metal and cement that guards the approach road to the complex looking down from a giant pedestal.

MONEY

ATMs are easy to find.

Banco Financiero Internacional (31-34-62-02; cnr Vicente García & 24 de Febrero; 9am-3pm Mon-Fri)

Cadeca (31-34-63-82; Colón No 141) Money changing.

POST

Post Office (31-34-38-63; Vicente García No 6; 8am-8pm) In the center.

TOURIST INFORMATION

Infotur (31-37-27-17; infotur@tunas.infotur.tur.cu; Francisco Varona No 298; 8:15am-4:15pm Mon-Fri & alternate Sat) Provides good information on local attractions.

TRAVEL AGENCIES

Ecotur (31-34-20-73; Av 2 de Diciembre, Hotel Las Tunas; 9am-4:30pm Mon-Fri, to noon Sat) Books visits to Monte Cabaniguan (CUC$20), though you will also need a separate 4WD transfer.

Getting There & Away

BUS

The main **bus station** (Francisco Varona) is 1km southeast of the main square. **Víazul** (31-37-42-95; www.viazul.com) buses have daily departures; tickets are sold by the *jefe de turno* (shift manager). Get tickets one hour early or days before during high season.

Havana-bound buses stop at Camagüey (CUC$7, 2½ hours), Ciego de Ávila (CUC$13, 4¼ hours), Sancti Spíritus (CUC$17, 5½ to six hours), Santa Clara (CUC$22, seven hours) and Entronque de Jagüey (CUC$26, 9¼ hours). Service to Holguín (CUC$6, 70 minutes) leaves at 2:40am, 6:35am, 8:30am and 3:30pm.

Santiago buses stop at Bayamo (CUC$6, 1¼ hours). To get to Guantánamo or Baracoa, you have to connect through Santiago de Cuba.

TRAIN

The **train station** (31-34-81-46; Terry Alomá, btwn Lucas Ortíz & Ángel de la Guardia) is near Estadio Julio Antonio Mella on the northeast side of town.

Getting Around

Taxis hang around outside the bus station, Hotel Las Tunas and the main square. Horse carts run along Frank País near the baseball stadium to the town center; they cost 10 pesos.

For car and scooter rentals try **Cubacar** (31-34-68-99; cnr Angel de la Guardia & Maceo; 8am-5pm Mon-Fri, to noon Sat) at Hotel Las Tunas. An **Oro Negro gas station** (cnr Francisco Varona & Lora) is a block west of the bus station.

The **Servi-Cupet gas station** (Carretera Central; 24hr) is at the exit from Las Tunas toward Camagüey.

Puerto Padre

POP 93,700

Languishing in a half-forgotten corner of Cuba's least spectacular province, it's hard to believe that Puerto Padre – or the 'city of mills' as it is locally known – was once the largest sugar port on the planet. But for die-hard travelers the wanton abandonment inspires a wistful sense of curiosity. Blessed with a Las Ramblas–style boulevard, a miniature Malecón, and a scrawny, forlorn statue of Don Quixote beneath a weathered windmill that has registered one too many hurricanes, the town is the sort of place where you stop to ask the way at lunchtime and end up, a couple of hours later, tucking into fresh lobster at a bayside restaurant.

Sights

Fuerte de la Loma FORT

(31-51-52-24; Av Libertad; CUC$1; 9am-4pm Tue-Sat) This fort at the top of the sloping Av Libertad, also known as the Salcedo Castle, is testimony to Puerto Padre's former strategic importance. There's a small military museum with temperamental opening hours.

Museo Fernando García Grave de Peralta MUSEUM

(31-51-53-08; Yara 45, btwn Av Libertad & Maceo; CUC$1; 9am-4pm Tue-Sat) Lashed regularly by hurricanes, the municipal museum – when it's not being renovated – contains the usual round of fallen revolutionaries, stuffed animals and antiques. Look out for the antique record players.

Courses

Silverio Cuevas Vargas DANCING

(mobile 53-26-66-39; silcuevas@nauta.cu; Martires de la Herradura No 109; per hour CUC$10) Salsa, rumba and popular Cuban dances: years of rigid Teutonic form will limber up under Silverio's warm tutelage. Classes are usually one-on-one and can even be held in Las Tunas. His house is across from the taxi area.

Sleeping & Eating

Roberto Lío Montes de Oca CASA PARTICULAR $

(Los Chinos; 31-51-57-22; Francisco V Aguilera No 2, btwn Jesús Menéndez & Conrrado Benítez;

r CUC$25; ❄) This bright coral facade shines amid the ubiquitous dilapidation and portends cozy digs inside. There's a sweets shop downstairs and two prettily decorated bedrooms in the second-story home of a young couple. Breakfast and dinner are available. Street signs don't exist. It's one block from Parque Martin and three blocks from the boardwalk.

El Bodegón de Polo CUBAN $
(☎31-51-23-57; Lenin No 54; meals CUC$2-5; ⏲11am-11pm) Keen-to-please local restaurant serving delicacies such as crab, octopus and swordfish on a breezy upstairs terrace. The best deal in town and friendly to boot.

La Sicilia ITALIAN $$
(☎mobile 54-40-91-66; Paco Cabrera No 47; mains CUC$5-10; ⏲6:30pm-midnight Mon-Sat) It's hard to beat the ambience of this restored seafront mansion. The owner Lili spent time in Italy and offers hearty fare such as baked fish, spicy chicken and lasagna with white sauce or rich tomato ragu. The restaurant is on the 2nd floor with glorious water views.

☆ Entertainment

Casa de la Cultura CULTURAL CENTER
(☎31-51-54-63; Parque de la Independencia) Nighttime activities are held at the municipal culture house.

1913 Ballroom DANCE
(☎31-51-68-97; Jesus Menendez, btwn 24 de Febrero & Av Ameijeres; ⏲hours vary) Have a drink or bite to eat and work up a sweat dancing at this downtown venue.

ℹ Getting There & Away

The 52km between Las Tunas and Puerto Padre are well paved. Puerto Padre is best accessed by truck ($10 *moneda nacional*), leaving from Las Tunas train station, or with your own wheels. A taxi from the provincial capital should cost approximately CUC$30.

Punta Covarrubias

Situated 49 rutted kilometers northwest of Puerto Padre, Punta Covarrubias has a spotless sandy beach. It's a haven for scuba diving off the beaten path.

Las Tunas Province's only all-inclusive resort, **Brisas Covarrubias** (☎31-51-55-30; s/d CUC$41/82; P❄@≋), with 122 comfortable rooms in cabin blocks, with one for disabled guests, is also one of the island's most isolated. Scuba diving at the coral reef 1.5km offshore is the highlight. Packages of two dives per day start at CUC$45 at the Marina Covarrubias. There are 12 dive sites here.

Self-sufficient travelers can turn in to the beach at the *mirador* (lookout), 200m before the hotel, or procure a hotel day pass for CUC$25.

ℹ Getting There & Away

Almost all guests arrive on all-inclusive tours and are bused in from Frank País Airport in Holguín, 115km to the southeast. It's very secluded.

The road from Puerto Padre to Playa Covarrubias is what Cuban taxi drivers call *mas o menos* (more or less) due to regular hotel traffic. West to Manatí and Playa Santa Lucía is an African-style hole-fest. Drive slowly and carefully!

You may find a taxi in Las Tunas (one-way CUC$45, plus CUC$10 per hour to wait).

Playas la Herradura, la Llanita & las Bocas

This wild string of northern beaches hugs the Atlantic coast 55km from Holguín. Come to read, relax and lose yourself in the vivid colors of traditional Cuban life.

From Puerto Padre it's 30km to the rustic Playa la Herradura. Enjoy this delicious scoop of golden sand with no resort in sight. In this attractive small town everyone knows everyone.

Continue west 11km to Playa la Llanita. The road was abused by Hurricane Matthew; drive with care. There's a long, straight beach and the water is somewhat shallow. The sand here is softer and whiter than in La Herradura, but the beach lies on an unprotected bend and there's sometimes a vicious chop.

Just 1km beyond, Playa las Bocas marks the end of the road with a few houses, a convenience store and open-air bar. You can usually catch a local ferry to El Socucho (CUC$1) to continue to Puerto Padre.

🛏 Sleeping & Eating

★**Villa Carolina** CASA PARTICULAR $
(☎mobile 52-38-72-72; Casa No 99, La Herradura; r CUC$20-25; ❄) On the way into town look for this yellow two-story home. The rooms are all upstairs along a long shaded terrace with rockers and sea views. There are three rooms, all impeccable, with refrigerators and TV. Breakfast is CUC$2.50 extra.

THE BALCONY OF THE ORIENTE

Thanks to the nature of its colonization and the vast array of outside influences that have washed up intermittently on its shores, Cuba exhibits distinct regional differences. The most marked are those between the west (Occidente) and east (Oriente), demarcated by a line that runs roughly through Las Tunas, a province popularly known as El Balcón del Oriente (the Balcony of the Oriente).

Prior to 1976, Las Tunas and the four provinces to the east (Guantánamo, Santiago de Cuba, Granma and Holguín) were encased in a single culturally distinct province known simply as 'Oriente.' Although the political barriers were removed in the 1976 provincial shake-up, regional identity remains strong, especially among the traditional 'underdogs' from the east.

Geographically closer to Haiti than Havana, Cuba's Oriente has often looked east rather than west in its bid to cement an alternative Cuban identity, absorbing myriad influences from Jamaica, the Lesser Antilles and, in particular, French Haiti. It is this soul-searching, in part, which accounts for the region's rich ethnic diversity and long-standing penchant for rebellion.

It's no accident that all of Cuba's revolutionary movements have been ignited in the Oriente, inspired by such fiery easterners as Carlos Manuel de Céspedes (from Bayamo), Antonio Maceo (from Santiago) and Fidel Castro (from Birán near Holguín). The region has also been a standard-bearer for the lion's share of Cuba's hybrid musical genres, from *son* and *changüí* to *nueva trova*. Cuban hip-hop might have had its genesis in Alamar, a suburb of Havana, but most of its instigators were eastern migrants from Santiago de Cuba.

Today, Cuba's east–west rivals continue to trade humorous insults on all number of topics. Listen carefully and you'll notice that people from the Oriente have a strong 'singsong' accent. They are also generally less well-off economically, resulting in the long-standing trend for easterners to migrate west for work. More subtle are the musical and religious nuances. The Oriente hides copious Afro-Haitian traditions left over from the era of slavery. These are most clearly manifested in Santiago's folkloric dance troupes and its manic July carnival.

Casa Reinold CASA PARTICULAR **$**
(☎52-38-04-68; entrada Playa La Llanita, La Llanita; r CUC$25; ❄) Let's be clear. There is little else to do here than dig your feet into the white sand and watch the lapping surf. For some, that will be enough. This beachfront electric-pink house has two average rooms for rent, electric showers and meals when you want them. There are two Adirondack chairs alongside a sea-grape tree and shallow waters.

The location is just at the entrance to La Llanita, to the right of a fork in the road.

Restaurante Roberto SEAFOOD **$$**
(☎31-54-71-26; Las Bocas, Playa Las Bocas; mains CUC$3-12; ❄) A coral wall surrounds this small home courtyard with a couple of open-air tables and friendly service. The shady patio is pleasant but there's no sea view. Seafood is offered at all hours, there are also a couple of dark rooms for rent.

ℹ Getting There & Away

There are trucks ($3 *moneda nacional*) that can take you as far as Puerto Padre from Las Tunas. From Puerto Padre, other trucks ($2 *moneda nacional*) make the trip. It's much easier to get up this way from Holguín, changing at the town of Velasco.

Driving is the best shot, though after Puerto Padre the road can be in poor condition. Taxis from Puerto Padre cost CUC$20, or more due to road conditions. Taxis from Las Tunas to the beaches cost CUC$61 to CUC$66, depending on the distance.

1

MIAMI2YOU/SHUTTERSTOCK ©

2

4

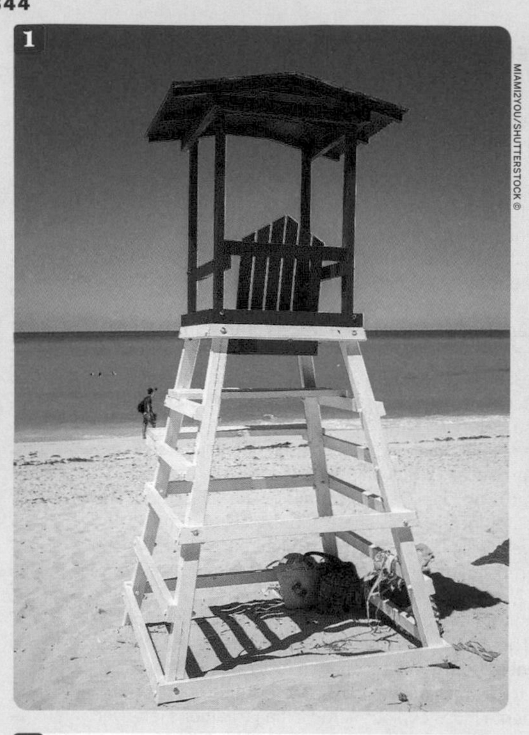

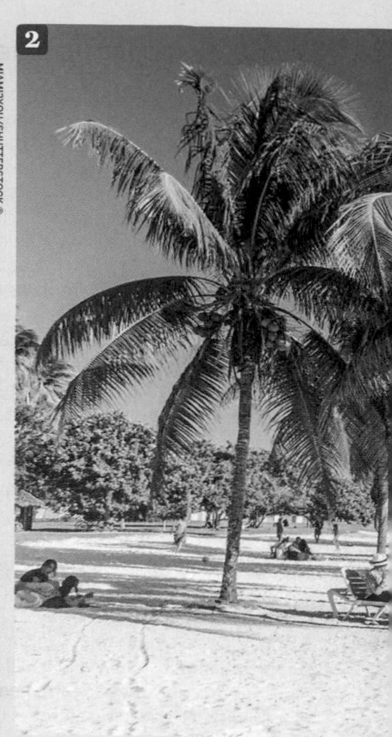

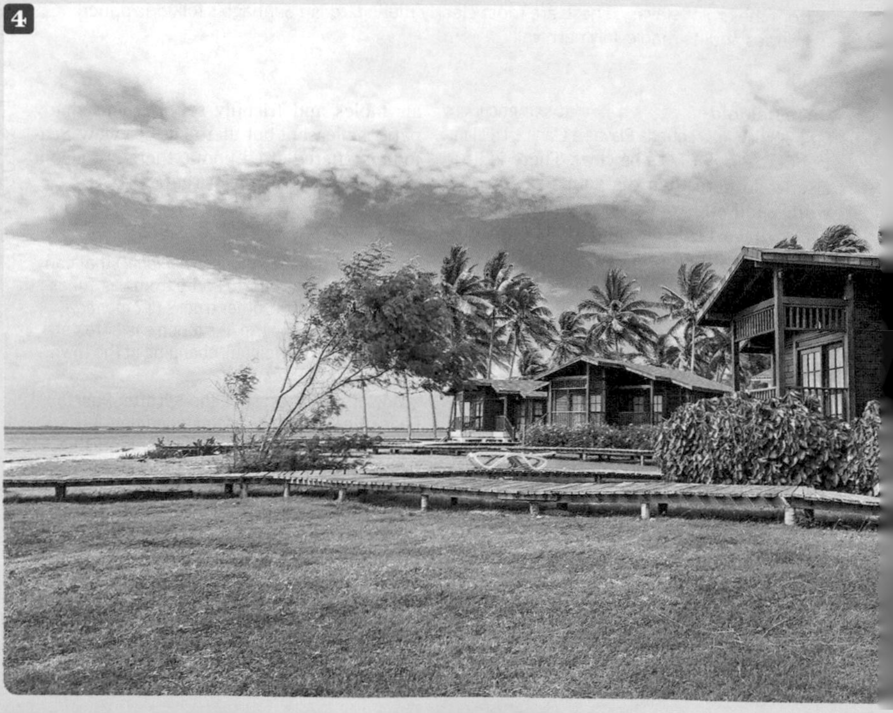

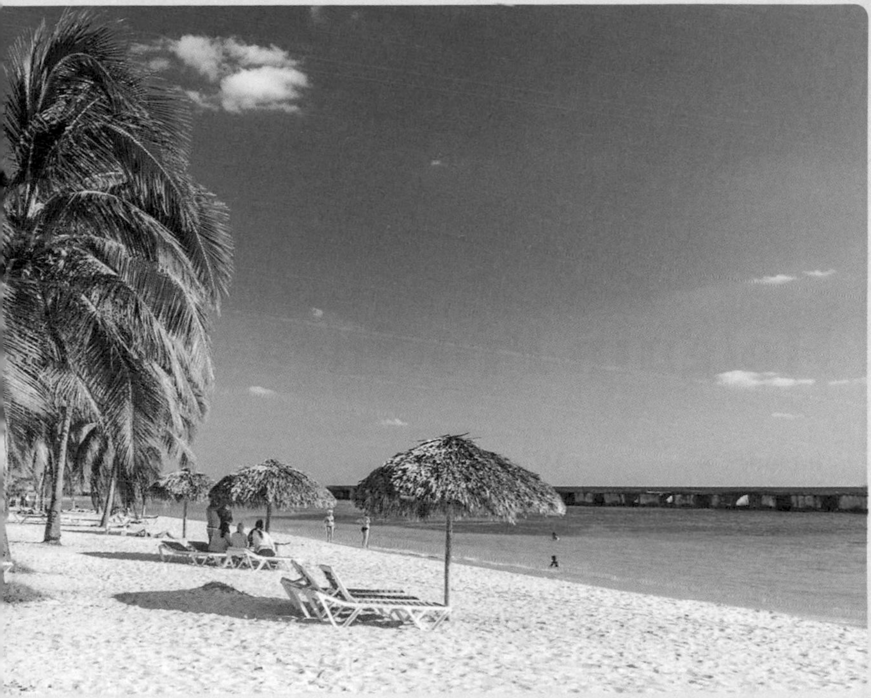

MATYAS REHAK/SHUTTERSTOCK ©

VVITAL/SHUTTERSTOCK ©

FINDELMUNDO/SHUTTERSTOCK ©

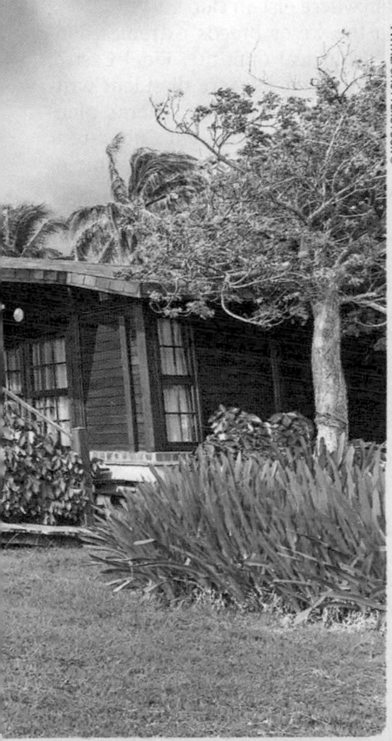

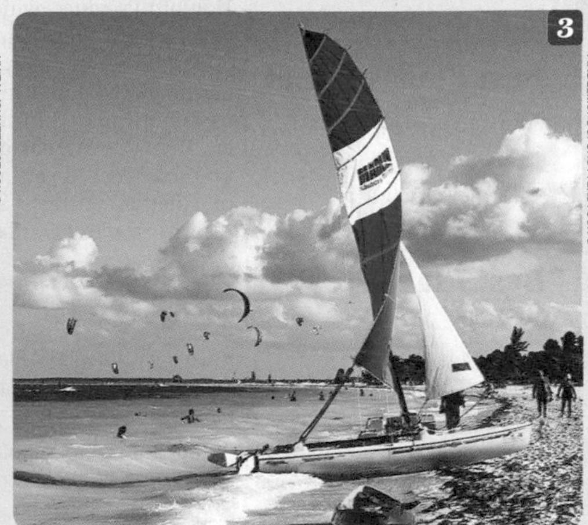

1. Varadero (p200)
Home to Cuba's largest resort area, on 20kms of uninterrupted blond sand.

2. Playa Girón (p231)
One of Cuba's best spots for diving and snorkeling, Playa Girón nestles peacefully on the eastern side of the infamous Bay of Pigs.

3. Cayo Guillermo (p314)
Cayo Guillermo has recently morphed into one of Cuba's most prized kiteboarding locations.

4. Secortel Club Cayo Guillermo (p315)
The oldest hotel on the Sabana-Camagüey archipelago, Sercotel sits in a quiet beachside location.

Holguín Province

☎24 / POP 1,037,600

Includes ➜

Best Places to Eat

- ➜ Restaurante 1910 (p353)
- ➜ El Ancla (p366)
- ➜ La Cueva (p359)

Best Places to Sleep

- ➜ Villa Pinares del Mayarí (p369)
- ➜ Villa Cayo Saetía (p369)
- ➜ Villa Don Lino (p362)
- ➜ Campismo Silla de Gibara (p362)

Why Go?

In this beautiful hill-studded hinterland, Cuba's contradictions are magnified. For the visitor, there's rich landscapes ranging from the pine-scented mountains of the Sierra Cristal to the palm-fringed beaches around Guardalavaca. Holguín's beauty was first spied by Christopher Columbus who, by most accounts, docked near Gibara in October 1492 where he was met by a group of curious Taíno natives. The Taínos didn't survive the ensuing Spanish colonization, though fragments of their legacy can be reconstructed in Holguín Province, which contains more pre-Columbian archaeological sites than anywhere else in Cuba.

Perhaps something in the water breeds extremes. Fulgencio Batista, and his ideological opposite, Fidel Castro, were both reared in this province, as were dissident writers Reinaldo Arenas and Guillermo Infante. There's plenty of contrast in settings as well: the inherent Cuban-ness of Gibara contrasts sharply with the tourist swank of resort-complex Guardalavaca.

When to Go

- ➜ Guardalavaca and Playa Pesquero resorts are at their best during the prime tourist season from December until early March.
- ➜ Latin music fans should hit Holguín in late October for the Fiesta de la Cultura Iberoamericana
- ➜ In April movie aficionados take over the sleepy town of Gibara for the offbeat Festival Internacional de Cine Pobre.
- ➜ The city of Holguín shows off its religious spirit during the Romerías de Mayo in early May, culminating with a procession up the steep Loma de la Cruz.
- ➜ To avoid the peak storm period, don't travel during the hurricane season from July to mid-November.

Holguín

POP 288,400

The nation's fourth-largest city serves up authentic provincial Cuba without the wrapping paper. Though the city of San Isidoro de Holguín barely features in Cuba's tourist master plan, there's magic and mystery here for a certain type of traveler. There's an overabundance of shiny vintage Chevys, plazas filled with uniformed school children sharing wi-fi and interactions not marred by rushing or selling. Use it as a window to life in the interior: from the religious solemnity of the annual procession climbing Loma de la Cruz to the exuberant cheers pouring forth from the oversized baseball stadium.

Although Guardalavaca is nearby, there's little focus on tourism in the provincial capital. You won't find tour groups milling the streets in migratory herds, but you will find an easy authenticity. Think eager-to-please casas particulares, cheap food in pioneering restaurants and a city that loves – and brews – its own beer.

Sights

Base yourself around the city's four central squares and you'll see most of what's on offer. However, no walk is complete without a climb up the emblematic Loma de la Cruz – a little off the grid, but well worth the detour.

★Museo de Historia Provincial — MUSEUM

(Map p352; ☎24-46-33-95; Frexes No 198; CUC$1; ⌚8am-4:30pm Tue-Sat, 8am-noon Sun) Now a national monument, the building on the northern side of Parque Calixto García was constructed between 1860 and 1868 and was used as a Spanish army barracks during the independence wars. It was nicknamed La Periquera (Parrot Cage) for the red, yellow and green uniforms of the Spanish soldiers who stood guard.

The prize exhibit is an old axe-head carved in the likeness of a man, known as the Hacha de Holguín (Holguín Axe), thought to have been made by indigenous inhabitants in the early 1400s and discovered in 1860. Looking even sharper in its polished glass case is a sword that once belonged to national hero and poet, José Martí.

★La Loma de la Cruz — LANDMARK

At the northern end of Maceo, a stairway built in 1950 ascends 465 steps to top a hill (275m) with panoramic views, a restaurant and a 24-hour bar. It's a 20-minute walk from the center or go via bici-taxi (CUC$1) to the base. This walk is best tackled early in the morning when the light is pristine and temperature cooler.

A cross was raised here in 1790 in the hope of relieving a drought. During Romerías de Mayo, devotees climb to the summit on May 3 where a special Mass is held.

★Catedral de San Isidoro — CATHEDRAL

(Map p352; Manduley) Dazzling white and characterized by its twin domed towers, the Catedral de San Isidoro, one of the town's original constructions, dates from 1720. Added over the years, the towers are of 20th-century vintage. A hyper-realistic statue of Pope John Paul II stands right of the main doors. If it's open, take a peek inside at the relatively austere interior.

Parque Céspedes — PARK

(Parque San José; Map p352) Holguín's youngest park is also its shadiest. Named for 'Father of the Motherland' Carlos Manuel de Céspedes – his statue stands center stage next to a monument honoring the heroes of the War of Independence – the cobbled central square is dominated by the Iglesia de San José.

The church, with its distinctive mezzanine floor, dome and belltower, was once used by the Independistas as a lookout tower. Locals still refer to the park by its old name, San José.

Parque Peralta — SQUARE

(Parque de las Flores; Map p352) This square is named for General Julio Grave de Peralta (1834–72), who led an uprising against Spain in Holguín in October 1868. His marble statue (1916) faces the imposing Catedral de San Isidoro. On the western side of the park is the Mural de Origen, depicting the development of Holguín and of Cuba from indigenous times to the end of slavery.

Fábrica de Órganos — FACTORY

(Carretera de Gibara No 301; ⌚8am-4pm Mon-Fri) Visitors can tour the only mechanical music-organ factory in Cuba. This small factory produces about six organs a year, as well as guitars and other instruments.

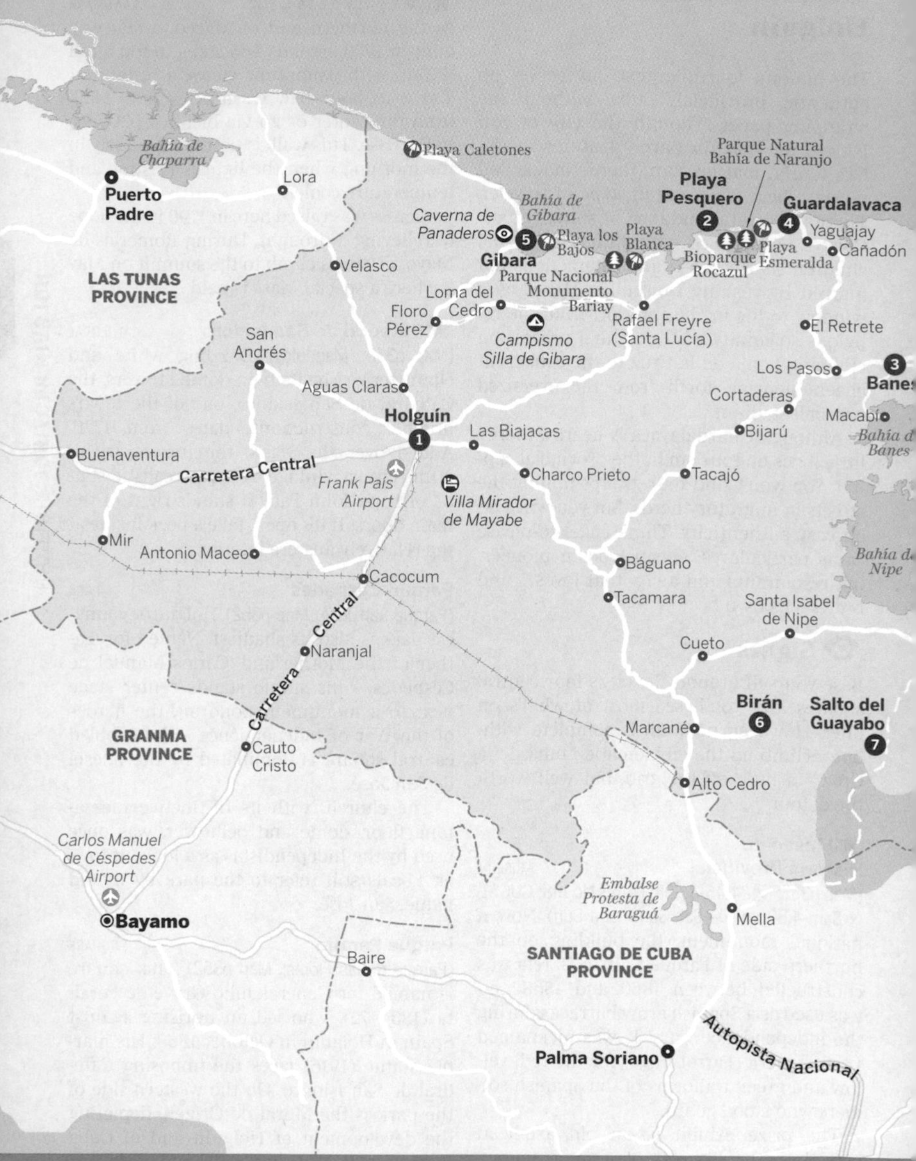

Holguín Province Highlights

1. **Loma de la Cruz** (p347) Seeing Holguín spread out like a map beneath you from the heights of this city peak.
2. **Playa Pesquero** (p363) Reveling in luxuriant beach time at one of several plush resorts.
3. **Banes** (p366) Pedaling leisurely through bucolic villages to this quintessential *holguiñero* town.
4. **Museo Chorro de Maita** (p363) Discovering Taíno treasures in one of Cuba's most important archaeological sites in Guardalavaca.

5 **Gibara** (p359) Relaxing in gorgeous colonial accommodations in this enigmatic seaside town.

6 **Museo Conjunto Histórico de Birán** (p370) Peeping behind the scenes of the Castro family compound while touring Fidel's childhood home.

7 **Salto del Guayabo** (p369) Gazing upon a spectacular waterfall in Cuba's little Switzerland.

Holguín

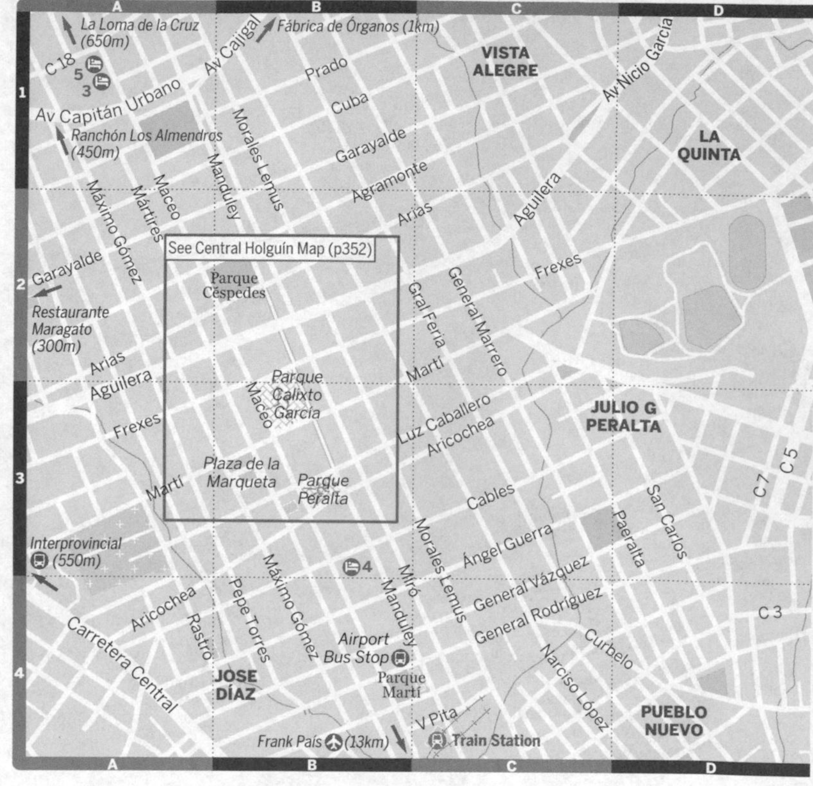

A good organ costs between US$10,000 and US$28,000. Eight professional organ groups exist in Holguín (including the Familia Cuayo, based at the factory): if you're lucky, you can hear one playing on Parque Céspedes on Thursday afternoon or Sunday morning.

Plaza de la Marqueta SQUARE

(Map p352) Laid out in 1848, rebuilt in 1918 and renovated only recently, this gleaming square is dominated by bronze busts and an impressive covered marketplace housing a cafe and artisan stalls. Running along the north and south sides of the plaza are myriad shops selling music, crafts and cigars.

Parque Calixto García SQUARE

(Map p352) This wide, expansive square is more about atmosphere than architecture. It was laid out in 1719 as the original Plaza de Armas and served for many years as the town's meeting point and marketplace. The centerpiece today is a 1912 statue of General Calixto García, where you'll find a mixture of old sages, baseball naysayers and teenagers on the prowl.

In the southwestern corner of Parque Calixto García is the **Centro de Arte** (Map p352; 24-42-23-92; Maceo No 180; 9am-4pm Mon-Sat) FREE, a gallery for temporary exhibitions that shares space with **Biblioteca Alex Urquiola** (24-46-25-62; 8am-9pm Mon-Sat), named after a local revolutionary, and housing Holguín's biggest book collection.

Casa Natal de Calixto García MUSEUM

(Map p352; 24-42-56-10; Miró No 147; CUC$1; 9am-5pm Tue-Sat) To learn more about the militaristic deeds of Holguín's local hero, head to this house situated two blocks east of the namesake park. The hugely underestimated García – who stole the cities of Las Tunas, Holguín and Bayamo from Spanish

Holguín

Sights

Sleeping

Drinking & Nightlife

Entertainment

control between 1896 and 1898 – was born here in 1839.

This small collection gives a reasonable overview of his life: military maps, old uniforms and even a spoon he ate with on the campaign trail in 1885.

Plaza de la Revolución SQUARE
(Map p350) Holguín is a city most *fiel* (faithful) and its bombastic revolutionary plaza, east of the center, is a huge monument to the heroes of Cuban independence, bearing quotations from José Martí and Fidel Castro. Massive rallies are held here every May 1 (Labor Day). The tomb and ashes of Calixto García are also here, as is as a smaller monument to García's mother.

Iglesia de San José CHURCH
(Map p352; Manduley No 116) In Parque Céspedes, the Iglesia de San José features a distinctive dome with a bell tower (1842), once used by the Independistas as a lookout.

Festivals & Events

★ Fiesta de la Cultura Iberoamericana MUSIC
(www.casadeiberoamerica.cult.cu; late Oct) Musicians from all over Latin America and beyond take over the city for a week of concerts (many free) in venues throughout the city. Some big Cuban acts play, too. Forty countries and diverse genres are represented. There are also workshops for musicians and a nod to the arts and dance.

Romerías de Mayo RELIGIOUS
(May) Holguín's big annual pilgrimage is held the first week of May: devotees climb Loma de la Cruz for a special mass. The whole city turns out to follow the procession from the Catedral de San Isidro, a custom dating back to the 1790s. In recent times the parade has become livelier with arty contributions from the Hermanos Saíz youth organization.

Sleeping

La Palma Casa Enrique CASA PARTICULAR $
(Map p350; 24-42-46-83; lapalmaenrique@nauta.cu; Maceo No 52a, btwn Calles 16 & 18, El Llano; r CUC$25;) Resembling a little piece of Florida, this smart, detached neocolonial with requisite palm tree dates from 1945. It sits in the shadow of the Loma de la Cruz, a calm location worth the minor inconvenience. Two spacious guest rooms occupy their own wing of the house, offering ample privacy. Enrique is a thoughtful and helpful host.

Check out the skilled artwork of Enrique's son: a terra-cotta bust of Che Guevara in the living room next to an unusual 3m-long canvas copy of Da Vinci's *The Last Supper* with

St John as a woman. There's wi-fi in a plaza one block away.

Villa Liba CASA PARTICULAR **$**
(Map p350; ☎24-42-38-23, 52-89-69-31; Maceo No 46, cnr Calle 18; s/d CUC$25/30; ❄) The *alma* (soul) bubbles over at this smart, soulful bungalow invoking a 1950s North American suburb. At the center are welcoming hosts: Jorge is a modern-day Pablo Neruda with whimsical anecdotes aplenty on Holguín life; and Mariela is an accomplished massage and Reiki specialist offering on-site treatment (CUC$25). It's worth dining in. Meals (CUC$4 to CUC$8), including vegetarian fare, have a Lebanese flair.

Villa Janeth CASA PARTICULAR **$**
(Map p350; ☎24-42-93-31, mobile 53-14-03-13; filihlg@infomed.sld.cu; Cables No 105; CUC$20-25; ❄) With great spaces, Janeth's clean, spacious house is a solid choice. Guests have the run of a full floor with balcony. There's classic Cuban style: one princess pink room and another featuring a king-sized bed with a leather headboard. There's kitchen use, TV and electric showers. She's also a welcoming host.

Central Holguín

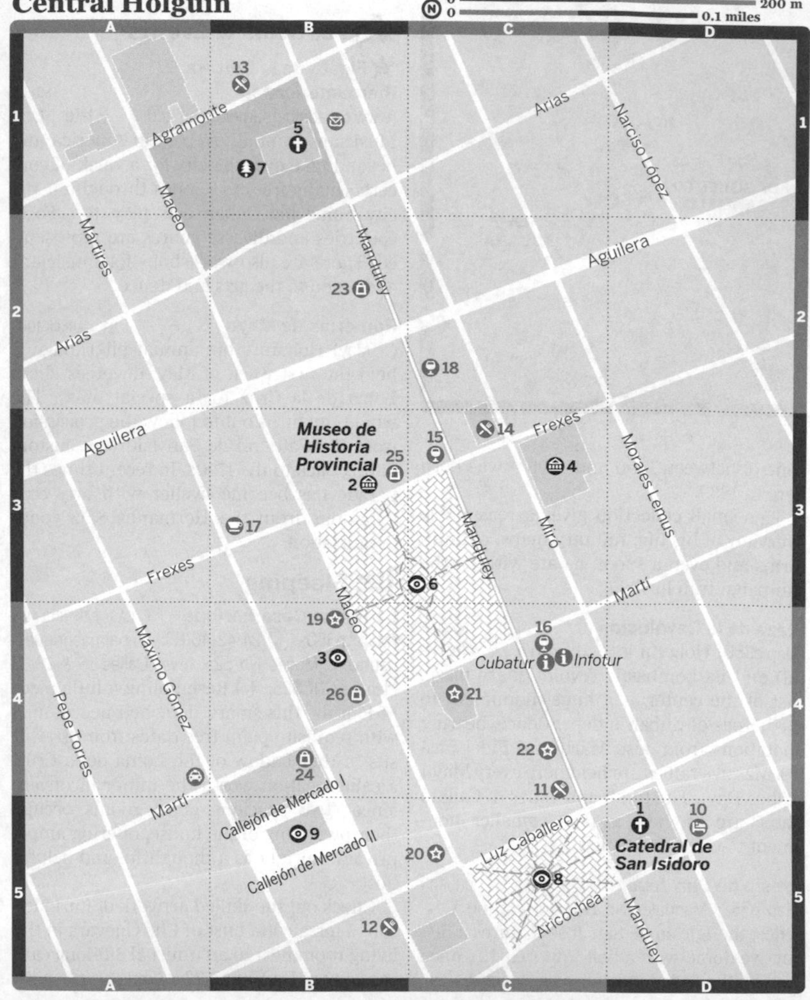

Villa Mirador de Mayabe HOTEL **$$**
(☎24-42-21-60; director@mayabe.islazul.tur.cu; Alturas de Mayabe Km8; s/d/ste CUC$69/81/102; P ❄ 📶 🏊) Cresting the Loma de Mayabe, 10km southeast of Holguín, this large hilltop compound includes adorable bungalows tucked into lush grounds. The views, taking in vast mango plantations, are especially good from the pool. For families, it's a welcome retreat. Pastel bungalows are small but pleasant, but the thatched restaurant is unremarkable.

Hotel Pernik HOTEL **$$**
(Map p350; ☎24-48-10-11; cnr Avs Jorge Dimitrov & XX Aniversario; s/d incl breakfast CUC$40/65; P ❄ @ 📶 🏊) The nearest decent hotel to the city center is another dose of Soviet-inspired '70s nostalgia. Its dour reputation is partially offset by edgy art by local artists. The breakfast buffet is plentiful and there's an information office, Cadeca (money exchange) and internet cafe. However, the hotel suffers from the usual foibles of interminable renovations and blaring late-night music.

★**Hotel Caballeriza** BOUTIQUE HOTEL **$$$**
(Map p352; ☎24-42-91-91; www.hotelescubanacan.com; Calle Miró No 203; s/d incl breakfast CUC$100/130; ❄ 📶) A renovated 1846 mansion that's seen it all. After the original owner went bankrupt it was turned into stables. Now it sports contemporary interiors with a grand colonial facade. The grand entrance features a lobby bar and restaurant. Branching off a central courtyard, big rooms have 19th-century decor and flat-screen TVs. There's 24-hour reception, attentive service and money changing services.

It's part of the elite Encanto hotel line represented by Cubanacán.

Eating

The 2011 relaxing of restrictions on private restaurants benefited Holguín more than most cities: there's a stash of reasonable private restaurants here more frequented by locals than tourists.

Restaurante-Bar San José CUBAN **$**
(Map p352; ☎24-42-48-77; Agramonte No 188; meals CUC$3-7; ⏱noon-11pm) A hub of locals slap-bang in the central square (Parque Céspedes) with mismatched paint and uniformed servers. The menu is nothing fancy, but this is where you come for *comida criolla* (Creole food) not duck á l'orange.

Cremería Guamá ICE CREAM **$**
(Map p352; ☎24-46-26-22; cnr Luz Caballero & Manduley; ice cream CUC$1; ⏱10am-10:45pm) Havana's famous ice-cream parlor. Lose an hour underneath the striped red-and-white awning overlooking pedestrianized Calle Manduley and enjoy peso treats alfresco.

★**Restaurante 1910** INTERNATIONAL **$$**
(Map p352; ☎24-42-39-94; www.1910restaurantebar.com; Mártires No 143, btwn Aricochea &

Central Holguín

Top Sights
1 Catedral de San Isidoro D5
2 Museo de Historia Provincial B3

Sights
3 Biblioteca Alex Urquiola B4
4 Casa Natal de Calixto García C3
Centro de Arte .... (see 3)
5 Iglesia de San José B1
6 Parque Calixto García C3
7 Parque Céspedes B1
8 Parque Peralta C5
9 Plaza de la Marqueta B5

Sleeping
10 Hotel Caballeriza D5

Eating
11 Cremería Guamá C4
12 Restaurante 1910 .... B5
13 Restaurante-Bar San José B1
14 Salón 1720 .... C3

Drinking & Nightlife
Bar Terraza .... (see 14)
15 Casa de la Música C3
16 Disco Cristal C4
17 Las 3 Lucías B3
18 Taberna Mayabe C2

Entertainment
19 Casa de la Trova B4
20 Salón Benny Moré C5
21 Teatro Comandante Eddy Suñol C4
22 Uneac C4

Shopping
23 Bazar – Proyecto de Desarollo Local B2
24 El Jigue B4
25 Fondo de Bienes Culturales B3
26 Pentagrama B4

Cables; meals CUC$8-11; ⌚ noon-midnight) Among Cuba's best offerings, count this elegant wood-trimmed colonial in. Guests tuck into thick steaks as if it were their last day on earth. There's also tender grilled octopus with garlic sauce, lovely chocolate *torta* (cake) and an extensive wine and liquor menu. Courteous service to boot. The restaurant is filled with locals and travelers alike. Come early or reserve.

Restaurante Maragato CUBAN **$$**
(☎ mobile 52-46-68-02; Calle Carbo, btwn Garayalde & Agramonte; mains CUC$4-11) Worth getting off the beaten path for, this easygoing restaurant does *comida criolla* (Creole food) with style. It also has the best cocktail bar in town, thanks to the barman owner. Dine on grilled meats, tender lamb shanks, yams and fresh salad. It's in front of the Hospital Lenin on a breezy 3rd-floor terrace.

Ranchón Los Almendros PARRILLA **$$**
(☎ 24-42-96-52; José A Cardet No 68, btwn Calles 12 & 14; mains CUC$10-12; ⌚ 10am-11pm) With excellent smoked meats with copious trimmings, *tostones* (fried plantain) and huge stuffed peppers filled with *ropa vieja* (shredded beef), this restaurant is worth the little bit extra it costs. Located near the Loma de la Cruz, it doesn't look much from the outside but rest assured – inside is a different story.

Salón 1720 CARIBBEAN **$$**
(Map p352; ☎ 24-46-81-50; Frexes No 190, cnr Miró; meals CUC$6-9; ⌚ noon-10:30pm) A painstakingly restored wedding cake mansion with a full, social atmosphere. Tuck into paella or chicken stuffed with vegetables and cheese; there's even complimentary crackers. In the same colonial-style complex there's a cigar shop, bar, boutique, car rental and a terrace with nighttime music. Check out the wall plaques that give interesting insights into Holguín's history.

Drinking & Nightlife

Welcome to beer city. The local bars aren't too flash, but you can cobble together a decent pub crawl here.

Casa de la Música CLUB
(Map p352; ☎ 24-42-95-61; cnr Frexes & Manduley; ⌚ Tue-Sun) There's a young, trendy vibe at this place on Parque Calixto García. If you can't dance, stay static sinking beers on the adjacent Terraza Bucanero (entry via Calle Manduley).

Bar Terraza BAR
(Map p352; Frexes, btwn Manduley & Miró; ⌚ 8pm-1am) Perched above Salón 1720, this is the city's poshest spot. Cocktails are in order as you drink in the views over Parque Calixto García (p350) while listening to live music.

Terraza del Pernik CLUB
(Map p350; ☎ 24-48-10-11; Hotel Pernik, cnr Avs Jorge Dimitrov & XX Aniversario; guest/nonguest CUC$2/4; ⌚ 10pm-2am Tue-Sun) Holguín's premier disco at Hotel Pernik. If you're staying there, the music will visit you – in your room – like it or not, until 1am.

Disco Cristal CLUB
(Map p352; ☎ 24-42-10-41; 3rd fl, Edificio Pico de Cristal, Manduley No 199; CUC$1; ⌚ 9pm-2am Tue-Thu) A nexus for Holguín's skilled dancers (most of whom are young, cool and determined to have a good time), this place is insanely popular at weekends when you'll find lots of inspiration for the salsa/rap/reggaeton (Cuban hip-hop) repertoire.

El Nocturno CLUB
(☎ 24-42-93-45; Av Cajígal; CUC$8; ⌚ 10pm-2am) This is a Tropicana-style cabaret club beyond the Servi-Cupet gas station, 3km out on the road to Las Tunas.

Las 3 Lucías CAFE
(Map p352; ☎ 24-45-18-72; cnr Mártires & Frexes; ⌚ 7am-11pm) Decorated in Cuban film memorabilia, this fancy cafe evokes a classy atmosphere of yesteryear – save for the big wall-mounted TV. It's known locally as a cheap outing. The cocktails are good, the coffee's alright and the atmosphere is pretty unique.

Lucía was a 1968 classic Cuban film about the lives of three women, each named Lucía, in different periods: the War of Independence, the 1930s and the 1960s.

Taberna Mayabe BAR
(Map p352; Manduley, btwn Aguilera & Frexes; ⌚ noon-6pm & 8-11pm Tue-Sun) A grotty tavern on pedestrian-only Manduley, where wooden tables and ceramic mugs create a hearty olden days atmosphere. Solo travelers elicit more than one sideways glance. Best for pairs or groups. The eponymous local brew is served.

Entertainment

★Uneac
THEATER, MUSIC

(Map p352; ☎24-47-40-66; Manduley, btwn Luz Caballero & Martí) There's at least one National Union of Cuban Writers and Artists per province in Cuba, but if you visit only one, make it here. Situated in the lovingly restored Casa de las Moyúas (1845) on car-free Calle Manduley, this friendly establishment offers literary evenings with famous authors, music nights, patio theater (including Lorca) and cultural reviews. There's an intermittent bar on a gorgeous central patio and an on-site art gallery-studio called La Cochera.

★Teatro Comandante Eddy Suñol
THEATER

(Map p352; ☎24-42-79-94; Martí No 111; ♿) Holguín's premier theater is an art deco treat from 1939 on Parque Calixto García. It hosts both the Teatro Lírico Rodrigo Prats and the Ballet Nacional de Cuba, and is renowned both nationally and internationally for its operettas, dance performances and Spanish musicals.

Check here for details of performances by the famous children's theater Alas Buenas and the Orquesta Sinfónica de Holguín (Holguín Symphony Orchestra).

★Casa de la Trova
LIVE MUSIC

(Map p352; ☎24-45-31-04; Maceo No 174; ⊙Tue-Sun) Old guys in Panama hats croon under the rafters, musicians in *guayaberas* (Caribbean dress shirts) blast on trumpets, while ancient couples in their Sunday best map out a perfect *danzón* (traditional Cuban ballroom dance). So timeless, so Holguín.

Salón Benny Moré
LIVE MUSIC

(Map p352; ☎24-42-35-18; cnr Luz Caballero & Maceo; ⊙show 10:30pm) Holguín's impressive outdoor music venue is the best place to round off a bar crawl with some live music and dancing.

Estadio General Calixto García
SPECTATOR SPORT

(Map p350; ☎24-42-26-14; off Av de los Libertadores; CUC$1-2) Mosey on down to this stadium to see Holguín's baseball team, former giant-killers the Perros (dogs) who snatched the national championship from under the noses of the 'big two' in 2002, but haven't barked much since. The stadium also houses a small but interesting sport museum.

Shopping

Fondo de Bienes Culturales
ARTS & CRAFTS

(Map p352; ☎24-42-37-82; Frexes No 196; ⊙10am-3pm Mon-Fri, 9am-noon Sat) This state-run shop on Parque Calixto García sells small, affordable paintings and similar handicrafts to the private vendor market a few blocks away.

Bazar – Proyecto de Desarollo Local
MARKET

(Map p352; Manduley, btwn Aguilera & Arias; ⊙8am-6pm Mon-Sat) The local private market as opposed to the nearby government-run affair. This Bazar sells a similar stash of trinkets, Afro-Cuban masks and clothing, but the money goes directly into the pockets of the vendors. *Capitalismo* or *socialismo* – take your pick.

Pentagrama
MUSIC

(Map p352; ☎24-45-31-35; cnr Maceo & Martí; ⊙8am-noon & 12:30-4:30pm) Official outlet of the Cuban state record company Egrem, selling a small but decent stash of CDs.

El Jigue
BOOKS, SOUVENIRS

(Map p352; ☎26-46-85-21; cnr Martí & Mártires; ⊙9am-5pm) Well-stocked bookstore and souvenir outlet adjacent to Plaza de la Marqueta.

Information

INTERNET ACCESS

There is a wi-fi hotspot in Parque Calixto García.

Etecsa Telepunto (☎24-47-40-67; Calle Martí No 122, btwn Martires & Máximo Gómez; internet per hr CUC$1.50; ⊙8:30am-7:30pm) Branch of Cuban phone company selling wi-fi scratchcards.

MEDICAL SERVICES

Farmacia Turno Especial (☎24-42-57-90; Maceo No 170; ⊙8am-10pm Mon-Sat) Pharmacy on Parque Calixto García.

Hospital Lenin (☎24-42-53-02; Av Vl Lenin) Will treat foreigners in an emergency.

MONEY

Banco de Crédito y Comercio (☎24-46-73-89; Arias; ⊙9am-3pm Mon-Fri) Bank on Parque Céspedes with ATM.

Banco Financiero Internacional (☎24-46-85-02; Manduley No 167, btwn Frexes & Aguilera; ⊙9am-3pm Mon-Fri) Has an ATM.

Cadeca (☎24-46-86-63; Manduley No 205, btwn Martí & Luz Caballero) Money-changing.

POST

Post Office (Map p352; Maceo No 114, Parque Céspedes; 8am-6pm Mon-Sat)

TOURIST INFORMATION

A number of agencies near the main plaza offer similar services for reservations, tickets and tours.

Infotur (Map p352; 24-42-50-13; 1st fl, Edificio Pico de Cristal, cnr Manduley & Martí; 8am-4pm Mon-Fri & alternate Sat) Tourist information on the 2nd floor above Cafetería Cristal.

TRAVEL AGENCIES

Cubatur (Map p352; Edificio Pico de Cristal, cnr Manduley & Martí) Travel agent bivouacked inside the Cafetería Begonias at a guest table. Useful for Viazul tickets.

Getting There & Away

AIR

Frank País Airport (HOG; 24-47-46-30) There are frequent international flights into Holguín's well-organized airport, 13km south of the city, including from Amsterdam, Düsseldorf, London, Montreal and Toronto. Almost all arrivals bus directly to Guardalavaca.

BUS

A daily bus, run by Transtur, connects to the Guardalavaca resorts (round-trip CUC$15). It departs from outside the Museo de Historia Provincial (p347) daily at 1pm, returning from Guardalavaca at 8am.

Interprovincial Bus Station (cnr Carretera Central & Independencia) West of the center near Hospital Lenin, this station houses **Víazul** (www.viazul.com).

CAR

Colectivos (shared taxis) run to Gibara (CUC$4) and Puerto Padre in Las Tunas Province from Av Cajígal. Those going to Guardalavaca (CUC$5) leave from outside Estadio General Calixto García (p355).

TRAIN

For starters, no one recommends the train. The only service that operates with any regularity is the train to Havana. The service to Santiago de Cuba is rather irregular. Research beforehand.

For Havana, change trains at the Santiago–Havana mainline junction in Cacocum, 17km south of Holguín. Theoretically, there's one daily morning train to Las Tunas (CUC$3, two hours), an 8am train every three days to Guantánamo, three daily trains to Santiago de Cuba (CUC$5, 3½ hours) and two daily trains (10:19pm and 5:28am) to Havana (CUC$26, 15 hours). This train stops in Camagüey (CUC$6.50), Ciego de Ávila (CUC$10.50), Santa Clara (CUC$15.50) and Matanzas (CUC$22.50).

Train Station (24-42-23-31; Calle V Pita 3) The train station is on the southern side of town.

TRUCK

Terminal Dagoberto Sanfield Guillén (Av de los Libertadores) Opposite Estadio General Calixto García (p355), this area has at least two daily trucks to Gibara, Banes and Moa.

Getting Around

TO/FROM THE AIRPORT

Airport Bus Stop (Map p350; General Rodríguez No 84; departs 2pm) The public bus to the airport leaves from the airport bus stop on Parque Martí near the train station.

BICI-TAXI

Definitely worth a try, the sidecar bici-taxi, resembling a bike with a wheelchair fused on, was invented here. Holguín's ubiquitous bici-taxis charge CUC$1 for a short trip, CUC$2 for a long one.

CAR

You can rent or return a car at Cubacar, with branches at Hotel Pernik (24-46-84-14; Av Jorge Dimitrov; 8am-9pm), Aeropuerto Frank País (24-46-84-14) and Cafetería Cristal (24-46-85-59; cnr Manduley & Martí; 8am-9pm).

A **Servi-Cupet gas station** (Av Cajigal; 24hr) is 3km out of town toward Las Tunas; another station is just outside town on the road to Gibara. An **Oro Negro gas station** (Carretera Central) is on the southern edge of town. The road to Gibara is north on Av Cajígal; also take

VÍAZUL BUS DEPARTURES FROM HOLGUÍN

DESTINATION	COST (CUC$)	DURATION (HR)	DAILY DEPARTURES
Havana	44	12	7:45am, 10:10am, 8:20pm, 9:15pm
Santiago	11	3.5	3:55am, 9:50am, 4:45pm
Trinidad	26	7¾	11:15pm
Varadero	38	11¼	11:45pm

this road and fork left after 5km to reach Playa la Herradura.

TAXI

A **Cubataxi** (Map p352; ☎24-47-35-35; Máximo Gómez cnr Martí) to Guardalavaca (54km) costs around CUC$35. To Gibara one way should cost no more than CUC$20.

Gibara

POP 73,000

Matched only by Baracoa for its wild coastal setting, half-forgotten Gibara, with its faded pastel facades and surging ocean rollers, conspires to seduce you. Close to Holguín, there's a cultural life here that seems big for a small town. In 2008, Hurricane Ike almost wiped the town off the map. Luckily, it did not.

Situated 33km from Holguín via a scenic road that undulates through villages, Gibara is a small, intimate place receiving a lift from much-needed investment. Unlike nearby Guardalavaca, development here is low-key and focused on renovating the town's beautiful but dilapidated architecture. The saddle-shaped Silla de Gibara that so captivated Columbus creates a wild, scenic backdrop. Nearby is the site of one of Cuba's first wind farms.

Each April Gibara hosts the Festival Internacional de Cine Pobre (p359), which draws films and filmmakers from all over the world.

History

Columbus first arrived in the area in 1492 and called it Río de Mares (River of Seas) for the Ríos Cacoyugüín and Yabazón that drain into the Bahía de Gibara. The current name comes from *jiba,* the indigenous word for a bush that still grows along the shore.

Refounded in 1817, Gibara prospered in the 19th century as the sugar industry expanded and the trade rolled in. To protect the settlement from pirates, barracks and a 2km wall were constructed around the town in the early 1800s, making Gibara Cuba's second walled city (after Havana). The once sparkling-white facades earned Gibara its nickname, La Villa Blanca.

Holguín's outlet to the sea was once an important sugar-export town that was linked to the provincial capital via a railway. With the construction of the Carretera Central in the 1920s, Gibara lost its mercantile importance and, after the last train service was axed in 1958, the town fell into a sleepy slumber from which it has yet to fully awaken.

Sights

Gibara has seen a small renaissance with government investment aimed at restoring and renovating the city's architecture. Though the specific attractions are few, rather like Baracoa, this is more a town to stroll the streets and absorb the local flavor. There are a couple of decent beaches within striking distance of Gibara, however.

In Town

El Cañonazo MUSEUM

(Map p361; ☎53-81-26-72; elpatriotaflores@gmail.com; ⏲hours vary) There's nothing else quite like this in Cuba. Known as the patriot, Miguel Flores has a quirky collection of homemade satire memorabilia featuring the Pope, Obama, 1950s movie stars and others. He is even considering a parody slave auction targeting Cuba's history. Refusing to take sides in politics, he calls all art 'a statement for peace.'

Iglesia de San Fulgencio CHURCH

(Map p361; ⏲8am-noon & 2-4:30pm Tue-Sun) Built in 1850, this church was recently the recipient of a gleaming renovation.

Parque Calixto García SQUARE

(Map p361) A central plaza lined with weird *robles africanos,* African oaks with large pods. The Statue of Liberty in front commemorates the Spanish-Cuban-American War.

Spanish Forts FORT

(Map p361) At the top of Calle Cabada, this crumbling brick Spanish fort with graceful arches provides stunning town and bay views. Continue on this street for 200m to Restaurante el Mirador for an even better vantage point. You'll see remnants of the old fortresses here and at the Fuerte Fernando VII, on the point beyond Parque de las Madres, a block over from Parque Calixto García. There's also a sentinel tower at the entrance to the town, coming in from Holguín.

Museo de Historia Natural MUSEUM

(Map p361; Luz Caballero No 23; CUC$1; ⏲8am-noon & 1-5pm Tue-Sat, 1-4pm Mon) Housed in a worn colonial palace (more interesting than the stuffed stuff it collects), is the Museo de

DON'T MISS

THE POOR PERSON'S FILM FESTIVAL

There's no red carpet, no paparazzi and no Hollywood stars, but what the Festival Internacional de Cine Pobre lacks in glitz it makes up for in raw, undiscovered talent. Then there's the setting – ethereal Gibara, Cuba's crumbling Villa Blanca, a perfect antidote to the opulence of Hollywood and Cannes.

Inaugurated in 2003, the Cine Pobre was the brainchild of late Cuban director Humberto Solás, who fell in love with this quintessential fisherman's town after shooting his seminal movie *Lucía* here in 1968.

Open to independent filmmakers of limited means, the festival takes place in April and, despite limited advertising, attracts up to US$100,000 in prize money. Lasting for seven days, proceedings kick off with a gala in the Cine Jiba (p360) followed by film showings, art exhibitions and nightly music concerts. The competition is friendly but hotly contested, with prizes used to reward and recognize an eclectic cache of digital movie guerrillas drawn from countries as varied as Iran and the US.

Historia Natural. Through barred windows you can watch women rolling cheroots in the cigar factory across the square.

Outside Town

Playa Caletones BEACH

A lovely little beach 17km west of Gibara. The apostrophe-shaped stretch of white sand and azure sea here is a favorite of Holguín vacationers. The town is ramshackle, with no services except a rustic restaurant. Ask here about freshwater *pozas* (pools) where you can go swimming. Get here by bike, taxi (round-trip with wait CUC$25) or rental car.

Guided *cenote* (sinkhole) diving (CUC$10), 5km further along, purportedly visits some of Cuba's best cave diving sites. You'll need your own equipment. With crystalline waters, the cave system goes back some 3000m, with water depth about 15m.

On the beachfront road, Restaurante La Proa serves up some of Cuba's most delectable fresh seafood on an upstairs terrace overlooking the water.

Caverna de Panaderos CAVE

(Map p361; Independencia; excursion CUC$5) This complex cave system with 19 galleries and a lengthy underground trail is close to town at the top end of Calle Independencia. Guides are required as there are no installations or signs here. Go with a qualified local guide who can offer helmets and headlamps. The walk to the cave is 1km. Those who are not too claustrophobic can squeeze into an inner chamber with a lake where you can swim. Reserve at least two hours for the excursion.

Locals have been working arduously to clean up this trail and remove an improvised trash dump from near the entrance, but it's still a work in progress, particularly before and near the entrance.

Playa Blanca BEACH

(Map p361) Located across the bay, this small sandy beach begs for bathers. From the Gibara dock, take a local *lancha* (open boat ferry; CUC$2) across the Bahía de Gibara to Juan Antonio, from where it's 400m on to Playa Blanca. There's a casa particular but no services so bring your own picnic.

Activities

Silla de Gibara CLIMBING

(Map p361) Silla de Gibara, the saddle-shaped limestone crag 35km southeast of Gibara, has around 20 'mapped' climbing routes on its shadowy north face, best tackled in the cooler months between November and February. With little government support, climbing here is similar to Viñales. Bring your own gear and use a guide.

Tours

Jose Corella TOURS

(☎mobile 53-97-90-96; joselin54@nauta.cu; city tour CUC$5) Professional and friendly, Gibara's resident historian also guides tours on weekends to Caverna de Panaderos and guides dives to the cave system near Playa Caletones. He also offers short historic city tours.

Alexis Silva García TOURS

(☎24-84-44-58) Local guide for Gibara-based climbing and caving excursions. Find him at the Museo de Historia Natural (p357).

Festivals & Events

★Festival Internacional de Cine Pobre FILM

(International Low-Budget Film Festival; www.cinepobre.com; ⊙Apr) Open to independent filmmakers of limited means, this festival in Gibara takes place in April. Despite limited advertising, it attracts up to US$100,000 in prize money.

Sleeping

Hotel offerings are slowly improving in Gibara, while casas particulares have solid offerings.

★Hostal Sol y Mar CASA PARTICULAR $

(☎52-40-21-64; J Peralta No 59; r CUC$25; ❄) With wonderful sea breezes and romantic sea views, this big yellow waterfront home beats all competition on ambience. The multiple terraces are conducive to privacy. Five rooms are well-equipped and modern with electric showers. The young host, who can speak French, English, Dutch and German, will make your stay a pleasant one. There's a self-catering kitchen.

★Hostal El Patio CASA PARTICULAR $

(☎24-84-42-69; oceanomg@nauta.cu; J Mora No 19, btwn Cuba & J Agüero; r CUC$30; ❄) Tucked away behind this high-walled patio are Gibara's coziest digs: a lovely, partially covered, plant-strewn patio leading to airy renovated rooms. Think updated '50's style, white with bright accents. There's also a rooftop terrace. Mealtimes are magical in this little getaway and the family is very helpful with local information.

Bayview CASA PARTICULAR $

(Map p361; ☎52-24-55-70; Playa Blanca; r CUC$25-30; ❄) Location, location, location. With boat access only, this small house is 900m from Playa Blanca, a comma of white sand blissfully free of development. There are hammocks and the possibility of home-cooked meals. To get here, take the 10-minute ferry from Gibara. It's not to be confused with the Playa Blanca near Guardalavaca. Reservations only – call Jimmy.

La Luz del Norte CASA PARTICULAR $

(☎58-60-64-49; anabeatriziberia@nauta.cu; Donato Marmol No 69; r CUC$25; ❄ 📶) Crafted for the millennial crowd, this cool refurbished home maintains its plank wooden floors with sparse furnishings and trompe l'oeil murals showing vivid sunsets or a Magritte-worthy wall of clouds surrounding an open window. There's five rooms and ample living space, a bit uphill from the action. The host Ana speaks English and has hotel experience.

Hotel Arsenita BOUTIQUE HOTEL $$

(☎24-84-44-00; reservas.arsenita@cubanacan.gibara.tur.cu; s/d incl breakfast CUC$80/110; ❄@) This brand-new colonial remodel infuses old-time glamour into staid old Parque Calixto García. There's an adorable three-seat lobby bar with a bow-tied barman mixing daiquiris, a gorgeous wall mural in the vaulted entry and 12 modern rooms with flat-screen TVs. In truth, it's the second-best hotel in town but we like its can-do spirit.

★Hotel Ordoño HOTEL $$$

(☎24-84-44-48; recepcion@hotelordono.tur.cu; J Peralta, cnr Donato Mámol & Independencia; s/d/ste incl breakfast CUC$100/130/160; ❄@) Once a general store, this majestic three-story colonial oozes character. Renovated recently with designs by young architects, it has maintained enormous rooms, particularly on the 3rd floor, some with details like filigree pillars. There's 27 in total plus a lovely roof terrace. Run by Cubanacán.

Throw in exemplary service and an ethereal Gibara setting and you'll feel like Louis XIV kicking back in Versailles (without the guilty conscience). Best hotel in Cuba? Definitely a contender.

Eating

At the speed of a Cadillac on a potholed track, things are modernizing. Some enterprising casas particulares operate as private restaurants.

★La Cueva PARRILLA $

(☎24-84-53-33; Calle 2da, cnr Carretera & Playa Caletones; dishes CUC$6; ⊙noon-midnight Tue-Sun) Gibara's eating scene becomes imaginative with this private place that grows its own herbs to garnish those grilled meats. It even has a small farm. There's a *ranchón*-style part and a more formal restaurant area above. It's at the northern end of town; you can get there by horse cart (CUC$2).

La Perla del Norte SEAFOOD $

(Céspedes; mains $3-11; ⊙11am-11pm) For above average seafood fare, this 2nd-story restaurant is a godsend. Go for the crab, *camarones enchilados* (shrimp in garlicky-tomato sauce), tasty fried rice and crisp plantain chips. There's a bit of outdoor seating or a chilly dining room. It's ultra-clean.

La Casa de Los Amigos SEAFOOD **$$**
(☎24-84-41-15; Céspedes 15, btwn J Peralta & Luz Caballero; meals CUC$5-10) Both casa and private restaurant, this place has an amazing interior patio with frescoes, a gazebo and hand-painted Gibara doors. It rents rooms, but the dining is more notable – a profusion of local fish dishes with ample trimmings.

Drinking & Nightlife

Bar La Loja BAR
(☎24-84-44-85; Calle J Agüero; ⏲9am-midnight Wed-Sun, 4pm-midnight Mon-Tue; 📶) Another quiver in Gibara's freshly renovated bow, this bar next to the Casa de la Cultura hosts live music on Friday and Sunday nights, but is always a good place to hang with the locals. They also feature a wine cave and a huge interior patio.

Entertainment

As in most Cuban seaside towns, the local 'yoof' hang around in the vicinity of the Malecón on weekend evenings. Spontaneous outbreaks of music are likely at any time in and around Parque Calixto García (p357) and Parque Colón.

Siglo XX CULTURAL CENTER
(☎24-84-54-75; Calle Martí; ⏲8am-5pm Mon-Tue, 8am-11pm Wed-Sun) A fine cultural center in the main square that hosts live traditional music on a Saturday night and provides the taped stuff at other times. The courtyard is a good place to chill with an icy *refresco* on a hot afternoon.

Cine Jiba CINEMA
(☎24-84-46-89; Parque Calixto García) Cuba's improbable poor person's film festival hosts most of its cutting-edge movies (some in English) in this small but quirky cinema covered with distinctive art-house movie posters. If you're going to go to the cinema anywhere in Cuba, it should be in Gibara – it's a local rite of passage.

Information

MONEY

Change money in nearby Holguín.

Bandec (☎24-84-41-01; cnr Independencia & J Peralta; ⏲9am-3pm Mon-Fri) Also changes traveler's checks.

POST

Post Office (Map p361; ☎24-84-43-95; Independencia No 15; ⏲8am-8pm Mon-Sat) Postal services.

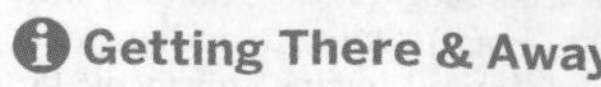

Getting There & Away

There are no Víazul buses to Gibara. Travelers can tackle the route with Cuban transport on a truck or *colectivo* (shared taxi; CUC$5) from Holguín. The bus station is 1km out on the road to Holguín. There are two daily buses (CUC$1) in each direction. It's possible to taxi to Holguín airport (CUC$40) or Guardalavaca (CUC$40).

For drivers heading toward Guardalavaca, the link road from the junction at Floro Pérez is hell at first, but improves just outside Rafael Freyre. There's an Oro Negro gas station at the entrance to town.

To get to Playa Blanca, take the ferry (CUC$2) to Juan Antonio and the beach is 400m further. It leaves the dock at 6:30am, 8:30am, 10:10am, 1pm, 3:40pm and 5pm.

Playa Pesquero & Around

With a luxury Caribbean sheen missing elsewhere on the island, these lesser-known beaches make for one serious getaway. The beach is sublime, with golden sand, shallow, warm water and great opportunities for snorkeling. You won't find a lot of action: besides a small shopping center, there is little to do beyond lounging. Of Holguín's three northern resort areas, Playa Pesquero (Fisher's Beach) is the most high-end. There are four tourist colossi here, including the five-star Hotel Playa Pesquero (p362).

Nearby Playa Esmeralda occupies the middle ground between Guardalavaca's economy and Playa Pesquero's opulence. Two megaresorts line this superior stretch of beach, 6km to the west of Guardalavaca and accessed by a spur just east of the Cayo Naranjo boat launch.

Sights

Bioparque Rocazul, Parque Nacional Monumento Bariay and Las Guanas at Playa Esmeralda are part of the Parque Natural Cristóbal Colón.

★**Bioparque Rocazul** NATURE RESERVE
(Map p361; ☎115 24-43-33-10; ejecutivo.comercial@pncolon.co.cu; Playa Esmeralda; ⏲9am-5:30pm; 👪) Located just off the link road that joins Playa Turquesa with the other Pesquero resorts, this protected park in

Guardalavaca & Playa Pesquero

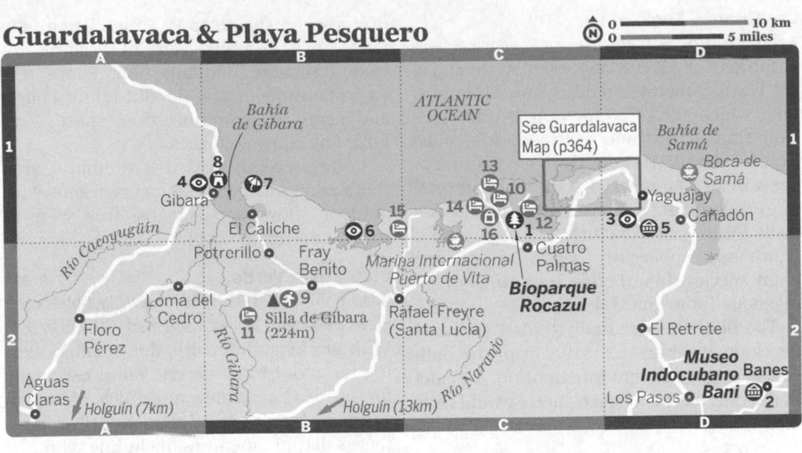

Guardalavaca & Playa Pesquero

Top Sights
1 Bioparque Rocazul C1
2 Museo Indocubano Bani D2

Sights
3 Aldea Taína D1
4 Caverna de Panaderos A1
El Cañonazo .... (see 8)
Iglesia de Nuestra Señora de la Caridad .... (see 2)
Iglesia de San Fulgencio .... (see 8)
5 Museo Chorro de Maita D1
Museo de Historia Natural .... (see 8)
Parque Calixto García .... (see 8)
6 Parque Nacional Monumento Bariay B1
7 Playa Blanca B1
8 Spanish Forts B1

Activities, Courses & Tours
9 Silla de Gibara B2

Sleeping
Bayview .... (see 7)
10 Blau Costa Verde C1
11 Campismo Silla de Gibara B2
12 Casa de Compay Kike C1
13 Hotel Playa Costa Verde C1
14 Hotel Playa Pesquero C1
15 Villa Don Lino B1

Shopping
16 Centro Comercial Playa Pesquero C1

Parque Natural Cristóbal Colón offers the usual hand-holding array of outdoor activities under the supervision of a nonnegotiable government guide. It's a commendable environmental effort in a major resort area, but the limitations can be a little stifling (and costly).

There's leisurely walking excursions (first hour CUC$8, per extra hour CUC$2), horseback riding (per hour CUC$16) and reef fishing (CUC$49). If you plan to stay the whole day, opt for the 'day in the country' (package CUC$40). The park is extensive with hills, trails, a minizoo aimed at kids and ocean access. You can also overnight in a **cabin** (r incl 3 meals CUC$59). There's a friendly bar at the entrance to the park where you can weigh up the options.

Parque Nacional Monumento Bariay HISTORIC SITE

(Map p361; ☎24-43-07-66; Playa Blanca; CUC$8; ⏰9am-5pm) Ten kilometers west of Playa Pesquero and 3km west of Villa Don Lino is Playa Blanca. Columbus landed somewhere near here in 1492. The meeting of two cultures is commemorated with a goofy reenactment and through varied sights including an impressive Hellenic-style monument designed by Holguín artist Caridad Ramos for the 500th anniversary of the landing in 1992.

Other points of interest include an information center, the remains of a 19th-century Spanish fort, three reconstructed Taíno Indian huts and an archaeological museum. It makes a pleasant afternoon's sojourn.

Las Guanas Eco-Archaeological Trail NATURE RESERVE
(Map p364; CUC$3; ⏰8am-4:30pm) At the end of the Playa Esmeralda road is this self-guided hike, which at CUC$3 for 1km, is quite possibly Cuba's (and one of the world's) most expensive trail. Walk slowly to get your money's worth! The marked route (with several more kilometers of bushwhacking on fire trails leading to a picturesque bluff with a lighthouse) apparently boasts 14 endemic plant species. Inauthentic sculptures of indigenous Taíno guard the route.

The bluff was originally touted for hotel development, but was saved from the bulldozers by government intervention. A model at the start shows what the hotel would have looked like.

Sleeping

Playa Pesquero

Campismo Silla de Gibara CABIN $
(Map p361; 24-42-28-81; Rafael Freyre; s/d CUC$18/36; P 🏊) Recently renovated, this *campismo* (cheap rustic accommodation) sits on sloping ground beneath Gibara's signature saddle-shaped hill. Reached via a rough road between Floro Pérez and Rafael Freyre, it's 35km southeast of Gibara itself and 1.5km off the main road. There are 42 rooms sleeping two, four or six people, but come for the views, not the comfort.

There's also a cave you can hike to, 1.5km up the hill, and horses for rent. It's best to make reservations with Cubamar (p417) in Santiago de Cuba rather than just turn up.

Villa Don Lino CABIN $$
(Map p361; 24-43-03-08; director@donlino.co.cu; Rafael Freyre; s/d from CUC$49/78; P ❄ 🏊) The bargain alternative to Playa Pesquero's 'big four,' Don Lino's refurbished wooden *cabañas* are planted right on a diminutive white beach. It makes for a romantic retreat. There's a small pool, nighttime entertainment and an element of Cuban-ness missing in the bigger resorts. Villa Don Lino is 8.5km north of Rafael Freyre along a spur road.

★ **Hotel Playa Pesquero** RESORT $$$
(Map p361; 24-43-35-30; Playa Pesquero; all-inclusive s/d CUC$175/280, premium CUC$430; P ❄ @ 📶 🏊) Among Cuba's biggest hotels, Playa Pesquero has 933 rooms, prime real estate on a beautiful beach. It was opened by Fidel Castro in 2003, and his speech is displayed in the reception area. Beautifully landscaped grounds over 30 hectares include Italianate fountains, fancy shops, seven restaurants, a spa, floodlit tennis courts and acres of swimming pool space – all linked by zippy golf carts.

It has recently added a premium area that's adult only, with 56 luxury rooms with outdoor showers, spa tubs, free wi-fi in rooms and iPhone docks.

Blau Costa Verde RESORT $$$
(Map p361; 24-43-35-10; www.blauhotels.com; Playa Pesquero; all-inclusive s/d CUC$107/184) With blocky architecture, this smaller offering turns out to be decent value, especially for divers who can take advantage of the on-site dive center. Beyond attractive tile rooms, there's decent amenities, including wi-fi.

Hotel Playa Costa Verde RESORT $$$
(Map p361; 24-43-05-20; reservationsmanager@playacostaverde.co.cu; Playa Pesquero; all-inclusive s/d CUC$130/210; P ❄ @ 📶 🏊) Despite the faux veneer, the Costa Verde has top-notch facilities including a Japanese restaurant, a gym, colorful gardens and a lagoon you cross to get to the beach. Run by hotel group Gaviota, the atmosphere is ticky-tacky but far more subdued than the hotels in Guardalavaca proper.

Playa Esmeralda

★ **Paradisus Río de Oro** RESORT $$$
(Map p364; 24-43-00-90; www.melia.com; Playa Esmeralda; all-inclusive s/d CUC$431/615, day pass CUC$115; P ❄ @ 📶 🏊) You may need a wallet of gold to access the river of gold resort by Meliá. Oft touted as Cuba's best resort, this 356-room resort shines with five-star pedigree. There's cliffside massage, a Japanese restaurant floating on a koi pond, and garden villas with private pools. Palm groves and thick foliage keep the property protected and private. Adults only.

While it is promoted as an ecoresort, its only sustainable distinction is keeping the property forested. High rollers should bid for the newer luxury area within the compound, featuring only several hundred rooms.

Sol Río Luna Mares Resort RESORT $$$
(Map p364; 24-43-00-30; Playa Esmeralda; all-inclusive s/d CUC$182/280; P ❄ @ 📶 🏊) This two-in-one hotel is an amalgamation of two resorts. Without a required reservation, its presentation is a bit stale. There's nearly

500 large rooms featuring a few extras such as coffee machines. Its main advantages over Guardalavaca are the superior food at the on-site French and Italian restaurants and the truly sublime beach, with beach toys included in the price.

Shopping

Centro Comercial Playa Pesquero MALL
(Map p361; Playa Pesquero entry; 9am-11pm Sun-Thu, 24hr Fri & Sat) A new mall with fast food, money exchange and shops.

Getting There & Away

The four resorts of Playa Pesquero are accessible from the main Holguín–Guardalavaca road via a spur road 12km west of Guardalavaca proper. Playa Esmeralda and its two resorts lie at the end of a short spur road 4km west of Guardalavaca. Hotels rent mopeds and bicycles.

A shuttle bus (CUC$5) run by Transtur links Playa Pesquero with Playa Esmeralda and Guardalavaca. Departures and returns are spaced two hours apart. There's also a trolley making the rounds of hotel grounds and Guardalavaca.

Taxis (to Guardalavaca CUC$10), including classic cars and horse carriages, wait outside the resorts.

Guardalavaca

Guardalavaca is a string of megaresorts draped along a succession of idyllic beaches backed by verdant hills, 54km northeast of Holguín. Before the rows of sunloungers and poolside bingo, Columbus described this stretch of coast as the most beautiful place he ever laid eyes on.

There are also sheltered turquoise coral reefs teeming with aquatic action. More spread out than Varadero and less isolated than Cayo Coco, it has enduring popularity. There's also long been beach access for Cubans, which helps provide a more local atmosphere.

In the early 20th century, this region was a rural village and important cattle-rearing area (Guardalavaca means 'shelter the cow'). The tourism boom moved into first gear in the late 1970s when local *holguiñero* Fidel Castro inaugurated Guardalavaca's first resort – the sprawling Atlántico – with a quick dip in the hotel pool. The local economy hasn't looked back since.

Sights

The resort area is split into three separate enclaves: Playa Pesquero, Playa Esmeralda and, 4km to the east, Guardalavaca proper, the original hotel strip that is already starting to peel around the edges.

Museo Chorro de Maita MUSEUM
(Map p361; 24-43-02-01; CUC$2; 9am-5pm Tue-Sat, 9am-1pm Sun) This archaeological-site-based museum protects the remains of an excavated Indian village and cemetery, including the well-preserved remains of 62 human skeletons and the bones of a barkless dog. The village dates from the early 16th century and is one of nearly 100 archaeological sites in the area. New evidence suggests indigenous peoples were living here many decades after Columbus' arrival.

Across from the museum is a reconstructed **Aldea Taína** (Taíno village; Map p361; 24-43-02-01; CUC$5; 9am-5pm Mon-Sat, 9am-1pm Sun;) that features life-sized models of native dwellings in a replicated indigenous village. Native dance rituals are staged here and there's also a restaurant.

Activities

You can arrange horseback riding in Playa Esmeralda or privately: CUC$10 per hour is the going rate.

You can rent mopeds at all the hotels for up to CUC$27 per day. Some all-inclusive resorts include bicycle use, but the bikes are fairly basic (no gears). The road between Guardalavaca and Playa Esmeralda, and on to Playa Pesquero, is flat and quiet and makes an excellent day excursion. For a bit more sweat you can make it to Banes and back (66km round-trip).

Diving

Guardalavaca has some excellent diving (better than Varadero and up there with Cayo Coco). The reef is 200m out and there are 32 dive sites, most of which are accessed by boat. Highlights include caves, wrecks, walls and La Corona, a giant coral formation said to resemble a crown.

Eagle Ray Marlin Dive Center DIVING
(Cubanacán Náutica; Map p364; 24-43-03-16; dives from CUC$45; 8:30am-4:30pm Mon-Sat) Guardalavaca beach's one dive center abuts the sand about 300m west of the Club Amigo Atlántico–Guardalavaca. There are open-water certification courses for

Guardalavaca

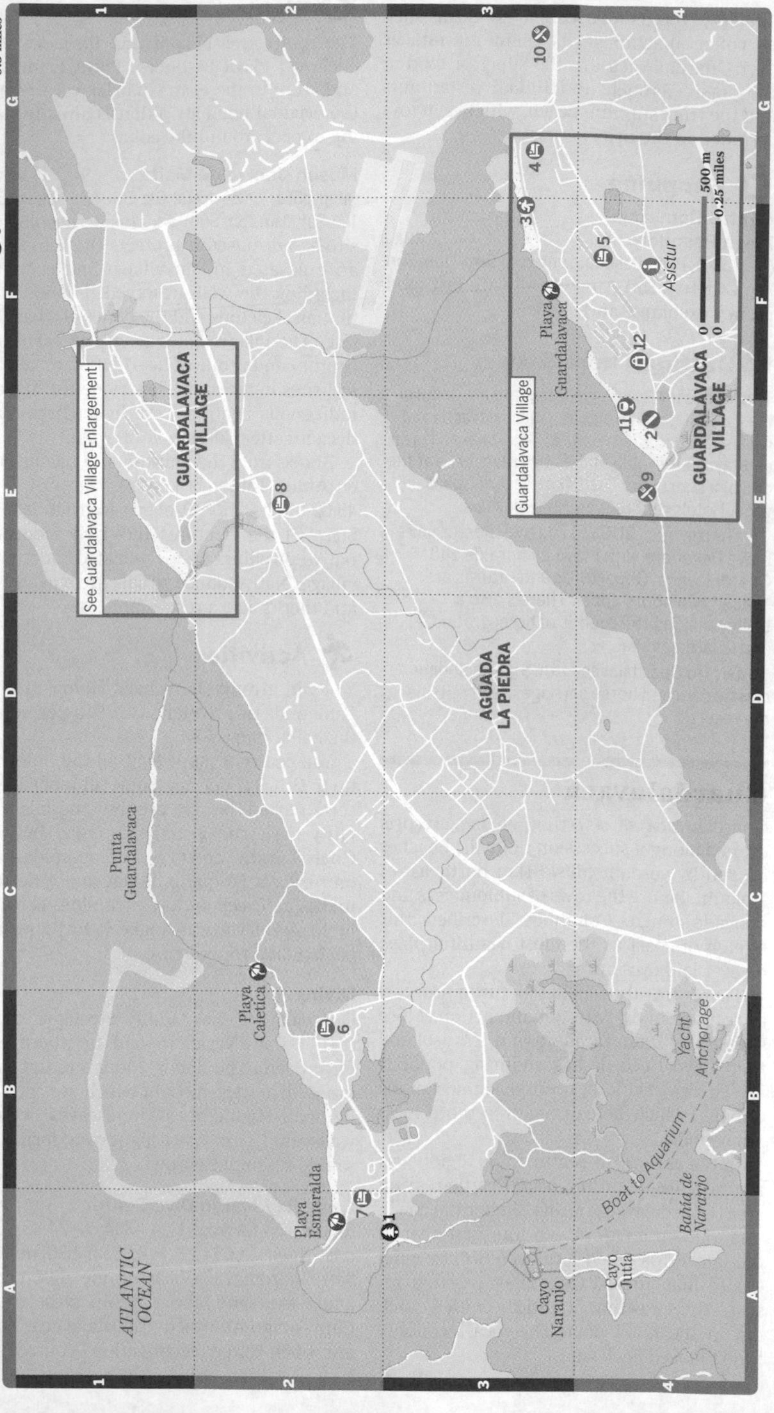

Guardalavaca

Sights
1 Las Guanas Eco-Archaeological Trail ... A3

Activities, Courses & Tours
2 Eagle Ray Marlin Dive Center ... E4
3 Luís Riveron ... F3

Sleeping
4 Brisas Guardalavaca ... G3
5 Club Amigo Atlántico – Guardalavaca ... F4
6 Paradisus Río de Oro ... B2
7 Sol Río Luna Mares Resort ... A2
8 Villa Bely ... E2

Eating
9 El Ancla ... E4
10 El Uvero ... G3

Drinking & Nightlife
11 Bar Pirata ... E4

Shopping
12 Boulevard ... F4

CUC$365 and two-hour Discover courses for CUC$70. Immersions start at CUC$45, with discounts for multiple dives. They do not offer snorkel tours.

Kitesurfing

Luís Riveron KITESURFING
(Map p364; 53-78-48-57; luiskitesurf@nauta.cu; kitesurfing lessons per hour CUC$50, rental per hour CUC$30) Cuba's newest sport has sprouted a private Guardalavaca operator that offers private lessons (discounts for more participants) and board rental. His perch is on the beach of Brisas Guardalavaca.

Boat Trips

Many water-based excursions leave from the **Marina Internacional Puerto de Vita** (Marina Gaviota; Map p361; 24-43-04-75) and can be booked through the hotels. There's another newer, but smaller marina at **Boca de Samá** (Map p361), 9km east of Guardalavaca and run by Cubanacán.

Aside from the ubiquitous sunset cruise possibilities (CUC$60), you can organize deep-sea fishing (up to six people CUC$360), and occasional catamaran trips across Bahía de Vita with snorkeling and open bar.

Sleeping

Guardalavaca now offers private rooms, so you are not obliged to shell out for the all-inclusives. There are dozens of apartments to rent in Guardalavaca village opposite the entrance to the all-inclusive zone. A new five-star hotel – the Albatros – is in the process of being built.

★Villa Bely CASA PARTICULAR $
(Map p364; 52-61-41-92; www.villabely.orgfree.com; entrance to Guardalavaca; r CUC$25-30; P ❄) The resort alternative, this casa has a top-floor apartment that's bigger and better than your average hotel room. It works for small families, with a tiny balcony and a lovely sleeping area raised on a dais. There are two smaller rooms below. It's just opposite the last highway exit from the all-inclusive zone.

Also offers snorkeling equipment and arranges guided horseback riding.

Brisas Guardalavaca RESORT $$$
(Map p364; 24-43-02-18; Playa Guardalavaca; all-inclusive s/d CUC$110/160; P ❄ @ 🛜 ≋) Attracting Canadians and trans-Atlantic snowbirds, this 437-room resort is a package-tour paradise stirring memories of 1970s British holiday camps. Bonuses are huge rooms, floodlit tennis courts and general lack of pretension. The setup is a bit reminiscent of a retirement home, with the kitsch never far from the surface, but it's quieter than nearby offerings and has a decent beach.

Club Amigo Atlántico – Guardalavaca RESORT $$$
(Map p364; 24-43-01-21; Playa Guardalavaca; all-inclusive s/d CUC$90/140; P ❄ @ 🛜 ≋) As cheap getaways go, this is Guardalavaca's bargain offering, but it's not for particular guests. Cleanliness is not always paramount in this 600-room village, a bog-standard mishmash of villas, bungalows and standard rooms. An extensive kids activities program makes it popular with families. There's more rocky inlets here than further down the beach and inland rooms are quieter.

This hard-to-fathom resort fused the former Guardalavaca and Atlántico hotels. The latter was Guardalavaca's oldest resort, completed in 1976 and christened by Fidel Castro with a swim in the pool.

Eating

There are a handful of options outside of the all-inclusive resorts, mainly in Guardalavaca itself.

★**El Ancla** SEAFOOD $$
(Map p364; ☎24-43-03-81; meals CUC$4-20; ⊙noon-9:30pm) On a rocky promontory of land at the far western end of Guardalavaca beach, this glass-walled restaurant is a fine spot to spend a few hours dining and sea gazing. The 180-degree view is outrageous. Somehow it didn't get blown away by Hurricane Ike in 2008. Come here for excellent lobster served on white linens and decent service.

El Uvero CUBAN $$
(Map p364; ☎52-39-35-71; Carretera Guardalavaca-Banes; meals $10-18; ⊙noon-11pm) Four kilometers and a short taxi ride east of Guardalavaca's main resort strip, this modest-looking local house in the village of Cuatro Caminos is well worth the small effort to get here. Pride of the menu is the *tres hermanos* (three brothers) consisting of prawns, lobster and white fish.

The place is guarded by an uvero (sea grape tree) as the name implies.

Drinking & Nightlife

Bar Pirata BAR
(Map p364; Playa Guardalavaca; ⊙9am-9pm) Right on the sand at Guardalavaca's liveliest strip of beach, Pirata is your standard beach shack with beer, music and enough ingredients to muster up a sand-free sandwich lunch. It's accessed via the flea market just west of Club Amigo Atlántico.

Shopping

Boulevard GIFTS & SOUVENIRS
(Map p364; entrance Playa Guardalavaca; ⊙7am-5pm) This touristy, open-air handicraft market caters to resort clients from the surrounding area. It flogs crafts, postcards, cheap clothing and Che Guevara – there's nothing much outside the knickknack box.

ℹ Information

EMERGENCIES

Asistur (Map p364; ☎24-43-01-48; Centro Comercial; ⊙8:30am-5pm Mon-Fri, to noon Sat) Provides insurance, medical assistance, repatriation and financial help for traveler emergencies.

MEDICAL SERVICES

The Clinica Internacional is a 24-hour pharmacy. Resorts have drugstores and offer medical services.

MONEY

Euros are accepted in all the Guardalavaca, Playa Esmeralda and Pesquero resorts. Additionally, all the big hotels have money-changing facilities.

Banco Financiero Internacional (☎24-43-02-17; Centro Comercial los Flamboyanes; ⊙9am-3pm Mon-Fri) In the shopping complex just west of Club Amigo Atlántico – Guardalavaca (p365). Has no ATM.

TOURIST INFORMATION

Infotur is adding a desk at the Centro Comercial los Flamboyantes in the Club Amigo complex. Resorts have tour desks offering information.

ℹ Getting There & Away

Transtur (☎24-43-04-90; comercialhlg@transtur.cu; round-trip CUC$15) runs a tourist bus from Guardalavaca to Holguín via Playa Esmeralda and Playa Pesquero once a day.

You can also take a taxi from Guardalavaca to Holguín (one way CUC$20). For radio taxis, call **Cubataxi** (☎24-43-01-39) or **Transgaviota** (☎24-43-49-66). Shared *colectivos* or *maquinas* – often classic cars – run from Guardalavaca village to Holguín for CUC$5.

ℹ Getting Around

A Transtur shuttle bus (day pass CUC$5) in Guardalavaca links the three beach areas and the Aldea Taína (p363). Theoretically it runs three times a day in either direction, but check at your hotel to see if there are any glitches. Drop-offs include Parque Rocazul, Playa Pesquero, Playa Costa Verde, Playa Esmeralda hotels, Club Amigo Atlántico – Guardalavaca and the Aldea Taína.

Coches de caballo (horse carriages) run between Playas Esmeralda and Guardalavaca, or you can rent a moped (per day CUC$25) or bicycle (free at all-inclusives) at the resorts. You can also taxi to Playa Esmeralda or Playa Pesqueros (CUC$10).

For car rental, try **Cubacar** (☎24-43-03-89; Club Amigo Atlántico – Guardalavaca). A **Servi-Cupet gas station** (⊙24hr) is situated between Guardalavaca and Playa Esmeralda.

Banes

POP 81,300

Former sugar town, Banes is the site of one of Cuba's oddest historical moments. Cuban president Fulgencio Batista was born here in 1901. Some 47 years later, Fidel Castro and Birta Díaz Balart tied the knot in the local clapboard church of Nuestra Señora de la Caridad. Generous, and surely unsuspecting the groom would one day overthrow him, Batista gave the couple a honeymoon present of US$500.

Founded in 1887, this effervescent company town was a virtual fiefdom of the US-run United Fruit Company until the 1950s. Many of the old American company houses still remain. These days, the sun-streaked streets and squares feature cigar-smoking cronies slamming dominoes and mums carrying meter-long loaves of bread; in short, everything Cuban that is missing from the all-inclusive resorts.

Thanks to its Taíno museum and the various indigenous sites nestled in the surrounding countryside, Banes is known as the archaeological capital of Cuba.

Sights

If you're coming from the resorts, Banes' biggest attraction may be enjoying the street life provided by a stroll through town. Don't miss the fine old company houses that once provided homes for the fat cats of United Fruit. If you're fit and adventurous, getting here from Guardalavaca by bicycle is a rare treat through undulating, bucolic terrain.

★Museo Indocubano Bani MUSEUM
(Map p361; General Marrero No 305; CUC$1; ⌚9am-5pm Tue-Sat, 8am-noon Sun) This museum's small but rich collection of indigenous artifacts is one of the best on the island. Don't miss the tiny golden fertility idol unearthed near Banes (one of only 20

CUBA'S ARCHAEOLOGICAL CAPITAL

Cuba's pre-Columbian history can be traced back over 8000 years, yet it rarely receives more than a passing mention in contemporary history books. Those interested in padding out the details should come to Holguín Province where the region around Banes has the highest concentration of pre-Columbian archaeological sites in the country.

Most archaeological remains unearthed so far in Cuba date from around 1050 to the early 1500s. The Taínos were the third wave of immigrants to reach the isles, in the footsteps of the less sophisticated Guanahatabeys and Siboneys with whom they ultimately coexisted. Primarily peace-loving, they were skilled farmers, weavers, ceramicists and boat-builders, and their complex society exhibited an organized system of participatory government that was overseen by a series of local *caciques* (chiefs).

Sixty percent of the crops still grown in Cuba today were pioneered by Taíno farmers, who planted cotton to use in hammocks, fishing nets and bags. Adults practiced a form of artificial cranial deformation by flattening the soft skulls of their young children, and groups lived together in villages characterized by their thatched *bohios* (living huts) and *bateys* (communal 'plazas'). A reconstructed Taíno village can be seen at the Aldea Taína (p363) near Guardalavaca. Next door in Chorro de Maita (p363), Cuba's most extensive archaeological site, some of the exhumed skeletons exhibit cranial deformation.

Columbus described the Taíno with terms such as 'gentle,' 'sweet,' 'always laughing' and 'without knowledge of what is evil,' which makes the genocide that he inadvertently unleashed even more horrendous. Estimates vary wildly as to Cuba's indigenous population pre-Columbus, though 100,000 is a good consensus figure. Within 30 years, 90% of the Taínos had been wiped out.

As Taíno villages were built of wood and mud they left no great towns or temples. Instead, the most important and emblematic artifacts unearthed are of *cemis* or idols, small figurines depicting Taíno deities. *Cemis* were cult objects that represented social status, political power or fertility.

The *hacha* del Holguín, a 600-year-old god-like figure made of peridotite rock, is on display in Holguín's Museo de Historia Provincial (p347). The ídolo del oro, a rare 10-carat gold fertility symbol from the 13th century or earlier, is in Banes' Museo Indocubano Bani. The oldest cemi found to date in Cuba was discovered near Maisí in Guantánamo Province in the 1910s. Called the Ídolo de Tabaco, it dates from the 10th century and is made of Cuban hardwood. It is currently on display at the Museo Antropológico Montané (p85) in Havana University.

gold artifacts ever found in Cuba). Excellent guides will enthusiastically show you round. La Plaza Aborigen outside has replicas of local cave paintings.

The museum's resident expert, **Luis Quiñones García** (☎24-80-26-91; luisq1962@nauta.cu; tours CUC$2), will fill you in on every facet of indigenous culture and local archaeology. He also offers tours of the town.

Playa de Morales BEACH

One day in the not-too-distant future (after its been Cancun-ized), we'll all wax nostalgic about this precious strip of sand situated 13km east of Banes along the paved continuation of Tráfico. For the time being enjoy this fishing village, whiling away an afternoon dining with locals and watching the men mend their nets. A few kilometers to the north is the even quieter Playa Puerto Rico.

Iglesia de Nuestra Señora de la Caridad CHURCH

(Map p361; Parque Martí) On October 12, 1948, Fidel Castro Ruz and Birta Díaz Balart were married in this unusual art deco church on Parque Martí in the center of Banes. After their divorce in 1954, Birta remarried and moved to Spain. Through their only child, Fidelito, Fidel has several grandchildren.

Sleeping

There are no hotels in the town proper, but Banes has some superfriendly private renters.

Villa Lao CASA PARTICULAR $

(☎24-80-30-49; Bayamo No 78, btwn José M Heredia & Augo Blanco; r CUC$25; ❄) Shimmering clean, professionally run house with two rooms; grab the upstairs one with its kitchen and plant-laden terrace if possible. It's got the front porch rocker thing going on, too, overlooking the central park.

Villa Gilma CASA PARTICULAR $

(☎24-80-22-04; Calle H No 15266, btwn Veguitas & Francisco Franco; r CUC$25; ❄) This classic colonial abode stands guard at the entrance to the town center and has one huge room (those ceilings must be 7m high) with private bath and fridge.

Casa 'Las Delicias' CASA PARTICULAR $

(☎24-80-29-05; Augo Blanca No 1107, btwn Bruno Merino & Bayamo; r CUC$25; ❄) One spick-and-span room, a private entrance, friendly owners and decent food in the downstairs private restaurant – what more could you ask from tranquil Banes?

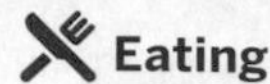

Eating

Restaurante Don Carlos CUBAN $

(☎24-80-21-76; Veguitas No 1702, cnr Calle H; meals CUC$3-8; ⏲noon-10pm) Salt-of-the-earth, meet-the-locals private restaurant where you can discover the other side of Cuba over some pretty decent seafood. Not 30 minutes from Guardalavaca's gigantic resorts.

Restaurant el Latino CARIBBEAN $

(General Marrero No 710; mains CUC$5-8; ⏲11am-11pm) A long-standing Banes favorite, this state-run place has all the usual Creole dishes delivered with a little extra flair and charm. Service is good and the accompanying musicians unusually talented and discreet.

Entertainment

Cafe Cantante LIVE MUSIC

(☎24-80-46-58; General Marrero No 320) This gregarious, music-filled patio is the top spot in Banes, with honking municipal band rehearsals, discos, *son* septets and Zen-inducing jazz jams. It's colloquially known as the Casa de la Trova.

Getting There & Away

From the **bus station** (cnr Tráfico & Los Ángeles) there are two daily buses (MN$1) to Holguín (72km). There are no timetables; check the chalkboards. Trucks (MN$5) leave Banes for Holguín more frequently.

A taxi from Guardalavaca (33km) will cost around CUC$25 one way. Or tackle it with a moped (easy) or bicycle (not so easy) in a fantastic DIY day trip from Guardalavaca.

Sierra del Cristal

Cuba's own 'Little Switzerland' is a rugged amalgam of the Sierra del Cristal and the Altiplanicie de Nipe, with two important national parks. Parque Nacional Sierra Cristal, Cuba's oldest, was founded in 1930 and harbors 1213m Pico de Cristal, the province's highest summit. Of more interest to travelers, the piney 53-sq-km Parque Nacional la Mensura, 30km south of Mayarí, protects the island's highest waterfall. Notable for its cool alpine microclimate and 100 or more species of endemic plants, La Mensura offers hiking and horseback riding and accommodation in a Gaviota-run ecolodge. It also hosts a mountain research center run by Academia de Ciencias de Cuba.

Flanking the Sierra del Cristal, the landscape inspired Buena Vista Social Club's hit 'Chan Chan'. Now frequented by aficionados of lead singer Compay Segundo, the route is often dubbed Ruta de Chan Chan.

Sights

★ Salto del Guayabo WATERFALL
(entry CUC$5) At just over 100m in height, Guayabo (15km from the Villa Pinares del Mayarí) is considered the highest waterfall in Cuba. There's a spectacular overlook and the guided 1.2km hike to its base through fecund tropical forest includes swimming in a natural pool.

Salto de Capiro WATERFALL
A short 2km trail from Villa Pinares del Mayarí brings you to this hidden waterfall in lush forest.

Activities

Most activities can be organized at Villa Pinares del Mayarí or via 4WD excursions from Guardalavaca's or Santiago de Cuba's hotels.

Sendero la Sabina HIKING
(entry CUC$3) A short interpretive trail at the Centro Investigaciones para la Montaña, located 1km from Villa Pinares del Mayarí. Check out the vegetation of eight different ecosystems, including a 150-year-old tree the 'Ocuje Colorado' – and rare orchids.

Hacienda la Mensura HORSEBACK RIDING
Eight kilometers from Villa Pinares del Mayarí is this breeding center for exotic animals such as antelope. Horseback riding can be arranged here.

Sleeping

★ Villa Pinares del Mayarí HOTEL $
(☎24-45-56 28; s/d CUC$25/35; P ❄ ≋) Ensconced in one of Cuba's largest pine forests, Pinares del Mayarí stands between the Altiplanicie de Nipe and Sierra del Cristal at 600m. Part chalet resort, part mountain retreat, this isolated alpine-style rural hideaway features two- and three-bedroom cabins with hot showers and comfortable beds. There's a large restaurant (mains CUC$4 to CUC$9), bar, sports court, gym and sublime pool.

El Cupey, a small natural lake, sits 300m away. It's great for an early morning dip. The compound, 30km south of Mayarí on a rough dirt road, is run by Gaviota.

Getting There & Away

The only way to get to Villa Pinares del Mayarí and Parque Nacional la Mensura outside an organized tour is via car, taxi (from Holguín CUC$50) or bicycle (if you're adventurous and it's not a Cuban one).

The access road is mostly a rough collection of holes with the odd bit of asphalt thrown in, but it's passable in a hire car if driven with care. You'll need at least 1½ hours to cover the 30km.

Cayo Saetía

East of Mayarí the road becomes increasingly potholed and the dusty rural surroundings are progressively more remote. The culmination of this rustic drive is lovely Cayo Saetía, a small, flat, wooded island in the Bahía de Nipe that's connected to the mainland by a small bridge. During the 1970s and '80s this was a favored hunting ground for communist apparatchiks who enjoyed spraying lead into the local wildlife. Now Cayo Saetía is a protected wildlife park with 19 species of exotic animals, including camels, zebras, antelopes, ostriches and deer.

Bisected by grassy meadows and adorned by hidden coves and beaches, it's the closet Cuba gets to an African wildlife reserve. However, it's also still run by the military and not overly friendly to visitors – particularly those just out to explore. The gorgeous beach is often commandeered by organized catamaran groups from Guardalavaca.

Sleeping

Villa Cayo Saetía RESORT $$
(☎24-51-69-00; s/d incl breakfast CUC$43/62; ❄) This rustic cay resort, on a 42-sq-km island at the entrance to the Bahía de Nipe, is small, remote and more upmarket than the price suggests. The 12 rooms are split into rustic and standard *cabañas* with a minimal price differential. You'll feel as if you're 1000 miles from anywhere.

The in-house restaurant (mains CUC$5 to CUC$12), La Güira sits decked out Hemingway-style with hunting trophies mounted on the wall like gory art. It's fully in tune with the exotic meats, such as antelope, on the menu.

WORTH A TRIP

FIDEL'S CHILDHOOD HOME

Fidel Castro Ruz was born on August 13, 1926, at the Finca las Manacas near the village of Birán, south of Cueto. The sprawling ranch, bought by Fidel's father Ángel in 1915, includes its own workers village (a cluster of small thatched huts for the mainly Haitian laborers), a cockfighting ring, butcher's shop, post office, store and telegraph. The several large, yellow wooden houses surrounded by lush cedars housed the Castro family.

The farm opened as **Museo Conjunto Histórico de Birán** (admission/camera/video CUC$10/10/10; ⌚9am-3:30pm Tue-Sat, 9am-noon Sun) in 2002, its unassuming name intending to downplay any Castro 'personality cult.' This gaggle of attractive wooden buildings on expansive grounds constitutes a *pueblito* (small town) and makes a fascinating excursion. It appears as a backwater today, but once sat on the *camino real*, Cuba's main east–west road in colonial times. Tours are thorough and very worthwhile.

Around the various houses, you can see more than a hundred photos, assorted clothes, Fidel's childhood bed and his father's 1918 Ford motorcar. Perhaps most interesting is the schoolhouse where Fidel first studied before moving on to Santiago as an outstanding pupil. Fidel sat in the middle of the front row. There are pictures of young Fidel and Raúl and Fidel's birth certificate, made out in the name of Fidel Casano Castro Ruz.

A cemetery contains the grave of Fidel and Raúl's father, Ángel, and siblings. The site illustrates, if nothing else, the extent of the inheritance that this hot-headed ex-lawyer gave up when he absconded to the Sierra Maestra for two years, surviving on a diet of crushed crabs and raw horse meat. Finca Las Manacas was the first property to be appropriated by the government after the revolution.

Getting There & Away

Road conditions are poor in the final 20km approaching the key (separated by a bridge). Those arriving by car hit a control post 15km off the main road at the bridge; every visitor must pay CUC$7 here for access. It's another 8km along a rough, unpaved road to the resort.

If it hasn't been raining, a rental car will make it with care. Don't attempt the drive in rain as the clay surface becomes impossibly slippery. Be warned that without reservations you will be in for a world of harassment by the guards.

From Guardalavaca there are catamaran day tours (per person CUC$120), arranged through travel agencies and resorts.

Getting Around

There are three ways to explore Cayo Saetía, aside from the obvious two-legged sorties from the villa itself. A one-hour, 4WD safari costs CUC$9 per person, while there are also excursions by horse and boat, arranged directly through the resort.

Granma Province

☎23 / POP 836,000

Includes ➡

Best Places to Eat

- Meson La Cuchipapa (p379)
- Restaurante San Salvador de Bayamo (p378)
- Fiesta de la Cubanía (p379)

Best Places to Sleep

- Villa La Paz (p378)
- Adrián & Tonia (p385)
- Villa Santo Domingo (p383)

Why Go?

Few parts of the world get named after yachts, which helps explain why in Granma (christened for the boat that delivered Fidel Castro and his bedraggled revolutionaries ashore to kick-start a guerrilla war in 1956) Cuba's *viva la Revolución* spirit burns most fiercely. This is the land where José Martí died and where Granma native Carlos Manuel de Céspedes freed his slaves and formally declared Cuban independence for the first time in 1868.

The alluringly isolated countryside helped the revolutionary cause. Road-scarce Granma is one of Cuba's remotest regions, with lofty tropical mountains dense enough to harbor fugitive Fidel Castro for more than two years in the 1950s.

Its isolation has bred a special brand of Cuban identity. Granma's settlements are esoteric places enlivened with weekly street parties (with outdoor barbecues and archaic hand-operated street organs), and provincial capital Bayamo is among the most tranquil and cleanest places in the archipelago.

When to Go

- Pockets of Granma already have a balmy climate, but from January to February the beach area of Marea del Portillo becomes the warmest place in Cuba.
- To see provincial traditions at their finest, don't miss Bayamo's biggest celebration, the Incendio de Bayamo on January 12.
- In the far wetter Sierra Maestra mountains, March and April are the driest times for hiking the trails, with bearable nighttime temperatures.
- December 2 is the anniversary of the historic Granma landing, which put the Revolution in motion; it's celebrated with festivities and a ceremony at Las Coloradas.

Granma Province Highlights

1. **Marea del Portillo** (p390) Enjoying one of Cuba's balmiest climates in this secluded beach resort.
2. **Comandancia de la Plata** (p381) Trekking up to Fidel's wartime headquarters in Gran Parque Nacional Sierra Maestra.
3. **Parque Nacional Desembarco del Granma** (p388) Exploring marine terraces and archaeological remains.
4. **Santo Domingo** (p382) Getting a dose of fresh mountain air at the bucolic Gran Parque Nacional Sierra Maestra with horseback riding or a stroll to a swimming hole.
5. **Fiesta de la Cubanía** (p379) Immersing yourself in the inimitable Bayamo party spirit with pork roast, street organs and a chess game.
6. **Museo Histórico la Demajagua** (p385) Visiting the site where the Cubans uttered their first cry of independence.

History

Stone petroglyphs and remnants of Taíno pottery unearthed in Parque Nacional Desembarco del Granma suggest the existence of native cultures in the Granma region long before the Spanish arrived.

Columbus, during his second voyage, was the first European to explore the area, taking shelter from a storm in the Golfo de Guacanayabo. All other early development schemes came to nothing, and by the 17th century Granma's untamed coast had become the preserve of pirates and corsairs.

Granma's real nemesis didn't come until October 10, 1868, when sugar-plantation owner Carlos Manuel de Céspedes called for the abolition of slavery from his Demajagua sugar mill near Manzanillo, freed his own slaves by example and incited the First War of Independence.

Drama unfolded again in 1895 when the founder of the Cuban Revolutionary Party, José Martí, was killed in Dos Ríos just a month and a half after landing with Máximo Gómez off the coast of Guantánamo to ignite the Spanish-Cuban-American War.

Then on December 2, 1956, Fidel Castro and 81 rebel soldiers disembarked from the yacht *Granma* off the province's coast at Playa las Coloradas (ironically, the boat that literally launched the Revolution – and later gave the province its present name – was purchased from an American, who had named it in honor of his grandmother). Routed by Batista's troops shortly after landing in a sugarcane field at Alegría del Pío, 15 or so survivors managed to escape into the Sierra Maestra, establishing headquarters at Comandancia de la Plata. From there they coordinated the armed struggle, broadcasting their progress and consolidating their support among sympathizers nationwide. After two years of harsh conditions and unprecedented beard growth, the forces of the M-26-7 (July 26 Movement) triumphed in 1959.

Bayamo

POP 157,400

Elegant and old, this relatively hush city spells oasis to the traveler weary of confrontation. Predating both Havana and Santiago, it has been cast for time immemorial as the city that kick-started Cuban independence. Yet self-important it isn't. The *ciudad de los coches* (city of horsecarts) is an easygoing, slow-paced, trapped-in-time place, where you're more likely to be quoted literature than sold trinkets. Cuba's balmiest provincial capital, it resounds to the clip-clop of hooves; nearly half the population use horses for daily travel.

Bayamo has played a sacrificial role in Cuba's convoluted historical development. *'Como España quemó a Sagunto, así Cuba quemó a Bayamo,'* (As the Spanish burnt Sagunto, the Cubans burnt Bayamo) wrote José Martí in the 1890s. While an 1869 arson blaze destroyed many of the city's classic colonial buildings, there's still plenty left. Neither did it undermine Bayamo's intransigent spirit or its long-standing traditions.

Sights

In Town

★Plaza de la Revolución SQUARE

(Parque Céspedes) One of Cuba's leafiest squares, Bayamo's central meeting point is surrounded by pedestrian-only streets, making it a rare and peaceful spot. Despite its friendly airs and secondary role as the city's best outdoor music venue (orchestras regularly play here), the square is loaded with historical significance.

In 1868 Céspedes proclaimed Cuba's independence for the first time in front of the columned **Ayuntamiento** (City Hall; General García). The square is surrounded by grand monuments and big trees loaded with bird life at dusk. Facing each other in the center are a bronze statue of Carlos Manuel de Céspedes, hero of the First War of Independence, and a marble bust of Perucho Figueredo, with the lyrics of the Cuban national anthem (which he wrote), carved upon it.

★Casa Natal de Carlos Manuel de Céspedes MUSEUM

(Maceo No 57; CUC$1; ⌚9am-5pm Tue-Fri, 9am-5pm & 8-10pm Sat, 10am-1:30pm Sun) Birthplace of the 'father of the motherland,' this museum is where Céspedes was born (on April 18, 1819) and spent his first 12 years. Inside, Céspedes memorabilia is complemented by a collection of period furniture. It's notable architecturally as Bayamo's only remaining two-story colonial house: one of the few buildings to survive the 1869 fire.

Bayamo

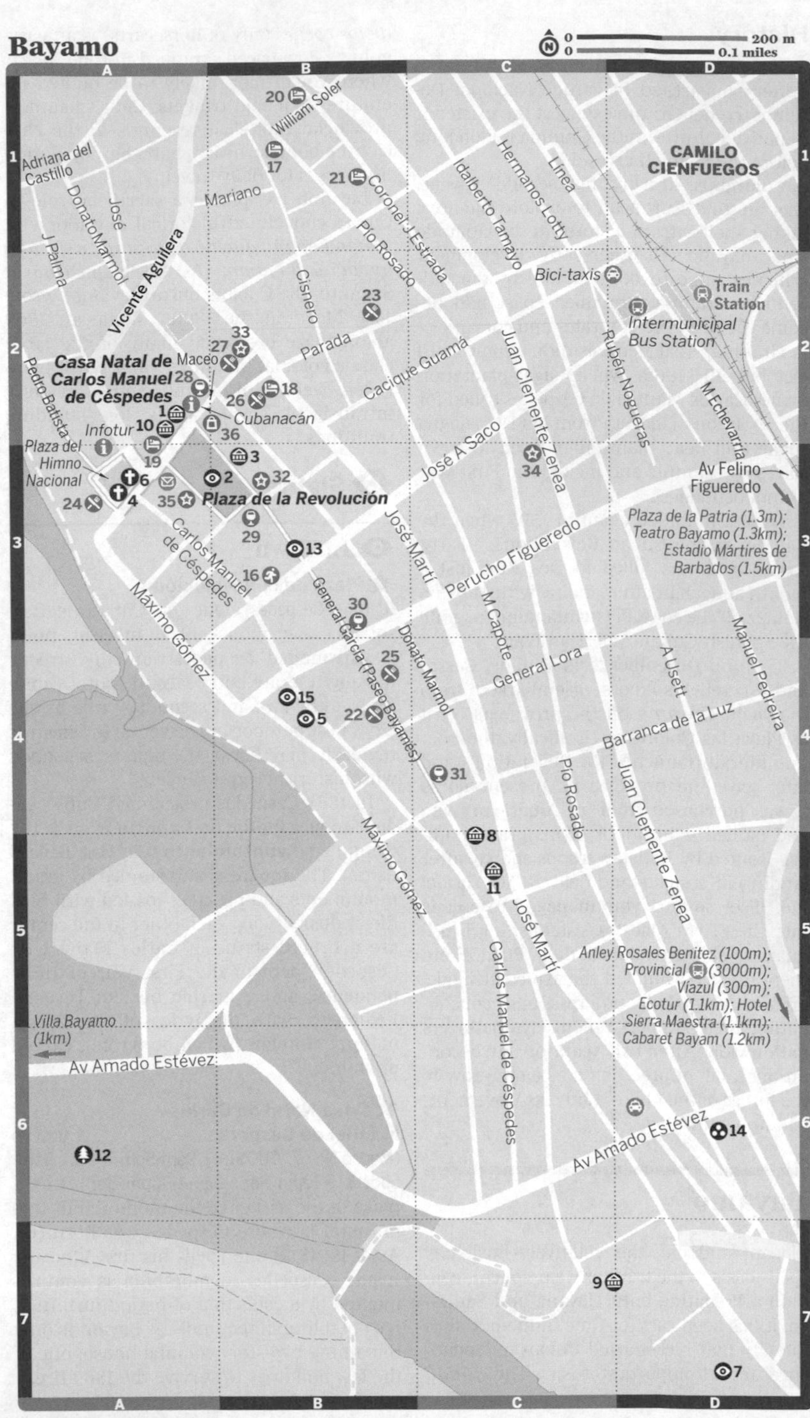
0 200 m
0 0.1 miles
A
B
C
D
1
2
3
4
5
6
7
CAMILO CIENFUEGOS
William Soler
Adriana del Castillo
Donato Marmol
José
J Palma
Mariano
Vicente Aguilera
Cisnero
Coronel J Estrada
Pío Rosado
Idalberto Tamayo
Hermanos Lotty
Línea
Bici-taxis
Train Station
Intermunicipal Bus Station
Parada
Cacique Guamá
Juan Clemente Zenea
Rubén Nogueras
M Echevarría
Casa Natal de Carlos Manuel de Céspedes
Maceo
Cubanacán
Pedro Batista
Infotur
Plaza del Himno Nacional
Plaza de la Revolución
José A Saco
Av Felino Figueredo
Plaza de la Patria (1.3m); Teatro Bayamo (1.3km); Estadio Mártires de Barbados (1.5km)
Carlos Manuel de Céspedes
Máximo Gómez
General García (Paseo Bayamés)
José Martí
Perucho Figueredo
M Capote
Donato Marmol
General Lora
A Usett
Manuel Pedreira
Barranca de la Luz
Pío Rosado
Juan Clemente Zenea
Máximo Gómez
José Martí
Carlos Manuel de Céspedes
Anley Rosales Benitez (100m); Provincial (3000m); Víazul (300m); Ecotur (1.1km); Hotel Sierra Maestra (1.1km); Cabaret Bayam (1.2km)
Villa Bayamo (1km)
Av Amado Estévez
Av Amado Estévez
GRANMA PROVINCE

Bayamo

Top Sights
1 Casa Natal de Carlos Manuel de Céspedes ... A2
2 Plaza de la Revolución ... B3

Sights
3 Ayuntamiento ... B3
4 Capilla de la Dolorosa ... A3
5 Casa de Estrada Palma ... B4
6 Catedral de San Salvador de Bayamo ... A3
7 Fabrica de los Coches ... D7
8 Museo de Cera ... C5
9 Museo Ñico López ... C7
10 Museo Provincial ... A2
11 Oficina de Arqueología ... C5
12 Parque Chapuzón ... A6
13 Paseo Bayamés ... B3
14 Torre de San Juan Evangelista ... D6
15 Ventana de Luz Vázquez ... B4

Activities, Courses & Tours
16 Academia de Ajedrez ... B3

Sleeping
17 Casa de la Amistad ... B1
18 Casa Olga ... B2
19 Hotel Royalton ... A3
20 Villa La Paz ... B1
21 Villa Pupi & Villa América ... B1

Eating
22 Cuadro Gastronómica de Luz Vázquez ... B4
23 El Polinesio ... B2
24 La Bodega ... A3
25 La Sevillana ... B4
26 Meson La Cuchipapa ... B2
Restaurante Plaza ... (see 19)
27 Restaurante San Salvador de Bayamo ... B2

Drinking & Nightlife
28 Bar la Esquina ... A2
29 Café Literario Ventana Sur ... B3
30 La Taberna ... B3
31 Piano Bar ... C4

Entertainment
32 Casa de la Cultura ... B3
33 Casa de la Trova la Bayamesa ... B2
34 Centro Cultural Los Beatles ... C3
35 Cine Céspedes ... A3
Uneac ... (see 5)

Shopping
36 ARTex ... B2

Paseo Bayamés AREA
(Calle General García) Bayamo's main shopping street was pedestrianized in the 1990s and reconfigured with benches and funky artwork. Here you'll find wax museum **Museo de Cera** (☎23-42-54-21; General García No 261; CUC$2; ⏰9am-5pm Tue-Fri, 10am-1pm & 7-10pm Sat, 9am-noon Sun), various public utilities and plenty of Cuban-style commerce, including food stalls at night.

Plaza de la Patria PLAZA
(Av Felino Figueredo) This square is where Fidel Castro gave his final, rousing public speech in July 2006 before being taken ill and stepping down as president. The monument to the Cuban greats here features Manuel de Céspedes, Antonio Maceo, Máximo Gomez, Perucho Figueredo and, subtly placed left of center, Fidel: it's the only monument he appears on in Cuba.

It's six blocks northeast of the bus station.

Parque Chapuzón PARK
(Av Amado Estevez; 👪) Greenery beckons not a kilometer from Bayamo's center where the Bayamo River has carved a lush belt through the urban grid. Locals come to this blissful spot to water their horses or have a family barbecue. Footpaths and gazebo-shaped stalls selling food and drink embellish the banks, but never detract from the all-pervading mood of tranquility.

Oficina de Arqueología MUSEUM
(☎23-42-15-91; General García No 252; CUC$1; ⏰9am-5pm Tue-Fri, 9am-noon & 6-10pm Sat, 9am-1pm Sun) Features Pre-Colombian stone tools and objects such as shells, bones and ceramics.

Catedral de San Salvador de Bayamo CHURCH
(☎23-42-25-14; Jose Joaquin Palma No 130) There's been a church on this site since 1514. The current edifice dates from 1740 but got devastated in the 1869 fire, so much of what you see results from building work in 1919. One original section surviving the fire is the **Capilla de la Dolorosa** (J Palma; donations accepted; ⏰9am-noon & 3-5pm Mon-Fri, 9am-noon Sat) with its gilded wooden altar.

A highlight of the main church is the central arch, which exhibits a mural depicting the blessing of the Cuban flag in front of the revolutionary army on October 20, 1868.

Outside, Plaza del Himno Nacional is where the Cuban national anthem, 'La Bayamesa,' was sung for the first time in 1868.

Museo Provincial MUSEUM
(☎23-42-41-25; Maceo No 55; CUC$5; ⊙8am-5pm Tue-Fri, 9am-5pm Sat, 9am-1pm Sun) Directly next door to Céspedes' ex-home, this provincial museum completes Bayamo's historical trajectory with a yellowing city document dating from 1567 and a rare photo of Bayamo immediately after the fire.

Torre de San Juan Evangelista RUINS
(cnr José Martí & Amado Estévez) A church dating from Bayamo's earliest years stood at this busy intersection until it was destroyed in the great fire of 1869. Later, the church's tower served as the entrance to the first cemetery in Cuba, closed in 1919. The cemetery was demolished in 1940 but the tower survived.

A monument to local poet José Joaquín Palma (1844–1911) stands in the park diagonally across the street from the tower, and beside the tower is a bronze statue of Francisco Vicente Aguilera (1821–77), who led the independence struggle in Bayamo.

Ventana de Luz Vázquez LANDMARK
(Céspedes, btwn Figueredo & Luz Vázquez) A forerunner of the national anthem, cowritten by Céspedes (and, confusingly, also called 'La Bayamesa') was first sung from here on March 27, 1851. A memorial plaque has been emblazoned onto the wall next to the wood-barred colonial window.

Casa de Estrada Palma CULTURAL CENTER
(Céspedes No 158) Cuba's first postindependence president, Tomás Estrada Palma, was born here in 1835. One-time friend of José Martí, Estrada Palma was disgraced post-Revolution for his perceived complicity with the US over the Platt Amendment. His birth house is now the seat of Uneac (Unión Nacional de Escritores y Artistas de Cuba; National Union of Cuban Writers and Artists).

You'll find little about the famous former occupant inside, but the courtyard contains a palm (dating from 1837) that would (probably) have come into contact with Palma.

Museo Ñico López MUSEUM
(☎23-42-31-81; Abihail González; CUC$1; ⊙9am-noon & 1:30-5:30pm Tue-Sat, 9am-1pm Sun) This museum is in the former officers' club of the Carlos Manuel de Céspedes military barracks, 1km southeast of Parque Céspedes. On July 26, 1953, this garrison was attacked by 25 revolutionaries led by Ñico López in tandem with the assault on Moncada Barracks in Santiago de Cuba in order to prevent reinforcements from being sent.

López escaped to Guatemala and was the first Cuban to befriend Ernesto 'Che' Guevara, but was killed shortly after the *Granma* landed in 1956.

Fabrica de los Coches FACTORY
(☎23-41-16-44; Prolongacion General García No 530; CUC$1 donation; ⊙8am-3pm Mon-Fri & every 2nd Sat) It's worth the jaunt to observe the goings-on at Cuba's only handcrafted *coche* (horse cart) production line. Most horse carts you'll see in Cuba are metal, but these are fashioned in wood and take far longer (up to three months per cart) to produce.

You'll see horse carts in various stages of completion, meet the workers and be able to buy Bayamo's best souvenir: miniature model horse carts with incredible attention to detail. The big ones cost about 8000 pesos (CUC$325) and don't fit quite so well into a suitcase.

Outside Town

Jardín Botánico de Cupaynicu GARDENS
(Carretera de Guisa, Km 10; CUC$2; ⊙8am-4:30pm Tue-Sun) For a floral appreciation of Bayamo's evergreen hinterland, head to this botanic garden about 16km outside the city off the Guisa road. It's on very few itineraries, so you can have the serene, serendipitous 104 hectares more or less to yourself. There are 74 types of palms, scores of cacti, blooming orchids and sections for endangered and medicinal plants.

The guided tour (Spanish only) gains you access to greenhouses, notable for the showy ornamentals. To get here, take the road to Santiago de Cuba for 6km and turn left at the signposted junction for Guisa. After 10km you'll see the botanic garden sign on the right. From Bayamo, trucks (MN$10) heading in this direction leave from the intermunicipal bus station in front of the train station.

Academia de Ajedrez CHESS SCHOOL
(José A Saco No 63, btwn General García & Céspedes; ⊙9am-noon, 2pm-3:30pm & 8-10pm Mon-Fri) Catering to adorable students in school

uniforms, the Academia de Ajedrez is the place to go to improve your pawn-king-four technique. Pictures of Cuban heroes emblazoned onto the walls of this cerebral institution offer plenty of inspiration.

Tours

Anley Rosales Benitez TOURS

(52-92-22-09; www.bayamotravelagent.com; Carretera Central No 478) Anley coordinates trips to the Sierra Maestra, which can be difficult to find transport for on your own. Since he doesn't make all trips personally, confirm bilingual guide services ahead. The highlight tour takes in the revolutionary sites of the 1956–58 years when the rebels were holed up hereabouts, such as the village where Fidel famously played baseball with locals.

Services include everything from day trips to the Jardín Botánico Cupaynicu to Bayamo airport pick-up and all-inclusive Comandancia de la Plata excursions (two people CUC$115).

Festivals & Events

Incendio de Bayamo CULTURAL

(Jan 12) The biggest annual event is the Incendio de Bayamo, on January 12, remembering the city's 1869 burning with live music and theatrical performances in Parque Céspedes, and culminating in fireworks launched from nearby buildings.

Sleeping

Bayamo has a good mix of hotel and private lodgings, with the long-awaited addition of Hotel Telegrafo set to reopen in 2017.

AND THEN THERE WERE THREE...

It seemed like an ignominious defeat. Three days after landing in a crippled leisure yacht on Cuba's southeastern coast, Castro's expeditionary force of 82 soldiers had been decimated by Batista's superior army. Some of the rebels had fled, others had been captured and killed. Escaping from the ambush, Castro found himself cowering in a sugarcane field along with two ragged companions: his 'bodyguard,' Universo Sánchez, and diminutive Havana doctor, Faustino Pérez. 'There was a moment when I was commander-in-chief of myself and two others,' said the man who would one day go on to overthrow the Cuban government, thwart a US-sponsored invasion, incite a nuclear standoff and become one of the most enduring political figures of the 20th century.

Hunted by ground troops and bombed from the air by military planes, the trio lay trapped in the cane field for four days and three nights. The hapless Pérez had inadvertently discarded his weapon; Sánchez, meanwhile, had lost his shoes. Wracked by fatigue and plagued by hunger, Fidel continued to do what he always did best. He whispered incessantly to his beleaguered colleagues – about the Revolution, about the philosophies of José Martí. Buoyantly he pontificated about how 'all the glory of the world would fit inside a grain of maize.' Sánchez, not unwisely, concluded that his delirious leader had gone crazy and that their grisly fate was sealed – it was just a matter of time.

At night, Fidel – determined not to be caught alive – slept with his rifle cocked against his throat, the safety catch released. One squeeze of the finger and it would have been over. No Cuban Revolution, no Bay of Pigs, no Cuban Missile Crisis.

Fatefully, the moment didn't arrive. With the army concluding that the rebels had been wiped out, the search was called off. Choosing their moment, Fidel and his two companions crept stealthily northeast toward the safety of the Sierra Maestra, sucking on stalks of sugarcane for nutrition.

It was a desperate fight for survival. For a further eight days the rebel army remained a bedraggled trio as the fugitive soldiers dodged army patrols, crawled through sewers and drank their own urine. It wasn't until December 13 that they met up with Guillermo García, a *campesino* sympathetic to the rebel cause, and a corner was turned.

On December 15 at a safe meeting house, Fidel's brother, Raúl, materialized out of the jungle with three men and four weapons. Castro was ecstatic. Three days later a third exhausted band of eight soldiers – including Che Guevara and Camilo Cienfuegos – turned up, swelling the rebel army to an abject 15.

'We can win this war,' proclaimed an ebullient Fidel to his small band of not-so-merry men. 'We have just begun the fight.'

★Villa La Paz CASA PARTICULAR $

(52-77-34-59, 23-42-39-49; anyoleg2005@yahoo.es; Coronel J Estrada No 32, btwn William Soler & Av Milanés; r CUC$20-25;) Any visitor to Cuba would consider this spotless modern home with attractive renovated rooms great value. Guests have flat-screen TVs, wi-fi and their own separate dining area. While the house is short on outdoor spaces, the indoor ones are extra pleasant, as are the hosts, who speak English and Russian.

Casa Olga CASA PARTICULAR $

(23-42-38-59, mobile 54-95-59-54; olgacr@nauta.cu; Parada No 16, cnr Martí; r CUC$25;) With a balcony gazing out on the plaza, these three 2nd-floor rooms couldn't be more central. Olga is a welcoming host who prepares substantial breakfasts. Open your window and suave sounds from the Casa de la Trova (situated opposite) waft in.

Casa de la Amistad CASA PARTICULAR $

(23-42-57-69; gabytellez2003@gmail.com; Pío Rosado No 60, btwn Ramíriez & N López; r CUC$25;) Gabriel and Rosa let out two spacious apartments on the upper floor of their pastel-shaded house. Guests have a private entrance, kitchen, sitting area, bedroom and bathroom. They are fine and helpful hosts who speak excellent English, and there's even wi-fi.

Villa Pupi & Villa América CASA PARTICULAR $

(23-42-30-29; yuri21504@gmail.com; Coronel J Estrada No 76-78; r CUC$20-25;) This family-run enterprise in two adjacent homes offers three rooms – the better ones flank a spacious 2nd-floor terrace where good local cooking is served (mains CUC$5 to CUC$10). Be warned, reservations are not always respected.

Villa Bayamo HOTEL $$

(23-42-31-02; s/d CUC$58/64;) This out-of-town option (it's 3km southwest of the center on the road to Manzanillo) offers a definitive rural feel and a pleasant swimming pool overlooking fields at the back. With well-appointed rooms and a reasonable restaurant.

Hotel Sierra Maestra HOTEL $$

(23-42-79-70; Carretera Central; s/d CUC$56/64;) With a ring of the Soviet '70s about it, the Sierra Maestra hardly merits its three stars, although rooms have had some much-needed attention. Three kilometers from the town center, it's OK for an overnighter. Let the mojitos at the bar be your consolation.

★Hotel Royalton HOTEL $$$

(23-42-22-90; Maceo No 53; s/d CUC$120/135;) Bayamo's best hotel has 33 rooms upgraded to boutique standard with power showers and flat-screen TVs; there's also a roof terrace. Downstairs an attractive bar complements the reception area with seats spilling out onto a sidewalk terrace overlooking Parque Céspedes. The on-site restaurant is a good eating option.

Eating

There's some unique street food in Bayamo, sold from Calle Saco and Parque Céspedes. Otherwise you're dealing with mainly local restaurants with prices in Cuban pesos.

El Polinesio CUBAN $

(23-42-24-49; Parada No 125, btwn Pío Rosado & Cisnero; meals CUC$6-8; noon-11pm) This longtime staple debuted in the days when private restaurants could only seat 12 people and serve pork and chicken. Today's menu ventures into seafood with wine sauce and chicken with vegetables.

What hasn't changed is the venue – upstairs in an open-fronted family dining room with five or six tables – and the service. Big smiles all round.

La Sevillana SPANISH $

(23-42-14-72; General García, btwn General Lora & Perucho Figueredo; mains CUC$1-4; noon-2pm & 6-10pm) Come and see Cuban chefs attempt Spanish cuisine – paella and *garbanzos* (chickpeas). This is a new kind of peso restaurant, with a dress code (no shorts), a doorman in a suit, and a reservations policy. Press your trousers, brush up on your Spanish, but don't expect *sevillano* creativity.

Cuadro Gastronómica de Luz Vázquez FAST FOOD $

(off General García, btwn Figueredo & General Lora; dishes from MN$10; hours vary) Along this short lane are parked at least a dozen clean-looking food carts selling *bayamés* street snacks (pay in Cuban pesos). Bank on hot dogs, croquettes, ice cream, sardines and empanadas.

★Restaurante San Salvador de Bayamo CARIBBEAN $$

(23-42-69-42; Maceo No 107; mains CUC$3-9; noon-11pm) Who isn't in the mood to be serenaded by violins in a splendid colonial place? Thanks to the knowledgeable owner, dishes avoid the obvious to tap into indigenous/bucaneer influences on regional cuisine. Try tortilla with cassava and local cheese or shrimp in garlic sauce – also try the *cerveza mambisa,* jagua juice fermented in a sugarcane stalk.

There's a cheaper menu in *moneda national* (MN$; Cuban pesos) or set meals in pesos convertibles.

★Meson La Cuchipapa CUBAN **$$**

(☎52-39-89-05; lacuchipapa@gmail.com; Parada btw Marmol & Martí; mains CUC$6-10; ⏲11am-midnight) Real *comida Cubana* (Cuban food) fashioned on reviving traditions rarely known to visitors. At wooden picnic benches, try cassava bread originally consumed by native Taínos, fragrant bean stews and big portions of regular fare such as smoked pork chops. You can also brave *frutanga,* a cocktail starring the local firewater sweetened with sugarcane crushed by your own hand on an old handcrank mill.

Restaurante Plaza CUBAN **$$**

(☎23-42-22-90; Maceo No 53, Hotel Royalton; mains CUC$6-10; ⏲7:30am-10:30pm) Bayamo's finest hotel (the Royalton) also hosts one of its best restaurants; nothing legendary mind you, but with an excellent setting including the option to sit outside overlooking one of Cuba's most pleasant squares. Food is generously labeled 'international' with a strong meat, rice and beans bias. Service is officious on a bad day, quietly polite on a good one.

La Bodega CARIBBEAN **$$**

(☎23-42-10-11; Plaza del Himno Nacional No 34; meals CUC$5-15, cover after 9pm CUC$3; ⏲11am-1am) On Bayamo's main square, head to the rear terrace overlooking Río Bayamo, fringed by a bucolic backdrop worthy of an isolated country villa. Set menus offer pork or *vaca frita* (a kind of shredded beef) with sides and dessert. Try the beef and taste the coffee, or simply relax before the tour groups arrive. Has live music on some afternoons.

Drinking & Nightlife

Café Literario Ventana Sur BAR

(Figueredo No 62; ⏲10am-midnight) Join the town's poets, artists and musicians imbibing strong coffee and swapping ideas. You'll see them at the alfresco tables strumming their guitars before launching into spontaneous outbreaks of music – Silvio Rodríguez meets Radiohead.

Bar la Esquina BAR

(☎23-42-17-31; cnr Donato Marmol & Maceo; ⏲12pm-12am) International cocktails are served in this tiny corner bar replete with plenty of local atmosphere.

Piano Bar BAR

(☎23-42-40-27; Bartholomé Masó btw General García & Barranca de la Luz; MN$10; ⏲12pm-12am Mon-Fri, 2pm-2am Sat & Sun) Ice-cold air-con, starched tablecloths, stern waiters, good live music from piano recitals to *trovadores* (folk singers) and crooners of *musica romantica.* So plush it's sometimes invite-only. Music is daily, except for Mondays.

La Taberna BAR

(General García, btwn Saco & Figueredo; ⏲10am-10pm) This busy local place on the main shopping street has beer on tap in ceramic mugs and a constant buzz of conversation. Pay in Cuban pesos.

☆ Entertainment

Teatro Bayamo THEATER

(☎23-42-51-06; Reparto Jesús Menéndez) Six blocks northeast of the bus station, opposite Plaza de la Patria, lies one of the Oriente's most impressive theaters. Constructed in 1982, the theater was converted into its current function only in 2007. The

DON'T MISS

FIESTA DE LA CUBANÍA

Bayamo's quintessential nighttime attraction is an ebullient and unique street party, the likes of which you'll find nowhere else in Cuba. It includes the locally famous pipe organs, whole roast pig, an eye-watering oyster drink called *ostiones* and – incongruously in the middle of it all – rows of tables laid out diligently with chess sets. Dancing is, of course, de rigueur. The action kicks off at 8pm-ish on Saturday. Traditionally the fiesta has been held in Calle Saco close to the main square but, to the chagrin of many locals, it has been moved to a site just outside the center in Plaza de la Fiesta. Check its current status at Infotur (p380).

vitrales (stained glass windows) in the lobby are sensational. Performances are usually Wednesday, Saturday or Sunday.

Casa de la Trova la Bayamesa TRADITIONAL MUSIC
(☎23-42-56-73; Maceo No 111; CUC$1; ⌚10am-1am) One of Cuba's best *trova* houses, in a lovely colonial building on Maceo. Pictures on the wall display the famous '70s afro of Bayamo-born *trova* king Pablo Milanés. There's an ARTex gift shop onsite.

Uneac ARTS CENTER
(☎23-42-36--70; Céspedes No 158; ⌚vary) You can catch heartfelt boleros (ballads) on the flowery patio here in the former home of disgraced first president Tomás Estrada Palma, the man invariably blamed for handing Guantánamo to the *yanquis* (Yankees).

Centro Cultural Los Beatles LIVE MUSIC
(☎23-42-17-99; Zenea, btwn Figueredo & Saco; CUC$1; ⌚6am-midnight Tue-Sun) Just as the rest of the world fell for the exoticism of the Buena Vista Social Club, Cubans fell for the downright brilliance of the Fab Four. This quirky place hosts Beatles tribute bands (in Spanish) every weekend. Unmissable!

Cine Céspedes CINEMA
(☎23-42-42-67; Libertad No 4; MN$5) This cinema is on the western side of Parque Céspedes by the post office. It offers everything from Gutiérrez Alea to the latest Hollywood blockbuster (occasional English-language films with Spanish subtitles).

Casa de la Cultura ARTS CENTER
(☎23-42-59-17; General García No 15) Wide-ranging cultural events, including art expos, on the east side of Parque Céspedes.

Estadio Mártires de Barbados SPECTATOR SPORT
(☎23-42-57-47; Av Granma) From October to April there are baseball games at this stadium, approximately 2km east of the center.

Cabaret Bayam CABARET
(☎23-48-16-98; Carretera Central, Km 2; ⌚7pm-midnight Tue-Sun) Bayamo's glittery nightclub/cabaret opposite the Hotel Sierra Maestra draws out the locals on weekends in their equally glittery attire. It's the largest indoor cabaret in Cuba.

Shopping

Paseo Bayamés is the main pedestrian shopping street but, with few tourists, stores are mainly aimed at locals.

ARTex GIFTS & SOUVENIRS
(☎23-48-79-56; General García No 7; ⌚9am-4:30pm Mon-Sat) The usual mix of Che Guevara T-shirts and bogus Santería dolls in Parque Céspedes.

Information

INTERNET ACCESS

There is wi-fi in the Plaza de la Revolucion and the small park in front of the Casa de la Trova.

Etecsa Telepunto (☎23-42-83-53; General García, btwn Saco & Figueredo; internet per hr CUC$1.50; ⌚8:30am-7pm) Buy Internet scratch cards here or use the internet terminals; it's rarely busy.

MEDICAL SERVICES

Farmacia Internacional (☎23-42-95-96; General García, btwn Figueredo & Lora; ⌚8am-noon & 1-5pm Mon-Sat) Pharmacy.

Hospital Carlos Manuel de Céspedes (☎23-42-50-12; Carretera Central, Km 1) For medical emergencies.

MONEY

There are plenty of ATMs.

Banco de Crédito y Comercio (☎23-42-63-40; cnr General García & Saco; ⌚8am-4pm Mon-Fri, 8am-11am Sat) Bank with ATM.

Cadeca (☎23-42-72-22; Saco No 101; ⌚8:30am-4pm Mon-Sat) Money changing.

POST

Post office (☎23-42-32-72; cnr Maceo & Parque Céspedes; ⌚8am-8pm Mon-Sat)

TOURIST INFORMATION

Cubanacán (Maceo; ⌚9am-noon, 1pm-4:30pm Mon-Sat) Arranges hikes to Pico Turquino and Parque Nacional Desembarco del Granma, among other places.

Ecotur (☎23-48-70-06 ext 639; Hotel Sierra Maestra) Helpful office booking excursions to Pico Turquino and Parque Nacional Desembarco de Granma. Ask about the Ruta de la Revolución hike.

Infotur (☎23-42-34-68; Plaza del Himno Nacional, cnr Joaquín Palma; ⌚8:30am-noon & 1-5pm Mon-Fri) Take advantage of this courteous, helpful information office – a rare find. It offers bilingual city tours by bicycle taxi (CUC$4) and sells the same tours as Ecotour and Cubanacán. Use hashtags #Infotur #Bayamo on Facebook site to find city events.

Getting There & Away

AIR

Bayamo's Carlos Manuel de Céspedes Airport (airport code BYM) is about 4km northeast of town, on the road to Holguín. There are no international flights to or from Bayamo.

BUS & TRUCK

The **provincial bus station** (cnr Carretera Central & Av Jesús Rabí) has **Víazul** (☎23-42-74-82; www.viazul.com; cnr Carretera Central & Av Jesús Rabí) buses to several destinations.

Buses heading west also stop at Las Tunas (CUC$6), Camagüey (CUC$11), Ciego de Ávila (CUC$17), Sancti Spíritus (CUC$21) and Santa Clara (CUC$26).

Passenger trucks leave from an adjacent terminal for Santiago de Cuba, Holguín, Manzanillo, Pilón and Niquero several times per day. You can truck it to Bartolomé Masó, as close as you can get on public transport to the Sierra Maestra trailhead. Trucks leave when full and you pay as you board.

The **intermunicipal bus station** (☎23-42-40-40; cnr Saco & Línea), opposite the train station, receives mostly local buses of little use to travelers, although trucks to Guisa leave from here.

TAXI

State taxis can be procured for hard-to-reach destinations such as Manzanillo (CUC$30), Pilón (CUC$75) and Niquero (CUC$80). Prices are estimates and will depend on the current price of petrol. Nonetheless, it is usually cheaper to reach all these places by taxi than by rental car.

TRAIN

The **train station** (☎23-42-30-56; cnr Saco & Línea; train to Havana CUC$25) is 1km east of the center. There are three local trains a day to Manzanillo (via Yara). Other daily trains serve Santiago and Camagüey. The long-distance Havana–Manzanillo train passes through Bayamo every fourth day.

Getting Around

Cubataxi (☎23-42-43-13) can supply a taxi to Bayamo airport for CUC$5 or to Aeropuerto Frank País in Holguín for CUC$35. A taxi to Villa Santo Domingo (setting-off point for the Alto del Naranjo trailhead for Sierra Maestra hikes) or Comandancia la Plata will cost approximately CUC$35 one way. There's a taxi stand in the south of town near Museo Ñico López.

Cubacar (☎23-59-70-05; Carretera Central) rents cars at the Hotel Sierra Maestra, and the **Servi-Cupet gas station** (Carretera Central) is between Hotel Sierra Maestra and the bus terminal as you arrive from Santiago de Cuba.

The main horse-cart route (MN$1) runs between the train station and the hospital, via the bus station. Bici-taxis (a few pesos a ride) are also useful for getting around town. There's a stand near the train station.

Gran Parque Nacional Sierra Maestra

Comprising a sublime mountainscape of verdant peaks and humid cloud forest, and home to honest, hardworking *campesinos* (country folk), **Gran Parque Nacional Sierra Maestra** (CUC$15; ⏲closes at 4pm) is an alluring natural sanctuary that still echoes with the gunshots of Castro's guerrilla campaign of the late 1950s. Situated 40km south of Yara, up a very steep 24km concrete road from Bartolomé Masó, this precipitous, little-trammeled region contains the country's highest peak, Pico Turquino (1972m; just over the border in Santiago de Cuba Province), unlimited birdlife and flora, and the rebels' one-time wartime headquarters, Comandancia la Plata.

Sights

★Comandancia de la Plata — LANDMARK

Topping a crenellated mountain ridge amid thick cloud forest, this pioneering camp was established by Fidel Castro in 1958 after a year on the run in the Sierra Maestra. Well camouflaged and remote, the rebel HQ was chosen for its inaccessibility and it served its purpose well – Batista's soldiers never found it.

Today it remains much as it was left in the '50s, with 16 simple wooden buildings providing an evocative reminder of one of the most successful guerrilla campaigns in history. It's easy to appreciate the site's strategic location. The main site, culminating in the Casa de Fidel (Fidel's House) is approached via an open space, then a climb through thick trees.

Highlights include the small museum, near the beginning of the complex, the masterfully designed Casa de Fidel with its seven concealed escape routes in case the Revolution's leaders got discovered, and the steep climb up Radio Rebelde to the radio-communications buildings where the rebel's early broadcasts were aired. The hospital buildings, a wake-up call to the brutality of guerilla medical care, lie far below along a separate path (positioned here so

Gran Parque Nacional Sierra Maestra

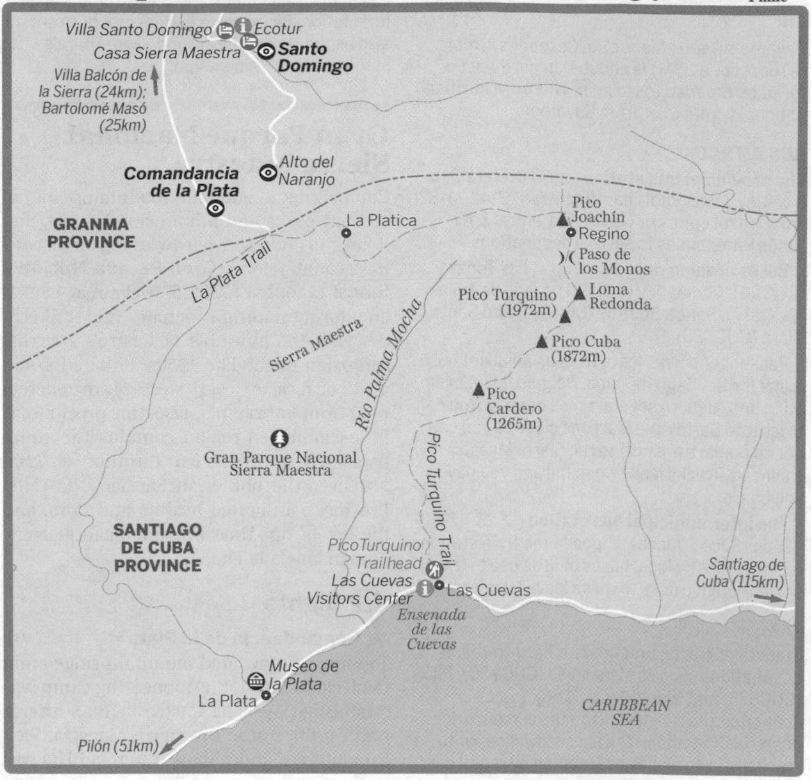

the injured wouldn't give the camp location away in their agony).

Comandancia de la Plata is controlled by the Centro de Información de Flora y Fauna in Santo Domingo. Aspiring guerrilla-watchers must first hire a guide at the park headquarters, then get transport (or walk) 5km up to Alto del Naranjo and then proceed on foot along a muddy track for the final 4km. The guided excursion costs CUC$33 including transport, water and a snack (CUC$5 extra for cameras). You can organize it at the Ecotur (p384) office in Villa Santo Domingo.

★ Santo Domingo VILLAGE

(museum admission CUC$1; ⏲ museum hours vary) This tiny village nestles in a deep green valley beside the deliciously clean Río Yara. Communally it provides a wonderful slice of peaceful Cuban *campesino* life that has carried on pretty much unchanged since Fidel and Che prowled these shadowy mountains in the 1950s. If you decide to stick around, you can get a taste of rural socialism at the local school and medical clinic, or ask at Villa Santo Domingo about the tiny village museum.

Locals also offer horseback riding (CUC$10 per hour), pedicure treatments, hikes to natural swimming pools and some classic old first-hand tales from the annals of revolutionary history.

The park closes at 4pm but rangers won't let you pass after mid-morning, so set off early to maximize your visit.

Alto del Naranjo LANDMARK

All trips into the park begin at the end of the near-vertical, corrugated-concrete access road at Alto del Naranjo (after Villa Santo Domingo the road gains 750 vertical meters in less than 5km). To get there, it's an arduous two-hour walk or zippy ride in a 4WD.

There's a wondrous view of the plains of Granma from this 950m-high lookout, otherwise it's a launching pad for La Plata (3km) and Pico Turquino (13km).

Sleeping

Casa Sierra Maestra CASA PARTICULAR **$**
(☎23-56-44-91; Santo Domingo; r CUC$15-40; ❄) Rustic heaven! Across the river from the park entrance in Santo Domingo (cross on the stepping stones), this place has four perfectly decent rooms (two in separate cabins) and an atmospheric *ranchón*-style bar-restaurant (mains CUC$4 to CUC$8). Chickens cluck, and rural bliss descends.

★ **Villa Santo Domingo** HOTEL **$$**
(☎23-56-55-68, 23-56-58-34; s/d CUC$38/50, bungalow CUC$63; P❄) This villa, 24km south of Bartolomé Masó, flanks the gateway to Gran Parque Nacional Sierra Maestra. There are 40 cabins (20 cheaper concrete ones and 20 newer ones in smart wooden buildings) next to the Río Yara. The setting, among cascading mountains and *campesino* huts, is idyllic and the best

WORTH A TRIP

CLIMBING PICO TURQUINO

Towering 1972m above the calm Caribbean, Pico Turquino – so named for the turquoise hue that colors its steep upper slopes – is Cuba's highest and most regularly climbed mountain.

Carpeted in lush cloud forest and protected in a 140-sq-km national park, the peak's lofty summit is embellished by a bronze bust of national hero José Martí. In a patriotic test of endurance, the statue was dragged to the top in 1953 by a young Celia Sánchez and her father, Manuel Sánchez Silveira, to mark the centennial of the apostle's birth.

Four years later, Sánchez visited the summit again, this time with a rifle-wielding Fidel Castro in tow to record an interview with American news network CBS. Not long afterwards, the rebel army pitched their permanent headquarters in the mountain's imposing shadow, atop a tree-protected ridge near La Plata.

Best tackled as a through trek from the Santo Domingo side, the rugged, two- to three-day grind up Turquino starts from Alto del Naranjo above Santo Domingo and ends at Las Cuevas on the Caribbean coast (an out-and-back Alto del Naranjo–Pico Turquino hike is also possible). Guides are mandatory and can be arranged through Flora y Fauna employees at Villa Santo Domingo or at the small hut at Las Cuevas. The cost varies, depending on how many days you take. If you organize it through Ecotur/Cubanacán in Bayamo, bank on CUC$68 per person for two days. You'll also need to stock up on food (dinner/breakfast at the overnight shelters are included but nothing in-between), warm clothing, candles and some kind of sleeping roll or sheet. Even in August it gets cold at the shelters, so be prepared. Water is available along the trail, but is scarce: carry reserves.

The trail through the mountains from Alto del Naranjo passes the village of La Platica (water), Palma Mocha (campsite), Lima (campsite), Campismo Joachín (shelter and water), El Cojo (shelter), Pico Joachín, Paso de los Monos, Loma Redonda, Pico Turquino (1972m), Pico Cuba (1872m; with shelter/water at 1650m), Pico Cardero (1265m) and La Esmajagua (600m; with basic refreshments) before dropping down to Las Cuevas on the coast. The first two days are spent on the 13km section to Pico Turquino (normally overnighting at the Campismo Joachín and/or Pico Cuba shelters), where a prearranged guide takes over and leads you down to Las Cuevas. As with all guide services, tips are in order. Prearranging the second leg from Pico Cuba to Las Cuevas is straightforward and handled by park staff.

These hikes are well coordinated and the guides efficient. The sanest way to begin is by overnighting at Villa Santo Domingo and setting out in the morning (you should enter the park gate by 10am). Transport from Las Cuevas along the coast is sparse, with one scheduled truck on alternate days. Arrange onward transport from Las Cuevas in advance. Approaching from Santo Domingo, you will not (officially) be able to do the Comandancia de la Plata and Pico Turquino hikes the same day, but must stay overnight in the village then begin the Pico Turquino hike the following day.

jumping-off point for Comandancia de la Plata and Pico Turquino.

You can also test your lungs by going for a challenging early-morning hike up a painfully steep road to Alto del Naranjo (5km; 750m of ascent). Other attractions include horseback riding, river swimming and traditional music in the villa's restaurant. Fidel stayed here on various occasions (in hut 6) and Raúl dropped by in 2001 after scaling Pico Turquino at the ripe old age of 70. Breakfast is included.

Villa Balcón de la Sierra HOTEL **$$**
(☎23-56-55-13; s/d incl breakfast CUC$62/72; P ❄ 🏊) One kilometer south of Bartolomé Masó and 16km north of Santo Domingo, this simple hotel is nestled in the mountain foothills somewhat far for easy park access. A swimming pool and restaurant are perched on a small hill with killer mountain views, while 20 air-conditioned cabins are scattered below. Lovely natural ambience juxtaposed with the usual basic but functional Islazul furnishings.

ℹ Information

Ecotur (☎23-56-58-34; ⏰8am-noon, 2-5pm) maintains a very handy desk at Villa Santo Domingo. If you want to book in advance try Ecotur in Bayamo or Santiago.

The park closes at 4pm, but rangers won't let you pass after mid-morning, so set off early to maximize your visit.

ℹ Getting There & Away

There's no public transport from Bartolomé Masó to Alto del Naranjo (and trucks to Bartolomé Masó from Bayamo are infrequent and uncomfortable). A taxi from Bayamo to Villa Santo Domingo should cost around CUC$35 one way. Ensure it can take you all the way; the last 7km before Villa Santo Domingo is extremely steep but passable in a (decent) normal car. Returning, the hotel should be able to arrange onward transport for you to Bartolomé Masó, Bayamo or Manzanillo.

A 4WD vehicle with good brakes is necessary to drive the last 5km from Santo Domingo to Alto del Naranjo; it's the steepest road in Cuba with 45% gradients near the top. Powerful 4WDs pass regularly, usually for adventurous tour groups, and you may be able to find a space on board for approximately CUC$5 – ask at Villa Santo Domingo (p383). Alternatively, it's a tough but rewarding 5km hike (or a gut-wrenching morning run!).

Manzanillo

POP 131,000

Bayside Manzanillo isn't exactly pretty but it does find its way under your skin. Hang out in the semiruined central park with its old-fashioned street organs and distinctive neo-Moorish architecture. With bare-bones transport links, few travelers make it here. Off the standard guidebook trail, you can see how Cubans have learned to live with decades of austerity.

Founded in 1784 as a small fishing port, Manzanillo's early history was dominated by smugglers and pirates trading in contraband. The subterfuge continued into the late 1950s, when the city's proximity to the Sierra Maestra made it an important supply center for arms and men joining Castro's revolutionaries in their secret mountaintop headquarters.

Manzanillo's famous hand-operated street organs were first imported from France in the early 20th century. The city's musical legacy was solidified further in 1972 with a government-sponsored *nueva trova* festival that culminated in a solidarity march to Playa las Coloradas.

👁 Sights

👁 In Town

Manzanillo is well known for its striking architecture, a psychedelic mélange of wooden beach shacks, Andalusian-style town houses and intricate neo-Moorish facades. Check out the ramshackle wooden abodes around Perucho Figueredo, between Merchán and JM Gómez.

Parque Céspedes PARK
Manzanillo's central square is notable for its priceless *glorieta* (gazebo/bandstand), an imitation of the Patio de los Leones in Spain's Alhambra, where Moorish mosaics, a scalloped cupola and arabesque columns set off a theme that's replicated elsewhere. Nearby, a permanent statue of Carlos Puebla, Manzanillo's famous homegrown troubadour, sits contemplatively on a bench.

On the eastern side of Parque Céspedes, is Manzanillo's Museo Histórico Municipal whilst the Iglesia de la Purisma Concepción is a neoclassical beauty from 1805, with an impressive gilded altarpiece.

Celia Sánchez Monument MONUMENT

About eight blocks southwest of the park lies Manzanillo's most evocative sight. Built in 1990, this terra-cotta-tiled staircase embellished with colorful ceramic murals runs up Calle Caridad between Martí and Luz Caballero. The birds and flowers on the reliefs represent Sánchez, lynchpin of the M-26-7 (July 26 Movement) and longtime aid to Castro, whose visage appears on the central mural near the top of the stairs. It's a moving memorial with excellent views out over the city and bay.

City Bank of NY Building NOTABLE BUILDING

(cnr Merchán & Dr Codina) For an example of the city's striking architecture, check out the old City Bank of NY building, dating from 1913.

Museo Histórico Municipal MUSEUM

(☎23-57-20-53; Martí No 226; ⏰8am-noon & 2-6pm Tue-Fri, 8am-noon & 6-10pm Sat & Sun) FREE On the eastern side of Parque Céspedes, Manzanillo's Museo Histórico Municipal gives the usual local history lesson with a revolutionary twist

Outside Town

★Museo Histórico la Demajagua MUSEUM

(☎52-19-40-80; CUC$1; ⏰8am-5pm Tue-Sat, 8am-2pm Sun) Ten kilometers south of Manzanillo is the moving sight of the sugar estate of Carlos Manuel de Céspedes, whose outcry, known as 'Grito de Yara', and the subsequent freeing of his slaves on October 10, 1868, marked the opening of Cuba's independence wars. There's a small museum and the Demajagua bell that Céspedes tolled to announce Cuba's (then unofficial) independence.

In 1947 an as-yet-unknown Fidel Castro 'kidnapped' the bell and took it to Havana in a publicity stunt to protest against the corrupt Cuban government.

Also at La Demajagua are the remains of Céspedes' original *ingenio* (sugar mill) and a poignant monument (with a quote from Castro). To get here, travel south 10km from the Servi-Cupet gas station in Manzanillo, in the direction of Media Luna, and then another 2.5km off the main road, towards the sea.

WORTH A TRIP

MEDIA LUNA

One of a handful of small towns punctuating the swaying sugar fields between Manzanillo and Cabo Cruz, Media Luna is worth a pit stop on the basis of its Celia Sánchez connections. The revolution's 'first lady' was born here in 1920 in a small clapboard house that is now the fastidiously curated **Celia Sánchez Museum.** (☎23-59-34-66; Raúl Podio No 111; admission CUC$1; ⏰9am-5pm Mon-Sat, 8am-noon Sun).

If you have time, take a stroll around this quintessential Cuban sugar town dominated by a tall soot-stained mill (now disused) and characteristic clapboard houses decorated with gingerbread embellishments. There is also a lovely *glorieta* (gazebo/bandstand), almost as outlandish as Manzanillo's. The main park is the place to get a take on the local street theater while supping on quick-melting ice cream.

A signposted road from Media Luna leads 28km to Cinco Palmas.

Criadero de Cocodrilos WILDLIFE RESERVE

(Crocodile Farm; ☎23-53-22-11; CUC$5; ⏰7am-6pm Mon-Fri, 7-11am Sat) The nearby Cauto River delta is home to a growing number of wild crocodiles, so it's no surprise to encounter one of Cuba's half dozen or so crocodile farms here. There are close to 1000 crocs at this breeding farm, although they're all of the less-endangered 'American' variety. The farm is 9km south of Manzanillo on the road to Media Luna. The farm can be reached by taxi (CUC$10) from Manzanillo.

Sleeping

Manzanillo – thank heavens – has great quality casas particulares, as there's not much happening on the hotel scene.

★Adrián & Tonia CASA PARTICULAR $

(☎23-57-30-28; ato700714@gmail.com; Mártires de Vietnam No 49; r CUC$20-25; P ❄ ≋) This fabulous *casa* would stand out in any city, let alone Manzanillo. The position, on the terra-cotta staircase to the Celia Sánchez monument, obviously helps. But Adrián and Tonia have gone beyond the call of duty with a vista-laden terrace, plunge pool and five separate suites, including one with private entrance and kitchen facilities.

La Roca CASA PARTICULAR **$**
(58-15-18-21, 23-57-79-80; mercyandraca@nauta.cu; Martires de Vietnam No 68; r CUC$25;) Climb the Celia Sánchez staircase to this smart multistory home with two guest rooms. Rooms are ample and bright and there are great city views. The recommended onsite restaurant (mains CUC$5 to CUC$10) is for guests only. You can catch wi-fi from the balcony.

Casa Peña CASA PARTICULAR **$**
(52-46-61-51, 23-57-26-28; mherrerar@grannet.sld.cu; Maceo No 189 cnr Loma; r CUC$25) A pleasant *casa* run by Dolli. The public areas resemble a refined museum and the one ample room and quiet plant-filled terrace don't disappoint.

Hotel Guacanayabo HOTEL **$**
(23-57-40-12; Circunvalación Camilo Cienfuegos; s/d CUC$25/40;) The austere Islazul-run Guacanayabo resembles a tropical reincarnation of a Gulag camp. Stay if you must. It's 3km from the center.

Eating

The city's renowned for its fish, including the delicious *liseta*, but overall restaurant choices are dire: if in doubt eat at your casa particular or drop in on the weekend Sábado en la Calle when the locals cook up traditional whole roast pig.

Paladar Rancho Luna CUBAN **$**
(23-57-38-58; José Miguel Gómez No 169; meals CUC$3-5; noon-11pm) A passable restaurant blaring reggaetón, it's nonetheless your best option for reasonably priced fare. A decorative, typically Manzanillan facade sets the tone. The food, though never legendary, is perfectly OK as long as you stick to the local specialty – prawns.

Cayo Confite SEAFOOD **$$**
(Malecón; mains CUC$8; 9am-9pm) Utter simplicity – sit on this shady deck facing the waterfront for whole fried fish served with plantain chips. It's on the edge of town at the far end of the Malecón (boardwalk).

Complejo Costa Azul PARRILLA **$$$**
(mains MN$15-30; food noon-9:30pm daily, cabaret 8pm-midnight Tue-Sun) Down by the bay is this grillhouse and cabaret thrown into one. It's highly likely neither amenity will blow your mind but, nevertheless, the eating/entertainment are nigh on as good as it gets here. Pay in pesos.

Drinking & Nightlife

Bodegón Pinilla BAR
(Martí No 212; 9am-8pm Mon-Thu, to 2am Fri & Sat) A new two-level place on the *peatonal* (pedestrianized section) and a good bet for a beer.

Entertainment

Manzanillo's best 'gig' takes place on Saturday evening in the famed Sábado en la Calle, a riot of piping organs, roasted pigs, throat-burning rum and, of course, dancing locals. Don't miss it! The local 'yoof' prefer the Malecón.

Teatro Manzanillo THEATER
(23-57-25-39; Villuendas, btwn Maceo & Saco; shows 8pm Fri-Sun) Touring companies such as the Ballet de Camagüey and Danza Contemporánea de Cuba perform at this lovingly restored venue. Built in 1856 and restored in 1926 and again in 2002, this 430-seat beauty is packed with oil paintings, stained glass and original detail.

Casa de la Trova TRADITIONAL MUSIC
(23-57-54-23; Merchán No 213; MN$1) In the spiritual home of *nueva trova* (traditional singing), a renovation of the local *trova* house was long overdue. Pay a visit to this hallowed and freshly painted musical shrine where Carlos Puebla once plucked his strings.

Information

INTERNET ACCESS

There's a wi-fi signal on the plaza. Purchase wi-fi scratchcards at **Etecsa** (23-57-88-91; cnr Gomez & Codina; internet per hour CUC$1.50; 8:30am-7pm).

MONEY

Banks are plentiful, with ATMs.

Banco de Crédito y Comercio (23-57-71-25; cnr Merchán & Saco; 9am-3pm Mon-Fri) Has an ATM.

Cadeca (23-57-74-67; Martí No 188) Two blocks from the main square. With few places accepting convertibles here, you'll need some Cuban pesos.

POST

Post office (☎23-57-29-21; cnr Martí & Codina; ⏰8am-8pm Mon-Sat) One block from Parque Céspedes.

TOURIST INFORMATION

Infotur (☎23-57-44-12; Maceo btwn Maran & Gomez; ⏰8am-5:30pm Mon-Fri) Helpful information desk facing the plaza. If you are interested in *espiritismo* (rituals with Taíno roots that integrate Catholic saints), they can help arrange a visit to the largest *espiritismo* center in Cuba called Centro la Ville.

ℹ Getting There & Away

AIR

Manzanillo's Sierra Maestra Airport (airport code MZO) is on the road to Cayo Espino, 8km south of the Servi-Cupet gas station in Manzanillo. In winter, **Sunwing** (www.sunwing.ca) flies direct from Toronto and Montreal and **Silver Airways** (www.silverairways.com) flies from Fort Lauderdale, USA.

A taxi between the airport and the center of town should cost approximately CUC$10, though may be more if you have ordered a taxi from your lodging to wait for your flight.

BUS & TRUCK

The **bus station** (☎23-57-27-27; Av Rosales) is 2km northeast of the city center. There are no Víazul services. This narrows your options down to *guaguas* (local Cuban buses, MN$3 for regional destinations) or trucks (no reliable schedules and long queues; MN$10 to MN$15 for regional destinations).

Services run several times a day to Yara (20 minutes) and Bayamo (two hours) in the east and Pilón (two hours) and Niquero (1¾ hours) in the south. For the latter destinations you can also board at the crossroads near the Servi-Cupet gas station and the hospital, which is also where you'll find the *amarillos* (transport officials).

CAR

Cubacar (☎23-57-77-36; Hotel Guacanayabo) has an office at the Hotel Guacanayabo. There's a sturdy road running through Corralito up into Holguín, making this the quickest exit from Manzanillo toward points north and east.

TRAIN

All services from the train station on the north side of town are via Yara and Bayamo. All are painfully slow.

ℹ Getting Around

Horse carts (MN$2) to the bus station leave from Dr Codina between Plácido and Luz Caballero. Horse carts to the shipyard leave from the bottom of Saco (MN$6).

WORTH A TRIP

CINCO PALMAS

At the hamlet of Cinco Palmas, pristine natural landscapes are doused in poignant revolutionary history. This is where Castro's rebels regrouped on December 18, 1956, after their baptism of fire at Alegrio de Pio, 28km away. A bronze monument of three *campesinos* who helped the beleaguered rebel army, then down to a dozen men, was erected in 2008. The monument guards the *finca* of Ramón 'Mongo' Pérez where Castro and others sought shelter. There's also a small, free museum with a 3D map of the hilly terrain.

Cinco Palmas lies 28km southeast of the town of Media Luna along a rough but passable dirt road. Trails from the site lead west to Alegria de Pio and east to Comendancia La Plata. Ask about guided hikes at Ecotur (p380) in Bayamo.

Niquero

POP 41,252

A good launchpad to Parque Nacional Desembarco del Granma, Niquero is a small fishing port and sugar town in the isolated southwest corner of Granma. It's dominated by the Roberto Ramírez Delgado sugar mill. Built in 1905 and nationalized in 1960, it is one of the few regional mills still in operation. Like many Granma settlements, Niquero is characterized by its distinctive clapboard houses.

Ostensibly, there isn't much to do in Niquero, but you can explore the town park, where there's a cinema, and visit a small museum. Look out for the monument commemorating the oft-forgotten victims of the *Granma* landing, who were hunted down and killed by Batista's troops in December 1956.

There are two Servi-Cupet petrol stations and a bank.

But here's a surprise, and a far-from-unpleasant one. Nestled in Niquero's center, is **Hotel Niquero** (☎23-59-23-68; Esquina Martí; s/d CUC$25/28; P ❄ 📶), a low-key, out-on-a-limb hotel situated opposite the local sugar factory with substantially sized, amenable rooms, and little balconies overlooking the street. The affordable on-site restaurant can rustle up a reasonable beef steak with sauce.

Getting There & Away

There are buses to Manzanillo several times per day, but no Viazul services.

Parque Nacional Desembarco del Granma

Mixing unique environmental diversity with heavy historical significance, the **Parque Nacional Desembarco del Granma** (CUC$5) consists of 275 sq km of forest, peculiar karst topography and uplifted marine terraces. A shrine to the Cuban Revolution, Castro's stricken leisure yacht *Granma* limped ashore here in December 1956.

This Unesco World Heritage Site protects some of the Americas' most pristine coastal cliffs. Of 512 plant species identified thus far, about 60% are endemic, with a dozen found only here. Fauna is equally rich, with 25 species of mollusk, seven species of amphibian, 44 types of reptile, 110 bird species and 13 types of mammal.

In El Guafe, archaeologists have uncovered Cuba's second-most important community of ancient agriculturists and ceramic-makers. Thousand-year-old artifacts include altars, carved stones and earthen vessels along with idols guarding a water goddess inside a ceremonial cave.

There's two main access points: Las Coloradas and the village of Alegrio de Pio.

Sights

Alegría de Pío HISTORIC SITE

(CUC$5) Considered hallowed revolutionary ground, this is the spot where Castro's shipwrecked rebels were intercepted by Batista's army in 1956 and forced to split up and flee. It's also the official finishing point for the 18km hike from Las Coloradas following the rebels' route in December 1956. There's guided hiking, birdwatching and exploration of a fascinating cave system. It's accessed via 28km of potholed purgatory from a turn-off in Niquero. Bring plenty of drinking water.

There's a monument in the sugar cane field where the rebels were surprised. It's emblazoned with the names of the fallen and the words '*Nadie se rinde aqui, cojone!*' (No one surrenders here, bollocks!), supposedly shouted by Camilo Cienfuegos and repeated by Juan Almeida as all hell broke loose. A guide will show you around the site, which includes various graves, billboards and a cave where Che Guevara and Juan Almeida hid for two days.

The highlight for outdoors enthusiasts will be the cave system. Morlotte-Fustete is a 2km trail that traverses the spectacular marine terraces (sometimes using wooden ladders) and takes in the Cueva del Fustete – a 5km-long cavern replete with stalagmites and stalactites – and the Hoyo de Morlotte, a 77m deep karstic hole caused by water corrosion. El Samuel is a 1.3km trail to the Cueva Espelunca, another cave thought to have been used by indigenous people for religious ceremonies. Boca de Toro is a 6km trail to high cliffs overlooking a river valley and takes in the Farallón de Blanquizal, a beautiful natural lookout.

From here the rebel trail from Las Coloradas continues east to Cinco Palmas and, ultimately, Comendancia La Plata.

Cabo Cruz VILLAGE

Three kilometers beyond the El Guafe trailhead is a tiny fishing community with skiffs bobbing offshore and sinewy men gutting their catch on the golden beach. The 33m-tall Vargas lighthouse here (erected 1871) now belongs to the Cuban military. There are plans to install a diving center to take advantage of incredible diving opportunities nearby.

There's good swimming and shore snorkeling east of the lighthouse; bring your own gear as there are no facilities.

Museo las Coloradas MUSEUM

(CUC$5; 8am-6pm) A large monument just beyond the park gate marks the *Granma's* landing spot. A small museum outlines the routes taken by Castro, Guevara and the others into the Sierra Maestra, and there's a full-scale replica of the *Granma,* which – if you're lucky – a machete-wielding guard will let you climb inside to wonder how 82 men ever made it.

The entry ticket includes a visit to the simple reconstructed hut of the first *campesino* (a poor charcoal-burner) to help Fidel after the landing. An enthusiastic guide will also accompany you along a 1.3km path

WORTH A TRIP

PILÓN

Pilón is a small, isolated settlement wedged between the Marea del Portillo resorts and the Parque Nacional Desembarco del Granma. With the sugar mill shut down, its reason for being is the **Casa Museo Celia Sánchez Manduley** (CUC$1; ⌚9am-5pm Mon-Sat), a museum in honour of the revolution's 'first lady' who briefly lived at this address in Pilón.

If you happen here on a Saturday, attend the lively Sábado de Rumba, a weekly street party with whole roast pig, shots of rum and plenty of live music. This is your best chance of seeing the popular Cuban dance called the *pilón* (named after the town), which imitates the rhythms of pounding sugar.

The hotels at Marea del Portillo 11km away run a weekly Saturday evening transfer bus to Pilón for CUC$5 return. Getting here otherwise will involve a car, long-distance bike or winging it with the *amarillos* (transport officials).

through dense mangroves to the ocean and the spot where the *Granma* ran aground, 70m off-shore.

Activities

Sendero Arqueológico Natural el Guafe HIKING

(CUC$5) About 8km southwest of Las Coloradas is this well-signposted, 2km-long trail, the park's headline nature-archaeological hike. An underground river here has created 20 large caverns, one of which contains the famous Ídolo del Agua, carved from stalagmites by pre-Columbian Indians; there's also a 500-year-old cactus, butterflies, 170 different species of birds (including the tiny colibrí) and multiple orchids.

Guides are required but included in the entry cost. You should allow two hours for the stroll in order to take in everything. There are hundreds of flies here. Bring repellent.

The park is flecked with other trails, the best of which is the 30km trek to Alegria del Pio, replicating the journey of the 82 rebels who landed here in 1956. Due to its length and lack of suitable signage, this rarely tackled trail is best done with a guide (the trail actually runs on a further 70km into the Sierra Maestra, if you're feeling energetic). Inquire at Ecotur (p380) in Bayamo beforehand. You'll need to arrange for transport to meet you at Alegria del Pio.

Sleeping

Campismo las Colorados CAMPISMO $

(Carretera de Niquero Km 17; s/d CUC$8/12; ❄) A Category 3 campismo with 28 duplex cabins standing on 500m of murky beach, 5km southwest of Belic, just outside the park. All cabins have air-con and baths and there's a restaurant, a games hall and watersport rental on-site. You can book through **Campismo Popular** (☎23-42-24-25; General García No 112; ⌚8am 5pm) in Bayamo.

Eating

Restaurante el Cabo SEAFOOD $

(Cabo Cruz; meals CUC$3; ⌚7am-9pm Tue-Sun) The cheapest seafood in Cuba comes straight out of the Caribbean behind this restaurant that lies in the shadow of the Vargas lighthouse. Expect fresh fillets of snapper and swordfish, and prices in Cuban pesos.

Ranchón las Colorados CARIBBEAN $

(Los Colorados; meals CUC$2-4; ⌚noon-7pm) A traditional thatched-roof restaurant selling fairly basic *comida criolla* (Creole cooking) just before the park gates. This place does the business if you're hungry after a long drive.

Getting There & Away

Ten kilometers southwest of Media Luna the road divides, with Pilón 30km to the southeast and Niquero 10km to the southwest. Belic is 16km southwest of Niquero. It's another 6km from Belic to the national park entry gate. The turn-off for Alegria de Pio is just after the Servi-centro in Niguero.

If you don't have your own transport, getting here is tough. Irregular buses go as far as the Campismo las Coloradas daily and there are equally infrequent trucks from Belic. As a last resort, you can try the *amarillos* (transport officials) in Niquero. The closest gas station is in Niquero.

Marea del Portillo

There's something infectious about Marea del Portillo, a tiny south-coast village bordered by two low-key all-inclusive resorts. Wedged into a narrow strip of dry land between the glistening Caribbean and the cascading Sierra Maestra, it occupies a spot of great natural beauty – and great history.

The problem for independent travelers is getting here. There is no regular public transport, which means that you may, for the first time, have to take a long distance taxi or brave sporadic truck transport. Another issue for beach lovers is the sand, which is of a light gray color and may disappoint those more attuned to the brilliant whites of Cayo Coco.

The resorts themselves are affordable and well-maintained but isolated; the nearest town of any size is lackluster Manzanillo 100km to the north. Real rustic Cuba, however, is right outside the hotel gates.

Activities

There's plenty to do here, despite the area's apparent isolation. Horseback riding to El Salto, village tours to Sevilla, Pilón and Mota or jeep tours to El Macio River can be arranged. You can also visit Parque Nacional Desembarco del Granma from here. Book trips at Cubanacán desks in Hotel Marea del Portillo and Hotel Farallón del Caribe.

Hiking

El Salto HIKING

This wondrous DIY 20km out-and-back hike takes you through fields and valleys, a small village, past a lake, across a river and, finally, to El Salto, where there's a small waterfall, a shady thatched shelter and an inviting swimming hole.

Starting right outside the hotel complex, turn right onto the coast road and then, after approximately 400m, hang left onto an unpaved track just before a bridge. The track eventually joins a road and traverses a dusty, scattered settlement. On the far side of the village a dam rises above you. Rather than take the paved road up the embankment to the left, branch right and, after 200m, pick up a clear path that rises steeply up above the dam and into view of the lake behind. This beautiful path tracks alongside the lake before crossing one of its river feeds on a wooden bridge. Go straight on and uphill here and, when the path forks on the crest, bear right. Heading down into a verdant tranquil valley, pass a *casa de campesino* (the friendly owners keep bees and will give you honey, coffee and a geographical reorientation), cross the river (Río Cilantro) and then follow it upstream to El Salto.

Salto de Guayabito HIKING

Starting in the village of Mata Dos about 20km east of Marea, this hike is normally done as part of an organized trip from the hotels. Groups – who often embark on horseback – follow the Río Motas 7km upstream to an enchanting waterfall surrounded by rocky cliffs, ferns, cacti and orchids. It's a leisurely day trip.

Diving

Centro Internacional de Buceo Marea del Portillo DIVING, FISHING

(☎23-59-71-39; Hotel Marea del Portillo) Adjacent to Hotel Marea del Portillo, this Cubanacán-run dive center offers affordable scuba diving. For real excitement, dive to the *Cristóbal Colón* wreck (sunk in the 1898 Spanish-Cuban-American War). The open-sea fishing excursion includes bar and lunch. There have been complaints about reliability (the excursions will not leave if the center doesn't have fuel for the boats).

Other water excursions include a seafari (with snorkeling), a sunset cruise and a trip to uninhabited Cayo Blanco.

Sleeping

New casas particulares are an interesting alternative to all-inclusive resorts.

Casa Particular Barbara Mendez CASA PARTICULAR $

(☎23-59-71-62; Marea del Portillo No 14; r CUC$30) For a private option, Barbara lets out two rooms in her apartment that's 200m from the beach.

Hotel Marea del Portillo HOTEL $$

(☎23-59-70-08; all-inclusive s/d/tr CUC$40/80/90; P ❄ @ ≋) It's not Cayo Coco, but it barely seems to matter here. In fact, Marea's all-round functionalism and lack of big-resort pretension seem to work well in this traditional corner of Cuba. The 74 rooms are perfectly adequate, the food buffet does a good job and the dark sandy arc of beach is within baseball-pitching distance of your balcony-patio.

Servicing loyal repeat-visit Canadians and some Cuban families means there is a mix of people here, plus interesting excursions to some of the island's less-heralded sights.

★Hotel Farallón del Caribe HOTEL $$$
(☎23-59-70-82; all-inclusive s/d CUC$95/120, day pass CUC$25; ⏲Nov-Apr; P❄@🛜≋) Perched on a low hill with the Caribbean on one side and the Sierra Maestra on the other, the modern Farallón is the most impressive option in Marea de Portillo. Three-star, all-inclusive facilities are complemented by five-star surroundings. The food is superior to the competition's and views are great, though it is the furthest resort from the actual beach.

The resort is popular with snow-fleeing Canadians bused in from Manzanillo and is only open seasonally (November to April).

ℹ Getting There & Away

The journey east to Santiago is one of Cuba's most spectacular, but the road quality is awful and regularly affected by the weather. Options are your own car (check ahead regarding road conditions), a taxi (bank on at least CUC$160 for Marea to Santiago de Cuba), bicycle (a two- to three-day view-loaded rollercoaster) or winging it with 'public transport' (possibly one of Cuba's greatest adventures, but only for the hardy who are not averse to long waits and some hitchhiking).

Warning: the road sees very little traffic and has virtually no facilities and no gas stations (the nearest is in Pilón). Travel with supplies.

ℹ Getting Around

The hotels rent out scooters for approximately CUC$25 a day. **Cubacar** (☎23-59-70-05; 🛜) has a desk at Hotel Marea del Portillo, or you can join in an excursion with Cubanacán. The route to El Salto can be covered on foot.

Santiago de Cuba Province

☎22 / POP 1,043,200

Includes ➡

Best Battle Sites

- ➡ Cuartel Moncada (p398)
- ➡ Loma de San Juan (p402)
- ➡ El Uvero (p428)
- ➡ Museo de la Lucha Clandestina (p399)

Best Natural Sites

- ➡ La Gran Piedra (p420)
- ➡ Pico Turquino (p427)
- ➡ El Saltón (p425)
- ➡ Laguna Baconao (p422)

Why Go?

Lovely Santiago. Far from the capital in Cuba's mountainous 'Oriente' region, this perennial hotbed of rebellion and sedition is Cuba's most 'Caribbean' enclave. The difference is invigorating and sometimes overwhelming. Cultural influences here have often come from the east, imported via Haiti, Jamaica, Barbados and Africa. There's a raucous West Indian–style carnival and a cache of *folklórico* dance groups that owe as much to French-Haitian culture as they do to Spanish.

As the focus of Spain's new colony in the 16th and early 17th centuries, Santiago de Cuba enjoyed a brief spell as Cuba's capital until it was usurped by Havana in 1607. The subsequent slower pace of development has some distinct advantages. Drive 20km or so along the coast in either direction from the provincial capital and you're on a different planet, one of rugged coves, crashing surf, historical coffee plantations and emerald hills riotous with endemism.

When to Go

➡ July is the key month in Santiago de Cuba's cultural calendar, when the city is *caliente* (hot) in more ways than one and the streets are bursting with revelers. The fun begins with the vibrant Festival del Caribe and ends with the justifiably famous Carnaval.

➡ More excellent music is on offer in March at the Festival Internacional de Trova, when the city rediscovers its musical roots.

➡ March through to June is renowned for its high water clarity, ensuring excellent diving conditions for wreck diving off the south coast.

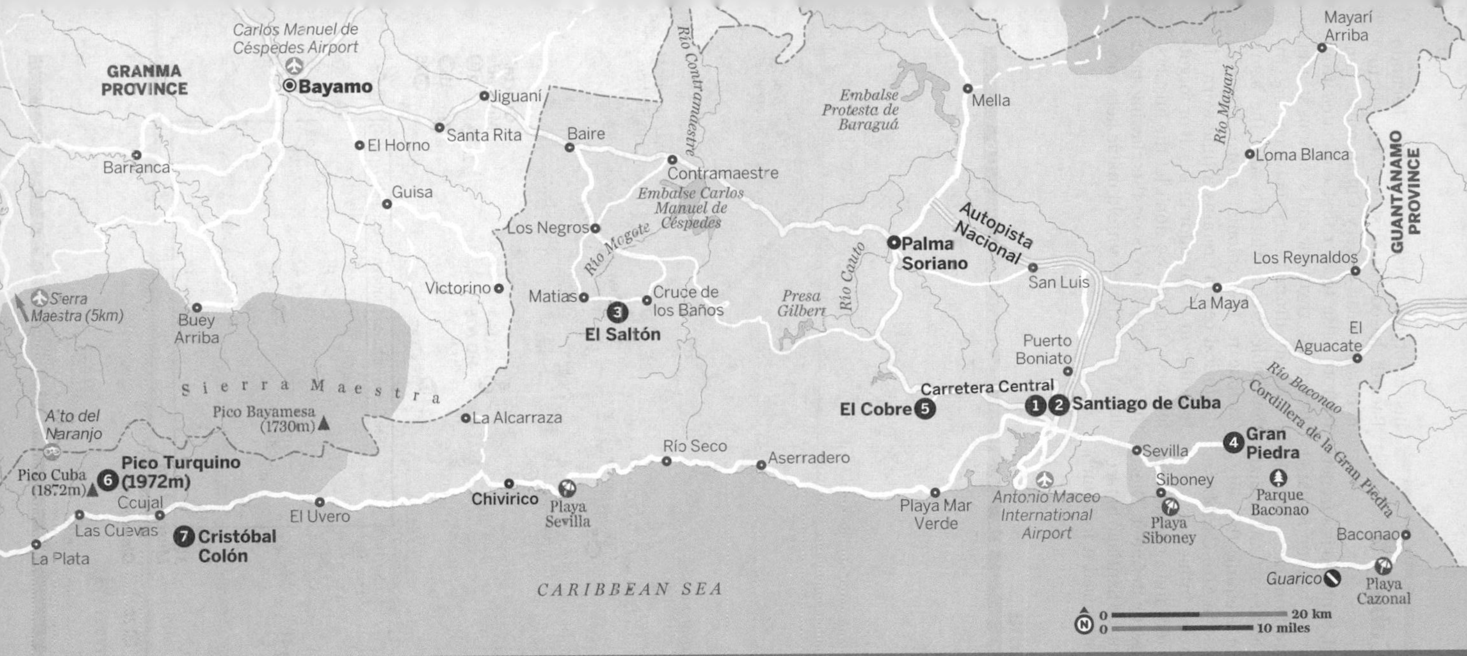

Santiago de Cuba Province Highlights

1. **Cementerio Santa Ifigenia** (p402) Paying your respects to the nation's heroes at this gorgeous Santiago de Cuba cemetery.

2. **Cuartel Moncada** (p398) Taking in the audacity (or folly) of Castro's 1953 insurrection at this Santiago de Cuba landmark.

3. **El Saltón** (p425) Making an eco-escape to a luscious mountain getaway.

4. **Cafetal la Isabelica** (p420) Tracing the history of Cuba's French-inspired coffee culture in Gran Piedra.

5. **El Cobre** (p424) Undertaking a pilgrimage with countless believers visiting the shrine of Cuba's patron saint, La Virgen de la Caridad.

6. **Pico Turquino** (p427) Standing atop Cuba's highest mountain alongside the bust of José Martí and taking in the gaping panorama.

7. **Cristóbal Colón** (p428) Diving to the wreck of a Spanish warship off the wild coast near Chivirico.

Santiago de Cuba

POP 431,500

Cuba's cultural capital, Santiago is a frenetic, passionate and noisy beauty. Situated closer to Haiti and the Dominican Republic than to Havana, it leans east rather than west, a crucial factor shaping this city's unique identity, steeped in Afro-Caribbean, entrepreneurial and rebel influences.

Trailblazing characters and a resounding sense of historical destiny define it. Diego Velázquez de Cuéllar made Santiago his second capital, Fidel Castro used it to launch his embryonic revolution, Don Facundo Bacardí based his first-ever rum factory here, and nearly every Cuban music genre from salsa to *son* first emanated from these dusty, rhythmic and sensuous streets.

Caught dramatically between the indomitable Sierra Maestra and the azure Caribbean, the colonial *casco histórico* (historical center) retains a time-worn air reminiscent of Salvador in Brazil or forgotten New Orleans. So don't let the hustlers, the speeding Chevys or the clawing heat defeat you. There's untold magic here too.

Santiago de Cuba

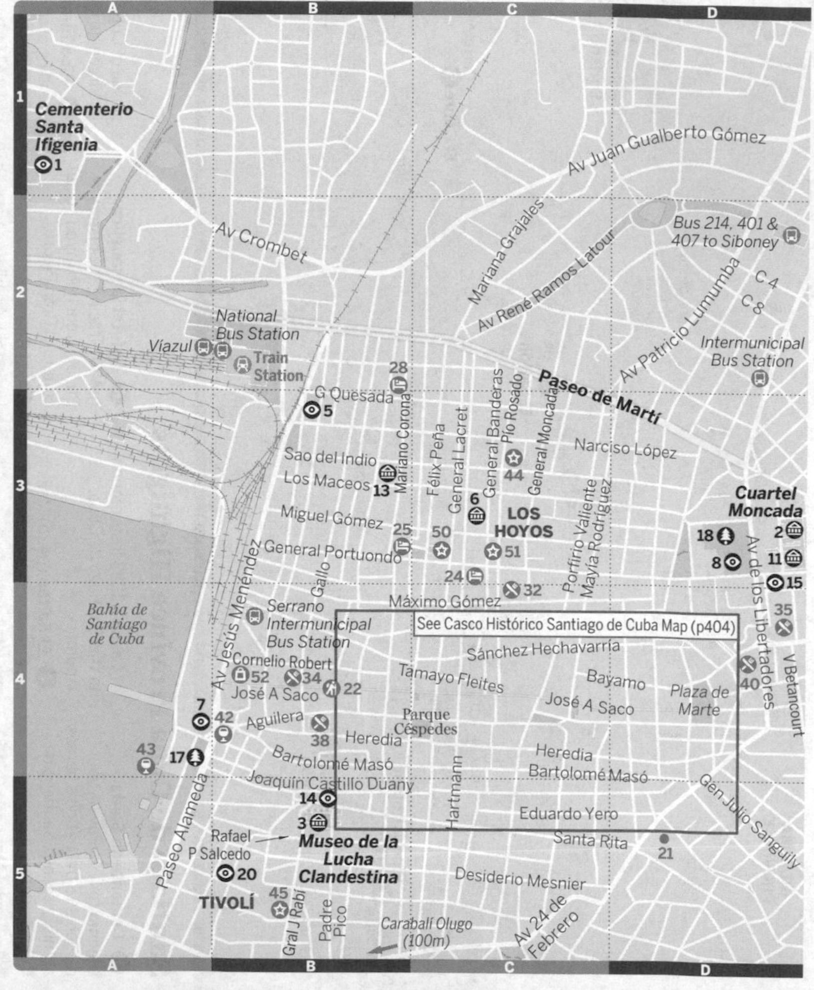

Sights

Casco Histórico

★Museo de Ambiente Histórico Cubano MUSEUM

(Casa de Diego Velázquez; Map p404; ☎22-65-26-52; Felix Peña No 602; CUC$2; ⏱9am-5pm Mon-Sun) The oldest house still standing in Cuba, this arresting early colonial abode dating from 1522 was the official residence of the island's first governor, Diego Velázquez. Restored in the late 1960s, the Andalusian-style facade with fine, wooden lattice windows was inaugurated in 1970 as a museum.

The ground floor was originally a trading house and gold foundry, while the upstairs was where Velázquez lived. Today, rooms display period furnishings and decoration from the 16th to 19th centuries. Check the two-way screens, where you could look out without being observed: a Turkish influence (Turkey had a big influence on European style at this time). Visitors are also taken through an adjacent 19th-century neoclassical house.

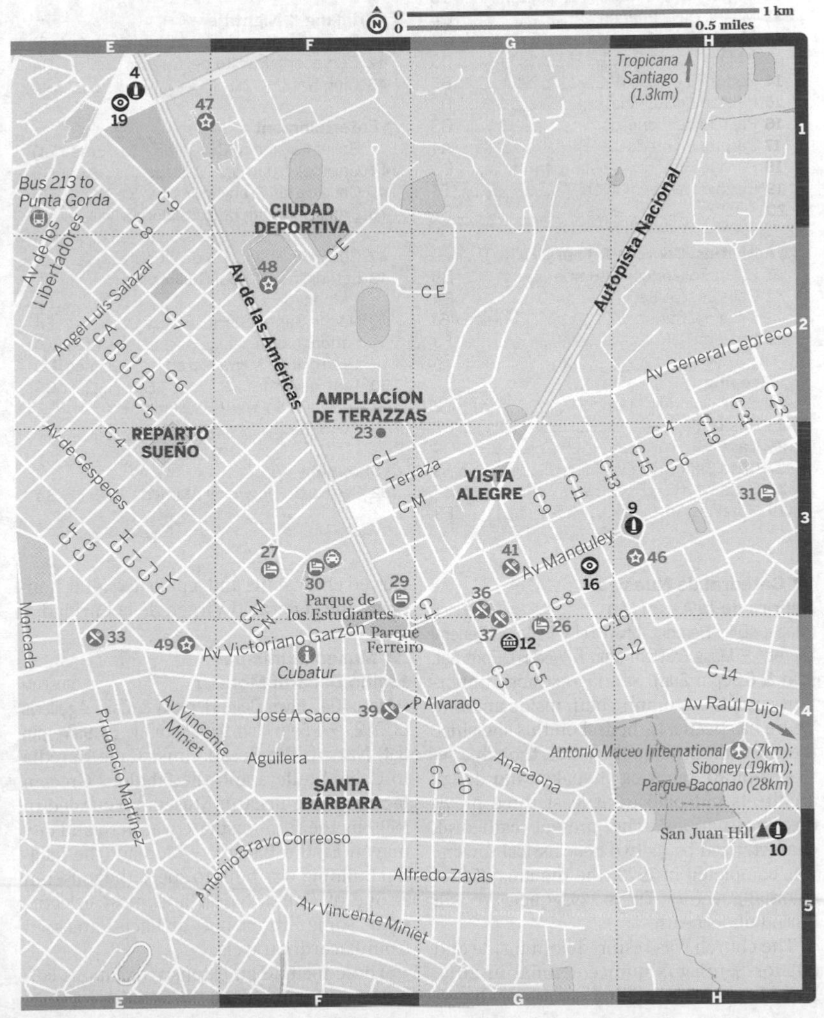

Santiago de Cuba

Top Sights

1 Cementerio Santa Ifigenia A1
2 Cuartel Moncada D3
3 Museo de la Lucha Clandestina B5

Sights

4 Antonio Maceo statue E1
5 Bacardí Rum Factory B3
6 Casa Museo de Frank y Josué País C3
7 Clock Tower A4
8 Fountain of Martí & Abel Santamaría D3
9 José María Heredia y Heredia Statue H3
10 Loma de San Juan H5
11 Moncada Museum D3
12 Museo de la Imagen G4
13 Museo-Casa Natal de Antonio Maceo B3
14 Padre Pico Steps B5
15 Palacio de Justicia D3
16 Palacio de Pioneros G3
17 Parque Alameda A4
18 Parque Histórico Abel Santamaría D3
19 Plaza de la Revolución E1
20 Tivolí B5

Activities, Courses & Tours

21 Ballet Folklórico Cutumba D5
22 Calle José A Saco B4
Casa del Caribe .... (see 46)
23 UniversiTUR F3

Sleeping

24 Casa Colonial 'Maruchi' C3
25 Casa Lola B3
26 Casa Mili G4
27 Casa Señora Inalvis F3
28 Casa Yoyi B2
29 Hotel las Américas F3
30 Meliá Santiago de Cuba F3
31 Villa Gaviota H3

Eating

32 Compay Gallo C4
33 El Barracón E4
34 Jardín de los Enramadas B4
35 La Arboleda D4
36 La Fortaleza G3
37 Madrileño G4
38 Municipal Market B4
39 Ranchon Los Naranjos F4
40 Restaurante España D4
41 Restaurante Zunzún G3
Ristorante Italiano la Fontana .... (see 30)

Drinking & Nightlife

Barrita de Ron Havana Club .... (see 5)
42 Cervecería Puerto del Rey B4
43 Club Nautico A4

Entertainment

Ballet Folklórico Cutumba .... (see 21)
44 Carabalí Izuama C3
45 Casa de las Tradiciones B5
46 Compañia Danzaría Folklórica Kokoyé H3
47 Conjunto Folklórico de Oriente E1
48 Estadio de Béisbol Guillermón Moncada F2
49 Noche Santiagüera E4
Santiago Café .... (see 30)
Teatro José María Heredia .... (see 47)
50 Teatro Martí C3
51 Tumba Francesa la Caridad de Oriente C3

Shopping

52 Centro de Negocios Alameda B4

★ Catedral de Nuestra Señora de la Asunción CHURCH

(Map p404; Heredia, btwn Felix Peña & General Lacret; Mass 6:30pm Mon & Wed-Fri, 5pm Sat, 9am & 6:30pm Sun) Santiago's most important church is stunning both inside and out. There has been a cathedral on this site since the city's inception in the 1520s, though a series of pirate raids, earthquakes and dodgy architects put paid to at least three previous incarnations. The present cathedral, characterized by its two neoclassical towers, was completed in 1922; the remains of first colonial governor, Diego Velázquez, are still buried underneath.

The church was restored both inside and out for Santiago's quincentennial in 2015. Expect intricate ceiling frescoes, hand-carved choir stalls and a polished altar honoring the venerated Virgen de la Caridad.

★ Museo Municipal Emilio Bacardí Moreau MUSEUM

(Map p404; btwn Calle Heredia & Calle Aguilera; CUC$2; 1-5pm Mon, 9am-5pm Tue-Fri, 9am-1pm Sat) Narrow Pío Rosado links Calle Heredia to Calle Aguilera and the fabulous Grecian facade of the Bacardí Museum. Founded in 1899 by the rum-magnate war hero and city mayor, Emilio Bacardí y Moreau (the palatial building was built to spec), the museum is one of Cuba's oldest and most eclectic, with some absorbing artifacts amassed from Bacardí's travels.

These include an extensive weapons collection, paintings from the Spanish *costum-*

brismo (19th-century artistic movement that predates Romanticism) school and the only Egyptian mummy on the island.

Memorial de Vilma Espín Guillois MUSEUM

(Map p404; ☎22-65-54-64; Sánchez Hechavarría No 473; CUC$2; ⏰9am-12:30pm Mon-Sat, 1-5pm Sun) This erstwhile home of Cuba's former 'first lady,' Vilma Espín, the wife of Raúl Castro, and instrumental force in the success of the Cuban Revolution, opened in 2010, three years after her death. This house, where she lived from 1939 to 1959, is packed with lucid snippets of her life.

The daughter of a lawyer to the Bacardí clan, Vilma was first radicalized after a meeting with Frank País in Santiago in 1956. Joining the rebels in the mountains, she went on to found the influential Federation of Cuban Women in 1960.

Calle Heredia STREET

(Map p404) The music never stops on Calle Heredia, Santiago's most sensuous street and also one of its oldest. Melodies waft from the paint-peeled Casa de Cultura Josue País García (p414), where *danzón*-(ballroom dance) strutting pensioners mix with svelte teen rap artists. One door up is Cuba's original Casa de la Trova (p414), a beautiful balconied townhouse redolent of New Orleans' French Quarter.

The Casa is dedicated to pioneering Cuban *trovador*, José 'Pepe' Sánchez (1856–1928) and first opened as Cuba's orginal *trova* (traditional poetic singing-songwriting) house in March 1968.

Museo del Ron MUSEUM

(Map p404; ☎22-62-88-84; Bartolomé Masó No 358; CUC$2; ⏰9am-5pm Mon-Sat) While not as impressive as its Havana equivalent, this museum is also refreshingly devoid of the Havana Club sales bias. It offers an insightful outline of the history of Cuban rum (old machinery, examples of bottlings throughout the last century) along with a potent shot of the hard stuff *(añejo)*.

Encased in a handsome townhouse, it has a bar below (same hours as the museum) that is so hidden away it's reminiscent of a speakeasy, but with a knowledgeable bartender on hand to serve you up their 'recommendations.'

Parque Céspedes PARK

(Map p404) Archetype for romantic Cuban street life, Parque Céspedes is a throbbing kaleidoscope of walking, talking, hustling, flirting, guitar-strumming humanity. Surrounded by colonial architecture, this most ebullient of city squares is a sight to behold day or night. See the bronze bust of Carlos Manuel de Céspedes, who kick-started Cuban independence in 1868, and Cubans enjoying the open wi-fi signal.

Museo del Carnaval MUSEUM

(Map p404; ☎22-62-69-55; Heredia No 303; CUC$1; ⏰2-5pm Mon, 9am-5pm Tue-Fri & Sun; 9am-10pm Sat) A worthwhile museum, this is a quick visit to study the history of Santiago's biggest shindig, the oldest and biggest carnival between Río and Mardi Gras. Drop in to see floats, effigies and the occasional *folklórico* dance show on the patio.

Balcón de Velázquez VIEWPOINT

(Map p404; cnr Bartolomé Masó & Mariano Corona; donation CUC$1) The alfresco Balcón de Velázquez is the site of an old Spanish fort. It offers ethereal views over the terracotta-tiled roofs of the Tivolí neighborhood toward the harbor. If a historian gives you an abbreviated history of the city, it's best to tip.

Plaza de Dolores SQUARE

(Map p404; cnr Aguilera & Porfirio Valiente) East of Parque Céspedes is the pleasant and shady Plaza de Dolores, a former marketplace now dominated by the 18th-century **Iglesia de Nuestra Señora de los Dolores** (Map p404; cnr Aguilera & Porfirio Valiente). Many restaurants and cafes flank this square. It's also Santiago's most popular gay cruising spot.

Iglesia de San Francisco CHURCH

(Map p404; Juan Bautista Sagarra No 121) This three-nave, 18th-century ecclesiastical gem is situated three blocks north of Parque Céspedes.

Plaza de Marte SQUARE

(Map p404) Guarding the entrance to the *casco histórico,* motorcycle-infested Plaza de Marte formerly served as a macabre 19th-century Spanish parade ground where prisoners were executed publicly for revolutionary activities. Today, the plaza is the city's *esquina caliente* (hot corner), where local baseball fans plot the imminent downfall of Havana's Industriales. The tall column topped with a red cap symbolizes liberty.

Has a public wi-fi signal.

SANTIAGO DE CUBA STREET NAMES

Welcome to another city where the streets have two names.

OLD NAME	NEW NAME
Calvario	Porfirio Valiente
Carniceria	Pío Rosado
Enramadas	José A Saco
José Miguel Gómez	Havana
Paraíso	Plácido
Reloj	Mayía Rodríguez
Rey Pelayo	Joaquín Castillo Duany
San Félix	Hartmann
San Francisco	Sagarra
San Gerónimo	Sánchez Hechavarría
San Mateo	Sao del Indio
Santa Rita	Diego Palacios
Santo Tómas	Felix Peña
Trinidad	General Portuondo

Casa Natal de José María Heredia y Heredia MUSEUM

(Map p404; ☎22-62-53-50; Heredia No 260; CUC$1; ⏲9am-7pm Tue-Sat, to 2pm Sun) A minuscule museum illustrating the life of one of Cuba's greatest Romantic poets and the man after whom the street is named, José María Heredia y Heredia (1803–39). Heredia's most notable work, 'Ode to Niagara,' is inscribed outside; it attempts to parallel the beauty of Canada's Niagara Falls with his personal feelings of loss about his homeland. Like many Cuban independence advocates, Heredia was forced into exile, dying in Mexico in 1839.

Maqueta de la Ciudad MUSEUM

(Map p404; Mariano Corona No 704; CUC$1; ⏲9am-5pm Mon-Sat) Cuba is obsessed with scale city models and Santiago, with this incredibly detailed *maqueta,* is no exception. Interesting historical and architectural information is displayed on illustrated wall panels and you can climb up to a mezzanine gallery for a true vulture's-eye view. For more views, gravitate to the cafe-terrace at the back.

Ayuntamiento HISTORIC BUILDING

(Map p404; cnr General Lacret & Aguilera) The neoclassical Ayuntamiento was erected in the 1950s using a design from 1783 and was once the site of Hernán Cortés' mayoral office. Fidel Castro appeared on the balcony of the present building on the night of January 2, 1959, trumpeting the Revolution's triumph.

Iglesia de Nuestra Señora del Carmen CHURCH

(Map p404; Félix Peña No 505) You can dig deeper into Santiago's ecclesiastical history in this tumbledown construction, a hall church dating from the 1700s that is the final resting place of Christmas-carol composer Esteban Salas (1725–1803), one-time choir master of Santiago de Cuba's cathedral.

Casa de la Cultura Miguel Matamoros MUSEUM

(Map p404; General Lacret No 651) The Casa de la Cultura Miguel Matamoros, on Parque Céspedes' eastern aspect, is the former San Carlos Club, a social center for wealthy *santiagüeros* until the Revolution. Next door British novelist Graham Greene once sought literary inspiration in the terrace-bar of the Hotel Casa Granda (p409), built in 1914.

North of Casco Histórico

★Cuartel Moncada MUSEUM

(Moncada Barracks; Map p394; ☎22-66-11-57; Av Moncada) Santiago's famous Moncada Barracks, a crenellated art-deco building completed in 1938, is now synonymous with one of history's greatest failed putsches. Moncada earned immortality on July 26, 1953, when more than 100 revolutionaries led by then little-known Fidel Castro stormed Batista's troops at what was then Cuba's second-most important military garrison.

After the Revolution, the barracks, like all others in Cuba, was converted into a school called Ciudad Escolar 26 de Julio, and in 1967 a **museum** (Map p394; CUC$2; ⊙9am-5pm Mon-Sat, to 1pm Sun) was installed near gate 3, where the main attack took place. As Batista's soldiers had cemented over the original bullet holes from the attack, the Castro government remade them (this time without guns) years later as a poignant reminder. The museum (one of Cuba's best) contains a scale model of the barracks plus interesting and sometimes grisly artifacts, diagrams and models of the attack, its planning and its aftermath. Most moving, perhaps, are the photographs of the 61 fallen at the end.

The first barracks on this site was constructed by the Spanish in 1859, and actually takes its name after Guillermón Moncada, a War of Independence fighter who was held prisoner here in 1874.

Parque Histórico Abel Santamaría PARK

(Map p394; cnr General Portuondo & Av de los Libertadores) This is the site of the former Saturnino Lora Civil Hospital, stormed by Abel Santamaría and 60 others on that fateful July day (they were later tortured and killed). On October 16, 1953, Fidel Castro was tried in the Escuela de Enfermeras for leading the Moncada attack. It was here that he made his famous *History will Absolve Me* speech.

The park contains a giant Cubist fountain, engraved with the countenances of Abel Santamaría and José Martí, which gushes out a veritable Niagara Falls of water.

Museo-Casa Natal de Antonio Maceo MUSEUM

(Map p394; ☎22-62-37-50; Los Maceos No 207; CUC$1; ⊙9am-5pm Mon-Sat) This important museum is where the *mulato* general and hero of both Wars of Independence was born, on June 14, 1845, and exhibits highlights of Maceo's life with photos, letters and a tattered flag that was flown in battle. Known as the Bronze Titan in Cuba for his bravery in battle, Maceo was the definitive 'man of action.'

In his 1878 Protest of Baraguá, he rejected any compromise with the colonial authorities and went into exile rather than sell out to the Spanish. Landing at Playa Duaba in 1895, he marched his army as far west as Pinar del Río before being killed in action in 1896.

Plaza de la Revolución SQUARE

(Map p394) As with all Cuban cities, Santiago has its bombastic Revolution Square. This one's placed strategically at the junction of two sweeping avenues and anchored by an eye-catching **statue** (Map p394; Plaza de la Revolución) of dedicated city hero (and native son), Antonio Maceo, atop his horse and surrounded by 23 raised machetes. Underneath the giant mound/plinth a small reverential museum contains info on his life. Other notable buildings bordering the square include modern Teatro José María Heredia and the National Bus Station.

Palacio de Justicia LANDMARK

(Map p394; cnr Av de los Libertadores & General Portuondo) On the opposite side of the street to Parque Histórico Abel Santamaría, this court building was taken by fighters led by Raúl Castro during the Moncada attack. They were supposed to provide cover fire to Fidel's group from the rooftop but were never needed. Many of them came back two months later to be tried and sentenced in the court.

Casa Museo de Frank y Josué País MUSEUM

(Map p394; ☎22-65-27-10; General Banderas No 226; CUC$1; ⊙9am-5pm Mon-Sat) Integral to the success of the Revolution, the young País brothers organized the underground section of the M-26-7 (26th of July Movement) in Santiago de Cuba until Frank's murder by the police on July 30, 1957. The exhibits in this home-turned-museum tell the story. It's located about five blocks southeast of Museo-Casa Natal de Antonio Maceo.

South of Casco Histórico

★**Museo de la Lucha Clandestina** MUSEUM

(Map p394; ☎22-62-46-89; General Jesús Rabí No 1; CUC$1; ⊙9am-5pm Tue-Sun) This gorgeous yellow colonial-style building houses a museum detailing the underground struggle against Batista in the 1950s. It's a fascinating, if bloody, story enhanced by far-reaching views from the balcony. Across the street is the house where Fidel Castro lived from 1931 to 1933, while a student in Santiago de Cuba (not open for visits).

The museum was a former police station attacked by M-26-7 activists on November 30, 1956, to divert attention from the arrival of the tardy yacht *Granma*, carrying Fidel Castro and 81 others. It's up the slope from the western end of Diego Palacios.

Parque Alameda PARK

(Map p394; Av Jesús Menéndez) Below the Tivolí quarter, this narrow park embellishes a dockside promenade opened in 1840 and redesigned in 1893. Recent refurbishment for the 2015 quincentennial has made it the center of the Malecón (boardwalk) in the style of Havana's, also featuring a playground, palm trees and public wi-fi. The north end features the old clock tower, aduana (customs house) and cigar factory. With smart architecture, sea air and a dash of port-side sketchiness, it's good for a stroll.

Tivolí AREA

(Map p394) Santiago's old French quarter was first settled by colonists from Haiti in the late 18th and early 19th centuries. Set on a south-facing hillside overlooking the shimmering harbor, its red-tiled roofs and hidden patios are a tranquil haven these days, with old men pushing around dominoes and ebullient kids playing stickball amid pink splashes of bougainvillea.

The century-old **Padre Pico steps** (cnr Padre Pico & Diego Palacios), cut into the steepest part of Calle Padre Pico, stand at the neighborhood's gateway.

Bacardí Rum Factory LANDMARK

(Fábrica de Ron; Map p394; ☎22-65-12-12; Av Jesús Menéndez, opposite train station; ⊙9am-6pm) While it's not as swanky as its modern Bermuda HQ, the original Bacardí factory, which opened in 1868, oozes history. Spanish-born founder Don Facundo dreamed up the world-famous Bacardí bat symbol after discovering a bat colony in the factory's rafters. The Cuban government continues to make traditional rum here – the signature Ron Caney brand, Ron Santiago and Ron Varadero.

The Bacardí family fled the island post-Revolution. In total, the factory knocks out nine million liters of rum a year, 70% of which is exported. There are currently no factory tours, but the Barrita de Ron Havana Club (p413), a tourist bar attached to the factory, offers rum sales and tastings. A billboard opposite the station announces Santiago's modern battle cry:

City Walk
A Walk Through History

START PARQUE ALAMEDA
END CUARTEL MONCADA
LENGTH 2KM; THREE TO FOUR HOURS

Against a backdrop of verdant mountains and a steely blue bay, a walking tour of Santiago's *casco histórico* (historical center) is an obligatory rite of passage for first-time visitors keen to uncover the steamy tropical sensations that make this city tick.

Start beside the bay with your sights set uphill. Parque Alameda inhabits the rundown thoroughfare facing Santiago's not-so-busy port. Most of the excitement lies to the east in a hilly neighborhood colonized by French-Haitians in the early 1800s and baptized **1 El Tivolí**. Tivolí is one of Santiago's most picturesque and traffic-lite quarters where red-roofed houses and steep streets retain a time-warped Cuban atmosphere. The neighborhood's only real 'sight' is the **2 Museo de la Lucha Clandestina** reached by following Calle Diego Palacios uphill from the port. From the museum take the famous **3 Padre Pico steps** – a terracotta staircase built into the hillside – downhill to Calle Bartolomé Masó where a right turn will deposit you on the breeze-lapped **4 Balcón de Velázquez** site of an ancient fort. This stupendous view once inspired less calming contemplations; early Spanish colonists used it to look out for meddlesome pirates.

Head east next, avoiding the angry roar of the motorbikes, until you resurface in **5 Parque Céspedes**. The **6 Casa de Diego Velázquez**, with its Moorish fringes and intricate wooden arcades, is believed to be the oldest house still standing in Cuba and anchors the square on its west side. Contrasting impressively on the south side is the mighty, mustard facade of the **7 Catedral de Nuestra Señora de la Asunción**. This building has been ransacked, burned, rocked by earthquakes and rebuilt, then remodeled and restored and ransacked again. Statues of Christopher Columbus and Fray Bartolomé de las Casas flank the entrance in ironic juxtaposition.

If you need a break, step out on to the lazy terrace bar at **8 Hotel Casa Granda** on the southeastern corner of the park, for mojitos

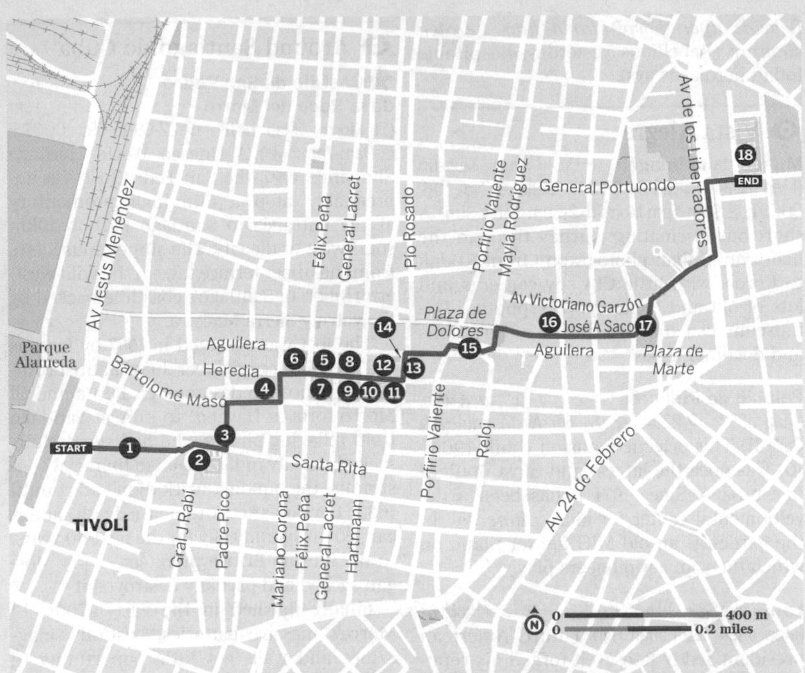

and Montecristo cigars. Graham Greene came here in the 1950s on a clandestine mission to interview Fidel Castro. The interview never came off, instead he managed to smuggle a suitcase of clothes up to the rebels in the mountains.

Follow the music as you exit and plunge into the paint-peeled romance of Calle Heredia, Santiago's – and one of Cuba's – most atmospheric streets, which rocks like New Orleans at the height of the jazz era. Its centerpiece is the infamous 9 **Casa de la Trova**.

Heading upstream on Heredia, you'll pass street stalls, cigar peddlers, a guy dragging a double bass, and countless motorbikes. That yellowish house on the right with the poem emblazoned on the wall is 10 **Casa Natal de José María Heredia y Heredia**, birthplace of one of Cuba's greatest poets. You might find a living scribe in 11 **Uneac**, the famous national writers' union a few doors down. Stick your head inside and check out the *cartelera* (culture calendar) advertising the coming week's offerings. Plenty more dead legends are offered up in print in funky 12 **Librería la Escalere de Edy**, an unkempt but roguish bookstore across the street where busking musicians often crowd the stairway. Cross the street next (mind that motorbike) and stick your nose into the 13 **Museo del Carnaval**. Divert along Pío Rosado one block to Aguilera where you'll be confronted by the sturdy Grecian columns of the 14 **Museo Municipal Emilio Bacardí Moreau**. Back outside, narrow Aguilera winds uphill to the shady 15 **Plaza de Dolores**, which remains amazingly tranquil, considering the ongoing motorcycle mania. There are benches to relax on underneath the trees while you weigh up if you have enough energy to keep going or abort into one of the nearby bars or restaurants.

Skip north a block to 16 **Calle José A Saco**, a steep pedestrian street with pet shops and *churro* (fried dough) salespeople that will lead you directly east to 17 **Plaza de Marte**, the third of the *casco histórico's* pivotal squares and far more manic than the other two.

The walk ends in what is perhaps Santiago's most politically significant site, the art-deco 18 **Cuartel Moncada**, a one-time military barracks where the first shots of Cuba's Castro-led Revolution were fired in 1953. Today it functions more innocuously as a school, but a preserved section at the rear where the short skirmishes between the soldiers and the rebels took place is now one of Cuba's most interesting and poignant museums.

Rebelde ayer, hospitalaria hoy, heroica siempre (Rebellious yesterday, hospitable today, heroic always).

Vista Alegre

Museo de la Imagen MUSEUM

(Map p394; ☎22-64-22-34; Calle 8 No 106; CUC$1; ⏲9am-5pm Mon-Fri, 2-5pm Sat & Sun) A short but fascinating journey through the history of Cuban photography from Kodak to Korda, with little CIA spy cameras and lots of old and contemporary photos. The museum also guards a library of rare films and documentaries.

Palacio de Pioneros LANDMARK

(Map p394; ☎22-64-22-18; cnr Av Manduley & Calle 11) This eclectic mansion (built 1906–10) was once the largest and most opulent in Santiago. Since 1974 it has been a developmental center for kids *(pioneros)*. In the garden is an old MiG fighter plane on which the younger pioneers play.

Loma de San Juan MONUMENT

(Map p394; San Juan Hill) Future American president Teddy Roosevelt forged his reputation on this small hillock where, flanked by the immortal rough riders, he supposedly led a fearless cavalry charge against the Spanish to seal a famous US victory. Protected on pleasantly manicured grounds adjacent to the modern-day Motel San Juan, Loma de San Juan marks the spot of the Spanish-Cuban-American War's only land battle (July 1, 1898).

In reality, it is doubtful Roosevelt even mounted his horse in Santiago, while the purportedly clueless Spanish garrison – outnumbered 10 to one – managed to hold off more than 6000 American troops for 24 hours. Cannons, trenches and numerous US monuments, including a bronze rough rider, enhance the classy gardening, while the only acknowledgement of a Cuban presence is the rather understated monument to the unknown Mambí soldier.

José María Heredia y Heredia Statue MONUMENT

(Map p394; cnr Av Manduley & Calle 13) The traffic circle at the corner of Av Manduley and Calle 13 contains an impressive marble statue of poet José María Heredia y Heredia.

Around Santiago de Cuba

★Castillo de San Pedro de la Roca del Morro FORT

(El Morro; Map p418; ☎22-69-15-69; CUC$5; ⏲9am-7pm; 👪) A Unesco World Heritage Site since 1997, the San Pedro fort sits impregnably atop a 60m-high promontory at the entrance to Santiago harbor, 10km southwest of the city. The stupendous views from the upper terrace take in the wild western ribbon of Santiago's coastline backed by the velvety Sierra Maestra.

The fort was designed in 1587 by famous Italian military engineer Juan Bautista Antonelli (who also designed La Punta and El Morro forts in Havana) to protect Santiago from pillaging pirates who had successfully sacked the city in 1554. Due to financial constraints, the building work didn't start until 1633 (17 years after Antonelli's death) and it carried on sporadically for the next 60 years. In the interim British privateer Henry Morgan sacked and partially destroyed it.

Finally finished in the early 1700s, El Morro's massive batteries, bastions, magazines and walls got little opportunity to serve their true purpose. With the era of piracy in decline, the fort was converted into a prison in the 1800s and it stayed that way – bar a brief interlude during the 1898 Spanish-Cuban-American War – until Cuban architect Francisco Prat Puig mustered up a restoration plan in the late 1960s.

Today, the fort hosts the swashbuckling Museo de Piratería, with another room given over to the US-Spanish naval battle that took place in the bay in 1898.

The fort, like Havana has a cañonazo ceremony (firing of the cannon) each day at sunset when actors dress up in Mambises regalia.

To get to El Morro from the city center, take bus 212 to Ciudamar and walk the final 20 minutes. Alternatively, a round-trip taxi ride from Parque Céspedes with wait should cost no more than CUC$25.

★Cementerio Santa Ifigenia CEMETERY

(Map p394; Av Crombet; CUC$3; ⏲8am-6pm) Nestled peacefully on the city's western extremity, the Cementerio Santa Ifigenia is second only to Havana's Necrópolis Cristóbal Colón (p83) in its importance and grandiosity. Created in 1868 to accommodate the victims of the War of Independence and a simultaneous yellow-fever outbreak, the Santa Ifigenia includes many great historical figures among its 8000-plus tombs, notably the mausoleum of José Martí and final resting place of Fidel Castro.

Names to look out for include Tomás Estrada Palma (1835–1908), Cuba's now disgraced first president; Emilio Bacardí y Moreau (1844–1922) of the famous rum dynasty; María Grajales, the widow of independence hero Antonio Maceo; and

MONCADA – THE 26TH OF JULY MOVEMENT

Glorious call to arms or poorly enacted putsch – the 1953 attack on Santiago's Moncada Barracks, while big on bravado, came to within a hair's breadth of destroying Castro's nascent revolutionary movement before the ink was even dry on the manifesto.

With his political ambitions decimated by Batista's 1952 coup, Castro – who had been due to represent the Orthodox Party in the canceled elections – quickly decided to pursue a more direct path to power by swapping the ballot box for a rifle.

Handpicking and training 116 men and two women from Havana and its environs, the combative Fidel, along with his trusty lieutenant, Abel Santamaría, began to put together a plan so secret that even his younger brother Raúl was initially kept in the dark.

The aim was to storm the Cuartel Moncada, a sprawling military barracks in Santiago (in Cuba's seditious Oriente region) with a shabby history as a Spanish prison. Rather than make an immediate grab for power, Castro's more savvy plan was to capture enough ammunition to escape up into the Sierra Maestra from where he and Santamaría planned to spearhead a wider popular uprising against Batista's malignant Mafia-backed government.

Castro chose Moncada because it was the second-biggest army barracks in the country, yet distant enough from Havana to ensure it was poorly defended. With equal sagacity, the date was set for July 26, the day after Santiago's annual carnival when both police and soldiers would be tired and hungover from the boisterous revelries.

But as the day of attack dawned, things quickly started to go wrong. The plan's underlying secrecy didn't help. Meeting in a quiet rural farmhouse near the village of Siboney, many recruits arrived with no idea that they were expected to fire guns at armed soldiers and they nervously balked. Secondly, with all but one of the Moncadistas drawn from the Havana region (the only native *santiagüero* was an 18-year-old local fixer named Renato Guitart), few were familiar with Santiago's complex street layout and after setting out at 5am in convoy from the Siboney farm, at least two cars became temporarily lost.

The attack, when it finally began, lasted approximately 10 minutes from start to finish and was little short of a debacle. Splitting into three groups, a small contingent led by Raúl Castro took the adjacent Palacio de Justicia, another headed by Abel Santamaría stormed a nearby military hospital, while the largest group led by Fidel attempted to enter the barracks itself.

Though the first two groups were initially successful, Fidel's convoy, poorly disguised in stolen military uniforms, was spotted by an outlying guard patrol and only one of the cars made it into the compound before the alarm was raised.

In the ensuing chaos, five rebels were killed in an exchange of gunfire before Castro, seeing the attack was futile, beat a disorganized retreat. Raúl's group also managed to escape, but the group in the hospital (including Abel Santamaría) were captured and later tortured and executed.

Fidel escaped into the surrounding mountains and was captured a few days later; but, due to public revulsion surrounding the other brutal executions, his life was spared and the path of history radically altered.

Had it not been for the Revolution's ultimate success, this shambolic attempt at an insurrection would have gone down in history as a military nonevent. But viewed through the prism of the 1959 Revolution, it has been depicted as the first glorious shot on the road to power.

It also provided Fidel with the political pulpit he so badly needed. 'History will absolve me,' he trumpeted confidently at his subsequent trial. Within six years it effectively had.

Casco Histórico Santiago de Cuba

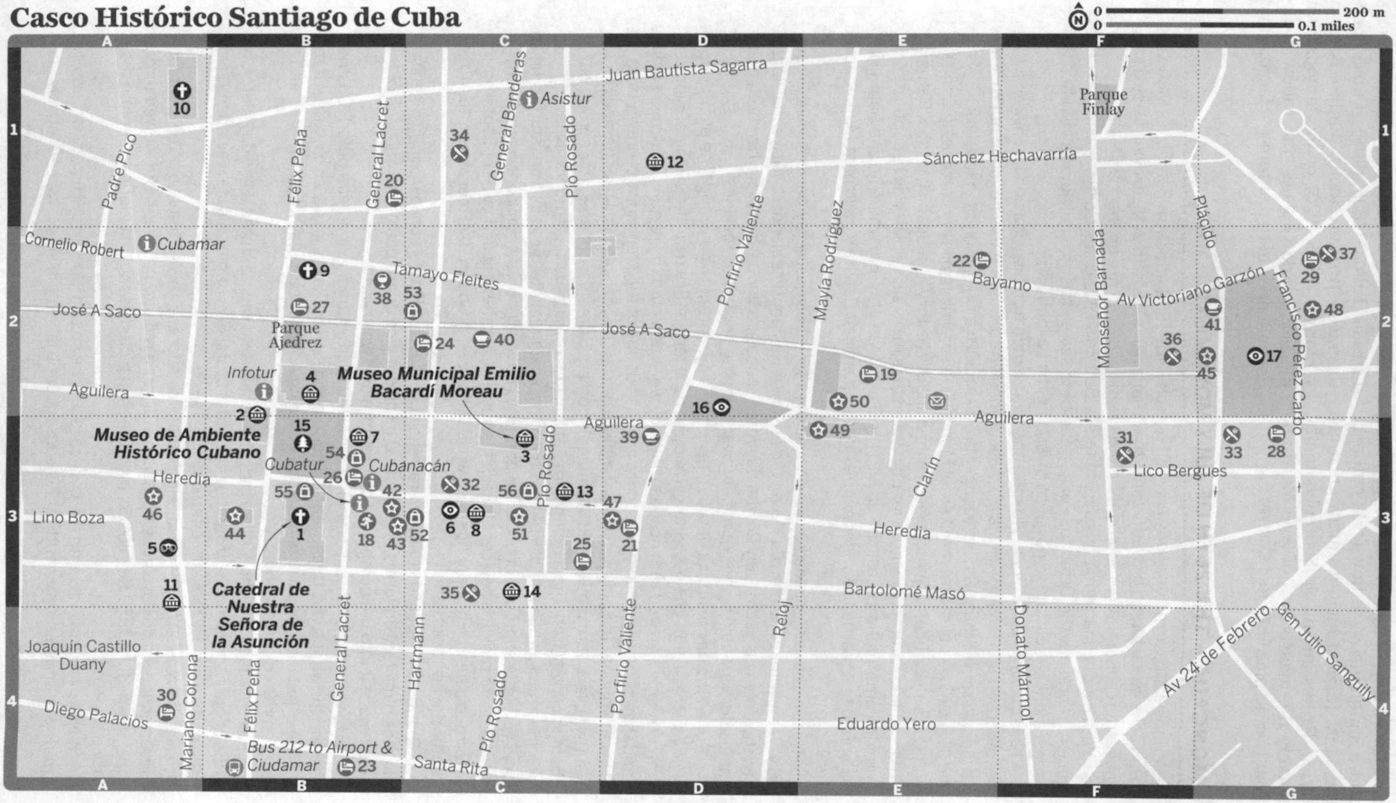

0 200 m
0 0.1 miles

Museo Municipal Emilio Bacardí Moreau
Museo de Ambiente Histórico Cubano
Catedral de Nuestra Señora de la Asunción
Parque Finlay
Parque Ajedrez
Asistur
Cubamar
Infotur
Cubatur
Cubanacán
Bus 212 to Airport & Ciudamar

Juan Bautista Sagarra
Sánchez Hechavarría
Padre Pico
Félix Peña
General Lacret
General Banderas
Pío Rosado
Porfirio Valiente
Mayía Rodríguez
Monseñor Barnada
Plácido
Cornelio Robert
Tamayo Fleites
Bayamo
Av Victoriano Garzón
Francisco Pérez Carbo
José A Saco
Aguilera
Heredia
Lino Boza
Lico Bergues
Clarín
Bartolomé Masó
Joaquín Castillo Duany
Mariano Corona
Hartmann
Reloj
Donato Mármol
Av 24 de Febrero
Gen Julio Sanguily
Diego Palacios
Eduardo Yero
Santa Rita

A B C D E F G
1 2 3 4

10, 34, 12, 20, 9, 38, 53, 27, 24, 40, 22, 37, 29, 48, 41, 36, 45, 17, 19, 4, 2, 16, 50, 49, 15, 7, 3, 39, 31, 33, 28, 54, 26, 32, 56, 13, 47, 42, 55, 46, 44, 18, 43, 52, 6, 8, 51, 21, 25, 1, 5, 11, 35, 14, 30, 23

Casco Histórico Santiago de Cuba

Top Sights
1 Catedral de Nuestra Señora de la Asunción ... B3
2 Museo de Ambiente Histórico Cubano ... B2
3 Museo Municipal Emilio Bacardí Moreau ... C3

Sights
4 Ayuntamiento ... B2
5 Balcón de Velázquez ... A3
6 Calle Heredia ... C3
7 Casa de la Cultura Miguel Matamoros ... B3
8 Casa Natal de José María Heredia y Heredia ... C3
Iglesia de Nuestra Señora de los Dolores ... (see 49)
9 Iglesia de Nuestra Señora del Carmen ... B2
10 Iglesia de San Francisco ... A1
11 Maqueta de la Ciudad ... A3
12 Memorial de Vilma Espín Guillois ... D1
13 Museo del Carnaval ... C3
14 Museo del Ron ... C3
15 Parque Céspedes ... B3
16 Plaza de Dolores ... D2
17 Plaza de Marte ... G2

Activities, Courses & Tours
18 Ecotur ... B3

Sleeping
19 Alchel & Corrado ... E2
20 Casa Colonial 1893 ... B1
21 Casa Milena ... D3
22 Casa Nelson & Deisy ... E2
23 Casa Terraza Pavo Real ... B4
24 Gran Hotel ... C2
25 Hostal San Basilio ... C3
26 Hotel Casa Granda ... B3
27 Hotel Imperial ... B2
28 Hotel Libertad ... G3
29 Hotel Rex ... G2
30 Roy's Terrace Inn ... A4

Eating
31 Bendita Farándula ... F3
Cafe Hotel Casa Granda ... (see 26)
32 El Holandes ... C3
33 Panadería Doña Neli ... G3
Roy's Terrace Inn Roof Garden Restaurant ... (see 30)
34 Rumba Café ... C1
35 Santiago 1900 ... C3
36 St Pauli ... F2
37 Supermercado Plaza de Marte ... G2

Drinking & Nightlife
38 Bar Sindo Garay ... B2
39 Café la Isabelica ... D3
40 Café Ven ... C2
Casa Granda Roof Garden Bar ... (see 26)
41 La Gran Sofía ... G2

Entertainment
42 Casa de Cultura Josué País García ... B3
43 Casa de la Trova ... B3
44 Cine Rialto ... B3
45 Iris Jazz Club ... G2
46 Orfeón Santiago ... A3
47 Patio ARTex ... D3
48 Patio los Dos Abuelos ... G2
49 Sala de Conciertos Dolores ... E3
50 Subway Club ... E2
51 Uneac ... C3

Shopping
52 ARTex ... C3
53 Discoteca Egrem ... C2
54 Galería de Arte de Oriente ... B3
55 Librería Internacional ... B3
56 Librería la Escalera de Edy ... C3

Mariana Grajales, Maceo's mother; 11 of the 31 generals of the independence struggles; the Spanish soldiers who died in the battles of San Juan Hill and Caney; the 'martyrs' of the 1953 Moncada Barracks attack; M-26-7 activists Frank and Josué País; father of Cuban independence, Carlos Manuel de Céspedes (1819–74); and international celebrity-cum-popular-musical-rake, Compay Segundo (1907–2003) of Buena Vista Social Club fame.

Many visitors come to pay homage at the quasi-religious mausoleum to national hero José Martí (1853–95). Erected in 1951 during the Batista era, the imposing hexagonal structure is positioned so that Martí's wooden casket (draped solemnly in a Cuban flag) receives daily shafts of sunlight. This is in response to a comment Martí made in one of his poems that he would like to die not as a traitor in darkness, but with his visage facing the sun. A round-the-clock guard of the mausoleum is changed, amid much pomp and ceremony, every 30 minutes.

Now, the cemetery's most famous resident is a recent arrival, situated alongside his hero, José Martí. After a cross-country procession that re-created the revolutionary's 1959 victory march in reverse, the ashes of Fidel Castro Ruz (1926–2016) were interred here on December 4, 2016. The private ceremony featured a 21-gun salute and no speeches. Castro has famously insisted that he wants no tributes, statues or honors in his name. This simple monument takes the form of an enormous boulder bearing a plaque with just the name Fidel.

Horse carts go along Av Jesús Menéndez, from Parque Alameda to Cementerio Santa Ifigenia; otherwise it's a hearty leg-stretching walk.

Jardín de los Helechos GARDENS

(Map p418; ☎22-60-83-35; Carretera de El Caney No 129; CUC$3; ⏰9am-5pm Mon-Fri) This peaceful garden is a lush haven of 350 types of ferns and 90 types of orchids. It's the erstwhile private collection of *santiagüero* Manuel Caluff, donated in 1984 to the Academia de Ciencias de Cuba (Cuban Academy of Science), which continues to keep the 3000-sq-meter garden in psychedelic bloom. The center of the garden has an inviting dense copse-cum-sanctuary dotted with benches.

For the orchids, the best time is November to January. Bus 5 (20 centavos) from Plaza de Marte in central Santiago passes this way, or you can hire a taxi. It's 2km from downtown Santiago de Cuba on the road to El Caney.

Cayo Granma ISLAND

A small, populated key near the jaws of the bay, Cayo Granma is a little fantasy island of red-roofed wooden houses – many of them on stilts above the water – that guard a traditional fishing community. You can hike up to the small whitewashed Iglesia de San Rafael at the key's highest point, or walk around the whole island in 15 minutes.

The best thing about this place, however, is just hanging out and soaking up a bit of the real Cuba. Eat at seafood haven Restaurante el Cayo or the clapboard Palmares restaurant jutting out over the water on the Cayo's far side.

To get to the key, take the regular ferry (leaving every one to 1½ hours) from Punta Gorda just below El Morro fort. The boat stops en route at La Socapa (actually still the mainland; the western jaw of the Bahia de Santiago) where there are decent swimming beaches.

Activities

Calle José A Saco WALKING

(Map p394) A pedestrian-only street stretching from Plaza de Marte to the Paseo Alameda on the waterfront. Heaps of locals browse the shops and restaurants.

For extra credit, detour on to pedestrian alley Tamayo Fleites (aka Callejon del Carmen), an ambient three-block stretch between Felix Peña and Pío Rosado where you'll find stands selling crafts and souvenirs.

Ecotur OUTDOORS

(Map p404; ☎22-68-72-79; General Lacret No 701, cnr Hartmann) The best bet for guided summit attempts on Pico Turquino.

Courses

Opportunities for courses abound in Santiago; everything from architecture to music, either official or unofficial. You can sign up for something beforehand, or jump on the bandwagon when you arrive.

Ballet Folklórico Cutumba MUSIC, DANCE

(Map p394; Teatro Galaxia, cnr Avs 24 de Febrero & Valeriano Hierrezuelo) Santiago's *folklórico* groups are highly inclusive and can organize dance and percussion lessons either in groups or individually. Start with the Cutumba who often perform at Hotel las Américas (p410). Also helpful are Conjunto Folklórico de Oriente (p414).

Casa del Caribe MUSIC, DANCE

(Map p394; ☎22-64-22-85; Calle 13 No 154) The portal of all things Santería and *folklórico,* this cultural institution can arrange dance lessons in conga, *son* and salsa for CUC$10 per hour. Resident staff member Juan Eduardo Castillo can also organize lessons in percussion. Real aficionados can inquire about in-depth courses on Afro-Cuban religions and culture. These guys are experts and they're very flexible.

UniversiTUR LANGUAGE

(Map p394; ☎22-64-31-86; www.uo.edu.cu; Universidad de Oriente, cnr Calle L & Ampliación de Terrazas) Arranges Spanish courses. Monthly rates for 60-hour courses (three hours a day, five days a week) start at CUC$280.

Festivals & Events

Few cities can match the variety and vivacity of Santiago de Cuba's annual festivals.

★Carnaval CULTURE, MUSIC

(⏰Jul) One of the largest and most authentic in the Caribbean, Santiago de Cuba's

CARNAVAL CRAZINESS: A VERY VIVID HISTORY

Santiago's cultural complexity ensures its raucous July Carnaval is one of the largest and most authentic in the Caribbean with a kaleidoscope of costumes, copious food stalls, and enough music and noise to summon up the dead. If you can brave the heat of summer and don't mind a bit of neck-craning and jostling, this is the real deal.

Unlike most Latin American carnivals, Santiago's annual knees-up did not develop around a Lent-based celebration of deep religious significance. Instead, it was an amalgam of several separate days of fun and diversion called *mamarrachos* which fell around the time of saint's days such as San Juan on June 24 or Santa Ana on July 26 (but lacked any further religious significance). The festivities gave laborers downtime after the January to May period of sugar-cane harvesting. At one time, they were even dubbed *'festivales de las clases bajas'* (festivals of the lower classes).

Spanish authorities tolerated the festivities as a means of distracting the poor from other more serious forms of rebellion and quickly Carnaval became synonymous with debauchery and scandal. In a delicious touch of modern-day irony, Carnaval now culminates in the Día de la Rebeldía Nacional (July 26), honoring Cuba's most famous (albeit failed) rebellion: the assault on the Moncada Barracks.

Santiago's carnivals blossomed in the late 19th century, although people back then knew them only as *mamarrachos:* a byword for parties where anything goes: horse races, large-scale bonfires, food fights, copious alcohol consumption, *cantos de pullas* (mocking, satirical songs) and what the Spanish authorities considered overly sensual dancing.

These days Carnaval has toned down. A bit.

Don't miss the *comparasas,* parades that are satirical or even antiestablishment in origin. They subdivide into the *congas,* simpler but feistier performances by poorer people in large groups with somewhat manic percussion. Also on show are more-elaborate *paseos,* usually horse-drawn parades, lavish in scale and similar to European-style carnival floats. The freshly inaugurated Malecón is the hub of parade action.

Santiago's Museo del Carnaval (p397) offers some background on the carnival's culture and history.

version of Carnaval lets loose with fantastic costumes, food stalls, and music round the clock. The whole city spills out onto the streets to absorb it.

★Fiesta del Fuego CULTURAL

(⏲early Jul) The literal firing up for Carnaval, this early-July celebration includes a ceremony where the devil is burned to the glee of huge crowds on the Malecón.

Fiesta de San Juan CULTURAL

(⏲Jun 24) The summer season begins with the Fiesta de San Juan, celebrated with processions and conga dancing by cultural associations called *focos culturales.*

Festival Internacional Matamoros Son MUSIC

(⏲Oct) A tribute to one of Santiago de Cuba's musical greats, Miguel Matamoros, kicks off in late October with dances, lectures, concerts and workshops. Main venues include the Casa de la Trova (p414) and the Teatro José María Heredia (p415).

Festival Internacional de Coros MUSIC

(⏲Nov) The international choir festival brings in some strong international singing groups for some cultural cross-fertilization and spirit-lifting music.

Festival del Caribe CULTURAL

(⏲Jul) Festival of Caribbean culture held in July. Together with the Fiesta del Fuego, it's a warm-up for Carnaval.

Boleros de Oro MUSIC

(⏲Jun) Arrive in mid- to late June for this crooner's extravaganza that is replicated in various cities throughout the country.

Sleeping

★Roy's Terrace Inn CASA PARTICULAR $

(Map p404; ☎22-62-05-22; roysterraceinn@gmail.com; Diego Palacios No 177, btwn Padre Pico & Mariano Corona; r CUC$35; P❄📶) From the hanging rooftop garden to wall murals and impeccable rooms, every fiber gleams.

Run by an enthusiastic team of well-traveled Cubans and local mamas who woo you with their warmth and cooking, this spot is tops. Rooms are filled with modern amenities, including TV, hairdryers and information packets. Service – in English, Spanish, French and some German – is a highlight.

Guests are given preference for dinner reservations at the tiny rooftop restaurant. Consider it a must.

Casa Colonial 1893 CASA PARTICULAR **$**
(Map p404; ☎22-62-24-70; casacolonial1893@gmail.com; Hechavarría No 301; r CUC$25-30; ❄) In a lovely, well-preserved colonial, this home features seven rooms gathered around a huge interior patio with original tiles. Rooms feature bright satin bedcovers. Not unusual for casas where renting is important to the household, but still unsettling, the family congregates off to the side, beyond a partial wall in the front room.

Casa Señora Inalvis CASA PARTICULAR **$**
(Map p394; ☎22-65-11-13, 53-08-80-20; nalviscasado@nauta.cu; Calle 6ta No 660; r CUC$25-30; ❄) Located on a convenient corner near Meliá Santiago de Cuba hotel, this cute suburban home has just a couple of rooms and a shady back patio. Your host Sra Inalvis is a gem, a former journalist who is unusually helpful and quick to offer fresh juice or coffee.

Casa Milena CASA PARTICULAR **$**
(Map p404; ☎22-62-88-22, mobile 53-19-58-14; penelope1212@nauta.cu; Heredia No 306; r CUC$25-30; ❄) Smack in the heart of the street renowned for live music, this welcoming family home features three huge rooms in a colonial home. It's very clean and central.

Casa Terraza Pavo Real CASA PARTICULAR **$**
(Map p404; ☎22-65-85-89; juanmarti13@yahoo.es; Santa Rita No 302, cnr San Félix; r CUC$25-30; ❄📶) The meticulously maintained family home of Juan Martí has a palatial quality, with a riot of antique furniture, light-filtering *vitrales* (stained-glass windows) and coiled spiral staircases. The crowning glory is a huge Alhambra-esque patio with a sleep-invoking fountain and an expansive roof terrace with exotic orchids. Yet, many might feel at odds with the tropical birds and peacocks in cages. Breakfast spreads are noteworthy.

Casa Nelson & Deisy CASA PARTICULAR **$**
(Map p404; ☎22-65-63-72, mobile 53-65-81-33; casanelsonydeysi@yahoo.es; Donato Marmol No 476 1/2; r CUC$20-25; ❄) Decked in white, this thoroughly modern casa sits in a renovated building in the colonial core. There are three smart rooms and a private terrace. Nelson and Deisy are famous for their cooking, with good vegetarian fare and cocktails to boot. Has very cordial service.

Casa Lola CASA PARTICULAR **$**
(Map p394; ☎22-65-41-20; Mariano Corona No 309, btwn General Portuondo & Miguel Gómez; r CUC$20-25; ❄) With a large private garden crowned by a gazebo, who needs plaza chill-out time? The young resident hosts go out of their way to be helpful. Rooms are basic but clean, one with a large balcony overlooking the street. As the surrounding streets are poorly lit, coming home from the bar can seem like a long walk – better take a taxi.

Casa Colonial 'Maruchi' CASA PARTICULAR **$**
(Map p394; ☎22-62-07-67, mobile 52-61-37-91; maruchib@yahoo.es; Hartmann No 357, btwn General Portuondo & Máximo Gómez; r CUC$30; ❄) This 19th-century colonial with brick walls and museum-worthy furniture is a temple to all things Santería. The three guest rooms feature brass beds with quilts, the upstairs option the most private. All types stay here: *santeros* (priests of Santería), backpackers and foreign students studying for PhDs on the Regla de Ocha. With encyclopedic knowledge of Afro-Cuban religions, Maruchi can organize presentations.

The food is legendary and the fecund courtyard equally sublime.

Hotel Libertad HOTEL **$**
(Map p404; ☎22-62-77-10; reserva@libertad.tur.cu; Aguilera No 658; s/d CUC$61/66; ❄@📶) Cheap Cuban hotel chain Islazul breaks out of its Soviet-themed concrete-block obsession and goes colonial in this venerable beauty on Plaza de Marte. It has positive staff and 17 clean (if sometimes dark) high-ceilinged rooms featuring narrow singles. It's quirky in novel ways – don't be surprised if a Chinese salesperson is selling clothes out of suitcases in the hall.

The pleasant street-side restaurant is volumes better than the rooftop disco – if you're trying to sleep at 1am, that is.

Casa Yoyi CASA PARTICULAR $
(Map p394; ☎22-62-31-66; eulogiadelosmilagros@nauta.cu; Mariano Corona No 54; r CUC$25-30; ❄) A 10-minute walk from the center in the Los Hoyos neighborhood, cheerful Casa Yoyi is modern and tranquil. There are large 1st-floor rooms and an apartment decked out with flat-screen TVs and bright flower prints. Beds vary in quality – some sag – so it pays to see a few rooms. Has a great roof terrace. English and Russian are spoken.

Casa Mili CASA PARTICULAR $
(Map p394; ☎22-66-74-56; mileidis.rodriguez@nauta.cu; Calle 8 No 156, btwn Av 5 & 7; r incl breakfast CUC$25; ❄) If you can't bear the motorcycle madness of the city center, escape to the residential quarter of Vista Alegre and this spacious, high-ceiling casa with its fine frontal columns and shiny floors. Run by the determined Clara, there are five rooms, with more private ones behind the patio, including an ample family room.

Villa Gaviota HOTEL $
(Map p394; ☎22-64-13-70; jefe.recepcion@gaviota.co.cu; Calle 21, Vista Alegre; s/d CUC$38/50; P❄≋) Santiago's quiet suburban Vista Alegre district is either an oasis of calm – or a ghost town. Odd duck Villa Gaviota has a number of attractive clustered properties and apartments here with bare-bones furnishings. With ample greenery, it's private and fairly priced but service can be achingly slow. Features include a swimming pool, bar-restaurant, a billiards room and laundry.

There's wi-fi at the bar-restaurant on Manduley.

Hotel Balcón del Caribe HOTEL $
(Map p418; ☎22-69-10-11, 22-69-15-06; Carretera del Morro Km 7.5; s/d incl breakfast CUC$34/56; P❄ᯤ≋) The tremendous setting next to El Morro fort (p402) is counterbalanced by the usual humdrum Islazul hotel-chain foibles: flowery curtains, ancient mattresses and furnishings salvaged from a 1970s garage sale. But there's a pool and the view is stunning. Get a room inside the complex; not a grottier external cabin. It's located 10km from the city center, making transport a headache.

Aichel & Corrado CASA PARTICULAR $
(Map p404; ☎22-62-27-47; www.casaparticularsantiago.com; José A Saco No 516, btwn Mayía Rodríguez & Donato Mármol; r CUC$20-25; ❄ᯤ) Owners at this 2nd and 3rd floor walk-up on the pedestrian street seem more interested in doing a brisk business than greeting guests. You might love the location (and the rooftop room seems promising) but get ready for a slight aura of chaos. The downstairs Italian restaurant is part of the business.

Hotel Rex HOTEL $$
(Map p404; Victoriano Garzón; s/d incl breakfast CUC$96/100; ❄ᯤ) The hotel that once served as a pre-raid base for the Moncadistas in 1953 has been reborn as a comfortable midrange accommodation option. Suspended above the motorcycle madness and musical backbeat of central Santiago, it maintains a very Cuban flair – rare for hotels here. There's a pleasant roof terrace and an interior bar with soccer on the TV.

Tranquil it isn't; unmistakably Cuba, it most definitely is.

Hotel Versalles HOTEL $$
(Map p418; ☎22-69-10-16; Alturas de Versalles; s/d incl breakfast CUC$69/79; P❄@≋) Not to be confused with the namesake rumba district of Matanzas, or the resplendent home of Louis XIV, this modest hotel is on the outskirts of town off the road to El Morro. There's a dose of style in its inviting pool and the comfortable rooms with small terraces.

Hotel Casa Granda HOTEL $$
(Map p404; ☎22-65-30-24; Heredia No 201; s/d CUC$92/128; ❄@ᯤ) This elegant 1914 hotel, artfully described by Graham Greene in his book *Our Man in Havana,* has 58 rooms and classic atmosphere. Greene stayed here in the late 1950s when he enjoyed relaxing on the street-side terrace while his famous pen captured the nocturnal essence of the city. Half a century later, rooms are serviceable but the atmosphere remains potent.

Aside from Che Guevara posters and some seriously erratic service on reception, not much has changed.

Hostal San Basilio BOUTIQUE HOTEL $$
(Map p404; ☎22-65-17-02; www.cubatravelnetwork.com; Bartolomé Masó No 403, btwn Pío Rosado & Porfirio Valiente; d incl breakfast CUC$100; ❄@) The lovely eight-room San Basilio (named for the original name of the street on which it lies) is cozy and refreshingly contemporary – with a romantic colonial setting including a petite patio dripping with ferns. Rooms come with DVD

players, umbrellas, bathroom scales and mini bottles of rum. Alas, some mattresses need replacing. A small restaurant serves breakfast and lunch.

Hotel las Américas HOTEL **$$**

(Map p394; ☎22-64-20-11; jcarpeta@hamerica.seu.tur.cu; cnr Avs de las Américas & General Cebreco; s/d CUC$92/102; P ❄ @ ≋) The 70 rooms here offer the usual lackluster Islazul interiors, probably not worth it unless you are after the standard hotel amenities. It does offer comprehensive facilities, with a restaurant, 24-hour cafe, small pool and nightly entertainment.

★**Hotel Imperial** HISTORIC HOTEL **$$$**

(Map p404; ☎22-62-82-30; José A Saco, btwn Felix Peña & General Lacret; s/d CUC$97/138; ❄ ⊜) The return of a Santiago landmark, the eclectic-style 1915 Hotel Imperial has been refurbished to sparkling condition with some welcome concessions to modernity. The 39 rooms are smartly furnished and spanking new, with flat-screen TVs, tall windows and glass showers. Features an elevator to an elegant roof-terrace bar with great city views and live music on weekends.

There's also an on-site restaurant and street-level snack bar open late.

Meliá Santiago de Cuba HOTEL **$$$**

(Map p394; ☎22-68-70-70; www.meliacuba.com/cuba-hotels/hotel-melia-santiagodecuba; cnr Av de las Américas & Calle M; s/d incl breakfast CUC$174/224; P ❄ @ ⊜ ≋) Sleek on the inside, a blue-mirrored monster on the outside, the 1990s-designed Meliá is Santiago's only 'international' hotel with a laundry list of amenities hard to find elsewhere. Count on real bathtubs in every room, three pools, four restaurants, various shopping facilities and an elegant 15th-floor bar. The downsides are its location on the outskirts and lack of genuine Cuban charm.

Nonguests can get a day pass (CUC$20) for the pool.

Gran Hotel HOTEL **$$$**

(Map p404; ☎22-28-71-71; José A Saco, btwn General Lacret & Hartmann; s/d incl breakfast CUC$95/134; ❄ @) Opened in 2016, this remake of a classic downtown hotel falls slightly short. The 42 rooms are generally large and there's a pleasant roof terrace and cyber cafe but staff is either sleepwalking or indifferent. Guests can choose from rooms with a balcony overlooking the pedestrian street or interior rooms without windows.

For now, reservations are made through Casa Granda (p409).

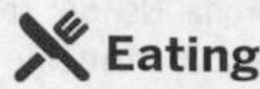

Eating

Despite having more than one million inhabitants and a medley of cultures, the restaurant scene is lean. The outlook is mediocre with the odd get-out-of-jail card, though the situation has improved slightly in the last few years.

In the *casco histórico,* Calle José A Saco is a pedestrian-only street with mobile food units selling *comida ligera* (light food).

Ranchon Los Naranjos CUBAN **$**

(Map p394; ☎22-71-40-68; Pedro Alvarado No 16; MN$6-10) On a hilly residential street by Meliá, this open-air restaurant offers great-value meals. Grilled fish and lamb stewed in tomato sauce come recommended. Maybe it's the out-of-the-way location, but it's conducive to chilling. Beware the neon cocktails which run a little too sweet. Prices are in *moneda nacional,* the local currency.

Rumba Café CAFE **$**

(Map p404; ☎58-02-21-53; Hartmann No 455; sandwiches CUC$3-7; ⊙9:30am-10:30pm Mon-Sat; ✎) You can escape the frenetic pace of downtown Santiago by ducking into this sleek, air-conditioned cafe that seems like an alternate reality. Lattes? Vegetarian sandwiches? It's real. There are inviting spaces, satisfying grilled sandwiches and beautiful omelettes.

Bendita Farándula CARIBBEAN **$**

(Map p404; ☎22-65-37-39; Monseñor Barranda No 513; meals CUC$5-9; ⊙noon-11pm) You would probably never wander in here unbidden, but with an ambience reminiscent of a provincial French bistro, this cozy two-floored place with guests' musings on the walls does Santiago's only *pescado con leche de coco* (fish with coconut sauce; a Barracoan specialty) and a really nice *bistek de cerdo con jamon y queso* (pork steak with ham and cheese).

Jardín de los Enramadas ICE CREAM **$**

(Map p394; ☎22-65-22-05; cnr José A Saco & Gallo; ice cream CUC$1-2; ⊙9:45am-11:45pm) Occupying a block just down from the *casco histórico* en route to the port, this garden is devoted to ornamental plants and great ice cream (which comes with marshmallows and biscuits). Service is exemplary.

La Fortaleza CUBAN $
(Map p394; ☎22-64-62-96; cnr Av Manduley & Calle 3; meals CUC$3-7; ⊙noon-11:30pm) In a conducive setting amid Vista Alegre's mansions, a spacious, inviting shady patio serving above-average food (pay in pesos) alongside live music at lunchtime. But? A big fat zero for the quality of service.

La Arboleda ICE CREAM $
(Map p394; cnr Avs de los Libertadores & Victoriano Garzón; ice cream CUC$1; ⊙10am-11:40pm Tue-Sun) Santiago's ice-cream cathedral is a little out of the center, not that this lessens the queue length. Yell out *¿Quién es último?* (who is last?) and take your place on the Av de los Libertadores side of the parlor. Milkshakes are sometimes sold from the outside window.

Cafe Hotel Casa Granda CAFE $
(Map p404; ☎22-65-30-21; Heredia No 201, Casa Granda; snacks CUC$2-8; ⊙9am-midnight; 📶) Positioned like a whitewashed theater box overlooking the unscripted cabaret of Parque Céspedes, the Casa Granda's Parisian-style terrace cafe has to be one of the best people-watching locations in Cuba. Food-wise, you're talking snacks (burgers, hot dogs, sandwiches etc) and service-wise you're talking impassive, verging on grumpy; but with this setting, who cares?

Restaurante España SEAFOOD $
(Map p394; Av Victoriano Garzón; meals CUC$3-7; ⊙noon-4pm, 6-10pm) Get ready for the Arctic blast of air-con and readjust your Cuban-food preconceptions before you walk into España. It specializes in seafood cooked with panache and – on occasion – fresh herbs. Try the lobster or tangy prawns, but bypass the Cuban wine which is almost undrinkable.

Santiago 1900 CARIBBEAN $
(Map p404; ☎22-62-35-07; Bartolomé Masó No 354; meals CUC$2-8; ⊙noon-midnight) In the former Bacardí residence you can dine on the standard chicken, fish or pork for Cuban pesos in a plush dining room that recently recovered its fin de siècle colonial airs. Beware the draconian dress code: no shorts or T-shirts.

El Barracón CARIBBEAN $
(Map p394; ☎22-66-18-77; Av Victoriano Garzón; meals CUC$3-9; ⊙noon-11pm) El Barracón tries to reignite the roots of Afro-Cuban culture and cuisine with mixed results. The state-run restaurant's interior, a mix of atmospheric Santería shrine and *cimarrón* (runaway slave) is intriguing, but the food can't match its private competition. Stick to the delicious *tostones* (fried plantain patties) filled with chorizo and cheese, or opt for the lamb special.

Panadería Doña Neli BAKERY $
(Map p404; ☎22-64-15-28; cnr Aguilera & Gen Serafin Sánchez; breads/snacks CUC$0.50-1; ⊙7am-7pm) Hard-currency bakery on Plaza de Marte, vending divine-smelling bread and cakes with a scowl.

Supermercado Plaza de Marte SUPERMARKET $
(Map p404; ☎22-68-60-45; Av Victoriano Garzón; ⊙9am-6pm Mon-Sat, to noon Sun) One of the better-stocked supermarkets in town, with a great ice-cream selection and cheap bottled water. It's just beyond the northeastern corner of Plaza de Marte.

Municipal Market MARKET $
(Map p394; cnr Aguilera & Padre Pico) The main market, two blocks west of Parque Céspedes, has a poor selection considering the size of the city. Show up early to find more produce.

★Roy's Terrace Inn Roof Garden Restaurant CUBAN $$
(Map p404; ☎22-62-05-22; roysterraceinn@gmail.com; meals CUC$10-15; ⊙7-9.30pm; 📶🖉) If only the rest of Cuba could harness this formula: quality homemade food, caring service and excellent atmosphere. Reserve one day ahead for one of only six rooftop tables surrounded by tumbling flowers in candlelight. Cocktails deliver and family-style servings come overflowing. Fish, chicken or pork are served with sides such as crispy *tamal*es or sautéed eggplant. Vegans and vegetarians welcome.

★St Pauli INTERNATIONAL $$
(Map p404; ☎22-65-22-92; José A Saco No 605; meals CUC$4-15; ⊙noon-11pm Mon-Thu, noon-midnight Fri-Sun) In a city of no great culinary tradition, St Pauli arrived like a hurricane. Walk the long mural decorated corridor off Calle Saco to a bright room featuring blackboard menus and a glass-wall kitchen. Everything is consistently good, particularly the cocktail glass gazpacho, *pulpo al ajillo* (octopus with garlic) and pineapple chicken fajitas. If you've come behind a group: patience!

DON'T MISS

SEEING A FOLKLÓRICO DANCE GROUP

Seeing a *folklórico* dance group is a definitive Santiago de Cuba cultural experience. The city is home to a dozen such groups (more than anywhere else in Cuba), which exist to teach and perform traditional Afro-Cuban *bailes* (dances) and pass their traditions on to future generations. Most of the groups date from the early 1960s and all enjoy strong patronage from the Cuban government.

A good place to find out about upcoming *folklórico* events is at the Casa del Caribe (p406) in Vista Alegre where many of the groups hang out and perform.

Santiago's oldest folklórico group is the Conjunto Folklórico de Oriente (p414) formed in 1959. They perform a huge range of Afro-Cuban dance genres from *gagá* and *bembé* to *tumba francesa* at the Teatro José María Heredia. The **Ballet Folklórico Cutumba** (Map p394; 22-62-32-01; Teatro Galaxia, cnr Avs 24 de Febrero & Valeriano Hierrezuelo; CUC$2; from 8pm Fri & Sun) is an offshoot of the Oriente group formed in 1976. You can usually see them rehearsing at their HQ, the Teatro Galaxia, from 9am to 1pm, Tuesday to Friday.

For pure *tumba francesa* dancing check out the **Tumba Francesa La Caridad de Oriente** (Map p394; Pio Rosado No 268), one of only three of these French-Haitian groups left in Cuba. They can be seen in their rehearsal rooms on Tuesday and Thursday at 9pm.

The **Carabalí Olugo** (Map p418; Carretera del Morro, cnr Av 24 de Febrero) and the **Carabalí Izuama** (Map p394; Pío Rosado No 107) are *comparsas* (carnival music and dance groups) who represent the Tivolí and Los Hoyos neighborhoods in Santiago's July carnival. They are both descendants of 19th-century *cabildos* or mutual aid societies formed along ethnic lines, a factor still reflected in their music.

Compañia Danzaría Folklórica Kokoyé (Map p394) is a more modern group, formed in 1989 to promote Afro-Cuban dance to tourists. They can be seen performing on Saturday evening and Sunday afternoon in the Casa del Caribe.

Madrileño CUBAN **$$**
(Map p394; 22-64-41-38; Calle 8 No 105; meals CUC$4-15; noon-11pm) A well-respected, good-quality option, Madrileño occupies a classy colonial abode in Vista Alegre with interior patio dining with chirping birds. Contrary to the name, this is Cuban *comida criolla* (creole food). Succulent odors waft from the kitchen. There's an extensive menu with an emphasis on grilled meats. Forgo the seafood skewers which are on the dry side.

There's dependable Italian fare such as pasta, or Caribbean flavors that have been marinated on the barbecue and glazed and trussed to spicy perfection. The succulent smoked steaks or seafood *brochetas* are both good. No harm in booking early: it's popular.

El Palenquito PARRILLA **$$**
(Map p418; 22-64-52-20; Av del Río No 28, btwn Calle 6 & Carretera de Caney; mains CUC$6-12) Barbecue is the specialty of this casual backyard restaurant on the outskirts of Santiago. Grilled pork and chicken are served with the typical sides, but the real star is dessert. Try rich zapote or coconut ice cream in the shells of the original fruit – portions are huge, but you suddenly might not want to share. With good service.

El Holandes CUBAN **$$**
(Map p404; 22-62-48-78; Heredia No 251; mains CUC$6-15; 12pm-midnight) A small, pleasing paladar (privately owned restaurant) with seating indoors or on a pleasant elevated terrace. The food is classic Cuban, the setting clean and the location is right in the thick of things.

Restaurante el Morro CARIBBEAN **$$**
(Map p418; 22-69-15-76; Castillo del Morro; mains CUC$6-12; noon-5pm) Bravo to the spectacular cliffside location sporting huge sea views. Think classics: roast chicken and pork are nicely presented. A busload of European/North American 50-somethings can really slow down service, so time your visit. Not that this put off Paul McCartney, who ate here during a whistle-stop 2000 visit (his plate is proudly mounted on the wall).

According to the waiters, the world's most famous vegetarian made do with an omelet. For meat-eaters, the set *comida criolla* (Creole food) lunch is a better bet, a filling spread with soup, main, a small dessert and one drink. Take bus 212 to Ciudamar and walk the last 20 minutes, or take a taxi and combine it with a fort visit.

Compay Gallo CUBAN **$$**
(Map p394; ☎22-65-83-95; Máximo Gómez No 503 altos; meals CUC$4-10; ⊙noon-11pm) Upstairs in a typical narrow Santiago street on the cusp of the city center, Compay Gallo does classic Cuban food with mixed results. Try the prawn-cocktail starter and the *ragout de codero* (lamb ragu) with ample vegetables.

Ristorante Italiano la Fontana ITALIAN **$$$**
(Map p394; cnr Av de las Américas & Calle M, Meliá Santiago de Cuba; mains CUC$6-18; ⊙noon-11pm) Pizza *deliciosa* and lasagna *formidable,* ravioli and garlic bread; *mamma mía,* this has to be the number-one option for breaking away from all that chicken and pork! Prices are jacked up on Chilean wines, but it might be worth it anyway.

Restaurante Zunzún CARIBBEAN **$$$**
(Map p394; ☎22-64-15-28; Av Manduley No 159; meals CUC$12-18; ⊙noon-10pm) Dine in bygone bourgeois style in this mansion turned restaurant, Zunzún, in the once upscale Vista Alegre neighborhood. It has always been lauded, though overpriced. Exotic dishes include chicken curry, paella or a formidable cheese plate and cognac. Expect professional, attentive service and entertaining troubadours.

Drinking & Nightlife

★Casa Granda Roof Garden Bar BAR
(Map p404; top fl, Heredia No 201; cover CUC$3-10; ⊙11am-1am) Slip up to the 5th-floor roof of Casa Granda for the most breathtaking sunset in Cuba. Views of the scene in Parque Céspedes and the dramatically lit cathedral are well worth the minimum consumption charge for nonguests (it increases after 7pm), which credits toward your first drink. So what if drinks are double than elsewhere? You're well above the fray.

Cerveceria Puerto del Rey MICROBREWERY
(Map p394; ☎22-68-60-48; Paseo Alameda & Aguilera; ⊙noon-midnight) You know Cuba is changing when you find an actual warehouse-style brewpub filled with locals quaffing pints brewed on-site. If your taste runs stronger and darker than Buccanero, come to this noisy, fun spot. Flavors aren't yet perfected, but who cares? There's decent pub food, including popular *caldo del rey* (a broth with a pork-rib base).

Best after a walk on the new Malecón.

La Gran Sofía CAFE
(Map p404; Paraíso; snacks CUC$1-2; ⊙24hr) A local hangout where the coffee is good and *bocaditos* (snacks) won't set you back.

Bar Sindo Garay BAR
(Map p404; ☎22-65-15-31; cnr Tamayo Fleites & General Lacret; ⊙11am-11pm) As much a museum to one of Cuba's most famous *trova* musicians (Sindo Garay, most renowned for his composition *Perla marina*) as a bar, this is a smart, usually packed place with two levels, serving great cocktails on pedestrianized Tamayo Fleites.

Café Ven CAFE
(Map p404; ☎22-62-26-60; José A Saco, btwn Hartmann & Pío Rosado; ⊙24hr) Small cafe tucked into busy Saco (Enramadas) with lung-enriching air-con, interesting coffee *cafetal* (plantation) paraphernalia and enough Italiano clientele to keep the cappuccino-making staff on their toes.

Café la Isabelica CAFE
(Map p404; ☎22-66-95-46; cnr Aguilera & Porfirio Valiente; ⊙7am-11pm) Forget the coffee – you've had better at truck stops. It's all about atmosphere: 100% authentic. This smoky, dark cantina-type cafe sells cups of java with prices in pesos.

Club Nautico BAR
(Map p394; off Paseo Alameda; ⊙noon-midnight) Enlivening Paseo Alameda with its lively *ranchón*-style bar suspended over the water with a great view over the bay, this is a breezy locale to escape the sizzling Santiago heat. Food isn't a highlight – come here for the drinks and the views. Pay in pesos or CUC.

Barrita de Ron Havana Club BAR
(Map p394; Av Jesús Menéndez No 703; ⊙9am-6pm) A tourist bar attached to the Bacardi Rum Factory (p400), offers rum sales and tastings. There are no factory tours.

☆ Entertainment

'Spoiled for choice' would be an understatement in Santiago. For what's happening, look for the biweekly *Cartelera Cultural*. The reception desk at Hotel Casa Granda (p409) usually has copies.

★Casa de las Tradiciones LIVE MUSIC
(Map p394; ☎22-65-38-92; General J Rabí No 154; CUC$1; ⏲5pm-midnight) The most discovered 'undiscovered' spot in Santiago still retains its smoke-filled, foot-stomping, front-room feel. Hidden in the gentile Tivolí district, some of Santiago de Cuba's most exciting ensembles, singers and soloists take turns improvising. Friday nights are reserved for straight-up classic *trova*, à la Ñico Saquito and the like. There's a gritty bar and some colorful artwork.

★Iris Jazz Club JAZZ
(Map p404; General Serafin Sánchez, btwn José A Saco & Bayamo; CUC$5; ⏲shows 9:30pm-2am) When Santiago gets too hot, noisy and agitated, you need a dose of Iris, one of Cuba's suavest and best jazz clubs where you can sit in a comfy booth surrounded by pictures of puffing jazz greats and watch some incredibly intuitive exponents of Santiago's small but significant jazz scene.

Noche Santiagüera LIVE PERFORMANCE
(Map p394; Av Victoriano Garzón, btwn Moncada & Parque los Estudiantes; ⏲6pm-midnight Sat) FREE Every Saturday night, the side streets branching off this main thoroughfare teem with street food, music and crowds for a city-wide outdoor party.

Conjunto Folklórico de Oriente DANCE
(Map p394; ☎22-64-31-78; Teatro José María Heredia, cnr Avs de las Américas & de los Desfiles) Santiago's oldest *folklórico* group was formed in 1959; they are currently bivouacked at the Teatro Heredia (p415). They perform a huge range of Afro-Cuban dance genres from *gagá* and *bembé* to *tumba francesa*.

Casa de la Trova LIVE MUSIC
(Map p404; ☎22-65-38-92; Heredia No 208; ⏲hours vary) Santiago's shrine to the power of traditional music is still going strong five decades on, continuing to attract big names such as Buena Vista Social Club singer Eliades Ochoa. Warming up on the ground floor in the late afternoon, the action slowly gravitates upstairs where, come 10pm, everything starts to get a shade more *caliente*.

Santiago Café CABARET
(Map p394; ☎22-68-70-70; cnr Av de las Américas & Calle M; CUC$5; ⏲10pm-2am Sat) This is the hotel Meliá Santiago de Cuba's (p410) slightly less spectacular version of the Tropicana. Cabarets take place on Saturday with a disco afterward. It's on the hotel's 1st floor. Head up to the 15th floor for the exciting Bello Bar.

Uneac CULTURAL CENTER
(Unión Nacional de Escritores y Artistas de Cuba, Union of Cuban Writers & Artists; Map p404; ☎22-65-34-65; Heredia No 266) First stop for art fiends seeking intellectual solace in talks, workshops, encounters and performances – all in a gorgeous colonial courtyard.

Casa de Cultura Josué País García LIVE MUSIC
(Map p404; ☎22-62-78-04; Heredia No 204; CUC$1; ⏲from 9pm Wed, Fri & Sat, 1pm Sun) Grab a seat (or stand in the street) and settle down for whatever this spontaneous place can throw at you: orchestral *danzón* (ballroom dance), folkloric rumba, lovelorn *trovadores* (traditional singers) or rhythmic reggaeton (Cuban hip-hop).

Tropicana Santiago CABARET
(Map p418; ☎22-68-70-20; from CUC$35; ⏲from 10pm Wed-Sun) Anything Havana can do, Santiago can do better – or at least cheaper. Styled on the Tropicana original, this 'feathers and baubles' Las Vegas–style floor show is heavily hyped by all the city's tour agencies who offer it for CUC$35 plus transport (Havana's show is twice the price, but no way twice as good).

It's located out of town, 3km north of the Hotel las Américas, so a taxi or rental car is the only independent transport option, making the tour-agency deals a good bet. The Saturday-night show is superior.

Patio ARTex LIVE MUSIC
(Map p404; ☎22-65-48-14; Heredia No 304; ⏲11am-11pm) Art lines the walls of this shop-and-club combo that hosts live music both day and night in a quaint inner courtyard; a good bet if the Casa de la Trova is full, or too frenetic.

LOCAL KNOWLEDGE

LA TUMBA FRANCESA

The specter of Haiti, Cuba's Gallic eastern neighbor loomed large over the isles throughout the late colonial period, especially in the Oriente. The reason? Revolution! Haiti's 1791 slave rebellion sent thousands of terrified French-Haitian landowners scurrying west to the safer climes of Cuba's eastern mountains, bringing their black slaves with them.

As the displaced entrepreneurs set about building sugar mills and coffee plantations in their new home, their indentured slaves were put to work on nascent rural estates where they continued to celebrate the music and cultural practices of the land they had left behind. Descended from slaves originally brought to Haiti from the French colony of Dahomey (now Benin) in Africa, the centerpiece of Cuban-Haitian culture is a hybrid music and dance style known as *tumba francesa*.

An unusual marriage between 18th-century French ballroom dancing and the frenetic drum rhythms of West Africa, *tumba francesa* is perhaps best described as a kind of voodoo meets Versailles. Picture a trio of drummers accompanied by a chorus of female singers chanting words in a barely decipherable French-African patois. The music provides accompaniment to two key dances. The *masón*, a stately couples' dance that parodies the high society balls of the erstwhile slave owners wouldn't have looked out of place in the corridors of Louis XIV-era Paris. The *yuba* is a more improvised and athletic dance also partaken by couples. Both are performed by dancers dressed in elegant 19th-century garb: white shirts and colored shawls for men, and wide ankle-length dresses and fans for ladies.

When freed slaves started migrating to Cuba's cities from the countryside in the late 1800s, they took their music with them and *tumba francesa* societies quickly sprang up all over the Oriente. At one time there were over a hundred such societies.

Today, just three remain: the Santa Catalina de Ricci Pompadour founded in 1902 in the city of Guantánamo, La Caridad de Oriente (p412) dating from the 1870s in Santiago de Cuba, and the Bejuco de Sagua de Tánamo in Holguín Province. Witnessing a performance is a unique insight into an increasingly rare art. In 2008 the endangered *tumba francesa* was declared an intangible cultural heritage by Unesco.

Subway Club LIVE MUSIC
(Map p404; ☎22-66-91-19; cnr Aguilera & Mayía Rodriguez; CUC$5; ⏰8pm-2am) Stylish venue with interesting solo acts singing their hearts out to great piano music come nightfall. Good fun.

Estadio de Béisbol Guillermón Moncada SPECTATOR SPORT
(Map p394; ☎22-64-26-55; Av de las Américas) During the baseball season, from October to April, this stadium hosts games at 7:30pm Tuesday, Wednesday, Thursday and Saturday, and 1:30pm Sunday (1 peso). The Avispas (Wasps) are the main rivals of Havana's Industriales, with National Series victories in 2005, 2007, 2008 and 2010. On the northeastern side of town.

Cubanacán runs trips to Avispa games with a visit to the dressing room afterward to meet the players.

Teatro José María Heredia THEATER
(Map p394; ☎22-64-31-90; cnr Avs de las Américas & de los Desfiles; ⏰box office 9am-noon & 1-4:30pm) Santiago's huge, modern theater and convention center went up during the city refurbishment in the early 1990s. Rock and folk concerts often take place in the 2459-seat Sala Principal, while the 120-seat Café Cantante Niagara hosts more esoteric events. The Conjunto Folklórico de Orient is based here.

Patio los Dos Abuelos LIVE MUSIC
(Map p404; ☎22-62-32-67; Francisco Pérez Carbo No 5; CUC$2; ⏰10pm-2am Mon-Sat) The old-timers label (*abuelos* means grandparents) carries a certain amount of truth. This relaxed live-music house is a bastion for traditional *son* sung the old-fashioned way. The musicians are seasoned pros and most of the patrons are perfect ladies and gentlemen.

Sala de Conciertos Dolores LIVE MUSIC
(Map p404; cnr Aguilera & Mayía Rodríguez; ⏰from 8:30pm) You can catch the Sinfónica del Oriente at this former church on Plaza de Dolores, plus the impressive children's

choir (at 5pm). The event calendar is posted outside.

Teatro Martí THEATER
(Map p394; ☎22-62-05-07; Félix Peña No 313; 👪) Children's shows are staged at 5pm on Saturday and Sunday at this theater near General Portuondo, opposite the Iglesia de Santo Tomás.

Orfeón Santiago LIVE MUSIC
(Map p404; ☎22-62-07-52; Heredia No 68; ⏰9am-11am Mon-Fri) This classical choir sometimes allows visitors to attend its practice sessions from 9am to 11am Monday to Friday.

Cine Rialto CINEMA
(Map p404; ☎22-62-30-35; Félix Peña No 654) This cinema, next to the cathedral, is one of only a few currently operating in Santiago de Cuba. Occasional English-language films.

Shopping

Creativity is inscribed into the louvers in colonial Santiago, and a brief sortie around the *casco histórico* will reveal snippets of eye-catching art. Decent craft stalls are set up in Calle Heredia most days.

Galería de Arte de Oriente ARTS & CRAFTS
(Map p404; ☎22-65-38-57; General Lacret No 656; ⏰9:30am-6pm Mon-Fri, 9:30am-noon Sat, 10am-10pm Sun) Probably the best gallery in Santiago de Cuba, the art here is consistently good.

Librería la Escalera de Edy BOOKS
(Map p404; Heredia No 265; ⏰10am-10pm) A veritable museum of old and rare books stacked ceiling high, plus vinyl records. Sombrero-clad *trovadores* often sit on the stairway and strum.

Discoteca Egrem MUSIC
(Map p404; ☎22-62-61-91; José A Saco No 309; ⏰9am-6pm Mon-Sat, to 2pm Sun) The definitive Cuban specialist-music store; this retail outlet of Egrem Studios has a good selection from local musicians.

ARTex GIFTS & SOUVENIRS
(Map p404; ☎22-65-48-14; Patio ARTex, Heredia No 208; ⏰11am-7pm Tue-Sun) Focuses on musical souvenirs, with a respectable selection of CDs and cassettes.

Librería Internacional BOOKS
(Map p404; ☎22-68-71-47; Heredia, btwn General Lacret & Félix Peña) On the southern side of Parque Céspedes. Decent selection of political titles in English; sells postcards and stamps.

Centro de Negocios Alameda SHOPPING CENTER
(Map p394; Av Jesus Menéndez, cnr José A Saco; ⏰8:30am-4:30pm) The port's latest regeneration project is opening this shopping center in a colonial building: internet, a pharmacy, the immigration office and a Cubanacán desk, plus shops.

Information

DANGERS & ANNOYANCES

Santiago is well known, even among Cubans, for its overzealous *jinteros* (touts), all working their particular angle – be it cigars, private restaurants, *chicas* (girls) or unofficial 'tours.' Sometimes it can seem impossible to shake off the money-with-legs feeling, but a firm 'no' coupled with a little light humor ought to keep the worst of the touts at bay.

Santiago's traffic is second only to Havana's in its environmental fallout. Making things worse for pedestrians is the plethora of noisy motorcyclists weaving for position along the city's sinuous 1950s streets. Narrow or non-existent sidewalks throw further obstacles into an already hazardous brew. Always look before you cross.

EMERGENCIES

Police (☎116; cnr Mariano Corona & Sánchez Hechavarría)

INTERNET ACCESS

There's wi-fi in public plazas, major hotels and a few casas particulares. Buy wi-fi credit on scratchcards at Etecsa Telepunto centers, where there's usually a line out the door, or hotel lobbies, though the latter frequently run out.

Etecsa Multiservicios (☎22-62-47-84; cnr Heredia & Félix Peña; internet per hour CUC$1.50; ⏰8:30am-7:30pm) Internet terminals and wi-fi scratchcards in a small office on Plaza Céspedes.

Etecsa Telepunto (☎22-65-75-21; cnr Hartmann & Tamayo Fleites; internet per hour CUC$1.50; ⏰8:30am-7:30pm) Internet terminals, plus sells wi-fi scratchcards.

MEDICAL SERVICES

Santiago has the best access to medicine and related services in the region.

Clínica Internacional Cubanacán Servimed (☎22-64-25-89; cnr Av Raúl Pujol & Calle 10,

Vista Alegre; 24hr) Capable staff speak some English. A dentist is also present.

Farmacia Clínica Internacional (22-64-25-89; cnr Av Raúl Pujol & Calle 10; 24hr) Best pharmacy in town, selling products in convertibles.

Farmacia Internacional (22-68-70-70; Meliá Santiago de Cuba, cnr Av de las Américas & Calle M; 8am-6pm) In the lobby of the Meliá Santiago de Cuba, it sells products in convertibles.

MONEY

The city has plenty of banks and currency-exchange centers.

Banco de Crédito y Comercio (22-62-80-06; Felix Peña No 614; 9am-3pm Mon-Fri) In the jarring modern building in Plaza Céspedes.

Banco Financiero Internacional (22-68-62-52; cnr Av de las Américas & Calle I; 9am-3pm Mon-Fri) Has an ATM.

Bandec (cnr José A Saco & Mariano Corona; 9am-3pm Mon-Fri) Has an ATM.

Cadeca Has two branches. Aguilera (22-65-13-83; Aguilera No 508; 8:30am-4pm Mon-Fri, to 11:30am Sat), with long lines for currency exchange; José A Saco (José A Saco No 409; 8:30am-4pm Mon-Fri, to 11:30am Sat)

POST

Post Office (Map p404; 22-62-21-08; Aguilera No 519; 9am-5pm Mon-Fri) Has telephones too.

TOURIST INFORMATION

As all tour agencies are government-run, they offer overlapping services and consistent prices.

Asistur (Map p404; 22-65-68-47; www.asistur.cu; Sagarra 204; 9am-5pm Mon-Fri) Situated under the Hotel Casa Granda (p409), this office specializes in helping foreigners, mainly in the insurance and financial fields.

Cubamar (Map p404; 22-65-36-39; comercial@scu.campismopopular.cu; Cornelio Robert 163 bajo; 8:30am-5pm Mon, Wed & Fri, 10am-6pm Tue & Thu, 9am-1pm Sat) For reservations at campismos in the province such as Caletón Blanco, Las Golondrinas, El Salton and La Mula. Study the varied opening hours before stopping by.

Cubanacán (Map p404; 22-68-64-12; Heredia No 201; 8am-6pm) Very helpful; sells tours in the Hotel Casa Granda.

Cubatur Has several branches. Heredia (Map p404; Heredia No 701; 8am-8pm); **Av** Victoriano Garzón (Map p394; 22-65-25-60; Av Victoriano Garzón No 364, cnr Calle 4; 8am-8pm) Sells all number of excursions, for everything from La Gran Piedra to El Cobre.

Infotur (Map p404; 22-68-60-68; Felix Peña 562; 8am-8pm) Helpful location and staff. There's also a branch in Antonio Maceo International Airport.

Getting There & Away

AIR

Antonio Maceo International Airport (SCU; Map p418; 22-69-10-53) is 7km south of Santiago de Cuba, off the Carretera del Morro. International flights arrive from Santo Domingo (Dominican Republic), Toronto and Montreal on **Cubana** (22-65-15-77; cnr José A Saco & General Lacret; 9am-5pm). Toronto and Montreal are also served by **Sunwing** (www.sunwing.ca). With mostly charter service, **AeroCaribbean** flies weekly between here and Port Au Prince, Haiti. **American Eagle** (www.aa.com) runs regular charters to and from Miami serving the Cuban-American community.

Internally, Cubana flies nonstop from Havana to Santiago de Cuba two or three times a day (about CUC$136 one-way, 1½ hours). There are also services to Holguín with g distanc.

BUS

The **National Bus Station** (Map p394; Paseo de Martí), behind train station and opposite the Heredia Monument, is 3km northeast of Parque Céspedes. **Víazul** (Map p394; 22-62-84-84; www.viazul.cu) buses leave from the same station.

The Havana bus stops at Bayamo (CUC$7, two hours), Holguín (CUC$11, 3½ to 4 hours), Las Tunas (CUC$11, five hours), Camagüey (CUC$18, 7½ hours), Ciego de Ávila (CUC$24, 9½ hours), Sancti Spíritus (CUC$28, 10 to 10½ hours) and Santa Clara (CUC$33, 11 to 12 hours). The Trinidad bus can drop you at Bayamo, Las Tunas, Camagüey, Ciego de Ávila and Sancti Spíritus. The Baracoa bus stops in Guantánamo.

VÍAZUL BUS DEPARTURES FROM SANTIAGO DE CUBA

DESTINATION	COST (CUC$)	DURATION (HR)	DAILY DEPARTURES
Baracoa	15	4¾	1:50am, 8am
Havana	51	13-14½	12:30am, 6:30am, 4pm
Trinidad	33	11½	7:30pm
Varadero	49	15	8pm

Greater Santiago de Cuba

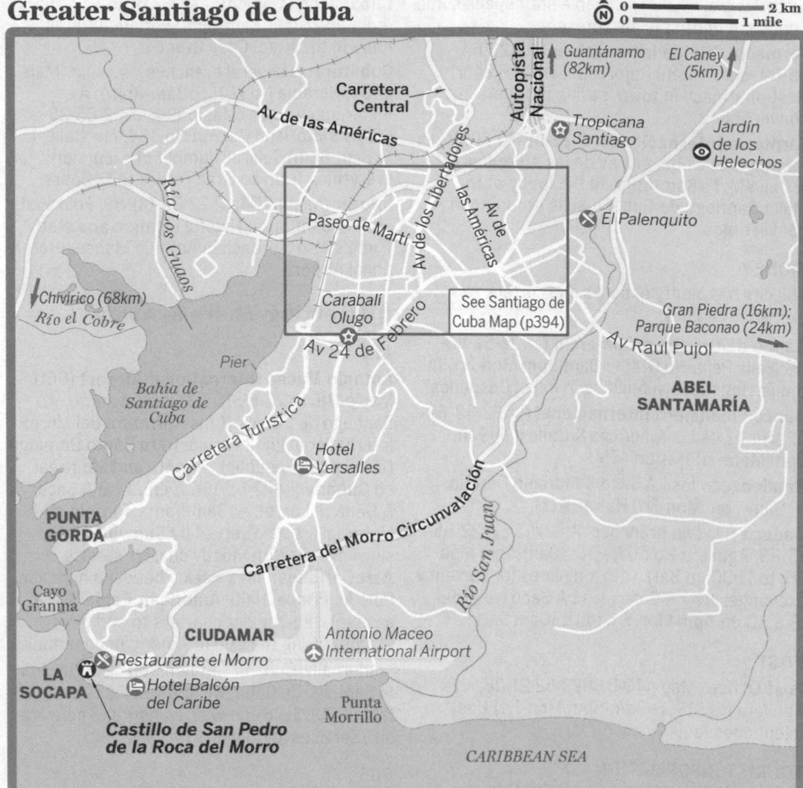

TRAIN

The modern French-style **train station** (☎22-62-28-36; cnr Av Jesús Menéndez & Martí; to Havana CUC$30) is situated near the rum factory northwest of the center. The *Tren Francés* leaves every fourth day for Havana (minimum 16 hours) stopping at Camagüey and Santa Clara en route. Check ahead regarding departure times.

Another slower *coche motor* (cross-island) train plies the route to Havana when a *Tren Francés* isn't running, additionally stopping at Las Tunas, Ciego de Ávila, Guayos and Matanzas.

Cuban train schedules are fickle, so you should always verify beforehand what train leaves when and get your ticket as soon as possible thereafter.

TRUCK

Intermittent passenger trucks leave **Serrano Intermunicipal Bus Station** (Map p394; cnr Av Jesús Menéndez & Sánchez Hechavarría; MN$5) near the train station to Guantánamo and Bayamo throughout the day. Prices are a few pesos and early morning is the best time to board. For these destinations, don't fuss with the ticket window; just find the truck parked out front going your way. Trucks for Caletón Blanco and Chivirico also leave from here.

The **Intermunicipal Bus Station** (Map p394; Terminal Cuatro, cnr Av de los Libertadores & Calle 4; MN$1), 2km northeast of Parque Céspedes, has two buses a day to El Cobre. Two daily buses also leave for Baconao from here.

Getting Around

TO/FROM THE AIRPORT

A taxi to or from the airport should cost CUC$10, but drivers will often try to charge you more. Haggle hard before you get in.

You can also get to the airport on bus 212, which leaves from Av de los Libertadores opposite the Hospital de Maternidad. Bus 213 also goes to the airport from the same stop, but visits Punta Gorda first. Both buses stop just beyond the west end of the airport car park to the left of the entrances.

Another option to Havana is **Conectando Cuba** (to Havana incl lunch CUC$51), a long-distance tourist shuttle.

BUS & TRUCK

Useful city buses include **bus 212** to Airport & Ciudamar (Map p404; MN$1), **bus 213** to Punta Gorda (Map p394; MN$1) (both of these buses start from Av de los Libertadores, opposite Hospital de Maternidad, and head south on Felix Peña in the *casco histórico*), and **bus 214, 401 & 407** (Map p394; MN$1) to Siboney (from near Av de los Libertadores No 425). **Bus 5** to El Caney stops on the northwestern corner of Plaza de Marte and at General Cebreco and Calle 3 in Vista Alegre. These buses run every hour or so; more frequent trucks serve the same routes.

Trucks to points north leave from Av de las Américas near Calle M. On trucks and buses you should be aware of pickpockets and wear your backpack in front.

CAR & MOPED

Santiago de Cuba suffers from a chronic shortage of rental cars (especially in peak season). You might find there are none available; though the locals have an indefatigable Cuban ability to *conseguir* (to manage or get) and *resolver* (to resolve or work out). The airport offices usually have better availability than those in town.

Cubacar (☎22-68-71-60; Hotel las Américas, cnr Avs de las Américas & General Cebreco; ⏲8am-10pm) rents out mopeds for CUC$25 per day.

The **Servi-Cupet gas station** (cnr Avs de los Libertadores & de Céspedes; ⏲24hr) is open 24 hours. There's an **Oro Negro gas station** (cnr Av 24 de Febrero & Carretera del Morro) on the Carretera del Morro.

TAXI

There's a **Transtur** (Map p394; ☎22-68-71-60) taxi stand in front of Meliá Santiago de Cuba. Taxis also wait on Parque Céspedes near the cathedral and hiss at you expectantly as you pass. Hammer out a price beforehand. To the airport, costs range between CUC$8 and CUC$10 depending on the state of the car.

Bici-taxis charge about 5 pesos per person per ride.

Siboney

Playa Siboney is Santiago's answer to Havana's Playas del Este, a low-key seaside town 19km east that's more rustic village than deluxe resort. Guarded by precipitous cliffs and dotted with a mixture of craning palms and weather-beaten clapboard houses, the setting here is laid-back. The beach scene that mixes fun-seeking Cuban families and young *santiagüeras* with their older, balder foreign partners. Unfortunately, as of late the town is full of *jejenes* (sand fleas) and *jinteros* (touts). Both will bother you.

While the small crescent of grayish sand is none too inspiring, there's consolation in cheap prices and a good location (on the doorstep of Parque Baconao). For those craving a break from Santiago, it's an okay hideaway.

Sights

Granjita Siboney MUSEUM

(Map p422; CUC$1; ⏲9am-5pm Tue-Sun, to 1pm Mon) Had the Revolution been unsuccessful, this unassuming red-and-white farmhouse 2km inland from Playa Siboney on the road to Santiago de Cuba would be the forgotten site of a rather futile putsch. As it is, it's another shrine to the glorious national episode that is Moncada. From this spot, at 5:15am on July 26, 1953, 26 cars under the command of Fidel Castro left to attack the military barracks in Santiago de Cuba.

The house retains many of its original details, including the dainty room used by the two *compañeras* (female revolutionaries) who saw action, Haydee Santamaría and Melba Hernández. There are also displays of weapons, interesting documents, photos and personal effects related to the attack. Notice the well beside the building, where weapons were hidden prior to the attack.

Overlooking the stony shoreline nearby is an American war memorial dated 1907, recalling the US landing here on June 24, 1898.

Sleeping

There are a good dozen casas particulares in this small seaside settlement.

Ovidio González Salgado CASA PARTICULAR $

(Map p422; ☎22-39-93-40; Av Serrano; r CUC$25-35; ⏲Nov-Apr; ❄) A spacious place with three rooms and multiple terraces. Your best bet is the private top-floor apartment with views of town and sea. With a pleasant owner and great meals.

María González CASA PARTICULAR $

(Map p422; ☎22-39-92-00; rafaelrg47@nauta.cu; Obelisco No 10; CUC$25; P ❄ ≋) Three slightly disheveled rooms are outshone by the terrace with rockers and giant sea views. The swimming pool may or may not be operating. With busy family life, it can be a bit chaotic, but the owner has a 1968 Peugeot available as a taxi – handy in these parts.

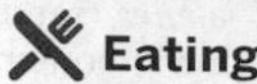

Eating

Eat at the restaurant, or hit the cheap peso food stalls on the beachfront (with care!). There is also an open-air bar on the beach that sells drinks – pay in convertibles.

Sitio del Compay CARIBBEAN **$$**
(Map p422; Av Serrano; meals CUC$5-10; ⏲11am-7pm) Siboney's only real dining option serves no-frills *comida criolla* with friendly service and good beach views. It's in the former house of musical sage turned international icon, Francisco Repilado, aka Compay Segundo, the man responsible for writing the immortal song 'Chan Chan,' which visitors hear on replay across Cuba.

Born in a small shack by this site in 1907, Compay Segundo shot to superstardom at the age of 90 as the guitarist/winking joker in Ry Cooder's Buena Vista Social Club.

Getting There & Away

Bus 214 runs from Santiago de Cuba to Siboney from near Av de los Libertadores No 425, opposite Empresa Universal, with a second stop at Av de Céspedes No 110. It leaves about once hourly between 4am and 8:45am (hit-and-miss thereafter), and bus 407 carries on to Juraguá three times a day. Passenger trucks also shuttle between Santiago de Cuba and Siboney.

A taxi to Playa Siboney will cost CUC$25 to CUC$30, depending on whether it's state or private.

La Gran Piedra

Crowned by a 63,000-ton boulder that perches like a grounded asteroid high above the Caribbean, the Cordillera de la Gran Piedra forms part of Cuba's greenest and most biodiverse mountain range. Not only do the mountains have a refreshingly cool microclimate, they also exhibit a unique historical heritage based on the legacy of some 60 or more coffee plantations set up by French farmers in the latter part of the 18th century.

On the run from a bloody slave rebellion in Haiti in 1791, enterprising Gallic immigrants overcame arduous living conditions and terrain to turn Cuba into the world's number-one coffee producer in the early 19th century. Their craft and ingenuity have been preserved for posterity in a Unesco World Heritage Site centered on the Cafetal la Isabelica. The area is also part of Baconao Unesco Biosphere Reserve, instituted in 1987.

Sights & Activities

The steep 12km road up the mountain range becomes increasingly beautiful as the foliage closes in and the valley opens up below. Mango trees are ubiquitous.

You can visit the ruins of many of the surrounding 60-plus coffee plantations on foot. Trails lead out from Cafetal la Isabelica, but there are no signs.

Cafetal la Isabelica MUSEUM
(Map p422; Carretera Gran Piedra; CUC$2; ⏲8am-4pm) The hub of the Unesco World Heritage Site bestowed in 2000 upon the First Coffee Plantations in the Southeast of Cuba is this impressive two-story stone mansion, with its three large coffee-drying platforms, built in the early 19th century by French émigrés from Haiti. It's a 2km hike beyond La Gran Piedra on a rough road.

The complex includes a workshop and numerous metal artifacts. You can also stroll around the pine-covered plantation grounds at will. It's worth using a guide (for a tip) to show you around as there are no explanatory notices. There were once more than 60 such coffee *cafetales* in the area.

La Gran Piedra MOUNTAIN
(Map p422; Carretera Gran Piedra; CUC$2) It's worth huffing and puffing the 459 stone steps to the summit of La Gran Piedra at 1234m. The huge rock on top measures 51m long and 25m high and weighs...a lot. Its popularity and commercialization goes a little unchecked (cue the eager trinket salespeople on top).

On a clear day there are excellent views out across the Caribbean and on a dark night you are supposedly able to see the lights of Jamaica.

Sleeping

Villa la Gran Piedra HOTEL **$$**
(Map p422; ☎22-68-61-47; Carretera Gran Piedra Km 14.5; s/d CUC$60/68; P ❄) At 1225m, Cuba's highest hotel has rebooted its wooden cabins that were damaged in the 2012 hurricane. They are plain but comfortable, with tile floors and sparse furniture. Their best feature is the abundant vegetation that surrounds them (and views!) Reception is

HISTORIC COFFEE PLANTATIONS

The Cubans have always been enthusiastic coffee drinkers. But, while the shade-loving national coffee crop thrives in the cool tree-covered glades of the Sierra del Escambray and Sierra Maestra, it's not indigenous to the island.

Coffee was first introduced to Cuba in 1748 from the neighboring colony of Santo Domingo, yet it wasn't until the arrival of French planters from Haiti in the early 1800s that the crop was grown commercially.

On the run from Toussaint Louverture's slave revolution, the displaced French found solace in the mountains of Pinar del Río and the Sierra Maestra, where they switched from sugarcane production to the more profitable and durable coffee plant.

Constructed in 1801 in what is now the Sierra del Rosario Reserve in Artemisa Province, the Cafetal Buenavista was the first major coffee plantation in the New World. Not long afterward, planters living in the heavily forested hills around La Gran Piedra began constructing a network of more than 60 *cafetales* (coffee plantations) using pioneering agricultural techniques to overcome the difficult terrain. Their stoic efforts paid off and, by the second decade of the 19th century, Cuba's nascent coffee industry was thriving.

Buoyed by high world coffee prices and aided by sophisticated new growing techniques, the coffee boom lasted from 1800 to about 1820, when the crop consumed more land than sugarcane. At its peak, there were more than 2000 *cafetales* in Cuba, concentrated primarily in the Sierra de Rosario region and the Sierra Maestra to the east of Santiago de Cuba.

Production began to slump in the 1840s with competition from vigorous new economies (most notably Brazil) and a string of devastating hurricanes. The industry took another hit during the War of Independence, though the crop survived and is still harvested today on a smaller scale using mainly traditional methods.

The legacy of Cuba's pioneering coffee industry is best evidenced in the Archaeological Landscape of the First Coffee Plantations in the Southeast of Cuba, a Unesco World Heritage Site dedicated in 2000 that sits in the foothills of the Sierra Maestra close to La Gran Piedra.

at the on-site restaurant, right by the entrance to the La Gran Piedra viewpoint.

Getting There & Away

A steep, winding paved road climbs 1.5 vertical kilometers from the junction with the coast road near Siboney (on the 214 bus route) through *muchos* potholes.

A taxi from Santiago de Cuba will cost approximately CUC$80 to CUC$90 (bargain hard) for the round-trip. Sturdy Cubans and the odd ambitious foreigner hike up 12km from the bus stop at the road junction in Las Guásimas.

Parque Baconao

Wondrous and weird, Parque Baconao covers 800 sq km between Santiago de Cuba and the Río Baconao. The Unesco Biosphere Reserve acts as an important haven for a whole ecosystem, and sports an outdoor car museum and a park of life-sized dinosaur sculptures.

Encased in a shallow chasm fenced in by the Sierra Maestra on one side and the placid Caribbean on the other, Baconao's biodiversity is nothing short of remarkable. There are more than 1800 endemic species of flora – from craning royal palms to prickly cliffside cacti. Fauna includes many types of endangered bats and spiders.

Beaches are smaller than those on the northern coast but there's fishing and some 70 scuba-diving sites nearby, including the *Guarico,* a small steel wreck just south of Playa Sigua. Baconao is also famous for its crabs. From mid-March to early May, tens of thousands of large land crabs fill the coast beyond Playa Verraco.

Sights

Valle de la Prehistoria AMUSEMENT PARK

(Map p422; ☎22-39-92-39; CUC$1; ⏱8am-5pm) The oddest in a plethora of bizarre attractions in Parque Baconao, this Cuban Jurassic Park mixes giant Apatosauruses with concrete cavemen and women, no matter that 57 million years separated their existence. Take in the full 11 hectares of this surreal kitsch park with its 200 life-size concrete

La Gran Piedra & Parque Baconao

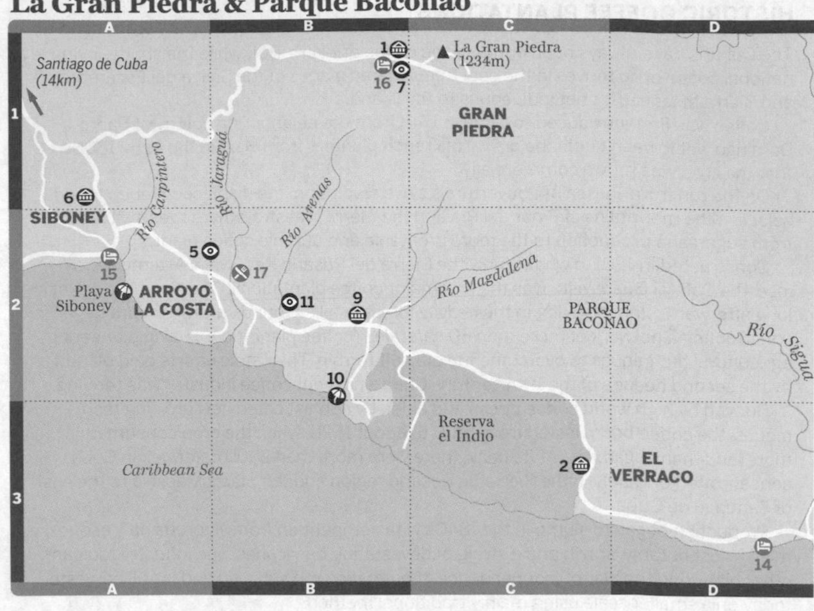

La Gran Piedra & Parque Baconao

Sights

1 Cafetal la Isabelica........B1
2 Comunidad Artística Verraco........C3
3 Criadero de Cocodrilos........E3
4 Exposición Mesoamericana........E3
5 Fiesta Guajira........A2
6 Granjita Siboney........A1
7 La Gran Piedra........B1
8 Laguna Baconao........F3
9 Museo Nacional de Transporte Terrestre........B2
10 Playa Daiquirí........B2
11 Valle de la Prehistoria........B2

Activities, Courses & Tours

12 Centro Internacional de Buceo Carisol los Corales........E3

Sleeping

13 Club Amigo Carisol – Los Corales........E3
14 Hotel Costa Morena........D3
15 María González........A2
Ovidio González Salgado........(see 15)
16 Villa la Gran Piedra........B1

Eating

Fiesta Guajira........(see 5)
17 Finca el Porvenir........B2
Sitio del Compay........(see 15)

dinosaurs built by inmates from a nearby prison. There is a rather lame natural-history museum on-site, as well as a basic Fred Flintstone–style cafe.

Comunidad Artística Verraco GALLERY
(Map p422; 9am-6pm) Ten kilometers past the Playa Daiquirí turn-off lies another village of painters, ceramicists and sculptors who maintain open studios (turn-off unsigned). Here you can visit the artists and buy original works of art. All it lacks is a good organic cafe.

Laguna Baconao LAKE
(Map p422; guided hiking CUC$2) At Laguna Baconao, 2km northeast of Los Corales, you'll find a restaurant, rowboats for hire and several short lakeside hikes, plus a forlorn-looking zoo with crocodiles and the like. The lake supposedly contains 'wild' dolphins. Various trails ply the lakeshore including one that circumnavigates it completely (8km). As it's a flora and fauna reserve you must first hire a guide. Multilingual Norge Ramos Barroso is your main man. Horse riding may also be available.

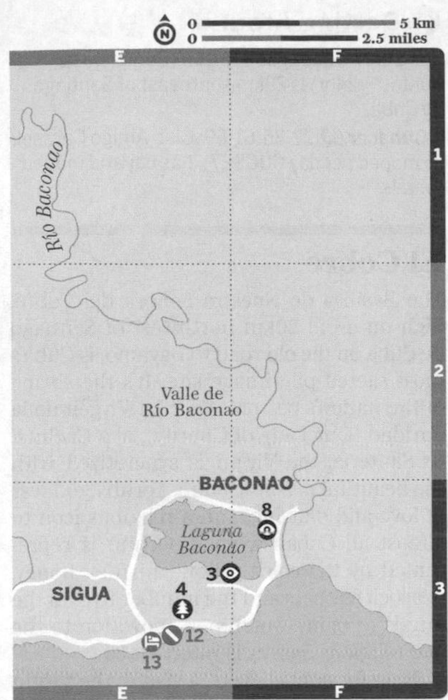

From Playa Baconao at the eastern corner of the lake, the paved road continues 3.5km up beautiful Valle de Río Baconao before turning into a dirt track. Soldiers at a checkpoint at the village turn back vehicles from the direct coastal road to Guantánamo because it abuts the US Naval Base. To continue east, backtrack 50km to Santiago de Cuba and take the inland road.

Museo Nacional de Transporte Terrestre MUSEUM
(Map p422; ☎22-39-91-97; La Punta Km 8.5; CUC$1; ⌚8am-5pm) Anywhere besides Cuba, this alfresco car museum 2km east of Valle de la Prehistoria would impress. There's Benny Moré's 1958 Cadillac, the Chevrolet Raúl Castro got lost in on the way to Moncada Barracks and Cuban singer Rosita Fornés' lovely Ford T-Bird. But where '50s car relics are as common as cheap cigars, it's like a Toyota Yaris museum in Kyoto.

Exposición Mesoamericana PARK
(Map p422; CUC$1) Every Cuban resort area seems to have an attraction replicating indigenous scenes. Here it's the Exposición Mesoamericana, just east of Club Amigo Carisol – Los Corales (p424). Indigenous cave art from Central and South America is arranged in caves along the coastal cliffs.

Fiesta Guajira RANCH
(Map p422; CUC$5; ⌚9am & 2pm Wed & Sun) Situated in the El Oasis artists' community, this Ecotur-run *finca* (farm) formerly ran rodeos but post-hurricane is focused round a rustic restaurant, and a cockpit.

Playa Daiquirí BEACH
(Map p422) Entry to this landmark is prohibited. The main US landings during the Spanish-Cuban-American War took place on June 24, 1898, at this beach, 2km down a side road from the Museo Nacional de Transporte Terrestre. They might have named a cocktail after it, but the area is now a holiday camp for military personnel.

Criadero de Cocodrilos FARM
(Map p422; Laguna Baconao; CUC$1; ⌚8am-5pm) At the Laguna Baconao, 2km northeast of Los Corales, you'll find the Criadero de Cocodrilos, a dozen crocodiles kept in pens below a restaurant, plus other caged animals such as lizards and *jutías* (tree rats). Horses may be for hire, as well as boats to ply the lake.

Activities

Centro Internacional de Buceo Carisol los Corales DIVING
(Map p422; ☎22-35-61-21; www.nauticamarlin.com; Club Amgio Carisol – Los Corales) Situated in the hotel of the same name 45km east of Santiago, this center nevertheless picks up divers at the other hotels daily. Two boats can take up to 20 people to any of the 24 local dive sites. The open-water certification course is CUC$375. There are shipwrecks close to shore and you can feed black groupers by hand.

The water off this bit of coast is some of Cuba's warmest (25°C to 28°C); best visibility is between February and June.

Sleeping

All-inclusives usually close in low season (May to October). Check ahead.

Hotel Costa Morena HOTEL $$
(Map p422; ☎22-35-61-26; all-inclusive s/d CUC$59/80; P ❄ ≋) At the time of writing this longtime hotel was under renovation. It has attractive architecture and a large terrace right on the cliffs but no direct beach access. There is good sea swimming, with protection afforded by a reef. A shuttle takes guests to the beach at Club Amigo Carisol –

Los Corales, at Sigua, 44km southeast of Santiago de Cuba.

Club Amigo Carisol – Los Corales RESORT $$$
(Map p422; ☎22-35-61-21; all-inclusive s/d/tr CUC$98/140/188; P ❄ @ ≋) There's the swim-up bar, umbrellas in the piña coladas, and the government-sponsored band knocking out 'Guantanamera' as you tuck into your lukewarm buffet dinner: you must be back in all-inclusive land. This two-piece Cubanacán resort is situated 44km east of Santiago on the coast's best section of beach (although it's been damaged by successive hurricanes).

Bonuses are a tennis court, a disco, multiple day trips on offer and bright spacious clean rooms. Nonguests can purchase a day pass for CUC$25 including lunch.

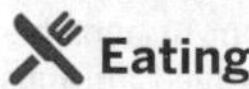

Eating

You'll find resort dining plus scattered roadside restaurants, most active on weekends.

Finca el Porvenir CARIBBEAN $$
(Map p422; ☎22-68-64-94; Carretera de Baconao Km 18; meals CUC$8-12; ⏲9am-5pm) Situated on the left of the main road about 4km east of El Oasis, this Palmares-run *finca* knocks out no-frills *comida criolla* with a great swimming pool and horseback-riding excursions. Dining selection is sparse but the smoked pork chops are surprisingly tasty washed down with a cold Buccanero. The only obstacle to chillaxing is the blaring reggaeton: sound familiar?

Fed by river water constantly circulating out, the swimming pool is clean and refreshingly cool.

Fiesta Guajira CARIBBEAN $$
(Map p422; ☎22-39-95-86; Carretera Baconao, El Oasis; meals CUC$7-10; ⏲9am-5pm) Once a rodeo; now mainly just a restaurant serving *comida criolla* (Creole food).

Getting There & Away

Most people access Baconao's spread-out sights by private car, taxi or as part of an organized tour from Santiago de Cuba.

Bus 415 from the municipal bus terminal in Santiago's Av de los Libertadores plies this route three times a day, but the bus timetables are not set in stone. Check ahead.

When planning your visit, remember the coastal road from Baconao to Guantánamo is closed to nonresidents.

Getting Around

The **Servi-Cupet gas station** (Complejo la Punta; ⏲24hr) is 28km southeast of Santiago de Cuba.

Cubacar (☎22-35-61-69; Club Amigo Carasol; ⏲moped per day CUC$27) has car and moped rentals.

El Cobre

The Basílica de Nuestra Señora del Cobre, high on a hill 20km northwest of Santiago de Cuba on the old road to Bayamo, is Cuba's most sacred pilgrimage site. It's the shrine of the nation's patron saint: La Virgen de la Caridad (Our Lady of Charity), aka Cachita. In Santería, the Virgin is syncretized with the beautiful *orisha* Ochún, Yoruba goddess of love and dancing, and a religious icon to almost all Cuban women. Ochún is represented by the color yellow, mirrors, honey, peacock feathers and the number five. In the minds of many worshipers, devotion to the two religious figures is intertwined.

Even for nonbelievers, a visit to the Virgin is a fascinating look in to local culture. The road to the basilica is lined with sellers of elaborate flower wreaths, intended as offerings to La Virgen, and hawkers of miniature 'Cachitas'.

Sights

Basílica de Nuestra Señora del Cobre CHURCH
(⏲6am-6pm) Stunning as it materializes above the village of El Cobre, Cuba's most revered religious site shimmers against the verdant hills behind. Recently renovated – along with many other of Cuba's churches – the church's interior is impressive; light, but not ostentatious with some vivid stained glass. The existing basilica dates to 1927, though a sanctuary has existed on this site since 1648. There's an unending line of pilgrims, many of whom will have traveled from as far as the US.

Visitors maintain a respectful silence and light prayer candles (purchased outside). La Virgen resides in a glass case high above the altar. For such a powerful entity, she's absolutely diminutive, some 40cm from crown to the hem of her golden robe. Check out the fine Cuban coat of arms in the center, a wondrous work of embroidery.

Most of the donations left here (crutches no longer needed, awards gained through prayer) have been removed. In a small chapel at the side of the basilica, there's a small collection drawn from thousands of offerings giving thanks for favors bestowed by the Virgin. Clumps of hair, a TV, a thesis, a tangle of stethoscopes, a raft inner-tube sculpture (suggesting they made it across the Florida Straits safely) and floor-to-ceiling clusters of teeny metal body parts crowd the room.

Monumento al Cimarrón MONUMENT
A 10-minute hike up a stone staircase brings you to this anthropomorphic sculpture commemorating the 17th-century copper-mine slave revolt. It's now the location of one of Cuba's most important Santería gatherings in July, Ceremonia a las Cimarrones (part of the Fiesta del Caribe). Views are superb from up here; walk to the far side of the sculpture for a vista of copper-colored cliffs hanging over the aqua-green reservoir.

The way here is signposted in El Cobre.

Festivals & Events

Ceremonia a las Cimarrones RELIGIOUS
(Jul) As part of Santiago's Fiesta del Caribe, there's a Santería religious service at the Monumento al Cimarrón.

Sleeping

Hospedaría el Cobre HOSTEL $
(22-34-62-46; r MN$30) This large building behind the basilica has a pleasant sitting room and 15 basic rooms with one to three beds with bath charged in *moneda nacional* (not CUC). Meal times are 7am, 11am and 6pm. The nuns are very hospitable. House rules include no drinking or unmarried couples. Convertible donations to the sanctuary are appreciated. Reserve up to 15 days ahead.

The downstairs lobby displays information about the history of the Virgin and the church from the 1600s through to the visit of Pope Benedict XVI in 2012.

Getting There & Away

Bus 2 goes to El Cobre (MN$1) twice a day from Santiago's Intermunicipal Bus Station (p418). Trucks (MN$5), charged in *moneda nacional*, are more frequent on this route.

You can also take Cubataxi from Santiago de Cuba (around CUC$25 round-trip).

If you're driving toward Santiago de Cuba from the west, you can join the Autopista Nacional near Palma Soriano but, unless you're in a hurry, it's better to continue on the Carretera Central via El Cobre, which winds through picturesque hilly countryside.

El Saltón

Basking in well-earned eco-credentials, El Saltón is a tranquil mountain escape in the Tercer Frente municipality. Hills that once echoed with the sound of crackling rifle fire now reverberate to the twitter of tropical birds. Secluded and hard to reach, it consists of a lodge, a hilltop *mirador* (viewpoint) and a 30m cascading waterfall with an adjacent natural pool ideal for swimming. Eco-guides can offer horseback riding, hiking to thermal baths or tours into the nearby coffee and cocoa plantations. Alternatively, you can just wander off on your own through myriad mountain villages with alluring names such as Filé and Cruce de los Baños. While access is difficult, the reward is ample for nature lovers. Check the state of the waterfall with Cubamar (p417) in Santiago, it can seasonally run dry.

Sleeping

Villa el Saltón HOTEL $$
(22-56-63-26; Carretera Puerto Rico a Filé; s/d with breakfast CUC$45/65; P) Run by Cubamar, this 22-room lodge spreads over three blocks, nestled like hidden tree houses amid thick foliage. Invigorating extras include a sauna, hot tub, massage facilities and the hotel's defining feature, a refreshing natural waterfall and pool. The OK restaurant/bar is popular for billiards, adjacent to a gushing river. Rooms themselves are nothing special.

Getting There & Away

To get to El Saltón, continue west from El Cobre to Cruce de los Baños, 4km east of Filé village. El Saltón is 3km south of Filé. With some tough negotiating in Santiago de Cuba, a sturdy taxi will take you here for CUC$90.

Chivirico & Around

POP 5800

Chivirico, 75km southwest of Santiago de Cuba and 106km east of Marea del Portillo, is the only town of any significance on the enticing south-coast highway, a roller-coaster of plummeting mountains, crinkled bays and crashing surf that makes up one of Cuba's loveliest road trips. Transport links are

OFF THE BEATEN TRACK

CUBA'S BEST & WORST ROAD

The 180km-long coastal road that connects Santiago de Cuba with the small isolated village of Pilón in Granma Province is the best in Cuba for raw natural beauty, but the absolute *worst* for drivers weaned on smooth asphalt instead of endless gaping potholes.

Not surprisingly, traffic on the road is extremely light, and no regular buses operate west of Chivirico. Sturdy taxis and rental cars can ply the route if road conditions are agreeable, but make sure the car is well-maintained and check ahead to see if the road is blocked, closed or washed away. Taxi drivers were asking approximately CUC$160 for the one-way trip between Santiago and the Marea del Portillo hotels at last visit.

Another option is to use a bicycle. Caught between escarpment and sea, the road makes for a truly epic ride, but beware: there are very few facilities, scant places to eat and drink along the way and, should you have bike problems in the remoter areas, only occasional vehicles pass by. Although the route generally hugs the coast, it periodically ascends and descends steep headlands requiring proper gears and a good level of fitness.

Fortunately, the magnificence of the scenery makes slow travel highly desirable. This remote segment of southeast Cuba has remained completely and utterly unspoiled, a glorious ribbon of hidden bays and crashing surf backed by precipitous cloud-covered mountains. On the land side the road skirts the foothills of Cuba's two highest mountain massifs topped by Pico Turquino and Pico Bayamesa. The mountains create a rain shadow effect rendering their southern slopes dry and speckled with dwarf foliage.

Settlements are bucolic and etched in revolutionary folklore. El Uvero and La Plata were the sites of guerrilla attacks in the 1950s by Castro's nascent army, while just off the coast lie the wrecks of two Spanish destroyers sunk in the Cuban-Spanish-American war.

Those attempting a cycling journey should stock up on food and water in Santiago, and spread the ride over three days with planned stops in Brisas Sierra Mar, Campismo La Mula (p428; check availability in Santiago) and **Hotel Marea del Portillo** (☎23-59-70-08; all-inclusive s/d/tr CUC$40/80/90).

relatively good up until Chivirico but, heading west, they quickly deteriorate.

Chivirico itself has little to offer, although there's some rugged hiking across the Sierra Maestra if you can get permission.

Sleeping

Campismo Caletón Blanco CABIN $

(☎22-62-57-97; Caletón Blanco Km 30, Guamá; d incl breakfast CUC$20; P ❄) One of two handy campismos situated along this route (the other is La Mula). This is one of Cubamar's top campismos, the closest to Santiago (30km) and the newest. Twenty-two bungalows sleep two to four people. There's also a restaurant, snack bar, bike rental and facilities for campervans. Make your reservations with Cubamar's Santiago de Cuba office (p417) before arrival.

Brisas Sierra Mar RESORT $$

(☎22-32-91-10; all-inclusive s/d CUC$69/98, day pass CUC$27; P ❄ @ ≋) Isolated but inviting, this big, pyramid-shaped resort sits on Playa Sevilla, 63km west of Santiago de Cuba and a two-hour drive from the airport. Built into a terraced hillside, a novel elevator leads to a brown-sand beach famous for sand fleas. The highlight: a remarkable coral wall superb for snorkeling is just 50m offshore. Dolphins can frequent these waters too.

As for activities, there are plenty. Horseback riding is available here, there's a Marlin Dive Center on the premises, and plenty of special kids' programs (kids under 13 stay free). The hotel gets a lot of repeat visits. Nonguests can buy a day pass that includes lunch, drinks and sport until 5pm. For those cycling the south coast, it's a nice indulgence.

Getting There & Away

Trucks run to Chivirico throughout the day from the Serrano Intermunicipal Bus Station (p418) opposite the train station in Santiago de Cuba. There are also three local buses a day.

Theoretically, one daily truck trundles along to Campismo la Mula and the Pico Turquino trailhead. Transport on to Marea del Portillo is almost unheard of and road conditions vary from bad to downright impassable.

Pico Turquino Area

Near the border of Granma and Santiago de Cuba Provinces, the pinprick settlement of Las Cuevas is the starting point for arduous ascents of Cuba's highest mountain. It's possible in a very long day trip. With guides, visitors can through-hike to Alto del Naranjo and Santo Domingo in Granma Province with an overnight.

Sights

Museo de la Plata MUSEUM

(Map p382; CUC$1; Tue-Sat) Five kilometers west of Las Cuevas (which is 40km west of El Uvero) is this small museum at La Plata, just below the highway. The first successful skirmish of the Cuban Revolution happened here on January 17, 1957. Museum exhibits include the piece of paper signed by the 15 *Granma* survivors who met up at Cinco Palmas in late 1956.

Marea del Portillo is 46km to the west. Don't confuse this La Plata with Comandancia La Plata, Fidel Castro's Sierra Maestra Revolutionary headquarters.

Activities

Hiking Turquino

There are two routes to access **Pico Turquino** (Map p382). Access via Las Cuevas requires a long ascent to traverse to the trailhead in Santo Domingo in Granma Province.

If summiting the mountain is your main aim, this is probably the quickest, easiest route. If you want to immerse yourself in the area's history and hike to Comandancia la Plata, set out from Santo Domingo. Both options can be linked in a spectacularly thorough trek with Ecotur (p406). Onward transportation is better from the Santo Domingo side).

Ecotur in Santiago offers an intensive day trip (per person CUC$130), an overnight (CUC$171) and a three-day expedition which includes Comandancia de la Plata (CUC$201) Costs include entrance fee, transportation from Santiago, food, basic lodging and guides. It's possible to arrange it as a through-hike, ending in Santo Domingo, or out-and-back. The hike from Las Cuevas may also be organized at relatively short notice at the trailhead.

Camps & Shelters

Located 12km east of the trailhead, Campismo la Mula (p428) is handy for those entering the area late or on their way out. Self-sufficient hikers can also pitch tents or use the basic accommodations at Las Cuevas Visitors Center (p428). Paid here, the entry fee includes a compulsory Cuban guide.

You can stay overnight at the rudimentary shelter on Pico Cuba (an additional CUC$30) if you don't want to descend the same day. There's a basic kitchen, wood-fired stove and plank beds (no mattresses) or, if those are taken, floor space.

The Route

The trail from Las Cuevas begins on the south-coast highway, 7km west of Ocujal and 51km east of Marea del Portillo. This trek also passes Cuba's second-highest peak, Pico Cuba (1872m). Allow at least six hours to go up and four hours to come down, more if it has been raining, as the trail floods and turns slick with mud.

The hike is grueling: you're gaining almost 2km in elevation across only 9.6km of trail. But shade and peek-a-boo views provide plenty of respite. Fill up on water before setting out.

Be sure you're on the trail by 6:30am at the latest for the out-and-back day hike.

The well-marked route leads from Las Cuevas to La Esmajagua (600m; 3km; there's water here), Pico Cardero (1265m; quickly followed by a series of nearly vertical steps called Saca la Lengua, literally 'flops your tongue out'), Pico Cuba (1872m; 2km; water and shelter here) and Pico Turquino (1972m; 1.7km). When the fog parts and you catch your breath, you'll behold a bronze bust of José Martí standing on the summit of Cuba's highest mountain.

Record-breakers should note that the (unofficial) summit record by a guide is two hours, 45 minutes.

What to Bring

Trekkers should bring sufficient food, warm clothing, a sleeping bag and a poncho – precipitation is common up here (some 2200mm annually), from a soft drizzle to pelting hail. Carry everything you need plus extra food to share if you can carry it and a little something for the *compañeros*

WORTH A TRIP

EL UVERO

A major turning point in the revolutionary war took place in this nondescript settlement 23km west of Chivirico, on May 28, 1957, when Castro's rebel army – still numbering less than 50 after six months on the run – audaciously took out a government position guarded by 53 of Batista's soldiers. By the main road are two red trucks taken by the rebels and nearby a double row of royal palms leads to a large monument commemorating the brief but incisive battle. It's a poignant, little-visited spot. To visit, take a taxi from Chivirico or consult Ecotur (p406) in Santiago.

(comrades) who take 15-day shifts up on Pico Cuba.

Ask ahead if you would like an English-speaking guide (there are several, but most are based on the Santo Domingo side). Also ask about food provision at Pico Cuba. Drinks are available for purchase at the Las Cuevas trailhead. Tipping the guides is mandatory – CUC$3 to CUC$5 is sufficient.

Diving

Cristóbal Colón DIVING
Cuba's greatest wreck dive, the well-preserved Spanish cruiser *Cristóbal Colón* sank in 1898, about 15m down and only 30m offshore at La Mula. This is a genuine remnant of the Spanish-Cuban-American War. Visit with dive centers from Brisas Sierra Mar (p426) or Club Amigo Carisol-Los Corales (p424) (in Parque Baconao). Without scuba gear you can see the wreck with a mask and snorkel.

Sleeping

Campismo la Mula CABIN $
(☎22-32-62-62; Carretera Granma Km 120; r CUC$16) On a remote pebble beach, 12km east of the Pico Turquino trailhead, La Mula has 50 small cabins popular with holidaying Cubans, hikers destined for Turquino and the odd hitchhiking south-coast adventurer. It's pretty much the only option on this isolated stretch of coast. Check with Cubamar (p417) in Santiago before turning up.

There's a rustic cafe and restaurant onsite.

Information

Las Cuevas Visitors Center (Map p382; Las Cuevas; entry CUC$15, camera fee CUC$5) At the coastal trailhead to Pico Turquino.

Getting There & Away

The Las Cuevas trailhead is located 130km west of Santiago de Cuba on the remote coastal road. If you are headed here with **Ecotur** (p406), ensure that transportation is included.

Private trucks and the odd rickety bus connect La Mula to Chivirico, but they are sporadic; don't bank on more than one per day. A taxi from Santiago costs CUC$100 to CUC$120 – at this point you see why booking the trip as a tour offers little price difference. Traffic is almost nonexistent in this neck of the woods, but the views are fabulous.

Guantánamo Province

☎21 / POP 511,000

Includes ➡

Best Places to Eat

- Restaurante Las Terrazas Casa Nilson (p443)
- El Buen Sabor (p443)
- Sabor Melián (p433)
- Restaurante La Punta (p443)

Best Places to Sleep

- Villa Maguana (p445)
- Casa Colonial Ykira Mahiquez (p440)
- La Casona (p440)

Why Go?

A fantasy land of crinkled mountains and exuberant foliage, the Cuban Guantánamo remains a galaxy away from modern America in ambience. That doesn't stop most people associating it with the United States Guantanamo Bay Naval Base, which continues in operation, though downsized. Off the base, the region's isolated valleys and wild coastal microclimates (arid in the south, lush in the north) are Cuba at its most mysterious and esoteric. Herein lie primitive musical subgenres, little-known Afro-Cuban religious rites, and echoes of an indigenous Taíno culture supposedly wiped out by the Spanish centuries ago – or so you thought.

Though brutally battered by Hurricane Matthew in October, 2016, Baracoa and its rural surroundings remain the regional highlight, closely followed by the vibrant endemism of the semivirgin Parque Nacional Alejandro de Humboldt. Further west, the city of Guantánamo, perennially bypassed by most travelers, represents the Cuba rarely tasted by tourists.

When to Go

- Baracoa's biggest festival, the Semana de la Cultura Baracoesa, takes place in late March/early April with an eruption of music, dance and cultural activities.
- Non-touristy Guantánamo lights a fire in mid-December for the sultry Festival Nacional de Changüí, the ancestor of the modern salsa.
- Hurricanes and bad storms mar the months of September and October, making this period the best time to avoid Baracoa.
- Guantánamo's climate varies hugely, but it's dependent more on geography than the seasons, meaning mountain passes and lush parks stay wetter than the dry coastal areas.

Guantánamo Province Highlights

1. **Parque Nacional Alejandro de Humboldt** (p445) Searching for the world's smallest frog in the most diverse national park in the Caribbean.
2. **Baracoa** (p442) Sampling the exotic culinary delights of the city.
3. **La Farola** (p436) Cycling the ultra-scenic lighthouse road from Cajobabo to Baracoa.
4. **Zoológico de Piedras** (p435) Getting an eyeful of the homespun artistry of these stony statues.
5. **El Yunque** (p444) Ascending tropical jungle to summit Baracoa's mysterious flat-topped mountain.
6. **Guantánamo** (p431) Uncovering multiple music genres belonging to this forgotten city.
7. **Boca de Yumurí** (p436) Boating upstream from the river mouth to the jaws of a narrow river gorge.

Guantánamo

POP 217,400

Famous for all the wrong reasons, Guantánamo is most often bypassed by travelers on the Santiago–Baracoa bus. The malnourished grid of crusty buildings might not look appealing, but employ some Sherlock Holmes-style sleuthing and a little faltering Spanish and you will find Cuban soul aplenty.

Guantánamo created its own indigenous music genre *(changüí)*, claims one of Cuba's three legendary Tumba Francesa (French-Haitian song and dance) troupes; supports an active West Indian social club; and exhibits a distinct subgenre of eclectic architecture spearheaded by the intricate work of Leticio Salcines.

'Discovered' by Columbus during his second voyage in 1494, the settlement wasn't built until 1819, when French plantation owners evicted from Haiti founded the town of Santa Catalina del Saltadero del Guaso. In 1843, the burgeoning city became Guantánamo. In 1903, the US Navy took up residence in the bay next door. Sparks have been flying ever since.

Sights

Guantánamo's geometric city grid is easy to navigate. Tree-lined Av Camilo Cienfuegos, a few blocks south of Bartolomé Masó, with its bizarre sculptures and central Rambla-style walkway, is the best place for a walk.

Parque Martí SQUARE

Anchored by the tiny Parroquia de Santa Catalina de Riccis (1863), the renovated Parque Martí features information boards and a clutch of interesting shops, restaurants and entertainment nooks strung along vibrant boulevards. Sitting timelessly amid the action is a seated statue of 'El Maestro', from whom the square takes its name.

Palacio Salcines NOTABLE BUILDING

(cnr Pedro A Pérez & Prado; hours vary) Local architect Leticio Salcines (1888–1973) left a number of impressive works around Guantánamo, including his personal residence built in 1916, a lavish monument said to be the building most representative of the city. The palacio is now a museum of colorful frescoes, Japanese porcelain and the like. Opening times can be sporadic

On the palace's turret is La Fama, a sculpture designed by Italian artist Americo Chine that serves as the symbol of Guantánamo, her trumpet announcing good and evil.

Plaza Mariana Grajales SQUARE

The huge, bombastic Monument to the Heroes, glorifying the Brigada Fronteriza 'that defends the forward trench of socialism on this continent,' dominates Plaza Mariana Grajales, 1km northwest of the train station and opposite Hotel Guantánamo. It's one of the more impressive 'revolution squares' on the island.

Biblioteca Policarpo Pineda Rustán LIBRARY

(21-32-33-52; cnr Los Maceos & Emilio Giro; 8am-5pm Mon-Sat) Another architectural gift from Leticio Salcines is this beautiful provincial library that was once the city hall (1934–51). Trials for Fulgencio Batista's thugs were held here in 1959, and a number were killed when they snatched a rifle and tried to escape.

Museo Provincial MUSEUM

(21-32-58-72; cnr José Martí & Prado; CUC$1; 8am-noon & 12:30-4:30pm Mon-Fri, 8am-noon Sat) Housed in an old jail guarded by two canons, the city museum has *salas* (rooms) dedicated to aboriginal culture, local nature, weapons (lots of Mambí swords) and decorative arts.

Parroquia de Santa Catalina de Riccis CHURCH

(Parque Martí) This unspectacular but noble church dates from 1863. In front is a statue of local hero, Mayor General Pedro A Pérez, erected in 1928, opposite a tulip fountain and diminutive *glorieta* (bandstand).

Tours

Oficina de Patrimonio WALKING

(21-35-14-37; Los Maceos, btwn Emilio Giro & Flor Crombet; 8:30am-4:30pm Mon-Fri) For a fuller exposé of Guantánamo's interesting architectural heritage, ask here about walking tours. There are various offered, including 'In the Footsteps of José Lecticio Salcines' (the architect).

Festivals & Events

Festival Nacional de Changüí MUSIC

(mid-Dec) Mid-December celebration of *changüí* music, a regional style considered a predecessor of *son montuno* and modern salsa that employs African rhythms and Spanish guitar.

Noches Guantanameras FIESTA

(⌚8pm Sat) Saturday night is reserved for this local coming together, when Calle Pedro A Pérez closes to traffic and stalls are set up in the street: come and enjoy whole roast pig, belting music and copious amounts of rum.

Sleeping

The upside of Guantánamo having little tourism means that hotels come cheap here, though casas particulares are probably the best option.

Casa Norka CASA PARTICULAR $

(☎21-35-45-12; Calixto García No 766, btwn Prado & Jesús del Sol; r CUC$25; ❄🏊) With just enough quirk to keep you interested (hello, Beyoncé and JLo posters). Rooms are large and well-kept and there's a very nice inner patio with plants and tiny pool.

Lissett Foster Lara CASA PARTICULAR $

(☎21-32-59-70; Pedro A Pérez No 761, btwn Prado & Jesús del Sol; r CUC$25; ❄) Like many *guantanameras,* Lissett speaks perfect English and her house is polished, comfortable and decked out with the kind of plush fittings that wouldn't look amiss in a North American suburb. There are three rooms, including a delightful one on the substantial roof terrace.

Hotel Brasil HOTEL $

(☎21-32-43-32; Calixto García btw Miro & Crombet; s/d CUC$13/20; ❄) At these prices, how much can you expect? The 35 economical, clean rooms smell only slightly musty, a pleasant surprise given the dark reception area blaring reggaeton. In case you wondered, staff is indifferent.

Hotel Guantánamo HOTEL $$

(☎21-38-10-15; Calle 13 Norte, btwn Ahogados & 2 de Octubre; s/d incl breakfast CUC$54/64; P❄📶🏊) Hotel Guantánamo is some-

Guantánamo

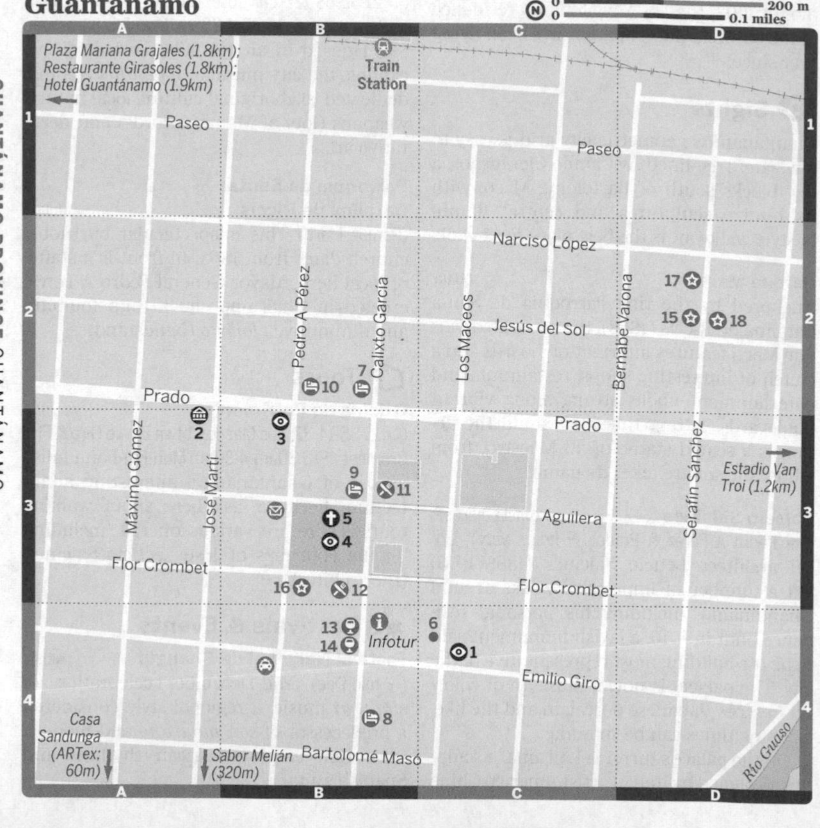

thing approaching comfortable. The generic rooms are clean, the pool has water in it, and there's a good lobby bar-cafe mixing up tempting mojitos and serving coffee. It's 1km northwest of the train station.

Hotel Martí HOTEL **$$**
(☎21-32-95-00; magdalaine.borges@hotelmarti.tur.cu; cnr Aguilera & Calixto García; s/d CUC$74/85; ❄📶) Overlooking Parque Martí, this somewhat refurbished colonial exudes some elegance, but buyer beware: check your room carefully for potential leaks (note water stains on the walls). Entertainment-wise, there's the rooftop-terrace restaurant with deafening music and the street-level bar circled by *jinteras* (female touts). Islazul sells discounted rooms through agencies.

Eating

★ Sabor Melián CARIBBEAN **$**
(☎21-32-44-22; Camilo Cienfuegos No 407; meals CUC$3-7; ⊙noon-midnight) With a discreet entrance on a busy avenue, this locals' favorite features good service and quality Caribbean chow. Don't fear going face-to-face with the whole fried snapper – under crisp skin the meat is incredibly moist. Less inspiring is the dark, air-conditioned interior with original art and reggaeton videos.

Restaurante 1870 CUBAN **$**
(☎21-32-05-40; Flor Crombet; meals CUC$2-5; ⊙7am-9am, noon-3pm & 6-11pm) If not for this place opposite Parque Martí, Guantánamo's colonial heyday would go unnoticed. Climb a sweeping marble staircase to the plush balcony-bar gazing down on the main eating area. Prices are more than reasonable and the *ropa vieja* (shredded beef in a tangy sauce) is not bad. Dress code is no shorts or tank tops.

Restaurante Girasoles CARIBBEAN **$**
(☎21-38-41-78; Calle 15 Norte, cnr Ahogados; meals CUC$1-5; ⊙10am-10pm) A nude statue rather than a *girasol* (sunflower) marks the entrance to what is, by process of elimination, one of Guantánamo's best restaurants. Behind the Hotel Guantánamo, Girasoles serves up (albeit at a snail's pace) chicken and fish, occasionally in interesting sauces. The terrace is popular for an afternoon drink.

Bar-Restaurante Olimpia BURGERS **$**
(cnr Calixto García & Aguilera; mains CUC$2; ⊙9am-midnight) A celebration of Guantánamo's remarkable Olympic Games performances, this bar-restaurant displays baseball shirts, athletics memorabilia and the boxing vest of three-time Olympic gold medalist Félix Savón (a local boy). Inside there's a small open patio and a mezzanine bar where you can enjoy beers and Cuban-style burgers, all with a vista of adjacent Parque Martí.

Drinking & Nightlife

Casa de las Promociones Musicales 'La Guantanamera' CLUB
(☎21-32-72-66; Calixto García, btwn Flor Crombet & Emilio Giro; ⊙hours vary) Another well-maintained concert-orientated venue, with Thursday rap *peñas* (performances) and Sunday *trova* (traditional poetic singing) matinees.

La Ruina BAR
(☎21-32-95-65; cnr Calixto García & Emilio Giro; ⊙9:30am-midnight) This shell of a ruined

Guantánamo

Sights
1 Biblioteca Policarpo Pineda Rustán C4
2 Museo Provincial A3
3 Palacio Salcines B3
4 Parque Martí B3
5 Parroquia de Santa Catalina de Riccis B3

Activities, Courses & Tours
6 Oficina de Patrimonio C4

Sleeping
7 Casa Norka B2
8 Hotel Brasil B4
9 Hotel Martí B3
10 Lissett Foster Lara B2

Eating
11 Bar-Restaurante Olimpia B3
12 Restaurante 1870 ..... B3

Drinking & Nightlife
13 Casa de las Promociones Musicales 'La Guantanamera' B4
14 La Ruina B4

Entertainment
15 Casa de Changüí D2
16 Casa de la Trova B3
17 Casa del Son D2
18 Tumba Francesa Pompadour D2

colonial building has 9m ceilings and there are plenty of benches to prop you up after you've downed your nth beer. There's a popular karaoke scene for those with reality-TV ambitions. The bar menu's good for a snack lunch.

☆ Entertainment

Guantánamo bleeds music. The city's own distinctive musical culture is enshrined in a subgenre of *son* known as *changüí*.

★ Tumba Francesa Pompadour LIVE MUSIC
(Serafín Sánchez No 715; ⌚9:30am-1pm, from 7pm 2nd & 4th Tue) One of only three Tumba Francesa societies left in Cuba, this house, situated four blocks east of the train station, specializes in a unique form of Haitian-style dancing. Programs include *mi tumba baile* (dance) on Tuesdays, *encuentro tradicional* (traditional get-together) and *peña campesina* (country music). If closed, consult showtimes at the Casa de Changüí opposite.

Casa de Changüí LIVE MUSIC
(☎21-32-41-78; Serafín Sánchez No 710, btwn N López & Jesús del Sol; ⌚9am-noon, 2-6pm & 7pm-midnight Tue-Sun) As primary pulpit for Guantánamo's indigenous music, this is *the* place to experience *changüí* and is a shrine to its main exponent, local *timbalero* (percussionist) Elio Revé. There's a small Sala de Historia museum onsite.

Casa Sandunga (ARTex) LIVE MUSIC
(☎21-35-54-99; Máximo Gómez No 1062; CUC$1; ⌚8pm-1am Tue-Sun) Housed in a royal-blue building on a quiet street, this spot for variety shows and humor is openly referred to as 'the place.'

Casa del Son LIVE MUSIC
(☎21-32-41-78; cnr Serafin Sánchez & Prado; ⌚5pm-midnight) A new venue for old music, this *casa* shares lovingly restored digs with the Casa de Changüí in Calle Serafin Sánchez, the city's boisterous 'music street.'

Casa de la Trova LIVE MUSIC
(cnr Pedro Pérez & Flor Crombet; CUC$1; ⌚9am-noon, 2-6pm & 7pm-midnight) It's hard not to love this scene: a traditional music house with old men in Panama hats casting aside their arthritis to dance athletically.

Estadio Van Troi SPECTATOR SPORT
(☎21-32-71-13) Baseball games are played from October to April at this stadium in Reparto San Justo, 1.5km south of the Servi-Cupet gas station. Despite a strong sporting tradition, Guantánamo – nicknamed Los Indios – are perennial underachievers who seldom make the play-offs.

ℹ Information

INTENET ACCESS

There's wi-fi in Parque Martí and on the surrounding pedestrian-only blocks.

Etecsa Telepunto (☎21-32-78-78; cnr Aguilera & Los Maceos; internet per hour CUC$1.50; ⌚8:30am-7:30pm) Four computers plus hardly any tourists equals no queues. Sells wi-fi scratchcards.

MEDICAL SERVICES

Hospital Agostinho Neto (☎21-35-54-50; Carretera de El Salvador Km 1; ⌚24hr) This hospital at the west end of Plaza Mariana Grajales near Hotel Guantánamo will help foreigners in emergencies.

Farmacia Internacional (☎21-35-11-29; Flor Crombet No 305, btwn Calixto García & Los Maceos; ⌚9am-5pm) Pharmacy on the northeast corner of Parque Martí.

MONEY

Banco de Crédito y Comercio (☎21-32-73-21; Calixto García, btwn Emilio Giro & Bartolomé Masó; ⌚9am-3pm Mon-Fri) One of two branches on this block, with ATM.

Cadeca (☎21-35-59-09; cnr Calixto García & Prado; ⌚8am-4pm) Money changing.

POST

Post Office (☎21-38-20-11; Pedro A Pérez; ⌚8am-1pm & 2-6pm Mon-Sat) On the west side of Parque Martí.

TOURIST INFORMATION

Infotur (☎21-35-19-93; infotur@guantanamo.infotur.tur.cu; Calixto García btwn Flor Crombet & Emilio Giro; ⌚8:30am-5pm Mon-Sat) Helpful tourist information office, closes for an (unspecified) hour for lunch.

TRAVEL AGENCIES

Havanatur (☎21-32-63-65; Aguilera, btwn Calixto García & Los Maceos; ⌚8am-noon & 1:30-4:30pm Mon-Fri, 8:30-11:30am Sat) Travel agency.

ℹ Getting There & Away

AIR

Cubana (☎21-35-54-53; Calixto García No 817) flies four times a week (CUC$159 one way, 2½ hours) from Havana to Mariana Grajales Airport (also known as Los Canos Airport). There are no international flights.

BUS

The rather inconveniently placed Terminal de Ómnibus (bus station) is 5km west of the center on the old road to Santiago (a continuation of Av Camilo Cienfuegos). A taxi from the Hotel Guantánamo should cost CUC$3 to CUC$4.

There are two daily **Víazul** (☎21-32-96-40; www.viazul.com; bus terminal) buses to Baracoa (CUC$10, three hours, 3:30am and 9:30am) and one to Santiago de Cuba (CUC$6, 1¾ hours, 11:30pm).

CAR

The Autopista Nacional to Santiago de Cuba ends near Embalse la Yaya, 25km west of Guantánamo, where the road joins the Carretera Central (work to extend this road continues).

To drive to Guantánamo from Santiago de Cuba, follow the Autopista Nacional north about 12km to the top of the grade, then take the first turn to the right. Signposts are sporadic and vague, so take a good map and keep alert.

TRAIN

The **train station** (☎21-32-55-18; Pedro A Pérez; trains to Havana CUC$32), several blocks north of Parque Martí, has one departure for Havana (CUC$32, 19 hours) every fourth day via Camagüey, Ciego de Ávila, Santa Clara and Matanzas.

Purchase tickets in the morning of the day the train departs at the office on Pedro A Pérez.

TRUCK

Trucks to Santiago de Cuba and Baracoa leave from the Terminal de Ómnibus and allow you to disembark in the smaller towns in between.

Trucks for Moa park on the road to El Salvador north of town near the entrance to the Autopista.

Cost for any trip is generally CUC$1 or less.

Getting Around

Taxis hang out around Parque Martí. Bus 48 (20 centavos) runs between the center and the Hotel Guantánamo every 40 minutes or so. There are also plenty of bici-taxis (around CUC$2).

South Coast

The long, dry coastal road from Guantánamo to the island's eastern extremity, Punta de Maisí, is Cuba's spectacular semidesert region, where cacti nestle on rocky ocean terraces and prickly aloe vera pokes out from the scrub. Several little stone beaches between Playa Yacabo and Cajobabo make refreshing pit stops for those with time to linger, while the diverse roadside scenery – punctuated at intervals by rugged purple mountains and impossibly verdant riverside oases – impresses throughout.

WORTH A TRIP

ZOOLÓGICO DE PIEDRAS

Surreal even by Cuban standards, the **Zoológico de Piedras** (CUC$1; ⏲9am-6pm Mon-Sat) is an animal sculpture park set amid thick foliage in the grounds of a mountain coffee farm, 20km northeast of Guantánamo. Carved quite literally out of the existing rock by sculptor Angel Iñigo Blanco, starting in the late 1970s, the sculptures now number more than 300 and range from hippos to giant serpents. Señor Blanco passed away in 2014, but the stone zoo continues in his memory.

To get here you'll need your own wheels or a taxi. Head east out of town and fork left toward Jamaica and Honduras. The 'zoo' is in the settlement of Boquerón.

Sights

Playita de Cajobabo BEACH

Cajobabo's main beach is stony and flanked by dramatic cliffs, but nonetheless makes a good snorkeling spot. Follow the road at its far end over a headland and the asphalt deadends at another beach. Walk east along this beach for 400m and you'll come to a boat-shaped monument commemorating the spot where José Martí landed in 1895 to launch the Second War of Independence.

Martí and Gómez arrived in a rowing boat with four others at 10pm on the night of April 11. The disembarkation served as inspiration for Fidel Castro's subsequent landing in *Granma* 61 years later.

Museo de 11 Abril MUSEUM

(☎21-88 63-15; ⏲8am-noon & 1:30-5:30pm) FREE Set in a tiny *casa* on the approach road to Cajobabo beach is the former home of Salustiano Leyva who, at the age of 11 in 1895, helped the freshly landed José Martí and Máximo Gómez to rest and plan their subsequent march west. The museum charts the events with maps and mementos. Leyva lived into the 1970s and was one of the few people to have met both Martí and Castro.

Activities

★La Farola SCENIC DRIVE

One of the seven modern engineering marvels of modern Cuba, the so-called 'Lighthouse road' runs 55km from Cajobabo all the way to Baracoa, connecting cacti-sprinkled semidesert with lush rain forest. There are soaring pines and a lookout at its highest point, Alto de Cotilla.

Sleeping

Campismo Cajobabo CABIN $

(☎21-88-63-04; CUC$12) These rustic cabins at Cajobabo beach are reserved through **Cubamar** (Campismo Popular; ☎21-64-27-76; comercial.baracoa@campismopopular.cu; Martí No 225) in Baracoa

Getting There & Away

Buses between Guantanamo and Baracoa ply this road twice daily; otherwise you can get here via bicycle, private transportation or a taxi.

Punta de Maisí

From Cajobabo, the coastal road continues 51km northeast to La Máquina. As far as Jauco, the road is good; thereafter less so. Coming from Baracoa to La Máquina (55km), it's a good road as far as Sabana, then rough in places from Sabana to La Máquina. Either way, La Máquina is the starting point of the very rough, 13km track down to Punta de Maisí. It's best covered in a 4WD but also popular with cyclists.

This is Cuba's easternmost point and there's a lighthouse (1862) and a small, fine white-sand beach. You can see Haiti 70km away on a clear day.

After a long time as an off-limits military zone, the Maisí region has opened up to travelers with day tours to the lighthouse, camping and a new hotel in 2017.

Four-wheel drive safaris (CUC$64 per person, two-person minimum) are run by Infotur (p444) in Baracoa.

For somewhere to stay, the new Islazul hotel, **Faro de Maisí** (☎21-68-96-20; adrian.rivas@hotelgtmo.tur.cu; La Asunción; r incl breakfast $40-60; ❄📶), with an onsite restaurant is a decent choice in an outstanding location. Modern rooms feature generic graphic images, TVs and phones. Superior rooms have mini fridges with refreshments.

Getting There & Away

Visitors can come on a day tour from Baracoa or by private 4WD transportation.

Boca de Yumurí

Five kilometers south of Baracoa a road branches east off La Farola and travels 28km along the coast to Boca de Yumurí at the mouth of Río Yumurí. Near the bridge over the river is the Túnel de los Alemanes (German Tunnel), an amazing natural arch of trees and foliage. Though lovely, the dark-sand beach here has become the day trip from Baracoa. Hustlers hard-sell fried-fish meals, while other people peddle colorful land snails called *polymitas*. They are endangered as a result of their wholesale harvesting for tourists, so refuse all offers.

Activities

Boca de Yumurí makes a superb bike jaunt from Baracoa (56km round-trip): hot but smooth and flat with great views and many potential stopovers (try Playa Bariguá at Km 25). You can arrange bikes in Baracoa – ask at your casa particular.

Boat Taxis BOATING

(CUC$3) From beneath the bridge at the mouth of Río Yumurí, boat taxis head 400m upstream where the steep river banks narrow into a haunting natural gorge. You can arrange to be dropped off here for a picnic on an island in the river delta.

Playa Cajuajo HIKING

Near Boca de Yumurí, this little-visited sandy expanse is accessible via a 5km trail from the Río Mata through biologically diverse woodland. Ecotur (p439) in Baracoa runs trips here.

Eating

Restaurant Tato SEAFOOD $$

(mains CUC$5-9; ⏲8am-midnight) On delightful little Playa Mangalito, this beach-abutting restaurant will prepare you fresh octopus caught in the shallows just yards from your plate.

Getting There & Away

Visitors can access this area via rental car or taxi from Baracoa, though taxis usually cost more than a tour. Organize an excursion either privately or with **Cubatur** (CUC$22) in Baracoa (p439).

GITMO – THE STORY SO FAR

Procured in the aftermath of the Spanish-Cuban-American War via the infamous Platt Amendment in 1903, US naval base in Guantánamo Bay (dubbed Gitmo by US Marines) was first established primarily to protect the eastern approach to the strategically important Panama Canal.

In 1934, an upgrade of the original treaty reaffirmed the lease terms and agreed to honor them indefinitely unless both governments accorded otherwise. It also set an annual rent of US$4085, a sum that the US continues to cough up, but which the Cubans won't bank on the grounds that the occupation is illegal (Fidel Castro allegedly stored the checks in the top drawer of his office desk).

The US naval base sits at the jaws of Guantánamo Bay with military installations on both sides and the interior of the bay actually inside Cuban territory. Facilities include a dozen beaches, a water desalination plant, two airstrips and Cuba's only McDonald's, KFC and Starbucks. Approximately 9500 military personnel have been based here.

The facility's recent history is notorious. In the early '90s, it held thousands of Haitian migrants and Cuban *balseros* (rafters) picked up by the US Coast Guard while trying to reach Florida.

Since 2002 the US has held more than 770 prisoners with suspected Al-Qaeda or Taliban links at Camp Delta in Guantánamo Bay without pressing criminal charges. Denied legal counsel and family contact while facing rigorous interrogations, the detainees mounted hunger strikes. Several committed suicide. In 2004, Amnesty International and the UN called to close the base down amidst Red Cross reports that aspects of the camp regime were tantamount to torture. The US released 420 prisoners, charging just three of them.

In January 2009, President Barack Obama promised to shut down Guantánamo's detention camps, ending what he termed 'a sad chapter in US history.' Bipartisan opposition in Congress prevented the shutdown. International condemnation of the force-feeding of some 100 inmates on hunger strike in May 2013 renewed pressure, yet Congress successively blocked all further attempts to move prisoners to the US for trial.

As of late 2016, 60 prisoners remained in Guantánamo. At least half of them are cleared to leave but, so far, the authorities have struggled to find a country to take them. Meanwhile, the Trump administration has announced plans to reinstate the base as a detainment center.

Baracoa

POP 82,000

Beguiling, outlandish and surreal, Baracoa's essence is addictive. On the wet and windy side of the Cuchillos del Toa mountains, Cuba's oldest and most isolated town exudes original atmosphere.

Feast your eyes upon deep green foliage that's wonderfully abundant after the stark aridity of Guantánamo's south coast. Delve into fantastical legends, and acquaint yourself with an unorthodox cast of local characters. There's Cayamba, the self-styled 'Guerrilla troubadour' who once claimed he was 'the man with the ugliest voice in the world;' La Rusa, an aristocratic Russian émigré who inspired a novel by magic-realist author Alejo Carpentier; and Enriqueta Faber, a French woman who passed herself off as a man to practice as a doctor and marry a local heiress in Baracoa's cathedral in 1819 – likely Cuba's first same-sex marriage. Baracoa – what would Cuba be without you?

While 2016's Hurricane Matthew hit Baracoa hard, the town is already on the rebound.

Sights

In Town

★Museo Arqueológico 'La Cueva del Paraíso' MUSEUM

(Moncada; CUC$3; ⌚8am-5pm) Baracoa's most impressive museum, Las Cuevas del Paraíso is a series of caves that were once Taíno burial chambers. Among nearly 2000 authentic Taíno pieces are unearthed skeletons, ceramics, 3000-year-old petroglyphs and a replica of the Ídolo de Tabaco, a sculpture found in Maisí in 1903 and considered to be one of the most important Taíno finds in the Caribbean.

One of the staff will enthusiastically show you around. The museum is 800m southeast of Hotel El Castillo. Tickets can be purchased at Ecotur.

Casa del Cacao MUSEUM

(☎21-64-21-25; Antonio Maceo, btwn Maraví & Frank País; ⏰7am-11pm) FREE Baracoa, you will quickly ascertain (via your nose), is the center of Cuba's chocolate industry; cocoa is grown hereabouts and subsequently chocolate-ized in a local factory. Thus this museum with cafe chronicles the history of cacao and its importance in eastern Cuba as well as offering cups full of the pure, thick stuff (hot or cold) in a pleasant indoor cafe. It also sells bars of dark, agreeably bitter Baracoan chocolate.

Fuerte Matachín FORT

(Museo Municipal; ☎21-64-21-22; cnr José Martí & Malecón; CUC$1; ⏰8am-noon & 2-6pm) Baracoa is protected by a trio of muscular Spanish forts. This one, built in 1802 at the southern entrance to town, houses the Museo Municipal. The small but beautiful building showcases an engaging chronology of Cuba's oldest settlement including *polymita* snail shells, the story of Che Guevara and the chocolate factory, and the particular strand of music Baracoa gave birth to: *kiribá,* a forefather of *son*.

There are also exhibits relating to Magdalena Menasse (née Rovieskuya, 'La Rusa'), after whom Alejo Carpentier based his famous book, *La Consagración de la Primavera* (The Rite of Spring).

El Castillo de Seboruco FORT

(Loma del Paraíso) Baracoa's highest fort was begun by the Spanish in 1739 and finished by the Americans in 1900. Barely recognizable as a fort these days, it serves as Hotel El Castillo. There's an excellent view of El Yunque's flat top over the shimmering swimming pool. A steep stairway at the southwest end of Calle Frank País climbs directly up.

Bust of Hatuey STATUE

(Antonio Maceo) Facing the cathedral is the Bust of Hatuey, a rebellious Indian *cacique* (chief) who was burned at the stake near Baracoa in 1512 after refusing to convert to Catholicism.

Catedral de Nuestra Señora de la Asunción CHURCH

(☎21-64-30-05; Antonio Maceo No 152; ⏰7am-11am & 4-9pm Tue-Sun) After years of neglect, Baracoa's hurricane-battered historic cathedral has been lovingly restored using primarily Italian funding. There's been a building on this site since the 16th century, though this present, much-altered, incarnation dates from 1833.

The church's most famous artifact is the priceless Cruz de la Parra, the only survivor of 29 wooden crosses erected by Columbus in Cuba on his first voyage in 1492. Carbon dating has authenticated the age of the cross (it dates from the late 1400s), but has indicated it was originally made out of indigenous Cuban wood, thus disproving the legend that Columbus brought the cross from Europe.

Fuerte de la Punta FORT

This Spanish fort has watched over the harbor entrance at the northwestern end of town since 1803. The super-thick, hurricane-resistant walls now hide a restaurant.

Outside Town

Parque Natural Majayara PARK

(CUC$2, lookout CUC$5) Southeast of town in the Parque Natural Majayara are a couple of magical hikes and swimming opportunities plus an archaeological trail in the grounds of a lush family farm. It's a very low-key, DIY diversion. Alternatively, Ecotur (p439) leads trips here (CUC$20).

Passing the Fuerte Matachín, hike southeast past the baseball stadium and along the dark-sand beach for 20 minutes to the Río Miel, where a long low bridge crosses the river.

On the other side, bear left following a track up through a cluster of rustic houses to another junction. A guard-post here is sometimes staffed by a park official collecting entry fees. Turn left again and continue along the vehicle track until the houses clear and you see a signposted, single-track path leading off left to Playa Blanca, an idyllic spot for a picnic.

Staying straight on the track, you'll come to a trio of wooden homesteads. The third of these houses belongs to the Fuentes family. For a donation, Señor Fuentes will lead you on a hike to his family finca, where you can stop for coffee and tropical fruit. Further on he'll show you the Cueva de Aguas, a cave

OFF THE BEATEN TRACK

KIRIBÁ & NENGÓN: THE ROOTS OF SON

Those on a mission to unravel the complex family tree of Cuban music shouldn't skip the tiny village of Güirito, 18km southeast of Baracoa. Herein lie two of the primitive precursors to Cuba's national music, *son*. While *son* and its rhythmic cousin, salsa, got exported around the world, the orphic genres of *kiribá* and *nengón* never got much further than Güirito.

So what exactly are these rugged and rootsy musical forms? Both *kiribá* and *nengón* are rustic antecedents of *son* (rather than variants) passed down orally from generation to generation since the First Independence War in the mid-19th century. Thanks to a local revival in 1982, *kiribá* and *nengón* are still widely practiced in Güirito by a 21-person music and dance group who have meticulously safeguarded the old traditions.

Kiribá's fast beat and relatively free choreography incorporates a couples' dance in which partners move together in broad circular steps. *Nengón* is a slower dance with a distinctive foot-dragging motion said to imitate erstwhile farm-workers who stamped their feet on dried coffee and cacao beans to grind them.

The accompanying music is invariably played by a septet consisting of *tres* (Cuban-style guitar), *güiro* (a ridged, hollowed-out gourd), claves, marimbula, bongos, maracas and voice. *Nengón* has 22 registered songs but in *kiribá* singers make up the words as they go along. The costumes worn at musical gatherings are equally distinctive. Women wear white blouses and long flower-patterned skirts. Men wear *guayabera* (Caribbean dress) shirts and straw *yarey* hats, and carry handkerchiefs.

On most Saturday afternoons the group gets together in Güirito for a traditional fiesta, an informal affair with a wide interchange of Baracoan food. There's *bacán* (crab and plantain tamales), *frangollo* (dried banana mixed with sugar and wrapped in a banana leaf) and rice cooked inside the stomach of a whole roasted pig. Fuelled by rum drawn from oak barrels, the dancing can go on until the small hours. Anyone is welcome.

with a sparkling, freshwater swimming hole inside. Tracking back up the hillside you'll come to an archaeological trail with more caves and marvelous ocean views.

Playa Duaba BEACH

Heading north on the Moa road, take the Hotel Porto Santo/airport turnoff and continue for 2km past the airport runway to a black-sand beach at the river mouth where Antonio Maceo, Flor Crombet and others landed in 1895 to start the Second War of Independence. There's a campismo (cheap rustic accommodation), memorial monument and close-up views of El Yunque, though the beach itself isn't sunbathing territory.

Tours

Organized tours are a good way to view Baracoa's hard-to-reach outlying sights, and the **Cubatur** (☎61-32-83-42; Antonio Maceo No 181; ⏰8am-noon & 2-5pm Mon-Fri) and **Ecotur** (☎21-64-24-78; Antonio Maceo; ⏰8am-noon & 2-6pm Mon-Sat) offices on Plaza Independencia can book excursions, including to El Yunque (CUC$16 to CUC$20), Parque Nacional Alejandro de Humboldt (CUC$22 to CUC$25) and Boca de Yumurí (CUC$22).

★ **José Ángel Delfino Pérez** TOURS

(☎21-64-13-67, mobile 54-25-58-19; joseguia@nauta.cu; day tours CUC$25-27) Walking plant encyclopedia and enthusiastic geological expert, José has to be Baracoa's best private guide. His professional tours visit El Yunque, Punta de Maisí, Humboldt and – best of all – Boca de Yumurí, a trip that takes in cacao plantations, chocolate tastings and visits to isolated beaches. Per-person prices drop for larger groups.

Ask to see José's ID, as he has some unwelcome local impersonators. You can contact him by phone, email or at the casa particular of Nilson Abad Guilaré.

Festivals & Events

★ **Semana de la Cultura Baracoesa** CULTURAL

(⏰late Mar) Locals hit the streets to celebrate the 1895 landing of Antonio Maceo. There are feasts and fairs featuring genuine traditions: musical styles and dancing influenced

Baracoa

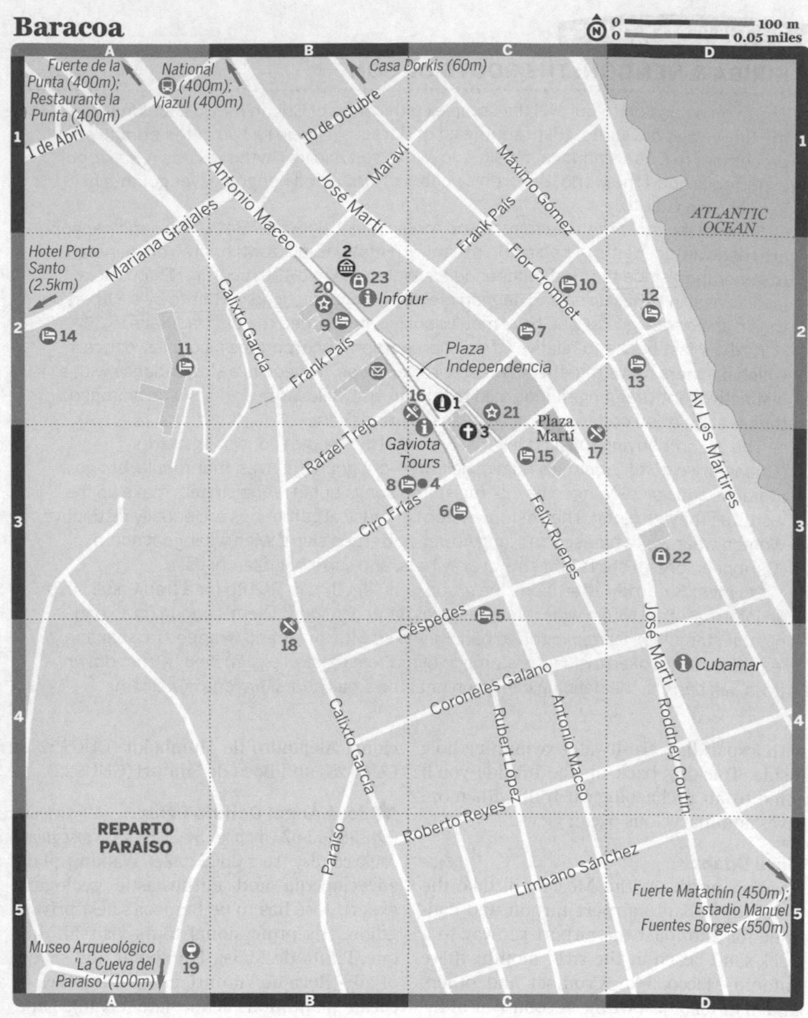

by both indigenous and modern rhythms. It ends with an April 1st pilgrimage.

Sleeping

★Casa Colonial Ykira Mahiquez CASA PARTICULAR $
(☎21-64-38-81; ykiram@nauta.cu; Antonio Maceo No 168A, btwn Ciro Frías & Céspedes; r CUC$25; ❄) Welcoming and hospitable, Ykira is Baracoa's premier hostess. She also serves a mean dinner made with homegrown herbs. With a lovely mural lining the entrance walk, there are two rooms set in the bosom of family life but with plenty of personal space. Guests enjoy terraces and a *mirador* (viewpoint) with sea views.

★La Casona CASA PARTICULAR $
(☎21-64-21-33; Félix Ruenes No 1 altos; r CUC$20-25; ❄) Rarely is a city's most central casa among its best, but thus have the young hosts made this place: two spotless 2nd-floor rooms and a knockout terrace where you can enjoy a cocktail or two.

Isabel Castro Vilato CASA PARTICULAR $
(☎21-64-22-67, mobile 53-55-36-34; rosellocastro@gmail.com; Mariana Grajales No 35; r CUC$25; P❄) You can't tell from the busy street out-

Baracoa

Sights
1 Bust of Hatuey ... C2
2 Casa del Cacao ... B2
3 Catedral de Nuestra Señora de la Asunción ... C3
El Castillo de Seboruco ... (see 11)

Activities, Courses & Tours
4 Ecotur ... C3

Sleeping
5 Casa Colonial Lucy ... C3
6 Casa Colonial Ykira Mahiquez ... C3
7 Casa Yamicel ... C2
8 Hostal 1511 ... B3
9 Hostal la Habanera ... B2
10 Hostal Nilson ... C2
11 Hotel El Castillo ... A2
12 Hotel la Rusa ... D2
13 Hotel Río Miel ... D2
14 Isabel Castro Vilato ... A2
15 La Casona ... C3

Eating
16 Cafetería el Parque ... C2
17 Dorado Café ... C3
18 El Buen Sabor ... B4
Restaurante Las Terrazas Casa Nilson ... (see 10)

Drinking & Nightlife
19 El Ranchón ... A5

Entertainment
20 Casa de la Cultura ... B2
21 Casa de la Trova Victorino Rodríguez ... C2

Shopping
22 ARTex ... D3
23 Taller Mirate ... B2

side, but this elegant green clapboard-and-stone house has lovely country style and a tranquil atmosphere. There are four massive rooms with minibars and a beautiful backyard garden growing breakfast provisions for your table. The hosts are helpful and wonderful. Unusually for Baracoa, there's a secure garage/car parking space.

Casa Yamicel CASA PARTICULAR $
(☎21-64-11-18; ncc.gtm@infomed.sld.cu; Martí No 145A, btwn Pelayo & Ciro Frias; r CUC$25, mains CUC$6-12; ❄) Doctor-proprietors that make killer mojitos? You'd better believe it. This colonial house offers four pleasant rooms with gorgeous wooden window bars (the best are on the top floor). There's wonderful hospitality, good meals (mains CUC$6 to CUC$12) and a roof terrace with reviving sea breezes.

Casa Dorkis CASA PARTICULAR $
(☎21-64-34-51, 52-38-53-16; dorkistd72@yahoo.es; Flor Crombet No 58 altos; r CUC$25; ❄) Though a bit of a walk from the plaza, this is one of your best bets for lodging. This quiet 2nd-story apartment has clean rooms with lovely decor flooded with natural light. There's an *azulejo*-tiled terrace with Atlantic views – ideal for a couple of days of lazy relaxation.

Casa Colonial Lucy CASA PARTICULAR $
(☎21-64-35-48; astralsol36@gmail.com; Céspedes No 29, btwn Rubert López & Antonio Maceo; r CUC$20; ❄) This welcoming 1840 home effuses character with patios, porches and flowering begonias, though cleanliness could score a little higher. There are two rooms here as well as terraces on different levels, and the atmosphere is quiet and secluded. Lucy's son speaks four languages and offers salsa lessons.

Hostal Nilson CASA PARTICULAR $
(☎21-64-31-23, 52-71-85-56; www.hostalnilson.baracoa.co; Flor Crombet No 143, btwn Ciro Frías & Pelayo Cuervo; d CUC$20-25, ste CUC$35-50; ❄) A super clean house with three quirky rooms stacked on several floors. Ideal for close groups or families, a spacious, very private suite features a bathroom with two showers and two toilets, face-to-face. No waiting at the door here! Above the restaurant there's a roof terrace with sea views.

Hostal 1511 HOTEL $$
(☎21-64-57-00; reservas@gavbcoa.co.cu; Ciro Frías, btwn Rubert López & Maceo; s/d CUC$59/64; ❄📶) The year 1511 is Baracoa's foundation date, and this diminutive place is a landmark, too, for offering dead-central accommodations with an abundant colonial vibe. The model ship in the lobby sets the tone for an overtly nautical decor that works best in the more charming upstairs rooms.

Hostal la Habanera HOTEL $$
(☎21-64-52-73; Antonio Maceo No 126; s/d CUC$59/64; ❄📶) Atmospheric and inviting in a way only Baracoa can muster, La Habanera sits in a restored and regularly repainted

colonial mansion. The four front bedrooms share a street-facing balcony replete with tiled floor and rocking chairs: perfect for imbibing that quintessential Baracoa ambience (street-hawkers, hip-gyrating music, and seafood a-frying in the restaurants).

The downstairs lobby has a bar, a restaurant and a handy Gaviota tour desk.

Hotel El Castillo HOTEL **$$**

(☎21-64-52-24; reservas@gavbcoa.co.cu; Loma del Paraíso; s/d CUC$59/80; P ❄ ☜ ≋) Recline like a colonial-era conquistador in this historic fort-turned-hotel in the hilltop Castillo de Seboruco. Choose your room well: there's some wear and tear, though conquistadors never boasted the privilege of a swimming pool or housekeeping fashioning towels into ships and swans. The 28 newer rooms in a separate block offer jaw-dropping El Yunque views.

Hotel Río Miel HOTEL **$$**

(☎21-64-12-07; reservas@gavbcoa.co.cu; Ave Malecón, cnr Ciro Frias; s/d CUC$59/64; ❄ ☜) Stylish and sturdy, this hotel withstood Hurricane Matthew with honors. It's on the Malecón where it faces some of the most inclement weather in Cuba. Run by Gaviota, the service can be slack, but there are remodeled rooms with large safes that fit a laptop.

Hotel Porto Santo HOTEL **$$**

(☎21-64-51-06; ejecutivo.comercial@gavbcoa.co.cu; Carretera del Aeropuerto; s/d CUC$59/80; P ❄ ☜ ≋) On the bay where Columbus allegedly planted his first cross is this peaceful, well-integrated low-rise hotel. Situated 4km from the town center and 200m from the airport, there are 36 more-than-adequate rooms all within earshot of the sea. A steep stairway leads down to a tiny, wave-lashed beach. Unfortunately, Hurricane Matthew downed most of the palms shading it.

Hotel la Rusa HOTEL **$$**

(☎21-64-30-11; reservas@gavbcoa.co.cu; Máximo Gómez No 161; s/d CUC$46/55; ❄ ☜) Russian émigré Magdalena Rovieskuya once posted aid to Castro's rebels up in the Sierra Maestra. La Rusa hit Baracoa in the 1930s, built a seafront hotel and welcomed guests like Errol Flynn, Che Guevara and Fidel Castro. After her death in 1978, it became a more modest government-run joint with sad little single beds and a rundown lobby.

Eating

Dorado Café CAFE **$**

(☎52-38-53-16; Martí No 171; snacks CUC$3; ⌚10am-2pm & 6-10pm) Small private cafe in the center of Baracoa that sells pizza, sandwiches and the like.

BARACOA'S UNIQUE FOOD CULTURE

Unlike more complex cuisines, Cuban cooking doesn't really have a strong *regional* identity, at least not until you arrive in Baracoa. Here everything – including the food – is different. Home to the country's most fickle weather, Baracoa has used its wet microclimate and geographic isolation to jazz up notoriously unambitious Cuban cuisine with spices, sugar, exotic fruits and coconut. Fish anchors most menus yet even the seafood can pull some surprises. Count on tasting tiny tadpole-like *teti* fish drawn from the Río Toa between July to January during a waning moon.

The biggest taste explosion is a locally concocted coconut sauce known as *lechita*, a mixture of coconut milk, tomato sauce, garlic and a medley of spices best served over prawns, *aguja* (swordfish) or dorado. Other main-course accompaniments include *bacán*, raw green plantain melded with crabmeat and wrapped in a banana leaf, or *frangollo*, a similar concoction where the ground bananas are mixed with sugar.

Sweets are another Baracoa *tour de force* thanks largely to the ubiquity of the cocoa plant and the presence of the famous Che Guevara chocolate factory. Baracoan chocolate is sold all over the island, but the local Casa del Cacao (p438) is an obvious sampling point. You're likely to get it for breakfast in your casa particular, stirred into a local hot-chocolate drink made with banana powder known as *chorote*.

Baracoa's most unique culinary invention is undoubtedly *cucurucho*, a delicate mix of dried coconut, sugar, honey, papaya, guayaba, mandarin and nuts (no concoction is ever quite alike) that is wrapped in an ecologically friendly palm frond. The best stuff is sold by the *campesinos* on La Farola coming into town from Guantánamo, a stop usually made by buses.

Cafetería el Parque FAST FOOD $
(☎21-64-12-06; Antonio Maceo No 142; snacks CUC$1-3; ⏲24hr;) The favored meeting place of just about everyone in town, you're bound to end up at this open terrace at some point, if only to crack open a Bucanero beer and tune into the wi-fi.

★Restaurante Las Terrazas Casa Nilson CUBAN $$
(☎21-64-31-23; Flor Crombet No 143, btwn Ciro Frías & Pelayo Cuervo; meals CUC$6-15; ⏲noon-3pm & 6:30-11pm) Up above his house on a spectacular two-level terrace decorated in quirky Afro-Caribbean style, owner Nilson serves some of the best authentic Baracoan food in town, and hence Cuba. You can't miss with wonderfully rich *pescado con leche de coco* (fish fillet in coconut milk) or the melt-in-your-mouth octopus with basil ink with homemade *patacon guisado,* a plantain dish. Unforgettable!

Reserve ahead to ensure a table.

★El Buen Sabor CUBAN $$
(☎21-64-14-00; Calixto García No 134 altos; meals CUC$6-15; ⏲noon-midnight) Served on a spotless and breezy upstairs terrace, meals come with salad, soup and side included. You can expect the best of Baracoan cuisine at this private restaurant, including swordfish in a coconut sauce, *bacán* (raw green plantain melded with crabmeat and wrapped in a banana leaf) and chocolate-y deserts. Service is attentive.

★Restaurante la Punta CARIBBEAN $$
(☎21-64-14-80; Fuerte de la Punta; meals CUC$5-12; ⏲10am-11pm) Cooled by Atlantic breezes (and the occasional full-on gale), the Gaviota-run La Punta aims to impress with well-prepared, garnished food in the lovely historical surrounds of the La Punta fort. Go on a Saturday night for live music.

Drinking & Nightlife

El Ranchón CLUB
(☎21-64-23-64; CUC$1; ⏲from 9pm) Atop a long flight of stairs at the western end of Coroneles Galano, popular El Ranchón mixes an exhilarating hilltop setting with taped disco and salsa music and legions of resident *jinteras* (female touts). Watch your step on the way down – it's a scary 146-step drunken tumble.

Entertainment

★Casa de la Trova Victorino Rodríguez TRADITIONAL MUSIC
(Antonio Maceo No 149A; CUC$1; ⏲matinee 5:30pm, 9pm-midnight) Cuba's smallest, zaniest, wildest and most atmospheric *casa de la trova* (*trova* house) rocks nightly to the voodoo-like rhythms of *changüí-son*. One night the average age of the band is 85, the next it's 22. The common denominator? It's all good. Matinees are usually free. Order a mojito in a jam jar and join in the show.

Casa de la Cultura CULTURAL CENTER
(☎21-64-23-64; Antonio Maceo No 124, btwn Frank País & Maraví) This venue does a wide variety of shows including some good rumba incorporating the textbook Cuban styles of *guaguancó, yambú* and *columbia* (subgenres of rumba). Go prepared for *mucho* audience participation. There's a good *spectaculo* (show) on the terrace, La Terraza, every Saturday at 11pm: expect rumba, Benny Moré, and the local hairdresser singing Omara Portuondo.

Estadio Manuel Fuentes Borges BASEBALL
Pummeled by Hurricane Matthew, the stadium, now mostly a ruin, may or may not host baseball games from October to April. Literally on the beach, it's possibly the only ground in Cuba where players come in to bat with the taste of fresh sea spray on their lips.

Shopping

Interesting art is easy to find in Baracoa and, like most things in this whimsical seaside town, it has its own distinctive flavor.

Taller Mirate ART
(Antonio Maceo; ⏲10am-8pm) An artist's co-op where you'll always find one of the young creative painters sitting at a palette in the window. The very local painting style is best described as Gauguin meets Van Gogh in the pages of a Gabriel García Márquez novel.

ARTex GIFTS & SOUVENIRS
(☎21-64-53-73; José Martí No 197; ⏲9am-4:30pm Mon-Sat) For the usual tourist trinkets, check out this place.

Information

INTERNET ACCESS

There's wi-fi access on the Plaza Independencia.

Etecsa Telepunto (☎21-64-31-82; Antonio Maceo No 182; internet per hr CUC$1.50; ⏰9am-7pm) Sells wi-fi internet scratchcards and offers internet on computer terminals. Little to no line.

MEDICAL SERVICES

Clínica Internacional (☎21-64-10-37; cnr José Martí & Roberto Reyes; ⏰8am-8pm) A newish place that treats foreigners; there's also a hospital 2km out of town on the road to Guantánamo.

MONEY

Cadeca (☎21-64-53-45; José Martí No 241; ⏰8:15am-4pm Mon-Fri, 8:15am-11:30am Sat & Sun) Short queues for currency exchange.

Banco Popular de Ahorro (☎21-64-52-09; José Martí No 166; ⏰8-11:30am & 2-4:30pm Mon-Fri) Has an ATM.

Banco de Crédito y Comercio (Antonio Maceo No 99; ⏰8am-2:30pm Mon-Fri) Has an ATM.

POST

The **post office** (☎21-64-24-15; Antonio Maceo No 136; ⏰8am-8pm) is located near the main plaza.

TOURIST INFORMATION

Tour destinations and roads may have been affected by Hurricane Matthew, so ask ahead before traveling further afield.

Infotur (☎21-64-17-81; Antonio Maceo No 129a, btwn Frank País & Maraví; ⏰8:30am-noon & 1-4:45pm Mon-Sat) Very helpful.

TRAVEL AGENCIES

Gaviota Tours (☎21-64-51-64; Cafeteria El Parque; ⏰8am-noon, 2-6pm Mon-Sat) Helpful in arranging stays at Gaviota properties, airline tickets and general tours.

Getting There & Away

AIR

Gustavo Rizo Airport (airport code BCA) is 4km northwest of the town, just behind the Hotel Porto Santo. Book flights to Havana with one of the travel agencies.

The planes (and buses) out of Baracoa can be fully booked, so don't arrive on a tight schedule without outbound reservations.

BUS

The **National Bus Station** (☎21-64-38-80; cnr Av Los Mártires & José Martí) has service with **Víazul** (☎21-64-38-80) to Guantánamo and Santiago de Cuba. Reserve your tickets a day in advance (more in high season).

The bus departs for Santiago (CUC$15, five hours) at 8:15am, stopping in Guántanamo. A later bus at 2pm goes to Guantánamo (CUC$10, three hours) only.

TRUCK

Trucks to Moa (departures from 6am) leave from the National Bus Station, traveling along the very bumpy road northwest.

Getting Around

The best way to get to and from the airport is by taxi (CUC$8 to CUC$10), or bici-taxi (CUC$5) if you're traveling light.

There's a helpful **Via Gaviota** (☎21-64-16-65) car-rental office at the airport. The **Servi-Cupet gas station** (José Martí; ⏰24hr) is at the entrance to town 4km from the center, on the road to Guantánamo. If you're driving to Havana, note that the northern route through Moa and Holguín is the most direct but the road disintegrates rapidly after Playa Maguana – for this reason taxi prices can be astronomical. Most locals prefer the La Farola route.

Bici-taxis around Baracoa charge foreigners CUC$2 to CUC$5.

Most casas particulares will be able to procure you a bicycle (CUC$5 per day). The ultimate bike ride is the 20km ramble down to Playa Maguana, one of the most scenic roads in Cuba. Or rent mopeds for CUC$25 at either Gaviota Tours or Hotel El Castillo (p442).

Northwest of Baracoa

The rutted road heading out of town toward Moa is a green paradise flecked with palm groves, rustic farmsteads and serendipitous glimpses of the ocean. There's windswept beaches, coffee farms and rain forest. In 2016, Hurricane Matthew hit this area hard, knocking a principle bridge out, but access has been restored.

Much of this region lies within the Cuchillas Toa Unesco Biosphere Reserve, an area of 2083 sq km that incorporates the Alejandro de Humboldt World Heritage Site. Here is Cuba's largest rain forest, with many precious hardwoods and a high number of endemic species.

Sights

★**El Yunque** MOUNTAIN

(CUC$13) Baracoa's rite of passage is the 8km (up and down) hike to the top of this moody, mysterious mountain. Views from the summit (575m) and the flora and birdlife along the way are stupendous. Bank on seeing *tocororo* (Cuba's national bird), *zunzún* (the world's smallest bird), butterflies and *polymitas* (colorful endangered snails). The hike is hot (bring 2L of water) and usually muddy. It starts from the campismo 3km past the Finca Duaba (4km from the Baracoa–Moa road).

All visits must be guided. Cubatur offers this tour almost daily (CUC$16 person, minimum four people). The fee covers admission, guide, transport and a sandwich. If you're not up to bagging the peak itself, ask Ecotur about the 7km Sendero Juncal-Rencontra that bisects fruit plantations and rain forest between the Duaba and Toa rivers.

Río Toa RIVER

Ten kilometers northwest of Baracoa, the Toa is the third-longest river on the north coast of Cuba and the country's most voluminous. It's also an important bird and plant habitat. Cocoa trees and ubiquitous coconut palms grow in the Valle de Toa.

A vast hydroelectric project on the Río Toa was abandoned after a campaign led by the Fundación de la Naturaleza y El Hombre convinced authorities it would do irreparable ecological damage; engineering and economic reasons also played a part.

Playa Maguana BEACH

There's some magic in this relatively undeveloped Caribbean beach where fun-seeking Cubans roll up in their vintage American cars and haul their prized music boxes out of the boot. Beyond a food shack there's little infrastructure here and that's part of the attraction. Watch your valuables!

Finca Duaba FARM

(CUC$2; 8am-7pm) Five kilometers out of Baracoa on the road to Moa and then 1km inland, Finca Duaba offers a fleeting taste of the Baracoan countryside. It's a verdant farm surrounded with profuse tropical plants and embellished with a short *cacao* (cocoa) trail that explains the history and characteristics of chocolate. There's also a good *ranchón*-style restaurant and the opportunity to swim in the Río Duaba. A bici-taxi can drop you at the road junction.

Sleeping

Finca la Esperanza FARMSTAY $

(52-18-07-35; r incl breakfast CUC$13, lunch CUC$8) Located at Km 8 on the Baracoa–Moa road, this lovely farmstay also offers meals and excursions. There are boat rides (CUC$2) and walks on the Sendero Cayo los Chinos (CUC$5) trail.

Campismo Duaba CABIN $

(CUC$18) A recent addition with 10 lovely dollhouse cabins with bathrooms and air-conditioning. From Baracoa, it's on the road to Moa just before the Río Duaba.

Campismo el Yunque CABIN $

(21-64-52-62; r CUC$12) Simple Cuban-style campismo offering very basic cabins at the end of the Finca Duaba road, 9km outside of Baracoa. The El Yunque hike starts here.

★ Villa Maguana HOTEL $$

(21-64-12-04; Carretera a Moa Km 20; s/d CUC$86/103; P) Knocking the socks off any Cuban all-inclusive resort is this delightful place 22km north of Baracoa. Four rustic wooden villas house 16 rooms in total. Guarded by two rocky promontories, it clings precariously to Maguana's famously dreamy setting above a bite-sized scoop of sand. There's a restaurant and amenities such as satellite TV, fridge and air-con.

Eating

Playa Maguana Snack Bar CARIBBEAN $

(snacks CUC$2-5; 9am-5pm) Right on the beach, this open-sided snack bar is good for cheese sandwiches, beer and rum.

Rancho Toa CUBAN $$

(meals CUC$10-12, boat rides CUC$5-10) A Palmares restaurant reached via a right-hand turnoff just before the Toa bridge. You can organize boat or kayak trips here and watch acrobatic Baracoans scale *cocotero* (coconut palms). A traditional Cuban feast of whole roast pig is available if you can rustle up enough people (eight, usually).

This attraction closed after Hurricane Matthew but should be operational again.

Getting There & Away

A Moa-bound truck can drop you in this area or you can go via taxi to Playa Maguana (around CUC$25 round-trip), Campismo el Yunque (CUC$18 round-trip) and other destinations.

Parque Nacional Alejandro de Humboldt

These steep pine-clad mountains and creeping morning mists guard an astonishing ecosystem that's unmatched in the Caribbean. Cuba's most dramatic and diverse national park was named after German naturalist-explorer Alexander von Humboldt who first visited in 1801. It was designated a Unesco World Heritage Site in 2001 as 'one of the most biologically diverse tropical island sites on earth.'

Perched above Bahía de Taco, 40km northwest of Baracoa, lies 600-odd sq km of pristine forest and 2641 hectares of lagoon and mangroves. With 1000 flowering plant species and 145 ferns, it's the Caribbean's most diverse plant habitat. The toxic nature of the underlying rocks in the area has forced plants to survive by adaptation. As a result, 70% of the plants are endemic, as are nearly all 20 species of amphibians, 45% of the reptiles and many birds. Endangered bird species include Cuban Amazon parrots, hook-billed kites and ivory-billed woodpeckers.

Activities

The park has a network of trails leading to waterfalls, a *mirador* (lookout) and a massive karst cave system around the Farallones de Moa. Four trails are currently open to the public, taking in only a tiny segment of the park's 594 sq km. Typically, you can't just wander around on your own.

Ecotur recently added 4WD and ATV excursions. The longest hike features an eight-hour reconnoiter deeper into the forest, featuring bird and orchid observation.

Each option is accompanied by a highly professional guide. If you're showing up independently, get to the visitor center before 10am to secure one. Prices range from CUC$5 to CUC$10, depending on the hike, but most people organize an excursion through Ecotur, Cubatur or Gaviota in Baracoa, which includes transport and a pit stop on Playa Maguana on the way back (CUC$24). Hurricane Matthew passed through here, and as a result, some tour options might be curtailed for a period.

Balcón de Iberia HIKING
The park's most challenging loop (7km) bisects both agricultural land and pristine rain forest. It includes a swim in a natural pool near the Salto de Agua Maya waterfall.

Bahía de Taco HIKING
A circuit hike that incorporates a boat trip through the mangroves and the idyllic horseshoe-shaped bay, plus a 2km hike. Boats use a manatee-friendly motor developed by scientists here.

El Recreo WALKING
This trail is an easy 2km stroll around the bay.

Information

Visitors Center (Carretera a Moa; park entry CUC$10) The small visitors center is staffed with biologists.

Getting There & Away

The park visitors center is approximately halfway between Baracoa and Moa. You can arrange a tour through an agency in Baracoa or get here independently. The gorgeously scenic road is a collection of holes but passable in a hire car if driven with care. This road continues into Holguín Province, improving just before Moa.

At present, a provisional bridge connects the park after hurricane damage, but this situation should improve.

Understand Cuba

Cuba Today

On the big, blue horizon a new chapter in Cuban history is being written. The death of long-time leader Fidel Castro has put the island into twin moods of reflection and anticipation. Meanwhile, his brother, President Raúl Castro, has dedicated his tenure to balancing party ideology with reforms to restore economic health. This has meant green-lighting business start-ups, Internet access, travel abroad, and the right to sell homes. In no time, Cuba's window on the world has expanded exponentially.

Best on Film

Four Seasons in Havana (Félix Viscarret; 2016) Netflix mini-series based on the acclaimed detective series by Leonardo Padura.

Che: The Argentine (Steven Soderbergh; 2008) First part of the classic biopic focuses on Che's Cuban years.

Before Night Falls (Julian Schnabel; 2000) The life and struggles of Cuban writer Reinaldo Arenas.

Fresa y Chocolate (Tomás Gutiérrez Alea; 1993) Marries the improbable themes of homosexuality and communism.

El Ojo del Canario (Fernando Pérez; 2010) This atmospheric biopic of José Martí earned numerous Latin film awards.

Best in Print

Our Man in Havana (Graham Greene; 1958) Lampoons both the British Secret Service and Batista's corrupt regime.

Cuba and the Night (Pico Iyer; 1995) The most evocative book about Cuba ever written by a foreigner.

Dirty Havana Trilogy (Pedro Juan Gutiérrez; 2002) Dirty, itchy study of life and sex in Havana during the Special Period.

Che Guevara: A Revolutionary Life (Jon Lee Anderson; 1997) Anderson's meticulous research helped unearth Che's remains in Bolivia.

New Chapter in US–Cuba Relations

Cuba's tentative rapprochement with the United States gained traction when the two countries brokered a prisoner swap in 2014. On December 17, 2014, Barack Obama appeared on television to announce the most significant thaw in US–Cuban relations in 54 years, measures that included US telecommunications aid to Cuba, the authorization of American credit and debit cards, a gentle easing of US travel restrictions, and – most importantly – the reestablishment of diplomatic relations between the two countries for the first time since 1961.

In July 2015, the US and Cuba reopened their respective embassies in Havana and Washington. In May of 2016, Obama became the first sitting president to visit Cuba since the 1959 revolution, meeting with entrepreneurs, Cuban dissidents and President Raul Castro. Whether the thaw will confine the embargo to the history books is hard to predict, but President Obama unequivocally opened up a new chapter in US–Cuba relations.

Yet ending the embargo requires US Congressional approval still pending under the Trump administration. Despite strong pockets of resistance in the Senate and House of Representatives, polls suggest that a majority of Americans and an increasing number of Cuban-Americans want the embargo to end. However, with an unpredictable new administration and a solid block of long-established Cuban exiles still determined not to negotiate, it could be a tough political fight.

New Class of Entrepreneurs

It's not quite democratic socialism, but the 2011–15 reforms have helped unleash the creativity and entrepreneurship of a generation of economically stifled Cubans. Private business has rocketed in numerous trades, especially for those with ready access to hard currency, often with the aid of remittances sent home from abroad.

With less bureaucratic regulations, some casas particulares (Cuban homestays) have morphed into mini-hotels employing dozens of staff, and advertising via websites and street signage (unheard of under Fidel). Restaurants have improved exponentially, both in cuisine and imaginative decor. Voguish cafes, hip bars and swanky nightclubs, particularly in Havana, appeal both to the newly monied class and visitors. Places such as Havana's Fábrica de Arte Cubano, an avant-garde art co-op with impromptu concerts, are the mark of a trend. Equally creative are budding vintage magazine shops, retro barbers, private hiking guides and genre-bending artists – private businesses that were just pipe-dreams five years ago.

Yet change brings mixed results. Those working in the private sector suddenly have far better prospects than their government-employed counterparts, a not-so-equal system. The buying and selling of homes has introduced gentrification: neighbors no longer know each other and top real estate has become the exclusive domain of the foreign rental market.

Testing the Limits

While most discussions about Cuba's reforms focus on economic matters, there's also a cultural transformation. Subtle attitude shifts question the unwavering authoritarianism of yore. In 2014, Havana quietly opened its first recognizably gay-friendly bar. The LGBTIQ community has also benefited from an annual pride parade and its first openly transgender elected official.

Even before Pope Francis' popular visit in 2015, Cuba has been going through a religious renaissance of sorts, with many more citizens openly attending church services and others practicing Santería traditions. Freedom to travel has also opened doors for those who can afford it. While some people have sold up and left the isles permanently, there has been no mass exodus, although plenty of Cubans have returned home from trips abroad loaded with ideas, inspiration and boxes of fancy consumer goods.

For every opening in Cuba, there is always a niggling back-shuffle, a notion that breeds cynicism among the majority of Cubans and keeps them constantly on their toes. Raúl Castro answered Obama's speech in December 2014 by stressing that Cuba would neither stray from its socialistic economic path nor yield to US pressure to change its political system. True to form, the Cuban government has shown no real appetite for extending political liberties beyond their current limits and given no indication as to what might happen when Raúl relinquishes the presidency in 2018. The future, as ever, is uncertain.

POPULATION: **11.2 MILLION**

AREA: **110,860 SQ KM**

DOCTOR TO PATIENT RATIO: **1:149**

LIFE EXPECTANCY: **79.1 YEARS**

INFANT MORTALITY: **4.6 PER 1000**

if Cuba were 100 people

65 would be White
25 would be Mixed
10 would be Black

belief systems

(% of population)

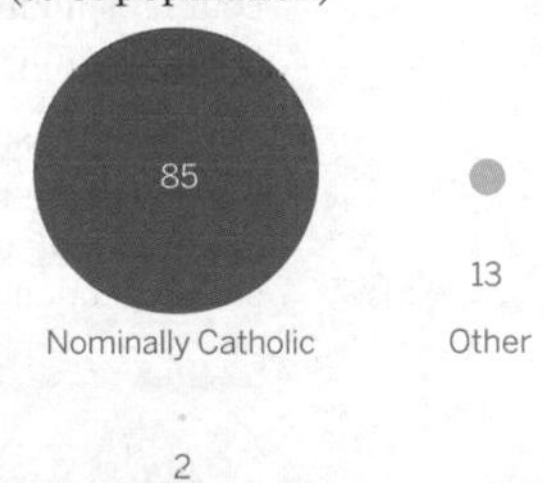

population per sq km

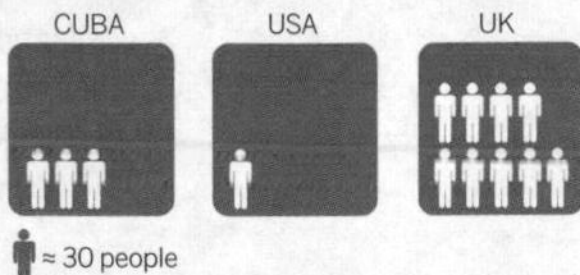

History

Embellished by extraordinary feats of revolutionary derring-do, and plagued routinely by the meddling armies of foreign invaders, Cuba has achieved a historical importance far greater than its size would suggest. The underlying and – until the 1960s – ongoing historical themes have been outside interference and internal rebellion, and the results of both have often been bloody.

A Turbulent Historical Trajectory

Since the arrival of Columbus in 1492, Cuba's turbulent historical trajectory has included genocide, slavery, two bitter independence wars, a period of corrupt and violent quasi-independence, and, finally, a populist revolution that, despite early promise, hit a metaphoric pause button. The fallout has led to the emigration of almost one-fifth of the Cuban population, mostly to the US.

For the sake of simplicity, the country's historical eras can be divided into three broad categories: pre-colonial, colonial and post-colonial. Before 1492 Cuba was inhabited by a trio of migratory civilizations that originated in the Orinoco Basin of South America before island-hopping north. Their cultures have been only partially evaluated to date, primarily because they left very little behind in the way of documentary evidence.

Cuba's colonial period was dominated by the Spanish and the divisive issue of slavery, which spanned the whole era from the 1520s until abolition in 1886. Slavery left deep wounds on Cuba's collective psyche, but its existence and final quashing was integral to the evolution of the country's highly distinctive culture, music, dance and religion. Understand this and you're halfway to understanding the complexities of the contemporary nation.

Post-colonial Cuba has had two distinctive sub-eras, the second of which can be further subdivided in two. The period from the defeat of Spain in 1898 to the Castro coup of 1959 is usually seen as an age of quasi-independence with a strong American influence. It was also a time

TIMELINE

BC 2000

The Guanahatabeys, Cuba's earliest known Stone Age civilization, live in the caves along the coast of present-day Pinar del Río Province.

AD 1100

Taíno people start arriving in Cuba after leapfrogging their way across the islands of the Lesser Antilles from the Orinoco Basin in present-day Venezuela.

1492

Christopher Columbus lands in Cuba in modern-day Holguín Province. He sails for a month along the coast, as far as Baracoa, planting religious crosses and meeting with the indigenous Taínos.

characterized by violence, corruption and frequent insurrection on the part of opposition groups intent on toppling the government.

The post-1959 Castro epoch breaks conveniently into two stages: the age of Soviet domination from 1961 to 1991, and the modern era that stretches from the Special Period to the present day, when Cuba, despite its devastating economic difficulties, became a truly independent power for the first time.

Pre-Colonial Cuba

The first known civilization in Cuba was that of the Guanahatabeys, a primitive Stone Age people who lived in caves and eked out a meager existence as hunter-gatherers. At some point over a 2000-year period, the Guanahatabeys were gradually pushed west into what is now Pinar del Río Province, displaced by the arrival of another pre-ceramic culture known as the Siboneys. The Siboneys were a slightly more developed group of fishers and small-scale farmers who settled down comparatively peacefully on the archipelago's sheltered southern coast. By the second millennium AD they were similarly displaced by the more sophisticated Taíno, who liked to use Siboneys as domestic servants.

The Taínos first started arriving in Cuba around AD 1050 in a series of waves, concluding a migration process that had begun on mainland South America several centuries earlier. Related to the Greater Antilles Arawaks, the new peace-loving natives were escaping the barbarism of the cannibalistic Caribs who had colonized the Lesser Antibes, pushing the Taínos northwest into Puerto Rico, Hispaniola and Cuba.

Colonial Cuba

Columbus & Colonization

Columbus neared Cuba on October 27, 1492, describing it as 'the most beautiful land human eyes had ever seen.' He named it 'Juana' in honor of a Spanish heiress. But deluded in his search for the kingdom of the Great Khan, and finding little gold in Cuba's lush and heavily forested interior, Columbus quickly abandoned the territory in favor of Hispaniola (modern-day Haiti and the Dominican Republic).

The colonization of Cuba didn't begin until nearly 20 years later in 1511, when Diego Velázquez de Cuéllar led a flotilla of four ships and 400 men from Hispaniola to conquer the island for the Spanish Crown. Docking near present-day Baracoa, the conquistadors promptly set about establishing seven *villas* (towns) on the main island – Havana, Trinidad, Baracoa, Bayamo, Camagüey, Santiago de Cuba and Sancti

Independence War Heroes

Carlos Manuel de Céspedes (1819–74)

Máximo Gómez (1836–1905)

Calixto García (1839–98)

Ignacio Agramonte (1841–73)

Antonio Maceo (1845–96)

1494

Columbus returns to Cuba on his second voyage, docking briefly at various points along Cuba's south coast and 'discovering' La Isla de la Juventud.

1508

Spanish navigator Sebastián de Ocampo circumnavigates Cuba, establishing that it's an island and disproving Columbus' long held idea that it might be a peninsula of the Asian continent.

1511

Diego Velázquez lands at Baracoa with 400 colonizers, including Hernán Cortés (the future colonizer of Mexico). The new arrivals construct a fort and quickly make enemies of the local Taínos.

1519

Havana, the last of Cuba's seven founding *'villas'*, is moved to its present site at the mouth of a fine natural harbor. It is inaugurated with a solemn mass under a ceiba tree in what is now Plaza de Armas.

US Presidents Who Tried to Buy Cuba

1808 – Thomas Jefferson (undisclosed sum)

1848 – James Polk ($100 million)

1854 – Franklin Pierce ($130 million)

1898 – William McKinley ($300 million)

Spíritus – in a bid to bring their new colony under strong central rule. Watching nervously from the safety of their *bohíos* (thatched huts), a scattered population of Taínos looked on with a mixture of fascination and fear.

Despite Velázquez' attempts to protect the local Taínos from the gross excesses of the Spanish swordsmen, things quickly got out of hand and the invaders soon found that they had a full-scale rebellion on their hands. Leader of the embittered and short-lived Taíno insurgency was the feisty Hatuey, an influential *cacique* (chief) and archetype of the Cuban resistance, who was eventually captured and burned at the stake, Inquisition-style, for daring to challenge the iron fist of Spanish rule.

With the resistance decapitated, the Spaniards set about emptying Cuba of its relatively meager gold and mineral reserves, using the beleaguered natives as forced labor. As slavery was nominally banned under a papal edict, the Spanish got around the various legal loopholes by introducing a ruthless *encomienda* system, whereby thousands of natives were rounded up and forced to work for Spanish landowners on the pretext that they were receiving free 'lessons' in Christianity.

The brutal system lasted 20 years before the 'Apostle of the Indians,' Fray Bartolomé de Las Casas, appealed to the Spanish Crown for more humane treatment, and in 1542 the *encomiendas* were abolished for the indigenous people. For the unfortunate Taínos, the call came too late. Those who had not already been worked to death in the gold mines quickly succumbed to fatal European diseases such as smallpox, and by 1550 only about 5000 scattered survivors remained.

The Independence Wars

With its brutal slave system established, the Spanish ruled their largest Caribbean colony with an iron fist for the next 200 years, despite a brief occupation by the British in 1792. Cuba's creole landowners, worried about a repetition of Haiti's brutal 1791 slave rebellion, held back when the rest of Latin America took up arms against the Spanish in the 1810s and 1820s. As a result, the nation's independence wars came more than half a century after the restyears war of Latin America had broken away from Spain. But when they arrived, they were no less impassioned – or bloody.

The Ten Years' War

Fed up with Spain's reactionary colonial policies and enviously eyeing Lincoln's new American dream to the north, *criollo* (Spaniards born

1522

The first slaves arrive in Cuba from Africa, ushering in an era that is to last for 350 years and have a profound effect on the development of Cuban culture.

1555

The age of piracy is inaugurated. French buccaneer Jacques de Sores attacks Havana and burns it to the ground. In response, the Spanish start building a huge network of forts.

1607

Havana is declared capital of Cuba and becomes the annual congregation point for Spain's Caribbean treasure fleet, loaded up with silver from Peru and gold from Mexico.

1741

A British Navy contingent under the command of Admiral Edward Vernon briefly captures Guantánamo Bay during the War of Jenkins' Ear, but is sent packing after a yellow fever epidemic.

in the Americas) landowners around Bayamo began plotting rebellion in the late 1860s. On October 10, 1868, Carlos Manuel de Céspedes, a budding poet, lawyer and sugar-plantation owner, launched an uprising from his Demajagua sugar mill near Manzanillo in the Oriente.

Calling for the abolition of slavery and freeing his own slaves as an example, Céspedes proclaimed the famous *Grito de Yara,* a cry of liberty for an independent Cuba, encouraging other disillusioned separatists to join him. For the colonial administrators in Havana, such an audacious bid to wrest control was an act tantamount to treason. The furious Spanish reacted accordingly.

Fortunately for the loosely organized rebels, the cagey Céspedes had done his military homework. Within weeks of the historic *Grito de Yara,* the diminutive lawyer-turned-general had raised an army of more than 1500 men and marched defiantly on Bayamo, taking the city in a matter of days. But initial successes soon turned to lengthy deadlock. A tactical decision not to invade western Cuba, along with an alliance between *peninsulares* (Spaniards born in Spain but living in Cuba) and the Spanish, soon put Céspedes on the back foot.

Temporary help arrived in the shape of *mulato* general Antonio Maceo, a tough and uncompromising Santiagüero, nicknamed the 'Bronze Titan' for his ability to defy death on countless occasions, and the equally formidable Dominican Máximo Gómez. But despite economic disruption and the periodic destruction of the sugar crop, the rebels lacked a dynamic political leader capable of uniting them behind a singular ideological cause.

With the loss of Céspedes in battle in 1874, the war dragged on for another four years, reducing the Cuban economy to tatters and leaving an astronomical 200,000 Cubans and 80,000 Spanish dead. Finally, in February 1878 a lackluster pact was signed at El Zanjón between the uncompromising Spanish and the exhausted separatists, a rambling and largely worthless agreement that solved nothing and acceded little to the rebel cause. Maceo, disgusted and disillusioned, made his feelings known in the antidotal 'Protest of Baraguá,' but after an abortive attempt to restart the war in 1879, both he and Gómez disappeared into a prolonged exile.

The Spanish-Cuban-American War

Cometh the hour, cometh the man. José Martí – poet, patriot, visionary and intellectual – had grown rapidly into a patriotic figure of Bolívarian proportions in the years following his ignominious exile in 1871, not just

Of the 12 or so men that survived the disastrous *Granma* landing in December 1956, only two were still alive in 2017: Raúl Castro and Ramiro Valdés.

1762

Spain joins France in the Seven Years' War, provoking the British to attack and take Havana. They occupy Cuba for 11 months before exchanging it for Florida in 1763.

1791

A bloody slave rebellion in Haiti causes thousands of white French planters to flee west to Cuba, where they set up the earliest coffee plantations in the New World.

1808

Pre-empting the Monroe Doctrine, US president Thomas Jefferson proclaims Cuba 'the most nteresting addition which could be made to our system of states,' thus beginning a 200-year US fixation.

1850

Venezuelan filibuster Narciso López raises the Cuban flag for the first time in Cárdenas during an abortive attempt to 'liberate' the colony from Spain.

Cuba's First Three Presidents

Tomás Estrada Palma (1902–06)

José Miguel Gómez (1909–13)

Mario García Menocal (1913–21)

in Cuba but in the whole of Latin America. After his arrest at the age of 16 during the First War of Independence for a minor indiscretion, Martí had spent 20 years formulating his revolutionary ideas abroad in places as diverse as Guatemala, Mexico and the US. Although impressed by American business savvy and industriousness, he was equally repelled by the country's all-consuming materialism and was determined to present a workable Cuban alternative.

Dedicating himself passionately to the cause of the resistance, Martí wrote, spoke, petitioned and organized tirelessly for independence for well over a decade and by 1892 had enough momentum to coax Maceo and Gómez out of exile under the umbrella of the Partido Revolucionario Cubano (PRC; Cuban Revolutionary Party). At last, Cuba had found its spiritual leader.

Predicting that the time was right for another revolution, Martí and his compatriots set sail for Cuba in April 1895, landing near Baracoa two months after PRC-sponsored insurrections had tied down Spanish forces in Havana. Raising an army of 40,000 men, the rebels promptly regrouped and headed west, engaging the Spanish for the first time on May 19 in a place called Dos Ríos.

On this bullet-strafed and strangely anonymous battlefield, Martí, conspicuous on his white horse and dressed in his trademark black suit, was shot and killed as he charged suicidally toward the Spanish lines. Had he lived he would certainly have become Cuba's first president; instead, he became a hero and a martyr whose life and legacy would inspire generations of Cubans in years to come.

Conscious of mistakes made during the First War of Independence, Gómez and Maceo stormed west with a scorched-earth policy that left everything from the Oriente to Matanzas in flames. Early victories quickly led to a sustained offensive and, by January 1896, Maceo had broken through to Pinar del Río, while Gómez was tying down Spanish forces near Havana.

The Spaniards responded with an equally ruthless general named Valeriano Weyler, who built countrywide north–south fortifications to restrict the rebels' movements. In order to break the underground resistance, *guajiros* (country people) were forced into camps in a process called *reconcentración,* and anyone supporting the rebellion became liable for execution.

The brutal tactics started to show results. On December 7, 1896, the Mambís (the name for the 19th-century rebels fighting Spain) suffered a major military blow when Antonio Maceo was killed south of Havana trying to break out to the east.

1868

Céspedes frees his slaves in Manzanillo and proclaims the *Grito de Yara,* Cuba's first independence cry and the beginning of a 10-year war against the Spanish.

1878

The Pact of El Zanjón ends the First War of Independence. Cuban general Antonio Maceo issues the Protest of Baraguá and resumes hostilities the following year before disappearing into exile.

1886

After more than 350 years of exploitation and cross-Atlantic transportation, Cuba becomes the second-last country in the Americas to abolish slavery.

1892

From exile in the US, José Martí galvanizes popular support and forms the Cuban Revolutionary Party, laying the groundwork for the resumption of hostilities against Spain.

Enter the Americans

By this time Cuba was a mess: thousands were dead, the country was in flames, and William Randolph Hearst and the US tabloid press were leading a hysterical war campaign characterized by sensationalized, often inaccurate reports about Spanish atrocities.

Preparing perhaps for the worst, the US battleship *Maine* was sent to Havana in January 1898, on the pretext of 'protecting US citizens.' Its touted task never saw fruition. On February 15, 1898, the *Maine* exploded out of the blue in Havana Harbor, killing 266 US sailors.

The Spanish claimed it was an accident, the Americans blamed the Spanish, and some Cubans accused the US, saying it provided a convenient pretext for intervention. Despite several investigations conducted over the following years, the real cause of the explosion may remain one of history's great mysteries, as the hulk of the ship was scuttled in deep waters in 1911.

After the *Maine* debacle, the US scrambled to take control. They offered Spain US$300 million for Cuba and, when this deal was rejected, demanded a full withdrawal of the Spanish from the island. The long-awaited US–Spanish showdown that had been simmering imperceptibly beneath the surface for decades had finally resulted in war.

The only important land battle of the conflict was on July 1, when the US Army attacked Spanish positions on San Juan Hill just east of Santiago de Cuba. Despite vastly inferior numbers and limited, antiquated weaponry, the under-siege Spanish held out bravely for over 24 hours before future US President Theodore Roosevelt broke the deadlock by leading a celebrated cavalry charge of the Rough Riders up San Juan Hill. It was the beginning of the end for the Spaniards, and an unconditional surrender was offered to the Americans on July 17, 1898.

Post-Colonial Cuba

Independence or Dependence?

On May 20, 1902, Cuba became an independent republic – or did it? Despite three years of blood, sweat and sacrifice during the Spanish-Cuban-American War, no Cuban representatives were invited to the historic peace treaty held in Paris in 1898 that had promised Cuban independence *with conditions*.

The conditions were contained in the infamous Platt Amendment, a sly addition to the US 1901 Army Appropriations Bill that gave the US the right to intervene militarily in Cuba whenever it saw fit. The US also used its significant leverage to secure itself a naval base in Guantánamo

In the 1880s there were over 100,000 Chinese people living in Cuba, mainly as cheap labor on sugar plantations in and around the Havana region.

1895

José Martí and Antonio Maceo arrive in Cuba to ignite the Second Independence War. Martí is killed at Dos Ríos in May and is quickly elevated to martyr status.

1896

After sustaining more than 20 injuries in a four-decade military career, Antonio Maceo meets his end at Cacahual, Havana, where he is killed in an ambush.

1898

Following the loss of the battleship USS *Maine*, the US declares war on Spain and defeats its forces near Santiago. A four-year US occupation begins.

1902

Cuba gains nominal independence from the US and elects Tomás Estrada Palma as its president. US troops are called back three times within the first 15 years of the republic.

Bay in order to protect its strategic interests in the Panama Canal region.

Despite some opposition in the US and a great deal more in Cuba, the Platt Amendment was passed by Congress and was written into Cuba's 1902 constitution. For Cuban patriots, the US had merely replaced Spain as the new colonizer and enemy. The repercussions have been causing bitter feuds for over a century and still continue today.

The Batista Era

Fulgencio Batista, a *holguiñero* of mixed race from the town of Banes, was a wily and shrewd negotiator who presided over Cuba's best and worst attempts to establish an embryonic democracy in the 1940s and '50s. After an army officers' coup in 1933, he had taken power almost by default, gradually worming his way into the political vacuum it left amid the corrupt factions of a dying government. From 1934 onwards, Batista served as the army's chief of staff and, in 1940 in a relatively free and fair election, he was duly elected president.

Given an official mandate, Batista began to enact a wide variety of social reforms and set about drafting Cuba's most liberal and democratic constitution to date. But neither the liberal honeymoon nor Batista's good humor were to last. Stepping down after the 1944 election, the former army sergeant handed power over to the politically inept President Ramón Grau San Martín, and corruption and inefficiency soon reigned like never before.

The Revolutionary Spark is Lit

Aware of his erstwhile popularity and sensing an easy opportunity to line his pockets with one last big paycheck, Batista cut a deal with the American Mafia, promising to give them carte blanche in Cuba in return for a cut of their gambling profits, and positioned himself for a comeback.

Che Guevara – whose father's family name was Guevara Lynch – can trace his Celtic roots back to a Patrick Lynch, born in Galway in Ireland in 1715, who emigrated to Buenos Aires via Bilbao in 1749.

On March 10, 1952, three months before scheduled elections that he appeared he would lose, Batista staged a military coup. Wildly condemned by opposition politicians inside Cuba, but recognized by the US government two weeks later, Batista quickly let it be known, when he suspended various constitutional guarantees including the right to strike, that his second incarnation wouldn't be as enlightened as his first.

After Batista's coup, a revolutionary circle formed in Havana around the charismatic figure of Fidel Castro, a lawyer by profession and a gifted orator who had been due to stand in the canceled 1952 elections. Supported by his younger brother Raúl and aided intellectually by his

1920
Sharp increases in world sugar prices after WWI spearhead the so-called 'Dance of the Millions' in Cuba. Huge fortunes are made overnight. A heavy economic crash quickly follows.

1925
Gerardo Machado is elected president and institutes a massive program of public works, but his eight-year reign turns increasingly despotic as his declining popularity leads to resentful unrest.

1933
The 1933 revolution is sparked by an Army Officers' Coup that deposes the Machado dictatorship and installs Fulgencio Batista in power.

1940
Cuba adopts the '1940 Constitution', considered one of the most progressive documents of its era, guaranteeing rights to employment, property, minimum wage, education and social security.

HUMAN RIGHTS

'Human rights' in Cuba has long been the revolution's Achilles heel. To speak out against the government in this tightly controlled, politically paranoid society is a serious and heavily punishable crime that – if it doesn't first land you in jail – is likely to lead to job stagnation, petty harassment and social ostracism.

The Castro era got off to a bad start in January 1959 when the revolutionary government – under the auspices of Che Guevara – rounded up Batista's top henchmen and summarily executed them inside Havana's La Cabaña fort with barely a lawyer in sight. Within a matter of months the Cuban press had been silenced and worried onlookers in the US were vociferously calling 'foul.'

In the years since, Cuba has scored badly on most global human rights indices with the world's two most respected human rights bodies, Amnesty International and Human Rights Watch, regularly berating the government for its refusal to respect the rights of assembly, association and expression, and other basic civil liberties.

Cuba's international image took another hit during 2003's 'Black Spring' when the government rounded up 75 dissidents, who they claimed were agents of the US, and handed them all lengthy jail terms. After an international outcry, all of the dissidents were eventually released, the last in 2011. Notwithstanding, harassment and intimidation of dissidents, including peaceful protesters such as the 'Ladies in White,' continues.

Cuba's supporters often justify the alleged human rights violations with tit-for-tat arguments. When the US questioned the 2011 jailing of American development contractor Alan Gross, they pointed to the incarceration of the 'Cuban Five' (five Cubans imprisoned in the US on equally flimsy spying charges). Gross and the Cuban Five were finally released in a prisoner swap in December 2014.

There have been other improvements in recent years. Gay persecution, once rife at all levels of Cuban society, is largely a thing of the past. Religious persecution is similarly rare. Freedom of expression and the press, however, remain frustratingly stifled, although, in the internet age, some high-profile bloggers, most notably Yoani Sánchez, have managed to reach an international audience.

trusty lieutenant Abel Santamaría (later tortured to death by Batista's thugs), Castro saw no alternative to the use of force in ridding Cuba of its dictator.

Low on numbers but determined to make a political statement, Castro led 119 rebels in an attack on the strategically important Moncada army barracks in Santiago de Cuba on July 26, 1953. The audacious and poorly planned assault failed dramatically when the rebels' driver (who was from Havana) took the wrong turning in Santiago's badly signposted streets and the alarm was raised.

1952

Batista stages a b loodless military coup, canceling the upcoming Cuban elections in which an ambitious young lawyer named Fidel Castro was due to stand.

1953

Castro leads a band of rebels in a disastrous attack on the Moncada army barracks in Santiago. He uses his subsequent trial as a platform to expound his political plans.

1956

The *Granma* yacht lands in eastern Cuba with Castro and 81 rebels aboard. Decimated by the Cuban Army, only about a dozen survive to regroup in the Sierra Maestra.

1958

Che Guevara masterminds an attack against an armored train in Santa Clara, a military victory that finally forces Batista to concede power. The rebels march triumphantly on Havana.

Fooled, flailing and hopelessly outnumbered, 64 of the Moncada conspirators were rounded up by Batista's army and brutally tortured and executed. Castro and a handful of others managed to escape into the nearby mountains, where they were found a few days later by a sympathetic army lieutenant named Sarría, who had been given instructions to kill them. 'Don't shoot, you can't kill ideas!' Sarría is alleged to have shouted on finding Castro and his exhausted colleagues.

By taking Castro to jail instead of murdering him, Sarría ruined his military career, but saved Fidel's life. (One of Fidel's first acts after the revolution triumphed was to release Sarría from prison and give him a commission in the revolutionary army.) Castro's capture soon became national news, and he was put on trial in the full glare of the media spotlight. Fidel defended himself in court, writing an eloquent and masterfully executed speech that he later transcribed into a comprehensive political manifesto entitled *History Will Absolve Me.*

Basking in his newfound legitimacy and backed by a growing sense of dissatisfaction with the old regime in the country at large, Castro was sentenced to 15 years imprisonment on Isla de Pinos (a former name for Isla de la Juventud). Cuba was well on the way to gaining a new national hero.

In February 1955 Batista won the presidency in what were widely considered to be fraudulent elections and, in an attempt to curry favor with growing internal opposition, agreed to an amnesty for all political prisoners, including Castro. Believing that Batista's real intention was to assassinate him once out of jail, Castro fled to Mexico, leaving Baptist schoolteacher Frank País in charge of a fledgling underground resistance campaign that the vengeful Moncada veterans had christened the 26th of July Movement (M-26-7).

A 1976 book entitled *How the Battleship Maine Was Destroyed* concluded that the explosion of the *Maine* in Havana Harbor in 1898 was caused by the spontaneous combustion of coal in the ship's bunker.

The Revolution

In Mexico City, Castro and his compatriots plotted and planned afresh, drawing in key new figures such as Camilo Cienfuegos and the Argentine doctor Ernesto 'Che' Guevara, both of whom added strength and panache to the nascent army of disaffected rebel soldiers. On the run from the Mexican police and determined to arrive in Cuba in time for an uprising that Frank País had planned for late November 1956 in Santiago de Cuba, Castro and 81 companions set sail for the island on November 25 in an old and overcrowded leisure yacht named *Granma.*

After seven dire days at sea they arrived at Playa Las Coloradas near Niquero in Oriente on December 2 (two days late). Following a catastrophic landing – 'It wasn't a disembarkation; it was a shipwreck,' a wry

1959
Castro is welcomed ecstatically in Havana. The new government passes the historic First Agrarian Reform Act. Camilo Cienfuegos' plane goes missing over the Cuban coast off Camagüey.

1960
Castro nationalizes US assets on the island, provoking the US to cancel its Cuban sugar quota. Castro immediately sells the sugar to the Soviet Union.

1961
US-backed Cuban mercenaries stage an unsuccessful invasion at the Bay of Pigs. The US declares a full trade embargo. Cuba embarks on a highly successful literacy campaign.

1962
The discovery of medium-range nuclear missiles in Cuba, installed by the Soviet Union, brings the world to the brink of nuclear war in the so-called Cuban Missile Crisis.

Guevara later commented – they were spotted and routed by Batista's soldiers in a sugarcane field at Alegría de Pío three days later.

Of the 82 rebel soldiers who had left Mexico, little more than a dozen managed to escape. Splitting into three tiny groups, the survivors wandered around hopelessly for days half-starved, wounded and assuming that the rest of their compatriots had been killed in the initial skirmish. 'At one point I was Commander in Chief of myself and two other people,' Fidel commented years later. However, with the help of the local peasantry, the dozen or so hapless soldiers finally managed to reassemble two weeks later in Cinco Palmas, a clearing in the shadows of the Sierra Maestra, where a half-delirious Fidel gave a rousing and premature victory speech. 'We will win this war,' he proclaimed confidently. 'We are just beginning the fight!'

The comeback began on January 17, 1957, when the guerrillas scored an important victory by sacking a small army outpost on the south coast in Granma Province called La Plata. This was followed in February by a devastating propaganda coup when Fidel persuaded *New York Times* journalist Herbert Matthews to come up into the Sierra Maestra to interview him. The resulting article made Castro internationally famous and gained him much sympathy among liberal Americans.

By this point he wasn't the only anti-Batista agitator. On March 13, 1957, university students led by José Antonio Echeverría attacked the Presidential Palace in Havana in an unsuccessful attempt to assassinate Batista. Thirty-two of the 35 attackers were shot dead as they fled, and reprisals were meted out on the streets of Havana with a new vengeance. Cuba was rapidly disintegrating into a police state run by military-trained thugs.

Elsewhere passions were running equally high. In September 1957 naval officers in the normally tranquil city of Cienfuegos staged an armed revolt and set about distributing weapons among the disaffected populace. After some bitter door-to-door fighting, the insurrection was brutally crushed and the ringleaders rounded up and killed, but for the revolutionaries the point had been made. Batista's days were numbered.

Back in the Sierra Maestra, Fidel's rebels overwhelmed 53 Batista soldiers at an army post in El Uvero in May and captured more badly needed supplies. The movement seemed to be gaining momentum and despite losing Frank País to a government assassination squad in Santiago de Cuba in July, support and sympathy around the country was starting to mushroom. By the beginning of 1958 Castro had established a fixed headquarters in a cloud forest high up in the Sierra Maestra he christened 'La Plata', and was broadcasting propaganda messages

Castro's government passed over 1000 laws in its first year (1959), including rent and electricity cost reductions, the abolition of racial discrimination and the First Agrarian Reform Act.

1967

Che Guevara is hunted down and executed in Bolivia in front of CIA observers after a 10-month abortive guerrilla war in the mountains.

1968

The Cuban government nationalizes 58,000 small businesses in a sweeping socialist reform package. Everything falls under strict government control.

1970

Castro attempts to achieve a 10-million-ton sugar harvest. The plan fails and Cuba begins to wean itself off its unhealthy dependence on its mono-crop.

1976

Terrorists bomb a Cuban jet in Barbados, killing all 73 people aboard. A line is traced back to anti-Castro activists with histories as CIA operatives working out of Venezuela.

THE SPECIAL PERIOD

Following the demise of the Soviet Union in 1991, the Cuban economy – reliant since the 1960s on Soviet subsidies – went into freefall. Almost overnight half of the country's industrial factories closed, the transport sector ground to a halt, and the national economy shrunk by as much as 60%.

Determined to defend the revolution at all costs, Fidel Castro battened down the hatches and announced that Cuba was entering a 'Special Period in a Time of Peace' *(período especial),* a package of extreme austerity measures that reinforced widespread rationing and made acute shortages an integral part of everyday life. It was an unprecedented turnaround that quickly resonated throughout all levels of society. Suddenly Cubans, who had been relatively well-off a year or so earlier, faced a massive battle just to survive.

The stories of how ordinary Cubans got through the darkest days of the Special Period are as remarkable as they are shocking. In three fearsome years the average Cuban lost over a third of their body weight and saw meat pretty much eradicated from their diet. In the social forum, the Special Period invented a whole new culture of conservation and innovation, and elements of this communal belt-tightening still characterize the Cuban way of life today.

The worst years of the Special Period were 1991–94, though the recovery was slow with proper progress only possible after Cuba forged closer ties with Venezuela (and its oil) in the early 2000s.

from Radio Rebelde (710AM and 96.7FM) all across Cuba. The tide was starting to turn.

Sensing his popularity waning, Batista sent an army of 10,000 men into the Sierra Maestra in May 1958, on a mission known as Plan FF (*Fin de Fidel* or End of Fidel). The intention was to liquidate Castro and his merry band of loyal guerrillas who had now burgeoned into a solid fighting force of 300 men. The offensive became something of a turning point as the rebels – with the help of the local *campesinos* (country people) – gradually halted the onslaught of Batista's young and ill-disciplined conscript army.

With the Americans increasingly embarrassed by the no-holds-barred terror tactics of their one-time Cuban ally, Castro sensed an opportunity to turn defense into offense and signed the groundbreaking Caracas Pact with eight leading opposition groups calling on the US to stop all aid to Batista. Che Guevara and Camilo Cienfuegos were promptly dispatched to the Escambray Mountains to open up new fronts in the west, and by December, with Cienfuegos holding down troops in Yagua-

1980

Following an incident at the Peruvian embassy, Castro opens the Cuban port of Mariel. Within six months, 125,000 have fled the island for the US in the so-called Mariel Boatlift.

1988

Cuban forces play a crucial role in the Battle of Cuito Cuanavale in Angola, a serious defeat for the white South African army and its system of apartheid.

1991

The Soviet Union collapses and Cuba heads toward its worst economic collapse of modern times, entering what Castro calls a 'Special Period in a Time of Peace.'

1993

Attempting to revive itself from its economic coma, Cuba legalizes the US dollar, opens up the country to tourism and allows limited forms of private enterprise.

jay (the garrison finally surrendered after an 11-day siege) and Guevara closing in on Santa Clara, the end was in sight.

It was left to Che Guevara to seal the final victory, employing classic guerrilla tactics to derail an armored train in Santa Clara and split the country's battered communications system in two. By New Year's Eve 1958, the game was up: a sense of jubilation filled the country, and Che and Camilo were on their way to Havana unopposed.

In the small hours of January 1, 1959, Batista fled by private plane to the Dominican Republic. Meanwhile, materializing in Santiago de Cuba the same day, Fidel made a rousing victory speech from the town hall in Parque Céspedes before jumping into a 4WD and traveling across the breadth of the country to Havana in a Caesar-like cavalcade. The triumph of the revolution was seemingly complete.

In December 1946 the Mafia convened the biggest ever get-together of North American mobsters in Havana's Hotel Nacional, under the pretense that they were going to see a Frank Sinatra concert.

Post-Revolutionary Realities

Cuba's history since the revolution has been a David and Goliath tale of confrontation, rhetoric, Cold War stand offs and an omnipresent US trade embargo that has featured 11 US presidents and two infamous Cuban leaders – both called Castro. For the first 30 years, Cuba allied itself with the Soviet Union as the US used various retaliatory tactics (all unsuccessful) to bring Fidel Castro to heel, including a botched invasion, 600-plus assassination attempts and one of the longest economic blockades in modern history.

When the Soviet bloc fell in 1989–91, Cuba stood alone behind an increasingly defiant and stubborn leader surviving, against all odds, through a decade of severe economic austerity known as the Special Period. GDP fell by more than half, luxuries went out the window, and a wartime spirit of rationing and sacrifice took hold among a populace that, ironically, had prized itself free from foreign (neo)colonial influences for the first time in its history.

In the 17th century the Spanish forced the remaining indigenous population into towns known as *pueblos indios*. Old and New World cultures cross-fertilized, allowing Indian practices and words to seep into everyday Cuban life.

Enter Raúl

In July 2006, the unimaginable happened. Fidel Castro, rather than dying in office and paving the way for an American-led capitalistic reopening (as had long been predicted), retired from day-to-day governing due to poor health and passed power quietly onto his younger brother, Raúl. Inheriting the country's highest office on the cusp of a major worldwide recession, Raúl began a slow package of reforms.

It kicked off modestly in 2008 when Cubans were permitted access to tourist hotels, and allowed to purchase mobile phones and myriad electronic goods; rights taken for granted in most democratic countries, but long out of reach to the average Cuban. These moves were followed

1996

Miami 'Brothers to the Rescue' planes are shot down by Cuban jets, provoking Bill Clinton to sign the Helms-Burton Act, further tightening the terms of the US embargo.

2002

Half of Cuba's sugar refineries are closed, signaling the end of a three-century-long addiction to the boom-bust mono-crop. Laid off sugar workers continue to draw salaries and are offered free education.

2003

The Bush administration tightens the noose for US citizens traveling to Cuba. Many political dissidents are arrested by Cuban authorities in an island-wide crackdown.

2006

Castro is taken ill just before his 80th birthday with diverticulitis disease and steps down from the day-to-day running of the country. He is replaced by his brother Raúl.

THE US & CUBA

What next? Cuba-watchers continue observing and speculating about the future of Cuba and US relations after the death of Fidel Castro followed the first tentative moves on behalf of the US to reinstate relations.

Despite its location 90 miles off the shores of Florida, Cuba remains, in the eyes of most Americans, one of the last great travel mysteries. Since 1963, when the US government instituted a de facto Cuban travel ban, visits by US nationals have been problematic. While the Obama administration opened the doors considerably, all bets are off whether relations will continue to thaw as the Trump administration seeks a stricter policy. See p511 and 519 for more information.

Putting Pressure on the Embargo

While the US reduced restrictions on travel and trade with Cuba under the Obama administration, the US Congress has yet to approve lifting the embargo, termed *el bloqueo* in Spanish. Surveys in the US suggest that a majority of Americans are opposed to the US embargo. The UN General Assembly passes annual resolutions against the US embargo. The most recent passed by a margin of 188 votes, with the US and Israel voting against a lift in 2016.

The Cuban-American Dream

With economic migrants currently outnumbering older politicized exiles in the US, a small majority of Cuban-Americans is now less vociferously anti-Castro and more in favor of ending the embargo that inadvertently helped keep Castro in power. After 50 years of squabbling, the Cubans and their exiled counterparts remain a divided populace. What part could the exile community play in a new Cuban government? How much are they in the pockets of the Americans? And would Cuba compensate them for property and goods confiscated in 1960?

Emigrating to the US has become tougher than ever. As one of his last acts in office, President Obama ended the 'wet foot, dry foot' policy that guaranteed all Cuban migrants the possibility of US residency.

in January 2011 by the biggest economic and ideological shake-up since the country waved *adiós* to Batista. Radical new laws laid off half a million government workers and tried to stimulate the private sector by granting business licenses to 178 state-recognized professions – everything from hairdressers to disposable-lighter refillers.

In October 2011, car sales were legalized and Cubans were allowed to buy and sell their homes for the first time in half a century. Even bolder was a decree announced in late 2012 that allowed Cubans to

2008

Raúl Castro is officially inaugurated as Cuban president and embarks on his first set of reforms, permitting Cubans access to tourist hotels and allowing them to purchase mobile phones and electronic goods.

2009

The inauguration of Barack Obama signifies a long-awaited thaw in Cuba-US relations. In an early act of rapprochement, Obama loosens restrictions for Cuban-Americans returning to the island to visit relatives.

2011

Raúl Castro signals an economic thaw by announcing that the government plans to cut half a million jobs from the state sector and open up private enterprise to more than 175 licensed businesses.

2014

Following a prisoner swap, Barack Obama announces the reestablishment of diplomatic ties with Cuba and a raft of measures including telecommunications aid and the easing of financial restrictions.

travel freely abroad, a basic right that had been barred to all but the favored few since 1961.

By 2013, Cuba had witnessed its most dramatic economic shift in decades with nearly 400,000 people working in the private sector, 250,000 more than in 2010, though it was still far from anything like Western-style capitalism.

The Passing of Fidel

Fidel's omnipresence for the past half-century made the man seem invincible, yet on November 25th, 2016, Raúl Castro announced his brother's passing at the age of 90. His cremated remains were laid to rest in Santiago de Cuba after a cross-island procession that recalled the march of his revolutionary triumph, done in reverse. Throughout Cuba, crowds lined the streets to pay homage to their longtime leader as exiles celebrated in Miami.

The Observer noted that Fidel Castro was 'as divisive in death as he was in life.' His cremated remains were laid to rest under a large boulder-shaped stone simply engraved 'Fidel.' Orders were left to not use his likeness for statues or souvenirs, nor his name for streets, institutions or public sites (perhaps the commodification of Che Guevara rested heavy on his shoulders).

Yet 2016 had already been a year for further transition for Cuba. In March, US President Barack Obama had visited, meeting with Raúl Castro and local entrepreneurs, promising that change would come to the island. The first sitting US president to visit since the 1959 revolution, his visit heralded telecom agreements, mutual cooperation in law enforcement and the environment and the reinstatement of commercial flights to and from the US.

A new chapter of history was beginning. Fidel Castro responded at the time via the communist party newspaper *Granma*: 'We don't need the empire to gift us anything.'

Fidel's proclamations and reflections continue to pour forth from the grave, published in *Granma* posthumously.

2016

Fidel Castro dies on November 25th, 2016 at the age of ninety. After one week of mourning and a cross-island procession during which the vehicle carrying his remains breaks down, he is laid to rest in Santiago de Cuba.

2017

Before leaving office, US President Obama ends the 'wet foot, dry foot' policy that gave sanctuary to all Cuban immigrants, a policy long opposed by the Cuban government.

2017

While not nearly a full rollback of his predecessor's Cuba policies, US President Donald Trump's directives limit travelers from the US to group tours and seek to clampdown on travel-related transactions with the Cuban military.

Food & Drink

Until recently Cuba was a country where rationing dictated the menu. Only in recent years did change incrementally start. Inspired and enabled by the ongoing political and economic reform, the nation's long-suppressed chefs started innovating. Sure, creativity in part comes from facing limitations, but there's no denying that a culinary revolution is coming.

Above Lamb stew

The Culinary Challenge

Señores and señoras, we are pleased to announce that Cuba is no longer the proverbial 'leftover' plate of the culinary world. The turnaround has been astronomical and unprecedented. The economic reforms of 2011, when the Cuban government allowed private restaurants (until then limited to 12 people) to expand and diversify, has been a massive game-changer.

Taste-deprived travelers who once wisely elected to skip the first few courses to proceed directly to rum and cigars, now have honey-glazed chicken, lovingly prepared béchamel sauces, and new takes on old Cuban favorites such as *ropa vieja* (spicy shredded beef). Feeding the trend, Havana and other cities are awash with creative new private restaurants experimenting with cooking methods and ingredients previously unheard of on the island. Free from the shackles of austere 1990s rationing, Cuban chefs bandy around words like 'fusion' and 'medium-rare', and inscribe their menus with dishes such as eggplant caviar.

For first-time visitors accustomed to French-style creativity or American abundance, the food might not seem very remarkable. But if you last visited Cuba in the early 2000s, in the days when all chickens were fried to smithereens and soggy cheese-and-ham sandwiches spelled lunch, you're in for a rather pleasant surprise.

The 'holy trinity' of cocktails consists of the mojito, the daiquiri and the Cuba Libre.

Stewing 500 Years

The pain and shortages of the 1990s didn't do Cuban cuisine any favors, starving it of all but the most basic of ingredients and obscuring what, beneath the surface, has always been a rich and surprisingly diverse food culture.

Cuba's cuisine is a creative stew of selective morsels, recipes and cooking techniques left behind by successive travelers since the epoch of Columbus and Velázquez. Imagine a bubbling cauldron filled with ingredients plucked from Spain, Africa, France, pre-colonial Taínos, and cultures from various other islands in the Caribbean that has been left to intermingle and marinate for 500 years.

From the original Taínos came indigenous root vegetables such as yucca and sweet potato, and native fruits such as guava; from the Spanish came pork, rice, flavor-enhancing spices and different frying techniques; African slave culture brought plantains in their various guises along with *congrí* (rice and beans cooked together with spices in the same pot); while, from its island neighbors, Cuba shares the unmistakable taste of the Caribbean enshrined in *sofrito,* a base sauce of tomatoes seasoned with onions, peppers, garlic, bay leaf and cumin.

Mix it all together for 'Cuban' cuisine: simple, hearty but healthy food that's light on spice (cumin and oregano predominate), but has no shortage of flavor. Whole roast pork is the meat of choice, closely followed by chicken, fried or roasted and often flavored with citrus sauces or honey.

REGIONAL SPECIALTIES

➡ **Caibarién** This small town in Villa Clara Province is Cuba's crab capital.

➡ **Baracoa** A completely different food universe to the rest of Cuba. Specialties include *cucurucho* (sweet blend of honey, coconut, guava and nuts), *bacán* (tamale with mashed banana, crab and coconut), *teti* (tiny fish indigenous to Toa River), and *lechita* (spicy coconut sauce).

➡ **Playa Larga & Zapata Peninsula** Crocodiles are farmed and consumed in stews in hotels and casas particulares in southern Matanzas Province.

➡ **Bayamo** *Ostiones* (oysters usually served in a tomato sauce) are a staple street-food in Granma's main city.

➡ **Oriente** *Congrí* – rice and red beans seasoned with cumin, peppers and pork chunks – has its roots in the African-influenced culture of eastern Cuba. In the west, you're more likely to get *moros y cristianos* (with black beans but no pork).

➡ **Las Tunas** Birthplace of *La Caldosa,* a soup-like stew made with root vegetables, chicken and spices.

Tamales

Never far from the sea, the Cubans love fish: lobster, crab, prawns, *aguja* (swordfish) and *pargo* (snapper) are common. The key starch is rice usually mixed with beans as either *moros y cristianos* (made with black beans) or *congrí* (made with red beans). Root vegetables are another mainstay and are complemented by plantains, cooked many ways. In season, Cuban avocados are sublime and tropical fruit is abundant.

Don't leave Cuba without trying the national dish, *ropa vieja* (spicy shredded beef), whole roast pork with all the trimmings, *picadillo* (ground beef with olives and capers), *tostones* (twice-fried plantains), and *moros y cristianos*.

Rum Tales

Pioneers in the field of rum manufacture in the mid-19th century, the Cubans successfully transformed *aguardiente,* the coarse and unrefined 'fire water' imbibed by sailors and pirates on the Spanish Main, into the smooth, clear 'Ron Superior' used today in sophisticated cocktails such as mojitos and daiquiris. The man behind the metamorphosis was a Spanish immigrant from Catalonia called Don Facundo Bacardí Massó (1814-86). Don Facundo's Santiago de Cuba rum factory was inaugurated in a bat-infested dockside warehouse in 1862 where he experimented with the region's high-quality sugarcane to create a new kind of aged rum that was delicate, crisp and fruity on the palate. Winning instant popularity, Bacardí's name quickly became a byword for rum and the family emerged as powerful and influential voices in Cuban politics.

Guarapo is pure sugarcane juice mixed with ice and lemon that is served from quaint little roadside stalls called *guaraperos* all over rural Cuba.

Yet the Bacardís ultimately fell out with the Castro regime in the early 1960s and fled abroad, moving their headquarters to Bermuda. Although you won't find any Bacardí rum sold in Cuba today, the company's old factory in Santiago still produces the domestically popular Ron Caney (the so-called 'rum of the revolution'), stored in Don Facundo's barrels.

Mojito

The other famous Cuban rum dynasty, Havana Club was founded by José Arechabala in the town of Cárdenas in 1878. The Arechabala family also fled Cuba after the revolution although they were less successful in maintaining their trademark, seized by the Cuban government in 1973. Today, Havana Club accounts for 40% of Cuba's alcohol market.

Aside from the Ron Caney factory in Santiago and the Havana Club operation now based in Santa Cruz del Norte near Havana, Cuba supports more than 100 rum factories. Tap a local and they'll probably wax poetically about Ron Santiago de Cuba, Ron Mulata (made in Villa Clara) or Ron Varadero.

Rum is made from molasses, a by-product of sugarcane. Its fabrication in Cuba has been overseen by generations of skillful *maestros romeros* ('rum masters'), who must have a minimum of 15 years of rum-tasting experience. The drink is classified by both color (dark, golden or clear) and age *(añejo)*. Good rums can range from anything from three years to 14 years in age. As a rule, rum cocktails (always made with clear rum) are more popular with tourists than Cubans. Cubans prefer to drink their rum dark and neat (without ice) in order to enjoy the full flavor.

FRUIT, GLORIOUS FRUIT

Stay in a Cuban casa particular and you'll nearly always be offered a massive breakfast. The first thing to arrive is usually an ambrosial plate of tropical fruit. Its contents vary according to season and location, but the classic selection consists of a juicy quintet of banana, papaya, mango, pineapple and guava. Of these only guava and pineapple predate the arrival of the Spanish on the isles. Bananas and mangoes, both Asian in origin, were brought to Cuba during the colonial period, where they thrive in the tropical climate. The papaya is indigenous to South America.

Cuban Way of Life

Blurring past the outskirts of a provincial city on a tour bus, Cuba can seem bleak and austere. But what you see isn't always what you get on this island. Try observation, patience and a little sleuthing to glimpse beneath Cuba's hard and opaque surface. You'll see that elaborate codes keep vibrant local life ticking. Crack them to find the irrepressible energy and inventiveness, the culture's non-stop dance to carry on in spite of everything.

A Recipe for Being Cuban

Just try to understand life on this ever-contradictory island. Your first impression may be that it is solid and immutable. But the truth is that Cuba is a moving target that evades easy definition.

For starters, it's like nowhere else. For those familiar with Latin America, there's close-knit families and an ease with unpredictability. But there are differences too. Cuba's strong educational system has created erudite citizens more likely to quote the classics than pop songs. They are playful, even raucous, but also intimate with hardship and austerity, skilled but as languorous as any Caribbean outport.

The best way to get to know Cuba is to reserve comment and watch it unfold before you. While long lines and poor service infuriate tourists, Cubans remain unflappable. Rushing doesn't make things happen any faster. But there are richer ways to pass the time: shooting the breeze in rocking chairs, spending Sundays with families or inviting their cousins, friends and neighbors over when a bottle of rum comes your way.

Lifestyle

Survivors by nature and necessity, Cubans have long displayed an almost inexhaustible ability to bend the rules and 'work things out' when it matters. The two most overused verbs in the national phrasebook are *conseguir* (to get, manage) and *resolver* (to resolve, work out). Cubans are experts at doing both. Their intuitive ability to bend the rules and make something out of nothing is borne out of economic necessity. In a small nation bucking modern sociopolitical realities, where monthly salaries top out at around the equivalent of US$25, survival can often mean getting innovative as a means of supplementing personal income.

Cruise the crumbling streets of Centro Habana and you'll see people *conseguir*-ing and *resolver*-ing wherever you go. There's the off-duty doctor using his car as a taxi, or the street cartoonist scribbling sketches of unsuspecting tourists in the hope of earning a tip. Other schemes may be ill-gotten or garnered through trickery, such as the *compañero* (comrade) who pockets the odd blemished cigar from the day job to sell to unsuspecting Canadians. Old Cuba hands know one of the most popular ways to make extra cash is working with (or over) tourists.

In Cuba, hard currency (ie convertible pesos) rules, primarily because it is the only way of procuring the modest luxuries that make living in this austere socialist republic more comfortable. Paradoxically, the post-

Main Cuban Crops

- *Bananas*
- *Citrus fruit*
- *Coffee*
- *Mangos*
- *Pineapples*
- *Rice*
- *Sugarcane*
- *Tobacco*

1993 double economy has reinvigorated the class system the Revolution worked so hard to neutralize, and it's no longer rare to see Cubans with access to convertibles touting designer clothing while others beg tourists for bars of soap. This stark re-emergence of 'haves' and 'have-nots' is striking.

Other social traits that have emerged since the Revolution are more altruistic and less divisive. In Cuba sharing is second nature and helping out your *compañero* with a lift, a square meal or a few convertibles when they're in trouble is considered a national duty. See the way that strangers interact in queues and neighbors share everything from tools, to food, to babysitting time without a second thought.

Cubans are informal. The *tú* form of Spanish address is much more common that the formal *usted,* and people greet each other with a variety of friendly addresses. Don't be surprised if a complete stranger calls you *mi amor* (my love) or *mi vida* (my life), and expect casa particular owners to regularly open the front door shirtless (men), or with their hair in rollers (women). To confuse matters further, Cuban Spanish is rich in colloquialisms, irony, sarcasm and swears.

Cuba leads the world with the lowest patient to doctor ratio. It has almost three times as many doctors to patients as in the United States.

The Home Front

While Cuban homes sport the basics (fridges, cookers, microwaves), they still lack the expensive trappings of 21st-century consumerism. Car ownership is approximately 38 per 1000, compared to 800 per 1000 in the US; few households sport clothes dryers (spot the flapping clothes lines). That impressive breakfast laid out by your casa particular owner at 8am probably took three hours of searching and queuing to procure (Cuban supermarkets have nothing like the variety and abundance of goods as their counterparts in the US or Europe).

Not that this dents home pride; gathered ornaments and mementos, however old and kitschy, are displayed with love and kept ruthlessly clean. To most outsiders, the local lifestyle seems old-fashioned and austere.

What makes Cuba different from somewhere like Mexico City or Philadelphia, though, is the government's heavy subsidising of every facet of life, meaning there are few mortgages, no health-care bills, no college fees and fewer taxes. Expensive nights out cost next to nothing in Cuba, where tickets for the theater, the cinema, the ballpark or a music concert are state-subsidized and considered a right of the people.

CUBAN CIGARS

From the sombrero-clad *guajiros* in the tobacco fields of Pinar del Río to the high-end smoking rooms and cigar-pushing hustlers of Havana, cigars are deeply embedded in Cuban culture. Here are some local favorites:

Cohiba The cigar championed by Fidel Castro. Made with Cuba's finest Pinar del Río Province tobacco; production allegedly comes from a coveted 10 fields from the princedom of the nation's plantations, the Vuelta Abajo region around San Juan y Martínez.

Vegas Robaina Hard to come by outside Cuba, the brand is named after tobacco-growing legend Alejandro Robaina, famous for the outstanding quality of the tobacco used, which heralds from the Alejandro Robaina Tobacco Plantation outside Pinar del Río.

Partagás One of the best-loved cuban cigars since before the Revolution, known now for its annual *ediciones limitada* (limited editions).

Puro Cubano An unbranded cigar that Cubans prefer because of its vastly cheaper price, but nevertheless rolled with some of Pinar del Río Province's best leaves.

The Winds of Change

Fueled by cautious reform, the Cuban way of life has been changing slowly and subtly since Raúl Castro took the reins from Fidel in 2008. Though the progress may seem sluggish to insiders, a returning exile who has spent the last decade in Miami or Madrid would have some illuminating epiphanies.

Barely anyone had a cell phone in Cuba in the mid-2000s; today, the devices are almost as ubiquitous as they are in the rest of the world. The recent addition of public wi-fi hotspots has turned parks into vibrant collective one-sided conversations held loudly with relatives abroad. A diaspora of families separated for decades are getting to know one another again.

Electronic goods legalized in 2008 have also found their way into Cuban households. These days, it is not unusual to see a DVD player and a modern flat-screen TV beneath a yellowing picture of José Martí. The ability of Cubans to travel abroad since January 2013 has enabled a lucky few who can afford it to shop overseas. Consequently, some of the more successful casas particulares come equipped with shiny sandwich-makers and coffee machines.

Cuba's improved culinary scene (p464) is one of the most visible changes for people who remember the hunger of the 1990s. Notwithstanding, the dilemma of any new private restaurant owner is how to pitch their pricing – at foreigners or Cubans, or a mix of both? Some keep two menus with different pricing in both currencies. Top restaurants in Havana are still generally the preserve of tourists and diplomats, while private restaurants in the smaller provincial towns are patronized primarily by locals and are thus more reasonably priced.

Until 2008, Cubans were inexplicably barred from staying in tourist hotels. While high prices still keep out many, some of the more economical resorts like Playa Santa Lucía welcome plenty of Cuban guests during the long hot summer holiday.

A quick drive around the Cuban countryside will induce further surprises. While it's hardly LA yet, there are noticeably more cars on the road than there were in the early 2000s. That said, the new law permitting Cubans to buy and sell their own vehicles is little more than a political gesture. Precious few people can afford Toyotas and Audis, meaning 'yank tanks' and Ladas remain the cars of necessity.

Agriculture has also registered significant improvements. Pre-2008, Cuba's notoriously emaciated and unproductive cows wandered around pathetically in twos or threes. Now whole fields full of plump healthy-looking livestock populate the farms of Las Tunas and Camagüey Provinces.

Markets and shops, though still far from lavish, have fewer empty shelves these days and there has been a surge in shops selling large household items such as fridges and washing machines. In urban centers, private business resonates everywhere, from street-side barbers to sophisticated tour guides with their own business cards and websites. You'll even see professional street-signs advertising casas particulares or restaurants – something that was unheard of (and prohibited) until recently.

Inevitably these changes, while almost universally welcomed, have accentuated income divisions in a country long accustomed to socialism. People with ready access to convertibles – primarily those working in the tourist sector – have prospered; indeed, some casas particulares in Havana (who were limited to renting just two rooms until 2011) have morphed into mini-hotels in all but name. Meanwhile, the lives of people in the more isolated parts of rural Cuba have changed little. In small towns in the Oriente, the foibles that have haunted Cuba since the Special Period – shortages of bottled water, crumbling public buildings and awful roads – continue to bite.

Elements of French culture imported via Haiti in the 1790s are still visible in Cuba today, particularly in the French-founded settlements of Guantánamo and Cienfuegos.

Sport

Considered a right of the masses, professional sport was abolished by the government after the Revolution. Performance-wise it was the best thing the new administration could have done. Since 1959, Cuba's Olympic medal haul has rocketed into the stratosphere, though in recent years its flagging performance is blamed on lack of funding.

The crowning moment came in 1992 when Cuba – a country of 11 million people languishing low on the world's rich list – brought home 14 gold medals and ended fifth on the overall medals table. It's a testament to Cuba's high sporting standards that their 11th-place finish in Athens in 2004 was considered something of a national failure.

Characteristically, the sporting obsession starts at the top. Fidel Castro was once renowned for his baseball-hitting prowess, but what is lesser known was his personal commitment to the establishment of a widely accessible national sporting curriculum at all levels. In 1961 the National Institute of Sport, Physical Education and Recreation (INDER) founded a system of sport for the masses that eradicated discrimination and integrated children from a young age. By offering paid leisure-time to workers and dropping entrance fees to major sports events, the organization caused participation in popular sports to multiply tenfold by the 1970s and the knock-on effect to performance was tangible.

Cuban *pelota* (baseball) is legendary and the country is riveted during the October to March regular season, turning rabid for the play-offs in April. You'll see passions running high in the main square of provincial capitals, where fans debate minute details of the game with lots of finger-wagging in what is known as a *peña deportiva* (fan club) or *esquina caliente* (hot corner).

Cuba is also a giant in amateur boxing, as indicated by champions Teófilo Stevenson, who brought home Olympic gold in 1972, 1976 and 1980, and Félix Savón, another triple medal winner, most recently in 2000. Every sizable town has an arena called *sala polivalente,* where big boxing events take place, while training and smaller matches happen at gyms, many of which train Olympic athletes.

Multiculturalism

A convergence of three different races and numerous nationalities, Cuba is a multicultural society that, despite difficult challenges, has been relatively successful in forging racial equality.

The annihilation of the indigenous Taíno by the Spanish and the brutality of the slave system left a bloody mark in the early years of colonization, but the situation had improved significantly by the second half of the 20th century. The Revolution guaranteed racial freedom by law, though black Cubans are still far more likely to be stopped by the police for questioning, and over 90% of Cuban exiles in the US are of white descent. Black people are also under-represented in politics; of the victorious rebel army officers that took control of the government in 1959, only a handful (Juan Almeida being the most obvious example) were black or mixed race.

According to the most recent census, Cuba's racial breakdown is 27% *mulato* (mixed race), 64% white, 8% black and 1% Chinese. Aside from the obvious Spanish legacy, many of the so-called 'white' population are the descendants of French immigrants who arrived on the island in various waves during the early part of the 19th century. Indeed, the cities of

Cuba high-jumper Javier Sotomayor has held the world record (2.45m) for the event since 1993, and has recorded 17 of the 24 highest jumps ever.

Guantánamo, Cienfuegos and Santiago de Cuba were all either pioneered or heavily influenced by French *émigrés,* and much of Cuba's coffee and sugar industries owe their development to French entrepreneurship.

The black population is also an eclectic mix. Numerous Haitians and Jamaicans came to Cuba to work in the sugar fields in the 1920s and they brought many of their customs and traditions with them. Their descendants can be found in Guantánamo and Santiago in the Oriente or places such as Venezuela in Ciego de Ávila Province, where Haitian voodoo rituals are still practiced.

Religion

Religion is among the most misunderstood and complex aspects of Cuban culture. Before the Revolution, 85% of Cubans were nominal Roman Catholics, though only 10% attended church regularly. Protestants made up most of the remaining church-going public, though a smattering of Jews and Muslims have always practiced in Cuba and still do. When the Revolution triumphed, 140 Catholic priests were expelled for reactionary political activities and another 400 left voluntarily, while the majority of Protestants, who represented society's poorer sector, had less to lose and stayed.

When the government declared itself Marxist-Leninist and therefore atheist, life for *creyentes* (literally 'believers') took on new difficulties. Though church services were never banned and freedom of religion never revoked, Christians were sent to Unidades Militares de Ayuda a la Producción (UMAPs; Military Production Aid Units), where it was hoped hard labor might reform their religious ways; homosexuals and vagrants were also sent to the fields to work. This was a short-lived experiment, however. More trying for believers were the hard-line Soviet days of the '70s and '80s, when they were prohibited from joining the Communist Party and few, if any, believers held political posts. Certain university careers, notably in the humanities, were off-limits as well.

Things have changed dramatically since then, particularly in 1992 when the constitution was revised, removing all references to the Cuban state as Marxist-Leninist and recapturing the laical nature of the government. This led to an aperture in civil and political spheres of society for religious adherents, and to other reforms (eg believers are now eligible for party membership).

Cuba is one of the few small nations graced with the visit of the past three popes. Since Cuban Catholicism gained the papal seal of approval with Pope John Paul II's visit in 1998, church attendance surged, rewarded further with the arrival of his successor Pope Benedict XVI in 2012. Pope Francis, the first pontiff from Latin America, was received by a thrilled public in a nine-day visit in 2015 as he urged more freedom to worship. He also is credited with brokering the diplomatic thaw in US–Cuba relations.

It's worth noting that church services have a strong youth presence. There are currently 400,000 Catholics regularly attending Mass and 300,000 Protestants from 54 denominations. Other denominations such as the Seventh Day Adventists and Pentecostals are rapidly growing in popularity.

Santería

Of all Cuba's cultural mysteries (and there are many), Santería is the most complex, cloaking an inherent 'African-ness' and leading you down an unmapped road that is at once foggy and fascinating.

A syncretistic religion that hides African roots beneath a symbolic Catholic veneer, Santería is a product of the slave era, but remains deeply embedded in contemporary Cuban culture, where it has had a major

THE REVOLUTION WILL BE BLOGGED

Ever-literary Cuba is producing a growing number of eloquent bloggers with views across the political spectrum, despite poor internet access. Note that you probably shouldn't access these sites from Cuba.

Generación Y (Yoani Sánchez; www.desdecuba.com/generaciony) Sánchez is Cuba's most famous blogger (and dissident) and her gritty blog 'Generación Y' has been testing the mettle of Cuba's censorship police since April 2007. An unapologetic critic of the Cuban government, she has attracted a huge international audience (US President Barack Obama once replied to one of her posts) and won numerous awards, including the Ortega & Gasset prize for digital journalism.

Havana Times (www.havanatimes.org) A website and 'blog cooperative' started by American writer Circles Robinson in 2008 that positions itself as anti-Castro and anti-embargo.

Café Fuerte (www.cafefuerte.com; Spanish only) Blog spot set up by four Cuban writers and journalists with international experience in 2010. It reports independently on Cuban-related news matters both inside and outside Cuba.

impact on the evolution of the country's music, dance and rituals. Today more than three million Cubans identify as believers, including numerous writers, artists and politicians.

Santería's misrepresentations start with its name; the word is a historical misnomer first coined by Spanish colonizers to describe the 'saint worship' practiced by 19th-century African slaves. A more accurate moniker is Regla de Ocha (way of the *orishas*), or Lucumí, named for the original adherents who hailed from the Yoruba ethno-linguistic group in southwestern Nigeria, a prime looting ground for brutal slave-traders.

Fully initiated adherents of Santería (called *santeros*) believe in one God known as Oludomare, the creator of the universe and the source of Ashe (all life forces on earth). Rather than interact with the world directly, Oludomare communicates through a pantheon of *orishas*, various imperfect deities similar to Catholic saints or Greek gods, who are blessed with different natural (water, weather, metals) and human (love, intellect, virility) qualities. *Orishas* have their own feast days, demand their own food offerings, and are given numbers and colors to represent their personalities.

Unlike Christianity or Islam, Santería has no equivalent to the Bible or Koran. Instead, religious rites are transmitted orally and, over time, have evolved to fit the realities of modern Cuba. Another departure from popular world religions is the abiding focus on 'life on earth' as opposed to the afterlife, although Santería adherents believe strongly in the powers of dead ancestors, known as *egun*, whose spirits are invoked during initiation ceremonies.

Santería's syncretism with Catholicism occurred surreptitiously during the colonial era when African animist traditions were banned. In order to hide their faith from the Spanish authorities, African slaves secretly twinned their *orishas* with Catholic saints. Thus, Changó the male *orisha* of thunder and lightning was hidden somewhat bizarrely behind the feminine form of Santa Bárbara, while Elegguá, the *orisha* of travel and roads became St Anthony de Padua. In this way an erstwhile slave praying before a statue of Santa Bárbara was clandestinely offering his/her respects to Changó, while Afro-Cubans ostensibly celebrating the feast day of Our Lady of Regla (September 7) were, in reality, honoring Yemayá. This syncretization, though no longer strictly necessary, is still followed today.

Literature & the Arts

Leave your preconceptions about 'art in a totalitarian state' at home. The breadth of Cuban cinema, painting and literature could put many far more politically libertarian nations to shame. The Cubans seem to have a habit of taking almost any artistic genre and reinventing it for the better. You'll pick up everything here from first-class flamenco and ballet through to classical music and alternative cinema to Shakespearean theater and Lorca plays.

Literary Cuba

Cubans *love* conversation and extend their loquaciousness to the page. Maybe it's something in the rum, but since time immemorial, writers in this highly literate Caribbean archipelago have barely paused for breath, telling and retelling their stories with zeal. In the process they have produced some of Latin America's most groundbreaking, influential literature.

The Classicists

Any literary journey should begin in Havana in the 1830s. Cuban literature found its earliest voice in *Cecilia valdés*, a novel by Cirilo Villaverde (1812–94), published in 1882 but set 50 years earlier in a Havana divided by class, slavery and prejudice. It's widely considered to be the greatest 19th-century Cuban novel.

Preceding Villaverde, in publication if not historical setting, was romantic poet and novelist Gertrudis Gómez Avellaneda. Born to a rich Camagüeyan family of privileged Spanish gentry in 1814, Avellaneda was a rare female writer in a rigidly masculine domain. Eleven years before *Uncle Tom's Cabin* woke up America to the same themes, her novel *Sab,* published in 1841, tackled the prickly issues of race and slavery. It was banned in Cuba until 1914 due to its abolitionist rhetoric. What contemporary critics chose not to see was Avellaneda's subtle feminism, which depicted marriage as another form of slavery.

Further east, neoclassical poet and native *santiagüero*, José María de Heredia lived and wrote mainly from exile in Mexico. He was banished for allegedly conspiring against the Spanish authorities. His poetry, in-

MARTÍ – A CATEGORY OF HIS OWN

The writing of José Julián Martí Pérez (1853–95) stands alone. A pioneering philosopher, revolutionary and modernist writer, Martí broadened the political debate in Cuba beyond slavery (which was abolished in 1886) to issues such as independence and – above all – freedom. His instantly quotable prose remains a rare unifying force among Cubans around the world, whatever their political affiliations. He is similarly revered by Spanish speakers globally for his internationalism, which has put him on a par with Simón Bolívar.

Martí's writing covered a huge range of genres: essays, novels, poetry, political commentaries, letters and even a hugely popular children's magazine called *La edad de oro* (Golden Age). An accomplished master of aphorisms, his powerful one-liners still crop up in everyday Cuban speech. His two most famous works, published in 1891, are the political essay *Nuestra América* (Our America) and his collected poems, *Versos sencillos* (Simple Verses), both of which laid bare his hopes and dreams for Cuba and Latin America.

cluding the seminal *Himno del desterrado,* is tinged with a nostalgic romanticism for his homeland.

The Experimentalists

Cuban literature grew up in the early 1900s. Inspired by a mixture of Martí's modernism and new surrealistic influences wafting over from Europe, the first half of the 20th century was an age of experimentation for Cuban writers. The era's literary legacy rests on three giant pillars: Alejo Carpentier (1904–1980), a baroque wordsmith who invented the much-copied style of *lo real maravilloso* (magic realism); Guillermo Cabrera Infante (1929–2005), a Joycean master of colloquial language who pushed the parameters of Spanish to barely comprehensible boundaries; and José Lezama Lima (1910–1976), a gay poet of Proustian ambition, whose weighty novels are rich in layers, themes and anecdotes.

None are easy to read, but all broke new ground inspiring erudite writers far beyond Cuban shores (Márquez and Rushdie among them). Swiss-born Carpentier's magnum opus was *El siglo de las luces* (Explosion in a Cathedral), which explores the impact of the French revolution in Cuba through a veiled love story. Many consider it to be the finest novel ever written by a Cuban author. Infante, from Gibara, rewrote the rules of language in *Tres tristes tigres* (Three Trapped Tigers), a study of street life in pre-Castro Havana. Lezama, meanwhile, took an anecdotal approach to novel writing in *Paradiso* (Paradise), a multilayered, widely interpreted evocation of Havana in the 1950s with homoerotic undertones.

Grasping at the coattails of this verbose trio was Miguel Barnet, an anthropologist from Havana, whose *Biografía de un cimarrón* (Biography of a Runaway Slave), published in 1963, gathered testimonies from 103-year-old former slave Esteban Montejo and crafted them into a fascinating written documentary of the brutal slave system nearly 80 years after its demise.

Enter Guillén

Born in Camagüey in 1902, *mulato* (mixed race) poet Nicolás Guillén was far more than just a writer: he was a passionate and lifelong champion of Afro-Cuban rights. Rocked by the assassination of his father in his youth, and inspired by the drum-influenced music of former black slaves, Guillén set about articulating the hopes and fears of dispossessed black laborers with the rhythmic Afro-Cuban verses that would ultimately become his trademark. Famous poems in a prolific career included the evocative *Tengo* (I Have) and the patriotic *Che comandante, amigo* (Commander Che, Friend).

Working in self-imposed exile during the Batista era, Guillén returned to Cuba after the revolution whereupon he was given the task of formulating a new cultural policy and setting up the Writer's Union, Uneac (Unión de Escritores y Artistas de Cuba).

The Dirty Realists

In the 1990s and 2000s, baby boomers that had come of age in the era of censorship and Soviet domination began to respond to radically different influences in their writing. Some fled the country, others remained; all tested the boundaries of artistic expression in a system weighed down by censorship and creative asphyxiation.

Stepping out from the shadow of Lezama Lima was Reinaldo Arenas, a gay writer from Holguín Province, who, like Guillermo Cabrera Infante, fell out with the revolution in the late '60s and was imprisoned for his efforts. Arenas finally escaped to the US in 1980 during the Mariel Boatlift. He went on to write his hyperbolic memoir, *Antes que anochezca* (Before

Heberto Padilla (1932–2000) was a Cuban poet whose dissident writings in the 1960s led to his imprisonment, inspiring the 'Padilla Affair'.

PRIZE-WINNING PAZ

Senel Paz, author of *El Lobo, El Bosque y El Hombre nuevo* (The Wolf, the Forest and the New Man), the book that inspired famed movie *Fresa y Chocolat*, returned to international attention in 2008 with the publication of his novel *En el cielo con diamantes* (In the Sky with Diamonds) – a poignant tale of friendship in 1960s Havana. This garnered him literary prizes and status as Cuba's most widely read contemporary writer.

Night Falls), about his imprisonment and homosexuality. Published in the US in 1993, it met with huge critical acclaim.

The so-called 'dirty realist' authors of the late '90s and early 2000s took a more subtle approach to challenging contemporary mores. Pedro Juan Gutiérrez earned his moniker, 'tropical Bukowski', for the *Dirty Havana Trilogy*, a sexy, sultry study of Centro Habana during the Special Period. The trilogy held a mirror up to the desperate economic situation but steered clear of direct political polemics.

Zoé Valdés, born the year Castro took power, has been more direct in her criticism of the regime, particularly since leaving Cuba for Paris in 1995. Her most readily available novels (translated into English) are *I Gave You All I Had* and *The Weeping Woman*.

The Fascinated Foreigners

Cuba also inspires foreign writers to pen fiction, most notably Ernest Hemingway and Graham Greene. Hemingway first visited Cuba in the late 1930s on his boat *El Pilar*, partly as a break from his soon-to-be ex-wife. His love affair with the country continued until his death. His novels *The Old Man and the Sea* (1952; a portrayal of an old man's quest to bag a giant fish) and *Islands in the Stream* (1970; a harrowing trilogy following the fortunes of writer Thomas Hudson) were based on his experiences fishing – and, during WWII, hunting for German submarines – off Cuba's coast.

Greene visited the island several times in the 1950s and it became the setting for his book *Our Man in Havana* (1958), a tongue-in-cheek look at espionage that casts an interesting light on pre–Cuban Missile Crisis Havana.

Whilst none of his novels take place in Cuba, Colombian author Gabriel García Márquez developed a long-standing friendship with Fidel Castro during the 1960s, and wrote several articles on Cuba including *Memories of a Journalist* (1981) which recalls the Bay of Pigs invasion.

Cinema

Cuban cinema has always been closer to European art-house traditions than to the formula movies of Hollywood, especially since the Revolution, when cultural life veered away from American influences. Few notable movies were made until 1959, when the new government formed the Instituto Cubano del Arte e Industria Cinematográficos (Icaic), headed up by longtime film sage and former Havana University student, Alfredo Guevara, who held the position on and off until 2000.

Graham Greene originally set his comic take on British espionage in Soviet-occupied Tallinn, Estonia. But a chance visit to Havana changed his mind. The novel ultimately became *Our Man in Havana*.

The 1960s were Icaic's *Década de oro* (golden decade) when, behind an artistic veneer, successive directors were able to test the boundaries of state-imposed censorship and, in some cases, gain greater creative license. Innovative movies of this era poked fun at bureaucracy, made pertinent comments on economic matters, questioned the role of intellectualism in a socialist state and, later on, tackled previously taboo gay issues. The giants behind the camera were Humberto Solás, Tomás

Gutiérrez Alea, and Juan Carlos Tabío, who, working under Guevara's guidance, put cutting-edge Cuban cinema on the international map.

Cuba's first notable post-revolutionary movie, the joint Cuban-Soviet *Soy Cuba* (I am Cuba; 1964) was directed by a Russian, Mikhail Kalatozov, who dramatized the events leading up to the 1959 Revolution in four interconnecting stories. Largely forgotten by the early '70s, the movie was resurrected in the mid-1990s by American director Martin Scorsese, who was astounded by its cinematography, atmospheric camera work and technically amazing tracking shots. The film gets a rare 100% rating on the Rotten Tomatoes website and has been described by one American film critic as 'a unique, insane, exhilarating spectacle.'

Contemporary writer Leonardo Padura Fuentes is well known for his quartet of Havana-based detective novels, *Los cuatro estaciones* (Four Seasons), now a riveting Netflix miniseries.

Serving his apprenticeship in the 1960s, Cuba's most celebrated director, Tomás Gutiérrez Alea, cut his teeth directing art-house movies such as *La muerte de un burócrata* (Death of a Bureaucrat; 1966), a satire on excessive socialist bureaucratization; and *Memorias de subdesarrollo* (Memories of Underdevelopment; 1968), the story of a Cuban intellectual too idealistic for Miami, yet too decadent for the austere life of Havana. Teaming up with fellow director Juan Carlos Tabío in 1993, Gutiérrez went on to make another movie classic, the Oscar-nominated *Fresa y chocolate* (Strawberry and Chocolate) – the tale of Diego, a skeptical homosexual who falls in love with a heterosexual communist militant. It remains Cuba's cinematic pinnacle.

Humberto Solás, a master of low budget *(cine pobre)* movies, first made his mark in 1968 with the seminal *Lucía.* It explored the lives of three Cuban women at key moments in the country's history: 1895, 1932 and the early 1960s. Solás made his late-career masterpiece, *Barrio Cuba,* the tale of a family torn apart by the revolution, in 2005.

Since the death of Gutiérrez Alea in 1996 and Solás in 2008, Cuban cinema has passed the baton. Fernanado Pérez, who leapt onto the scene in 1994 with the Special Period classic *Madagascar,* focusing on an inter-generational struggle between a mother and daughter, and followed it up with 2003's *Suite Habana,* a moody documentary about a day in the life of 13 real people in the capital that uses zero dialogue. Pérez's closest 'rival' is Juan Carlos Cremata, whose 2005 road movie *Viva Cuba,* a study of class and ideology as seen through the eyes of two children, garnered much international praise.

COLONIAL ART

Just as Rome wasn't built in a day, so Cuba's art culture took a long time to establish itself. The first true Cuban artist of note was José Nicolás de la Escalera. Born in Havana in 1734, he was a religious painter who closely aped the baroque works of Spanish master Esteban Murillo. While the style of Escalera's paintings was far from groundbreaking, his subject matter proved to be more revealing. He was the first Cuban artist to depict black slaves in his paintings – a concept considered revolutionary in the late 18th century. Much of Escalera's work is still very visible in Havana, not just in galleries but also in several municipal churches including the Iglesia de Nuestra Señora del Rosario (p134) in outer Havana. His dark oil paintings are also well represented in the Museo Nacional de Bellas Artes (p76).

Many Cuban painters of the 19th century were strong advocates of independence. Guillermo Collazo (1850–96), a landscape painter from Santiago, kept a studio in Havana and was a close friend of José Martí who he helped get his first writing post. Armando Menocal (1863–1942) was a light impressionist painter and graduate of Havana's San Alejandro Academy who fought in the Independence War of 1895–98. But while revolution swept across the battlefields, the revolution on canvas had to wait until the early 20th century to reveal itself.

RAÚL MARTÍNEZ & THE GRUPO DE LOS ONCE

Ciego de Ávila–born Raúl Martinez (1927–1995) spearheaded the Cuban pop art movement during the 1950s and '60s with iconic depictions of José Martí, Camilo Cienfuegos and Che Guevara, although much of his work was inspired by Soviet socialism as much as by the American pop art movement. Martinez was a member of the Grupo de los Once, a group of groundbreaking abstract painters and sculptors who exhibited together between 1953 and 1955 and left a lasting impression on Cuban art. You can see much of the work of Martínez in Ciego de Ávila's Centro de Promoción Cultural Guiarte (p303).

The last few years have seen few classics of the same clout, but 2011's *Juan of the Dead*, Cuba's version of UK horror-comedy *Shaun of the Dead*, broke ground as Cuba's first zombie movie. In a thinly-veiled critique on the regime, an idler-turned-slayer-of-the-undead fights for survival in a Havana overrun by zombies.

Reflecting the expanded options of distribution in the digital age, director Arturo Sotto's entertaining 2014 comedy *Boccaccerías Habaneras* is available in its entirety on YouTube.

Havana's significant influence in the film culture of the American hemisphere is highlighted each year in the Festival Internacional del Nuevo Cine Latinoamericano held every December in Havana. Described as the ultimate word in Latin American cinema, this annual get-together of critics, sages and filmmakers has been fundamental in showcasing recent Cuban classics to the world.

Painting & Sculpture

Thought-provoking and visceral, modern Cuban art combines lurid Afro-Latin American colors with the harsh reality of the revolution. For foreign art lovers visiting Cuba, it's a unique and intoxicating brew. Forced into a corner by the constrictions of the culture-redefining Cuban Revolution, modern artists have invariably found that, by co-opting (as opposed to confronting) the socialist regime, opportunities for academic training and artistic encouragement are almost unlimited. Encased in such a volatile, creative climate, abstract art in Cuba – well established in its own right before the revolution – has flourished.

The first flowering of Cuban art took place in the 1920s when painters belonging to the so-called Vanguardia movement relocated temporarily to Paris to learn the ropes from the avant-garde European school then dominated by the likes of Pablo Picasso. One of the Vanguardia's earliest exponents was Victor Manuel García (1897–1969), the genius behind one of Cuba's most famous paintings, *La gitana tropical* (Tropical Gypsy; 1929), a portrait of an archetypal Cuban woman with her luminous gaze staring into the middle distance. The canvas, displayed in Havana's Museo Nacional de Bellas Artes, is often referred to as the Latin Mona Lisa.

Victor Manuel's contemporary, Amelia Peláez (1896–1968), also studied in Paris, where she melded avant-gardism with more primitive Cuban themes. Though Peláez worked with many different materials, her most celebrated work was in murals, including the 670-sq-meter tile mural on the side of the Hotel Habana Libre.

After the high-water mark of Wifredo Lam, Cuban pop art was a major influence during the 1950s and 1960s. Art has enjoyed strong government patronage since the revolution (albeit within the confines of strict censorship), exemplified with the opening of the Instituto Superior de Arte in the Havana neighborhood of Cubanacán in 1976.

Top Contemporary Artists

- *José Villa*
- *Joel Jover*
- *Flora Fong*
- *José Rodríguez Fúster*
- *Tomás Sánchez*
- *Julia Valdéz*

Architecture

There is nothing pure about Cuban architecture. Rather like its music, the nation's eclectic assemblage of buildings exhibits an unashamed hybrid of styles, ideas and background influences. The resulting architecture riffs on themes and variations, making imported genres into something uniquely Cuban. Going forward, Cuba is facing the loss of much of its great architectural heritage due to a lack of resources to maintain these structures. At present the widespread demolition of precarious buildings is wiping out Cuba's valuable heritage.

Styles & Trends

Emerging relatively unscathed from the turmoil of three revolutionary wars and buffered from modern globalization by its peculiar economic situation, the nation's well-preserved cities have survived into the 21st century with the bulk of their colonial architectural features intact. The

Above Habana Vieja (p62), Havana

Rare examples of Cuban Gothic architecture can be seen at Iglesia del Sagrado Corazón de Jesús in Havana and its namesake church in the nation's most devoutly religious city, Camagüey.

preservation has been helped by the nomination of Havana Vieja, Trinidad, Cienfuegos and Camagüey as Unesco World Heritage sites, and aided further by foresighted local historians who have created a model for self-sustaining historical preservation that might well go down as one of the revolutionary government's greatest achievements.

Cuba's classic and most prevalent architectural styles are baroque and neoclassicism. Baroque designers began sharpening their quills in the 1750s; neoclassicism gained the ascendency in the 1820s and continued, amid numerous revivals, until the 1920s. Trademark buildings of the American era (1902–59) exhibited art deco and, later on, modernist styles. Art nouveau played a cameo role during this period influenced by Catalan *modernisme;* recognizable art nouveau curves and embellishments can be seen on pivotal east–west axis streets in Centro Habana. Ostentatious eclecticism, courtesy of the Americans, characterized Havana's rich and growing suburbs from the 1910s onwards.

Building styles weren't all pretty, though. Cuba's brief flirtation with Soviet architectonics in the 1960s and '70s threw up plenty of breeze-block apartments and ugly utilitarian hotels that sit rather jarringly alongside the beautiful relics of the colonial era. Havana's Vedado neighborhood maintains a small but significant cluster of modernist 'skyscrapers' constructed during a 10-year pre-revolutionary building boom in the 1950s.

Coastal Fortifications

While European kings were hiding from the hoi polloi in muscular medieval castles, their Latin American cousins were building up their colonial defenses in a series of equally colossal Renaissance forts.

The protective ring of fortifications that punctuates Cuba's coastline stretching from Havana in the west to Baracoa in the east forms one of the finest ensembles of military architecture in the Americas. The construction of these sturdy stone behemoths by the Spanish in the 16th, 17th and 18th centuries reflected the colony's strategic importance on the Atlantic trade routes and its vulnerability to attacks by daring pirates and competing colonial powers.

As Cuban capital and the primary Spanish port in the Caribbean, Havana was the grand prize to ambitious would-be raiders. The sacking of the city by French pirate Jacques de Sores in 1555 exposed the weaknesses of the city's meager defenses and provoked the first wave of fort building.

Havana's authorities called in Italian Military architect Bautista Antonelli to do the job and he responded with aplomb, reinforcing the harbor mouth with two magnificent forts, El Morro and San Salvador de la Punta. The work, which started in the 1580s, was slow but meticulous; the forts weren't actually finished until after Antonelli's death in the 1620s. Antonelli also designed the Castillo de San Pedro de la Roca del Morro in Santiago, started around the same time but, thanks to ongoing attacks, most notoriously by British buccaneer Henry Morgan in 1662, not finished until 1700.

More forts were added in the 18th century, most notably at Jagua (near present-day Cienfuegos) on the south coast and Matanzas in the north. Baracoa in the far east was encircled with a bulwark of three small fortifications, all of which survive.

With their thick walls, and polygon layout designed to fit in with the coastal topography, Cuba's forts were built to last (all still survive) and largely served their purpose at deterring successive invaders until 1762. In that year the British arrived during the Seven Years War, blasting a hole in San Severino in Matanzas and capturing Havana after a

Castillo de la Real Fuerza (p65), Havana

44-day siege of El Morro. Spain's response when it got back Havana from the British in 1763 was to build the humungous La Cabaña, the largest fort in the Americas. Not surprisingly, its heavy battlements were never breached.

In the 1980s and '90s, Havana's and Santiago's forts were named Unesco World Heritage sites.

Theatrical Architecture

Attend a dance or play in a provincial Cuban theater and you might find your eyes flicking intermittently between the artists on the stage and the equally captivating artistry of the building.

As strong patrons of music and dance, the Cubans have a tradition of building iconic provincial theaters and most cities have an historic venue where you can view the latest performances. By popular consensus, the most architecturally accomplished Cuban theaters are the Teatro Sauto (p217) in Matanzas, the Teatro la Caridad (p257) in Santa Clara, and the Teatro Tomás Terry (p237) in Cienfuegos.

All three gilded buildings were constructed in the 19th century (in 1863, 1885 and 1890 respectively) with sober French neoclassical facades overlaying more lavish Italianate interiors. A generic defining feature is the U-shaped three-tiered auditoriums which display a profusion of carved wood-paneling and wrought iron, and are crowned by striking ceiling frescos. The frescos of angelic cherubs in the Caridad and Tomás Terry were painted by the same Philippine artist, Camilo Salaya, while the Sauto's was the work of the theater's Italian architect, Daniele Dell'Aglio. Other features include ornate chandeliers, gold-leafed mosaics and striking marble statues: the Sauto's statues are of Greek goddesses, while the Tomás Terry sports a marble recreation of its eponymous financier, a Venezuelan-born sugar baron.

Notable Art Deco Buildings

- *Edificio Bacardí (p74), Havana*
- *Teatro América (p115), Havana*
- *Iglesia de Nuestra Señora de la Caridad (p368), Banes*
- *Cuartel Moncada (p398), Santiago de Cuba*

Camagüey (p318)

Philanthropy played a major part in many Cuban theaters in the 19th century, none more so than Santa Clara's Caridad (the name means 'charity') which was paid for by local benefactor, Marta Abreu. In an early show of altruism, Abreu, who donated to many social and artistic causes, ensured that a percentage of the theater's ongoing profits went to charity.

Lack of funds in recent times has left many Cuban theaters in dire need of repair. Some buildings haven't survived. The Colesio, Cuba's earliest modern theater built in 1823 in Santiago de Cuba, was destroyed by fire in 1846. The Teatro Brunet in Trinidad built in 1840 is now a ruin used as an atmospheric social center. Havana's oldest theater, the Tacón, survives, but was overlaid by a Spanish social center (the Centro Gallego) in the 1910s. Pinar del Río's recently refurbished Teatro Milanés (1838) has a lovely Sevillan patio, while the neoclassical Teatro Principal (1850) in Camagüey is the home of Cuba's most prestigious ballet company.

Cuban Baroque

Baroque architecture arrived in Cuba in the mid-1700s, via Spain, a good 50 years after its European high-water mark. Fueled by the rapid growth of the island's nascent sugar industry, nouveau riche slave-owners and sugar merchants plowed their juicy profits into grandiose urban buildings. The finest examples of baroque in Cuba adorn the homes and public buildings of Habana Vieja, although the style didn't reach its zenith until the late-1700s with the construction of the Catedral de la Habana (p62) and the surrounding Plaza de la Catedral (p62).

Due to climatic and cultural peculiarities, traditional baroque (the word is taken from the Portuguese noun *barroco,* which means an 'elaborately shaped pearl') was quickly 'tropicalized' in Cuba, with local architects adding their own personal flourishes to the new municipal structures that were springing up in various provincial cities. Indigenous features included: *rejas,* metal bars secured over windows to protect against burglaries and allow for a freer circulation of air; *vitrales,* multicolored glass panes fitted above doorways to pleasantly diffuse the tropical sun's rays; *entresuelos,* mezzanine floors built to accommodate live-in slave families; and *portales,* galleried exterior walkways that provided pedestrians with shelter from the sun and the rain.

Signature baroque buildings, such as the Palacio de los Capitanes Generales (p63) in Plaza de Armas in Havana, were made from hard local limestone dug from the nearby San Lázaro quarries and constructed using slave labor. As a result, the intricate exterior decoration that characterized baroque architecture in Italy and Spain was noticeably toned down in Cuba, where local workers lacked the advanced stonemasonry skills of their more accomplished European cousins.

Some of the most exquisite baroque buildings in Cuba are found in Trinidad and date from the early decades of the 19th century when designs and furnishings were heavily influenced by the haute couture fashions of Italy, France and Georgian England.

Best Colonial Plazas

Plaza de la Catedral (p62), Havana

Plaza Mayor (p277), Trinidad

Parque José Martí (p243), Cienfuegos

Parque Ignacio Agramonte (p319), Camagüey

Plaza Martí (p266), Remedios

Neoclassicism

Neoclassicism first evolved in the mid-18th century in Europe as a reaction to the lavish ornamentation and gaudy ostentation of baroque. Conceived in the progressive academies of London and Paris, the movement's early adherents advocated sharp primary colors and bold symmetrical lines, coupled with a desire to return to the perceived architectural 'purity' of ancient Greece and Rome.

The style eventually reached Cuba at the beginning of the 19th century, spearheaded by groups of French émigrés who had fled west from Haiti following a violent slave rebellion in 1791. Within a couple of decades, neoclassicism had established itself as the nation's dominant architectural style.

By the mid-19th century sturdy neoclassical buildings were the norm among Cuba's bourgeoisie in cities such as Cienfuegos and Matanzas, with striking symmetry, grandiose frontages and rows of imposing columns replacing the decorative baroque flourishes of the early colonial period.

Havana's first true neoclassical building was El Templete, a diminutive Doric temple constructed in Habana Vieja in 1828 next to the spot where Father Bartolomé de las Casas is said to have conducted the city's first Mass. As the city gradually spread westward in the mid-1800s, outgrowing its 17th-century walls, the style was adopted in the construction of more ambitious buildings, such as the famous Hotel Inglaterra overlooking Parque Central. Havana grew in both size and beauty during this period, bringing into vogue new residential design features such as spacious classical courtyards and rows of imposing street-facing

TRINIDAD'S COLONIAL ARCHITECTURE

Trinidad is one of the best-preserved colonial towns in the Americas. Most of its remarkably homogenous architecture dates from the early 19th century when Trinidad's sugar industry reached its zenith. Typical Trinidad houses are large one-story buildings with terracotta-tiled roofs held up by wooden beams. Unlike in Havana, the huge front doors usually open directly into a main room rather than a vestibule. Other typical Trinidadian features include large glass-less windows fronted with wooden (or iron) bars, wall frescos, verandas, and balconies with wooden balustrades raised above the street. Larger Trinidad houses have Mudejar-style courtyards with trademark *aljibes* (storage wells).

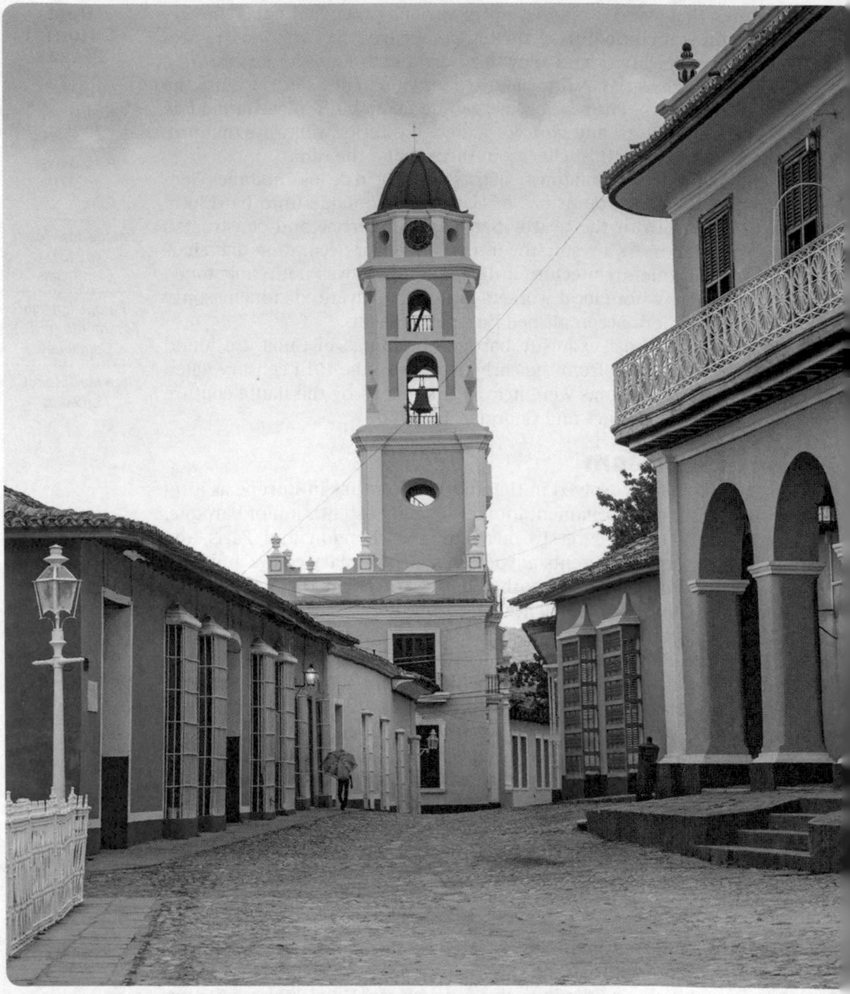

TUPUNGATO/SHUTTERSTOCK ©

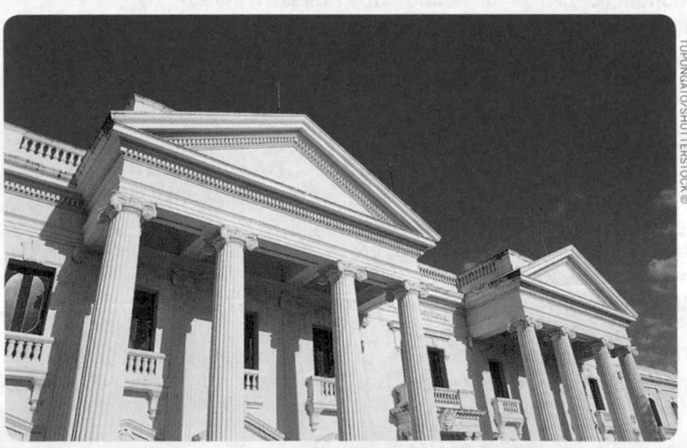

Top Plaza Major (p277), Trinidad **Bottom** Palacio Provincial (p259), Santa Clara

Edificio Bacardí (p74), Havana

colonnades, leading seminal Cuban novelist Alejo Carpentier to christen it the 'city of columns.'

A second neoclassical revival swept Cuba at the beginning of the 20th century, spearheaded by the growing influence of the US on the island. Prompted by the ideas and design ethics of the American Renaissance (1876–1914), Havana underwent a full-on building explosion, sponsoring such gigantic municipal buildings as the Capitolio Nacional and the Universidad de la Habana. In the provinces, the style reached its high-water mark in a series of glittering theaters.

Art Deco

Art deco was an elegant, functional and modern architectural movement that originated in France at the beginning of the 20th century and reached its apex in America in the 1920s and '30s. Drawing from a vibrant mix of Cubism, futurism and primitive African art, the genre promoted lavish yet streamlined buildings with sweeping curves and exuberant sun-burst motifs such as the Chrysler building in New York and the architecture of the South Beach neighborhood in Miami.

From the United States it came to Cuba, which quickly acquired its own clutch of 'tropical' art-deco buildings with the lion's share residing in Havana. One of Latin America's finest examples of early art deco is the Edifico Bacardí in Habana Vieja, built in 1930 to provide a Havana headquarters for Santiago de Cuba's world-famous rum-making family.

Another striking creation was the 14-story Edificio López Serrano in Vedado, constructed as the city's first real *rascacielo* (skyscraper) in 1932, using New York's Rockefeller Center as its inspiration. Other more functional art-deco skyscrapers followed, including the Teatro América on Av de la Italia, the Teatro Fausto on Paseo de Martí and the Casa

Best Examples of Architectural Styles

Early Colonial *Museo de Pintura Mural (p73)*

Baroque *Catedral de la Habana (p62)*

Neoclassical *Capitolio Nacional (p77)*

Art Deco *Edificio Bacardí (p74)*

Art Nouveau *Palacio Cueto (p69)*

Eclectic *Palacio de Valle (p239)*

Modernist *Edificio Focsa (p86)*

Gothic *Iglesia del Sagrado Corazón de Jesús (p78)*

Palacio de Valle (p239), Cienfuegos

de las Américas on Calle G. A more diluted and eclectic interpretation of the genre can be seen in the famous Hotel Nacional, whose sharp symmetrical lines and decorative twin Moorish turrets dominate the view over the Malecón.

Architectural Hotels

- Hotel Ordoño (p359), Gibara
- Hotel Raquel (p89), Havana
- Hostal del Rijo (p296), Sancti Spíritus
- Hotel Camino de Hierro (p324), Camagüey
- Hotel Caballeriza (p353), Holguin

Eclecticism

Eclecticism is the term often applied to the non-conformist and highly experimental architectural zeitgeist that grew up in the United States during the 1880s. Rejecting 19th-century ideas of 'style' and categorization, the architects behind this revolutionary new genre promoted flexibility and an open-minded 'anything goes' ethos, drawing their inspiration from a wide range of historical precedents.

Thanks to the strong US presence in the decades before 1959, Cuba quickly became a riot of modern eclecticism, with rich American and Cuban landowners constructing huge Xanadu-like mansions in burgeoning upper-class residential districts. Expansive, ostentatious and, at times, outlandishly kitschy, these fancy new homes were garnished with crenellated walls, oddly shaped lookout towers, rooftop cupolas and leering gargoyles. For a wild tour of Cuban eclecticism, head to the neighborhoods of Miramar in Havana, Vista Alegre in Santiago de Cuba and the Punta Gorda in Cienfuegos.

Music & Dance

Rich, vibrant, layered and soulful, Cuban music has long acted as a standard-bearer for the sounds and rhythms emanating out of Latin America. This is the birthplace of salsa, where elegant European dances adopted edgy black rhythms, and where the African drum first courted the Spanish guitar. From the down-at-heel docks of Matanzas to the bucolic villages of the Sierra Maestra, the amorous musical fusion went on to fuel everything from *son*, rumba, mambo, *cha-cha-chá, charanga, changüí, danzón* and more.

Into the Mix

Aside from the obvious Spanish and African roots, Cuban music has drawn upon a number of other influences. Mixed into an already exotic melting pot are genres from France, the US, Haiti and Jamaica. Conversely, Cuban music has also played a key role in developing various melodic styles and movements in other parts of the world. In Spain they called this process *ida y vuelta* (return trip) and it is most clearly evident in a style of flamenco called *guajira*. Elsewhere the 'Cuban effect' can be traced back to forms as diverse as New Orleans jazz, New York salsa and West African Afrobeat.

Described by aficionados as 'a vertical representation of a horizontal act,' Cuban dancing is famous for its libidinous rhythms and sensuous close-ups. Inheriting a love for dancing from birth and able to replicate perfect salsa steps by the age of two or three, most Cubans are natural performers who approach dance with a complete lack of self-consciousness – a notion that can leave visitors from Europe or North America feeling as if they've got two left feet.

Best Places for Música Cubana

Son *Casa de la Trova (p414), Santiago de Cuba*

Nueva Trova *Casa de la Trova (p286), Trinidad*

Salsa/Timba *Casa de la Música (p133), Centro Havana*

Rumba *Callejón de Hamel (p113), Havana*

Jazz *Jazz Club La Zorra y El Cuervo (p113), Havana*

Classical *Basílica Menor de San Francisco de Asís (p113), Havana*

Danzón Days

The invention of the *danzón* is usually credited to innovative Matanzas band leader, Miguel Faílde, who first showcased it with his catchy dance composition *Las Alturas de Simpson* in Matanzas in 1879. Elegant and purely instrumental in its early days, the *danzón* was slower in pace than the *habanera*, and its intricate dance patterns required dancers to circulate in couples rather than groups, a move that scandalized polite society at the time. From the 1880s onward, the genre exploded, expanding its peculiar syncopated rhythm, and adding such improbable extras as conga drums and vocalists.

By the early 20th century, the *danzón* had evolved from a stately ballroom dance played by an *orchestra típica* into a more jazzed-up free-for-all known alternatively as *charanga, danzonete* or *danzón-chá*. Not surprisingly, it became Cuba's national dance, though since it was primarily a bastion of moneyed white society, it was never considered a true hybrid.

Africa Calling

While drumming in the North American colonies was ostensibly prohibited, Cuban slaves were able to preserve and pass on many of their musical traditions via influential Santería *cabildos,* religious brotherhoods that re-enacted ancient African percussive music on simple *batá* drums or *chequeré* rattles. Performed at annual festivals or on special Catholic saints' days, this rhythmic yet highly textured dance music was offered up as a form of religious worship to the *orishas* (deities).

Over time the ritualistic drumming of Santería evolved into a more complex genre known as rumba. Rumba was first concocted in the docks of Havana and Matanzas during the 1890s when ex-slaves, exposed to a revolving series of outside influences, began to knock out soulful rhythms on old packing cases in imitation of various African religious rites. As the drumming patterns grew more complex, vocals were added, dances emerged and, before long, the music had grown into a collective form of social expression for all black Cubans.

Spreading in popularity throughout the 1920s and '30s, rumba gradually spawned three different but interrelated dance formats: *guaguancó,* an overtly sexual dance; *yambú,* a slow dance; and *columbia,* a fast, aggressive dance often involving fire torches and machetes. The latter originated as a devil dance of the Náñigo rite, and today it's performed only by solo males.

Pitched into Cuba's cultural melting pot, these rootsy yet highly addictive musical variants slowly gained acceptance among a new audience of middle-class whites, and by the 1940s the music had fused with *son* in a new subgenre called *son montuno,* which, in turn, provided the building blocks for salsa.

Indeed, so influential was Cuban rumba by the end of WWII that it was transposed back to Africa with experimental Congolese artists, such as Sam Mangwana and Franco Luambo (of OK Jazz fame), using ebullient Cuban influences to pioneer *soukous,* their own variation on the rumba theme.

Raw, expressive and exciting to watch, Cuban rumba is a spontaneous and often informal affair performed by groups of up to a dozen musicians. Conga drums, claves, *palitos* (sticks), *marugas* (iron shakers) and *cajones* (packing cases) lay out the interlocking rhythms, while the vocals alternate between a wildly improvising lead singer and an answering *coro* (chorus).

DANCE FUSION

Cuban dance is as hybridized as the country's music; indeed many dance genres evolved from popular strands of Cuban music.

Early dance forms mimicked the European-style ballroom dances practiced by the colonizers, but added African elements. This unorthodox amalgamation of styles can be seen in esoteric genres such as the French-Haitian tumba francesa, a marriage between 18th-century French court dances and imported African rhythms: dancers wearing elegant dresses wave fans and handkerchiefs while shimmying to the drum patterns of Nigeria and Benin.

Other dances reflected the working lives of Cuban slaves. The *pilón* in Granma Province copies the motion of pounding sugarcane. *Nengón* and *kiribá* in Baracoa mimic the crushing of cocoa and coffee beans beneath the feet.

The first truly popular dance hybrid was the *danzón*, a sequence dance involving couples whose origins lay in the French and English *contradanza*, but whose rhythm contained a distinctive African syncopation.

The mambo and *chachachá* evolved the *danzón* further, creating dances that were more improvised and complicated. Mambo's creator, Pérez Prado, specifically pioneered mambo dancing to fit his new music in the 1940s, while the *cha-cha-chá* was codified as a ballroom dance in the early 1950s by a Frenchman named Monsieur Pierre.

Rising Son

Cuba's two most celebrated 19th-century sounds, rumba and *danzón*, came from the west – specifically the cities of Havana and Matanzas. But as the genres remained largely compartmentalized between separate black and white societies, neither can be considered true hybrids. The country's first real musical fusion came from the next great sound revolution, *son*.

Son emerged from the mountains of the Oriente region in the second half of the 19th century, though the earliest known testimonies go back as far as 1570. It was one of two genres to arise at around the same time (the other was *changüí*), both of which blended the melodies and lyricism of Spanish folk music with the drum patterns of recently freed African slaves. *Son's* precursor was *nengón*, an invention of black sugar-plantation workers who had evolved their percussive religious chants into a form of music and song.

The leap from *nengón* to *son* is unclear and poorly documented, but at some point in the 1880s or '90s the *guajiros* (country folk) in the mountains of present-day Santiago de Cuba and Guantánamo Provinces began blending *nengón* drums with the Cuban *tres* guitar while over the top a singer improvised words from a traditional 10-line Spanish poem known as a *décima*.

In its pure form, *son* was played by a sextet consisting of guitar, *tres* (guitar with three sets of double strings), double bass, bongo and two singers who played maracas and claves (sticks that tap out the beat). Coming down from the mountains and into the cities, the genre's earliest exponents were the legendary Trio Oriental, who stabilized the sextet format in 1912 when they were reborn as the Sexteto Habanero. Another early *sonero* was singer Miguel Matamoros, whose self-penned *son* classics such as 'Son de la Loma' and 'Lágrimas Negras' are de rigueur among Cuba's ubiquitous musical entertainers, even today.

In the early 1910s *son* arrived in Havana, where it adopted its distinctive rumba clave (rhythmic pattern), which later went on to form the basis of salsa. Within a decade it had become Cuba's signature music, gaining wide acceptance among white society and destroying the myth that black music was vulgar, unsophisticated and subversive.

By the 1930s the sextet had become a septet with the addition of a trumpet, and exciting new musicians such as blind *tres* player Arsenio Rodríguez – a songwriter who Harry Belafonte once called the 'father of salsa' – were paving the way for mambo and *chachachá*.

The *danzón* was originally an instrumental piece. Words were added in the late 1920s and the new form became known as the *danzonete*.

Barbarians of Rhythm

In the 1940s and '50s the *son* bands grew from seven pieces to eight and beyond, until they became big bands boasting full horn and percussion sections that played rumba, *chachachá* and mambo. The reigning mambo king was Benny Moré, who with his sumptuous voice and rocking 40-piece all-black band was known as El Bárbaro del Ritmo (The Barbarian of Rhythm).

Mambo grew out of *charanga* music, which itself was a derivative of *danzón*. Bolder, brassier and more exciting than its two earlier incarnations, the music was characterized by exuberant trumpet riffs, belting saxophones and regular enthusiastic interjections by the singer (usually in the form of the word *dilo!* or 'say it!').

The style's origins are mired in controversy. Some argue that it was invented by native *habanero* Orestes López after he penned the new rhythmically dextrous 'Mambo' in 1938. Others give the credit to Matanzas band leader Pérez Prado, the first musician to market his songs under the increasingly lucrative mambo umbrella in the early '40s. Whatever the case, mambo soon spawned the world's first universal dance craze, and from New York to Buenos Aires, people couldn't get enough of its infectious rhythms.

A variation on the mambo theme, the *cha-cha-chá*, was first showcased by Havana-based composer and violinist Enrique Jorrín in 1951 while playing with the Orquesta América. Originally known as 'mambo-rumba,' the music was intended to promote a more basic kind of Cuban dance that less-coordinated North Americans would be able to master, but it was quickly mambo-ized by overenthusiastic dance competitors, who kept adding complicated new steps.

Salsa & Its Offshoots

Salsa is an umbrella term used to describe a variety of musical genres that emerged out of the fertile Latin New York scene in the 1960s and '70s, when jazz, *son* and rumba blended to create a new, brassier sound. While not strictly a product of Cubans living in Cuba, salsa's roots and key influences are descended directly from *son montuno* and indebted to innovators such as Pérez Prado, Benny Moré and Miguel Matamoros.

The self-styled Queen of Salsa was Grammy-winning singer and performer Celia Cruz. Born in Havana in 1925, Cruz served the bulk of her musical apprenticeship in Cuba before leaving for self-imposed exile in the US in 1960. But due to her longstanding opposition to the Castro regime, Cruz' records and music have remained largely unknown on the island, despite her enduring legacy elsewhere.

Far more influential on their home turf are the legendary salsa outfit Los Van Van, a band formed by Juan Formell in 1969 and one that still performs regularly at venues across Cuba. With Formell at the helm as the group's great improviser, poet, lyricist and social commentator, Los Van Van were one of the few modern Cuban groups to create their own unique musical genre – that of songo-salsa. The band also won top honors in 2000 when it memorably took home a Grammy for its classic album, *Llego Van Van*. Despite the death of Formell in 2014, the band continues to play, record and tour.

Modern salsa mixed and merged further in the '80s and '90s, allying itself with new cutting-edge musical genres such as hip-hop, reggaeton and rap, before coming up with some hot new alternatives, most notably *timba* and songo-salsa.

Timba is, in many ways, Cuba's own experimental and fiery take on traditional salsa. Mixing New York sounds with Latin jazz, *nueva trova*, American funk, disco, hip-hop and even some classical influences, the music is more flexible and aggressive than standard salsa, incorporating greater elements of the island's potent Afro-Cuban culture. Many *timba* bands such as Bamboleo and La Charanga Habanera use funk riffs and rely on less-conventional Cuban instruments such as synthesizers and kick drums. Others – such as NG La Banda, formed in 1988 – have infused their music with a more jazzy dynamic.

Filin' is a term derived from the English word 'feeling.' It was a style of music showcased by jazz crooners in the 1940s and '50s. In Cuba *filin'* grew out of bolero and *trova*.

Traditional jazz, considered the music of the enemy in the Revolution's most dogmatic days, has always seeped into Cuban sounds. Jesús 'Chucho' Valdés' band Irakere, formed in 1973, broke the Cuban music scene wide open with its heavy Afro-Cuban drumming laced with jazz and *son*, and the Cuban capital boasts a number of decent jazz clubs. Other musicians associated with Cuban jazz include pianist Gonzalo Rubalcaba, Isaac Delgado and Adalberto Álvarez y Su Son.

Nueva Trova – the Soundtrack of a Revolution

The 1960s were heady days for radical new forms of musical expression. In the US Dylan released *Highway 61 Revisited,* in Britain the Beatles concocted *Sgt Pepper* while, in the Spanish-speaking world, musical activists such as Chilean Víctor Jara and Catalan Joan Manuel Serrat were turning their politically charged poems into passionate protest songs.

Charangas were Cuban musical ensembles that showcased popular *danzón*-influenced pieces.

Determined to develop their own revolutionary music apart from the capitalist West, the innovative Cubans – under the stewardship of Haydee Santamaría, director at the influential Casa de las Américas – came up with *nueva trova.*

A caustic mix of probing philosophical lyrics and folksy melodic tunes, *nueva trova* was a direct descendent of pure *trova*, a bohemian form of guitar music that had originated in the Oriente in the late 19th century. Post-1959, *trova* became increasingly politicized and was taken up by more sophisticated artists such as Manzanillo-born Carlos Puebla, who provided an important bridge between old and new styles with his politically tinged ode to Che Guevara, 'Hasta Siempre Comandante' (1965).

Nueva trova came of age in February 1968 at the Primer Encuentro de la Canción Protesta, a concert organized at the Casa de las Américas in Havana and headlined by such rising stars as Silvio Rodríguez and Pablo Milanés. In a cultural context, it was Cuba's mini-Woodstock, an event that resounded forcefully among leftists worldwide as a revolutionary alternative to American rock 'n' roll.

In December 1972, the nascent *nueva trova* movement gained official sanction from the Cuban government during a music festival held in

CONTEMPORARY SOUNDS

Orishas From 2006, '537 Cuba' remixed Buena Vista Social Club's hit *Chan Chan* into a most addictive reggaeton beat. And there's more.

Jacob Forever A hot young reggaeton artist originally from Camagüey; his hit 'Hasta Que Se Seque El Malecón' (Until the boardwalk dries up) made waves in 2016.

Gente de Zona Collaborating with Marc Anthony and Enrique Iglesias, this reggaeton-salsaton group hit the roof winning Latin Grammys and other awards with recent energy-infused hits.

Interactivo An artist's collective that has showcased countless individual talent since its formation in 2001, including hip hop artist Kumar, jazzy poet and instrumentalist Yusa and founder, the jazz pianist Roberto Carcassés. Cuban fusion personified.

Buena Fe Creative rock duo from Guantánamo whose penetrating lyrics appeal to Cuba's awakening youth movement.

Haydée Milanés Jazzy singer and daughter of *trova* great, Pablo Milanés.

X-Alfonso The man behind Havana's exciting new Fábrica de Arte Cubano is a king of many genres from Hendrix-style rock to Latin hip hop. Listen out also for his sister M-Alfonso, another great fusion singer.

Diana Fuentes Singer with an R&B and funk bent who has worked with everyone who's anyone in the Cuban music scene, including X-Alfonso.

Yissy Probably Cuba's most talented drummer, Yissy García lays down her beat with a strong nod to Yoruba tradition.

Doble Filo Pioneering Cuban hip hop artists with outspoken lyrics. They once rapped with Fidel Castro.

Manzanillo city commemorating the 16th anniversary of the *Granma* landing. Highly influential throughout the Spanish-speaking world during the '60s and '70s, *nueva trova* has often acted as an inspirational source of protest music for the impoverished and downtrodden populations of Latin America, many of whom looked to Cuba for spiritual leadership in an era of corrupt dictatorships and US cultural hegemony. This solidarity was reciprocated by the likes of Rodríguez, who penned numerous internationally lauded classics such as 'Canción Urgente para Nicaragua' (in support of the Sandinistas), 'La Maza' and 'Canción para mi Soldado' (about the Angolan War).

Rap, Reggaeton & Beyond

The contemporary Cuban music scene is an interesting mix of enduring traditions, modern sounds, old hands and new blood. With low production costs, solid urban themes and lots of US-inspired crossover styles, hip-hop and rap are taking the younger generation by storm.

Born in the ugly concrete housing projects of Alamar, Havana, Cuban hip-hop, rather like its US counterpart, has gritty and impoverished roots. First beamed across the nation in the early 1980s when American rap was picked up on homemade rooftop antennae from Miami-based radio stations, the new music quickly gained ground among a young urban black population who were culturally redefining themselves during the inquietude of the Special Period. By the '90s groups such as Public Enemy and NWA were de rigueur on the streets of Alamar and by 1995 there was enough hip-hop to throw a festival.

Tempered by Latin influences and censored by the parameters of strict revolutionary thought, Cuban hip-hop has shied away from US stereotypes, instead taking on a progressive flavor all its own. Instrumentally the music uses *batá* drums, congas and electric bass, while lyrically the songs tackle important national issues such as sex tourism and the difficulties of the stagnant Cuban economy.

Despite being viewed early on as subversive and anti-revolutionary, Cuban hip-hop has gained unlikely support from inside the Cuban government, whose art-conscious legislators consider the music to have played a constructive social role in shaping the future of Cuban youth. Fidel Castro went one step further, describing hip-hop as 'the vanguard of the Revolution' and – allegedly – trying his hand at rapping at a Havana baseball game.

Cuba's first hybrid musical genre was the *habanera*, a traditional European-style dance with a syncopated drumbeat, that rose to the fore in the mid-19th century and lasted until the 1870s.

The same cannot be said for reggaeton, a melding of hip hop, Spanish reggae and Jamaican dance hall that emerged out of Panama in the 1990s and gained mainstream popularity in Puerto Rico in the mid-2000s. The Cuban government banned explicit reggaeton songs from TV and radio in 2012, and many hip hop artists have expressed their discomfort with the genre's overtly sexist and narcissistic lyrics that glorify sex, violence and drug culture.

Nonetheless, reggaeton is the soundtrack of Cuban youth, who idolize homegrown artists such as Osmani Garcia, Jacob Forever and Gente de la Zona.

Landscape & Wildlife

Some 1250km long and between 31km and 193km wide, Cuba is the Caribbean's largest island with a total land area of 110,860 sq km. Shaped like one of its signature crocodiles and situated just south of the Tropic of Cancer, the country is actually an archipelago made up of 4195 smaller islets and coral reefs. Its unique ecosystems have been fascinating and perplexing scientists and naturalists ever since Alexander von Humboldt first mapped them in the early 1800s.

The Cuban Landscape

Formed by a volatile mixture of volcanic activity, plate tectonics and erosion, Cuba's landscape is a lush, varied concoction of mountains, caves, plains and *mogotes* (flat-topped hills). The highest point, Pico Turquino (1972m), is situated in the east among the Sierra Maestra's lofty triangular peaks. Further west, in the Sierra del Escambray, ruffled hilltops and gushing waterfalls straddle the borders of Cienfuegos, Villa Clara and Sancti Spíritus Provinces. Rising like purple shadows in the far west, the 175km-long Cordillera de Guanguanico is a more diminutive range that includes the protected Sierra del Rosario Biosphere Reserve and the distinctive pincushion hills of the Valle de Viñales.

Lapped by the warm turquoise waters of the Caribbean Sea in the south, and the chop of the Atlantic Ocean in the north, Cuba's 5746km of coastline shelters more than 300 natural beaches and features one of the world's largest tracts of coral reef. Home to approximately 900 reported species of fish and more than 410 varieties of sponge and coral, the country's unspoiled coastline is a marine wonderland and a major reason why Cuba has become renowned as a diving destination.

The 7200m-deep Cayman Trench between Cuba and Jamaica forms the boundary of the North American and Caribbean plates. Tectonic movements have tilted the island over time, creating uplifted limestone cliffs along parts of the north coast and low mangrove swamps on the south. Over millions of years Cuba's limestone bedrock has been eroded by underground rivers, creating interesting geological features including the 'haystack' hills of Viñales and more than 20,000 caves countrywide.

As a sprawling archipelago, Cuba contains thousands of islands and keys (most uninhabited) in four major offshore groups: the Archipiélago de los Colorados, off northern Pinar del Río; the Archipiélago de Sabana-Camagüey (or Jardines del Rey), off northern Villa Clara and Ciego de Ávila; the Archipiélago de los Jardines de la Reina, off southern Ciego de Ávila; and the Archipiélago de los Canarreos, around Isla de la Juventud. Most visitors will experience one or more of these island idylls, as the majority of resorts, scuba diving and beaches are found in these regions.

As a narrow island, Cuba is never wider than 200km north to south. The longest river, the 343km-long Río Cauto, flows from the Sierra Maestra in a rough loop north of Bayamo, only navigable by small boats for 110km. To compensate, 632 *embalses* (reservoirs) or *presas* (dams), covering an area of more than 500 sq km altogether, have been created for irrigation and water supply; these supplement the almost unlimited groundwater held in Cuba's limestone bedrock.

Cuba's Longest River

Name *Río Cauto*

Length *343km*

Navigable length *110km*

Basin area *8928 sq km*

Source *Sierra Maestra Mountains*

Mouth *Caribbean Sea*

Parque Nacional Alejandro de Humboldt is named for the German naturalist Alexander von Humboldt (1769–1859) who visited the island between 1801 and 1804.

Lying in the Caribbean's main hurricane region, Cuba has been hit by some blinders in recent years, notably 2012's Sandy, which wrought more than US$ 2billion in damage and Hurricane Matthew, which touched down in Baracoa in 2016.

Unesco & Ramsar Sites

The highest level of environmental protection in Cuba is provided by Unesco, which has created six biosphere reserves over the last 25 years. Biosphere reserves are areas of high biodiversity that rigorously promote conservation and sustainable practices. After a decade and a half of successful reforestation, the Sierra del Rosario became Cuba's first Unesco Biosphere Reserve in 1985. It was followed by Cuchillas del Toa (1987), Península de Guanahacabibes (1987), Baconao (1987), Ciénaga de Zapata (2000) and the Bahía de Buenavista (2000). Additionally, two of Cuba's nine Unesco World Heritage sites are considered 'natural' sites, ie nominated primarily for their ecological attributes. They are Parque Nacional Desembarco del Granma (1999), hailed for its uplifted marine terraces, and Parque Nacional Alejandro de Humboldt (2001), well known for its extraordinary endemism. Complementing the Unesco sites are half a dozen Ramsar Convention sites earmarked in 2001–02 to conserve Cuba's vulnerable wetlands. These lend added protection to the Ciénaga de Zapata and Bahía de Buenavista, and throw a lifeline to previously unprotected regions such as Isla de la Juventud's Lanier Swamp (prime crocodile territory), the expansive Río Cauto delta in Granma/Las Tunas, and the vital flamingo nesting sites on the north coasts of Camagüey and Ciego de Ávila Provinces.

National Parks

The definition of a national park is fluid in Cuba (some are referred to as natural parks or flora reserves) and there's no umbrella organization as in Canada or the USA. A handful of the 14 listed parks – most notably Ciénaga de Zapata – now lie within Unesco biosphere reserves or Ramsar Convention sites, meaning their conservation policies are better monitored. The country's first national park was Sierra del Cristal, established in 1930 (home to Cuba's largest pine forest), though it was 50 years before the authorities created another, Gran Parque Nacional Sierra Maestra (also known as Turquino), which safeguards Cuba's highest mountain. Other important parks include Viñales, with its *mogotes*, caves and tobacco plantations and Gran Piedra, near Santiago de Cuba, which is overlaid by the Baconao Unesco Biosphere Reserve. Two important offshore national parks off the south coast are the Jardines de la Reina, an archipelago diving haven off Ciego de Ávila Province's coast; and the rarely visited Cayos de San Felipe off the coast of Pinar del Río Province.

Agriculture

Agricultural land accounts for some 30% of the Cuban landmass and one in every five Cubans is engaged in some form of agricultural work.

Tobacco, grown primarily in prosperous Pinar del Río Province, is Cuba's third-most important industry for the embattled Cuban economy. Like most farming in Cuba, it's still carried out in a way that's changed little in centuries, with fields plowed by yoked oxen, and is as photogenic to watch as it is gut-busting to do.

Sugar was an economic powerhouse before the US embargo and, despite the many closed sugar mills across the island, is becoming more important again, with China the major importer. The other big crop grown is rice, whilst coffee is cultivated on the Cordillera de la Gran Piedra near Santiago de Cuba.

Wildlife

Cuba has an unusual share of indigenous fauna to draw serious animal-watchers. Birds are the biggest draw and Cuba has over 350 different varieties, two dozen endemic. Head to the mangroves of Ciénaga de Zapata in Matanzas Province or to the Península de Guanahacabibes in Pinar del Río for the best sightings of *zunzuncito* (bee hummingbird), the world's smallest bird. At 6.5cm, it's not much longer than a toothpick. These areas are also home to the *tocororo* (Cuban trogon), Cuba's national bird. Other popular bird species include *cartacubas* (indigenous to Cuba), herons, spoonbills, parakeets and rarely seen Cuban pygmy owls.

Flamingos are abundant in Cuba's northern keys, though the largest nesting ground in the western hemisphere, located in Camagüey Province's Río Máximo delta, has been compromised by contamination.

Land mammals have been hunted almost to extinction with the largest indigenous survivor the friendly *jutía* (tree rat), a 4kg edible rodent that scavenges on isolated keys living in relative harmony with armies of inquisitive iguanas. The vast majority of Cuba's other 38 species of mammal are from the bat family.

Cuba harbors a species of frog so small and elusive that it wasn't discovered until 1996 in what is now Parque Nacional Alejandro de Humboldt near Baracoa. Still lacking a common name, the endemic

Cuba's Isla Grande (main island) is the 17th-largest island in the world by area; slightly smaller than Newfoundland, but marginally bigger than Iceland.

CUBA'S PROTECTED AREAS

AREA NAME	YEAR DESIGNATED	OUTSTANDING FEATURES
UNESCO BIOSPHERE RESERVES		
Sierra del Rosario	1985	eco practices
Cuchillos Ioa Biospehere Reserve	1987	primary rainforest
Península de Guanahacabibes	1987	turtle nesting site
Baconao	1987	coffee culture
Ciénaga de Zapata	2000	largest wetlands in Caribbean
Buenavista	2000	karst formations
RAMSAR CONVENTION SITES		
Ciénaga de Zapata	2001	largest wetlands in Caribbean
Buenavista	2002	karst formations
Ciénaga de Lanier	2002	unusual mosaic of ecosystems
Humedal del Norte de Ciego de Ávila	2002	unique coastal lakes
Humedal Delta del Cauto	2002	large population of aquatic birds
Humedal Río Máximo-Cagüey	2002	significant flamingo nesting site
'NATURAL' UNESCO WORLD HERITAGE SITES		
Parque Nacional Desembarco del Granma	1999	pristine marine terraces
Parque Nacional Alejandro de Humboldt	2001	high endemism

amphibian is known as *Eleutherodactylus iberia*; it measures less than 1cm in length, and has a range of only 100 sq km.

Other odd species include the *mariposa de cristal* (Cuban clear-winged butterfly), one of only two clear-winged butterflies in the world; the rare *manjuarí* (Cuban alligator gar), an ancient fish considered a living fossil; the *polimita*, a unique land snail distinguished by its festive yellow, red and brown bands and, discovered only in 2011, the endemic *Lucifuga*, a blind troglodyte fish.

Reptiles are well represented in Cuba. Aside from iguanas and lizards, there are 15 species of snake, none poisonous. Cuba's largest snake is the *majá*, a constrictor related to the anaconda that grows up to 4m in length; it's nocturnal and doesn't usually mess with humans. The endemic Cuban crocodile *(Crocodylus rhombifer)* is relatively small but agile on land and in water. Its 68 sharp teeth are specially adapted for crushing turtle shells. Crocs have suffered from major habitat loss in the last century though greater protection since the 1990s has seen numbers increase. Cuba has established a number of successful crocodile breeding farms *(criaderos)*, the largest of which is at Guamá near the Bay of Pigs. Living in tandem with the Cuban croc is the larger American crocodile *(Crocodylus acutus)* found in the Zapata Swamps and in various marshy territories on Cuba's southern coast.

Cuba's marine life compensates for what the island lacks in land fauna. The manatee, the world's only herbivorous aquatic mammal, is found in the Bahía de Taco and the Península de Zapata, and whale sharks frequent the María la Gorda area at Cuba's eastern tip from November to February. Four turtle species (leatherback, loggerhead, green and hawksbill) are found in Cuban waters and they nest annually in isolated keys or on protected beaches in Península de Guanahacabibes.

Endangered Species

Due to habitat loss and persistent human hunting, many of Cuba's animals and birds are listed as endangered species. These include the critically endangered Cuban crocodile, which has the smallest habitat range of any crocodile, existing only in 300 sq km of the Ciénaga de Zapata (Zapata Swamp) and in the Lanier Swamp on Isla de la Juventud. Protected since 1996, wild numbers now hover at around 6000.

Other vulnerable species include the *jutía,* which was hunted mercilessly during the Special Period, when hungry Cubans tracked them for their meat (they still do – in fact, it is considered a delicacy); the tree boa, a native snake that lives in rapidly diminishing woodland areas; and the elusive *carpintero real* (ivory-billed woodpecker) spotted after a 40-year gap in the Parque Nacional Alejandro de Humboldt near Baracoa in the late 1980s, but not seen since.

The seriously endangered West Indian manatee, while protected from illegal hunting, continues to suffer from a variety of human threats, most notably from contact with boat propellers, suffocation caused by fishing nets and poisoning from residues pumped into rivers from sugar factories.

Cuba has an ambiguous attitude toward turtle hunting. Hawksbill turtles are protected under the law, though a clause allows for up to 500 of them to be captured per year in certain areas (Camagüey and Isla de la Juventud). Travelers will occasionally encounter *tortuga* (turtle), caught illegally, on the menu in places such as Baracoa.

The Caribbean manatee can grow 4.5m long and weigh up to 600kg. It can consume up to 50kg of plant life a day.

Plants

Cuba is synonymous with the palm tree; through songs, symbols, landscapes and legends the two are inextricably linked. The national tree is the *palma real* (royal palm), and it's central to the country's coat of arms and the Cristal beer logo. It's believed there are 20 million royal palms in Cuba and locals will tell you that wherever you stand on the island, you'll always be within sight of one of them. These majestic trees reach up to 40m in height and are easily identified by their lithe trunk and green stalk at the top. There are also *cocotero* (coconut palm); *palma barrigona* (big-belly palm) with its characteristic bulge; and the extremely rare *palma corcho* (cork palm). The latter is a link with the Cretaceous period (between 65 and 135 million years ago) and is cherished as a living fossil. You can see examples of it on the grounds of the Museo de Ciencias Naturales Sandalio de Noda in Pinar del Río. Cienfuegos' Jardín Botánico also boasts some 280 different palm varieties. Cuba itself has 90 palm-tree types.

It is estimated that Cuba harbors between 6500 and 7000 different species of plant, almost half of which are endemic.

Other important trees include mangroves which protect the Cuban shoreline from erosion and provide an important habitat for small fish and birds. Mangroves account for 26% of forests and cover almost 5% of the coast; Cuba ranks ninth in the world in terms of mangrove density, with the most extensive swamps situated in the Ciénaga de Zapata.

The largest native pine forests grow on Isla de la Juventud (the former Isle of Pines), in western Pinar del Río, in eastern Holguín's Sierra Cristal and in central Guantánamo. These forests are especially susceptible to fire damage, and pine reforestation has been a particular headache for Cuba's environmentalists.

Rainforests exist at higher altitudes – between approximately 500m and 1500m – in the Sierra del Escambray, Sierra Maestra and Macizo de Sagua-Baracoa mountains. Original rainforest species include ebony and mahogany, but today most reforestation is in eucalyptus, which is graceful and fragrant, but invasive.

Dotted liberally across the island, ferns, cacti and orchids contribute hundreds of species, many endemic, to Cuba's cornucopia of plant life. For the best concentrations check out the botanical gardens in Santiago de Cuba for ferns and cacti and Pinar del Río for orchids. Most orchids bloom from November to January, and one of the best places to see them is in the Reserva Sierra del Rosario. The national flower is the graceful *mariposa* (butterfly jasmine); you'll know it by its white floppy petals and strong perfume.

Medicinal plants are widespread in Cuba due largely to shortages of prescription medicines. Pharmacies are well stocked with effective tinctures such as aloe (for cough and congestion) and a bee by-product *propólio*, used for everything from stomach amoebas to respiratory infections. On the home front, every Cuban patio has a pot of *orégano de la tierra* (Cuban oregano), a cold remedy whipped up into a wonder elixir with lime juice, honey and hot water.

Environmental Issues

Most of Cuba's environmental threats are of human origin and relate either to pollution or habitat loss, often through deforestation. Efforts to conserve the archipelago's diverse ecology really began in 1978, when Cuba established the National Committee for the Protection and Conservation of Natural Resources and the Environment (Comarna).

To reverse 400 years of deforestation and habitat destruction, the body created green belts and initiated ambitious reforestation campaigns. Comarna oversees national and international environmental legislation, including adherence to international treaties that govern Cuba's Unesco Biosphere Reserves and Unesco World Heritage sites.

Cuba's greatest environmental problems are aggravated by an economy struggling to survive. As the country pins its hopes on tourism, a contradictory environmental policy has evolved. There is added strain on the environment with increased tourism as US relations open. With ally Venezuela ailing, Cuba's oil supply has destabilized. The government has plans to start drilling for oil off the northwest coast, though a spill would be devastating. Therein lies the dilemma: how can a developing nation provide for its people *and* maintain ecological standards?

Deforestation

At the time of Columbus' arrival in 1492, 95% of Cuba was covered in virgin forest. By 1959, thanks to wholesale land-clearing for sugarcane and citrus plantations, this area had been reduced to 16%. Large-scale tree-planting and the organization of protected parks has seen this figure creep back up to 24%, but there is still a lot of work to be done.

Las Terrazas in Pinar del Río Province provided a blueprint for reforestation in the late 1960s, restoring hectares of denuded woodland to prevent ecological disaster. More recent efforts have focused on safeguarding the Caribbean's last virgin rainforest in Parque Nacional Alejandro de Humboldt and adding protective forest fringes to wetlands in the Río Cauto delta.

Causeways

An early blip in Cuba's economy-versus-ecology struggle was the 2km-long stone *pedraplén* (causeway) constructed to link offshore Cayo Sabinal with mainland Camagüey in the late 1980s. This massive project, which involved piling boulders in the sea and laying a road on top (without any bridges), interrupted water currents and caused irreparable damage to bird and marine habitats.

And to what end? No resorts, as yet, inhabit deserted Cayo Sabinel. Other longer causeways were later built connecting Jardines del Rey to Ciego de Ávila (27km long) and Cayo Santa María to Villa Clara (a 48km-long monster). This time more ecofriendly bridges have enabled a healthier water flow, though the full extent of the ecological damage won't be known for another decade at least.

Wildlife & Habitat Loss

Maintaining healthy animal habitats is crucial in Cuba, a country with high levels of endemism and hence a higher threat of species extinction. The problem is exacerbated by the narrow range of endemic animals, such as the Cuban crocodile that lives almost exclusively in the Ciénaga de Zapata, or the equally rare *Eleutherodactylus iberia* (the world's smallest frog). The latter has a range of just 100 sq km and exists only

NATURAL SPAS

Cuban spas look more like utilitarian hospitals than candlelit retreats – not that this detracts from their restorative powers. The nation's most popular spas are fed by thermal, mineral-rich water sources and are connected to economical Islazul hotels. They offer a mixture of baths, gymnasiums and assorted therapies.

Balneario San Diego (p188) In Pinar del Río Province. The nation's oldest spa, opened in 1951 and finally getting a long-overdue makeover. Water temperatures of 32°C to 38°C and numerous mud-therapy treatments. Good for treating rheumatism.

Hotel & Spa Elguea (☎42-68-62-90; s/d incl breakfast CUC$45/65; P❄≋) Villa Clara Province. Cuba's hottest thermal waters (45°C to 50°C).

Villa San José del Lago (p300) In Sancti Spíritus Province; a more physically attractive spa, with a hotel and assorted outdoor pools rich in bicarbonate/calcium. Good for treating psoriasis.

in the Parque Nacional Alejandro de Humboldt, whose formation in 2001 undoubtedly saved it from extinction. Other areas under threat include the giant flamingo nesting sites on the Archipiélago de Sabana-Camagüey, and Moa, where contaminated water runoff has played havoc with the coastal mangrove ecosystems favored by manatees.

Building new roads and airports, and the frenzied construction of giant resorts on virgin beaches, exacerbate the clash between human activity and environmental protection. The grossly shrunken extent of the Reserva Ecológica Varahicacos in Varadero due to encroaching resorts is one example. Cayo Coco – part of an important Ramsar-listed wetland that sits adjacent to a fast-developing hotel strip – is another.

Overfishing (including turtles and lobster for tourist consumption), agricultural runoff, industrial pollution and inadequate sewage treatment have contributed to the decay of coral reefs. Diseases such as yellow band, black band and nuisance algae have begun to appear. The rounding up of wild dolphins as entertainers in tourist-oriented *delfinarios* has also rankled many activists.

Ageing Infrastructure & Pollution

As soon as you arrive in Havana or Santiago de Cuba, the air pollution hits you like a sharp slap on the face. Airborne particles, old trucks belching black smoke and by-products from burning garbage are just some of the culprits. Havana's century-old sewer system – built for a population that has since quadrupled – is on the point of complete breakdown. Sewage blockages affect over half of city residents and drinking water leaks sabotage conservation efforts. Cement factories, sugar refineries and other heavy industries have also made their (dirty) mark.

The nickel mines engulfing Moa serve as stark examples of industrial concerns taking precedence: some of Cuba's wildest landscape has turned into a barren wasteland of lunar proportions. Unfortunately there are no easy solutions; nickel is one of Cuba's largest exports, a raw material the economy couldn't do without.

While old American cars paint a romantic picture to tourists, they're hardly fuel efficient. Add to that the use of substandard fuels due to economic constraints. Then there's the public transport – even Fidel went on the record to lament the adverse health effects of Cuba's filthy buses.

Environmental Successes

On the bright side of the environmental equation is the Cuban government's enthusiasm for reforestation and protecting natural areas – especially since the mid-1980s – along with its willingness to confront mistakes from the past. It's most stunning achievement is reef conservation in Marine Protected Areas. Cuba has also taken on climate change and rising sea levels with preparatory measures.

Havana Harbor, once Latin America's most polluted, has been undergoing a massive cleanup, as has the Río Almendares, which cuts through the heart of the city. Sulfur emissions from oil wells near Varadero have been reduced, and environmental regulations for developments are now enforced by the Ministry of Science, Technology and the Environment. Fishing regulations have become increasingly strict. Striking the balance between Cuba's immediate needs and the future of its environment is a pressing challenge.

Las Terrazas is the nation's most obvious eco-success, though there have been others, including the implementation of windfarm sites and the first solar farm, opened in Cienfuegos Province in 2014. In terms of fauna, the nation can point to major crocodile reintroduction programs and successful sea turtle conservation. Strides are also being made in urban organic gardening.

Cuba's Highest Mountains

Pico Turquino
1972m, Santiago de Cuba Province

Pico Cuba
1872m, Santiago de Cuba Province

Pico Bayamesa
1730m, Granma Province

Survival Guide

Directory A–Z

Accommodations

Cuban accommodations run the gamut from CUC$10 beach cabins to five-star resorts. Solo travelers are penalized price-wise, paying 75% of the price of a double room.

Budget

In this price range, the accommodation consists almost entirely of casas particulares (private homestays) and campismos (rural cabins).

Although casa prices have crept up a little in the last few years, there are still only a handful of deluxe places (mainly in Havana) that will cost more than CUC$50. In cheaper casas particulares (CUC$20 to CUC$25) in the provinces you may have to share a bathroom and will have a fan instead of air-con.

There are around a dozen campismos countrywide that welcome international travelers and most are under CUC$50 a night. Accommodation is in old-fashioned cabins akin to a one- or two-star hotel.

Midrange

Cuba's scant midrange category is a lottery, with some boutique colonial hotels (run by Cubanacán) and some awful places with spooky Soviet-like architecture and atmosphere to match (run by Islazul). In midrange hotels you can usually expect air-con, private hot-water bathrooms, clean linens, satellite TV, a swimming pool and a restaurant, although the food won't exactly be gourmet.

Some of the more deluxe casas particulares now fall into this price bracket and they are nearly always pretty plush.

Top End

Cuba's state-run hotels and resorts have hiked up their prices two- or three-fold in the last couple of years. As a result, hotels in this bracket are somewhat overpriced.

The most comfortable top-end hotels are usually partly foreign-owned and maintain international standards (although service can sometimes be a bit lax). Rooms have everything that a midrange hotel has, plus big, quality beds and linens, a minibar, international phone service, and perhaps a terrace or view. Wi-fi is a prerequisite in these places, although it may be temperamental and only work in the reception area.

Practically all of Cuba's all-inclusive resorts fall into this price category.

Cuba's hotel star rating also includes half-star categories (eg 4½ stars).

Price Differentials

Factors influencing rates are time of year, location, hotel chain and whether the accommodations are state-run or private (the latter is nearly always cheaper). Low season is generally mid-September to late November and April to June (except for Easter week). Christmas and New Year is what's called extreme high season, when rates are 25% more than high-season rates. Bargaining is sometimes possible in casas particulares – though as far as foreigners go, it's not really the done thing. The casa owners in any given area pay generic taxes, and the prices you will be quoted reflect this. You'll find very few casas in Cuba less than CUC$20, unless you're up for a long stay. Prearranging Cuban accommodation has become easier with better wi-fi connections. It is now possible to make bookings on airbnb (www.airbnb.com) and pay with your credit card.

BOOK YOUR STAY ONLINE

For more accommodations reviews by Lonely Planet authors, check out http://lonelyplanet.com/hotels/. You'll find independent reviews, as well as recommendations on the best places to stay. Best of all, you can book online.

Types of Accommodations

CAMPISMOS

Campismos are where Cubans go on vacation (an estimated one million use them annually). Hardly camping, most of these installations are simple concrete cabins with bunk beds, foam mattresses and cold showers. There are over 80 of them sprinkled around the country in rural areas. Campismos are ranked either *nacional* or *internacional*. The former are (technically) only for Cubans, while the latter host both Cubans and foreigners and are more upscale, with air-con, hot water and/or linens. There are currently a dozen international campismos in Cuba ranging from the hotel-standard **Aguas Claras** (☎48-77-84-27; www.campismopopular.cu; s/d incl breakfast CUC$44/58; P 🏊) in Pinar del Río to the more basic **La Mula** (☎22-32-62-62; Carretera Granma Km 120; r CUC$16) in Santiago de Cuba province.

Listings can be found on the website www.campismopopular.cu. Every provincial city in Cuba has a campismo office where you can book ahead. Cabin accommodations in international campismos cost CUC$20 to CUC$60 per bed.

CASAS PARTICULARES

Private rooms are the best option for independent travelers in Cuba and a great way of meeting the locals on their home turf. Furthermore, staying in these venerable, family-orientated establishments will give you a far more open and less censored view of the country, and your understanding and appreciation of Cuba will grow far richer as a result. Casa owners also often make excellent tour guides and can often arrange all-number of extra activities from taxis to nature walks.

You'll know houses renting rooms by the blue insignia on the door marked 'Arrendador Divisa.' There are thousands of casas particulares all over Cuba; well over 2000 in Havana alone and over 800 in Trinidad. From penthouses to historical homes, all manner of rooms are available from CUC$15 to CUC$60. Most houses are family homes who rent out a few rooms. Some of the more successful houses have become larger and more businesslike in recent years, operating more like small private hotels.

Government regulation has eased since 2011, and renters can now let out multiple rooms if they have space. Owners pay a monthly tax per room depending on location (plus extra for off-street parking) to post a sign advertising their rooms and to serve meals. These taxes must be paid whether the rooms are rented or not. Owners must keep a register of all guests and report each new arrival within 24 hours. For this reason, you will also be requested to produce your passport (not a photocopy) on arrival. Regular government inspections ensure that conditions inside casas remain clean, safe and secure Most proprietors offer breakfast and dinner for an extra rate (usually CUC$5). Hot showers are a prerequisite. In general, rooms these days provide at least two beds (one is usually a double), fridge, air-con, fan and private bathroom. Bonuses could include a terrace or patio, private entrance, TV, security box, mini-bar, kitchenette and parking space.

Despite the abundance of casas particulares in Cuba, the recent spike in tourist numbers means they get very busy, especially in peak season (November to March). Whole towns can fill up fast. It is advisable to book ahead.

BOOKINGS & FURTHER INFORMATION

Due to the plethora of casas particulares in Cuba, it is impossible to include even a fraction of the total. The ones we have chosen are a combination of reader recommendations and local research. If one casa is full, they'll almost always be able to recommend to you someone else down the road.

The following websites list a large number of casas across the country and allow online booking. Cuban casas can now be booked internationally with a credit card on **Airbnb** (www.airbnb.com). Most casas will also accept reservations via text, phone or email.

➡ **Cubacasas** (www.cubacasas.net) The best online source for casa particular information and booking; up to date, accurate and with colorful links to hundreds of private rooms across the island (in English and French).

➡ **Casa Particular Organization** (www.casaparticularcuba.org) Reader-recommended website for prebooking private rooms.

SLEEPING PRICE RANGES

The following price ranges refer to a double room with bathroom in high season.

Havana

$ less than CUC$70

$$ CUC$70–150

$$$ more than CUC$150

Rest of Cuba

$ less than CUC$50

$$ CUC$50–120

$$$ more than CUC$120

HOTELS

All tourist hotels and resorts are at least 51% owned by the Cuban government and are administered by one of four main organizations. Islazul is the cheapest and most popular with Cubans (who pay in Cuban pesos). Although the facilities can be variable at these establishments and the architecture a tad Sovietesque, Islazul hotels are invariably clean, cheap, friendly and attract a mainly Cuban clientele. They're also more likely to be situated in the island's smaller provincial towns. One downside are the blaring on-site discos that often keep guests awake until the small hours. Cubanacán is a step up and offers a nice mix of midrange and top-end options in cities and resort areas. The company has also rolled out a clutch of reasonably priced boutique-style hotels (the Encanto brand) in attractive city centers such as Sancti Spíritus, Remedios, Camagüey and Santiago.

Gaviota manages higher-end resorts in the all-inclusive zone, though the chain also has a smattering of cheaper 'villas' in places such as Santiago and Cayo Coco. Gran Caribe does midrange to top-end hotels, including the emblematic Hotel Nacional in Havana. Except for Islazul properties, tourist hotels are for guests paying in convertible pesos only. Since May 2008, Cubans have been allowed to stay in any tourist hotel, although financially most of them are still out of reach.

At the top end of the hotel pyramid you'll often find foreign chains such as the Spanish-run Meliá and Iberostar brands running hotels in tandem with Cubanacán, Gaviota or Gran Caribe – mainly in the resort areas.

Climate

Havana

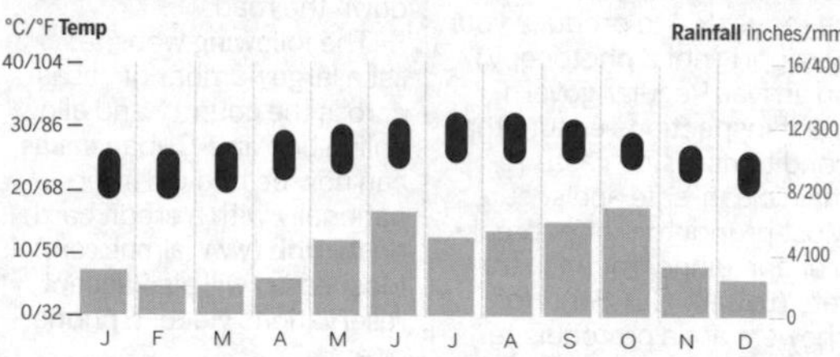

Sancti Spíritus

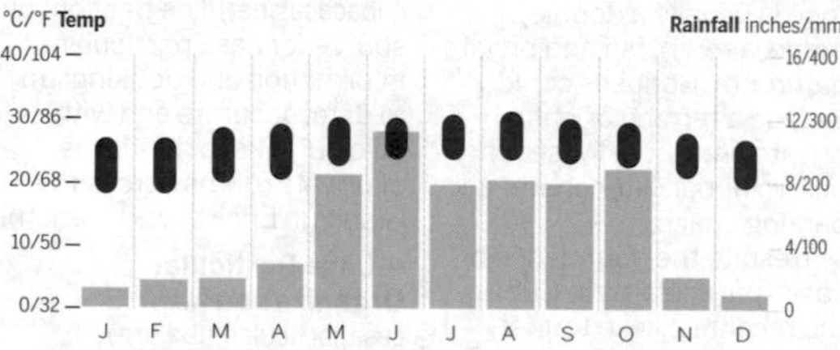

Santiago De Cuba

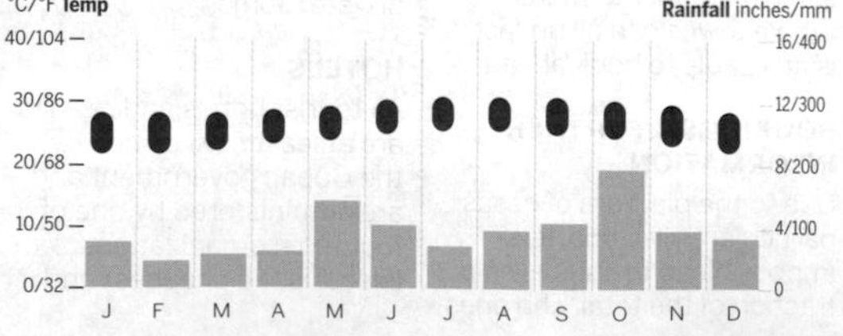

The standards and service at these types of places are not unlike resorts in Mexico and the rest of the Caribbean.

Customs Regulations

Cuban customs regulations are complicated. For the full up-to-date scoop see www.aduana.co.cu.

Entering Cuba

Travelers are allowed to bring in personal belongings including photography equipment, binoculars, a musical instrument, radio, personal computer, tent, fishing rod, bicycle, canoe and other sporting gear, and up to 10kg of medicines. Canned, processed and dried food are no problem, nor are pets (as long as they have veterinary certification and proof of rabies vaccination).

Items that do not fit into the categories mentioned above are subject to a 100% customs duty to a maximum of CUC$1000.

Items prohibited from entry into Cuba include narcotics, explosives, pornography, electrical appliances broadly defined, light motor vehicles, car engines and products of animal origin.

Leaving Cuba

You are allowed to export 50 boxed cigars duty-free (or 23 singles) and up to US$5000 (or the equivalent) in cash.

Exporting undocumented art and items of cultural patrimony is restricted and involves fees. Normally, when you buy art you will be given an official 'seal' at the point of sale. Check this before you buy. If you don't get one, you'll need to obtain one from the **Registro Nacional de Bienes Culturales** (Map p96; Calle 17 No 1009, btwn Calles 10 & 12, Vedado; ⌚9am-noon Mon-Fri) in Havana. Bring the objects here for inspection, fill in a form, pay a fee of between CUC$10 and CUC$30, which covers from one to five pieces of artwork and return 24 hours later to pick up the certificate.

Travelers should check local import laws in their home country regarding Cuban cigars. Some countries, including Australia, charge duty on imported Cuban cigars.

Discount Cards

Students who can provide proof of enrollment at a Cuban university or college for a minimum stay of six months are issued a *carnet* – the identification document that allows foreigners to pay for museums, transport (including *colectivos* – collective taxis) and theater performances in Cuban pesos (CUP), thus saving a bundle of money.

Electricity

The electrical current in Cuba is 110V with 220V in many tourist hotels and resorts.

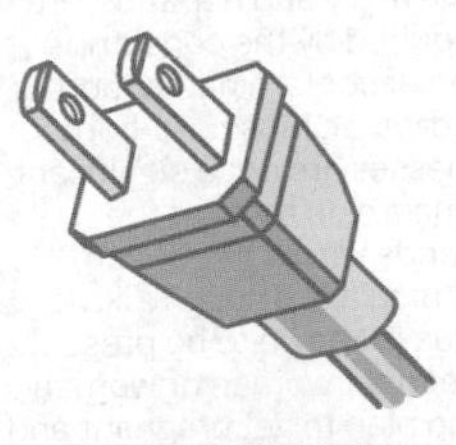

110V/220V/60Hz

Embassies & Consulates

All embassies are in Havana, and most are open from 8am to noon on weekdays. Australia is represented in the Canadian Embassy. New Zealand is represented in the UK Embassy. Canada has additional consulates in Varadero and Guardalavaca.

Austrian Embassy (☎7-204-2825; Av 5A No 6617, cnr Calle 70, Miramar)

Canadian Embassy (☎7-204-2516; Calle 30 No 518, Playa) Also represents Australia.

Danish Consulate (☎7-866-8128; Paseo de Martí No 20, 4th fl)

Dutch Embassy (☎7-204-2511; Calle 8 No 307, btwn Avs 3 & 5, Miramar)

French Embassy (☎7-201-3131; Calle 14 No 312, btwn Avs 3 & 5, Miramar)

German Embassy (☎7-833-2539; Calle 13 No 652, Vedado)

Italian Embassy (☎7-204-5615; Av 5 No 402, Miramar)

Japanese Embassy (☎7-204-3508; Miramar Trade Center, cnr Av 3 & Calle 80, Playa)

Mexican Embassy (☎7-204-7722; Calle 12 No 518, Miramar)

Spanish Embassy (☎7-866-8025; Cárcel No 51)

Swedish Embassy (☎7-204-2831; Calle 34 No 510, Miramar)

Swiss Consulate (☎7-204-2611; Av 5 No 2005, btwn Avs 20 & 22, Miramar)

UK Embassy (☎7-214-2200; Calle 34 No 702, Miramar) Also represents New Zealand.

US Embassy (☎7-833-3543; Calzada, btwn Calles L & M, Vedado)

Food & Drink

Cuban cuisine - popularly known as *comida criollla* - has improved immensely since new privatization laws passed in 2011 inspired a plethora of pioneering restaurants to take root, particularly in Havana. Travel outside the bigger cities, however,and Cuban food can still be limited and insipid.

Where to Eat & Drink

GOVERNMENT-RUN RESTAURANTS

Government-run restaurants operate in either *moneda nacional* or convertibles. *Moneda nacional* restaurants are often pretty grim and are notorious for handing you a nine-page menu (in Spanish) when the only thing available is fried chicken. There are, however, a few newer exceptions to this rule. *Moneda nacional* restaurants will normally accept payment in CUC$, though sometimes at an inferior exchange rate to the standard 25 to one.

Restaurants that sell food in convertibles are generally more reliable, but this isn't capitalism: just because you're paying more doesn't necessarily mean better service. Food is often limp and unappetizing and discourse with bored waiters can be worthy of a *Monty Python* sketch (whatever you do, don't complain about a dirty fork). That said, things have got progressively better in the last seven years. The state-run Palmares group manages a wide variety of excellent restaurants countrywide from bog-standard beach shacks to the *New York Times*–lauded **El Aljibe** (Map p126; ☎7-204-1583/4; Av 7, btwn Calles 24 & 26; mains CUC$12-15; ⏲noon-midnight) in Miramar, Havana. The government-run restaurants in Habana Vieja are some of the best in Cuba, and Gaviota has recently tarted up some of its old staples. Employees of state-run restaurants will not earn more than CUC$20 a month (the average Cuban salary), so tips are highly appreciated.

PRIVATE RESTAURANTS

First established in 1995 during the economic chaos

of the Special Period, private restaurants owe much of their success to the sharp increase in tourist traffic in Cuba, coupled with the bold experimentation of local chefs who, despite a paucity of decent ingredients, have heroically managed to keep the age-old traditions of Cuban cooking alive. They have proliferated since new business laws were passed in 2011, especially in Havana. Private restaurant meals are generally more expensive than their state-run equivalents, costing anything between CUC$8 and CUC$30.

In the last five years or so, private restaurants have become more adventurous, plying an increasing array of international and fusion dishes. Italian-themed and, to a lesser extent, Spanish-themed restaurants are popular all over the island. Havana has recently sprouted places specializing in Korean, Russian and Iranian food.

Vegetarians

In a land with a recent history of rationing and food shortages, strict vegetarians (ie no lard, no meat bullion, no fish) will have a hard time. Cubans don't traditionally understand vegetarianism, and when they do (or when they *say* they do), it can be summarized rather adroitly with one key word: omelet – or, at a stretch, scrambled eggs. However, things are changing. Cooks in casas particulares, who may already have have had experience cooking meatless dishes for other travelers, are usually pretty good at accommodating vegetarians. The same goes for private restaurants, many of which have started to develop menus with vegetarian sections. Havana and Viñales have recently sprouted Cuba's first decent full-blown vegetarian restaurants.

> **EATING PRICE RANGES**
>
> It will be a very rare meal in Cuba that costs over CUC$25. Restaurant listings use the following price brackets for main dishes.
>
> **$** less than CUC$7
>
> **$$** CUC$7–15
>
> **$$$** more than CUC$15

Staples & Specialties

Cuban meals are characterized by *congrí* (rice flecked with black beans), meat (primarily pork, closely followed by chicken and beef), fried plantains (green bananas), salad (limited to seasonal ingredients) and root vegetables, usually *yuca* (cassava) and *calabaza* (pumpkin-like squash).

Pescado (fish) is also readily available. Though you'll come across dorado, *aguja* (swordfish), and occasionally octopus and crab in some of the specialist seafood places, you're more likely to see *pargo* (red snapper), lobster or prawns.

Cubans are also aficionados of ice cream and the nuances of different flavors are heatedly debated. Coppelia ice cream is legendary, but ridiculously cheap tubs of other brands (440g for CUC$1) can be procured almost everywhere, and even the machine-dispensed peso stuff ain't half bad.

LGBTIQ Travelers

While Cuba isn't a queer destination (yet), it's more tolerant than many other Latin American countries. The hit movie *Fresa y Chocolate* (Strawberry and Chocolate, 1994) sparked a national dialogue about homosexuality. Activist Mariela Castro, the daughter of Raúl, has led the way in much-needed LGBTIQ reforms and changing social perceptions. Today Cuba is pretty tolerant, all things considered.

People from more accepting societies may find this tolerance too 'don't ask, don't tell' or tokenistic but Cuba remains ahead of most of Latin America in this respect.

Lesbianism is less tolerated and seldom discussed and you'll see very little open displays of gay pride between female lovers. There are occasional *fiestas para chicas* (not necessarily all-girl parties but close); ask around at the **Cine Yara** (Map p96; cnr Calles 23 & L) in Havana's gay cruising zone.

Cubans are physical with each other and you'll see men hugging, women holding hands and lots of friendly caressing. This type of casual, non-sensual touching shouldn't be a problem.

Health

From a medical point of view, Cuba is generally safe as long as you're reasonably careful about what you eat and drink. The most common travel-related diseases, such as dysentery and hepatitis, are acquired by the consumption of contaminated food and water. Mosquito-borne illnesses are not a significant concern on most of the islands within the Cuban archipelago, though Zika virus is known to be present. Pregnant women or women who plan to get pregnant and their partners should check travel advisories before going to Cuba.

Prevention is the key to staying healthy while traveling around Cuba. Travelers who receive the recommended vaccines and follow commonsense precautions usually come away with nothing more than a little diarrhea.

Health Insurance

Since May 2010, Cuba has made it obligatory for all foreign visitors to have medical insurance. Random checks are made at the airport, so ensure you bring a printed copy of your policy.

Should you end up in hospital, call **Asistur** (☎7-866-4499, emergency 7-866-8527; www.asistur.cu; Paseo de Martí No 208; ⏰8:30am-5:30pm Mon-Fri, 8am-2pm Sat) for help with insurance and medical assistance. The company has regional offices in Havana, Varadero, Cayo Coco, Guardalavaca and Santiago de Cuba.

Outpatient treatment at international clinics is reasonably priced, but emergency and prolonged hospitalization gets expensive (the free medical system for Cubans should only be used when there is no other option).

Should you have to purchase medical insurance on arrival, you will pay from CUC$3 per day for coverage of up to CUC$25,000 in medical expenses (for illness) and CUC$10,000 for repatriation of a sick person.

Health Care for Foreigners

The Cuban government has established a for-profit health system for foreigners called **Servimed** (☎7-240-141; www.servimedcuba.com), which is entirely separate from the free, not-for-profit system that takes care of Cuban citizens. There are more than 40 Servimed health centers across the island, offering primary care as well as a variety of specialty and high-tech services. If you're staying in a hotel, the usual way to access the system is to ask the manager for a physician referral. Servimed centers accept walk-ins. While Cuban hospitals provide some free emergency treatment for foreigners, this should only be used when there is no other option. Remember that in Cuba medical resources are scarce and the local populace should be given priority in free health-care facilities.

Almost all doctors and hospitals expect payment in cash, regardless of whether you have travel health insurance or not. If you develop a life-threatening medical problem, you'll probably want to be evacuated to a country with state-of-the-art medical care. Since this may cost tens of thousands of dollars, be sure you have insurance to cover this before you depart.

There are special pharmacies for foreigners also run by the Servimed system, but all Cuban pharmacies are notoriously short on supplies, including pharmaceuticals. Be sure to bring along adequate quantities of all medications you might need, both prescription and over the counter. Also, be sure to bring along a fully stocked medical kit. Pharmacies marked *turno permanente* or *pilotos* are open 24 hours.

Tap Water

Tap water in Cuba is not reliably safe to drink and outbreaks of cholera have been recorded in the past few years. Bottled water called Ciego Montero rarely costs more than CUC$1, but is sometimes not available in small towns. Stock up in the cities when going on long bus or car journeys.

Internet Access

State-run telecommunications company Etecsa has a monopoly as Cuba's internet service provider. For public internet access, almost every provincial town has an Etecsa *telepuntos* center where you can wait in line to enter and buy a one-hour user card (CUC$1.50) with scratch-off *usuario* (code) and *contraseña* (password) to use at computers onsite or in a public wi-fi area (usually the central plaza of a town). Cards can be used for multiple internet sessions.

There are few, if any, independent internet cafes outside the *telepuntos*. As a general rule, most three- to five-star hotels (and all resort hotels) have wi-fi and internet terminals. They also can be a more convenient place to buy scratchcards, though some hotels charge abusive rates for them (sometimes as much as CUC$7 per hour).

Very few casas particulares offer internet, but their numbers are growing.

Warning: connections are often slow and temperamental, particularly at peak times (late afternoon and early evening).

Legal Matters

Cuban police are everywhere and they're usually very friendly – more likely to ask you for a date than a bribe. Corruption is a serious offense in Cuba, and typically no one wants to get mixed up in it. Getting caught out without identification is never good; carry some around just in case (a driver's license, a copy of your passport or a

PRACTICALITIES

Electrical current 110V with 220V in many tourist hotels and resorts.

Newspapers Three state-controlled, national newspapers: *Granma*, *Juventud Rebelde* and *Trabajadores*.

TV Five national television channels with some imported foreign shows on the newer Multivisión channel.

Smoking Technically banned in enclosed spaces but only sporadically enforced.

Weights and measures Metric system except in some fruit and vegetable markets, where imperial is used.

student ID card should be sufficient).

Drugs are prohibited in Cuba, though you may still get offered marijuana and cocaine on the streets of Havana. Penalties for buying, selling, holding or taking drugs are serious, and Cuba is making a concerted effort to treat demand and curtail supply; it is only the foolish traveler who partakes while on a Cuban vacation.

Maps

Signage is awful in Cuba, so a good map is essential for drivers and cyclists alike. The comprehensive *Guía de Carreteras*, published in Italy, includes the best maps available in Cuba. If it doesn't come free when you rent a car, you can usually buy it. It has a complete index, a detailed Havana map and useful information in English, Spanish, Italian and French. Handier is the all-purpose *Automapa Nacional*, available at hotel shops and car-rental offices.

The best map published outside Cuba is the Freytag & Berndt 1:1.25 million *Cuba* map. The island map is good, and it has indexed town plans of Havana, Playas del Este, Varadero, Cienfuegos, Camagüey and Santiago de Cuba.

For good basic maps, pick up one of the provincial *Guías* available in Infotur offices.

Money

This is a tricky part of any Cuban trip, as the double economy takes some getting used to. As of early 2017, two currencies were still circulating in Cuba: convertible pesos (CUC$) and Cuban pesos (referred to as *moneda nacional*, abbreviated MN$).

Most things tourists pay for are in convertibles (eg accommodation, rental cars, bus tickets, museum admission and internet access). At the time of writing, Cuban pesos were selling at 25 to one convertible, and while there are many things you can't buy with *moneda nacional*, using them on certain occasions means you'll see a bigger slice of authentic Cuba. The prices we list are in convertibles unless otherwise stated.

Making everything a little more confusing, euros are also accepted at the Varadero, Guardalavaca, Cayo Largo del Sur, Cayo Coco and Cayo Guillermo resorts, but once you leave the resort grounds you'll still need convertibles.

The best currencies to bring to Cuba are euros, Canadian dollars or pounds sterling. The worst is US dollars, for which you will be penalized with a 10% fee (on top of the normal commission) when you buy convertibles (CUC$). Since 2011, the Cuban convertible has been pegged 1:1 to the US dollar, meaning its rate will fluctuate depending on the strength/weakness of the US dollar. Australian dollars are not accepted anywhere in Cuba.

Cadeca branches in every city and town sell Cuban pesos (MN$). You won't need more than CUC$10 worth of pesos a week. There is almost always a branch at the local *agropecuario* (vegetable market). If you get caught without Cuban pesos and are drooling for that ice-cream cone, you can always use convertibles; in street transactions such as these, CUC$1 is equal to 25 pesos and you'll receive change in pesos. There is no black market money changing in Cuba, only hustlers trying to fleece you with money-changing scams.

CURRENCY UNIFICATION

In October 2013, Raúl Castro announced that Cuba would gradually unify its dual currencies (convertibles and *moneda nacional*). As a result, prices are liable to change. At the time of writing, the unification process had yet to begin and no further details had emerged as to when or how the government will go about implementing the complex changes. Check www.lonelyplanet.com for updates.

ATMs & Credit Cards

Cuba is primarily a cash economy. Credit cards are accepted in resort hotels and some city hotels. There are a growing number of ATMs.

US residents must note: as of early 2017, debit and credit cards from the USA could still not be used.

The acceptance of credit cards has become more widespread in Cuba in recent years and was aided by the legalization of US and US-linked credit and debit cards in early 2015. However, change is still a work in process.

While services can still be booked with credit cards from the USA on the internet, in the country it's another story. Residents of the US can wire money via Western Union, though this requires help from a third party and hefty fees.

When weighing up whether to use a credit card or cash, bear in mind that the charges levied by Cuban banks are similar for both (around 3%). However, your home bank may charge additional fees for ATM/credit card transactions. An increasing number of debit cards work in Cuba, but it's best to check with both your home bank and the local Cuban bank before using them.

Ideally, it is best to arrive in Cuba with a stash of cash and a credit and debit card as back-up.

Almost all private business in Cuba (ie at casas particulares and paladares) is still conducted in cash.

Cash advances can be drawn from credit cards, but the commission is the same. Check with your home bank before you leave, as many banks won't authorize large withdrawals in foreign countries unless you notify them of your travel plans first.

ATMs are becoming more common. This being Cuba, it is wise to only use ATMs when the bank is open, in case any problems occur.

Cash

Credit cards don't have the importance or ubiquity that they do elsewhere in the western hemisphere. Although carrying just cash is far riskier than the usual cash/credit card/debit card mix, it's infinitely more convenient. As long as you use a concealed money belt and keep the cash on you or in your hotel's safety deposit box at all times, you should be OK.

It's better to ask for CUC$20/10/5/3/1 bills when you're changing money, as many smaller Cuban businesses (taxis, restaurants etc) can't change anything bigger (ie CUC$50 or CUC$100 bills) and the words *no hay cambio* (no change) echo everywhere. If desperate, you can always break big bills at hotels.

DENOMINATIONS & LINGO

One of the most confusing parts of a double economy is terminology. Cuban pesos are called *moneda nacional* (abbreviated MN) or *pesos Cubanos* or simply pesos, while convertible pesos are called *pesos convertibles* (abbreviated CUC), or simply pesos (again!). More recently people have been referring to them as *cucs*. Sometimes you'll be negotiating in *pesos Cubanos* and your counterpart will be negotiating in *pesos convertibles*. It doesn't help that the notes look similar as well. Worse, the symbol for both convertibles and Cuban pesos is $. You can imagine the potential scams just working these combinations.

The Cuban peso comes in notes of one, five, 10, 20, 50 and 100 pesos; and coins of one (rare), five and 20 centavos, and one and three pesos. The five-centavo coin is called a *medio*, the 20-centavo coin a *peseta*. Centavos are also called *kilos*.

The convertible peso comes in multicolored notes of one, three, five, 10, 20, 50 and 100 pesos; and coins of five, 10, 25 and 50 centavos, and one peso.

Post

Letters and postcards sent to Europe and the US take about a month to arrive. While *sellos* (stamps) are sold in Cuban pesos and convertibles, correspondence bearing the latter has a better chance of arriving. Postcards cost CUC$0.65 to all countries. Letters cost CUC$0.65 to the Americas, CUC$0.75 to Europe and CUC$0.85 to all other countries. Prepaid postcards, including international postage, are available at most hotel shops and post offices and are the surest bet for successful delivery. For important mail, you're better off using DHL, which is located in all the major cities; it costs CUC$55 for a 900g letter pack to Australia, or CUC$50 to Europe.

Public Holidays

Officially Cuba has nine public holidays. Other important national days to look out for include January 28 (anniversary of the birth of José Martí); April 19 (Bay of Pigs victory); October 8 (anniversary of the death of Che Guevara); October 28 (anniversary of the death of Camilo Cienfuegos); and December 7 (anniversary of the death of Antonio Maceo).

January 1 Triunfo de la Revolución (Liberation Day)

January 2 Día de la Victoria (Victory of the Armed Forces)

May 1 Día de los Trabajadores (International Worker's Day)

July 25–27 Día de la Rebeldía Nacional (Commemoration of Moncada Attack)

October 10 Día de la Indepedencia (Independence Day)

December 25 Navidad (Christmas Day)

December 31 New Year's Eve

Safe Travel

Cuba is generally safer than most countries, with violent attacks extremely rare. Petty theft (eg rifled luggage in hotel rooms or unattended shoes disappearing from the beach) is common, but preventative measures work wonders. Pickpocketing is preventable: wear your bag in front of you on crowded buses and at busy markets, and only take the money you will need when you head out at night.

Begging is more widespread and is exacerbated by tourists who hand out money, soap, pens, chewing gum and other things to people on the street. If you truly want to do something to help, pharmacies and hospitals will accept medicine donations, schools happily take pens, paper, crayons etc, and libraries will gratefully accept books. Alternatively pass stuff onto your casa particular owner or leave it at a local church. Hustlers are called *jinteros/jinteras* (male/female touts), and can be a real nuisance.

Telephone

Cell phone usage has become relatively widespread in Cuba in the last few years. Normally a recorded message will inform you of phone number changes. Etecsa *telepuntos* have air-conditioned phone and internet terminals in almost every provincial town.

Cell Phones

Check with your service provider to see if your phone will work (GSM or TDMA networks only). International calls are expensive. You can pre-buy services from the state-run phone company, Cubacel.

You can use your own GSM or TDMA phones in Cuba, though you'll have to get a local chip and pay an activation fee (approximately CUC$30) at Etecsa *telepunto*. Bring your passport. There are numerous offices around the country (including at the Havana airport) where you can do this.

Costs run between CUC$0.35 per minute for calls within Cuba, CUC$0.10 for texts. You pay the same amount if a fixed line calls you. International calls start at CUC$1.10 per minute. To rent a phone in Cuba costs from CUC$8 plus a CUC$3 daily activation fee. You'll also need to pay a CUC$100 deposit. Charges after this amount to around CUC$0.35 per minute. For up-to-date costs and information see www.etecsa.cu.

Phone Codes

➡ To call Cuba from abroad, dial your international access code, Cuba's country code (☎53), the city or area code (minus the '0,' which is used when dialing domestically between provinces), and the local number.

➡ To call internationally from Cuba, dial Cuba's international access code (☎119), the country code, the area code and the number. To the US, you just dial ☎119, then 1, the area code and the number.

➡ To call cell phone to cell phone just dial the eight-digit number (which always starts with a '5').

➡ To call cell phone to landline (or landline to landline) dial the provincial code plus the local number.

➡ To call landline to cell phone dial '01' (or '0' if in Havana) followed by the eight-digit cell phone number.

➡ To call landline to landline dial '0' plus the provincial code plus the local number.

Phone Rates

Local calls cost from five centavos to 75 centavos per minute depending on the time of day and distance. Since most coin phones don't return change, common courtesy means that you should push the 'R' button so that the next person in line can make their call with your remaining money.

International calls made with a card cost CUC$1 per minute regardless of destination.

Hotels with three stars and up usually offer slightly pricier international phone rates.

Phonecards

Etecsa is where you buy phonecards, use the internet and make international calls. Blue public Etecsa phones accepting magnetized or computer-chip cards are everywhere. The cards are sold in convertibles (CUC$5, CUC$10 and CUC$20), and in *moneda nacional* (five and 10 pesos). You can call nationally with either, but you can call internationally only with convertible cards.

You will also see coin-operated phone booths good for Cuban pesos *(moneda nacional)* only.

Tourist Information

Cuba's official tourist information bureau is called **Infotur** (www.infotur.cu). It has offices in all the main provincial towns and desks in most of the bigger hotels and airports. Travel agencies, such as **Cubanacán** (☎7-833-4090; www.cubanacan.cu), **Cubatur** (☎7-838-4597; www.cubtur.cu), **Gaviota** (☎7-204-5708; www.gaviota-grupo.com) and **Ecotur** (☎7-273-1542; www.ecoturcuba.tur.cu) can usually supply some general information.

Travelers with Disabilities

Cuba's inclusive culture extends to disabled travelers, and while facilities may be lacking, the generous nature of Cubans generally compensates when it can. Sight-impaired travelers will be helped across streets and given priority in lines. The same holds true for travelers in wheelchairs, who will find the few ramps ridiculously steep and will have trouble in colonial parts of town where sidewalks are narrow and streets are cobblestone. Elevators are often out of order. Etecsa phone centers have telephone equipment for the hearing-impaired, and TV programs are broadcast with closed captioning.

Visas & Tourist Cards

Regular tourists who plan to spend up to two months in Cuba do not need visas. Instead, you get a *tarjeta de turista* (tourist card) valid for 30 days, which can be extended once you're in Cuba (Canadians get 90 days plus the option of a 90-day extension).

Package tourists receive their card with their other travel documents. Those going 'air only' usually buy the tourist card from the travel agency or airline office that sells them the plane ticket, but policies vary (eg Canadian airlines give out tourist cards on their airplanes), so you'll need to check ahead with the airline office via phone or email.

In some cases you may be required to buy and/or pick up the card at your departure airport, sometimes at the flight gate itself some minutes before departure. Some independent travelers have been denied access to Cuba flights because they inadvertently haven't obtained a tourist card.

Once in Havana, tourist-card extensions or replacements cost another CUC$25. You cannot leave Cuba without presenting your tourist card. If you lose it, you can expect to face at least a day of frustrating Cuba-style bureaucracy to get it replaced.

You are not permitted entry to Cuba without an onward ticket.

Fill the tourist card out clearly and carefully, as Cuban customs are particularly fussy about crossings out and illegibility.

Business travelers and journalists need visas. Applications should be made through a consulate at least three weeks in advance (longer if you apply through a consulate in a country other than your own).

Visitors with visas or anyone who has stayed in Cuba longer than 90 days must apply for an exit permit from an immigration office. The Cuban consulate in London issues official visas (£22 plus two photos; £47 by mail). They take two weeks to process, and the name of an official contact in Cuba is necessary.

Licenses for US Visitors

At the time of research, most visitors have been traveling under general licenses.

General licenses are self-qualifying and don't require travelers to notify the Office of Foreign Assets Control (OFAC) of their travel plans. Travelers sign an affidavit stating the purpose of travel and purchase a Cuban visa at check-in when departing the United States via flights. Visas average $50, purchased through airlines or established third parties.

Note that in June 2017 the Trump administration eliminated individual travel under the 'educational purpose' license category, and policy is still in the process of being formally changed. For the most up-to-date information on current travel requirements, review the US Treasury department Cuba policy fact sheet (**www.treasury.gov/resource-center/sanctions/Programs/pages/cuba.aspx**).

Extensions

For most travelers, obtaining an extension once in Cuba is easy: you just go to the *inmigración* (immigration office) and present your documents and CUC$25 in stamps. Obtain these stamps from a branch of Bandec or Banco Financiero Internacional beforehand. You'll only receive an additional 30 days after your original 30 days (apart from Canadians who get an additional 90 days after their original 90), but you can exit and re-enter the country for 24 hours and start over again (some travel agencies in Havana have special deals for this type of trip).

Attend to extensions at least a few business days before your visa is due to expire and never attempt travel around Cuba with an expired visa.

US CITIZENS & CUBA

When President Obama decided to restore diplomatic relations with Cuba, decades of regulations started to shift, though some measures still await change (like banking). To further complicate matters, the Trump administration has already signaled a partial rollback of the new policies.

In conjunction with the US embargo against Cuba, the US government 'travel ban,' which had prevented US citizens from visiting Cuba, relaxed under the Obama administration. Technically a treasury law prohibiting Americans from spending money in Cuba, it squelched leisure travel for more than 45 years. Currently, visitors undertaking non-tourism related activities are allowed to visit Cuba provided they meet the requirements of special categories.

A little history: The 1996 Helms-Burton Act, which was signed into law by President Clinton on March 12, 1996, imposes without judicial review fines of up to US$50,000 on US citizens who visit Cuba without US government permission. It also allows for confiscation of their property. In addition, under the Trading with the Enemy Act, violators may face up to US$250,000 in fines and up to 10 years in prison.

Under the Obama administration there was considerable progress in Cuban relations. Bilateral agreements have eased travel restrictions for Cuban-Americans, direct commercial flights are operating between the US and Cuba, there's a postal service between the two countries, restrictions on goods brought from Cuba has relaxed, and there is greater leniency in the granting of legal licenses. However, the Trump administration has moved to limit self-directed, individual travel and direct economic activity away from the Cuban military. See p519 for more information.

Cuban Immigration Offices

Nearly all provincial towns have an immigration office (where you can extend your visa), though the staff rarely speak English and aren't always overly helpful. Try to avoid Havana's office if you can, as it gets ridiculously crowded.

Baracoa (Antonio Maceo No 48)

Bayamo (☎23-57-25-84; Carretera Central, Km 2; ⏰8am-7pm Mon, Wed & Fri, 8am-5pm Tue, 8am-noon Thu & Sat) In a big complex 200m south of the Hotel Sierra Maestra.

Camagüey (Calle 3 No 156, btwn Calles 8 & 10, Reparto Vista Hermosa; ⏰8am-7pm Mon, Wed & Fri, 8am-5pm Tue, 8am-noon Thur & Sat)

Ciego de Ávila (Map p304; cnr Delgado & Independencia; ⏰8am-7pm Mon, Wed & Fri, 8am-5pm Tue, 8am-noon Thu & Sat)

Cienfuegos (☎43-52-10-17; Av 46, btwn Calles 29 & 31)

Guantánamo (Calle 1 Oeste, btwn Calles 14 & 15 Norte; ⏰8am-7pm Mon, Wed & Fri, 8am-5pm Tue, 8am-noon Thu & Sat) Directly behind Hotel Guantánamo.

Havana (Calle 17 No 203, btwn Calles J & K, Vedado; ⏰8am-7pm Mon, Wed & Fri, 8am-5pm Tue, 8am-noon Thu & Sat)

Holguín (Calle Fomento No 256, cnr Peralejo; 8am-7pm Mon, Wed & Fri, 8am-5pm Tue, 8am-noon Thu & Sat)

Las Tunas (Av Camilo Cienfuegos, Reparto Buenavista; ⏰8am-7pm Mon, Wed & Fri, to 5pm Tue, to noon Thu & Sat)

Sancti Spíritus (☎41-32-47-29; Independencia Norte No 107; ⏰8am-7pm Mon, Wed & Fri, to 5pm Tue, to noon Thu & Sat)

Santa Clara (cnr Av Sandino & Sexta; ⏰8am-7pm Mon, Wed & Fri, to 5pm Tue, to noon Thu & Sat) Three blocks east of Estadio Sandino.

Santiago de Cuba (☎22-64-19-83; Av Pujol No 10, btwn Calle 10 & Anacaona; ⏰8am-7pm Mon, Wed & Fri, to 5pm Tue, to noon Thu & Sat) Stamps for visa extensions are sold at the Banco de Crédito y Comercio at Felix Peña No 614 on Parque Céspedes.

Trinidad (Julio Cueva Díaz; ⏰8am-7pm Mon, Wed & Fri, to 5pm Tue, to noon Thu & Sat) Off Paseo Agramonte.

Varadero (cnr Av 1 & Calle 39)

Volunteering

There are a number of bodies offering volunteer work in Cuba, though it is always best to organize things in your home country first. Just turning up in Havana and volunteering can be difficult, if not impossible. Those with a people-to-people license work with US visitors.

Canada-Cuba Farmer to Farmer Project (www.farmertofarmer.ca) Vancouver-based sustainable agriculture organization.

Cuban Solidarity Campaign (www.cuba-solidarity.org) Head office in London, UK.

Global Volunteers (https://globalvolunteers.org/cuba) With programs in Havana, Ciego de Avila and Sancti Sprírítus.

Go Overseas (www.gooverseas.com) A catalog of 22 programs in Cuba organized by length of stay, area and program rating, many officially licensed by the US.

Pastors for Peace (www.ifconews.org) Collects donations across the US to take to Cuba.

Witness for Peace (www.witnessforpeace.org) People-to-people licensed. Brings delegations to Cuba, some studying the impact of US policy.

Women Travelers

In terms of physical safety, Cuba is a dream destination for women travelers. Most streets can be walked alone at night, violent crime is rare and the chivalrous part of machismo means you'll never step into oncoming traffic.

But machismo cuts both ways, protecting on one side and pursuing – relentlessly – on the other. It can be tiresome to go out alone at night and steel yourself against the onslaught of *pretendientes* (men courting), unless you're really keen on them or improving your Spanish. There's also relatively few solo travelers in Cuba and no youth hostels which means fewer travelers to keep company with.

Cuban women are used to *piropos* (the whistles, kissing sounds and compliments constantly ringing in their ears), and might even reply with their own if they're feeling frisky. For foreign women, however, it can feel like an invasion.

Ignoring *piropos* is the first step. But sometimes ignoring isn't enough. Learn some rejoinders in Spanish so you can shut men up. *No me moleste* (don't bother me), *está bueno ya* (all right already) or *que falta respeto* (how disrespectful) are good ones, as is the withering 'don't you dare' stare that is also part of the Cuban woman's arsenal. Wearing plain, modest clothes might help lessen unwanted attention; topless sunbathing is out. An absent husband, invented or not, seldom has any effect. If you go to a disco, be very clear with Cuban dance partners what you are and are not interested in.

Women must bring their own tampons (non-existent in Cuba) or pads (called *intimos*, literally 'intimates').

Transportation

GETTING THERE & AWAY

Entering the Country

Whether it's your first or 50th time, descending low into José Martí International Airport, over rust-red tobacco fields, is an exciting and unforgettable experience. Entry procedures are relatively straightforward, and with approximately three million visitors a year, immigration officials are used to dealing with foreign arrivals.

Outside Cuba, the capital city is called Havana, and this is how travel agents, airlines and other professionals will refer to it. Within Cuba, it's almost always called La Habana. For the sake of consistency, we use the former spelling.

Flights, tours and rail tickets can be booked online at lonelyplanet.com/bookings.

Air

Airports & Airlines

INTERNATIONAL AIRPORTS

Cuba has 10 international airports. The largest by far is **Aeropuerto Internacional José Martí** (www.havana-airport.org; Av Rancho Boyeros) in Havana. The only other sizable airport is **Juan Gualberto Gómez International Airport** (☎45-61-30-16, 45-24-70-15) in Varadero.

AIRLINES FLYING TO & FROM CUBA

In Havana most airline offices are situated in one of two clusters: the **Airline Building** (Calle 23 No 64) in Vedado, or in the **Miramar Trade Center** (Map p126; Av 3, btwn Calles 76 & 80, Miramar; ⏲hours vary) in Playa.

Cubana (www.cubana.cu), the national carrier, operates regular flights to Bogotá, Buenos Aires, Mexico City, Cancún, Caracas, Madrid, Paris, Toronto, Montreal, São Paulo, San José (Costa Rica) and Santo Domingo (Dominican Republic). Its airfares are usually among the cheapest, though overbooking and delays are nagging problems. Overweight baggage is strictly charged for every kilogram above the 20kg allowance.

For safety recommendations, check the latest at www.airsafe.com. Cubana had back-to-back crashes in December 1999, with 39 fatalities, but it hasn't had any major incidents since.

AFRICA

Direct flights from Africa originate in Luanda, Angola with **TAAG** (☎in Angola 9231-90-000; www.taag.com). From all other African countries you'll need to connect in London, Paris, Madrid, Amsterdam or Rome.

ASIA & AUSTRALIA

There are no direct flights to Cuba from Australia. Travelers can connect through

CLIMATE CHANGE & TRAVEL

Every form of transport that relies on carbon-based fuel generates CO_2, the main cause of human-induced climate change. Modern travel is dependent on airplanes, which might use less fuel per mile per person than most cars but travel much greater distances. The altitude at which aircraft emit gases (including CO_2) and particles also contributes to their climate change impact. Many websites offer 'carbon calculators' that allow people to estimate the carbon emissions generated by their journey and, for those who wish to do so, to offset the impact of the greenhouse gases emitted with contributions to portfolios of climate-friendly initiatives throughout the world. Lonely Planet offsets the carbon footprint of all staff and author travel.

DOCUMENTS REQUIRED ON ENTRY

- Passport valid for at least one month beyond your departure date
- Cuba 'tourist card' filled out correctly
- Proof of travel medical insurance (random checks at airport)
- Evidence of sufficient funds for the duration of your stay
- Return air ticket

Europe, Canada, the US or Mexico. **Air China** (www.airchina.com) has weekly flights between Havana and Beijing.

CANADA

Flights from Canada serve 10 Cuban airports from 22 Canadian cities. Toronto and Montreal are the main hubs. Other cities are served by direct charter flights.

Airlines include:

Air Canada (in Canada 844-347-4268; www.aircanada.com)

Air Transat (in Canada 877-872-6728; www.airtransat.com)

Sunwing (in Canada 877-877-1755; www.flysunwing.com)

Westjet (in Canada 888-937-8538; www.westjet.com)

Travel agency **A Nash Travel** (in Canada 905-755-0102; www.anashtravel.com) can be helpful with bookings.

CARIBBEAN

Cubana is the main airline serving the Caribbean, in addition to **Air Caraibes Airlines** (in Guadeloupe 0820-835-835; www.aircaraibes.com), **Bahamas Air** (in the Bahamas 1-242-702-4140; https://bahamasair.com) and **Cayman Airways** (www.caymanairways.com; Miramar Trade Center).

EUROPE & UK

Regular flights to Cuba depart from Belgium, France, Germany, the Netherlands, Italy, Russia, Spain, Switzerland and the UK. The following airlines serve Europe:

Aeroflot (in Havana 72-043-200, in Moscow +7-495-223-55-55; www.aeroflot.ru; Miramar Trade Center)

Air Europa (in Spain 902-401-502; www.aireuropa.com; Miramar Trade Center)

Air France (in France 09-69-39-02-15, in Havana +537-206-4444; www.airfrance.com; Calle 23 No 64; 8:30am-4:30pm Mon-Fri)

Blue Panorama (in Italy 06-9895-6666; www.blue-panorama.com)

Condor (in Germany 49-180-676-7767; www.condor.com)

Edelwiess (www.flyedelweiss.com)

KLM (www.klm.com)

Neos (in Italy 800-325-955; www.neosair.it)

Thomas Cook (www.thomascook.com)

TUI Netherlands (www.tui.nl)

Virgin Atlantic (in Cuba 7204-0747, in the UK 0344-874-7747; www.virgin-atlantic.com; Miramar Trade Center)

MEXICO

Mexico City and Cancún are good places to connect with a wide number of US cities.

Interjet (in Mexico 01800-011-2345; www.interjet.com.mx) serves Mexico.

SOUTH & CENTRAL AMERICA

There are good connections to airports throughout South America. Central American airports provide the best link to other parts of the Caribbean. The following airlines serve Latin America:

Avianca (www.avianca.com)

Conviasa (in Venezuela 500-266-8427; www.conviasa.aero)

Copa Airlines (in Panama 217-2672; www.copaair.com)

LATAM (in Chile 600-526-2000; www.latam.com)

UNITED STATES

The first commercial flights between the US and Cuba started in November, 2016, following moves by the Obama administration to ease travel restrictions. Those traveling on a US passport still must be traveling under the authorized travel categories. The following airlines now serve Cuba:

Alaska Airlines (in the USA 800-252-7522; www.alaskaair.com)

American Airlines (in the USA 800-433-7300; Miramar Trade Center)

Delta Airlines (in the USA 800-241-4141; www.delta.com)

Jet Blue (in the USA 800-538-2583; https://book.jetblue.com)

Southwest Airlines (in the USA 800-435-9792; www.southwest.com)

Spirit Airlines (in the USA 801-401-2222; www.spirit.com)

United Airlines (in the USA 800-864-8331; www.united.com)

Sea

Cruises

With US–Cuban relations evolving, many more cruise ships are calling at Cuban ports. **Oceania Cruises** (www.oceaniacruises.com), **Norweigan Cruise Line** (www.ncl.com), **Pearl Seas Cruises** (www.pearlseascruises.com) and **Royal Caribbean** (www.royalcaribbean.com) are all adding Cuba itineraries.

Canadian company **Celestyal** (www.yourcubacruise.com) circumnavigates the island calling in at Havana, Holguín, Santiago, Montego Bay (Jamaica), Cienfuegos and La Isla de la Juventud.

Another option is with British-based **Thomson** (www.thomson.co.uk), whose

Commercial Air Routes

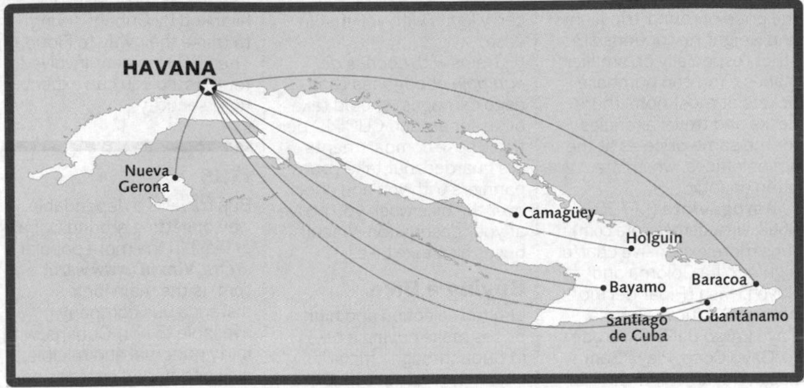

seven-night *Cuban Fusion* trip runs out of Montego Bay, Jamaica.

Private Yacht

If you have your own private yacht or cruiser, Cuba has eight international entry ports equipped with customs facilities:

- Marina Hemingway (Havana)
- Marina Dásena (Varadero)
- Marina Cienfuegos
- Marina Cayo Guillermo
- Marina Santiago de Cuba
- Puerto de Vita (near Guardalavaca in Holguín province)
- Cayo Largo del Sur
- Cabo San Antonio (far western tip of Pinar del Río province)

Boat owners should communicate with the Cuban coast guard on VHF 16 and 68 or the tourist network 19A. There are no scheduled ferry services to Cuba.

Tours

Cuba is popular on the organized-tour circuit, especially in the realm of soft adventure. There are also specialist tours focusing on culture, the environment, adventure, photography, cycling, bird-watching, architecture and hiking. Some popular agencies include:

Cuban Adventures (in Australia 4305-04636; www.cubagrouptour.com)

Exodus (in England 0203-553-1385; www.exodus.co.uk)

Explore (in Great Britain 01-252-883-914; www.explore.co.uk)

GETTING AROUND

Air

Airlines in Cuba

There are no internal connections between the airports, except via Havana. At the time of writing, these flights were plagued by delays and cancellations.

Cubana de Aviación (www.cubana.cu) has flights between Havana and 11 regional airports. The company's aging aircraft are spread thin across routes and often in need of last-minute maintenance. If you are scheduling to meet an international

DOMESTIC FLIGHTS FROM HAVANA

DESTINATION	FREQUENCY	DURATION (HR)
Baracoa	1 weekly	2½
Bayamo	2 weekly	2
Camagüey	daily	1½
Guantánamo	5 weekly	1½
Holguín	1–2 daily	1½
Nueva Gerona	2 daily	35 min
Santiago de Cuba	1–2 daily	1½

flight, build in extra time in case you have to travel by bus.

One-way flights are half the price of round-trip flights and weight restrictions are strict (especially on smaller planes). You can purchase tickets at most hotel tour desks and travel agencies for the same price as at the airline offices, which are often chaotic.

Aerogaviota (☎7-203-0668; www.aerogaviota.com) runs more expensive charter flights to La Coloma and Cayo Levisa (Pinar del Río province), Nueva Gerona, Cayo Largo del Sur, Varadero, Cayo Coco, Playa Santa Lucía, Bayamo, Manzanillo, Baracoa and Santiago de Cuba. It also plans to add commercial routes within Cuba.

Bicycle

Cuba is a cyclist's paradise, with bike lanes, bike workshops and drivers accustomed to sharing the road countrywide. Spare parts are difficult to find – you should bring important spares with you. Still, Cubans are grand masters at improvised repair and, though specific parts may not be available, something can surely be jury-rigged. *Poncheros* (puncture repair stalls) fix flat tires and provide air; every small town has one.

Helmets are unheard of in Cuba, except at upscale resorts, so you should bring your own. A lock is imperative, as bicycle theft is rampant. *Parqueos* are bicycle parking lots located wherever crowds congregate (eg markets, bus terminals, downtown etc); they cost one peso.

Throughout the country, the 1m-wide strip of road to the extreme right is reserved for bicycles, even on highways. It's illegal to ride on sidewalks and against traffic on one-way streets and you'll be ticketed if caught. Road lighting is deplorable, so avoid riding after dark (over one-third of vehicle accidents in Cuba involve bicycles); carry lights with you just in case.

Trains with *coches de equipaje* or *bagones* (baggage carriages) should take bikes for around CUC$10 per trip. These compartments are guarded, but take your panniers with you and check over the bike when you arrive at your destination. Víazul buses also take bikes.

Buying a Bike

Limited selection and high prices make buying a bike in Cuba through official channels unattractive. Better to ask around and strike a deal with an individual to buy their *chivo* (Cuban slang for bike) and trade it or resell it when you leave. With some earnest bargaining, you can get one for around CUC$40 – although the more you pay, the less your bones are likely to shake. Despite the obvious cost savings, bringing your own bike is still the best bet by far.

Rental

Official bike rental places are scant in Cuba, but with the private economy taking off so rapidly, this could change. You can usually procure something roadworthy for between CUC$5 per hour or CUC$20 per day. Bikes are usually included as a perk in all-inclusive resort packages, but beware of bad brakes and zero gears.

Boat

The most important ferry services for travelers are the **catamaran** (Map p162; cnr Calle 24 & Calle 33; ⏲8am-5:30pm) from Surgidero de Batabanó to Nueva Gerona, Isla de la Juventud, and the passenger ferry from Havana to Regla and Casablanca Ferry Terminal (☎7-867-3726). These ferries are generally safe, though in 1997 two hydrofoils crashed en route to Isla de la Juventud. In both 1994 and 2003, the Regla/Casablanca ferry was hijacked by Cubans trying to make their way to Florida. The 2003 incident involved tourists, so you can expect tight security.

Bus

Bus travel is a dependable way of getting around Cuba, at least in the more popular areas. **Víazul** (www.viazul.com) is the main long-distance bus company available to non-Cubans, with fairly punctual and reliable air-conditioned coaches going to destinations of interest to travelers.

Víazul charges for tickets in convertibles. Buses schedule regular stops for lunch/dinner and always carry two drivers. Bring warm layers – the air conditioning blasts an Arctic chill. Reserve ahead on the more popular routes, particularly in high season. A handy new route from Trinidad goes daily to Santa Clara, Remedios, Caibarien and Cayo Santa Maria.

Note that the demand in high season outstrips availability. If you can't get a seat on the bus you want, look for other stranded travelers to join for a shared taxi to your destination.

Conectando, run by Cubanacán, is a newer option set up to relieve some of Víazul's overcrowding. The pros are that they run between city center hotels and can be booked head of time at Infotur and Cubanacán offices. The cons are that the schedules aren't as reliable or extensive as Víazul. Check ahead that your bus is running.

Many of the popular tourist areas now have 'bus tours,' hop-on, hop-off buses that link all the main sights in a given area and charge CUC$5 for an all-day ticket. The services are run by government transport agency Transtur. Havana and

VÍAZUL ROUTES

ROUTE	DURATION (HR)	PRICE (CUC$)	STOPPING AT...
Havana–Holguín	10½	44	Santa Clara, Sancti Spíritus, Ciego de Ávila, Camagüey, Las Tunas
Havana–Santiago de Cuba	15½	51	Entronque de Jaguey, Santa Clara, Sancti Spíritus, Ciego de Ávila, Camagüey, Las Tunas, Holguín, Bayamo
Havana–Trinidad	6	25	Entronque de Jaguey, Cienfuegos
Havana–Varadero	3	10	Matanzas, Varadero Airport
Havana–Viñales	3¼	12	Pinar del Río
Santiago de Cuba–Baracoa	4¾	15	Guantánamo
Trinidad–Santiago de Cuba	12	33	Sancti Spíritus, Ciego de Ávila, Camagüey, Las Tunas, Holguín, Bayamo
Trinidad–Varadero	6	20	Cárdenas, Colón, Entronque de Jaguey, Cienfuegos
Varadero–Santiago de Cuba	16	49	Cárdenas, Colón, Santa Clara, Sancti Spíritus, Ciego de Ávila, Camagüey, Las Tunas, Holguín, Bayamo

Varadero both have open-topped double-decker buses. Smaller minibuses are used in Viñales, Trinidad, Cayo Coco, Guardalavaca, Cayo Santa María and Baracoa (seasonal).

Cubans travel over shorter distances in provincial buses. These buses sell tickets in *moneda nacional* and are a lot less comfortable and reliable than Víazul. They leave from the provincial bus stations in each province. Schedules and prices are usually chalked up on a board inside the terminal. Sometimes travelers are not allowed on these buses or preference is given to locals getting a seat.

Reservations

Reservations with Víazul are necessary during peak travel periods (June to August, Christmas and Easter) and on popular routes (Havana–Trinidad, Trinidad–Santa Clara, and Santiago de Cuba–Baracoa). You can usually book a day or two beforehand.

The Víazul bus out of Baracoa is almost always booked, so reserve a seat on this service when you arrive. It is now possible to make reservations online at www.viazul.com if you register with the site. However, like all Cuban websites, it is prone to 'crashing.'

Car & Motorcycle

Renting a car in Cuba is easy, but once you've factored in gas, insurance, hire fees etc, it isn't cheap. Prices vary with car size, season, and length of rental. Bank on paying an average of CUC$70 per day for a medium-sized car. It's actually cheaper to hire a taxi for distances of under 150km (at the time of writing taxis were charging CUC$0.55 per kilometer for intercity routes).

Driving Licences

Your home license is sufficient to rent and drive a car in Cuba.

Fuel

Gas sold in convertibles (as opposed to peso gas) is widely available in stations all over the country (the north coast west of Havana being the notable exception). Gas stations are often open 24 hours and may have a small parts store on site. Gas is sold by the liter and comes in *regular* (CUC$1 per liter) and *especial* (CUC$1.20 per liter) varieties. Rental cars are advised to use *especial*. All gas stations have efficient pump attendants, usually in the form of *trabajadores sociales* (students in the process of studying for a degree).

Rental

Renting a car in Cuba is straightforward. You'll need your passport, driver's license and a refundable deposit of between CUC$150 and CUC$250 (cash or credit card). You can rent a car in one city and drop it off in another for a reasonable fee, which is handy. If you're on a tight budget, ask about diesel cars – some agencies stock a few and you'll save bundles in gas money. Note that there are very few rental cars with automatic transmission.

If you want to rent a car for three days or fewer, it will come with limited kilometers, while contracts for three days or more come with

RENT A CAR & DRIVER

Sure, there's not a lot of traffic on the roads, but driving in Cuba isn't as easy as many people think, especially when you factor in teetering bicyclists, baseball-chasing children, galloping horses, pedestrians with limited or no peripheral vision, and – worst of all – a serious lack of signposts.

To avoid hassle, you can hire both a comfortable, modern car and a driver with a growing number of companies, most notably **Car Rental Cuba** (☎54-47-28-22; www.carrental-cuba.com; Maceo No 360-1, btwn Serafin García & EP Morales; per day CUC$75 plus CUC$0.30 per km).

unlimited kilometers. In Cuba, you pay for the first tank of gas when you rent the car and return it empty (a suicidal policy that sees many tight-fisted tourists running out of gas a kilometer or so from the drop-off point). You will not be refunded for any gas left in the tank.

Petty theft of mirrors, antennas, taillights etc is common, so it's worth it to pay someone a convertible or two to watch your car for the night. If you lose your rental contract or keys you'll pay a CUC$50 penalty. Drivers under 25 pay a CUC$5 fee, while additional drivers on the same contract pay a CUC$3 per day surcharge.

Check over the car carefully with the rental agent before driving into the sunset, as you'll be responsible for any damage or missing parts. Make sure there is a spare tire of the correct size, a jack and a lug wrench. Check that there are seatbelts and that all the doors lock properly.

We have received many letters about poor or nonexistent customer service, bogus spare tires, forgotten reservations and other car-rental problems. Reservations are only accepted 15 days in advance and are still not guaranteed. While agents are usually accommodating, you might end up paying more than you planned or have to wait for hours until someone returns a car. The more Spanish you speak and the friendlier you are, the more likely problems will be resolved to everyone's satisfaction (tips to the agent might help). As with most Cuban travel, always have a Plan B.

Insurance

Rental cars come with a required CUC$15 to CUC$30 per day insurance, which covers everything but theft of the radio (store in the trunk at night) and tires.

If you do have an accident, you must get a copy of the *denuncia* (police report) to be eligible for the insurance coverage, a process which can take all day. If the police determine that you are the party responsible for the accident, say *adiós* to your deposit.

Spare Parts

While you cannot count on spare parts per se to be available, Cubans have decades of experience keeping old wrecks on the road without factory parts and you'll see them do amazing things with cardboard, string, rubber and clothes hangers to keep a car mobile.

If you need air in your tires or you have a puncture, use a gas station or visit the local *ponchero*. They often don't have measures, so make sure they don't overinflate them.

Road Hazards

Driving here isn't just a different ballpark, it's a different sport. The first problem is that there are no signs – almost anywhere. Major junctions and turnoffs to important resorts or cities are often not indicated at all. Not only is this distracting, it's also incredibly time-consuming. The lack of signage also extends to highway instructions. Often a one-way street is not clearly indicated or a speed limit not highlighted, which can cause problems with the police (who won't understand your inability to telepathically absorb the road rules), and road markings are nonexistent everywhere.

The Autopista, Vía Blanca and Carretera Central are generally in a good state, but be prepared for roads suddenly deteriorating into chunks of asphalt and unexpected railroad crossings everywhere else (especially in the Oriente). Rail crossings are particularly problematic, as there are hundreds of them and there are never any safety gates. Beware: however overgrown the rails may look, you can pretty much assume that the line is still in use. Cuba's trains, rather like its cars, defy all normal logic when it comes to mechanics.

While motorized traffic is refreshingly light, bicycles, pedestrians, oxcarts, horse carriages and livestock are a different matter. Many old cars and trucks lack rearview mirrors and traffic-unaware children run out of all kinds of nooks and crannies. Stay alert, drive with caution and use your horn when passing or on blind curves.

Driving at night is not recommended due to variable roads, drunk drivers, crossing cows and poor lighting. Drunk-driving remains a troublesome problem despite a government educational campaign. Late night in Havana is particularly dangerous, as it seems there's a passing lane, cruising lane and drunk lane.

Traffic lights are often busted or hard to pick out

and right-of-way rules are thrown to the wind. Take extra care.

Road Rules

Cubans drive how they want, where they want. It seems chaotic at first, but it has its rhythm. Seatbelts are supposedly required and maximum speed limits are technically 50km/h in the city, 90km/h on highways and 100km/h on the Autopista, but some cars can't even go that fast and those that can, go faster still.

With so few cars on the road, it's hard not to put the pedal to the floor and just fly. Unexpected potholes are a hazard, however, and watch out for police. There are some clever speed traps, particularly along the Autopista. Speeding tickets start at CUC$30 and are noted on your car contract; the fine is deducted from your deposit when you return the car. When pulled over by the police, you're expected to get out of the car and walk over to them with your paperwork. An oncoming car flashing its lights means a hazard up ahead (and usually the police).

The Cuban transportation crisis means there are a lot of people waiting for rides by the side of the road. Giving a *botella* (a lift) to local hitchhikers has advantages aside from altruism. With a Cuban passenger you'll never get lost, you'll learn about secret spots, and you'll meet some great people. There are always risks associated with picking up hitchhikers; giving lifts to older people or families may reduce the risk factor. In the provinces, people waiting for rides are systematically queued by the *amarillos* (roadside traffic organizers), and they'll hustle the most needy folks into your car, usually an elderly couple or a pregnant woman.

Hitching & Ride-Sharing

The transportation crisis, culture of solidarity and low crime levels make Cuba a popular hitchhiking destination. Here, hitchhiking is more like ride-sharing, and it's legally enforced. Traffic lights, railroad crossings and country crossroads are regular stops for people seeking rides.

In the provinces and on the outskirts of Havana, the *amarillos* (official state-paid traffic supervisors, so-named for their mustard yellow uniforms) organize and prioritize ride seekers, and you're welcome to jump in line. Rides cost five to 20 pesos depending on distance. Travelers hitching rides will want a good map and some Spanish skills. Expect to wait two or three hours for rides in some cases.

Hitchhiking is never entirely safe in any country in the world, and we don't recommend it. Travelers who decide to hitchhike should understand that they are taking a small but potentially serious risk. People who do choose to hitchhike will be safer if they travel in pairs and let someone know where they are planning to go.

Local Transport

Bici-Taxi

Bici-taxis are big pedal-powered tricycles with a double seat behind the driver. They are common in Havana, Camagüey, Holguín and a few other cities. In Havana drivers want a CUC$2 minimum fare (Cubans pay five or 10 pesos). Some

US TRAVELERS

Since January 2011, Americans have been able to travel legally to Cuba on government sanctioned people-to-people trips. While the Obama administration permitted self-directed, individual travel for educational purposes and 'in support of the Cuban people', the Trump administration announced a stricter policy toward US-Cuba relations in June 2017 that will end individual people-to-people travel. Americans will now be limited to group travel through licensed tour operators.

Travel agencies going to Cuba from the US include:

Cuba Travel Services (☎in the USA 1-800-963-2822; www.cubatravelservices.com)

Insight Cuba (☎in the USA 1-800-450-2822; www.insightcuba.com)

GeoEx (☎in the USA 415-922-0448; www.geoex.com)

Moto Discovery (☎1-800-233-0564; www.motodiscovery.com)

Overseas Aventure Travel (☎in the USA 1-800-955-1925; www.oattravel.com)

Before booking a trip, US travelers should consult the US Treasury department **Cuba policy fact sheet** (www.treasury.gov/resource-center/sanctions/Programs/pages/cuba.aspx) to review travel requirements. See p511 also for more information.

bici-taxistas ask ridiculous amounts. The fare should be clearly understood before you hop aboard.

Boat

Some towns, such as Havana, Cienfuegos, Gibara and Santiago de Cuba, have local ferry services that charge in *moneda nacional*.

Bus

Very crowded, very steamy, very challenging, very Cuban – *guaguas* (local buses) are useful in bigger cities. Buses work fixed routes, stopping at *paradas* (bus stops) that always have a line, even if it doesn't look like it. You have to shout out *¿el último?* to find out who was the last in line when you showed up as Cuban queues form in loose crowds.

Buses cost a flat MN$0.40 or five centavos if you're using convertibles. Havana and Santiago de Cuba have recently been kitted out with brand new fleets of Chinese-made metro buses.

You must always walk as far back in the bus as you can and exit through the rear. Make room to pass by saying *permiso*, always wear your pack in front and watch your wallet.

Colectivo

Colectivos are taxis running on fixed, long-distance routes, leaving when full. They are generally pre-1959 American cars that belch diesel fumes and can squash in at least three people across the front seat. State-owned taxis that charge in convertibles hang about bus stations and are faster and usually cheaper than the bus.

Horse Carriage

Many provincial cities have *coches de caballo* (horse carriages) that trot on fixed routes, often between train/bus stations and city centers. Prices in *moneda nacional* cost around one peso. Many horses are overworked and in lamentable condition. It's best to give your business to healthy ones if there's an option (or better yet, a bici-taxi!)

Taxi

Car taxis are metered and cost CUC$1 to start and CUC$1 per kilometer in cities. Taxi drivers are in the habit of offering foreigners a flat, off-meter rate that usually works out very close to what you'll pay with the meter. The difference is that with the meter, the money goes to the state to be divided up; without the meter it goes into the driver's pocket.

Train

Public railways operated by Ferrocarriles de Cuba serve all of the provincial capitals and are a unique way to experience Cuba, as long as you have the patience of a saint and the stamina of a prize fighter.

Old trains and fuel shortages set you up for delays. Travelers report long delays, non-functional bathrooms, police removing passengers for on-board offenses and other passengers having fits or getting kicked off. It is not for the faint of heart. Cubans who have the budget to travel by other means do so.

The departure information provided is purely theoretical. Getting a ticket is usually no problem, as there's a quota for tourists paying in convertibles.

Foreigners must pay for their tickets in cash, but prices are reasonable and the carriages, though old and worn, are fairly comfortable. The toilets are foul – bring toilet paper. Watch your luggage on overnight trips and bring your own food. Only the Tren Francés has snack facilities, although vendors often come through the train

CUBA'S TRAIN SERVICES FROM HAVANA

The following information is liable to changes or cancellations. Always check ahead.

DESTINATION	TRAIN NO	FREQUENCY
Bayamo	13	every 4th day
Camagüey	5, 15	every 4th day
Cienfuegos	73	every other day
Guantánamo	15	every 4th day
Manzanillo	28	every 4th day
Matanzas	5, 7, 15	every 4th day
Morón	29	daily
Pinar del Río	71	every other day
Sancti Spíritus	7	every other day
Santa Clara	5, 7, 9, 15	every 4th day
Santiago de Cuba	5, 11, 12	every 4th day

THE TREN FRANCÉS

Cuba's best and fastest train is the *Tren Francés* (train number 11), which runs between Havana and Santiago de Cuba in both directions every fourth day (CUC$30, 15½ hours, 861km). The trains use secondhand French carriages (hence the name), which formerly operated on the Paris–Brussels–Amsterdam European route. They were bought by the Cubans in 2001. The carriages are relatively comfortable, if a little worn, with frigid air-conditioning, a limited cafe, a purser (one per carriage) and decidedly dingy toilets. As with many things in Cuba, it's not so much the quality of the carriages that's the problem, but their upkeep – or lack thereof. The *Tren Francés* has only 1st class, which by the way, is nothing like 1st class.

selling coffee (you supply the cup).

For Cuban train times and types, consult The Man in Seat Sixty-One (www.seat61.com), run by Mark Smith in the UK.

At time of research the Estación Central of Havana was closed until mid-2018 for renovation. In the meantime, most departures are leaving through the La Coubre station.

Classes

Trains are either *especial* (air-conditioned, faster trains with fewer departures), *regular* (slowish trains with daily departures) or *lecheros* (milk trains that stop at every little town on the line). Trains on major routes such as Havana–Santiago de Cuba will be *especial* or *regular* trains.

Costs

Regular trains cost under CUC$3 per 100km, while *especial* trains cost closer to CUC$5.50 per 100km. The Hershey Train (between Havana and Matanzas) is priced like the *regular* trains.

Rail Network

Cuba's train network is comprehensive, running almost the full length of the main island from Guane in Pinar del Río province to Caimanera, just south of the city of Guantánamo. There are also several branch lines heading out north and south and linking up places such as Manzanillo, Nuevitas, Morón and Cienfuegos. Baracoa is one of the few cities without a train connection. Other trainless enclaves are the Isla de la Juventud, the far west of Pinar del Río province and the northern keys. Trinidad has been detached from the main rail network since a storm brought down a bridge in 1992. Trinidad's small branch line along the Valle del los Ingenios was under repair at the time of writing.

Reservations

In most train stations, you just go to the ticket window and buy a ticket. In La Coubre train station in Havana, there's a separate waiting room and ticket window for passengers paying in convertibles. Be prepared to show your passport when purchasing tickets. It's always wise to check beforehand at the station for current departures because things change.

Services

Many additional local trains operate at least daily and some more frequently. There are also smaller trains linking Las Tunas and Holguín, Holguín and Santiago de Cuba, Santa Clara and Nuevitas, Cienfuegos and Sancti Spíritus, and Santa Clara and Caibarién.

The Hershey Train is the only electric railway in Cuba and was built by the Hershey Chocolate Company in the early years of the 20th century; it's a fun way to get between Havana and Matanzas.

Train Stations

Cuban train stations, despite their occasionally grandiose facades, are invariably dingy, chaotic places with little visible train information. Departure times are displayed on black chalkboards or handwritten notices; there are no electronic or printed timetables. Always check train info two to three days before your intended travel.

Truck

Camiones (trucks) are a cheap, fast way to travel within or between provinces. Every city has a provincial and municipal bus stop with *camiones* departures. They run on a (loose) schedule and you'll need to take your place in line by asking for *el último* to your destination; you pay as you board. For many destinations, the majority of departures leave in the early morning.

Camion traveling is hot, crowded and uncomfortable, but is a great way to meet local people, fast; a little Spanish will go a long way. A truck from Santiago de Cuba to Guantánamo costs five pesos (CUC$0.20), while the same trip on a Víazul bus costs CUC$6.

Sometimes terminal staff tell foreigners they're prohibited from traveling on trucks. As with anything in Cuba, smile and never take 'no' as your final answer. Striking up a conversation with the driver or appealing to other passengers for aid usually helps.

Language

Spanish pronunciation is pretty straightforward – Spanish spelling is phonetically consistent, meaning that there's a clear and consistent relationship between what you see in writing and how it's pronounced. Also, most Latin American Spanish sounds are pronounced the same as their English counterparts. Note though that the kh in our pronunciation guides is a throaty sound (like the 'ch' in the Scottish *loch*), v and b are similar to the English 'b' (but softer, between a 'v' and a 'b'), and r is strongly rolled. If you read our colored pronunciation guides as if they were English, you'll be understood just fine. The stressed syllables are in italics.

Spanish nouns are marked for gender (masculine or feminine). Endings for adjectives also change to agree with the gender of the noun they modify. Where necessary, both forms are given for the phrases in this chapter, separated by a slash and with the masculine form first, eg *perdido/a* (m/f).

Spanish has two words for the English 'you': an informal (*tú*) and polite form (*Usted*) which are accompanied by a different form of the verb. When talking to people familiar to you or younger than you, use the informal form of 'you', *tú*, rather than the polite form *Usted*. In all other cases use the polite form. The polite form is used in the phrases provided in this chapter; where both options are given, they are indicated by the abbreviations 'pol' and 'inf'.

WANT MORE?

For in-depth language information and handy phrases, check out Lonely Planet's *Latin American Spanish Phrasebook*. You'll find it at **shop.lonelyplanet.com**, or you can buy Lonely Planet's iPhone phrasebooks at the Apple App Store.

BASICS

Hello.	*Hola.*	o·la
Goodbye.	*Adiós.*	a·*dyos*
How are you?	*¿Qué tal?*	ke tal
Fine, thanks.	*Bien, gracias.*	byen *gra*·syas
Excuse me.	*Perdón.*	per·*don*
Sorry.	*Lo siento.*	lo *syen*·to
Yes./No.	*Sí./No.*	see/no
Please.	*Por favor.*	por fa·*vor*
Thank you.	*Gracias.*	*gra*·syas
You're welcome.	*De nada.*	de *na*·da

My name is ...
Me llamo ... — me *ya*·mo ...

What's your name?
¿Cómo se llama Usted? — *ko*·mo se *ya*·ma *oo*·ste (pol)
¿Cómo te llamas? — *ko*·mo te *ya*·mas (inf)

Do you speak English?
¿Habla inglés? — *a*·bla een·*gles* (pol)
¿Hablas inglés? — *a*·blas een·*gles* (inf)

I don't understand.
Yo no entiendo. — yo no en·*tyen*·do

ACCOMMODATIONS

I'd like to book a room.
Quisiera reservar una habitación. — kee·*sye*·ra re·ser·*var oo*·na a·bee·ta·*syon*

How much is it per night/person?
¿Cuánto cuesta por noche/persona? — *kwan*·to *kwes*·ta por *no*·che/per·*so*·na

Does it include breakfast?
¿Incluye el desayuno? — een·*kloo*·ye el de·sa·*yoo*·no

campsite	*terreno de cámping*	te·*re*·no de *kam*·peeng
hotel	*hotel*	o·*tel*
guesthouse	*pensión*	pen·*syon*
youth hostel	*albergue juvenil*	al·*ber*·ge khoo·ve·*neel*

I'd like a ... room.	*Quisiera una habitación ...*	kee·*sye*·ra *oo*·na a·bee·ta·*syon* ...
single	*individual*	een·dee·vee·*dwal*
double	*doble*	*do*·ble

air-con	*aire acondicionado*	*ai*·re a·kon·dee·syo·*na*·do
bathroom	*baño*	*ba*·nyo
bed	*cama*	*ka*·ma
window	*ventana*	ven·*ta*·na

DIRECTIONS

Where's ...?
¿Dónde está ...? don·de es·*ta* ...

What's the address?
¿Cuál es la dirección? *kwal* es la dee·rek·*syon*

Could you please write it down?
¿Puede escribirlo, por favor? *pwe*·de es·kree·*beer*·lo por fa·*vor*

Can you show me (on the map)?
¿Me lo puede indicar (en el mapa)? me lo *pwe*·de een·dee·*kar* (en el *ma*·pa)

at the corner	*en la esquina*	en la es·*kee*·na
at the traffic lights	*en el semáforo*	en el se·*ma*·fo·ro
behind ...	*detrás de ...*	de·*tras* de ...
far	*lejos*	*le*·khos
in front of ...	*enfrente de ...*	en·*fren*·te de ...
left	*izquierda*	ees·*kyer*·da
near	*cerca*	*ser*·ka
next to ...	*al lado de ...*	al *la*·do de ...
opposite ...	*frente a ...*	*fren*·te a ...
right	*derecha*	de·*re*·cha
straight ahead	*todo recto*	*to*·do *rek*·to

EATING & DRINKING

What would you recommend?
¿Qué recomienda? ke re·ko·*myen*·da

What's in that dish?
¿Que lleva ese plato? ke *ye*·va e·se *pla*·to

I don't eat ...
No como ... no *ko*·mo ...

That was delicious!
¡Estaba buenísimo! es·*ta*·ba bwe·*nee*·see·mo

Please bring the bill.
Por favor nos trae la cuenta. por fa·*vor* nos *tra*·e la *kwen*·ta

Cheers!
¡Salud! sa·*loo*

KEY PATTERNS

To get by in Spanish, mix and match these simple patterns with words of your choice:

When's (the next flight)?
¿Cuándo sale (el próximo vuelo)? *kwan*·do *sa*·le (el *prok*·see·mo *vwe*·lo)

Where's (the station)?
¿Dónde está (la estación)? don·de es·*ta* (la es·ta·*syon*)

Where can I (buy a ticket)?
¿Dónde puedo (comprar un billete)? don·de *pwe*·do (kom·*prar* oon bee·*ye*·te)

Do you have (a map)?
¿Tiene (un mapa)? *tye*·ne (oon *ma*·pa)

Is there (a toilet)?
¿Hay (servicios)? ai (ser·*vee*·syos)

I'd like (a coffee).
Quisiera (un café). kee·*sye*·ra (oon ka·*fe*)

I'd like (to hire a car).
Quisiera (alquilar un coche). kee·*sye*·ra (al·kee·*lar* oon *ko*·che)

Can I (enter)?
¿Se puede (entrar)? se *pwe*·de (en·*trar*)

Could you please (help me)?
¿Puede (ayudarme), por favor? *pwe*·de (a·yoo·*dar*·me) por fa·*vor*

Do I have to (get a visa)?
¿Necesito (obtener un visado)? ne·se·*see*·to (ob·te·*ner* oon vee·*sa*·do)

I'd like to book a table for ...	*Quisiera reservar una mesa para ...*	kee·*sye*·ra re·ser·*var* *oo*·na *me*·sa *pa*·ra ...
(eight) o'clock	*las (ocho)*	las (*o*·cho)
(two) people	*(dos) personas*	(dos) per·*so*·nas

Key Words

appetisers	*aperitivos*	a·pe·ree·*tee*·vos
bottle	*botella*	bo·*te*·ya
bowl	*bol*	bol
breakfast	*desayuno*	de·sa·*yoo*·no
children's menu	*menú infantil*	me·*noo* een·fan·*teel*
(too) cold	*(muy) frío*	(mooy) *free*·o
dinner	*cena*	*se*·na
food	*comida*	ko·*mee*·da
fork	*tenedor*	te·ne·*dor*
glass	*vaso*	*va*·so

highchair	*trona*	tro·na
hot (warm)	*caliente*	kal·*yen*·te
knife	*cuchillo*	koo·*chee*·yo
lunch	*comida*	ko·*mee*·da
main course	*segundo plato*	se·*goon*·do *pla*·to
market	*mercado*	mer·*ka*·do
menu (in English)	*menú (en inglés)*	me·*noo* (en een·*gles*)
plate	*plato*	*pla*·to
restaurant	*restaurante*	res·tow·*ran*·te
spoon	*cuchara*	koo·*cha*·ra
vegetarian food	*comida vegetariana*	ko·*mee*·da ve·khe·ta·*rya*·na
with/without	*con/sin*	kon/seen

Meat & Fish

beef	*carne de vaca*	*kar*·ne de *va*·ka
chicken	*pollo*	*po*·yo
duck	*pato*	*pa*·to
fish	*pescado*	pes·*ka*·do
lamb	*cordero*	kor·*de*·ro
pork	*cerdo*	*ser*·do
turkey	*pavo*	*pa*·vo
veal	*ternera*	ter·*ne*·ra

Fruit & Vegetables

apple	*manzana*	man·*sa*·na
apricot	*albaricoque*	al·ba·ree·*ko*·ke
artichoke	*alcachofa*	al·ka·*cho*·fa
asparagus	*espárragos*	es·*pa*·ra·gos
banana	*plátano*	*pla*·ta·no
beans	*judías*	khoo·*dee*·as
beetroot	*remolacha*	re·mo·*la*·cha
cabbage	*col*	kol
carrot	*zanahoria*	sa·na·*o*·rya
celery	*apio*	*a*·pyo
cherry	*cereza*	se·*re*·sa
corn	*maíz*	ma·*ees*
cucumber	*pepino*	pe·*pee*·no
fruit	*fruta*	*froo*·ta
grape	*uvas*	*oo*·vas
lemon	*limón*	lee·*mon*
lentils	*lentejas*	len·*te*·khas
lettuce	*lechuga*	le·*choo*·ga
mushroom	*champiñón*	cham·pee·*nyon*
nuts	*nueces*	*nwe*·ses
onion	*cebolla*	se·*bo*·ya
orange	*naranja*	na·*ran*·kha
peach	*melocotón*	me·lo·ko·*ton*
peas	*guisantes*	gee·*san*·tes
(red/green) pepper	*pimiento (rojo/verde)*	pee·*myen*·to (*ro*·kho/*ver*·de)
pineapple	*piña*	*pee*·nya
plum	*ciruela*	seer·*we*·la
potato	*patata*	pa·*ta*·ta
pumpkin	*calabaza*	ka·la·*ba*·sa
spinach	*espinacas*	es·pee·*na*·kas
strawberry	*fresa*	*fre*·sa
tomato	*tomate*	to·*ma*·te
vegetable	*verdura*	ver·*doo*·ra
watermelon	*sandía*	san·*dee*·a

Other

bread	*pan*	pan
butter	*mantequilla*	man·te·*kee*·ya
cheese	*queso*	*ke*·so
egg	*huevo*	*we*·vo
honey	*miel*	myel
jam	*mermelada*	mer·me·*la*·da
oil	*aceite*	a·*sey*·te
pasta	*pasta*	*pas*·ta
pepper	*pimienta*	pee·*myen*·ta
rice	*arroz*	a·*ros*
salt	*sal*	sal
sugar	*azúcar*	a·*soo*·kar
vinegar	*vinagre*	vee·*na*·gre

Drinks

beer	*cerveza*	ser·*ve*·sa
coffee	*café*	ka·*fe*
(orange) juice	*zumo (de naranja)*	*soo*·mo (de na·*ran*·kha)
milk	*leche*	*le*·che
tea	*té*	te

Signs

Abierto	Open
Cerrado	Closed
Entrada	Entrance
Hombres/Varones	Men
Mujeres/Damas	Women
Prohibido	Prohibited
Salida	Exit
Servicios/Baños	Toilets

(mineral) water	*agua (mineral)*	a·gwa (mee·ne·*ral*)
(red/white) wine	*vino (tinto/ blanco)*	vee·no (*teen*·to/ *blan*·ko)

EMERGENCIES

Help!	*¡Socorro!*	so·*ko*·ro
Go away!	*¡Vete!*	ve·te

Call ...!	*¡Llame a ...!*	*ya*·me a ...
a doctor	*un médico*	oon *me*·dee·ko
the police	*la policía*	la po·lee·*see*·a

I'm lost.
Estoy perdido/a. es·*toy* per·*dee*·do/a (m/f)

I'm ill.
Estoy enfermo/a. es·*toy* en·*fer*·mo/a (m/f)

I'm allergic to (antibiotics).
Soy alérgico/a a (los antibióticos). soy a·*ler*·khee·ko/a a (los an·tee·*byo*·tee·kos) (m/f)

Where are the toilets?
¿Dónde están los servicios? *don*·de es·*tan* los ser·*vee*·syos

SHOPPING & SERVICES

I'd like to buy ...
Quisiera comprar ... kee·*sye*·ra kom·*prar* ...

I'm just looking.
Sólo estoy mirando. so·lo es·*toy* mee·*ran*·do

May I look at it?
¿Puedo verlo? *pwe*·do *ver*·lo

I don't like it.
No me gusta. no me *goos*·ta

How much is it?
¿Cuánto cuesta? *kwan*·to *kwes*·ta

That's too expensive.
Es muy caro. es mooy *ka*·ro

Can you lower the price?
¿Podría bajar un poco el precio? po·*dree*·a ba·*khar* oon *po*·ko el *pre*·syo

There's a mistake in the bill.
Hay un error en la cuenta. ai oon e·*ror* en la *kwen*·ta

Question Words

How?	*¿Cómo?*	*ko*·mo
What?	*¿Qué?*	ke
When?	*¿Cuándo?*	*kwan*·do
Where?	*¿Dónde?*	*don*·de
Who?	*¿Quién?*	kyen
Why?	*¿Por qué?*	por ke

ATM	*cajero automático*	ka·*khe*·ro ow·to·*ma*·tee·ko
credit card	*tarjeta de crédito*	tar·*khe*·ta de *kre*·dee·to
internet cafe	*cibercafé*	see·ber·ka·*fe*
post office	*correos*	ko·*re*·os
tourist office	*oficina de turismo*	o·fee·*see*·na de too·*rees*·mo

TIME & DATES

What time is it?	*¿Qué hora es?*	ke o·ra es
It's (10) o'clock.	*Son (las diez).*	son (las dyes)
It's half past (one).	*Es (la una) y media.*	es (la oo·na) ee *me*·dya

morning	*mañana*	ma·*nya*·na
afternoon	*tarde*	*tar*·de
evening	*noche*	*no*·che
yesterday	*ayer*	a·*yer*
today	*hoy*	oy
tomorrow	*mañana*	ma·*nya*·na

Monday	*lunes*	*loo*·nes
Tuesday	*martes*	*mar*·tes
Wednesday	*miércoles*	*myer*·ko·les
Thursday	*jueves*	*khwe*·ves
Friday	*viernes*	*vyer*·nes
Saturday	*sábado*	*sa*·ba·do
Sunday	*domingo*	do·*meen*·go

January	*enero*	e·*ne*·ro
February	*febrero*	fe·*bre*·ro
March	*marzo*	*mar*·so
April	*abril*	a·*breel*
May	*mayo*	*ma*·yo
June	*junio*	*khoon*·yo
July	*julio*	*khool*·yo
August	*agosto*	a·*gos*·to
September	*septiembre*	sep·*tyem*·bre
October	*octubre*	ok·*too*·bre
November	*noviembre*	no·*vyem*·bre
December	*diciembre*	dee·*syem*·bre

TRANSPORTATION

Public Transportation

boat	*barco*	*bar*·ko
bus	*autobús*	ow·to·*boos*
plane	*avión*	a·*vyon*
train	*tren*	tren

Numbers

1	*uno*	oo·no
2	*dos*	dos
3	*tres*	tres
4	*cuatro*	*kwa*·tro
5	*cinco*	*seen*·ko
6	*seis*	seys
7	*siete*	*sye*·te
8	*ocho*	o·cho
9	*nueve*	nwe·ve
10	*diez*	dyes
20	*veinte*	*veyn*·te
30	*treinta*	*treyn*·ta
40	*cuarenta*	kwa·*ren*·ta
50	*cincuenta*	seen·*kwen*·ta
60	*sesenta*	se·*sen*·ta
70	*setenta*	se·*ten*·ta
80	*ochenta*	o·*chen*·ta
90	*noventa*	no·*ven*·ta
100	*cien*	syen
1000	*mil*	meel

first	*primero*	pree·*me*·ro
last	*último*	*ool*·tee·mo
next	*próximo*	*prok*·see·mo

I want to go to ...
Quisiera ir a ... kee·*sye*·ra eer a ...

Does it stop at ...?
¿Para en ...? *pa*·ra en ...

What stop is this?
¿Cuál es esta parada? kwal es *es*·ta pa·*ra*·da

What time does it arrive/leave?
¿A qué hora llega/ sale? a ke *o*·ra *ye*·ga/ *sa*·le

Please tell me when we get to ...
¿Puede avisarme cuando lleguemos a ...? *pwe*·de a·vee·*sar*·me *kwan*·do ye·*ge*·mos a ...

I want to get off here.
Quiero bajarme aquí. *kye*·ro ba·*khar*·me a·*kee*

a ... ticket	*un billete de ...*	oon bee·*ye*·te de ...
1st-class	*primera clase*	pree·*me*·ra *kla*·se
2nd-class	*segunda clase*	se·*goon*·da *kla*·se
one-way	*ida*	*ee*·da
return	*ida y vuelta*	*ee*·da ee *vwel*·ta

airport	*aeropuerto*	a·e·ro·*pwer*·to
aisle seat	*asiento de pasillo*	a·*syen*·to de pa·*see*·yo
bus stop	*parada de autobuses*	pa·*ra*·da de ow·to·*boo*·ses
cancelled	*cancelado*	kan·se·*la*·do
delayed	*retrasado*	re·tra·*sa*·do
platform	*plataforma*	pla·ta·*for*·ma
ticket office	*taquilla*	ta·*kee*·ya
timetable	*horario*	o·*ra*·ryo
train station	*estación de trenes*	es·ta·*syon* de *tre*·nes
window seat	*asiento junto a la ventana*	a·*syen*·to *khoon*·to a la ven·*ta*·na

Driving & Cycling

I'd like to hire a ...	*Quisiera alquilar ...*	kee·*sye*·ra al·kee·*lar* ...
4WD	*un todo-terreno*	oon to·do·te·*re*·no
bicycle	*una bicicleta*	*oo*·na bee·see·*kle*·ta
car	*un coche*	oon *ko*·che
motorcycle	*una moto*	*oo*·na *mo*·to

child seat	*asiento de seguridad para niños*	a·*syen*·to de se·goo·ree·*da* *pa*·ra *nee*·nyos
diesel	*petróleo*	pet·*ro*·le·o
helmet	*casco*	*kas*·ko
hitchhike	*hacer botella*	a·*ser* bo·*te*·ya
mechanic	*mecánico*	me·*ka*·nee·ko
petrol/gas	*gasolina*	ga·so·*lee*·na
service station	*gasolinera*	ga·so·lee·*ne*·ra
truck	*camion*	ka·*myon*

Is this the road to ...?
¿Se va a ... por esta carretera? se va a ... por *es*·ta ka·re·*te*·ra

(How long) Can I park here?
¿(Por cuánto tiempo) Puedo aparcar aquí? (por *kwan*·to *tyem*·po) *pwe*·do a·par·*kar* a·*kee*

The car has broken down (at ...).
El coche se ha averiado (en ...). el *ko*·che se a a·ve·*rya*·do (en ...)

I have a flat tyre.
Tengo un pinchazo. *ten*·go oon peen·*cha*·so

I've run out of petrol.
Me he quedado sin gasolina. me e ke·*da*·do seen ga·so·*lee*·na

GLOSSARY

altos – upstairs apartment; caps when in an address
agropecuario – vegetable market; also sells rice, fruit
amarillo – a roadside traffic organizer in a yellow uniform
americano/a – in Cuba this means a citizen of any Western hemisphere country (from Canada to Argentina); a citizen of the US is called a *norteamericano/a* or *estado- unidense*; also gringo/a and yuma
Arawak – linguistically related Indian tribes that inhabited most of the Caribbean islands and northern South America
Autopista – the national highway that has four, six or eight lanes depending on the region

babalawo – a *Santería* priest; also *babalao*; see also *santero*
bahía – bay
bailes – dances
barbuda – name given to Castro's rebel army; literally 'bearded one'
barrio – neighborhood
bici-taxi – bicycle taxi
bodega – stores distributing ration-card products
bohío – thatched hut
bolero – a romantic love song
botella – hitchhiking; literally 'bottle'

cabaña – cabin, hut
cabildo – a town council during the colonial era; also an association of tribes in Cuban religions of African origin
cacique – chief; originally used to describe an Indian chief and today used to designate a petty tyrant
Cadeca – exchange booth
cafetal – coffee plantation
caliente – hot
calle – street
camión – truck
campesinos – people who live in the *campo*
campismo – national network of 82 camping installations, not all of which are open to foreigners
casa particular – private house that lets out rooms to foreigners (and sometimes Cubans); all legal casas must display a green triangle on the door
casco histórico – historic center of a city (eg Trinidad, Santiago de Cuba)
CDR – Comités de Defensa de la Revolución; neighborhood-watch bodies originally formed in 1960 to consolidate grassroots support for the Revolution; they now play a decisive role in health, education, social, recycling and voluntary labor campaigns
chachachá – cha-cha; dance music in 4/4 meter derived from the rumba and mambo
Changó – the *Santería* deity signifying war and fire, twinned with Santa Barbara in Catholicism
chivo – Cuban slang for 'bike'
cimarrón – a runaway slave
claves – rhythm sticks used by musicians
coches de caballo – horse carriages
Cohiba – native Indian name for a smoking implement; one of Cuba's top brands of cigar
colectivo – collective taxi that takes on as many passengers as possible; usually a classic American car
comida criolla – Creole food
compañero/a – companion or partner, with revolutionary connotations (ie 'comrade')
congrí (rice flecked with black beans)
conseguir – to get, obtain
convertibles – convertible pesos
coppelia – Cuban ice creamery
criollo – Creole; Spaniard born in the Americas
Cubanacán – soon after landing in Cuba, Christopher Columbus visited a Taíno village the Indians called Cubanacán (meaning 'in the center of the island'); a large Cuban tourism company uses the name
danzón – a traditional Cuban ballroom dance colored with African influences, pioneered in Matanzas during the late 19th century
décima – the rhyming, eight-syllable verse that provides the lyrics for Cuban son
duende – spirit/charm; used in flamenco to describe the ultimate climax to the music

El Lider Máximo – Maximum Leader; title often used to describe Fidel Castro
el último – literally 'the last'; this term is key to mastering Cuban queues (you must 'take' *el último* when joining a line and 'give it up' when someone new arrives)
entronque – crossroads in rural areas

finca – farm

Gitmo – American slang for Guantánamo US Naval Base
Granma – the yacht that carried Fidel and his companions from Mexico to Cuba in 1956 to launch the Revolution; in 1975 the name was adopted for the province where the Granma arrived; also name of Cuba's leading daily newspaper
guajiros – country folk
guarapo – fresh sugarcane juice

habanero/a – someone from Havana
herbero – seller of herbs, natural medicines and concocter of remedies; typically a wealth of knowledge on natural cures

ingenio – an antiquated term for a sugar mill; see central
inmigración – immigration office

jardín – garden
jinetera – a female tout; a woman who attaches herself to male foreigners
jinetero – a male tout who hustles tourists; literally 'jockey'

M-26-7 – the '26th of July Movement,' Fidel Castro's revolutionary organization, was named for the abortive assault on the Moncada army barracks in Santiago de Cuba on July 26, 1953
maqueta – scale model
máquina – private peso taxi
mercado – market

mirador – lookout or viewpoint

mogote – a limestone monolith found at Viñales

Moncada – a former army barracks in Santiago de Cuba named for General Guillermo Moncada (1848-95), a hero of the Wars of Independence

moneda nacional – abbreviated to MN; Cuban pesos

mudéjar – Iberian Peninsula's Moorish-influenced style in architecture and decoration that lasted from the 12th to 16th centuries and combined elements of Islamic and Christian art

nueva trova – philosophical folk/guitar music popularized in the late '60s and early '70s by Silvio Rodríguez and Pablo Milanés

Operación Milagros – the unofficial name given to a pioneering medical program hatched between Cuba and Venezuela in 2004 that offers free eye treatment for impoverished Venezuelans in Cuban hospitals

Oriente – the region comprised of Las Tunas, Holguín, Granma, Santiago de Cuba and Guantánamo provinces; literally 'the east'

orisha – a *Santería* deity

paladar – a privately owned restaurant

parada – bus stop

parque – park

PCC – Partido Comunista de Cuba; Cuba's only political party, formed in October 1965 by merging cadres from the Partido Socialista Popular (the pre-1959 Communist Party) and veterans of the guerrilla campaign

peña – musical performance or get-together in any genre: son, rap, rock, poetry etc; see also esquina

período especial – the 'Special Period in Time of Peace' (Cuba's economic reality post-1991)

pregón – a singsong manner of selling fruits, vegetables, brooms, whatever; often comic, they are belted out by *pregoneros/as*

puente – bridge

quinceañera – Cuban rite of passage for girls turning 15 *(quince)*, whereby they dress up like brides, have their photos taken in gorgeous natural or architectural settings and then have a big party with lots of food and dancing

ranchón – rural farm/restaurant

reggaetón – Cuban hip-hop

Regla de Ocha – set of related religious beliefs popularly known as *Santería*

resolver – to resolve or fix a problematic situation; along with *el último*, this is among the most indispensable words in Cuban vocabulary

río – river

salsa – Cuban music based on son

salsero – salsa singer

Santería – Afro-Cuban religion resulting from the syncretization of the Yoruba religion of West Africa and Spanish Catholicism

santero – a priest of *Santería*; see also babalawo

santiagüero – someone from Santiago de Cuba

s/n – *sin número;* indicates an address that has no street number

son – Cuba's basic form of popular music that jelled from African and Spanish elements in the late 19th century

Taíno – a settled, Arawak-speaking tribe that inhabited much of Cuba prior to the Spanish conquest; the word itself means 'we the good people'

tambores – *Santería* drumming ritual

telepunto – Etecsa (Cuban state-run telecommunications company) telephone and internet shop/call center

temporada alta/baja – high/low season

Behind the Scenes

SEND US YOUR FEEDBACK

We love to hear from travelers – your comments keep us on our toes and help make our books better. Our well-traveled team reads every word on what you loved or loathed about this book. Although we cannot reply individually to your submissions, we always guarantee that your feedback goes straight to the appropriate authors, in time for the next edition. Each person who sends us information is thanked in the next edition – the most useful submissions are rewarded with a selection of digital PDF chapters.

Visit **lonelyplanet.com/contact** to submit your updates and suggestions or to ask for help. Our award-winning website also features inspirational travel stories, news and discussions.

Note: We may edit, reproduce and incorporate your comments in Lonely Planet products such as guidebooks, websites and digital products, so let us know if you don't want your comments reproduced or your name acknowledged. For a copy of our privacy policy visit lonelyplanet.com/privacy.

OUR READERS

Many thanks to the travelers who used the last edition and wrote to us with helpful hints, useful advice and interesting anecdotes:

A Adam Wereszczynski, Adrian Lange, Alison Douglas, Andreas Jansen, Ann Barrett, Anne Schneider, Annegret Krüger, Annette Brook, Antonio Cascos, Ayal Weiner-Kaplow **B** Beth Handman, Birgit Einzenberger, Brian Dargan, Bruno Selun **C** Cédric Quatannens, Claire Liboureau, Claudia Krapp **D** Daniel Drury, Daniela D'Alessio, Detlef Greiner, Djoeke Geijs, Duane Marxen **E** Elitsa Matsanova, Emilio Muñoz, Emma Åsenius, Eric Labonne, Erik de Brouwer, Erin Lindsey **F** Federica Gallo, Felix Kallenberg, Florian Güster, Franky Knoechel **G** Gavin Dixon **H** Hank Raymond, Hannes Holst, Helmut Ninaus, Hendrik Mueller-Ide, Hilary Duffy, Hind Benkirane, Holly Maltby **I** Ivan Chang **J** Jack Edwards, Jakob Merljak, Jan Keymis, Jan van Dok, Jana Gehlen, Janna Pape, Jaroslav Sirotek, Jenni Williams, Jenny Cottle, Joachim Hertz, Joe Pundek, Johan Borchert, John Kilgannon, John Sturt, Jon Groner, Jonathan Hales, Jonathan Pattenden, Jörg Deppe, Josh Levin, Judy Rubin **K** Kalev Mändmaa, Karl Manco, Kerstin Thunwall, Kristen Smith, Kristin Gjersdal, Kwassi Dadzie **L** Lars Bendtsen, Lesley Bayliss, Lindley Owen, Louise Heseltine, Lucas Bornschlegl, Ludo Teunissen **M** Marco Catalano, Margje van Weerden, Melanie Luangsay, Mette Hedegaard **N** Nicolas Combremont, Nicole Rochat **O** Oli Taylor, Othmar Kyas **P** Patrizia Bertini, Paul Lewis, Peter Tesche, Pinar Sayin **R** Rafael Gonzalez, Ray Weglehner, Rebecca Vaughan, Rhonda Keen, Richard Creel, Richard Heins, Robin van der Griend, Ross More, Rui Lopes **S** Samantha Bond, Sandra Engblom, Sandra Schrammel, Scott Schamber, Stephanie Kirichek, Stephanie Matse, Steve Struthers, Stuart Kandell **T** Tasha Stephenson, Tim Beswick, Tim Laslavic, Tim Micklinghoff, Tobias Eigenmann, Tony Mortlock, **U** Ursula Berlinchamp **V** Valerio Pieri **W** Wil Bennett, Will Hudson **Y** Yi Zhao, Yolande Hachez **Z** Zsolt Bogoti

WRITER THANKS

Brendan Sainsbury

Thanks to all my Cuban *amigos*, many of whom helped me immensely during this research (and have been doing so for years). Special thanks to Carlos Sarmiento, Luis Miguel, Maité and Idolka in Morón, Julio and Elsa Roque, Joel in Matanzas, Beny in Varadero, Ramberto on the Isla de la Juventud, and to my wife, Liz, and son, Kieran, for accompanying me on the road.

Carolyn McCarthy

Heartfelt thanks to those who made my work in Cuba possible: from my host Luis Miguel in Havana to Domingo Cuza in Bayamo, the Muñoz family, Rafael in Camagüey, Nilson and Infotur. Brendan Sainsbury, Diego y Roy: *para su ayuda y buenos consejos, no hay suficiente Havana Club en el mundo para compensarles, pero intentamos!*

ACKNOWLEDGEMENTS

Climate map data adapted from Peel MC, Finlayson BL & McMahon TA (2007) 'Updated World Map of the Köppen-Geiger Climate Classification', Hydrology and Earth System Sciences, 11, 163344.

Cover photograph: Taxi, Havana. Grant Faint/Getty Images ©

Illustrations p70–1 by Michael Weldon

THIS BOOK

This 9th edition of Lonely Planet's *Cuba* guidebook was researched and written by Brendan Sainsbury and Carolyn McCarthy. The previous two editions were also written by Brendan, and Luke Waterson. This guidebook was produced by the following:

Destination Editor Bailey Freeman

Product Editor Amanda Williamson

Senior Cartographers Mark Griffiths, Corey Hutchison

Book Designer Clara Monitto

Assisting Editors Nigel Chin, Melanie Dankel, Bruce Evans, Carly Hall, Kellie Langdon, Jodie Martire, Louise McGregor, Gabrielle Stefanos

Assisting Cartographer Valentina Kremenchutskaya

Cover Researcher Naomi Parker

Thanks to Evan Godt, Paul Harding, Liz Heynes, Elizabeth Jones, Sandie Kestell, Kate Mathews, Catherine Naghten, Lauren O'Connell, Kirsten Rawlings, Tony Wheeler

Index

Map Pages **000**
Photo Pages **000**

Map Pages **000**
Photo Pages **000**

Map Pages **000**
Photo Pages **000**

G

H

I

J

K

L

M

Map Pages **000**
Photo Pages **000**

Map Pages **000**
Photo Pages **000**

T

Map Pages **000**
Photo Pages **000**

Map Legend

Sights
- Beach
- Bird Sanctuary
- Buddhist
- Castle/Palace
- Christian
- Confucian
- Hindu
- Islamic
- Jain
- Jewish
- Monument
- Museum/Gallery/Historic Building
- Ruin
- Shinto
- Sikh
- Taoist
- Winery/Vineyard
- Zoo/Wildlife Sanctuary
- Other Sight

Activities, Courses & Tours
- Bodysurfing
- Diving
- Canoeing/Kayaking
- Course/Tour
- Sento Hot Baths/Onsen
- Skiing
- Snorkeling
- Surfing
- Swimming/Pool
- Walking
- Windsurfing
- Other Activity

Sleeping
- Sleeping
- Camping

Eating
- Eating

Drinking & Nightlife
- Drinking & Nightlife
- Cafe

Entertainment
- Entertainment

Shopping
- Shopping

Information
- Bank
- Embassy/Consulate
- Hospital/Medical
- Internet
- Police
- Post Office
- Telephone
- Toilet
- Tourist Information
- Other Information

Geographic
- Beach
- Gate
- Hut/Shelter
- Lighthouse
- Lookout
- Mountain/Volcano
- Oasis
- Park
- Pass
- Picnic Area
- Waterfall

Population
- Capital (National)
- Capital (State/Province)
- City/Large Town
- Town/Village

Transport
- Airport
- Border crossing
- Bus
- Cable car/Funicular
- Cycling
- Ferry
- Metro station
- Monorail
- Parking
- Petrol station
- Subway/Subte station
- Taxi
- Train station/Railway
- Tram
- Underground station
- Other Transport

Note: Not all symbols displayed above appear on the maps in this book

Routes
- Tollway
- Freeway
- Primary
- Secondary
- Tertiary
- Lane
- Unsealed road
- Road under construction
- Plaza/Mall
- Steps
- Tunnel
- Pedestrian overpass
- Walking Tour
- Walking Tour detour
- Path/Walking Trail

Boundaries
- International
- State/Province
- Disputed
- Regional/Suburb
- Marine Park
- Cliff
- Wall

Hydrography
- River, Creek
- Intermittent River
- Canal
- Water
- Dry/Salt/Intermittent Lake
- Reef

Areas
- Airport/Runway
- Beach/Desert
- Cemetery (Christian)
- Cemetery (Other)
- Glacier
- Mudflat
- Park/Forest
- Sight (Building)
- Sportsground
- Swamp/Mangrove

OUR STORY

A beat-up old car, a few dollars in the pocket and a sense of adventure. In 1972 that's all Tony and Maureen Wheeler needed for the trip of a lifetime – across Europe and Asia overland to Australia. It took several months, and at the end – broke but inspired – they sat at their kitchen table writing and stapling together their first travel guide, *Across Asia on the Cheap*. Within a week they'd sold 1500 copies. Lonely Planet was born.

Today, Lonely Planet has offices in Franklin, London, Melbourne, Oakland, Dublin, Beijing and Delhi, with more than 600 staff and writers. We share Tony's belief that 'a great guidebook should do three things: inform, educate and amuse'.

OUR WRITERS

Brendan Sainsbury
Havana, Artemisa & Mayabeque, Isla de la Juventud (Special Municipality), Valle de Viñales & Pinar del Río, Varadero & Matanzas, Cienfuegos, Villa Clara, Ciego de Ávila Originally from Hampshire, England, Brendan has been going to Cuba for more than 20 years as a travel guide and writer. He has explored every corner of the country from Cabo de San Antonio to Punta de Maisí using every known method of transportation from cycling to hitchhiking. Now based in Vancouver, Canada, Brendan has contributed to more than 50 Lonely Planet guides, including six editions of the one you are holding. He also wrote the latest Pocket guide to Havana. For more information visit https://auth.lonelyplanet.com/profiles/brendansainsbury

Carolyn McCarthy
Trinidad & Sancti Spíritus, Camagüey, Las Tunas, Holguín, Granma, Santiago de Cuba, Guantánamo Carolyn specializes in travel, culture and adventure in the Americas. She has written for *National Geographic*, *Outside*, *BBC Magazine*, *Boston Globe* and other publications. A former Fulbright fellow and Banff Mountain Grant recipient, she has documented life in the most remote corners of Latin America. Carolyn gained her expertize by researching guidebooks in diverse destinations. She has contributed to more than 30 guidebooks for Lonely Planet, including *Colorado*, *USA*, *Argentina*, *Chile*, *Trekking in the Patagonian Andes*, *Panama*, *Peru* and *USA's National Parks*. For more information, visit www.carolynmccarthy.org or follow her Instagram travels at @masmerquen

Published by Lonely Planet Global Limited
CRN 554153
9th edition – Oct 2017
ISBN 978 1 78657 149 6

10 9 8 7 6 5 4 3 2 1
Printed in China